Police Training Manual

Police Training Manual

Tenth Edition

Jack English and Brian English

The *McGraw·Hill* Companies

London Boston Burr Ridge, IL Dubuque, IA Madison, WI New York
San Francisco St. Louis Bangkok Bogotá Caracas Kuala Lumpur Lisbon Madrid
Mexico City Milan Montreal New Delhi Santiago Seoul
Singapore Sydney Taipei Toronto

The **McGraw·Hill** Companies

Police Training Manual, tenth edition
Jack English and Brian English
ISBN 007710 7314

 **Professional**

Published by McGraw-Hill Professional
Shoppenhangers Road
Maidenhead
Berkshire
SL6 2QL
Telephone: 44 (0) 1628 502 500
Fax: 44 (0) 1628 770 224
Website: www.mcgraw-hill.co.uk

British Library Cataloguing in Publication Data
A catalogue record for this book is available from the British Library

Library of Congress Cataloguing in Publication Data
The Library of Congress data for this book has been applied for from the Library of Congress

Text design and typeset by Gray Publishing, Tunbridge Wells, Kent
Cover design by Fielding Design Ltd
Printed and bound in the UK by Bell and Bain Ltd, Glasgow

Contents

Preface   vii

Stage 1

Pocket notebook rules   3
Lost and found property   7
Computer misuse and data protection   10
Police Regulations and conditions of service   16
Complaints against the police   22
Police Federation and negotiating machinery   52
Constitutional position of the police   59

Stage 2

Common law and statute law   77
Functions of, and evidence accepted by, courts   84
Summonses and warrants   122
Making an arrest and powers of entry without a search
   warrant to arrest   131
Classification of offences and powers to arrest without warrant   150
Stop and search   159
Questioning and treatment of persons   182
Road checks   213
Safe custody of prisoners   216
Theft   220
Burglary   234
Criminal deception   242
Report writing rules   254
Robbery   257
Taking conveyances   259
Handling stolen goods   265
Application of road traffic law   273
Motor vehicles – registration and licensing   281
Driving licences, insurance and test certificates   305
The law relating to highways   337
Motor traffic offences by owners and drivers   344
Road traffic – associated offences   352
Lights on vehicles   355
Fixed-penalty procedure   367
Road vehicles – construction and use   375
Traffic signs and pedestrian crossings   399
Introduction to statement writing   409
Further development of statement writing skills   415
Scenes of crime – management   421
Loss of memory and illness in the street   425
Missing persons, absconders, deserters and escapees   427

Breath specimens and drinking and driving 432
Public order 464
Criminal damage 491
Dogs 499
Assaults and woundings 507
Domestic disputes 517
Drugs 525
Statutory preventive measures 533
Sudden death 546
Accidents – law 551
Accidents – police action 557
Firearms 562
Indecent language, exposure and telephone calls 577
Indecent assault 580
Railways 583
How to give evidence 586
Crime prevention 589

Stage 3

Crime reporting and the *modus operandi* system 595
Police National Computer 600
Identification methods 605

Stage 5

Major incidents – fires and carriage of dangerous substances 635

Stage 6

Licensed premises, registered clubs, refreshment houses and
   drunkenness 643
Control of alcohol at sporting events 661
'Street offences' 674
Sexual offences including rape 679
Indecent literature through the post 690
Goods vehicles – plating and testing: driving licences and
   operators' licences 694
Dangerous and careless driving and exceeding speed limits 707
Foreign citizens in the United Kingdom 722
Wildlife and countryside 730
Animals 735
Children and young persons 740
Offences of entering and remaining on property 756
Appendix: Licensed premises, licensed persons, clubs, places of
   entertainment and offences of drunkenness 761
Index 785

Note: Stage 4 is concerned with gaining practical experience of police work and therefore sits outside the scope of this book.

Preface

A review was conducted into the Police Probationer Training Programme during 1995–96. Following that review, the Police Training Council approved the basis of a new training programme for general introduction.

The aim of the new training programme is to provide probationers with the necessary skills, knowledge, attitudes and understanding to enable them to fulfil their future roles as police officers in accordance with the Police Training Council strategy within police forces and Police Training Centres. The stages of the probationary training programme are:

Stage 1: a minimum of 2 weeks in force, induction and in-force familiarisation.
Stage 2: 15 weeks' classroom-based training at a Police Training Centre.
Stage 3: a maximum of 2 weeks in force dealing with local procedures.
Stage 4: work experience comprising 10 weeks in force, undertaking supervised patrol with a designated tutor constable.
Stage 5: 2 weeks in force to extend knowledge of local procedures.
Stage 6: the development stage, comprising a minimum of 20 days leading to confirmation in rank.

We have attempted, so far as is possible, to separate the subject matter related to law and police procedure which will be considered within the various stages involving formal teaching. It will be appreciated, however, that it is not always possible to draw a distinct line between matters which will arise within one discussion as opposed to another, or within one stage as opposed to another. Each subject has, therefore, been dealt with completely on the first occasion upon which it is introduced into the training programme wherever it is realistic to do so; on other occasions, subjects have been separated whenever it appeared to be realistic to do so.

There are exceptions to these general guidelines.

Where training undertaken in a particular stage represents a continuation of the consideration of subjects which have previously been encountered, for the sake of completeness, all of the material will appear in one place, usually at the point where the subject is first offered for consideration.

This book seeks to provide police officers who are undergoing probationer training with details of the law and police procedures which are included within the probationary training programme. The 'law' content of the book has been considerably increased within this edition in the hope that it will be of value well beyond probationer training. It does not attempt to deal with the complex issues which surround policing; such social issues are best left to specialist trainers who combine knowledge of the subject with sound experience of policing at the front line. The inclusion of such subjects would considerably increase the size of the book and its cost. The only exceptions to the rule that the book will confine itself to matters related to the law and approved procedures is where it is considered that 'background' material (unrelated to social issues) is not readily available elsewhere.

This book is written in recognition of the terms of s 6 of the Interpretation Act 1978, which seeks to avoid the constant use of the terms 'he' and 'she'. The Act provides that, in all respects, words importing the feminine gender include the masculine and words importing the masculine gender include the feminine. The provisions of s 6 are explained more fully at the commencement of the book.

This book includes changes in law and procedures which occurred before 1 July 2003, although it has been possible to take into account some changes which have occurred since that date when such changes could be made without affecting the printer's page setting.

Jack English
Brian English

The use of gender pronouns

The use of gender pronouns within law books presents a particular problem. In most books, for most of the time, the writer will be referring to a particular person and the following use of a pronoun will refer, therefore, particularly to a man or to a woman. This is not so in the case of law. The law refers to 'a person' when describing the way in which offences can be committed and this leads to difficulties in relation to gender pronouns. Because the 'person' could be either a man or a woman, it would be necessary subsequently to refer to both possibilities. The frequency with which this would occur in a 'law book' is such that it would become irritating to a reader.

This was recognised by Parliament, which consequently included in the Interpretation Act 1978, s 6 which provides:

In any Act, unless the contrary intention appears –

(a) words importing the masculine gender include the feminine;
(b) words importing the feminine gender include the masculine;
(c) words in the singular include the plural and words in the plural include the singular.

Within this book, where matters of law and statutory procedures are being considered, the approach which is generally adopted in law books has been followed by referring to only one gender pronoun as the 1978 Act makes it clear that such a reference is an inclusive reference. In some places where the subject matter sits outside statutory procedures, pairs of gender pronouns follow references to 'person', etc. The authors appreciate that there may be occasions upon which the rule has not been perfectly applied.

Stage 1

Pocket notebook rules

Introduction

The constable's pocket notebook is issued to enable written notes of an occurrence to be made either at the time or as soon after the occurrence as practicable. These notes will often form the basis of a written report or statement and it is, therefore, essential for a police officer to observe certain basic rules when making entries in his pocket notebook. They represent an officer's immediate recollection of an occurrence and although neatness is desirable it is secondary to the accuracy achieved by the immediate note made at the first opportunity. Accuracy is most important. All entries in a pocket notebook must be accurate whether they refer to times of duties performed or to facts connected with an offence or incident. Often a pocket notebook will be produced in court when a constable wishes to refresh his memory. In such a case the court is then entitled to examine the relevant entries, and if the notes are found to be inaccurate or untrustworthy this will detract considerably from the value of any evidence given by the constable.

In order to achieve accuracy, all entries in a pocket notebook must be made at the time an incident occurs or as soon after it happened as practicable, while the details of the event are still fresh in the officer's mind. Thus notes must be made, so far as possible, contemporaneously, but the courts recognise the fact that the nature of police duties is such that notes cannot always be made 'at the time'. The purpose of the notes is that they will be available at a later date to assist the officer, if necessary, when giving evidence in court. The rule is that a witness may refresh his memory by reference to any writing made or verified by that person concerning the facts to which he testifies provided that the record is made contemporaneously. However, it is sufficient for the purposes of the rule if the writing was made or verified at a time when the facts were still fresh in the witness' memory. Where notes were made 2 hours following an unsolicited conversation with a woman who was later charged with aiding and abetting her husband to drive while disqualified, the Divisional Court supported the justices' finding that the notes were made at the first practical opportunity (the officer had been dealing with her husband's arrest and subsequent procedures) and that they had been made while the events were still fresh in the officer's mind.

All notes must be made in the pocket notebook; scraps of paper should only be used in exceptional circumstances and should be carefully preserved as the true record of an event. An example would be when a police officer in plain clothes is keeping observations inside premises and recording breaches of the law. Obviously, notes could not be made in a pocket notebook but could be made on the side of a newspaper or magazine or even on a scrap of paper, later to be transferred and written out in full in the pocket notebook, the newspaper, magazine or scrap of paper being carefully preserved as the true record made at the time of observations.

Details required

At the start of a police officer's tour of duty, the officer should commence pocket book entries with the day and date in block capitals and this entry should be underlined. Whatever the entries which follow may illustrate, surnames should be written in capital letters so that they stand out when the entry is referred to. All matters of significance which occur during the tour of duty should be recorded and a note made of the time of occurrence or the time at which it was reported, or both. At the conclusion of the tour of duty, entries for the day should be finalised by the drawing of a continuous line across the page, immediately below the final entry.

It is essential to check force procedures in this respect as there are variations in requirements as to 'standard information' which should be recorded in pocket books. Many booklets and forms exist for immediate completion and the entries made within those documents become the officer's original entry which must be referred to when evidence is being given.

Omissions and errors

The pages of pocket notebook are numbered and a page should never be deliberately left blank. If a page is inadvertently left blank then a diagonal line should be drawn across the page from the top to the bottom and a note added indicating the reason why it was left blank, e.g. 'omitted in error'.

It would not be human to expect every entry to be free from mistakes, but no alterations or erasures should be made in a pocket notebook. If a mistake is made the offending word or words should be struck out neatly with a single line in such a way that the word or words can still be read and the deletion should be initialled. If the mistake is discovered before any further notes are made the correct words can then be substituted immediately after the entry, but where the mistake is followed by other notes, an asterisk should be made close to the struck-out words and repeated at the end of the entries, followed by the correction.

Collaboration by police officers in preparing notes

Where two or more police officers are present at the same interview, there is no objection to their consulting together when preparing their notes of the interview. However, as interviews which take place at police stations are now tape recorded, this is of less significance. Similarly, if two or more police officers have been keeping observations then collaboration may properly take place over the preparation of notes on the observations, but such notes must only reflect a genuine personal observation and recollection. In either case, where this is done the officers concerned should record in their pocket notebooks that such collaboration took place.

Off-duty note taking

It frequently occurs that a police officer is off duty when that officer sees something which is important, or the need for action arises. The officer will not be in possession of his pocket notebook on many of these occasions and will be compelled to make notes upon pieces of paper. The important factor to remember is that it is the notes made upon the pieces of paper which represent the primary evidence for production in court.

Any notes later made in a pocket notebook which are copied from, or are based upon these notes taken at the scene, are merely secondary evidence and are not admissible unless the court can be satisfied of good reason why the original notes cannot be produced. Original notes must be carefully preserved. It is good practice to pin such notes to the pages of the pocket notebook upon which copy entries have been made, unless otherwise instructed by a supervisory officer. Reports or statements should refer to the fact that such loose notes exist, and the manner of their preservation should be described. The originals must be taken to court in the event of a subsequent hearing. On occasions, orders require that the original notes be attached to the report.

Various forms of note taking

The form of note taking will vary with the nature of the incident but there are some general rules which assist.

Non-offence occurrence

The police are called upon to deal with such a variety of incidents that it would be impossible to compile a comprehensive list of notes which should be made covering every eventuality; however, there are certain basic details which must always be recorded. Where the incident is not connected with any offence but will later be the subject of a report, e.g. a person collapsing in the street because of a serious illness, notes on the following matters will provide the basic information for a subsequent report:

(a) Time, day and date.
(b) The exact place where the occurrence took place, giving the name of the street or road and the township or area, e.g. outside 21, High Street, Whitehaven.
(c) Details of the particular occurrence in narrative form.
(d) Identity of the person concerned, that is name, age (date of birth), occupation, address and telephone number where possible.
(e) Identity of any witness or informant including all of the particulars set out above. Details of witnesses should be obtained as soon as possible after an occurrence (otherwise a valuable witness may leave the scene before his identity can be established). Arrangements should be made for the taking of a statement if it cannot be taken then.
(f) Action taken by police officer. A brief but accurate account should be included of all action taken both at the scene and subsequently.
(g) Any other factors which need to be brought to the attention of supervisory officers.

Offence occurrence

Where an incident involves the commission of an offence or suspected offence, extra details will be needed covering the various points which it is necessary to prove for that offence. Although the following list is not designed to cover every type of offence, if these details are recorded correctly, together with the points to prove for the offence, they will provide the necessary data for any subsequent report:

(a) Time, day and date.
(b) The exact place where the offence took place, giving the name of the street or road or township or area.
(c) Abbreviated reference to the offence, that is, a description of the offence.
(d) The exact reply made by the offender, in direct speech, after the caution has been given in accordance with the Code of Practice. This should be recorded in capital letters for ease of reference at a later stage.

(e) Name, age (date of birth), occupation and address of the offender. If the offender is a child or young person, the name of the school which the offender attends, or last attended, should also be obtained together with the full name of the parent, or guardian where appropriate. If the offender is a commercial company, the full name of the company and the address of that company should be obtained together with the name of the company secretary.

(f) Details of any article connected with the offence, e.g. the make, model and registered number of any motor vehicle involved.

(g) Documents produced which relate to an offence disclosed or if they are required for any other purpose, e.g. driving licence, excise licence, certificate of insurance or test certificate.

(h) Note, using block capitals, any reply made by the offender when told that he will be reported for the offence. This should be noted in direct speech. The Code of Practice states that it is not necessary to give or repeat a caution when informing a person who is not under arrest of the possibility of prosecution for an offence. If already cautioned when the offence was pointed out, do not repeat the caution.

(i) Name and full particulars of any witness or the complainant in appropriate circumstances. This is extremely important in offence-based incidents as the evidence of such witnesses is likely to be essential to proving aspects of the offence. If the offence is of a sexual nature, it is important to note the condition, appearance and general demeanour of the complainant.

(j) A final entry in narrative form describing what the officer saw, heard or did, including all of the relevant facts which will be required in evidence.

Arrest occurrence

The record made of an arrest is very similar in character to that made in relation to an offence, which is not surprising since most arrests will be in respect of offences. However, there are certain additional factors to be taken into account. The reason for the arrest must be explained to the offender, who must be cautioned in accordance with the Code of Practice if the arrest is to be lawful. This process should be carefully recorded, for example, 'I said to him, "I AM ARRESTING YOU FOR STEALING MONEY FROM A GAS METER AT A HOUSE AT 10, HIGH STREET", I cautioned him and he replied, "NOT ME"'.

It is recognised that entries will not be made at the time of effecting an arrest as it will be neither practical nor sensible to try to do so. The entries should be made as soon as practicable. When prisoners have been taken to a police station following an arrest, the time of arrival at the police station should be recorded.

Lost and found property

Obligations and duties

There is no statutory duty imposed on a person to report to the police the finding of any property, or on the police to record and deal with lost or found property, but by custom the police have become the central agency for dealing with such property. It is the duty of the police to keep accurate records of all reports of property lost and found and to ensure that property coming into their possession is stored safely. For these purposes lost and found property registers are maintained by the police.

The owner of property always retains the best claim to it; the finder has the next best claim. A finder, although not required by law to hand over found property to the police, is under a duty to take steps to trace or contact the owner where this is possible. If this is not done, there is an exposure to allegations of theft.

Report of lost property

Where a police officer in the street receives a report that property has been lost, the officer should, at the time, enter in the pocket notebook the time, date and place the report was received, the name and address of the person making the report and a detailed description of the property, including any identifying means. If the lost property is likely to cause danger – for example, controlled drugs, firearms or explosives – then the station should be informed immediately; in any other case a report will be made when the officer returns to the station. If the substance is dangerous, the officer in charge of the station will consider circulation of details and notification to the Police National Computer (PNC).

Where the report is received at the station, or where a police officer has received a report in the street and has returned to the station, the above details will be entered in the lost property register. An examination should be made of the entries in the found property register for any record of the property having been reported as found. The person reporting the loss, whether in the street or at the station, should be asked to inform the police if the missing property is subsequently found.

Where a report is received in one police area relating to property lost in another police area, the officer should record the required details as described above and, in addition, a message containing the recorded details should be sent to the police area concerned. The lost property register should be endorsed to show the action taken.

Where lost property is found and restored to the owner, the entry in the lost property register should be endorsed accordingly. If the property comes into the possession of the police and it is returned to the loser by the police it should be treated as found property and the entries in the found property register and the lost property register should be cross-referenced.

Report of found property

When a report of found property is made to a police officer in the street, the officer should, at the time, enter in the pocket notebook the time, date and place the report was received, the name and address of the finder and the time, date and place found. A full description of the property should be entered in the pocket notebook in the presence of the finder. Particulars of any money or valuables should be carefully noted.

When describing valuable articles, precise descriptions should be avoided. It is better to describe an article as gold-coloured than as gold, and stones as stones of a particular colour, rather than as diamonds, etc. Once an article has been recorded as consisting of a precious metal or as containing precious stones, that is what an auditor would expect to find when found property is inspected.

Sealed pay packets or similar containers apparently containing money or other valuables should be opened in the presence of the finder so that the contents may be verified. If the finder does not wish to retain the property, that person should be asked to sign the entry in the pocket notebook. On return to the police station, the officer will immediately record the details of the finding, etc., in the found property register. If the property is retained by the finder a note is made of the address at which the property is being kept.

Keys, cheques, firearms, ammunition or any other form of explosive are not, of course, returned to a finder; nor are gambling instruments, hypodermic syringes, medicines, tablets or weapons of any kind. Official documents which have been found and handed to the police should be forwarded to the appropriate authority and not returned to individual losers.

If letters, including registered, recorded or express letters, or bundles of letters or parcels are found which, although they appear to have passed through the post, do not seem to have reached the addresses, they should be deposited immediately at the police station. This course should also be adopted if a mail bag containing letters is handed in as found property. Unopened letters, whether stamped or otherwise, which have not been through the post, should, in the absence of any suspicious circumstances, be posted by the police officer who finds the letters or by the police officer to whom they are handed, and such action should be reported and recorded at the police station in the normal way.

Where the found property consists of perishable articles, the general police practice is to sell the property and retain the proceeds for the owner. If no claimant comes along, the proceeds of the sale may be paid to the finder after the lapse of the appropriate period, usually 3 months, although this may vary according to local procedures.

Property in public transport

Where a person finds property in a public service vehicle, there is a legal requirement to hand it over immediately to the conductor or, if there is no conductor, to the driver or operator's representative. The property is then deposited with the operator of the public service vehicle.

If a police officer is called to a case where a person has lost property on a public service vehicle and has claimed the property from the conductor or driver before either has deposited it with the operator, the driver or conductor should be told that there is a requirement to restore the property to the loser, without fee, if the loser can give satisfactory proof of ownership of the property.

Particulars of found property must be recorded by the operator and made available for inspection by the police and traffic examiners at reasonable times. Unclaimed property vests in the operator after 3 months. Perishable goods found in public service vehicles may be destroyed by the operator or sold after 48 hours. Property found on railway property must be handed to the railway company and that found in public hackney carriages to the driver.

Property found by police officers

Property found by police officers must be handed in at the police station. A police officer finding property is not allowed to receive either the unclaimed property or the proceeds from the sale of such property. If the property is not claimed after the lapse of the appropriate period, the property is sold and the proceeds are credited to official funds.

Restitution of property to loser

When a person claims property that has been found and handed to the police, the officer dealing with the matter should satisfy himself that the person claiming the property is the owner before handing the property over. A receipt should be obtained when the property is handed over, and the finder should be notified that the property has been returned to the owner. The name and address of the finder may be given to the owner.

Where the property has been retained by the finder, the name and address of the finder may be given to a person claiming the property who should be asked to notify the police if the property is identified and restored to him. This will enable the lost property and found property registers to be endorsed accordingly.

Restitution of property to finder

If found property is not claimed after the prescribed period has elapsed, which varies according to local procedure, it may be restored to the finder against his signature on a receipt and the found property register should be endorsed accordingly. If the finder does not want the property it may be disposed of by the police, by auction if the property is of any value, or destruction if worthless. Property found by a police officer is not returned to the police officer although there is nothing to prevent the purchase of the property where it is sold by auction.

Treasure Act 1996

This act deals with property which may be described as 'treasure', that is, an object at least 300 years old when found and, if not a coin, has a metallic content of which at least 10 per cent is precious metal, and if a coin, is either one of at least two having that percentage of precious metal, or is one of at least 10 coins found at that time. Such property belongs to the holder of the franchise, if there is one (person to whom a right has been granted by a public authority), and otherwise to the Crown, unless some other ownership can be proved.

The Treasure (Designation) Order 2002 extended the meaning of 'treasure' to include two classes of objects as being of outstanding historical, archaeological or cultural importance. The first class of object is one of at least two base metal objects (other than coins), from the same find which are of prehistoric date. The second class of object is any object (other than a coin) of prehistoric date, any part of which is gold or silver.

Computer misuse and data protection

Computer misuse

The misuse of computers is a common occurrence. So much valuable, confidential information is now stored electronically that some of best minds are applied to procedures whereby such information can be accessed. There is a lot of legislation which is aimed at those who 'steal' information which is stored on a computer. This legislation is concerned with those who do so for a commercial or ideological purpose. The industrial 'spy' is now well established. Information which might be described as 'secret' is a target not only for those whom we might describe as 'spies', but also for those who see access as a challenge. However, there are additional problems and these are associated with the fact that confidential information is stored in most computers which are available to employees of organisations in both the public and private sectors. The misuse of such computers is controlled by the Computer Misuse Act.

The misuse of computer hardware or software may involve one or more of three offences under the Computer Misuse Act 1990:

(a) unauthorised access to computer material;
(b) unauthorised access with intent to commit or facilitate commission of a further offence;
(c) unauthorised modification of computer material.

Unauthorised access to computer material

By s 1(1) of the 1990 Act, a person commits an offence if:

(a) that person causes a computer to perform any function with intent to secure access to any program or data held in the computer;
(b) the access that person intends to secure is unauthorised; and
(c) that person knows at the time when he causes the computer to perform the function that that is the case.

The intended access need not relate to any particular program or data or any particular type of program or data, or to a program or data held in any particular computer. It is immaterial whether the program or data is unauthorisedly accessed directly from the computer containing them or indirectly via another computer.

The scope of this offence is wide, since it covers all forms of computer hacking. Indeed, actual access to any program or data held in a computer is not required, since it is enough that the accused simply causes a computer to perform a function with intent to secure access to a program or data held in it, that intended access being unauthorised to his knowledge.

Access to a program or data is secured by a person if, by causing a computer to perform any function, he:

(a) alters or erases the program or data;
(b) copies or moves it to any storage medium other than that in which it is held or to a different location in the storage medium in which it is held;
(c) uses it; or
(d) has it output from the computer in which it is held (whether by having it displayed or in any other manner).

Intent to secure access to a program or data is to be understood accordingly.

Despite its width, the offence does not cover computer eavesdropping; mere surveillance of data displayed on a VDU is not enough since the accused must cause the computer to perform a function if the accused is to be guilty.

In relation to the requirement that the intended access to any program or data held in a computer must be unauthorised, access of any kind by a person is unauthorised if the person is not entitled to *control* access of the kind in question to the program or data *and* he does not have consent to such access from any person who is so entitled. Thus all hackers, honest or dishonest, are caught; it does not matter that the accused was seeking access merely out of curiosity or for the challenge and excitement of breaking through a security system designed to restrict access. It is important to stress that access by a person is only authorised where there is appropriate entitlement or consent to access of the kind in question to the program or data. Access by a person entitled to control access of the kind in question is not unauthorised even though he accesses the program or data for an unauthorised purpose.

Unauthorised access with intent

By s 2(1) of the 1990 Act, a person commits an arrestable offence if he commits the unauthorised access offence under s 1 with intent:

(a) to commit an offence to which this section applies; or
(b) to facilitate the commission of such an offence (whether by himself or by any other person).

Section 2 applies to any offence where sentence is fixed by law (e.g. murder) or for which an offender of 21 years or over may be sentenced to imprisonment for 5 years (18 will be substituted when an amendment in the Criminal Justice and Court Services Act 2000 is in force) (e.g. the various deception offences under the Theft Acts, theft, forgery and criminal damage).

It is immaterial whether the further offence is to be committed on the same occasion as the unauthorised access offence or on any future occasion, and it is also immaterial that the facts are such that the commission of the further offence is impossible.

Unauthorised modification of computer material

By s 3(1) of the 1990 Act, a person is guilty of an arrestable offence if:

(a) he does any act which causes an unauthorised modification of the contents of any computer; and
(b) at the time at which he does the act he has the requisite intent and the requisite knowledge.

A modification of the contents of a computer takes place if, by the operation of any function of the computer concerned or any other computer, any program or data held in the computer are altered or erased, or any program or data are added to its contents. Thus, the offence can be committed in a variety of ways, for example by the addition or deletion of material contained in a computer or software held in a computer or by interfering with a computer or software by introducing a computer virus by means of an infected disc or some other means. Any act which contributes towards causing a modification is regarded as causing it.

A modification is unauthorised if the person whose act causes it is not entitled to determine whether it should be made and he does not have consent to the modification from anyone who is so entitled.

The 'requisite intent' is an intent to cause a modification of the content of a computer and by so doing to impair its operation, or to prevent or hinder access to any program or data held in it or to impair the operation of any such program or the reliability of any such data. An example would be where someone, by misusing or bypassing a password, places in the files of a computer a bogus e-mail pretending that the password holder was the author, since an addition would result in an unauthorised modification of the contents of the computer and would clearly be done with intent to cause such modification and by so doing to impair the reliability of the data in the computer. The intent need not be directed at any particular computer program or data, or a particular kind of program or data, or at any particular modification or particular kind of modification.

The 'requisite knowledge' is knowledge that any modification which the accused intends to cause is unauthorised.

It is immaterial whether an unauthorised modification or any intended effect of it is, or is intended to be, permanent or merely temporary.

Data Protection Act 1998

The 1998 Act is concerned with the regulation of processing of information relating to individuals, including the obtaining, holding, use or disclosure of such information.

Principles

Unless exempted by the provisions of the Act, a 'data controller' is obliged to comply with certain 'data protection principles' in relation to all 'personal data' in relation to which he is data controller. A 'data controller' is a person who (alone or jointly or in common with others) determines the purposes for which and the way in which any personal data are, or are to be, processed. It follows that each chief constable is a data controller.

The 'data protection principles' are:

1. Personal data shall be processed fairly and lawfully and, in particular, shall not be processed unless:
   (a) the data subject has given his consent, or the processing is required by law, or is necessary in the interests of the administration of justice, or in certain other cases; and
   (b) in the case of 'sensitive personal data' [e.g. an individual's racial origin, his political or religious belief, his health or his commission (or alleged commission) of an offence], the data subject has given his explicit consent or the processing is necessary for the data controller to exercise or perform any right or duty imposed by law on the controller in connection with employment, or the processing is necessary in the interests of justice, or in certain other cases.
   This principle does not usually apply to the processing of personal data for the purpose of preventing or detecting crime.
2. Personal data shall be obtained only for one or more specified and lawful purposes, and shall not be further processed in any manner incompatible with that purpose or those purposes.

3. Personal data shall be adequate, relevant and not excessive in relation to the purpose or purposes for which they are processed.
4. Personal data shall be accurate and, where necessary, kept up to date.
5. Personal data processed for any purpose or purposes shall not be kept longer than is necessary for that purpose or those purposes.
6. Personal data shall be processed in accordance with the rights of data subjects under the Data Protection Act 1998.
7. Appropriate technical and organisational measures shall be taken against unauthorised or unlawful processing of personal data and against accidental loss or destruction of, or damage to, personal data.
8. Personal data shall not be transferred to a country or territory outside the European Economic Area unless that country or territory ensures an adequate level of protection for the rights and freedoms of data subjects in relation to the processing of personal data.

'Data' means information which:

(a) is being processed by means of equipment operating automatically in response to instructions given for that purpose;
(b) is recorded with the intention that it should be processed by means of such equipment;
(c) is recorded as part of a relevant filing system or with the intention that it should form part of a relevant filing system; or
(d) does not fall within paragraphs (a), (b) or (c) but forms part of an educational, health or public record of a prescribed type.

'Personal data' means data which relate to a living individual who can be identified:

(a) from those data or
(b) from those data and other information which is in the possession of, or is likely to come into the possession of, the data controller.

It includes any expression of opinion about the individual and any indication of the intentions of the data controller or any other person in respect of the individual.

Registration

'Data controllers' must register with the Data Protection Commissioner in order for personal data to be processed if the data fall within type (a) or (b) above, but not (normally) in the case of the other types of data. Thus, the manual files retained within command and control systems do not require registration, but data stored on the Police National Computer do.

By s 21(1) of the 1998 Act, it is an offence to process personal data unless an entry in respect of that data controller has been registered.

Unlawful obtaining, etc., of personal data

Section 55(1) of the 1998 Act provides that a person must not knowingly or recklessly, without the consent of the data controller:

(a) obtain or disclose personal data or the information contained in personal data or

(b) procure the disclosure to another person of the information contained in personal data.

Breach of s 55(1) is an offence.

Section 55(1) does not apply to a person who shows:

(a) interest that the obtaining, disclosing or procuring
   (i) was necessary for the purpose of preventing or detecting crime (as where the data are passed from one police force to another for this purpose) or
   (ii) was required or authorised by or under any enactment, by any rule of law or by the order of a court;
(b) that he acted in the reasonable belief that he had in law the right to obtain or disclose the data or information or, as the case may be, to procure the disclosure of the information to the other person;
(c) that he acted in the reasonable belief that he would have had the consent of the data controller if the data controller had known of the obtaining, disclosing or procuring and the circumstances of it; or
(d) that in the particular circumstances the obtaining, disclosing or procuring was justified as being in the public interest.

By s 55(3), a person who sells personal data is guilty of an offence if he obtained the data in contravention of s 55(1). Section 55(4) provides that a person who offers to sell personal data commits an offence they have been obtained in contravention of s 55(1) or if subsequently so obtained.

Prohibition of requirement as to production of certain records

Section 56(1) of the 1998 Act provides that a person must not, in connection with:

(a) the recruitment of another person as an employee;
(b) the continued employment of another person; or
(c) any contract for the provision of services by another person,

require that other person or a third party to supply a relevant record or to produce a relevant record.

Likewise, s 56(2) provides that a person concerned with the provision (for payment or not) of goods, facilities or services to the public or a section of the public must not, as a condition of providing or offering to provide any goods, facilities or services to another person, require that other person or a third party to supply a relevant record or to produce a relevant record to him.

Breach of either of these provisions is an offence.

A 'relevant record' in these provisions includes any record of a conviction or caution obtained by a data subject from a data controller who is a chief officer of police or the Director General of the National Crime Intelligence Service or National Crime Squad.

Sections 56(1) and (2) do not apply to a person who shows:

(a) that the imposition of the requirement was required or authorised by or under any enactment, by any rule of law or by the order of a court; or
(b) that in the particular circumstances the imposition of the requirement was justified as being in the public interest (which it will not be if the alleged justification is that it would assist in the prevention or detection of crime; in such a case a certificate of criminal record will be available from the Criminal Records Agency).

Section 56 is the only section of the 1998 Act still to be brought into force. It is associated with ss 112, 113 and 115 of the Police Act 1997 (which provide for the issue by the Secretary of State of criminal conviction certificates, criminal record certificates and enhanced criminal record certificates). Provision has now been made in respect of such certificates and the introduction of s 56 should soon follow.

Police Regulations and conditions of service

Governing legislation

The Police Act 1996 s 50 empowers the Home Secretary to make regulations in respect of police officers. The Police Regulations 1995 deal with the organisation of police forces, the appointment, promotion, retirement, personal records, duty, overtime, leave, allowances, housing, uniform and equipment and pay of police officers. Discipline within the service is dealt with by the Police (Conduct) Regulations 1999 and, to some extent, by the Police (Efficiency) Regulations 1999. The main areas with which we are concerned are:

(a) conditions of service;
(b) promotion;
(c) discipline.

Disciplinary matters are dealt with in a later section of this book.

Conditions of service

We shall examine the following matters which are included in Police Regulations.

Restrictions on the private lives of members

It may, at first consideration, appear to be unfair that citizens who are appointed as constables and swear to uphold the peace should be subjected to additional restrictions upon their private lives. We tend to divorce our work from our home life and to think of them as separate matters. The labour organisations guarding the interests of workers in other fields would be unlikely to accept the idea of rules restricting, in any way, the private lives of their members, but it is important to recognise the unique position of a police constable.

The Police Regulations state that a constable shall at all times abstain from any activity which is likely to interfere with the impartial discharge of his duties, or which is likely to give rise to the impression among members of the public that it may so interfere. The importance of public confidence in the police is emphasised by the final words of this sentence within which it is made clear that nothing must be undertaken which suggests that a police officer may owe a certain allegiance to any section of society. If a constable was known to be working in the evenings as a steward in the local golf club, members of the public, knowing that in that capacity he was a servant of the members of the club, must doubt that constable's willingness to enforce the law in circumstances involving one of the members.

It is therefore not surprising to find that regulations also control a police officer's involvement in business, the term 'business interest' being so widely defined as to include any employment for hire or gain outside the police service which is not compatible with the office of constable, unless the previous consent of the appropriate chief officer of police has been gained. This regulation also applies to any shop or like business which is kept or carried on by a constable's spouse (not being separated from him) at any premises within the police area, or by any relative included in the family, at the premises where he resides as any business interests in which they were involved which were not compatible with a police officer's duties could be seen to have a similar effect upon the officer's willingness to discharge duties impartially. In particular, the regulation prohibits the constable or spouse (not being separated from him) or any relative in the family living with him, from holding a liquor licence, licences and permits associated with betting and gaming or places of public entertainment, or holding a pecuniary interest in any such licence or permit. It is apparent, without the necessity for regulations to repeat it, that it is undesirable for police officers or their families to be responsible for the conduct of betting offices, public houses, night clubs and dance halls. These are some of the establishments in which breaches of the law are likely to take place from time to time, and it is inconceivable that a police officer should be directly connected with them. Although the regulation also includes a shop within the area of the police force in which the officer is serving, it is unlikely that a chief officer of police would refuse permission for an officer's husband or wife to open a shop which dealt with standard commodities, provided that the officer concerned did not intend to identify himself or herself with it. It would be embarrassing to sell goods to a customer on one day and to report that person for an offence on the following day. The purpose of such regulations is not to prevent police officers or their families from having other interests, but rather to ensure that their impartiality can never be questioned.

When a chief officer of police receives written notice of an intention to acquire a business interest, he must determine whether it is compatible with service as a constable and, within 28 days, notify the constable of the decision. Within 10 days of that notification (or such longer period as the police authority may allow) the constable may appeal to the police authority by written notice. On receipt of such notice the police authority must require the chief officer of police to provide it with a notice within 10 days setting out the reasons for refusal, together with any documents which are relied upon in support of the decision. The police authority must send copies of the notice and documents to the constable and afford a reasonable time (not less than 14 days) to comment. Within 28 days of receipt of such comments, the police authority must determine the appeal. If they support refusal, a further appeal lies to the Secretary of State.

Active participation in politics is prohibited absolutely, although this does not preclude police officers from exercising their democratic right to vote at elections. Successive governments have always taken care to avoid legislation which suggested, even to the smallest degree, that police officers were subject to the dictates of central government or any political party temporarily in power. If police officers were to be seen adding vocal support at political meetings, the public could not be blamed for becoming alarmed at the significance. At times of industrial unrest, officers must be particularly careful to avoid identification with either side involved in the dispute, otherwise they will be accused of political bias.

Further restrictions with which we are concerned relate to a police officer's place of residence. The areas policed by most forces are considerable and it is the duty of a chief officer of police to ensure that all parts of the force area are efficiently policed. It is therefore essential that there is some control over the place at which a police officer shall live. In consequence, police officers were provided with free accommodation some years ago, or were granted an allowance if they were owner-occupiers of residential property or had rented property on their own behalf. The practice of providing such an allowance has now been discontinued in respect of new entrants to the service but an allowance to assist in relation to house purchase is payable in some forces, predominantly in the south east. It is therefore understandable that a police officer must obtain the approval of the chief officer of police as to his or her place of residence. In addition, an officer must not, without the previous consent of the chief officer of police, receive a lodger in a house or quarters which is provided by the police authority, nor must he sub-let any part of the premises. The situation is slightly different if the officer owns the house in which a lodger is received, or sub-lets part of the property; in such a case *written notice* must be given to the chief officer before doing so. This allows the chief officer to make any adjustment to the allowance payable in respect of the property which recognises such an arrangement.

The final requirement is that a police officer shall not wilfully refuse or neglect to discharge any lawful debt. This part of the regulations was not intended to discourage police officers from obtaining advances from building societies or buying motor cars or house furnishings under hire purchase agreements. The intention is to prevent officers from incurring debts with local individuals who will then be in a position to exert some influence over them in the discharge of their duties, particularly if they are not in a position to clear the debt at the time.

Although not representing a 'restriction', Police Regulations provide that every member of a police force must, on appointment, have a sample of hair or saliva taken. Such a specimen must be kept separate from specimens obtained under the provisions of the Police and Criminal Evidence Act 1984 (PACE), s 63, and must be destroyed when the officer leaves the service.

Sick leave

It is essential that force areas are efficiently policed for 24 hours each day. The right to strike has always been denied to the police service as the public have a right to expect to be protected from the criminal section of society at all times. In the same way, steps have been taken to ensure that unnecessary absences from duty are prevented by requiring that all such absences are supported by a medical certificate.

All police authorities have taken advantage of the provisions of Police Regulations which permit them to consent to absence of not more than 7 days on any one occasion without a medical certificate. The Regulations make provision for a medical practitioner appointed or approved by the police authority to examine a police officer who is absent and in respect of whom a medical certificate is in force. If it is considered that the officer is fit for duty, with the consent of the medical practitioner who issued the certificate, a third doctor may examine the officer within 28 days of the difference of opinion occurring. If the third medical practitioner considers the officer fit for duty, he must return to duty. Police forces now maintain detailed records of absences through sickness so that procedures may be fashioned to meet existing circumstances.

Police Regulations also impose limits upon the time which a police officer may continue on full salary while on sick leave.

Personal records

In any efficient organisation, it is essential that up-to-date records of employees are kept. Police Regulations require that such records be kept containing a constable's personal particulars together with details of service. This will include place and date of birth, particulars of any marriage or children, military service or service in another force and passes or failures in qualifying examinations for promotion. When an officer, for example, is being considered for promotion to a higher rank, details of previous promotions, the stations and departments in which he has served, his commendations by a chief officer or officers of courts of law, together with records of any punishments awarded under discipline regulations, must be readily available. A member of a police force is entitled, on request, to inspect a personal record. Punishments of a fine or reprimand shall be expunged after 3 years free of punishment other than a caution, or 5 years in other cases.

Probationary period and discharge of a probationer

A police constable is on probation for the first 2 years of service in a police force or for a longer period, not exceeding 12 months, where, in the opinion of the chief officer of police, the period of probation was seriously interrupted by a period of absence from duty by reason of injury or illness. Probation may also be extended by the chief officer of police for other reasons, but this must be with the consent of the Secretary of State. The power to extend a constable's period of probation may be delegated to an assistant chief constable, but a decision to dispense with the services of a probationer constable should only be taken by the chief officer himself. If an officer transfers from one force to another and has already successfully completed a probationary period in the first force, that officer may not be required to undergo probationary service once again. There are other exceptions to the rule which can be exercised at the discretion of a chief officer of police, but the basic principle is that a constable in one way or another must undergo a full term of probationary service at the commencement of his police career.

This requirement is not surprising as it is impossible to determine, with certainty, that an applicant will be suited to a career in a police force on appointment to the office of constable. The police service is a disciplined service but peculiar in that the discipline required from individuals is mainly a self-discipline. The job is demanding. A constable patrols alone at all hours of the day and night, he is required to deal with distressing situations which can have some effect upon the individual, and there is a requirement to enforce laws which are not always popular with members of the public. It is therefore necessary to have a period during which a fair assessment can be made of suitability to hold the office of constable.

At any time during this probationary period a constable can be discharged if the chief officer considers that he is not fit mentally or physically to perform the duties of the office, or is not likely to become an efficient or well-conducted officer. By using the term 'mentally' it is not suggested that the officer is found to be of low IQ or unstable, but, as described above, the office of constable makes high demands upon men and women and not all are mentally equipped to hold such office. It can also be appreciated that the outdoor nature of police work demands some physical endurance, caused by changing tours of duty, peculiar hours of work and the typical British winter season.

A constable whose services are dispensed with under these provisions may give notice to the police authority of an intention to retire. If this is done before the date upon which his services are to be dispensed with, he shall not be considered to have had his services dispensed with under these provisions.

A chief constable does not have an absolute discretion to dismiss a probationer constable at will. The action must be fair and in accordance with the rules of natural justice and must give the probationer constable an opportunity to offer any explanation or defence. In addition, it is only the chief constable, or an assistant commissioner in the case of the Metropolitan Police, who can so dismiss; this function cannot be delegated to an assistant chief constable. The enquiry into the issue need not be conducted by the chief constable, who can delegate administrative matters, but the decision must be that of the chief constable alone.

Where a chief constable is considering dispensing with the services of a probationer constable under these regulations, the probationer constable must be shown any report containing judgements and opinions on the probationer. If the allegations amount to a disciplinary offence the probationer must be charged and a disciplinary hearing held.

Qualification for promotion

Matters concerning promotion are dealt with by the Police (Promotion) Regulations 1996. These regulations are fairly brief and deal with qualification, selection, probationary service in the rank of sergeant, temporary promotion and promotion of officers selected to take part in the high potential development scheme which was introduced in April 2002. This scheme will allow police officers participating in it to be promoted to the ranks of sergeant, inspector and chief inspector as soon as their chief officer of police determines that they are competent to carry out the duties of those ranks. Such promotions may take place whether or not there is a vacancy in the rank concerned and do not affect any existing or subsequent vacancy unless the person promoted is designated to fill it. Sergeants participating in this scheme may be promoted to inspector after only 1 year's service in the rank of sergeant.

The regulations require that to be qualified for promotion to the rank of sergeant, a constable must have passed the qualifying examination for promotion to the rank of sergeant, have completed 2 years' service and have completed probationary service, and that sergeants, similarly, must have passed the sergeant's qualifying examination for promotion to the rank of inspector and have completed 2 years' service in the rank of sergeant. Having been promoted to the rank of inspector, there are no further qualifying examinations to be undertaken before being advanced to higher rank, nor are there minimum periods of service laid down to be completed within any rank. Further promotion is by selection. Chief officers of police are usually assisted in this task by appraisal reports submitted by supervisory officers and the observations of members of interview boards set up by the chief officers for the purpose.

The Police (Promotion) Regulations prescribe two-part examinations, the first a written paper and the second a practical test. A constable who will before 1 December in any year have completed probationary service is eligible to take the first part of the examination. A member of a police force who on 1 July in any year holds the rank of sergeant (other than on temporary promotion under reg. 6) is eligible to take the first part of the qualifying examination for promotion to the rank of inspector. Officers who fail Part I in the year immediately preceding are not eligible to sit within the following year without leave of the examinations board. Part II of the examinations may not be taken before Part I has been passed and must be taken within 12 months of the pass in Part I unless the Board specifically permits it to be taken outside that time. Candidates who successfully complete the Part I examination will be permitted three attempts to pass Part II but, if unsuccessful, must then re-sit Part I.

Passes in examinations taken prior to the establishment of the current system remain valid.

The content, form, pass mark and assessment criteria for each of the examinations are a matter for consideration by the Police Promotion Examinations Board. The Board is appointed by the Home Secretary and includes persons of suitable academic standing, a Home Office representative, representatives from police authorities, local government management board (which has undertaken the administrative arrangements in respect of the examinations), one of HM Inspectors of Constabulary, a representative from the Metropolitan Police and representatives from the ranks of the chief officers, superintendents and the federated ranks.

A member of a police force who is promoted to the rank of sergeant shall be on probation in that rank for a period of 1 year or for such longer period as the chief officer of police determines in the circumstances of a particular case and may be reduced to the rank of constable at any time during the period of probation if the chief officer of police considers that the officer is not likely to perform satisfactorily the duties of a sergeant. This regulation merely provides an opportunity to examine an officer's potential to lead and direct people in an operational setting before confirming the rank.

Complaints against the police

Police complaints and discipline

The foundations of the system

These procedures, at the time of going to press, are dealt with by the Police Act 1996, the Police (Conduct) Regulations 1999 and the Police (Efficiency) Regulations 1999. However, changes are proposed within the Police Reform Act 2002, the relevant provisions of which are expected to be brought into force on 1 April 2004, shortly after this edition was published. The provisions set out below are therefore those of the new system brought into being by the Police Reform Act 2002 and readers should be aware that the old system may still be in force for a short period following publication.

The Police Reform Act 2002 established a body corporate known as 'the Independent Police Complaints Commission', which has wider powers than the Police Complaints Authority that it replaces. The investigation of many complaints may continue to be carried out by police forces but those investigations may be carried out by a person serving with the police (of the force concerned or any other force), the National Crime Intelligence Service or the National Crime Squad. There is no requirement that the investigator must be a police officer. In addition, the Commission is empowered to carry out its own investigation of complaints and to supervise or manage other investigations. Section 9 of the Act of 2002 has been brought into force to permit the setting up of the Commission.

The functions of the Commission include the maintenance by the Commission itself, and by police authorities and chief officers, of suitable arrangements for the handling of complaints about the conduct of persons serving with the police, the recording of those complaints and the manner of their investigation. The Commission is required to enter into arrangements with the chief inspector of constabulary for the purpose of securing co-operation between the Commission and the Inspectorate. However, the 2002 Act does not confer any function on the Commission in relation to any part of a complaint or conduct matter which relates to the direction and control of a police force by a chief officer of police.

The Commission is required to make an annual report to the Secretary of State, copies being sent to police authorities and service authorities (e.g. National Crime Intelligence Service and National Crime Squad).

Under s 19, an order may be made by the Home Secretary authorising the use of directed or intrusive surveillance and the conduct and use of covert human intelligence sources to assist the Commission in carrying out its functions.

Complaints

The Independent Police Complaints Commission and complaints generally

Section 9 of and Schedules 2 and 3 to the Police Reform Act 2002 deal with the constitution of a body corporate known as 'the Independent Police Complaints Commission' (hereafter 'the Commission'), which consists of a chairman (who is appointed by the Queen) and not less than 10 other members (who are appointed by the Home Secretary). The Home Secretary may appoint not more than two deputy chairmen from the membership. These appointments are for a maximum period of 5 years at a time.

The Home Secretary may remove these members from office for various reasons. With the consent of the Home Secretary, the Commission may set up regional offices in any part of England and Wales.

The rules below apply whatever the rank of the officer against whom the complaint is made. As will be seen, various functions relating to complaints are carried out by the 'appropriate authority'. The 'appropriate authority is the chief officer of police of the officer, etc., who is subject to the complaint. Where a complaint relates to the chief officer, the police authority is the appropriate authority.

Handling of complaints

Schedule 3, Part I, to the Police Reform Act 2002 requires that, where a complaint about the conduct of a person serving under his direction or control is submitted to a chief officer of police, or that chief officer becomes aware that such a complaint has been made to the Commission or to a police authority, he must take, as soon as is reasonably practicable, any steps that appear to be desirable for the purpose of obtaining or preserving evidence relating to the conduct complained of. The term 'a person serving under control and direction' includes members of a police force, police authority employees under the direction and control of a chief officer and special constables.

Section 12 of the Act of 2002 provides that a 'complaint' is any complaint about the conduct of a person serving with the police which is made (whether in writing or otherwise) by:

(a) a member of the public who claims to be the person in relation to whom the conduct took place;
(b) any other member of the public who claims to have been adversely affected by the conduct;
(c) a member of the public who claims to have witnessed the conduct;
(d) a person acting on behalf of such persons in categories (a) to (c) above.

However, there is no 'complaint' where an allegation is made *by or on behalf* of a person who claims to have been adversely affected only as a result of having seen or heard the conduct or any of its alleged effects, unless it was only because that person was physically present, or sufficiently nearby, when the conduct took place or the effects occurred that it was possible to see or hear the conduct or its effects, or unless the adverse effect is attributable to, or was aggravated by, the fact that the person in relation to whom the conduct took place was already known to the person claiming to have suffered the adverse effect. A person is taken to have witnessed conduct only if knowledge was acquired in a manner which would make him a competent witness capable of giving admissible evidence, or if he has in possession or under control anything which would constitute admissible evidence.

In order to be authorised for the purposes of (d), to act on behalf of another, a person must be either designated by the Commission as a person through whom a complaint may be made, or a person who has been authorised in writing by the person on behalf of whom that person is acting.

Initial handling and recording of complaints

Where a complaint is made to the Commission, it must determine whether the complainant consents to the police authority or appropriate chief officer being notified;

if this is so, it must give that notification. Where no consent is given, but the Commission believes that it is in the public interest for the subject matter of the complaint to be brought to the attention of the appropriate authority and recorded, the Commission may bring the matter to the attention of the appropriate authority as if it were a 'recordable conduct matter' (as to which term, see page 27); where this is done the provisions of Schedule 3 have effect as if it were such a matter.

When it receives a complaint about a police officer, etc., a police authority must notify the chief officer who is 'the appropriate authority' in relation to the officer, etc., against whom the complaint was made. A chief officer must do likewise in respect of a complaint for which he is not the appropriate authority. Where notification of a complaint is given to an appropriate authority, the person who gave the notification or, as the case may be, the Commission, must notify the complainant. If the chief officer determines that he is not the appropriate authority, because the complaint relates to an officer in another force or to a senior officer, he must notify the 'appropriate authority' and inform the complainant that this has been done.

Schedule 3 provides that if a chief officer determines that he is the appropriate authority in relation to a complaint, or if notified that is so, he must record the complaint. However, a complaint need not be recorded where the subject matter of the complaint has been, or is already being, dealt with by means of criminal or disciplinary proceedings or the complaint has been withdrawn.

Non-notification or recording of a complaint

Where a complaint has been received by, or notified to, an appropriate authority and the authority decides to take no action in relation to recording it, or notifying the appropriate authority, it must notify the complainant of the decision, the grounds for reaching it and the complainant's right of appeal. The complainant has a right of appeal to the Commission against that decision. The Commission must decide whether action should have been taken and, if it thinks that it should, give directions to the appropriate authority, which is bound to comply with such directions. All parties must be notified. Regulations may be made governing the procedures to be followed.

Reference of complaints to the Commission

A complaint must be referred to the commission if:

(a) it alleges that the conduct complained of has resulted in death or serious injury;
(b) it is of a description specified in regulations; or
(c) the Commission notifies the appropriate authority that it requires it to be referred to it for consideration.

In cases other than those in which reference is mandatory, an appropriate authority may refer a complaint to the Commission if it considers that it would be appropriate to do so in view of the gravity of the subject matter or other exceptional circumstances. Such references may be made regardless of the fact that the complaint is already been considered by the Commission. Such action must be notified to the complainant and, except where any future investigation may be prejudiced, to the person complained against.

Where a complaint is referred to the Commission it must determine whether or not it is necessary for the complaint to be investigated. Where it considers that investigation is not necessary, it may, if it thinks fit, refer the complaint back to the appropriate authority for 'local resolution' and inform the complainant and (unless it considers that this may prejudice a possible future investigation of the complaint) the person complained against that it has done so.

When these provisions of the Police Reform Act 2002 are brought into force, the existing Police (Complaints) (Mandatory Referrals etc.) Regulations 1985 will be replaced.

Handling of complaints by the appropriate authority

Having recorded a complaint which does not need to be referred, the appropriate authority must then consider whether the complaint is suitable for local resolution. If it determines that it is suitable for local resolution, and the complainant consents (after having been informed of the right to appeal), it may make suitable arrangements. Any consent so given may not be withdrawn after the procedure has begun. If it is not so suitable, the appropriate authority must take steps to investigate it formally.

A determination that a complaint is suitable for local resolution is dependent upon the appropriate authority being satisfied that the conduct complained of (even if it were proved) would not justify the bringing of any criminal or disciplinary proceedings or the Commission has approved such resolution. In order to approve a 'local resolution', the Commission must be satisfied that any disciplinary proceedings which might be justified would be unlikely to result in a dismissal, a requirement to resign or retire, a reduction in rank or other demotion or the imposition of a fine. Alternatively, the Commission must be satisfied that it would not be practicable for criminal proceedings which would be likely to result in a conviction, or disciplinary proceedings leading to one of those results, to be brought.

Dispensation by the Commission (other action or no action)

Where a complaint has been recorded, and not referred to the Commission, and the appropriate authority considers that it should be handled otherwise than in accordance with procedures set out in Schedule 3 or that no action should be taken in relation to that complaint, and that the complaint falls within a description of complaints specified in regulations, it may apply to the Commission for permission to handle the complaint in an alternative manner. It must notify a complainant that this application has been made. The Commission must inform the authority and the complainant of its decision. Where the Commission gives permission for an appropriate authority to handle the complaint in whatever manner the authority considers to be fit, the authority need do no more under Schedule 3 than preserve the evidence, and take any action which it considers appropriate, or take no action at all.

Where the Commission does not grant permission, the appropriate authority must consider whether the complaint is suitable for local resolution.

Local resolution of complaints

Where there is to be a local resolution of a complaint, the arrangements made by the appropriate authority for subjecting a complaint to local resolution may include the appointment of *a person who is serving with the police* and is under the direction and control of the chief officer of police of the relevant force, to secure the local resolution of the complaint. The requirement is not that it shall be *a police officer*. The Secretary of State is authorised to make regulations dealing with the manner of local resolution of complaints. Any statement made for the purpose of such resolution is not admissible in any subsequent criminal, civil or disciplinary proceedings except to the extent that it consists of an admission relating to a matter which has not been subjected to local resolution.

If, after attempts to achieve local resolution, it appears to an appropriate authority that such resolution is impossible, or that the matter is unsuitable for such resolution, it must arrange for an investigation. In such a case, any attempt at local resolution must be discontinued. Such an attempt must also be discontinued if there is a requirement for the matter to be referred to the Commission or it is otherwise referred. Any person who has been involved in an attempt at local resolution shall be barred from participation in subsequently investigating the complaint.

Appeals relating to local resolution

A complainant has a right of appeal to the Commission against the conduct of the local resolution of a complaint. Where this is done, the only matter to be considered is whether there have been contraventions of procedural requirements relating to local resolution. The Commission must consider representations from both sides. Where the Commission rules in the complainant's favour, it must give binding directions to the appropriate authority as to the future handling of the complaint. This may take the form of requiring an investigation. Both parties must be informed.

Regulations may be made concerning the appeal procedure.

When these provisions of the Police Reform Act 2002 are brought into force, the Police (Complaints) (Informal Resolution) Regulations 1985 will be replaced.

Handling of conduct matters

Schedule 3, Part 2, to the 2002 Act deals with this. A 'conduct matter' (a term used by the 2002 Act) is a matter which is not and has not been the subject of a complaint in respect of which there is, in the substance, an indication that the person serving with the police may have committed a criminal offence or may have behaved in a manner which would justify disciplinary proceedings.

Conduct matters arising in civil proceedings

Where a police authority or a chief constable has received notification that civil proceedings have been brought by a member of the public against them or are likely to be brought and it appears that these proceedings would involve a conduct matter, it or he should follow the same procedure in relation to recording that matter or notifying the appropriate authority about it and in relation to the Commission. There is no requirement to record where the matter has already been dealt with by means of criminal or disciplinary proceedings.

Regulations may be made dealing with such matters.

Recording, etc., of conduct matters in other cases

Where a conduct matter comes to the attention of a police authority or chief officer of police in some other way from that just mentioned and it is conduct:

(a) which appears to have resulted in the death of any person;
(b) as a result of which a member of the public has been adversely affected by it; or
(c) which is of a description specified in regulations,

the matter must be recorded and the appropriate authority must consider whether it is a matter which must be referred to the Commission, or is one which it would be appropriate to refer. If it is not required to refer the matter and does not do so, it may deal with the matter in such other manner (if any) as it may determine. No such matter which has already been dealt with by means of criminal or disciplinary proceedings need be recorded.

The Commission may direct an appropriate authority to record a matter that has come to its attention and that it considers to be a 'recordable conduct matter' if it has not otherwise been recorded.

Duties to preserve evidence relating to conduct matters

The appropriate authority has a duty, as soon as practicable, to obtain and preserve evidence related to a recordable conduct matter.

Reference of conduct matters to the Commission

The same matters *must be referred* as in the case of complaints and there are similar arrangements in respect of voluntary references. Similar conditions apply in relation to notifications to interested parties.

Where reference has been made, it is the duty of the Commission to decide whether or not an investigation is necessary. Where it does not consider such an investigation to be necessary, it may refer the matter back to the appropriate authority to be dealt with in such manner (if any) as the authority determines.

Investigations and subsequent proceedings

Power of the Commission to determine the form of an investigation

Schedule 3, Part 3, of the 2002 Act applies where a complaint or recordable conduct matter has been referred to the Commission and it decides that an investigation is necessary. The form of the investigation will depend upon the seriousness of the case and the public interest but must consist of:

(a) an investigation by the appropriate authority on its own behalf;
(b) an investigation by that authority under the supervision of the Commission;
(c) an investigation by that authority under the management of the Commission;
(d) an investigation by the Commission.

The form of the investigation may be changed by the Commission any time and the Commission may give directions to that effect.

Investigations by the appropriate authority on behalf of the Commission

The appropriate authority must appoint a person serving with the police (whether under the direction and control of the chief officer of police of the relevant force or of the chief officer of another force) or a member of the National Criminal Intelligence Service or the National Crime Squad to investigate the complaint or matter.

In the case of an investigation into the conduct of a chief officer, the investigating officer may not be a person under that chief officer's direction or control. In the case of the Commissioner of Police of the Metropolis or the Deputy Commissioner, it must be a person nominated by the Home Secretary.

Investigations supervised by the Commission

The Commission may require that no appointment as an investigating officer may be made without its approval. If an appointment has already been made a further, approved appointment must be made as soon as practicable.

The same conditions apply in relation to the investigation of chief officers.

The person appointed to investigate the complaint or matter must comply with directions from the Commission which are authorised by regulations.

Investigations managed by the Commission

The same conditions apply as apply in the case of supervised investigations with the addition that the investigator must be under the direction and control of the Commission.

Investigations by the Commission itself

The Commission must designate a member of its own staff to take charge of the investigation on behalf of the Commission; it must also designate other members of its staff to assist that person. Any member of the Commission's staff so designated who does not already have all the powers and privileges of a constable throughout England and Wales and the adjacent UK waters shall have, for the purposes of carrying out the investigation and all purposes connected with it, all those powers and privileges of a constable. The 2002 Act authorises an order specifying that provisions of PACE may apply subject to specified modifications.

Restrictions on proceedings pending the conclusion of an investigation

No criminal or disciplinary proceedings may be brought in relation to any matter subject to an investigation (unless the investigation has been discontinued) until a report has been submitted to the Commission or appropriate authority. However, these provisions do not apply to proceedings by the Director of Public Prosecutions in exceptional cases where delay is undesirable.

Power of the Commission to discontinue an investigation

The Commission may order the discontinuance of any investigation in relation to a complaint or matter specified in regulations made by the Home Secretary. Where an investigation is so discontinued, the Commission may give the appropriate authority directions, as authorised by regulations, or may act, as authorised by regulations, on its own behalf.

Final reports on investigations

Where the investigation is carried out on behalf of an appropriate authority, the investigating officer must submit a report to that authority. Where the investigation was supervised or managed by the Commission, the investigating officer must send a report to the Commission and a copy to the appropriate authority. Where the Commission carries out the investigation itself, the investigating officer must report to the Commission. In all of these cases, the investigator is not prevented by any obligation of secrecy from including all such matters in the report as considered fit.

Action by the Commission in response to an investigation report

Where the Commission receives a report submitted to it in respect of an investigation which it has supervised, managed or carried out itself, it must send a copy to the appropriate authority and determine whether or not a criminal offence is disclosed. If it considers that such an offence is disclosed it must notify the Director of Public Prosecutions (DPP) and send a copy of the report, and it must notify the appropriate authority of this notification. The DPP must notify the Commission of the decision to take, or not to take, action in respect of the matter or matters investigated. If criminal proceedings are brought by the DPP, the Commission must inform, in the case of a complaint, the complainant and every person entitled to be kept informed in relation to the complaint as required by s 21 of the 2002 Act; in the case of a recordable conduct matter, every person entitled to be kept informed of that matter under s 21 must be informed. Where the Commission has determined that there is no indication of a criminal offence having been committed, or where it is notified that the DPP (having been sent the report) has decided to take no action, or where it is satisfied that any criminal proceedings have been concluded, the Commission must inform the appropriate authority requiring it to determine what action (if any) it will take in respect of matters dealt with in the report.

On being required to determine what action it will take, the appropriate authority must determine what action it will take and submit a memorandum to the Commission giving its decision and details of any proposed action. Where it decides that no disciplinary proceedings should follow, the reasons must be set out. The Commission must then consider whether the proposed action is appropriate and whether or not to make recommendations. It may make recommendations to the appropriate authority. The complainant and other entitled persons must be informed of those recommendations.

Action by appropriate authority in response to investigation report

The appropriate authority must decide whether the report submitted or sent to it indicates that a criminal offence may have been committed by the person whose conduct has been investigated. If it determines that it has, it must notify the DPP and send a copy of the report. If the DPP brings criminal proceedings, the appropriate authority must notify the complainant of this and every other person entitled to be kept informed under s 21.

If the appropriate authority decides that the report does not indicate a criminal offence or (where a copy of the report has been sent to the DPP) it is notified that the DPP does not propose to bring criminal proceedings, the authority must decide upon what action (if any) it will take and make similar notifications in this respect. It must also do this once it is satisfied that any criminal proceedings in respect of matters in the report have been concluded (apart from any appeal). The notification must set out the report's findings, whether the appropriate authority has decided to take action, what action (if any) it has decided to take and the complainant's right of appeal.

Except so far as it may be otherwise directed by regulations, an appropriate authority may (notwithstanding any obligation to secrecy imposed by any rule of law) give such a person notification of the findings by sending the person a copy of the report.

Appeals to the Commission with respect to an investigation

A complainant has a right of appeal to the Commission:

(a) on the grounds that he has not been provided with adequate information about the findings of the investigation or any proposals in relation to the taking or not taking of action;
(b) against the findings of the investigation; and
(c) against any proposal of the appropriate authority to take, or not to take, action in respect of any of the matters dealt with in the report.

The Commission must notify all persons concerned that such an appeal has been lodged.

If such an appeal is brought, the Commission may require the appropriate authority to submit a memorandum specifying whether any action is proposed to be taken, and, if it is, specifying the nature of that action; and, where no disciplinary proceedings are proposed, specifying the reasons for so deciding. In addition, where the investigation was carried out by the appropriate authority on its own behalf, and the Commission so requires, it must be supplied with a copy of the report. If the Commission considers that the complainant has not been provided with sufficient information it must direct the appropriate authority to provide such information.

Where the Commission determines that the findings of the investigation need to be reconsidered it may review those findings without further investigation, or direct that the complaint be reinvestigated.

Where the Commission considers that the appropriate authority is not proposing to take action which the Commission considers to be appropriate it must make such recommendations as it considers appropriate. Any direction or recommendation made by the Commission as a result of determining an appeal must be notified to all persons concerned. An appropriate authority must comply with any directions.

The 2002 Act empowers the Home Secretary to make regulations concerning the appeals procedure.

Review and reinvestigations following an appeal

On review of the findings of an investigation based upon the existing report, the Commission may:

(a) uphold the findings in whole or in part;

(b) direct the appropriate authority in relation to a review by the authority of the findings, the information provided for the complainant and generally in respect of the handling of the matter in future; or

(c) direct that the complaint be reinvestigated in a specified form.

All persons concerned must be informed by the Commission of any such determination or direction.

Duties with respect to disciplinary proceedings

Certain duties are imposed on the appropriate authority in the case of any investigation where it has given, or is required to give, notification to entitled persons of the action which it is proposing to take, or it has submitted, or is required to submit, a memorandum setting out the action which it is proposing to take.

Subject to any recommendations or directions given by the Commission, the authority must take any action notified and, where that action consists of or includes disciplinary proceedings, it must secure that those proceedings are taken to a proper conclusion.

Where a memorandum has been submitted to the Commission, the Commission may make recommendations that disciplinary proceedings, or specified disciplinary proceedings, are brought against the person concerned, or that proposed disciplinary proceedings should be modified so as to include specified charges. The appropriate authority is then obliged to notify the Commission as to whether it accepts the recommendation and (if it does) to set out the steps which it is proposing to take. Where the appropriate authority does not take steps to carry out the recommendations of the Commission, the Commission may direct the authority to do so, setting out the steps to be taken, and the authority must comply. The Commission must supply a statement of its reasons for giving such a direction. The appropriate authority must keep the Commission informed of the action which it takes.

Information for complainant, etc., about disciplinary recommendations

The complainant and all other persons entitled to be informed of such matters must be notified by the Commission of any steps which it recommends to be taken by the appropriate authority unless the authority has not notified its acceptance of the recommendation. If the appropriate authority notifies the Commission that it does not accept the recommendations, or fails to effect them, the Commission must determine what further steps, if any, should be taken. The Commission must also notify such persons of any determination not to take further steps or of the outcome of a determination to take further steps.

However, as stated above, the Independent Police Complaints Commission had not been set up at the time of writing. The following matters are not affected by the proposed new system.

Public interest immunity

It can happen that a complainant, having failed under the complaints procedure, will wish to bring a civil action against the police officer or the chief constable, or that the officer in question will wish to sue the complainant for defamation.

Documents which come into existence in relation to the investigation of a complaint will not be available for the preparation of the case and for use as evidence, if they are covered by public interest immunity, unless the court orders their disclosure. The law is as follows. Documents relating to the police complaints procedure are not as a class entitled to public interest immunity. However, particular documents may be entitled to public interest immunity on the grounds of their contents, and it is possible for a sub-category of documents relating to police complaints to be immune as a 'class'. An example of such a sub-category is a report prepared by an investigating officer for the Complaints Authority. A 'contents claim' to immunity, or a 'class claim' of a recognised sub-category, will not necessarily succeed, because the court will order disclosure where the public interest in the administration of justice outweighs the public interest in preserving the confidentiality of the documents in question. In deciding whether a claim of public interest immunity should be upheld, the court is entitled to inspect the document if it wishes to do so.

Regulations governing complaints

Section 23 of the Police Reform Act 2002 empowers the Secretary of State to make regulations as to procedure, particularly in relation to the appropriate authority, in the case of a complaint against any person, to be required, in accordance with prescribed procedures:

(a) to supply the person complained against with a copy of the complaint and to supply the complainant with a copy of the record made of that complaint;

(b) for matters to be taken into account in making any determination as to which procedure to adopt for the handling complaints and dealing with recordable conduct matters;

(c) for procedures to be discontinued where a complaint is withdrawn, the complainant indicates that he does not wish any further steps to be taken or the whole or part of the investigation of the complaint has been postponed until the conclusion of criminal proceedings and the complainant fails to indicate after the conclusion of those proceedings that he wishes the investigation to be resumed, and for the manner in which any such withdrawal or indication is to be effected or given, and for the circumstances in which it is to be taken as effected or given;

(d) for requiring the subject matter of the complaint that has been withdrawn to be treated for the purposes of the Act, in the cases and to the extent specified in the regulations, as a recordable conduct matter;

(e) for the manner in which any procedure is to be discontinued and for the consequences of such discontinuance;

(f) for the circumstances in which any investigation or other procedure must be suspended to allow another investigation to proceed and for the consequences of such suspension;

(g) for the appointment of persons to carry out investigations and for the regulation of the carrying out of such investigations;

(h) for combining into a single investigation the investigation of different complaints (whether relating to the same or different conduct and the investigation of those matters);

(i) procedure where the Commission relinquishes the supervision or management of an investigation and for the manner in which a reference of a complaint or conduct matter should be made;

(j) for applying the provisions where a person has ceased to be a person serving with the police;

(k) for dealing with cases where the identity of the person whose conduct is subject to a complaint remains unascertained;

(l) for notifications to be made by and records to be kept by police authorities and chief officers, for the establishment and maintenance of Commission records;

(m) for chief officers to delegate; and

(n) for the manner of notification and its form.

The Police (Complaints) (Informal Resolutions) Regulations 1985 were made under the previous legislation dealing with some of these matters together with the Police (Dispensation from Requirement to Investigate Complaints) Regulations 1989. At the time of writing the provisions permitting new regulations to be made had been brought into force, but no regulations had been made. As can be seen from the information set out above, new regulations are likely to be extensive.

Discipline regulations

The police officer occupies a unique role within society and it is fitting that the highest possible standards are demanded of a constable, who, in addition to being answerable to the laws of the land in the same way as any other citizen, is also answerable to a disciplinary code. In the case of chief superintendents and below, the Code is set out in the Police (Conduct) Regulations 1999.

The Police (Conduct) Regulations 1999

Suspension from membership of a police force

Regulation 5 of these Regulations provides that where a report, complaint or allegation indicates that the conduct of a member of a police force does not meet the appropriate standard, the chief officer of the force concerned may suspend the member concerned from membership of the force and from the office of constable whether or not the matter has been investigated. These powers may be exercised at any time following receipt of the report, complaint or allegation until:

(a) the supervising officer decides not to refer the case to a hearing;

(b) the notification of a finding that the conduct of the member concerned did not fail to meet the appropriate standard;

(c) the time limit under reg. 34 (request for a review) for giving notice of intention to seek a review has expired; or

(d) any review under reg. 35 (conduct of the review) has been completed.

Suspension will continue until such events occur, or until the chief officer decides to lift the suspension, whichever occurs first. Where a suspended member is subsequently required to resign, he will remain suspended during the period of notice.

This power to suspend may be delegated to an assistant chief constable (or commander).

The *appropriate standard* referred to in reg. 5 means the standard set out in the Code of Conduct which is included in Schedule 1 to the Regulations. This Code of Conduct replaces the disciplinary offences which were included in the replaced disciplinary regulations. Although the Code is expressed in a way which suggests that it is concerned with the achievement of desirable objectives, this is not so. Failure to comply with any of the 'aims' of the Code amounts to an offence. A finding that an officer is guilty of any of the offences described in the code as *appropriate standards* may face any of the sanctions set out in reg. 31:

(a) dismissal from the force;
(b) requirement to resign from the force as an alternative to dismissal taking effect either forthwith or on such date as may be specified in the decision;
(c) reduction in rank;
(d) fine;
(e) reprimand;
(f) caution.

However, s 84(1) of the Police Act 1996 provides that the penalties of dismissal, requirement to resign or reduction in rank cannot be imposed unless the member concerned has been given the opportunity to elect to be legally represented at the hearing. The provisions concerning legal representation may need to be looked at in consequence of a decision of the European Court of Human Rights which held that it was a breach of a prisoner's human rights for prison governors to deny them legal representation within disciplinary proceedings. It would be inconsistent to find that a police officer should be denied a protection afforded to prisoners.

In addition, reg. 32 requires that those conducting the hearing must have regard to an officer's personal record and may receive evidence from witnesses. The member concerned, or his representative, must be given an opportunity to make oral or, if appropriate, written representations as respects the question or to adduce evidence relevant thereto.

Conduct of investigations

Where there are criminal proceedings outstanding against a member, proceedings under the Regulations (other than suspension) must not take place unless the chief officer believes that exceptional circumstances make it appropriate to do so.

Where a report, complaint or allegation received by the chief officer indicates that the conduct of the member did not meet the appropriate standard, the chief officer may refer the case to an officer to supervise the investigation of the case. The officer is called the 'supervising officer'.

The supervising officer

The 'supervising officer' must be:

(a) at least one rank above that of the member concerned;
(b) of at least the rank of superintendent;
(c) a member of the same force as the member concerned; and
(d) not an interested party (i.e. not a witness or any person involved in the conduct which is the subject of the case or anyone who has a direct interest in the case).

The investigating officer

The supervising officer may appoint an investigating officer, who must be:

(a) a member of the same police force as the member concerned or, if at the request of the supervising officer the chief officer of some other force agrees to provide an investigating officer, a member of that other force;

(b) of at least the rank of inspector or, if the member concerned is a superintendent or chief superintendent, of at least the rank of assistant chief constable or, if the investigating officer is a member of the City of London or Metropolitan Police force, of at least the rank of commander;

(c) of at least the same rank as the member concerned; and

(d) not an interested party.

However, this is subject to the Police Complaints Authority's right to require that where they supervise the investigation they may require that no appointment is made without their approval.

The investigation

The investigating officer must, as soon as practicable (without prejudicing that or any other investigation), cause the member concerned to be given written notice:

(a) that there is to be an investigation into the case;

(b) of the nature of the report, complaint or allegation;

(c) informing the member that he is not obliged to say anything concerning the matter, but that he may, if so desired, make a written or oral statement concerning the matter to the investigating officer or to the chief officer concerned;

(d) informing the member that if such a statement is made it may be used in any subsequent proceedings under these Regulations;

(e) informing the member that there is a right to seek advice from the staff association; and

(f) informing the member that there is a right to be accompanied by a member of a police force, who shall not be an interested party, at any meeting, interview or hearing.

The investigating officer must submit a written report on the case to the supervisory officer and, if the Complaints Authority (or Commission) is supervising the investigation, also to the Authority (or Commission). If at any time during the investigation it appears to the investigating officer that it is likely that the case is a *special case* (as defined by Schedule 2, Part I, viz.

(a) conduct is of a serious nature and that an imprisonable offence may have been committed;

(b) if referred to a hearing under reg. 11 and proved, it may lead to dismissal from the force;

(c) the allegation is supported by written statements, documents or other material which is, in the opinion of the *appropriate officer*, sufficient without further evidence to establish on the balance of probabilities that the conduct of the member did not meet the appropriate standard; and

(d) the *appropriate officer* is of the opinion that it is in the public interest for the member concerned to cease to be a member of a police force without delay) the investigating officer must, whether or not the investigation is at an end, submit to the supervising officer:

(a) a statement of the belief that the case may be one to which reg. 39 (the regulation which deals with special cases) applies and the grounds for that belief; and

(b) a written report on the case so far as it has then been investigated.

The *appropriate officer* is an assistant chief constable or an assistant commissioner.

When an investigation has been completed, the supervising officer may refer the case to a hearing. Where the chief officer has a duty to proceed (a memorandum has been sent to the Complaints Authority (or Commission) stating that he intends to bring disciplinary proceedings), or the member has received two written warnings about his conduct within the previous 12 months and has admitted that the conduct failed to meet the required standard [see proceedings under Police (Efficiency) Regulations 1999 below], the supervising officer must refer the case to a hearing.

Where a supervising officer, on receipt of an investigating officer's report, is of the opinion that the case is a *special case*, he must refer the case to the appropriate officer. If the appropriate officer does not consider it to be a *special case*, he must return it to the supervising officer. If he considers it to be a *special case*, he must certify it as such and refer it to a hearing or, if the circumstances make such certification inappropriate, return the case to the supervising officer.

Where a case is not referred to a hearing, it must not be referred to in a member's personal record.

A supervising officer may direct withdrawal of a case at any time before a hearing unless the chief officer is under a duty to proceed.

The disciplinary hearing

Arrangements for hearing

Before any of the sanctions set out in reg. 31 may be applied, there must be a disciplinary hearing. The supervising officer must inform the member concerned in writing of the decision to refer the case to a hearing as soon as practicable and must supply the member, not less than 21 days before the date of the hearing, with details of the time and place of the hearing and with any statement which the member may have made to the investigating officer and any relevant statement (if an oral one an account of it), document or other material obtained during the course of the investigation. The conduct which allegedly amounts to a failure to meet the appropriate standard, together with the paragraph of the Code of Conduct in respect of which the appropriate standard is alleged not to have been met, must be specified.

A hearing may take place before the expiry of 21 days where a member is given written notice of a decision to refer a case to a hearing and is at the time detained in prison in consequence of a sentence of a court, or has received a suspended sentence of imprisonment and that member has not elected to be legally represented at the hearing.

Legal representation

Where a supervising officer is of the opinion that a hearing should have available the sanctions of dismissal, requirement to resign or reduction in rank, he must cause the member to be informed in writing at the time at which the notice of the hearing is received of the right to elect to be legally represented at the hearing and that this may be by either counsel or solicitor. The member must also be informed that alternatively, representation may only be by a member of a police force.

Notice of hearing – procedure following receipt

A member must be invited to state in writing within 14 days of receipt of the notice and documents:

(a) whether or not the member accepts that the conduct did not meet the appropriate standard;

(b) where representation is allowed by these Regulations, whether there is a wish to be legally represented at the hearing;

(c) where the member proposes to call any witnesses to relevant facts at the hearing, that fact together with the names and addresses of any such witnesses whose attendance the supervising officer is to arrange.

Police officers will be ordered to attend and other witnesses will be informed that their attendance is desired. The Regulations do not require that a hearing be adjourned where a witness is unable or unwilling to attend a hearing.

Where the allegation is accepted, the member concerned will be supplied with a prepared summary of the facts of the case at least 14 days before the hearing. If the facts are not accepted, he may respond within 7 days. Where the allegation is not accepted, no summary of the facts shall be prepared.

The hearing itself

The case must be heard by three officers appointed by the chief officer. They must not be interested parties. The presiding officer must be an assistant chief constable or a commander. The other officers must be of at least the rank of superintendent, each of whom shall be a member of a police force maintained under s 2 of the Police Act 1996. If the member concerned is a superintendent or chief superintendent, the presiding officer must be assisted by assistant chief constables (or commanders) from a different force or forces than the member concerned.

The officers conducting the hearing will be supplied with a copy of the supervising officer's written notice to the member of the decision to refer the case to a hearing and any summary of the facts together with any response made by the member concerned. The case will be presented by a member of a police force appointed by the supervising officer (unless the member concerned has given written notice in an appropriate case that he is to be legally represented). The member concerned may conduct his own case either in person or by a member of a police force selected by him, or where, in an appropriate case, notice has been given of legal representation, by counsel or solicitor.

The officers conducting the hearing determine their own procedure. They must review the facts of the case and decide whether or not the conduct of the member concerned met the appropriate standard and, if it did not, whether in all the circumstances it would be reasonable to impose any, and if so which, sanction. Before there may be a finding that the conduct of a member concerned failed to meet the appropriate standard, the conduct must be either admitted or proved by the person presenting the case on the *balance of probabilities* to have failed to meet that standard. We return to the standard of proof later.

Police officers should give careful consideration to their actions when confronted by a number of suspects. The 'balance' of probability can be influenced by the number of persons who assert that a particular fact is true. Actions taken should be carefully recorded as soon as possible after the event and subsequent events should also be recorded and witnessed where possible.

The member concerned must be ordered to attend the hearing and if there is a failure to attend the case may proceed. Where absence makes it impossible to comply with any of the procedures set out in the regulations, that procedure shall be dispensed with. The case may be adjourned where non-attendance is due to ill health or some other unavoidable reason.

Where the case for hearing is as a result of a complaint, the complainant must be allowed to attend the hearing while witnesses are being examined or cross-examined and may, at the discretion of the presiding officer, be accompanied by a friend or relative. However, if that complainant is to give evidence, the complainant or the associate may not be present before giving evidence. If the member concerned gives evidence, following any cross-examination by the presenting officer, the presiding officer must put to the member any questions posed by the complainant which might have been properly put by the presenting officer. However, the presiding officer has the discretion to allow the complainant to put such questions directly to the member concerned.

The presiding officer is empowered by the Regulations to exclude such a complainant and any person accompanying him if they intervene in or interrupt the hearing, or behave in a disorderly or abusive manner, or otherwise misconduct themselves.

With the exceptions set out above, the hearing must be in private although the presiding officer has the discretion to allow a solicitor or any such other persons as considered desirable to attend the whole or part of the hearing, subject to the consent of all parties to the hearing. Where the hearing is as a result of a complaint, any member of the Police Complaints Authority (or Commission) is entitled to attend the hearing. This also applies where an investigation has been supervised by the Authority as required by the Police Act 1996, s 72 (conduct resulting in death, serious injury, etc.). In addition, the member concerned may be accompanied at the hearing by a member of a police force and the presiding officer may allow witnesses to be accompanied by a friend or relative. However, where it appears that a witness may disclose information which it is not in the public interest to disclose, the presiding officer may require any member of the public, including the complainant and any person accompanying him, to withdraw while the evidence is given.

The presiding officer may determine issues of admissibility or the relevance of questions. With the consent of the member concerned, evidence may be admitted consisting of any document notwithstanding that a copy has not been supplied in advance as required by the Regulations.

The hearing may be adjourned if it appears to the officers conducting the hearing to be necessary or expedient to do so.

The decision of the officers conducting the hearing can be a majority decision. There will be no indication as to whether the decision was taken unanimously or by a majority.

The standard of proof

In 1991, the Police Complaints Authority, in its Triennial Review, voiced concern about the police complaints procedure. One of the concerns was the high standard of proof required to secure the conviction of a police officer for a disciplinary offence. The Authority called for the level of proof required in minor cases to shift from 'beyond reasonable doubt' to 'the balance of probabilities'.

In the event, the Police (Conduct) Regulations 1999 provide for proof to be limited to the 'balance of probabilities' for all disciplinary offences including those in respect of which the punishments of dismissal from a police force and the office of constable; requirement to resign and reduction in rank may follow a finding of guilt based upon such a balance. The 'balance' in favour of finding the charge proved need only exist in the minds of two of the three members of the disciplinary panel. This appears to be a little 'unbalanced'. It may be that it will be challenged in the course of time.

Remission of cases for hearing

Where the presiding officer is an interested party, or it appears that the sanctions of dismissal, requirement to resign or reduction in rank ought to be available and the member concerned has not been given the opportunity to elect to be legally represented and that it would be desirable for there to be another hearing at which the member could be so represented, the case must be remitted for hearing by an officer of equivalent rank in the force concerned or to such an officer in another force. Where a case is so remitted, notice in writing must be served on the member concerned inviting him to elect, within 14 days of receipt, to be legally represented at that hearing. The officer to whom such a case is remitted must not be given any indication as to the presiding officer's assessment of the case or the sanction which might be imposed.

The Presiding Officer may remit any other case if, either before or during the hearing, it is considered that remission is appropriate.

Record of hearing

There must be a verbatim record of the entire proceedings. A transcript of the record or a copy of it must be supplied to a member if requested within the time limit for any appeal and an appeal has been lodged.

Procedure following a hearing

The member must be informed orally of the finding and sanction imposed at the conclusion of the hearing and must receive written notification, together with a summary of reasons, within 3 days.

Review of a hearing

Where a sanction is imposed in consequence of a disciplinary hearing, a member may request in writing, stating the grounds on which the review is requested, within 14 days of the receipt of the written summary of reasons (unless this period is extended by the reviewing officer), that the chief officer (or assistant commissioner) review the *finding or sanction* imposed or both the *finding and sanction*.

The reviewing officer should, if requested to do so, hold a meeting with the member, who may be accompanied by a member of a police force and, where appropriate, by counsel or solicitor. The member must be informed of the finding of the reviewing officer within 3 days. The reviewing officer may confirm the original decision, or impose a different sanction, but not one which is greater than that originally imposed. If the decision of the reviewing officer is such that the member is dismissed, required to resign or reduced in rank, he must be notified in writing of the right to appeal to a Police Appeals Tribunal.

The role of the reviewing officer may be undertaken by an assistant chief constable (or commander) designated to act on the chief officer's behalf where the chief officer is an interested party, or is suspended, or that post is vacant. Where the designated assistant chief constable is for any reason unavailable, the review will be conducted by the chief officer of another force. Where the Commissioner of the City of London Police is either absent or is an interested party, the review must be conducted by the chief officer of another force or an assistant commissioner of the Metropolitan Police force.

Record of disciplinary proceedings

A book of record must be kept, including details of every case brought against a member of a police force, with the finding and the record of the decision in any further proceedings.

Alternative procedures in special cases

The procedures are modified by Schedule 2 to the Regulations where the case is *a special case*.

In such a case the *appropriate officer* may direct that the case be returned to the supervising officer at any time before the beginning of the hearing.

The *appropriate officer* must ensure that, as soon as practicable, the member concerned is invited to an interview with the appropriate officer at which written notice must be given of the decision to refer the case to a hearing and be supplied with the relevant documentation. Where a member fails or is unable to attend the interview, the notice and documentation may be delivered personally or left with some person at, or sent by recorded delivery to, the address at which the member is, with the approval of the chief constable, residing.

The date of any hearing must not be less than 21 or more than 28 days from the date of any notice. The appropriate officer must ensure that the member concerned is notified forthwith of the time, date and place of the hearing. The member must also be informed of the right to elect to be legally represented at the hearing and of the effect of s 84(1) to (3) of the Police Act 1996 (representation at disciplinary and other proceedings).

A *special case* must be heard by the chief officer concerned. However, where the chief officer is an interested party, it must be heard by the chief officer of another force. The officer conducting the hearing may adjourn the proceedings if it appears to be necessary or expedient to do so, but shall not do so more than once or for a period of more than 1 week or, on the application of the member concerned, 4 weeks.

The complainant must be allowed to attend the hearing and may at the discretion of the presiding officer be accompanied by a friend or relative. Such persons shall neither intervene in nor interrupt the hearing and if they behave in a disorderly or abusive manner, or otherwise misconduct themselves, the officer conducting the hearing may exclude them from the remainder of the hearing. However, the provisions which apply in cases other than special cases, which prohibit a complainant from being present before giving evidence, do not apply, nor do those which allow the presiding officer, in other cases, to put questions to the member on the complainant's behalf, or to allow the complainant to do so directly at the presiding officer's discretion. Regulation 27 (which, in other cases, allows the presiding officer to exclude members of the public if information may be disclosed by a witness which it is not in the public interest to disclose) does not apply to special cases.

In relation to the admission of statements in lieu of oral evidence, reg. 28 is modified to recognise that witnesses will not be involved in the proceedings.

The regulation concerning the remission of cases is modified to recognise the different situation existing in a special case. The officer conducting the hearing may return the case to the supervising officer if, either before or during the hearing, the officer conducting the hearing considers it appropriate to do so.

In relation to the receipt of evidence of a member's personal record, the regulation is altered to permit the introduction of documentary evidence only.

The written notice of the finding must be provided within 24 hours where the case is a special one. So far as a request for a review is concerned, the regulation is adapted so that the request is for a review by the chief officer of another force. The member must be informed of the finding of any such review within 24 hours. In such a case, where the reviewing officer considers that the officer conducting the hearing should have returned the case to the supervising officer, the case must be so returned.

The 'Code of Conduct'

The Code of Conduct contained in Schedule 1 to these Regulations replaces the 'Discipline Code' which appeared in Schedule 1 to the repealed Police (Discipline) Regulations 1985. The notes to the schedule draw attention to the extraordinary powers granted to the police and the high standards expected from police officers. They state that the Code does not seek to restrict an officer's discretion. It defines the parameters of conduct within which that discretion should be exercised. A breach of the principles in the Code may result in action being taken which in serious cases, may involve dismissal. The Code applies whilst on duty, or whilst off duty if the conduct is serious enough to indicate that an officer is not fit to be a police officer. The notes indicate that the Code will be applied in a reasonable and objective manner.

However, it is important to remember that there is no basic difference between the old 'Discipline Code' and the new 'Code of Conduct'. Under the replaced Discipline Code offences were described as offences. Under the Code of Conduct the offences are set out in such a way that they have the appearance of performance objectives. They are not. They continue to be offences. Regulation 13(2) requires that a notice of hearing shall specify the conduct of the member concerned which it is alleged failed to meet the appropriate standard and the paragraph of the Code of Conduct in respect of which the appropriate standard is alleged not to have been met. Thus, abuse of authority remains an offence but must now be described as failing to meet the appropriate standard by abuse of authority as required by paragraph 4 of the Code of Conduct.

The paragraphs of the Code of Conduct are as follows.

Honesty and integrity

1. It is of paramount importance that the public has faith in the honesty and integrity of police officers. Officers should therefore be open and truthful in their dealings;

avoid being improperly beholden to any person or institution; and discharge their duties with integrity.

Fairness and impartiality

2. Police officers have a particular responsibility to act with fairness and impartiality in all their dealings with the public and their colleagues.

Politeness and tolerance

3. Officers should treat members of the public and colleagues with courtesy and respect, avoiding abusive or deriding attitudes or behaviour. In particular, officers must avoid: favouritism of an individual or group; all forms of harassment, victim-isation or unreasonable discrimination; and overbearing conduct to a colleague, particularly to one junior in rank or service.

Use of force and abuse of authority

4. Officers must never knowingly use more force than is reasonable, nor should they abuse their authority.

Performance of duties

5. Officers should be conscientious and diligent in the performance of their duties. Officers should attend work promptly when rostered for duty. If absent through sickness or injury, they should avoid activities likely to retard their return to duty.

Lawful orders

6. The police service is a disciplined body. Unless there is good and sufficient cause to do otherwise, officers must obey all lawful orders and abide by the provisions of Police Regulations. Officers should support their colleagues in the execution of their lawful duties, and oppose any improper behaviour, reporting it where appropriate.

Confidentiality

7. Information which comes into the possession of the police should be treated as con-fidential. It should not be used for personal benefit and nor should it be divulged to other parties except in the proper course of police duty. Similarly, officers should respect, as confidential, information about force policy and operations unless author-ised to disclose it in the course of their duties.

Criminal offences

8. Officers must report any proceedings for a criminal offence taken against them. Conviction of a criminal offence may of itself result in further action being taken.

Property

9. Officers must exercise reasonable care to prevent loss or damage to property (excluding their own personal property but including police property).

Sobriety

10. Whilst on duty officers must be sober. Officers should not consume alcohol when on duty unless specifically authorised to do so or it becomes necessary for the proper discharge of police duty.

Appearance

11. Unless on duties which dictate otherwise, officers should always be well turned out, clean and tidy whilst on duty in uniform or plain clothes.

General conduct

12. Whether on or off duty, police officers should not behave in a way which is likely to bring discredit upon the police service.

The Police (Efficiency) Regulations 1999

These Regulations make provision with respect to the efficiency of members of a police force and establish procedures by which members of a police force may be required to resign or may be reduced in rank. The provisions are additional to those contained in the Police (Conduct) Regulations 1999. They follow concern expressed by both the Government and chief officers that there existed no means by which chief officers could rid themselves of officers whom they considered to be lazy or incompetent. The Regulations were amended in 2003 to include unsatisfactory attendance by members of a police force.

The Regulations do not apply to a probationer constable who has not completed the period of probation.

First interview concerning performance

Circumstances and arrangement

Where a reporting officer (the police officer who has the immediate supervisory responsibility for the officer concerned or the person employed under the Police Act 1996, s 15, who has such responsibility) is of the opinion that the performance or attendance of a member is unsatisfactory the member concerned may be required to attend an interview (first interview) to discuss the member's performance or attendance (or both). Where the reporting officer is a civilian employee, any other member of the force who has supervisory responsibility for that first member may, if of the opinion that the performance of that member is unsatisfactory, require attendance at a first interview to discuss performance. In such circumstances, references to a reporting officer will be taken to include references to that member with that supervisory responsibility.

The reporting officer must send a notice in writing to the member concerned:

(a) requiring attendance at a specified time and place, for an interview with the reporting officer or, if the member concerned so requests, the countersigning officer (a supervisor who is senior in rank to the reporting officer);

(b) stating the reasons why performance is considered unsatisfactory;

(c) informing the member that advice may be sought from a representative of the staff association and be accompanied at the interview by a member of a police force selected by him; and the reporting officer must send a copy of the notice to the countersigning officer.

Not later than 7 days after receipt (or such longer period as the reporting officer may permit), the member concerned may request by notice in writing that the interview be conducted by the countersigning officer. If there is such a request, the interview will be so conducted.

Procedure at interview

The interviewing officer must explain the reasons why the reporting officer is of the opinion that performance or attendance is unsatisfactory and provide the member, or the officer who has accompanied him, or both, with an opportunity to make a response. If after considering any representations the interviewing officer is satisfied that performance has been unsatisfactory, he must:

(a) inform the member concerned in what respects performance or attendance is considered unsatisfactory;

(b) warn the member of any specific action which is required to be taken to achieve an improvement in performance; and

(c) warn the member that, if a sufficient improvement is not made within such reasonable period as the interviewing officer shall specify, there may be a requirement to attend a second interview.

He may recommend that the member concerned seek assistance in relation to any matter affecting health or welfare. The interviewing officer is also empowered to adjourn the interview to a specified later time or date if it appears necessary or expedient to do so.

Not later than 7 days after the first interview, the reporting officer must:

(a) cause to be prepared a written record of the substance of the matters discussed at the interview; and

(b) send a copy to the member (two if he was accompanied) together with a written notice informing the member that written comments may be submitted, or an indication may be given that there is no comment to be made, not later than 7 days after the date of receipt.

Where the first interview is required in relation to attendance and the member has failed to attend the interview, the interviewing officer shall, if satisfied that the attendance of the member has been unsatisfactory, not later than 7 days after the date on which the first interview was to take place, send a written notice (or two where the member representing the officer involved attended the interview) informing the member in what respects attendance is considered unsatisfactory, warning of any specific action which is required to be taken and warning that if sufficient improvement is not made within a specified period, there may be a requirement to attend a second interview.

A notice must also be sent informing the member concerned that he may submit written comments, or indicate that he has no comments to make, not later than 7 days after the date upon which the notice is received by him.

If made, such comments must be retained within the record of the interview. On application by the member, the interviewing officer may extend that period.

The interviewing officer must then send a copy of the record and any written comments to:

(a) the senior manager (the supervisory officer of the countersigning officer or where the member concerned is a superintendent or chief superintendent, his supervising officer);

(b) the personnel officer (a person employed under the Police Act 1996, s 15, which authorises civilian employees) or a member of a police force who, in either case, has responsibility for personnel matters relating to members of the police force concerned; and

(c) (i) if the interview was conducted by the reporting officer, the countersigning officer; or

(ii) if the interview was conducted by the countersigning officer, the reporting officer.

Where a member has been required to attend a first interview in relation to performance, attendance or both of those categories of behaviour, any second interview must only relate to the category or categories of behaviour that was or were the subject of the first interview.

Second interview concerning performance or attendance

Circumstances and arrangement

Where a reporting officer is of the opinion that a member who has been warned concerning performance or attendance has failed to make sufficient improvement in performance or attendance within the time specified, the case may be referred to the countersigning officer where the countersigning officer is a member of the police force concerned who may, after consultation with the personnel officer, require the member concerned to attend a second interview to discuss performance, or as the case may be, attendance.

(a) A notice must be sent:
    (i) requiring attendance, at a specified time and place, at an interview with the countersigning officer and the personnel officer;
    (ii) stating the reason why performance or attendance is considered unsatisfactory and that further action will be considered in the light of the interview; and
    (iii) informing the member that advice may be sought from a representative of the staff association and that he may be accompanied at the interview by a member of a police force selected by him; and

(b) a copy of the notice must be sent to the reporting officer, the senior manager and the personnel officer.

Procedure at second interview

The second interview will be conducted by the countersigning officer and the personnel officer. The countersigning officer must explain the reasons why the reporting officer is of the opinion that the member concerned has failed to make a sufficient improvement in performance or attendance or, as the case may be, that performance or attendance is unsatisfactory. He must provide the member, or the accompanying member, or both, with an opportunity to make representations. If after considering any such representations, it is considered that performance has been unsatisfactory during the period under review, the countersigning officer shall:

(a) inform the member concerned in what respects performance or attendance is considered unsatisfactory;
(b) warn that an improvement in performance or attendance is required in any such respect;
(c) inform the member of any specific action which is required to be taken to achieve such improvement; and
(d) warn the member concerned that, if a sufficient improvement is not made within such reasonable period as the countersigning officer shall specify, there may be a requirement to attend an inefficiency hearing at which the officers conducting the hearing will have the power, if appropriate, to require the member to resign from the force or to order reduction in rank.

The countersigning officer may adjourn the interview if it appears necessary or expedient to do so.

Procedure following second interview

The countersigning officer must, not later than 7 days after the interview, prepare, in consultation with the personnel officer, a written record of the matters discussed at interview and send a copy (or two copies where the member was accompanied) of that record to the member concerned, together with a notice confirming the terms of any warning given during the interview and informing the member that he may submit written comments, or indicate that there are no such comments, not later than 7 days after receipt of the notice. However, this time limit may be extended by the countersigning officer. Any comments received must be retained in records. Where a member fails to attend a second interview related to attendance, the countersigning officer must if satisfied that the attendance of the member has been unsatisfactory during the specified period, not later than 7 days after the date on which the interview was due to take place:

(a) prepare a written notice informing and warning the member of the unsatisfactory nature of performance or attendance; of the improvement required and action necessary to achieve it; and stating that if sufficient improvement is not made within a specified period, there may a requirement to attend an inefficiency hearing at which the tribunal will have the power to require resignation or reduction in rank; and
(b) send a copy (two copies if member representing officer attended interview), together with a notice informing the member that written comments may be submitted, or an indication may be given that there are no comments to be made, not later than 7 days after the date on which the copy is received by him.

The countersigning officer must send a copy of the record and any comments by the member, to the reporting officer, the personnel officer and the senior manager.

Any subsequent efficiency hearing must be restricted to matters related to the second performance or attendance interview. Not later than 14 days after the end of the specified period for improvement, the countersigning officer and reporting officer must assess performance or attendance during that period and inform the member in writing whether they are of the opinion that there has been a sufficient improvement in performance or attendance. If the countersigning officer is of the opinion that there has been an insufficient improvement, the member must be informed in writing, within that period of 14 days, that there may be a requirement to attend an inefficiency hearing, to be notified separately, at which performance will be considered. That hearing must not be sooner than 21 days and not later than 56 days after receipt of notice. The matter must then be referred to the senior manager who may, if it is considered appropriate to do so, direct that such a hearing be arranged.

The inefficiency hearing

Arrangements

The personnel officer must send a notice, not less than 21 days before the hearing, giving the time and place of the hearing and stating the reasons why performance or attendance is considered to be unsatisfactory. It must also inform the member of the right to be represented at the hearing by counsel or solicitor, or a member of a police force selected by him. It must warn that if the officers conducting the hearing find that performance or attendance during the relevant period has been unsatisfactory they may:

(a) require the member concerned to resign from the force either 1 month after the date of receipt of a copy of the decision, or such later date as may be specified;

(b) order reduction in rank with immediate effect and issue a written warning that unless sufficient improvement in performance is made within a specified period, the member may, following consideration of performance following the hearing (see below), be required to attend a first interview in respect of that performance; or

(c) issue such a written warning as is mentioned in (b).

Where there is a requirement to resign and the member does not do so, the effect of the decision shall be that the member is dismissed from the time specified.

The member concerned must give 7 days' notice to the personnel officer if there is a requirement to call witnesses, giving their names and addresses.

The hearing

The chairman must be an assistant chief constable (or commander, or in the case of the City of London either an assistant commissioner or commander) and will be assisted by two assessors. None of them must have been involved with the first or second interviews. Where the member concerned is a superintendent or chief superintendent, the other assessors must be assistant chief constables or commanders. Where the member is below the rank of superintendent, they will be superintendents. The personnel officer must send the chairman a copy of any document available to the interviewing officer at the first interview, any document which was available to the countersigning officer at the second interview or any documents which have been prepared within the procedure following the second interview. The member concerned must receive copies of all such documents.

The procedure shall be decided by the chairman and the hearing must be in private unless the chairman, with the consent of the member, decides otherwise. The member must be given an opportunity to make representations about any matter contained in the written notice sent with the arrangements for the hearing and to call any witnesses in respect of whom notice has been given. A verbatim record of the proceedings must be made and a transcript must be supplied to the member within the time limit for any appeal, notice of which has been lodged under the Police Act 1996, s 85. In the event of non-attendance of the member, the hearing may take place in his absence if the chairman considers it proper to do so. In such a case, it may be assumed that any procedure involving the member has been complied with.

In the case of an inefficiency hearing other than one in respect of which the member concerned has been sent a notice stating the reasons why attendance is unsatisfactory, the chairman may postpone or adjourn the hearing if notified by the member that he is unable to attend, or where satisfied that there is a good reason for non-attendance. The hearing may also be adjourned if the chairman considers, following representations made by the member, that it is appropriate to allow a further period of assessment of performance or attendance. A date must be fixed for resumption which allows further assessment by the reporting officer and the countersigning officer over a period not exceeding 3 months. Not later than 14 days after the conclusion of the additional period of assessment, the reporting officer must prepare a report of the member's performance or attendance during that period and the countersigning officer must send it to the chairman and a copy of it to the member.

At the resumed hearing the chairman must allow the member to make representations and to call witnesses in respect of whom notice has been provided. Should the chairman be absent, incapacitated or suspended and the situation is likely to continue for more than 28 days, the chief officer may arrange a suitable replacement.

The officers conducting the hearing must decide whether the performance or attendance of the member during the period considered following the second interview (or during any further period allowed within the period of adjournment together with the period following the second interview) has been satisfactory or not. It shall be a majority decision and no indication will be given of whether it was taken unanimously or by a majority. The decision may be deferred. Their decision must state the finding and the reasons why performance or attendance was considered to be unsatisfactory and the sanction imposed. A written copy of the decision must be sent to the member, senior manager and personnel officer within 3 days after the finding. The copy sent to the member must be accompanied by a notice explaining the right to have the decision reviewed.

Where there is a finding of unsatisfactory attendance they may:

(a) require the member to resign;
(b) where it is established that insufficient support has been given during the relevant period in order to assist return to work, specify the measures which must be taken to give sufficient support in order to assist return to work;
(c) issue a written warning that unless sufficient improvement in attendance is made within a specified period, there may be a requirement to attend a second inefficiency hearing at which there may be a requirement to resign;
(d) where it is established that the member's duties contribute directly to an unsatisfactory attendance record, order redeployment to alternative duties (which may involve a reduction in rank).

In the case of finding (b) or (d), a written warning must be issued that unless a sufficient improvement in attendance is made within a specified period, the member may be required to attend a first interview, a second interview or an inefficiency hearing as specified by the officers conducting the hearing.

Assessment of performance following an inefficiency hearing

The Regulations, as explained above, permit the officers conducting an inefficiency hearing to issue a warning, where their decision has been to reduce the member in rank, or in any other circumstances other than a finding of requirement to resign, that unless sufficient improvement in performance is made within a specified period, there may be a requirement to attend a first interview in respect of that performance. Performance, in such a case, must be assessed and reported upon not later than 14 days after the conclusion of the appropriate period and a copy must be sent to the member. If performance has been satisfactory, no further action will be taken in respect of performance during that period. Where this is not so, the reporting officer must request the member to attend a first interview.

Where the inefficiency hearing has been considering the attendance of the member, and a written warning has been given that unless sufficient improvement in attendance is made within a specified period there may be a requirement to attend a second inefficiency hearing at which there may be requirement to resign, not later than 14 days after the specified period the countersigning officer must assess attendance and prepare a report, a copy of which must be sent to the member concerned. Where it is concluded that attendance has been satisfactory no further action shall be taken in respect of attendance during that period. Where attendance has been unsatisfactory or insufficient improvement has been made, the countersigning officer may, where the member has already been given a written warning as set out in (c) above, require the member to attend an inefficiency hearing. Where steps under (b) or (d) have been taken, the member must be issued with a written warning that unless a sufficient improvement in attendance is made within a specified period, there may be a requirement to attend a first interview, second interview or an inefficiency hearing as specified by the officers conducting the inefficiency hearing.

Review of a decision by an inefficiency hearing

The member has a right to request a review by the chief officer (or an assistant commissioner) of any finding or sanction (or both) imposed by such a hearing. A request for a review must be made within 14 days of receipt (but this time may be extended by the reviewing officer) of a notice of the decision, state the grounds and indicate whether a meeting is required. The member may be accompanied at any meeting by a member of a police force and by counsel or solicitor.

The member must be informed of the finding of the reviewing officer within 3 days. The reviewing officer may confirm the decision of the hearing or impose a different sanction but not one which is greater than that originally imposed. If the decision involves a requirement to resign, the member must be told in writing of the right of appeal to a Police Appeals Tribunal.

Where the chief officer is an interested party, or is absent, incapacitated or suspended, or during any vacancy in the rank of chief constable, the assistant chief constable designated to act as chief officer (or designated commander or an alternative assistant commissioner) shall act as reviewing officer. Where the Commissioner of the City of

London police force is so absent, the review must be conducted by the chief officer of another force or by an assistant commissioner of the Metropolitan Police force.

If the designated assistant chief constable of a provincial force is also absent the review must be carried out by the chief officer of another force.

Maintenance of records of findings

Under the Police (Efficiency) Regulations 1999

Any sanction imposed under the Police (Efficiency) Regulations 1999, reg. 17 is expunged after 2 years free from any such sanction.

Under both the Police (Efficiency) Regulations 1999 and the Police (Conduct) Regulations 1999

Regulation 17(2A) of the Police Regulations 1995 provides that if, following any review of a sanction imposed under either set of Regulations, the reviewing officer substitutes a decision of the conduct hearing or inefficiency hearing, with a finding that the member concerned had not failed to meet the appropriate standard, or that the performance of the member concerned was not unsatisfactory, the sanction shall be expunged forthwith.

Disciplinary appeals

Section 85 of the Police Act 1996 provides that a member of a police force who is dismissed, required to resign or reduced in rank may appeal to a police appeals tribunal against such a decision. This appeal lies only after any other appeal has been exhausted, that is, an application for a review by a chief officer. If the reviewing officer decides that the sanction imposed shall remain, this further appeal lies to a tribunal.

Where a police appeals tribunal allows an appeal it may, if it considers it appropriate to do so, make an order dealing with the appellant in a way which appears to the tribunal to be less severe, and in which the member could have been dealt with by the person making the original decision.

Schedule 6 to the 1996 Act deals with appeals to police appeals tribunals.

A police appeals tribunal must consist of four members:

(a) a chairman chosen from a list of persons with a 7-year general qualification within the meaning of the Courts and Legal Services Act 1990 (currently only barristers and solicitors have this) who have been nominated by the Lord Chancellor;
(b) a member from the police authority (or a person nominated by the Home Secretary where he is the police authority);
(c) a member from a list of persons maintained by the Home Secretary who are (or within the past 5 years have been) chief officers of police, other than those of the authority concerned; and
(d) a retired police officer of appropriate rank.

Where there is an equality of vote, the casting vote is that of the chairman.

An appeals tribunal may determine an appeal without a hearing but may not do so unless both the appellant and the respondent (chief officer of police concerned) have been afforded an opportunity to make written or, if either so requests, oral representations and any such representations have been considered. At such a hearing the appellant has a right to be represented by a serving member of a police force or by counsel or solicitor. The respondent has similar rights and may also be represented by the clerk or other officer of the authority.

Any decision by a tribunal is final; there is no further appeal.

The Home Secretary has made the Police Appeals Tribunal Rules 1999. Notice of appeal must be given within 21 days from the date on which the decision appealed against was notified to the appellant. The time limit is extended to 28 days in certain circumstances if the case is a special case and criminal proceedings are involved. Rule 7 permits extension of the time limits where a police authority is satisfied that there are special circumstances and that it is just to do so.

Double jeopardy

The previous rule that, save where the disciplinary offence was that of being convicted of an offence, a member of a police force who had been convicted or acquitted of a criminal offence would not be liable to be charged with any offence against discipline which, in substance, was the same as the offence in respect of which the member had been convicted or acquitted has now been removed. Disciplinary proceedings may now be taken, in any circumstances, following such conviction or acquittal.

Police Federation and negotiating machinery

Terms of reference

The current legislation governing the Police Federation is s 59 of the Police Act 1996, and under the authority of this section the Home Secretary may make regulations which prescribe the constitution and proceedings of the Police Federation. The Police Federation is the representative organisation of most members of police forces and stands in place of the usual trade union membership which is met in outside bodies. It is responsible for representing members of police forces in England and Wales in all matters affecting their welfare and efficiency other than questions of discipline and promotion affecting individuals. In a disciplined service, such as the police, it can be appreciated that matters of discipline and promotion affecting individuals must be excluded from the matters with which the Federation may make representation. The hearing of disciplinary proceedings, the decision to be made and the selection of officers for promotion to a higher rank are matters solely for chief constables and tribunals. Members of a police force may be represented at the disciplinary hearing by another police officer, and appointed officers of the Police Federation may also accept this role but only in their capacity as members of a police force, not as officers of the Federation. Many chief constables allow Federation representatives to sit with the panel of senior officers charged with the task of interviewing candidates for promotion, on occasions to participate in the proceedings and at other times to act as observers.

Membership

The Home Secretary, in consultation with the Joint Central Committee of the Police Federation, makes provisions in regulations concerning membership. Currently, all members of police forces below the rank of superintendent and all police cadets are permitted to become members of the Federation. Superintendents have their own representative body, as do chief and assistant chief constables.

A branch of the Federation exists in every police force and in each are constituted three branch boards representing, separately, constables, sergeants and inspectors. Female officers are represented by these three boards in the same way as their male colleagues. The Police Federation also protects the interests of police cadets. Meetings are held at force, divisional or subdivisional level to establish the feelings of members upon matters then under consideration. Annual central conferences are also held, to which all forces send representatives at constable, sergeant and inspector levels, and such conferences provide an opportunity for discussion at national level on problems then existing for the federated ranks.

Having established a policy at national level, it next becomes necessary to present the view of the federated ranks to the Home Office. This is not done directly; it is necessary to form a smaller body of officers to discharge this duty. The Joint Central Committee has already been mentioned in the context of negotiation with the Home Secretary and is fairly small in number. Its members are elected at the annual conference.

Although the procedure for ensuring that matters receive attention at national level has been outlined, it must be appreciated that local matters can be effectively dealt with at force level and local branch boards are usually afforded the opportunity to discuss problems with chief constables.

Desborough Committee

The Desborough Committee was set up in 1919, at a time when there was serious unrest in the police service. Prior to that date, police officers had no right to make any form of representation to their superiors, and between 1909 and 1919 the situation had deteriorated rapidly. In 1909, a promising young inspector in the Metropolitan Police became involved in a dispute with his superiors and accused them of oppressive conduct. His grievance received much attention from the national press and Inspector Syme, being an expressive individual, made public knowledge much material that was embarrassing to his superiors. Disciplinary charges were heard and he was dismissed from the force, but he continued to make allegations. He formed the National Union of Police and Prison Officers and, as a result of continued libellous statements aimed at the Commissioner, together with his attempts to cause disaffection among the police in wartime, found himself in and out of prison, being finally admitted to Broadmoor. In 1931 he received, from the Government, substantial compensation for his treatment.

To be a member of this Police Union was to risk dismissal, but conditions were rife for discontent, with police pay falling well below that of industrial workers, until it reached a stage at which the families of police officers could not be adequately clothed and fed. When a police officer was sacked for his Union activities in 1918, certain demands were made of the Home Secretary by the Union. The demands were not met and a strike was called. It was partly successful in that it resulted in a substantial pay rise for the Metropolitan Police, the constable who had been dismissed was reinstated, but the Prime Minister would not accept a police union. A form of representation for inspectors, sergeants and constables was permitted but the scheme was not a success. The Union began to gain in strength and once again demanded recognition, which was refused. By this time the Desborough Committee had begun its work: an announcement had been made of a rise in the constable's starting pay from £1 10s to £3 10s per week and of the Government's intention to introduce an alternative form of representation, other than through a union. It was also made clear that police officers who went on strike would be dismissed, but the Union was determined to force its recognition and when the Police Bill was introduced into the House of Commons on 8 July 1919, providing for the establishment of a police federation and banning police officers from becoming members of a trade union, they called a second strike. It was doomed from the beginning. Many police officers felt that the service had achieved all it could hope for, a substantial pay increase and a representative body. The strike, by 2364 men from seven forces, soon collapsed. All strikers were dismissed from the service and none was ever reinstated.

It is probably fair to say that the sympathetic attitude of the members of the Desboough Committee avoided a period of major disruption in the police service. They accepted the description of a constable's duties as earlier reported by the Royal Commission of 1906–08:

> We are satisfied that a policeman has responsibilities and obligations which are peculiar to his calling and distinguish him from other public servants and municipal employees – the burden of individual discretion and responsibility placed upon a constable is much greater than that of any other public servant of subordinate rank

and as a result recommended:

(a) improvements in pay and conditions,
(b) that these should be standardised and, perhaps more importantly,
(c) that they should be matters for the Home Secretary.

For the first time, pay and conditions of service were standardised and brought under central control. However, the large issue as to whether or not there should be a national police force resulted in a complete rejection of nationalisation on the grounds that such large organisations frequently get themselves into a groove. Perhaps these findings are just as relevant today!

At the same time, the subsequent Police Act 1919 established the Police Council as a central advisory body to the Home Secretary and the Police Federation as the representative organisation of the police service. The structure of the Police Federation has already been considered.

The first meeting of the Police Council was a historic occasion. The Council was made up of representatives of the Home Office, local authorities, commissioners and policemen of all ranks, and the Home Secretary himself took the chair. The Council proved to be the ideal medium for implementing the recommendations of the Desborough Committee and the advantages to be gained by assembling together representatives of all bodies affected by proposals ensured the efficient formation of the first police regulations. As was expected, local authorities were reluctant to surrender any measure of their control over police forces and the volume of their protests ensured that small borough forces survived until 1946, and watch committees – the public authorities for borough forces – retained control of appointment, promotion and discipline until the passing of the Police Act 1964.

Oaksey Committee

Following the Desborough Committee and the 1919 Act, there was a long period of contentment in the police service, for although the service suffered two small reductions in pay as part of general government economic measures in 1922 and 1931, pay scales generally remained high in comparison with average incomes and the cost of living. The Second World War and its aftermath benefited the industrial worker at the expense of those in public service, and the low pay of police officers severely affected recruiting. The position had become so grave that the Metropolitan force had fewer men than in 1901 and an immediate pay increase was granted by the Government in 1946, which placed the constable 17 per cent above the average earnings in industry. Part of the agreement was that a further increase would not be sought before 1950, but the effects of inflation were such that the value of this award was quickly eroded. The Police Federation pressed for an earlier review and initial government opposition was overcome by rising discontent within the service. In May 1948, a committee was set up under the chairmanship of Lord Oaksey to consider the need for the recruitment and retention of an adequate number of men and women for the police forces in England, Wales and Scotland, and to report on pay, emoluments, allowances, pensions, promotion, methods of representation and negotiation and other conditions of service.

Two reports were presented by the Oaksey Committee, in April and November 1949. The first dealt with pay, pensions and conditions of service (and these findings proved to be disappointing, resulting in pay increases of about 15 per cent, which had such a small effect upon recruitment that a further increase of 20 per cent became necessary within 2 years); the second dealt with appointments, training, promotion, discipline, housing, amenities and the establishment of negotiating machinery.

The Committee recommended the setting up of a Police Council for Great Britain, which came into being in 1953. The Police Federation had for some time been dissatisfied with the Police Council, for although it had been successful in ensuring that representatives of all interested parties met regularly to discuss police affairs, it was considered that the Home Secretary could be over-sympathetic towards the views of police authorities in relation to pay, as both had an interest in keeping costs down. This new Council, which was not established on a statutory basis, consisted of three separate panels representing chief officers, superintendents and federated ranks. In turn, each panel consisted of a staff side and an official side, but provision was made to allow the whole Council to sit together to consider general questions. Prior to the Police Council for Great Britain being set up, pay claims had not been permitted to be referred to arbitration, but provision was now made for a panel of three arbitrators to be appointed by the Prime Minister. An independent chairman was appointed and the official side was to include representatives of all police authorities and the Home Office. The Police Federation was also permitted at this time to collect voluntary subscriptions. It can be appreciated that previously, when all Federation activity was dependent upon official funds, the scope of such activities was limited. Subscriptions currently made by members to Federation funds are allocated proportionately to the national and local organisations.

Police Act 1964

By the time the Royal Commission reported in 1962, the scene had been set. The Federation had already made known its suspicion of the Police Council established by the Police Act 1919 and had indicated its support of the Police Council for Great Britain. The 1964 Act, therefore, gave statutory authority to the Police Council for Great Britain as the negotiating body and the old Police Council was replaced by the Police Advisory Board, which was set up to advise the Home Secretary on general questions affecting the service. The title was later changed to the Police Council for the United Kingdom.

Edmund Davies Committee

This Committee of Inquiry was appointed in 1977 to review the machinery for negotiating police pay following a period of discontent in which some members felt it was necessary to demand the right to strike in order to press claims which would otherwise be ignored. The inquiry led to a formula by which future pay settlements would be established and resulted in the eclipse of the old Police Council, which was replaced by the Police Negotiating Board. The Board has an independent chairman and secretariat. The Police Federation ensures that the views of all federated ranks are made known to the Board, in all matters.

The Sheehy Inquiry

The Sheehy Inquiry into Police Responsibilities and Rewards, under the chairmanship of Sir Patrick Sheehy, produced a report which was presented to the Home Secretary in 1993. One of its recommendations was concerned with establishing a means by which police officers might be rewarded in accordance with their performance, skills and the job which they were asked to do. Whilst the issue of performance-related pay is restricted in the Police Act 1996 to officers of the rank of superintendent and above (although the provisions in respect of superintendents are merely permissive), the report provided a means by which assessment of pay within the formula established by Lord Edmund Davies was broken.

The efforts of the Police Federation, and those of the Association of Chief Police Officers and the Superintendent's Association, were largely instrumental in ensuring that many of the proposals of this group were ignored by the Home Secretary. Perhaps the most significant of the proposals which were not taken up were those which would have led to fixed-term appointments for all police officers and a common retirement age of 60 years. Although the Home Secretary included the proposals which would have led to the abolition of the ranks of both chief superintendent and chief inspector within the original Bill that led to the 1994 Act, strong opposition in both Houses of Parliament led to the retention of the rank of chief inspector. These provisions were repeated in the Police Act 1996. The Criminal Justice and Police Act 2001, s 125, reintro-duced the rank of chief superintendent, thus finally reinstating the position which had existed prior to the findings of this Inquiry. The ranks of deputy chief constable (in provincial forces) and deputy assistant commissioner (in the Metropolitan Police) were also reintroduced by the Act of 2001.

Thus, many of the recommendations of the Sheehy Inquiry which were implement-ed have since been reversed. However, it is probably fair to say that the provisions which remain in place are the most damaging. The payment of housing allowance was denied to new entrants. This has led to police officers being faced with accommoda-tion costs which they are unable to meet from the salary offered to a probationer con-stable. The problem has been answered by providing special allowances for officers serving in certain areas (mainly in the south east) and at different rates depending upon circumstances. These allowances, being fairly substantial in some instances, have led to the beginnings of different rates of pay for officers serving in different areas. Although this may assist in recruitment to some forces covering areas in which prop-erty prices are high, it nevertheless loses sight of the fact that at the end of an officer's service in one of these 'chosen' areas, that officer ends up with a much more valuable house than that of fellow officers serving elsewhere. The Metropolitan Police officer who sells up and retires to the provinces will certainly end up with a more substantial bounty than provincial colleagues.

The other relic of the Sheehy Inquiry is the fixed-term contract, currently restricted to chief officers.

Role of the Police Federation

The Police Federation has moved a long way since its formation following the demand for a police union during and after the First World War. It is clear that the Home Secre-tary and chief constables welcome the active participation of the Federation in matters affecting the welfare and efficiency of the service.

As has already been discussed, the Police Council for the United Kingdom was the usual medium through which the views of the Federation, the Association of Chief Police officers and the Superintendents' Association were made known. It had five standing committees: (A) for matters affecting chief and assistant chief officers (ranks above chief superintendents); (B) for matters affecting chief superintendents and superintendents; (C) for matters affecting the federated ranks; (D) to consider problems peculiar to all ranks of the service; and finally (E) to consider police pensions. Before making regula-tions concerned with these matters, the Home Secretary had to take into account any recommendations made by the Council and had to provide the Council with a draft of such regulations.

The Police Advisory Board, which may consider any issues affecting the police service, is made up of the Home Secretary, who is its chairman, representatives of local authorities (police authorities), the Commissioner of the City of London Police, the receiver for the Metropolitan Police District, the Association of Chief Police Officers, the Superintendents' Association, the Police Federation and the Home Office. The Police Federation is, therefore, able to have matters which it wishes to be discussed considered by the Police Advisory Board.

One might consider the Advisory Board as being a group of advisers immediately available to offer advice to the Home Secretary on general matters affecting the police, many of which would not need to be consolidated in Police Regulations. In contrast, the Police Council for the United Kingdom was very much a debating chamber in which would be discussed all matters affecting, for example, pay, allowances, promotion and discipline – all being matters dealt with by existing Police Regulations.

It is now standard practice for members of the Police Federation to be invited to join working parties and committees set up on behalf of the Advisory Board or the Home Office. In this way it is possible for such groups to be aware of the feelings of the members of the service on matters which are being considered.

The Police Council for the United Kingdom was abolished by the Police Negotiating Board Act 1980, which replaced the Council with the Police Negotiating Board for the United Kingdom. This Board is charged with the duty to consider the interest of police authorities, members of police forces and police cadets of the United Kingdom in questions related to hours of duty, leave, pay and allowances, pensions or the issue, use and return of police clothing, personal equipment and accoutrements.

Each police force has a Joint Negotiating and Consultative Committee which was set up following recommendations of the Edmund Davies Committee. It consists of representatives of all ranks of the force and provides a medium by which local problems can be easily resolved.

Assistance given to individuals

The Police Federation Regulations 1969 permit Federation funds to be used, within Police Federation rules, for any purpose which the Federation considers to be necessary or expedient in the interests of the Federation or its members. The only ban upon the use of such funds is in the support of a political party or a person's candidature in an election, or the making of a contribution to the funds of such a party, or a trade union or an organisation unconnected with the police service, its welfare or a charity. Such funds are often used to provide legal assistance to members charged with traffic offences arising in the course of police duty while driving or in charge of a motor vehicle with proper authority. Often the police authority, having an interest in such matters, arranges for an accused officer's defence after consultation with the Police Federation.

Legal charges incurred by members in proceedings brought against them for causing death or injury to any person or for any assault are frequently met by the Police Federation. The Joint Central Committee may impose terms and conditions upon use in such circumstances.

The Police Federation is particularly helpful in proceedings concerning claims for damages or injuries or in relation to national insurance and pension matters. It can usefully be approached concerning any matter affecting welfare and deals sympathetically with appeals for assistance for officers who occasionally find themselves in financial difficulty. Although there is no suggestion that Federation funds can be used for such purposes, many branch boards manage schemes which allow loans to be made to members in particular circumstances. A personal liability group insurance scheme is maintained by the Police Federation on behalf of its members. A death benefit is payable to serving officers who contribute to the funds of the Police Federation. It also operates a return of premium group insurance scheme for those who wish to participate.

The Police Federation will also provide assistance and will guide an officer in the correct procedure to be followed in the completion of a claim of compensation from the state-financed Criminal Injuries Compensation Board, should an officer be injured in the course of his duties.

Constitutional position of the police

The origins of the police system

Collective responsibility

The Danish and Anglo-Saxon invaders provided the foundation of the English police system. The nearest parallel to our modern police officer in those times was the Saxon 'tythingman' or 'headborough'. During the reign of King Alfred, the system of collective responsibility was developed which has as its basis a form of mutual protection against serious crime. The 'tuns' or 'vills', which are roughly equivalent to modern parishes, were each required to assume responsibility for their own policing and groups of about 10 families were formed and put in the charge of a tythingman. Every male of the age of 12 years or over was listed by the tythingman and was required to make himself available for police purposes. In this way, all adult male members of the community were made responsible for the good conduct of their fellows. If the group failed to produce a criminal for trial, it could be fined or forced to pay compensation. It is apparent that one of the weaknesses of the system was that minor crimes which did not appear to be easily solved might well be concealed.

The system was further developed by grouping the tything into 'hundreds', which were supervised by the hundred man, or royal reeve. At this stage a judicial function was introduced, as the hundred man exercised administrative and judicial powers through a hundred court and could, therefore, hear and determine offences. The hundred man was, in turn, under the control of a shire reeve, or sheriff, who was directly responsible to the King for the maintenance of the 'King's peace' within his shire. This system of policing was tribal in origin and could only be effectively carried out while there was little movement of population. In any particular area it was essential that each person was known to the remainder of the community. Strangers were looked upon with considerable suspicion; if they committed crime in the vill and moved on quickly to escape capture, the members of the particular community concerned were required to make good the loss. To give some protection against this type of situation, the shire reeve, in the King's name, was permitted to raise a *posse comitatus*, which consisted of every enrolled male in the shire. The system of hue and cry was developed which involved the posse setting off in pursuit of a felon and continuing such pursuit until the felon was apprehended or the chase was abandoned. With the necessity to pay compensation or a fine, the individuals of the community concerned were not likely to abandon pursuit prematurely.

The emergence of the office of constable

The Norman invaders revised the Saxon system of collective responsibility by introducing the 'frankpledge'. As conquerors they were mainly concerned with the Saxon population, and the language difficulty did nothing to ease their task. The Normans required the sheriffs to ensure that all were pledged to enforce the peace, and the sheriffs held twice-yearly sessions of the hundred court to ascertain that all had enrolled and had given their pledge to keep the peace under fixed penalties. The Norman sheriffs were ruthless and savage men who imposed fines at the slightest excuse and, after showing little concern for available evidence, did not hesitate to hang those reported for petty theft.

The Assize of Clarendon in 1166 made matters much worse for the Saxon population as, in addition to surrendering thieves, they were required to report suspicions they might have concerning one another. Such suspicions were presented by the tythingman to a jury of 12 free men of the hundred, who, in turn, informed the sheriff of the more serious accusations.

In the course of time, resentment of the barbaric practices of the Normans, together with some intermarriage, caused much of the older system to return. The courts of the hundred were replaced by manorial courts, or 'courts leet' as they became known. The term 'constable', which had previously referred to officers of the court, keepers of castles, etc., now began to describe the constable of the vill, tything or manor. However, the system of collective responsibility continued but the courts leet were given three distinct functions:

(a) they maintained the system of frankpledge;
(b) they awarded punishment against either an individual or a community;
(c) they appointed officers of the manor.

In exercising their functions, the courts leet relied upon the constables to present details of their suspicions in relation to offenders and crime generally within the area. Their status was considerably enhanced in 1252 by equating their authority to that of mayors and bailiffs, the office being recognised as a Crown appointment with responsibility for maintaining the peace. Such officers were appointed annually.

The Statute of Winchester in 1285 brought about the next significant development in our system of policing. It reinforced, but nevertheless confirmed, the best of previous systems and introduced 'watch and ward' in towns. The watch would consist of up to 16 men, stationed at the various gates to towns between sunset and sunrise, their duties being controlled by the constable. They had the power to arrest strangers at night and hand them over to the constable. All men of the town were required to perform these duties at the direction of the constable and were placed in the stocks if they refused. In addition to these measures, all male persons between the ages of 15 and 60 years were to keep arms, according to their status, to enforce the 'peace'.

The breakdown of collective responsibility

There was no significant change in the methods of law enforcement from this time until the nineteenth century, which saw the introduction of modern police forces. The role of the justice of the peace emerged in 1195 when King Richard I commissioned knights to ensure that the peace was kept by all over 16 years of age. The knights, in time, became known as keepers of the peace and were given the authority to hear and give judgement for minor offences. The Justice of the Peace Act 1361 provided the new title of 'justices'. Justices were appointed by the Crown and their functions were partly judicial, partly administrative and partly concerned with enforcement. In general practice the justice was often the lord of the manor, who effectively controlled the court leet and, therefore, was responsible for the appointment of the constable. It is not surprising, therefore, that the constable was looked upon as almost a servant of the justice. The constable, being without uniform, was recognised by the staff or baton of his office.

From this time onwards, the status of the office of constable began to decline, although it was still held in some esteem until the latter part of the sixteenth century. This erosion of dignity was caused by the reluctance of the better educated citizens to accept such an unpaid appointment for a period of 1 year. A stage was soon reached at which the office was recognised as being suitable for the old or infirm. If someone of higher status was appointed, he invariably paid a deputy to carry out his duties, which, by this time, involved a considerable amount of work. In 1827, a statute abolished the constable's duty to present matters connected with crime, vagabonds, etc., and the feudal system of policing was withdrawn without a substitute being offered.

It is interesting to note that recent Home Secretaries have been attracted by the possibility of a reintroduction of the 'parish constable' in one form or another to provide a focal point for rural communities in the fight against crime. The use of special constables for such purposes has also been considered. Perhaps we are witnessing a return to collective responsibility. The Police Reform Act 2002 introduced various forms of auxiliary personnel to assist police officers in law enforcement (see page 71). A high incidence of crime within the twentieth century created a situation in which collective responsibility of citizens was insufficient by itself and led to the appearance of the 'professional'. Perhaps we have now reached the stage at which only a sound professional service, fully supported by members of the public who accept the need for collective responsibility, will be sufficient to keep crime under control.

Formation of police forces

It might be imagined that in the years leading up to this situation there would have been an outcry for some effective form of policing, but the reverse was generally the case. Henry and John Fielding, as chief magistrates at Bow Street, made every effort to educate the public as to the dangers which faced society, but as late as 1820 many still believed that any organised form of policing would have a serious effect upon the liberty of the individual and that the state of considerable lawlessness which then existed was preferable.

The Metropolitan Police

The Home Secretary, Robert Peel, introduced the Metropolitan Police Force Act 1829, having been given authority by Parliament to create an office of police under the control of the Home Secretary, who would be responsible for the policing of the metropolitan area, but not the City of London. Two justices were to take charge of the police office and were authorised to appoint sufficient men to police the district effectively. The justices later came to be known as commissioners, and a receiver was also appointed with a duty to provide the financial management of the force. The first commissioners were Lt-Col. Charles Rowan, an army officer of distinction and a stern disciplinarian, and Richard Mayne, a young barrister with the legal knowledge necessary to administer such a new venture. The original force consisted of 3000 men organised into 17 divisions under the control of superintendents. Each superintendent was assisted by four inspectors and 16 sergeants, each sergeant commanding nine constables. The origins of our present rank structure were established at that time. Realising that such an organisation was unlikely to be well received by a population which had previously been subject to little effective control, care was taken to select constables from all sections of the public, except the upper classes, and to introduce a uniform which, although distinctive, was not too military in appearance. This was a wise decision, but in spite of these efforts the first policemen to patrol the streets received a hostile reception.

Borough police

The ultimate success of the Metropolitan Police Force ensured the general adoption of organised systems of policing. Criminals who found life difficult within the metropolitan area could not resist the temptation to operate within the comparatively unprotected boroughs, and this situation led to the passing of the Municipal Corporations Act 1835. This Act not only required boroughs to establish police forces but also reformed local government. Watch committees were appointed consisting of not more than one-third of the council members, and these committees were required to swear in a sufficient number of constables to preserve the peace in the borough. In England and Wales, 178 boroughs which had charters of self-government were affected by this Act, and the significance of the establishment of police forces in this way is that local authorities were made responsible for the policing of their areas, thus preventing a national police force from being formed. The Home Secretary was given no authority to interfere with local arrangements and chief constables, when appointed, were therefore in no way responsible to central government. The situation is still in existence. Although having assumed an advisory role in the interests of standardisation and efficiency, the Home Secretary is still unable to dictate to chief constables or police authorities (although he may determine priorities in relation to law enforcement). However, as central government is responsible for the payment of the major part of local authorities' expenditure in respect of police forces, the Home Secretary reserves the right to suspend exchequer payments if HM Inspectors of Constabulary feel that a particular police force is inefficient.

The original arrangements made by watch committees for the policing of their boroughs were somewhat haphazard and this was almost inevitable as no direction was given concerning rates of pay or the types of men to be recruited. Many boroughs merely used their existing watchmen and gave little thought to their appointment of chief officers, while others looked to the existing Metropolitan Police for assistance.

County police

One of the primary reasons for establishing police forces in counties was the sudden rise of Chartism. The Chartist Movement represented the discontent of the working classes, and when this discontent led to serious disorders it was at first necessary to use troops to suppress demonstrations. Even the Chelsea Pensioners were armed to act as a reserve unit. It was found then, and is still apparent today, that the armed services are well equipped to suppress disorder but are ill equipped to carry out a true policing function as they are not trained in the processes of law.

The County Police Act 1839 empowered, but did not compel, county authorities to establish police forces. The magistrates in quarter sessions were given the authority to appoint constables for the whole, or a part, of their area. The number of constables appointed was not to exceed one for every 1000 of population. The cost of running police forces was to be met by local rates and the Home Secretary was given power to make rules concerning the pay of constables and the appointment of the chief constables. An element of central government control was thus established within this Act. Attempts at this stage to exercise more governmental control over police forces were bitterly resisted by the Tory Party, which represented the view of the aristocracy, who were well represented in the ranks of the magistrates and preferred to retain local control.

County and borough police

The County and Borough Police Act 1856 insisted upon the establishment of police forces in all areas. Approximately half of the counties had taken advantage of the permissive provisions of the 1839 Act and others had appointed constables only in some areas within their jurisdiction. Considerable lawlessness was becoming apparent in parts of England and Wales and the 1856 Act was passed by Parliament to ensure an efficient police force in all areas. Further control by central government was ensured by the appointment of three inspectors of constabulary who were to assess the efficiency of all forces. Those found to be efficient would be given an exchequer grant of one-quarter of the cost of pay and uniform, and encouragement was given to smaller boroughs to amalgamate by withholding financial assistance to forces serving populations of less than 5000.

The modern police service

The constable

The modern police service has evolved since then, but although there have been many changes in the service itself, the office of constable has always retained the independence of a Crown appointment, which probably originated in 1662 when Charles II transferred to justices of the peace the power to appoint constables. The justices required constables to take the oath to preserve the King's peace and thus established their individual responsibility for their actions. Being also 'members of police forces', they are made subject to control by chief officers of police.

Progress throughout the 100 years which followed saw the appointment of policewomen, the provision of rest days, an increase to 50 per cent of the cost of police forces being provided by central funds and, following an unsuccessful strike by a number of police officers in support of a union, the formation of the Police Federation as a representative body. The process of the amalgamation of smaller forces was continued after the Second World War as a result of the Police Act 1946. Police training centres were also established, at first as a temporary measure, in order to train the large number of recruits available. In this way, responsibility for the initial training of recruits came for the first time within the scope of central government, as previously chief constables had been responsible for the training of their own constables on appointment.

County and borough police forces

The Royal Commission which reported in 1962 was set up to examine a number of important factors, including the control of police forces, a fair rate of pay for police officers, the state of police/public relations and the manner in which complaints were dealt with. The members of the Commission inevitably found themselves considering the desirability of local control of police forces as opposed to national control. The resulting Police Act 1964 abolished, or partly repealed, 61 Acts of Parliament, rejected the principle of national control (although they found many arguments in favour) and resolved that control should be exercised by a partnership involving the Home Secretary, police authorities and chief constables.

The Act gave the Home Secretary powers to promote efficiency in individual forces, to call for reports from chief constables, to approve the appointment of senior police officers, to compel the retirement of an inefficient chief constable and to require the amalgamation of police areas. This final power has resulted in major reorganisations of police areas in the late 1960s and again in 1974.

The first series of amalgamations – made sometimes under voluntary and at other times under compulsory schemes – resulted in a number of combined police forces consisting of previous counties and county boroughs. In Nottinghamshire, for example, the new force thus created even took the title of Nottinghamshire Combined Constabulary. The second series of amalgamation schemes followed the Local Government Act 1972, as a result of which the county borough disappeared. Police areas were once again changed, but whereas in the first instance amalgamation schemes were prepared with a view to increasing the size of forces, the second schemes were necessary to allow police areas to remain compatible with those of the local authorities. The Police and Criminal Evidence Act 1984 made further provisions in relation to the powers and duties of the police.

Types of police force

(a) *Provincial police forces* – The existing provincial police forces have developed through a series of stages. In the beginning, a large number of county borough and city police forces existed, each with its own chief constable. Many of these forces employed fewer police officers than are likely to be found in a modern police division. Within a series of amalgamation of police forces, the Home Office acted as midwife to the birth of the present police forces. This was done in the interests of efficiency. As the processes of law enforcement become more complex, it becomes increasingly necessary for forces to combine their resources in the interests of good service to the public. However, the policing provided tended to become less personal and the forces lost something by way of 'family' relationship.

(b) Usually, the area covered by a police force roughly corresponds with a local authority boundary, but this is not universally true. Experiments in the 1970s gave birth to some police forces which policed areas governed by new local authorities created to serve the 'metropolitan areas', or large city conurbations. Although these metropolitan authorities were later dismantled, the police forces created to police those areas have remained.

(c) The Police Act 1996, ss 1, 2, 3 and 4, requires that England and Wales shall be divided into police areas. The 'police areas' will be those referred to in Schedule 1 and for the Metropolitan Police District. It also provides that the Schedule may be amended by an Order under the 1996 Act or the Local Government Acts. Thus, the process of altering the boundaries of police forces is simplified for the future.

(d) The police authorities for provincial police forces are composed of members of local councils, magistrates and independent members appointed by the Home Secretary.

(e) *The City of London Police* – The City of London Police are responsible for the policing of an area of approximately one square mile of the old City of London. It is commanded by a Commissioner and its police authority is the Common Council of that City.

(f) *The Metropolitan Police Force* – The Metropolitan Police Force operates within the Greater London area and its functions are not controlled by the Police Act 1996. The force is commanded by a Commissioner and has its own police authority, which is appointed under legislation applying specifically to the Metropolitan Police District, that authority being responsible for the efficiency of that force and assuming a similar role to that fulfilled by police authorities in the provinces.

(g) *Private police forces* – Certain organisations have been allowed by statute to form police forces of their own. The British Transport Police, Ministry of Defence Police and the United Kingdom Atomic Energy Authority Constabulary are private forces which have been so created. The powers of officers appointed to those forces are generally limited to establishments in the occupation of those organisations, and a limited area which surrounds those establishments. However, recent legislation affecting the police has gone some way towards standardising law enforcement by embracing these police forces within the general system of policing.

Organisation and administration of police forces

Central Government

The Secretary of State for the Home Department, generally known as the Home Secretary, is responsible for the internal security of the nation. Certain aspects are delegated to other departments but, in the main, internal security is a matter for the police. It is plain that the Home Secretary is finally responsible for ensuring that sufficient constables are appointed to ensure that law and order are maintained. To advise the Home Secretary upon this factor and the efficiency of police forces, Her Majesty's Inspectors of Constabulary and a Chief Inspector of Constabulary are appointed. The Chief Inspector of Constabulary is required to make an annual report to the Home Secretary, which is laid before Parliament and subsequently published.

The Home Secretary's control of police forces is exercised directly under powers provided by the Police Act 1996 and the Police Reform Act 2002. He is responsible for the appointment of independent members of police authorities, for fixing the major objectives of policing in any year, for approving the appointment of chief officer, for allocating grants to police authorities towards the maintenance of their police forces and for making regulations concerning the conditions of service, pay and discipline affecting members of police forces. Although the Home Secretary no longer exercises direct control over the number of police officers employed by particular police authorities, he may find that a police force is not efficient or effective owing to a deficiency of police officers. The number of officers in a police force is very much dependent upon the number of people within the police areas, the acreage to be policed and local conditions including the incidence of crime and the presence of traffic. Chief officers of police, in turn, have administrative responsibilities of the highest order, as they must ensure that the members of their forces are deployed effectively throughout their police areas and that there is a satisfactory command structure.

Although chief officers of police and police authorities have retained control of their respective police forces, it is important to realise the significance of the powers of the Home Secretary. The Common Services Fund, to which forces contribute, is managed by the Home Office and finances police training, the Police College, research, wireless depots, central promotion examinations, the Police National Computer, the national co-ordination of regional crime squads, the Drugs and Illegal Immigration Intelligence Units, the National Crime Squad, National Crime Intelligence Service and many other bodies.

The 1996 Act permits the 'privatisation' of some specialist services. Where the Home Secretary feels that the best means of providing support to all forces is not the setting up of a service under his control, he may direct forces to use facilities provided by another agency. Forensic science services, one of the original common services provided by the Home Secretary, is well on the road to recovering its costs through direct charges to forces.

Although the courts have ruled that chief constables must carry out their duties independently, so that there may be no suggestion of direct government control in relation to law enforcement, the Police Act 1996 empowered the Home Secretary to determine objectives for the policing of the areas of all police authorities. However, the determination of such objectives falls short of direct interference in matters relating to law enforcement, in that it does not place restrictions upon those persons who may be investigated or prosecuted. The Police Reform Act 2002 extends the 1996 Act to introduce further elements of control, by authorising the Home secretary to prepare annually a 'National Policing Plan' setting out whatever the Secretary of State considers to be the strategic policing priorities for the year. However, provision is made for consultation with police authorities and chief officers. The Home Secretary is also empowered to issue codes of practice relating to the discharge of their functions by chief officers of police and to require police authorities, in conjunction with chief officers, to produce a 3-year strategy plan setting out the authority's medium- and long-term strategies. The Crime and Disorder Act 1998 additionally makes provision for crime and disorder reduction partnerships in a police area involving councils, chief officers, police authorities and fire authorities, Primary Care Trusts and health authorities in Wales, giving the Secretary of State power to make an order merging two or more partnership areas. An order may require the reduction of crimes and forms of disorder described within it.

The Home Secretary may require inspectors of constabulary, in addition to carrying out their normal annual inspections of forces, to carry out a specific inspection of a police force, the National Criminal Intelligence Service or the National Crime Squad. Where such an inspection leads to a conclusion that the force, or a part of it, is not efficient or effective, or will cease to be so unless remedial action is taken, the Home Secretary may direct the police authority to take such action as is specified in the direction. Such action must be reported to Parliament. Reasons for his conclusion must be given to both the police authority and the chief officer. The Police Reform Act 2002 also extends the provisions of the Police Act 1996 to permit the making of regulations requiring police forces in England and Wales to adopt particular procedures or practices. Before making such regulations, the Home Secretary must, after consultation, seek advice from the chief inspector of constabulary and the Central Police Training and Development Authority. Similar provisions are made in respect of the National Crime Intelligence Service and National Crime Squad. The Act also extends the powers of the Secretary of State and police authorities in relation to requiring the retirement of chief officers in the interests of efficiency and effectiveness and for the suspension of such officers. It also amends the 1996 Act to allow the making of disciplinary regulations for special constables.

The Home Secretary frequently appoints working parties to examine in depth differing aspects of police work, and the advantages of planning on a national level – as opposed to within individual forces – are apparent.

In addition, the Police Act 1997 set up a National Crime Intelligence Service (NCIS) and a National Crime Squad (NCS). The Criminal Justice and Police Act 2001 established a Central Police Training and Development Authority which will provide police training and promote best practice in policing matters generally. Their respective functions are set out below.

National Crime Intelligence Service

The functions of the NCIS are to:

(a) gather, store and analyse information in order to provide criminal intelligence;
(b) provide criminal intelligence to police forces in Great Britain and Northern Ireland to the NCS and to other law enforcement agencies; and
(c) act in support of such police forces, the NCS and other law enforcement agencies carrying out their criminal intelligence activities.

The Director General of the NCIS is appointed by the Secretary of State. Provision is made for the Director General and police service members to retain their status as constables. The NCIS is under the direction and control of the Director General, who must have regard to the service plan issued by the NCIS Service Authority. The Director General must submit an annual report of the activities of NCIS to the Service Authority and may obtain the views of chief officers of police, the Director General of the NCS and the Commissioners of Customs and Excise, as considered appropriate. Collaboration agreements may be made.

The Secretary of State may determine objectives for the NCIS, may set performance targets and may issue codes of practice.

The 1997 Act makes provision for the making of discipline regulations relating to the conduct of the NCIS and the maintenance of internal discipline.

National Crime Squad

The 1997 Act also provides for the setting up of a National Crime Squad and the appointment of its Director General and its Supervising Authority. It will similarly be under the form of control outlined above in relation to the NCIS and subject to similar complaints and disciplinary procedures.

The function of the NCS is to prevent and detect serious crime which is of relevance to more than one police area in England and Wales. The NCS may also, at the request of a chief officer of police in England and Wales, act in support of the activities of his or her force in the prevention and detection of serious crime. It may also similarly support the NCIS and co-operate with other police forces or other law enforcement agencies in the United Kingdom.

Central Police Training and Development Authority (Centrex)

This authority was established under the Criminal Justice and Police Act 2001, s 87, and its functions are:

(a) to provide police training and facilities for the provision of police training;
(b) to promote the value of the provision of police training;
(c) to give advice about the provision of police training to persons other than the Authority who provide it or are proposing to do so;

(d) to provide such persons with all such assistance in relation to the provision of police training as the Authority considers appropriate;

(e) to provide persons serving or employed for policing purposes in England and Wales with advice and consultancy services with respect to police matters generally and with respect to best police practice and the handling of incidents requiring police involvement.

In carrying out its functions, the Authority must have regard to any objectives set by the Secretary of State under s 89, after consultation with representative bodies. Performance targets may be set. The Authority must issue annual objectives and a 'Training and Development Plan' dealing with its priorities and the allocation of resources and specifying the objectives of the Secretary of State together with the Authority's own objectives. Copies will be sent to the Secretary of State, police authorities and chief officers of police in England and Wales.

Appointments to the Authority will be made by the Secretary of State after consultation with police representative bodies. It will consist of not less than 11 members including a chairman, two representing police authorities, two representing chief officers of police and at least one Crown servant.

The Secretary of State is authorised by s 97 to make regulations concerning police training and the qualification for deployment to perform particular tasks of persons employed for policing purposes in England and Wales. If inspection reports indicate that a training need exists within a police force, or that there is a need for the provision of opportunities for professional development, the Secretary of State may direct the police authority to take appropriate measures.

Police authorities

The 1996 Act, s 2, requires that a police authority shall be maintained for every police area. Police authorities shall consist of 17 members: nine from relevant councils, five independent members appointed by the Home Secretary and three magistrates of the area. The Home Secretary is empowered to provide, by order, that the number of members shall be a specified number greater than 17. At the time of writing, the Home Secretary has made such orders in respect of Devon and Cornwall, Greater Manchester and Dyfed Powys.

It is the duty of a police authority to secure the maintenance of an efficient and effective police force for its area. In discharging its functions, a police authority must have regard to objectives determined by the Secretary of State, its own declared objectives, performance targets established by the authority and a local policing plan issued by the authority. An authority must also have regard to any official 'Code of Practice' and it is required, in conjunction with chief officers, to produce a 3-year strategy plan setting out the authority's medium- and long-term strategies. The Police Reform Act 2002 additionally makes provision for crime and disorder reduction partnerships involving councils, chief officers, police authorities and fire authorities, Primary Care Trusts and health authorities in Wales, giving the Secretary of State power to make an order applying to any two or more areas. An order may require the reduction of crimes and forms of disorder described within it.

Local policing objectives must be determined for each year and these must be consistent with the objectives determined by the Secretary of State. Before setting the objectives, an authority must consult its chief constable and consider any views of the community on policing. The authority is also required to produce a 'local policing plan', which must include a statement of the authority's priorities for the year, the resources to be allocated, the objectives set by both the Secretary of State and the authority and the performance targets set. The authority must consider a draft of a policing plan produced by the chief constable and before issuing a plan which differs from that draft, it must consult the chief constable. Policing plans must be published.

A police authority is required to publish an annual report, which must include an assessment of the extent to which the local policing plan has been carried out. Police authorities are independent bodies.

The police authority appoints the chief constable, deputy chief constable and assistant chief constables and must determine the establishment of the force. It is also responsible for the maintenance of buildings, provisions, etc., of vehicles, apparatus, clothing and equipment and the selection of the deputy and assistant chief constables.

Police authorities form various liaison groups and committees to keep themselves informed of matters affecting the police force. Lord Scarman, in a report following inner city disturbances, placed considerable emphasis upon the need for police authorities to discharge their responsibilities firmly, ensuring that there is adequate liaison between police forces and the local communities.

The chief officer of a police force

By s 10 of the 1996 Act, a police force shall be under the direction and control of its chief constable. A chief constable is required to have regard to a police authority's policing plan. He is appointed by the police authority (subject to the Home Secretary's approval) and that authority may, with the approval of the Home Secretary, call upon him or her to retire in the interests of efficiency or effectiveness. The chief constable has complete control over the day-to-day policing operations carried out in the area and operational priorities related to law enforcement. He also has complete control over civilian personnel.

The Police Act 1996 also defines the powers and duties of chief constables and places forces directly under their control by insisting that chief constables in all forces have the power to appoint, discipline and promote subordinate ranks. The City of London Force is controlled by its commissioner and its police authority, the Court of Common Council, and the Metropolitan Force is controlled by its commissioner and its police authority appointed under legislation applicable to the Metropolitan Police Area. The chief officer of police is in close liaison with the police authority throughout the year and attends meetings of that authority and reports upon policing within the area. An annual report is also prepared for members of the police authority.

The policeman

The rank structure of the police service, being so associated with areas of responsibility, provides a chief constable with a command structure which, although allowing him to retain full control of the force, provides a medium for ensuring that his orders and policies are effectively implemented. At the same time, it is important to remember that the unique nature of the office of constable demands that the holder of that office bears full personal responsibility for actions taken. This is the major distinction which can be drawn between the police service, the armed services and other public bodies. A constable can never claim that he was merely acting upon orders if he performs acts which are legally or morally unacceptable.

General functions of a constable

The primary function of a constable is the preservation of the Queen's peace. It is essential that all police officers remember their oath as set out in Schedule 4 of the Police Act 1996 as amended by the Police Reform Act 2002 to take account of its provisions allowing a person of any nationality to be a member of a police force:

> I ... of ... do solemnly and sincerely declare and affirm that I will well and truly serve the Queen in the office of constable, with fairness, integrity, diligence and impartiality, upholding fundamental human rights and according equal respect to all people, and that I will, to the best of my power, cause the peace to be kept and preserved and prevent all offences against people and property, and that while I continue to hold the said office I will, to the best of my skill and knowledge, discharge all of the duties thereof faithfully according to law.

The appointment to the office of constable is a Crown appointment and the nature of that oath overrides all other considerations. The officer is appointed to protect life and property, maintain order, prevent and detect crime and to bring about the prosecution of those who offend against the peace. When appointed to the office of constable, a police officer has the power and privileges of that office throughout England and Wales.

The role of a constable

The words of Sir Robert Peel, the first commissioner, included in his first instructions to police officers, are always worth remembering:

> Therefore the constable will be civil and obliging to people of every rank and class. He must be particularly cautious not to interfere idly or unnecessarily in order to make a display of his authority; when required to act he will do so with decision and boldness. There is no qualification so indispensable to a police officer as perfect command of temper, never suffering himself to be moved in the slightest degree by any language or threat; if he does his duty in a quiet and determined manner, such conduct will probably excite the well disposed of the bystanders to assist him if he require them.

These words still reflect the nature of the office of constable. A constable is a citizen, locally appointed, but having authority under the Crown to carry out appointed duties. He is essentially a member of the community served and the nature of the oath to the Sovereign demands that duties are carried out impartially and correctly. A rank structure exists in police forces to permit greater efficiency and a degree of organisation and control to the peace-keeping functions, but a constable remains responsible for the actions which he takes as an independent officer of the Crown. The continuing support of members of the public is essential to the peace-keeping function. Criminals seldom commit offences within view of a constable but they are frequently seen by other members of the public. If the police service commands the respect and the trust of the society it serves, such members of the public will co-operate in bringing offenders to justice.

Traffic wardens

To assist the police with the control of traffic and pedestrians in towns, the police authorities are permitted to appoint traffic wardens who are required to operate under the control of the chief officer of police of that force. They are empowered to enforce certain aspects of road traffic law, but only while in uniform and on foot. They are only permitted to act in respect of a limited number of fixed penalty offences. They are permitted to stop vehicles for the purpose of testing under s 67(3) of the Road Traffic Act 1988 and to stop vehicles generally under s 163 of that Act.

Exercise of police powers by civilians

The Police Reform Act 2002 authorises chief officers of police to designate an employee of the police authority who is under his or her direction and control as:

(a) a community support officer;
(b) an investigating officer;
(c) a detention officer;
(d) an escort officer.

A person designated has the powers and duties conferred or imposed by the designation.

Each of these types of designated officer is given specific powers as set out in Schedule 4 to the 2002 Act.

A community support officer

A community support officer has power to issue prescribed fixed penalty notices and may require a person to give his or her name and address where there is reason to believe that a person has committed a 'relevant offence'. It is an offence to fail to do so.

A 'relevant offence' is such a fixed penalty offence or an offence which appears to the community support officer to have caused injury, alarm or distress to any other person, or the loss of, or any damage to, any other person's property. However, the chief officer's 'designation' may exclude offences from treatment as 'relevant offences' in specified circumstances. The designation may embrace similar powers in relation to persons reasonably believed to have been acting, or be acting, in an antisocial manner; alcohol consumption in designated public places; confiscation of alcohol or tobacco; entry to save life or limb or prevent serious damage to property; seizure of vehicles used to cause alarm, etc.; abandoned vehicles; power to stop vehicles for testing; power to control traffic for the purpose of escorting heavy loads; carrying out road checks; powers in cordoned areas; and power to stop and search vehicles, etc., in authorised areas.

Currently, within the police areas of Devon and Cornwall, Gwent, Lancashire, Northamptonshire, West Yorkshire and the Metropolitan Police district, where the person concerned fails to comply with a requirement to give his name and address and the community support officer has reasonable grounds for suspecting a false or inaccurate name or address, that other person may be required to remain with the support officer for a period not exceeding 30 minutes, for the arrival of a constable. The alleged offender may elect to accompany the community support officer to a police station as an alternative to waiting. Failure to wait, or making off, is an offence.

A designation can give a power to use reasonable force in exercising the power to detain in respect of a relevant offence. At the time of writing, such a designation can only be given in the six force areas referred to above.

In relation to these powers (other than within the areas specified above), powers to detain persons are not in force at the time of writing and this applies to all auxiliary personnel.

An investigating officer

An investigating officer may apply for a warrant to enter and search premises under s 8 of PACE and has the powers of a constable under s 8(2) to seize and retain articles found during a search. The safeguards, etc., provided by PACE in relation to searches apply equally to him. The powers of a constable under s 9(1) of PACE (access to excluded and special procedure material) may be designated to an investigating officer. The various procedural matters prescribed by PACE in relation to such matters will apply to such an officer. Powers under ss 18, 19 and 21 of PACE to enter, search, seize and copy things seized may also be designated, as may powers to arrest for a further offence at a police station for another offence. In addition, a designation may include powers under the Criminal Justice and Public Order Act 1994 to require arrested persons to account for certain matters.

A detention officer

A designation may authorise a detention officer to require a person to attend a police station for the taking of a sample, photograph or fingerprints (and to take those fingerprints without consent), to photograph a detained person and to carry out intimate or non-intimate searches of detained persons and searches and examinations to establish identity (including the taking of a photograph of an identifying mark).

An escort officer

An escort officer may be authorised to take an arrested person to a police station and to escort a person in police detention. Where those powers are such that, in the case of a constable, there is a provision for the use of reasonable force, such force may be used by the designated person. However, in relation to entry to premises by force, such a power may only be exercised in the company and under the supervision of a constable or for the purpose of saving life or limb or preventing serious damage to property.

Community safety accreditation schemes

The Act also authorises a chief officer to establish and maintain a 'community safety accreditation scheme' for the exercise in the area, by accredited persons, of powers related to community safety and security and, in co-operating in combatting crime and disorder, public nuisance and other forms of antisocial behaviour. Any such scheme must contain provisions for arrangements to be made with employers who are carrying on a business in the police area for those employers to supervise the carrying out of such functions for the purpose of which powers are provided. Chief officers must also ensure that the employer has made satisfactory arrangements for the handling of complaints relating to the exercise of those powers.

Powers and the exercise of those powers

All such personnel exercising powers following designation or accreditation shall produce evidence of that designation or accreditation if requested to do so by the person concerned. In addition, such persons may be restricted in the exercise of powers to times when wearing approved uniform or badge. The Police Reform Act 2002, s 46, creates offences of assault upon designated persons, accredited persons or other persons assisting such persons, in the execution of their duties, resisting or wilfully obstructing such persons, and with intent to deceive, impersonating, making a statement or doing an act calculated falsely to suggest that a person is designated or accredited, or making any statement or doing any act calculated falsely to suggest that that person has powers as a designated or accredited person which exceed the powers which have actually been given.

All such auxiliary personnel must, in the discharge of their duties, have regard to the provisions of the Codes of Practice. A person lawfully in the custody of such a person must be treated as in police detention.

Where any power exercised by one of the above types of person includes power to use reasonable force to enter premises, that power may only be exercised in the company, and under the supervision of a constable, or to save life or limb or prevent serious damage.

Stage 2

Common law and statute law

Law

The law of the land now falls into two categories – common law and statute law – and it is interesting to trace the process by which our laws have come into being. In modern times, when Parliament is so frequently in session, it is always possible to set down rules which members of the community must obey, and to include these rules in Acts of Parliament prescribing particular punishments which law breakers shall suffer. If we consider the position in the earliest times, when people began to live together in villages or communities, we realise that this was not possible. Citizens began to make their own rules to enforce a code of morality; as such, customs began to gain acceptance and the origins of an ordered society began to appear. When recognising these origins, it is not difficult to understand that the Sovereign, foreign Sovereigns and their ambassadors were held to be above the law, for we are considering a time when Sovereigns and their official representatives were all-powerful.

Common law

The common customs of the people were recognised and developed by the judges of the Court of King's Bench between the twelfth and fourteenth centuries. Whilst judges no longer claim the right to declare acts to be contrary to common law, this recognition, that the right no longer exists, is recent. Although many of the old common law offences have now been included in various Acts of Parliament, some offences still exist in common law only. No statutory definition of these offences can be found and the most notable of them is murder. Judges have so frequently defined the offence that no problems exist in relation to its recognition. The interesting factor is that the penalty for murder has often been a matter for Parliamentary debate. Manslaughter, similarly, remains a common law offence, although the maximum penalty is set out in the Offences Against the Person Act 1861, and authority is given to the courts to pass such minimal sentences as that of a fine, conditional, or even absolute discharge, by the Powers of Criminal Courts (Sentencing) Act 2000. The authority of the common law has, therefore, been firmly established. Although concerned on many occasions with the penalties for these common law offences, Parliament has acknowledged that their basis is firmly established in our common law and requires no further definition. Perhaps the most common example of the use of common law offences today is in respect of certain offences of conspiracy.

The common law has been built up on the doctrine of precedent. Decisions of the High Court are reported and officially set down, and subordinate courts are subsequently compelled to acknowledge the precedent which has been set. The majority of such rulings made by High Courts involve a question of interpretation of the law. The power of High Court judges is considerable; Parliament may express its will by statute, but the meaning of all sections of any statute is a matter for interpretation by the High Court. Within the history of the common law, judges have frequently exercised a power to create new crimes, and having recognised that our common law consists of rules of conduct which have been acknowledged and approved by the courts, this is not surprising.

In the nineteenth century, it had almost been recognised that judges would no longer exercise their power to declare new offences, in view of the relatively simple process of declaring acts to be contrary to statutes. In *R v. Price* (1884), Stephen J. refused to declare it to be a criminal offence to cremate a dead body instead of burying it on the grounds that nothing should be punishable unless it is contrary to the law, and this seemed to be the end of judge-made law. However, in 1932, one Elizabeth Manley reported to the police that she had been robbed and provided them with a description of the man responsible. The police spent a considerable time in enquiries which rendered innocent people liable to suspicion. Mrs Manley was charged with a common law offence of causing a public mischief by wasting the time of the police and placing innocent persons in peril of arrest. She was convicted on the grounds that all such acts or attempts as tend to the prejudice of the community are indictable, and once again judges of the High Court had exercised their right to declare such actions contrary to law. Many years later, the Criminal Law Act 1967 included the offence of causing the wasteful employment of the police, which can be punishable by 6 months' imprisonment. The offence of causing wasteful employment of the police under s 51(2) of the Act of 1977 is a 'penalty offence' for the purposes of Part I of the Criminal Justice and Police Act 2001 and may be dealt with under a fixed penalty procedure (see page 478).

In 1953, the Court of Criminal Appeal criticised the findings in *R v. Manley* and Lord Chief Justice Goddard gave the opinion that new crimes could only be created by statute. The position then seemed to be clear until *Shaw v. DPP* in 1962, when, in the House of Lords, Lord Simonds said:

> I entertain no doubt that there remains in the courts of law a residual power to enforce the supreme and fundamental purpose of the law, to conserve not only the safety and order but also the moral welfare of the state, and that it is their duty to guard it against attacks that may be the more insidious because they are novel and unprepared for.

There is some merit in this point of view. It is no bad thing to have an independent chamber in which such matters can be impartially considered. It seems that our judges have reserved the right to consider acts which appear to be contrary to the common interest and, in circumstances of necessity, to declare such acts to be unlawful. Recently, judges have on a number of occasions ruled that Ministers have acted outside the powers provided by legislation. Most recently, the House of Lords held that it was an offence for a man to rape his wife, although it had always previously been considered that consent to marriage amounted to a consent to intercourse.

Statute law

The majority of crimes are set out in Acts of Parliament, approved by both Houses and given Royal assent. Most offences were first created in this manner, but many common law offences have been given statutory backing. It is common for statute law to change the definition of common law offences considerably.

As our society has become more complex, Parliament has found it increasingly necessary to regulate our way of life. Common law crimes can usually be described as acts which are in some way morally wrong, and for many years the freedom of the individual was so jealously guarded that matters outside this broad definition were not punishable. As our way of life, particularly in urban communities, became much more affected by the actions of others, the necessity to impose further controls became compelling. To prevent epidemics, legislation requiring the notification of certain diseases was passed and, in a similar way, the coming of the motor vehicle made further demands to impose restrictions upon the individual. The necessity to provide public services has led to an ever-increasing volume of social legislation, much of which restricts the freedom of members of the public to exercise an individual choice, in the interests of the majority. On occasions such individual choice has been eliminated by Parliament in circumstances in which the act required has no bearing upon the safety of the public at large, for example, the requirement for an adult to wear a seat belt. In addition, the multi-cultural nature of society has led to legislation which limits the right to free expression in the interests of maintaining the 'peace'. With the passing of each statute, the responsibility of the police service increases.

The process of passing an Act of Parliament through both the House of Commons and the House of Lords before seeking Royal assent is a much quicker process than having customs recognised by the courts as common law offences. There is, however, considerable pressure upon Parliamentary time and each Act requires three readings before the House and some debate in committee stage. For these reasons, Acts of Parliament may give power to some body such as the Queen in Council, a Minister of the Crown or a local authority to make subordinate legislation and prescribe penalties for their breach.

All Acts of Parliament are divided into sections, each section dealing with specific offences, definitions of terms used within the Act and particular classes of persons who may be exempted from provisions or particular circumstances in which a person may be exempt.

Subordinate legislation

The term 'subordinate' is almost self-explanatory and when applied to law it should be given this ordinary meaning. Because of the pressure of Parliamentary time, an Act of Parliament will frequently give a Minister authority to make regulations governing certain matters. The regulations may be called statutory instruments, byelaws or some other form of regulations, but they all have in common a parent Act, in which authority has been given for their making. At first sight it may seem to be a procedure which allows a Minister of the Crown to assume the full powers of both Houses of Parliament, but a safeguard is provided in that such regulations in draft form must be made available for examination before they become law. We have already described how the Police Act 1996 authorises the Home Secretary to make Police Regulations. Discipline regulations made in this way provide some punishments which are much more severe than those prescribed by Parliament for very serious offences. Dismissal, or a requirement to resign as an alternative to dismissal, is the heaviest of punishments and fines imposed under the Regulations can amount to a much more substantial fine that is usually imposed by magistrates' courts. Although classed as subordinate legislation, it is important to recognise that this form of legislation is just as necessary in our modern society as the common law and Acts of Parliament themselves. The frequency with which police officers enforce regulations, for example, made under the Road Traffic Acts, is ever-increasing.

A good example of the need for subordinate legislation is provided by the need to prescribe standards to which motor vehicles must be constructed. To debate before both Houses every detail of 'the safe motor vehicle' would be such a time-consuming process that the business of government would be seriously affected. Section 41 of the Road Traffic Act 1988 now provides authority for the Secretary of State to make regulations governing the use of motor vehicles and trailers on roads, their construction and equipment, and conditions under which they may be used. The Secretary of State for Transport has made, in consequence of the authority given to him, a statutory instrument (SI 1986 No. 1078) which is given the title Road Vehicles (Construction and Use) Regulations 1986.

Subordinate legislation is, therefore, frequently referred to as delegated legislation and can be of two kinds. The more important, including Orders in Council (made in an emergency by the Queen in Privy Council) and such regulations as the Road Vehicles (Construction and Use) Regulations 1986, are known as statutory instruments and are made subject to Parliamentary control by the Statutory Instruments Act 1946, which deals with their publication, approval and annulment. The less frequent and less important type of delegate legislation is the by-law. Particular statutes provide the power under which differing bodies may make by-laws. In certain instances Ministers are given power to make regulations by some means other than statutory instruments, but generally, if the problem is a national one, these forms of delegated legislation have little place.

Legislation of the European Union

The main effect of legislation of the European Union is that there is a requirement that such laws become incorporated into our own legislative programme. The best example is that provided by Regulation (EEC) 3820/85, which sets out maximum permitted driving periods for drivers of goods vehicles and large passenger-carrying vehicles.

European Convention on Human Rights

Under the Human Rights Act 1998, English and Welsh courts are legally obliged, so far as possible, to read, and give effect to, Acts of Parliament, Orders in Council and subordinate legislation in general in a way which is compatible with the rights and fundamental freedoms set out in the European Convention on Human Rights (ECHR) and the First Protocol to it ('the Convention rights').

This obligation, however, does not affect the validity or enforcement of any incompatible Act of Parliament or Order in Council made under the royal prerogative, or of any incompatible Order in Council, regulation, by-law or the like made under statutory powers if primary legislation prevents removal of the incompatibility.

Where a superior court determines that a provision in an Act of Parliament or Order in Council made under the royal prerogative is incompatible with a Convention right, it may make a declaration of that incompatibility. In addition, if a court determines that a provision of subordinate legislation made under statutory powers is incompatible with a Convention right, and it is satisfied that the primary legislation concerned prevents removal of the incompatibility, it may make a declaration of that incompatibility. The effect of such a declaration will be that a government minister may, by order, amend the legislation, as he thinks appropriate, to remove the incompatibility.

The Court of Appeal has upheld a declaration of incompatibility in respect of regulations which impose a liability upon the drivers and owners of lorries in which illegal immigrants are discovered. The Court said that it was not possible to read and give effect to the Immigration and Asylum Act 1999 and its subordinate regulations in a manner which was compatible with the convention rights recognising obligations under the Human Rights Act 1998, s 3. The Regulations which were under examination have since been replaced.

Such an amendment will also be possible without a declaration of incompatibility if a government minister or the Queen in Council thinks that a piece of legislation is, in the light of a finding of the European Court of Human Rights, incompatible with the United Kingdom's obligations under the Convention.

The 1998 Act gives the judges a new role:

(a) primary legislation and subordinate legislation must, so far as possible, be read and given effect to in a way which is compatible with the Convention rights, and this is so even if there is contrary authority on the question;
(b) if an appellate court is unable to interpret primary legislation so as to make it compatible with a Convention right it may make a declaration of incompatibility. It can also make such a declaration in circumstances involving secondary legislation where primary legislation prevents the removal of the incompatibility;
(c) it is unlawful for a public authority such as a court, local authority or police officer to act in a way which is incompatible with a Convention right.

Hence legislation must, as far as possible, be read and acted upon in a way which is compatible with the Convention rights and this must be done even if there is contrary authority concerning the point in question. Where it is necessary to correct a defect in terms of ambiguity or omission, a court will be able to insert words into a statute to recognise a Convention right. However, a court cannot interpret a statute in a way which Parliament could not have intended. Perverse interpretation or extensive redrafting is not permissible. Where the mismatch is too great, a court will have to make a declaration of incompatibility. This can have the effect of causing a Crown Court to ignore the rulings of a superior court in order to recognise a Convention right.

The effect of the Act is likely to be far-reaching. The Convention provisions mentioned in (c) above apply unless:

(a) as a result of one or more provisions of primary legislation, the authority could not have acted differently; or
(b) in the case of one or more provisions of, or provisions made under, primary legislation which cannot be read or brought into effect in a way which is compatible with the Convention rights, the authority was acting so as to give effect to or enforce those provisions.

This provides some protection for police officers who act in accordance with the law as it stands at the moment in question.

An individual may bring legal proceedings against any public authority in respect of any act which he considers to be unlawful in terms of the Convention rights. A court may grant such relief or remedy (including compensatory damages) or make an order as it considers appropriate within the terms of the Act of 1998. The actions of police officers are therefore subject to additional scrutiny, not only in relation to the direct exercise of powers, but also in relation to orders which may be made by police officers in respect of processions or directions to persons to quit land, etc. However, it is provided that damages in respect of a judicial act done in good faith may not be made otherwise than to compensate a person for arrest and detention in contravention of the terms of art. 5. See page 176 in relation to the implications of the Act of 1998 upon aspects of the law of evidence obtained by surveillance and page 489 in relation to public order offences.

The Convention rights specified in Schedule 1 to the 1998 Act include:

(a) the right not to be deprived of liberty save in specified cases, e.g. after conviction or lawful arrest, and in accordance with a procedure prescribed by law (art. 5 of ECHR);
(b) the right to a fair trial (including the presumption of innocence) (art. 6);
(c) the right to respect for private and family life (art. 8);
(d) the freedom of expression (art. 10); and
(e) the freedom of assembly and association (art. 11).

The exercise of the last three rights or freedoms mentioned may be restricted by the law on specified grounds if this is necessary in a democratic society (for example) in the interests of national security, for the prevention of disorder or crime, for the protection of health or morals, or for the protection of the rights and freedoms of others.

By art. 14 of the ECHR, the enjoyment of the Convention rights must be secured without discrimination on any ground such as sex, race, opinion, national or social origin or other status.

Studying the law

The form of legal textbooks can be somewhat frightening to the student who is opening their pages for the first time, but there are some simple rules which can make their exploration much more easily achieved. Immediately following the title of the book and its preface, one usually finds a table of contents of the items as they occur, chapter by chapter. A general heading is normally given to the chapter, and if we consider the subject matter with which we have just dealt, we can imagine a general heading of 'English law' under which might be included the subheadings 'Common law', 'Statute law', 'Subordinate legislation' and 'Studying the law'. In this way, a table of contents gives a reader a quick reference to matters which are dealt with in each chapter.

Students of law will frequently know the particular Act of Parliament to which they must refer. A table of statutes is, therefore, usually found in one of two forms: either in chronological order according to the year, month, and date of the passing of the Act, or in alphabetical order. For example, in the chronological table of statutes, older textbooks might begin with the Justices of the Peace Act 1361. Knowing the date of the Act to which you wish to refer is therefore essential to its quick location in the book. In the case of alphabetical ordering, one would find, for example, under the heading 'Criminal Justice Act', references to all sections of the Acts of 1925, 1948, 1961, 1967, 1972, 1982, 1987, 1988, 1991 and 1993 listed in that order. With this type of table, the reader must be aware of the title of the Act and it is not so necessary to be certain of the date of its passing.

As the study of law intensifies, it becomes necessary to refer to particular cases, and the decisions of the High Court are identified by the title given at the time at which they were reported; for example, *Morton v. Chaney* (1960), a case which is concerned with the meaning of 'sporting purposes' for the purposes of the exemption from the necessity to possess a firearm certificate, appears in the table before *Morton v. Confer* (1963), which is concerned with the burden of proof placed upon a defendant.

An alphabetical index is included in all legal textbooks and usually appears at the end. To form such an index, the key words likely to spring to the mind of the student are taken as the identifying factor. For example, research may be intended upon the law relating to brakes on motor cars, and recognising that there are likely to be two approaches in the minds of readers, either through the term 'motor car' or the term 'brakes', one usually finds that reference is made to the matter under both headings. In one instance it will be traced under the main heading 'Motor car' and the subheading 'Brakes', and in the other, under the main heading 'Brakes' and the subheading 'Motor car'. A good index to a law book will lead you to the information which you require whatever the approach adopted.

Functions of, and evidence accepted by, courts

Introduction

It is the responsibility of the police to enforce the law, whether it is statute law laid down by Parliament in Acts and Regulations or the common law, which recognises certain conduct as being criminal. It is not part of that responsibility to decide the guilt or the innocence of a person accused of a breach of the law; this is for the courts of justice to determine. Police officers are required to bring offenders before the court. Criminal proceedings, with rare exceptions, commence in a magistrates' court. There are certain instances in which discretion is allowed in relation to reporting persons for offences and guidance is usually given in force orders. Proceedings are instituted on behalf of the police by the Crown Prosecution Service. The head of that service is the Director of Public Prosecutions. The evidence gathered by police officers is used as a basis for a decision by Crown Prosecutors in respect of criminal proceedings against persons or bodies.

It is presumed in law that a person is innocent of any offence until proven guilty. It is the function of the courts to establish guilt or innocence and persons alleged to have committed offences will appear before courts by way of answering a summons, or having being arrested on the authority of a warrant or having been arrested where authorised by law without a warrant. The nature of these courts and their functions are described in some detail to assist understanding of the legal processes.

Magistrates' court

This is a court which is usually composed of two or three justices of the peace, which sits in a court-house known as a petty sessional court-house. The county is divided into petty sessional areas, each having its own magistrates' court and, although these courts deal mainly with matters arising in their own petty sessional areas, in certain circumstances they have the power to deal with criminal offences committed outside those areas. Where it appears to justices to be necessary or expedient, with a view to the better administration of justice, that a person charged with an offence should be tried jointly with, or in the same place as, some other person who is charged with an offence in that area, and who is in custody or is being proceeded against within their area, they have jurisdiction to try an offence committed outside their area. This could occur where a person is charged with driving a goods vehicle and failing to keep records of work and the operators of the vehicle are charged with associated offences connected with records kept at their premises.

Justices of the peace are generally not legally qualified and are members of the community appointed to the unpaid office of magistrate. The appointment is for life although most retire at the age of 70. A district judge (magistrates' court), a legally qualified magistrate appointed on a salaried basis, when sitting alone has all of the power of a bench of lay magistrates. Lay magistrates receive advice from a legally qualified justices' clerk who advises upon points of law, procedure and sentencing. There is also a justices' chief executive, appointed by a magistrates' courts committee, who is responsible for allocating responsibility to justices' clerks in relation to matters affecting particular courts.

In criminal matters, a magistrates' court has jurisdiction in relation to the following.

Offences triable only summarily

A magistrates' court hears and determines informations alleging any of the numerous statutory offences referred to as summary offences. These include all minor traffic offences such as exceeding the speed limit and contravention of the Road Vehicle (Construction and Use) Regulations. These summary offences form the bulk of all criminal offences. Although a single justice is empowered to deal with a few summary offences such as simple drunkenness, or with idle and disorderly persons, they have a limited power to impose punishment in such circumstances.

Offences triable only on indictment

Magistrates' courts have two alternative functions in respect of these offences. First, and this has been the traditional function, they conduct committal proceedings in respect of a person charged before them with an indictable-only offence. Of course, there is no question of that person electing trial by a magistrates' court; the magistrates' court will move straight to committal proceedings. The proceedings will be conducted in the same way as described above. Second, there is the 'sending for trial' procedure. Section 51 of the Crime and Disorder Act 1998 provides that, where an adult appears or is brought before a magistrates' court charged with an indictable-only offence, the court must send him forthwith to the Crown Court for trial:

(a) for that offence; and
(b) for any either-way or summary offence with which he is charged which fulfils the 'requisite conditions'. The 'requisite conditions' are that:
　(i) the either-way or summary offence appears to the court to be related to the indictable-only offence; and
　(ii) in the case of a summary offence, it is punishable with imprisonment or involves obligatory or discretionary disqualification from driving.

Section 51 deals with the situation where an adult who has been sent for trial subsequently appears before or is brought before a magistrates' court charged with an either-way offence or summary offence which fulfils the 'requisite conditions' described above. Section 51 provides that the magistrates' court may send the accused forthwith to the Crown Court for trial for the either-way or summary offence.

There are also provisions for an adult co-accused (or, in some cases, a juvenile co-accused) of an adult satisfying the above criteria to be sent for trial with that person, even though that co-accused is not charged with an offence which – in relation to him – must be tried on indictment.

Notice of transfer procedures – offences involving children in sex, violence or cruelty

By the Criminal Justice Act 1991, s 53, where a person has been charged with a sexual offence or an offence of violence or cruelty, the Director of Public Prosecutions may serve a 'notice of transfer' on the magistrates' court in whose jurisdiction the offence has been charged. To be valid, the notice must be served before the magistrates begin committal proceedings. The effect of a notice of transfer is to transfer the case directly to the Crown Court, without committal proceedings taking place. The Director may only serve such a notice if of the opinion that:

(a) there is sufficient evidence to warrant committal;
(b) a child who is the alleged victim, or who is alleged to have witnessed the commission of the offence, will be called as a witness at the trial; and
(c) that such transfer is necessary to avoid any prejudice to the welfare of the child.

Where such a notice of transfer is served, the proposed place of trial must be a Crown Court centre equipped with live television link facilities. Those so equipped are listed in a Practice Direction issued in 1992. In areas where the 'sending for trial' procedure operates, the provisions relating to notice of transfer do not apply in respect of an 'indictable only' offence.

Offences triable either way

Certain offences listed in Schedule 1 of the Magistrates' Courts Act 1980 are triable either way, that is, they may be tried either summarily or on indictment. Certain statutory offences are specified by the statute creating them as being triable either way.

Where a person appears or is brought before a magistrates' court on information charging him with an offence triable either way, the court, in the presence of the accused, must cause the charge to be written down if this has not already been done, and to be read to the accused. The court must then explain to the accused in ordinary language that if he indicates that he would plead guilty:

(a) the court must proceed as if the proceedings constituted from the beginning the summary trial of the information, and the court had asked whether he pleaded guilty or not guilty; and
(b) he may be committed for sentence to Crown Court if the court is of the opinion that one of the grounds set out below exists.

The court must then ask the accused whether (if the offence were to proceed to trial) he would plead guilty or not guilty. If he indicates that he would plead guilty the court must proceed as if the proceedings constituted from the beginning the summary trial of the offence and the accused had pleaded guilty. If the court is of the opinion:

(a) that the offence or the combination of the offence and other offences associated with it was so serious that greater punishment should be inflicted for the offence than the court has power to impose; or
(b) in the case of a violent or sexual offence, that a sentence of imprisonment for a term longer than the court has power to impose is necessary to protect the public from serious harm from him,

the court may commit the offender in custody or on bail to the Crown Court for sentence.

If the accused indicates that he would plead not guilty, or fails to indicate how he would plead, the court must afford first the prosecutor and then the accused an opportunity to make representations as to which mode of trial would be more suitable. The court must consider the nature of the case, whether the circumstances make the offence one of a serious character, whether the punishment which a magistrates' court could inflict would be adequate and any other relevant circumstances.

If, having considered these issues, the magistrates' court decides that trial on indictment is more suitable, it will commence to hold committal proceedings. If the court decides that summary trial is more suitable, it must explain to the accused that the offence appears more suitable for summary trial and that he can either consent to such trial or, if he wishes, be tried on indictment. He must be warned that if he is tried summarily and convicted, he may be sent to a Crown Court for sentence if one of the grounds set out above exists. If he consents to summary trial, the court must proceed summarily; if he does not, committal proceedings will be held.

Binding over

A magistrates' court may require a person to enter into a recognisance, that is, an undertaking, with or without sureties, either to keep the peace or to be of good behaviour. Justices have always had a power to bind over to keep the peace any person who it is feared will cause another, or his family, bodily harm, if that other person declares on oath that he is in fear of such harm and has good cause for his fear. The power to bind over to be of good behaviour is more comprehensive than binding over to keep the peace. The Justice of the Peace Act 1361 gives justices the power to make an order binding over not only persons who have disturbed the peace but also those whose conduct is likely to cause a breach of the peace, even though no person is in fear of bodily harm. Protesters who put the Queen's peace at risk by their disorderly activities may be bound over where their conduct would have the natural consequence of provoking others to violence. It is not necessary to show that they put any person in bodily fear. However, where the person concerned is taking part in a lawful activity, e.g. a demonstration, it must be shown that the natural consequence of the continuation of such conduct would be to provoke another to violence and that, in all the circumstances, it was the defendant who was acting unreasonably rather than some other person. The same arguments apply where protesters interfere with an angling competition by throwing stones into the water and at fishing lines. Although the activity itself is lawful, it is likely to provoke a violent reaction from competitors. The demonstrators should have desisted when requested to do so by police officers.

Such orders are for a fixed period, usually 12 months, and if a person fails to comply with such an order the court may commit him to custody for a period not exceeding 6 months, or until he sooner complies with the order.

Open court

Hearings in a magistrates' court, as a general rule, must be in open public court. The public may have access to the court-house to the extent to which the premises will contain them, but children under the age of 14 years must not enter the court unless they are babes in arms or are involved in the proceedings before the court. Examining justices enquiring into a case shall also sit in open court except where there is a statutory provision which permits the proceedings to be held in camera, and except where it appears to the court that the ends of justice would not be served by sitting in open court.

Advance disclosure of evidence

The Criminal Procedure and Investigations Act 1996 contains provisions relating to the advance disclosure of information which apply where:

(a) a person charged with a summary offence pleads not guilty;

(b) a person of 18 or over charged with an either-way offence, in respect of which a court proceeds to summary trial, pleads not guilty;

(c) a person under 18 charged with an indictable offence, in respect of which a court proceeds to summary trial, pleads not guilty.

The provisions also apply where a person is charged with an indictable offence and is committed for trial, or proceedings are transferred for trial, to the Crown Court.

The 1996 Act sets out a procedure which is summarised below.

Primary disclosure by prosecutor – The prosecutor must disclose previously undisclosed prosecution material to the accused if the prosecutor considers that the material might undermine the prosecution case. At the same time, he must give the accused a document specifying any non-sensitive prosecution material which has not been disclosed to the accused.

Compulsory disclosure by the accused – Where cases are to be tried on indictment, the accused is required to provide the prosecutor with a defence statement containing specified information concerning his defence. This must be provided after the accused has received information about the prosecution case and after primary disclosure by the prosecutor.

Voluntary disclosure by the accused – Where the case is to be tried summarily, the accused may give a defence statement to the prosecutor.

Secondary disclosure by the prosecutor – The prosecutor has a duty to provide additional prosecution material which might reasonably assist the defence disclosed by the accused.

Application by accused for disclosure – Following secondary disclosure by the prosecutor, the accused may apply for the disclosure of material which has not at that time been disclosed and which he reasonably believes may assist his defence.

Continuing duty of prosecutor to disclose – The prosecutor must continually keep under review (until the trial is concluded) the question of whether there is a need for further disclosure to the accused because certain evidence undermines the prosecution case, or because it may assist a defence disclosed by the accused.

Protected material – Material such as photographs or pseudo-photographs of victims of sexual offences or reports of medical examinations must only be disclosed to an accused's legal representative, who must give an undertaking that the material will not be retained by the accused or shown to unauthorised persons. Such material may be shown in connection with the proceedings or for the assessment or treatment of a defendant (whether before or after conviction). Where an accused has no legal representative disclosure must be made by an authorised person such as a prison governor or his nominated representative or the officer-in-charge of a police station or any other person appearing to the prosecutor to be an appropriate person.

Inferences where there are faults in disclosure by accused – Where an accused fails to give a defence statement, gives one out of time, puts forward inconsistent defences, puts forward at his trial a defence which differs from that set out in his defence statement, puts forward an undisclosed alibi or calls a witness to support an alibi about whom he made no disclosure in his defence statement, the court, or any other party with the leave of the court, may make such comment as appears appropriate. In such circumstances, the court or jury may draw such inferences as appear proper in deciding whether the accused is guilty of the offence concerned. In such matters the court must have regard to the extent of the differences between the actual defence and that disclosed in advance and as to whether there is any justification for it.

A person shall not be convicted of an offence solely on such an inference.

The Criminal Procedure and Investigations Act 1996 (Defence Disclosure Time Limits) Regulations 1997 require disclosure by the accused within 14 days after disclosure by the prosecutor. That period may be extended by the court, on the application of the accused, if the court is satisfied that the accused could not reasonably have acted within that period. There is no limit upon such an extension, or further extensions.

Where such a period expires on a bank holiday or at a weekend, it is extended so as to expire on the next day which is not such a day.

The Regulations do not prescribe a particular period in relation to disclosure by the prosecution. However, the Criminal Procedure and Investigations Act 1996, s 13, requires such disclosure as soon as is reasonably practicable in the particular circumstances described in the section.

Special circumstances in which there may be controlled access to material

There may be circumstances in which the uncontrolled disclosure of exhibits may prejudice the safety of some person. The Divisional Court has said that, in circumstances in which audio and video surveillance material might prejudice the safety of an undercover police officer if disclosed without control, a stipendiary magistrate was right to reject a defence application for a stay of proceedings as an abuse of process.

The Court said that there was a strong presumption in favour of the defence being supplied with all copiable exhibits. It is for the prosecution to displace that presumption. It must normally be a matter for the trial judge to determine in the particular circumstances of each case whether fairness could be achieved by the prosecution permitting the defence to inspect originals or copies of original exhibits, rather than providing copies. Protection of the safety and future usefulness of an undercover police officer is clearly a valid consideration and it is a matter of judgment whether, in the circumstances, that which was proposed was necessary and would not prejudice the defence.

Police procedure

Police procedure is controlled by the Disclosure: Criminal Procedure and Investigation Act 1996: Code of Practice under Part II. It can be summarised as follows.

The officer in charge of the case

The officer in charge of the case is responsible for the recording and retention of materials and this includes negative material resulting from the interview of persons who could give no positive evidence. The officer must make such material available to the disclosure officer.

The disclosure officer

The duties of the disclosure officer may be carried out by the officer in charge of the case. Where this is not done, there must be full consultation between both officers. The disclosure officer is the link between the investigators and the Crown Prosecution Service and is responsible for providing the material for 'primary disclosure' and performing any other tasks required by the prosecutor. He must ensure, by liaison with the officer in charge of the case where that is a different person, that all material is made available for examination.

Separate schedules of all non-sensitive material and sensitive material (if there is none, this fact should be noted) which may be relevant to the investigation should be prepared. The schedule of sensitive material should exclude that which is a part of the prosecution case. In the first instance, such schedules need only be prepared in the case of an indictable or either-way offence or where there is likely to be a not guilty plea at summary trial. Where an offence has been witnessed by a police officer, or an either-way or a summary offence has been admitted, such a schedule is not required unless there is a subsequent not guilty plea. Material which is extremely sensitive may be disclosed to the prosecutor separately.

The disclosure officer must then identify material which might undermine the prosecution case. He must also make available any record of a first description of an alleged offender, any explanation for the offence which may have been given by the accused, material which casts doubt upon the reliability of a confession and any material casting doubts upon the reliability of a witness. In addition, he must draw the attention of the prosecutor to any other material retained by the investigator or other parties which may fall within the requirements for primary disclosure. This is the material which the defence will wish to inspect at this stage. The prosecutor may request additional information.

When the defence statement has been received, the disclosure officer must review the material and inform the prosecutor of any material which might assist the defence. If this duty is carried out by the prosecutor, the disclosure officer remains responsible for ensuring that it is done. When this has been done, secondary disclosure can be made. Even after this has been done, the disclosure officer is under a continuing duty to review material to identify items which should be disclosed. A disclosure officer may be directly involved in the disclosure of material, which the prosecutor has agreed to disclose, to the defence.

The Code requires investigating officers to pursue all reasonable lines of enquiry whether they point towards or away from the suspect. Records should be made of all such enquiries. Such officers are also under a duty to review material continually with a view to disclosure. It is therefore important that they are made aware of any defence statement.

Youth court

A youth court is a court of summary jurisdiction. It is composed of justices chosen because of their special qualifications for dealing with juvenile cases. Not more than three justices may sit in a youth court and one of them must be a woman and one a man; however, in exceptional circumstances, a court may sit without a woman or, as the case may be, without a man. A district judge (magistrates' court) may sit alone. There is no public right of access to a youth court.

A magistrates' court before which a person under 18 appears charged with an offence which, in the case of an adult, is triable only on indictment or triable either way must deal with it summarily unless:

(a) the charge is one of homicide; or
(b) the offence is so grave that under specific statutory powers he, if found guilty, may be sentenced to be detained for a long period; or
(c) he is jointly charged with an adult (i.e. a person who has attained the age of 18) and the court considers it necessary in the interests of justice to commit them both for trial.

Jurisdiction

The general rule is that no charge against a child or young person may be heard by a magistrates' court other than a youth court. The exceptions to this general rule, which allow trial by a magistrates' court, are:

(a) where the juvenile is charged jointly with an adult;
(b) where an adult is charged with aiding, abetting, counselling, procuring, allowing or permitting an offence with which a juvenile is charged;
(c) where the fact that the person is a juvenile is discovered in the course of proceedings in a magistrates' court, the court may hear and determine the proceedings;
(d) where a juvenile is charged with aiding, etc., an offence committed by an adult; and
(e) where the charge against a juvenile arises out of circumstances which are the same as, or connected with, those which give rise to an offence by an adult (e.g. theft by a juvenile and handling by an adult).

Any court by or before which a child or young person is found guilty of an offence other than homicide in any of the circumstances set out above must send the case to a youth court to be dealt with as if he had been tried and found guilty by that court. In other words, they must send the case to a youth court for sentence.

The Act also gives an adult court discretion to remit a juvenile, who has been jointly charged with an adult, to a youth court for trial if the adult pleads guilty, is committed for trial or is discharged and the juvenile pleads not guilty.

When the offences charged are indictable, problems arise when these offences are committed by juveniles who have reached the age of 18 years when the offences come to trial. In such cases the appropriate date in relation to determining whether an accused has turned 18 for the purpose of proceedings is the date of his appearance before the court when it determines which mode of trial is to be adopted, which is not necessarily his first appearance.

The Crown Court

The Crown Court is part of the Supreme Court and may sit in any place in England and Wales. For administrative purposes the various locations of the Crown Court are grouped in six circuits, and within each circuit there are three tiers of the Crown Court. The first-tier centres deal with both civil and criminal cases and are served by High Court, circuit judges or recorders; second-tier centres deal with criminal cases only but are served by both High Court and circuit judges; third-tier centres deal with criminal cases only and are served only by circuit judges. Offences are classified into one of four classes and, depending upon this classification, a magistrates' court when committing a person for trial shall specify the most convenient location of the Crown Court to deal with the offence.

The judge sits with a jury of 12 members of the public selected from the electoral register, advising the jury concerning legal matters and the extent of evidence required to prove offences. It is for the jury to decide guilt or innocence. The judge imposes the sentence upon those persons found guilty for a jury.

Jurisdiction

In criminal matters the Crown court has jurisdiction in relation to the following:

(a) All proceedings on indictment. These are either indictable offences or offences where an accused person has exercised a right to claim trial by jury, and a magistrates' court has committed the accused to the Crown Court for trial or for sentence.

(b) Appeal against the decision of a magistrates' court. A person convicted by a magistrates' court may appeal to the Crown Court against his sentence if he pleaded guilty, or against his conviction or sentence if he pleaded not guilty. The convicted person may also appeal against the making of certain 'orders'.

When the Crown Court sits in the City of London it is known as the Central Criminal Court.

Certain summary offences may be dealt with by a Crown Court where a person is committed for an offence which is triable either way, if such offences are punishable by imprisonment or involve obligatory or discretional disqualification from driving and arise from the same or connected circumstances.

Court of Appeal (Criminal Division)

This court consists of the Lord Chief Justice, Lords Justice of Appeal and judges of the Queen's Bench Division of the High Court. A circuit judge may take up one of these positions in certain specified circumstances. A person convicted of an offence on indictment may appeal to the Court of Appeal against conviction with the leave of the Court of Appeal or trial judge. On an appeal against conviction, the Court of Appeal can dismiss the appeal, allow it and quash the conviction or substitute a conviction for another offence if it appears that the accused should have been convicted of that offence, rather than the one of which he was actually convicted. If fresh evidence has come to light, the court may order a new trial. It may also do so in any other case where the interests of justice so require.

A person convicted on indictment before a Crown Court may appeal against sentence with the leave of the Court of Appeal, and so may a person who has been sentenced by a Crown Court on committal for sentence. In the case of an appeal against sentence, the Court of Appeal may vary it but cannot increase the sentence. However, the Attorney-General may (in certain circumstances) refer a sentence to the Court of Appeal with its leave if it appears to be unduly lenient. In these circumstances, the Court of Appeal may impose a more severe sentence.

Queen's Bench Division of the High Court

This Court's jurisdiction is normally exercised by two or more judges, one of whom is usually a Lord Justice of Appeal and the other a judge of the Queen's Bench Division. One function of a Divisional Court is to hear appeals on points of law from magistrates' courts or from the Crown Court in respect of appeals from magistrates' courts to the Crown Court. Such appeal is known as appeal by case stated, since the magistrates' court or Crown Court is asked to 'state a case', i.e. set out its reasons for its finding on the basis of its interpretation of the law in relation to the facts found by it. The High Court is not concerned with any form of retrial.

Another function of a divisional court relates to the issue of habeas corpus. This is a writ to secure the release of a person who is unlawfully or unjustifiably detained, whether in a prison or in some private place. It is available in any case in which it is alleged that a person has been deprived of his liberty without authority.

Administrative Court

A new branch of the Queen's Bench Division is the Administrative Court. This deals with the judicial review of the decisions of an inferior court or other body. In such cases the Administrative Court will examine whether there was authority or power by which the decision made could have been properly reached; whether the procedure followed the rules of natural justice, or whether the exercise of discretion on the part of the decision-making body was lawful. Thus the court is not examining the correctness of the decision but whether it was lawfully and reasonably reached. Applications for judicial review in criminal cases are heard by a divisional court. Applications in such cases are heard by a single judge, unless the court directs a hearing by a divisional court.

Following such a review, the Administrative Court may issue certain orders or writs, as follows.

Mandatory order – This is an order of the Court demanding that a person, inferior court or other body carries out a duty. It could be that a magistrates' court might refuse to hear a charge because the members of the court were in sympathy with the actions of the defendants. A mandatory order could be obtained in such a case to require that court to hear the case and decide it on its facts, disregarding any personal views which might be held.

Prohibiting order – This order requires an inferior court or tribunal not to do something improper.

Quashing order – This order is used to quash a decision made by an inferior court or tribunal. Such an order could be made where it is alleged that the justices had an interest or a bias in a particular case.

House of Lords

This is the highest court in the land and is composed of the Lord Chancellor, ex-Lord Chancellors, Lords of Appeal in Ordinary and any other peers holding or who have held high judicial office. The court hears appeals only from the Court of Appeal or the Queen's Bench Division on questions of law which are certified by the Court of Appeal or Queen's Bench Division to be questions of law involving general public importance, and the court is satisfied that the point of law is one which ought to be considered by the House, and leave to appeal has been given by the Court or the House itself.

European Court

Where, at a trial or on an appeal, a question is raised which involves the interpretation of a piece of EU law, the matter can be referred to the European Court. If the question is raised within an appeal in the House of Lords, such a matter must be referred for a 'preliminary ruling'.

The functions of a court

When dealing with courts of justice, it was stated that a magistrates' court has jurisdiction in relation to summary offences. Persons accused of such offences appear before the court either by arrest with or without warrant, or by having received a summons to attend the court. There is a statutory provision enabling persons to plead guilty in certain cases without appearing before the court, but this procedure will be dealt with later.

When a person appears before the court, the substance of the offence that he is alleged to have committed will be read out to him and he will be asked by the court whether he pleads guilty or not guilty. It is for the court to decide whether an offence has been committed and, if it was, whether or not it was committed by the defendant. The procedure which the court follows depends upon the plea.

Procedure on plea of guilty

The court must be satisfied that this is a clear, unequivocal plea. If the accused pleads guilty and then says, for example, 'but I still don't think I was doing anything wrong', then clearly this is not a true plea of guilty and the court will, in practice, enter this plea as being 'not guilty'.

In the case of a guilty plea, the court may convict him without hearing any evidence although, in practice, the prosecution will usually give a brief outline of the facts in the case. If the accused wishes to dispute those facts, the court will normally require evidence on oath regarding the disputed facts. After the facts have been outlined or the evidence has been given, the accused will be asked whether he wishes to say anything, and this gives the accused an opportunity to put forward any mitigating facts which he wishes the court to consider when deciding his sentence. The court will hear any evidence of character and antecedents presented by the prosecution before reaching a decision as to the appropriate method of dealing with the accused, e.g. fine and/or imprisonment, probation, or discharge whether absolutely or conditionally and, where appropriate, endorsement of any driving licence or disqualification from driving.

Procedure on plea of not guilty

When an accused pleads not guilty to the offence with which he is charged, the court will hear the evidence before arriving at a decision and the presentation of evidence and speeches made to the court will follow a certain order.

Witnesses out of court

The court will, at the request of either party, make an order requiring the witnesses in the case to leave the court. This is done to ensure that each witness may be examined without having heard the evidence of previous witnesses, so that his testimony will not be influenced by what he has heard. In some courts it is an established practice for witnesses to leave the court during a hearing without the court making such an order, in others application is made to the court for an order. Should a witness remain after the making of an order to leave, the court must still hear his evidence but the value of his evidence may be diminished by his conduct in failing to leave the court.

Case for the prosecution

Prosecutions are now undertaken by the Crown Prosecution Service. The accused having made his plea of 'not guilty', the prosecutor may address the court when he will usually give a brief outline of the facts of the case. The witnesses for the prosecution will then be called one by one to give their evidence.

Examination-in-chief

A witness, having taken the oath or affirmation, will then give his evidence. As soon as the examination-in-chief reaches the facts in issue in the case, leading questions, that is, questions suggesting the answer which the prosecutor wishes or expects, may not be put to the accused. An example of such a leading question would be, 'This occurred, did it not, at the junction of High Street with Maple Avenue?' Such leading questions can usually be answered by a 'yes' or 'no'. The question, to be asked properly, should have been, 'Where did this incident occur?'

Cross-examination

When a witness has finished giving his evidence, the defence may then cross-examine him on the evidence he has given. At this stage, the defence is permitted to ask leading questions, and the object of cross-examination is to test the accuracy, veracity and credibility, or to diminish the value of his evidence.

Re-examination

At the conclusion of the cross-examination, the prosecutor has a right to re-examine the witness upon any new facts which have come to light or to clear up any ambiguity which has arisen during cross-examination. There is no right to ask leading questions or to introduce new evidence at this stage.

Written statements

In any proceeding, a written statement by any person is admissible in evidence to the same extent as oral evidence if certain conditions and provisions are complied with. This means that instead of a witness attending court and giving oral evidence from the witness box, his written statement may be admitted without the need for him to attend court. By using this method, the evidence of witnesses which is not disputed by the defence or prosecution can be put before the court in the absence of the witnesses. The conditions which must be complied with before such a statement can be tendered in evidence are laid down in s 9 of the Criminal Justice Act 1967, and are as follows:

(a) the statement purports to be signed by the person making it;
(b) the statement contains a declaration by that person to the effect that it is true to the best of his knowledge and belief and that he made the statement knowing that, if it were tendered in evidence, he would be liable to prosecution if he wilfully stated in it anything which he knew to be false or did not believe to be true;
(c) before the hearing at which the statement is tendered in evidence, a copy of the statement is served by, or on behalf of, the party proposing to tender it (i.e. the prosecution or the defence) on each of the other parties to the proceedings;
(d) none of the other parties or their solicitors, within 7 days from the service of the copy of the statement, serves a notice on the party so proposing objecting to the statement being tendered in evidence.

If the parties agree either before or during the hearing, the conditions in (c) and (d) above shall not apply. However, the following provisions also apply to such a statement:

(a) if it is made by a person under the age of 18, it shall give his age;
(b) it is made by a person who cannot read it, it shall be read to him before he signs it and shall be accompanied by a declaration by the person who so read the statement to the effect that it was read to the person making it;
(c) if it refers to any other document as an exhibit, the copy served on any other party to the proceedings shall be accompanied by a copy of that document or by such information as may be necessary in order to enable the other party to inspect or copy the document.

The court may, notwithstanding that a person's evidence is tendered by means of a written statement, require the witness to attend and give oral evidence.

Submission of 'no case to answer'

At the conclusion of the case for the prosecution, the accused or his legal representative may make a submission to the court that the prosecution has failed to establish a prima facie case, that is, sufficient evidence has not been produced to show that the accused may have committed the offence charged. If the court is satisfied that the prosecution has failed to make out a case to be answered, it may dismiss the information.

Case for the defence

It is important to consider the general position of the accused in relation to the issue of 'right to silence' before going on to consider the presentation of his case. It is possible that the prosecution will have already offered evidence of his failure or refusal to answer questions and may have invited the court to draw inferences from such failure.

Inferences from accused's silence

When questioned or charged

Section 34 of the Criminal Justice and Public Order Act 1994 provides that where, in any proceedings against a person for an offence, evidence is given that the accused:

(a) at any time before he was charged with the offence, on being questioned under caution by a constable trying to discover whether or by whom the offence had been committed, failed to mention any fact relied on in his defence in those proceedings; or

(b) on being charged with the offence or officially informed that he might be prosecuted for it, failed to mention any such fact,

being a fact, which in circumstances existing at the time, the accused could reasonably have been expected to mention when so questioned, charged or informed, as the case may be, a court may draw such inferences from the failure as appear proper. The Court of Appeal has held that a person who declines to answer questions at a police interview but who gives the interviewing officers a prepared statement containing all the facts relied on by him at his subsequent trial has 'mentioned facts' and therefore falls outside s 34. This rule does not apply in a case where an accused was at an authorised place of detention (a police station or other prescribed place) at the time of the failure if he had not been allowed an opportunity to consult a solicitor prior to being questioned, charged or informed that he might be prosecuted.

The Court of Appeal has described the formal conditions to be met before any inferences may be drawn by a jury from a failure to mention a fact later relied upon:

(a) there must be proceedings against a person for an offence;

(b) the alleged failure must occur before a person is charged;

(c) the alleged failure had to occur during questioning under caution by a constable;

(d) the questioning had to be directed to trying to discover whether, or by whom, the alleged offence had been committed;

(e) the alleged failure by the defendant had to be to mention any fact relied on in his defence in those proceedings; and

(f) the fact that the defendant had failed to mention a fact which, in the circumstances existing at the time, he could reasonably have been expected to mention when so questioned.

Where it was submitted, in relation to (d), that at the time of the interview the police were not attempting to discover who was responsible for the offence as they were already in possession of sufficient evidence upon which to charge the interviewee, the Court of Appeal said that the issue was not clear as the police had come into possession of documents at the time of the arrest and the origin of these documents required investigation. It was desirable that police officers should have the opportunity to question suspects as explanations may be put forward which indicated that no offence had been committed, or that it had been committed by someone else. It is only where the officer is truly of the opinion that there is sufficient evidence upon which a successful prosecution may be based that an interview should not take place or should be discontinued.

The Court of Appeal said that in relation to (e), two questions were raised:

(i) was there some fact which the defendant had relied upon in his defence?; and
(ii) did the defendant, when he was being questioned in accordance with s 34, fail to mention it?

It added that, while it was open to a judge to give guidance to a jury on its approach to evidence and, in proper circumstances, to warn a jury against drawing an inference, he must bear in mind that the jury was the tribunal of fact. The power to draw inferences, as appear proper, is one which is given to a jury because a jury is the tribunal of fact and the drawing of appropriate inferences from fact was the task of the tribunal of fact.

The accused persons were charged with offences of supply and possession of Class A drugs and were advised by their solicitor not to answer questions as the solicitor considered that they were suffering from withdrawal symptoms. A force medical officer considered that they were fit to be interviewed. They gave no explanation for conduct which had been observed by the police. At trial they gave innocent explanations for their conduct and, at the request of the prosecutor, the trial judge admitted evidence of the 'no comment' interviews, telling the jury that it was a matter for them whether any adverse inference should be drawn from their failure to mention these innocent explanations when interviewed. His decision was endorsed by the Court of Appeal.

Where a solicitor merely advises a client to say 'no comment', the solicitor's statement is not hearsay as it is not a statement of fact and its truth is not, therefore, in issue. That statement may be relevant to the issue then before the court as it is relevant to the question of why the accused did not give an explanation. However, if it is not supported with evidence of reasons why no comment should be made which may be valid in the circumstances, it is insufficient reason for an accused's failure to give an explanation.

However, the section has no application where there has been a 'no comment' interview (whether on the advice of a solicitor or not) and a defendant calls no witnesses and does not give evidence on his own behalf. The failure must be to mention some fact relied upon in his defence.

The European Court of Human Rights has held that the fact that an accused has been given legal advice to remain silent must be given appropriate weight by a domestic court because there may be good reason for such advice, and that a good reason for not drawing an inference was bona fide legal advice. The European Court has held that an accused's right to a fair trial under art. 6 of the European Convention on Human Rights was violated where the judge's direction to the jury failed to strike the right balance between the right to silence and the circumstances in which an adverse inference may properly be drawn; in particular, the jury should have been directed that if they were satisfied that the accused's silence at interview could not sensibly be attributed to his having no answers that would stand up to questioning or investigation, they should not draw an adverse inference. It added that particular caution was required before an adverse inference could be drawn from silence during questioning.

The Court of Appeal has stressed that the effect of this decision is that a jury can only draw an adverse inference if they are satisfied that an accused's silence was for a non-innocent reason. Thus, it stated, if the jury is satisfied that the accused had no answer, or no answer which would stand up to questioning or investigation, and simply latched on to the legal advice as a convenient shield behind which to hide, an adverse inference could be drawn. However, if the jury thinks that an innocent reason given by the accused may be true it may not draw an adverse inference against him from his silence.

These special provisions of the Criminal Justice and Public Order Act 1994, s 34, do not affect the admissibility of evidence of silence or other reaction of an accused to things said in his presence relating to the conduct in respect of which he is charged, where such matters are admissible under other provisions. Nor do they preclude the drawing of any inference from any such silence or other reaction of the accused which could properly be drawn apart from the section. Thus, where an accused nods in response to a question, evidence of his seeming acceptance of the statement made to him continues to be admissible as direct evidence.

Failure to account for objects, etc.

Section 36 of the 1994 Act provides that where:

(a) a person is arrested by a constable and there is
      (i) on his person; or
      (ii) in or on his clothing or footwear; or
      (iii) otherwise in his possession; or
      (iv) in any place at which he is at the time of his arrest,
      any object, substance or mark, or there is any mark on any such object; and
(b) that or another constable investigating the case reasonably believes that the presence of the object, substance or mark may be attributable to the participation of the person arrested in the commission of an offence specified by the constable; and
(c) the constable informs the person arrested that he so believes, and requests him to account for the presence of the object, substance or mark; and
(d) the person fails or refuses to do so,

then, if in any proceedings for the offence so specified evidence of those matters is given, the court or jury may draw such inferences from the failure or refusal as appear proper.

Thus, an arrested person may be required to account for the presence of objects, substances or marks on his person, clothing, footwear or possessions. These provisions apply to the condition of clothing or footwear in addition to substances or marks thereon.

Such a person must be told in ordinary language of the consequences of his failure or refusal to comply with such a request. The section does not preclude the drawing of other inferences in these circumstances which could properly be drawn apart from the section.

Failure to account for presence in a particular place

Section 37 of the 1994 Act makes similar provisions in respect of such a person failing or refusing to account for his presence at a particular place, where:

(a) a person arrested by a constable was found by him at that place at or about the time the offence for which he is arrested is alleged to have been committed; and
(b) that or another constable investigating the offence reasonably believes that the presence of that person at that place and at that time may be attributable to his participation in the commission of the offence; and

(c) the constable informs the person that he so believes, and requests him to account for his presence; and

(d) the person fails or refuses to do so.

The term 'place' includes any building or part of a building, any vehicle, vessel, aircraft or hovercraft and any other place whatsoever.

The position of the accused at trial

Section 35 of the 1994 Act provides that at the trial of any person the court shall, at the conclusion of the evidence for the prosecution, satisfy itself (in the presence of the jury where appropriate) that the accused is aware that the stage has been reached at which evidence can be given for the defence. He must also be made aware that he can, if he wishes, give evidence and that, if he chooses not to give evidence, or having been sworn, without good cause refuses to answer any question, it will be permissible for the court or jury to draw such inferences as appear proper from his failure to give evidence or his refusal, without good cause, to answer any question. However, the Divisional Court has said that although it is mandatory to give such a warning, where a court omits to do so but does not draw any adverse inference from failure to give evidence, the omission does not render the conviction unsafe.

This does not apply where the accused's guilt is not in issue (so that where there is a guilty plea an accused cannot be required to give an account of his actions) or where the court considers that the accused's physical or mental condition is such that it is undesirable for him to give evidence. Nor does it apply where, at the conclusion of the evidence for the prosecution, it is established that the accused will give evidence. In addition, the section makes it clear that an accused's right to silence remains, in that he is not compellable to give evidence and will not be in contempt by failure to do so. However, where a person has been sworn and then refuses to answer any question, he shall be considered to have done so without good cause unless he is entitled to do so on the grounds of privilege, or by some enactment, or the court in the exercise of its general discretion excuses him from answering it.

The Court of Appeal has examined and rejected a submission that 'reasons or excuses' for silence might exist which could properly be advanced by defence counsel without the need for supporting evidence. It was suggested that where, for example, a defendant with previous convictions had attacked the character of a prosecution witness and did not want to give evidence as he would then be liable to cross-examination concerning his criminal record, this would apply. The Court of Appeal said that this would lead to a situation where a defendant with a record would be in a more privileged position than one with a clean record.

The Court of Appeal also said that, apart from exceptions included in s 35(1) (guilt not in issue/physical or mental condition of accused), it is open to a court to decline to draw an inference from silence where the circumstances of the case justified such a course. However, there must be some evidential basis, or exceptional factors, making that a fair course to take. The inferences permitted by s 35 are only those which 'appear proper'.

The Court highlighted the need for a jury to be told that:

(a) the burden of proof remained upon the prosecution;

(b) the defendant was entitled to remain silent;

(c) an inference could not by itself prove guilt;

(d) the prosecution must have established that there was a case to answer before drawing such an inference; and

(e) if, despite any evidence relied upon to explain silence or in the absence of any such evidence, the jury concluded that silence could only sensibly be attributed to the defendant's having no answer, or none that would stand up to cross-examination, they might draw an adverse inference.

Where a man was convicted of eight counts of theft and attempted theft but had only been interviewed by the police in respect of one offence, the Court of Appeal held that he could not claim that the police had deprived him of his right to comment while matters were fresh in his mind and that the judge should not, therefore, have allowed the jury to draw inferences from his silence at trial. The Court of Appeal said that nothing had prevented him from making a statement to his legal advisers while matters were fresh in his mind.

The accused or his representative may at this stage address the court whether or not evidence is called. If there are any witnesses for the defence, they are called one by one to give evidence in exactly the same way as the witnesses for the prosecution during examination-in-chief, cross-examination and re-examination. The accused person may also give evidence on his own behalf, but he cannot be compelled to give evidence. He must give evidence first unless the court in its discretion allows otherwise.

An accused person who does give evidence may be asked questions in cross-examination about the offence with which he is charged, but he may not be questioned about any other offences he may have committed, or as to his character, unless:

(a) he has given evidence of his good character; or

(b) the defence has asked questions of the prosecution witnesses with a view to establishing the good character of the accused; or

(c) he has given evidence against another person charged in the same proceedings; or

(d) the fact that he has committed other offences is admissible in evidence against him.

The Court of Appeal has held that, when rebutting a claim of good character, the prosecution may rely on attested copies of convictions by a foreign court. Fingerprint evidence went to the necessary objective of establishing that the person convicted and the defendant were the same person.

Rebutting evidence

At the conclusion of the evidence for the defence, the prosecution may, with leave of the court, call evidence to rebut new evidence introduced by the defence, but such rebutting evidence must be confined to a matter which has arisen unexpectedly in the course of the defence.

Unsworn statement by accused

When the accused does not give evidence on oath in his own defence, he does not have the right to make an unsworn statement to the court. However, if unrepresented he may address the court or jury in any way which would have been allowed to his solicitor or barrister.

Final address

The accused or his representatives may address the court at the conclusion of the evidence for the defence, but only if he has not previously addressed the court, or where the court grants permission. Where the court grants leave to one party to address the court twice, it shall not refuse leave to the other. Where both the prosecution and the defence have been granted leave to address the court twice, the prosecution will address the court first, leaving the accused or his representative to have the last word.

Decision of the court

After hearing all the evidence, the court will come to a decision and either convict the accused or dismiss the information. The court may adjourn before reaching a decision and may seek the advice of the justices' clerk; the executive should not retire with the magistrate as a matter of course, but only where his advice is required, and even then he should leave the magistrates to arrive at a decision.

Where the court convicts the accused, the court will ask if there is anything known about the accused, and the court may be given details of any previous convictions that the accused may have and details of his character and antecedents.

The accused may ask the court to take into consideration other offences committed by him over which the court has jurisdiction. He may also call evidence of his character and put before the court any mitigating facts which he wishes the court to consider when determining his sentence.

The court may then proceed to sentence the accused, or the court may adjourn the case before sentencing for enquiries to be made as to the most suitable method of dealing with the accused. Such an adjournment must not be for more than 4 weeks, or 3 weeks if the accused is remanded in custody.

Plea of guilty by post in magistrates' court

A great many of the cases heard in a magistrates' court involve minor summary offences where a defendant pleads guilty to the charge made against him, and in order to allow a defendant to plead guilty by post, and for the case against him to be heard at a magistrates' court in his absence, the Magistrates' Courts Act 1980 sets out a procedure which the prosecution can initiate. This permits such cases, where a defendant pleads guilty, to be heard without the need for the defendant to appear, or for any witnesses to be called.

The trial of such a case may take place in the absence of a defendant if:

(a) the case is one to be heard on summons (it does not apply to cases where a person has been arrested and bailed to appear before the court);

(b) the offence is not one for which the accused is likely to be sentenced to be imprisoned for a term exceeding 3 months, or an offence specified by the Secretary of State;

(c) the clerk of the court has been notified by the prosecutor that the accused, when served with the summons for the offence, was also served with
  (i) a notice explaining the procedure under the Magistrates' Courts Act 1980;
  (ii) *either* a concise statement of the facts of the case which will be put before the court in the event of him notifying the clerk of his plea of guilty *or* a copy of

such written statement or statements complying with the Criminal Justice Act 1967, ss 9(2)(a), (2)(b) and (3) (proof by written statement), as will be so placed in those circumstances;

    (iii) if any information relating to the accused will or may in the circumstances, be placed before the court by or on behalf of the prosecutor, a notice containing or describing the information; and

(d) the accused or his solicitor must have notified the clerk of the court that he wishes to plead guilty. On receipt of this information, the clerk will inform the prosecutor.

This procedure may be followed where a summons is issued in respect of a person who has attained the age of 16 or 17 years at the time when it is issued to appear before a youth court.

Where this procedure has been followed and the accused does not appear and it is proved to the satisfaction of the court, on oath or in such manner as may be prescribed, that the documents mentioned above have been served upon the accused with the summons, the court may proceed to hear and dispose of the case in the absence of the accused, whether or not the prosecutor is also absent, in like manner as if both parties had appeared and the accused had pleaded guilty. The court must cause the various documents referred to above, together with any submission which the accused wishes to be brought to the attention of the court with a view to mitigation of the sentence, to be read out by the clerk of the court. However, in the case of a statement under the Criminal Justice Act 1967, s 9, this is subject to any direction given by the court. Where such a direction is given, the clerk of the court must give an account of so much of the statement which is not read aloud. No other information may be put before the court. Such an absent defendant cannot be sentenced to imprisonment or any disqualification in his absence.

If the defendant, after giving notice that he will have the case dealt with in his absence, appears before the court, the court may, with his consent, proceed as if he were absent and this also applies where no notification of an intention to plead guilty has been received and the defendant appears before the court. However, in such cases, before accepting the plea of guilty and convicting the accused under this procedure, the court must afford the defendant the opportunity to make an oral submission with a view to mitigation of sentence and where that is done any statement of mitigating circumstances submitted becomes invalid.

Offences triable on indictment

Where:

(a) a person is charged before a magistrates' court with an offence which is triable only on indictment; or

(b) a person is charged before a magistrates' court with an offence triable either way and

    (i) the court has decided that the offence is more suitable for triable on indictment, or

    (ii) the accused has not consented to be tried summarily,

the court and the prosecutor shall proceed with a view to committing the proceedings for the offence to the Crown Court for trial.

The committal proceedings

The magistrates sit as examining justices, their duty being to conduct a preliminary enquiry into the offence. They must decide whether there is sufficient evidence upon which a reasonable jury, properly directed, could convict. They may act as examining justices in respect of any indictable offence wherever it was committed. This permits an offender to be dealt with at one court for offences committed anywhere in England or Wales. The law concerning committal proceedings was most recently amended by the Criminal Procedure and Investigation Act 1996. Oral evidence is not admitted in committal proceedings. The only evidence which is admitted is:

(a) *Written statement* – If it purports to be signed by the person who made it and it contains a declaration by that person to the effect that it is true to the best of his knowledge and belief and that he made the statement knowing that, if it were to be tendered in evidence, he would be liable to prosecution if he wilfully stated in it anything which he knew to be false or did not believe to be true. A copy must be given, by or on behalf of the prosecutor, to each of the other parties to the proceedings.

   Where such a statement is made by a person under 18 years of age, it must give his age; if it is made by a person who cannot read it, it must have been read to him before he signs it and it must be accompanied by a declaration by the person who so read the statement to the effect that it was so read; and if it refers to any other document as an exhibit, the copy given to the other parties to the proceedings must be accompanied by a copy of that document or by such information as may be necessary to enable the party to whom it is given to inspect that document or a copy of it.

(b) *Deposition* – A justice of the peace may issue a summons addressed to a reluctant witness who is likely to be able to make a statement containing material evidence, or produce a document or other exhibit likely to be material to committal proceedings. Such a person may have his evidence taken before a justice as a deposition. Such a deposition and documents and other exhibits to which it refers are admissible in committal proceedings provided that a copy has been given to the other parties and, if there is a reference to any other document as an exhibit, it is accompanied by a copy of that document or such information as will enable those parties to inspect it.

(c) *Documents or other exhibits referred to in written statements or depositions of the type referred to above* – These are admissible in committal proceedings.

(d) *Statements made by witnesses who are unlikely to attend trial* – The Criminal Justice Act 1988, ss 23 and 24 (see page 114), makes provision for the admissibility at trial, in certain circumstances, of statements made by persons who are, for various reasons, unlikely to be able to attend the trial of an accused. These provisions also apply to committal proceedings.

(e) *Other documents* – The Criminal Procedure and Investigation Act 1996 makes provision for certain documents which are provided for by statute to be admissible in committal proceedings.

   A magistrates' court enquiring into an offence as examining justices must, after consideration of the evidence,

   (i) commit the accused for trial if it is of the opinion that there is sufficient evidence to put him on trial for any indictable offence;

   (ii) discharge him if it is of the opinion that he is in custody for no other cause than the offence under inquiry, subject to other provisions of the Magistrates' Courts Act 1980 relating to the summary trial of indictable offences.

Where examining justices are satisfied that all the evidence tendered by or on behalf of the prosecutor falls within the provisions relating to written statements and documents, they may commit the accused for trial without consideration of the contents of any statements, etc., unless the accused, or one of the accused, has no legal representative acting for him in the case, or such a legal representative has requested the court to consider a submission that there is insufficient evidence to put the accused on trial by jury for the offence.

(f) *Committal for sentence* – The Criminal Justice Act 1988, s 41, makes provision for a person committed for trial in the Crown Court for an offence triable either way to be committed additionally for a summary offence if such offence is

   (i) punishable by imprisonment or involves obligatory or discretional disqualification from driving, and

   (ii) arises from the same or connected circumstances as the offence triable either way.

Notice of transfer

The Criminal Justice Act 1991, s 53, provides that where a person has been charged with a sexual offence or an offence of violence or cruelty, the Director of Public Prosecutions may serve a 'notice of transfer' on the magistrates' court in whose jurisdiction the offence has been charged. The effect of such a notice is to transfer the case directly to the Crown Court without committal proceedings taking place. The Director may only serve such notice if he is of the opinion that:

(a) there is sufficient evidence to warrant committal;

(b) a child who is the alleged victim, or who is alleged to have witnessed the commission of the offence, will be called as a witness at the trial; and

(c) that such a transfer is necessary to avoid any prejudice to the welfare of the child.

Trial by jury

Before a criminal charge can be tried at the Crown Court, a written accusation of the crime with which the accused is to be charged must be preferred before the Crown Court by delivering it to the appropriate officer of the court. This written accusation is called an indictment. An indictment may contain a number of charges, each of which is referred to as a count.

The accused is called to the bar of the court by name and the indictment is read over to him and explained if necessary. He is then asked whether he pleads guilty or not guilty to each count contained in the indictment. If the accused pleads not guilty to any charge, a jury must be sworn to try the issue of whether or not he is guilty of the offence.

All trials on indictment take place before a jury consisting of 12 individuals chosen at random from a panel of jurors. Arrangements for these panels or list of persons liable for jury service are made by the Lord Chancellor, who is responsible for the summoning of jurors to attend for service at the Crown Court. An accused has certain rights to challenge the jury as a whole or individual persons summoned for jury service at his trial. If, during the course of the trial, a juror dies or has to be discharged through illness, but the number of jurors left does not fall below nine, the trial may still continue and a verdict

▄▀

may be reached. However, in a trial for murder or any offence punishable with death, this provision will not apply unless both the prosecution and defence agree in writing to continue to trial.

When an accused pleads not guilty, the witnesses give evidence for the prosecution and for the defence and the jury decides whether he is guilty or not. The jury in criminal proceedings need not be unanimous in reaching its verdict if:

(a) in a case where there are not less than 11 jurors, 10 of them agree on the verdict; and
(b) in a case where there are 10 jurors, nine of them agree on the verdict;

and a verdict so reached is referred to as a majority verdict. Such a verdict shall not be accepted by the court unless the foreman of the jury states in open court the number of jurors who respectively agreed to and dissented from the verdict. Two hours must have elapsed between the time when the last member of the jury left the jury box to go to the jury room and the time when the jury returned to the jury box and is questioned concerning its verdict. The Crown Court may insist upon a longer period, bearing in mind the nature and complexity of the case.

If the accused is found guilty, the court will hear evidence of his character generally and of any previous convictions. The accused may ask the court to take into consideration other offences committed by him which are still untried, and the judge may properly take such offences into consideration when sentencing the accused.

Evidence

The basic functions of a court dealing with criminal matters are to determine:

(a) whether or not an offence has been committed, and if it is proved that an offence has been committed,
(b) whether or not the person accused before the court committed that offence, and finally, if this is proved,
(c) the most appropriate way of dealing with that person, i.e. by fine, by imprisonment, by conditional or absolute discharge, or by placing him on probation.

The proceedings before the court follow a process of enquiry: the prosecution attempting to prove certain facts and points to the court beyond reasonable doubt, and the defence attempting to disprove the same facts or points on the balance of probabilities. Like most other human activities, the proceedings are governed by certain rules as to the manner in which any fact or point in issue or question may be proved or disproved, and these rules are known as the rules of evidence.

Any evidence brought before a court must relate to the 'facts in issue'; by this we mean the facts which the prosecution alleges constitute the offence charged, and which the defence disputes. If the police bring proceedings against a person for a minor summary offence, e.g. riding a pedal cycle on a road between sunset and sunrise without showing obligatory lights to the front and rear, the facts in issue in such a case would be:

(a) *identity* – that the person before the court was the person seen riding the pedal cycle;
(b) *the place* – that the offence took place on a road;
(c) *the time* – that the incident took place between sunset and sunrise; and

(d) *the statutory provision breached* – that the cycle was not showing the lights required by law.

An accused person may dispute all these facts in issue, in which case the prosecution must bring evidence of all such facts before the court and convince the court, beyond reasonable doubt, that the facts alleged are true.

The accused may also bring evidence to show that the facts in issue have not been proved against him. Because it is for the prosecution to prove to the court the facts it alleges, an accused only has to show to the court that on the balance of probabilities, the facts are not true; this is called 'the burden of proof', and the burden of proving an offence rests on the prosecution throughout criminal proceedings.

Direct and circumstantial evidence

Direct evidence may be given of a particular fact which is in issue. If a person is found to be in possession of an explosive device, direct evidence will be given of this fact by the person who found him in possession of the device. The device will be produced to the court as direct evidence of its existence.

Circumstantial evidence is evidence of a fact, from which the existence of another fact, can be inferred. Where a person is charged with murder, evidence from a witness who saw him shoot the victim would be direct evidence. Evidence from a witness who did not see the actual shooting, but who saw the accused entering the victim's house carrying a gun shortly before the shot was fired, would be circumstantial evidence. It is evidence of a related fact from which the fact in issue (the accused's firing of the gun) may be inferred.

Presenting evidence

Evidence may be given to the court in the following manner.

(a) *Oral evidence* – This is a statement made by a witness before the court. In the example quoted, relating to the pedal cycle, it could be a police officer who, having been lawfully sworn, gives oral evidence that at a certain time, date and place, he saw the accused person riding the pedal cycle and at that time it was not displaying the obligatory lights required by law. Oral evidence is usually given by a witness concerning matters of which that person has knowledge; something they have seen, or heard, or felt, or smelt or touched.

(b) *Documentary evidence* – This is where the contents of a document are given in evidence to the court. Generally the document itself is also produced to the court, but in certain circumstances a verbal account of the contents may be given without the document itself being produced. An example of where the document is produced and the contents are given is where an accused person has made a written statement under caution to a police officer and he produces the statement and reads it to the court.

(c) *Real evidence* – This is where an article connected with the circumstances of the case is produced to the court by a witness who usually gives a verbal account of the article and its connection with the case. In an offence of theft it could be that a police officer produces to the court certain property which the accused is charged with stealing, and the officer states that he found the property in the possession of the accused, thus connecting the accused with the stolen property. Such articles are exhibits to be produced to the court and are the responsibility of the officer in charge of the case.

On occasions, difficulty is experienced in deciding whether certain types of documents are documentary or real evidence. This can be established by examining the reason why the evidence is produced. If, for example, a computer printout of telephone calls made at a hotel is produced merely to prove that certain calls were made, the printout would be real evidence; it would be documentary evidence if the printout was offered as evidence of the contents of the telephone calls.

It can be seen that these three methods overlap each other; verbal or oral evidence is generally given in connection with documents and articles produced before a court.

Special measures directions in case of vulnerable and intimidated witnesses

The relevant provisions are in the Youth Justice and Criminal Evidence Act 1999.

Witnesses who are eligible for special measures

A witness may be eligible for special measures under s 16 or 17 of the 1999 Act to help him in giving his evidence.

The Youth Justice and Criminal Evidence Act 1999, s 16, provides that a witness (other than the accused) is *eligible* for special measures if:

(a) the witness is under 17 at the time of the hearing (the time at which a court must decide whether he is eligible for such assistance); or
(b) if the court considers that the quality of the evidence given by the witness is likely to be diminished by reason of the witness
  (i) suffering from a mental disorder within the meaning of the Mental Health Act 1983, or
  (ii) otherwise having a significant impairment of intelligence and social functioning, or
  (iii) having a physical disability or suffering from a physical disorder.

References to the quality of a witness's evidence are to its quality in the terms of completeness, coherence and accuracy. 'Coherence' refers to a witness's ability in giving evidence to give answers which address the questions put to him and can be understood both individually and collectively (i.e. in relation to a particular question as to his evidence generally).

Section 17 of the 1999 Act provides that a witness (other than the accused) is *eligible* for assistance where the court is satisfied that the quality of evidence given by him is likely to be diminished by reason of fear or distress on his part in connection with testifying in the proceedings. In determining whether it is so satisfied, the court must consider in particular:

(a) the nature and the alleged circumstances of the offence to which the proceedings relate;
(b) the age of the witness;

(c) such of the following matters which appear relevant –
  (i) the social and cultural background and ethnic origins of the witness,
  (ii) the domestic and employment circumstances of the witness,
  (iii) any religious beliefs or political opinions of the witness;
(d) any behaviour towards the witness on the part of
  (i) the accused,
  (ii) members of the family or associates of the accused, or
  (iii) any other person who is likely to be an accused or a witness in the proceedings.

Where the complainant in a sexual offence (under the Sexual Offences Act 1956; the Indecency with Children Act 1960, the Sexual Offences Act 1967, the Criminal Law Act 1977, s 54, or the Protection of Children Act 1978) is a witness in proceedings relating to that offence (or other offence), there is a presumption that that person is *entitled* to 'assistance' unless the witness waives that entitlement.

Thus, s 16 applies 'special measures' in relation to persons who are under 17 at the time of the hearing, whereas s 17 is concerned with a witness of any age whose quality of evidence is likely to be affected by fear or distress. In either case, the court must consider any views expressed by the witness unless the witness is under 17.

Section 21 of the 1999 Act provides special protection for one type of person eligible for 'special measures' under s 16: 'a child witness' (i.e. someone under 17).

Where a court determines that a witness is a 'child witness', it must first have regard to the 'primary rule' that it must give in respect of that witness a special measures direction providing for a video recording of his evidence-in-chief to be admitted (unless this is contrary to the interests of justice) and providing for any evidence given by him which is not by means of video recording (whether in-chief or otherwise) to be given by means of a live link. This primary rule does not apply to the extent that the court is satisfied that compliance with it would not be likely to maximise the quality of the witness's evidence so far as practicable (whether because the application to that evidence of one or more other special measures available in relation to the witness would have that result or for any other reason). However, this exception does not apply where the child witness is in need of 'special protection', which he will be if the offence (or one of them) in question is:

(a) a sexual offence, as defined at page 685 (s 17); or
(b) kidnapping, false imprisonment, an offence under the Child Abduction Act 1984, s 1 or 2, an offence under the Children and Young Persons Act 1933, s 1 (cruelty), or any other offence which involves an assault on, or injury or a threat of injury to, any person.

Where a child is in need of special protection because the offence is a sexual offence, any special measure direction providing for video-recorded examination in chief must also provide for video-recorded cross-examination and re-examination otherwise than by the accused in person, unless the witness informs the court that he does not want that special measure to apply.

The essential point about s 21 is that where a child witness is in need of *special protection*, a court will not have to consider (as it normally must) whether the special measures mentioned will improve the quality of his evidence. That requirement is treated as satisfied.

By s 18 of the 1999 Act, a range of special measures is made potentially available to witnesses who are eligible for special measures under s 16 or 17. The 'special measures' are set out in detail by ss 23 to 28 of the 1999 Act. Once a court has determined that a witness is eligible for special measures, it must then determine whether any of those measures (or a combination of them) would be likely to improve the quality of the witness's evidence and, if so, determine which of those measures would be likely to maximise so far as practicable the quality of his evidence. Having made this second determination, it must give a 'special measures' direction in relation to the measure or measures so determined.

The special measures are:

(a) *Screening* – Screens may be authorised to shield a witness from the defendant (but the judge, jury, justices, a legal representative from each side, any interpreter and any person appointed to assist the witness must be able to see the witness).

(b) *Evidence by live link* – Usually this will be done by closed-circuit television but the terms of the section are wide enough to permit any technology. Where a direction is given that evidence will be given in this way, evidence may not be given in any other way without the consent of the court. Where facilities are not available at a petty-sessional court house, the court may sit elsewhere where such facilities exist. A Divisional Court has held that evidence being given in this way does not breach an accused's human right to a fair trial.

(c) *Evidence given in private* – The court may be cleared of non-essential personnel but this measure will only be available in relation to a sexual offence or when the court reasonably believes that someone has tried to intimidate, or will try to intimidate, the witness. At least one member of the press must be allowed to remain in court.

(d) *Removal of wigs and gowns* – This will apply to both the judiciary and legal representatives.

(e) *Video-recorded evidence-in-chief* – Where this special measure is directed, it will provide for a video recording of an interview of the witness to be admitted in evidence-in-chief. However, the direction may not provide for a video recording, or part of it, to be admitted if its admission would not be in the interests of justice. If it is decided to permit only an edited version to be shown, the court must consider whether the exclusion of part of the recording is prejudicial. A court may later exclude a recording if its making is not properly proved, but may nevertheless admit it in such circumstances. The party tendering the evidence must call the witness, unless a special measures direction provides for cross-examination otherwise than in court or the parties have agreed to non-attendance. The witness may not give evidence-in-chief otherwise than by means of the recording as to any matter adequately dealt with in the recording or, without the court's permission, as to any other matter dealt with in the recording.

(f) *Video-recorded cross-examination or re-examination* – Where a video recording of a witness's evidence-in-chief has been admitted, the special measures direction may also provide that the witness may be cross-examined before trial and that that cross-examination (and any re-examination) may be recorded for use at trial. This will not occur in the physical presence of the accused, although he will be able to see and hear it and to communicate with his legal adviser (live link). Nor need it take place in the physical presence of the judge or magistrates and the defence and prosecution legal representatives, although they must be able to see and hear the examination and to communicate with those present. However, a judge or magistrate must control the proceedings and it is intended that this person will normally be the trial judge or magistrate. The witness may not be subsequently cross-examined or re-examined in respect of his evidence unless the court so directs. This may only be done where a party to the proceedings has come into possession of additional material which he could not with reasonable diligence have ascertained since the time of the recording, or where it is in the interests of justice to do so.

The following additional measures are available only in the case of someone eligible for special measures under s 16:

(a) *Examination of witness through intermediary* – The relevant provisions were not in force at the time of writing. For convenience they are described as if they were. An intermediary is an interpreter or someone else whom the court approves to communicate to the witness the questions that the court, the defence and the prosecution ask, and then to communicate the answers which the witness gives in reply. He may also explain such questions or answers should that be necessary to facilitate understanding. It is foreseen that such an intermediary will normally be a specialist. An intermediary can act however and wherever the examination is conducted. The judge or magistrates and at least one legal representative for each side should be able to see and hear the witness and be able to communicate with the intermediary. The jury must be able to see and hear the witness unless the evidence is video recorded. An intermediary must declare that he will faithfully perform his function.

(b) *Aids to communication* – A special measures direction may require a witness to be provided with an appropriate device to assist communication.

The status of evidence given under special measures

Evidence given using any of the special measures set out above must be treated in the same way as oral evidence. However, the judge may give such warning to the jury as he considers necessary to ensure fairness to the accused.

If the evidence of a witness who would normally be sworn is given unsworn by means of a video recording, that evidence will be admissible at trial. However, where a person authorised to administer an oath is present, the evidence could be taken under oath in appropriate cases.

The Practice Direction (*Crime: children's video evidence*) then required that the party who made the application to admit the video recording must edit the recording in accordance with the judge's directions and send a copy of the edited recording to the appropriate officer of the Crown Court and to every other party to the proceedings.

Where a video recording is to be adduced during proceedings before a Crown Court, it must be produced and proved by the interviewer, or any other person who was present at the interview with the child, at which the recording was made. The parties may agree to accept a written statement in lieu of the attendance of such a person. The party adducing the video recording must arrange for the operation of the video playing equipment.

Failure to so prepare, which leads to an adjournment for this to be done, may lead to an appropriate award for costs.

Live television links at preliminary hearings

Section 57 of the Crime and Disorder Act 1998 provides for the use of live television links at preliminary hearings before a court, where an accused is being held in custody.

The use of such a link (where it is possible) does not require the consent of the accused, or his legal adviser, but is a matter for the discretion of the court.

By s 57(1) of the 1998 Act, in any proceedings for an offence, a court may, after hearing representations from the parties, direct that the accused shall be treated as being present in the court for any particular hearing before the start of the trial, if, during that hearing:

(a) he is held in custody in a prison or other institution; and
(b) whether by means of a live television link or otherwise, he is able to see and hear the court and to be seen and heard by it.

The term 'particular hearing' used in s 57(1) refers to any hearing before either a magistrates' court or Crown Court before the start of the trial.

Evidence by means of certificate

A further way in which evidence can be presented is by means of a statement or a certificate. Statements taken in accordance with s 2 or 9 of the Criminal Justice Act 1967 can be put in evidence and be admissible to the same extent as oral evidence without the witness himself appearing before the court. This procedure is designed to avoid the necessity for a witness to appear at court when his evidence is not disputed. A police officer carrying out an enquiry for another force in connection with a criminal offence usually submits the result of his enquiries in the form of a statement under the Criminal Justice Act 1967 so that he does not have to attend any subsequent court proceedings if his statement is accepted in evidence by the court and the other party to the proceedings.

Certain certificates are accepted in evidence by a court, for example, a certificate, under s 41 (1) of the Criminal Justice Act 1948, certifying a drawing made to scale; a certificate, under s 11 of the Road Traffic Offenders Act 1988, signed by a constable, certifying that a person made a statement to him regarding the driving, ownership or use of a motor vehicle on a particular occasion; and, of course, the analyst's certificate of his findings in relation to a laboratory specimen provided in a case of a person who has more than the prescribed limit of alcohol in the blood, driving, attempting to drive, or being in charge of a motor vehicle.

Having outlined the ways in which evidence may be presented to the court, it is time to examine the extent to which evidence is acceptable by a court, i.e. its admissibility and the restrictions placed on the testimony of a witness.

Hearsay evidence

The general rule is that a witness may only testify to facts he perceived with his own senses, such facts being relevant to the proceedings before the court. This general rule excludes a witness giving in evidence a statement made by another person, not the accused. An example of this would be where a pedestrian, who has seen the driver of a motor vehicle commit an offence, writes down the registration number of the offending vehicle and later passes this information to a police officer. If proceedings are taken against the offending driver, the police officer could not give in evidence the statement of the pedestrian, or produce the paper on which the pedestrian took down the registered number, as this would be hearsay evidence. The only person who could give such evidence is the pedestrian, who could then be cross-examined by the defence. Thus, we might define hearsay evidence as being evidence of what someone else expressly or impliedly asserted orally, in writing or by conduct, when the object of that evidence is to establish the truth of what was said or written.

However, there is a difference between a person stating a fact and giving hearsay evidence. If a police officer says that a person complained to him of an indecent assault, this is a fact and the officer is entitled to say that the event took place. It would be different if he then attempted to give details of the allegation made, as those details are best given by the person assaulted. Where a police officer offered evidence, as a statement of fact, that a person whom he saw receiving a package was a heroin addict, the evidence was held to be hearsay unless the officer had first-hand knowledge of that fact based upon previous convictions or the observation of needle marks or of that person's receipt of medical attention for drug addiction. That person's general reputation as an addict, without particular proof of addiction, was inadmissible hearsay.

Like many general rules in law, there are a number of exceptions to the rule that hearsay evidence is not admissible, the more important of which are:

(a) *Dying declaration* – In cases of murder or manslaughter, any statement made by the victim as to the fact and circumstances which caused his injuries is admissible in evidence. Such a declaration should give the actual words used and contain the fact that it is made in the hopeless expectation of imminent death. The person taking the declaration should date it, sign it and get any other person present who had heard the declaration to sign to this effect. A judge will receive such a declaration in evidence if he is satisfied that
  (i) the declarant is dead and would have been a competent witness had he lived and the manner of his death was the subject of the declaration;
  (ii) at the time it was made the declarant realised he was dying and had no hope of recovery.
(b) *Recent complaint in sexual offences* – In such cases, the words of a complaint made by the victim of a sexual offence to some other person as soon as possible after the offence may be given by the person who received the complaint, not as proof of the act alleged or to corroborate other evidence but as evidence of the conduct of the victim and of the fact that the victim did not consent to the act. An example of this is where the victim of a rape runs to the nearest house, knocks on the door, and says to the householder, 'A man has just attacked and raped me.' The householder could give this statement in evidence.
(c) *Statements made by persons now deceased* – Such statements, to be admissible in evidence, must have been made contemporaneously in the regular course of duty or business. An example of such a written statement would be entries made in a police officer's notebook or an official police report.
(d) *Statements forming part of the* res gestae – These are things done, or relevant to the matter before the court. Thus, if the victim in a poisoning case was heard by someone to say, 'I think the apple I just ate was poisoned', this could be put in evidence by the person who heard it. Police officers saw a man being jostled by two others. The assailant went into a shop doorway where the victim's wallet was found. The victim lunged at the men and said, 'They're the ones; these two mugged me of my wallet.' The victim did not give evidence. Could these statements (which were hearsay when repeated by the officers) be admitted as part of the res gestae? It was

held that, looking at the incident as a whole, the statements were relevant and properly admitted.

Although the length of time after the event is important, it is not critical. In one case where evidence was admitted as part of the *res gestae*, the victim had crawled for an hour to reach a house where he named his attacker. The important point is that the thoughts of the person concerned should be, at the time, so dominated by what had happened that they could be seen as being unaffected by later reasoning or fabrication.

(e) *First-hand hearsay* – Sections 23 and 24 of the Criminal Justice Act 1988 deal with these matters, which are set out below.

(i) *First-hand hearsay* – Section 23 permits a statement made in a document to be admissible as evidence of any fact stated therein of which direct oral evidence would be admissible if:

(1) any condition relating to the person who made the statement which is specified below is satisfied: (i) that the person who made the statement is dead or by reason of his bodily or mental condition, unfit to attend as a witness, or is outside the United Kingdom and it is not reasonably practicable to secure his attendance; or (ii) that all reasonable steps have been taken to find the person who made the statement but he cannot be found; or

(2) the statement was made to a police officer or some other person charged with the duty of investigating offences or charging offenders, and the person who made it does not give oral evidence through fear or because he is kept out of the way.

The words 'unfit to attend as a witness' apply not only to a person's physical inability to attend court but also to his mental capacity. The Court of Appeal has said that there is nothing to prevent the written evidence of a witness being admitted when he is too ill to give evidence at the time of the trial. Even where such evidence is evidence upon which the prosecution predominantly relies (eye-witness evidence of a burglary being committed by persons well known to the witness), there is nothing in the wording of the relevant sections to prevent such evidence from being admitted. Where it is necessary to consider allowing a witness statement to be read on the grounds that it is not reasonably practicable to secure a witness's attendance, the judge must consider the matter as existing on the date of the application. It would be difficult to apply s 23 with any certainty if the judge was required to consider future possibilities in relation to attendance.

The test of fear does not have to be based on reasonable grounds so long as the court is satisfied that the witness is in fear. There is no reason for a court to enquire into the basis for the fear, provided that fear is established. However, it is important to establish that the fear existed at the time of the trial. The Court of Appeal has said that it is not sufficient that the witness made a statement some months previously in which he said that he was afraid to give evidence because he feared repercussions against himself and his family.

(ii) *Business, etc., records* – Section 24 is concerned with documents created or received by a person in the course of a business, profession or other occupation, or as the holder of a paid or unpaid office. If the information contained in such a document was supplied by a person who had, or may reasonably be supposed to have had, personal knowledge of the matter dealt with, a statement in the document is admissible in evidence in the same way as oral evidence would be admissible. The Court of Appeal has ruled that records created at the time of the manufacture of a motor vehicle which identify a particular vehicle chassis with the various parts which were later added to it are admissible under these provisions.

(iii) *General* – Particular rules are prescribed for written statements prepared in respect of pending or contemplated criminal proceedings or of a criminal investigation. Such statements are admissible if the requirements of s 23(a) or (b) have been satisfied, or if the person who made the statement cannot reasonably be expected (having regard to the time that has elapsed and all the circumstances) to have any recollection of the matters dealt with in the statement.

Statements under s 23 or 24 may be contested in the same way as oral testimony can be challenged. In estimating the weight to be attached to such a statement, a court must consider all of the circumstances in assessing the accuracy or otherwise of the statement.

Statements which are prepared for the purpose of pending or contemplated criminal proceedings, etc., must not be admitted without the leave of the court which must not be given unless the court is of the opinion that the statement should be admitted in the interests of justice.

(iv) *Evidence from computer records* – The Youth Justice and Criminal Evidence Act 1999, s 60, repealed the Police and Criminal Evidence Act 1984 (PACE), s 69, which required that evidence by means of a document produced by a computer, to be used in evidence, had to be accompanied by proof that the computer was operating correctly at the time and was being properly used.

The effect of the repeal is that it will be presumed that a computer was operating correctly at the time in question in the absence of proof to the contrary. However, where there is a challenge to the reliability of the computer, the fact that it was working correctly will have to be established. It would therefore appear to be advisable that police practice continues to recognise the need for recording the fact that the computer appeared to be working correctly and that breath analysers calibrated correctly, although any references to the requirements of the Police and Criminal Evidence Act 1984, s 69, should be removed.

Where the necessity for proof arises because the reliability of a computer is challenged, proof by the prosecution that the computer has been operating satisfactorily can be satisfied by the evidence of a person familiar with the operation of the computer, who need not be a computer expert. The House of Lords has held that evidence by a store detective that computerised cash tills were working satisfactorily was admissible where it was apparent from the nature of her evidence that she was thoroughly familiar with the operation of the tills and the central computer, even though she did not understand the technical operation of the computer. Lord Griffiths said that he suspected that it would rarely be necessary to call an expert and that in the vast majority of cases it would be possible to discharge the burden by calling a witness who was familiar with the operation of the computer in the sense of knowing what the computer was required to do, and who could say that it was doing it properly.

(f) *Statements made by the accused* – Such statements are admissible as evidence when given by another person. For example, a police officer cautions a person and tells him he is being arrested on suspicion of theft. The prisoner's reply, 'OK, I broke in and stole the gear', is hearsay evidence but may be given in evidence by the police officer.

(g) *Statement made in the presence and hearing of the accused* – Such statements are admissible but only to the extent to which the accused, by words or conduct, appeared to accept the statement as true. If he immediately denied the implication of the statement, the court would ignore the statement. For example, if a man is arrested at his home on suspicion of handling stolen property and his wife says, 'I told you not to bring that stuff here, you knew it was stolen', and the husband replies, 'I know, I am sorry', the evidence of the statement made by the wife and the reply of the accused could be given in evidence by the arresting officer.

(h) *Evidence by certificate* – See 'Presenting evidence', page 107.

(i) *Entries in certain public documents* – When a person has a public duty to keep records, such as the Registrar of Births and Deaths, etc., the records may be given in evidence as proof of the facts contained in the record which the person recording has a public duty to satisfy himself is correct.

Expert reports

An expert report is admissible as evidence in criminal proceedings, whether or not the person making it attends to give oral evidence. However, if it is proposed that the maker of the report shall not give oral evidence, the report is only admissible with the leave of the court. Such a report must be written by a person dealing with matters on which he is (or would if living be) qualified to give expert evidence.

Evidence of opinion

The general rule is that the opinion of a witness is inadmissible as it is the function of the court or jury to draw conclusions from the facts presented. However, evidence of opinion from experts is admissible:

(a) where an expert gives an opinion on matters which are outside the knowledge or experience of a court or jury, on points of science or art; or

(b) he is a witness who is familiar with the handwriting of a person and is giving evidence as to that handwriting; or

(c) he is a lawyer shown to have knowledge of a particular system of foreign law.

For example, blame in relation to the driving of a motor car involved in an accident is a matter for the court or jury to decide. Thus, evidence of opinion to the effect that X was to blame for the accident is inadmissible because that is the matter to be determined by the court or jury. Evidence of the opinion as to the speed at which the vehicle was travelling at the time of the accident may be admitted if given by an expert; being based upon scientific calculations, from evidence available at the scene of the accident or as a result of it. Examples of occasions when a police officer may give evidence of opinion are:

(a) the speed of a motor vehicle where it is alleged to have been exceeding the speed limit, and

(b) the condition of a person who is intoxicated.

Matters which need not be proved

A court, when hearing a case, will decide the matter on the facts put before it. Generally such facts must be proved by the side which places them before the court, but in relation to certain matters the court is obliged to take judicial notice of certain well-known facts such as the common law, statutes, the ordinary course of nature and many other facts which it would be tedious to list, without the need to prove those facts. For example, it would not be necessary to prove that Christmas Day fell on 25 December each year.

When breath-testing devices were first introduced it was necessary to prove in each case that the Home Secretary had approved the use of the particular device. With the passage of time, the courts ruled that judicial notice could be taken of that approval.

Who may give evidence

So far, we have covered the various types of evidence and the ways in which such evidence may be presented, and now we must examine the question of competency, i.e. who can be called to give evidence, and compellability, i.e. who can be ordered by the court to attend and give evidence.

Competence and compellability

Competence

Sections 53 to 57 of the Youth Justice and Criminal Evidence Act 1999 provide that anyone, of whatever age, will be competent to give evidence unless he is unable to understand questions put to him as a witness, or unable to answer them in a way which can be understood. A witness may need the assistance of 'special measures' as set out at page 107. However, an accused person is not competent to give evidence for the prosecution (whether or not he is the only accused, or is a co-accused in the proceedings). This does not preclude a person who is no longer liable to be convicted of the offence whether because of a guilty plea or otherwise.

Questions of competence will be decided by the court and in the absence of the jury if there is one. The party calling the witness must satisfy the court that the witness, on the balance of probabilities, is competent to give evidence. Any questioning of the witness must be conducted by the court.

Compellability

Schedule 4 to the 1999 Act amended the Police and Criminal Evidence Act 1984, s 80, in relation to the 'compellability' of the spouse of an accused to give evidence.

In any proceedings, the wife or husband (X) of a person charged in the proceedings is compellable to give evidence on behalf of that person, unless he or she (i.e. X) is also charged in those proceedings. In addition, provided that he or she is not also charged in those proceedings, the husband or wife of a person charged in the proceedings is compellable to give evidence on behalf of any other person charged in those proceedings, but only in respect of any specified offence with which that other person is charged, or to give evidence for the prosecution, but only in respect of any specified offence with which such person is charged in the proceedings. In relation to the wife or husband of a person charged in any proceedings, an offence is a specified offence for these purposes if:

(a) it involves an assault on, or injury or a threat of injury to, the wife or husband or a person who was at the material time under the age of 16;
(b) it is a sexual offence alleged to have been committed in respect of a person who was at the material time under that age; or
(c) it consists of attempting or conspiring to commit, or of aiding, abetting, counselling, procuring or inciting the commission of, an offence under (a) or (b).

For the purposes of (b), a 'sexual offence' is an offence under:

(a) the Sexual Offences Acts 1956 and 1967;
(b) the Indecency with Children Act 1960;
(c) the Criminal Law Act 1977, s 54 (inciting a girl under 16 to have an incestuous relationship); or
(d) the Protection of Children Act 1978 (taking indecent photographs of a person under 16).

The references above to a person charged in any proceedings do not include a person who is not, or is no longer, liable to be convicted of any offence in the proceedings (whether as a result of pleading guilty or for any other reason).

The failure of a wife or husband of a person charged in any proceedings to give evidence in the proceedings must not be made the subject of any comment by the prosecution.

An ex-spouse is compellable to give evidence as if he or she had never been married to the accused.

Mentally handicapped persons

Such a person is incompetent to give evidence if, at the time, he is incapable of understanding the seriousness of the occasion and of realising that taking the oath involves something more than the duty to tell the truth in ordinary everyday life.

Privilege

We have covered the ways of presenting evidence and the persons who are competent and compellable to give evidence before a court, but before leaving this subject we must examine the question of privilege, that is, the right of a person to refuse to give evidence on the grounds of privilege. Generally, a person who refuses to give evidence can be treated as if he was in contempt of the court and would be liable to punishment, but in the following circumstances, where privilege is claimed, that person cannot be compelled to give evidence on the facts for which privilege is claimed. It is interesting to note that the confession of a person to a priest is not privileged and, theoretically, a priest could be compelled to give in evidence the details of such a confession. Similarly, communications between doctor and patient are not protected, but a court would have an overriding discretion to allow a doctor not to answer questions. The situations in which such privilege can be claimed are as follows:

(a) *Husband and wife* – There is *no* privilege in respect of communications between husband and wife. However, an answer to a question, or the production of a document that would tend to expose the witness or his or her spouse to a criminal charge is protected by privilege.

(b) *Self-incrimination* – A person cannot be compelled to answer any questions which might, in the opinion of the court, expose him to risk of punishment, penalty or forfeiture. This does not apply to an accused giving evidence on his own behalf. A number of statutes create exceptions to this rule and are primarily concerned with the protection of children and investigations carried out by the Serious Fraud Office. However, the Youth Justice and Criminal Evidence Act 1999 provides restrictions in relation to the use of evidence obtained within such investigations.

(c) *Legal representative and client* – Communications between a client and his solicitor or counsel for the purpose of the proceedings before the court are confidential. However, privilege does not extend to communications in the furtherance of crime or fraud. There is no privilege where disclosure of communications is from another source, such as documents coming into the possession of the police.

(d) *Public policy* – This is a matter for the court to decide, and a court will not compel a witness to give evidence of certain facts if it considers that to give such evidence would be contrary to the interest of the public, e.g. a police officer who does not wish to disclose an informant's identity should ask the court for a direction, and usually the court will rule that such information is privileged unless it is directly material to the case or necessary in the interests of the accused.

Corroboration

Corroboration is evidence from a source independent of the witness whose evidence is being corroborated which tends to confirm or support such evidence in a material particular. It is not generally required, but is always useful. However, the prosecution can discharge its burden of proof by the evidence of one witness whose evidence is not so supported.

A judge has a discretion to give a warning to the jury in respect of the uncorroborated evidence of one witness where the offence is a sexual offence or where the uncorroborated evidence is that of an accomplice in just the same way as he may give such a warning in any other case.

Where corroboration is required by statute, a court cannot convict on the uncorroborated evidence of one witness. Such corroboration is required in the following cases:

(a) perjury (Perjury Act 1911); and
(b) speeding (Road Traffic Regulation Act 1984).

Character of the defendant

An accused may always give evidence of his own good character. When he does so, the judge must direct the jury that evidence of good character is relevant in relation to their assessment of the credibility of the accused's evidence. It is also obligatory for the judge to direct that the previous good character of the accused may be regarded by them as a relevant factor when they are considering whether he is the kind of person who was likely to have behaved in the manner alleged.

The prosecution may generally not give evidence of the accused's bad character. However, such evidence may be admitted as evidence of similar facts (e.g. that the accused committed a previous offence which followed a particular and exclusive form which tends to identify him as the person responsible for the current offence), or where the accused seeks to establish his own good character during proceedings, either by giving direct evidence of that good character, or by cross-examination of a witness in order to establish it. In such circumstances, the accused has raised the issue of good character and it is therefore permissible for the prosecution to offer evidence of his bad character.

In addition, there are certain statutes which permit evidence to be given of an accused's bad character, but these instances are rare.

Refreshing memory

A police officer will normally be called to give evidence about the facts of a case and he should ensure that he has refreshed his memory before attending court. There is nothing less professional than a police officer reading his evidence straight from his notebook as if he was reading a story for the first time, and while there is no objection to a police officer referring to his official notebook to refresh his memory on a specific point, this does not mean he can read all the evidence from his notebook.

A police constable, and any other witness, may refresh his memory while giving evidence by referring to a document or notebook provided that:

(a) the entry was made or verified at the time of the event when the witness had a distinct recollection of the facts contained in the document or notebook; and

(b) the entry was made by the witness, or under his supervision if not made by him, and read over to him at a time when he had a distinct recollection of the facts contained in the document or notebook.

Where police officers refer to entries in their notebook when giving evidence, defending solicitors who wish to challenge credibility by discovering inconsistencies may ask to examine relevant entries. Where this is done, examination should be restricted to 'relevant entries', those associated with matters then before the court. Magistrates refused a defending solicitor's request to be allowed to remove clips put in place in an officer's notebook to mark the places at which relevant entries occurred. The officer had objected on the grounds that the book contained sensitive and confidential information unrelated to the case. The Divisional Court supported the officer's refusal.

There is no objection to two witnesses who have acted together refreshing their memories from notes they collaborated in making; thus, two police officers engaged on observations together may later collaborate when making a record of their observations. If a witness refreshes his memory from a written statement before giving evidence, it is desirable that the defence is informed.

In relation to (a), the Divisional Court held that a record made of a conversation which took place 2 hours after it occurred was made 'contemporaneously', where throughout that period, the officer had been dealing with a person arrested for the offence which the person concerned was charged with aiding and abetting. Being constantly involved with the circumstances of the offence, the court considered that the events which were then recorded must have been fresh in the officer's mind.

Exclusion of unfair evidence

The court has a right, provided by the Police and Criminal Evidence Act 1984, s 78, to exclude any evidence (including confessions) if it appears to the court that, having regard to all the circumstances, including the circumstances in which the evidence was obtained, the admission of the evidence would have such an adverse effect upon the fairness of the proceedings that the court ought not to admit it. 'Fairness of the proceedings' is directed primarily to fairness of the actual conduct of the proceedings but it is not strictly limited to this.

Where a man was convicted upon evidence obtained by way of a confession, after he had been falsely told by police that his fingerprints had been found at the scene of a crime, the confession was excluded because it posed a threat to the fairness of the proceedings. Similarly, breaches of the various codes of practice whilst collecting evidence have led to its exclusion. However, it has been held that a breach by the police of the European Convention on Human Rights does not necessarily render evidence inadmissible under s 78, but it is a matter which the judge must take into account when deciding whether to exclude the evidence.

Where, following an incident of serious disorder on a bus, from which a man jumped and was killed, police arrested and properly recorded statements after caution which contained admissions from some of those involved in the disorder, the Court of Appeal accepted their claims that they had made the admissions because they thought that they were assisting police enquiries into the death and did not realise that they were in peril of prosecution for offences of serious disorder, and excluded those admissions. With respect to the Court it is difficult to believe that a person arrested and told of the reason for that arrest could be in any doubt that facts which he disclosed in a statement after caution might be used within proceedings subsequent to that arrest.

Where police officers were examining a sub-post office at which there had been a robbery, they found a box containing £4390. Being suspicious, they obtained consent to the installation of a video camera to monitor the premises. When the sub-postmaster was allowed back into the premises, he was seen to examine the contents of the box. It was submitted that this evidence should not be admitted as the evidence had been obtained without consent to search the premises and this was a breach of the provisions of the Search Code. The judge admitted the evidence. The Court of Appeal supported the judge's decision. There had been no suggestion of bad faith and, in the circumstances, where an offence had been committed on the premises, there was no reason to think that consent would not have been given. Discretion must be exercised in fairness not only to the defendant, but also to the prosecution.

Summonses and warrants

Introduction

The subject of 'summonses and warrants' is associated with the process of prosecution of those who offend against the law. They provide a means by which such persons may be brought before a court. However, the procedure does not begin there; the responsibility for the conduct of criminal proceedings lies with the Director of Public Prosecutions, who is head of the Crown Prosecution Service. With the exception of various minor traffic offences, where the defendant wishes to plead guilty by post (see page 102), the Crown Prosecution Service will conduct criminal proceedings instituted by the police.

Summons

One of the ways in which a person can be brought before a court is by way of a summons. This is a written order issued by a magistrate or a justices' clerk on behalf of a magistrate, directing the person named in the order to appear at a given time and date before a specified court to answer the allegation contained in the order.

A summons is obtained by the prosecutor laying information before a justice of the peace or the justices' clerk on behalf of the justice and this process is explained below under the heading 'Defendant summons'. An information need not be in writing (although it always is in practice), or on oath. However, a summons may also be issued by way of a complaint. A complaint is a written or verbal allegation to the effect that a person has committed a breach of the law which is not a criminal offence. A common example is a complaint to the effect that some person has committed, or is threatening to commit, a breach of the peace. If the justices find that this is so, the person against whom the complaint has been made may be asked to find surety of the peace, but he will not be punished in the accepted sense that he will not be fined or imprisoned, etc.

Contents of a summons

All summonses contain the full name of the person to whom they are addressed. They also contain a directive for that person to appear at a named court on a specified date at a particular time. If the summons is directed to an offender it will contain details of the offence, sufficient to make it clear to the defendant that he is answering a particular allegation. In the case of a witness summons, it will direct him to give evidence in relation to a particular offence and perhaps to produce exhibits.

Defendant summons

This is the most usual method of bringing a person before a court to answer an allegation that he has committed an offence or act for which he is liable to be punished. The first stage in the sequence of events leading to the issue of a summons is the commission of the alleged offence. To take a simple example: a constable sees a motor car being driven on a road between sunset and sunrise, without displaying lights. The constable stops the vehicle and, after pointing out the offence to the driver, records in his pocket notebook or process book particulars of the driver and his vehicle and the necessary evidence relating to the offence. The constable then submits a report to the supervisory officer and, on the basis of this report, the Crown Prosecution Service will make a decision as to whether or not the driver should be prosecuted for the offence. If it is decided that there should be a prosecution, information will be laid before a magistrate, his justices' clerk (or authorised assistant) to the effect that the driver, now called the defendant, has committed the offence of driving a motor car on a road between sunset and sunrise without showing the necessary lights required by law. The information will specify the time, date and place where the offence is alleged to have occurred. The magistrate, justices' clerk (or authorised person) may then issue a summons directing the defendant to appear at the time, date and court named in the summons to answer the allegation that he has committed the offence specified.

Service of a summons

Once a summons has been issued, it then has to be served on the person to whom it is addressed, and generally it is the responsibility of the police to perform this task.

Whenever a constable is given a summons to serve, he should first check the contents for errors and should check that there is an original and a copy of the summons. The copy to be given to the defendant must be signed by the issuing magistrate, justices' clerk or authorised person. Details of the summons should then be entered in the constable's pocket notebook. If there is an error, it should be returned to a supervisory officer.

The summons, if a defendant summons, can then be served by:

(a) delivering it to the defendant; or
(b) leaving it for him with some person at his last known or usual address; or
(c) sending it by post in a letter addressed to him at his last known or usual place of abode.

It is no longer necessary that, where a person fails to appear after service of a summons either by leaving it for him with some person at his last or usual place of abode, or by sending it by post to him at his last known usual place of abode, it is proved that the summons came to his knowledge.

Service of a summons on a corporation may be effected by delivering it at, or sending it by post to:

(a) the registered office of the corporation, if that office is in the United Kingdom; or
(b) any place in the United Kingdom where the corporation trades or conducts its business, if there is no registered office in the United Kingdom.

The Magistrates' Courts Rules provide that, in any instance in which a summons may be sent by post to a person's last known or usual place of abode, the rules shall have effect as if they provided also for the summons to be sent in the manner specified to an address given by that person for that purpose. In the case of summary offences, postal service will be satisfactorily proved if the summons was sent by post.

When the original summons has been served, the constable should then complete the certificate of service on the back of the copy summons, showing the method of service, the date, and the signature of the person who effected the service, i.e. the constable. He should then make an entry in his pocket notebook of the service of the summons.

Postal service of a summons issued in England and Wales is permitted throughout the United Kingdom. The Scots use a 'citation' instead of a summons and this may be served by post in England and Wales. Northern Irish summonses cannot be served by post in England and Wales.

Witness summons

The object of this type of summons is, once again, to bring a person before a court, not to answer an allegation that he has committed an offence, but in order that he may give or produce evidence as a witness in proceedings before a magistrates' court. Such a summons is issued by a justice if he is satisfied that the person to whom it is addressed is likely to give material evidence or produce anything as evidence, and that this person will not voluntarily attend the court and give or produce such evidence. Unlike other summonses, a witness summons may not be served by post.

A justice may refuse to issue a witness summons if he is not satisfied that the application was made as soon as reasonably practicable after the accused pleaded not guilty. Crown Courts are also empowered to issue witness summonses.

Warrants

A warrant is a written authority, signed by a magistrate, directing the person or persons named in the warrant to carry out the purpose for which it was issued, the purpose being stated in the warrant. This may be to arrest a person and bring him before a court, to take a person to prison or to search premises and seize evidence.

Warrants to search premises

There are many statutes which provide particular powers to enter and search premises under the authority of a warrant. The Police and Criminal Evidence Act 1984 does not affect these provisions but additionally provides justices with a general power to issue warrants to enter and search premises. 'Premises' includes any place, vessel, aircraft or hovercraft or any off-shore installation and any tent or moveable structure. The Act of 1984 also standardises procedure in relation to the obtaining of such warrants and the procedures to be followed.

Section 8 (1) of the Act provides that if, on application made by a constable, a justice is satisfied that there are reasonable grounds for believing that:

(a) a serious arrestable offence or a 'relevant offence' under the Immigration Act 1971 has been committed; and
(b) there is material on premises specified in the application which is likely to be of substantial value (whether by itself or with other material) to the investigation of the offence; and
(c) the material is likely to be relevant (i.e. admissible) evidence; and
(d) it does not consist of or include items subject to legal privilege, excluded material or special procedure material; and
(e) any of the conditions specified in subsection (3) applies (see below),

the justice may issue a warrant authorising a constable to enter and search the premises. Subsection (2) authorises a constable to seize and retain anything for which a search has been authorised. All warrants to search, regardless of the statute which authorises them, must now be obtained by this procedure.

The conditions set out in subsection (3) are:

(a) that it is not practicable to communicate with a person entitled to grant entry to the premises;
(b) that it is practicable to communicate with a person entitled to grant entry to the premises but it is not practicable to communicate with any person entitled to grant access to the evidence;
(c) that entry to the premises will not be granted unless a warrant is produced;
(d) that the purpose of the search may be frustrated or seriously prejudiced unless a constable arriving at the premises can secure immediate entry to them.

The term 'serious arrestable offence' is not concerned with the term 'arrestable offence'. Schedule 5 to PACE defines certain offences as always being serious arrestable offences:

(a) treason;
(b) murder;
(c) manslaughter;
(d) rape;
(e) kidnapping;
(f) incest with a girl under 13;
(g) buggery with a boy under 16;
(h) an indecent assault which constitutes an act of indecency;
(i) causing an explosion likely to endanger life or property (Explosive Substances Act 1883, s 2);
(j) intercourse with a girl under 13 (Sexual Offences Act 1956, s 5);
(k) possession of a firearm with intent to endanger life, or use to resist arrest and carrying a firearm with criminal intent (Firearms Act 1968, ss 16, 17 and 18);
(l) hostage taking (Taking of Hostages Act 1982, s 1);
(m) hijacking (Aviation Security Act 1982, s 1);
(n) torture (Criminal Justice Act 1988, s 134);
(o) causing death by dangerous driving (Road Traffic Act 1988, s 1);
(p) causing death by careless driving when under the influence of drink or drugs (Road Traffic Act 1988, s 3A);
(q) endangering safety at aerodromes, hijacking ships, seizing or exercising control of fixed platforms (Aviation and Marine Security Act 1990, ss 1, 9 and 10);
(r) hijacking Channel Tunnel trains and seizing or exercising control of the tunnel system [Channel Tunnel (Security) Order 1994];
(s) taking, making, etc., indecent photographs or pseudo-photographs of children (Protection of Children Act 1978, s 1);
(t) the publication of obscene matter (Obscene Publications Act 1959, s 2); and
(u) an offence under s 170 of the Customs and Excise management Act 1979 (knowingly concerned, in relation to any goods, in any fraudulent evasion or attempt at evasion of a prohibition in force concerning importation of indecent or obscene articles).

In addition, s 116 of the 1984 Act specifies certain drug trafficking offences as serious arrestable offences.

Section 116 states that any other arrestable offence is serious only if its commission has led to any of the consequences set out below, or is intended to lead to any of those consequences:

(a) serious harm to the security of the State or to public order;
(b) serious interference with the administration of justice or with the investigation of offences or of a particular offence;
(c) the death of any person;
(d) serious injury to any person;
(e) substantial financial gain to any person; and
(f) serious financial loss to any person.

If the arrestable offence consists of making a threat, it is 'serious' if the consequences of carrying out the threat would be likely to lead to one of the consequences set out above in (a) to (f).

The term 'injury' includes any disease and any impairment of a person's physical or mental condition.

A loss is 'serious' for the purposes of the section if, having regard to all the circumstances, it is serious for the person who suffers it. The term 'injury' includes any disease and any impairment of a person's physical or mental condition. The seriousness of a loss is dependent upon the financial or other circumstances of the individual against whom the crime is committed. A theft of a large sum of money may not amount to a serious loss in the case of a multi-millionaire, while the theft of the small life-savings of a pensioner could be extremely serious in some cases.

Items subject to legal privilege are communications between lawyer and client and items enclosed with or referred to in such communications.

Excluded material includes personal records (medical, trade, business, etc.), human tissue or fluid taken for medical purposes, journalistic material, etc.

The information supplied by the constable in order to obtain a warrant shall identify, so far as is practicable, the articles or persons to be sought. Where the description of the articles provided by the warrant differed from that included in the information, the description not being so precisely phrased, the warrant was declared invalid. It will be insufficient in most circumstances to specify 'all records of the financial dealings of [company]' unless all dealings are under investigation. This is most improbable. If it is only the company's dealings with a particular body which are being examined, the information and the warrant should specify those dealings.

The conditions under which searches may be conducted are covered on page 146 dealing with mode of arrest.

Commitment or distress warrant

Such warrants are issued by a magistrates' court where a person has defaulted in the payment of a fine or order of a magistrates' court. A warrant of distress is for the purpose of levying the sum which is unpaid. Such a warrant is usually executed by a civilian enforcement officer or an approved enforcement agency but it may be directed to constables of that police area. It requires that goods be seized by labelling. Once labels are attached the goods are in legal custody. Property owned by public utilities cannot be seized, nor can clothes, bedding, or tools or implements of a person's trade. It is an offence to move goods once they have been labelled. A warrant of commitment orders the defaulter to be arrested and taken to prison unless he pays the amount specified in the warrant. When such an arrest has been effected, the person arrested should be taken to a designated police station for detention until transportation to the place specified in the warrant can be arranged. A receipt will be issued for the prisoner when he is handed over to the prison authorities.

Commitment warrants are usually issued where it appears that, on the return of a warrant of distress, the defaulter's assets are insufficient to satisfy the sum adjudged to be paid.

Arrest warrant

This type of warrant authorises the arrest of the person named or described in the warrant for the reason stated. To obtain a warrant to arrest, a written, sworn information is laid before a magistrate, who may then issue the warrant. A warrant to arrest for an offence shall not be issued in the first instance unless the offence to which it relates is an indictable offence, or punishable with imprisonment, or the address of the defendant is not sufficiently established for a summons to be served.

A warrant to arrest an adult for failing to appear at a magistrates' court after being summoned for an offence shall not be issued unless there is proof of the service of the summons and the offence is punishable with imprisonment, or the court having convicted the defendant proposes to impose a disqualification on him.

If a magistrate is satisfied by evidence on oath that any person should give or produce evidence as a witness in criminal proceedings before a magistrates' court, and either that person has been served with a witness summons or the magistrate is satisfied at the outset that such a summons would not procure his attendance at court, he may issue a warrant to arrest that person and bring him before the magistrates' court at a time and place specified in the warrant.

A warrant may be issued by a magistrate when a person has failed to pay a fine imposed after conviction. If this fine is paid in full, the person concerned should not be arrested.

Execution of warrants

Arrest warrants

A warrant is executed by carrying out the instructions contained in the warrant. If the warrant is to arrest for an offence and bring before the court, it is executed when the person named in the warrant is arrested. A warrant to arrest may be executed at any time anywhere in England and Wales by any constable for the police area in which the warrant is issued. Alternatively, it may be executed by a constable for another police area, within his police area. It may also be executed by a civilian enforcement officer or an approved enforcement agency. An arrest warrant remains in force until it is withdrawn, even if the magistrate who issued the warrant dies or ceases to be a magistrate. If the warrant is for the arrest of a person for an offence, and in some other circumstances set out on page 130, it need not be in the possession of the police officer making the arrest, provided that the warrant is shown to the person as soon as possible after his arrest; in any other case, the warrant is shown to that person as soon as possible after his arrest. In all other cases, the warrant must be in the possession of the police officer who executes it.

The most common form of warrant with which a constable has to deal is a warrant to arrest either for an offence or for non-payment of money which a court has ordered a person to pay. As with a summons, a constable receiving a warrant for execution must ensure that the warrant is in order and is signed. One particular point to check is whether the warrant specifies that the person arrested should be taken before a court at a specified time and date. On occasions, because of difficulty in execution, this date is passed and it becomes necessary to return the warrant unexecuted so that a new warrant may be issued specifying a new time and date. This difficulty is avoided in most cases by the warrant merely specifying that the arrested person is brought before the next court after his arrest. Having checked the warrant, the constable should enter brief details of the document in his pocket notebook.

The procedure for actually executing the warrant is that the constable should tell the person to whom is refers that he has a warrant for his arrest and show it to that person. In no circumstances must the warrant be handed over to him. It must be kept in the constable's possession. If the warrant is to arrest for an offence, that person should then be told he is being arrested for the offence specified in the warrant, and cautioned in accordance with relevant Code of Practice. If the warrant is to arrest in default, then the person should be asked whether he can pay the amount specified. If he can pay, the amount should be recorded in the constable's pocket notebook and he should ask the person to sign it. An official receipt will be delivered to him later, unless the constable is at the police station at this time, when a receipt will be made out and handed over to the person paying the money. The full amount must be paid to satisfy the demand made by the warrant; if a smaller amount is offered, this should be accepted, recorded and a receipt given, but the person must still be arrested. The part payment may result in a reduction in the period of imprisonment.

When a person is arrested on warrant, it will frequently be found that the warrant will contain specific directions on the reverse. These are often concerned with directions to release the person arrested on bail to appear at a specified court. These directions should be studied carefully as the Police and Criminal Evidence Act 1984 makes provisions for such persons to be released on bail without being brought to a police station. If such a direction is not included, the person must be taken to a police station at which the sergeant or officer in charge of the police station will arrange for the person to be released on bail.

Search warrants

The Police and Criminal Evidence Act 1984, s 16, permits a search warrant to be executed by any constable. Other persons may be authorised to accompany a constable. Entry and search must be within 1 month of the issue of the warrant and must be at a reasonable hour unless the purpose of the search may be frustrated by entry at such a time. Code A provides that these powers to search premises also authorise the search of a person, who is not under arrest, who is found on the premises during a search where the search is under the Criminal Justice Act 1988, s 139B, under which a constable may enter school premises to search for persons with weapons or under a warrant issued under the Misuse of Drugs Act 1971 to search premises for drugs or documents but only if the warrant specifically authorises the search of persons found on the premises.

Where the occupier of the premises is present, the constable must, before the search begins:

(a) identify himself (by warrant number in the case of terrorism enquiries) and, if not in uniform, show his warrant card (but in so doing in the case of terrorism enquiries, he need not reveal his name);
(b) produce the warrant to him; and
(c) supply him with a copy of it.

In the absence of the owner, the same procedure will be followed in relation to a person in charge of the premises.

See pages 144–147 for further information concerning the procedure to be followed when executing search warrants.

Action after execution of warrant and powers

Having executed a warrant, the constable must endorse on the back of the warrant the time, date, place and manner of execution and sign the endorsement. He should then enter brief details of the arrest in his pocket notebook. If money is received as directed in a warrant, this must be handed over to the sergeant or officer in charge of the police station as soon as practicable on arrival at the station, together with the endorsed warrant.

The Police and Criminal Evidence Act 1984, s 17, permits a constable to enter and search premises including any vehicle, vessel, aircraft or tent for the purpose of executing any warrant of arrest issued in connection with or arising out of criminal proceedings, or a warrant of commitment issued under the Magistrates' Courts Act 1980, s 76. The power is only exercisable where the constable has reasonable grounds for believing that the person he is seeking is on the premises. Where the premises consist of two or more separate dwellings, the entry and search is restricted to any common part of the building and the dwelling in which the constable reasonably believes that person may be.

See page 148 for action to be taken after executing a search warrant and page 144 in relation to forcible entry to premises.

Certain warrants may be executed by a constable who does not have possession of the warrant at the time:

(a) warrants to arrest a person in connection with an offence;
(b) warrants under the Army Act 1955, Air Force Act 1955, Naval Discipline Act 1957 or Reserve Forces Act 1996 (desertion, etc.); and
(c) warrants relating to the non-appearance of a defendant, warrants of distress, warrants of commitment, warrants issued in 'sending for trial' proceedings to arrest a potentially unwilling witness and warrants to arrest someone for non-compliance with a summons to make a deposition in connection with committal proceedings or 'sending for trial' proceedings (under the Magistrates' Courts Act 1980, ss 55, 76, 93, 97 and 97A, and the Crime and Disorder Act 1998, Schedule 3); and
(d) warrants issued under para. 3(2) of Schedule 1 to the Youth Justice and Criminal Evidence Act 1999 (offender referred to court by youth offender panel).

However, in such cases the warrants must, on the demand of the person concerned, be shown to him as soon as practicable (Magistrates' Courts Act 1980, s 125 D).

Except in the above cases, a warrant may not be executed by a constable who does not have it in his possession at the time. Thus, for example, a constable must be in possession of the warrant when executing a search warrant.

Cross-border enforcement of warrants

The Criminal Justice and Public Order Act 1994, s 136, provides that warrants issued in respect of offences in England and Wales, Scotland and Northern Ireland may be executed without endorsement throughout the United Kingdom by constables of the country of issue or the country of execution or by officers of the British Transport Police. The provisions also apply to warrants of commitment, warrants to arrest a witness and warrants to imprison (or to apprehend and imprison) issued in Scotland. This also applies to a warrant issued under paragraph 3(2) of Schedule 1 to the Youth Justice and Criminal Evidence Act 1999 (warrant for arrest of offender referred back to court by a youth offender panel).

Making an arrest and powers of entry without a search warrant to arrest

Arrest – factors for consideration

Now that so general a power of arrest is available to police officers, the 'necessity' to arrest must be carefully considered. The members of the Royal Commission whose recommendations led to the passing of the Police and Criminal Evidence Act 1984 stressed the 'necessity principle'. It was not anticipated that every refusal to give a name and address would lead to an arrest on the occasion of the first refusal of an offender to provide these particulars. A refusal should lead to the officer explaining the consequences of continued refusal to provide a satisfactory name and address. Only in the event of continued refusal should an arrest be effected.

In addition to these factors, officers should also consider their power to arrest in those particular circumstances, as s 25 of the Act of 1984 demands that a constable has reasonable grounds for suspecting that an offence has been committed or attempted, or is being committed or attempted. It is also essential that the gravity of the offence is taken into account before extreme measures are adopted. Most people who have committed a trivial offence will not continue to refuse to provide satisfactory evidence of identity if they are aware of the possibility of arrest in consequence of such failure. The intention of s 25 is clearly to ensure that all offenders are given every opportunity to make themselves answerable for their offence by way of summons, and arrest should be looked upon as an exceptional measure in most circumstances.

If an arrest is effected, s 30(7) of the Act of 1984 demands that a person arrested by a constable at a place other than a police station must be released if a constable is satisfied, before the person arrested reaches the police station, that there are no grounds for keeping him under arrest. If a person is arrested because of a failure to provide evidence of identity or a satisfactory address for the service of a summons and such information is subsequently provided, or the person is identified in some other way, that person must be instantly released. A record of such a release must be made as soon as practicable afterwards.

Object of arrest

An arrest consists of the seizing or touching of a person's body with a view to restraint. It amounts to the deprivation of a person's liberty to go where he pleases. It is possible to effect an arrest merely by words if they bring to a person's notice that he is under restraint and will be compelled to remain, and he submits to that compulsion. The purpose of such an arrest is to ensure that the person will answer an alleged offence. An arrest may also be effected by the automatic activation of door locks inside a car designed as a trap.

Information to be given on arrest

Section 28 of the Act of 1984 provides that where a person is arrested, otherwise than by being informed that he is under arrest, the arrest is not lawful unless the person arrested is informed that he is under arrest as soon as practicable after his arrest. This is so whether or not the reason for his arrest is obvious.

In addition, the section requires that, if an arrest is to be lawful, the person arrested must be informed of the grounds for his arrest at the time it takes place, or as soon as it practicable thereafter and this is an absolute requirement in that it must be done regardless of the fact that the grounds must be obvious. There are two essential factors, therefore: a person must be clearly told that he is under arrest, and he must also be told of the grounds for that arrest. In spite of television's assurances to the contrary, the words 'You are nicked' have no place in this procedure. These requirements will, on occasions, be easily satisfied. If a thief is seen leaving the premises of a jeweller carrying stolen property, it would be sufficient to say, 'I am arresting you for an offence of burglary which I have seen you commit'. If that person was seen leaving the grounds of a dwelling house and found to be in possession of property which was not normally carried about the person, it would be sufficient to say, 'I am arresting you on reasonable suspicion of having committed an offence of burglary, having seen you leave the grounds of a dwelling house which is not your own and having found you in possession of articles which I believe to have been taken from that dwelling house.' Such persons are frequently stopped by an officer and found, on being searched, to be in possession of many household articles which are not normally carried in a street. The section requires that the officer makes it clear that such a person is being arrested, and why, and any explanation, which must be clear to the person arrested, will be satisfactory: 'I am arresting you on reasonable suspicion of an offence of burglary. I have found you to be in possession of household articles concerning which you are unable to provide a satisfactory explanation. I believe that these articles have been taken from the dwelling house of some person, which you entered as a trespasser.'

The section provides an exception to these rules and this is limited to circumstances in which it was not reasonably practicable to do so by reason of the person's escape before the information could be given. Although this appears at first sight to be unimportant, the person who so escapes before being given this information is considered, for practical purposes, to have been arrested.

The Court of Appeal has held that the requirements are satisfied where a suspect is arrested by one officer, but informed by another of the reason for his arrest.

A constable who is in plain clothes at the time of an arrest must state that he is a police officer and show his warrant card.

Violence during arrest

If an arrest is effected outside, it is likely that some form of physical restraint will be applied as it is essential that a prisoner is not allowed to escape. However, when a quiet, elderly person is arrested it may be sufficient to effect that arrest merely by words which clearly indicate restraint as the issue of escape is unlikely and the possibility of successful escape remote.

It is important to remember that when unreasonable force is used in carrying out an arrest, the arrest is unlawful, whether or not the laid down procedures are followed. This is understandable. The person who is subjected to unnecessary and unreasonable force will not submit to such an arrest and to make such a person responsible for resisting a lawful arrest would be unrealistic.

An officer must use no more than reasonable force, that is, that which is necessary in the particular circumstances existing at the time. If violence is offered towards the constable he should request assistance so that the arrest may be made as effectively as possible. In any case, 'control' should be made aware of all occasions in which a police officer expects to find himself in trouble. The use of handcuffs should be restricted to exceptional circumstances and handcuffs should never be used on women and children.

Use of the truncheon

A police truncheon is capable of causing considerable injury. Its use should, therefore, be restricted to situations of extreme emergency when the officer has no other means of defending himself against violent attack. The truncheon is issued for the officer's protection and not as a weapon of offence. Its use should be restricted to circumstances in which the officer is dealing with a violent person or persons, to prevent the escape of a violent prisoner or where the officer is being overpowered.

When a truncheon is used, it should be used, with all of the care which the situation allows, if possible on the arms or legs of the assailant, particular care being taken to avoid a blow to the head. Many violent situations make the use of a truncheon, in any predetermined way, an impossibility, but it is always possible to make every conscious effort to use it as a weapon of defence. The defensive use of a truncheon has been studied and perfected by the advisers in methods of self-defence and forms an essential part of police training programmes.

Following any occasion upon which a truncheon has been used, the police officer concerned must make a record of that use as soon as practicable and must inform the custody officer immediately upon his arrival at the police station. The use of the truncheon must be mentioned when evidence is given in relation to the arrest of the offender.

Plain-clothes arrests

It is important that a person who is to be arrested is certain that the person who is carrying out the arrest is a police officer. If such a person assaults the officer, the issue of whether or not the person arrested knew that he was being arrested by a police officer is likely to be important.

It is essential, therefore, that an officer who is dressed in plain clothes at the time of the arrest clearly identifies himself as a police officer and produces his warrant card as proof of his identity.

Arrest – other than at a police station

Where a person is arrested by a constable for an offence, or is taken into custody by a constable having been arrested for an offence by some other person, at any place other than a police station, he shall be taken to a police station as soon as practicable. This is required by s 30(1) of the Act of 1984.

The words 'as soon as practicable' allow for circumstances in which it would be unrealistic to take the person arrested immediately to a police station. Section 30 (10) permits a delay in taking an arrested person to a police station if that person's presence elsewhere is necessary in order to carry out such investigations as it is reasonable to carry out immediately. This could occur where a person was seen to steal property from a motor car and, on being arrested after a chase, was found to have disposed of the stolen property along the route of the chase. In such circumstances it would be both sensible and proper to take the prisoner back along that route for the purpose of recovering the property, provided that he was not resisting arrest and was securely held. It would be important to do this to recover valuable property which had been thrown away in a public place where it was likely to be quickly discovered by other persons. If the chase had been across private fields, the recovery of the property immediately would not be so important. If property is not in danger of being lost, the prisoner should be taken immediately to a police station.

If there is any delay in taking an arrested person to a police station, the reason for that delay must be recorded on first arrival there.

It must also be remembered that a person arrested elsewhere than at a police station must be released if the constable is satisfied at any time before they reach the police station that there are no grounds for keeping him in custody. If this occurs, the constable must make a record of that release as soon as practicable after it occurs.

Arrest – category of police station

Generally, a person arrested must be taken to a 'designated police station'. A 'designated police station' is one which the chief officer of police of the area has designated to be used for the purpose of detaining arrested persons. The chief officer of police has a duty to designate those stations which appear to him to have sufficient accommodation for that purpose. The Chief Constable of the British Transport Police may designate police stations which (in addition to those designated under s 35) may be used for the purpose of detaining arrested persons. One or more custody officers must be appointed for each designated police station. A custody officer must be of at least the rank of sergeant. However, an officer of any rank may perform the functions of a custody officer at a designated police station if a custody officer is not readily available to perform them.

There are exceptional circumstances in which a person arrested may be taken to any police station. These are:

(a) where the constable is working in a locality covered by a police station which is not a designated police station; or

(b) where he is a constable belonging to a police force maintained by an authority other than a police authority (e.g. the British Transport Police).

The exception in (a) recognises that many officers, in county forces in particular, may patrol a beat many miles from a designated police station. If the offence is such that the person arrested is likely to be released on bail more or less immediately, it would be unrealistic to require that he be transported many miles to a 'designated police station', only to be released on bail. There are limitations placed upon detention in non-designated police stations and a constable must not take a prisoner to such a station if it appears to him that it may be necessary to keep the arrested person in police detention for more than 6 hours.

Any constable may take an arrested person to any police station if:

(a) the constable has arrested him without the assistance of any other constable and no other constable is available to assist him; or

(b) the constable has taken him into custody from a person other than a constable without the assistance of any other constable and no other constable is available to assist him, and (in either case) it appears to the constable that he will be unable to take the arrested person to a designated police station without the arrested person injuring himself, the constable or some other person.

There will be many occasions in which a police officer, acting upon his own, will encounter sufficient difficulty in attempting to take a resisting prisoner to the nearest police station. It would be unrealistic to require him to extend his journey in such circumstances.

When a person who is arrested is taken to a non-designated police station, that police station will not have any appointed 'custody officer'. This means that another police officer must perform the duties of a custody officer while that prisoner remains in police detention.

Section 36 (7) of the Act of 1984 allows that where an arrested person is taken to a police station which is not a designated police station, the functions of a custody officer shall be performed:

(a) by an officer who is not involved in the investigation of an offence for which he is in police detention, if such an officer is readily available; and
(b) if no such officer is readily available, by the officer who took him to the station, or any other officer.

Where the arresting officer is required to perform the duties of a custody officer at a police station to which he takes his prisoner, he shall inform an officer who is attached to a designated police station and is of at least the rank of inspector.

Arrest under the authority of a warrant

A warrant of arrest or of commitment (or of distress, or a search warrant) may be executed anywhere in England and Wales by a constable acting in his police area. In addition, by the Criminal Justice and Public Order Act 1994, s 136, a warrant issued in England, Wales or Northern Ireland for the arrest or commitment (or a like warrant issued in Scotland) of a person may, without endorsement, be executed by anyone to whom it is directed or by a constable acting within his police area.

Certain warrants may be executed by a constable who does not have possession of the warrant at the time. These are:

(a) warrants to arrest a person in connection with an offence;
(b) warrants under the Army Act 1955, Air Force Act 1955, Naval Discipline Act 1957 or Reserve Forces Act 1996 (desertion, etc.);
(c) warrants relating to the non-appearance of a defendant, warrants of distress, warrants of commitment, warrants to arrest a witness and warrants to arrest someone for non-compliance with a summons to make a deposition in connection with committal proceedings (under the Magistrates' Courts Act 1980, ss 55, 76, 93, 97 and 97A and the Crime and Disorder Act 1998, Schedule 3); and
(d) warrants issued under para. 3(2) of Schedule 1 to the Youth Justice and Criminal Evidence Act 1999 (offender referred to court by youth offender panel); see Magistrates' Courts Act 1980, s 125(4)(c)(v),

but, in such cases, the warrants must, on the demand of the person concerned, be shown to him as soon as practicable. The person arrested must be told of the existence of the warrant at the time of his arrest, as this is the reason for his arrest.

Where a warrant to arrest is in the possession of the officer at the time of the arrest, it must be shown to the person who is being arrested, but must not be given to him.

Searching of detained persons

The Police and Criminal Evidence Act 1984 removed all previous powers to search persons in custody. Section 54 of that Act charges a custody officer with a duty to ascertain the property which a person has with him when he is:

(a) brought to a police station after being arrested elsewhere or after being committed to custody by an order or a sentence of a court; or
(b) arrested at a police station or detained there when answering police bail or is arrested under s 46A (failure to answer police bail),

and to record particulars of that property in the person's custody record.

To discharge these responsibilities, a person may be searched to the extent considered necessary by the custody officer, but an intimate search may not be carried out under this section and a strip search may only be carried out in specified circumstances. A strip search must be carried out by a constable who must be of the same sex as the person searched. An authorised detention officer may carry out such searches.

Articles other than those subject to legal privilege (e.g. letters from solicitors, etc.) may be seized and retained but clothes and personal effects may only be seized if the custody officer believes that they may be used by that person:

(a) to cause physical injury to himself or another person;
(b) to damage property;
(c) to interfere with evidence;
(d) to assist him to escape,

or if the custody officer has reasonable grounds for believing that there may be evidence of an offence.

A person in custody at a police station or elsewhere may be searched at any time by a constable in order to ascertain whether he is in possession of any such articles. A constable may seize and detain anything found in such a search, except that clothes and personal effects may only be seized in the circumstances outlined above.

Persons must be told the reason why articles are being seized unless they are violent, or likely to be violent, or are incapable of understanding. All such items in (a) to (d) must be returned to such a person when he is released from custody.

A detained person may retain clothing and 'personal effects' (which does not include cash) at his own risk subject to a custody officer's discretion to retain them if there is risk of harm to others or to property, or to interfere with evidence, or of their use in an escape. The level of responsibility placed on a custody officer is high. Is the mirror in a woman's make-up case dangerous? Obviously it is not when it remains in its original condition, but it is, if it is subsequently broken. Is the woman likely to attempt to take her own life?

All such property must be recorded whether it is retained by the prisoner or retained by the custody officer. The detained person must be allowed to check the property record and to sign it. If articles are retained by the custody officer, the reason for doing so must be recorded.

The Anti-terrorism, Crime and Security Act 2001 (which is subject to review on 14 December 2003) adds a s 54A to PACE which permits an officer of at least the rank of inspector to authorise the search and/or examination of a detained person in a police station for the purpose of ascertaining whether he has any mark that would tend to identify him as a person involved in the commission of an offence, or for the purpose of facilitating the ascertainment of his identity. An authorisation for the purpose of ascertaining whether the person has an identifying mark may only be given where the appropriate consent has been withheld, or it is not practicable to obtain it. Otherwise, such authorisation may only be given if the person concerned has refused to identify himself or the officer has reasonable grounds for suspecting that the person is not who he claims to be. An authorisation may be given orally but must be conformed in writing as soon as is practicable.

Any identifying mark (including features and injuries) which is found may be photographed with consent or, if such consent is withheld or it is not practicable to obtain it, without consent. 'Photographed' covers the use of any means by which a visual image may be produced.

Such searches, examinations and taking of photographs may be conducted or taken by constables (or other people authorised by the chief officer of police) of the same sex as the person concerned, who may use reasonable force. An intimate search may not be carried out under the authority of s 54A.

Photographs taken under the section may be used for any purpose related to the prevention or detection of crime, the investigation of an offence or the conduct of a prosecution. They may be retained after use or disclosure but may not be used or disclosed except for a related purpose.

The references to 'crime' include conduct (whether under United Kingdom law or the law of a country or territory outside the United Kingdom) or which correspond to conduct which would be an offence in the United Kingdom if it all took place in any one part of the United Kingdom.

Release of detained persons

The Police and Criminal Evidence Act 1984, s 46, requires that where a person:

(a) is charged with an offence; and
(b) after being charged, is kept in police detention (or in the case of a juvenile) is detained by the local authority,

he must be brought before a magistrates' court as soon as practicable and in any event not later than the first sitting after he is charged (or, if he is brought before a magistrates' court in another area, not later than the first sitting of that court after his arrival in the area).

If there is no court due to sit on the day the person is charged, or on the next day, the custody officer must inform the justices' chief executive that there is a person in the area who has been detained after charge, and the justices' chief executive must arrange for a sitting of the court not later than the day next following the day on which he is charged. Christmas Day, Good Friday and any Sunday do not count as 'days next following'. An exception to the rule is where a person is in hospital and is not well enough to appear.

Police bail of person charged – general

Section 38 of the 1984 Act requires that where a person who is arrested otherwise than under a warrant endorsed for bail is charged with an offence, the custody officer must (subject to the Criminal Justice and Public Order Act 1994, s 25, which states that there must be no bail for defendants charged with homicide, rape or attempts to commit such offences, after a previous conviction for such an offence unless there are exceptional circumstances justifying bail) order his release from police detention, either on bail or without bail, unless:

(a) his name and address cannot be ascertained or the custody officer has reasonable grounds for doubting the truth of a name and address provided by him;
(b) the custody officer has reasonable grounds for believing that the person arrested will fail to appear in court to answer bail;
(c) in the case of a person arrested for an imprisonable offence (one punishable with imprisonment), the custody officer has reasonable grounds for believing that the detention of the person arrested is necessary to prevent him from committing an offence;
(d) in the case of a person who has attained the age of 18, the custody officer has reasonable grounds for believing that the detention of the person is necessary to enable a sample to be taken from him under s 63B (testing for presence of Class A drug);
(e) in the case of a person arrested for an offence which is not an imprisonable offence, the custody officer has reasonable grounds for believing that the detention of the person arrested is necessary to prevent him from causing physical injury to any other person or from causing loss of or damage to property;
(f) the custody officer has reasonable grounds for believing that the detention of the person arrested is necessary to prevent him from interfering with the administration of justice or the investigation of offences or of a particular offence; or
(g) the custody officer has reasonable grounds for believing that the detention of the person arrested is necessary for his own protection.

If the person charged is a juvenile it is also sufficient that the custody officer has reasonable grounds for believing that the juvenile should be detained in his own interests.

This section also requires that where a custody officer authorises an arrested juvenile to be kept in police detention, the custody officer shall secure that the arrested juvenile is taken to local authority accommodation unless the custody officer certifies:

(a) that by reason of such circumstances as are specified in the certificate, it is impracticable to do so; or
(b) in the case of a boy aged 12 or over, that no secure accommodation is available and that keeping him in other local authority accommodation would not be adequate to protect the public from serious harm from him.

In the case of juveniles charged with violent or sexual offences, references to protecting the public from serious harm refer to protection from death or serious personal injury, whether physical or psychological, occasioned by further offences.

'Sexual offence' means one under the Sexual Offences Act 1956 (other than a man living on earnings of prostitution, a woman exercising control over prostitutes, keeping a brothel, a landlord letting premises for use as a brothel, a tenant permitting premises to be used as a brothel and a tenant permitting premises to be used for prostitution);

s 128 of the Mental Health Act 1959 (sexual intercourse with patients); an offence under the Indecency with Children Act 1960; an offence under s 9 Theft Act 1968 of burglary with intent to commit rape; an offence under s 54 of the Criminal Law Act 1977 (inciting girl under 16 to incestuous sexual intercourse); an offence under the Protection of Children Act 1978 (indecent photographs); an offence under s 1 of the Criminal Law Act 1977 of conspiracy to commit any of the above offences; an attempt to commit any of those offences; or inciting another to commit any of those offences.

A 'violent offence' is one which leads, or is intended or likely to lead, to a person's death or physical injury, and includes an offence which is required to be charged as arson (whether or not it would otherwise fall within this definition).

By s 47 of the 1984 Act, a release on bail under the detention provisions of the Act shall be a release on bail granted in accordance with ss 3, 3A, 5 and 5A of the Bail Act 1976 as they apply to bail granted by a constable. The normal powers to impose conditions of bail shall be available to him where a custody officer releases a person on bail under s 38(1) (duties of custody officer after charge) or s 40(10) [which applies s 39(1) to review situations] *but not in any other case.*

Bail may be subject to a duty to appear before a magistrates' court or to attend at a police station at a time and date appointed by the custody officer. A person so bailed promises to appear as prescribed. The Bail Act 1976 includes penalties for those who fail to appear in answer to bail. In serious cases, an accused may be required to find one or more 'sureties', that is, persons who undertake to secure his attendance. In such a case each surety enters into a recognisance to forfeit a specified sum to the Crown should the accused fail to appear. The parent or guardian of a juvenile may be required to act as a surety for a sum not exceeding £50 to secure a juvenile's compliance with a condition attached to bail, but he must consent to be so bound.

A record must be made of the decision to grant bail and the accused must be supplied with a copy of the record if he so requires. The Criminal Justice and Police Act 2001 added ss 5(A) and (5B) to the Bail Act 1976, which have the combined effect of requiring a magistrates' court or a Crown Court to give reasons for granting bail after hearing representations from the prosecutor in favour of withholding it, to record those reasons and make a copy of the record available to the prosecutor on request.

The Bail Act s 3(6ZAA) provides the power for a court to impose conditions upon a child or young person which involve the electronic monitoring of his compliance with bail conditions. A person made subject to such monitoring must be at least 12 years of age, and have been charged with or convicted of a violent or sexual offence or an offence punishable by 14 years' imprisonment or more, or one or more imprisonable offences which amount to a recent history of repeatedly committing imprisonable offences while on bail. In such a case, a youth offending team must be of the opinion that the imposition of such a requirement will be suitable and some person must be required to monitor the person subject to that condition.

A magistrates' court may alter police bail to require attendance at a later time or to enlarge sureties.

Before a person is released on bail, the court or the custody officer may require him to comply with specified conditions. A custody officer may impose requirements as appear to be necessary to secure that the person surrenders to custody, does not commit an offence whilst on bail and does not interfere with witnesses or otherwise obstruct the course of justice whether in relation to himself or another person. However, he may not impose a requirement to live in a bail hostel. Where such conditions are imposed, a record must be made of the reasons for doing so which will be available if requested by the person concerned. The same applies to variations which may be made to such conditions.

Before a custody officer decides to grant bail, he may wish to take into account the provisions of para. 2A to Schedule 1 of the Bail Act 1976, which state that a court need not grant bail if the offence being considered is an indictable one or is triable either way and it appears to the court that the person was on bail in criminal proceedings on the date of that offence. It would seem to be good practice in such cases to put that person before a court to allow such consideration to be given to the matter.

Where a custody officer has granted bail in criminal proceedings, he or another custody officer serving at the same police station may, at the request of the person to whom it was granted, vary the conditions of bail, and in doing so he may impose conditions or more onerous conditions.

Delayed charges

Where a custody officer decides, when an accused is brought before him, that there is insufficient evidence at that stage to charge the prisoner, but that there probably will be when further enquiries have been made, he may release a prisoner on bail, such bail being conditioned upon his appearance at a police station at a given time, as opposed to appearing at court. In such a way, an accused can be brought before a custody officer at a later stage, for the situation to be re-assessed. This form of bail may be cancelled at any time by notice in writing from the custody officer. Where a person is detained, any previous time in custody must be included in any calculation of detention time. In practice, his old custody record will be continued.

No conditions may be attached to such bail.

Police powers

Section 46A was added to the 1984 Act by the Criminal Justice and Public Order Act 1994. It provides that a constable may arrest without warrant any person who, having been released on bail under these provisions subject to a duty to attend at a police station, fails to attend at that police station at the time appointed for him to do so.

A person who is arrested under this section shall be taken to a police station appointed as the place at which he is to surrender to custody as soon as practicable after his arrest.

Powers of entry without a search warrant to effect an arrest

The Act of 1984 abolishes all of the previous common law rules which gave a constable power to enter premises without a warrant for the purpose of effecting an arrest with the exception that the common law power still exists to enter premises to deal with a breach of the peace, or to prevent it. A constable may enter in such circumstances provided that he clearly states who he is and demands admission from the occupant. A power to enter in these circumstances merely recognises the urgency of certain situations. If urgent cries for help are heard coming from a dwelling, it would be unrealistic if a police officer was not entitled to enter. However, the power extends to 'preventing a breach of the peace'. This should be borne in mind when, having entered, the officer is required to leave by an occupant, other than the one in distress. The officer is entitled to remain to prevent a further breach of the peace.

Section 17 of the Police and Criminal Evidence Act 1984 provides that, without prejudice to any other enactment, a constable may enter and search any premises for the purpose:

(a) of executing a warrant of arrest issued in connection with or arising out of criminal proceedings, or a warrant of commitment issued under s 76 of the Magistrates' Courts Act 1980;

(b) of arresting a person for an arrestable offence;

(c) of arresting a person for an offence under s 1 of the Public Order Act 1936 (prohibited uniforms), or any enactment contained in ss 6–8 or 10 of the Criminal Law Act 1977 (offences of entering or remaining on property) – in the latter case the arresting officer must be in uniform; s 4 Public Order Act 1986 (fear or provocation of violence), or an offence under s 163 Road Traffic Act 1988 (failure to stop when required to do so by a police constable in uniform), or an offence under the Criminal Justice and Public Order Act 1994, s 76 (failure to comply with an interim possession order);

(d) of arresting, in pursuance of the Children and Young Persons Act 1969, s 32(1A), any child or young person who has been remanded or committed to local authority accommodation under s 23(1) of that Act;

(e) of recapturing any person who is, or is deemed for any purpose to be, unlawfully at large while liable to be detained
  (i) in a prison, remand centre, young offender institution or secure training centre, or
  (ii) in pursuance of the Powers of Criminal Courts (Sentencing) Act 2000, s 92 (dealing with children and young persons guilty of grave crimes), in any other place;

(f) of recapturing a person who is unlawfully at large and whom he is pursuing; or

(g) of saving life or limb or preventing serious damage to property.

With the exception of the instances involving the saving of life or limb or preventing serious damage, powers of entry and search under s 17 may only be exercised where the constable has reasonable grounds for believing that the person whom he is seeking is on the premises. A search under these provisions may only be to an extent that is reasonably required for the purpose.

A police officer must, when effecting an entry by force, inform any occupant on the premises at the time of the reason why he is seeking entry, unless the circumstances make it impossible, impracticable or undesirable.

In relation to premises consisting of two or more separate dwellings, the power to search is limited to those parts used commonly by the residents and the particular dwelling in which the constable has reasonable grounds for believing that the person whom he is seeking may be.

Entry and search after arrest

Prior to the Police and Criminal Evidence Act 1984, there was no general right to enter a dwelling house without a warrant to search for or to seize evidence after an arrest had been made. If the occupier would not consent to such a search, in most circumstances a warrant was necessary. Section 18 of the Act of 1984 allows a constable to enter and search any premises occupied or controlled by a person who is under arrest for an arrestable offence, if there are reasonable grounds for suspecting that there is evidence on the premises which relates to that offence or to some other arrestable offence which is connected with, or is similar to, that offence. (The evidence must be such that it is not subject to legal privilege.) The section, therefore, authorises the search of the dwellings of those arrested for offences such as burglary, drug pushing or thefts from motor vehicles, to recover evidence of the offence and further similar offences which might have been committed by the person arrested. A search of any person who has not been arrested, which is carried out during a search of premises, shall be carried out under the Stop and Search Code. The Divisional Court has held that the power provided by s 18 is limited to police enquiries into domestic offences and does not apply when an arrest is effected for an offence committed abroad.

A constable is also authorised by the section to seize and retain articles found on premises in consequence of such a search which relate to the offences for which a person has been arrested or to some other arrestable offence which is connected with or similar to that offence. The Court of Appeal considered circumstances in which a known sex offender was alleged to have committed a number of sexual offences against children in his motor car. The police seized the car as evidence as the children had identified various items which were in the car and had described the car itself. The Court said that it was clear that there was a power of seizure at common law and this had not been removed by the Police and Criminal Evidence Act 1984. However, there was in addition, a power of seizure under the 1984 Act. Sections s 19(2) and (3) provide a power to seize 'anything which is on those premises' and s 18(2) provides a power to seize and retain 'anything for which he may search under subsection (1)'.

Neither section provides a power to seize the premises themselves. Such premises could not be seized where they were immovable, but that barrier does not exist where the premises are movable. A vehicle, tent or caravan could be moved. The Court said that there was no reason why 'anything' should not include 'everything' where the nature of the premises allowed seizure.

The extended powers of seizure under s 50 of the Criminal Justice and Police Act 2001 (of articles which cannot be separated) apply to a search under s 18 of PACE.

A search under the authority of s 18 may only be made if it has been authorised in writing by an officer of the rank of inspector or above, unless it is carried out before a person is taken to a police station in circumstances where the presence of that person at the place in question is necessary for the effective investigation of the offence. Such an authorisation must be given on a document 'Notice of Powers and Rights', which should be given to or left for the occupier of the premises (see below). However, if a search is made in such circumstances without a written authority, the constable carrying out the search must inform an officer of the rank of inspector or above that the search has been made, as soon as practicable.

Thus, where a constable arrests a man who is a retailer of electrical goods in the living quarters above the shop, for thefts of electrical goods, the constable may search not only the living quarters, but also the shop premises as both are 'occupied and controlled' by the person arrested. If the shop premises are searched before the man is taken to the police station, the arresting officer must inform an officer of the rank of inspector or above that he has done so, as soon as practicable.

Where a search under the authority of a s 18 written authorisation is to be conducted, the officer conducting the search must explain to the occupier of the premises, in so far as it is practicable to do so, the reason why he intends to conduct the search. In circumstances in which police officers were asked to slide the authority to search under the door (the occupier's son had been arrested for burglary) and the officers offered to show it through the window but the occupier did not come to the window, the Divisional Court said that the officers were not entitled to force entry without explaining to the occupier the reason for requiring entry to search.

An officer who authorises a search or who is informed that a search has been made must record in writing, in the custody record if there is one, otherwise in his notebook or in the search record, the grounds for the search and the nature of the evidence which was being sought. If the occupier of the premises is, at the time, in police custody, the record must be made in the custody record.

Use of force to enter and search

The Code of Practice for the Searching of Premises by Police Officers, etc., states that reasonable force may be used, if necessary, to enter premises if the officer in charge is satisfied that the premises are those specified in any warrant or other written authority. There are certain conditions which must be satisfied, which are explained below. On any occasion upon which force is used, the use of such force must be justified. These provisions apply to all entries effected for the purpose of a search being made whether such entry is permitted by the Act of 1984 or any other statute.

The term 'premises' is defined by s 23 of the Act of 1984 as including *any place* and, in particular, includes:

(a) any vehicle, vessel, aircraft or hovercraft;
(b) any offshore installation; and
(c) any tent or moveable structure.

The term 'offshore installation' has the meaning given to it by s 1 of the Mineral Workings (Offshore Installations) Act 1971. It is, therefore, concerned with oil rigs, etc.

The local police/community consultative group or its equivalent should be informed as soon as practicable after a search where there is reason to believe that it might have an adverse effect on relations between the police and the community.

Code C provides that where the power to use force to enter premises is conferred upon a 'designated person' (designated under the Police Reform Act 2002) that power shall not be exercised unless that person is accompanied by, and is under the supervision of, a police officer.

Searching premises with consent

If it is proposed to obtain consent to search premises, the officer in charge shall state the purpose and extent of the proposed search to a person entitled to grant entry. This information should be as specific as possible, particularly regarding the articles or persons being sought and the parts of the premises to be searched. He must also be informed that he is not obliged to consent and that anything which is seized may be produced in evidence. In addition, if, at that time, such person is not suspected of an offence, the officer shall tell him so when stating the purpose of the search. An officer cannot enter and search premises or continue to search premises if consent has been given under duress or is withdrawn before the search is completed. The consent of the person entitled to grant entry to the premises must, if practicable, be given in writing on the Notice of Powers and Rights before the search takes place. Such consent in writing is unnecessary where the consent is obtained although there is a warrant in force or if there is a power of entry and search without warrant.

It is unnecessary to seek consent, however, where in the circumstances this would cause disproportionate inconvenience to the person concerned. This might occur where it is reasonable to assume that innocent occupiers would agree to, and expect that, police would take the proposed action. Examples are where a suspect has fled from the scene of a crime or to evade arrest and it is necessary quickly to check surrounding gardens and readily accessible places to see whether he is hiding; or where police have arrested someone in the night after a pursuit and it is necessary to make brief checks of gardens along the route of the pursuit to see whether stolen or incriminating articles have been discarded.

It is important that officers consult their supervisors before conducting such searches. It would be easy to forget that the searches of such gardens in other circumstances, in which the issue of inconvenience did not arise, should be consented to in writing. A garden is a 'place' which is included in the definition of the term 'premises'.

In the case of a lodging house or similar accommodation, a search should not be made on the basis solely of the landlord's consent unless the tenant is unavailable and the matter is urgent.

Notice of powers and rights

An officer who conducts a search of premises under the above powers (or under the Terrorism Act 2000) must, unless it is impractical to do so, provide the owner with a notice in standard format:

(a) specifying whether the search is made under warrant, or with consent or in the exercise of statutory powers under ss 17, 18 and 32 of PACE to search without warrant or consent;

(b) summarising the extent of the powers of search and seizure conferred in the Act;

(c) explaining the right of the occupier and the owner of property seized;

(d) explaining that compensation may be payable in appropriate cases for damage caused in entering and searching premises, and giving the address to which an application for compensation should be directed; and

(e) stating that a copy of the Search Code is available to be consulted at any police station.

If the occupier is present, copies of the notice and of the warrant (if the search is made under warrant) should if practicable be given to the occupier before the search begins, unless the officer in charge of the search reasonably believes that to do so would frustrate the object of the search or endanger the officers concerned or other persons. If the occupier is not present, copies of the notice, and of the warrant where appropriate, should be left in a prominent place on the premises or appropriate part of the premises and endorsed with the name of the officer in charge of the search, the name of the police station to which he is attached and the date and time of the search. A warrant or other identification number will suffice where there is a terrorist connection. The warrant itself should be endorsed to show that this has been done.

Entry other than with consent

Searches made under the authority of a warrant must be made within 1 month from the date of issue of the warrant. They must be made at a reasonable hour unless this might frustrate the purpose of the search.

The officer in charge shall first attempt to communicate with the occupier or any other person entitled to grant access to the premises by explaining the authority under which he seeks to enter the premises, and ask the occupier to allow him to do so. Where the premises are occupied, the officer shall identify himself (by warrant or other identification number in the case of enquiries linked to terrorism) and, if not in uniform, produce his warrant card (but in so doing in the case of enquiries linked to the investigation of terrorism, the officer need not reveal his name). He must state the purpose of the search and the grounds for undertaking it, identify and introduce any person accompanying the officer on the search (such persons should carry identification for production on request) and briefly describe that person's role in the process, and produce the warrant and supply the occupier with a copy of it before a search begins, unless there are reasonable grounds to believe that to alert the occupier or any other person entitled to grant access would frustrate the search or endanger the officers concerned or other persons. Where warrants were issued which referred to schedules setting out the property to be seized, the search was held to be unlawful in consequence of the fact that the schedules had been removed before the copies were supplied to the occupier of the premises. The warrants were no longer 'complete'.

There are, therefore, technically two stages to the process: first, there should be an attempt to communicate and explain the authority to enter, then, when entry has been gained, the officer should identify himself and state the purpose of the search and the grounds for making it. The logic of this is easy to establish – it would be unrealistic to demand that the constable shouted out the second stage information in the street, or through a letter box.

While there is no need for a constable to fulfil his obligations to identify himself, or to produce the various documents before entering if there are reasonable grounds to believe that this would frustrate the search or endanger the officer or others in such a case, he must do so at the earliest opportunity after entry and before starting to search (except that it is enough if he gives the copy of the warrant at the first reasonable opportunity thereafter).

The Code relating to Entry and Search states that it will not be necessary to carry out the above procedure if:

(a) the premises to be searched are known to be unoccupied;
(b) the occupier or any other person entitled to grant access is known to be absent;
(c) there are reasonable grounds to believe that to alert the occupier or any other persons entitled to grant access by attempting to communicate with him would frustrate the object of the search or endanger the officers concerned or other persons.

The circumstances embraced by (a) and (b) are self-explanatory. The provisions at (c) will cover a number of possibilities. The premises to be searched may be suspected to be housing a known, armed fugitive. To attempt to communicate with anyone inside the building would be likely to lead to the escape of such a fugitive, or to injury to the officers, or to the fugitive himself if the officers were armed. The provisions would also cover circumstances in which such warning of entry would provide the occupier with an opportunity to dispose of evidence, e.g. flushing drugs down a lavatory.

Reasonable and proportionate force may be used if necessary to enter premises if the officer in charge is satisfied that the premises are those specified in any warrant or other written authority and where:

(a) the occupier or any other person entitled to grant access has refused a request to allow entry to his premises;
(b) it is impossible to communicate with the occupier or any other person entitled to grant access; or
(c) any of the conditions set out in (a) to (c) above apply.

Where premises have been entered by force, the officer in charge shall, before leaving the premises, satisfy himself that they are secure either by arranging for the occupier or his agent to be present, or by any other appropriate means. This means that, in no circumstances, should premises which have been searched be left insecure.

The local police/community consultative group or its equivalent should be informed as soon as practicable after a search where there is reason to believe that it might have an adverse effect on relations between the police and the community.

Searching of premises

All searches must be carried out at a reasonable hour, unless this would frustrate the purposes of the search. For example, if it was known that a criminal who was to be arrested was armed and dangerous, the purpose of the search would be to locate him and arrest him without injury being occasioned to any person. In such circumstances, a search during the daylight hours would be unlikely to be effective in this respect. One conducted at 3 a.m. would be much more likely to achieve that aim.

Premises may be searched only to the extent necessary to achieve the object of the search, having regard to the size and nature of whatever is being sought. If the search is for stolen television sets, it would be unrealistic to search small drawers and bedside cabinets. A search under warrant may not continue under the authority of that warrant once all of the things specified in it have been found. If the warrant specifies three television sets of particular serial numbers, once these have been discovered and seized, the search must stop. On the other hand, once the officer in charge of the search is reasonably satisfied that the specified property or articles are not on the premises, the search must stop.

All searches must be conducted with due consideration for the property and the privacy of the occupier of the premises searched, with no more disturbance than necessary. If the search is for a stolen wallet or handbag, there is no necessity to remove personal articles of clothing from drawers. The presence or otherwise of the articles searched for can be established without the removal of such articles from the drawer. Reasonable force may be used only where this is necessary because the co-operation of the occupier cannot be obtained or is insufficient for the purpose. It may be that the occupier, after admittance has been gained, obstructs the conduct of the search and some reasonable force may have to be used to effect a search within the terms of the authority. If the occupier of such premises wishes to ask a friend, neighbour or other person to witness the search, he must be allowed to do so, unless the officer has reasonable grounds to believe that this would seriously hinder the investigation or endanger the officers concerned or other people. A search need not be delayed for this purpose. A person need not be cautioned before being asked questions which are solely concerned with the proper and effective conduct of a search, for example, to locate the key to a locked drawer or otherwise to seek co-operation. If questioning goes beyond this point it may amount to an interview and would require the associated safeguards.

No search may continue once the officer in charge is satisfied that what is being sought is not on the premises.

Seizure of property

The Police and Criminal Evidence Act 1984, s 10, defines 'items subject to legal privilege' as:

(a) communications between a professional legal adviser and his client or any person representing his client made in connection with the giving of legal advice to the client;

(b) such communications made in connection with or in the contemplation of legal proceedings which are for the purpose of these proceedings; and

(c) items enclosed with, or referred to in such communications and in connection with the giving of legal advice or in contemplation of such legal proceedings.

An officer who is conducting such a search may seize anything covered by the warrant, other than an item which is subject to legal, professional privilege. However, he may also seize anything which he has reasonable grounds for believing is evidence of an offence, or has been obtained in consequence of the commission of an offence, where seizure is necessary to prevent its concealment, alteration, loss or destruction. It is apparent, therefore, that although warrants, etc., will specify material to be searched for, there is an authority to seize evidence of other offences if such evidence is discovered *in the course of searching for the specified articles*. This must be so, as the Code of Practice for the Searching of Premises, etc., allows a search only to the extent necessary to locate the specified articles. In the example previously quoted, of searching premises for stolen television sets, it could be accepted that the officers conducting the search would be likely to find stolen video recorders in the places which they would be likely to search for television sets. They would be searching cupboards, wardrobes, etc. In searching for such television sets, they could not realistically discover stolen postage stamps in a small drawer. In most circumstances, the seizure of property discovered will be necessary to prevent concealment, alteration, loss or destruction.

Should an officer decide that it is not appropriate to seize property because of an explanation given by the person holding it, but nevertheless has reasonable grounds for believing that it has been obtained in consequence of the commission of an offence by some person, he shall inform the holder of his suspicions and shall explain that, if he disposes of the property, he may be liable to civil or criminal proceedings. This would most probably occur where a person has innocently come into possession of property stolen by someone else.

A constable may photograph or copy, or have photographed or copied, any document or other article which he has power to seize. Where he considers that information may be stored in any electronic form and that it could be used in evidence, he may require the information to be produced in a form which can be taken away and in which it is visible and legible.

Such articles which have been seized can be retained as long as is necessary in the circumstances. They may be required for use as evidence, for forensic examination or for other investigation in connection with an offence or when stolen, etc., to establish their lawful owner. Property (other than that resulting from an offence) should not be retained if a photograph or copy would suffice (e.g. trading records).

Where seized property is retained, the person who had custody or control of it immediately prior to its seizure must, on request, be provided with a list or description of the property within a reasonable time. He, or his representative, must be allowed supervised access to the property to examine it or have it photographed or copied, or must be provided with a photograph or copy, in either case within a reasonable time of any request and at his own expense, unless the officer in charge of any investigation has reasonable grounds for believing that this would prejudice the investigation of the offence or any criminal proceedings. In such a case, a record of the grounds must be made.

Action to be taken after searches

Where premises have been searched (other than when searched without consent because to seek it would cause disproportionate inconvenience, etc.), the officer in charge of the search shall, on arrival at a police station, make, or have made, a record of the search. The record shall include:

(a) the address of the premises searched;
(b) the date, time and duration of the search;
(c) the authority under which the search was made; where the search was made in exercise of a statutory power to search premises without a warrant, the record shall include the power under which the search was made; and where the search was made under warrant or with written consent, a copy of the warrant or consent shall be appended to the record or kept in a place identified in the record;
(d) the names of the officer in charge of the search and all other officers who conducted the search except in cases of enquiries linked to the investigation of terrorism, where the record must state the warrant or other identification number and the duty station of each officer;
(e) the names of any persons on the premises if they are known;
(f) any grounds for refusing the occupier's request to have someone present during the search;
(g) either a list of any articles seized or a note of where such a list is kept and, if not covered by a warrant, the reason for their seizure;
(h) whether force was used and, if so, the reason;
(i) details of any damage caused during the search, and the circumstances in which it was caused;
(j) if applicable, the reason why it was not practicable to give the occupier a copy of the 'Notice of Powers and Rights'; and
(k) when the occupier was not present, the place where the copies of the Notice of Powers and Rights and search warrant were left on the premises.

A search register shall be maintained at each sub-divisional police station. All records which are required to be made by the Code of Practice for the Searching of Premises, etc., shall be made, copied or referred to in that register. If the wrong premises are searched by mistake, everything possible must be done at the earliest opportunity to allay any sense of grievance. In appropriate cases, assistance should be given to obtain compensation.

In instances in which premises have been searched under warrant, the warrant must be endorsed to show:

(a) whether any articles specified in the warrant were found;
(b) whether any other articles were seized;
(c) the date and time at which it was executed;
(d) the names of the officers who executed it (except in the case of enquiries linked to terrorism, in which case the warrant or other identification number and duty station of each officer shall be shown);
(e) whether a copy, together with the Notice of Powers and Rights, was handed to the occupier or whether it was enclosed with the date and time of the search and left on the premises and, if so, where on them.

It is essential to ensure that premises which have been entered by force are properly secured when the search has been completed. This will no doubt be done by the owner of the property or his agent, if present, but if they are not it will be the responsibility of the officer in charge of the search to ensure that adequate steps are taken to safeguard the premises.

Any warrant which has not been executed within 1 month of its issue shall be returned to the justices' clerk.

Classification of offences and powers to arrest without warrant

Classification of offences

An offence is a disobedience of the common law or statute law which is punishable by the courts. It could be described as an act or omission which is forbidden by law on pain of punishment. Offences are divided into classes which indicate their mode of trial and the Interpretation Act 1978 defines the various classes of offences as:

(a) 'indictable offence' means an offence which, if committed by an adult, is triable on indictment, whether such an offence is exclusively so triable, or triable either way;
(b) 'summary offence' means an offence which, if committed by an adult, is triable only summarily; and
(c) 'an offence triable either way' means an offence which, if committed by an adult, is triable either on indictment or summarily.

Section 22 of the Magistrates Courts Act of 1980 provides special circumstances in which certain offences set out in Schedule 2 to the Act, which are triable either way, must be dealt with summarily if the 'value' involved in the offence is small.

Unless it is particularly provided by the statute creating the offence, a magistrates' court shall not try any information or hear a complaint in relation to a summary offence unless the information was laid or the complaint made within 6 months from the date when the offence was committed, or the complaint arose. A number of statutes do extend the period within which information may be laid. There is no time limit in relation to indictable offences unless such a time limit is directly imposed by the statute. There is, therefore, no time limit upon a magistrates' court hearing an 'indictable offence' unless the statute particularly creates that limitation. The same provisions are applied to offences 'triable either way'.

Powers of arrest without a warrant

An arrest is the taking or depriving of a person of his liberty in order that he will be available to answer an alleged or suspected crime or offence. Powers to arrest are provided by the common law, the provisions of the Police and Criminal Evidence Act of 1984 which relate to 'arrestable offences', and a general, conditional power of arrest which is provided by the 1984 Act. A few powers to arrest are still provided by particular statutes.

Common law powers of arrest

There are powers to arrest at common law in certain circumstances and these are unaffected by the provisions of the Police and Criminal Evidence Act 1984. These powers are associated with a 'breach of the peace'. A breach of the peace occurs whenever and wherever (even on private premises):

(a) harm is *actually done*, or is *likely* to be done, to a person, whether by the conduct of the person against whom a breach of the peace is alleged or by someone whom it provokes; or

(b) harm is *actually* done, or is *likely* to be done, to a person's property in his presence; or

(c) a person is genuinely in fear of harm to himself or to his property in his presence as a result of an assault, affray, riot or other disturbance.

At common law any person may arrest without warrant where:

(a) a breach of the peace is committed by the person arrested in the presence of the person making the arrest; or

(b) where no breach of the peace has occurred in the presence of the person making the arrest, but he reasonably believes that such a breach by the person arrested is about to occur or is imminent; he will not have such a belief if there is no real and present threat to the peace;

and a constable may arrest without warrant any person who assaults, or resists, or wilfully obstructs him in the lawful execution of his duty in circumstances which are likely to cause a breach of the peace.

These common law powers of arrest in relation to breaches of the peace are most important to police officers. They are not limited by the nature of the place in which the 'breach' occurs and arrests may be effected in public or private places. Once a constable reasonably foresees a breach of the peace, he is entitled to remain on the premises in which, until that time, he has been a trespasser. If persons fight, then regardless of all other considerations, a breach of the peace has occurred and an arrest is justified if it is necessary in the particular circumstances which are prevailing. If the stage of fighting has not been reached, the situation may exist in which it is apparent that the only way in which a fight will be prevented is to arrest some person. In other circumstances the fight may be over when a police officer arrives on the scene but it may be apparent that it will resume in the near future. The reason for the arrest is always to ensure the preservation of the peace.

The Court of Appeal has set out four factors to be considered before effecting an arrest under these common law powers:

1. Only a sufficiently real and present threat to the peace justifies depriving a citizen, not at the time acting unlawfully, of his liberty.

2. The threat must come from the person arrested.

3. The conduct must clearly interfere with the rights of others and its natural consequence must be 'not wholly unreasonable violence' from a third party.

4. The conduct of the person to be arrested must be unreasonable.

Arrestable offence

Section 24(1) of the Police and Criminal Evidence Act of 1984 defines the term 'arrestable offence' as being:

(a) an offence for which the sentence is fixed by law (essentially murder); or

(b) offences for which a person of 21 years of age or over (not previously convicted) may be sentenced to imprisonment for a term of 5 years, or might be so sentenced but for the restriction imposed by s 33 of the Magistrates' Courts Act 1980 (18 will be substituted when an amendment in the Criminal Justice and Court Services Act 2000 is in force); and

(c) an offence to which s 24(2) of the Police and Criminal Evidence Act 1984 applies (offences declared to be 'arrestable offences').

Generally, then, we are concerned with offences which are punishable by 5 years' imprisonment or more and this embraces a large proportion of the 'serious offences'. The powers given by s 24(1) apply equally to common law and statutory offences.

Examples of arrestable offences under (b) are manslaughter, rape, indecent assaults, assault occasioning actual bodily harm, wounding, grievous bodily harm, theft, burglary, deception and handling stolen goods.

Section 24(2) declares that the offences listed in Schedule 1A are arrestable although they do not come within the provisions set out in (a) or (b).

The offences listed in schedule are:

1. Offences for which a person may be arrested under the Customs and Excise Acts, as defined in the Customs and Excise Management Act 1979, s 1(1) (viz. that Act and a series of other 1979 Acts).
2. Offences under the Official Secrets Act 1920 which are not arrestable offences by virtue of the term of imprisonment for which a person may be sentenced in respect of them.
3. An offence under the Prevention of Crime Act 1953, s 1(1) (prohibiting the carrying of offensive weapons without lawful authority or reasonable excuse).
4. Offences under the Sexual Offences Act 1956, s 22 (causing prostitution of a woman) or 23 (procuration of girl under 21).
5. An offence under the Obscene Publications Act 1959, s 2 (publication of obscene articles).
6. Offences under the Theft Act 1968, s 12(1) (taking motor vehicle or other conveyance without authority, etc.) or 25(1) (going equipped for stealing, etc.).
7. An offence under s 3 of the Theft Act 1978 (making off without payment).
8. An offence under the Protection of Children Act 1978 (indecent photographs and pseudo-photographs of children).
9. An offence under s 1(1) or (2) or (6) of the Wildlife and Countryside Act 1981 (taking, possessing, selling, etc., of wild birds) in respect of a bird included in Schedule 1 to that Act or any part of, or anything derived from, such a bird.
10. An offence under s 1(5) of the Wildlife and Countryside Act 1981 (disturbance of wild birds); s 9 or 13(1)(a) or (2) of that Act (taking, possessing, selling, etc., of wild animals or plants; or s 14 of that Act (introduction of new species).
11. An offence under s 39(1) of the Civil Aviation Act 1982 (trespass on aerodrome).
12. An offence under s 21C(1) or 21D(1) of the Aviation Security Act 1982 (unauthorised presence in restricted zone or on aircraft).
13. An offence under s 1 of the Sexual Offences Act 1985 (kerb-crawling).
14. An offence under the Public Order Act 1986, s 19 (publishing, etc., material intended or likely to stir up racial or religious hatred).
15. An offence under the Criminal Justice Act 1988, s 139(1) (offence of having article with blade or point in public place); or s 139A(1) or (2) [offence of having article with blade or point (or offensive weapon) on school premises].
16. An offence under s 103(1)(b) of the Road Traffic Act 1988 (driving while disqualified).
17. An offence under s 170(4) of the Road Traffic Act 1988 (failure to stop and report an accident) in respect of an accident to which that section applies by virtue of s 170(1)(a) (accidents causing personal injury).
18. An offence under the Official Secrets Act 1989 other than subsection (1), (4) or (5) of s 8 of that Act.

19. An offence under s 14J or 21C of the Football Spectators Act 1989 (failure to comply with requirements imposed by or under a notice under s 21B).
20. Any offence under the Football (Offences) Act 1991.
21. An offence under the Criminal Justice and Public Order Act 1994, s 60AA(7) (failing to comply with requirement to remove disguise), an offence under s 166 of that Act (sale of tickets by unauthorised persons) or s 167 (touting for car hire services).
22. An offence under s 89(1) of the Police Act 1996 (assaulting a police officer in the execution of his duty or a person assisting such an officer).
23. An offence under the Protection from Harassment Act 1997, s 2 (harassment).
24. An offence under the Crime and Disorder Act 1998, s 32(1)(a) (racially or religiously aggravated harassment).
25. An offence under the Criminal Justice and Police Act 2001, s 12(4) (alcohol consumption in designated public place) or an offence under s 46 of that Act (placing of advertisement relating to prostitution).

The powers of arrest without warrant conferred in respect of arrestable offences also apply to the offences of:

(a) conspiracy to commit any of the offences listed in Schedule 1A;
(b) attempting to commit any such offence, other than one which is a summary offence;
(c) inciting, aiding, abetting, counselling or procuring any such offence.

These offences are deemed to be arrestable offences for the purposes of PACE.

Arrestable offences – powers of arrest without warrant

Section 24 of the Act of 1984 provides that any person may arrest without warrant:

(a) anyone *who is in the act of committing* an arrestable offence; and
(b) anyone whom he has reasonable grounds for suspecting *to be committing* such an offence,

and that where an arrestable offence *has been committed*, any person may arrest without warrant:

(a) anyone who is guilty of the offence; or
(b) anyone whom he has reasonable grounds for suspecting to be guilty of it.

It is important to note that it has been held that an arrest purportedly on the basis that an arrestable offence has been committed will not be covered by the latter provisions and will therefore be unlawful, where it transpires that no 'act' of theft was committed, and also if it transpires that, whilst there was such an act, the person carrying it out lacked the necessary guilty intent to commit that act. With respect to the Court, this is a bad decision as it is not possible for a person to appreciate what is going on in the mind of the person who carries out the act, which is apparently an unlawful act, and amounts to an arrestable offence.

The section provides further powers for a constable to arrest without warrant as follows:

(a) where a constable has reasonable grounds for suspecting that an arrestable offence has been committed, he may arrest without warrant anyone whom he has reasonable grounds for suspecting to be guilty of the offence;

(b) anyone who is about to commit an arrestable offence;

(c) anyone whom he has reasonable grounds for suspecting to be about to commit an arrestable offence.

Understanding of these powers is assisted if practical circumstances are examined. It is predictable that constables and other citizens will have the power to arrest persons found, or believed to be in the act of committing, arrestable offences. They obviously could not be expected to ignore such activities. Where a constable, or a member of the public, observes someone in the act of stealing articles, or inflicting grievous bodily harm on another person, both are empowered to arrest such a person. It may be that a thief cannot be seen to be *in the act* of stealing. He may be standing at an unattended counter on which jewellery is displayed and may be seen to be placing some articles, the nature of which cannot be identified in the circumstances, into an inside pocket. In such circumstances it would be reasonable to suspect that he was committing an arrestable offence. In both of these situations the common factor is that *he is in the act of doing something*. But what if, having completed these various actions, the perpetrator runs away? He is no longer *in the act* or *reasonably suspected of being in the act*. However, his pursuers know that an arrestable offence has been committed, or reasonably suspect that this is so. In the circumstances of the first example, they know that the person committed it and in the circumstances of the second, have reasonable grounds for suspecting that he has committed it. Both the constable and the member of the public are therefore empowered to arrest that person without warrant.

The powers of arrest without warrant which may only be exercised by a constable are those set out finally at (a), (b) and (c) above. These powers are restricted to constables because the acts described are such that there, generally, may only be a *suspicion* that an arrestable offence has been, or is about to be, committed. If a constable stops a motor car owned and driven by X and finds that the boot is full of the type of silverware which one expects to find in a stately home, and X alleges that someone sold the silverware to him for a sum of £5, the constable will have reasonable grounds for suspecting that the property is stolen or unlawfully obtained (thus suspecting that an arrestable offence has been committed). In the absence of a satisfactory explanation he will no doubt suspect that X has committed an offence of burglary, theft or handling (each of which is an arrestable offence). It will be appreciated that members of the public, who have no suitable training, would be unlikely to be able to carry out a meaningful interrogation of X in these circumstances. If the powers of arrest were extended to members of the public, it is possible that unlawful arrests would be made in circumstances where a member of the public was offered an opportunity to buy goods cheaply.

Constables may also arrest without warrant any person who is about to commit an arrestable offence. Once again, there is a question of judgement. If, for example, a person is about to throw a brick through a jeweller's window (which would amount to an offence of criminal damage which is an arrestable offence), a constable is empowered to arrest as he would be expected to know this. A member of the public is unlikely to know those offences which are 'arrestable' as opposed to merely being offences. In the same way, acts which constitute attempts to commit arrestable offences will only be identifiable as such by police officers who have been trained to recognise acts which are more than merely preparatory to the commission of an arrestable offence.

The term 'reasonable grounds' means an honest belief founded on reasonable suspicion leading an ordinary, cautious person to the conclusion that the person arrested is guilty.

The European Court of Human Rights has held that there were 'reasonable grounds for suspicion' on the facts established where a police officer had reasonable grounds to suspect that the person arrested was guilty of a terrorist murder, even though the suspicion was formed as a result of a police briefing by a superior officer, because the information in that briefing specifically linked the person arrested to the murder. The Court of Appeal has held that where an arresting officer's suspicion is formed on the basis of a Police National Computer (PNC) entry, that entry is likely to provide him with a reasonable suspicion.

There may be grounds for arresting a suspect on the sole basis of the word of an informer, but police officers must treat such information with considerable reserve. Where a store detective informed police officers that a woman had stolen property in the store, the Court of Appeal ruled that the employers of the detective were not liable in damages for false imprisonment where the police officers, acting upon that information, arrested the woman. The officers, acting upon that information, had acted in their own discretion.

The purpose of an arrest is to make a person answerable to a charge. Where a person is arrested on reasonable suspicion that he has committed an arrestable offence and the person arrested is able to prove that the arresting officer knew, at the time of the arrest, that there was no possibility of a charge being made, then the arrest would be unlawful because the arresting officer had acted on some irrelevant consideration or for an improper purpose. There is no reason why an arrest should not be made for the purpose of interviewing a person suspected of committing an arrestable offence in the hope of obtaining a confession as, in such a case, the possibility of prosecution still exists. However, arrests should not be made to 'teach a person a lesson' where there is no possibility of prosecution.

General conditional power to arrest

The power to arrest for other than arrestable offences and those offences specially mentioned is provided by s 25 of the Act of 1984. The section states:

> Where a constable has reasonable grounds for suspecting that any offence which is not an arrestable offence has been committed or attempted, or is being committed or attempted, he may arrest the *relevant person* if it appears to him that service of a summons is impracticable or inappropriate because any of the general arrest conditions is satisfied.

The Act, therefore, provides a conditional power of arrest which can be applied to all other offences, while at the same time repealing all but a few statutory powers which previously existed. The section refers to 'relevant persons' and to the 'general arrest conditions'.

A 'relevant person' is any person whom the constable has reasonable grounds to suspect of having committed or having attempted to commit the offence, or who has been in the course of committing or attempting to commit it. Therefore, such a person, committing any offence, may be arrested if the service of a summons is impracticable or inappropriate because any of the general arrest conditions are satisfied.

The general arrest conditions are:

(a) that the name of the relevant person is unknown to, and cannot be ascertained by, the constable;

(b) that the constable has reasonable grounds for doubting whether the name furnished by the relevant person as his name is his real name;
(c) that
    (i) the relevant person has failed to furnish a satisfactory address for service; or
    (ii) the constable has reasonable grounds for doubting whether an address furnished by the relevant person is a satisfactory address for service;
(d) that the constable has reasonable grounds for believing that arrest is necessary to prevent the relevant person
    (i) causing physical harm to himself or some other person;
    (ii) suffering physical injury;
    (iii) causing loss of or damage to property;
    (iv) committing an offence against public decency; or
    (v) causing an unlawful obstruction of the highway;
(e) that the constable has reasonable grounds for believing that arrest is necessary to protect a child or other vulnerable person from the relevant person.

An arrest may, therefore, be made if identity or address cannot be established satisfactorily or if it is necessary to prevent harm to anyone, damage to property, a continuing affront to public decency, an obstruction of the highway or for the protection of a child or other vulnerable person. Such arrests are necessary, either to prevent an offender from escaping the consequences of his acts, or for the protection of persons or property.

This general arrest provision is extremely helpful to police officers as such a power did not exist prior to the Act of 1984. Difficulties were encountered when persons gave names and addresses which were suspected of being false in respect of offences for which no power of arrest existed. In cases of doubt 'control' will be able to give considerable assistance in checking names and addresses given by offenders. Persons reasonably suspected of such offences should be given every opportunity to provide evidence of identity and address and the consequences of continued refusal should be explained to them. However, an arrest will be valid if the questions 'What is your name' and 'What is your address' lead to a refusal to answer, provided that the offender is told that he is being arrested in relation to a particular offence *and* for refusing to provide his name and address.

It is important to remember that the section does not require an offender to provide his residential address, it requires him to provide a satisfactory address for service of a summons. The section provides that an address is satisfactory if it appears to the constable that the relevant person will be at it for a sufficiently long period for it to be possible to serve him with a summons, or that some other persons specified by the relevant person will accept service of the summons for the relevant person, at that address. Thus, if a foreign goods vehicle driver who commits an offence can give a satisfactory address at which service of a summons will be accepted on his behalf, that is all that the section requires. Such a form of service is authorised by Regulation 99(8) of the Magistrates' Courts Rules 1981.

The section also limits arrest for an offence against public decency. Such an arrest must not be made unless members of the public going about their normal business cannot reasonably be expected to avoid the person to be arrested.

There are, therefore, in effect, three major factors to be considered before effecting an arrest in respect of offences for which the power of arrest is conditional:

(a) Has an offence been committed or attempted (other than an arrestable offence or one for which a statutory power of arrest is provided, in which case the 'conditional' provisions would not apply)?

(b) Are there reasonable grounds to suspect that person of being responsible?
(c) Is the service of a summons impracticable or inappropriate because any of the general arrest conditions apply?

However, these questions need not be asked if the arrest is carried out in consequence of any of the circumstances set out at d(i) to (v) above. Where the constable has reasonable grounds for believing that an arrest is necessary in such circumstances, his decision to arrest is not dependent upon doubts in relation to identification, or the existence of a satisfactory address for the service of a summons. If, for example, a man who was found in possession of indecent photographs of children threatened to kill himself rather than face the consequences of his act, and the constable reasonably believed that he was likely to do so, the constable is empowered by this section to arrest the man even though his name and address are known. The same would apply if his threat was to do some harm to the person who supplied him with the photographs.

Where a person is found drunk upon a highway, a constable may have reasonable grounds to believe that he may cause himself injury by falling down or by walking into the roadway and, in such circumstances, he may arrest that person. Similarly, it may be that there is such loss of bodily control that the person affected by alcohol may cause damage to property if he is allowed to continue by, for example, falling into flower beds or gardens or even through shop windows. Where a man insists on sunbathing in the nude on a crowded beach, in an area where this is not permitted, it is obvious that it will be necessary to arrest him as members of the public cannot reasonably be expected to avoid him. Perhaps most importantly, the commission of the offence of unlawful obstruction of the highway may merit arrest where the person or persons causing the obstruction refuse to move. Thus, 'sit-down' protesters may be removed and, if they persist, arrested.

Finally, the arrest of a person, where a constable has reasonable grounds to believe that arrest is necessary to protect a child or vulnerable person from the person who has committed an offence which is only subject to a provisional power of arrest, is authorised.

On none of these occasions is the establishment of the identity of the accused a central issue in relation to the arrest.

Statute law – powers to arrest without warrant

Section 26 of the Police and Criminal Evidence Act 1984 repeals all previous statutory powers to arrest (including those provided by local Acts) with the exception of certain powers which are specifically retained. These are listed in schedule 2 to the Act, and are concerned with:

(a) the arrest of absentees and deserters from HM Forces and Visiting Forces;
(b) the arrest of persons under emergency powers or terrorism legislation;
(c) the arrest of persons who are absent from places of detention or who have broken bail;
(d) the arrest of trespassers on some military lands;
(e) offences relating to remaining on property contrary to ss 6 to 10 of the Criminal Law Act 1977;
(f) the arrest of persons reasonably suspected of committing offences of drinking and driving, and driving when reasonably suspected of being disqualified;
(g) the arrest of persons reasonably suspected of committing offences contrary to s 1 of the Public Order Act 1936 (prohibited uniforms); and

(h) the power to arrest a person suspected of personation, at the direction of a presiding officer, at a polling station.

Further statutory powers to arrest have been provided in a number of Acts of Parliament passed since the repeal of all previous powers in 1984.

In addition, it has been held by the Divisional Court that, because s 26 conflicts with another provision in the 1984 Act in this respect, a constable's power under the Criminal Justice Act 1967, s 91(1), to arrest a person for the offence of being drunk and disorderly in a public place has not been repealed by s 26.

The Court of Appeal considered the power to arrest provided by the Vagrancy Act 1824, s 6. It held that the power to arrest given by the section to 'any person' to arrest a person who had committed an offence under the Act, applied to 'any person' whether a police constable or a citizen. While the Court was specifically examining the lawfulness of an arrest under the Vagrancy Act, it considered the 'any person' powers in general and found that s 26 did not take away a constable's power to arrest where a power was given in a statute to 'any person'. It considered that s 26 affects only those powers which were given specifically to a constable within a statute. If this was not so, the absurd position would arise in which a citizen would be empowered to arrest and a constable would not.

Cross-border powers of arrest

Under the Criminal Justice and Public Order Act 1994, s 137, where:

(a) the suspected offence is an arrestable offence; or
(b) in the case of another offence, it appears to the constable that the service of a summons is impracticable or inappropriate (the general arrest conditions),

a constable of an English or Welsh police force, who has reasonable grounds for suspecting that an offence has been committed or attempted in England and Wales and that the suspected person is in Scotland or Northern Ireland, may arrest without warrant the suspected person wherever he is in Scotland or Northern Ireland. Scottish officers and those of the Northern Irish Police Service have a similar power of arrest within England and Wales in respect of offences committed or attempted in Scotland or Northern Ireland, respectively.

These powers may be exercised in England and Wales and Scotland (but not Northern Ireland) by a British Transport Police Officer.

Where a person is arrested in Scotland or Northern Ireland under this power, he must be taken to the nearest convenient designated police station in England or Wales or to a designated police station in the police area where the offence is being investigated. This must be done as soon as reasonably practicable.

In addition, s 140 provides that where a constable in England and Wales would have a power to arrest a person under the Police and Criminal Evidence Act 1984, s 24(6) or (7) or 25 (arrestable offences and general arrest conditions), those powers are also given to constables of Scotland and Northern Ireland. The same applies to powers which would exist in Northern Ireland under parallel provisions and to powers to arrest given to a constable in Scotland.

The Anti-terrorism, Crime and Security Act 2001, extended all of these powers to officers of the British Transport Police.

Stop and search

Introduction

There was no general power given to constables to stop and search persons before the Police and Criminal Evidence Act 1984. The Codes of Practice which accompany the Act lay down strict safeguards to ensure that these powers are not abused. The power to stop and search is in reality provided to give an officer an opportunity to establish whether or not certain types of offence have been committed without the necessity to arrest such a person on reasonable suspicion of his having committed an offence. A search, carried out in good faith, may render such an arrest unnecessary if no evidence of the suspected offence is found.

The Act provides special power for 'statutory undertakers', that is, bodies authorised by enactments to carry out railway, road transport, water transport, canal, inland navigation, dock or harbour undertakings. Such constables may stop, detain and search any vehicle before it leaves a goods area wholly or mainly used for storage or handling of goods. In addition, existing powers to stop and search under s 23 of the Misuse of Drugs Act 1971, s 47 of the Firearms Act 1968 and s 2 of the Poaching Prevention Act 1862 have been retained.

The Criminal Justice and Public Order Act 1994, s 60 (as amended by s 8 of the Knives Act 1997), authorises a stop and search based on a reasonable belief on the part of an officer of the rank of inspector that an incident involving serious violence may take place within a specific locality and it is expedient to give an authorisation under the section to prevent such occurrence, or that persons are carrying dangerous instruments or offensive weapons in the locality without good reason. A stop and search may be authorised under s 44 of the Terrorism Act 2000. The provisions of the Search Code are applied to such stops and searches which may only be carried out by an officer in uniform. With these exceptions, a police officer's powers to stop and search are prescribed by the Act of 1984.

Code A, the Code of Practice for the Exercise by Police Officers of Statutory Powers of Stop and Search (the Stop and Search Code), applies to the exercise of powers to stop and search, other than those given to 'statutory undertakers' or powers under the Aviation Security Act 1982, s 27 (hijacking). The Code applies to stops and searches under powers:

(a) requiring reasonable grounds for suspicion that articles unlawfully obtained or possessed are being carried or under s 43 of the Terrorism Act 2000 that a person is a terrorist;
(b) authorised under the Criminal Justice and Public Order Act, 1994, s 60;
(c) authorised under the Terrorism Act 2000, ss 44(1) and (2);
(d) to search a person who has not been arrested in the exercise of a power to search premises.

Powers to stop and search

General

In addition to the legislative provisions relating to stop and search, the Code of Practice for the Exercise by Police Officers of Statutory Powers of Stop and Search, Code A, and the Code of Practice for Searches of Premises by Police Officers and the Seizure of Property Found by Police Officers on Persons or Premises, Code B, deal, together with the various provisions of the Police and Criminal Evidence Act 1984, with the search of persons or vehicles without first making an arrest and the search of premises and the seizure of property. Some aspects of the search of premises have been dealt with above. Whenever these codes of practice require the prior authority or agreement of an officer of at least inspector or superintendent rank, that authority may be given by a sergeant or chief inspector authorised to perform the function of the higher rank under the Police and Criminal Evidence Act, s 107.

Section 1(2) of the Police and Criminal Evidence Act 1984 states that subject to subsections (3) to (5) of the section a constable may search any person or vehicle (vehicle includes vessel, aircraft and hovercraft) *and* anything which is in or on a vehicle, for stolen or prohibited articles or articles to which s 1(8A) applies and he may detain a person or vehicle for the purpose of such a search.

Subsection (3) requires that a constable must have *reasonable grounds for suspecting* that he will find stolen or prohibited articles or articles to which s 1(8A) applies before carrying out such a search. Reasonable force may be used but every effort must be made to persuade a person to co-operate. His willingness to co-operate must be established before a compulsory search is made.

Conduct in breach or in excess of a relevant statutory or common law power may constitute a breach of a 'Convention right' under the Human Rights Act 1998 and may cause the police officer concerned to be liable in civil law or in criminal law. It may also render inadmissible evidence obtained as a result.

It is important to understand what is meant by 'reasonable suspicion'. The Code of Practice sets out a number of considerations which must be applied.

Where a police officer has reasonable grounds to suspect that a person is in innocent possession of a stolen or prohibited article, the power to stop and search exists, notwithstanding that there would be no power of arrest. However, every effort should be made to secure the voluntary production of the article before the power is resorted to.

Reasonable suspicion

The Stop and Search Code gives the following guidance on what may be 'reasonable suspicion' for the purposes of statutory powers of stop and search which require a reasonable suspicion.

Whether reasonable grounds for suspicion exist will depend on the circumstances in each case, but there must be some objective basis for it based on facts, information and/or intelligence which are relevant to the likelihood of finding an article of a relevant kind, or showing that a person is a terrorist. Reasonable suspicion can never be supported on the basis of personal factors alone without reliable supporting intelligence or information or some specific behaviour by the person concerned. For example, a person's race, age or appearance or the fact that the person is known to have a previous conviction cannot be used alone or in combination with each other as the reason for searching that person. Reasonable suspicion cannot be based on generalisations or stereotypical images of certain groups or categories of people as more likely to be involved in criminal activity.

Reasonable suspicion can sometimes exist without specific information or intelligence and on the basis of some level of generalisation stemming from the behaviour of a person. For example, if an officer encounters someone on the street at night who is obviously trying to hide something, the officer may (depending on the other surrounding circumstances) base such suspicion on the fact that this kind of behaviour is often linked to stolen or prohibited articles being carried. Similarly, for the purposes of the Terrorism Act 200, s 43, suspicion that a person is a terrorist may arise from the person's behaviour at or near a location which has been identified as a potential target for terrorists.

However, reasonable suspicion should normally be linked to accurate and current intelligence or information, such as information describing an article being carried, a suspected offender or a person who has been seen carrying a type of article known to have been stolen recently from premises within the area. Searches based on accurate and current intelligence or information are more likely to be effective. Targeting searches in a particular area at specified crime problems increases their effectiveness and minimises inconvenience to law-abiding members of the public. It also helps in justifying the use of searches both to those who are searched and to the general public. This does not, however, prevent stop and search powers being exercised in other locations where such powers may be exercised and reasonable suspicion exists.

Searches are more likely to be effective and legitimate and secure public confidence when reasonable suspicion is based upon a range of factors. The overall use of these powers is more likely to be effective when up-to-date and accurate intelligence or information is communicated to officers and they are well informed about local crime patterns.

Where there is reliable information or intelligence that members of a group or gang habitually carry knives unlawfully or weapons or controlled drugs, and wear a distinctive item of clothing or other means of identification to indicate their membership of the group or gang, that distinctive item of clothing or other means of identification may provide reasonable grounds to stop and search a person. Other means of identification might include jewellery, insignias, tattoos or other features which are known to identify members of the particular gang or group.

A police officer may have reasonable grounds to suspect that a person is in innocent possession of a stolen or prohibited article or other item for which he is empowered to search. In that case, the officer may stop and search the person even though there would be no power to arrest.

An officer who has reasonable grounds for suspicion may detain the person concerned for the purpose of carrying out a search. Before doing so, he may ask questions about the person's behaviour or presence in circumstances which gave rise to suspicion. As a result of questioning the detained person, the reasonable grounds for suspicion necessary to detain that person may be confirmed or, because of a satisfactory explanation, be eliminated. Questioning may also reveal reasonable grounds to suspect the possession of a different kind of unlawful article from that originally suspected. Reasonable grounds for suspicion, however, cannot be provided retrospectively by such questioning during a person's detention or by refusal to answer any questions put.

If, as a result of questioning before a search, or other circumstances which come to the attention of the officer, there cease to be reasonable grounds for suspecting that an article is being carried of a kind for which there is a power to stop and search, no search may take place. In the absence of any other lawful power to detain, the person is free to leave at will and must be so informed.

There is no power to stop and detain in order to find grounds for a search. Police officers have many encounters with members of the public which do not involve detaining people against their will. If reasonable grounds for suspicion emerge during such an encounter, the officer may search the person, even though no grounds existed when the encounter began. If an officer is detaining someone for the purpose of a search, he should inform the person as soon as the detention begins.

The guidance in the Stop and Search Code on what might be 'reasonable suspicion' has been stated fully because of its importance to police officers. The issue of whether or not an officer had reasonable grounds for suspecting possession of stolen or prohibited articles will frequently arise and, as we have indicated already, failure to observe the provisions of the Code may amount to a disciplinary offence, regardless of any other liability which might arise. The important factor is that the issue will be judged objectively in the light of the knowledge which was available to the police officer when he made his decision. This may be a description given to the officer when briefed for duty of a person suspected of offences. However, such a general description of a person would not allow a search by itself; the officer would have to apply his mind to the circumstances surrounding the particular person under observation. The fact that such person appeared to be seeking an opportunity to commit a similar type of crime might reinforce suspicion sufficiently to satisfy the objective test.

Again, although information received from a member of the public may constitute a basis for reasonable suspicion, whether it actually does so depends on the content and nature of the information and the credibility of the informant. If the manager of a filling station tells a police officer that a man, of whom he gives a description, stole two cartons of cigarettes from the kiosk before driving off in a green Escort which was damaged on the front offside wing, the issue is fairly clear. If the officer sees an Escort of that description, driven by a man of the description given by the station manager, he may accept that the information which he was given was clear and that it was given by a reliable witness. He may reasonably act upon that information since it provides him with the necessary reasonable suspicion.

The Stop and Search Code does not affect the ability of an officer to speak to or question a person in the ordinary course of his duties (and in the absence of reasonable suspicion) without detaining him or exercising any element of compulsion. It is not the purpose of the Code to prohibit such encounters between the police and the community with the co-operation of the person concerned, nor does it affect the principle that all citizens have a duty to help police officers to prevent crime and discover offenders.

Principles governing stop and search

There should be no discrimination. The Race Relations (Amendment) Act 2000 makes it unlawful for police officers to discriminate on the grounds of race, colour, ethnic origin, nationality or national origins when using these powers. The primary purpose is to allow officers to allay or confirm suspicions without the necessity for an arrest. It is important to explain such actions to the member of the public concerned.

An officer must not search a person, even with his consent, where no power to search is applicable. The Code specifies, as a sole exception, that an officer does not require a specific power when searching persons entering sports grounds or other premises carried out with their consent given as a condition of entry. This is now a provision of the Code. Previous editions of this Code made this proviso in a note of guidance.

Under the Criminal Justice and Public Order Act 1994 s 60

Where a police officer of or above the rank of inspector reasonably believes that:

(a) incidents involving serious violence may take place in any area in his locality, and that it is expedient to give an authorisation under the section to prevent their occurrence; or

(b) persons are carrying dangerous instruments or offensive weapons in any locality in his police area without good reason,

he may give an authorisation that the powers conferred by this section shall be exercisable at any place within that locality for a period not exceeding 24 hours. In circumstances where an inspector gives such an authorisation he must, as soon as it is practicable to do so, cause an officer of or above the rank of superintendent to be informed. Where such an authorisation has been given a constable in uniform has power:

(a) to stop any pedestrian and search him and anything carried by him for offensive weapons or dangerous instruments;

(b) to stop any vehicle and search the vehicle, its driver and any passenger for offensive weapons or dangerous instruments.

In these circumstances, the constable may stop any person or any vehicle he thinks fit, whether or not he has grounds for suspecting that the person or vehicle is carrying weapons or articles of that kind. He may seize dangerous instruments or articles which he has reasonable grounds for suspecting to be offensive. These powers apply to ships, aircraft and hovercraft (with the necessary modifications).

A person who fails to stop or (as the case may be) to stop the vehicle when required to do so commits an offence under the section which is punishable by 1 month's imprisonment, a level 3 fine, or both.

Such an authorisation must be in writing and must specify the grounds on which it is given and the locality and the validity of the authorisation. There is power, where an officer of or above the rank of superintendent feels that it is expedient to do so, having regard to offences which have, or are reasonably suspected to have been committed in connection with any incident falling within the authorisation, to extend it for a further 24 hours.

In addition, where an authorisation is in force under s 60 of the 1994 Act, s 60AA provides a constable in uniform with the power:

(a) to require any person to remove any item (e.g. a face mask) which the constable reasonably believes that person is wearing wholly or mainly for the purpose of concealing his identity;

(b) to seize any item which the constable reasonably believes any person intends to wear wholly or mainly for that purpose.

In addition, where an officer of or above the rank of inspector (who must, as soon as it is practicable, inform a superintendent) reasonably believes that activities may take place in any locality in his police area that are likely (if they take place) to involve the commission of offences and that it is expedient, in order to prevent or control the activities, he may give an authorisation that these powers shall be exercisable at any place within that locality for a specified period not exceeding 24 hours. Where it then appears to a superintendent that in view of offences which have been, or are reasonably suspected to have been, committed in connection with the activities to which the authorisation relates, he may direct that the authorisation continues in force for a further 24 hours.

Such an authorisation must be in writing and signed and specify the grounds for it, the locality and the period during which the powers are exercisable.

It is an offence against s 60AA(7) to fail to remove such an item when required by a constable to do so in the exercise of his powers under the section.

The Divisional Court examined circumstances in which an animal-rights protester assaulted a police officer who demanded that she remove her mask. The justices had found that the officer was not acting in the execution of his duty when demanding the removal of the mask as ss 2(2) and (3) of PACE required that where a search was being conducted, other than following an arrest, the power to search could not be exercised unless the person concerned had been told the constable's name, the name of his police station and the grounds for the search. The Court held that the exercise of this power did not give rise to a search.

Persons who are affected by the above power to search are entitled to the usual written statement of stop and search within 12 months.

The term 'dangerous instruments' means instruments which have a blade and are sharply pointed. The term 'vehicle' includes a caravan.

Under the Terrorism Act 2000, ss 44 to 47

By s 44 of the Terrorism Act where it appears to him that it is expedient to do so in order to prevent acts of terrorism, a police officer of or above the rank of assistant chief constable (or equivalent) may give an authorisation in writing which is signed, dated and timed (it may be given orally at first but should be confirmed in writing by the officer who gave it as soon as possible) that the powers set out in s 44(1) to stop and search vehicles and persons shall be exercisable at any place within his area, or a specified locality within his area, for a specified period not exceeding 28 days. Although an assistant chief constable of the British Transport Police or the Ministry of Defence Police may give such an authorisation, it may only be given in respect of specified places or areas policed by that force. Within the revised procedure, the person who gives the authorisation must inform the Secretary of State as soon as is reasonably practicable. If the authorisation is not confirmed it will cease to have effect after 48 hours but this will not affect the lawfulness of things done before the end of that period. Where an authorisation is confirmed, the Secretary of State may substitute an earlier date or time at which it must end. Such an authorisation may be renewed provided that the same procedure is followed once more. Authority may only be given to search for articles which may be connected with terrorism. The officer should set the minimum period he considers necessary in the circumstances, and a geographical area no wider than is necessary.

An authorisation under this section cannot be extended. A new authorisation is required.

The extended powers of seizure under s 51 of the Criminal Justice and Police Act 2001 (page 174) apply to searches under s 44(1) or (2) of the 2000 Act.

The powers set out in s 44 which are exercisable if an authorisation is given under the section are as follows. A constable in uniform may:

(a) stop any vehicle;
(b) search any vehicle, its driver or passenger or anything in or on the vehicle or carried by the driver or passenger for articles of a kind which could be used in connection with terrorism.

In the exercise of these powers, the constable may stop and carry out searches whether or not he has grounds for suspecting that the particular person or vehicle is carrying such articles. He may seize and retain any articles which he reasonably suspects to be used in connection with terrorism. The person or vehicle may be retained for a reasonable time to enable the search to be carried out.

The driver of a vehicle which has been stopped is entitled to obtain a written statement to that effect if he applies within 12 months.

A constable may not require a person to remove any of his clothes in public other than any headgear, footwear, outer coat, jacket or gloves.

A person who fails to stop his vehicle when required to do so by a constable in the exercise of these powers, or who wilfully obstructs him in the exercise of these powers, commits an offence.

Pedestrians

Section 44 of the 2000 Act authorises an officer of or above the rank of assistant chief constable (or equivalent), where it appears to him to be expedient to do so in order to prevent acts of terrorism, to give an authorisation [in the same manner as specified above in relation to s 44(1) and maybe in combination with an authorisation under that section] that the powers to stop and search persons conferred by the section shall be exercisable at a place specified in that authorisation. Those powers are to stop any pedestrian and to search him, or anything carried by him, for articles of a kind which could be used in connection with terrorism. The constable does not need to have grounds for suspecting the presence of such articles before exercising his powers. The requirement to remove clothing in public must be limited to headgear, footwear, outer coat, jacket or gloves. An offence is committed by a person who fails to stop for a constable exercising these powers or who wilfully obstructs such a constable.

Where an authorisation is given under s 44(2), the officer giving that authorisation must cause the Secretary of State to be informed, as soon as reasonably practicable, that such an authorisation has been given. The authorisation may take effect before the Secretary of State has decided whether to confirm it, but it ceases to have effect if not confirmed by the Secretary of State within 48 hours of it having been given. The Secretary of State may cancel such an authorisation immediately, or with effect from some other stated time, confirm it but for a shorter period or confirm it as given. An officer authorising the use of powers under s 44 must take immediate steps to send a copy of the authorisation to the National Joint Unit, Metropolitan Police Special Branch, who will forward it to the Secretary of State. The Secretary of State should be informed of the reasons for the authorisation. The National Joint Unit will inform the force concerned, within 48 hours of the authorisation being made, whether the Secretary of State has confirmed, cancelled or altered the authorisation.

An authorisation under this section cannot be extended. A new authorisation is required. A person stopped by a constable under this section shall be entitled to obtain a written statement that he was stopped under these powers if he applies for such a statement within 12 months.

A person who fails to stop when required to do so by a constable in the exercise of these powers, or who wilfully obstructs him in the exercise of these powers, commits an offence.

Exercise of these powers

The selection of persons stopped under powers provided by ss 44 to 46 should reflect an objective assessment of the threat posed by the various terrorist groups active in Great Britain. The powers should not be used to stop and search persons for reasons unconnected with terrorism. Particular care must be taken not to discriminate against members of ethnic minorities. There may be circumstances, however, where it is appropriate for officers to take account of a person's ethnic origin in selecting persons to be stopped in response to a specific terrorist threat (some international terrorist groups are associated with particular ethnic identities).

The powers provided by s 60 of the Criminal Justice and Public Order Act 1994 were extended by s 25 of the Crime and Disorder Act 1998 to provide a power to demand the removal of face coverings. An officer exercising such a power must reasonably believe that someone is wearing the face covering wholly or mainly for the purpose of concealing his identity. There is also a power to seize face coverings in such circumstances. There is no power to stop and search for face coverings. However, such an item may be seized if discovered when searching for something else, or which is seen to be carried in circumstances in which an officer reasonably believes it is intended to be used for such a purpose.

The period during which these powers may be exercised must be the minimum considered necessary to deal with the risk of violence, the carrying of knives or offensive weapons or terrorism.

The area within which these powers may be exercised must be carefully specified and officers must be aware of the geographical area enclosed. If the powers are to be used in response to a threat or incident which straddles police force areas, an officer from each of the forces affected must give an authorisation.

It is important for national monitoring purposes to specify in any record of a search under these provisions whether a stop and search was carried out under s 44(1) or (2).

Exercise of powers generally

It is important to ensure that powers to stop and search are used responsibly by those who exercise and those who authorise them. An officer should bear in mind that he may be required to justify the use of the powers to a senior officer and in court, and also that misuse of the powers is likely to be harmful to the police effort in the long term. This can lead to mistrust of the police by the community. Regardless of the power exercised, all police officers should be careful to ensure that the selection and treatment of those questioned or searched are based upon objective factors and not upon personal prejudice. It is also particularly important to ensure that any person searched is treated courteously and considerately. Where there may be religious sensitivities about asking someone to remove a face covering using the powers in s 25 of the Crime and Disorder

Act 1998, for example in the case of a Muslim woman wearing a face covering for religious purposes, the officer should permit the item to be removed out of public view. Where practicable, the item should be removed in the presence of an officer of the same sex as the person and out of sight of anyone of the opposite sex. In all cases the officer must reasonably believe that the person is wearing the item in question *wholly or mainly* to conceal his or her identity.

The actions of police officers will be examined objectively in the light of the knowledge available to the officer at the time of his decision. The officer may have been given a *general description* of a person suspected of committing burglaries and, if he exercises a power to stop and search, the court will examine the issue objectively, by assuming that that person also had that general description. However, such a general description would be unlikely, in itself, to constitute sufficient grounds for search, but observations of the actions of the suspect for a period of time may heighten the suspicion that he may be the person suspected of the offences of burglary.

It must be recognised that there is no power to stop and detain a person against his will in order to find grounds for a search.

The Stop and Search Code does not restrict an officer's right to speak to or question a person in the ordinary course of his duties (and in the absence of reasonable suspicion) without detaining him or exercising any element of compulsion, provided that the person concerned co-operates. It does not affect the principle that all citizens have a duty to help police officers prevent crime and discover offenders.

Where searches may be carried out

Section 1(1) of the Act of 1984 states that a constable may exercise these powers:

(a) in any place to which at the time when he proposes to exercise the power, the public or any section of the public has access, on payment or otherwise, as of a right or by virtue of express or implied permission; or
(b) in any other place to which people have ready access at the time when he proposes to exercise the power but which is not a dwelling.

The public have a general right of access to, and use of, a highway. They certainly have express permission to enter places of entertainment as they are invited to pay a fee for entry to cinemas, sporting grounds, etc. A part of their express permission is conditioned on such persons remaining only for the duration of the particular entertainment; it is not a general permission to be there. By implication, people may enter supermarkets, stores, business premises and public buildings. They also have 'implied' permission to enter the grounds of dwelling houses to visit lawfully the householder or to call upon him. The term 'ready access' does not concern itself with lawful presence. It is concerned with whether or not ready access was in fact available to the building, premises or land. The entry may well be a trespassory entry.

Section 1(4) of the Act of 1984 provides that persons in a garden or yard occupied with and used for the purpose of a dwelling, or on other land so occupied and used, may not be searched by a constable unless he has reasonable grounds for believing that such a person does not reside in the dwelling and that he is not in the place in question with the express or implied permission of a person who resides in the dwelling. These provisions also apply to vehicles which are in such grounds unless they are not there with express or implied permission.

Stolen or prohibited articles

A 'prohibited article' is defined by the section as:

(a) an offensive weapon, which is any article made or adapted for use for causing injury, or intended by the person having it with him for such use by him or by some other person; or

(b) an article made or adapted for use in the course of or in connection with an offence of burglary, theft, taking a motor vehicle or other conveyance without authority and obtaining property by deception, or intended by the person having it with him for such use by him or by some other person.

(See 'Statutory preventive measures' on page 535 for an explanation of these terms. The term 'stolen' is not defined and should be given its ordinary meaning.)

An 'article to which s 1(8A) applies' is any article in relation to which a person has committed, or is committing or is going to commit an offence under s 139 of the Criminal Justice Act 1988. This section deals with possession in a public place of an article which has a blade or is sharply pointed, except for a folding pocket knife. This section also applies to folding pocket knives if the cutting edge of its blade exceeds 3 inches. These provisions are discussed in greater depth under 'Offensive weapons' (see pages 535–537).

Section 51 of the Criminal Justice and Police Act 2001 provides for circumstances in which a person carrying out such a search finds something which he has reasonable grounds for believing may be, or may contain, something for which he is authorised to search and to seize and in the circumstances there existing, it is not reasonably practicable for the contents to be determined. The power conferred by the section permits seizure of so much of that which he has found, as it is necessary to remove from that place, to enable that to be determined. The details of this power and the circumstances in which it applies are set out below in relation to the seizure of property on premises. The powers are the same, with the modifications necessary to recognise that s 51 applies to a search of a person.

Written notice must be given to the person from whom such property is seized specifying what has been seized, the grounds under which the power was exercised, explaining the effect of ss 59 to 61 of the 2001 Act (remedies and safeguards), the name and address of the person to whom any application for remedy must be made in respect of the seized property and the name and address of the person to whom an application may be made to be allowed to attend the initial examination of the seized property, to determine how much of the property was such that there had been a power to search for it. The basis of the provisions related to 'remedies and safeguards' lies in the right of application to a Crown Court judge by any person with a relevant interest in the seized property on the grounds that there was no power of seizure, or that the seized material contains matter subject to legal privilege or contains excluded or special procedure material.

Searches connected with sports grounds

This is perhaps the moment at which to examine the current police practice of searching persons on football coaches for offensive weapons before allowing them into the ground. First, the Act and Code require that the officer should, before carrying out the search of a particular person, ask himself whether that person (not the persons on the coach as a whole) is reasonably suspected of possessing such a weapon. The Code does not allow a search if the suspicion is merely based upon the fact that he is a member of a group of disorderly soccer hooligans. There would have to be reason to suspect that person of possessing a weapon and little short of seeing him to be in such possession is likely to satisfy these requirements. There is no doubt that the Code was not drafted with the intention of stopping this desirable practice in view of the attitude of Parliament to the problems caused by soccer hooligans but, nevertheless, this is the effect of the Code of Practice. In recognition of this, Code A, para. 1.5, generally prohibits a search, even with consent, where no power to search exists in law. The paragraph exempts from this provision the searches of persons entering sports grounds or other premises carried out with their consent given as a condition of entry.

However, it should be noted that this does not extend beyond entry to premises and the search of 'soccer specials' would not be covered. In any case, such searches as a condition of entry should be carried out by persons other than police officers. It is no part of a police officer's duties to enforce a civil contract between the proprietors of football grounds and other places of entertainment and those who seek entry to such premises.

Information received from a third party may be taken into account when forming a reasonable suspicion, but the nature of the information and the credibility of the informant must be taken into account.

If such an article is found during a search, an officer must satisfy himself that an offence has been committed, there is a reasonable suspicion that the person committed it and that a power to arrest exists in respect of that offence.

The Sporting Events (Control of Alcohol, etc.) Act 1985 gives a constable power to search a person at any time during the period of a designated sporting event when such a person is in the area of a designated sports ground from which the event may be directly viewed, or while entering or trying to enter at such times, if he has reasonable grounds to suspect that person of having intoxicating liquor, or a bottle, can or other portable container (even if crushed or broken) which is for holding drink, which is of a kind which, when empty, is normally discarded or returned, or left to be recovered by the supplier, or part of such an article.

The 1985 Act also empowers a constable to stop and search:

(a) public service vehicles; and
(b) vehicles adapted to carry more than eight passengers, which are being used for the principal purpose of carrying passengers for the whole or part of a journey to or from a designated sporting event,

[in the case of (b) at least two persons must be carried], if he has reason to suspect that an offence is being committed in relation to the carriage of alcohol or an offence of drunkenness.

The Code's description of 'reasonable suspicion' must be applied to such searches.

The period of a designated sporting event is the period beginning 2 hours before the start of the event or (if earlier) 2 hours before the time at which it is advertised to start and ending 1 hour after the event. In the event of a postponement, the period is 2 hours before the advertised start to 1 hour after it.

Action to be taken on detaining a person for a search

In the first instance, an officer should remember that if a person is detained for the purpose of a search, that search need not be carried out if it subsequently appears to him that no search is required or that a search is impracticable. It is possible that, although a person was stopped and detained for the purpose of a search, he easily satisfies the officer that there are no grounds for suspicion. In such a case it is unnecessary to search. The detention will not be unlawful merely because the search was not carried out.

Before a search of a detained person or attended vehicle takes place, a police officer must:

(a) if he is not in uniform show his warrant card (if the search is linked to terrorism he need not reveal his name);

(b) give his name and the name of the police station to which he is attached (except in the case of enquiries linked to the investigation of terrorism, in which case he shall give his warrant or other identification number);

(c) explain the object of the proposed search;

(d) specify his grounds or authorisation for making that search; and

(e) inform that person that he is entitled to a copy of the record of the search if he asks for it within 1 year. (On occasions this will not be possible in a particular sense as it will not be practicable to make such a record – perhaps following multiple searches.) If the person wishes to have a copy, he should be advised to apply to the police officer's station.

Officers were carrying out searches under an authorisation to search members of the public entering a park where a fair was being held, that authorisation being given under the Criminal Justice and Public Order Act 1994, ss 60(4) and (5). They were assaulted by a man who appeared to consent to the search and then objected and asked to be taken to a police station. The officers continued their search suspecting that, because of his reaction, he was carrying a weapon. The Divisional Court held that they were not assaulted in the course of their duties as the search had been unlawful. The powers of search are conferred by the Police and Criminal Evidence Act 1984, s 2. The failure of police officers to supply their names and station rendered the search of a person unlawful. With respect to the court, their Lordships' suggestion that officers in such situations could carry slips of paper containing such details which could be handed out fails to recognise the pressures existing in such multiple search situations.

Code A requires that before any search of a detained person or unattended vehicle takes place, the officer must take reasonable steps to explain to the person that he is being detained for the purpose of a search, give his name (with the alternative provided in cases of terrorism), explain the legal search power being exercised and give a clear explanation of the purpose, the grounds for reasonable suspicion where that is a factor or, where that is not an essential, the nature of the power and any authorisation and the fact that it has been given. Warrant cards must be shown by officers not in uniform.

If the person to be searched, or in charge of a vehicle to be searched, does not understand what is being said, or there is any doubt about his ability to understand English, the officer must take reasonable steps to bring the information to his attention. If that person is deaf or does not understand English and has someone with him, the officer must establish whether that person can interpret or otherwise help him to give the required information.

Record of search

Code A requires that a record of a search must be made at the time, unless exceptional circumstances exist (e.g. in public order situations or where a constable is urgently required elsewhere). In such cases the record must be made as soon as practicable. There may be occasions where it is not practicable to obtain the information, but reasonable efforts must be made to do so. A copy must be given immediately to the person concerned. The officer must ask for the name, address and date of birth of the person searched, but there is no obligation for that information to be provided and no power to detain a person for that purpose. Where a search is carried out by more than one officer, all should be identified. There is nothing to prevent an officer who is present but not involved in the search from completing the record.

A note for guidance requires a record to be made of the self-defined ethnicity of every person stopped according to the categories listed in Annex B to Code A. The person concerned should be asked to select a main category and a sub-category (e.g. White/British). The code number shown in Annex B should also be recorded. The purpose of obtaining such information should be explained. If an apparently incorrect response is given (a person who appears to be white says that he is black), the response given should still be recorded but the officer should give his own perception of the ethnic background of *every person* stopped by using the PNC/Phoenix classification system. If the 'not stated' category is used, the reason for doing so must be stated.

The following information should always be included in the record of a search even if the person does not wish to identify himself or give his date of birth:

(a) the name of the person searched or (if he withholds it) a description of him;
(b) a note of the person's self-defined ethnic background;
(c) where a vehicle is searched, its registration number;
(d) the date, time and place the person or vehicle was first detained;
(e) the date, time and place the person or vehicle was searched [if different from (d)];
(f) the purpose of the search;
(g) the grounds for making it or, in the case of those searches authorised in anticipation of serious violence or terrorism, the nature of the power and any necessary authorisation and the fact that it has been given;
(h) its outcome (e.g. arrest or no further action);
(i) a note of any injury or damage to property resulting from it; and
(j) the identity of the officers making it [except in the case of enquiries relating to terrorism, when the warrant or other identification number and duty station of the officer(s) should be recorded].

A record is required for each person and each vehicle searched. However, only one record is required where a person who is in a vehicle is searched in addition to the vehicle. Where the vehicle only is searched, the name of the driver and his self-defined ethnic background must be recorded unless the vehicle is unattended. Records should include the reasons for searching the person concerned by reference to his behaviour or other circumstances. They must be made even though, following questioning, the detained person was not searched.

The record of the grounds for making a search must, briefly but informatively, explain the reason for suspecting the person concerned, whether by his behaviour or other circumstances or, in the case of searches under the 1994 or 2000 Acts, by stating the authority provided to carry out such a search. It is important for national monitoring purposes to specify in the record whether a search under the Terrorism Act 2000 was made under s 44(1) or (2).

Supervising officers, in monitoring the exercise of stop and search powers, should consider in particular whether there is any evidence that officers are exercising their discretion on the basis of stereotyped images or inappropriate generalisations. Supervising officers should satisfy themselves that the practice of officers under their supervision in stopping, searching and recording is fully in accordance with the Code. Supervisors should also examine whether the records reveal any trends or patterns which give cause for concern and, if so, take appropriate steps to address the matter.

Senior officers with area or force-wide responsibilities must also monitor the broader use of stop and search powers and, where necessary, take action at the relevant level. Supervision and monitoring must be supported by the compilation of comprehensive statistical records of stops and searches at force, area and local level. Any apparently disproportionate use of the powers by particular officers or groups of officers or in relation to specific sections of the community should be identified and investigated.

In order to promote public confidence in the use of the powers, forces in consultation with police authorities must make arrangements for the records to be scrutinised by representatives of the community, and to explain the use of the powers at local level. The right of confidentiality of those stopped and searched must be recognised. Anonymised forms and/or statistics generated from records should be the focus of the examinations by members of the public.

Searching unattended vehicles

If an unattended vehicle or anything in or on such a vehicle is searched, the constable must leave a notice:

(a) stating that he searched it;
(b) giving the name of the police station to which he is attached;
(c) stating where a copy of the record of a search may be obtained at any time within 12 months;
(d) stating where any application for compensation should be directed.

A vehicle which has been searched must, if practicable, be left secure. The notice shall be left inside the vehicle if this can be done without damaging the vehicle.

A person may be detained for such time as is reasonably required to permit a search to be carried out either at the place where the person or vehicle was first detained, or nearby. The Code advises that the extent of the search will be related to the nature of the articles sought and the circumstances in which the search takes place. If a person is seen to place an article in a particular pocket, the search of that pocket should be sufficient. If the article sought is such that it may easily be concealed anywhere, the search may have to be more thorough.

The term 'nearby' is not defined. It should be interpreted narrowly. To move a vehicle off the main road to a side road would be reasonable. To move a person from the direct view of the general public, into a more private place, would similarly be reasonable. This approach to the practicalities of such a search would appear to provide the reason for the word 'nearby'.

Removal of clothing

A constable may not require a person to remove any of his clothing in public other than an outer coat, jacket or gloves (other than where the search is under s 44 of the

Terrorism Act 2000, which grants a constable in addition the power to require a person to remove in public any headgear or footwear, or under s 60 of the Criminal Justice and Public Order Act 1994 as amended by the Crime and Disorder Act 1998, which grants a constable power to require the removal of any item worn to conceal identity), but he may search a person's mouth. This does not prevent the search of other garments provided they are not removed.

The Code of Practice provides that a search of clothing which has not been removed must be restricted to a superficial examination of outer garments. This does not prevent the placing of the hands inside the pockets or outer clothing, or feeling around the inside of collars, socks or shoes if this is reasonably necessary. Subject to the restrictions upon removal of headgear, a person's hair may be searched in public. Any search involving more than the removal of an outer coat, jacket or gloves, headgear or footwear, or any other item concealing identity, may only be made by an officer of the same sex as the person searched and may not be made in the presence of anyone of the opposite sex unless the person being searched specifically requests it.

Searches which involve intimate parts of the body must not be made as a routine extension of a less through search simply because nothing is found in the course of the initial search. Searches involving such exposure may be carried out at a nearby police station or other nearby location which is out of the public view. Where there may be religious sensitivities about asking someone to remove headgear, the police officer should offer to carry out the search out of public view (for example, in a police van or police station if there is one nearby). Where practicable, the item should be removed in the presence of an officer of the same sex and out of sight of anyone of the opposite sex.

The Stop and Search Code restricts searches in public to a superficial examination of outer clothing. If, on reasonable grounds, a more extensive search is considered necessary (e.g. by requiring a person to take off a T-shirt or headgear) it must be done out of view of the public. Any search involving more than the removal of an outer coat, jacket or gloves, headgear or footwear, may only be made by an officer of the same sex and may not be made in the presence of anyone of the opposite sex unless the person being searched specifically requests it. Every reasonable effort must be made to reduce the embarrassment caused.

A search in the street itself should be regarded as being in public, even if the street is empty at the time the search begins. As a search of a person in public should be a superficial examination of outer clothing only, such searches should be completed as quickly as possible.

The Detention Code makes provision for 'strip searches' and 'intimate searches'. Both of these types of searches are matters for the custody officer. A 'strip search' is one involving the removal of more than outer clothing including shoes and socks. These searches are carried out where the custody officer reasonably suspects that a person has a concealed article which he should not be allowed to keep. An 'intimate search' consists of the physical examination of a person's body orifices other than the mouth. The term 'body orifices' includes the nose, ears, anus and vagina. The advice of a registered medical practitioner or registered nurse will usually be sought and a risk assessment made.

Seizure of articles

Articles which are suspected of being stolen or prohibited articles may be seized. The Code and the Act of 1984 require that the person who had the custody or control of the articles immediately before the search was carried out, or the person who occupied the vehicle is entitled, on request, to a record of the things seized and such a record must be supplied within a reasonable time. Persons from whom articles are seized are entitled to a photograph or copy of such articles.

In addition, the Criminal Justice and Police Act 2001, s 50(1), deals with situations in which a person who is lawfully on the premises finds objects there which he reasonably believes to contain something for which he is authorised to search and in respect of which there would be a power of seizure to which s 50 applies. Section 50 provides that where it is not reasonably practicable to establish the nature of the contents on the premises, or the extent to which the contents comprise something which there is power to seize, the power of seizure includes power to seize so much of that which has been found as it is necessary to remove to enable its nature to be determined.

Section 50(2) provides a power of seizure where a person lawfully on premises finds anything there ('the seizable property') which he would be entitled to seize but for its being comprised in something else that he has [apart from s 50(2)] no power to seize. Section 50(2) provides that where:

(a) the power under which that person would have power to seize the seizable property is a power to which s 50 applies; and
(b) in all the circumstances it is not reasonably practicable for the seizable property to be separated in those premises from that in which it is comprised,

that person's power of seizure includes power to seize both the seizable property and that from which it is not reasonably practicable to separate it.

Section 50 requires that factors to be taken into account in considering whether it is reasonably practicable should be confined to:

(a) how long it would take to carry out the determination or separation on those premises;
(b) the number of persons who would be required to carry out that determination or separation on those premises within a reasonable period;
(c) whether the determination or separation would (or would if carried out on those premises) involve damage to property;
(d) the apparatus or equipment that it would be necessary or appropriate to use for the carrying out of the determination or separation; and
(e) in the case of separation, whether the separation
  (i) would be likely, or
  (ii) if carried out by the only means that are reasonably practicable on those premises, would be likely,

to prejudice the use of some or all of the separated seizable property for the purpose for which something seized under the power in question is capable of being used.

Section 50 of the 2001 Act applies to powers set out in Schedule 1 to that Act. More than 100 powers are specified, including all of the powers of seizure with which police forces are concerned in their day-to-day work. The usual restrictions on seizure of anything that a person has reasonable grounds for believing is legally privileged do not apply to the power of seizure under s 50(2). This is an essential change, as a person seizing property under the powers conferred by s 50 will not know the particular nature of the contents of the object seized. However, the 2001 Act requires that at a subsequent examination, which must take place as soon as reasonably practicable, property must be separated into that in respect of which there was a power of seizure, that in respect of which there was no power of seizure and any which appears to be subject to legal privilege or to be special procedure material (see page 173). Everything other than that in respect of which a power of seizure existed must be returned. Property which may be retained is that which there are reasonable grounds for believing to have been obtained in consequence of an offence, or is evidence in relation to any offence, which needs to be retained to prevent it from being concealed, lost, altered or destroyed.

Where such a power has been exercised, written notice must be given to the occupier of the premises, or some other person on the premises who is in charge. Where there is no person on the premises, a notice must be attached to the premises, in a prominent place.

Perhaps the best example would be the finding of a safe which was reasonably believed to contain seizable material and there was no means of gaining entry to the safe on the premises.

The Code provides that officers should be aware of the need for confidentiality in relation to the contents of any document and property must be returned as soon as possible. Delay may only be justified where the person to whom the material is to be returned is unavailable or where there are difficulties in making arrangements for the return of a large quantity of material.

Anything seized in accordance with the above provisions may be retained for as long as is necessary for:

(a) use as evidence at a trial for an offence;
(b) facilitating the use in an investigation or proceedings of anything to which it is inextricably linked (e.g. on a computer disc) without damaging evidential integrity;
(c) forensic examination or other investigation in connection with an offence;
(d) establishing its lawful owner where there are reasonable grounds for believing it has been stolen or obtained by commission of an offence.

The person who has custody or control of such property immediately before seizure must, on request, be provided with a list or description of the property and he, or his representative, must be allowed supervised access to examine the property or have it photographed or copied, or must be provided with a photograph or copy, within a reasonable time and at his own expense, unless the officer in charge of the investigation has reasonable grounds for believing that this would prejudice the investigation of the offence or criminal proceedings, or lead to the commission of an offence by providing access to unlawful material such as pornography. A record of such grounds must be made.

Summary of major notes for guidance

Before stop and search procedures are carried out, an officer must have reasonable grounds to suspect that the person is in possession of stolen or prohibited articles. That suspicion must be a reasonable one which is based on a foundation of fact. Having stopped such a person who has directed such suspicion towards himself, it may be that an acceptable explanation may be given for that conduct which eliminates the need for a search. If that search must be carried out, everything that it is possible to do to remove likely causes of embarrassment should be done. Wherever possible, the person should be removed from the view of the general public before the search is carried out.

Most members of the public, although they are unlikely to be attracted to the idea of being searched, will accept the necessity for such a procedure if it is properly explained.

Nothing in the Code affects the ability of an officer to speak to or question a person in the course of his duties without detaining him or exercising any element of compulsion.

If a person to be searched, or in charge of a vehicle which is to be searched, does not understand what is being said or there is any doubt about his ability to understand English, the officer must take reasonable steps to bring the required information to his attention. If the person has someone with him, then the officer must establish whether that person can interpret or otherwise help him to give the required information.

Regulation of investigatory powers and public postal services

This information is included here because of its close association with police powers to stop and search and police powers in general.

Telecommunications

The Regulation of Investigatory Powers Act 2000 repeals the Interception of Communications Act 1985 and makes new provisions which recognise the requirements of the European Convention on Human Rights. Article 8 deals with the right to respect for private and family life and requires that:

1. Everyone has the right to respect for his private and family life, his home and his correspondence.
2. There shall be no interference by a public authority with the exercise of this right except such as in accordance with the law and is necessary in a democratic society in the interests of national security, public safety or the economic well-being of the country, for the prevention of disorder or crime, for the protection of health and morals or for the protection of the rights and freedoms of others.

The provisions of the Act also recognise Article 5 of Council Directive 97/66, the Telecommunications Data Protection Directive, which requires that the confidentiality of communications is safeguarded.

Most of the provisions of the Act are aimed at protecting the confidentiality of public postal services and public telecommunications systems and some private systems which are attached to a public system. It is an offence intentionally and without lawful authority to intercept a communication in the course of its transmission by one of these means. The inclusion of such private systems means that someone who unlawfully intercepts a telephone conversation between a fellow employee and some other person may incur a liability under the Act. However, in the case of a private system, an interceptor does not commit an offence if he has a right to control the operation or use of the system *or* has the express or implied consent of such a person to make the interception.

The Act makes special provisions for the issue of interception warrants and provides for the lawful interception without an interception warrant where one or more of the parties has consented (for example, calls received from kidnappers). Such an interception will be authorised as surveillance, rather than by means of an interception warrant.

The Regulation of Investigatory Powers (Maintenance of Interception Capability) Order 2002 sets out the obligations which the Home Secretary considers to be reasonable to impose on the providers of public postal services or a public telecommunications service for the purpose of securing that it is practicable for requirements to provide assistance in relation to interception warrants to be imposed and complied with. The Order enables the Home Secretary to ensure compliance with the obligations by providing that he may give a service provider a notice requiring it to take the steps described in the notice and specifies the period within which a person served with a notice may refer it to the Technical Advisory Board.

The Regulation of Investigatory Powers (Interception of Communications: Code of Practice) Order 2002 implemented a Code of Practice relating to the interception of communications, to which anyone exercising or performing a power or duty to which the Code applies must have regard.

The Part of the Act which is of most direct concern to the police is Part II, which deals with surveillance and 'covert human intelligence sources', which is an attractive way of describing an informant.

Surveillance

The forms of surveillance covered by the Act are:

(a) *directed surveillance*, which is covert, but not intrusive surveillance and is undertaken for the purpose of a specific investigation or a specific operation in such a manner as is likely to result in the obtaining of *private information* about a person (whether or not one specifically identified for the purposes of the investigation or operation), and is otherwise than by way of an immediate response to events or circumstances the nature of which is such that it would not be reasonably practicable for an authorisation under this part to be sought for the carrying out of the surveillance; 'private information' includes any information relating to a person's private or family life;

(b) *intrusive surveillance*, which is covert surveillance that that is carried out in relation to anything taking place on any residential premises or in any private vehicle and involves the presence of an individual on the premises or in the vehicle or is carried out by means of a surveillance device.

These terms are defined by s 26 of the Act. However, the Act provides that surveillance will not be intrusive if it involves no more than the placing of a vehicle location device, or it is surveillance involving the interception of a communication which is one sent by, or intended for, a person who has consented to the interception. In addition, it will not be intrusive if it is carried out by a device which is not present upon the premises or vehicle concerned. However, this does not apply if the device is such that it consistently provides information of the same quality and detail as might be expected to be obtained from a device which was actually present on the premises or in the vehicle. The Act also, of course, exempts devices designed to catch TV licence dodgers!

Surveillance is covert if it is carried out in a manner that is calculated to ensure that the persons who are subject to the surveillance are unaware that it is or may be taking place.

The conduct of a covert human intelligence source

The 'conduct of a covert human intelligence source' refers to any conduct of a person who:

(a) if he establishes or maintains a personal or other relationship with a person, for the covert purpose of facilitating the obtaining of information or the provision of access to information to another person,

(b) covertly uses such a relationship to obtain information or to provide such access; or

(c) covertly discloses information obtained by the use of such a relationship, or as a consequence of the existence of such a relationship.

The 'use of a covert human intelligence source' refers to inducing, asking or assisting a person to engage in the conduct of such a source, or to obtain information by means of such a source.

A purpose is covert in relation to the establishment or maintenance of a personal or other relationship only if the relationship is conducted in a manner that is calculated to ensure that one of the parties to the relationship is unaware of the purpose. A relationship is used covertly, and information obtained is disclosed covertly, only if it is used or disclosed in a manner that is calculated to ensure that one of the parties to the relationship is unaware of the use or disclosure in question.

The Regulation of Investigatory Powers (Covert Human Intelligence Sources: Codes of Practice) Order 2002 introduced a Code of Practice which must be observed by a person exercising or performing a power or duty to which that Code applies.

Lawful surveillance, etc.

Authorisation of surveillance and covert human intelligence sources

Section 27 of the Act of 2000 provides that such conduct will be lawful if it is authorised and carried out in accordance with the authorisation. No civil liability will be incurred in respect of conduct 'incidental' to such lawful conduct and which is not in itself conduct in respect of which an authorisation or warrant is capable of being granted under a relevant enactment and might reasonably have been expected to be sought. A 'relevant enactment' means the Act of 2000, s 5 of the Intelligence Services Act 1994 (warrants for the intelligence services) or an enactment contained in Part III of the Police Act 1997 (powers of covert entry and interference with property by the police and customs officers).

Authorisation of directed surveillance and covert human intelligence sources

These matters are controlled by ss 28 and 29 of the 2000 Act.

A 'designated person' may grant authorisations for the carrying out of directed surveillance. A designated person must believe that the authorisation is necessary:

(a) in the interests of national security;

(b) for the purpose of preventing or detecting crime or of preventing disorder;

(c) in the interests of the economic well-being of the United Kingdom;

(d) in the interests of public safety;

(e) for the purpose of protecting public health;

(f) for the purpose of assessing or collecting any tax, duty, levy or other imposition, contribution or charge payable to a government department; or

(g) for any other purpose which is specified for the purpose by order made by the Secretary of State,

and that the authorised surveillance is proportionate to what is sought to be achieved by carrying it out.

In the case of an authorisation of covert human intelligence source, a designated officer must not only have the two beliefs just referred to but must also believe that there are arrangements for the source's case that satisfy the following requirements:

(a) that there will be at all times a person holding an office, rank or position with the relevant investigating authority who will have day-to-day responsibility for dealing with the source on behalf of that authority, and for the source's security or welfare;

(b) that there will be at all times another person holding an office rank or position with the relevant investigating authority who will have general oversight of the use made of the source;

(c) that there will be at all times a person holding an office, rank or position with the relevant investigating authority who will have responsibility for maintaining a record made of the use of the source;

(d) that the records relating to the source that are maintained by the relevant investigating authority will always contain particulars of all such matters (if any) as may be specified for the purposes of this paragraph in regulations;

(e) that records maintained by the relevant investigating authority that disclose the identity of the source will not be available to persons except to the extent that there is a need for access to them to be made available to those persons; and

(f) that any other requirement imposed by order by the Home Secretary is satisfied.

The 'relevant investigating authority' in relation to the use of an informant is the public authority that handles him. If the informant's activities are to be for the benefit of more than one public authority, one of them must assume these duties.

An authorisation will specify the conduct which is authorised and require that it is carried out in accordance with the authorisation. In the case of informants the authorisation will be specific to the individual and the particular investigation.

Persons entitled to grant authorisations for directed surveillance and covert human intelligence sources

By s 30 of the 2000 Act, the particular persons designated for the purposes of ss 28 and 29 are the individuals holding such offices, ranks and positions with the relevant public authorities as are prescribed by order. The Regulation of Investigatory Powers (Prescription of Offices, Ranks and Positions) Order 2000 as amended specifies who is designated. So far as police forces are concerned it specifies the rank of superintendent (inspector in urgent cases as provided by s 30). In the case of an authorisation combining an authorisation under s 28 or 29 and of an authorisation by the Secretary of State for carrying out intrusive surveillance (see below), the Secretary of State is the person designated for the purpose.

For the purposes of authorisations for directed surveillance, an authorisation may be granted by any public authority included in Schedule 1 to the 2000 Act. The Schedule, in addition to including any police force, the National Crime Intelligence Service, the National Crime Squad and the Serious Fraud Office, lists all government departments, local authorities, customs and excise, Ministry of Defence, post office and financial services and personal investment authorities, in addition to the Health and Safety Executive, NHS bodies in England and Wales and the Royal Pharmaceutical Society for Great Britain.

Authorisations of covert human intelligence sources may be granted by any public authority included in Schedule 1 (which includes all of the bodies listed in the paragraph above, except the Health and Safety Executive, NHS bodies in England and Wales and the Royal Pharmaceutical Society for Great Britain).

Special provisions in relation to intrusive surveillance

In relation to intrusive surveillance authorisations, s 32 requires that authorisations may only be granted by the Secretary of State and senior authorising officers (chief constables and equivalents, plus Assistant Commissioners of the Metropolitan Police). Such authorisations will only be granted where it is believed that they are necessary:

(a) in the interests of national security;
(b) for the purpose of preventing or detecting serious crime; or
(c) in the interests of the economic well-being of the United Kingdom,

and that the authorised surveillance is proportionate to that which is sought to be achieved. In considering whether these requirements are satisfied, account must be taken of whether the information to be obtained could reasonably be obtained by other means. Any such authorisation must specify the conduct which is authorised.

Authorisations for intrusive surveillance may be granted under s 34, by assistant chief constables or their equivalents in urgent cases where it is not reasonably practicable, in view of the urgency, for the senior authorising officer or his designated deputy to do so.

When an authorisation for intrusive surveillance is granted or cancelled, notice must be given to an ordinary Surveillance Commissioner. The Regulation of Investigatory Powers (Notification of Authorisations, etc.) Order 2000 provides details of those matters which must be notified to an ordinary Surveillance Commissioner when such events occur.

Sections 36 to 40 of the Act deal with the need for the approval of an ordinary Surveillance Commissioner before an authorisation for intrusive surveillance, other than one made by the Home Secretary, may take effect, the quashing of such an authorisation, appeals against decisions of a Surveillance Commissioner to the Chief Surveillance Commissioner (appointed under the Police Act 1997) and the information which is to be provided to Surveillance Commissioners.

The Regulation of Investigatory Powers (Covert Surveillance: Code of Practice) Order 2002 brought into force a Code of Practice relating to covert surveillance which came into force on 1 August 2002.

Retention of communications data held by communications providers

The Anti-terrorism, Crime and Security Act 2001, Part 11, empowers the Secretary of State to issue a code of practice relating to the retention by communications providers of communications data obtained by or held by them. A 'communications provider' is a person who provides a postal service or a telecommunications service. The code may contain such provisions as appear to the Secretary of State to be necessary for the purpose of safeguarding national security, or for the purpose of prevention or detection of crime or the prosecution of offenders which may relate directly or indirectly to national security. A failure to comply with a provision of the code does not, by itself, render a provider liable to criminal or civil proceedings. However, the contents of the code will be admissible in evidence in any related legal proceedings.

The Act of 2001 authorises the review of the operation of the requirements included in the code. Where the Secretary of State considers it to be necessary, he may by order authorise the giving of directions concerning the retention of communications data to communications providers generally, to providers of a specified description or to particular providers or a provider. The power to make such an order will lapse after the 'initial period' (2 years beginning with the day of Royal Assent, 14 December 2001) unless an order authorising the giving of such directions is made before the end of that time. In addition, the 'initial period' may be extended by statutory instrument.

Questioning and treatment of persons

Introduction

The questioning and treatment of persons by the police is now controlled by ss 53 to 65 of the Police and Criminal Evidence Act 1984, the Code of Practice for the Detention, Treatment, and Questioning of Persons by Police Officers and the Code of Practice on Tape Recording Interviews with Suspects. References throughout this chapter to the Act of 1984 will be references to 'the Act', the Code of Practice for the Detention, Treatment, and Questioning of Persons by Police Officers will be referred to as the Detention Code and the Code of Practice on Tape Recording Interviews with Suspects will be referred to as the Tape Recording Code.

These provisions replace all former controls upon police practice. Although references in the Detention Code are to persons 'detained' in police stations, those who are voluntarily in attendance must be treated with at least equal consideration. The procedures described must be carefully followed. Evidence which is obtained in a manner which breaches any provisions of the Code of Practice may be excluded at the trial judge's discretion. The breach may also involve the commission of a disciplinary offence if committed in such a way that the provisions of the disciplinary code are breached.

The Police Reform Act 2002, s 51, requires police authorities to make arrangements for detainees to be visited by persons appointed (independent custody visitors). They must be independent of both the police authority and the chief officer. The arrangements may provide rights of access to police stations, examination of records, meetings with detainees and the inspection of facilities. Access to a detainee may be denied if it appears to an officer of or above the rank of inspector that there are grounds for doing so at the time, those grounds being specified within the arrangements, and the procedural requirements imposed in relation to denial of access are complied with.

The Secretary of State may issue a code of practice as to the carrying out by police authorities and independent custody visitors of their functions under the arrangements.

The purpose of the Detention Code is to ensure that all persons in custody are dealt with expeditiously and are released as soon as the need for detention has ceased to apply. This and other Codes must be readily available at all police stations for consultation by police officers, detained persons and members of the public. The Codes issued under the authority of the Act contain within them advice which is headed 'Notes for Guidance'. These notes are not provisions of the Codes themselves and are only intended to assist application and interpretation. There are also a number of Annexes to the Codes and these *are* parts of the Codes themselves and compliance with these provisions is essential.

Whenever the Detention Code requires a person to be given certain information, he does not have to be given it if he is incapable at the time of understanding what is said to him or is violent or likely to become violent or is in urgent need of medical attention, but he must be given it as soon as practicable.

It is essential that police officers carefully follow the provisions of the Codes of Practice. There is nothing in the Codes which prevents a custody officer from allowing civilian support staff (who are not designated persons) to carry out individual procedures or tasks but, where this is done, the custody officer remains responsible for that person's compliance with the Code. The term 'designated person' has the meaning given by the Police Reform Act 2002 and references in the Code to a 'police officer' include a designated person acting within that designation.

The Code *does not apply* to:

(a) persons arrested on warrants issued in Scotland by police officers under the Criminal Justice and Public Order Act 1994, s 136(2), or arrested or detained without warrant by officers from a police force in Scotland under s 137(2). In these cases, police powers and duties and the person's rights and entitlements whilst at a police station in England and Wales are the same as those in Scotland;

(b) persons arrested for fingerprinting under the Asylum and Immigration Act 1999, s 142(3);

(c) persons whose detention is authorised by an immigration officer under the Immigration Act 1971;

(d) convicted or remanded prisoners held in police cells on behalf of the prison service;

(e) persons detained for examination under the Terrorism Act 2000, Schedule 7, and to whom the Code of Practice issued under Schedule 14, para. 6, applies; or

(f) persons detained for searches under stop and search powers except as required by Code A.

The Code *does apply* to all other persons who are in custody in police stations in England and Wales, whether or not they have been arrested for an offence, and to those who have been removed to a police station as a place of safety under ss 135 and 136 of the Mental Health Act 1983. However, s 15 of the Code (reviews of extensions of detention) applies solely to people in police detention, for example, those brought to a police station under arrest or arrested at a police station for an offence after attending there voluntarily.

Nothing in the Tape Recording Code shall be taken as detracting in any way from the requirements of the Detention Code.

Where the Codes require the prior authority or agreement of an officer of at least the rank of inspector or superintendent, that authority may be given by a sergeant or chief inspector authorised to perform the functions of the higher rank.

Enquiries prior to arrest

The Detention Code makes it clear that it does not affect the general principle that all citizens have a duty to help the police to prevent crime and discover offenders. It stresses that this is a civic, rather than a legal duty, but that when a police officer is trying to discover whether, or by whom, an offence has been committed he is entitled to question any person from whom he thinks useful information can be obtained, subject to the restrictions which the Code imposes. A person's declaration that he is unwilling to reply does not alter the entitlement.

Thus, the citizen's duty to assist the police is declared; the constable's right to ask questions is stated; that right continues to exist even though the person to whom the questions are addressed refuses to answer; and it is made clear that although a duty to assist exists, there is no requirement on the citizen's behalf to answer any of the questions addressed to him. These provisions provide a starting point to the process of criminal investigation. Whenever a person not under arrest is initially cautioned before or during an interview, he must at the same time be told that he is not under arrest and is not obliged to remain with the officer. A person who accompanies a police officer voluntarily, when taken to a police station, or who is at a police station voluntarily is not under arrest and is free to leave at any time. In addition, the Codes of Practice do not prevent a police officer from asking questions at the scene of a crime to elicit an explanation which could provide the arrested person with the opportunity to show that he was innocent.

If in the process of this questioning a point is reached at which there are grounds to suspect a person of an offence, that person must be cautioned before any questions about it (or further questions if it is his answers to previous questions that provide grounds for suspicion) are put to him regarding his involvement or suspected involvement in that offence if his answers or his silence (i.e. failure to answer a question or failure to answer satisfactorily) may be given in evidence in a court in a prosecution. The Court of Appeal has held that the term 'grounds to suspect' means 'reasonable grounds to suspect'. Thus, cautions will be required:

(a) at the stage of reasonable grounds to suspect that a person who has not been arrested has committed an offence (no matter how trivial);
(b) on the arrest of a person (unless it is impracticable or he has already been cautioned); and
(c) after arrest (in the circumstances described below).

Statements made under caution may be used only for the purposes for which they are provided. To use them for an extraneous purpose, for example, to leak to the press whether or not for reward, is legally actionable as a breach of confidence.

A person, therefore, need not be cautioned if questions are put to him for other purposes, for example,

(a) solely to establish his identity, or the ownership of any vehicle;
(b) to obtain information in accordance with any relevant statutory requirement (where his refusal to supply a name or address may render him liable to detention, or where refusal to provide a specimen for analysis under the Road Traffic Act 1988, s 7, may amount to an offence or make him liable to arrest);
(c) in furtherance of the proper and effective conduct of a search, for example to determine the need to search in the exercise of powers of stop and search or to seek co-operation while carrying out a search;
(d) to seek verification of a written record of any comments made, including unsolicited comments which are outside the context of an interview which might be significant; and
(e) when examining a person in accordance with the Terrorism Act 2000, Schedule 7, and the Code of Practice for Examining Officers issued under that Act.

For these purposes, a 'significant' statement or silence means one which appears capable of being used in evidence against the suspect, in particular a direct admission of guilt, or failure or refusal to answer a question (or failure to answer it satisfactorily) which might give rise to an inference under Part III of the Criminal Justice and Public Order Act 1994.

The Detention Code, therefore, requires police officers to administer a caution if the answer to the question posed is likely to be offered in evidence from the moment at which it is recognised that there are reasonable grounds to suspect that a particular person is guilty of an offence. It will be appreciated that questions which are put to establish identity or the ownership of a vehicle are questions the answers to which would merely establish that that person was the person who had committed the offences. If a motor car is found illegally parked and a person approaches that vehicle, it is not known that he is the person who parked the vehicle until the answers to such preliminary questions are obtained. Once it is established that he is the person responsible he must be cautioned or, put another way, advised to be careful concerning any further statements which he makes. It should be noted that if a person is under arrest, he must be cautioned when told that he will be prosecuted for an offence.

The Code also provides that when a person who is not under arrest is initially cautioned or is reminded that he is under caution, he must at the same time be told that he is not under arrest and is not obliged to remain with the officer. An 'interview' is the questioning of a person regarding his involvement or suspected involvement in a criminal offence or offences which the Code of Practice would require to be carried out under caution. Any person attending a police station voluntarily for the purpose of assisting with an investigation may leave at will unless placed under arrest. If it is decided that he should not be allowed to do so then he must be informed at once that he is under arrest and brought before the custody officer, who is responsible for ensuring that he is notified of his rights in the same way as other detained persons. If he is not placed under arrest, but is cautioned, the officer who gives the caution must at the same time inform him that he is not under arrest, that he is not obliged to remain at the police station, but that if he remains at the police station he may obtain free legal advice if he wishes. If he asks about his entitlement to legal advice, he should be given a copy of the notice explaining the arrangements for obtaining legal advice. These provisions are difficult to understand. The process of investigation will frequently be hampered by the necessity almost to invite a suspect to leave at the moment at which the truth of the matter is beginning to emerge. If the interviewing officer, as he must be, is absolutely fair to the person by cautioning him immediately a suspicion arises, and at the same time advising him that he may leave, this may lead to difficulties. However, the provisions of the Code must be complied with.

Action upon arrest

A person must be cautioned on arrest for an offence unless:

(a) it is impracticable to do so by reason of his condition or behaviour at the time; or
(b) he has already been cautioned prior to arrest as described above.

Action following arrest

Following an arrest, a police officer must caution that person (or cause him to be cautioned, or remind him that he remains under caution):

(a) before putting to him any questions or further questions for the purpose of obtaining evidence which may be given to a court in a prosecution (unless the questioning immediately follows arrest);
(b) when arresting him for any further offence in accordance with s 31 of the Act;
(c) when charging him with an offence (or informing him that he may be prosecuted for it);
(d) when bringing to his notice a written statement or questioning him as permitted by the Detention Code.

The requirement to remind a person that he remains under caution applies particularly where there has been a break within an interview. If there is any doubt that the person being questioned appreciates that he is still under caution, the caution should be given again in full. Although it was obviously the intention of the writers of the Code that the reference to 'breaks' was a reference to official breaks for meals, etc., where a police officer cautioned the driver of a car who admitted possessing cannabis and 2 minutes later questioned him about the presence of heroin in the car, it was claimed that he should have been cautioned once more, or reminded that he was under caution, before questions were put concerning the heroin. The Court of Appeal held that the caution administered during the first period of questioning was sufficient to cover the second series of questions. However, the case illustrates the need for the utmost care in ensuring that an accused remains aware that he is under caution.

The officer who administers a caution must ensure that the significance of the caution is understood by the suspect. The person should not, however, be left with a false impression that non-cooperation will have no immediate effect upon his treatment as this may not be so. For example, his refusal to establish his identity may prevent his release from police detention. However, if such a person asks the officer directly what action will be taken in the event of his answering questions, making a statement or refusing to do either, then the officer may inform the person what action the police propose to take in that event provided that the action is itself proper and warranted.

The caution shall be in the following terms:

> You do not have to say anything. But it may harm your defence if you do not
> mention when questioned something which you later rely on in court. Anything you
> do say may be given in evidence.

However, the Code provides that minor verbal deviations do not constitute a breach of this requirement provided that the sense of the caution is preserved. It has long been the practice of defending solicitors and counsel, when all else appears to be failing, to ask a police office to recite the words of a caution. Other forms of caution are prescribed by Annex C to Code C for use where the restriction on drawing adverse inferences from silence applies (see page 201).

If a person does not understand the meaning of the caution, a constable should explain it to him. (See under the heading 'Tape-recorded interviews' below concerning special cautions which apply to all interviews, not merely those which are tape recorded, although interviews are, almost invariably, tape recorded.)

A person detained or cautioned during an interview must be told that he is entitled to free independent legal advice and that he can speak to his solicitor on the telephone. If the suspect declines such advice, he should be invited to explain his reasons for doing so, which must be recorded. If such advice is requested, he may not be interviewed, or continue to be interviewed, until he has received it.

The exercise of the right to legal advice may be delayed only in accordance with the provisions of the Code (Annex B). Whenever legal advice is requested (unless Annex B below applies), the custody officer must act without delay to secure the provision of such advice to the person concerned. If, on being informed or reminded of the right to legal advice, the person declines to speak to a solicitor in person, the officer shall point out that the right to legal advice includes the right to speak to a solicitor on the telephone and ask him whether he wishes to do so. If the person continues to waive his right to legal advice, the officer shall ask him the reasons for doing so, and any reasons shall be recorded on the custody record or the interview record as appropriate. Reminders as to the right to legal advice are required in many parts of the Code. Once it is clear that a person does not want to speak to a solicitor either in person or by telephone, he should cease to be asked his reasons. A person is not obliged to give such reasons and should not be pressed to do so.

Generally, the 'delay' provisions of Annex B are concerned with persons in police detention in connection with a serious arrestable offence and who has not yet been charged with the offence. They permit an officer of the rank of superintendent or above (where the delay is concerned with legal advice) or inspector rank or above (where the delay is concerned with the right to have someone informed of his detention) to authorise a delay where he has reasonable grounds for believing that the exercise of the respective rights:

(a) will lead to interference with or harm to evidence connected with a serious arrestable offence or interference with or physical injury to other people; or
(b) will lead to the alerting of other people suspected of having committed such an offence but not yet arrested for it; or
(c) will hinder the recovery of property obtained as a result of such an offence.

The detention Code requires that superintendents should authorise such delays only after careful consideration.

Where a person asks for legal advice and the solicitor nominated by him or selected from a list cannot be contacted, or has previously indicated that he does not wish to be contacted, or having been contacted has declined to attend, and the person concerned has been told of the duty solicitor scheme but has declined to ask for the duty solicitor, or the duty solicitor is unavailable, the interview must be started or continued without further delay provided that an officer of the rank of inspector or above has agreed. However, where a solicitor chosen by a suspect is unavailable, the suspect may choose up to two alternatives. If these are unsuccessful, the custody officer may allow further attempts.

The same applies where a person who wanted legal advice changes his mind. Where this occurs, the inspector or above must enquire into the reasons for the change of mind before authorising the interview to proceed. All such details must be recorded on tape or in a written record.

When a detainee exercises his right to legal advice by consulting or communicating with a solicitor, he must be allowed to do so in private. This is a fundamental right. Except as allowed by the Terrorism Act 2000, Schedule 8, para. 9, if the requirement for privacy is compromised because what is said or written by the detainee or the solicitor for the purpose of the giving or receiving of legal advice is overheard, listened to or read by others without the informed consent of the detainee, the right will effectively have been denied. Where a person speaks to a solicitor on the telephone, he should be allowed to do so in private unless this is impractical because of the design and layout of the custody area or the location of the telephones. The normal expectation should be that facilities are available, unless they are being used, at all police stations to enable such private communication to be made.

For the purposes of the Code, an 'interview' is the questioning of a person regarding his involvement or suspected involvement in a criminal offence or offences which by virtue of the Code, is required to be carried out under caution. Procedures undertaken under s 7 of the Road Traffic Act 1988 (provisions of specimens for analysis) do not constitute 'interviews' for the purposes of the Code.

A poster advertising the right to have legal advice must be prominently displayed in the charging area of every police station. See also 'Urgent interviews' below.

An accurate record must be made of each interview with a person suspected of an offence, whether or not the interview takes place at a police station.

Tape-recorded interviews

Special caution to be given at beginning of interview

When a suspect who is interviewed at a police station or authorised place of detention after arrest fails or refuses to answer certain questions, or to answer them satisfactorily, *after due warning*, a court or jury may draw such inferences as appear proper, under the Criminal Justice and Public Order Act 1994, ss 36 and 37. This applies when:

(a) a suspect is arrested by a constable and there is found on his person or in or on his clothing or footwear, or otherwise in his possession or in the place where he was arrested, any objects, marks or substances, or marks on such objects, and the person fails or refuses to account for the objects, marks or substances found; or
(b) an arrested person was found by a constable at a place at or about the time the offence for which he was arrested is alleged to have been committed, and the person fails or refuses to account for his presence at that place.

For an inference to be drawn from a suspect's failure or refusal to answer a question about one of these matters, or to answer it satisfactorily, the interviewing officer must first tell him in ordinary language:

(a) what offence he is investigating;
(b) what fact he is asking the suspect to account for;
(c) that he believes this fact may be due to the suspect's taking part in the commission of the offence in question;
(d) that a court may draw a proper inference from his silence if he fails or refuses to account for this fact; and
(e) that a record is being made of the interview and that it may be given in evidence if he is brought to trial.

These provisions, when first enacted, led to lawyer-driven media hype concerning the alleged intention of the Home Secretary to remove a suspect's 'right to silence'. These provisions do not remove that right. They merely provide that proper cognisance can be taken of the circumstances surrounding the exercise of that right, which is a different matter. If a police officer tells a suspect that he is investigating an offence of burglary and asks him to account for the fact that he was seen in the garden of the attacked dwelling-house at the approximate time at which the offence was committed, and that he therefore believes that such presence in the garden may be due to his involvement in that offence, the magistrates or jury may draw a proper inference from his silence if he fails or refuses to account for his presence. It will be important for police officers to ensure that the information as set out in (a) to (e) above is properly given and that a record is made of it.

Procedural rules, and the extent to which they are followed, are becoming much more important than the question of guilt or innocence. It is certain that much time will be spent in the cross-examination of police officers concerning the nature of the warning given.

Nature of taped record

Such a record, if it occurs at a police station, must be made in accordance with the Code of Practice on Tape Recording Interviews with Suspects:

(a) with a person who has been cautioned in accordance with the Detention Code (grounds to suspect him of an offence) in respect of an indictable offence (including an offence triable either way);

(b) if it takes place as a result of an interviewer exceptionally putting further questions to a suspect about such an offence in (a) after he has been charged with, or informed that he may be prosecuted for, that offence; or

(c) in which an interviewer wishes to tell a person, after he has been charged with, or informed that he may be prosecuted for, such an offence in (a), any written statement made by another person, or the content of in interview with another person. (This may be done by playing a tape recording.)

However, tape recordings at police stations may be made of interviews with persons cautioned for other offences, at police discretion, provided that the Code is complied with. This also applies to responses after charge in such situations. The Terrorism Act 2000 makes separate provision for the tape recording of interviews in relation to terrorism.

A custody officer may authorise the interviewing officer not to tape record an interview in two cases: where it is not reasonably practicable to do so because of failure of the equipment or the non-availability of a suitable interview room or recorder, and the custody officer considers on reasonable grounds that the interview should not be delayed; or where it is clear from the outset that no prosecution will ensue he may authorise the interviewing officer not to tape record the interview. Priority should be given to tape recording in interviews with persons who are suspected of more serious offences. In other cases the interview must be recorded in writing and in accordance with the Detention Code. The custody officer must make a note, in specific terms, of the reason for not tape recording.

Where a person refuses to enter a room or remain in an interview room and the custody officer considers that the interview should not be delayed, the interview may be conducted in a cell using portable recording equipment or, if such equipment is not available, it should be recorded in writing.

The tape recording of an interview shall be carried out openly but unobtrusively and it must be made clear to the suspect that there is no opportunity to interfere with the tape recording or tapes. The 'master' tape will be sealed before it leaves the presence of the suspect. A 'master' tape may be either one of two tapes used in a twin-decked machine or the only tape used in a single-deck machine. A second tape will be used as a working copy and it may be either the other tape in the case of a twin-deck machine or a copy of the master used in a single-deck machine. Such a copy must be made in the presence of the suspect and without the master tape having left his sight.

In considering tape-recorded interviews (and all other forms of interview), it must be borne in mind that the Criminal Justice and Public Order Act 1994, ss 34, 36 and 37, describe the conditions under which adverse inferences may be drawn from a person's failure or refusal to say anything about his involvement in the offence when interviewed, after being charged or informed that he may be prosecuted. In effect, in the case of such a detainee at a police station who has asked for legal advice but has not yet been allowed an opportunity to consult a solicitor (including the duty solicitor), adverse inferences may not be drawn from his failure to say anything concerning his involvement in an offence. It would therefore be wrong to use the normal caution which includes the words 'But it may harm your defence if you do not mention when questioned something which you later rely on in court' as that simply would not be true. It has been held that no adverse inferences may be drawn where a person who has asked for legal advice has not received it. In such circumstances, the words cited above are omitted from the caution. However, it must be remembered that when legal advice becomes available to the detainee, the full caution must then be given as any failure then to respond may create circumstances which will permit adverse inferences to be drawn.

When a suspect is brought into the *interview* room, the police officer will without delay, but in the sight of the suspect, load the tape recorder with previously unused tapes and set it to record. The tapes must be unwrapped or otherwise opened in the presence of the suspect. The police officer will then:

(a) say that the interview is being recorded;
(b) say his name and rank and the name and rank of any other police officer present except in the case of enquiries linked to terrorism, when the warrant or other identification number should be stated rather than names;
(c) ask the suspect and any other person present (e.g. a solicitor) to identify themselves;
(d) say the date, time of commencement and place of the interview; and
(e) say that the suspect will be given a notice about what will happen to the tapes.

The police must then caution the suspect in the usual way (see page 185). He must remind the suspect of his right to free and independent legal advice, that he can speak to a solicitor on the telephone in accordance with the provisions of the Detention Code, and of any statements previously made.

At the beginning of an interview carried out at a police station, the interviewing officer, after cautioning the suspect, shall put to him any significant statement or silence which occurred before his arrival at the police station, and shall ask him whether he confirms or denies that earlier statement or silence and whether he wishes to add anything.

A 'significant' statement is one which appears capable of being used in evidence against the suspect, in particular a direct admission of guilt. A 'significant silence' is a failure or refusal to answer a question or to answer it satisfactorily, which might, allowing for the restriction on drawing inferences from silence, give rise to an inference under Part III of the Criminal Justice and Public Order Act 1994.

The reader is reminded that a special warning must be given before inferences can be drawn under the Criminal Justice and Public Order Act 1994, s 36 or 37, and of the fact that adverse inferences cannot be drawn where legal advice has been requested but has not been received.

If the suspect raises objections to such tape recording either at the outset, or during the interview, the officer shall explain the fact that the interview is being tape recorded and that the provisions of the Tape Recording Code require that the suspect's objections should be recorded on tape. When any objections have been recorded on tape or the suspect has refused to have his objections recorded, the police officer may turn off the recorder. In this eventuality, he must say that he is turning off the recorder and give his reasons for doing so and then turn it off. The police officer must then make a written record of the interview in accordance with the Detention Code (see below). If, however, the police officer reasonably considers that he may proceed to put questions to the suspect with the tape recorder still on, he may do so. He should bear in mind that a decision to continue recording against the wishes of the suspect may be subject to comment in court.

If a suspect indicates that he wishes to tell a police officer about matters not directly connected with the offence of which he is suspected and that he is unwilling for these matters to be recorded on tape, he must be given the opportunity to tell the police officer about these matters after the conclusion of the formal interview.

Where a requirement to caution arises at a time when the restriction on drawing adverse inferences from silence applies, the caution must be:

> You do not have to say anything, but anything you do say may be given in evidence.

Whenever the restriction begins or ceases to apply after a caution has been given, the person shall be re-cautioned in the appropriate terms. The changed position in relation to inferences and the fact that the previous caution no longer applies must be explained to the detainee in ordinary language. The Code suggests, in a note for guidance, that where the restriction on drawing adverse inferences begins to apply (because legal advice has been requested but not yet received), it should be explained that the caution previously given no longer applies (because it related to failure to account for prescribed matters) because after caution:

(a) the detainee asked to speak to a solicitor but has not yet had an opportunity to do so; or

(b) the detainee has been charged with or informed that he will be prosecuted for the offence, and he should be informed that this means that from now on, adverse inferences cannot be drawn at court and his defence will not be harmed just because he chose to say nothing. He should be asked to note that the new caution does not say anything about his defence being harmed.

Where any such restriction ceases to apply before or at the time the person is charged or informed that he may be prosecuted, the detainee should be told that the caution he was previously given no longer applies. This is because after that caution he has been allowed an opportunity to speak to a solicitor. He should be told to listen carefully as the caution now being given explains how his defence at court may be affected by him choosing to say nothing. The important factor is that where legal advice has been requested all bets are off in relation to silence until the detainee has had an opportunity to speak to a solicitor. This follows a ruling of the European Court of Human Rights.

Changing tapes and breaks

Where a tape is coming to an end, the interviewer must inform the suspect and round off that part of the interview, remove the tapes and insert new tapes which will be unwrapped or otherwise opened in the suspect's presence. Tapes should be marked with an identification number immediately they are removed from the tape recorder. A suspect must not be left unattended in the interview room.

A break involving the suspect vacating the interview room must be recorded together with the reason for it and the time it was taken. The tape must then be removed from the machine and dealt with in the same manner as if the interview had been concluded (see below). A short break, in which both the suspect and the police officer remain in the room, must be recorded on the tape. The recorder may be switched off, but there is no need to remove the tapes. Recommencement should be recorded and the interviewing officer must ensure that the person being questioned is aware that he remains under caution. If there is a doubt, it must be renewed.

Equipment failure

In the event of failure of equipment which can be rectified quickly, e.g. by inserting new tapes, this must be done following the procedures laid down in relation to the changing of tapes. The officer must record the reason and the time the interview recommences. Where the further use of the tape recorder is impossible and no alternative is readily available, the interview may continue without being tape recorded. The authority of the custody officer must be obtained.

Interview conclusion

At the conclusion of an interview, including the taking and reading back of any written statement, the suspect must be offered the opportunity to clarify anything he has said and to add anything he wishes. The time must be recorded and the tape recorder switched off. The 'master tape' must then be sealed with a master tape label and treated as an exhibit. The police officer must sign the label and ask the suspect or any third party to sign it also. If either, or both, refuse to sign the label, an officer of at least the rank of inspector or, if one is not available, the custody officer, shall be called into the interview room and asked to sign it. In the case of enquiries linked to terrorism, an officer who signs the label shall use his warrant or other identification number. The suspect will be given a notice explaining the use which will be made of the tape recording and the arrangements for access to it.

Broken tape

If one of the tapes breaks during an interview, it should be sealed as a master tape in the presence of the suspect and the interview should be resumed where it left off. The unbroken tape should be copied and the original sealed in the usual way. If equipment for copying the unbroken tape is not readily available, both tapes must be sealed and the interview begun again. If a single-deck machine is being used and it is one on which a broken tape cannot be copied, the tape should be sealed in the usual way and the interview begun again.

Visual recording of interviews

Under the provisions of PACE, s 60A(1)(a), the Secretary of State has issued a Code of Practice for the visual recording of interviews held by police officers at police stations which came into force on 8 May 2002. The provisions of the Code apply experimentally for 12 months to police interviews at Basingstoke, Portsmouth, Southampton, Chatham, Gravesend, Tonbridge, Bromley, Colindale, Edmonton, Redditch, Telford and Worcester, Southend, Colchester and Harlow police stations. The application of the Code to further areas will be brought about by order.

Written records following interviews

The police officer must make a note in his notebook of the fact that the interview has taken place and has been recorded on tape, its time, duration and date and the identification number of the master tape.

Where no proceedings follow in respect of the person whose interview was recorded the tapes must nevertheless be kept securely in accordance with the Code.

Where proceedings follow, the officer must prepare a written record of the interview and sign it. Any such written record of a tape-recorded interview shall be made in accordance with national guidelines approved by the Secretary of State. The officer may refresh his memory by listening to the working copy of the tape to check its accuracy. The interview record shall be 'exhibited' to any written statement prepared by the officer. If the officer's evidence of the interview is accepted by the defence, the evidence shall refer to the fact that the evidence was tape recorded and may be presented to the court in the form of the interview record. However, acceptance of an agreed summary of a tape-recorded interview does not exclude the later admission of the tapes before a jury. An issue may arise which can only be resolved by admitting the full tapes in evidence. Where such evidence is not so accepted, the officer must refer to and produce the master tape of the whole interview as an exhibit, informing the court of any transcription which has been made, of which he is aware.

An interview record enables the prosecutor to make informed decisions, is capable of use as an exhibit to an officer's witness statements and used pursuant to the Criminal Justice Act 1967, s 9, enables the prosecutor to comply with the rules of advance disclosure and, where the record is accepted by the defence, facilitates the conduct of the case by the prosecution, the defence and the court. Such a record must, therefore, comprise a balanced account of the interview including points in mitigation, and/or defence, made by the suspect. Where an admission is made, both the question and the answer containing the admission shall be recorded verbatim in the record. Matters considered to be prejudicial or inadmissible should be brought to the attention of the prosecutor by means of a covering report.

It must be stressed that the general rules concerning the giving of a caution apply in the case of tape-recorded interviews and the appropriate records of such cautions must be made.

Written records of interviews (non-tape-recorded)

Any written record (where such a procedure may be followed) must be made during the interview, unless in the investigating officer's view this would not be practicable or would interfere with the conduct of the interview. An accurate record must be made of each interview with a person suspected of an offence, whether or not the interview takes place at a police station. The record must state:

(a) the place of the interview;
(b) the time it begins and ends;
(c) details of breaks (including times); and
(d) the names of those present (subject to the provisions set out above in relation to terrorist offences);
(e) where legal advice is requested and interview proceeds without a solicitor, that fact,

and must be made and completed during the interview, unless this would not be practicable or would interfere with the conduct of the interview, and must constitute either a verbatim record of what has been said or, failing this, an account of the interview which adequately and accurately summarises it. Where it is not made during the interview it must be made as soon as practicable afterwards and the reason must be recorded. The record must be timed and signed by the maker.

Unless it is impracticable, the person interviewed must be given the opportunity to read the interview record and to sign it as correct or indicate the respects in which he considers it inaccurate. If the person concerned cannot read or refuses to read the record or sign it, the senior police officer present must read it over to him and ask him whether he would like to sign it as correct or to indicate the respects in which he considers it inaccurate. The police officer must then certify on the interview record itself what has occurred.

A written record should also be made of any comments made by a suspected person, including unsolicited comments which are outside the context of an interview but which might be relevant to the offence. Any such record must be timed and signed by the maker. Where practicable, the person must be given the opportunity to read the record and to sign it as correct or to indicate the respects in which he considers it inaccurate. Any refusal to sign shall be recorded. Where an appropriate adult or the person's solicitor is present during an interview, he should also be given the opportunity to read and sign the interview record (or any statement written down by a police officer).

Where a suspect agrees to read records of interviews and of other comments and to sign them as correct, he should be asked to endorse the record with words such as, 'I agree that this is a correct record of what was said', and add his signature. Where a suspect does not agree with the record, the officer should record the details of any disagreement and then ask the suspect to read these details and then sign them to the effect that they accurately reflect his disagreement. Any refusal to sign when asked to do so shall be recorded.

All entries in custody and written interview records (except those identifying the person to whom the record relates) must be timed and signed by the maker. Any refusal by a person to sign either a custody or interview record when asked to do so in accordance with the provisions of the Detention Code must itself be recorded.

Decision to charge – procedure

The Detention Code also provides that the interview or further interview of a person about an offence with which that person has not been charged or for which he has not been informed that he may be prosecuted must cease when:

(a) the officer in charge of the investigation is satisfied all the questions he considers relevant to obtaining accurate and reliable information about the offence have been put to the suspect; this includes allowing the suspect an opportunity to give an innocent explanation and asking questions to test whether the explanation is accurate and reliable, e.g. to clear up ambiguities or clarify what the suspect has said;

(b) the officer in charge of the investigation has taken account of any other available evidence; and

(c) the officer in charge of the investigation or, in the case of a detained suspect, the custody officer reasonably believes that there is sufficient evidence to provide a realistic prospect of conviction for that offence if the person was prosecuted for it.

However, this does not prevent officers in revenue cases or acting under the confiscation provisions of the Criminal Justice Act 1988 or the Drug Trafficking Act 1994 from inviting suspects to complete a formal question and answer record after the interview is concluded. The giving of a warning or the service of a notice of intended prosecution required by the Road Traffic Offenders Act 1988, s 1, does not amount to warning a detainee that he may be prosecuted for an offence and does not preclude further questioning in relation to that offence.

The requirements set out above replaced, in the revised Codes of Practice introduced in 2003, a previous requirement that, with narrow exceptions, questioning must cease as soon as it was believed that there was sufficient evidence to justify a prosecution, following criticism by the Court of Appeal that the previous requirements deprived an accused of the opportunity to make any comment or offer an explanation.

A subsequent finding that the initial arrest was unlawful does not invalidate the decision of a custody officer to hold a person in custody. When a person is detained in respect of more than one offence it is permissible to delay bringing him before a custody officer until these conditions are satisfied in respect of all offences. A person in detention must be cautioned when charged or informed that he may be prosecuted for an offence. If charged, he must also be given at that time, a written notice showing particulars of the offence with which he is charged and including the name of the officer in the case (in terrorist cases, the officer's warrant or other identification number instead), his police station, and the station's reference number for the case. So far as possible the particulars of the charge shall be stated in simple terms, but they shall also show the precise offence in law with which he is charged. Thus, for practical purposes, although the nature of the offence may be simply stated, there should be a reference to the section and the Act offended against or a clear statement of the common law requirement which is breached. The notice which is given to a suspect shall begin with the following words:

> You are charged with the offence(s) shown below. You do not have to say anything. But it may harm your defence if you do not mention now something which you later rely on in court. Anything you do say may be given in evidence.

Questions relating to an offence may not be put to a person after he has been charged with that offence, or informed that he may be prosecuted for it, unless they are necessary:

(a) to prevent or minimise harm or loss to some person or to the public; or
(b) to clear up ambiguity in a previous answer or statement; or
(c) where it is in the interests of justice that the person should have put to him and have an opportunity to comment upon any information concerning the offence which has come to light since he was charged or informed that he might be prosecuted.

However, before any such additional questions may be put, the person shall be warned that he does not have to say anything but that anything he does say may be given in evidence and reminded of his right to legal advice in accordance with the provisions of the Code.

Item (a) above is concerned with instances, for example, in which a person in detention may say prior to being charged, 'Yes, I broke into the High Street Electrical Stores and stole the property'. The prisoner has certainly caused the officer to decide that he is guilty of the offence and that he must be charged. However, there remains a duty to recover the stolen property to minimise the loss to the owner and the officer would, therefore, be entitled to ask, 'What did you do with the property?' In the case of (b) the prisoner may have referred to the name of a street without stating in which town, or a day of the week without clearly indicating which week of the year. This leads to ambiguity which can only be removed by further questioning. The purpose of (c) is to allow the prisoner an opportunity to comment upon further matters which had come to light since he was charged if it is in the interest of justice. Certain additional evidence may come into the hands of the prosecution and it may well be that it is in the prisoner's interests to have the nature of that evidence brought to his notice and perhaps, additionally, that he should have the opportunity to comment upon it. It may be that a subsequent search of premises in the occupation of the prisoner, has revealed the presence of stolen property. It is possible that the prisoner will be able to give some account for its presence which relieves him of responsibility.

If any such questions are put after charge, the questions and answers given shall be contemporaneously recorded in full on the forms provided and the record shall be signed by that person. If he refuses, it shall be signed by the interviewing officer and any third parties present. In the case of tape-recorded questions and answers, the procedural guide must be followed.

Interviews at police stations and procedural points

The interview itself

An interview is the questioning of a person regarding his involvement or suspected involvement in a criminal offence or offences which by virtue of the Code is required to be carried out under caution. Procedures undertaken under s 7 of the Road Traffic Act 1988 or the Transport and Works Act 1992 s 31 do not constitute interviews for the purpose of the Code.

It is easy to fall into the trap of believing that an interview is a 'continuing' activity. It is not. The Court of Appeal has held that even one question, in appropriate circumstances, can constitute an interview. Where a police officer observed a suspect drop a packet containing drugs on the way to the custody suite, the subsequent conversation consisting of two questions and answers was held to be an interview.

At the beginning of an interview carried out in a police station, the interviewing officer, after cautioning the suspect, shall put to him any significant statement or silence (see page 190) which occurred before his arrival at the police station, and ask him whether he confirms or denies that earlier statement or silence and whether he wishes to add anything. Thus, at the beginning of an interview in a police station, there is an opportunity to 'tidy up' any previous statements which may have been made before the formal interview takes place.

If a police officer wishes to interview, or conduct enquiries which require the presence of a detained person, the custody officer is responsible for deciding whether to deliver that detained person into the police officer's custody.

Following a decision to arrest a suspect, he must not be interviewed about the relevant offence except at a police station (or other authorised place of detention) unless the consequent delay would be likely:

(a) to lead to interference or harm to evidence connected with an offence or interference or physical harm to other persons; or

(b) to lead to the alerting of other persons suspected of having committed an offence but not yet arrested for it; or

(c) to hinder the recovery of property obtained in consequence of the commission of the offence.

Interviewing in any of these circumstances should cease once the relevant risk has been averted or the necessary questions have been put in order to avert that risk.

Immediately prior to the commencement or recommencement of any interview at a police station or other authorised place of detention, the interviewing officer should remind the suspect of his entitlement to free legal advice and that the interview can be delayed for him to obtain legal advice, unless the exceptions provided by the Code apply. It is the responsibility of the interviewing officer to ensure that all such reminders are noted in the interview record.

The Court of Appeal has recommended that if notes of an interview have, for any reason, not been shown to a suspect before the arrival of his solicitor, fairness both to the accused and to the police themselves requires that they be shown in the presence of his solicitor. If shown before the arrival of his solicitor, the solicitor should be informed of the facts when he arrives. If a court concludes that the police have acted less than fairly, the chances that the evidence of the conversation noted will be excluded will be increased considerably.

Where a solicitor is present at an interview, he may seek to intervene in order to seek clarification or to challenge an improper question, or the manner in which it is put, or to advise his client not to reply to particular questions, or if he wishes to give his client further legal advice.

The solicitor may only be required to leave an interview if his conduct prevents or unreasonably obstructs proper questions being put to the suspect or his responses being recorded. Examples of unacceptable conduct include answering questions on a suspect's behalf or providing written replies for him to quote.

No police officer may try to obtain answers to questions or to elicit a statement by the use of oppression or shall indicate, except in answer to a direct question, what action will be taken on the part of the police if the person being interviewed answers questions, makes a statement or refuses to do either. If the person asks the officer directly what action will be taken in the event of his answering questions, making a statement or refusing to do either, then the officer may inform the person what action the police propose to take in that event provided that the action is itself proper and warranted.

Conditions of detention

The Code demands, among other things in relation to welfare, that at least two light meals and one main meal must be offered within any period of 24 hours. Drinks must be provided at meal times and, on reasonable request, between meal times. Meals should be offered at recognised meal times, so far as possible. Whenever necessary, advice should be sought from the appropriate health-care professional (clinically qualified person working within the scope of his practice) on medical and dietary matters. As far as possible, meals provided must meet any special dietary needs or religious beliefs that a person may have; he may also have meals supplied by his family or friends at his own expense. However, especially in the case of a person detained under the Terrorism Act 2000, immigration detainees and others likely to be detained for an extended period, a custody officer is entitled to take account of the risk of items being concealed in any food or package and his responsibilities under food-handling arrangements.

The custody officer must determine whether a detainee may be in need of medical treatment, or requires an appropriate adult, assistance to check documentation or an interpreter, and must record his decision in these respects. He must make a risk assessment in relation to himself or custody staff which should include a PNC check. It may be necessary for him to consult others, e.g. the arresting officer or a health-care professional. Chief officers are required to ensure that a structured process is in place in this respect. The custody officer is responsible for implementing responses to such risks.

Detainees should be visited at least every hour. If no foreseeable risk was identified in a risk assessment, a sleeping detainee need not be awakened. A person suspected of being intoxicated through drink or drugs or whose level of consciousness causes concern must, subject to any clinical directions given by the appropriate health-care professional, be visited and roused at least every half hour. His condition must be assessed by entering the cell, calling his name and shaking him gently before asking his name and where he lives as well as where he thinks he is. He should be asked to open his eyes and to lift his arms successively. The visitor must be aware of the possibility of illness, injury or the existence of a mental condition. A drowsy person who smells of drink may have diabetes, epilepsy, a head injury or drug intoxication, may have overdosed or may have suffered a stroke. Visits or rousing of detained persons made in accordance with the Detention Code or in accordance with medical advice do not amount to an interruption to a rest period such that a fresh period must be allowed. Nothing in the Code prevents the police from calling a police surgeon or appropriate health-care professional for the purpose of obtaining evidence relating to an offence.

A custody officer must ensure that a detainee receives appropriate clinical attention if that person appears to be suffering from any illness, injury or mental disorder. If a detainee requests a clinical examination an appropriate health-care professional must be called. If an appropriate care plan cannot be produced, a police surgeon must be called. This should not delay a transfer for the purpose of an assessment under the Mental Health Act 1983, s 136.

If a person is required to take or apply any medication in compliance with medical directions, but prescribed before his detention, the custody officer should consult the appropriate health-care professional prior to the use of the medication. No police officer may administer any controlled drugs subject to the Misuse of Drugs Regulations 2001, Schedule 1, 2 or 3. A person may administer controlled drugs to himself under the supervision of the registered medical practitioner authorising their use. Drugs listed in Schedule 4 or 5 may be distributed by the custody officer for self-administration if the authorising medical practitioner has been consulted. This may be done by telephone. Where a person has in his possession or claims to need medication relating to a heart condition, diabetes, epilepsy or a comparable condition, the advice of a police surgeon must be obtained.

A record must be made of the request for and the arrangements made for any examination by an appropriate health-care professional, of any complaint made and any relevant remarks, together with a record of any clinical attention received, together with a note of any injury, ailment or condition causing such arrangements to be made. A note should be made of any responses made when attempting to arouse a detainee. This could prove to be interesting in the case of drunks! If a health-care professional makes a record outside the custody record, a note should be made of where the record is kept. A note must be made of all medication in the possession of a detainee. Records should include the opinions of health-care professionals concerning risks or problems.

A person who appears to be drunk may be ill or suffering from the effects of drugs. Care must be taken and an officer should err on the side of caution when in doubt about calling a health-care professional.

A detained person may be dependent upon drugs, including alcohol, and may be suffering harmful effects. A health-care professional should be consulted or an ambulance called in such cases. A record must be made of any intoxicating liquor supplied.

Complaints concerning treatment

If a complaint is made by or on behalf of a detained person about his treatment since his arrest, or it comes to the notice of any officer that he may have been treated improperly, a report must be made as soon as practicable to an officer of the rank of inspector (or above) who is not connected with the investigation. If the matter concerns a possible assault or the unnecessary or unreasonable use of force, the appropriate health-care professional must also be called and a record must be made of the arrangements made.

The Police Reform Act 2002, s 51, requires police authorities to make arrangements for detainees to be visited by persons appointed (independent custody visitors). The arrangements may provide for right of access to police stations, examination of records, meetings with detainees and the inspection of facilities. Access to a detainee may be denied if it appears to an officer of or above the rank of inspector that there are grounds for doing so at the time, those grounds being specified within the arrangements and the procedural requirements imposed in relation to denial of access. The Secretary of State may issue a Code of Practice.

Nature of records and security of tapes

An accurate record must be made of all interviews, whether or not they take place at a police station. If this record is for any reason not made during the course of an interview, it must be made as soon as practicable after its completion and the reason for non-completion of the record during the interview must be recorded in the pocket notebook.

These records must state the place of the interview, the time it begins and ends, the time the record is made (if different), any breaks in the interview and the names of all those present (subject to the provisions set out above in relation to terrorist offences) and must be made on the forms provided for this purpose or in the officer's pocket notebook or in accordance with the Code of Practice on Tape Recording.

The security of master tapes is the responsibility of the officer in charge of each police station. Seals must not be broken on master tapes required for criminal proceedings, unless done in the presence of a representative of the Crown Prosecution Service. The defendant, or his legal adviser, shall be informed and shall be given a reasonable opportunity to be present. If either is present, he shall be invited to reseal and sign the master tape. If not present, or in the event of refusal, this will be done by the representative of the Crown Prosecution Service. If master tapes have been delivered to the Crown Court following committal, application must be made to the chief clerk of the Crown Court for the release of the tape for unsealing by the Crown Prosecutor.

Written interview records must be timed and signed by the maker. Any refusal by a person to sign an interview record when asked to do so in accordance with the provisions of the Code must itself be recorded.

Oppression and unreliability

It is important to remember that a constable must not at any time try to obtain answers to questions or to elicit a statement from a person by oppression. Regardless of disciplinary issues, the Police and Criminal Evidence Act 1984, s 76, states that statements obtained by oppression, or in consequence of anything said or done which was likely, in the circumstances existing at the time, to render unreliable any confession which might be made, shall be excluded by the court. If a prisoner is promised that if he is willing to give evidence against another he will not be prosecuted and is subsequently prosecuted, admissions made by him in consequence of that promise will not be admissible as they were gained by an inducement.

Where an accused was charged with theft in circumstances in which other offences may be discovered if other probable victims were interviewed, it was oppressive to threaten that such enquiries would be pursued in the absence of a confession, and any such confession must be excluded.

The inadmissibility of an original confession does not necessarily mean that any subsequent confession will be inadmissible. However, it is not sufficient that the second interview was conducted by a different police officer and that a caution was given. In such a case the suspect must have received appropriate legal advice between the first and second interviews.

The Court of Appeal has directed that 'oppression' should be given its ordinary dictionary meaning. It denotes the exercise of power or authority in a burdensome, harsh or wrongful manner, or unjust or cruel treatment, or the imposition of unreasonable or unjust burdens, in circumstances which would almost always entail some impropriety on the part of the interrogator. Recent decisions of the High Court in relation to the meaning of 'oppression' indicate a strong need for care in this respect. Confessions have been excluded even where conducted under independent, expert supervision but where forceful, repetitious questioning has taken place.

Section 76 also provides that a court may exclude a confession which was obtained in consequence of anything said or done which was likely, in the circumstances existing at the time, to render that confession unreliable. However, when considering whether a confession is unreliable because of the absence of an appropriate adult at an interview with a person who was mentally retarded, a court should hear evidence as to who was present at the interview and what had occurred during that interview. The Divisional Court has held that justices are not entitled to exclude relevant evidence, and evidence of what happened at an interview is relevant to the issue of admissibility.

Whether or not a drug addict is fit to be interviewed, in the sense that his answers could be relied upon in the circumstances, is a matter for those present at the time. Where experienced police officers considered a person fit to be interviewed and a doctor who saw him after the interview was of the same opinion, there was no reason to believe that a confession was unreliable.

It is frequently claimed that a confession or admission is unreliable because the person concerned is of low IQ. Expert evidence may be admitted only where it is alleged that a defendant was suffering from a personality disorder so severe as to be categorised as mental disorder. It may not be admitted to show that a defendant is of dull intelligence and very suggestible.

At the end of any interview with a detained person, the interviewing officer must inform the custody officer that the Code of Practice has been complied with.

If evidence of a fact is discovered as a result of a confession and that confession, or a relevant part of it, is subsequently excluded under s 76, evidence of that fact may nevertheless be offered by the prosecution. However, no reference should be made to the fact that the discovery was made as a result of the confession.

Tape recordings in evidence

A tape recording of a police interview with a defendant is primary evidence which, when produced at a trial, becomes an exhibit. If the jury wish to hear it rather than rely upon a transcript, there is no reason why they should not be allowed to do so. It should be listened to in open court.

Written statements under caution

All written statements made at police stations after caution must be written on the forms provided for the purpose and be taken in accordance with the rules in Annex D to the Detention Code. Before a person makes a written statement under caution at a police station, he must be reminded about the right to legal advice.

Written by a person under caution

A person shall always be invited to write down himself what he wants to say.

A person *who has not been charged with, or informed that he may be prosecuted for, any offence* to which the statement will relate, must *unless the statement is made at a time when the restrictions on drawing adverse inferences from silence applies*, be asked to write out and sign the following before writing what he wants to say:

> I make this statement of my own free will. I understand that I need not say anything but that it may harm my defence if I do not mention when questioned something which I later rely on in court. This statement may be given in evidence.

If the statement is *made at a time when the restriction on drawing adverse inferences from silence applies*, he must be asked to write out and sign the following before writing what he wants to say:

> I make this statement of my own free will. I understand that I do not have to say anything. This statement may be given in evidence.

When a person, on the occasion of being charged with or informed that he may be prosecuted for any offence, asks to make a statement which relates to any such offence and wants to write it, he must, unless the restriction on drawing adverse inferences from silence applied when he was so charged or informed that he would be prosecuted, be asked to write out and sign the following before writing what he wants to say:

> I make this statement of my own free will. I understand that I do not have to say anything but that it may harm my defence if I do not mention when questioned something which I later rely on in court. This statement may be given in evidence.

If *the restriction on drawing adverse inferences from silence applied* when that person was so charged or informed that he would be prosecuted, he must be asked to write out and sign the following before writing what he wants to say:

> I make this statement of my own free will. I understand that I do not have to say anything. This statement may be given in evidence.

Where a person who has *already been charged with or informed that he may be prosecuted for an offence* asks to make a statement which relates to any such offence and wants to write it, he must be asked to write out and sign the following before writing what he wants to say:

> I make this statement of my own free will. I understand that I do not have to say anything. This statement may be given in evidence.

Any person writing his own statement shall be allowed to do so without any prompting, except that a police officer or civilian interviewer may indicate to him which matters are material or question any ambiguity in the statement.

Written by a police officer

If a person says that he would like someone to write it for him, a police officer or civilian interviewer shall write the statement. If the person *has not been charged* with, or informed that he may be prosecuted for, any offence to which the statement he wants to make relates, he shall, before starting, be asked to sign or make his mark, to the following endorsement *unless the statement is made at a time when the restriction on drawing adverse inferences from silence applies*:

> I ... wish to make a statement. I want someone to write down what I say. I understand that I do not have to say anything but that it may harm my defence if I do not mention when questioned something which I later rely on in court. This statement may be given in evidence.

If the statement is made at a time when the restriction on drawing adverse inferences from silence applies:

> I ... wish to make a statement. I want someone to write down what I say. This statement may be given in evidence.

If, on the occasion of *being charged with or informed that he may be prosecuted for any offence*, the person asks to make a statement which relates to any such offence, he shall before starting be asked to sign, or make his mark, to the following *unless the restriction on drawing adverse inferences from silence applied when he was so charged or informed that he may be prosecuted*:

> I ... wish to make a statement. I want someone to write down what I say. I understand that I do not have to say anything but that it may harm my defence if I do not mention when questioned something which I later rely on in court. This statement may be given in evidence.

If the restriction on drawing adverse inferences from silence applied when he was so charged or informed that he may be prosecuted:

> I ... wish to make a statement. I want someone to write down what I say. This statement may be given in evidence.

If, *having already been charged with or informed that he may be prosecuted for any offence*, a person asks to make a statement which relates to such an offence, he shall before starting, be asked to sign or make his mark to:

> I … wish to make a statement. I want someone to write down what I say. This statement may be given in evidence.

Where a police officer writes the statement, he must take down the exact words spoken by the person making it and he must not edit or paraphrase it. Any questions that are necessary (e.g. to make it more intelligible) and the answers given must be recorded contemporaneously on the statement form.

When the writing of a statement by a police officer is finished the person making it shall be asked to read it and to make any corrections, alterations or additions he wishes. When he has finished reading it he shall be asked to write and sign or make his mark on the following certificate at the end of the statement:

> I have read the above statement, and I have been able to correct, alter or add anything I wish. This statement is true. I have made it of my own free will.

If the person making the statement cannot read, or refuses to read it, or to write the above-mentioned certificate at the end of it or to sign it, the senior police officer present shall read it over to him and ask him whether he would like to correct, alter or add anything and put his signature or make his mark at the end. The police officer shall then certify on the statement itself what has occurred.

Summary

A statement must begin with a declaration to the effect that the person wishes to make a statement. The Code requires that, where police officers write the statement, they must record the exact words said by that person and that they must not edit or paraphrase those words. However, for this latter provision, a shortened statement including only the words which a police officer considered to be important could still contain the exact words used, but perhaps not all of them. Provisions are made concerning alterations, corrections and signatures and that (in the event of an inability to read) *the senior officer present* shall read it over and deal with such matters. That officer must then certify on the statement what he has done.

Remember that the golden rule is that *where a detainee has asked for legal advice and has not received it*, the caution, whether verbal or written, will always be in the *shortened form*, omitting any reference to a silence possibly harming a later defence. *Immediately that legal advice is received, all previous cautions become redundant and the detainee must be cautioned in the fuller form*, indicating that silence may, in certain circumstances, harm a later defence.

General guidance – written statements made by alleged offenders

(a) All statements under caution should be written in ink on the statement form provided.
(b) An offender must be given the opportunity to write his own statement.
(c) If an offender dictates his statement, use only his words; do not edit or paraphrase.
(d) Do not leave spaces in the statement and avoid the use of paragraphs as this necessitates the leaving of spaces and admits the possibility of later allegations of words being inserted.

(e) Corrections should involve words being neatly crossed out, a single line being placed through the word, the correction being initialled by the person making the statement.

(f) The statement should be signed by the person making it at the bottom of each page.

(g) The purpose of an interview is to obtain from the person concerned his explanation of the facts, and not necessarily to obtain an admission.

Drug testing

Experimental work in relation to drug testing is currently being undertaken in the police areas of Staffordshire, Nottinghamshire the Metropolitan Police District, Bedfordshire, Devon and Cornwall, Lancashire, Merseyside, South Yorkshire, North Wales, Avon and Somerset, Greater Manchester, Thames Valley, West Yorkshire, Cleveland and Humber. Within those areas the Police and Criminal Evidence Act 1984 (Codes of Practice) (Modification) Order 2002 operates. The Order permits the taking of urine or non-intimate samples from someone who appears to be an adult for the purpose of ascertaining whether he has any *specified* Class A drug in his body where he has been charged:

(a) with a 'trigger offence' (theft, robbery, burglary, aggravated burglary, taking a motor vehicle or other conveyance without authority, aggravated vehicle-taking, obtaining property by deception, going equipped for stealing, etc., and under the Misuse of Drugs Act 1971 if committed in respect of a Class A drug associated with producing and supplying a controlled drug, possessing a controlled drug, possessing a controlled drug with intent to supply), or

(b) with any offence where an officer of the rank of inspector or above, who has reasonable grounds for suspecting that the misuse by that person of any specified Class A drug caused or contributed to the offence, has authorised such a sample to be taken.

Any samples so taken may not be used for identification purposes.

The specified Class A drugs are cocaine and diamorphine (heroin), their salts and any preparation or other product containing cocaine or diamorphine or its salts.

A request for a sample must be preceded by an explanation of its purpose (to ascertain whether there is a specified Class A drug in his body), that failure without good cause to provide such a sample may make the person requested liable to prosecution and, where authorised under (b) above, the grounds for giving the authorisation. In addition, the person requested must be reminded of his right to have someone informed of his arrest, of his right to consult privately with a solicitor, of the availability free of charge of independent legal advice and of the right to consult the relevant code of practice. Where a sample is taken following authorisation by an inspector (or above), the authorisation and the grounds for suspicion must be recorded in the custody records. Details of authorisations and the giving of warnings must be recorded, together with the time of charge and the time at which a sample was given. The Order suggests that when warning a person who is asked to provide a urine or non-intimate sample in these circumstances, the following form of words might be used:

> You do not have to provide a sample, but I must warn you that if you fail or refuse without good cause to do so, you will commit an offence for which you may be imprisoned, or fined, or both.

Custody officers may authorise continued detention for up to 6 hours from the time of charge to enable a sample to be taken.

The persons who may take such samples are prescribed by Order. They are a police officer, a person employed by a police authority for that purpose or an employee of a contractor under the terms of the contract with a police authority.

Statements by co-accused

If, after these procedures have been carried out, a police officer wishes to tell a detainee about any written statement or interview with another person relating to the offence, the detainee must be handed a true copy of the written statement or the content of the interview record. Nothing must be done to invite a reply or comment except to caution the detainee that he does not have to say anything, but anything he does say may be given in evidence and to remind him of his right to legal advice. If the detainee cannot read, the document may be read to him. In relevant cases, the appropriate adult must be given a copy of the document or it must be brought to his attention.

These provisions prevent verbal information being given to a person in detention concerning matters which are alleged to have been said by a co-accused who is also in detention. If such matters are to be brought to the attention of a prisoner, he must be shown and allowed to read the written record.

Persons at risk

A juvenile or someone who is mentally disordered or mentally vulnerable, whether suspected of crime or not, must not be interviewed in the absence of the 'appropriate adult' with the exception of the circumstances set out below, nor may he be asked to give or sign a written statement.

The 'appropriate adult' for the purpose of all Codes of Practice is:

(a) in the case of a juvenile, his parent or guardian or,
(b) if the juvenile is in local authority or voluntary organisation care, or is otherwise being looked after under the Children Act 1989, a person representing that authority or organisation, a social worker of a local authority social services department or, failing these, some other responsible adult aged 18 or over who is not a police officer or employed by the police.

A person, including a parent or guardian of a juvenile, should not be the appropriate adult if he is suspected of involvement in the offence in question, is the victim, is a witness, is involved in the investigation or has received admissions prior to attending to act as the appropriate adult. If a parent or guardian of a juvenile is estranged from the juvenile, he should not be asked to be the appropriate adult if the juvenile expressly and specifically objects to his presence.

If a juvenile admits an offence to or in the presence of a social worker other than during the time the social worker is acting as the appropriate adult for that juvenile, another social worker shall be the appropriate adult in the interests of fairness; and
(c) in the case of a person who is mentally disordered or mentally vulnerable, a relative, guardian or other person responsible for his care or custody, someone who has experience of dealing with mentally disordered or mentally vulnerable people who is not a police officer or employed by the police or, failing either of the above, some other responsible adult, aged 18 or over, who is not a police officer or employed by the police.

It may, in some cases, be more satisfactory if the appropriate adult is someone who has experience or training in the case rather than a relative lacking those qualifications. However, if the person himself prefers a relative to a better qualified stranger, his wishes should, if practicable, be respected.

A solicitor, or independent custody visitor who is present at the police station in a professional capacity, may not act as the appropriate adult.

Where a suspect is mentally vulnerable and is interviewed without such a person being present, the issue is not whether the confession obtained is true and can be relied upon; once it has been established that there has been a breach of the code of practice, the prosecution must prove beyond reasonable doubt that the confession was not obtained in breach of the Police and Criminal Evidence Act 1984, s 76(2), and the 'circumstances existing at the time' are all important in relation to reliability. If the absence of an appropriate adult was likely to result in a confession being unreliable, the confession should be excluded.

The only exceptions to the general rule that interviews may not be conducted in the absence of the 'appropriate adult' are when the need to carry out the interview is urgent and such an interview is authorised by a superintendent. Such instances will be rare.

These provisions do not prevent a police officer from asking questions at the scene of a crime to elicit an explanation which could provide an arrested person an opportunity to show that he was innocent. If, in the course of such questions, the suspect, even if a juvenile, made a confession, it is prima facie admissible even though no adult was present provided that no advantage was taken of that fact. For example, if a juvenile was seen attempting to gain entry to a residence in suspicious circumstances, it would be proper for a police officer to ask why, and if he knew anyone who lived there. If he replies that he does not, it would be equally proper to offer a further chance to explain his actions by asking why he was attempting to gain entry. A reply of, 'Just to have a look around', leads naturally to a question such as, 'For what?' However, such questions must not go beyond that necessary to provide such a suspect with a reasonable opportunity to provide an *immediate* explanation at the scene.

Interviews – juveniles

Juveniles may only be interviewed at their place of education in exceptional circumstances and then only when the principal or his nominee agrees. Every effort must be made to contact both the parent(s) or other person responsible for the juvenile's welfare and the appropriate adult (if a different person) and a reasonable time should be allowed to enable the appropriate adult to attend. Where this would cause undue delay and unless the offence is against the educational establishment, the principal or his nominee can act as the appropriate adult for the purposes of the interview. It is preferable that a juvenile is not arrested at his place of education unless this is unavoidable. In that case, the principal or his nominee must be informed.

Detention of juveniles following charge

The Police and Criminal Evidence Act 1984, s 38, requires that an arrested juvenile who is not released from custody after charge should be taken to local authority accommodation unless the custody officer certifies:

(a) that by reason of such circumstances as are specified in the certificate, it is impracticable to do so; or

(b) in the case of an arrested juvenile aged 12 or over that no secure accommodation is available and that keeping him in other local authority accommodation would not be adequate to protect the public from serious harm from that juvenile.

'Secure accommodation' is that provided for the purpose of restricting liberty. In the case of arrested juveniles who are charged with a violent or sexual offence, references to protecting the public from serious harm shall be construed as references to protection from death or serious bodily injury, whether physical or psychological, occasioned by further such offences.

The term 'sexual offence' in this context means an offence under the Sexual Offences Act 1956 (other than living on immoral earnings, a woman exercising control over a prostitute or offences connected with brothels); an offence under the Mental Health Act 1959, s 128 (sexual intercourse with patients); the Indecency with Children Act 1960; an offence under the Theft Act 1968, s 9, of burglary with intent to rape; an offence under the Criminal Law Act 1977, s 54 (inciting incest with girl under 16); the Protection of Children Act 1978 (indecent photographs); or a conspiracy or attempt to commit any of these offences or inciting such an offence.

A 'violent offence' is an offence which leads, or is intended or likely to lead, to a person's death or to physical injury to a person, and includes an offence which is required to be charged as arson (whether or not it would otherwise fall within this definition).

However, except for these circumstances, neither a juvenile's behaviour nor the nature of the offence with which he is charged provides grounds for the custody officer to retain him in police custody rather than to seek to arrange for his transfer to the care of the local authority on the grounds of impracticability. Similarly, the lack of secure local authority accommodation shall not make it impracticable for the custody officer to transfer him. The availability of secure accommodation is only a factor in relation to the whole issue. The obligation to transfer a juvenile to local authority accommodation applies as much to a juvenile charged during the daytime as it does to a juvenile to be held overnight, subject to a requirement to bring the juvenile before a court under s 46 of the Police and Criminal Evidence Act 1984.

Notes for guidance

All of these special groups may be particularly open to suggestion. Consequently, special care should always be exercised in questioning such a person, and it is important to obtain corroboration of any facts admitted wherever possible.

Foreign languages, the deaf and the blind

The Detention Code provides:

(a) If a person has difficulty in understanding English, the interviewing officer cannot himself speak the person's own language or the person wishes an interpreter to be present, he must not be interviewed in the absence of an adult capable of acting as an interpreter, unless the urgent situation exists as described below.

(b) The interviewing officer must ensure that the interpreter makes a note of the interview at the time, in the language of the person being interviewed, for use in the event of his being called to give evidence and that he certifies its accuracy. The interviewer should allow sufficient time for the interpreter to note each question and answer after each is put, given and interpreted. The person should be allowed to read the record or have it read to him and sign it as correct, or indicate the respects in which he considers it inaccurate. If the interview is tape recorded or visually recorded, the provisions of the respective codes apply.

(c) In the case of a person making a statement in a language other than English:
   (i) the interpreter must take down the statement in the language in which it is made;
   (ii) the person making the statement must be invited to sign the statement; and
   (iii) an official English translation must be made in due course.

The provisions merely follow the rules of common sense. It would be unrealistic to record a statement in a language which the person who was making the statement could not read. The Community Relations Council can supply a list of interpreters. If a person is deaf or there is a doubt about his hearing ability, he must not be interviewed in the absence of an interpreter unless he agrees in writing to be interviewed without one, or it is an 'urgent interview' as described above. An interpreter should also be called if a juvenile is interviewed and the parent or guardian present as the appropriate adult is deaf, unless he agrees in writing that the interview should proceed without one. The interviewing officer must ensure that the interpreter is given the chance to read the record of the interview and to certify its accuracy in the event of being called to give evidence. The person must be given an opportunity to read it and sign it as correct or indicate the respects in which he considers it inaccurate. Where an interview is being tape recorded and the suspect is deaf, or there is a doubt about his hearing ability, the police officer shall take a contemporaneous note of the interview in addition to tape recording it.

The Code directs that if a person appears to be blind or seriously visually impaired, deaf, unable to read or communicate orally with the officer dealing with him at the time, he should be treated as such for the purpose of the Code in the absence of clear evidence to the contrary.

If a person is blind or seriously visually impaired or is unable to read, the custody officer should ensure that his solicitor, relative, the appropriate adult or some other person likely to take an interest in him is available to help in any documentation. Where the Code requires consent or signification, then this person who is assisting may be asked to sign instead.

Where a person in detention cannot communicate with a solicitor, whether because of language or hearing difficulties, an interpreter must be called.

Interpreters should be provided at public expense and this must be made clear to the person concerned. The interpreter may not be a police officer when the interpretation is needed for the purpose of obtaining legal advice. In other cases a police officer may interpret if the detained person (or the appropriate adult) agrees in writing. The appropriate adult should not be the interpreter. If such an interview is tape recorded the appropriate rules must be followed.

Records are, once again, important. The action taken to call an interpreter must be recorded, together with any waiver of a right not to be interviewed in the absence of an interpreter. It must be remembered that as the interpreter will be required as a witness at the person's trial, a second interpreter will be needed to assist at the trial.

Urgent interviews

The Detention Code is concerned with urgent interviews of particularly vulnerable people in exceptional circumstances. It overrides the usual bar upon interviews taking place in the absence of the 'appropriate adult'. If, and only if, an officer of the rank of superintendent (or above) considers that delay will lead to interference with or harm to evidence connected with an offence, interference with or physical harm to other people, or serious loss of or damage to property, or lead to alerting other people suspected of committing an offence but not yet arrested for it, or hinder the recovery of property obtained in consequence of the commission of an offence, may such an interview take place. Interviewing in any of these circumstances must cease once the relevant risk has been averted or the necessary questions have been put in order to attempt to avert that risk.

A mentally disordered or mentally vulnerable person might be interviewed in the absence of the appropriate adult where it is suspected that she had stolen a child and was suspected of having abandoned that child in circumstances which involved risk to the life of the child. In such circumstances the primary aim of all concerned would be to find the child and a superintendent would, undoubtedly, authorise questioning to begin at once.

Questioning in these circumstances must not continue once sufficient evidence has been obtained to avert the immediate risk. In the example given above, this would occur when the location of the child had been discovered. At that point questioning would have to cease until the arrival of the 'appropriate adult'. A record must be made of the grounds for any decision to interview a person in the above circumstances.

In any circumstances in which such a 'person at risk' has been cautioned and interviewed prior to the attendance of the appropriate adult, then the caution must be repeated in the adult's presence upon arrival (unless the interview has by then finished).

The Detention Code also permits such urgent interviews of persons heavily under the influence of drink or drugs, or persons who have difficulty in understanding English or those with a hearing disability.

Access to solicitor

By s 58 of the Police and Criminal Evidence Act 1984, a person arrested and held in police custody is entitled, if he so requests, to consult a solicitor privately at any time; the consultation may be in person, in writing or by telephone. Where a suspect chooses to speak to a solicitor by telephone he should be allowed to do so in private unless this is impractical because of the design and layout of the custody area or the location of the telephones. If a person makes such a request he must be permitted to consult a solicitor as soon as practicable, and the custody officer must act without delay to secure the provision of such legal advice.

The European Court of Human Rights has held that a detained person has a right [arising from its interpretation of art. 6(3)(c) of the European Convention on Human Rights (page 685)] to communicate with his solicitor, etc., out of hearing of a third party unless there is good cause for restricting the right. If the detained person is not permitted to have private communication without good cause and this prejudices his defence and his chance to a fair hearing in court, there will be a breach of the Convention.

'Solicitor' means a solicitor who holds a current practising certificate, a trainee solicitor, a duty solicitor representative or an accredited representative included on the register of representatives maintained by the Legal Services Commission. If a solicitor wishes to send a non-accredited or probationary representative to provide advice on his behalf, then that person shall be admitted to the police station for this purpose unless an officer of the rank of inspector or above considers that such a visit will hinder the investigation of crime and directs otherwise. Hindering the investigation of crime does not include giving proper legal advice to a detained person in accordance with the Code.

In exercising his discretion, the officer should take into account in particular whether the identity and the status of the non-accredited or probationary representative have been satisfactorily established, whether he is of suitable character to provide legal advice (a person with a criminal record is unlikely to be suitable unless the conviction was for a minor offence and is not of recent date) and any other matter in any written letter of authorisation provided by the solicitor concerned. However, the Court of Appeal has held that a chief constable is not entitled to make a blanket order banning a particular probationary solicitor's representative from all police stations in his area. He may advise his officers that a particular representative is likely to hinder an investigation but the officer dealing with the case must decide whether, in the particular circumstances, the representative should be excluded.

No police officer shall at any time do or say anything with the intention of dissuading a person in detention from obtaining legal advice. Whenever legal advice is requested (unless delay is authorised) a custody officer must, without delay, secure the provision of such advice. If, on being informed of this right, a person declines to speak to a solicitor in person, the officer shall point out that the right to legal advice includes the right to speak to a solicitor on the telephone and ask him if he wishes to do so. If the person continues to waive his right, the officer shall ask him his reasons for doing so, and any reasons shall be recorded on the custody record, or interview record. Once it is clear that a person does not wish to speak to a solicitor either in person or by telephone, he should cease to be asked his reasons. He is not obliged to give such reasons.

A person who asks for legal advice should be given an opportunity to consult a specific solicitor, or another solicitor from that firm, or the duty solicitor. If advice is not available by these means, or he does not wish to consult the duty solicitor, he should be allowed to choose from a list. If his choice is unavailable, he may choose up to two alternatives. The custody officer has discretion to allow two further attempts. A police officer must not advise the suspect about any particular firm of solicitors. Delay is permissible, but only if the person is in police detention for a serious arrestable offence and an officer of the *rank of inspector or above authorises the delay.*

An arrested person must be informed of this right and must be given a notice to this effect. A record must be made of such matters in the custody records and the person should be asked to sign it. If video cameras are installed in the custody area, notices which indicate that cameras are in use should be prominently displayed. Any request by any person to have such cameras switched off will be refused.

Where the right to legal advice has been exercised, an interview may not be started or continued until such advice has been received unless special circumstances exist. A superintendent (or above) must decide whether such special circumstances exist.

However, where a person who wanted legal advice changes his mind, the interview may be started or continued without further delay, provided that the person concerned has given his agreement in writing or on tape to being interviewed without receiving legal advice and an officer of the rank of inspector or above, having enquired into the suspect's reasons for his change of mind, has given approval for the interview to proceed. Confirmation of the person's agreement, his change of mind, his reasons where given and the name of the authorising officer shall be recorded in the taped or written interview record, at the beginning or recommencement of interview. The authorisation may be given over the telephone if the authorising officer satisfies himself as to the reason for the change of mind.

Inform someone of arrest

The Police and Criminal Evidence Act 1984, s 56, provides that where a person has been arrested and is being held in custody at a police station or other premises, he shall be entitled, if he so requests, to have one friend or relative or other person who is known to him or is likely to take an interest in his welfare told, as soon as practicable, that he has been arrested and is being detained there. Where a person so chosen cannot be contacted, the person being detained can make up to two alternative choices. In the event of it being impossible to contact either of them, the person in charge of his detention or of the investigation has discretion to allow further attempts until the information has been conveyed. Where delay is authorised, that delay may not be authorised beyond 36 hours after his arrest.

In addition, where an enquiry as to the whereabouts of the person is made by such persons, this information shall be given if the person detained agrees and delay has not been authorised.

Delay is permitted where the person concerned is in police detention for a serious arrestable offence and has not been charged with it and an officer of at least the rank of inspector authorises that delay. He may only do so where he has reasonable grounds for believing that the exercise of the right will lead to interference with or harm to evidence connected with a serious arrestable offence or interference with or physical injury to other persons, or will lead to the alerting of other persons suspected of having committed such an offence but not yet arrested for it or will hinder the recovery of property obtained as a result of such an offence. The code of practice also extends the right of delay to drug trafficking offences (where proceeds of those crimes may be confiscated) and offences to which the Criminal Justice Act 1988, Part VI, applies (confiscation orders), where disclosure may prevent the recovery of the proceeds of such crimes.

In addition, the Children and Young Persons Act 1933, s 34, requires that where a child or young person is in police detention, his parent or guardian must be informed as soon as practicable that he has been arrested and of where he is being detained. The Detention Code requires that if a court order is in force under which a person or organisation is given any degree of statutory responsibility, reasonable steps must be taken to notify that person or organisation (the responsible officer), who will normally be a member of a youth offending team, except for a curfew order which involves electronic monitoring when the contractor providing the monitoring will normally be the responsible officer. If he is in care, the care authority or voluntary organisation must be informed in place of the parent or guardian.

Visits, letters and telephone calls

Generally, a person so detained shall be supplied with writing materials on request and allowed to speak on the telephone for a reasonable time to one person. However, where an officer of the rank of inspector or above considers that the sending of a letter or the making of a telephone call might result in the circumstances which are described in connection with the authorisation of a delay and the offence concerned is a serious arrestable offence, for which purpose any reference to a serious arrestable offence in Annex B (dealing with delay) includes an arrestable offence, or is one under the Terrorism Act 2000 and may lead to similar consequences, the exercise of the privilege can be delayed or denied.

Before letters are sent, or telephone calls are made, the person detained must be told that what he says in the letter or call or message (other than in the case of a communication to a solicitor) may be read or listened to as appropriate and may be given in evidence. Such a telephone call may be terminated if it is being abused.

Records must be kept of such requests which are made and the action which is taken in consequence of them.

Road checks

Statutory powers for road checks

The conduct of road checks is governed by the Police and Criminal Evidence Act 1984, s 4. They may be conducted for the purpose of finding out whether a vehicle is carrying:

(a) a person who has committed an offence other than a road traffic offence or a vehicle excise offence;
(b) a person who is a witness to such an offence;
(c) a person intending to commit such an offence; or
(d) a person unlawfully at large.

A 'road check' consists of the exercise in a locality of the power conferred by the Road Traffic Act 1988, s 163 (power of a constable to stop a mechanically propelled vehicle or pedal cycle on a road), in such a way as to stop all vehicles or vehicles selected by any criterion. They are therefore concerned with the apprehension of actual or intending criminals or escaped prisoners. The purpose of a road check is to stop all vehicles or all vehicles of a particular type if it is selective. If the person being sought is known to be in a particular model and colour of motor vehicle, it may be that only vehicles of that description will be stopped. However, the circumstances may be such that that person will have had ample opportunity to change vehicles and, in such a case, all vehicles will be stopped.

The powers given to a police officer to deal with traffic matters in the ordinary course of his duties are unaffected by this legislation. A constable may stop as many vehicles as he wishes if he has reason to do so under powers granted by the Road Traffic Acts. The 1984 Act is concerned with what might be described as 'road blocks'.

Authorisation of road checks

A road check must be authorised in writing by an officer of the rank of superintendent or above. Such authorisation may only be given:

(a) if the commission of an offence, or the intention to commit an offence, is involved, the officer must have reasonable grounds for believing that the offence is a serious arrestable offence and for suspecting that the person is, or is about to be, in the locality of the proposed check;
(b) if it is to trace a witness to an offence, the officer must have reasonable grounds for believing that the offence is a serious arrestable offence; and
(c) if it is to arrest a person who is unlawfully at large, the officer must have reasonable grounds for suspecting that the person is, or is about to be, in that locality.

The term 'serious arrestable offence' is defined. The offences are treason, murder, manslaughter, rape, kidnapping, incest with a girl under 13, buggery with a person under 16, an indecent assault which constitutes an act of gross indecency, causing an explosion likely to endanger life or property (Explosive Substances Act 1883, s 2), intercourse with a girl under 13 (Sexual Offences Act 1956, s 5), possession of a firearm with intent to endanger life or use to resist arrest or carrying a firearm with criminal intent (Firearms Act 1968, ss 16, 17 and 18), hostage-taking (Taking of Hostages Act 1982, s 1), hijacking (Aviation Security Act 1982, s 1), torture (Criminal

Justice Act 1988), causing death by dangerous driving and by careless driving when under the influence of drink or drugs (Road Traffic Act 1988, ss 1 and 3A), endangering safety at aerodromes, hijacking of ships and seizing or exercising control of fixed platforms (Aviation and Maritime Security Act 1990), indecent photographs and pseudo-photographs of children (Protection of Children Act 1978) and publication of obscene matter (Obscene Publications Act 1959). In addition, s 116 of the 1984 Act provides that any offence specified in para. 1 of Schedule 2 to the Proceeds of Crime Act 2002, or any offence under s 327, 328 or 329 of that Act (certain money laundering offences), is a serious arrestable offence.

By s 116 of the 1984 Act, any other arrestable offence is serious *only if its commission has led to, or is intended to lead to*:

(a) serious harm to the security of the State or to public order;
(b) serious interference with the administration of justice or with the investigation of offences or of a particular offence;
(c) the death of any person;
(d) serious injury to any person;
(e) substantial financial gain to any person; and
(f) serious financial loss to any person.

'Loss' is serious for the purposes of the section if, having regard to all the circumstances, it is serious for the person who suffers it. Thus, the life savings of a pensioner, although this may not be a large sum of money in a general sense, may represent the difference between 'subsistence' and 'meaningful existence' to such a person. A much larger sum would be less important to a wealthy person and may not represent a serious financial loss.

If any other *arrestable offence* consists of making a threat, it is 'serious' if the consequences of carrying out the threat would be likely to lead to one of the consequences set out above in (a) to (f).

Emergency authorisation

In an emergency situation in which there is insufficient time to obtain the authorisation of a superintendent, authorisation may be given by an officer below the rank of superintendent. Where this has been done, the officer who gives such emergency authorisation must, as soon as practicable:

(a) make a written record of the time of the authorisation; and
(b) cause a superintendent (or above) to be informed.

In such a case, the superintendent (or above) may then authorise, in writing, the road check to continue. Should he decide that it should not continue, he must record the fact that it took place, and its purpose (including the relevant serious arrestable offence).

Time limits for road checks

The maximum period for which a road check may be authorised is 7 days. However, written authorisation may be given for a further period not exceeding 7 days if a superintendent (or above) believes that a road check ought to continue.

There may be limitations in respect of the periods of a day in which such a check may be carried out, or no limitations may apply in the circumstances.

Records

A written authorisation will show:

(a) the period during which the road check is authorised to continue;
(b) the name of the officer who authorised it;
(c) the purpose of the road check (including any relevant serious arrestable offence); and
(d) the locality in which vehicles are to be stopped.

Persons in charge of vehicles which are stopped at a road check are entitled to obtain a written statement of the purpose of the road check if they apply for such a statement within 12 months of the road check. The notice need only contain information concerning the purpose of the road check.

Searches

Whilst the 1984 Act does not give a constable power to search vehicles which are stopped at a road check, the power exists to do so:

(a) if he has reasonable grounds for suspecting that it contains stolen or prohibited articles (s 1); or
(b) for the purpose of arresting someone for an arrestable offence if he has reasonable grounds to suspect that the person is there (s 17); or
(c) under powers granted by any other statute, e.g. the Firearms Act 1968.

Common law powers

It is submitted that s 4 of the 1984 Act does not affect the previously existing common law powers to set up road blocks which are related to apprehended breaches of the peace. If there is an *immediate threat of a breach of the peace*, the Divisional Court has ruled that if the police, on reasonable grounds, believe that a breach of the peace may be committed, the police officer is not only entitled but under a duty to take reasonable steps to prevent the breach occurring. Provided that they honestly and reasonably form the opinion that there is *a real risk of a breach of the peace in the sense that it is in close proximity in both time and place*, then the conditions exist for reasonable preventive action. The possibility of a breach must be real to justify preventive action. The imminence or immediacy of the threat to the peace determines what action is reasonable.

If a vehicle is stopped under this power an officer is also entitled to search it. A person in such a vehicle who insists on continuing his journey may be arrested under common law powers to prevent the apprehended breach of the peace.

This is not to say that where there is sufficient time in such circumstances a check should not be authorised under the provisions of s 4, but the circumstances existing at the time may not necessarily fall within the parameters of such a check.

Safe custody of prisoners

Preliminary search after arrest

A constable has power to search a person at the time of his arrest for an offence. Section 32 of the Police and Criminal Evidence Act 1984 states:

> A constable may search an arrested person in any case where the person to be searched has been arrested at a place other than a police station, if the constable has reasonable grounds for believing that the arrested person may present a danger to himself or others.

The inclusion of the words 'place other than a police station' recognises that any such search which was carried out in a police station would become the responsibility of the custody officer. The description of these powers extends to:

(a) the *search* of an arrested person for anything which he might use to assist him to escape from lawful custody, or which might be evidence relating to an offence; and
(b) *entry* and *search* of any premises in which he was when arrested or immediately before he was arrested for evidence relating to the offence for which he has been arrested.

These powers only extend to that which is reasonably required for the purpose of discovering any such thing or any such evidence and do not authorise the removal of clothing in a public place other than an outer coat, jacket or gloves. A constable must have reasonable grounds for believing, in the circumstances set out in (a), that the person may have concealed on him anything for which a search is permitted in those circumstances. The section is concerned with the search of an arrested person. It was held that the police acted beyond their powers under this section when they demanded the car keys of a person arrested for burglary. The keys did not relate to an offence of burglary. The same suspicion must exist in relation to the searching of premises as in (b). There must be reasonable grounds for believing that there is evidence to be found.

Thus a person may be searched 'on the spot' at the time of his arrest. Such a power is essential. The prisoner may be in possession of dangerous weapons or articles which may be used to injure the constable in order to effect an escape from custody. If a person who is arrested pulls out a knife and it is taken from him by a constable, the officer must have reason to believe that he may have some other concealed weapon and such a person must be searched. He has shown a will to escape and a willingness to use any article which might assist him. If that person has been arrested for a series of thefts it is probable that, on the way to the police station, he will attempt to dispose of any articles in his possession taken in the course of those thefts. If he is suspected of being in possession of such articles, he should be searched 'on the spot' to the extent necessary, but not further than that allowed by s 32, to take possession of such articles.

If an arrest is effected upon premises, similar considerations must apply. As a police officer approaches a building to arrest a person who is in it, it is certain that such person will quickly conceal any property associated with the commission of a crime. The position will not alter if the person to be arrested leaves the building immediately before the officer arrives at the door. He has been in that building and it is probable that the property or article will have been concealed within it. The section empowers a constable to enter and to search such premises to any reasonable extent, necessary for the discovery of such articles. If a search is being conducted for stolen television sets, a search of desk drawers would be outside these powers. In the case of searches of premises the powers are limited to searches for evidence of the offence 'for which he has been arrested' under the terms of s 32.

Some buildings will be found to be in 'communal occupation'. Bedsitters, hotels, etc., are such buildings. Where there are two or more separate dwellings the search must be limited to the premises in which the arrest took place, or in which the arrested person was immediately before his arrest, and any parts which are shared with the other occupants of the building. These would include common dining rooms, lounge, even shared kitchen facilities, but would not include the rooms of other occupants, unless the person arrested was known to have been in the room of one of the other occupiers immediately prior to his arrest. This could occur where a thief sees the approach of the officer and rushes into his neighbour's room and asks him to conceal property for him. If the officer knows this, he may search that other room also.

Constables exercising these powers may seize and retain anything which they find (other than an article subject to legal privilege), if they have reasonable grounds for believing:

(a) that it may be used to cause physical injury to the arrested person or to another; or
(b) that he might use it to assist him to escape from lawful custody; or
(c) that it is evidence of an offence or has been obtained in consequence of the commission of an offence.

The important factor in relation to the exercise of these powers is that the process should be reasonable. A man who is arrested for indecent assault who is known to be of a non-violent nature would not necessarily be searched 'on the spot'. There can be no evidence of the offence available and he is known to be non-violent.

Although a search may be carried out in the first instance to discover stolen property, the power set out in (c) above would allow the seizure of articles relating to other offences which were accidentally discovered during the course of that search. The extension of the power to things 'obtained in consequence of the commission of an offence' means that property obtained from the disposition of stolen goods, etc., may also be seized.

All searches must be carried out as soon as practicable and, as far as possible, out of the public view. The prime responsibilities of a constable when carrying out a preliminary search are to ensure that the prisoner does not escape during the process of that search, the preservation of evidence and his own protection and the protection of any other persons who may be present.

The extended powers of seizure under s 51 of the Criminal Justice and Police Act 2001 (where articles cannot be separated) apply to searches under s 32 of PACE.

Transport of a prisoner

All persons who are arrested should be taken to a police station as soon as possible. Section 30 of the Police and Criminal Evidence Act 1984 requires that the police station to which such a person is taken shall be a designated police station. There are special circumstances in which a prisoner may be taken to a police station other than a designated police station.

Where it is necessary to use a motor vehicle to transport a prisoner to a police station, the arresting officer should be accompanied by a driver. If escape is to be prevented and the possibility of harm eliminated, this is essential. However, it is recognised that certain non-violent criminals are 'picked up' by police officers on occasions when it is recognised that strict measures need not be taken. Where a prisoner is seated in a motor vehicle he should occupy a rear seat with the arresting officer alongside him. The prisoner should not be placed directly behind the driver. It is essential that a prisoner is carefully watched at all times while he is being transported to a police station. If given the opportunity he will dispose of all incriminating articles while on the journey. For these reasons, the vehicles must be thoroughly searched at the conclusion of the journey. Property is often concealed under the rear seat. It must be remembered that even though property may be discovered at this stage, the fact that the prisoner was allowed to dispose of it gives him the opportunity to allege that it was there as a result of another prisoner having been in the vehicle, or that it was planted by the police.

Arrival at the police station

The arresting officer, upon arrival at the police station, must report immediately with his prisoner to the custody officer. The custody officer will be at least of the rank of sergeant and he is responsible, in every respect, for the detention of persons in that police station. The arresting officer must satisfy the custody officer that there were grounds for making the arrest and that the arrest was correctly effected under existing powers. The custody officer should note on the detention record any comment made by the detained person in relation to the arresting officer's 'account' but should not invite comment. If the custody officer authorises his detention he must tell him why as soon as practicable and in any case before that person is questioned about any offence. The custody officer shall note any comment the person may make in respect of the decision to detain him but shall not invite comment. The custody officer must not put specific questions to the person regarding his involvement or in respect of comments made in response to the arresting officer's account, or the decision to place him in detention. Such an exchange is likely to constitute an interview.

Whilst a custody officer is required by the Code to deal with such a person as soon as it is practicable, the Code provides that a custody officer shall not be in breach in the event of delay provided that it is justifiable and all reasonable steps have been taken. This may occur where large numbers of suspects are brought to a police station simultaneously, or where all interview rooms are being used or solicitors are awaited.

The custody officer must tell such a person that he has:

(a) the right to have someone informed of his arrest;
(b) the right to consult privately with a solicitor and the fact that independent legal advice is available free of charge; and
(c) the right to consult the Codes of Practice.

He must also give such a person a written notice setting out such rights, the arrangements for obtaining legal advice, the right to a copy of the custody record, the caution and given an additional notice setting out his entitlements while in custody. Receipt, or refusal, must be noted on the custody record.

A custody officer is responsible for all persons in detention and for ensuring that they are properly treated in accordance with the Codes of Practice. He is also responsible for maintaining a chronological and contemporaneous record of every aspect of a person's treatment while in custody.

There are occasions upon which officers other than specially appointed custody officers will have to assume the duties of such an officer. As this will always be for a short period, it means that most of the complexities of such an officer's duties do not need to be fully studied by all officers, but recognition of the general principles of 'correct detention' is essential. In these circumstances, any officer at that police station may be called upon to carry out the duties of a custody officer during the brief detention of such a prisoner, or until he is transferred to a designated police station. Such an officer will be required to maintain the record of the prisoner's detention on the 'custody records' held in police stations. The Officer who carries out these duties should not be involved in the investigation of the offence.

In an emergency, where no other officer is available, the arresting officer is authorised to carry out these duties. In all circumstances in which an officer is required to perform the duties of a custody officer at a non-designated police station, such officer must inform an officer of at least the rank of inspector, at a designated police station, that he is doing so, as soon as it is practicable to do so. The officer will then act under the directions of such senior officer. The provisions of the Detention Code, which apply to a custody officer, apply to an officer who is performing the function of a custody officer.

Detention in police cells

When persons are confined in police cells, no additional restraints should be used within a locked cell unless absolutely necessary, and then only approved restraint equipment which is reasonable and necessary in the circumstances having regard to the detainee's demeanour and with a view to ensuring his safety and the safety of others. If the detainee is deaf, mentally disordered or otherwise mentally vulnerable, particular care must be taken when deciding whether to use any form of approved restraints.

Theft

The law relating to theft has generally followed the pattern of our society. At common law it was divided into petty larceny, the stealing of property not exceeding 12d in value, and grand larceny if the value was in excess of that figure. The Larceny Acts of 1861 and 1916 varied the offence and the punishment in accordance with the degree of aggravation and having regard to whether or not the person who committed the offence was in a position of trust, or if particular forms of property were involved.

The Theft Act 1968 repealed previous legislation and set out to deal with all forms of theft in a simplified manner.

Section 1 of the Theft Act 1968 provides:

A person is guilty of theft if he dishonestly appropriates property belonging to another with the intention of permanently depriving the other of it; and 'thief' and 'steal' shall be construed accordingly.

For there to be a theft it is not essential that the appropriation of property is made with a view to gain, or is made for the thief's own benefit. The person who appropriates a motor car and burns it, steals the car when he indicates his intention to deprive the owner permanently of his property by destroying it.

To be guilty of an offence of theft two main elements are necessary:

(a) the appropriation of property belonging to another (the *actus reus* of the offence); and
(b) the dishonest intention of permanently depriving the owner of his property (the *mens rea* of the offence).

Dishonesty

Whether or not an action was carried out dishonestly is a question of fact for a jury to decide.

Section 2 of the Act attempts to establish the dishonesty of the intention of the person who steals by describing circumstances in which there is no dishonest intention. A person's appropriation of property belonging to another is not to be regarded as dishonest:

(a) if he appropriates the property in the belief that he has in law the right to deprive the other of it, on behalf of himself or a third person; or
(b) if he appropriates the property in the belief that he would have the other's consent if the other knew of the appropriation and the circumstances of it; or
(c) (except where the property came to him as a trustee or personal representative) if he appropriates the property in the belief that the person to whom the property belongs cannot be discovered by taking reasonable steps.

A person's appropriation of property belonging to another may be dishonest notwithstanding that he is willing to pay for the property.

It will be helpful to consider each of these circumstances in greater detail.

Belief in lawful right to deprive

There is no dishonest intention if the act is done by someone in the belief that he has a legal right to do it. It is perhaps immaterial whether the belief is reasonable or not, or that there exists no basis in law for such a belief, if the person concerned honestly believed that he had a right. For practical purposes, the less reasonable a belief appears to be, the less likely it is that a court will accept it. Although the Act refers to a right in law, it does not necessarily imply that belief in a moral right will be sufficient to negate an allegation that an act is done dishonestly. Much will depend upon the nature of such belief, otherwise theft committed by anarchist organisations, the members of which believe that they have a moral right to finance their political activities with the money of other people, would become excusable.

Money is often taken by persons who have possession of it, but do not own it, with the intention of replacing it at some later date. Such persons may be employed as collectors and may use some of the money acquired on behalf of their employers in an emergency. It could be argued that this was not 'dishonest', if they knew with certainty that they could replace the money almost at once. This may occur if they used some of it on a Saturday while the banks were closed, knowing that they had more than sufficient in their account to replace it on Monday morning, but it certainly would be dishonest if the money was taken in circumstances in which it was not possible for them to replace it, or they merely enjoyed a vague hope that it would be possible, such as may occur if they had made a bet on the result of a horse race, which if successful would give them sufficient money to repay. A sound definition of dishonesty in such circumstances is: 'Does the person intend to act to the detriment of the owner against his wishes?'

Belief that the owner would have consented

A similar defence was provided to charges of taking motor vehicles without the consent of the owner or other lawful authority under a repealed section of the Road Traffic Act 1960. This defence was provided to protect persons who had a special relationship with the owner of such a vehicle who, on finding the owner absent on calling to borrow his motor car, may nevertheless take it in the knowledge that consent would be given. The taking of motor vehicles and other conveyances is now dealt with under the Theft Act 1968, and the former defence to such charges available under the Road Traffic Act 1960 has been included in that Act. However, having been included as a general defence to a charge of theft on the grounds that such an act would not be dishonest, it would apply in all circumstances and would equally apply if such a person removed an alarm clock in the absence of the owner, knowing that the property would have been handed over had the owner been present. In most circumstances of this nature, the taker would leave a note explaining what he had done, but on occasion reports of such thefts are received from the owner of the property, to be followed by a further report that a relative had since telephoned to inform him that he had removed the property in his absence.

Belief that the owner cannot be discovered by taking reasonable steps

The common law has always recognised the right of possession of property by the finder against all but the true owner or any other person having special rights in relation to such property. These rights have been preserved within the Theft Act 1968. Whether an owner is likely to be able to be traced is largely a question of fact. If a man finds £10 note on the footpath in a busy shopping area he may be considered to be acting reasonably if he assumes that the owner cannot be traced. Although the property can be identified by its serial number, very few people are aware of the numbers of bank notes in their possession at any time. If, on the other hand, the £10 note was in a wallet which also contained a business card, a banker's card, or some other means by which the owner could be traced, the finder is clearly guilty of theft if he uses the money for his own purposes. The nature of the property, coupled with the circumstances of the finding, determines the form of steps which would have to be taken in order to attempt to trace an owner. In the case of the single £10 note, little less than an extensive advertising campaign would have much hope of success, and this goes well beyond the term 'reasonable', whereas in the circumstances in which the bank note was contained in a wallet with some other personal, identifiable articles, a limited action would be sufficient to trace the owner and such action would certainly be within the term 'reasonable'. The question really turns upon the belief of the finder.

However, this defence is not limited to circumstances in which property if found. A person may be asked to take care of property for some other person who is subsequently not heard of for many years. In such circumstances, if he converts the property to his own use or even disposes of it for cash, the question of whether or not his act was 'dishonest' will have to be considered. If he believed that the owner could not be traced by taking reasonable steps, this defence will be open to him. In the circumstances in which he disposed of the property for cash, the owner of the property will have a claim upon it, but his belief that he could not be traced by taking reasonable steps is a defence to be considered in relation to a charge of theft.

Where the taker is willing to pay

Section 2(2), by stating that a person's appropriation of another's property may be dishonest notwithstanding that he is willing to pay for it, resolves the situation concerning whether or not an act can be dishonest when full payment is made for goods which are taken. Such protection is necessary, otherwise rare, valuable property could be taken from collectors by persons willing to pay the market value. Payment for goods taken can be a mitigating factor to be considered by the court when considering the sentence to be passed. However, this subsection does say that such an action 'may' be dishonest and we must differentiate between the man who takes a newspaper from an unattended news stand and leaves payment, where he obviously believes that the owner would welcome such a sale, and the man who, being disappointed at not being able to purchase a rare painting, removes it from the owner's house and leaves payment. In the first instance there was no dishonest intention but in the second there clearly is an intention to act dishonestly against the interests of the owner.

Dishonesty in a general sense

However, the Act merely describes particular acts which will not be dishonest. In a general sense, it is a matter for the justices or the jury to decide whether or not a particular act was carried out dishonestly. In deciding such an issue, they must consider whether or not a person's actions were dishonest according to the ordinary standards of reasonable and honest people.

If an employee in a grocery store takes provisions without paying for them, knowing that his employer would not consent, but claims that he intended to put the money in the till on the following day when he received his pay, he could not claim a belief in law that he had a right to take the provisions, or that he believed that he would have the owner's consent if he knew of the appropriation. However, he could claim that, in the circumstances, he did not believe that what he was doing was dishonest and it will be for the prosecution to show that he did not intend to pay. The magistrates or jury must then decide whether his actions were 'dishonest' in the light of evidence offered by the prosecution.

Appropriates

In considering the term 'dishonestly' we have looked at the guilty state of the person's mind or *mens rea*, but in considering the term 'appropriates' we are concerned with the guilty act, or *actus reus*.

Section 3(1) of the Theft Act 1968 defines appropriation as follows:

> Any assumption by a person of the rights of an owner amounts to an appropriation, and this includes where he has come by the property (innocently or not) without stealing it, any later assumption of a right
> to it by keeping or dealing with it as owner.

Previous to the Theft Act 1968, an intention to deprive the owner permanently had to exist at the time of taking the property, but s 3(1) now makes it clear that an appropriation can take place at any time, even if the property was acquired innocently in the first place. In most instances of theft reported to the police, the appropriation will have amounted to a straightforward removal of the property from the possession of the owner – for example, the stealing of a radio from a motor car, the removal of a wallet from a pocket or the taking of a bottle of milk from a doorstep.

Circumstances in which a later appropriation would amount to theft might involve a person handing over his radio to an acquaintance who, at that time, intended to repair it for him, but later decides to sell it and spend the money. The appropriation takes place at the time such person assumes the rights of the owner by disposing of the property. In determining when an appropriation has taken place, it is helpful to ask yourself the question, 'When did the accused first assume the rights of an owner?' This is not necessarily when property is sold or disposed of in circumstances in which original receipt of the goods was innocent. If, in the example given above, the accused had advertised the radio for sale, the offering of the goods for sale clearly indicates an assumption of the rights of an owner, and an offence of theft is complete. A mental decision to keep or dispose of the property will not normally be sufficient as there will be no '*actus reus*'; the accused must in some way, by his *actions*, indicate an appropriation of the property.

Similarly, where a man hands over a sum of money to a second party who is to invest it on his behalf, the money continues to be the property of the owner as the second party is merely acting as his agent. If the second party later uses the money for his own purposes, he appropriates it at that time as he then assumes ownership rights.

A lorry driver is to deliver 100 toy train sets to a customer. On delivering his load he finds that there are five sets too many and decides to keep them. He then drives to his home and leaves the train sets there. In the first instance he came into possession of the surplus sets innocently, as he was unaware that his vehicle had been overloaded and on discovering the mistake, decided to keep them. When he begins to drive them to his home, he assumes the rights of an owner and appropriates the property. In another example, a workman on a building site knows that he is due approximately £100 as his weekly pay, but is given a pay packet containing £160. He realises that the money is not his, but later spends it. Once again the appropriation takes place not at the moment at which he decides to keep the money, but immediately that he assumes ownership rights by putting the money to use.

This special type of appropriation where property is received initially due to another's mistake, but in circumstances in which that person is under an obligation to make restoration, is covered specifically by s 5(4) of the Act, which provides that the property shall be regarded as still belonging to the person who made that mistake. It can, therefore, be appropriated by the recipient.

When a man struck a woman causing her to drop her handbag, it was ruled that he was trying to exclude the woman from her possession of the bag and had, therefore, appropriated it, this being an unlawful assumption of the right of the owner.

An appropriation may take place through an innocent agent. If a person in authority signs a false invoice, intending that innocent people take further steps which result in money being debited, and thus appropriated from a bank account, he is guilty of theft.

There may be an appropriation by deception where the goods are obtained in circumstances in which the consent which is obtained could not be described as a valid consent. Where a man obtained his shop manager's consent to release goods to another party by alleging that he had checked the validity of cheques which he knew to be stolen, it was held that he had appropriated the goods. Similarly, where a taxi driver took money from the wallet of a foreign visitor, in addition to the £1 which was offered in payment for a fare which was less than £1, he was held to have appropriated that money although no objection to its removal had been offered by the person concerned. The common factor within both of these cases is that neither of the injured parties would have consented to the taking had they known of the true circumstances of that taking. However, in such circumstances the persons concerned would also commit an offence of obtaining property by deception and that is the charge which would usually be preferred. Deception is considered at page 242.

Where a person removes goods from a shelf in a supermarket and conceals them in his coat pocket to avoid having to pay for them, he clearly appropriates property as this amounts to an adverse interference with, or usurpation of, the rights of the owner (an unlawful act or *actus reus*). However, where an honest shopper takes goods from a shelf and puts them in a shopping trolley provided by the owner of the supermarket, there is no such interference or usurpation as this is an act which is authorised by the owner and is therefore not unlawful. If a person removes an article from a shelf and switches the price label for one indicating a lesser price and this is done with the intention of depriving the owner of a part of the true price of his goods, there is an appropriation with the required dishonest intent. A practical joker who switches labels for fun would not steal because he did not appropriate those articles and, in any case, had no dishonest intent.

Similarly, if a shop assistant sells goods to a friend at a price which is less than that fixed by the owner, she steals that property although she was in lawful possession of it at the outset, as what she does amounts to an assumption of the rights of an owner to fix the price at which goods should be sold.

The definition of the term 'appropriation' is such that a person who does not steal at the outset may steal in consequence of some later action. If a person 'borrows' a raincoat from a coat stand in a public house because it is raining, intending to return it on the following evening, he does not steal at that time as he does not intend to deprive the owner permanently of his property. If he later sells the coat, he appropriates it dishonestly at that time, as he has assumed an ownership right; the right of disposal.

Section 3(2) of the Act is designed to protect the purchaser who innocently buys goods in good faith, paying full value, only to discover later that the seller had no title to the goods which still belonged to another person. It provides:

> Where property or a right or interest in property is or purports to be transferred for value to a person acting in good faith, no later assumption by him of rights which he believed himself to be acquiring shall, by reason of any defect in the transferor's title, amount to theft of the property.

In the normal circumstances in which such a transaction may occur, the facts will be straightforward. A man may buy a watch from a market trader, paying full value for it, and it is later found that it is one of a consignment stolen at an entry port. This subsection protects him fully if he assumes the rights of an owner, thus 'appropriating' the property, as the act of appropriation in such circumstances is declared not to be contrary to the law. It is important to realise that this is so regardless of the mental state of the person concerned, which in normal circumstances will be innocent enough, as most people would feel that having paid a fair price they had a good claim to ownership; but even if the person who had come into innocent possession of the property, on discovering that it was the property of some other person, continued to use it as an owner or even gave it away, he is not guilty of an offence of theft. If such a person sold the goods after discovering that they had been stolen, he may be found guilty of obtaining money by deception, the deception being that he pretends to be the true owner of the property.

The original receipt of property must be innocent in every sense of the word before the protection of s 3(2) is valid. Property is frequently purchased in circumstances in which the buyer must have realised that it was stolen. Currently there is considerable illegal traffic in stolen home entertainment equipment and purchasers who receive such equipment at much reduced prices must be fully aware that there is some question as to title. However, where a man buys motor cycle parts for value and issues a receipt, but later suspects that such parts are stolen when he discovers that engine numbers have been removed, there can be no theft if he decides to keep them. Although such an act is clearly an appropriation, s 3(2) prevents it from being theft.

Appropriation can be by act or omission, and acts of appropriation have already been discussed. An example of appropriation by omission is provided by the following circumstances. A child under the age of criminal responsibility brings home a pedal cycle which does not belong to him. The child commits no offence as it is conclusively presumed that he cannot commit crime. The child's father knows that the cycle must be stolen but does nothing about it, being content to allow his child to keep it, and, therefore, assumes ownership rights through the innocent agency of the child.

Property

Section 4(1) describes what is meant by the term 'property':

> 'Property' includes money and all other property, real or personal, including things in action and other intangible property.

This definition deals with forms of property which we might describe as the tangible and the intangible, or perhaps the things we can hold in our hands and the things which we cannot hold. Money requires no further description, and the terms 'real or personal' property may include articles, things, houses or estates or may be used to indicate the owner's rights over that article or estate. Things 'personal' are usually moveable, whereas those 'real' are not. 'Things in action' are intangibles. They include a debt, a copyright or a trademark in respect of which a person has ownership rights which may be dishonestly assumed by another person.

When a person has money in a bank account, the bank acknowledges that it owes that person a debt (the extent of the current balance). If a person dishonestly draws a cheque on that account, he steals from it as he has appropriated a part of the bank's debt to that person. It will be appreciated that in such circumstances, the drawer of the cheque could not steal money belonging to the holder of the bank account, as the money in the cashier's till which would be handed over, does not belong to the holder of the account. The debt is a 'thing in action'.

Land and things forming part of the land

Subsection (2) provides:

> A person cannot steal land, or things forming part of land and severed from it by him or by his directions, except:
>
> (a) when he is a trustee or personal representative, or is authorised by power of attorney, or as a liquidator of a company, or otherwise to sell or dispose of land belonging to another, and he appropriates the land or anything forming part of it by dealing with it in breach of the confidence reposed in him; or
> (b) when he is not in possession of the land and appropriates anything forming part of the land by severing it or causing it to be severed, or after it has been severed; or
> (c) when, being in possession of the land under a tenancy, he appropriates the whole of part of any fixture or structure let to be used with the land.

The subsection begins with a general statement to the effect that a person cannot steal land, or things which he detaches from it, or causes to be detached, and then gives various exceptions to the rule which cover many possibilities. Thus, a person who moves his boundary fence in order to enclose land belonging to a neighbour does not steal that land. Other remedies are open to him.

In the first instance this section deals with persons put in a position of trust in relation to land, who deal with it wrongfully by selling it or otherwise disposing of it in breach of the confidence placed in them. It may be, for example, that a firm of solicitors is authorised to act as agents on behalf of the owner in relation to the administration of an estate, and may be permitted to deal with tenancies and to appoint estate officers on behalf of the land owner. If a member of the firm sells sections of the land, or in any other way assumes rights of ownership, he is guilty of theft.

Second, it is concerned with people other than persons who are in possession of, or have a special responsibility for, the land. Such persons may steal fixtures, things growing or even the land itself, provided that they sever them first. Examples would be the unauthorised removal of gravel from a pit, the cutting of hay and its immediate removal from the land, the removal of stones fixed into land such as marker stones indicating the borders between England, Wales and Scotland, which are occasionally dug up and removed by nationalist organisations. It will be noticed that both severance and the assumption of ownership rights are essential before an offence of theft is committed.

Finally, the subsection is concerned with persons who are in possession of land as tenants, and who are, therefore, in a position of trust. If the tenancy includes the right to use buildings and fixtures which are situated on the land, use and occupation of the building is permitted, but the removal of such buildings or fixtures would amount to the assumption of the rights of the owner and would make the tenant liable to prosecution for an offence of theft.

Things growing wild

Subsection (3) provides protection for persons who pick mushrooms, blackberries, elderberries or any other wild produce of the field or hedgerow. The protection of this subsection does not apply if the gathering of such wild produce is done for some commercial purpose, and one can appreciate the law makers excepting the casual hollypicker who requires one or two sprigs of holly to decorate his house at Christmas, but wishing to punish the trader who strips the hedgerows in order to make a big profit. The subsection provides:

> A person who picks mushrooms growing wild on any land, or who picks flowers, fruit or foliage from a plant growing wild on any land, does not (although not in possession of the land) steal what he picks, unless he does it for reward or for sale or other commercial purpose.

This subsection is interesting: by permitting only the picking of flowers, fruit or foliage, the removal of the plant by the roots is still prohibited. Such actions would, in any case, offend against the Wildlife and Countryside Act 1981, s 13, in the case of 'protected plants'. The term 'picking' is clear; it permits the normal actions of the country rambler who wishes to pick flowers or berries, but would not be wide enough to permit someone to saw off the top of a Christmas tree. As Christmas approaches many police forces organise special patrols to prevent thefts of poultry, Christmas trees and holly by thieves looking for a readily saleable commodity. Certain vehicles are checked as they leave the rural districts of counties and drivers are asked to provide documentary evidence to show that any poultry, trees or large quantities of holly found in their vehicle have been purchased from recognised sources.

Wild animals

Finally, subsection (4) explains the law of theft in relation to wild animals. The common law always differentiated between tame and wild animals, and the position in relation to tame or domestic animals has always been clear; they are the property of some person and, therefore, may be stolen. In contrast, wild animals have no owner and being free to roam from place to place are not generally the subject of theft at common law. The Poaching Prevention Act and Game Laws have the effect of making the killing and taking of such animals offences in many cases, and the Theft Act 1968 continues to recognise that such offences exist and it is, therefore, unnecessary to make the taking of wild animals punishable as theft:

> Wild creatures, tamed or untamed, shall be regarded as property; but a person cannot steal a wild creature not tamed nor ordinarily kept in captivity, or the carcass of any

such creature, unless either it has been reduced into possession by or on behalf of another person and possession of it has not since been lost or abandoned, or another person is in the course of reducing it into possession.

The meaning of this subsection is clear: wild creatures cannot, in normal circumstances, be stolen, but let us consider instances in which birds or animals, which are wild by nature, may be stolen. Hawks and falcons are wild birds but are occasionally trained in captivity. Where this is so, they are capable of being stolen because they are ordinarily kept in captivity. The carcasses of wild birds or animals may be taken into the possession of particular persons. This could occur if a land owner had been shooting over his land and stored dead pheasants and partridges in his shed. When they have been reduced into the possession of an individual or individuals in circumstances such as these, the birds may be stolen from the shed by some other party. The same would apply if the birds had been taken by a poacher; they are capable of being stolen from the poacher as they have been reduced into his possession.

The reference to possession having since been lost or abandoned can refer to wild creatures which have been temporarily in captivity (but which are not ordinarily kept in captivity) and subsequently escape. A poacher may have driven games birds into a trap and in this way have reduced them into his possession, but if they are subsequently released or escaped they return to their wild state and are incapable of being stolen.

Special provisions in relation to deer

The Deer Act 1991 creates specific offences of entering upon land without the consent of the owner or occupier or other lawful authority, in search or pursuit of a deer with the intention of taking, killing or injuring it. There are further offences of taking, killing or injuring, searching for or pursuing with such intention, or removing the carcass of any deer, once again without consent of the owner, etc. If a constable suspects with reasonable cause that any person is committing or has committed any of these offences, the constable may without warrant stop and search, search or examine vehicles, animals, weapons or other things and arrest that person, if he fails to give his name and address to the constable's satisfaction (as required by s 25 Police and Criminal Evidence Act 1985) and seize or detain evidence of such offences. To exercise these powers a constable may enter any land other than a dwelling house.

The Deer Act replaces previous offences included in Schedule 1, Theft Act 1968.

Special provisions in relation to fish

Schedule 1 of the Theft Act 1968 deals with fish. It distinguishes between fish which are in a wild state and those which can almost be proved to have been reduced into possession. It is an offence for anyone unlawfully to take or destroy, or attempt to take or destroy, any fish in water which is private property and in respect of which there is a private right of fishing. It is probable that in either of these circumstances the water concerned has been stocked by the owner or those persons who have been granted the rights of fishing.

The penalties for such offences vary, taking into account a previous conviction and whether the offence was committed during the day or by night. Night is defined as the period beginning 1 hour after sunset and ending 1 hour before sunrise. Although distinctions by way of penalties are unimportant to police officers, there is also a difference in police powers. A person committing such offences by night may be arrested by anyone who reasonably suspects him of committing the offence, but no such power applies during the day. Articles used in the taking or destruction of fish may be seized and a court may subsequently order their forfeiture. See page 157 in relation to the powers of a constable in such cases. Thus, Schedule 1 creates special offences in relation to private fisheries within waters which are 'open' to the extent that is possible for the fish concerned to leave those waters because they are not enclosed.

However, fish which are securely contained within a pond or pool are the property of the owner of that pond or pool, or the person who, with the consent of the owner of that pond or pool, put them there. Where such fish are unlawfully taken, the offence is one of theft under the main provisions of the Act, and is an arrestable offence.

Belonging to another

Before property can be stolen it must belong to another. Section 5(1) states:

> Property shall be regarded as belonging to any person having possession or control of it, or having in it any proprietary right or interest.

It appears at first sight that everything which we can imagine will be capable of being owned by someone, but the notable exception is a human corpse, which is not the property of any person and, therefore, cannot be stolen. For this reason, special legislation was introduced many years ago to deal with 'body snatching' for medical experimentation. However, there have been convictions in magistrates' courts for the theft of products of the human body such as hair and urine specimens. Where a body, or part of a body, has undergone a process or other application of human skill, such as embalming or dissecting, for teaching or exhibition purposes, it thereby becomes property for the purposes of the Act.

In considering all other property which is clearly capable of ownership, the problem is one of determining the 'owner' for the purposes of the Theft Act 1968, so that a correct charge may be preferred. If it is no one's property, then it cannot be stolen as the section requires that property 'belonging to another' is involved. Property which has been abandoned cannot be stolen. If a man is riding his pedal cycle home late at night and the tyre becomes punctured, he may leave it and walk home intending to return for it the following morning. The cycle can still be stolen as he intends to return for it and he has not abandoned it. It would be different if he threw the cycle into a field without the intention of returning for it, having made up his mind that it was of so little value that it was not worth reclaiming. To abandon property means that the owner had made up his mind that it is of no further use to him and he does not intend to exclude others from the use of his property. The owner of a coal mine does not necessarily abandon minerals which are thrown on to a tip; he may wish to exclude others from taking such minerals and has every right to do so.

Circumstances may be met in which property which appears to have been abandoned is in fact still owned by some person and, in such cases, if the taker of the property believes that it has been abandoned his appropriation of it will not be 'dishonest' and no charge of theft will lie.

The term 'belonging to another' includes persons who have rights of ownership or possession or control. This is necessarily so to protect persons who have special interest in property. If a man buys a watch for £30, there is no difficulty in establishing that he has possession of it and that he is the owner, but if he subsequently takes the watch to a repairer, the repairer has a special interest in it. The owner can in these circumstances steal his own watch from the repairer if he recovers it by stealth to avoid paying the repair bill. It may appear strange that when the owner always has a better right of possession of his property than any other person, he may be charged with stealing it, but this must be so in certain circumstances. The example outlined above is clear because the possession of the article was transferred to another person who had a special interest in it, but it is possible for an owner to retain possession, merely giving control to another person, and to steal the property from that person. A jewellery store owner may provide his managers with goods to be sold in their departments and, although retaining possession of all the goods in his store, in the same way as he retains possession of all the goods in his home, he gives 'control' to his manager. He may then steal the goods from his manager as the meaning of the term 'belonging to another' extends to persons having 'control'. It may be that the store owner, having made his managers responsible for the value of their stock, wishes to avoid payment of wages, or that he wishes subsequently to make a false claim upon an insurance company.

Section 5(3) provides that, where a person receives property from or on account of another and is under an *obligation* (i.e. a legal obligation) to the other to *retain* and *deal* with that property, or *its* proceeds, *in a particular way*, the property or proceeds shall be regarded as belonging to the other. Section 5(3) makes it clear that where a person has received property in accordance with its terms, that property or its proceeds (i.e. things into which it has been converted) is regarded as belonging to another for the purposes of theft, even though ownership, possession and control of the property may have been transferred to the recipient.

Section 5(3) is clearly satisfied where a person receives money from another which he is legally obliged to use in a particular way (e.g. to pay it into a Christmas Club). Where money is collected for a charity, the donor gives money with the expectation that the collector is obliged to pay the money to that charity and that imposes a trust. Misappropriation of the money is to take money which belongs to the beneficiaries of the trust, that is, the charity. The property in the money passed from the person who put the money into the collecting tin, to the charity, at the time at which the donation was given.

Husbands and wives may prosecute one another for any offence under the Theft Act, even if they are living together. On many occasions it may be that the parties are in the position of joint owners, and charges of theft will be appropriate if one party assumes the ownership rights of the other. If two men buy a car and one sells it without the consent of the other, the seller has assumed the ownership rights of the other party and has, therefore, 'appropriated' the property. A turnstile operator was held to be not guilty of theft when he took £2 from a man who did not have a ticket and allowed him entry to the ground. The High Court ruled that he had taken a bribe, and this being so, at no time did the £2 'belong' to his employer. It would have been different if the operator had placed the money in the official till and then removed it later, as he would then have taken it out of the possession of the owner of the ground.

On occasions, property may be obtained by the mistake of some other person. Section 5(4) of the 1968 Act is concerned with such circumstances. However, the provisions of the subsection are limited to circumstances in which the property concerned is delivered to a person who is then under an immediate legal obligation to restore it, or its proceeds or value. This, in effect, limits the provisions to where a person receives ownership, possession or control of money under a mistake and he did not know of that mistake at the time. If he was aware of the mistake when he obtained the property he could be convicted of theft on the basis that the appropriation at the time was accompanied by the necessary *mens rea* of theft.

The mistake must be on the part of the owner who wrongly believes that the person who receives the money is legally entitled to it. Thus, where an employer, by mistake, overpays his employee and the employee is aware that this has occurred but nevertheless appropriates the money by spending it, that employee steals from his employer. This is so because s 5(4) provides that at the time at which the money was spent (appropriated) it still belonged to the employer. In other words, ownership of the money did not pass to the employee when he received the wage packet.

With the intention of permanently depriving the other of it

The common law and all previous legislation concerning theft have preserved the rule that appropriation of property must be accompanied by an intention to deprive the owner permanently of his property. If it is merely intended to deprive him of the use of it for a limited period, it is not theft.

In most cases of theft, the presence of an intention to deprive permanently is easily proved. Where a person takes a bicycle belonging to another person, sells it and spends the money, the nature of his subsequent conduct clearly illustrates that he did not 'borrow' the bicycle. Where a thief steals money and uses it to purchase something, his actions clearly indicate an intention to deprive the owner of that money. A claim of an intention to repay is irrelevant, although it may be of significance in some cases in relation to 'dishonesty'.

Two exceptions to the general rule are included in the Act as it has become necessary, owing in the first instance to legal difficulties and in the second to the prevalence of such action, to punish the removal of articles from place open to the public, for example, art galleries, and the taking of motor vehicles and other conveyances without authority. With these exceptions, 'unlawful borrowing' is not punishable under the Theft Act. If a man takes his neighbour's lawn mower without his permission, but intends to return it in due course, he is not guilty of theft although he may have committed a civil trespass.

If the Act were to leave matters as simply as this, many anomalies would arise as property could be appropriated and sold back to the owner, thus showing that there was no intention to deprive permanently. For many years, boys have removed empty lemonade bottles from storage yards of business premises and have then taken them into a shop to claim the deposit charge of each bottle. Section 6(1) provides:

> A person appropriating property belonging to another without meaning the other permanently to lose the thing itself is nevertheless to be regarded as having the intention of permanently depriving the other of it if his intention is to treat the thing as his own to dispose of regardless of the other's rights; and a borrowing or lending of it may amount to so treating it if, but only if, the borrowing or lending is for a period and in circumstances making it equivalent to an outright taking or disposal.

There are many examples of instances in which property can be returned to the owner in circumstances which would not deprive him permanently of his property but would certainly be dishonest, and this subsection is designed to protect owners from such actions. A man may take a £20 note from a bookmaker's satchel and immediately return it to him by placing a bet, but in such circumstances he would have treated the £20 note as his own and would have disposed of it regardless of the bookmaker's rights in the property, and thus be guilty of stealing it. Similarly, a thief may take a car and use it for a number of years until it is almost worthless and then return it to the owner, hoping to show that he did not intend to deprive him permanently of his car. This would amount to theft as his 'borrowing' was for such a period and in such circumstances that it is equivalent to an outright taking.

There can be certain complications when property which has been hired is unlawfully taken away as, if a man has hired a garden cultivator for a period of 1 week and his neighbour removes this without authority, returning it after the hire period is concluded, there is no doubt that he has permanently deprived the hirer of his interest in the machine. His interest is as one who has possession or control of the garden cultivator.

The meaning of the words 'regardless of others' rights' was considered where the tenant of a council house removed doors from another council house to replace those for which he was responsible in his own home. Whilst he had not, in a direct sense, deprived the council of the doors, he had treated them as his own to dispose of regardless of the other's rights. He had shown a clear intention to treat the doors as his own property.

Finally, s 6(2) of the 1968 Act is concerned with circumstances in which a person who is in possession or control (lawfully or not) of property belonging to another parts with the property under a condition as to its return which he may not be able to meet. This could occur where such a person pawns a valuable ring in circumstances in which it will be almost impossible for him to redeem it. Although in the absence of s 6(2), he might have claimed that the act of 'pawning' was such that it did not indicate an intention permanently to deprive, s 6(2) safeguards the owner's property by providing that the nature of the 'pawning' must be examined.

Abstracting electricity

The abstraction of electricity is dealt with separately because of difficulties which arise in alleging the theft of things which are not physical in form and cannot be held in the hand. Section 13 of the Theft Act 1968 provides:

> A person who dishonestly uses without due authority, or dishonestly causes to be wasted or diverted, any electricity shall, on conviction indictment, be liable to imprisonment for a term not exceeding 5 years.

The section has the effect of making electricity something which is as capable of being stolen as an apple or pear. Its dishonest use, waste or diversion amounts to an offence. If an unauthorised person, perhaps someone who has left home and has no fixed address, enters a building and switches on electric heaters to dry out his clothes, he has dishonestly used electricity. Police officers sometimes encounter circumstances in which householders reconnect an electricity supply which has been disconnected by the Electricity Company, bypassing the company's meter to avoid payment. Where a building is in joint occupation and each of the persons living there had equal opportunity to carry out such an act as bypassing a meter, it must be proved that one, both or all of those persons committed the offence, as the case may be.

The source of electrical power is immaterial; an offence will be equally committed if electricity that is provided by some form of battery is used, wasted or diverted dishonestly. However, it must be remembered that Parliament has made such offences separate from common offences of theft. It is not theft for the purposes of burglary, i.e. a man who enters premises as a trespasser and switches on a light will not be guilty of burglary in these circumstances only.

Offences of theft and the abstractions of electricity are arrestable offences.

Burglary

The Theft Act 1968 considerably simplified the law relating to burglary. The entry of premises with intent to steal was previously punishable according to the types of building which were attacked and the time of day or night at which the offence was committed. The offence of burglary, as defined by s 9 of the Act, now covers all illegal entries into all types of buildings:

By s 9(1), a person is guilty of burglary if:

(a) he enters any building or part of a building as a trespasser and with intent to commit any such offence as is mentioned in subsection (2) below; or

(b) having entered any building or part of a building as a trespasser he steals or attempts to steal anything in the building or that part of it or inflicts or attempts to inflict on any person therein any grievous bodily harm.

Subsection (2) provides that the offences referred to in subsection (a) above are offences of stealing anything in the building or part of a building in question, of inflicting on any person therein any grievous bodily harm or raping any person therein, and of doing unlawful damage to the building or anything therein.

Subsection (4) applies the above provision to inhabited vehicles or vessels and states that the provisions will apply equally whether the person is living there at the time, or he is not. The offences are considered so seriously that a maximum penalty of 14 years' imprisonment is provided by subsection (3) where the building is a dwelling and 10 years in any other case.

In considering fully the offences of burglary, it will be he helpful to examine the terms used separately.

Entry

The common law rule concerning 'entry' is that the insertion of any part of the body, however small, will constitute an entry, as will the insertion of any instrument into a building if it is to be used for the purpose of committing the offence. However, in relation to the modern law of burglary, the Court of Appeal has adopted the test of 'effective entry', which excludes minimal intrusions such as might occur where a thief puts his hand across the top of a window frame to pull it downwards. However, the Court of Appeal has held that there was an entry where a man was found stuck in a window of a house, having his head and arm inside the window whilst trapped by the neck by the window itself. It said that it was irrelevant that he could not steal property from the position in which he was trapped. Therefore, if a thief breaks a window and is seen to insert his hand, for the purpose of stealing goods, he has entered the building.

If, having broken the window, he pushes in a walking stick for the purpose of hooking out a shopping bag, he has again entered the building. It should be remembered that the instrument must be used or be intended to be used for the commission of a relevant further offence inside the building. It would be sufficient if a murderer broke a glass window, inserted a gun and shot the occupier, but it would be insufficient if a thief, in using a drill upon a door, allowed the bit of the drill to enter the building as the bit would not be used or be intended to be used for the commission of an offence inside. The old law recognised an entry by an innocent agent and there is little doubt that this will still apply. If a person uses a child, who is below the age of criminal responsibility, or a trained animal to enter a building and to bring out articles, that will amount to an entry by that person.

For an entry to be an entry for the purposes of this section, it must be effected in order to commit a relevant further offence, not merely to gain or facilitate entry to the building.

Building or part of a building

The term 'building' is likely to be widely defined and will probably include any building made of any material which has some degree of permanence. If we think of the typical country mansion and its immediate surrounds, the house itself will be protected, as will those of employees; garages, greenhouses, barns, stables or outhouses will also be buildings for the purpose of this section. In considering other buildings, shops, warehouses, factories and similar structures will be equally protected. It is probable that the building must be fairly complete and solid, perhaps to the extent that it has a roof, before it may be classed as a building, as it was obviously not the intention of the legislators to protect open structures such as walled gardens or bunkers. Tents, partially built houses without a roof and open-sided barns are clearly outside the protection of s 9.

The inclusion of the term 'part of a building' is to protect premises which are subdivided into separate occupation, so that a man who rents a room in a lodging house may enter the room of another lodger or of the landlord as a trespasser, and a hotel guest may similarly enter the rooms of others as a trespasser. However, it does have a wider meaning and can include any separate part of premises where there is a clear division. For example, the 'behind the counter area' in most shops is clearly separate and is a 'no go' area. Where that is so, a person who goes behind the counter and steals from the till is clearly guilty of burglary.

Whilst customers are clearly welcomed into shops, their permission to enter is restricted to public parts of the building. There is no implied permission to enter stockrooms, staff rest rooms, offices or any other part of the shop which is clearly 'private'.

Charges of burglary should indicate that the offence was committed against the person who is in possession or occupation of the building entered.

Inhabited vehicles or vessels

The adjective 'inhabited' is of extreme importance. Many people in our modern society live in caravans or on boats, and it is reasonable that their homes should be protected in the same way as one built of bricks and mortar. The importance of the use of such a word as 'inhabited' is that it means more than mere presence; there must be someone living in the vehicle or vessel. If they are absent at the time, perhaps abroad for a long holiday, their residence remains protected by the section as it is an inhabited vehicle or vessel. On other occasions the vehicle or vessel attacked may not be inhabited in the general sense in that it is not a man's permanent residence. It appears that it will only be inhabited during periods of permanent residence, for example, during a family's summer holiday when such vehicle or vessel is taken into use as a home. In such circumstances, it will remain an inhabited vehicle or vessel until such time as the holiday is over, regardless of whether or not the occupiers are present at the time. It may be that a family moves into a caravan for a period of 1 month but, at the time that is unlawfully entered and property is stolen, the family is spending the day at the seaside some miles away. The caravan will be an inhabited vehicle for the purposes of this section throughout the period of the annual holiday. The situation as it affects a motorised caravan is an interesting one, as it would seem that if it is used as a car for the majority of the year it cannot be classed as an 'inhabited vehicle', but immediately that the family load it up and move into it as a place of residence it becomes inhabited for the purposes of the section.

It was necessary to add these words to give some protection to places of residence which were not buildings. It can be seen that a tent, whether or not it is permanently occupied, is not within this section as it is not a building. If protection was to be given to tented families, it would be necessary to add the word 'tent' to the places mentioned in subsection (3).

Trespasser

If the building is in the possession of some other person who does not consent to entry, then entry is a trespass. To be charged with an offence of burglary it should be shown that the accused knew that he was a trespasser, or was at least unconcerned as to whether he was a trespasser or not. The section deals with criminal offences in respect of which *mens rea*, or guilty state of mind, should exist. For this reason it is submitted that the drunken man who enters his neighbour's house by mistake may be a trespasser at civil law but would not be so for the purposes of this section. Instances occur where estranged husbands return to the matrimonial home to beat up unfaithful wives and, even though the wives may be the owners of the houses, if those husbands believe that they have a right to enter, they may be a trespassers at civil law but do not necessarily have the guilty state of mind to make them so for the purposes of this section.

The law which was replaced by the 1968 Act recognised that where entry into premises was gained by means of deceit, it was unlawful. Although the Theft Act does not specify it, a 'constructive' illegal entry on such terms makes the person concerned a trespasser even though he has the householder's consent to enter. One television crime prevention film showed a lady answering the door in quick succession to bogus callers, each of whom falsely alleged that he represented an official organisation, so that when she finally opened the door to her husband, the living room of the house had been stripped bare of possessions. Although she had given permission to each of these men to enter, it was conditional upon their being official representatives of these organisations, and this not being so, the permission is null and void. As has been said by a judge of the High Court in considering trespass:

> When you invite a person into your house to use the staircase, you do not invite him to slide down the banisters. So far as he sets foot on to so much of the premises as lie outside the invitation or uses them for purposes which are alien to the invitation, he is not an invitee but a trespasser.

This appears to summarise the position fairly.

Whether or not a person is a trespasser on any particular occasion is a matter of fact for determination by a court. Permission to enter may be given directly, or it may be implied, as is the case with a shop, restaurant, etc. There is an implied consent to entry by members of the public to all such places for the purpose of business. Where a person enters a shop with permission during normal business hours, conceals himself upon the premises at closing time, then emerges from his place of concealment after the premises have closed and steals property, he does not necessarily commit burglary.

To commit burglary he must enter another 'part' of the premises and steal goods there. In 1979 the Court of Appeal ruled upon previously conflicting decisions concerning burglary in two important areas. The defendant entered the 'till area' of a supermarket, opened the till further and shut it when he found it to be empty. It was held, in supporting a conviction for burglary, that it was a matter for the jury to decide whether an area was part of a building from which the public were excluded and that in the case examined, there was ample evidence to show that customers were prohibited and that the defendant knew it. When a person enters such a part of a building as a trespasser intending at the time of entry to steal it, it is immaterial whether there is, in fact, anything worth stealing.

The owner of a dwelling-house either expressly or impliedly will have given permission to members of his family to enter. However, if persons enter a shop or restaurant for the purpose of damaging the property in order to induce the owner to pay protection money, they enter as trespassers as their entry is outside the limits of the permission given to enter. The same would be true where someone who had been given permission to enter and use a dwelling-house, entered by stealth in order to steal property.

On occasions, permission is given directly to a person to enter a building under a mistake as to identity. If a person dresses as a meter reader and is given permission to enter to read a meter, permission is given to a meter reader, not to a person pretending to be such.

The forms of the offence of burglary

It must be proved that a person entered a building or part of a building as a trespasser, knowing that he was a trespasser, or at least being reckless as to whether he was a trespasser or not (guilty state of mind), with intent to:

(a) steal;
(b) inflict grievous bodily harm;
(c) rape any person;
(d) commit unlawful damage to the building or anything therein,

or, having entered a building or part of a building as a trespasser, he

(a) steals or attempts to steal; or
(b) inflicts or attempts to inflict grievous bodily harm.

The offences set out in (a) to (d) above are set out in s 9(2) of the 1968 Act.

There are some important distinctions between the offences which may be committed by a trespasser who enters places protected by the section, with one of the specified intents [as set out in s 9(1)(a)] and those who subsequently commit offences [as set out in s 9(1)(b)]. The offences of stealing and inflicting grievous bodily harm are included in both instances, but those of rape and committing offences of unlawful damage are only relevant in the case of one who enters with the intention of carrying out those acts. As the punishment for rape is one of life imprisonment, the reason for its exclusion in the second instance is clear, and the exclusion of unlawful damage to buildings or their contents prevents charges of burglary being preferred where damage is incidental to the trespass. For practical circumstances, the prosecution frequently relies upon the fact that an offence was committed to prove that the accused entered the buildings with that intention.

If a trespasser is apprehended in a building, part of a building, inhabited vehicle or vessel and admits that he entered with the intention of stealing, inflicting grievous bodily harm, raping or committing damage to buildings or their contents, an offence of burglary is complete. Should he merely admit to entering as a trespasser, without other evidence to indicate a particular intent, it is necessary to prove that he stole property or attempted to steal it, or inflicted or attempted to inflict grievous bodily harm.

A tramp enters a building to find a place in which to sleep, but before leaving in the morning he makes himself a meal, eats it and leaves the premises. He is guilty of burglary because he entered as a trespasser and stole property. On the following evening he again enters a building for the same reasons but is discovered there by a night watchman. In order to escape he assaults the watchman, breaking his jaw, and thus commits an offence of burglary; having entered as a trespasser he inflicts grievous bodily harm. Had he been disturbed in the first instance and forced to leave before eating the meal (having prepared it), or having aimed a vicious blow at the watchman with a crowbar and missed, in the second, he would still have been guilty of burglary as he attempted to commit the specified offences in both cases. Attempts to commit the offences of theft or inflicting grievous bodily harm are specifically included in s 9(1)(b).

If a young man has a dispute with his girl friend and enters her flat as a trespasser with intent to steal some of her property, to beat her up, rape her or wreck the contents of her flat, he is guilty of burglary. (Since the Criminal Justice and Public Order Act 1994 extended the offence of rape to men, he would be equally guilty if he had entered with intent to rape his boy friend.) If he enters, still as a trespasser, but merely with the intention of talking matters over with her and, when she returns, does so without patching up his quarrel and, as a result of this lack of success, rapes her or wrecks the contents of her flat, he is not guilty of burglary. However, if he stole or attempted to steal a handbag, or caused grievous bodily harm, or attempted to do so, he would be guilty of burglary.

Where it is alleged that an offence has been committed against s 9(1)(b) (trespassory entry followed by the commission of an offence), as well as the *mens rea* required for theft, or an offence of inflicting grievous bodily harm (or an attempt to commit either of these offences), the accused must know or be reckless that he has entered as a trespasser.

Aggravated burglary

Section 10 of the Theft Act 1968 deals with offences known as aggravated burglary. The aggravating circumstances are related to the possession of articles which are likely to be frightening to people in the building and the use of which might lead to serious consequences. The section provides:

> A person is guilty of aggravated burglary if he commits any burglary and at the time has with him any firearm or imitation firearm, any weapon of offence, or any explosive.

The various terms are defined as follows:

(a) 'Firearm' includes an airgun or air pistol and 'imitation firearm' means anything which has the appearance of being a firearm, whether capable of being discharged or not.

(b) 'Weapon of offence' means any article made or adapted for use for causing injury to or incapacitating a person, or intended by the person having it with him for such use.

(c) 'Explosive' means any article manufactured for the purpose of producing a practical effect by explosion, or intended by the person having it with him for that purpose.

The use of weapons of all descriptions during the commission of offences of this nature is becoming common. The term 'firearm' includes air weapons, and all recognised forms of firearms are included. Bearing in mind that the aggravating circumstances are such that will cause fear or possible injury to persons, it is submitted that component parts of firearms, as defined in the Firearms Act 1968, would not be considered to be firearms for the purpose of this section. Things which have the appearance of being firearms are covered by the inclusion of the term 'imitation firearm'.

'Weapon of offence' could include all offensive weapons made or adapted for causing injury, for example, coshes, knuckledusters, razors and caps with razor blades in the peaks, but in these circumstances would also include articles made or adapted for incapacitating a person, such as handcuffs or even knotted tights to be used for strangulation. Examples of those weapons intended to be used to cause injury could include almost all objects, for example, walking sticks or a golf club, and those intended to incapacitate could include a chloroform pad, powder to be thrown in the face or a length of rope to be used for binding a person.

The definition of the term 'explosive' is equally wide and includes anything manufactured for the purpose of producing a practical effect by explosion, or intended for that purpose. The use of explosives by certain organisations is certainly increasing, and although other serious offences are included in the various Explosives Acts, it is nevertheless an offence of aggravated burglary to enter a building or anything in the building by use of explosives. Fireworks are not within this definition.

In each case of aggravated burglary, it is essential to prove that an offence of burglary has been committed and, at the time, the accused had with him a firearm, imitation firearm, weapon of offence or an explosive. It is not necessary that such a person was armed when he entered the building as a trespasser. The time at which a defendant must be proved to have with him a weapon of offence is the time at which he steals, attempts to steal, etc., where the burglary is contrary to s 9(1)(b).

A person who commits a burglary and has with him at the time of the offence a knuckleduster is guilty of aggravated burglary because a knuckleduster is an article made for use for causing injury or incapacitating a person. However, if he was in possession of a small pocket knife the offence of aggravated burglary would only be committed if he showed an intention to use it for such purposes, as a small pocket knife is not an article made for use for causing injury or incapacitating. (See page 535 for further information regarding weapons of offence.)

For the purposes of aggravated burglary, an article not made or adapted to cause injury or to incapacitate can be a weapon of offence even if the necessary intent is only formed an instant before it is used to injure or incapacitate (which is in contrast with the rule which applies to an offence of carrying an offensive weapon in a public place; see page 535).

A man used a screwdriver to break into a house. He was handling a video recorder when confronted by the occupier and another person. He took the screwdriver from his pocket and prodded the occupier in the stomach with the screwdriver. It was held that this was aggravated burglary as the screwdriver became an offensive weapon on proof that he intended to use it for injuring or incapacitating the occupier at the time of the theft, thereby aggravating the burglary.

Three men knocked on the door of a residential caravan and demanded money from the occupier. One of these man was armed with a stick. He assaulted the occupier with the stick when he said that he had no money and pursued him, outside the caravan, aiming further blows. One of the others entered the caravan intending to steal. The Court of Appeal said that he who entered the caravan could not be guilty of aggravated burglary as the armed man had at no time trespassed inside the building. The gravamen of the offence is entry into a building with a weapon.

All offences of burglary and aggravated burglary are arrestable offences.

Removal of articles from places open to the public

Where an art lover removes a valuable picture from an art gallery and alleges that he only did so to allow himself the luxury of enjoying it exclusively for a period of time before returning it to the gallery, there is a problem when attempting to prove theft or any associated offence. It would be necessary to show that this claim was false and that the taker intended to deprive the owner permanently of his property or that this was a 'borrowing' of such a nature that the period of time for which the article was 'borrowed' and the circumstances in which it had been kept were such that it amounted to an outright taking. To avoid these difficulties, the Theft Act 1968, s 11, creates a specific offence to cover such cases whilst providing a safeguard, by careful drafting, to limit the offence to particular circumstances. It provides:

> Where the public have access to a building in order to view the building or part of it, or a collection or part of a collection housed in it, any person who without lawful authority removes from the building or its grounds the whole or part of any article displayed or kept for display to the public in the building, or that part of it, or in its grounds, shall be guilty of an offence.

The place from which the article is removed

There are two major points to prove. First, it must be shown that the article was removed:

(a) from the *building* to which the public have access in order to view the building or part of it, or a collection or a part of a collection housed in it; or

(b) from the grounds of the building.

Thus, in dealing with this first point we are considering removal of articles from national galleries, stately homes, etc., *which are open to the public in order to view the building, etc.*, or from the grounds of such buildings. The offence cannot be committed, therefore, from public buildings such as the offices of local authorities which, whilst they are open to the public, are not open for the purpose of 'viewing'. They are open to the public to carry out the functions of local government. We are also concerned with 'public access' so that, where access is limited to a certain section, or sections of the public, the offence, once again, does not apply. If the particular building was open to members of a local historical society, or a group of architects, it would not be open to the public for the purposes of this offence.

However, the offence does not apply to circumstances in which a collection of art treasures has been brought together for display with a view to sale or for any other commercial purpose. The removal of articles from a commercial art gallery, therefore, is not covered by s 11. At the other extreme, articles which are merely brought together temporarily for display in a local village hall are protected by the section as they are displayed in a building to which the public has access in order to view.

In most instances, offences against s 11 can be committed whether or not the gallery, etc., is open to the public at the time. The removal of paintings from the National Gallery, for example, will offend against this section at any time and this can easily be appreciated. Such a gallery exists for no other purpose than to give a home to such treasures so that they may be viewed by the public. In contrast, this is not the case in relation to stately homes. Whilst they are open to the public the treasures which they contain are vulnerable to such removal, but when they are not open to the public, the offence does not apply as they then revert to being a dwelling house and the 'treasures' are merely a part of its decoration and are protected in the normal way.

The nature of the article

The second point is concerned with whether or not the article which was removed was *displayed or kept for display to the public*. If a member of the public is admitted to the building to examine articles and he takes one of them, for example an old sword, he commits an offence under the provisions of this section. If, however, it was a fur coat belonging to the owner of the house which was taken from a wardrobe in one of the bedrooms (an article which had not been on display), then the offence which was committed would be one of theft and it would not fall within the parameters of s 11.

The nature of the removal

The article concerned must be removed completely from the building or, as the case may be, its grounds. A visitor who places an article in his pocket with a view to removal does not commit an offence at that stage. He commits the offence when he walks out of the building and takes the article without lawful authority. If the article which he plans to remove is a statue which stands in the grounds, this offence is committed when it is removed from the grounds.

It is not essential that 'dishonesty' existed throughout the transaction as this is not a part of the offence. However, the section provides that a person does not commit the offence if he believes that he has lawful authority for the removal of the thing in question or that he would have it if the person entitled to give it knew of the removal and its circumstances. If, therefore, a man who had been asked by the owner or his agent to take certain items of furniture for restoration, took an item of furniture which was not meant to be taken for restoration, he would not commit an offence against s 11 if he believed that he had lawful authority for its removal.

Police powers

This is an arrestable offence.

Criminal deception

Obtaining property by deception

Section 15 of the Theft Act 1968 deals with the obtaining of property by deception:

(a) A person who by any deception obtains property belonging to another, with the intention of depriving the other of it, shall on conviction on indictment be liable to imprisonment for a term not exceeding 10 years.
(b) For the purposes of this section a person is to be treated as obtaining property if he obtains ownership, possession or control over it, and 'obtains' includes obtaining for another or enabling another to obtain or to retain.

Dishonestly

The deception must be made with a dishonest intention, and the meaning of the term has already been discussed when dealing with theft.

Obtains

Subsection (2) describes the extent of the meaning of this word, which includes obtaining ownership, possession or control for oneself, for another, or enabling another to obtain or retain it.

(a) *Ownership* – When a person buys an article in a shop, upon payment of the full agreed price he obtains the property in the article and has first claim to it. As opposed to everyone else he has the right of ownership and may do as he pleases with that particular article. If a person buys a car and pays full price for it, from the moment that the agreement is signed the retailer surrenders his rights of ownership to the purchaser. The purchaser may then do as he pleases with the car, provided that his actions do not conflict with the law, and he may change the colour of it, apply stickers to it or even destroy it, if that is his wish. The law recognises that property may be jointly owned by two or more persons and provides that offences may be committed by one owner who deals with the property in some way which is against the interests of the others, for example, by assuming full rights over the property.
(b) *Possession and control* – It is an advantage to examine these terms together as it is difficult, on occasions, to separate their meaning. Possession is often described in two forms, actual and constructive, and it is when considering forms of constructive possession that a certain identification with the term 'control' can become apparent. The man who buys a car from a retailer is in actual possession of it as he drives it home. If, on arriving home, he sends his gardener on an errand and instructs him to drive his car, the gardener is now in actual possession of the car, but the owner also retains possession through his servant, and such possession is frequently described as constructive possession. 'Control' is a word of more general meaning which could be fittingly applied to both the gardener and the owner in the circumstances described above, but can also be more extensive in meaning. If the gardener was allowed to take his master's car to his home for the evening and parked it outside his house, he would no longer be in actual possession of it, but it would still be under his control. The inclusion of all three words in the section illustrates clearly

the extent of the term 'obtains', which covers obtaining property from an owner or a person who, in any way, has a special interest in the property. Possession by an owner is identified by the fact that, no matter where the article may be, he retains control over it and can exercise his rights of ownership whenever he may wish to do so. For the purposes of the law relating to criminal deception, it is equally important to be aware of the term 'ownership' as, on occasions, the deception practised is such that an owner is induced to surrender his rights of ownership, in addition to his possession of the article, believing some false story to be true.

(c) *When does ownership pass?* – Property has been obtained for the purposes of this section immediately that ownership, possession or control has passed to another person. An owner of property may be induced by means of deception to sell 100 soccer balls to the party practising the deceit. The ownership in this property passes immediately that the deal has been completed, although no payment has been made and delivery has not been effected. This is normal business procedure: the ownership in articles being passed to retail traders on the promise of later payment. In examining circumstances which may include an offence of criminal deception, it is important not only to identify the passing of physical possession or control of property but also to look for a possible transfer of ownership, by the original owner surrendering his ownership at some particular moment, intending delivery at a later date. In most circumstances, a written contract will have been made out, but it is not necessary that it should be in writing. If an offer has been made by a person making false statements, or by a person whose conduct is misleading, and this has been accepted by the owner of the property, who surrenders his rights of ownership, then a contract has been completed, although this will later be voidable if the deceit is discovered.

(d) *Who may obtain?* – In most circumstances the offender will have acted in order to benefit himself, but subsection (2) makes it clear that an offence will equally have been committed if the act is done for another, or to enable another to obtain or retain possession, ownership or control.

A man may tell a false story to an official of a charitable body concerning the circumstances of his friend, thus inducing the charity to make a payment to the friend. In such circumstances the man concerned will have obtained money for another by means of deception. Similarly, it may be that a man is offering rings for sale to a group in a public house, when another party deceives the potential buyers as to the quality of the rings in order to allow the seller to obtain a better price. He is, therefore, guilty of enabling the seller to obtain money by means of deception. In such circumstances, it is possible that the man telling the false story and the seller were acting in concert and the seller is, therefore, also guilty of an offence under this section. It is less likely that circumstances will be met in which some form of deceit has been practised to enable someone to retain property. This could occur, for example, if the owner had allowed someone the use of valuable paintings, and upon requiring their return was falsely told by another party that the borrower has arranged for various interested parties to visit his home over the following months to view the paintings and that it would cause him considerable embarrassment to be unable to meet his obligations. In this way, as a result of deceit, another person would have been enabled to retain property belonging to someone else, but such circumstances may lead to action under the Theft Act 1978 (see below).

(e) *What may be obtained from whom?* – The terms 'property' and 'belonging to another' have already been examined under the heading of theft. Although there may be marginal differences in interpretation of the term 'property' for the purposes of the offence of criminal deception, all forms of property described by s 4 in relation to theft are included and persons to whom property may belong are as described by s 5 of the 1968 Act.

However, property cannot be obtained from a machine by deception. A machine has no mind and therefore cannot be deceived.

The deception

Subsection (4) of the Act states:

> For the purposes of this section, 'deception' means any deception (whether deliberate or reckless) by words or conduct as to fact or as to law, including a deception as to the present intentions of the persons using the deception or any other person.

(a) *Deliberate or reckless* – By including both of these words, the prosecution is not required to prove beyond reasonable doubt that the offender knew that his story was false; it is sufficient to show that he was at least reckless as to whether or not it was true. 'Reckless' means more than being careless or negligent and involves an indifference as to whether the statement is true or false. A man may say that the watch he is selling has an 18-jewel movement, knowing that this is untrue, but he also may make this claim without having any knowledge of its truth or falsity, therefore showing recklessness. If his statement proves to be untrue and, because of it, another person pays money for the watch, the seller is guilty of an offence under this section. It is important, however, to recognise the difference between recklessness as to the falsity of a statement and mere negligence, as the basis of offences of criminal deception is that the act is done dishonestly. If the statement is such that any reasonable person should have known that it was false, this is good evidence that the accused knew of its falsity or was at least reckless in this respect. In the same way, a court is expected to listen to the explanation given by the accused and, if he is considered to have genuinely believed that his claim in respect of the property was true, he is entitled to be acquitted. There must be a dividing line between criminal claims in relation to property and accepted forms of advertising. The Trade Descriptions Acts punish instances of using any misleading trade descriptions in forms of advertising.

(b) *By words or conduct* – Police officers experience little difficulty in identifying a deception by words. If a man tells another that the ring he is selling is gold, knowing that it is of some lesser metal, it is clearly a deception by words. Fortunately, most cases involve a deceit of this nature. However, the conduct of the man can be sufficient. If he wears a badge representing that he is an accredited bookmaker and receives bets from punters, that conduct inducing them to part with their money, his actions become dishonest if he has no intention of honouring the bets which are placed with him. A common form of criminal deception is the purchase of goods, by means of a cheque, by a person who knows that he has insufficient funds in his account. The signing of a cheque implies three things: that the drawer has authority to draw that sum; that he has a bank account with that particular bank; and that the cheque is good and valid for that amount of money. If the drawer of the cheque has been notified by his banker that he has a certain sum of money in his account (by bank statement, verbally or in answer to an enquiry) and he signs a cheque for an amount in excess of that sum knowing that no further funds are likely to be paid into his account, he has practised a deception, his actions are dishonest and he has obtained property as a result of his deception. It would be different if he had authority to overdraw. However, banks guarantee that cheques up to a certain amount will be honoured and consequently a person using a cheque guarantee card, as authorised by his bank, cannot be guilty of deception in representing that such a cheque will be met. It would be different if the bank had withdrawn his authority to use the card. However, it has been held that a *genuine* belief that a cheque would be honoured provides a defence to a charge of deception, even if the belief is not based on reasonable grounds. Where a cheque book and cheque card are stolen and the thief forges a signature on one of the cheques and supports it with the card, he obtains money by the deception that he has authority to use the card.

There can also be a deception by omission. If a woman is in receipt of benefits which are calculated on the basis that she is separated from her husband and is receiving no help from him, and she continues to draw those benefits after her husband has returned to her, she commits this offence. Her original representation is a continuing one existing on each occasion upon which she draws benefit.

Instances in which customers in restaurants have left without paying for their meal are frequently reported to the police and it can be a difficult matter to decide when such conduct is criminal and when it is not. A person who orders and consumes a meal in a restaurant has incurred a debt for which he is then obliged to pay. This can be described as a normal debt. If he then finds that he is unable to pay he may, by arrangement with the owner, defer payment until a later date. His conduct becomes criminal when his intentions are dishonest and he deceives the owner of the restaurant or his servant either by words or conduct. If it can be proved that he had no intention of paying when he sat down for the meal, he is clearly guilty of obtaining the meal, which is property, by deception, and he is therefore guilty of an offence against s 15. However, unless this is admitted, it is seldom possible to show that this was his intention at the time he ordered the meal.

(c) *Deception as to present intentions* – Promises concerning future conduct were not generally punishable under the legislation which was replaced by the 1968 Act. Section 15 is now wide enough to permit proceedings in such cases provided that it is possible to prove beyond reasonable doubt that the accused had no intention of fulfilling his promise at the time that he made it. If a man receives money as a deposit for the fitting of new guttering to a house and he has no intention of carrying out the work, he has obtained that money by deception as to his present intentions. It is important to differentiate between the man who intended to carry out the work at the time and later finds it impossible to do so, and he who did not intend to do the work at the time at which he received money in consideration of doing so.

(d) *Injured person must be deceived* – The person who is deprived of his property must believe that the false story is true, or be deceived by the conduct of the accused, before the full offence can be committed. The section requires that the accused 'obtains property by deception' and before this can be true, the owner must believe the falsehood and because of this, part with ownership, possession or control of his property. If he is not deceived, the person practising the deceit is guilty of attempting to obtain property by means of deception. Statements taken from injured parties should, therefore, include evidence of their belief in the particular deceit involved in the offence.

Where an unlicensed taxi driver picked up a foreign passenger at an airport, he falsely represented by his conduct that he was a licensed taxi driver and that his fares would be reasonable. When he charged a grossly excessive amount, although his passenger suspected by then that he was not a genuine taxi driver, the passenger felt obliged to pay the extortionate rate. It was held that he had obtained the money by deception. If the deception is the effective cause of the property being obtained it is irrelevant that, at the final moment, the victim suspected or even believed that he was being swindled. However, in such cases it would be better to charge theft, as theft can occur where an atmosphere of menace is the cause of a person parting with his property.

If a deception occurs after the property has been obtained, the person making the deception cannot be guilty of this offence because the deception must operate on the mind of the person deceived and be the effective cause of the thing in question being obtained. Thus, where a man obtained petrol at a self-service station, then told the attendant to charge the petrol to the account of his former employer, the offence was not committed as the representation was made subsequent to the obtaining of petrol.

The meaning of the term 'intention of permanently depriving' has already been discussed on page 231.

Obtaining a money transfer by deception

The Theft Act 1968, s 15A(1), provides that a person is guilty of an offence if by any deception he dishonestly obtains a money transfer for himself or another. The offence was added by the Theft (Amendment) Act 1996 in consequence of a decision by the House of Lords that no offence had been committed against s 15 where mortgage advances were obtained as a result of false representations contained in the mortgage applications on the grounds that there was no obtaining, or attempt to obtain, property *belonging to another*. The House decided that where an electronic transfer of cash took place, in the course of that transaction, a new 'account or chose in action' was created which did not belong to the lending institution at the time at which it was 'obtained'. Section 15A fills the gap which was so created.

The ingredients of the offence

Deception

The obtaining of the money transfer must have been by means of a deception and the meaning of the term 'deception' is explained above.

Obtains a money transfer

Section 15A(2) provides that a money transfer occurs when:

(a) a debit is made to one account;
(b) a credit is made to another; and
(c) the credit results from the debit or the debit results from the credit.

The references to 'credit' and 'debit' are references to amounts of money. It is immaterial whether these amounts correspond or whether the money transfer is effected by presentment of a cheque or by another method, whether delay occurs in the process, whether intermediate credits or debits are made or whether either of the accounts is overdrawn before or after the money transfer is effected.

Thus, the terms of s 15A are wide enough to cover any form of mortgage fraud or dishonest transfer of cash from one account to another which is brought about by deception. Where advances of cash are obtained from banks or building societies, as a result of mortgage applications which contain false statements concerning relevant matters, and such applications are dishonestly made, the offence will be made out. However, the terms of the offence are such that they will embrace any such transfer of cash from one account to another and there need be no connection with a mortgage application. Although the offence is primarily aimed at the transfer of funds by telegraphic or electronic transfer, it is not limited to such means.

See page 268 for the associated offence under s 24A of the 1968 Act of retaining a wrongful credit obtained by such a money transfer.

Obtaining pecuniary advantage by deception

Section 16 of the Theft Act 1968 provides:

> A person who by any deception dishonestly obtains for himself or another any pecuniary advantage shall on conviction on indictment be liable to imprisonment for a term not exceeding 5 years.

The offence is similar to that created by s 15, the difference being that for an offence to be committed contrary to s 15, property must be obtained as a result of the deception, whereas s 16 requires that a 'pecuniary advantage' be obtained.

Pecuniary advantage

Subsection (2) of s 16 defines 'pecuniary advantage':

> The cases in which a pecuniary advantage is to be regarded as obtained for a person are cases where:
>
> (a) (this subsection was repealed by the Theft Act 1978);
> (b) he is allowed to borrow by way of overdraft, or to take out any policy of insurance or annuity contract, or obtain an improvement of the terms on which he is allowed to do so; or
> (c) he is given an opportunity to earn remuneration or greater remuneration in an office of employment, or to win money by betting.

Although s 16 creates only one offence, it is essential that the charge specifies the pecuniary advantage which the accused is alleged to have obtained. It is, therefore, important to examine the meaning of each of these conditions. It is also important to recognise that these are the only forms of pecuniary advantage covered by the section.

Overdraft, insurance policy or improved terms

An authority to overdraw may be given by a bank manager upon being deceived by a customer into believing that he had assets which he did not in fact have. In addition, when a bank's customer with an overdrawn account uses a cheque card to obtain goods after a warning that no more cheques would be met, and after having been requested to return the bank card, the customer commits the offence of obtaining a pecuniary advantage from his bank by his deception of the owner of the goods. This was an interesting decision of the Court of Appeal as it had been submitted that the customer who obtained a railway ticket and a dog by use of her banker's card, had deceived the railway booking clerk and the pet shop owner, not the bank. It was held that her deception had indeed been practised upon these two individuals, but as the bank was bound to honour cheques which were supported by its card when presented, she had obtained a pecuniary advantage from the bank. It is not necessary that the person deceived is the person from whom the pecuniary advantage is obtained, although there should be some connection. Where a person uses a cheque card to obtain money in excess of the limit imposed by the bank, he is borrowing by way of an overdraft and if this is done dishonestly, he is guilty of this offence.

Policies of insurance or annuity contracts with insurance companies may be obtained by deception as to the past medical history of the applicant, or it may be that the terms offered are improved because of a similar deception.

Opportunity to earn remuneration, greater remuneration or win money by betting

Before the passing of the Theft Act 1968, there was no criminal offence of obtaining an office or employment by deceit. Section 16 now deals with such conduct. If a man obtains a post as a school teacher by dishonestly representing that he had successfully completed a training course at a college of education, he is guilty of an offence. Alternatively, it may be that he is a qualified teacher, but on appointment he falsely alleges that he is the holder of an honours degree in order to obtain a higher salary. Such conduct would amount to securing a greater remuneration by deception. There is a difference between applying for an office *carrying* remuneration and having an opportunity to *earn* remuneration. Thus, a man who makes a false statement to obtain a brewery tenancy does not commit this offence because, as a tenant, he would not be in the *employ* of the brewery company, nor could the post be described as an *office*. However, where a man falsely represented that he was a member of the Chartered Institute of Management Accountants and agreed to complete accounts and VAT returns for customers, and claimed that the nature of the contract existing between himself and his customers was such that he was self-employed, it was held that he would be an employee in the eyes of ordinary literate men and women. To say differently would offer the opportunity for dishonest persons to arrange matters so that they became self-employed and thus escape the consequences of their deceitful conduct.

A person may gain the opportunity to win money by betting, by deceiving a bookmaker into allowing credit betting. A pecuniary advantage is obtained – that is, the opportunity to win money – and that advantage is gained by deception.

Powers of arrest

All of the above offences of pecuniary advantage by deception are arrestable offences.

The Theft Act 1978

The Theft Act 1978 repealed s 16(2)(a) of the Theft Act 1968 in respect of which there had been many problems of interpretation. Although problems in relation to the dividing lines which might exist between offences may have been simplified for the courts, this short Act is not one which fits easily into the understanding of those who are required to enforce the law. The 1978 Act deals with three offences: obtaining services by deception, the evasion of liability by deception and making off without payment.

Obtaining services by deception

Section 1 makes it an offence for any person, by any deception, to obtain services dishonestly from another. The deception need not relate to the question of payment. It must be the cause of the services being obtained by the accused (the person making the deception) or another.

The deception may involve a failure to declare a change in circumstances. A man received approval from his council for a grant to provide a downstairs toilet for use by his elderly mother. Although she died 2 days later, he permitted the work to be carried out without notifying the council. The Court of Appeal ruled that his positive acquiescence in knowingly permitting the work to proceed was conduct which was capable of amounting to a deception.

We have already considered the obtaining of goods or pecuniary advantage by deception. The first is concerned with 'tangible' goods, the second with 'intangible' benefits in the sense that one cannot take hold of them. We now consider 'services' which are also intangible in the sense that they cannot be taken hold of. A ride in a taxi, a manicure or the services of a mechanic to start a troublesome car are all services provided by someone else; so is permitted entry to a theatre or a sports ground.

The section goes on to say that it is an obtaining of services where the other is induced to confer a benefit by doing some act, or causing or permitting some act to be done, on the understanding that the benefit has been, or will be, paid for. The essence of this offence is seated in 'deception', 'dishonesty' and the 'obtaining of services'. It is calculated to identify the criminal offences, as opposed to instances of debt. A man may, by means of a dishonest deception, induce a builder to carry out work on his behalf. If he issues a worthless cheque, he has then induced the builder to believe that his services *have been* paid for. If he induces him to believe that he will pay on completion of the work, knowing that he is not, and will not be, in a position to pay at that time, he has by deception, dishonestly caused the builder to believe that his services *will be* paid for. The prosecution must prove the dishonesty and the deception, which, in effect, converts a civil debt into a criminal offence.

There are certain factors to remember. The debt does not need to be one which is legally enforceable, the services must be for reward and there may be an offence even though the person practising the deception intends to pay, if the deception is concerned with some other related matter. In examining these factors in turn, it is realised that the obtaining of the services of a prostitute by deception (a debt which is not legally enforceable) is nevertheless an offence under this section. A man who pays a prostitute with a worthless cheque, knowing that it is worthless, in advance of receiving her services, is clearly liable under this section. There is a deception, his intentions are dishonest, and it does not matter that the debt is not legally enforceable. However, if he pays the prostitute after the event with a worthless cheque, it would be necessary to prove that he did not intend to pay from the outset, that is at the time at which he obtained the services. If he discovered afterwards that he had no money and paid with a worthless cheque merely to avoid embarrassment, there would be no offence under this section.

To illustrate the second point, if a man hires a car and deliberately pays for that hire with a worthless cheque, he is clearly guilty of this offence. However, if he paid for the hire, but produced a friend's driving licence with the intention of concealing the fact that he was disqualified from driving, he would still be guilty under this section, although he had paid for the services. The deception is not limited to matters concerning payment, it is broadly attached to the 'obtaining of services by deception'. The aim of the section is to limit consideration of things done commercially: a man who 'hires' a lawnmower by deception without an intention to pay is guilty, he who borrows one from his neighbour is not.

The term used in subsection (2) 'confer a benefit' as related to the services which may be obtained gives width to the section; we are not only considering a job done, but a benefit provided, for example the services of an estate agent or surveyor who does no physical work, or admission to theatres, soccer grounds, etc., by deception.

Section 1(3) provides that, without prejudice to the generality of subsection (2), it is an obtaining of services where the other is induced to make a loan, or cause or permit a loan to be made, on the understanding that any payment (whether by way of interest or otherwise) will be or has been made in respect of the loan. This subsection was added by the Theft (Amendment) Act 1996 to overcome a ruling that a mortgage advance could not be described as a service within the provisions of s 1 of the 1978 Act.

It must be shown that an accused made his deception deliberately or recklessly and that he obtained his services dishonestly.

If a man books into a hotel intending not to pay, he obtains accommodation (a service) by deception. If he then takes breakfast, although the food represents goods, he continues to obtain services by deception as the waiter is not deceived by any words or conduct on the guest's part; he supplies the food because he believes that person to be a guest in the hotel and that is true.

Evasion of liability by deception

Section 2 deals with three offences which are seated in securing remission of a liability by deception: dishonestly securing remission of liability, inducing a creditor to wait for or forgo payment and obtaining exemption from, or abatement of, an existing liability. In all such instances the liability must be a legally enforceable one and this represents the first difference from offences which we have considered contrary to s 1. Thus, the man who receives services from a prostitute by deception, or waiver of gambling debts, etc., by means of deception, cannot commit any of the offences outlined below. A non-accepted claim for compensation is in the same way not legally enforceable at that stage.

Remission of liability

Section 2(1)(a) makes it an offence for any person who, by means of any deception, dishonestly secures the remission of the whole, or part of an existing liability to make payment, whether his own liability or another's. To 'remit' means to 'refrain from exacting' so that any cancellation, whether in whole or in part, as a result of deception is sufficient for this offence. To separate this offence in our minds from that described in s 1, we must remember that s 1 was concerned with 'services', whereas s 2 is concerned with 'liabilities'. To commit offences contrary to s 1, the deception must be practised in order to obtain services, so that the man who deceives a radio dealer into repairing his radio by means of deception is guilty of an s 1 offence as he 'obtained services' by deception. A second man, who merely places a radio with the dealer for repair, practising no deception and even intending at that time to pay, has committed no offence. When the radio is returned to him he has a 'liability' to pay the repairer his charge. If he dishonestly, and by means of deception at this stage, secures remission either in full or in part, of that liability, he is guilty of an offence against s 2(1)(a). Similarly, a man may borrow money from a friend and thereby have a liability to repay. If he later tells a false story to the effect that his mother has died and that he is required to meet the funeral expenses, as a result of which his friend either cancels or reduces the debt, the man is guilty of this offence. The term 'existing liability' means that there must have been some previous transaction which has been completed. It may amount to a credit sale, a borrowing, or a debt in respect of repair, etc.

Wait for or forgo payment

Section 2(1)(b) deals with a person who, by means of a deception *with intent to make per-manent default* in whole or in part on any existing liability to make payment, or with intent to let another do so, dishonestly induces the creditor or any person claiming payment on behalf of the creditor, to wait for payment (whether or not the due date for payment is deferred) or to forgo payment. A person is induced by deception to forgo payment if the deception causes him to give up waiting for payment and (although he does not necessarily agree to extinguish it) to write off the debt, or he is convinced by deception that there is no liability to pay.

As these offences are all concerned with deception, understanding of the differences between particular offences becomes difficult. Previously we have been concerned with *services which are obtained* by deception and *debts which are cancelled or reduced* by means of deception. Now we are concerned with *criminal intentions*, deceptions practised 'with intent to make permanent default', which result in an inducement to persons to wait for pay-ment or to forgo it. The subsection is concerned with 'stalling debtors' who embark upon a course of conduct which tends to indicate an intention to make permanent default. There must come a time in the course of such processes when the reasonable man would decide that a debtor intended to make permanent default. This is the reason why subsec-tion (3) specifically declares that when a creditor takes a cheque in conditional satisfaction of a pre-existing liability, he is to be treated not as being paid, but as being induced to wait for payment. Therefore, a defendant who gives a creditor a worthless cheque com-mits an offence contrary to s 2(1)(b) if he is dishonest and intends never to pay. However, where a man pays off a debt with a cheque which he knows to be worthless merely to get the creditor 'off his back' and intends to pay when funds are available, he does not intend to make permanent default and does not, therefore, commit this offence.

If customers in a restaurant dishonestly deceive the proprietor by alleging that they have already paid the bill, they deceive with intent to make permanent default.

We have considered the first part of this offence, 'waiting for payment', in the light of the deception with intent to make permanent default, by a stalling debtor.

The second provision of this subsection uses the word 'forgo' and we are concerned with the man who by means of deception, with intent to make permanent default, dishonestly induces his creditor to 'decide' that he will never seek repayment. If we consider two stu-dents who rent a room from a landlord, and one of them informs the landlord that the other has left owing rent and without leaving a forwarding address and that story is false, the landlord may decide that it will not be worth his trouble to try to trace the student and may cancel the debt. If the student who left intended to make permanent default, he is guilty of this offence. So is the student who practised the deception if his intention was to allow his colleague to make permanent default. The words 'with intent to let another do so' make him a principal offender. In the same way, a man who is about to leave the country or the district, who pays a small garage bill by means of a worthless cheque and thereby similarly induces the garage owner to decide to cancel the debt, would be guilty if he intended to make permanent default. If the garage owner did not decide to cancel the debt, he would have been induced to wait for payment in these circumstances.

Exemption or abatement

Section 2(1)(c) makes it an offence for a person dishonestly, by any deception, to obtain an exemption from or abatement of liability to make a payment. Although this appears at first sight to bear many parallels with the offences already described, it adds a new dimension. So far we have been concerned with obtaining services, evasion of existing liabilities and inducing creditors to wait for or forgo payment. Now we are considering a dishonest deception which from the outset was concerned with securing some form of 'exemption' or 'abatement', the term 'abatement' signifying a reduction of liability. The offender may obtain services at a reduced rate, for example a railway ticket by use of a student's union card, to which he was not entitled, thus obtaining 'abatement of liability to make payment', or free passage on a public service vehicle by use of a pensioner's pass to which he was not entitled, which would amount to an 'exemption'. A consultant who had a duty to give information to an NHS hospital concerning patient services received by private patients, but who deliberately and dishonestly refrained from giving that information, was held to be guilty of this offence because, by his deception (by omission) he had obtained exemption from patient charges which otherwise would have arisen.

Section 1 could not apply to any of these offences as the benefit was not conferred on an understanding that it would be, or had been, paid for; it was given on a false belief that the offender was entitled to concessions. This subsection will also apply to the dishonest, deceptive claim made to a tax inspector or local authority council tax officer to secure allowances or rebates to which the person submitting the claim is not entitled. Perhaps this illustrates the purpose of ss 1 and 2 of the 1978 Act to cover deceptions related to concessions.

Making off without payment

The Theft Act 1978, s 3, makes it an offence for a person who, knowing that payment on the spot for any goods supplied or service done is required or expected from him, dishonestly makes off without having paid as required or expected and with intent to avoid payment of the amount due.

This offence was included to cover offences known as 'bilking', for example, leaving a restaurant or a self-service petrol station without paying. The previous theft law left gaps in relation to such activities as it was necessary to prove dishonest intentions at the beginning of the transaction and did not cover 'opportunist' offences. The section states that the term 'payment on the spot' includes payment at the time of collecting goods on which work has been done, or in respect of which a service has been provided. The payment must be one which is legally enforceable. Because the accused must make off 'without having paid *as required or expected*', an offence is not committed if the creditor has agreed that payment would be postponed, even if that postponement was procured as a result of a dishonest deception. However, this offence does not require 'deception' and the dishonesty need only be present at the time of 'making off'.

The offender must have known that payment on the spot was required or expected *of him*. This means immediate 'on the spot' payment. Therefore, if Jones takes two friends into a restaurant and orders meals on the clear understanding that it is his party and he will pay the bill, and the whole party leave without paying, only Jones commits this offence as payment was expected from him. The wording of the section is such that it distinguishes between instances in which an account may be settled at a later date and instances in which payment on the spot is required. If a garage mechanic goes to his firm's wholesalers and collects goods on behalf of his employer and leaves without signing for them, there can be no offence. A debt exists between his employer and the wholesaler. No one expected the mechanic to pay on the spot; his employer will settle the account and it is his employer who is expected to pay, but not on the spot. It would be different if the next customer is a private customer who has no account with the wholesaler and who wishes to make a credit card transaction. If the goods which he requires are supplied and he, seeing an opportunity, leaves without presenting his credit card so that the purchase can be recorded, he commits an offence. In this case, payment was clearly expected of him on the spot and such payment has not been made until the credit voucher has been made out.

This offence will frequently be associated with self-service garages, restaurants and taxis (where there is a clear requirement to pay on the spot), as opposed to the hiring of a car for a wedding, where payment is not required on the spot.

The section does not require the payment to be made at any particular spot. The words 'on the spot' relate to the knowledge which a customer must have of *when* payment must be made. The words 'dishonestly make off without payment' involve a departure without paying, from the place where payment would normally be made. Where a hotel customer arranged to postpone payment of his bill with a hotel proprietor, the Divisional Court said that the expectation that 'payment on the spot' would be made was removed, even if that agreement was obtained by deception.

Police powers

The offences against ss 1, 2 and 3 are arrestable offences.

Report writing rules

Introduction

The end product of the majority of police enquiries is a written report. A report is an official and confidential document containing all the relevant facts in a logical sequence. The skill in compiling a good report will only come with practice but, whether skilful or not, a report must always be legible, accurate, unambiguous and to the point. Many police forces have introduced special report forms for use in connection with particular incidents, for example, accident report books, process cards, minor incident reports and crime reports. All such documents are designed to ensure that a police officer obtains the required information by working through the various headings so that no detail is overlooked. The purpose of any report is to pass to others, usually senior officers, first-hand knowledge of an incident so that decisions can be made as to action which needs to be taken.

Occurrence and offence reports

Occurrence report

An occurrence report should accurately describe the details of an incident which does not involve the commission of an offence. It could refer to any street incident of such a nature that the attention of some other person needs to be drawn to it. Someone may collapse in the street and this may result in action being taken by a police officer which leads to that person being detained in a particular hospital. Apart from other considerations, the incident took place in public and it is likely that some form of enquiry will be made at the police station, perhaps by representatives of the local press or by relatives of the person concerned. It is important that supervisors and station officers are aware of such incidents. On occasions it may be necessary to do no more than make an entry in a station record book or update the command and control system; on many other occasions, a full report setting out the circumstances and detailing the action which was taken will be required. A patrolling officer may notice damaged road signs or road markings which are becoming obliterated and these matters need to be reported so that the highway authority can be informed. In such cases a record should be made or the command and control system should be updated.

These reports provide a permanent record in police stations of incidents which occur elsewhere. The matters so recorded are brought to the attention of any external agency involved or which may be interested. It must be remembered that even though an offence is not involved, proceedings may frequently take place in civil courts when damages are sought for injuries which result from such incidents. Frequently such proceedings occur long after the incident took place and it is, therefore, essential that an accurate record is made at the time.

Offence report

The purpose of this report is to report details of an offence committed by some person identified in the report. It is submitted to allow senior officers and the Crown Prosecution Service to decide whether proceedings should be taken before a court in respect of that offence. This report, in effect, forms the basis of the information which is given to a magistrate or to a justices' chief executive for a decision as to whether or not to issue a summons.

Two factors are very important in report writing:

(a) *Accuracy* – One of the purposes of a police officer's notebook is to allow essential information to be recorded accurately at the time of the incident. These entries will form the basis of any subsequent report. Offence reports form the basis of the prosecution's case in court and the report on the reverse of the offence report is in every respect an offence statement as the contents follow that form and recognise, as far as possible, the rules of evidence by containing only those facts which can be given in evidence. The contents of that report, supported by the oral evidence given by the constable, will to some considerable extent determine the guilt or innocence of the defendant.

It has already been said that occurrence reports may be referred to many years after their completion if proceedings arise in a civil court. Police officers may attend family disputes as a result of which there are no criminal proceedings. In most instances this will be an isolated incident, but on other occasions disputes will continue until some serious incident occurs and it becomes necessary to piece together events which have occurred over a number of years. It is therefore essential that reports are fully descriptive and accurate, sufficiently so to refresh the memory after the passage of a considerable time.

(b) *Legibility and clarity* – Reports are meant to be read by persons who have no direct knowledge of the incident described. It is therefore essential that the record is a written one and is legible. Many reports, which are of a standard type, are produced in a particular form to allow direct completion at the scene of an incident, e.g. an accident report. These are not subsequently typed or copied in another form. The original remains the permanent record. The clarity of any report must be proportionate to the circumstances of its completion. The correct use of the English language and the order in which the facts are assembled are important to its readability. Senior officers judge the efficiency of their constables to a marked degree by the quality of the written work which they submit.

Contents of occurrence and offence reports

Reports generally contain certain standard information, regardless of the nature of the incident which they describe. A police officer must ensure that certain factors are included in any report:

(a) Time, day, and date of incident or offence.
(b) The exact location of the incident, naming not only the street or road but the district or town. It is essential to be precise and it is usual to refer to a fixed spot which is identifiable, for example, at the junction of High Street with Elm Street.
(c) How the incident came to notice; was it seen or reported by some other person, etc.?
(d) Action taken by the police, including not only the action taken by the reporting officer but also action taken by any other police officers concerned with the incident. Where a person has been injured or property damaged, details of the persons concerned or the owner of the property should also be included. Where a person has been taken to hospital or some other establishment, the name of the hospital or building should be referred to in the report.

(e) Identities of all persons concerned. Surnames should be shown in capitals. Care must be taken to include ages and occupations as well as names and addresses. In relation to the person who is the subject of the report, the manner in which that person came to the notice of the officer should also be included. The exact age of juveniles, together with the parents' details and those of the school attended, should be included when offences are alleged to have been committed by juveniles.

(f) A clear account of events as they occurred and in the order of their happening is required. This gives the same sequence and flow to the report as the occurrence of the events themselves and this provides a clear picture to the reader.

(g) Any explanations given by persons must be in direct speech in the case of an offence report. It is helpful if this can be done in an occurrence report as the actual words used will always convey a clearer picture than any abstraction. However, when a lengthy occurrence has taken place requiring extensive and immediate action, this will not be possible.

(h) The officer submitting the report should sign it and include his rank and number.

(i) The report should be dated to show when it was submitted. On some occasions the time of submission will be extremely important as a matter of record.

Additional details

Occurrence reports

Occurrence reports are frequently addressed to particular persons, recognising the nature of the incident which is reported upon. They are submitted through the normal channels involving supervisory officers. Such reports should be given a clear general heading which indicates the nature of the incident being reported upon. If the officer completing the report wishes that any particular outside body or person be informed of any action or requirement, this should be indicated in the report. It may, for example, be necessary to inform a highway authority of the dangerous condition of a section of roadway. Administrative staff will prepare a letter for the authority based upon the substance of the report.

Offence reports

These must contain details of the full identity of all persons alleged to be offenders. Similar details should be included of witnesses. There must be an exact description of the offence committed and this is normally recorded on the front of the form. There must be a reference to the Act and section contravened. An example would be, 'Did use a motor vehicle, namely Ford motor car Registered Number A123 ABC on a certain road called Front Street, Dinnington, there not being in force in relation to the use of that vehicle such a policy of insurance or security in respect of third party risks as complies with the requirements of Part VI of the Road Traffic Act 1988, contrary to Section 143 Road Traffic Act 1988.'

When a registered company is the offender, for example when such a company is the owner of a defective vehicle, the name of the company secretary and the registered address of the company should also be included.

The basis of all good reports is a police officer's notebook. The essential details should always be noted carefully and an officer should rely upon remembering facts. The officer's notebook is issued primarily for the purpose of recording facts which may later be the subject of a report.

Robbery

Section 8(1) of the Theft Act 1968 provides:

> A person is guilty of robbery if he steals, and immediately before or at the time of doing so, and in order to do so, he uses force on any person or puts or seeks to put any person in fear of being then and there subjected to force.

Theft – an essential element

The subsection requires that in every offence of robbery there is a theft. It is probably more accurate to say that robbery is merely an aggravated form of theft, the person responsible being liable to a maximum sentence of life imprisonment. In considering charges of robbery it is helpful to examine the theft of the property first in order to ensure that all the essential points to prove are evident within the circumstances. A man who genuinely believes that he has the right to recover property to which he has a claim of right is not guilty of robbery if he does so by force provided that he genuinely believes that he has a claim of right as, in those circumstances, his actions are not dishonest. However, it is not sufficient merely for him to claim that he had *a* right to the property.

A previous tenant returned to the property to take goods forcibly from the landlord's possession to the value of his cash deposit which had not been returned to him. He accepted that he was aware that he had no legal right to the property which he took, but needed a bargaining counter to ensure that his property was returned. Whilst admitting that this was not the best way to achieve his aims, he claimed that what he did was fair and was not dishonest. His appeal against conviction for robbery was dismissed. The jury had been properly directed and came to the conclusion that his actions were dishonest. The facts of this case clearly illustrate the difference between a genuine claim of right and that which might be described as 'a convenient excuse'. Whatever else he might have believed he could not realistically have believed that he had a claim of right to the goods which he took.

A man who forcefully dispossesses another of his motor car and drives away does not commit robbery if he takes it for the purpose of escaping from a pursuer and with the intention of abandoning it when he has escaped from the scene. If he takes the car with the intention of permanently depriving the owner of it, he commits robbery.

The use of force

Having established that a theft has occurred, the circumstances should be examined for evidence of the use of force (which is the exercise of physical strength against another), or the threat to use force. There must be the use of force, or the threat of such use, in order to steal. The offence commonly known as 'mugging' provides a good example of robbery. The victim is assaulted and on occasions may be knocked unconscious before being relieved of his wallet and other valuables. On such occasions force is used for the purpose of making the completion of the theft much easier. If, however, two men fight outside a public house and one knocks the other unconscious, then later decides to relieve the other of his wallet, there is no robbery as the force was not used for the purpose of theft, the decision to steal having been made when the assault had been completed.

A threat of force must be directed at the person. To threaten the use of force against a man's home or his motor car is insufficient to justify a charge of robbery. Similarly, if the force used is merely sufficient to gain possession of the property, for example, to snap a watch chain, the offence will be one of theft rather than robbery as no force was directed against the person. The dividing line is frequently a fine one and it is a question of fact whether or not a charge of robbery should be preferred. If a man snatches a lady's handbag and runs away he has committed theft as the force was merely sufficient to gain possession of the property, but if the lady holds on to her handbag and it become necessary to use force to overcome her resistance, then force is used before or at the time of the theft and is directed against the person, and the offence is robbery. A threat of the future use of force is insufficient, it must be to use violence then and there.

Force must be used before or at the time of the theft

The force or threat of force must be used immediately before or at the time of the theft. If a threat is involved, it must refer to force which is to be used then and there, so that the property is given up while fear is acting upon the victim. Examples of force being used immediately before a theft have already been given. Instances of theft at the time at which force is applied are not so clear, as a theft occurs at the time at which property is appropriated. It may be argued that an appropriation has taken place immediately a thief grips property with a dishonest intention, but it is unlikely that the interpretation will be so narrow. If this view is taken, then as soon as a thief places his hand into a man's pocket and takes hold of his cigarette case an appropriation has taken place and if, on being discovered, he uses force against his victim to enable the removal of the cigarette case, a charge of robbery would not be possible. For this reason, it is more realistic to look at an act of appropriation as continuing until the property is completely removed. The distinction is important, as force offered after a theft has been completed will not constitute an offence of robbery in any circumstances. If a pickpocket steals a wallet and is pursued by his victim whom he subsequently assaults when he is caught, there is no robbery as the offence of theft was complete before the assault took place. In such circumstances it would be proper to charge theft and to include a separate charge of assault according to the degree of violence used, the intention of the assailant, and the injury caused to the victim.

The force or threatened use of force may be directed at any person. It is not essential that it is directed at the person from whom property is stolen. If a thief is about to steal property from a market stall and is seen by a shopper who has no connection with the stallholder, but who nevertheless attempts to prevent the completion of the theft, the use of force against him in order to steal would amount to robbery, provided that the theft is completed.

In circumstances in which a theft has not been completed, it may be possible to charge assault with intent to rob. It must be clearly shown that there was assault and that it was carried out with the intention of stealing property.

Police powers

The offences of robbery and assault with intent to rob are both arrestable offences.

Taking conveyances

Introduction

The offences concerned with the unlawful taking of conveyances in the Theft Act 1968 differ from the other offences of theft in that they do not require that the taker had an intention to deprive the owner permanently of his property. The motive for moving a conveyance is immaterial, if it is taken and moved in a way which involves its use as a conveyance, the offence is committed. Similar offences were dealt with by the Road Traffic Acts prior to the passing of the Theft Act. If a conveyance is appropriated with the intention of depriving the owner permanently of his property, then the offence is one of theft of a conveyance.

Taking conveyances

Section 12(1) of the Theft Act 1968 provides:

> A person shall be guilty of an offence if, without having the consent of the owner or other lawful authority, he takes any conveyance for his own or another's use or, knowing that any conveyance has been taken without such authority, drives it or allows himself to be carried in or on it.

Conveyance

Subsection (7) defines the term 'conveyance':

> 'conveyance' means any conveyance constructed or adapted for the carriage of a person or persons whether by land, water or air, except that it does not include a conveyance constructed or adapted for use only under the control of a person not carried in it or on it, and 'drive' shall be construed accordingly.

The term is a wide one and will include most motor vehicles, railway locomotives, aircraft, hovercraft, ships and dinghies. Some vehicles are excluded by the exception which describes forms of transport for the carriage of goods which are not controlled by a driver who is in or on the vehicle. Goods trailers, milk floats and trolleys such as those used by railway porters are not conveyances for the purpose of this section. The offence is an arrestable offence. The Criminal Justice Act 1988 made the offence a summary one. As there can be no offence of 'attempt' in relation to a summary offence, the previous offence of attempting to take a conveyance was removed by the 1988 Act.

Where there is an attempt to take conveyance, charges of 'vehicle interference' or 'criminal damage' will have to be considered as alternatives. Pedal cycles are dealt with separately.

Takes

The word 'takes' means to acquire possession. However, the mere unauthorised assumption of possession or control is not enough to constitute a 'taking' of a conveyance, there must be some movement of it.

A person who breaks into a car and is sitting in the driving seat has not taken it, but if he moves it only a few feet, he has taken it. A man who sits in a rowing boat and casts it adrift has taken it; he who stands on the shore and casts it adrift has not. Where two men pushed a motor car around a corner and hid it as a practical joke, this offence was not committed. The use did not involve use as a conveyance.

The necessity to acquire possession without being authorised means that no offence is committed by a person who merely uses a vehicle for some purpose which has not been specifically authorised by the owner, as he is already in possession of the vehicle and, therefore, cannot 'take' it.

It may be that a man is employed as a van driver and is authorised by his employer to use his motor vehicle for the purpose of delivering goods upon a prescribed route. If he decides to deviate without authority from this route, he is not guilty of taking the vehicle as it was already in his possession. The position is not so clear in circumstances in which the employee has completed his work for the day and parks his employer's vehicle outside his house and then returns to it later in the evening, outside his authorised working hours, and uses the vehicle for some private purpose. In such circumstances it has been held that when he parked the vehicle at the conclusion of his day's work, his authority to use it ceased and possession of the vehicle reverted to the employer, the employee merely having custody of it.

Although the distinction appears to be a fine one, it can be appreciated that Parliament did not intend to punish professional drivers who merely deviated from a prescribed route, but probably did intend to punish drivers who used their employer's vehicle for private purposes outside their hours of employment, against the wishes of the owner.

The High Court has also ruled that if a driver uses his employer's vehicle in a manner which is inconsistent with his terms of employment it may amount to a 'taking'.

In this instance, a driver had not only deviated from his route but had visited several public houses and had driven a number of friends to their homes, showing an intention to use the vehicle as he would his own. It has been held that merely to move a vehicle for convenience, because it was blocking a householder's doorway, does not in normal circumstances constitute an offence.

Without having the consent of the owner or other lawful authority

Section 12(6) provides that a person does not commit an offence under the section by anything done in the belief that he has lawful authority to do it or that he would have the owner's consent if the owner knew of his doing it and the circumstances involved.

The consent which is obtained from the owner must be a true consent and not one which has been given as a result of threats of violence or any other form of intimidation.

If a man with a pistol 'requests' permission to borrow a car, the consent which he obtains cannot be a valid one! On the other hand, a consent which has been obtained by fraud is nevertheless valid and prevents the offence from being committed. Where a hirer misrepresented his identity and falsely stated that he had a driving licence, he did not 'take' the car even though the consent was fraudulently obtained. If a man borrows his friend's car by alleging that he wishes to pick up his wife from the railway station, when in fact it was someone else whom he wished to meet, he does not take the car without consent. The consent gained is not invalidated by a deception as to the destination or purpose of the journey.

The term 'other lawful authority' recognises that the law authorises certain persons, including constables, to remove vehicles in certain circumstances without the consent of the owner and that an owner's representative, for example his wife, may on occasions give authority to some other person to use her husband's car.

If X hired a car to Y subject to a contractual requirement for Y to return it on a certain day, X would have lawful authority to take it in the event of its non-return.

The term 'other' means, in relation to a conveyance which is the subject of a hire purchase agreement, the person in possession under that agreement.

Drives it or allows himself to be carried in or on it, knowing it to have been taken without such authority

If special mention was not made of other persons who may knowingly use a conveyance which has been unlawfully taken by some other person, they would commit no offence provided that they were not a party to the original taking.

If a man takes a car without the owner's consent, drives it to the home of his friends, tells them what he has done and invites them to come for a drive with him, they cannot be charged with 'taking' the car as they were not present when it was taken, nor were they a party to its taking. However, having accepted the offer, each of them allows himself to be carried in the car and is, therefore, guilty of an offence. If one of them should subsequently drive the vehicle he may be charged with that offence.

When solo motor cycles are unlawfully taken it is not uncommon for others to drive the motor cycle at the taker's invitation, in the full knowledge that it has been so taken. On each occasion, the person concerned is guilty of driving the motor cycle knowing it to have been taken without authority; they cannot be charged with 'taking' as the act had previously been completed.

It may not always be possible to prove that the taker informed the persons concerned that the conveyance had been illegally acquired, but a court is entitled to take into account the surrounding circumstances which may make it clear that they must have known or, at least, have deliberately closed their eyes to the obvious.

Limitation upon proceedings for an offence against s 12(1)

Subsections (4A), (4B) and (4C) of s 12 of the Theft Act 1968 provide that proceedings for an offence of taking a conveyance without authority shall not be commenced after the end of the period of 3 years beginning with the day on which the offence was committed but, subject to that, may be commenced at any time within 6 months beginning with the 'relevant day'. The 'relevant day' is the day on which sufficient evidence to justify proceedings came to the knowledge of any person responsible for deciding whether to commence any proceedings.

For the purpose of proceedings conducted by a public prosecutor within 6 months of such evidence coming to his knowledge, a certificate to that effect will be conclusive evidence of the fact.

Aggravated vehicle taking

The Aggravated Vehicle Taking Act 1992 creates offences of aggravated vehicle taking by adding a s 12A to the Theft Act 1968. An offence is committed where a person has offended against s 12(1) in any way in relation to a mechanically propelled vehicle and it is proved that at any time after the vehicle was unlawfully taken (whether by himself or another) and before it was recovered, the vehicle was driven, or injury or damage was caused in one or more of the following circumstances:

(a) that the vehicle was driven dangerously (as defined by the Road Traffic Acts, see page 712) on a road or other public place;
(b) that, owing to the driving of the vehicle, an accident occurred by which injury was caused to any person;
(c) that, owing to the driving of the vehicle, an accident occurred by which damage was caused to any property other than the vehicle;
(d) that damage was caused to the vehicle.

However, it is a defence for such a person to prove that such driving, accident or damage occurred before he committed the basic offence, or that he was neither in, nor on, nor in the immediate vicinity of the vehicle when such driving, accident or damage occurred.

The Court of Appeal has held that, in relation to (c) above, the question must be, 'was the driving of the car a cause of the accident?' It was impossible to say that the words of s 12A(2)(b) import a requirement of fault in the driving of the vehicle. No word suggesting fault appears in the statutory language.

The Act extends the concept of 'joint enterprise' to these offences. All who commit an offence against the Theft Act 1968, s 12(1), where the motor vehicle is subsequently involved in one of the sets of circumstances set out in (a) to (d) above, are guilty of aggravated vehicle taking. Section 12(1) embraces those who drive and those who allow themselves to be carried in addition to those who 'take'. Thus, the difficult problem of proving who was actually driving at the time or who actually took the vehicle in the first instance is avoided as all offend against s 12(1). That those jointly involved in the enterprise should be similarly treated is reinforced by s 3 of the 1992 Act, which amends the Road Traffic Offenders Act 1988, s 34, to provide that the fact that a person who is convicted of an offence under the Theft Act 1968, s 12A, did not drive the vehicle in question at any particular time, or at all, shall not be regarded as a special reason for the purposes of s 34(1). The offences under s 12A require obligatory disqualification and obligatory endorsement of 3–11 penalty points. The offence is triable only on indictment and punishable with 2 years' imprisonment, or where the accident causes the death of some person, with 5 years' imprisonment. Where a person is found not guilty of aggravated vehicle taking he may be convicted of the basic offence and the Crown Court shall have the same powers as a magistrates' court in such circumstances.

The offences must be tried summarily if the 'value' of damage to the vehicle or to property is less than the 'relevant sum' specified in the Magistrates' Courts Act 1980, s 22, currently £5000. However, the restriction placed upon imprisonment by s 33 in such cases (maximum of 3 months) is removed in the case of aggravated vehicle taking.

Taking pedal cycles

As previously described, the taking of pedal cycles is dealt with separately by s 12(5) because of the nature of the punishment provided for the unlawful taking of other conveyances. The maximum penalty for offences involving pedal cycles is a fine at level 3, and these offences are not arrestable offences.

Subsection (5) provides that a person who, without having the consent of the owner or other lawful authority, takes a pedal cycle for his own or another's use, or rides a pedal cycle knowing it to have been taken without such authority, is guilty of a summary offence. The defence of belief in lawful authority, or that consent would have been given, also applies to offences involving pedal cycles.

Differences between taking conveyances or pedal cycles and theft

As described in the introduction to this subject, theft requires an intention to deprive the owner of his property permanently, but such an intention is deliberately excluded from these offences to make joyriding, in all forms of conveyances described in this section, punishable. Because at times, particularly when a conveyance has been kept by the accused person for a considerable period, the dividing line between theft and these offences will be a fine one, the section provides that on trial on indictment, an accused charged with theft of a conveyance may be found guilty of an offence under subsection (1).

Interference with vehicles

The Theft Act 1968 deals with offences of taking a conveyance, the term conveyance including motor vehicles. The offences under the Criminal Attempts Act deal with associated offences. If a person interferes with:

(a) a motor vehicle or trailer; or
(b) with anything carried in or on a motor vehicle or trailer, with the intention that an offence of
   (i) theft of the motor vehicle or trailer, or part of such vehicles, or
   (ii) theft of anything carried in or on the motor vehicle or trailer, or
   (iii) taking a conveyance, contrary to s 12 of the Theft Act 1968,

be committed either by himself or by another person, he shall be guilty of an offence of 'interference with vehicles', contrary to s 9 of the Criminal Attempts Act 1981.

These offences cover a wide range of activities.

A person interfering with the door locks of a vehicle is clearly interfering with the vehicle. As his actions develop and he enters the car, his intention should soon become apparent: he either intends to steal the car, or to steal property within the car or parts of the car. He may open the door to allow someone else to enter and steal property or the vehicle itself, and in such circumstances would be guilty of this offence of interference. Additionally, interference with the load on a vehicle or trailer with the intention of stealing is an offence. The removal of securing ropes and tarpaulins would amount to such interference. The terms 'motor vehicle' and 'trailer' have the meanings given to them by the Road Traffic Act 1988.

The distinction must be made between incidents of hooliganism and vandalism, and those involving theft or taking. Although those who 'rock' a vehicle to set off its alarm system or scratch the paintwork with a coin 'interfere' with a vehicle, they do not do so with the intention of theft or taking. He who breaks off a car aerial and throws it to the ground does not commit this offence, but he who pulls off a mirror with the intention of stealing it does.

Where an accused person can be shown to have intended to commit one of these offences, it is immaterial that it cannot be shown which offence it was.

Practical hints on investigation

Taking conveyances without authority is a common offence. It is unusual for conveyances to be taken before the eyes of a patrolling police officer, but this is not unknown. However, a much greater number *have* been taken when they are first observed by the police officer. There is always the possibility that the vehicle with which an officer is concerned may have been stolen or unlawfully taken.

Often the hour of the day and the circumstances of the use of the vehicle will attract suspicion, but the taking of motor vehicles is now a common occurrence at any time of the day or night. Particular care should be taken when checking ownership of a vehicle by questioning the driver. Has he any documentary proof of ownership? Not many drivers carry their vehicle registration documents but they frequently have other documents which carry their names and the registration mark of the vehicle, such as service schedules. If the ignition circuit has been bypassed then the driver must have a very good explanation for the need to have done so. Does the driver know the registration number? Surprisingly, many true owners do not, but they can usually give some indication of the range of the symbols. Is the driver conversant with the keys? Does he know which key fits which lock? Most drivers have a sound knowledge of the contents of the car and its boot. Even the unobservant must notice something in the course of using the vehicle daily. The details of the excise licence should be known, as should damage, marks or peculiarities affecting the vehicle. The driver and the occupants of the vehicle may be ill at ease if it has been unlawfully taken, although this need not necessarily be so as for many it is a daily pastime. Many habitual car thieves do not expect to be caught and are used to dealing with such checks. Familiarity with the controls is somewhat reassuring but the regular thief tends to take particular models of motor car with which he is familiar.

A PNC check can be helpful as there may be a record of the driver, occupants or the vehicle itself. However, it is important to remember that a negative response from the PNC does not mean that all is in order. It merely signifies that there is no record in the computer at that time.

Pedal cycles present additional difficulties because there is no registration system to assist enquiries. The observations to be made might include the size and suitability of the machine to the user. Does the user have cycle clips if wearing long trousers? The rider, if the owner, should have a knowledge of the make of the machine and the contents, if any, of the cycle bag. Are there any marks or peculiarities on the machine? Is the rider aware of these? Within many areas there is now a registration system in relation to pedal cycles. Many forces are involved in these schemes, which result in identifiable particulars of pedal cycles being recorded.

The art of easy conversation, which demands the stimulation of an exchange of information, will assist in such situations. A staccato, stilted form of questioning is artificial and unprofessional and leads conversation up a succession of blind alleys. Encourage suspects to be descriptive, give opportunities for them to enlarge upon their story, their explanation of where they have come from and where they are going to. The greater the opportunities given to allow them to talk, the greater the possibility of inconsistency.

Handling stolen goods

Offence

Section 22 of the Theft Act 1968 provides:

> A person handles stolen goods if (otherwise than in the course of stealing) knowing or believing them to be stolen goods he dishonestly receives the goods, or dishonestly undertakes or assists in their retention, removal, disposal or realisation by or for the benefit of another person, or if he arranges to do so.

It can be seen that there are a number of ways in which offences can be committed in respect of the handling of goods which have been stolen. It will be of assistance if the terms 'goods' and 'stolen goods' are examined before looking at the various forms of these offences.

Goods

Section 34 states that for the purposes of the Theft Act, 'goods', except in so far as the context otherwise requires, includes money and every other description of property except land and includes things severed from the land by stealing. It therefore seems that property which can be dishonestly handled is almost identical with property which may be stolen. There are, perhaps, minor differences which are restricted to things in action, e.g. assets handled by an executor.

Stolen goods

The meaning of 'stolen' is set out in s 24 of the Act and can be summarised as follows:

(a) goods which have been stolen in circumstances contrary to s 1;
(b) goods which have been obtained as a result of blackmail (s 21);
(c) goods which have been obtained by means of deception (s 15);
(d) goods which have been stolen abroad contrary to the law of that land, the stealing of which would, in England or Wales, have been contrary to ss 1, 15 or 21 of the Theft Act 1968.

References to stolen goods also include money which is dishonestly withdrawn from an account to which a 'wrongful credit' has been made, but only to the extent that the money derives from the credit. See page 268 for the definition of 'wrongful credit'. The circumstances set out above are likely to cover the dishonest handling of stolen goods in all circumstances in which police officers are likely to be involved.

The goods must be stolen goods at the time of the handling. When the taker of the property is under the age of criminal responsibility, the law conclusively presumes that such a person is incapable of theft and there being no original stealing, there cannot be a handling of stolen goods. It is not essential that the thief has been found guilty of stealing it; it is for the court to decide whether or not the property is stolen property. These issues can be some distance apart; it may frequently be clear to a court that property which is produced in the course of proceedings is stolen property, but it may be much more difficult to establish that a particular person is responsible for its theft. Frequently, offenders are dealt with for dishonestly handling stolen property when the person responsible for the original theft has not been apprehended or is perhaps unknown. In any case, evidence of the conviction of a thief is not admissible at the trial of a person charged with dishonestly handling, for the purpose of proving that the property is stolen. The status of the property is most frequently established by the evidence given by the owner of the property.

Goods ceasing to be stolen

It is extremely important that police officers realise that there comes a moment when goods cease to be stolen. Section 24(3) provides:

> But no goods shall be regarded as having continued to be stolen goods after they have been restored to the person from whom they were stolen or to other lawful possession or custody, or after that person and any other person claiming through him have otherwise ceased as regards those goods to have any right to restitution in respect of the theft.

It is obvious that if the owner discovers the whereabouts of his property and recovers it, it ceases to be stolen property, otherwise property once stolen would continue to be classified as stolen indefinitely. The addition of the words 'or to other lawful possession or custody' is most important to police officers. When, in the course of an investigation, a police officer recovers property on behalf of an owner, it ceases to be stolen property. The property has been taken into 'other lawful possession or custody'. This point is important, as no charge of dishonest handling will lie in circumstances in which police officers arrest a thief and take possession of stolen property on behalf of the owner, then subsequently allow the property to pass to a receiver.

If a police officer arrests a thief in his home and takes possession of the radio he has stolen and then discovers that a prospective purchaser, who knows that the radio is stolen, is about to call, and as a result returns the property to the thief before concealing himself, the purchaser does not handle stolen property when he 'buys' the radio. The property is in 'lawful possession and custody' of the police officer and is no longer stolen.

The words 'lawful possession or custody' are important. A thief stole cartons of cigarettes and loaded them on to a lorry. A security officer discovered them, initialled them for later identification and then informed the police, who allowed the lorry to be driven away. The goods were delivered to two men who admitted that they knew they were stolen. It was held that the security officer never took 'physical' possession of them; he merely wrote his name on them. He was, therefore, not exercising control over them and the goods at the material time remained stolen goods. At all material times the goods remained in the thief's possession and in his custody and he had full power to dispose of them as he saw fit. The goods remained stolen at the time of handling.

The moment at which an owner or other person with a title to goods ceases to have a right to restitution is not so apparent and is a question of fact. The owner himself can waive title at any time at which he chooses, and this occasionally occurs when property has been obtained as a result of deception. On discovering the deception, the owner may nevertheless be satisfied with the contract which has been made and give his approval. In such circumstances, although the property was originally classed as stolen property (having been obtained by deception contrary to s 15 of the Act), the owner has waived his title to it and no longer has a right to have the property restored to him (restitution). The passage of time has no bearing upon the matter; goods stolen today will remain the property of the owner as long as he does nothing to set aside his title.

The subsequent sale of stolen property to a person acting in good faith allows such a person to assume the rights of an owner without being guilty of theft, and he acquires a good title to the goods if bought in open market. In certain circumstances, it is possible for the original owner's right to restitution to become affected by later dealings in respect of the property.

Goods representing those originally stolen

It is possible for there to be a dishonest handling of goods other than those which were originally stolen, as s 24 also provides that references to stolen goods shall include, in addition to the goods originally stolen:

(a) any other goods which directly or indirectly represent or have at any time represented the stolen goods in the hands of the thief as being the proceeds of any disposal or realisation of the whole or part of the goods stolen or of goods so representing the stolen goods; and

(b) any other goods which directly or indirectly represent or have at any time represented the stolen goods in the hands of a handler of the stolen goods or any part of them as being the proceeds of any disposal or realisation of the whole or part of the stolen goods handled by him or of goods so representing them.

The effect of these provisions is that goods which an accused is charged with handling must, at the time of the handling or at some previous time:

(a) have been in the hands of the thief or of a handler; and

(b) have represented the original stolen goods in the sense of being the proceeds, direct or indirect, of a sale or other realisation of the original goods.

The 'thief' is the person by whose conduct the goods were originally stolen. A 'handler' is any person who has committed the act of handling with the necessary dishonest intention.

If a thief steals a transistor radio he is then in possession of a stolen radio set which may subsequently be dishonestly handled by some other person. Should he exchange the radio for a cigarette lighter, the lighter represents the stolen goods, being the proceeds of the disposal of the stolen property. Had the thief sold the radio set, then the money obtained as a result of the sale represents the stolen property, and if subsequently used to purchase a bicycle, the bicycle then represents the stolen property, being the proceeds of its disposal. The process is one which could continue indefinitely and police officers investigating handling offences frequently find the tasks of tracing the origin of any article in the possession of a thief or a receiver to be impossible.

The principle to bear in mind when dealing with such offences is that when a person's property is wrongfully converted into another form, he continues to own the property in its changed form. The only difficulty which can arise for police officers is in circumstances in which the actual stolen property is recovered from some other person who bought it innocently, and money is also recovered from the offender which represents the original property. The legal position is that immediately the stolen property is returned to the owner, it ceases to be stolen property and, at the same time, money, or other goods received in exchange for it, cease to represent 'stolen' property. In such cases, a court may give directions as to the disposal of money, or other goods representing this property, found in the possession of a thief or receiver.

Where an accused handles goods believing them to be stolen, although they were not stolen or those goods had lost their status as stolen goods, he may nevertheless be guilty of an attempt. The Criminal Attempts Act 1981 states that a person may be guilty of an attempt to commit an offence even though that offence could not, for some reason, be committed.

Status of 'wrongful credit' which is dishonestly obtained

Section 24A was added to the 1968 Act by the Theft (Amendment) Act 1996. This became necessary to overcome a ruling that wrongful credits could be created by electronic transfers of money in circumstances which did not involve an offence against the Theft Act 1968, s 15; see page 247. This meant that a wrongful credit could be created in circumstances in which, at least for a period of time, it was not the property of the person deceived. It could not therefore be 'handled'.

Section 24A provides that a person is guilty of an offence if:

(a) a wrongful credit has been made to an account kept by him or in respect of which he has any right or interest;
(b) he knows or believes that the credit is wrongful; and
(c) he dishonestly fails to take such steps as are reasonable in the circumstances to secure that the credit is cancelled.

The offence is concerned with 'money' credits and they are 'wrongful' if they represent the credit side of a money transfer obtained contrary to the provisions of s 15A.

However, the section goes further by stating that a credit to an account is also wrongful to the extent that it derives from:

(a) theft;
(b) an offence under s 15A of the Theft Act 1968;
(c) blackmail; or
(d) stolen goods.

As in the case of an offence against s 15A, it is immaterial (in particular) whether the account is overdrawn before or after the credit is made.

Where a person dishonestly, by deception, obtains a transfer of money from someone else's account to his own, he is guilty of an offence of obtaining a money transfer by deception contrary to s 15A. If he then retains that money, he commits an offence of dishonestly retaining a wrongful credit, contrary to s 24A. The offence is not, however, restricted to transfers of money and can be committed where a person knowing or believing that money is stolen, permits it to be paid into his account and takes no steps to cancel the credit. However, the offence covers circumstances in which a person causes a money transfer to be made to someone else's account, unknown to that person. If that person then fails to take reasonable steps to cancel the credit, he commits an offence as the credit is 'wrongful'.

Forms of handling

The term 'handling' is a collective term, describing different ways in which an offence can be committed contrary to s 22 of the Act. There is only one offence created by the section and it may be committed:

(a) by receiving stolen goods; or
(b) by dishonestly undertaking or assisting in their
    (i) retention;
    (ii) removal;
    (iii) disposal;
    (iv) realisation;
(c) by or for the benefit of another person, or arranging to do so.

Before the passing of the Theft Act 1968, the only offence known was that of receiving, one of the requirements of which was that the receiver must have had the goods in his possession or control. It is essential to remember that the section specifically excludes those who handle goods in the course of the original stealing. Such persons are guilty of theft.

Receiving

Receiving still remains somewhat distinct from the other forms of handling, as in all other instances the handling must have been by or for the benefit of another person. This provides a useful starting point in considering the correct form of charge in particular cases. If there is no evidence of handling for the benefit of another person, the only charge which will be appropriate is one of receiving or arranging to receive. Evidence must be available to show that the person concerned received the goods, and this might be done directly or by authorising employees to receive them on his behalf. It is not essential that the receiver acquires any profit or advantage from his actions, and it would be sufficient if he merely agreed to receive them into his warehouse for a short period to conceal them. However, it must be shown that he, knowing or believing the goods to be stolen, took them into his possession or under his control. If the stolen property has not yet been taken into possession or under control, the only charge to be considered would be one of arranging to receive stolen property. In considering charges of arranging to receive stolen property, it must be remembered that the arrangement must have been made after the theft had taken place, as it is essential that the receiver knows or believes the goods to be stolen.

Where goods are found on the premises of a particular person, but the premises are not in his sole occupation and there is no evidence that he received them, possession by that person can only be proved if it can be shown that the goods had come into the premises by arrangement and that an employee or agent had instructions from him to receive them. Such an employee or agent would also be guilty if he knew or believed that the goods were stolen.

A person may 'arrange to receive' stolen goods where there is an arrangement between him and another person (most frequently the thief) to receive stolen goods. If a person, having stolen property, approaches another and that person agrees to accept the property which he knows or believes to be stolen, he is guilty of arranging to receive those goods, whether or not they are subsequently delivered.

Undertaking and assisting

In cases other than receiving or arranging to receive the forbidden act must be done 'by or for the benefit of' a person other than the handler. 'Undertaking' and 'assisting' are the two key words which can be qualified by the words 'retention', 'removal', 'disposal' or 'realisation'. 'Retention' means keeping possession of, not losing, continuing to have. 'Removal' refers to the movement of stolen goods from one place to another, for example, taking stolen goods by means of a vehicle to another place. 'Disposal' is concerned with giving away, destroying, melting down or reducing to scrap. 'Realisation' means the exchange of the stolen goods for money or some other property.

If thieves take a motor lorry loaded with goods and, on arrival at a warehouse, are assisted with the unloading of the vehicle by others who know that the property is stolen, such persons have assisted in the removal of stolen goods, although they have no intention of receiving them. The person who lends the motor lorry for that purpose assists in the removal of those goods. Arranging to commit any of the offences of handling is also punishable, therefore, if the men had merely agreed to assist with the unloading of the vehicle but had not begun to do so, they would still be guilty of an offence. If a wife brings home household goods stolen from a shop and the husband allows such articles to remain in the house knowing that they have been so obtained, he is assisting in their retention, and if he later helps her to remove some of the goods, he is assisting in the disposal of the goods.

Verbal representation made for the purpose of concealing the identity of stolen goods, if made dishonestly and for the benefit of another, can amount to handling stolen goods by assisting in their retention. This might be so if a wife dishonestly denied that goods in the house were stolen and told lies about them to assist her husband to retain them.

For the benefit of another person

In all cases of undertaking and assisting in the retention, removal, disposal, or realisation of stolen goods (i.e. all charges other than those of receiving), it must be shown that such undertaking was for the benefit of another person, who should be named in the charge if his identity is known. If his identity is not known, the charge should indicate that the acts were done for the benefit of some person unknown.

Guilty knowledge

The guilty state of mind, or *mens rea*, necessary in handling offences is described by the words 'knowing or believing them to be stolen goods'. Before the Theft Act 1968, it was essential to prove actual knowledge that the property was stolen, and this was occasionally difficult to prove beyond doubt. If a man was offered property at a figure below the market price, he may have suspected that it had been stolen but may not have been sure. Now the question is simply: did he know or 'believe' that the property was stolen? A man might be said to 'know' that goods were stolen if he is told by someone with first-hand knowledge that this is so. 'Belief' is less than knowledge. It exists where a person says to himself, 'I do not know that these goods are stolen but there can be no other reasonable conclusion in the light of all the circumstances'. Mere suspicion is insufficient. If a man says to himself, 'I suspect that these goods are stolen but on the other hand they may not be stolen', this is insufficient as a 'belief' does not exist. The knowledge or belief must exist at the time that the goods are received, supervening belief or subsequent dishonesty is insufficient.

A second-hand dealer bought a watch worth £29 for £5. He admitted that he had taken a chance that the watch might be stolen. The Court of Appeal ruled that the prosecution must prove knowledge or belief.

It is not necessary to prove that the handler was aware of the precise nature of the goods. If he believes that crates contain stolen television receivers it is no defence that they in fact contained stolen radios.

The word 'dishonestly' qualifies 'knowing or believing' by requiring that the very act itself is criminal. It is possible that a man might handle property knowing that it is stolen, but may intend to return it to the owner. In such circumstances his act would not be dishonest.

In practice, when stolen property is found in the possession of some person other than the thief, full enquiries are made to establish the transactions which took place between the thief, handler and any other person. Factors which assist in establishing knowledge or belief that property had been stolen are: property which has been carefully concealed on premises, the owner having denied its presence prior to its being found; identification marks destroyed; immediate, furtive disposal (perhaps at night), or secret disposal; purchase of property at a price well below market value; or the lack of records by persons who normally keep records of all goods upon the premises.

Recognising the difficulty which may be encountered by the police in proving knowledge or belief that property had been stolen, s 27 of the Theft Act allows special evidence to be given in certain circumstances, but only in respect of handling charges. Provided that evidence has been given of possession, arranging, undertaking or assisting in the retention, removal, disposal or realisation, the following evidence may be given to help to prove knowledge, or belief, that the property was stolen:

(a) evidence that he has had in his possession or has undertaken or assisted in the retention, removal, disposal or realisation of stolen goods from any theft taking place not earlier than 12 months before the offence charged; and

(b) (provided that 7 days' notice in writing has been given to him of the intention to prove the conviction) evidence that he has, within the 5 years preceding the date of the offence charged, been convicted of theft or of handling stolen goods.

Although advantage is not always taken of the provisions of this section by the police, its value is readily apparent. If premises are raided upon which it is suspected that there is stolen property, it is likely that goods stolen upon many separate occasions will be recovered by the police. The court may be reluctant to accept that the owner of the premises knew or believed that property was stolen if property connected with only one offence of theft is found, but is unlikely to accept that the owner could innocently come into possession of property connected with a number of offences of theft. In the same way, the provisions outlined in (b) allow a court to take notice of the fact that the owner of the premises is either a thief or a receiver of stolen property. The Court of Appeal has ruled that (a) above does not permit the introduction of details of a previous conviction for an offence of handling and this seems to be a reasonable approach. It appears obvious that the Act at that point is concerned with other property found at the time.

Evidence of recent possession of stolen goods in the hands of receivers or handlers may be offered. A court may infer guilty knowledge if the defendant offers no explanation, or the court does not believe the explanation offered. However, where stolen goods are found in the premises of a particular person, to establish that those goods were in his actual or constructive possession it must be shown that the goods came to the premises by his arrangement and that he accepted the goods, or a servant or agent had instructions to accept them on his behalf.

Police powers

The handling of stolen property is an arrestable offence. Because of the nature of these offences, it is frequently necessary for premises to be searched for stolen property. Section 26, therefore, authorises a justice, on receipt of information on oath that there is reasonable cause to believe that a person has stolen goods in his custody or possession, to grant a search warrant authorising a constable to search for and seize the property at any time.

Application of road traffic law

Classification of vehicles subject to legislation

The Road Traffic Acts and regulations deal with the use of all vehicles on roads. The term 'vehicle' includes any kind of carrier or conveyance, not necessarily a motor vehicle. In order to apply the law correctly it is important to distinguish between the various types of motor vehicles, particularly in relation to the Road Vehicle (Construction and Use) Regulations, and the type of licence required to drive certain classes of motor vehicle. The term 'motor vehicle' is defined in s 185 of the Road Traffic Act 1988 as meaning: 'a mechanically propelled vehicle intended or adapted for use on roads'.

This definition applies for the purposes of the Road Traffic Acts 1988 and regulations made thereunder, but it does not necessarily apply under the Vehicle Excise and Registration Act 1994; for the purposes of that Act, a mechanically propelled vehicle does not need to be intended or adapted for use on a road. 'Mechanically propelled' means constructed so that the vehicle can be propelled by mechanical means; thus, a motor-assisted pedal cycle comes within the terms of the definition even while it is being propelled by the pedals. Similarly, a motor car with the engine removed is still classed as mechanically propelled if there is evidence that admits the possibility of the engine being restored. The term 'mechanically propelled' includes not only petrol and oil-driven vehicles but also steam and electricity-driven vehicles.

The test of whether a mechanically propelled vehicle is intended or adapted for use on roads is whether a reasonable person, looking at the vehicle, would say that its general use encompassed possible general use on a road. The particular use to which a particular person puts a vehicle is irrelevant. A vehicle which was originally manufactured for use on a road may cease to be a 'motor vehicle' for the purposes of s 185 if it is subsequently altered, but only if such alterations are very substantial.

Some motor vehicles are obviously 'mechanically propelled' but they are not 'intended or adapted for use on a road'. An obvious example is a go-kart. Whether or not some motor vehicles are intended or adapted for use on a road will depend upon the evidence as to their construction. The test is whether a reasonable person looking at the vehicle would say that its general use encompassed possible general road use, and the particular use to which a particular person put a vehicle is irrelevant. In contrast, a motorised scooter known as a 'go-ped' was held to be a motor vehicle in respect of which the rider must have a driving licence and insurance. The go-ped consisted of a small foot platform attached to a two-barred sub-frame on which the person using the go-ped would stand. The vehicle was powered by a 22.5-cc engine which was attached to the rear. It was capable of a maximum speed of 20 mph. The braking system was such that it could not stop the vehicle if it was travelling at any great speed, or when the brakes were applied in an emergency situation. Severe braking caused the rear wheel to lift from the road surface.

The Divisional Court said that the roadworthiness of a conveyance or its capability to be used safely on a road was not conclusive in relation to whether or not its use on a road was contemplated. There was no obvious place in which a go-ped could be used, other than on a road. It could not travel on rough ground or soft or uneven surfaces. It was not designed for use in a place other than a road, such as was the case with a dumper truck, which was specifically constructed for use in connection with road construction. Regardless of the fact that the manufacturers said that it was not to be used on a road, it would be and the reasonable person would recognise that to be so.

Classification of motor vehicles by unladen weight

Many motor vehicles are classified by means of their unladen weight, that is, the weight unladen of the vehicle inclusive of the body and all parts which are necessary to or ordinarily used with the vehicle when working on a road, but excluding the weight of water, fuel, batteries used for propulsion and of loose tools and loose equipment. Loose equipment does not include loose boards fitted in slots at the side of a lorry to enable it to carry a heavier load but it would include moveable shelves fitted to slide on brackets in a baker's van. For our consideration, vehicles can be divided into those which are solely used for the carriage of passengers, goods vehicles, those which carry permanent equipment (e.g. mobile cranes) and motor cycles. A description of all types of vehicle follows.

Types of motor vehicle

Invalid carriage

The term 'invalid carriage' is defined by s 185 Road Traffic Act 1988 as:

> a mechanically propelled vehicle, the weight of which unladen does not exceed 254 kg (5 cwt) and which is specially designed and constructed, and not merely adapted, for use of a person suffering from some physical defect or disability and is used solely by such a person.

When an invalid carriage exceeds 254 kg (5 cwt) in unladen weight, it is classified as a motor car or motor cycle, depending on its weight and number of wheels.

An invalid carriage must not only be specially designed and constructed for the sole use of a disabled person, but must only be used by such a person. When used by a person who is not disabled, the vehicle ceases to be an invalid carriage and any exemption granted by the Act or regulations to invalid carriages would cease to apply for the period when it was being used.

It should be noted, however, that for the purpose of driver licensing, the maximum weight of an invalid carriage is increased to 510 kg.

Motor cycle

The term 'motor cycle' is defined in s 185 as:

> a mechanically propelled vehicle, not being an invalid carriage, with less than four wheels and the weight of which unladen does not exceed 410 kg (8 cwt).

This general definition is sufficient for most purposes and covers all mechanically propelled vehicles with less than four wheels and not exceeding 410 kg.

An electrically assisted pedal cycle is not a motor cycle. It is not a motor vehicle of any description. In general terms, an electrically assisted pedal cycle is one fitted with pedals and an electric motor which will not propel the vehicle in excess of 15 mph.

Motor car

We are all familiar with this term, but again for the purposes of the Road Traffic Acts and Road Traffic Regulation Act and associated regulations the term is defined by s 185 as being:

> A mechanically propelled vehicle, not being a motor cycle or an invalid carriage, which is constructed itself to carry a load or passengers and the weight of which unladen:
>
> (a) if it is constructed solely for the carriage of passengers and their effects, is adapted to carry not more than seven passengers exclusive of the driver, and is fitted with tyres of such a type as may be specified in regulations made by the Secretary of State, does not exceed 3050 kg (3 tons);
> (b) if it is constructed or adapted for use for the conveyance of goods or burden of any description, does not exceed 3050 kg (3 tons), or 3500 kg (3½ tons) if the vehicle carries a container or containers for holding for the purpose of propulsion of any fuel which is wholly gaseous at 17.6 °C under a pressure of 1.013 bar or plant and materials for producing such fuel;
> (c) does not exceed 2540 kg (2½ tons) in a case falling within neither of the foregoing paragraphs.

Let us examine these three categories. Sub-paragraph (a) refers to the type of vehicle which we know as the private motor car, the important point being that such vehicles are constructed solely for the carriage of passengers and their effects. Sub-paragraph (b) covers two types of motor cars, the first being a motor vehicle constructed or adapted for the carriage of goods or burden of any description which would include such things as a small van or light lorry, neither of which would exceed 3050 kg unladen weight, and the second type being a motor vehicle which uses gas as a fuel and carries the gas in containers fitted to the vehicle, or carries the plant and materials used for producing gas to power the engine. Gas-fuelled motor vehicles not exceeding 3500 kg (3½ tons) and used for the carriage of goods are not common, although the incidence of the use of such vehicles has increased since the levels of fuel tax have increased sharply.

For the purpose of vehicle classification, articulated vehicles are declared to be goods vehicles, i.e. vehicles which are deemed to be constructed to carry a load. This applies to the towing unit when a trailer is not attached. In effect then at (b) we are talking about goods vehicles. Sub-paragraph (c) refers to vehicles which cannot be classified as (a) or (b), e.g. a minibus.

Heavy motor car

This type of vehicle is often confused with a motor car; in fact, the most common examples you will find of a heavy motor car are either lorries constructed to carry goods or motor coaches constructed to carry passengers. Examine the definition as given by s 195, and you will see that these two examples fit perfectly. The definition reads:

> a 'heavy motor car' means a mechanically propelled vehicle, not being a motor car, which is constructed itself to carry a load or passengers and the weight of which unladen exceeds 2540 kg (2½ tons).

This definition covers a wide range of vehicles, from the small lorry or a coach to the juggernaut or the large double-decked public service vehicle. The important distinction to be made between this class of vehicle and the following three classes is that a heavy motor car is constructed to carry a load or passengers whereas the next three classes are not constructed to carry any load.

Motor tractor

When one thinks of a motor tractor, immediately a picture of a tractor used on a farm springs to mind, but the term embraces a wider variety of vehicle than agricultural tractors. The important points to remember are that such a vehicle does not carry a load or passengers and has a maximum weight rather than a minimum weight as with heavy motor cars. If the vehicle exceeds this maximum weight then it falls into one of the next two classes of motor vehicle. The definition of a motor tractor is contained in s 185, and reads:

> a 'motor tractor' means a mechanically propelled vehicle which is not constructed itself to carry a load, other than the following articles, that is to say, water, fuel, accumulators and other equipment used for the purpose of propulsion, loose tools and loose equipment, and the weight of which unladen does not exceed 7370 kg (7¼ tons).

The type of motor tractor you will normally see used on roads is a large motor vehicle drawing a laden trailer. The drawing vehicle itself does not carry a load but provides the motive power to tow the trailer; a common example is the type used by travelling show-men to tow a trailer with fairground equipment, or the type used by a large haulage company to draw a trailer carrying a large, indivisible load.

Light locomotive

The term 'locomotive' conjures up a picture of a railway engine, but the term also extends to wheeled vehicles used on roads and, like the motor tractor, this type of vehicle is not constructed to carry a load but intended to draw heavily laden trailers or for other purposes unconnected with the carriage of a load.

The definition of a light locomotive is contained in s 185, and reads:

> a 'light locomotive' means a mechanically propelled vehicle which is not constructed itself to carry a load, other than articles used in connection with propulsion of the vehicle, loose tools and loose equipment, and the weight of which unladen does not exceed 11 690 kg (11½ tons) but does exceed 7370 kg (7¼ tons).

A light locomotive is thus distinguished from a motor tractor purely in terms of unladen weight.

Heavy locomotive

This term also applies to wheeled vehicles used on roads and the points made above under light locomotive apply equally to this class of vehicles. The definition of this class of motor vehicle is contained in s 185, which reads:

> a 'heavy locomotive' means a mechanically propelled vehicle which is not constructed itself to carry a load other than any of the articles aforesaid (see under 'Motor tractor'), and the weight of which unladen exceeds 11 690 kg (11½ tons).

This is the largest type of motor vehicle which will be found in use on a road, other than a special type of vehicle the use of which has been specifically authorised by the Secretary of State.

Other types of vehicle

The next group of motor vehicles is distinguished by their construction and not by unladen weight, although they will also, by reason of their unladen weights, fall into one of the classes of motor vehicle dealt with above.

Articulated vehicle

Generally, an articulated vehicle can be described as a vehicle so constructed that it can be divided into two parts, both of which are vehicles and one of which is a motor vehicle. When we think of this in terms of goods vehicles we see a tractive unit with a trailer attached to it in such a way that a substantial part of the weight of the trailer is borne by the motor vehicle. The trailer is, therefore, resting on the back of the towing vehicle by superimposition, rather than being attached in the normal way, by a tow bar.

An 'articulated bus' is a passenger vehicle similarly constructed, but usually incapable of being divided other than in a workshop. Passengers must be able at all times, when the vehicle is coupled up, to move from one part to another.

Dual-purpose vehicle

As the title suggests, this is a motor vehicle which can be used to carry either passengers or goods, or both, if the vehicle is capable of transmitting the driving power of the engine to all the wheels of the vehicle or it is constructed in accordance with certain specifications and in either case the unladen weight of the vehicle does not exceed that specified. This definition of a dual-purpose vehicle is contained in Regulation 3(2) of the Road Vehicles (Construction and Use) Regulations 1986 and reads:

> a 'dual-purpose vehicle' means a vehicle constructed or adapted for the carriage both of passengers and of goods or burden of any description, being a vehicle of which the unladen weight does not exceed 2040 kg which either:
>
> (a) satisfies the conditions as to construction, or
> (b) is so constructed or adapted that the driving power of the engine is, or by the appropriate use of controls of the vehicle can be, transmitted to all the wheels of the vehicle.

The types of motor vehicle referred to in (b) above are Land Rovers, Jeeps and vehicles, not being track-laying vehicles, which are designed to travel on both rough land and roads.

The types of vehicle referred to in (a) are mainly shooting brakes, estate cars and utility brakes, which comply with certain conditions as to construction. These are mainly concerned with such vehicles having a rigid roof and at least two passenger seats in the rear of the vehicle, together with side windows in the rear section of the vehicle.

Classification of offenders

When we examine road traffic provisions, we continually find that a person commits an offence if he 'uses, causes or permits' some act or omission. These three terms are used disjunctively and have different meanings. For example, when we report offenders for breaches of the statutory provisions relating to the construction and use of motor vehicles, we have to state which of the three terms applies, whether the offender 'used' the vehicle, 'permitted' the use, or 'caused' the vehicle to be used. We shall look at these terms in greater depth when we study offences which can be committed under the Road Vehicles (Construction and Use) Regulations where they are often given a wider interpretation. However, we shall now look at the general application of these terms to road traffic offences.

Use

The term 'use' should be given its everyday, ordinary meaning. A person who drives a motor vehicle uses it and so does the person who owns it if it is used by his employee upon his business. The offence is one of strict liability, that is, awareness of the defective condition of a vehicle is irrelevant, as is the fact concerning whether or not a person should have known about it. To 'use' a vehicle there must be an element of controlling, operating or managing the vehicle as such.

If a person drives a motor lorry which proves to have a defective tyre, he 'uses' the vehicle; so does the owner of the vehicle if it is used upon his business by an employee. However, a person who lends his motor car to a friend without conditions, allowing the friend to use the vehicle in any way which he pleases, does not 'use' the motor car when it is being used solely for a purpose relevant to the friend. In such circumstances it is not being used for any purpose relevant to the owner.

Where the statutory provisions relate to 'using, causing or permitting', the only persons who can be convicted of 'using' are the driver or the employer of the driver if the vehicle was being driven on the employer's business, or the owner when he is being driven in his own vehicle for his purposes. The Divisional Court has ruled that a person is the 'user' only if he is the owner or the driver of the vehicle, but it applies to the owner only if the driver is employed by the owner under a contract of service and at the material time he is driving on his employer's business. Thus, an owner is not 'using' where he employs a self-employed driver who is paid on a daily basis and who pays his own tax and national insurance, even though that person is driving that person's vehicle. Drivers provided by an employment agency are usually employees of that agency, not the owner of the vehicle. Where there is no strict employer/employee relationship, charges of 'causing' or 'permitting' must be preferred.

However, offences under the Vehicle Excise and Registration Act can relate to the user of a vehicle or the keeper of the vehicle. When considering whether or not a vehicle is being used on a road without insurance, one should ask two questions: is it a road in the ordinary sense, that is, a definable way between two points over which vehicles can pass?; and do the public, or a section of the public, have access to that path which appears to be a definable way?

Cause or permit

The term 'cause' involves some degree of dominance or control, and it involves some express or positive command or direction to the other person. A general manager of five depots, each of which was independently supervised, was held not to have 'caused' a vehicle to be used on a road in a dangerous condition. If the general manager had ordered one of the vehicles to be used for a specific purpose, he could have been 'causing' the use in those circumstances.

The term 'permit' is somewhat looser than 'cause'. There is not the same express or positive mandate as in 'cause'. It includes those cases when permission may be inferred, for example, where a person requests the loan of your vehicle and you tell him that he can use the vehicle any time he likes, and give him the keys. It cannot be said that you 'caused' him to use the vehicle, but you certainly 'permitted' him to use the vehicle.

'Causing' and 'permitting' always refer to another person. A person should not be reported for causing or permitting himself to commit an offence, although there are some offences involving a person causing a vehicle to be in a place in which it should not be. It is often difficult to differentiate between the two terms and if in doubt choose 'permitting', which does not require the control or positive mandate required by the term 'causing'. The essential element of each, as opposed to 'using', is that *mens rea* is necessary for these two offences.

Aid, abet, counsel or procure

If a person aids, abets, counsels or procures another to commit an offence, then he is liable to be tried and punished as if here were a principal, i.e. the offender himself. When the offence is summary, the relevant statutory provision is s 44 of the Magistrates' Courts Act 1980, and where the offence is indictable, it is s 8 of the Accessories and Abettors Act 1861. Now, let us examine these terms to get their true meaning in relation to offences.

A person aids and abets an offence if, knowing all the circumstances which constitute the offence, he assists the principal in committing the offence. In such circumstances he may be said to be an aider and abettor. It is not necessary for the defendant to realise that the facts known to him amount to an offence. To use a simple example: the holder of a provisional licence is riding his solo motor cycle with a pillion passenger who knows that the driver has a provisional driving licence. The motor cycle is not displaying 'L' plates. The driver commits the offences of (a) carrying a passenger and (b) failing to display 'L' plates as required by his licence. He could not commit the first offence unless the passenger actively assisted by being on the vehicle; thus, the passenger commits the offence of aiding and abetting the offence at (a), but unless there was evidence that he actively assisted the driver to remove the 'L' plates, or to persuade him to drive without the plates, he does not aid and abet the offence at (b) merely because he was being carried on the vehicle.

If a person shuts his eyes to the obvious, he may be guilty of aiding and abetting, although in most circumstances inactivity will be insufficient to constitute assistance. However, if a person deliberately refrains from making enquiries the results of which he may not wish to know and the nature of the offence is such that it is obvious, an aiding and abetting may occur.

In relation to the supervisor of a learner driver, the supervisor has a special relationship with the driver which places him under certain obligations. If the supervisor permitted the learner driver to drive without 'L' plates, he would be aiding and abetting the offence notwithstanding that he did not actively assist in the removal of the 'L' plates.

The words 'aid, abet, counsel or procure' create only one offence and all the words can be used in a charge.

See page 376 for further explanation of these terms.

Police powers to stop motor vehicles

Section 163 of the Road Traffic Act 1988 empowers a constable in uniform to require a person driving a mechanically propelled vehicle, or a cycle, on a road to stop. Failure to comply is an offence. A constable in uniform may arrest a person without warrant if he has reasonable cause to suspect that the person has committed this offence.

Motor vehicles – registration and licensing

Registration

The Secretary of State for Transport has a duty to register all mechanically propelled vehicles used or kept on public roads in Great Britain. All records related to mechanically propelled vehicles are held by the Driver and Vehicle Licensing Agency (DVLA) at Swansea and stored in a computer.

Registration is completed when the details of the vehicle, such as colour, body, chassis number and engine number, are recorded, together with the name and address of the person who is the owner or keeper of the vehicle. On registering a vehicle, the Secretary of State will assign a registration mark and issue a registration document which contains the registered particulars of the vehicle. The provisions in respect of motor dealers allow the Secretary of State to issue 'blocks' of registration numbers to suitable motor dealers who are then in a position to allocate particular numbers to vehicles purchased by customers, supply the necessary registration plates and send details of each vehicle and its owner to the DVLA. This registration document is not to be treated as proof that the person shown as the owner or keeper of the vehicle referred to in the registration document is the owner of the vehicle.

The Road Traffic (Vehicle Testing) Act 1999 provides a statutory basis for the establishment of a central computer database of motor vehicles and while this will be concerned with vehicle testing procedures at the outset, it is intended that the Act will provide, in due course, the option of a paperless form of vehicle relicensing.

The Motor Vehicles (Access to Driver Licensing Records) Regulations 2001 set out the conditions under which this information may be made available to the Police Information Technology Organisation.

Regulation 2 provides that the purposes for which constables may be given access to information made available to the Police Information Technology Organisation. They are:

(a) the prevention, investigation or prosecution of a contravention of any provision of the following enactments:
   (i) the RTA 1988;
   (ii) the RTOA 1988;
   (iii) the RT (Northern Ireland) Order 1981;
   (iv) the RT (Northern Ireland) Order 1995; and
   (v) the RTO (Northern Ireland) Order 1996;
(b) ascertaining whether a person has had an order made in relation to him under
   (i) s 40B(1) or (5) (disqualifications from driving: further provisions) of the Child Support Act 1991;
   (ii) s 248A(1) (general power to disqualify offenders) or s 248B(2) (power to disqualify fine defaulters) of the Criminal Procedure (Scotland) Act 1995; or
   (iii) s 39(1) (offenders) or 40(2) (fine defaulters) of the Crime (Sentences) Act 1997.

In relation to further disclosure, reg. 3 provides that information to which constables have been given access may be further disclosed to an employee of a police authority for any purpose ancillary to, or connected with, the use of the information by constables.

Mechanically propelled

The term 'mechanically propelled vehicle' is wider than the term 'motor vehicle' as defined in the Road Traffic Act 1988, which states that a motor vehicle is a mechanically propelled vehicle intended or adapted for use on a road. The Vehicle Excise and Registration Act 1994 and regulations made under that Act apply to all mechanically propelled vehicles used or kept on public roads, whether or not the vehicle was intended or adapted for such use. If, for example, a go-kart was seen being used on a public road, then, because such a vehicle has been held not to be a motor vehicle intended or adapted for use on a road, any breach of the provisions contained in the Road Traffic Act or regulations made under the Act would not be an offence, but, because the go-kart is a mechanically propelled vehicle, any use on a public road is a breach of the provisions contained in the Vehicle Excise and Registration Act 1994 or any regulations made under the Act.

Section 1(1A) of the Vehicle Excise and Registration Act 1994 provides that duty will be charged in respect of every *thing* (whether or not it is a vehicle) that has been, but has ceased to be, a mechanically propelled vehicle. Thus, the fact that something which has been a mechanically propelled vehicle has changed in character so that it will no longer fit within this definition is irrelevant to the issue if it is used or kept on a public road.

Used or kept

A person 'keeps' a mechanically propelled vehicle on a public road if he causes it to be on such a road for any period, however short, when it is not in use there. From this it appears that the mere sight of a vehicle stationary and unattended on a public road is sufficient evidence to show that the vehicle was kept there, and evidence of any 'use' is sufficient to show that the vehicle was being used on a public road.

Where the driver is an employee of the owner or keeper of the vehicle and is using it on his employer's business, but is not responsible for registering or licensing the vehicle, it was held that it would be oppressive to take action against the driver and proceedings should be limited to the owner or keeper, who would also be deemed to be using the vehicle in such circumstances. (See 'Vehicle excise licence', page 293.)

Public road

This means 'a road repairable at public expense', and it therefore does not include privately maintained roads such as those that may be found in a dock area or an enclosed factory complex. It should be noted that this definition is much narrower than the definition of road contained in the Road Traffic Act 1988. A situation may arise where a mechanically propelled vehicle is seen being used on a road in contravention of a provision contained in the Vehicle Excise and Registration Act 1994 or regulations made under the Act, but because the road is not repairable at public expense the statutory provisions would not apply. However, if it could be proved that there was public access to this road, the provision of the Road Traffic Act 1988 would apply and a check may reveal offences under that Act or associated regulations.

Vehicle registration document

When the Secretary of State registers a mechanically propelled vehicle, he issues a registration document and, unless a registration mark has already been assigned by a motor dealer who has received a 'block' of numbers, assigns a registration mark to that vehicle. Even if a vehicle is exempt from the requirement to be licensed, it must still be registered. A registration document contains the registered particulars of the vehicle and the name and address of the person shown in the register as the keeper of the vehicle.

Regulation 13 of the Road Vehicles (Registration and Licensing) Regulations 2002 provides that where a registration document has been, or may have been, lost, stolen, destroyed or damaged, or it contains any particulars that have become illegible, the registered keeper must apply for a replacement. In the case of damage or illegibility the document must accompany the application. In any other case an oral application by telephone may be accepted. Provided that he is satisfied as to the circumstances, the Secretary of State must issue a replacement document. Before doing so, he may require the keeper of the vehicle to produce the vehicle, or evidence that it accords with its currently registered particulars. Regulation 15(3) and Schedule 3 to the 2002 Regulations, which provide for the issue of a new registration document, have effect in certain circumstances where the vehicle concerned is one with regard to which an insurer has informed the Secretary of State that it has 'written off' the vehicle and destroyed the registration document, or the registration document has been surrendered under reg. 20(5): the schedule requires the production and examination of the vehicle in order to ascertain that it is the registered vehicle concerned.

By reg. 12, a police officer can require the owner to produce a registration document and he must produce it for inspection if he is at any reasonable time required to do so. There are no provisions for later production as there are in the case of licences or insurance certificates.

The registered owner of a mechanically propelled vehicle is not necessarily its legal owner, and possession of a registration document is not in itself proof of ownership.

In addition to the requirements already set out in relation to the Police Information and Technology Organisation, reg. 27 of the Road Vehicles (Registration and Licensing) Regulations 2002 authorises the Secretary of State to make available particulars contained in the register to a local authority investigating an offence or a decriminalised parking contravention, a chief officer of police or any person who can show satisfactory cause for requiring the information. Regulation 28 authorises the Secretary of State to sell such particulars to such persons as he considers fit, for a fee and within conditions which he considers appropriate, provided that the information does not identify any person or contain anything enabling such identification.

Notification of change of ownership

Where the registration book was issued before 24 March 1997

Regulation 21 of the Road Vehicles (Registration and Licensing) Regulations 2002 deals with the procedures to be followed when there is a change in the ownership of a mechanically propelled vehicle in respect of which the current vehicle registration book was issued before 24 March 1997. The registered keeper must deliver the part of the registration document which relates to a change of keeper to the new keeper and notify the Secretary of State forthwith on that part of the document which relates to notification of transfer (or otherwise in writing) of the change of keeper, giving the date of transfer, name and address of the new keeper, the registration mark of the vehicle and the make, model and colour of the vehicle.

The new keeper of the vehicle, if he intends to use or keep the vehicle upon public roads otherwise than under a trade licence (see below) or does not intend to use or keep the vehicle on public roads, must enter his name and address in the space provided in the document and send it to the Secretary of State, or notify him otherwise in writing. If the new owner intends to use the vehicle on public roads solely under a trade licence, he must notify the Secretary of State that this is his intention on or before whichever is the sooner of:

(a) the expiration of the period of 3 months beginning with the date on which he became keeper of the vehicle; or
(b) if a further change of keeper occurs, the date of the change.

Where the registration book was issued on or after 24 March 1997

Regulation 22 is concerned with changes of ownership affecting vehicles in respect of which the registration document was issued on or after 24 March 1997. The regulation recognises the change in the form of the registration document issued for such vehicles. In effect, where there is a 'private' sale or transfer of a vehicle, that is, to a person other than a motor vehicle trader, the registered keeper must give the new keeper the part of the registration document which provides for particulars of a new keeper, to that new keeper, and must forthwith send to the Secretary of State the remainder of the registration document giving:

(a) the name and address of the new keeper;
(b) the date of transfer;
(c) a signed declaration that this information is correct to the best of his knowledge; and
(d) a signed declaration made by the new keeper to the effect that this information is correct.

By reg. 23, where the new keeper in such a case is a vehicle trader, the registered keeper must notify the Secretary of State, on the part of the registration document which relates to the transfer to a vehicle dealer, of the name and address of the vehicle trader and of the date on which the transfer took place, and he must send declarations from both himself and the vehicle trader to the effect that the transfer occurred on a specified date.

In addition, reg. 24 deals with the duties of a vehicle trader in such circumstances. The trader must, on or before the 'appropriate date', notify the Secretary of State of the date of his acquisition of the vehicle. The 'appropriate date' is the earliest of the day of first use or keeping of the vehicle on a public road otherwise than under a trade licence, or the day following the expiration of a period of 3 months. If there is a transfer to another vehicle trader within the period of 3 months, the registration document must be transferred with the vehicle.

Where a vehicle trader transfers the vehicle to a person other than another vehicle trader or transfers the vehicle to another trader outside that period, he must, forthwith, on the appropriate part of the registration document inform the Secretary of State of:

(a) the name and address of the new keeper;
(b) the date of transfer;

(c) a signed declaration to the effect that he transferred the vehicle to the vehicle trader on the date specified; and

(d) a signed declaration from the new keeper that the vehicle was transferred to him on the date specified.

Failure to notify the Secretary of State is not a continuing offence and therefore the time limitation upon proceedings runs from the day of the transfer of the vehicle. If, therefore, a period of 6 months has passed since the transfer of a vehicle, no proceedings may be taken against either of the parties to the transaction if they have failed to comply with the requirement to notify the Secretary of State forthwith.

Notification of other changes

An owner of a registered vehicle who changes his name or address is required by reg. 18 of the Road Vehicles (Registration and Licensing) Regulations 2002 forthwith notify the Secretary of State and deliver the registration document to him.

In the event of a vehicle being broken up, destroyed or sent permanently out of Great Britain or Northern Ireland, reg. 17 requires notification of that fact and the surrender of the registration document.

Regulation 16 of the Road Vehicles (Registration and Licensing) Regulations 2002 is concerned with procedures which must be followed when there has been any alteration to a vehicle which renders the particulars in the registration document incorrect. Such alterations must be notified to the Secretary of State forthwith in writing by the owner and the registration document surrendered for amendment. This would apply, for example, if a motor car was resprayed or fitted with a new engine, since the details of colour and engine numbers are contained in the document. Should the alteration necessitate changes to the vehicle excise licence, it must also be surrendered by the owner for amendment.

Provisions of the Vehicles (Crime) Act 2001 concerning 'salvage'

The Vehicles (Crime) Act 2001 was passed to tackle the problem caused where vehicles are stolen, and then either broken up for their parts or 'ringed' (i.e. the true identity of the car is swapped for that of a written-off car). Part I deals with motor salvage operators. It requires that all persons who carry on a business as 'motor salvage operators' must be registered with the local authority. The term 'motor salvage operator' covers those who carry on a business consisting:

(a) wholly *or partly* in the re-use or sale of salvageable parts from vehicles and the subsequent sale and other disposal for scrap of the remainder of the vehicle concerned (which definition covers scrap metal dealers);

(b) wholly *or mainly* in the purchase of written-off vehicles and their subsequent repair and resale;

(c) wholly *or mainly* in the sale or purchase of motor vehicles which are to be subject to any of the activities at (a) or (b); or

(d) wholly *or mainly* in activities falling within (b) and (c).

It will be noted that the 2001 Act refers to *motor vehicles* to which the Act gives a special definition. In the present context a 'motor vehicle' is one whose function is or was to be used on a road as a mechanically propelled vehicle.

A local authority may refuse to register a person whom it considers to be unfit to carry on such a business. An appeal against such a decision lies to a magistrates' court.

The 2001 Act creates offences of failure to register, failure to keep appropriate records and failure to notify the Secretary of State of the destruction of a motor vehicle. A person commits an offence if he makes a false statement in an application for registration, or if he fails to give notice of any change in the registered information. Section 12 of the 2001 Act makes it an offence for any person to give a false name or address to a motor salvage operator when selling a vehicle to him.

Section 9 of the Act of 2001 provides a constable with a power of entry at any reasonable time into the registered premises which are occupied as a 'motor salvage yard' by a person carrying on a business as a motor salvage operator or are occupied by him in relation to that business. At any reasonable time a constable may require the production of, and inspect, motor vehicles, salvageable parts and records, and may take copies or extracts of entries. Provision is also made for the issue of a warrant authorising entry and inspection. Force may not be used in respect of general entry, but it may be used in association with the execution of a warrant. When effecting entry without a warrant, a constable must, if required by or on behalf of the owner or occupier or person in charge of the premises, produce evidence of identity, and of his authority for entering, before doing so.

Regulations are to be made under s 8 of the 2001 Act (not in force at the time of writing) requiring registered motor salvage operators to notify the Secretary of State of the destruction of motor vehicles. The Motor Salvage Operators Regulations 2002 require motor salvage operators to keep records of such vehicles passing through their hands. The records must contain a range of specified information about a vehicle: registration number, vehicle identification number, make, model, colour, identity of supplier or receiver of the vehicle, details of proof of his identity and the condition of the vehicle and the date on which the information was entered. It is an offence to fail to record any of this information, except information relating to proof of identity or the vehicle's condition.

Police powers

A police officer may require the owner of a mechanically propelled vehicle to produce the registration document for inspection at any reasonable time.

Failure to produce the registration document or to comply with any of the above requirements relating to changes in ownership, registered particulars, etc., is a summary offence. However, it should be noted that the offence by the previous owner is committed when the change is effected.

If there is ever any suspicion that a vehicle may be stolen or the documents forged, an examination of the registration document may provide evidence to confirm a suspicion. Thieves steal vehicles and either strip them of all parts and accessories or respray the body and pass it off as a newly built vehicle which had been previously written off. The engine number should tally with that given in the registration document and any evidence of filing or punching of the metal round an engine number should be viewed with suspicion. However, regulations to be made under the Vehicles (Crime) Act 2001 will provide for the detailed examination of vehicles at the time of re-registration and the production of documentary evidence of the legitimacy of vehicles.

Registration mark

The registration mark assigned to a vehicle is a combination of letters and figures which serve to identify the vehicle and is often referred to as the registered number of the vehicle. The size, shape and character of any registration mark are governed by the Road Vehicles (Display of Registration Marks) Regulations 2001.

General factors in relation to registration marks

The requirement to have a registration mark fixed to a vehicle is provided by the Vehicle Excise and Registration Act 1994, s 42, and is punishable under that section. The offence of displaying a plate which has become obscured, etc., is contrary to s 43 of that Act.

   The Road Vehicles (Display of Registration Marks) Regulations 2001 revoked the provisions of the Road Vehicles (Registration and Licensing) Regulations 1971 in this respect. The replaced regulations are those which dealt with the forms of registration mark which were authorised to be used on motor vehicles, works trucks, agricultural machines and trailers and the manner in which they were fixed to vehicles.

   The forms of registration mark differ depending upon the date of the first use of the vehicle concerned. Schedule 2 to the 2001 Regulations sets out the specifications of the approved registration plates. Vehicles registered on or after 1 September 2001 must conform with specifications set out in Part 1 to that Schedule; those registered on or after 1 January 1973 and before 1 September 2001 must conform with Part 2 (or with Part 1 if the plate is changed) and *may*, in any case, comply with Part 1 (plates authorised under Parts 1 and 2 must all show black characters on a white background at the front and black characters on a yellow background at the rear); and vehicles registered before 1 January 1973 must conform with Part 3 which provides optional specifications by requiring that where the plate is such that it may be illuminated from behind by virtue of the translucency of its characters, there must be white translucent characters on a black background, upon which, when illuminated, the characters appear white against a black background. Otherwise such plates must carry black characters on a white background at the front and black characters on a yellow background at the rear, or a plate displaying white, silver or grey letters and numbers on a black surface which are indelibly inscribed on the plate and cannot readily be detached.

Permitted layouts

Regulation 13 and Schedule 3, Parts 1 and 2 of the 2001 Regulations, introduced a new format for registration marks. Registration marks in any other format will be unlawful. The new marks may be, for example, a group consisting of two letters and two numbers followed by a group of three letters (DE51 ABC); a group consisting of a single letter and not more than three numbers followed by a group of three letters (A123 ABC); a group of three letters followed by a group consisting of not more than three numbers and a single letter (ABC 123A); a group of four numbers followed by a single letter or a group of two letters (1234 A, 1234 AB); a group of not more than three numbers followed by a group of not more than three letters (123 ABC, 123 AB, 12A); a group of not more than three letters followed by a group of not more than three numbers (ABC 123, AB 123, A12); a single letter or group of two letters followed by a group of four numbers (A 1234, AB 1234); and in Northern Ireland, a group of three letters followed by a

▚▚▚

group of four numbers (ABZ 1234) or a group of four numbers followed by a group of three letters (1234 ABZ).

It is not necessary that these letters and numbers all follow one another. The plates may be square, permitting the letters and characters to be placed in two or three rows as illustrated in the Schedule. Plates containing all of the letters and numbers in a straight line are not permitted on motor cycles. Plates containing three rows of characters are not permitted on vehicles first registered on or after 1 September 2001.

Character sizes and fonts

Regulation 14 of and Schedule 3 to the 2001 Regulations make provision in respect of character and size. They provide that the registration marks of vehicles first registered on or after 1 September 2001 or before 1 January 1973, and on vehicles registered on or after 1 January 1973 should the plate be replaced, must be 79 mm high. In respect of vehicles first registered on or after 1 January 1973 but before 1 September 2001, the registration marks may be 79 mm high instead of 89 mm, except where a plate is replaced after 1 September 2001. By way of exception to the above rules, the required height is 64 mm in relation to a motor cycle, motor tricycle, quadricycle, agricultural machine, works truck or road roller. The width of characters, spacing and margins are all precisely prescribed by Table B in Schedule 3.

Regulation 14A applies to a vehicle imported into the United Kingdom which does not have a European Community Whole Vehicle Type Approval and is so constructed that the area available for the fixing of the registration plate precludes the display on the plate of a registration mark in conformity with the requirements of reg. 14. In such a case the prescribed height of characters is 64 mm; the width (except for the letter 'I' or figure '1') must be 44 mm; the width of every part of a stroke and the spacing of characters within a group must be 10 mm, the vertical spacing between groups of characters and the width of a margin between the mark and the top and lateral sides of the registration plate must not be less than 5 mm and the space between the bottom of the mark and the bottom of the registration plate must not be less than 13 mm.

Regulation 12(2) of the 2001 Regulations permits deviation from the prescribed height of characters provided that the deviation is not more than 1 mm either way. In the case of other dimensions, including spaces, the permitted deviation is 0.5 mm either way.

Regulation 15 and Schedule 4 to the 2001 Regulations deal with the font of characters displayed on a registration plate fixed to a vehicle first registered on or after 1 September 2001, or on a new registration plate fixed to any other vehicle (except where the vehicle was first registered before 1 January 1973). They require that each of the characters must be in the prescribed font. In relation to other cases, characters must be in the prescribed font or in a style which is substantially similar to the prescribed font so that the character is easily distinguishable but in the latter case characters must not be formed in italic script (or other script which is not vertical), or in script in which the curvature or alignment of the lines of the strokes is substantially different from the prescribed font, or in script using multiple or a broken stroke or in such a way that a character, or characters, appear like a different character or characters. A character will not be treated as substantially different solely on the grounds that it has, or does not have, serifs (small lines at the extremity of a main stroke).

Fixing of rear registration plates: post-1938 vehicles

Regulation 5 of the 2001 Regulations (which applies to all vehicles first registered on or after 1 October 1938 other than works trucks, road rollers and agricultural machines) requires a rear registration plate to be fixed on the rear of the vehicle or (where it is towing a trailer) to the rear of the trailer or the rearmost trailer. However, where a vehicle or trailer has been constructed for rear plates to be fixed in accordance with relevant EC type-approval directives, the plate may be fixed in the space provided in accordance with the directives. Regulation 9 requires a vehicle or trailer of the present type to be lit in accordance with the regulation when used on a road between sunset and sunrise.

Unless fitted in a space provided in accordance with an EC type-approval directive, a rear registration plate must be fitted vertically (or, if that is not reasonably practicable, as close to vertical as is reasonably practicable) in such a position that the characters are easily distinguishable from a distance of 22 m (where the characters are of a width of 57 mm); 21.5 m (where the characters are of a width of 50 mm); and 18 m (where the characters are of a width of 44 mm). Regulation 9 provides that except where a plate is fitted and lit in accordance with EC type-approval requirements, the plate should be lit so that it is easily distinguishable from a distance of 18 m, but 15 m is substituted where the characters are of a width of only 44 mm.

Fixing of front registration plates: post-1938 vehicles

Regulation 6 of the 2001 Regulations deals with registration plates on a vehicle first registered on or after 1 October 1938, with the same exceptions as above in relation to rear plates. It requires that a front registration plate must be fixed vertically (or if that is not reasonably practicable, as close to vertical as is reasonably practicable) so that its characters are easily distinguishable from the rest of the plate in normal daylight.

Regulation 6 requires that, in the case of motor cycles or motor tricycles which do not have a body of a type which is characteristic of the body of a four-wheeled vehicle, there must not be a front registration plate if the vehicle was first registered on or after 1 September 2001. A front registration plate need not be fitted if such a vehicle was registered before that date.

Pre-1938 vehicles, works trucks, road rollers and agricultural machines

Regulation 7 of the 2001 Regulations deals with registration plates fitted to the front of vehicles registered before 1 October 1938 and to their rear (and the rear of any trailer or rearmost trailer). It requires vertically fitted plates which are easily distinguishable.

There are similar provisions in respect of reasonable practicability and distinguishability of the characters on the front plate as under reg. 6. Likewise, there is no need for a front plate to be fitted to a motor bicycle or motor tricycle. The lighting requirements of reg. 9 apply to the rear plates of these vehicles.

Regulation 8 is concerned with works trucks, road rollers and agricultural machines. Registration plates must be fitted vertically on both sides of the vehicle, and on its rear. When the vehicle is towing a trailer and the plate is not fitted to the sides of the vehicle, a plate must be fixed on the trailer (or rearmost trailer) so that the characters of the towing machine so that the mark are easily distinguishable from behind the trailer. In the case of a towing machine which is an agricultural machine (tractor, off-road tractor, light agricultural vehicle, agricultural engine or mowing machine), the plate displayed on the trailer may be that of any agricultural machine kept by the keeper of the towing vehicle. The lighting requirements of reg. 9 do not apply to these vehicles.

Use of reflex-reflecting material and other impediments to true photographs

Regulation 11 of the 2001 Regulations prohibits the application of reflex-reflecting material to any part of the registration plate or the treatment of the plate in such a way as to cause the registration mark to become retroreflective. In addition, it requires that the surface of a registration plate must not comprise or incorporate a design, pattern or texture, or be treated in any way which gives to any part of the plate the appearance of a design, pattern or texture. It also prohibits any treatment of a registration plate which has the effect of making it less distinguishable or would prevent or impair the making of a true photograph. The use of a screw or bolt or other fixing device in a manner which has the effect of changing the appearance or legibility of any characters of a registration mark, or would impair the making of a true photograph, is also prohibited.

GB plates and exemptions

Regulation 16 provides that no material other than a registration mark may be displayed on a registration plate other than the display of the international distinguishing sign of the United Kingdom adjacent to the registration mark in accordance with Council Regulation 2411/98.

Regulations 3 and 18 preserve the exemption of small invalid carriages and pedestrian-controlled vehicles from the requirement to carry registration marks. The use of old-style number plates on 'classic' vehicles is also preserved.

Offences

The offences are all summary offences and those contrary to the Vehicle Excise and Registration Act 1994, s 42 or 43 (registration plates not fixed in accordance with s 23 of that Act or obscured or rendered or allowed to become not easily distinguishable), are fixed penalty offences, as are offences under s 59 of VERA 1994 if they relate to a failure to fix prescribed registration marks to a vehicle in accordance with regulations made under s 23(4)(a) of that Act (which are concerned with the size, shape and character of registration marks).

Where a plate is not easily distinguishable, etc., the person driving the vehicle or, if it is not being driven, the person keeping it, commits an offence. It is a summary offence contrary to the Road Vehicles Lighting Regulations 1989 to use or keep such a vehicle on a public road and fail to illuminate the registration mark fixed to the rear of the vehicle. In instances where motor vehicles may be lawfully parked without lights within the period between sunset and sunrise, there is no legal requirement to have the registration mark illuminated.

The name and address of the registered keeper of a motor vehicle can be obtained from the Secretary of State for Transport or, more easily, through the Police National Computer on most occasions.

Registration plates

Regulation of suppliers of registration plates

Part 2 of the Vehicles (Crime) Act 2001 is concerned with the regulation of suppliers of registration plates.

By s 17 of the Act a person commits an offence if he carries on business as a registration plate supplier without being registered with the Secretary of State. A person carries on a business as a registration plate supplier if his business consists wholly or partly in selling registration plates and he is not an exempt person (as provided by regulations) from the provisions of the Act. At the time of writing, no such regulations had been made. However, the Vehicles (Crime) (Registration of Registration Plate Suppliers)(England and Wales) Regulations 2002 provide that the activity of selling a vehicle fitted with registration plates where the seller is a dealer in vehicles and has arranged the first registration in the United Kingdom of the vehicle on the intending purchaser's behalf is not an activity which consists in selling registration plates.

Under s 18, on payment of any prescribed fee, the Secretary of State *must* supply information from his register on request by any person (subject to exceptions provided by regulations). Where a request is so made, and subject to any prescribed exception and fee, the Secretary of State must supply the information in the form of a certified copy of the register or of an extract from it. Any such certified copy is evidence of the matters mentioned in it. The Secretary of State *may* make all the information contained in the register, or prescribed parts of it, available to the Police Information Technology Organisation for use by constables in the investigation of offences against Part 2. Regulations may limit the further disclosure by constables of information to which they have been given access.

Section 19 (3) provides that a person who, in making an application for registration, makes a statement which he knows to be false in a material particular, or recklessly makes a statement which is false in a material particular, commits an offence. On conviction for such an offence, a court may make an order under s 20 providing for the removal of the entry relating to him in the register, and/or prohibiting him from making an application for registration within a period not exceeding 5 years specified by the court.

Under s 21, the Secretary of State may cancel a person's registration if he is satisfied that a person is not carrying on the business of a registration plate dealer and has not, while registered, been doing so for the past 28 days, but may not do so without serving notice under s 22 and allowing time for representations. An appeal lies to a magistrates' court within 21 days.

The Vehicles Crime (Registration of Registration Plate Suppliers) (England and Wales) Regulations 2002 are concerned with the keeping of records by registered persons. Section 24 of the 2001 Act creates the offence of failure to comply with such provisions. A registered person is under various record-keeping requirements set out in reg. 7 of the Vehicles Crime (Registration of Registration Plate Suppliers) (England and Wales) Regulations 2002.

The 2002 Regulations also require registered persons who are in the course of selling registration plates to obtain prescribed information from the prospective purchasers before the completion of the sale. By s 25 of the 2001 Act, it is an offence to fail to comply with any provisions of such regulations. Both sections provide a defence where an accused can show that he took all reasonable steps and exercised all due diligence to avoid committing the offence.

The information to be obtained by a registered supplier from a prospective purchaser is prescribed by reg. 6. He is required to obtain:

(a) his name and usual address (or business address in the case of a firm);
(b) the name and address of any agent involved with the sale;
(c) the registration mark to be shown;
(d) where the request is from a vehicle body repairer on behalf of an insurance company, the name of that company and the number of the insurance policy (in such a case, if the record includes all of this information, no additional verification is needed);
(e) the connection of the purchaser with the registration mark or the vehicle on which it is to be affixed.

Identity must be verified by the registered person by production of a driving licence which contains a photograph. Alternatives are permitted but in each case there must be two documents:

(a) a bill issued within 6 months by an electricity, gas or water supplier or a bank or building society statement, together with;
(b) a second document which is:
  (i) another form of driving licence (not necessarily UK),
  (ii) a passport (whether or not UK),
  (iii) a national identity card of another state,
  (iv) a debit or credit card (with a photograph) issued by a bank or building society,
  (v) a travel pass with a photograph issued by a local authority, public service vehicle (PSV) operator or a railway operator.

In addition, the purchaser must establish his connection with the registration mark or the vehicle by a registration document, certificate of entitlement to a registration mark, document proving his right to a particular registration mark, vehicle licensing reminder to registered keeper, certificate of vehicle registration, an authorisation issued by the Secretary of State for the purchase of a number plate or an authorisation for the purchase of the number plate issued by a company owning more than one vehicle stating that he holds the registration document and containing either the reference number from the registration document or the vehicle identification number.

None of these requirements applies to a motor trader who is arranging a first registration on behalf of a purchaser.

Regulation 7 requires a registered person to keep records at his principal place of business or at any other premises at which he carries on the business of a registration plate supplier. Records must be retained for a period of 3 years from the date of registration. Such records shall contain:

(a) the information required by reg. 6;
(b) method of purchase;
(c) issuer and account number if a credit or debit card is used;
(d) if a cheque, the name of the bank and the account number;
(e) a statement of the document used to verify name and address and if a driving licence, the number;
(f) a statement of the document used to verify connection with a registration mark or the vehicle; and

(g) where the document is a registration document or authorisation for purchase issued by a company, either a reference number from that document or a vehicle identification number.

Failure to comply with these provisions is an offence against s 24(4) of the Vehicles (Crime) Act 2001.

Section 26 provides a power of entry and inspection to the registered premises of registered persons for a constable or authorised person (authorised by the local authority of the area in which the premises are situated) at any reasonable time. The constable or authorised person has power to require production, and to inspect, any plates kept at the premises and any records which are required to be kept under Part 2 and to take copies or extracts of those. Provision is also made for the issue to a constable or authorised person of a warrant. Although force may not be used to obtain entry in normal circumstances, it may be used in the exercise of the constable or authorised person's powers under the authority of a warrant. When effecting entry without a warrant, a constable must, if required by or on behalf of the owner or occupier or person in charge of the premises, produce evidence of identity and of his authority for entering, before doing so. This also applies to an 'authorised person', who must also produce such evidence when executing a warrant. The section also creates an offence of obstruction of an authorised person in the exercise of his powers under the section.

A person registered under Part 2 of the 2001 Act is required by s 27 to give notice of changes of circumstances. Section 27(4) creates the offence of failure to do so. The same defence as is set out above in relation to ss 24 and 25 is available to a person accused of this offence.

Section 28 is concerned with counterfeit registration plates. It creates offences of selling a plate or other device which is not a registration plate as a registration plate, knowing that it is not such a plate or being reckless as to whether it is a registration plate (hereafter 'unlawful activity'); of supplying such a plate, device or other object to a person who is carrying on a business which consists wholly or partly of such activities and he knows or reasonably suspects that the plate, device or other object will be used for the purposes of that other person's unlawful activities.

Section 29 creates the offence of supplying a plate, device or other object to an unregistered person (other than an exempt person to be defined by regulations) who is carrying on a business which consists wholly or partly in selling registration plates and knowing or reasonably suspecting that the plate, device or other object will be used for the purpose of that other person's business as a registration plate or as part of a registration plate.

Vehicle excise licence

With certain exceptions, every mechanically propelled vehicle used or kept on a public road must have in force in relation to that vehicle an excise licence issued by the Secretary of State. An application may be made for a licence up to 14 days before the licence is to have effect. The application form containing the prescribed particulars must be accompanied by a test certificate (if applicable), a certificate of insurance covering the use of that vehicle, the registration document relating to the vehicle (in some circumstances) and the amount of duty payable on the licence. However, amending regulations of 1999 provide that it may not be necessary to provide evidence of insurance if the insurance company concerned has agreed with the Secretary of State to make available for inspection an electronic database maintained by the insurer. In addition, the Vehicles (Crime) Act 2001 provides that the Secretary of State may require, by regulations, such documentary or other evidence of the legitimacy of a motor vehicle before issuing a licence.

Section 29 of the Vehicle Excise and Registration Act 1994 provides that if any person uses or keeps on a public road any vehicle for which a licence is not in force, not being a vehicle exempted from duty under the Act, he is guilty of an offence.

In addition, if a vehicle is unlicensed the registered keeper is guilty of an offence contrary to s 31A of the 1994 Act, unless it is an exempt vehicle. However, s 31B provides a number of exceptions. The registered keeper does not commit an offence under s 31A if *at the relevant time*:

(a) he is not the person keeping the vehicle and, if previously he was the person keeping it, he has by the relevant time complied with *any requirements to furnish particulars or make declarations which apply on surrendering or not renewing a licence, or when keeping an unlicensed vehicle*;
(b) he is keeping the vehicle, it is neither kept nor used on a public road and he has complied with any requirement italicised in (a);
(c) the vehicle has been stolen and has not been recovered, and he has notified the prescribed person with prescribed details about the theft; or
(d) the period of 'grace days' has not expired since the expiry of the last licence and a licence is taken out within the 'grace days'.

Vehicles exempt from licence duty

Under the Vehicle Excise and Registration Act 1994, a number of mechanically propelled vehicles are exempt from the requirement to have an excise licence when used or kept on public roads. The main exceptions are:

(a) police vehicles;
(b) fire engines and mine rescue vehicles;
(c) vehicles kept by a fire authority while being used or kept for the purposes of fire fighting;
(d) ambulances, including veterinary ambulances and vehicles being used as such by NHS-approved bodies;
(e) vehicles used on tram lines;
(f) vehicles used or kept on a road solely for haulage of lifeboats and their equipment;
(g) vehicles (including pedal cycles with an attachment for propelling them by mechanical power) which do not exceed 10 cwt (508 kg) and are adapted and used or left on a road, for invalids, or vehicles used or kept for use by or for the purposes of a disabled person who is in receipt of some form of mobility supplement;
(h) vehicles purchased by overseas residents;
(i) vehicles travelling to or from a previously arranged test in connection with a test certificate or vehicle identity check, or to or from a place where work is to be or has to be done on it to remedy defects for which a test certificate has been refused, or when towed to be broken up;
(j) during a test or identity check by an authorised person;

(k) vehicles used for agriculture, horticulture or forestry used on public roads only in passing between different areas of land occupied by the same person and the distance travelled on public roads in so passing does not exceed 1.5 km;

(l) electrically assisted pedal cycles; and

(m) off-road tractors and hedge- and verge-cutting tractors, mowing machines, snow ploughs and gritters.

In relation to (i), the exemption afforded will also apply to a vehicle parked on a road on its way to the testing station, provided that it is still reasonable to say that the purpose of the journey is, in effect, to submit it for a test. Thus, small deviations from a direct route may be permitted.

The Road Vehicles (Exemptions from Duty) Regulations 1986 exempt vehicles imported by members of visiting forces, members of a headquarters of an organisation, or dependants of such persons. This exemption lasts for a period of 12 months only.

Duration of licence

Vehicle excise licences for most vehicles may be issued for periods of 12 or 6 months. Licences valid for 6 months are limited to vehicles for which the annual rate of duty exceeds £50. The Secretary of State may also issue temporary licences for 14 days, or such other period as may be prescribed. Applications for a licence may be made by any person who makes out a declaration and furnishes the prescribed particulars. The licence is issued to the vehicle, not to any person, and must be either transferred with the vehicle if it is sold, or returned to the DVLA for a rebate. It has become a practice to allow up to 14 days after a licence has expired as a period of grace in which road users may make application for the renewal of a licence, but such a licence will commence on the first day of the month following the expiry of the previous licence. Regulation 26 and Schedule 4 to the Road Vehicles (Registration and Licensing) Regulations 2002 require that, where a vehicle licence expires or is surrendered and a new licence is not taken out, the keeper must make a 'required declaration' (as approved by the Secretary of State in writing, orally or by electronic means) not later than the day upon which the licence ceases to be in force (or 3 months after such expiry in the case of motor traders). The declaration is to the effect that the vehicle will not be used or kept on a public road and that a licence will be taken out before any such use. It is an offence to fail to make such a declaration. If there is a transfer of such a vehicle during an unlicensed period and a licence is not taken out, a 'required declaration' must be made by the new owner.

Exhibition of licence

An excise licence must be fixed to a vehicle in a holder sufficient to protect the licence from the effects of the weather to which it would otherwise be exposed. Consequently, an externally displayed licence must be completely enclosed in a waterproof container. Regulation 6 of the Road Vehicles (Registration and Licensing) Regulations 2002 sets out the requirements. An excise licence must be exhibited on the vehicle so that the particulars are clearly visible in daylight from the nearside of the road, as follows:

(a) on an invalid carriage, tricycle or bicycle, on the nearside of the vehicle;

(b) on a bicycle with sidecar, on the nearside of the handlebars or the nearside of the sidecar;

(c) on a vehicle with a windscreen extending across the vehicle, on or adjacent to the nearside of the windscreen; or

(d) on any other vehicle, on the nearside window of the driver's cab (if it has one), or on the nearside of the vehicle in front of the driver's seat and not less than 760 mm and not more than 1.8 m above the surface of the road.

Rates of duty

The cost of a licence varies with the type of vehicle. The Vehicle Excise and Registration Act 1994, Schedule 1, sets out the rate of duty in respect of all non-exempted vehicles. It sets the basic rate (which applies where no other provision is made by the Schedule) and this is the rate which applies to private cars. Buses are charged in relation to their seating capacity and goods vehicles according to their revenue weight. This is, in most circumstances, the plated gross or plated train weight, but where the vehicle is not plated it will be the design weight and a certificate of that weight will be in force.

Provision is made by reg. 5 of the Road Vehicles (Registration and Licensing) Regulations 2002 for reduced rates of vehicle excise duty to be applicable to certain buses, haulage vehicles and heavy goods vehicles which have been adapted to reduce pollution. Where this is so, a 'reduced pollution certificate' will be in force. In addition, changes have been made within annual Finance Acts for a reduced rate of duty to apply to motor cars with engines below a specified cubic capacity. Provision has also been made for new vehicles to be taxed in accordance with the level of carbon dioxide emissions caused by their engines.

Some vehicles attract lower rates than would otherwise apply because they are 'special'. The basic rate of goods vehicle duty is payable where the vehicle is 'special' (digging machines and mobile cranes used on-site at road works, etc., and 'works trucks'). A works truck is designed for use on private premises, which is used on public roads only for carrying goods between private premises and a vehicle or to another separate part of the private premises, or in connection with road works (e.g. dumper truck). However, such works trucks can only be used whilst enjoying this status, when used in the *immediate vicinity* of such premises or works, and this means a very considerable degree of closeness.

A recovery vehicle is a vehicle which is constructed or permanently adapted primarily for the purpose of lifting, towing and transporting a disabled vehicle or for any one or more of those purposes. The approved purposes are set out in Schedule 1 to the Vehicle Excise and Registration Act 1994 and Schedule 7 to the Road Vehicles (Registration and Licensing) Regulations 2002. For a vehicle to be classified as a recovery vehicle for the purpose of attracting a lower rate of duty, it must be used for:

(a) the recovery of a disabled vehicle;

(b) the removal of a disabled vehicle from the place where it became disabled to premises at which it is to be repaired or scrapped;

(c) the removal of a disabled vehicle from premises to which it was taken for repair, to other premises at which it is to be repaired or scrapped;

(d) carrying fuel and other liquids required for its propulsion and tools and other articles required for the operation or in connection with integral or permanently mounted apparatus designed to lift, tow or transport a disabled vehicle;

(e) repairing a disabled vehicle at the place where it became disabled or to which it had been removed in the interests of safety after becoming disabled; or

(f) drawing or carrying one trailer if the trailer was, immediately before a vehicle became disabled, being drawn or carried by the disabled vehicle.

The rate of duty which applies to a recovery vehicle is the basic goods rate where the revenue weight exceeds 3500 kg but does not exceed 25 000 kg, and 2.5 times that rate if the revenue weight exceeds 25 000 kg.

When recovering or removing a disabled vehicle, a recovery vehicle may carry the driver, any passenger and the load which was in the vehicle when it became disabled. It may also carry persons and their personal effects from a place where the vehicle is to be repaired to their destinations. Such a vehicle is not a recovery vehicle if it is being used to recover more than two vehicles at any time.

Offences

There are a number of offences which can be committed in connection with an excise licence, the most common of which can be summarised as follows:

(a) using or keeping a mechanically propelled vehicle on a public road without having in force an excise licence – s 29.
(b) failing to display an excise licence – s 33;
(c) to forge, fraudulently alter or use, or fraudulently lend or allow to be used by any other person, an excise licence – s 44.
(d) to exhibit anything which is intended to be or could be mistaken for a licence – Regulation 7 of the Road Vehicles (Registration and Licensing) Regulations 2002 and s 59;
(e) to make a false declaration in an application for the issue of a licence – s 45.
(f) supplying false information or producing false documents in relation to the design weight of a vehicle – s 45(3A); and
(g) forgery of, alteration or use of a design weight certificate or knowingly lending or allowing it to be used, or making or having such in possession – s 45(3B).

Where an excise licence is alleged to be forged, the issue does not surround whether there was an intention to avoid payment of excise duty. It must be proved that there was an intention by deceit to cause a person exercising a public duty to act or refrain from acting in a way which he would not otherwise have done. Thus, the alteration of an excise licence with the intention of avoiding the attention of police officers being drawn to the car whilst an application for a licence is pending contravenes the section.

Documentary evidence of commission of offence of using or keeping

Section 47 of the 1994 Act provides that proceedings for offences of using, etc., without a licence, of using a trade licence outside permitted uses (see later) and of using a licensed vehicle for a purpose which attracts a higher rate of duty than that paid can only be instituted by the Secretary of State or a constable; such a person is known as the authorised prosecutor. Moreover, no prosecution may be instituted by a constable for these offences without the approval of the Secretary of State; proof that such approval has been given is required at the outset of proceedings in court.

Proceedings instituted by an authorised prosecutor for one of the above offences or for an offence under s 44 or 45 of the 1994 Act (forgery or false statements, etc.) may be instituted within 6 months from the date on which sufficient evidence came to the prosecutor's knowledge to warrant proceedings, subject to a maximum limit of 3 years from the commission of the offence. This means that, if the Secretary of State institutes proceedings as the authorised prosecutor, the 6-month time limit runs from the time when the required evidence came to his knowledge. The 6-month limit replaces the normal rule requiring that proceedings for summary offences be taken within 6 months from the commission of the offence. Section 47 of the 1994 Act allows proof of the date upon which evidence came to the knowledge of the authorised prosecutor, or proof that the Secretary of State has approved the institution of a prosecution by a constable, to be given by means of a certificate signed by or on behalf of the authorised prosecutor or, as the case may be, the Secretary of State. Such a certificate is conclusive evidence of the facts stated, and is deemed to be properly signed unless the contrary is proved.

Section 52 of the 1994 Act allows certified extracts from DVLA records to be admissible to the same extent as oral evidence. Evidence may therefore be offered of the last date upon which a mechanically propelled vehicle was licensed by means of such a certified extract.

Section 46 of the 1994 Act requires that, where one of the offences mentioned above (except forgery) is alleged to have been committed in relation to a particular mechanically propelled vehicle, the person keeping the vehicle must give such information as he may be required by or on behalf of a chief officer of police or the Secretary of State to give as to the identity of the person or persons concerned in the offence. Failure to do so is an offence, unless the accused keeper satisfies the court that he did not know and could not with reasonable diligence have ascertained the identity of the person or persons concerned. A divisional court has held that where there is evidence of using or keeping a vehicle on a road and a notice has been sent in accordance with this section to which the keeper does not respond, the justices should draw an adverse inference from the fact that there was a failure to respond and that this, coupled with the other evidence of using or keeping, is sufficient to support a conviction under s 46. The requirement is also extended to any other person (besides a 'keeper') who may have such knowledge, and (in cases of unlicensed use) to the person alleged to have been using the vehicle. Both types of person commit an offence if they fail to give such information as to identity as it is in their power to give. A request under s 46 is, in practice, made by serving on a person a form requiring the specified information. A reply to such a request must be made in writing.

Section 20 of the Road Traffic Offenders Act 1988 provides that evidence of a fact relevant to proceedings for an offence to which the section applies may be given by the production of a record produced by a prescribed device which is accompanied by a certificate as to the circumstances in which the record was produced, signed by a constable or a person authorised by or on behalf of a chief officer of police. An offence under s 29 of the vehicle Excise and Registration Act 1994 is prescribed as an offence to which s 20 of the 1988 Act applies and in respect of it a prescribed device is one designed or adapted to register:

(a) an image of a vehicle and its registration mark; and
(b) the time at which the image is registered,

and to record that information if, according to data stored by or otherwise accessible by the device, that vehicle is unlicensed.

Police powers

Although there is no statutory power given to a police officer to seize any licence plate or registration document which he suspects to be forged, altered or otherwise fraudulently used, it is an accepted practice to seize such articles to ensure their availability as evidence of the offence in any subsequent court proceedings.

Where a police officer finds a mechanically propelled vehicle exhibiting an excise licence issued in respect of another vehicle, he should not only bear in mind offences under the Vehicles Excise and Registration Act 1994, but also remember that there could be a theft or handling of stolen property involved. If there is any suspicion of either offence, then there would be a power of arrest without warrant, both offences being arrestable offences. A common explanation given when a vehicle is found displaying a licence issued to another vehicle is that the owner of the vehicle bought the licence from a stranger in a public house, which could be an offence of handling stolen property, or that he had found it lying in the road, which would be theft.

In relation to certain offences under the Act, the most important of which is the offence under s 29 of using or keeping a mechanically propelled vehicle on a public road without having an excise licence in force, s 46 of the Act gives the police certain powers to require persons to give information. If it is alleged that a vehicle has been used or kept in breach of the provisions of s 29, then:

(a) the person keeping the vehicle shall give such information as he may be required by or on behalf of a chief officer of police (or the Secretary of State) to give as to the identity of the persons who were driving or using or keeping the vehicle at the time of the alleged offence;

(b) any other person shall, if required as above, give such information as it is in his power to give as to the identity of any of the persons concerned – i.e. the driver, user or keeper of the vehicle – at the time of the alleged offence;

(c) the person who is alleged to have used the vehicle at the time of the alleged offence shall, if required as above, give such information as it is in his power to give as to the identity of the person by whom the vehicle was kept at that time.

A failure to give this information when required to do so under the provisions of s 46 is a summary offence, but a person coming within (a) above shall not be convicted if he shows to the satisfaction of the court that he did not know and could not, with reasonable diligence, have ascertained the identity of the person or persons concerned.

The Divisional Court has held that where there is evidence of using or keeping a vehicle on a road and a notice has been sent in accordance with this section to which the keeper does not respond, the justices should draw an adverse inference from the fact that there was a failure to respond and this, coupled with the other evidence of using or keeping, is sufficient to support a conviction. The appeal courts have ruled that the requirement to provide information in this way is not in contravention of the European Convention in relation to Human Rights, in that it requires a person to give information which may be used in evidence against him. Although, in a case in which the person from whom the information is demanded was the driver at the relevant time, such an admission would amount to self-incrimination, the use of motor vehicles brings with it responsibilities for the good of the community at large.

Evidence of driving

Where it is proved that such a requirement has been made of such a person, the Vehicle Excise and Registration Act 1994, s 51, permits proof that a person was the driver, user or keeper of the vehicle on a particular occasion, by proof of service by post of a request under s 46, together with the production of a signed statement from the accused to the effect that he was the driver, user or keeper on that occasion. This does not apply, of course, where the recipient of the form identifies some other person.

Immobilisation of unlicensed vehicles

The Vehicle Excise Duty (Immobilisation, Removal and Disposal of Vehicles) Regulations 1997 authorise the wheelclamping of stationary vehicles which 'an authorised person' (a police officer may be so authorised) has reason to believe is unlicensed. The Regulations apply throughout England, Scotland, Wales and Northern Ireland. A 'clamped' vehicle will not be released until a valid vehicle excise licence is produced, or a 'surety payment' is made, and release charges have been paid. Where a surety payment has been made, a voucher will be issued.

A 'surety payment' will usually be made where it is not possible at that time to obtain an excise licence. Where such a payment has been made, no further offence of unlicensed use will be committed within the following 24 hours. The fee is returnable when a valid excise licence is produced. Where vehicles are clamped, an immobilisation notice must be fixed to the vehicle, warning against an attempt to move the vehicle and providing information concerning release.

The Regulations authorise the immediate removal of such a vehicle to the possession of an authorised 'custodian'. In addition, after a vehicle has been immobilised for a period of 24 hours, it may be removed to the custody of such a person. Where such a removal has been effected, a removal charge is additionally payable for release.

The 1997 Regulations create the following offences:

(a) unauthorised removal of or interference with an immobilisation notice – reg. 7(1) and (2);
(b) removal, or attempted removal, of an immobilisation device – reg. 7(3);
(c) false declaration to secure release of vehicle from immobilisation device – reg. 8;
(d) false declaration to secure possession of impounded vehicle – reg. 13;
(e) false declaration in obtaining voucher or a refund relating to a surety payment – reg. 16(1) and (3); and
(f) forgery, etc., of voucher relating to surety payment – reg. 16(2) and (3).

Trade licences

When dealing with the registration and licensing of mechanically propelled vehicles used or kept on public roads, it was stated that, with certain exceptions, all mechanically propelled vehicle must have a current excise licence in force in relation to that vehicle, one licence to each vehicle. Trade licences, however, can be used on vehicles and are a type of excise licence issued to a motor trader or vehicle tester by the Secretary of State for use in connection with his business as a motor trader or vehicle tester. The term 'motor trader' is defined in s 62(1) of the Vehicle Excise and Registration Act 1994 as:

(a) a manufacturer or repairer of, or dealer in, vehicles; or
(b) any other description of person who carries on a business of such description as may be prescribed by regulations made by the Secretary of State,

and a person is treated as a dealer in vehicles if he carries on a business consisting wholly or mainly of collecting and delivering vehicles, and not including any other activities except activities as a manufacturer or repairer of, or dealer in, vehicles.

In addition, a person whose business is that of modifying vehicles (by fitting accessories or otherwise) or of 'valeting' (i.e. thorough cleaning, including removing wax and grease) prior to first registration or in order to prepare them for sale is also a 'motor trader'. Thus, persons entitled to trade licences are clearly defined and private motorists and similar persons are clearly excluded.

The term 'vehicle tester' means a person, other than a motor trader, who regularly in the course of his business engages in the testing on roads of mechanically propelled vehicles belonging to other persons.

Applications for a trade licence or for two or more trade licences must be made to the Secretary of State and, if the licence is granted, the holder of the licence will be issued with two plates, referred to as 'trade plates', showing the general registration mark assigned to the holder of the licence, and one of the plates shall contain means whereby the licence can be fixed to that plate.

Trade licences are granted for periods of 12 months or such shorter period as may be prescribed. The annual duty payable for a 12-month licence is currently that for a vehicle excise licence for motor cars or for motor cycles as the case may be.

Trade plates

The holder of a trade licence is issued with two plates in respect of each licence held by him, and provided he satisfies the Secretary of State that the vehicles which he will use include bicycles as well as other vehicles, he shall be entitled to be issued free of charge with an additional plate for use on such bicycles. The plates remain the property of the Secretary of State and shall be returned to him when the person to whom they were issued ceases to be the holder of a trade licence. The plates themselves contain the registration mark assigned to the licence, the letters and figures of which are red against a white background. These plates should be exhibited to the front and rear of the vehicle in the same manner as the ordinary registration mark is displayed. It is an offence to fail to do so.

Display of licence

The trade licence is put in a holder fixed to the trade plate which is exhibited at the front of the vehicle so as to be at all times clearly visible by daylight. In addition to the contents of an ordinary excise licence, the trade licence contains the name and address of the person who holds the licence. Motor cycles may display a rear plate only and, if this is so, the licence will be contained on that plate. It is an offence, contrary to s 59 of the Act and reg. 42 of the Road Vehicles (Registration and Licensing) Regulations 2002, to fail to display a licence.

Use of a trade licence by its holder

The Vehicle Excise and Registration Act 1994, s 12, places limitations upon the use of the licence by its holder. He is not entitled:

(a) to use more than one mechanically propelled vehicle at any one time; or
(b) to use any vehicle for any purpose other than a permitted one (see below); or

(c) to keep any vehicle on a road if it is not being used thereon, except in such circumstances as may be prescribed.

However, this refers to a particular licence and there is nothing to prevent a trader from
holding more than one licence so that he may use plates on more than one vehicle at
any one time. It is an offence to use more than the number of vehicles permitted by
such licences.

It makes it clear in (c) above that a trade licence cannot be used in respect of a vehicle
which is being 'kept' rather than being 'used' on a road.

Restrictions on use of trade licences

Regulation 37 of and Schedule 6 to the Road Vehicles (Registration and Licensing) Regulations 2002 provide that the holder of a licence must not permit any person to display
trade licence or trade plates on a vehicle other than one which that person is using for
the purpose of the licence holder's business, or other than when the vehicle is being
used for one or more of the prescribed permitted purposes. However, this does not prevent a person driving a vehicle on a road with the consent of the licence holder, when
the vehicle is being used for the licence holder's business. Thus, an employee may drive
vehicles in the course of his employer's (the licence holder's) business.

Permitted purposes

The use of mechanically propelled vehicles by a motor trader under a trade licence is
controlled by regs 38 to 42 of the Road Vehicles (Registration and Licensing) Regulations 2002.

Regulation 38 of and Schedule 6 to the 2002 Regulations prescribe the purposes for
which the holder of a trade licence may use a vehicle by virtue of a trade licence.
Those purposes do not include the carrying of any person on the vehicle or any trailer
drawn by it except a person carried in connection with such a purpose. The prescribed
purposes are without prejudice to the provisions of ss 11(4) to (6) of the 1994 Act
which specify classes of vehicle which a trade licence is for, in relation respectively to a
motor trader who is a manufacturer of vehicles, any other motor trader and a vehicle
tester.

Schedule 6, para. 10, authorises the holder of a trade licence to use a vehicle on
a public road for:

(a) business purposes as specified by para. 11;
(b) purposes specified by para. 12; and
(c) purposes that do not include the conveyance of goods or burden of any description except specified loads (test load or built-in load which is returned to the place
of loading without having been removed).

Business purposes, para. 11

The paragraph authorises use:

(a) as a manufacturer or repairer of or dealer in vehicles;
(b) as a manufacturer or repairer or dealer in trailers carried on in conjunction with
his business as a motor trader;

(c) of modifying vehicles (whether by the fitting of accessories or otherwise); or

(d) of valeting vehicles.

Permitted purposes, para. 12

A vehicle is used for a para. 12 purpose if it is used:

(a) for the test or trial of the vehicle, or its accessories or equipment in the ordinary course of construction, modification or repair, or after completion;

(b) for proceeding to or from a public weighbridge to ascertain its unladen weight, or to or from any place for its registration or inspection by someone acting on the Secretary of State's behalf;

(c) for its test or trial for the benefit of a prospective purchaser, including going either to or from a place of such test or trial at the instance of the prospective purchaser;

(d) for its test or trial for the benefit of a person interested in promoting publicity in regard to the vehicle, including going either to or from a place of such test or trial at the instance of such a person;

(e) for delivering it to a purchaser;

(f) for demonstrating the operation of the vehicle or its accessories or equipment when handed over to a purchaser;

(g) for delivering it between parts of the motor trader's own premises or to the premises of another manufacturer, dealer or repairer, or bringing it back from there directly to his own premises;

(h) for proceeding to or from a workshop where a body, or a special type of equipment or accessories, is to be or has been fitted to it or where it is to be or has been painted, valeted or repaired;

(i) for proceeding from the premises of a manufacturer, repairer or dealer to a railway station, airfield or shipping dock for the purpose of transportation, or for proceeding to such premises from a railway station, etc., to which it has been transported;

(j) for proceeding to or from any garage, auction room or storage place where vehicles are usually stored or offered for sale and at which the vehicle is to be or has been stored or offered for sale as the case may be;

(k) for proceeding to or from a place of testing; or

(l) for proceeding to a place to be broken up or otherwise dismantled.

The use of a vehicle with a trailer is regarded as the use of a single vehicle under the licence.

Schedule 6, paras 14 and 15 to the 2002 Regulations deal respectively with manufacturers' research vehicles and use by vehicle testers. The first restricts use to manufacturers for research and development purposes and the second restricts testing to vehicles and trailers drawn thereby, or any accessory or equipment on the vehicle or trailer, in the course of a business as a vehicle tester.

The above purposes are the only purposes for which mechanically propelled vehicles may be used under a trade licence, and even then only in the course of the business of the holder. If an employee used the trade plates and licence to remove his own private car to a paint shop for spraying, not in the course of his employer's business, the use would be unlawful. If the holder of the licence used under trade plates a vehicle which was in his possession in the course of his business to visit a cinema in the evening, that use of the motor vehicle would be unlawful as it would not be in the course of his business as a motor trader.

Carriage of goods or burden

Schedule 6, para. 13 of the 2002 Regulations defines the 'special loads' referred to in para. 10 above. Regulations prohibit the use of a vehicle under trade plates for the conveyance of goods or burden of any description except:

(a) a load which is carried by a vehicle being used for the purpose of testing or demonstrating the vehicle, or its accessories or equipment, within the terms of (b), (d), (e) or (g), above, and is carried solely for that purpose, and which is returned to the place of loading without having been removed from the vehicle (except in the case of an accident or for demonstrating its operation to a purchaser when handed over to him, or when the load consists of water, fertiliser or refuse);

(b) in the case of a vehicle which is being delivered or collected and is being used for a relevant purpose [as described in (f) to (k) above], a load consisting of another vehicle used or to be used for travel to or from the place of delivery or collection;

(c) any load built in as a permanent part of the vehicle or permanently attached to it;

(d) in the case of a vehicle which is being used for a purpose falling within para. 12(h), (i) or (j), a load which consists of a trailer or of parts, accessories or equipment designed to be fitted to the vehicle and of tolls for fitting them.

Although these provisions appear to be complex at first, their effect is simply to prohibit the carriage of goods on vehicles being used under a trade licence in all but the narrowest of circumstances. It may be that a 'test and trial' will necessarily involve the use of a vehicle with a load. If so, provisions limit the carriage of the load to the duration of that trial. In most circumstances in which a goods vehicle is observed being used under a trade licence whilst carrying a load, an offence will be committed. Some vehicles have what might be described as built-in loads, such as essential engineering equipment, and vehicles which are on their way to have accessories, etc., fitted may carry these accessories, etc., with them for that purpose. None of these loads is being carried for a commercial purpose connected with the use of the vehicle in the accepted sense of the word 'commercial'. The regulation makes similar restrictions in respect of use by vehicle researchers and vehicle testers.

Trade plate and trade licence offences

We have already dealt with the offence under s 34(1) of the 1994 Act relating to non-permitted use of trade licences. Breach of the regulations relating to loads or passengers is also an offence.

Schedule 6, para. 3 of the 2002 Regulations provides that the holder of a licence must not, or must not permit any person, to exhibit on any vehicle any trade licence or trade plate which has been altered, defaced, mutilated or added to, upon which the figures or particulars have become illegible or upon which the colours have been altered by fading or otherwise.

Section 44 of the 1994 Act provides that the offences thereunder of forgery, fraudulent alteration or use, or fraudulent lending or allowing to be used by any other person, of excise licences and registration marks also apply to trade licences and trade plates.

Driving licences, insurance and test certificates

The general rule is that before a person can drive a motor vehicle on a road he must be the holder of a current driving licence covering the category of vehicle he is driving, and there must be in force in relation to the use of the vehicle a valid policy of insurance or other approved form of insurance. The object behind the need to hold a driving licence is to ensure that all drivers possess the necessary basic skill to drive a motor vehicle on a road in a manner which is not likely to endanger other road users. To enable persons to practise driving in order to reach the standard required to pass a driving test, a person may be granted a provisional driving licence but, when driving, such persons must conform to certain conditions, the object of which is to indicate to other drivers that the driver is a 'learner' and, in the case of most motor vehicles, to ensure that such a 'learner' is under the supervision of a competent driver in or on the vehicle who is in such a position that he can supervise the actions of the learner driver. We will examine the various types of driving licence, the grant and issue of licences, the conditions that may be imposed and the powers of the police as regards production and inspection. We will also examine the legal requirements relating to insurance and police powers relating to production, etc.

For the purposes of this legislation, the term 'road' includes any highway and any other road to which the public has access and includes bridges over which a road passes. We are, therefore, considering roads used by the public, who have a right of access to them. However, some roads, although they may be considered to be 'private' by their owners, may be public roads for the purpose of the Road Traffic Acts if there is an unrestricted access. A highway allows members of the public a right of way on foot, riding, accompanied by a beast of burden or with vehicles or cattle. The term, therefore, embraces all forms of 'public passage'. Car parks which surround superstores inevitably have access and egress roads which are open to the public for general use. When cars are parked, passengers leave those vehicles and walk along various paths to and from the store. By reason of such use, those 'ways' may be roads for the purposes of this legislation but they will not be roads merely because people so use them. If these 'roads' merely exist to serve access and egress from the parking bays, rather than to convey persons from one place to another (the purpose of a road within the meaning of the Road Traffic Acts), the nature of those 'roads' and their usage will have to be examined by a court. Even where it might be shown that a road exists within a car park, this does not mean that the whole of the car park, including the parking bays, becomes a part of that road. Roads exist for the purpose of permitting travel to a destination. Car parks are for the purposes of allowing vehicles to stand and wait. However, offences of driving without insurance can be committed on a road or 'other public place'. Such open car parks at superstores will certainly be public places for the purpose of such offences.

Vehicles such as motor cycles which use public paths may be subject to the provisions of the Road Traffic Acts if public usage can be proved. If it is possible to show that the place is a 'road' (which includes a highway), and that members of the public generally use it, without trespass, then the provisions of the Road Traffic Acts apply. The common offences are driving otherwise than in accordance with a licence for a particular category of vehicle and for some other person to cause or permit another to drive a motor vehicle on a road otherwise than in accordance with such licence. The essence of driving is using the controls of the vehicle to control its movements. Persons 'freewheeling' in a motor vehicle or being towed (provided they have steerage) are driving.

Someone who is pushing a vehicle is not driving it, even if his hand is placed through the window and on to the steering wheel.

Driving licences

A driving licence is an authority to drive a motor vehicle on a road, and the onus is upon a person to show that he has this authority if he is found driving a motor vehicle on a road. The offence of driving otherwise than in accordance with a driving licence is contained in s 87 of the Road Traffic Act 1988. The onus is upon a person found driving a motor vehicle on a road to prove that he is licensed to drive as this is a fact peculiarly within his own knowledge. It is *desirable* that there should be, where possible, a statutory demand for production. It is also an offence to cause or permit a person to drive on a road a motor vehicle of any class otherwise than in accordance with a licence authorising him to drive a motor vehicle of that class. It can be seen, therefore, that employers have a responsibility to ensure that persons employed as drivers must be licensed. However, notwithstanding these provisions, a person may drive or cause or permit another person to drive a vehicle of any class if:

(a) the driver has held:
   (i) a licence under Part III of the Act (which deals with driving licences) to drive vehicles of that or a corresponding class; or
   (ii) a Community licence to drive vehicles of that or a corresponding class; or
   (iii) a Northern Ireland licence to drive vehicles of that or a corresponding class; or
   (iv) a British External licence or British Forces licence to drive vehicles of that or a corresponding class; or
   (v) an exchangeable licence (community licence or that of an specified country) to drive vehicles of that or a corresponding class; and
(b) either:
   (i) a qualifying application by the driver for the grant of a licence to drive vehicles of that class for a period which includes that time has been received by the Secretary of State; or
   (ii) a licence to drive vehicles of that class granted to him has been revoked or surrendered (for endorsement or alteration of details) otherwise than by reason of a current disqualification or of its being granted in error; and
(c) in relation to a provisional driving licence, the conditions relating to such a licence are being complied with.

This exemption only applies to the renewal of a licence. A person applying for his first licence must not drive until the licence is issued.

The significance of these provisions was lessened by legislation extending the validity of driving licences until the age of 70. However, licences which authorise the holder to drive large goods or large passenger-carrying vehicles shall be renewable on the holder's 45th birthday, or after 5 years, whichever is the *longer*, or where the licence is issued to a person between 45 and 65, for the period ending on his 66th birthday or after 5 years, whichever is the shorter. After the age of 65, such a licence will remain in force for 1 year only.

The categories of vehicles embraced by the DVLA licence have been extended to include all categories of large goods vehicles and large passenger-carrying vehicles and the licensing provisions which relate to such vehicles will be separately explained in the chapters dealing specifically with such vehicles.

Minimum age for driving classes of motor vehicles

Section 101 of the Road Traffic Act 1988 provides that persons are disqualified from holding or obtaining a licence to drive a motor vehicle of a particular class if they are below the age specified as the minimum age for driving such a vehicle. The ages at which various classes of vehicles may be driven are set out against a description of those vehicles in a table included within the section. The Motor Vehicles (Driving Licences) Regulations 1999, reg. 9, makes a number of additions and variations to those ages in particular circumstances. If a person drives a vehicle while under the age specified as the minimum age to drive that class of vehicle, he drives otherwise than in accordance with a licence granted to him, as any licence granted to him is invalid. The classes of vehicles and minimum ages are as follows:

(a) *16 years*:
  - (i) *Invalid carriage*.
  - (ii) *Moped*. This means a motor vehicle which has fewer than four wheels and
    - (1) in the case of a vehicle the first use of which occurred before 1 August 1977, has a cylinder capacity not exceeding 50 cc and is equipped with pedals by means of which the vehicle is capable of being propelled, and
    - (2) in any other case, has a maximum design speed not exceeding 50 kph and, if propelled by an internal combustion engine, has a cylinder capacity not exceeding 50 cc.
  - (iii) *Agricultural or forestry tractor*, provided it is a wheeled vehicle not exceeding 2.45 m in width and driven without a trailer (other than a two-wheeled or close-coupled four-wheeled trailer not exceeding 2.45 m in width). The person must have passed a test for category F or be proceeding to or from such a test.
  - (iv) *Disability living allowance*. Sixteen-year-olds in receipt of a disability living allowance of the higher rate component under the Social Security Contributions and Benefits Act 1992 may drive a small vehicle if it is driven without a trailer.
(b) *17 years*:
  - (i) *Motor cycle*, other than a moped.
  - (ii) *Small vehicle*. This means a motor vehicle (other than an invalid carriage, moped or motor bicycle) which
    - (1) is not constructed or adapted to carry more than nine persons inclusive of the driver, and
    - (2) has a maximum gross weight not exceeding 3.5 tonnes, and includes a combination of such a vehicle and a trailer.
  - (iii) *Incomplete large vehicle* not exceeding 3.5 tonnes.
  - (iv) *Some road rollers* (not steam, not exceeding 11.69 tonnes, no soft tyres and not constructed or adapted to carry a load other than vehicle equipment).
(c) *18 years*:
  - (i) *Medium-sized goods vehicles*. This means a motor vehicle constructed or adapted to carry or haul goods and not adapted to carry more than nine persons

inclusive of the driver, with a permissible maximum weight exceeding 3.5 tonnes but not 7.5 tonnes and includes a combination of such a vehicle and a trailer where the relevant maximum weight of the trailer does not exceed 750 kg. However, the age of 21 applies if such a vehicle is drawing a trailer and the maximum authorised mass of the combination exceeds 7.25 tonnes.

(ii) *Small passenger-carrying vehicle* which is an ambulance owned or operated by a health service body or a National Health Service Trust or a Primary Care Trust.

(iii) *A motor vehicle and trailer combination of sub-category C1 + E* the maximum authorised mass of which does not exceed 7.5 tonnes.

(iv) *Other motor vehicles in special circumstances.* A person of 18 may drive a large goods vehicle of a category to which a training agreement applies, and which is owned by his employer or a registered heavy goods vehicle training establishment, provided that he is employed by a registered employer and that he is a registered employee in accordance with the Training Scheme. In addition, a person of 18 may drive a large passenger vehicle where:

(1) the driver of the vehicle holds a provisional licence authorising the driving of the vehicle and is not engaged in the carriage of passengers, or

(2) the driver holds a full passenger-carrying vehicle driver's licence and

  (i) is engaged in the carriage of passengers on a regular service over a route which does not exceed 50 km, or

  (ii) where he is not so engaged, is driving a vehicle of a class included in sub-category D1,

  (iii) and the vehicle is operated under a PSV operator's licence, a permit under the Transport Act 1985 (educational and other purposes), or a Community bus permit.

(v) *Incomplete large vehicle exceeding 3.5 tonnes but not exceeding 7.5 tonnes.*

(d) *21 years*:

(i) *Large passenger vehicle*, i.e. passenger vehicles with more than nine seats inclusive of the driver.

(ii) *Large goods vehicle*, i.e. exceeding 7.5 tonnes.

(iii) *Large motor bicycles* unless the person concerned passed a test on or after 1 January 1997 for a motor cycle in category A (but not A1) and the standard access period has elapsed (2 years from date of test for standard motor cycles less any periods of disqualification, etc., before the date in question excluding any period of disqualification or during which the licence has ceased to be in force), or in the case of a person who passed a test for a licence authorising the driving of a large motor bicycle before 1 January 1997.

(iv) *All other motor vehicles.* This residual category covers generally those motor vehicles which do not normally carry passengers or carry or haul a load, e.g. a mobile crane.

The regulations permit members of the armed services, aged 17 or over, to drive large motor cycles and medium and large goods vehicles which are owned by the Secretary of State for Defence and are being used subject to his orders. Clearly this exemption is not a general one and the nature of the use of the vehicle at the time must be taken into account.

Although these provisions appear to be complex at first sight, the vehicles with which police officers are generally concerned are motor cycles, private saloon cars, goods vehicles and public service vehicles. Mopeds may be ridden at 16, motor cycles (unless they are large motor cycles without a sidecar exceeding 25 kw or a power to weight ratio exceeding 0.16 kw/kg or sidecar combinations having a power to weight ratio exceeding 0.16 kw/kg) and private cars at 17, and public service vehicles and large goods vehicles generally at 21. Goods vehicles carry plates which show their permissible weights and those under 3.5 tonnes may be driven at 17, those between 3.5 and 7.5 tonnes at 18 and those in excess of 7.5 tonnes at 21 (18 when under an approved heavy goods vehicle training scheme) in most circumstances. Small passenger vehicles, which are generally private cars (as the seating of such a vehicle must not exceed nine), may be driven at 17. Passenger vehicles with more than nine seats may, with the exceptions outlined, only be driven by a person of 21 years; most vehicles of the 'Transit' type fall within this category.

Disqualification

Obligatory disqualification

Persons below the ages specified above in relation to particular classes of vehicle are disqualified by reason of their age from driving. However, while s 103 of the Road Traffic Act 1988 creates offences of obtaining a driving licence while disqualified for holding or obtaining such a licence, and driving a motor vehicle on a road while so disqualified, these offences do not apply where the disqualification is by reason of age. Sections 34–36 of the Road Traffic Offenders Act 1988 deal with disqualification for certain offences, disqualification for repeated offences and disqualification until a test is passed.

A person who is disqualified from driving until a test is passed is permitted, by s 37(3) of the Road Traffic Offenders Act 1988, to obtain a provisional licence in order to prepare for the test. The provisional licence only authorises that person to drive if he complies with all of the conditions applicable to a provisional licence. If he drives a motor vehicle on a road and does not so comply, he is driving whilst disqualified and commits an offence against the Road Traffic Act 1988, s 103(1).

By s 34 of the Road Traffic Offenders Act 1988, where a person is convicted of an offence involving obligatory disqualification, the court must order him to be disqualified for such period, not less than 12 months, as the court thinks fit unless the court for special reasons thinks fit to order him to be disqualified for a shorter period or not to order him to be disqualified. The term 'special reasons' relates to circumstances peculiar to the offence, rather than to the offender. A lorry driver who stands to lose his livelihood cannot plead that these are special reasons for non-disqualification where that disqualification is in respect of a particular offence. The reasons are peculiar to the driver not the offence. However, a doctor called out to a serious accident, or a police officer ordered back to duty in an emergency where instant attendance was essential, could plead that these amounted to special reasons for driving while a little over the prescribed limit. It would be a matter for the court to decide whether or not their conduct was such that it might be 'special' to the case.

The offences that involve obligatory disqualification are:

(a) manslaughter;
(b) causing death by dangerous driving;
(c) dangerous driving;

(d) causing death by careless driving when under the influence of drink;
(e) driving or attempting to drive when unfit through drink or drugs;
(f) driving or attempting to drive with alcohol concentration above the prescribed limit;
(g) failing to provide a specimen for analysis or failing to allow a specimen to be subjected to laboratory test in (e) and (f) above;
(h) motor racing or taking part in special trials on highways; and
(i) aggravated vehicle taking under the Theft Act 1968, s 12A.

The offences of manslaughter (or in Scotland culpable homicide), causing death by dangerous driving and causing death by careless driving while under the influence of drink or drugs involve obligatory disqualification for a period of 2 years. This will also apply where a person has been disqualified within the 3 years immediately preceding the commission of the offence, for more than one fixed period of 56 days. If the conviction is for any of the offences which are connected with the drink/driving laws, that is an offence under s 3A, 4(1), 5(1)(a) or 7(6) or 7A(6) of the 1988 Act, and there has been a previous conviction for such an offence within the preceding 10 years, a court must order disqualification for a period of not less than 3 years unless there are special reasons for not doing so.

Discretionary disqualification

There are a number of other offences in respect of which a court may, at its discretion, order disqualification for such period as the court may think fit, but this must not be an indefinite period although it may be for life. Examples of these offences are careless and inconsiderate driving, the offences of being in charge of vehicles while unfit, etc., failing to stop after an accident and give particulars, driving otherwise than in accordance with a licence, driving with uncorrected eyesight and using an uninsured vehicle. Offences which carry discretional disqualification usually carry obligatory endorsement. However, a court cannot order penalty points to be endorsed if it orders the offender to be disqualified in respect of any offence of which he is convicted on that occasion.

Penalty points and disqualification

Disqualification may also result from the accumulation of penalty points on conviction for certain offences. If, for any reason, persons who are convicted of offences for which there should be obligatory or discretional disqualification, are not disqualified, the particulars of the offence and the date upon which it was committed must be endorsed on the licence or counterpart together with the number of penalty points awarded by the court. Where a defendant is convicted of two or more offences committed on the same occasion, the number of penalty points to be awarded must be the number, or generally, the highest number which could be awarded for one of those offences. Where a person is convicted for aiding and abetting offences involving obligatory disqualification, the number of penalty points to be attributed is 10.

On conviction for an offence, when the penalty points awarded bring the total to 12 or more in respect of offences within the preceding 3 years, the court must order disqualification for a minimum of 6 months unless the court is satisfied, having regard to all the circumstances, that there are grounds for mitigating the normal consequences of the conviction and thinks fit to order disqualification for a shorter period or not to order disqualification at all. In such cases the magistrates may consider *all of the circumstances*, but no account must be taken of any circumstances which are alleged to make the offence other than a serious one, or of any hardship other than exceptional hardship. Once such a disqualification has been imposed, the driving licence is in effect wiped clean. However, 'wiping clean' is restricted to such disqualification for repeated offences. Where a disqualification is imposed under the Road Traffic Offenders Act 1988, s 34, for a specific offence, the penalty points previously accumulated are to remain effective at the end of the period of disqualification until the expiry of 3 years from the date of the offence for which they were imposed. The penalty points for particular offences are listed in Schedule 2 to Road Traffic Offenders Act 1988. Some examples are given in the table.

Dangerous driving	3–11	Motor vehicle insurance offences	6–8
Careless driving	3–9	Contravention of pedestrian crossing regulations	3
In charge of vehicle while unfit, etc.	10	Exceeding speed limit	3–6 (or fixed penalty 3)
Failure to comply with traffic directions	3	Construction and use offences – tyres, brakes or steering	3
Driving otherwise than in accordance with a licence	3–6	Failure to stop after accident	5–10

A constable in uniform may arrest without warrant any person driving a motor vehicle on a road whom he has reasonable cause to suspect of being disqualified. This power does not extend to circumstances in which the person is disqualified by reason of age.

Use of vehicle in commission of crime: discretion to disqualify

The Powers of Criminal Courts (Sentencing) Act 2000, s 147, provides that if the Crown Court is satisfied that a motor vehicle was used (by the person convicted or anyone else) for the purpose of committing or facilitating the commission of an offence, it may disqualify the person convicted for such a period as it thinks fit from holding or obtaining a licence to drive. 'Facilitation' will include use after the offence for disposal of property or avoiding apprehension or detection. This power may only be exercised by the Crown Court on convicting an offender of an offence punishable on indictment with imprisonment for a term of 2 years or more, or when sentencing such a person after his conviction before a magistrates' court.

Disqualification: offenders in general

The Powers of Criminal Courts Crime (Sentencing) Act 1997, s 146, empowers a court on conviction of any offence to order the offender to be disqualified from holding or obtaining a driving licence. A court may only make an order under s 39 if the Secretary of State has notified it that it may exercise the power to do so. The same restriction applies under s 40 of the 1997 Act to the power of a magistrates' court to order disqualification in a case of default in paying a fine.

Driving while disqualified

A person who drives whilst disqualified commits an offence. It is necessary not only to prove the disqualification of a person of the same name and date of birth; the offender must, if he does not admit that he is that person, be formally identified, preferably by someone who was present in court when the disqualification was imposed but identification can be proved by fingerprint [this method of proving previous convictions has since been abolished by the Criminal Justice and Police Act 2001, s 78(9), but that Act provides, in s 82(2), that fingerprints may be used for the purpose of the conduct of a prosecution and this provision should cover the proof of a previous conviction, where it is an essential element in an offence, such as driving while disqualified for the purposes of a prosecution] or by admission under the Criminal Justice Act 1967, s 10.

However, the Divisional Court has said that it would be absurd to consider that any admission other than a formal one was irrelevant, or that evidence linking the accused with 'driving' when the first offence in respect of which the disqualification was imposed was insufficient. In addition, a statement under the Criminal Justice Act 1967, s 9, which refers to a person whom the deponent knew and stating that he knew him under a particular name may be sufficient to entitle justices to find sufficient evidence of identification.

A disqualified driver, when stopped by police, produced a passport and photograph. A Deputy Justices' Clerk provided a statement under the Criminal Justice Act 1967, s 9, stating that a man of the same name, address and date of birth was sentenced to disqualification at a particular court. The statement was accompanied by a certificate of conviction relating to the same person. An s 9 statement was also accepted from the driver's employer giving the same personal details and stating that the driver had produced a licence to the company which contained the same details. The Divisional Court said that the s 9 statements, which had been properly served, carried the weight of oral evidence and were sufficient evidence upon which the justices could convict. The court also said that the accused's failure to answer questions posed by the police officer and his failure to give evidence meant that the justices were entitled to draw inferences from his failure to give evidence. The court was, however, satisfied that there was sufficient evidence without such inferences.

The offence is an arrestable offence as it is listed in Schedule 1A to PACE containing those offences which are declared to be arrestable. This power of arrest does not apply in relation to persons disqualified by reason of age.

Removal of disqualification

The Road Traffic Offenders Act 1988, s 42, provides that a person who has been disqualified by a court may apply to have the disqualification removed as follows:

(a) if the disqualification is for less than 4 years, after 2 years;
(b) if it is for less than 10 but more than 4 years, when half the disqualification has expired; or
(c) in any other case (life or 10 or more years), when 5 years have passed.

Disqualification until test is passed

The Road Traffic Offenders Act 1988, s 36, provides that where a person is disqualified under s 34 (obligatory disqualification) on conviction for manslaughter by the driver of a motor vehicle, or an offence of causing death by dangerous driving, or for dangerous driving, causing death by careless driving while under the influence of drink or drugs, or is disqualified under s 34 or 35 (repeated offences) in such circumstances or for such period as the Secretary of State may prescribe, or is convicted of an offence involving obligatory endorsement which may be prescribed by the Secretary of State, the court *must* order him to be disqualified until he has passed the appropriate driving test.

The term 'appropriate driving test' means an extended driving test where a person is convicted of an offence involving obligatory disqualification or an offence prescribed by the Secretary of State, or is disqualified under s 35, and the ordinary driving test in any other circumstances.

A person disqualified until he has passed a driving test is permitted to take out a provisional licence once any fixed period of disqualification has passed in order to prepare himself for the appropriate test. Such a driver who does not comply with the conditions applicable to a provisional driving licence commits the offence of driving while disqualified.

In any case not covered by the above paragraph, where a person is convicted of an offence involving obligatory endorsement, the court *may* order him to be disqualified until he passes the ordinary driving test (whether or not he has previously passed such a test).

Revocation of licence of 'new driver'

The Road Traffic (New Drivers) Act 1995 provides that where a qualified driver commits an offence involving obligatory endorsement during his 'probationary period' (2 years from the date of becoming a qualified driver) and the penalty points to be taken into account on that occasion number six or more, the court must send a notice to the Secretary of State, containing the particulars to be endorsed on the counterpart of the person's licence together with the licence and counterpart. A similar requirement is made of a fixed-penalty clerk, where a fixed-penalty offence is involved.

The Secretary of State must, by notice, revoke that licence. The licence must not be restored until such a person has passed a relevant driving test within the relevant period (not more than 2 years).

The prescribed probationary period will come to an end where an order is made under the Road Traffic Offenders Act 1988, s 36 (disqualification until test is passed), after revocation where the licence is restored after passing a test or after revocation under Schedule 1 [where a person at the time holds a licence used as a provisional licence and a 'test certificate' (evidence of having passed a test) he is granted a full licence following his passing of a test].

Regulations provide for the issue of temporary licences for the duration of any appeal.

Types of driving licence

The purpose of holding a driving licence is to be able to offer instant proof to a police officer of a qualification to drive a particular class of motor vehicle on a road. In order to become qualified, it is necessary to become used to driving motor vehicles on roads and to allow persons to gain the necessary experience, provisional licences are issued. Once a satisfactory degree of proficiency has been achieved and the test successfully completed, a full licence can be issued in respect of the category of vehicle concerned and any other categories which the regulations allow. The categories are generally as follows:

Category	Class of vehicle included in category	Additional
	Part 1	
A	Motor bicycles	B1, K and P
A1	A sub-category of category A comprising learner motor bicycles	P
B	Any motor vehicle, other than a vehicle included in category A, F, K or P, having a maximum authorised mass exceeding 3.5 tonnes and having not more than eight seats in addition to the driver's seat, including (i) a combination of such a vehicle and a trailer where the trailer has a maximum authorised mass not exceeding 750 kg, and (ii) a combination of such a vehicle and a trailer where the maximum authorised mass of the combination does not exceed 3.5 tonnes and the maximum authorised mass of the trailer does not exceed the unladen weight of the tractor vehicle	F, K and P
B1	A sub-category of category B comprising motor vehicles having three or four wheels, and an unladen weight not exceeding 550 kg	K and P
B + E	Combination of a motor vehicle and trailer where the tractor vehicle is in category B but the combination does not fall within that category	
C	Any motor vehicle having an authorised mass exceeding 3.5 tonnes, other than a vehicle falling within category D, F, G or H, including such a vehicle drawing a trailer having a maximum authorised mass not exceeding 750 kg	
C1	A sub-category of category C comprising motor vehicles having a maximum authorised mass exceeding 3.5 tonnes but not exceeding 7.5 tonnes including such a vehicle drawing a trailer having a maximum authorised mass not exceeding 750 kg	
D	Any motor vehicle constructed or adapted for the carriage of passengers having more than eight seats in addition to the driver's seat, including such a vehicle drawing a trailer having a maximum authorised mass not exceeding 750 kg	
D1	A sub-category of category D comprising motor vehicles having more than eight seats but not more than 16 seats in addition to the driver's seat and including such a vehicle drawing a trailer with a maximum authorised mass not exceeding 750 kg	

Category	Class of vehicle included in category	Additional
C + E	Combination of a motor vehicle and trailer where the tractor vehicle is in category C but the combination does not fall within that category	B + E
C1 + E	A sub-category of category C + E comprising any combination of a motor vehicle and trailer where (a) the tractor is in sub-category C1, (b) the maximum authorised mass of the trailer exceeds 750 kg but not the unladen weight of the tractor vehicle, and (c) the maximum authorised mass of the combination does not exceed 12 tonnes.	B + E
D + E	Combination of a motor vehicle and trailer where the tractor vehicle is in category D but the combination does not fall into that category	B + E
D1 + E	A sub-category of category D + E comprising any combination of a motor vehicle and trailer where (a) the tractor vehicle is in sub-category D1, (b) the maximum authorised mass of the trailer exceeds 750 kg but not the unladen weight of the tractor vehicle, (c) the maximum authorised mass of the combination does not exceed 12 tonnes, and (d) the trailer is not used for the carriage of passengers	B + E
F	Agricultural or forestry tractor, including any such vehicle drawing a trailer but excluding any vehicle included in category H	K
G	Road roller	
H	Track-laying vehicle steered by its tracks	
K	Mowing machine which does not fall within category A and vehicles controlled by a pedestrian	
P	Moped	

Part 2

C1 + E	A sub-category of category C + E comprising any combination of a motor vehicle and trailer in sub-category C1 + E, the maximum authorised mass of which does not exceed 8.25 tonnes.	
D1	A sub-category of category D comprising motor vehicles in sub-category D1 driven otherwise than for hire or reward	
D1 + E	A sub-category of D + E comprising motor vehicles in sub-category D1 + E driven otherwise than for hire or reward	
L	Vehicle propelled by electrical power	

Part 3

B1 (invalid carriage)	A sub-category of category B comprising motor vehicles which are invalid carriages	

So far as vehicles of category B1 (invalid carriages) are concerned, reg. 5 of the 1999 Regulations provides that no licence may be issued for that sub-category to a person who did not hold one on 12 November 1999.

The term 'maximum authorised mass' has the same meaning:

(a) in relation to goods vehicles as 'permissible maximum weight' in the Road Traffic Act 1988, s 108(1), and
(b) in relation to any other vehicle or trailer as 'maximum gross weight' in the Road Vehicles (Construction and Use) Regulations 1986, reg. 3(2), viz. the weight which the vehicle is designed or adapted not to be exceeded when travelling on a road.

The regulatory provisions concerning driving licences are set out in the Motor Vehicles (Driving Licences) Regulations 1999.

Regulation 43 provides that where a person passes a test prescribed in respect of a class of motor vehicle included in any category or sub-category, the licensing authority must grant him a licence which will authorise him to drive vehicles of all classes included in that category or sub-category unless his licence is restricted to such vehicles fitted with automatic transmission, or vehicles specially adapted for the disabled, in which cases his entitlement will be restricted to similar vehicles within that class. Such holders are also authorised to drive those vehicles shown in column 3 above as additional categories or sub-categories with the same limitations as set out above, should the test have been taken on those types of vehicles. Where the additional category is F, K or P, the restriction related to 'automatics' does not apply.

Regulation 43 has since been amended in two ways. First, in relation to a person passing the test of competence to drive a vehicle in category A after 1 February 2001, a licence to drive a vehicle in category A does not confer an entitlement to drive a vehicle in sub-category B1. Second, in relation to a person passing the test of competence to drive a vehicle in category B on or after 1 February 2001, a licence to drive a vehicle in category B does not confer an entitlement to drive vehicles in category P unless that person has successfully completed an approved training course for motor cyclists.

The 1999 Regulations parallel new categories of vehicles with the old categories which were described by 1987 Regulations. They provide that licences (whether full or provisional) granted before 1 January 1997 are valid in respect of the new categories of vehicle, as set out in the table to the regulations.

Full driving licences issued to those who have passed the appropriate test are granted until the holder achieves the age of 70 years. After that age, the licence can be renewed for periods of 3 years. When the time for renewal arrives, it is the duty of the licence holder to make application for renewal; there is no requirement for reminders, nor are there any days of grace in respect of renewal. Those licences which authorise the holder to drive prescribed goods or passenger carrying vehicles will be renewable on the holder's 45th birthday, or after 5 years, whichever is the *longer*, or where the licence is issued to a person between 45 and 65 for the period ending on his 66th birthday or after 5 years, whichever is the *shorter*. A licence granted after the age of 65 will remain in force for 1 year only.

When there is a prosecution for an offence under s 87, the issue is whether the accused was driving the vehicle otherwise than in accordance with the licence at the material time, and a licence taken out later in the day does not excuse unlicensed driving earlier in that day.

All licences must be signed in ink immediately on receipt unless they are of the photo-card type (see below), in which case a signature will have been provided in advance. Defaced or lost licences may be replaced by the licensing authority. If a lost licence is subsequently found it must be returned to the authority. All new licences will be of the photocard variety but previous licences remain valid until they expire. An applicant for photocard licences must supply the licensing authority with a photograph which is a current likeness of him and with a specimen signature which can be electronically recorded and reproduced on the licence.

Overseas visitors and overseas residents

The provisions set out above are concerned with the British national who produces either a full or provisional licence to a police officer. Not all drivers on our roads today are British nationals and, therefore, many drivers will produce a foreign document. The term 'Convention permit' refers to a driving licence issued under the authority of a country outside the United Kingdom within the terms of the Motor Vehicles (International Circulation) Order 1975 and issued in accordance with various international conventions on road traffic. The document will be headed 'International Driving Permit'.

A 'Domestic Driving Permit' is a document issued under the law of a country outside the United Kingdom authorising the holder to drive vehicles of a specified class or classes. It refers to a driving licence of that country.

Persons holding either of these documents or a 'British Forces Germany' document who is temporarily in Great Britain may drive vehicles of the classes authorised for a period of 12 months from the last date of entry into the United Kingdom. EEA (European Economic Area) residents who have the domestic driving permit of their own country or an international driving permit may drive any large goods vehicle or any large passenger-carrying vehicle if authorised to drive those categories of vehicle by their permit.

Other holders of such permits may only drive such vehicles brought temporarily into Great Britain. Holders of driving licences issued by States within the EEA, in effect, hold 'Community licences'. If they become resident in Great Britain they are authorised by those licences to drive here without the need to exchange those licences for British ones within 1 year of becoming resident (persons other than EEA residents must do so). Such person do, however, have a right to exchange their licences. Where matters of validity, standards of health and fit-ness and disqualification are concerned, the exchange of licences is mandatory. Resident Community licence holders are subject to the same medical requirements as holders of British licences. Counterpart licences *may* be issued to such persons upon which endorsements may be made. These will provide evidence of previous convictions for the purposes of the Road Traffic Offenders Act 1988, Part III.

The right to the issue of British driving licences is restricted to persons normally resident in the United Kingdom. Community licence holders resident in Great Britain with appropriate licences who wish to drive medium-sized or large goods vehicles and passenger-carrying vehicles of any class must, after a period of 12 months, deliver their licence to the Secretary of State and provide details prescribed by the Road Traffic Act 1988, s 99B. They will be issued with counterpart licences. Community licence holders are also entitled to be licensed to drive a taxi or private hire vehicle or to drive small buses for charitable purposes provided that their Community licence authorises them to drive cars.

Persons who become resident in Great Britain and who hold British external licences granted in the Isle of Man, Jersey or Guernsey authorising the driving of large- or medium-sized goods vehicles or passenger-carrying vehicles and who are not disqualified from holding or obtaining a licence in Great Britain may drive such vehicles under the authority of those licences for a period of 1 year from the date upon which they became resident.

Provisional driving licence

The object of a provisional driving licence is to enable a person to drive a motor vehicle on a road, subject to certain conditions, so that he can gain the necessary experience and be given the necessary tuition to prepare him for a test by a traffic examiner, the passing of which entitles such a person to be granted a full driving licence for certain classes of vehicles, specified in the licence, e.g. entitled to drive motor vehicles of certain categories.

The Motor Vehicles (Driving Licences) Regulations 1999, Part III, deals with the constituent parts of driving tests, and the certificates to be issued to those who take tests. The regulations require that tests be conducted in two parts, a theory and hazard perception test followed by a practical or unitary test. The theory and hazard perception test must be taken before the practical test. Schedule 7 to the Regulations sets out the matters to dealt with within a theory test and Schedule 8 similarly deals with matters to be included in a practical or unitary test. The hazard perception test is conducted by means of the exhibition of film clips which take the perspective of the driver of a motor vehicle and show, at some point during each film clip, one or more hazards to traffic occurring on or near the road and require the candidate (using electronic equipment capable of recording the exact moment of each response) to indicate during each film clip the moment he observed a hazard relating to traffic on a road. The 1999 Regulations include requirement that, where a person produces to an examiner an appropriate licence which does not include a photograph, he must satisfy the person conducting the test as to his identity by producing a document to establish his identity as prescribed by Schedule 6 (all of which have a photograph) or a document of a like nature. In addition, if the person's identity is clearly apparent from the facts known to, or other evidence in the possession of, the person conducting the test this will be satisfactory. A provisional licence is granted by the Secretary of State for Transport and lasts for such period as may be prescribed (usually 2 years).

Full licence used as a provisional

The Road Traffic Act 1988, ss 98(2) and 99A(5), provide that a full licence, other than a provisional licence or a prescribed licence, may be used as a provisional licence to drive motor vehicles of other classes provided that the holder is not disqualified by reason of age from driving such a vehicle. However, reg. 19 of the 1999 Regulations provides that a full licence restricted to a specially adapted vehicle for a person with a physical disability may not act as a provisional licence for any other classes of vehicle.

Sections 98(2) and 99A(5) do not apply to a licence in so far as it allows the holder to drive vehicles of a class included in category B + E, C + E, D + E, or K or in sub-category B1 (invalid carriages), C1 or D1 (not for hire or reward). In addition, holders of full licences restricted to vehicles with automatic transmissions may use those licences as provisional licences to drive manually controlled vehicles of a category or sub-category as specified in the table to reg. 19.

In the case of licences authorising the driving of motor bicycles of sub-category A1 (learner motor cycles including category P) or standard motor cycles (those which are not large motor bicycles), such licences do not authorise the driving of large motor cycles (exceeding 25 kW maximum net power output or power to weight ratio exceeding 0.16 kW/kg) by a person under the age of 21.

The holders of Community licences are similarly entitled to use such full licences as provisional licences.

Special factors in relation to motor bicycles

The Road Traffic Act 1988, s 97(3), provides that a provisional licence shall not authorise a person under the age of 21 years, before he has passed a test of competence to drive:

(a) a motor bicycle without a sidecar unless it is a 'learner motor cycle' or its first use occurred before 1 January 1982 and the cylinder capacity of the engine does not exceed 125 cc, or
(b) a motor bicycle with a sidecar unless its power to weight ratio is less than or equal to 0.16 kW/kg.

A 'learner motor bicycle' is one which either is propelled by electrical power or has the following characteristics:

(a) the cylinder capacity does not exceed 125 cc,
(b) the 'maximum net power output' of its engine does not exceed 11 kW.

The power to weight ratio is assessed on the basis of the relationship of the maximum power output to the actual weight of the machine with a full fuel tank and normal equipment. 'Maximum net power output' means the maximum net power output measured under full engine load. Provisional licence holders who ride motor bicycles in excess of the power specified commit the offence of riding otherwise than in accordance with the conditions of their licences. The reason is that the provisional licence which they hold does not authorise the riding of that particular class of vehicle.

A provisional licence does not authorise a person, before he has passed a test of competence to drive, to drive on a road a motor bicycle or moped, except where he has successfully completed an approved training course for motor cyclists or is undergoing training on such a course and is driving a motor cycle or moped on a road as part of the training. Certificates will be issued to those who have successfully completed such courses.

A certificate is not valid:

(a) if the person to whom it is issued is at the time of issue ineligible to undertake the training course; and
(b) after whichever is the earliest of the following dates, namely
    (i) in a case where the person to whom the certificate was furnished is subsequently disqualified by order of a court under s 36 of the Offenders Act, the date on which the order is made;

(ii) in a case where the licence of the person to whom the certificate was furnished is subsequently revoked by the Secretary of State under s 3(1) of the Road Traffic (New Drivers) Act 1995, the date on which the revocation has effect in accordance with s 3(2) of that Act;

(iii) in a case where the certificate was issued before 1 February 2001, the last day of the period of 3 years beginning with the date of the certificate; or

(iv) in a case where the certificate was issued on or after 1 February 2001, the last day of the period of 2 years beginning with the date of the certificate.

The first part is concerned with the basic handling and control of machines. The training for the first part of the test can be undertaken without the necessity to ride on a road. The second part of the test is the normal 'on the road' training to drive which takes place under the supervision of instructors.

Regulation 69 of the 1999 Regulations provides that the requirement that a person is not authorised to drive a motor bicycle on a road unless he has passed a test of competence to drive, without having successfully completed an approved training course, does not apply to a person who is a provisional entitlement holder by virtue of having passed a test in respect of category P (mopeds) on or after 1 December 1990 provided that he has not subsequently been disqualified from driving until a test has been passed. Nor shall such a person be required to produce such a certificate on applying for a test of competence to drive a motor bicycle. Similar exemptions exist in favour of persons resident on exempted islands.

Regulation 69 has been amended by the addition of paragraphs (2A), (2B) and (2C) to modify the exemptions from the requirements to complete such training courses. The general proposition is that no person shall be permitted to take a test of competence to drive a motor bicycle unless he produces the prescribed certificate of completion of an approved training course. The amended regulation provides that this will not apply to a person who is for the time being the holder of a full licence for a class of vehicle included in category A (motor bicycles) in respect of a test of competence to drive a vehicle of any other class included in that category. Such a holder shall also be exempt from the restrictions imposed by s 97(3)(e) of the Road Traffic Act 1988 (which prevents the driving of a motor bicycle or moped on a road by the holder of a provisional licence before he has successfully completed an approved training course for motor cyclists) of his driving of a vehicle of another class included in that category. However, these exemptions do not apply in relation to the holder of a full licence authorising him only to drive a vehicle in category A having automatic transmission in respect of a test to drive vehicles with manual transmission or the driving of such a vehicle.

Regulation 44 of the 1999 Regulations provides that where a person passes a test for a licence authorising the driving of motor bicycles of any class other than a class included in sub-category A1, the licensing authority shall grant:

(a) where the test was passed on a motor bicycle, without a sidecar, the engine of which has a maximum net power output of not less than 35 kW, a licence authorising the driving of all classes of motor bicycles included in category A;

(b) where the test was passed on any other motor bicycle without a sidecar, a licence authorising him to drive a standard motor bicycle (a motor bicycle which is not a large motor bicycle) but a licence granted under this provision shall authorise the driving of all classes of motor bicycles in category A upon the expiration of the 'standard access period' (see below);

(c) where the test was passed on a motor bicycle and sidecar combination and the engine of the bicycle has a maximum net power output of not less than 35 kW, a licence authorising him to drive all classes of motor bicycle and sidecar combinations included in category A;

(d) where the test was passed on a motor bicycle and a sidecar combination the power to weight ratio of which does not exceed 0.16 kW/kg, but does not fall within paragraph (c), a licence authorising the driving of standard motor bicycles and sidecar combinations, but such a licence will authorise such a person to drive all classes of motor bicycles and combinations after the expiration of the standard access period.

The 'standard access period' is the period of 2 years commencing on the date upon which a person passes a test for a licence authorising the driving of standard motor bicycles of any class other than a class included in sub-category A1 but disregarding any period of disqualification or other period during which the licence has ceased to be in force.

At 17 years or over, a person will be able to seek a licence to drive motor bicycles. If he is tested on a motor bicycle without a sidecar of 75 cc, but not more than 120 cc, success will bring a category A1 licence. Success in a test involving the use of a motor bicycle of 121 cc which is capable of a speed of 100 km/h will bring a full standard licence (which, of course, includes A1 entitlement). Before being permitted to drive a 'large motor cycle', a candidate must be at least 21 and must pass a test on a motor bicycle with a maximum net engine power output of 35 kW. However, a person of less than 21 may take a test for a 'large motor cycle' entitlement if he has held a full standard category A licence for a period of 2 years. In the case of persons over 21 they are permitted, after holding a full standard category A licence for a period of 2 years, to drive large motor cycles without undergoing a further test.

Conditions applicable to a provisional licence holder

Provisional licences are issued to those who wish to learn to drive motor vehicles and are issued subject to conditions set out in the Motor Vehicles (Driving Licences) Regulations 1999, reg. 16. These conditions are set out below.

Supervision

With the exceptions listed below, a provisional licence holder must not drive or ride a motor vehicle otherwise than under the supervision of a qualified driver who is present with him in or on the vehicle. A person is a qualified driver if he:

(a) is 21 years of age or over;
(b) holds a relevant licence;
(c) has the relevant driving experience; and
(d) in the case of a disabled driver, he is supervising a provisional licence holder who is driving a vehicle of a class included in category B and would in an emergency be able to take control of the steering and braking functions of the vehicle in which he is a passenger.

A relevant licence is:

(i) in the case of a disabled driver, a full licence authorising the driving of a vehicle in category B other than vehicles in sub-category B1 or B1 (invalid carriages); and

(ii) in any other case, a full licence authorising the driving of vehicles of the same class as the vehicle being driven by the provisional licence holder.

A person has 'relevant driving experience' if:

(i) he has held a relevant licence for a continuous period of not less than 3 years or for periods amounting in aggregate to not less than 3 years, or

(ii) where he is supervising a provisional licence holder who is driving a vehicle in category C, D, C + E or D + E, he held the relevant licence on 6 April 1998 and has held it continuously since that date and he has also held a full licence authorising the driving of vehicles in category B for a continuous period of not less than 3 years or for periods amounting in aggregate to not less than 3 years.

A 'disabled driver' is a person who holds a relevant licence which is limited by virtue of a notice under the Road Traffic Act 1988, s 92(5)(b), to vehicles of a particular class. The term 'full licence' includes a Northern Ireland licence and a Community licence.

The conditions requiring that a qualified driver be over the age of 21 and that he has relevant driving experience do not apply to a member of the armed forces of the Crown acting in the course of his duties for naval, military or air force purposes. In addition, such a member may drive a dual-purpose vehicle when it is being used to carry passengers for naval, military or air force purposes; where the vehicle does not exceed 3.5 tonnes, if he holds a relevant licence for category B (other than B1); where it is more than 3.5 tonnes but less than 7.5 tonnes, a category C1 licence; and in any other case, a licence in category C other than C1.

Notices served under s 95(2)(b) specify that the Secretary of State is satisfied that a person who took a test and was suffering from a disability would be a danger to the public unless driving is restricted to a particular class of vehicle.

The supervisor's duty is to make up for any deficiencies in the skill of the learner; as part of his duty he must participate in the driving to such extent as could reasonably be expected to prevent danger to other persons or property. Because he has a right of control over the learner driver, a supervisor can be convicted as an accomplice to a driving offence committed by the learner driver if he deliberately fails to prevent it when he could reasonably have done so. For example, if a learner drives with an excess alcohol level, his supervisor can be convicted as an accomplice, if he is aware that the learner has been drinking and may be 'over the limit', and deliberately refrains from stopping the learner driving.

A provisional licence holder is not required to be supervised whilst undergoing a test. Although an examiner will be with him, the examiner is there for the purpose of assessing his competence, not for the purpose of supervision (and therefore not for the purpose of interference when a lack of skill is evident). The examiner is not, therefore, similarly exposed to charges of aiding and abetting offences by the learner.

A provisional licence holder is not required to be supervised if he:

(a) is driving a motor vehicle of a class included in sub-category B1 or B1 (invalid carriages) or in category F, G, H or K which is constructed to carry only one person and not adapted to carry more than one person;

(b) is riding a moped or motor bicycle with or without a sidecar; or

(c) is driving a motor vehicle other than a vehicle of a class included in category C, C + E, D or D + E, on a road in an exempted island.

Category B1 vehicles may have three or four wheels and an unladen weight not exceeding 550 kg. It follows, for example, that a *small* three- or four-wheeler with two seats requires a supervisor in order to be driven by a provisional licence holder, whereas if it *is constructed* with only one seat it does not (unless it has since been adapted to carry more than one person). The removal of a seat from a two seater does not alter the position since it will have been constructed with two. It must be emphasised that there is a total exemption for two-wheeled motor bicycles, whether fitted with a sidecar or not.

Other conditions

Motor vehicles which are driven or ridden by persons holding a provisional driving licence must display on the front and on the back of the vehicle the letter 'L' (or 'D' in Wales) in such a manner that it is clearly visible from a reasonable distance to other persons using the road. It is an offence for the holder of a provisional licence to drive a vehicle which is not so marked.

The drawing of trailers by a motor vehicle driven by the holder of a provisional licence is prohibited, with the exception of the holder of a provisional licence authorising the driving of a vehicle of a class included in category B + E, C + E, D + E or F (combination vehicles where the tractor falls in category B, i.e. not exceeding 3.5 tonnes or nine seats or agricultural or forestry tractors) in relation to motor vehicles of that class.

Holders of provisional licences authorising the driving of mopeds or motor bicycles with or without a sidecar must not drive such a vehicle whilst carrying on it another person.

Regulation 16(7) deals with compulsory basic training on motor cycles. It requires that the holder of a provisional licence authorising the driving of a motor bicycle other than a learner motor bicycle must drive under the supervision of a 'direct access instructor' who is accompanying him on another motor bicycle, is able to communicate with him by means of a radio which is not hand-held, who is supervising only that person, or at the most, one additional provisional licence holder and is carrying a valid certificate issued by the licensing authority. However, this does not apply to a person who has impaired hearing, provided that a suitable means of communication with the instructor is arranged in advance. Direct access instructors hold additional qualifications in respect of large motor cycles and must carry certificates of authorisation.

It is a condition of a provisional licence to drive a moped or learner motor bicycle that, when undergoing 'relevant training' (receiving professional tuition from a paid instructor in driving on a road after compulsory basic training), the holder of the licence cannot be in a group of more than three other such learners. Such an instructor must be present with him and riding a moped, or learner motor bicycle or any other motor bicycle.

Offences

It has already been said that a person who drives a motor vehicle on a road otherwise than in accordance with a licence authorising him to drive the class of vehicle in question commits the offence of unlicensed driving, contrary to s 87(1) of the 1988 Act.

It should be noted that, when a police officer discovers an offence of driving without a driving licence in circumstances in which the offender's driving would not have been in accordance with any licence that could have been granted to him, the police officer should include in the report reference to whether or not the conditions applicable to that licence were being complied with. The reason is that this is important to the court in relation to the penalty points awarded for the offence.

Driver training courses generally

The Transport Act 2000 amended s 99 of the Road Traffic Act 1988 to provide for the making of regulations which will have the combined effect of providing that persons who have not successfully completed a driver training course:

(a) may not take a test of competence to drive motor vehicles of a prescribed class (or a prescribed part of such a test);

(b) are not authorised to drive motor vehicles of a prescribed class (before having passed a test of competence to drive them) by a provisional licence [or by s 98(2) or 99A(5) of the Act of 1988 use of full licence as provisional];

(c) are not granted a licence authorising the driving of motor vehicles of a prescribed class by virtue of regulations under s 89(6)(b) or (c) of that Act (authority to drive vehicles of other classes); and

(d) are not authorised to drive motor vehicles of a prescribed class in prescribed circumstances (despite having passed a test of competence to drive them).

Exemptions are made in respect of (b), (c) and (d) where the person is undergoing training on a driver training course and is driving a motor vehicle as a part of that training. Regulations may provide and limit exemptions and provide for evidence of the completion of a driver training course in addition to the nature of the courses themselves. The legislation providing the power to make such regulations has been brought into force and regulations are awaited at the time of writing.

Examination of driving licences

The Road Traffic Act 1988, s 97(1), requires the Secretary of State to issue a licence to a person who applies for one in the prescribed manner, pays the appropriate fee and supplies necessary evidence to support his application. Section 98 requires that the licence shall be in the form of a photocard of a description specified by the Secretary of State or such other form as he may specify. Thus, provision is made for the introduction of photocard licences but licences issued in another form continue to be valid.

Where a photocard licence is to be issued, the licensing authority may require a specimen signature which can be electronically recorded and reproduced on a licence. If another form of licence is issued, it must be signed forthwith by the recipient.

The following particulars should be noted: the type of licence (provisional or full), the serial number, the driver number which indicates date of birth and sex of holder, the name of the person to whom the licence was issued, date of issue, date of expiry, the categories of vehicles which may be driven and the signature of the holder. Holders must notify any change of address forthwith. Offences are committed if they do not.

Defective eyesight

If a person drives a motor vehicle on a road while his eyesight is such that he cannot comply with the eyesight requirements prescribed under s 96 of the Road Traffic Act

1988, he commits an offence. The requirements are that he must be able to read in good daylight (with the aid of corrective lenses if worn) a vehicle registration mark containing letters and figures of the prescribed size, that is, where the characters are 79 mm high and 57 mm wide at a distance of 20.5 m (registration mark is one provided before 1 September 2001) or where the characters are 79 mm high and 50 mm wide at a distance of 20 m (registration mark is one provided on or after 1 September 2003). In the case of mowing machines and pedestrian-controlled vehicles, the distance is 12.3 m in the former case and 12 m in the latter.

A police officer having reason to suspect that a person with defective eyesight is driving a motor vehicle may require the driver to submit to a test to ascertain whether, using no other means of correction than he used at the time of driving, he can comply with the requirements as to eyesight. Refusal to submit to a test is an offence against s 96 of the Road Traffic Act 1988. It should be noted that the test must be carried out in good daylight, and it is usual to request the assistance of the traffic branch to arrange for such a test to be carried out.

Forgery, false statements, etc.

Sections 173, 174 and 175 of the Road Traffic Act 1988 deal with the various offences of forgery and false statements in relation to certain documents, which include driving licences and certificates of insurance or documents purporting to be evidence of insurance, and we will deal with the various offences in order.

Section 173 states that a person shall be guilty of an offence, who, with intent to deceive:

(a) forges, or alters, or uses or lends to, or allows to be used by any other person, a document to which this section applies;

(b) makes or has in his possession any document or other thing so closely resembling a document or other thing to which this section applies as to be calculated to deceive.

The most common form of this offence is when a person produces a driving licence or certificate of insurance relating to another person, intending to pass it off as his own. It can be seen that in such circumstances there may be an offence of 'lending or allowing to be used with intent to deceive' as well as 'using with intent to deceive'. A Community licence is a licence for the purposes of the section.

Section 174 deals with false statements and withholding material information.
The relevant provisions are set out below:

(1) A person shall be guilty of an offence who knowingly makes a false statement for the purpose of:
   (a) obtaining the grant of a licence under any part of this Act to himself or any other person (this includes a driving licence); or
   (b) preventing the grant of any licence; or
   (c) procuring the imposition of a condition or limitation in relation to such licence – s 174(1).

(2) A person shall be guilty of an offence who makes a false statement or withholds any material information for the purpose of obtaining the issue:
   (a) of a certificate of insurance or certificate of security; or

(b) of any document issued under regulations made by the Secretary of State which may be produced in lieu of a certificate of insurance or a certificate of security – s 174(5).

The question of whether there is any gain or advantage derived from the making of a false statement is immaterial. Where a person whose name is 'Jones' shows another name, e.g. 'Brown', on a proposal form for insurance purposes he is guilty of an offence under this section. However, most road traffic offences are punished by a fine and are 'spent' after a period of 5 years. Questions on insurance proposal forms relating to convictions cannot relate to spent convictions and a person may answer accordingly.

The final offence under this heading deals with the issue of false documents, and by virtue of s 175 of the Act a person is guilty of an offence if he issues a certificate of insurance, certificate of security or any other document which may be produced in lieu of such certificates as evidence of insurance, if the document or certificate so issued is, to his knowledge, false in a material particular. The accused must know that the document or certificate is false. The most common form of this offence is where a person issues a cover note for insurance and back dates the issue of the cover note, falsely showing that a vehicle was covered prior to the note being issued. The section also covers test certificates.

Police powers

If a constable has reasonable cause to believe that a document which is produced to him under the provisions of the Road Traffic Act 1988 is a document in relation to which an offence has been committed under s 173, 174 or 175 of the Act, he may seize the document.

Section 164 of the Road Traffic Act 1988 authorises a constable to require a person to state his date of birth in circumstances which are now prescribed by the Motor Vehicles (Driving Licences) Regulations 1999:

(a) where that person fails to produce forthwith for examination his driving licence on being required to do so by a constable; or
(b) where, on being so required, that person produces a licence which the constable has reason to suspect
   (i) was not granted to that person, or
   (ii) was granted to him in error, or
   (iii) contains an alteration in its particulars made with intent to deceive; or
(c) where, on being required, that person produces a licence in which the driver number has been altered, erased or defaced;
(d) in the case of the supervisor of a learner driver; where the constable has reason to suspect that he is under 21 years of age.

It is an offence to fail to state a date of birth when so required.

Insurance

The requirement

The purpose of requiring every user of a motor vehicle on a road or public place to be insured is to ensure that monetary compensation is available for any injury or damage resulting from the use of a motor vehicle on a road or other public place.

Section 143(1) of the Road Traffic Act 1988 reads:

Subject to the provisions of this part of the Act:
(a) a person must not use a motor vehicle on a road or other public place unless there is in force in relation to the use of the vehicle by that person such a policy of insurance or such a security in respect of third-party risks as complies with the requirements of this part of this Act; and
(b) a person must not cause or permit any other person to use a motor vehicle on a road or other public place unless there is in force in relation to the use of the vehicle by that other person such a policy of insurance or such a security in respect of third-party risks as complies with the requirements of this part of the Act.

A person who acts in contravention of these provisions is guilty of an offence.

As in the case of driving licences, the onus is upon a person found using a motor vehicle on a road or other public place to prove the existence of insurance as this is a fact peculiarly within his knowledge. However, it is *desirable* that there should be a statutory demand for its production.

A policy must be issued by an authorised insurer and must provide the minimum third-party cover for such person, persons or classes of persons as may be specified in it in respect of the death or bodily injury to any person (other than the driver) or damage to property up to a maximum value of £250 000, caused by or arising out of the use of the vehicle, and also provide for emergency treatment. It must also cover a policy holder against any liability which may be incurred in respect of the use within the territory of any member of the EU of a vehicle normally based in Great Britain, according to the law on compulsory motor insurance against liability in that State or, if it would give higher cover, the law which would be applicable if the vehicle was used in Great Britain when the event occurred.

It is common to find that the use of a vehicle in particular circumstances, or by a particular person, is not covered by the certificate of insurance produced. If the certificate refers to social, domestic and pleasure purposes only, then the policy-holder is not covered if he uses the vehicle for his business. If it covers the policy-holder and his spouse, then this is precisely what it means and no one else may drive. It is the terms of the certificate which are important, as the test is whether or not the terms of the certificate cover the use, not whether the insurance company says it would have accepted the risk. Vehicles are frequently driven by persons not covered by the policy-holder's certificate, but they may be covered by their own certificate of insurance, which allows them to drive other vehicles which they do not own or have not hired.

The test to be applied is concerned with whether or not there is a binding contract of insurance in force and not with the opinion of insurers as to whether or not they are liable. When a man obtained a cover note without disclosing that he was disqualified from driving, it was held that this contract was not void from the outset, but merely voidable and that until the insurers took steps to void the contract, it remained in force.

'Use' in relation to insurance offences may be interpreted in its widest sense as previously discussed. It is not necessarily something done by a driver, or even an owner or a group of persons if acting in concert, in relation to their usage of a motor vehicle. There is a 'use' for the purposes of motor vehicle insurance if there is any element of controlling, managing or operating the vehicle as a vehicle. Thus, there may be a use by a passenger but there must be more than mere knowledge that the vehicle is uninsured. Where, however, there is a clear agreement to use a vehicle for a particular purpose and both persons take part, there may be a use by the passenger.

The Court of Appeal has said that there can be a 'user' of a motor vehicle by a person who is not the driver. The Court summarised factors established within appeal court hearings:

(a) A 'user' is by definition someone required to provide third-party cover and, if he fails to do so, is potentially liable both criminally and civilly.
(b) Not all passengers are users even when they know that the vehicle is being driven without insurance.
(c) There has to be present in the putative user some element of controlling, managing or operating the vehicle.
(d) That element can exist as a result of a joint venture to use the vehicle for a particular purpose or where the passenger procures the making of the journey.
(e) Not every joint venture or procurement, however, will involve the element of control or management necessary to constitute the passenger as a user.
(f) Whether in any given case there is sufficient element of control or management to constitute the passenger as a user is a question of fact and degree for the trial judge.

However, there may also be a use where a vehicle is parked even if, because of some defect, the vehicle is incapable of moving, for example, where the brakes are seized. The Divisional Court has ruled that a motor vehicle which is parked on a road is being used for the purposes of s 143 even if it is totally immobilised and could only be moved by being dragged away. Where the owner of a vehicle is charged with 'using' that vehicle without insurance when it is driven by his employee in the course of the owner's business, it must be proved that the vehicle was being so used. A statement by a police officer to the effect that the driver told him that he was so engaged is insufficient. Such a statement is hearsay in relation to any charge made against the owner in these circumstances.

It is worth noting that the Road Traffic Act 1988 requires, *inter alia*, that judgment in respect of third-party liabilities must be met by authorised insurers even where the vehicle has been illegally used. Where insurance is limited to use by specified persons, judgments in respect of use by other persons shall be met as if the policy related to 'all persons'. However, although insurers must meet such liabilities, the test in relation to offences of uninsured use is concerned with the risks which are covered by the terms of the policy of insurance.

A United Kingdom motor vehicle insurance covers the legal requirements in relation to use in any EU country or in countries with which we have an agreement. The use of vehicles from those countries in the United Kingdom is similarly covered, as is the use of Northern Ireland vehicles if they are properly insured in Northern Ireland. Other foreign visitors must have an international insurance card, known as the 'green card insurance'.

Permitting uninsured use

Where a person borrows a motor vehicle subject to an implied limitation, of which he is aware, and he uses the vehicle outside that limitation, the use is uninsured if the policy demands that the use was with the consent of the owner.

Where a person permits another to have the use of his vehicle subject to an express condition that sufficient insurance cover is obtained in relation to its use, he *may* or *may not* permit the use of the vehicle without insurance. The situation is that, if the condition is *directly* communicated to the person who uses the vehicle without insurance, the person imposing the condition does not permit uninsured use. This is clear: a person cannot be said to have permitted something which he has expressly forbidden. However, the Divisional Court has ruled that if such a condition as to use has not been *directly* communicated to the user but has been passed on by someone else (as would occur if the vehicle was borrowed by A, but subsequently driven by B who had not spoken to the owner), the owner will be guilty of permitting uninsured use by B. The rule appears to be that any condition which would rule out 'permitting' must be directly between the two parties concerned.

Particular use of vehicles and trailers

A policy which covers social, domestic and pleasure purposes only does not cover business use. However, giving a lift to a friend who is 'on business' does not amount to a business use by the user of the vehicle. Most non-business policies will exclude use 'for hire or reward' and it may be that a vehicle used to assist a friend to move personal possessions is used for hire or reward if payment is made in respect of that use. Whilst payments made to cover expenses may be considered to be outside the term 'hire or reward', the dividing line will often be a fine one.

Policies frequently permit a person to drive with the permission of the policy holder if such driver 'holds or has held a licence to drive' and is not disqualified. If that person has at any time held a licence, whether full or provisional, it is sufficient in law to satisfy that requirement. It may be that on other occasions, a policy will refer to a person holding or having held a licence in respect of that category of vehicle, which is more restrictive.

In Great Britain, the use of trailers does not expressly need to be covered in respect of third-party risks. This cover is essential in other EU countries. In practice, in most cases in Great Britain, the use of trailers is covered and in any case, such 'use' would appear to be within the 'use' of the motor vehicle. Any relevant injury or damage caused by a trailer must be due to the use of the towing motor vehicle on a road.

When a person is apprehended for taking a motor vehicle without consent, it is possible that his own motor vehicle insurance will cover him for use of the vehicle concerned. It is the terms of the policy which are important. If the policy covers the use by him of another vehicle not owned by him or hired to him under a hire purchase agreement, the policy will cover such use even though the vehicle has been illegally taken. It would be different if the use covered was similar but 'with the consent of the owner of that other vehicle'.

Proof of insurance

Depending on the type of insurance that a person has, any of the following documents may be produced as evidence that the use of a vehicle was lawfully covered for the purpose of s 143 of the Road Traffic Act 1988:

(a) a certificate of motor insurance signed by the insuring company and containing the date of commencement and expiry, the person or persons entitled to drive, the limitations as to use and a reference to the vehicle covered by the certificate;

(b) a cover note issued by an insurance company, pending the issue of a certificate of insurance;

(c) an international motor insurance card;

(d) a Northern Ireland certificate of insurance;

(e) any EU certificate of insurance.

There are other, fairly rare documents, which may be held by large undertakings.

A security, rather than a policy of insurance, can satisfy the provisions of Part VI of the Act if it satisfies certain conditions set out in s 146. The security must consist of an undertaking by the giver of the security (who must be an authorised insurer or some body of persons in the business of giving securities which has deposited with the Accountant General of the Supreme Court the sum of £500 000 in respect of that business). The undertaking must be to make good, subject to any conditions specified therein, any failure by the person covered by the security duly to discharge any third-party liability for which insurance would otherwise be required under Part VI of the Act. Use of securities is frequently made by large undertakings, such as bus companies, which would experience unnecessary difficulties in negotiating separate insurance in respect of a large fleet of vehicles. A security is of no effect for the purposes of Part VI unless there is a 'certificate of security' in force in relation to the vehicles.

Exemptions from insurance

The use, on a road or public place, of a motor vehicle which falls into one of the following classifications does not require to be covered by a policy of insurance:

(a) a vehicle owned by a local authority or a National Parks Authority at a time when it is being driven under the owner's control;

(b) a vehicle owned by a police authority, or the Receiver for the Metropolitan Police District, at a time when it is being driven under the owner's control;

(c) a vehicle when it is being driven for police purposes by or under the direction of a police constable or a person employed by a police authority;

(d) a vehicle owned by the Service Authority for the NCIS or the NCS (when being driven under the owner's control) or when being driven for the purposes of such an Authority by or under the direction of a constable (or an employee of such authority);

(e) a vehicle being used for salvage purposes pursuant to Part IX of the Merchant Shipping Act 1984;

(f) a vehicle being used for the purpose of it being provided under a direction of the Army Act 1955 or the Air Force Act 1955;

(g) a vehicle which is owned by a health service body or NHS trust, at a time when the vehicle is being driven under the owner's control; or

(h) a vehicle which is made available by the Secretary of State to any person, body or local authority under the National Health Service Act 1977 when used within prescribed terms.

It should be noted, however, that although a vehicle being driven for a police purpose by or under the direction of a police constable [see (c) above] does not require to be covered by a policy of insurance, the driver will be liable for any injury or damage caused by the use of such a motor vehicle on a road or other public place. Most police forces carry motor vehicle insurance and have standing instructions concerning police officers authorised to drive various classes of vehicle. Caution should, therefore, be exercised when stolen or abandoned motor vehicles are driven by police officers who, if not specifically authorised to drive such vehicles, may find themselves personally liable for any injury or damage caused arising out of the use of the vehicle on a road or other public place under their direction.

Particulars to note

When a certificate of insurance is examined, the following factors should be checked: the number of the certificate, date of issue, date of expiry, the name and address of the insurance company, the authorised uses of the vehicle as measured against the use to which it is being put, the vehicle which is insured and the persons entitled to drive the insured vehicle.

Defence

If a person is charged with using a motor vehicle without being covered by a policy of insurance he shall not be convicted if he proves that the vehicle does not belong him and was not in his possession under a contract of hiring or of loan, that he was using the vehicle in the course of his employment and that he neither knew nor had reason to believe that there was not in force in relation to the vehicle a valid policy of insurance or security. This provision is to safeguard a person who, if employed as a driver, should not be made responsible for the insurance in relation to his employer's vehicles.

Details of insurance may be disclosed to police by companies

Section 36 of the Vehicles (Crime) Act 2001 permits the Secretary of State to make regulations for relevant information which is required to be kept by reg. 10 of the Motor Vehicles (Third Party Risks) Regulations 1972 (keeping of records by companies issuing a policy or security of names and addresses, specified motor vehicles, dates of validity and any conditions affecting indemnity) or by any subsequent regulations made under the Road Traffic Act 1988, to be made available to the Police Information Technology Organisation. The term 'relevant information' means information relating to policies of insurance, securities or certificates issued with policies or securities, or information relating to motor vehicles to which s 143 of the Act does not apply, or to any certificates or other documents issued in connection with such vehicles.

Test certificate

The increased use of motorways places greater stress upon motor vehicles, and the consequences of mechanical defects occurring in vehicles using these roads can be so serious that legislation was introduced to ensure that older motor vehicles were examined from time to time and that no major defects existed which were likely to make their presence on a road a danger both to the driver and to others using the road.

Sections 45 to 47 of the Road Traffic Act 1988 authorise the Secretary of State for Transport to make regulations setting out the requirements for such examinations and testing generally. He is permitted to authorise particular persons to carry out these tests, and approved testing stations display a sign consisting of three white triangles on a blue background, carrying the words 'Vehicle Testing Station'. These sections were amended by the Road Traffic (Vehicle Testing) Act 1999 to provide a statutory basis for the establishment of a central computer database of the MOT status of motor vehicles. This will aid enforcement of the provisions of the Vehicle Excise and Registration Act 1994 and subordinate regulations. The revised sections permit the Secretary of State to supervise testing stations by nominating a supervisor for each testing station. A computer link will be created with all testing stations to enable the results of individual tests to be fed into the central database. The Secretary of State is empowered to release such information to prescribed persons on payment of a fee and to the police free of charge via the Police National Computer. Provision is also made for statements concerning the issue, and the date of issue of a test certificate to be admissible in evidence. The Motor Vehicles (Tests) Regulations 1981 have been modified to recognise the provisions relating to electronic testing and the authorisation of testers and examiners.

A person offends against the Road Traffic Act 1988, s 47(1), if he uses a motor vehicle, or causes or permits it to be used on a road, without an appropriate test certificate. A motor vehicle which is parked on a road is being used for the purposes of this section even if it is totally immobilised and could only be moved by being dragged away.

Examination of motor vehicles

The Motor Vehicles (Tests) Regulations 1981 require that certain parts of vehicles are tested. For the purposes of these tests, motor vehicles are divided into Classes I to VII and specific testing requirements are set out for each class of vehicle in Schedule 2 to the Regulations. The most commonly used vehicles are those falling within Class IV (motor cars and heavy motor cars not being vehicles which fall within other classes). The specified parts to be tested in relation to such vehicles include wheels and tyres, steering, audible warning instrument, front position lamps, rear retro reflectors, stop lamps, direction indicators, rear registration plate lamps, rear fog lamps, hazard warning signal devices, braking, glass and field of vision, mirrors, windscreen cleaning, fuel tanks and pipes, seat belts and anchorages, exhaust (general condition), exhaust (emissions), vehicle identification number, structure and suspension (body, chassis, subframe, mounting or suspension which prejudices steering, braking or seat belt mountings or may otherwise cause danger), seats, doors and other openings to the extent that their condition may cause danger, and registration marks.

Owing to the construction of the vehicles, the requirements in respect of vehicles in Classes I (light motor bicycles), II (motor bicycles) and III (light motor vehicles other than motor bicycles) regarding the parts to be tested differ on occasions.

The tests are even more extensive for vehicles which fall within Classes V and VI, including speedometers, speed limiters and speed limiter plates, in addition to examination of many interior fittings. Class VII vehicles are inspected in a similar but extended fashion to those in Class IV, the test including such items are tyre loads and speed ratings.

The tests have been extended in relation to vehicles in Classes III to VII to include seat belts and anchorages fitted to such vehicles other than those required to be fitted by law.

When a test certificate is refused, the examiner must give a notice of refusal stating the reasons for failure. He must also provide in relation to all vehicles, other than motor cycles, an inspection check list on an approved form, giving details of the examination. Test certificates must be embossed by the stamp of the examiner or council on whose behalf it is issued. There is a right of appeal to the Secretary of State for Transport.

Motor vehicles requiring test certificates

Motor vehicles which are more than 3 years old, following the date of their original registration, must be examined annually and may only be used on a road if a test certificate is issued. On some occasions it is their date of manufacture which is taken into consideration if the vehicle has been used for some time before registration. This might occur when the vehicle has been used in the United Kingdom by one of Her Majesty's Services and is not registered until sold by auction to a private individual. For these purposes, date of manufacture is taken to be the last day of the year in which the vehicle was finally assembled or modified.

The provisions apply to:

(a) passenger vehicles with not more than eight seats, excluding the driver's seat;
(b) rigid goods motor cars, the unladen weight of which does not exceed 1525 kg;
(c) dual-purpose vehicles;
(d) motor cycles (including three-wheelers and mopeds); and
(e) motor caravans.

Motor vehicles used for the carriage of passengers and with more than eight seats, excluding the driver's seat (mainly public service vehicles), taxis and ambulances should be tested when they are 1 year old and annually thereafter.

It is important, therefore, that when a person is reported for an offence of using a motor vehicle without there being a test certificate in force, the date of the vehicle's first registration is obtained. This will be recorded in the vehicle registration document and at DVLA Swansea.

Exemptions

Certain vehicles are exempt from these provisions, and on a number of occasions they are exempt because they are subject to other testing requirements, or are owned by public services which have their own rules concerning inspection. Examples of such vehicles are goods vehicles [most of which are subject to ss 49–53 of the 1988 Act and the Goods Vehicles (Plating and Testing) Regulations 1988] and taxis licensed to ply for hire, which are subject to local inspection.

Vehicles temporarily in Great Britain (but only for the first year of their stay) are also exempt from these requirements. Vehicles in respect of which a Northern Ireland Test Certificate has been issued are also exempt during its validity.

Special exemptions

In certain circumstances, the use of vehicles which require a test certificate is permitted without such a certificate being in force, but such use is limited and is always associated with the test itself. It is possible that the owner of a motor vehicle may forget that an annual test is due and, if there were no exceptions to the rule concerning use, he could not drive the vehicle to a testing station on realising his omission. Use of vehicles without a test certificate is, therefore, permitted when going to, coming from or during a pre-arranged test. The test must have been booked. On occasions a vehicle may fail the test and it may be necessary to remove it to some place for repair, and in these circumstances it may be driven directly to that place. If the owner decides to scrap the vehicle, it may be lawfully towed to a breaker's yard.

Police officers and customs officials must occasionally remove vehicles under statutory powers, for example, when abandoned on roads or when seized, and test certificates are unnecessary in such circumstances.

Contents of certificate

The form of test certificate is not set out within the regulations. It shall be in a form supplied by the Secretary of State. Each certificate will generally have a serial number and contain a statement to the effect that the vehicle complied with the statutory requirements on the date of the examination. The registration number, vehicle testing station number, date of issue, date of expiry and the signature of the person issuing the certificate are currently shown. The signature may be a facsimile of the signature of the examiner or of a person authorised by the Secretary of State. If the previous certificate was out of date at the time of examination, the number of that certificate may be included. The testing station name and address are embossed on the certificate.

It is an offence to use, cause or permit to be used a motor vehicle more than 3 years old (from the date of its first registration) on a road without a current test certificate.

Evidence of first registration

As the offences of using, causing or permitting a motor vehicle to be used on a road without a current test certificate apply to motor vehicles of age decided upon by the Secretary of State for Transport (currently 3 years old), it is important in each case to prove the date of the original registration of the vehicle. This information can be obtained from the registration document, and the Motor Vehicles (Registration and Licensing) Regulations 2002 require the registered owner of a mechanically propelled vehicle, in respect of which a vehicle registration document has been issued, to produce it for inspection at any reasonable time if required to do so by a police officer or a local taxation officer. In the event of such a document having been lost, the owner must apply for a duplicate.

Police powers; production of driving licences and other documents

Sections 164 and 165 of the Road Traffic Act 1988 give a constable or vehicle examiner power to demand production of driving licences and their counterparts, insurance and test certificates, from any person:

(a) driving a motor vehicle on a road; or
(b) whom a constable or vehicle examiner has reasonable cause to believe to have been the driver of a motor vehicle at a time when an accident occurred owing to its presence on a road or other public place; or

(c) whom a constable or vehicle examiner has reasonable cause to believe to have committed an offence in relation to the use of a motor vehicle on a road.

In addition, a constable or vehicle examiner may require a person who supervises the holder of a provisional driving licence, in the circumstances described in (a) to (c), to produce his driving licence and its counterpart.

Where a constable is demanding production of a driving licence under these provisions the person concerned must, in prescribed circumstances, state his date of birth. The prescribed circumstances are those involving that person's failure to produce his driving licence forthwith or where the constable has reason to suspect that the licence was not granted to that person, or was granted to that person in error, or that it contains an alteration made with intent to deceive, or contains a driver number which has been altered, removed or defaced.

The purpose of the production of a driving licence is to enable the constable or vehicle examiner to ascertain the name and address of the holder of the licence, its date of issue and the authority by which it was issued. A person so required to produce his certificate of insurance or test certificate may also be required to give his name and address and the name and address of the owner of the vehicle.

The 'counterpart' to a driving licence means a document in such a form as the Secretary of State may determine, issued with the licence, containing such information as he determines and designed for the endorsement of particulars relating to the licence.

A person so required to produce such documents who fails to do so is guilty of an offence, but a person shall not be convicted of such an offence by reason only of failure to produce any such document if in proceedings against him for any such offence he shows that:

(a) within 7 days after the production was required, that document (and in the case of a licence, its counterpart) was produced at such police station as may have been specified by him at the time when its production was required (in person in the case of a driving licence); or
(b) it was produced there as soon as reasonably practicable (in person in the case of a driving licence); or
(c) it was not reasonably practicable for it to be produced there before the day on which the proceedings were commenced.

The laying of the information shall, for the purposes of these requirements, be treated as the commencement of the proceedings.

The usual practice, where a person fails to produce his vehicle documents as required by these sections, on the demand of a constable, is to issue him with a form HO/RT 1, but this only represents police procedure and a failure to issue a person with a form HO/RT 1 does not affect the liability of the person concerned should he fail to produce in accordance with a police requirement. However, it is not an offence to fail to produce a driving licence if requested to do so by a constable for the purpose of issuing a fixed-penalty notice.

These offences are committed *at the time of the demand* which is made in relation to production. In the event of a subsequent non-production, the driver should be charged with driving a motor vehicle on a road without having such a document in force and with the offence of non-production. It will then be for him to prove to the court that such a document, or documents, were in force at the time as these are matters particularly within his knowledge. If he produces the relevant document(s) to the court, he will still be convicted of an offence of non-production should the circumstances described above not apply in his case.

There is no power to require the driver of an invalid carriage to produce a certificate of insurance or a test certificate, as these provisions do not apply to such vehicles.

Section 164 of the Road Traffic Act 1988 allows the production of a receipt for a driving licence in place of a driving licence subject to the same conditions as to production which are applied to the licence itself, provided that if the person producing such a receipt is required to do so, he produces the licence and its counterpart in person, immediately on its return, at such police station as may have been specified. Receipts are issued under the authority of s 56 of the Road Traffic Offenders Act 1988 where a licence is surrendered within the fixed-penalty procedure.

Where a provisional licence has been produced to a constable by a person driving a motor bicycle and the constable has reasonable cause to believe that the holder was not driving that motor bicycle as part of the training being provided on a training course for motor cyclists, the constable may require him to produce the prescribed certificate of a training course for motor cyclists. The provisions at (a) to (c) on page 335 apply to such production.

A traffic warden is empowered by s 164 to require the production of a driving licence where the offence is one concerned with stopping on a pedestrian crossing or leaving a vehicle in a dangerous position and, where employed to perform functions in connection with the custody of vehicles removed because they were illegally, obstructively or dangerously parked, and he has reasonable cause to believe that the offence was committed by that person.

The law relating to highways

Highway

The term 'highway' has many definitions, but is described most clearly in s 328 of the Highways Act 1980 as being the whole or part of a highway other than a ferry or waterway. We are, therefore, considering roads along which vehicles or people pass, until they arrive at a river or estuary, the crossing of which involves going aboard ship. Section 328 of the Act goes on to include, within the term 'highway', bridges and tunnels over which or through which traffic passes. It is, therefore, clear that any road over which traffic actually passes is a highway, but such traffic need not be vehicular.

The term 'bridleway' is defined as including a highway over which the public merely have a right of way on foot or on horseback. In addition, the Countryside Act 1968 has given pedal cyclists the right to use bridleways, in the absence of local by-laws prohibiting their use.

A 'footpath' is a highway over which the public have a right of way on foot only and a 'footway' means a way comprised in a highway which also comprises a carriageway (for the passage of vehicles), being a way over which the public have a right of way on foot only.

A highway may, therefore, consist of many things: carriageways for the passage of vehicles, bridleways for horses, pedal cyclists and pedestrians, and footpaths or footways which are reserved for use by pedestrians. It is important to recognise that the term does not merely describe a 'road' but is wide enough to include any form of way over which any form of traffic passes. Section 137 of the Act says that it is an offence for any person, without lawful authority or excuse, wilfully to obstruct in any way the free passage of the highway.

The test of whether a particular use of a highway, for example, by a vehicle, amounts to an obstruction is whether the use is reasonable in all the circumstances. This means taking into account the duration, position and purpose, and any actual as opposed to potential obstruction. Such obstruction is 'wilful' if it is done with free will and causes an obstruction. An obstruction of a footway may be caused by a shopkeeper who causes a queue outside his premises by carrying on business in an unusual way. Selling or exposing goods for sale on a footway would similarly amount to an obstruction, as would the driving of a motor vehicle at a slow speed on the crown of the road so that faster vehicles are unable to overtake, although such an act may amount to an offence under the Road Traffic Acts. (See offence of driving without reasonable consideration for other road users.)

However, where a local authority was carrying out work on an area with a view to pedestrianisation and vehicles were permitted access for loading or unloading, it was held that there could not be an obstruction of an area which had been a footpath by a shop blind, which, because of the presence of scaffolding opposite, prevented the passage of vehicles. There must be evidence that exclusive use of the footway had been extinguished by resolution or otherwise and proof (beyond reasonable doubt) that a footway which had existed for many years had ceased to exist.

Where a supermarket left trolleys in a pedestrian precinct for the convenience of shoppers, there was an unlawful obstruction even though no complaint had been made by a member of the public. In addition, the right to protest is not a reasonable excuse for obstruction of the highway.

'Lawful authority' exists, for example, where essential road works are carried out in a proper manner or where a road check is lawfully carried out by police officers.

Powers

Section 25 of the Police and Criminal Evidence Act 1984, which provides the general power of arrest to constables, makes specific provision in respect of highway obstructions. A constable who has reasonable grounds for believing that arrest is necessary to prevent a person causing an unlawful obstruction of the highway may arrest such a person without warrant. However, it should be recognised that this power was probably given to allow the police to deal with 'sit-down demonstrators' where such obstructions are caused on roads. Nevertheless, the power is not limited to such circumstances and it is for a constable to decide whether an arrest is necessary in accordance with the terms of s 25.

Games

It is an offence contrary to the Highways Act 1980, s 161, for any person to play at football or any other game on a highway to the annoyance of any user. Complaints are often received concerning children who are playing various ball games in the street. Frequently, the complaint is made by a householder who has viewed the nuisance through a window. Before there can be an offence, the game must cause annoyance to the *user of a highway*. In most instances, these matters are dealt with by way of advice.

Fires and fireworks

It is an offence contrary to the Highways Act 1980, s 161, without lawful authority or excuse, to light any fire on or over a highway which consists of or comprises a carriageway, or to discharge any firearm or firework within 50 feet of the centre of such a highway, if as a consequence a user of the highway is injured, interrupted or endangered. It is important to recognise that this offence is only committed if the highway includes a carriageway.

The Fireworks (Safety) Regulations 1997 prohibit the supply of fireworks of erratic flight and mini-rockets, aerial shells, shells-in-mortar, aerial maroons and maroons-in-mortar. These Regulations also prohibit the supply of bangers, including banger/combination fireworks but not wheels with bangers, and prohibit persons under 18 from purchasing fireworks other than caps, crackers, snaps, novelty matches, party poppers, serpents and throw-downs. There are exceptions in relation to the supply to 'professional' organisations who organise firework displays.

Retailers must not sell fireworks removed from a primary pack or selection pack.

It is an offence contrary to the Explosives Act 1875, s 80, to throw or fire a firework in or on to a street or public place. This is a 'penalty offence' for the purposes of Part I of the Criminal Justice and Police Act 2001 and may be dealt with under a fixed penalty procedure; see page 478.

The Highways Act 1980, s 161A, prohibits the lighting of fires on land not forming part of such a highway, or directing or permitting such a fire to be lit if as a consequence a user of the highway is injured, interrupted or endangered by, or by smoke from, that fire or any other fire caused by that fire. There is a statutory defence available to persons charged with this offence:

(a) that at the time the fire was lit, he was satisfied on reasonable grounds that such consequences were unlikely; and
(b) either
    (i) that both before and after the fire was lit he did all that he reasonably could to prevent users of any such highway from being so injured, etc.; or
    (ii) that he had reasonable excuse for not doing so.

Depositing litter

It is an offence to throw down, drop or otherwise deposit in, into or from any place specified in the Environmental Protection Act 1990, s 87, and to leave any thing whatsoever in such circumstances as to cause, contribute to, or tend to lead to, the defacement by litter of such a place, unless it was authorised by law or was done with the consent of the owner, occupier or person or authority having control over such place.

The Environmental Protection Act 1990, s 87, is concerned with the *place* 'from which, in which or into which' litter is deposited so that it causes defacement by litter of such a *place*. The term *place* means any public open place (place in the open air to which the public are entitled or permitted to have access without payment and any covered place open to the air on at least one side and available for public use), special roads, Crown land, relevant land of statutory undertakers or educational authorities, or relevant land of a principal litter authority or within a litter-controlled area.

Thus, the act of depositing litter must be made from, in or into a specified place. It has been held that 'depositing and leaving' is a single act with two elements and it is, therefore, necessary to prove that the litter was left by the person throwing it down. If it is subsequently picked up, then no offence will have been committed. It must be left and must cause, contribute to, or tend to lead to the defacement by litter of such a place. A covered place open to the air on at least one side, such as a bus shelter, is an open place. However, a telephone kiosk which is so constructed that it is enclosed with the exception of a 6-inch gap at the bottom, is not a public open place within the terms of the section, nor has it one side open to public use.

A person who deposits litter in a lay-by commits this offence. It is deposited in a public open place and leads to its defacement. If that person threw the litter over the hedge into a field he would not, unless the field was a place particularly specified by the section, for example Crown land, commit an offence contrary to s 87. Although the act of depositing was *from* a place specified by the section, it did not *lead to the defacement of such a place*. There would be an offence however, against the provisions of the Refuse Disposal (Amenity) Act 1978, s 2; see below.

Section 88 of the 1990 Act makes provisions for the payment of a fixed penalty in respect of an offence of depositing litter contrary to s 87. Power is given to an authorised officer of the litter authority (authorised in writing) to give to a person whom he finds and whom he has reason to believe has on that occasion committed an offence contrary to s 87 in the area of the authority, a fixed-penalty notice. Where this is done, no proceedings shall be instituted for that offence before the expiration of a period of 14 days following the issue of the notice. A person may not be convicted of such an offence if he pays the fixed penalty before the expiration of that period.

The 1990 Act has, therefore, placed a significant responsibility for the enforcement of the provisions of the Act which deal with litter upon local authorities. Whilst the fixed-penalty provisions are not extended to police officers, s 87 creates an offence which may be dealt with by police officers.

A man and his family were living in a tent in a lane. Nearby was a lorry against which was a pile of scrap metal and the man was found sorting through it. It was held that he was guilty of depositing litter as he intended only to remove the scrap which had value. The High Court stated that 'leaves' does not mean 'abandons'. The metal had been deposited and permitted to remain beside the road and had been left. An article deposited with no intention to remove it can be 'left' after being there for only a short time.

It has been held that 'depositing and leaving' is a single act with two elements and it is, therefore, necessary to prove that the litter was left by the person throwing it down. If it is subsequently picked up, then no offence will have been committed.

The Refuse Disposal (Amenity) Act 1978 s 2 creates the offence of abandoning, without lawful authority, on any land in the open air or on other land forming part of a highway, anything which has been brought to the land for the purpose of being abandoned there. There is no mention in this Act of depositing from particular places and prosecutions usually follow the discovery of identifiable waste which has been abandoned on any land in the open air. This offence is further described in relating to vehicles on page 349.

When dealing with offences in relation to litter, the court will require a full description of the nature of the litter and the extent of the defacement caused.

Interfering with litter bins and notice boards

Local authorities are empowered by the Public Health Act 1961 to provide and maintain litter bins and notices concerning their use. Section 51 of that Act creates the offences of wilfully removing or otherwise interfering with such a receptacle or a notice.

Builders' skips

The Highways Act 1980, s 139, allows builders' skips to be deposited on the highway with the permission of the highway authority. Such permissions must be in writing. Each skip must be authorised on each occasion; a general permission to place skips cannot be given. The owner of the skip must:

(a) ensure that it is properly lighted during the hours of darkness;
(b) ensure that the skip is clearly and indelibly marked with the owner's name and with his telephone number or address, and has attached to the sides which face in the direction of the carriageway two oblong plates of diagonal red and yellow fluorescent or reflective material, similar to those fitted to the rear of heavy goods vehicles;
(c) ensure that it is removed as soon as practicable after it has been filled;
(d) ensure that each of the conditions subject to which the permission was granted is complied with.

The requirement in (d) refers to the fact that the highway authority may grant permission with or without additional conditions. The additional conditions which may be attached to the use of a builder's skip may include conditions relating to:

(i) the siting of the skip;
(ii) its dimensions;

(iii) the manner in which it should be coated with paint or other material to make it immediately visible to traffic;

(iv) the care and disposal of its contents;

 (v) the manner in which it is to be lighted or guarded;

(vi) its removal at the end of the period of permission.

An offence will be committed by the owner of a builder's skip if it is deposited on the highway without permission. Offences are also committed by the owner if he fails to comply with any of the duties set out in (a) to (d) above, or any conditions attached by the highway authority under the headings shown in (i) to (vi). The term 'owner' in relation to a skip which is hired for 1 month or more, or one which is the subject of hire purchase agreement, means the person in possession of the skip under the hiring agreement. In most instances in which a skip is left on the highway beyond its authorised date, the offence of failure to comply with a condition, i.e. that it would be removed on a certain date, will have been committed. However, the term 'deposit' has been held to include 'leaving, remaining or leave lying' and it is, therefore, possible to charge depositing without permission if there are difficulties in relation to the particular conditions.

The highway authority or a police constable in uniform may require the owner of a skip to remove or reposition it, or cause it to be removed or repositioned and may either remove it or cause it to be removed. The expenses of removal may be recovered from the owner as a civil debt. It is an offence for the owner to fail to remove the skip as soon as reasonably practicable. A request by a constable must be made in person. A request by telephone, for example, is not sufficient.

Loudspeakers

Section 62 of the Control of Pollution Act 1974 states that loudspeakers shall not be operated in a street between 9 p.m. and 8 a.m. *for any purpose* or at any other time for the purpose of advertising any entertainment, trade or business.

There are certain exceptions, which include police, fire brigade, ambulance, the Environment Agency or a water undertaking in the exercise of its functions and travelling showmen using loudspeakers on land used as a pleasure fair and used in an emergency provided that the loudspeaker is so operated as not to give reasonable cause for annoyance to persons in the vicinity. For the purposes of this Act, a street is defined as being a highway or any other road, footway, court or square open to the public for the time being. The most usual exception to be encountered is the use of loudspeakers to broadcast chimes from travelling shops or ice cream vehicles. Their use is permitted if the following conditions are served:

(a) the loudspeaker is fixed to a vehicle used for carrying perishable foods; and

(b) is operated solely to inform the public that such food is for sale;

(c) no words are used;

(d) it is operated so as not to cause annoyance;

(e) it is only used between 12 noon and 7.00 p.m.

Parking by disabled persons

The Chronically Sick and Disabled Persons Act 1970, s 21, requires that a badge of the prescribed form be issued by local authorities for motor vehicles driven by, or used for the carriage of, disabled persons resident within their areas. A badge so issued may be displayed on a vehicle either inside or outside the area of the issuing authority, and exemptions afforded to such persons apply anywhere. Badges may also be issued to institutions concerned with the care of the disabled.

The Local Authorities Traffic Orders (Exemptions for Disabled Persons) (England) Regulations 2000 contain a requirement that all no waiting orders, etc., made by local authorities must contain exemptions in favour of disabled persons' vehicles. However, the requirement to include an exemption does not apply to orders which prohibit the waiting of vehicles of all other classes.

The Disabled Persons (Badges for Motor Vehicles) (England) Regulations 2000 follow Council Recommendation 98/376/EC which recommends a Community-wide parking card for people with disabilities. The Regulations deal with those persons who are eligible to receive badges, the grounds for refusal and the circumstances in which a disabled person's badge must be returned to the issuing authority. Regulation 11 prescribes the forms of the badges to be issued and the Schedules to the regulations show the contents and various forms of badges. The background on the front and reverse sides of the badge is coloured light blue and includes a background of wheelchair symbols. The square box which contains the wheelchair symbol and the rectangular box containing the country identifier are coloured dark blue. All other boxes contained within the badge are coloured white. Those badges issued under the previous 1982 Regulations will comply with the requirements of the 1982 Regulations and will contain similar information but will be coloured orange. These badges retain their validity until expiry.

Regulation 12 of the 2000 Regulations requires that a disabled person's badge is exhibited on the dashboard or facia of the vehicle or, where the vehicle is not fitted with a dashboard or facia, in a conspicuous position, in either case so that the front of the badge is clearly legible from outside the vehicle. Similar provisions are made by the Local Authorities' Traffic Orders (Exemption for Disabled Persons) (England) Regulations 2000 for the display of parking discs, so that the quarter-hour period during which the period of waiting begins is legible from outside the vehicle.

Regulation 13 of the Disabled Persons (Badges for Motor Vehicles) (England) Regulations 2000 sets out the circumstances in which an individual's disabled person's badge may be displayed while the vehicle is being driven. These are:

(a) the holder is either driving or being carried in the vehicle; or
(b) if the vehicle is being used solely to collect the holder; or
(c) if the vehicle is leaving the place where the holder has got out.

For (b) and (c) to apply, it is necessary that a disabled person's concession (other than one relating to parking) would be available to a vehicle displaying such a badge, and it would not have been practicable for the vehicle to be lawfully driven to, or to stop at, or to have left the place where the holder is collected. By reg. 14 of the 2000 Regulations the circumstances in which an individual's disabled person's badge may be displayed while the vehicle is parked are:

(a) if it has been driven by the holder, or has been used to carry him, to the place where he is parked; or
(b) if it is to be driven by the holder, or is to be used to carry him, from that place.

A disabled person's vehicle must therefore be displaying a badge, and for that badge to be lawfully displayed, the relevant conditions set out above must apply. The Regulations provide that badges issued in Scotland and Wales are valid in England.

The Chronically Sick and Disabled Persons Act 1970, s 21, makes it an offence for a person to drive a motor vehicle which is displaying such a badge otherwise than in a manner or in circumstances prescribed by the Regulations. It also creates the offence of displaying a badge which is not issued by a local authority.

The exemptions in favour of disabled persons' vehicles are in respect of orders prohibiting vehicles waiting beyond a specified period of time, of no waiting orders for vehicles generally (whether in relation to some types or all vehicles), of orders prohibiting waiting for more than a specified period in a street parking place, and of charges and time limit restrictions at parking meters. The only restriction which may apply to disabled persons' vehicles is where there is a prohibition on waiting for a period more than 3 hours. In such a case a disabled person's vehicle is exempt for a maximum of 3 hours (but then must not return for 1 hour to that place), provided that a badge is displayed showing the time of arrival (disc parking scheme).

Similar Regulations of 2000 exist in Wales and the offences which can be committed are identical.

The badge scheme does not permit

The badge scheme does not permit parking:

(a) during the time a ban on loading or unloading is in force (indicated by one, two or three yellow marks on a kerb, at a time shown on a post-mounted plate);
(b) where there is a double white line in the centre of the road even if one of the lines is broken;
(c) in a bus or cycle lane when it is in use;
(d) on zebra or pelican crossings or on the zigzag markings before or after these crossings;
(e) in parking places reserved for specific users, e.g. loading bays, residents, taxis or cycles; and
(f) in suspended meter bays or when the use of the meter is prohibited.

Wrongful use of disabled person's badge

The Road Traffic Regulation Act 1984, s 117, deals with the wrongful use of a disabled person's badge. It provides that a person is guilty of an offence if, when he commits some other offence under the Act (e.g. contravention of an order relating to parking made under it), the following conditions are satisfied:

(a) a disabled person's badge was displayed on the motor vehicle;
(b) he was using the vehicle in circumstances where a disabled person's concession would be available to a disabled person's vehicle; and
(c) the vehicle was not being used either by the person to whom the badge was issued or for institutional use.

Motor traffic offences by owners and drivers

Motor cycles and mopeds

For the definitions of the terms 'motor cycle' and 'moped', see page 274.

Passengers on motor cycles

The Road Traffic Act 1988, s 23, provides that no more than one person, in addition to the driver, shall be carried on a two-wheeled motor cycle. Such a passenger must be carried sitting astride the cycle, on a proper seat securely fixed to the cycle behind the driver's seat. It is important to recognise that the duties are those of the driver, who commits the offence of carrying more than one passenger, or of carrying a passenger otherwise than astride the machine on a seat securely fixed behind the driver. The person carried may be proceeded against for aiding, abetting, counselling, or procuring the commission of the offence, if sufficient evidence of 'joint enterprise' is available.

Footrests for passengers

The Road Vehicles (Construction and Use) Regulations 1986, reg. 102, provides that if any person, in addition to the driver, is carried astride any two-wheeled motor cycle (whether a sidecar is attached or not), suitable supports or rests for the feet shall be available on the cycle.

   The offence is one of using, causing or permitting a two-wheeled motor cycle to be used on a road, upon which a person in addition to the driver was carried astride, there not being available on the cycle for that person suitable supports or rests for the feet.

Protective headgear

Every person driving or riding a motor bicycle on a road (otherwise than in a sidecar) shall wear protective headgear of approved design. If he does not, he commits an offence under the Road Traffic Act 1988, s 16(4). The regulations which are contravened are the Motor Cycles (Protective Helmets) Regulations 1998. Turban-wearing followers of the Sikh religion are exempted. There is no requirement to wear a crash helmet when pushing a motor cycle. A driver is not liable in respect of a passenger who does not wear a crash helmet, unless that passenger is under 16 years.

Passengers on pedal cycles

By the Road Traffic Act 1988, s 24, it is not lawful for more than one person to be carried on a road on a bicycle not propelled by mechanical power unless it is constructed or adapted for the carriage of more than one person. If a cycle is ridden in contravention of this section, each of the persons carried is guilty of an offence. A tandem machine provides a good example of a cycle which is constructed for the carriage of more than one person. Cycles are frequently seen which have been adapted by the owner to allow a child to be carried by attaching a seat securely to the cross bar, with footrests provided below it. The test as to whether or not there has been an adaptation can be applied by asking the question, 'If the vehicle had been originally produced in this form, would it have been produced for the carriage of two persons?'

Riding on a footpath

The offence of wilfully riding a pedal cycle on a footpath by the side of a road and set apart for pedestrians is one contrary to s 72 of the Highways Act 1835. There are, frequently, local by-laws controlling the use of pedal cycles in particular places.

Brakes on pedal cycles

The Pedal Cycles (Construction and Use) Regulations 1983 are not the most easily understood regulations to appear in legal textbooks. It is helpful to imagine, in the first instance, the types of pedal cycle which are likely to be seen in use on a road and to consider in each case the braking systems which are required. We must think in terms of children's cycles, all forms of bicycles, passenger and goods tricycles and, since these regulations also deal with the later concept of electrically assisted pedal cycles, we must also consider the separate provisions made for such cycles. No person under 14 may ride an electrically assisted pedal cycle. Such a cycle is not a motor vehicle. In addition, the 1983 Regulations make different provisions in respect of cycles manufactured before 1 August 1984.

Let us first consider cycles manufactured before 1 August 1984. Generally in the case of two-wheeled machines with wheels exceeding 460 mm in outside diameter, including the fully inflated tyre, there are two types of pedal cycle to consider. The first has a fixed wheel (a wheel which cannot rotate independently of the pedals) and the other has two free wheels. The fixed wheel is really a braking system in itself and it is possible to bring the cycle to a halt by progressively slowing down the pedalling action. It is not surprising to find that such a cycle requires only one braking system operating on the front wheel. If such a bicycle is free wheel, then it is obvious that it will require two independent systems operating on each wheel.

Cycles with a lesser wheel diameter than that prescribed require only one braking system, e.g. a child's cycle, although some children's cycles are exempt entirely from these provisions.

Tricycles with wheels exceeding 460 mm are rarer than bicycles and most that still exist are passenger (that is non-goods) tricycles. In such cases it is sufficient to have two independent braking systems operating on the single wheel of the machine. Although it is now unusual to see a goods tricycle, some still do exist which are used for the sale of 'hot dogs', etc. They are tricycles which are constructed or adapted for the carriage of goods and they require, if fixed wheel, a system operating on all front wheels. (There may be one or two depending upon the construction of the tricycle.) If it is free wheel, it must have braking systems operating on both the front and rear wheels and the front system must act on all of the wheels (there may be one or two), but that fitted to the rear need only act on one wheel (whether one or two are fitted).

Pedal cycles manufactured on or after 1 August 1984 must be equipped with at least one braking system. If they have a saddle, the height of which is 635 mm (the part of the seat furthest from the ground) or more, or have four or more wheels they must in the case of fixed-wheel cycles have a braking system operating on the front wheel(s) and in the case of a free-wheel cycle, two independent systems, one operating on the front wheel(s) and the other on the rear wheel(s).

These provisions must apply to at least two wheels where there is more than one wheel, although perhaps this did not need to be said as the likelihood of finding a cycle with three wheels at either the front or the rear is at present remote. In general terms, as most cycles with which police officers deal are bicycles, those manufactured on or after 1 August 1984 are treated in the same way as those manufactured before that date, with the substitution of saddle height for wheel diameter as the criterion.

Offences are committed by those who ride, or cause or permit to be ridden on a road, a pedal cycle which does not comply with the regulations concerning the fitting of brakes on pedal cycles.

The regulations introduce legislation governing pedal cycles to which the Electrically Assisted Pedal Cycle Regulations 1983 apply. An electrically assisted pedal cycle is one which has pedals by which the cycle may be propelled and a kerbside weight not exceeding 40 kg and a continuously rated electrical output not exceeding 0.2 kW. All of these cycles must be such that the electric motor will not operate when the cycle is travelling at more than 15 mph. Tandems and tricycles may weigh 60 kg and their rated output may be 0.25 kW.

No person shall ride or cause or permit to be ridden on a road a pedal cycle to which the Electrically Assisted Pedal Cycle Regulations 1983 apply unless it is fitted with braking systems which are so designed and constructed that, in the case of a bicycle, they comply with clause 6 of the British Standard and in the case of a tricycle they comply with standards no less than those set out for a bicycle in that standard. These provisions are also included in the Pedal Cycles (Construction and Use) Regulations 1983 and, therefore, follow the pattern of the Road Vehicle (Construction and Use) Regulations in being directed towards manufacturers in matters regarding safety. It can be safely assumed that the braking requirements for electrically assisted pedal cycles will have been met by the manufacturers. It is only in instances of 'amateur conversions' that police officers may have to refer to the British Standard. Copies (which will be required for production in court in any case) can be obtained from the British Standards Institution at 195 Pentonville Road, London N1 9ND.

These cycles are also required to carry a securely fixed plate showing the name of the manufacturer, the voltage of the battery and the rated output. The battery must not leak and there must be a device, biased to the off position, which allows power from the battery only when it is operated. An offence is committed by anyone who rides, causes or permits the riding on a road of such a cycle if the plate is not fixed, or if the battery leaks or if there is not such a device.

The most likely offence is one of failure to maintain a braking system and this offence can be committed by a person who rides, causes or permits such an electrically assisted cycle to be ridden on a road when the braking systems are not in efficient working order.

Maintenance of brakes

All braking systems required by the Pedal Cycle (Construction and Use) Regulations must be efficient and kept in proper working order, and it is an offence if they are not. Any system fitted to a cycle which operates directly on the tyre of any wheel is not permitted.

Exemptions

Persons who are resident outside Great Britain, who are staying temporarily, may use cycles which do not comply with these regulations. However, certain safety standards are set down by the Geneva Convention on Road Traffic. There is also an exemption in respect of cycles which are so constructed that the pedals act directly upon any wheel or the axle of such wheel. Examples are the penny farthing bicycle and the small tricycles with solid wheels to which pedals are attached, used by small children.

Police powers

Any police officer in uniform may test and inspect the brakes of any cycle being used on a road at any time. Inspections may also be carried out on premises within 48 hours of an accident, provided that the owner of the premises consents.

Vehicles – dangerous position

A person in charge of a vehicle commits an offence if he causes or permits the vehicle or its trailer to remain at rest on a road in such a position, or in such a condition, or in such circumstances as to be likely to cause danger to other persons using the road. A person is in charge of a vehicle from the moment he takes it out on to the road until he puts it away again or hands it over to some person, thus surrendering his charge of it. This offence is committed in relation to vehicles (not necessarily motor vehicles). The common element is danger but the section describes three ways in which that danger might be caused. It may be the way it is parked, it may be its condition [although other offences contrary to the Road Vehicles (Construction and Use) Regulations might also be considered in such circumstances], or the total circumstances surrounding the presence of the vehicle and its condition may be taken cumulatively to cause that danger.

A traffic warden may require a person whom he has reasonable cause to believe to have committed such an offence to produce his driving licence.

Causing danger to road users

By section 22A of the 1988 Act, a person is guilty of an offence if he intentionally and without lawful authority or reasonable excuse:

(a) causes anything to be on or over a road; or
(b) interferes with a motor vehicle, trailer or cycle; or
(c) interferes (directly or indirectly) with traffic equipment,

in such circumstances that it would be obvious to a reasonable person that to do so would be dangerous.

The term 'danger' for the purposes of this offence relates to danger either of injury to any person while on or near a road or of serious damage to property on or near a road. In determining what would be obvious to a reasonable person in a particular case, regard shall be had not only to the circumstances of which he could be expected to be aware but also to circumstances shown to have been within the knowledge of the accused.

Where a person hangs out washing in a back street, that person certainly causes articles to be over a road. However, it could be argued that those actions were not 'dangerous' as opposed to being a nuisance. Washing can easily be seen and such danger is unlikely. Hooligans who intentionally throw objects on to a motorway obviously cause things to be on a road in such circumstances that it would be obvious to a reasonable person that to do so would be dangerous. He who deflates a tyre to a low pressure, or who interferes with the brakes or steering of a vehicle, clearly interferes with those parts for the purposes of (b) above in such circumstances that it would be obvious to a reasonable person that to do so would be dangerous.

'Traffic equipment' for the purposes of the section means anything placed on or near a road by a highway authority or some other person, or any fence, barrier or light so placed to protect street works or undertakings, or items placed by a constable or person acting on the instructions (whether general or specific) of a chief officer of police.

Things so placed shall be deemed to have been lawfully placed unless the contrary is proved. Thus, official road signs, those indicating temporary works or obstructions, road accidents or diversions are covered by the section. Interference with traffic equipment will almost invariably create an obvious danger but this may not always be so. A person may remove a light from road workings without causing such danger. If the lights were closely placed, it is unlikely that a court will find that the necessary element of danger was present. However, if a group of persons are together and each removes a light, their joint enterprise will be such that such danger could be caused. A person who removes a 'Stop' sign undoubtedly commits an offence against this section. He who removes a sign which merely indicates the direction of a town may have caused a nuisance, but he is unlikely to have caused obvious danger.

Removal of vehicles

The Removal and Disposal of Vehicles Regulations 1986, reg. 3, empowers a constable to move or require a vehicle to be removed by the owner, driver or other person in control or charge of any vehicle which:

(a) has broken down, or been permitted to remain at rest, on a road in such a position, condition or circumstances as to cause obstruction to other persons using the road, or as to be likely to cause danger to such other persons; or
(b) has been permitted to remain at rest or has broken down and remained at rest on a road in contravention of a prohibition or restriction in or under any enactment mentioned in Schedule 1 to the Regulations.

The statutory prohibitions or restrictions included in Schedule 1, referred to in (b), are concerned with parking in 'no waiting' areas, in the controlled areas of pedestrian crossings or in contravention of traffic signs, including police 'no waiting' signs. Part of the constable's requirement may be to remove the vehicle to some place which is not on a road.

It is an offence to fail to remove the vehicle as soon as practicable on being required to do so by a constable. Although the powers of removal are set out in the Removal and Disposal of Vehicles Regulations 1986, the offence is contrary to s 91 of the Road Traffic Offenders Act 1988.

Vehicles which have been left on a road in any of these circumstances are either a danger to other road users or likely to cause serious inconvenience, and the provisions allow a constable to ensure that vehicles are moved in addition to dealing with the driver for particular offences. A constable may remove or arrange for the removal of a vehicle which is on a road in the circumstances described above. He may also do so if the vehicle, having broken down on a road or on any land in the open air, appears to have been abandoned without lawful authority, or if the vehicle has been permitted to remain at rest on a road or on any land in the open air in such a position or circumstances as to appear to the constable to have been abandoned without lawful authority. The Court of Appeal has said that reg. 4 is not concerned with whether or not a vehicle has been abandoned, but whether it has been left in such a position as to appear to a constable to have been abandoned. If a complaint is to be made concerning such removal, it must be shown that in the particular circumstances the vehicle could not have appeared to the constable to have been abandoned. The burden of proof rests with the complainant.

The power to remove vehicles from land occupied by any person is subject to giving notice as prescribed by s 99 of the Road Traffic Regulation Act 1984 and reg. 8 of the Removal and Disposal of Vehicles Regulations 1986.

Traffic wardens, community support officers or persons accredited under a community safety accreditation scheme may remove a vehicle parked or broken down in a road in circumstances where it is causing an obstruction, it is likely to cause danger to road users or an offence is being committed under certain enactments by or under which prohibitions or restrictions are imposed upon the waiting of vehicles on roads.

It is now common to see vehicles which have apparently been abandoned at the side of motorways, many of them having been stripped of all identifying marks. In these circumstances, it is often impossible to trace the owner in order to require its removal and it was obviously not the intention of the legislators to have police officers acting as refuse collectors. Local authorities are, therefore, also empowered by these regulations to remove vehicles apparently abandoned on roads and on land in the open air, but in addition, the Refuse Disposal (Amenity) Act 1978 places upon them the duty to provide places where such vehicles may be deposited. This Act also gives local authorities the power to remove vehicles which appear to have been abandoned on open land or land which forms part of a highway, to dispose of them and to recover the expenses involved in doing so.

Section 2 of the Refuse Disposal (Amenity) Act 1978 makes it an offence for any person, without lawful authority, to abandon a motor vehicle or part of a vehicle removed during the course of dismantling it in these places or to abandon anything other than a motor vehicle. If motor vehicles or other things are left in circumstances or for such a period of time that they reasonably appear to have been abandoned, the burden of proof is upon the defendant to prove that there was no abandonment.

The provisions of the Refuse Disposal (Amenity) Act 1978 allow local authorities to remove such waste material and additionally enable the prosecution of those responsible. Police officers may institute proceedings under this Act.

Heavy commercial vehicles – parking on footways, etc.

An offence is committed by a person who parks a heavy commercial vehicle wholly or partly on the verge of a road or any land situated between two carriageways which is not a footway, or on any footways. For the purposes of s 19 of the Road Traffic Act 1988, which creates this offence, a heavy commercial vehicle is a goods vehicle with an operating weight exceeding 7.5 tonnes. The 'operating weight' is the maximum laden weight of the vehicle and all its trailers. Parking is banned on verges (grass strips), central reservations and footpaths because of the damage which may be caused.

The exceptions to this rule are logical. A police officer may give permission for such parking to take place. He may wish, for example, to authorise such parking to remove an obstruction caused by a broken down or damaged vehicle. Such vehicles may also park in such places in order to save life or extinguish fire. This provision allows usage by emergency vehicles. Finally, these vehicles may park on a verge or a footway for the purpose of loading or unloading, if that loading or unloading could not have been performed if the vehicle had not been so parked, provided that the vehicle is not left unattended at any time while so parked. This final exemption is not intended to author-ise such parking generally; the nature of the loading, etc., must be such that it could not be effectively carried out in any other way.

The Road Traffic Act 1991, ss 76 and 77 and Schedule 3, make provisions for 'spe-cial parking areas'. London and provincial authorities can apply to the Secretary of State for an order designating an area as a permitted parking area and a special park-ing area. Where such an order is in force it has the effect of making nominated park-ing offences within that area offences which lead to a parking penalty, recoverable by civil process. This offence becomes so punishable within a special parking area and the criminal offence ceases to apply.

Notice of intended prosecution

Section 1 of the Road Traffic Offenders Act 1988 requires that, for certain offences, the offender must have been:

(a) warned at the time of the possibility of prosecution for the offence; or
(b) served with a summons within 14 days of its commission; or
(c) a notice of intended prosecution specifying the nature of the alleged offence and the time and place where it is alleged to have been committed was served within 14 days on him or the person, if any, registered as the keeper of the vehicle at the time of the commission of the offence.

If the offence is one involving the use of a pedal cycle (dangerous or careless cycling), notice must be sent to the rider of the cycle. The requirements of s 1 are deemed to have been complied with unless and until the contrary is proved. The words 'at the time of the offence' mean at the time of the incident and not *the moment of the offence*.

The offences in respect of which such warning must be given are:

(a) *Road Traffic Act 1988*
  Section 2   Dangerous driving
  Section 3   Careless and inconsiderate driving
  Section 22   Leaving a vehicle in a dangerous position
  Section 28   Dangerous cycling
  Section 29   Careless and inconsiderate cycling
  Section 35   Failing to conform with the indication given by a constable engaged in the regulation of traffic
  Section 36   Failing to comply with the indication given by a traffic sign
(b) *Road Traffic Regulation Act 1984*
  Section 16   Exceeding temporary speed restrictions imposed under s 14
  Section 17(4)   Exceeding speed restriction on special road
  Section 88(7)   Exceeding temporary speed limit imposed by order
  Section 89(1)   Speeding offences generally.

A notice sent by post must be dispatched so that in the normal time of postal delivery it will arrive within 14 days. If it is so posted, but is held up in the post and is delivered outside the 14-day period, it will be deemed to have been served in the 14-day period; consequently the driver can still be convicted. It has been held that service of a notice on the wife of a defendant by a constable handing the notice to her was a valid service, since she was a person authorised to accept and deal with her husband's mail. It would be different if the notice was left with a hall porter, as he would not be so authorised. However, it is better to restrict service by hand to the offender. Where a notice is sent by post, it is advisable to send it by registered post or recorded delivery service since in such a case it is deemed to have been served if the notice was addressed to him at his last known address, notwithstanding that the notice is returned as undelivered or is for some other reason not received by him.

It is assumed that the provisions of this section of the Act have been complied with unless the contrary is proved.

To prevent offenders escaping the consequences of their acts, if the name and address of the driver or registered keeper could not with reasonable diligence have been discovered in time for service, or if the accused by his own conduct contributed to the failure, failure to serve a notice or a summons shall not be a bar to conviction.

Points of procedure

(a) A general warning at the time, which does not indicate the offence clearly, is insufficient. A constable must say, 'You will be reported for consideration of the question of prosecuting you for', followed by clear words describing the offence.

(b) A warning given 35 minutes after the offence was committed, but as soon as possible after the arrival of police officers on the scene, has been held to be sufficient. A warning given after a man had been in custody for 3 hours for driving while unfit through drink was also held to be satisfactory as there was an unbroken chain of circumstances taking place which was connected with the incident.

(c) Common sense should be used in determining whether or not there is sufficient information in the notice. The object is 'to take back the recollection of the motorist to the facts upon which reliance is to be placed'.

(d) A notice is deemed to have been served within 14 days if it is posted within that period.

(e) In considering the 14 days within which the notice must be served, the date of the commission of the offence is excluded.

(f) Some police forces send a written notice of intended prosecution in all cases although the driver may have been warned at the time. This provides an added safeguard against an allegation by a driver that he has not been warned.

(g) It is not necessary to comply with the provisions in relation to notices of intended prosecution if, at the time of the offence or immediately thereafter, an accident occurs owing to the presence on a road of the vehicle in respect of which the offence was committed. If any of the actions specified above results at the time, or immediately afterwards, in an accident, there is no need to comply with the provisions of this section. However, before this can apply, the offender must have been aware that the accident had occurred. In addition, where a driver who is seriously injured in an accident has no recollection of the accident occurring, there is no bar to prosecution because no notice has been given. The Divisional Court has ruled that Parliament cannot have intended oral warnings to be given to unconscious survivors of serious road accidents or the giving of written notices to survivors so badly injured as to be unable to read them or understand their effect.

(h) The provisions of this section need not be complied with in relation to an offence in respect of which a full or provisional fixed penalty notice has been given or fixed under the provisions of the Road Traffic Offenders Act 1988.

Road traffic – associated offences

Introduction

Whilst most of the offences which we have so far considered have been concerned with roads and places to which the public have access, there are other offences involving the use of vehicles which may be committed elsewhere. It is also important to consider how the identity of a driver may be discovered in circumstances in which that vehicle was not stopped at the time and the identity of the driver established.

Driving elsewhere than on a road

On common land, etc.

The Road Traffic Act 1988, s 34(1), creates an offence of, without lawful authority, driving a motor vehicle:

(a) on to or upon any common land, moorland or land of any other description, not being land forming part of a road, or
(b) on any road being a footpath or bridleway.

Subsection (2) provides that it is not an offence under the section to drive a motor vehicle on any land within 15 yards of a road, being a road on which a motor vehicle may lawfully be driven, for the purpose of parking the vehicle on the land.

The provisions of the section do not, therefore, prevent the parking of vehicles on the land immediately abutting upon a road, but are useful in preventing 'off-road' events which are unauthorised. Whilst motor rallies may be specifically authorised to use areas of such land, or parts of footpaths or bridleways which cross private land, the unauthorised use of trials motor cycles would amount to an offence. A 'footpath' means a way over which the public have a right of way on foot only, and a 'bridleway' means a way over which the public have a right of way on foot and a right of way on horseback or leading a horse, with or without a right to drive animals of any description along the way.

Subject to any orders made by a local authority and to any by-laws, the public have a right to ride a pedal cycle on a bridleway, but cyclist must give way to pedestrians and persons on horseback.

Subsection (3) provides that a person shall not be convicted of an offence against s 34 if he proves to the satisfaction of the court that the vehicle was driven in contravention of the section for the purpose of saving life or extinguishing fire or meeting any other like emergency.

The Police Reform Act 2002, ss 59 and 60, provide powers for the seizure of vehicles in prescribed circumstances; see page 718.

On a footpath

A person who wilfully drives a carriage on a footpath offends against the Highways Act 1835, s 72. The Road Traffic Act 1988, s 191, states that a motor vehicle or a trailer is a 'carriage' for the purposes of any Act of Parliament or any rule, regulation or by-law made under any such Act. Bicycles and tricycles and other similar machines are declared to be 'carriages' by the Local Government Act 1988, s 85.

Tampering with motor vehicles

The Road Traffic Act 1988, s 25, is concerned with persons who, while a motor vehicle is on a road or on a parking place provided by a local authority:

(a) get on to the vehicle; or
(b) tamper with the brake or other part of its mechanism,

without lawful authority or reasonable cause.

The vehicle must be on a road and/or on a 'parking place provided by a local authority'. For whom or for what purpose the parking place is provided is irrelevant. The word 'tamper' is not defined by the 1988 Act and should be given its ordinary meaning of improper interference. The words 'other part of its mechanism' are wide enough to refer to any mechanical part of the vehicle.

Information as to identity of driver

The requirement to give information

The Road Traffic Act 1988, s 172(2), provides that where the driver of a vehicle is alleged to be guilty of an offence to which the section applies:

(a) the person keeping the vehicle shall give such information as to the identity of the driver as he may be required to give by or on behalf of a chief officer of police; and
(b) any other person shall if required as stated above give any information which is in his power to give and may lead to the identification of the driver.

The section applies to:

(a) all offences against the provisions of the Road Traffic Act 1988 except an offence under Part V (driving instruction), or s 13 (promoting motoring events on highway), s 16 (wearing of protective headgear), s 51(2) (certain test conditions – goods vehicles), s 61(4) (certain type approval requirements), s 67(9) (obstructing a vehicle examiner), s 68(4) (failing to proceed to place of vehicle inspection), s 96 (driving with uncorrected defective eyesight), or s 120 (offence against regulations dealing with licensing of drivers of large goods vehicles and passenger-carrying vehicles);
(b) an offence under s 25 (information as to date of birth and sex after conviction), 26 (interim disqualification) or 27 (production of a licence on conviction) of the Road Traffic Offenders Act 1988;
(c) any offence relating to any other enactment relating to the use of vehicles on roads, except an offence under para. 8 of Schedule 1 to the Road Traffic (Driver Licensing and Information Systems) Act 1989 (relating to drivers' licences of large goods and passenger-carrying vehicles); and
(d) manslaughter by the driver of a motor vehicle.

A requirement may be made by way of written notice and served by post. Where it is so made:

(a) it shall have effect as a requirement to give the information within the period of 28 days beginning on the day on which the notice is served; and
(b) the person on whom the notice is served shall not be guilty of an offence under the section if he shows either that he gave the information as soon as reasonably

practicable after the end of that period or that it had not been reasonably practicable for him to give it.

The offence

A person who fails to comply with such a requirement commits an offence. However, he shall not be guilty of the offence if he shows that he did not know and could not with reasonable diligence have ascertained who the driver of the vehicle was.

Procedural points

There is no requirement that the police specify the nature of the offence which it is alleged has been committed. A notice signed by an inspector with the authority of his superintendent, that superintendent having implied delegated authority from the Commissioner of Police to delegate further to his inspector, has been held to be a good and valid notice. In addition, it has been held that where a notice has been produced from an official source and has every appearance of authenticity, justices may draw an inference as to the validity of the notice. However, at the other end of the scale, it cannot be said that a police officer acting in the course of his duties is necessarily acting on behalf of his chief officer of police.

The expression 'any other person' as used in the section includes the driver himself.

A Divisional Court held that a driver was guilty of an offence under s 172 where he had provided the required information by telephone to an employee in the relevant fixed-penalty office of the Constabulary concerned but outside the 28-day period allowed by the notice for a reply to be made. The Court said that the Road Traffic Act 1988, s 172(7), provides for a written notice to be sent and provides that where this is done it shall have effect as a requirement to give the information within a period of 28 days beginning with the date upon which the notice is served.

In all cases involving extended enquiries in order to trace a driver, it is important to ensure that any complainant is informed of what is being done.

The Privy Council has concluded that the use of an admission obtained in pursuance of s 172(2)(a) is not incompatible with the defendant's human rights under Article 6(1) of the Convention for the Protection of Human Rights and Fundamental Freedoms. The subsection merely provides for the putting of one simple question. The answer to that question cannot, by itself, incriminate the suspect. It does not permit prolonged questioning of a nature similar to that to which exception had been taken by the European Court. The Divisional Court, having been asked to consider the position of 'any person' under s 172(2)(b), concluded that the position was no different. Conclusive evidence should be admitted unless there is good reason for not doing so. The fact that, in this case, evidence could have been given by the driver's employer was not such a reason. It could not be unfair to admit the defendant's own answer to a requirement made under the section. Parliament had sought to facilitate the giving of evidence as to the identity of drivers by means of written statements.

Lights on vehicles

Introduction

The Act of Parliament which controls the lighting of vehicles used on roads during the hours of darkness is the Road Traffic Act 1988. It authorises the Secretary of State for Transport to make regulations. The Road Vehicles Lighting Regulations 1989 currently set out the details of road vehicle lighting requirements. There is a general requirement that all vehicles must display lights of various types while being driven or used on a road between sunset and sunrise (or, on occasions, during the hours of darkness). There are additional requirements when visibility is seriously reduced during times other than 'hours of darkness'. It will be appreciated that certain lights must be used at all times whether it is light or dark. Direction indicators are used at all times and the purpose of stop lights is not to make the vehicle visible when it is dark, it is to warn following drivers that the brakes are being applied. The regulations therefore seek to ensure the provision of satisfactory lighting so that vehicles may be seen at night, so that drivers can see the road ahead at night, so that manoeuvres of vehicles can be anticipated and to ensure the safety of other road users generally.

Roads

The term 'road' is defined as meaning any length of highway or of any other road to which the public has access, and includes bridges over which a road passes. The Act and regulations are concerned with vehicles which are 'on a road'. It has been established that a motor vehicle is on a road if it is partly on a road and partly on private land and that the forecourt of a hotel can be deemed to be part of a highway if there is no obstruction separating it from the road and it is frequently used by the public to pass from one street to another. However, other cases involving such private property have resulted in different rulings, but always on the grounds that where there was no separation from the highway, there was no evidence of public use.

Normally, a highway is described as the area of right of way as defined by its fences. Grass verges may be a part of the highway, but this is dependent upon who erected the fences. If they were erected by the highway authority, it raises a presumption that the fences define the extent of the highway itself. Whether a road is public or private is dependent upon the evidence available of public use, rather than ownership. A private road leading to a farmhouse which was maintained by the farmer, but had no gate, was held to be a road to which the public had access, evidence being given that it was used by people who had no business at the farm.

Daytime hours

This means the time between half an hour before sunrise and half an hour after sunset.

Hours of darkness

This means the time between half an hour after sunset and half an hour before sunrise. The term 'sunset' means sunset according to local, not Greenwich, time and as lighting-up times vary from place to place within Great Britain, lighting-up times are frequently published in force orders. Most local newspapers publish local lighting-up times.

Obligatory lights and reflectors

The term 'obligatory' is defined by the regulations. It means, in relation to a lamp, reflector, rear marking or device, a lamp, reflector, rear marking or device with which a vehicle, its load or equipment is required by the regulations to be fitted. The 1989 Regulations, and particularly the schedules to these regulations, specify precisely the lights, etc., the performance expected from those lights, etc., and the permitted uses of such lights, etc.

Optional lamps and reflectors

The regulations state that 'optional', in relation to a lamp, reflector, rear marking or device, means a lamp, reflector, rear marking or device with which a vehicle, its load or equipment is not required by the regulations to be fitted.

There are a number of lights which are permitted to be fitted by the regulations as 'optional extras', but if they are fitted, the nature of the lamps, etc., the positions in which they may be fitted, their performance and their use are nevertheless controlled by the regulations.

The situation generally is that certain lamps, etc., must be fitted to vehicles and certain additional lamps, etc., may be fitted. If additional optional lamps are fitted, they must comply with the provisions of the 1989 Regulations. In this way, the law ensures that a multiplicity of lamps, reflectors, etc., are not fitted to vehicles in such a way that confusion and danger may be caused to other road users.

Types of lamps and reflectors which are obligatory on most motor vehicles

Headlamps

The regulations define two types of headlamps, main beam and dipped headlamps. Although separately defined, most vehicles carry headlamps. A 'main beam' means a beam of light emitted by a lamp which illuminates the road over a long distance ahead of the vehicle. A 'dipped beam' means a beam of light emitted by a lamp which illuminates the road ahead of the vehicle without causing undue dazzle or discomfort to oncoming drivers or other road users.

In most circumstances, two dipped beam headlamps are required by motor vehicles with three or more wheels. The maximum permitted distance from the side of the vehicle is usually 400 mm (except vehicles first used before 1 January 1972, agricultural, engineering and industrial tractors). There is no minimum distance by which the two lamps need to be separated. Solo motor bicycles or combinations and three wheelers first used before 1 January 1972, and certain others, require only one headlamp on the centre line of the motor vehicle itself. Buses first used before 1 October 1969 need only have one dipped beam headlamp.

Dipped beam headlamps should generally be not more than 1200 mm and not less than 500 mm from the ground. There are no minimum requirements for vehicles first used before 1 January 1956 and no maximum for vehicles first used before 1 January 1952 or, regardless of date, for agricultural, emergency or home forces vehicles. They must be of the same colour and intensity and switch off and on together.

The light which must be emitted by a dipped beam headlamp must be either white or yellow. The lamp must be such that the direction of the beam of light can be adjusted while the vehicle is stationary. Where two dipped beam lamps are required to be fitted, they must form a matched pair and be capable of being switched on and off simultaneously and not otherwise.

The provisions concerning main beam headlamps are the same, with the exception that buses first used before 1 October 1969 are required to have two main beam head-lamps. They must have two headlamps but only one of them needs to be capable of dipping. Main beam headlamps must be such that they can be deflected at the will of the driver to become a dipped beam, or so that they can be extinguished by a device which at the same time switches on dipped beam, or causes another lamp to emit a dipped beam. 'Long-range' driving lamps are invariably fitted by manufacturers so that they are extinguished by the dip switch operating the normal headlamps.

The 1989 Regulations require that vehicles first used on or after 1 April 1987 shall be fitted with 'dim-dip' lighting devices. The devices are capable of causing a dipped-beam headlamp to operate at reduced intensity. Alternatively, vehicles may be equipped with a 'running lamp', which is a lamp used to make the presence of a moving vehicle readily visible from the front. Vehicles having a maximum speed of 40 mph, home forces vehicles and those complying with Community Directives are exempt.

Headlamps may not be used so as to cause undue dazzle or discomfort to other persons using the road and shall not be lit when a vehicle is parked.

Front and rear position lamps

A 'front position lamp' is one which is used to indicate the presence and width of a vehicle when viewed from the front. A 'rear position lamp' indicates its presence and width from the rear.

Vehicles with three or more wheels (other than invalid carriages and pedal tricycles) require two front and two rear position lamps. Front position lamps shall be white, unless they are incorporated in a yellow headlamp, in which case they may be yellow. All rear position lamps must be red.

Front position lamps on vehicles first used before 1 April 1986 must not be more than 510 mm from the side of the vehicle. Motor vehicles first used on or after that date must have front position lamps not more than 400 mm from the side. Pedal cycles, solo motor bicycles and invalid carriages require only one front position lamp which must be fitted on the centre line or offside of the vehicle. Motor cycle combinations with a headlamp on the motor bicycle require a front position lamp on the centre line of the sidecar or on the side of the sidecar furthest from the motor bicycle. Solo motor bicycles fitted with a headlamp need not be fitted with a front position lamp.

Certain vehicles do not require two rear position lamps. Those which require only one include buses first used before 1 April 1955, solo motor cycles, pedal cycles with less than four wheels, trailers drawn by pedal cycles, trailers (the overall width of which does not exceed 800 mm) drawn by solo or motor cycle combinations, invalid carriages having a maximum speed not exceeding 4 mph and vehicles propelled by hand. (There is a general exemption for some hand-propelled vehicles not exceeding 800 mm in width.)

Rear position lamps, where two are required to be fitted on vehicles first used before 1 April 1986, shall not be more than 800 mm from the side of the vehicle. After that date, the distance is reduced to 400 mm. In cases in which only one rear position lamp is required it must be fitted on the centre line of the vehicle or on its offside. Because of the tendency for enthusiasts to fit extra rear position lamps, it is helpful to know that the maximum permitted height of such lights on motor vehicles first used before 1 April 1986 other than buses, or trailers manufactured before 1 October 1985 and other specialist exemptions, is 2100 mm. Vehicles first used after 1 April 1986 have a permitted maximum of 1500 mm unless the structure of the vehicle makes this impracticable, when the height of 2100 mm applies.

The provisions concerning rear position lamps also apply to trailers.

Rear registration lamps

Every motor vehicle which is required to be fitted with a rear registration plate must have lighting that is capable of adequately illuminating the rear registration plate. The international distinguishing sign of the United Kingdom may be included within a rear registration plate notwithstanding that it comprises retro-reflective material which is not red.

Stop lamps

All motor vehicles having three or more wheels and trailers drawn by motor vehicles must, unless stated otherwise in the regulations, be fitted with two stop lamps. Solo motor bicycles, combinations, invalid carriages and trailers drawn by motor cycles and motor vehicles or trailers first used before 1 January 1971 need only be fitted with one stop lamp. Motor cycles of less than 50 cc, if first used before 1 April 1986, are exempt.

If two are fitted they should be one each side of the longitudinal axis of the vehicle. If there is only one it should be on the centre line or offside of the vehicle. Stop lights must be separated by a distance of at least 400 mm and they should not be more than 1500 mm from the ground or, if the structure of the vehicle makes this impracticable, 2100 mm. The minimum height is 350 mm. There are no maximum or minimum height specifications for vehicles first used before 1 January 1971. Those first used before 1 January 1936 do not require stop lamps, nor do vehicles with a maximum speed of 25 mph or less, or agricultural vehicles or works trucks first used before 1 April 1986.

Stop lamps must be operated by the application of a service braking system. If there are two, they must form a pair. It is common practice for enthusiasts to fit additional stop lamps and there is no restriction upon the number of such lights which may be fitted. If additional lights are fitted they must comply with all of the provisions of Schedule 12 to the regulations, except the requirements as to number, position and angles of visibility. Motor vehicles, other than motor bicycles, first used on or after 1 April 1991 are subject to control in relation to the intensity of the light projected through rear windows.

Direction indicators

Motor vehicles first used before 1 April 1936 and trailers manufactured before that date may have any arrangement of indicators which makes the intentions of the driver clear to other road users but they are not required to have any indicators at all. Motor vehicles first used on or after that date and before 1 April 1986 (or trailers manufactured between 1 January 1936 and 1 October 1985) must be provided with any arrangement of indicators so as to satisfy the requirements for angles of visibility.

Motor vehicles first used on or after 1 April 1986 and trailers manufactured on or after 1 October 1985, if having more than three wheels, must have a front and rear indicator and a side repeater indicator on each side of the vehicle. They must also have at least one side repeater indicator on each side. Trailers may have one or two rear indicators on each side. Motor bicycles and combinations, first used on or after 1 April 1986, must have one single front and one single rear indicator on each side of the vehicle.

All indicators shall be operated by one switch. There must be a tell-tale to show that the indicators are in operation. Flashing indicators must flash at a constant rate of not less than 60 and not more than 120 times per minute.

Rear retro reflectors

It is generally required that all vehicles and trailers will be equipped with two retro reflectors. Some vehicles only require one rear retro reflector: they are solo motor bicycles, pedal cycles with less than four wheels (with or without a sidecar), trailers drawn by pedal cycles generally, trailers not exceeding 800 mm drawn by solo motor cycles or combinations, invalid carriages having a maximum speed not exceeding 4 mph and hand-propelled vehicles. There are some vehicles which are restricted in respect of speed (maximum of 25 mph) which require four reflectors.

Reflectors must be fitted at or near the rear of the vehicle. Motor vehicles first used before 1 April 1986 and trailers manufactured before 1 October 1985 must have their obligatory reflectors fitted no more than 610 mm from the side. After these dates the distance is reduced to 400 mm. Where only one reflector is fitted it must be on the centre line or offside of the vehicle. Before the 1 April 1986 deadline, the maximum permitted height of reflectors is 1525 mm for motor vehicles. After that date the height is reduced to 900 mm unless the structure of the vehicle makes it impracticable (when it may be 1200 mm). All rear reflectors must be red.

Rear fog lamps

All motor vehicles manufactured on or after 1 October 1979 and first used on or after 1 April 1980, having three or more wheels, and all trailers drawn by motor vehicles must (unless specifically dealt with in some other way) have at least one rear fog lamp fitted, at or near the rear, on the centre line or offside of the vehicle. If there are two lamps fitted there is no requirement concerning the distance at which the lamps are placed from the sides of the vehicle. The maximum height from the ground is 1000 mm (except agricultural, engineering plant and motor tractors) and the minimum height is 250 mm. Rear fog lamps must be separated from the stop lamps of the vehicle by a minimum distance of 100 mm. No more than two lamps may be fitted.

Rear fog lamps must show a red light. They must not be fitted so that they are illuminated by the braking of the vehicle. There must be a tell-tale fitted to show that the light(s) are on. If two lamps are fitted to a motor vehicle first used on or after 1 April 1986, or a trailer manufactured on or after 1 October 1985, they must be a matched pair.

Vehicles first used before 1 April 1980 (or manufactured before 1 October 1979) are not required to have rear fog lamps and there are other, limited exceptions. If they do have them, there are no restrictions in respect of number, but they must be separated from stop lamps by a distance of at least 1000 mm and must not be capable of illumination by the braking system.

Motor vehicles either used or manufactured on or after these dates are not permitted to have more than two rear fog lamps and both must comply with all of the conditions set out above.

Rear fog lamps must not be used so as to cause undue dazzle or discomfort to other following drivers. They must not be used when a vehicle, other than an emergency vehicle, is parked. Their use generally is restricted to conditions of seriously reduced visibility.

Trailers, the overall width of which does not exceed 1300 mm, do not require rear fog lamps.

Hazard warning signals

A hazard warning signal device is one which is capable of causing all the direction indicators with which a vehicle, or a combination of vehicles, is fitted to operate simultaneously.

The device must be operated by one switch which causes all of the direction indicators with which the vehicle (or combination of vehicles) is equipped to flash in-phase. There must be a tell-tale in the vehicle and the device must be capable of operation without the ignition being switched on.

The fitting of hazard warning signal devices is obligatory on vehicles having three or more wheels and first used on or after 1 April 1986, with the exception of vehicles which are not required to be fitted with indicators.

Hazard warning signals may only be used on a motor vehicle while it is stationary to warn road users of a temporary obstruction or of the presence of a school bus which is loading or unloading, or on a motorway or unrestricted dual carriageway, to warn of a temporary obstruction ahead, or in the case of a bus to summon assistance. A bus which is fitted with a sign of yellow reflective material (including black figures of school children) may use hazard warning lights when it is stationary and children are entering or leaving the vehicle, or are about to enter or leave, or have just left the vehicle.

Types of lamp which are commonly found as 'optional lamps' on motor vehicles

Reversing lamps

A vehicle may not be fitted with more than two reversing lamps. They are fitted to vehicles to indicate when the vehicle is reversing and to illuminate the road to the rear. The light shown must be white.

The reversing lamps must be wired so that the only way in which the light can be switched on is by selecting reverse gear, or by using a switch which shows a tell-tale light when the lamps are in use. Such lamps may not be used for any purpose other than reversing the vehicle.

Front fog lamps

The term 'fog lamp' clearly indicates the intended use of these optional lamps. They are lamps used to improve the illumination of the road in front of a motor vehicle in conditions of seriously reduced visibility and are fitted in a low position to allow light to seek out the road in poor visibility conditions when a headlamp light tends to become scattered by fog or falling snow. They must be white or yellow lights. Where they are used in conditions of seriously reduced visibility in place of the obligatory headlamps they must not be more than 400 mm from the side of the vehicle. This is logical; they are being used as headlights and should give a clear indication of the approximate width of the vehicle. They may not be placed more than 1200 mm from the ground; there is no minimum height requirement. (The maximum height permits the usual exceptions, as with headlamps.)

If the front fog lamps are used in place of the obligatory headlamps they must be a matched pair. These lights may only be used when the vehicle is on a road, in conditions of seriously reduced visibility. They must not be lit if this causes undue dazzle or discomfort to other road users and must not be lit when the vehicle is parked. Motor vehicles (other than motor bicycles) first used on or after 1 April 1991 may not have more than two front fog lamps.

Warning beacons

Certain vehicles are permitted to show blue, amber, green or yellow (on limited occasions) rotating lights to indicate to other road users the presence of those vehicles on a road in special circumstances.

A blue and white chequered light is permitted from a domed lamp fitted to a police control vehicle and intended for use at the scene of an emergency; a blue lamp is permitted from a warning beacon, or rear special warning lamp on an emergency vehicle.

Amber lamps are authorised on road clearance, refuse, breakdown vehicles, vehicles when not exceeding 25 mph, those with an overall width exceeding 2.9 m, road service vehicles, special vehicles carrying abnormal loads (and escorts) and vehicles of HM Customs and Excise (fuel testing vehicles). Motor vehicles first used before 1 January 1947 with a maximum speed not exceeding 25 mph must show, or show on any trailer, at least one amber warning beacon when on an unrestricted dual carriageway road (other than a motorway). This does not apply to such vehicles merely crossing such a road.

Green lights are limited to registered medical practitioners, who may only use such lights in an emergency.

Yellow lights (as opposed to amber) are rare. They are used by airport vehicles.

All warning beacons must be mounted so that the centre of the lamp is not less than 1200 mm from the ground. They must flash between 60 and 240 times per minute at constant intervals.

Only authorised vehicles may be fitted with such warning beacons. However, where a vehicle is constructed or adapted as an emergency vehicle and is used as such, there is no requirement that the warning beacon should be removed or covered up when the vehicle is used for some other purpose (but the light may not be used). The regulation dealing with 'fitting' refers to vehicles which are 'used' as emergency vehicles, not to vehicles which are 'being' used.

Trailers – obligatory lights and reflectors

General rule

The general rule is that trailers require the same obligatory lamps as the towing vehicle, with the obvious exception of headlamps. On occasions, trailers do not require front position lamps; if they do not exceed 1600 mm width; pre-October 1985 vehicles if their length, excluding draw bar, does not exceed 2300 mm, or boat trailers. Obviously, there are no exceptions in respect of rear position lamps.

Trailers which are not fitted with lights may lawfully be used on a road during daylight hours.

Side marker lamps

Side marker lamps, that is, lamps fitted to the side of a vehicle or its load and used to render the vehicle more visible to other road users, must be fitted to some trailers (and motor vehicles). Exemption exists in favour of trailers the overall length of which, excluding any drawbar and any fitting for its attachment, does not exceed 6 m, or 9.15 m if manufactured before 1 October 1990. The obligatory requirements are to have two side marker lamps on each side and as many more as are sufficient to ensure that the maximum distance from the front of the vehicle (including any drawbar) to the first lamp is 4 m and the maximum distance from the rear in respect of the rearmost side marker lamp is 1 m. The maximum separation distance of adjacent obligatory side marker lamps on the same side of the vehicle is 3 m or, if this is not practicable, 4 m. (Motor vehicles first used before 1 April 1991 are exempt from these provisions.)

Additional side marker lamps are required to be fitted to a vehicle, or a combination of vehicles the overall length of which (including any load) exceeds 18.3 m, one lamp being no more than 9.15 m from the foremost part of the vehicle or vehicles and one lamp no more than 3.05 m from the rear (including loads in both instances). Other lamps must be placed to ensure that no more than 3.05 m separates lamps. Where the length exceeds 12.2 m but not 18.3 m and the load is supported by any two vehicles, there shall be lamps placed behind the rearmost part of the drawing vehicle, but not more than 1530 mm to the rear of that point. If the supported load extends more than 9.15 m to the rear of the drawing vehicle, the lamp shall not be forward of, or more than 1530 mm to the rear of, the centre of the length of the load. These last provisions do not apply to articulated vehicles. Lamps must be no more than 2300 mm from the ground. There is no minimum height restriction.

End-outline marker lamps

Trailers (and motor vehicles) with an overall width exceeding 2100 mm require end-outline marker lamps. These are lamps fitted near the outer edge of a vehicle in addition to the front and rear position lamps to indicate the presence of a wide vehicle. There must be two visible from the front and two visible from the rear. They must be no more than 400 mm from the side of the vehicle. These provisions apply to trailers manufactured on or after 1 October 1990 (and to motor vehicles first used on or after 1 April 1991). Any number *may* be fitted.

Side retro reflectors

Side retro reflectors are obligatory on certain trailers (and motor vehicles). The provisions do not apply to passenger vehicles, or to goods vehicles whose overall length does not exceed 6 m (if first used on or after 1 April 1986), or whose overall length does not exceed 8 m (if first used before that date). We are therefore considering long goods vehicles. In the case of such vehicles first used before 1 April 1986 and trailers manufactured before 1 October 1985, there must be two side retro reflectors on each side of the vehicle. In the case of those first used or manufactured on or after those dates, there must be two on each side of the vehicle and as many more as are required by para. 2(a) of Schedule 17 to the Regulations. Side retro reflectors must be amber or, within 1 m of the rear of the vehicle, they may be red. They must not be triangular in shape.

Rear markings

The provisions concerning *rear markings* are dealt with here as they are more commonly associated with articulated vehicles and are therefore primarily concerned with trailers. These are 'long vehicle' markings. Such long vehicles which were first used before 1 April 1996 which do not exceed 13 m in length need only carry marker boards with diagonal lines of fluorescent yellow and red. Those which exceed that length must have boards which also display the words 'long vehicle' in black on a yellow background surrounded by a red border or, as an alternative, boards of yellow retro reflective material surrounded by a red fluorescent border. Those used on or after 1 April 1996 which do not exceed 13 m must carry boards of red and yellow diagonal stripes and those which exceed 13 m, boards of yellow retro reflective material surrounded by a red fluorescent border. Trailers forming part of a combination of vehicles are similarly affected; if, in the case of a trailer manufactured before 1 October 1995, the overall length does not exceed 11 m the marking must be of the diagonal line variety, if between 11 and 13 m the marking may be of any approved variety, and if it exceeds 13 m it must be of the 'long vehicle' type, or a board of yellow reflective material surrounded by a red fluorescent border. In the case of a trailer manufactured on or after 1 October 1995 which does not exceed 11 m, it must carry a board of red and yellow diagonal stripes, if it exceeds 11 but not 13 m it may carry boards of such red and yellow stripes or of yellow surrounded by red and if it exceeds 13 m the boards must be of yellow surrounded by red.

General exceptions

Within the requirements set out above, there are a number of vehicles which are exempt, but those exemptions are predictable. They are, for example, works trailers, agricultural trailers, on occasions, boat trailers and incomplete trailers. Itemised provisions are set out in Schedule 1, Table VI concerning exceptions to the general rules and the particular provisions relating to each type of lamp are set out in following schedules.

Overhanging and projecting loads

Regulation 21 prohibits any person from using, or causing or permitting to be used on a road:

(a) any trailer which projects laterally beyond the preceding vehicle in the combination; or

(b) any vehicle or combination of vehicles which carries a load or equipment,

which (in either case) does not comply with the specifications set out in the regulation.

The specifications with which we are concerned are:

(a) a trailer which (or whose load) projects laterally more than 400 mm from the outer-most part of the obligatory front position lamp on that side of the vehicle in front of it must have white lights to the front which are not more than 400 mm from the outermost projection of the trailer (or, as the case may be, of the load);

(b) a vehicle whose load projects laterally more than 400 mm must have lights at the front and rear not more than 400 mm from the outermost projection of the load;

(c) a vehicle whose load projects more than 1 m to the front or to the rear must have a front or rear lamp not more than 1 m from the foremost or rearmost projection of the load (except that that distance is 2 m in the case of an agricultural vehicle or vehicle carrying a fire escape); or

(d) a vehicle carrying a load which obscures any obligatory lamps, reflector or rear markings must show a lamp, etc., in the prescribed position.

These restrictions only apply whilst the vehicle is being used between sunset and sunrise or in conditions of reduced visibility, except that in relation to stop lights and direction indicators in the circumstances set out in (d) the requirement applies at any time.

Pedal cycles – lamps and reflectors

There is no daytime requirement in relation to pedal cycles. They need only fitted with obligatory lamps and reflectors if used during the hours of darkness. They require one front position lamp which shows a white light, one rear position lamp which shows a red light and one rear, red reflex reflector.

Pedal cycles manufactured after September 1985 must be fitted with amber reflectors on the leading and trailing edge of each pedal.

Use of obligatory lamps during the hours of darkness

A person must not use, or cause or permit to be used, on a road, a vehicle which is fit-ted with obligatory dipped beam headlamps unless every such lamp is kept lit:

(a) during the hours of darkness, except on a road which is a restricted road by virtue of a system of street lighting with lamps not more than 200 yards apart which are lit; and

(b) in seriously reduced visibility (i.e. during daylight hours).

It must be remembered that in (b), front fog lamps, as previously discussed, may be used as an alternative to headlamps but only if they are fitted as described.

In addition, the regulations prohibit a person using, or causing or permitting to be used, a vehicle on a road between sunset and sunrise or (while the vehicle is in motion) during daytime hours in seriously reduced visibility unless every front position lamp, rear position lamp and rear registration plate lamp required by the regulations to be fitted is kept lit. The term 'seriously reduced visibility' is not defined by the regula-tions. Common sense requires that the various forms of lighting should be used when the daytime situation requires them in the interests of road safety.

The provisions do not apply to a solo motor cycle or pedal cycle which is being pushed along the left-hand edge of the carriageway, a pedal cycle waiting to proceed provided that it is kept to the left-hand or near-side edge of a carriageway or a vehicle which is parked in an area outlined by lamps or traffic signs so as to prevent the presence of the vehicle, its load or equipment being a danger to persons using the road.

The regulations also exempt vehicles of certain classes which are parked during the hours of darkness on roads which are subject to speed limits of 30 mph or less from showing such lights. The vehicles which are exempt are goods vehicles not exceeding 1525 kg, passenger vehicles other than buses, invalid carriages and motor cycles and pedal cycles (in either case with or without a sidecar). If a trailer is attached to such vehicles the exemption does not apply, nor does it apply if the vehicle is carrying a load which requires lamps. The regulations only apply to particular places:

(a) designated parking places on roads; or
(b) a lay-by which is clearly shown to be such; or
(c) elsewhere, provided, if the vehicle is parked on a one-way road, that it is facing in the correct direction on either side of the road as close as possible to the kerb or, if it is parked on an ordinary road, it is properly parked and facing the correct way, and in either case no part of the vehicle is less than 10 m from a junction with the road upon which it is parked, whether the junction is on the same side of the road or not. For the purposes of measuring the distance from a junction where a curving kerb exists, the junction is regarded as beginning where the kerb begins to curve.

Light goods vehicles, passenger vehicles, combinations, solo cycles and invalid carriages may therefore park on restricted roads provided that they are in a designated parking place, a lay-by or elsewhere on one-way streets or ordinary roads provided that they are not within 10 m of a junction on either side of the road.

The person who parks without lights outside the permitted exceptions commits the offence of allowing the vehicle to remain at rest, or cause or permit to be allowed to remain at rest, on a road, between sunset and sunrise, without the front and rear position lamps, and/or rear registration plate lamp, being kept lit.

General control on parking at night

The Road Vehicles (Construction and Use) Regulations prohibit any person, without the permission of a police constable in uniform, causing or permitting any motor vehicle to stand on any road between sunset and sunrise otherwise than with the left or nearside of the vehicle as close as may be to the edge of the carriageway. The usual exemptions apply in respect of emergency and public utility vehicles and, of course, in one-way streets.

This offence is not concerned with the Road Vehicles Lighting Regulations of 1989, it is concerned with vehicles being parked facing the wrong way at night. If the vehicles are unlit, in circumstances in which they should be lit, then a second offence is committed.

Maintenance of lamps and reflectors

It is an offence against reg. 23 for a person to use, or cause or permit to be used, on a road any vehicle unless every front position lamp, rear position lamp, headlamp, rear registration plate lamp, rear fog lamp and retro reflector with which it is required to be fitted, is in good working order and, in the case of a lamp, clean.

The regulations require the correct maintenance of all lamps, reflectors and devices which the vehicle is required to have fitted. Additionally, they demand that every stop lamp and direction indicator, even if they are in excess of the number required to be fitted, be maintained at all times. The provisions concerning rear fog lamps do not apply to a vehicle which is drawing a trailer (as the rear fog lamp will not show in any case). There is also a proviso which excuses a defective lamp of any character if the defect arose in the course of a daytime journey (but this would not excuse use at night), or if arrangements have been made to have the defect remedied with all reasonable expedition. Thus, a vehicle with a defective wiring loom might be used during the daytime if it had been 'booked in' for repair. Similarly, a vehicle may be driven to a garage to have a new bulb or fuse fitted.

Dipped beam headlamps, front fog lamps, rear fog lamps and reversing lamps must be so maintained so that their aim will not cause undue dazzle or discomfort to other persons using the road. These provisions apply to all lamps fitted, whether required by the regulations to be fitted or not. It is an offence to use, cause or permit to be used, on a road, a vehicle with such lamps not so maintained.

Fitting and use of lamps and reflectors

The 1989 Regulations require that obligatory lamps, reflectors, devices, etc., are fitted to vehicles and are performing satisfactorily at all times. These requirements, however, do not apply to incomplete vehicles which are proceeding to a works for completion, pedal cycles, pedestrian-controlled vehicles, horse-drawn vehicles, hand-propelled vehicles and certain combat vehicles of HM Forces.

The exemption also applies to a vehicle which is not fitted with any front or rear position lamps. If an enthusiast is building a car from parts and has not yet installed a lighting system, that person will not commit an offence by using the car during the daytime. (It would be committed, of course, if used at night.) For the purposes of the regulations, a lamp shall not be treated as a lamp if it is painted over or masked so that it is not capable of being immediately used or readily put to use, or if it is an electric lamp which is not provided with any system of wiring by means of which that lamp is (or can readily be) connected with a source of electricity. Headlamps, etc., which are masked over or are not wired up could not be used in such a way that they would cause undue dazzle or inconvenience, so the exemption during daylight hours is logical. The vehicle could not be used generally upon the roads at night as it could not display headlights in the circumstances required. Equally, it could not be used in conditions of seriously reduced visibility.

Fixed-penalty procedure

Introduction

The fixed-penalty procedure is concerned with offences in respect of which an offender's liability may be discharged by the payment of a fixed sum by way of penalty without the necessity for the offender to appear before a court. The police officer dealing with the offence issues a 'ticket' which is in a prescribed form. Depending upon circumstances, the ticket may be given to the offender or attached to the offender's vehicle.

The penalty with which we are concerned must be paid within a period of 21 days or such longer period as may be prescribed in the notice. If it is not paid and no request for a hearing before a court has been received, a penalty will be registered against that person equal to the fixed penalty, plus half of that penalty.

The fixed penalty to be paid in respect of an offence is such amount as the Secretary of State may by order prescribe, or half of the maximum amount of the fine to which the person committing the offence would be liable on summary conviction, whichever is the less. The amounts currently prescribed by the Secretary of State are contained in the Fixed Penalty Order 2000 as amended by the Fixed Penalty Offences Order 2003. Those amounts are shown in the table.

Offence	Fixed penalty (£)
A fixed-penalty offence under s 143 of the RTA 1988	200
A fixed-penalty offence under s 172 of the RTA 1988	120
Any other fixed-penalty offence involving obligatory endorsement	60
A fixed-penalty parking offence committed in Greater London on a red route	60
Any other fixed-penalty parking offence committed in Greater London	40
A fixed-penalty offence under s 47 of the RTA 1988	60
A fixed-penalty offence under s 33 of the VERA 1994	60
Any other fixed-penalty offence	30

The term fixed-penalty parking offence means an offence under the Road Traffic Regulation Act 1984 which does not involve obligatory endorsement and is committed in respect of a stationary vehicle and road obstruction offences under a variety of statutory provisions. A 'red route' means a length of road on which there are traffic signs bearing the words 'red route' or red lines or marks.

The Road Traffic Act 1991 authorises the extension of the Function of Traffic Wardens Order to permit traffic wardens to deal with offences which involve obligatory endorsement provided that they were committed while the vehicle concerned was stationary.

The issue of a fixed-penalty notice

Schedule 3 of the Road Traffic Offenders Act 1988 lists the offences which are fixed-penalty offences. It indicates the sections of the relevant enactments and describes the offences. However, for enforcement purposes, police fixed-penalty notices (tickets) are prepared separately to deal with those offences which are endorsable and those which are not.

Schedule 2 indicates the offences which carry obligatory endorsement. However, to assist in this respect, *aides-mémoire* have been prepared listing the various offences which are non-endorsable fixed-penalty offences and those which are endorsable. Those in relation to endorsable offences also indicate the number of penalty points which apply, and give a code number for each offence. Those for non-endorsable fixed-penalty offences include advice concerning enforcement policies existing within a police force, particularly where a vehicle rectification scheme is in force.

Section 54 of the Road Traffic Offenders Act 1988 authorises a constable in uniform on any occasion upon which he has reason to believe that a person is committing or has on that occasion committed a fixed-penalty offence to give him a fixed-penalty notice in respect of that offence. These provisions, therefore, apply where the constable finds the driver and gives him a notice at the time of the offence. A fixed-penalty notice for these offences must be issued at the time or immediately after the offence is committed and cannot be issued in circumstances involving the need for future enquiries to trace the driver. For example, a driver seen to enter a motor vehicle upon which there is no vehicle excise licence displayed may be dealt with by a constable who so 'finds' the driver committing the offence. If he drives away before the constable has an opportunity to speak to him, and it therefore becomes necessary to carry out certain enquiries to trace the driver before speaking to him, a fixed-penalty notice cannot be issued to him under s 54 as the driver is not *found on that occasion* to be committing the offence. In such a case the conditional offer of a fixed-penalty procedure (see below) will have to be used or a prosecution will have to be instituted.

Section 62 of the Road Traffic Offenders Act 1988 provides that where on any occasion a constable has reason to believe in the case of a stationary vehicle that a fixed-penalty offence is being or has been committed in respect of it on that occasion, he may fix a fixed-penalty notice in respect of that offence to the vehicle, unless the offence appears to him to involve obligatory endorsement.

One offence only – by fixed penalty

Only one fixed-penalty notice may be issued on any one occasion. If more than one offence is committed on a particular occasion, a constable should either:

(a) report the offender for all offences; or
(b) give a verbal warning for all offences; or
(c) issue a fixed-penalty notice for one offence and administer a verbal warning in respect of all other offences.

However, these restrictions would not apply to the instance where a constable has issued a fixed-penalty notice for one offence which he knows to exist at the time that the notice is issued and, subsequently, further offences are disclosed. This could occur where vehicle or driver documents were produced later and found to be defective. Where this occurs, those offences subsequently disclosed will be reported by the officer with a view to proceedings by way of summons even though a fixed-penalty notice has been issued for the original offence.

The issue of fixed-penalty notices for non-endorsable offences, by traffic wardens, is restricted to offences included in the Function of Traffic Wardens Order 1970 as amended. The schedule to this order provides that traffic wardens may be employed to enforce law with respect to:

(a) offences of parking without obligatory lights or reflectors during the hours of darkness;
(b) offences of obstruction of a road by vehicles waiting, or being left or parked, being loaded or unloaded, on a road or public place;
(c) offences against the Vehicle Excise and Registration Act 1994 (e.g. no vehicle excise licence);
(d) offences related to parking places on highways where charges are made (e.g. by meters or machines);
(e) offences committed by causing a vehicle, or any part of it, to stop in contravention of the pedestrian crossing regulations;
(f) to stop vehicles for the purpose of testing under s 67 of the Road Traffic Act 1988; and
(g) to escort vehicles or trailers carrying loads of exceptional dimensions.

Types of fixed-penalty notice

Fixed-penalty notices are of two types: those issued for non-endorsable offences, e.g. breaches of parking regulations, and those issued for endorsable offences, that is, those offences which attract penalty points, e.g. speeding.

Schedule 3 of the Road Traffic Offenders Act 1988 lists the offences to which the fixed-penalty provisions apply.

Generally, non-endorsable fixed-penalty offences are concerned with parking offences, failure to wear seat belts or crash helmets, offences connected with the display of vehicle excise licences and registration marks, driving elsewhere than on a road, failure to comply with certain traffic signs, obstruction and those offences against the Road Vehicles (Construction and Use) Regulations 1986 which are not concerned with the dangerous loading or condition of vehicles or any vehicle with defective braking, steering systems or tyres, and some offences committed by motorcyclists and cyclists. Endorsable fixed-penalty offences include the offences set out above in relation to the Road Vehicles (Construction and Use) Regulations 1986, failure to comply with 'Stop' signs, double white lines, traffic lights, directions of a constable, pedestrian crossing offences related to a motor vehicle in relation to stopping, overtaking, parking and failure to accord precedence under both the 'zebra' and 'pelican' regulations, breaches of the conditions of provisional licences, offences committed by passengers on motor cycles and leaving a vehicle in a dangerous position.

Fixed-penalty notice – non-endorsable offence

The issue of a fixed-penalty notice for a non-endorsable offence may either be issued to the offender or attached to the unattended vehicle which is parked in breach of the regulations, or is defective or is not displaying licences, etc. It is an offence for a person to interfere with or remove a fixed-penalty notice which has been fixed to a vehicle in respect of a fixed-penalty offence. Such a notice may only be removed by the driver, the person in charge of the vehicle, the person liable for the offence or any person acting on the authority of any of these persons.

Fixed-penalty notice – endorsable offence

For the purposes of the Road Traffic Offenders Act 1988, an endorsable offence is an offence involving obligatory endorsement (as set out in Schedule 2 to the Act), which is also specified in Schedule 3 (which lists fixed-penalty offences). Occasionally, Schedule 2 limits the endorsable provisions of certain enactments by specifying particular offences within regulations which involve obligatory endorsement.

When an offender is dealt with, either by a court or by way of a fixed penalty for such an offence, he is liable to have his driving licence endorsed with the appropriate number of penalty points for the offence. The number of penalty points to be set against each offence is prescribed by Schedule 2 to the Road Traffic Offenders Act 1988. The procedure involving the award of penalty points has, as its ultimate aim, the disqualification of persistent offenders. The penalty points to be taken into account on the occasion of a person committing an endorsable fixed-penalty offence are any which will be awarded for the existing offence and any which are already endorsed on the licence for offences committed not more than 3 years before that offence. In determining whether a person convicted of an offence would be liable to disqualification, it shall be assumed, in the case of an offence in relation to which a range of numbers is shown, that the number of penalty points to be attributed to the offence would be the lowest in the range. However, if a court has disqualified a driver within that period this has the effect of rubbing out penalty points added to the licence prior to the date of conviction which led to that disqualification. However, this 'wiping clean' of a driving licence is restricted to a disqualification for repeated offences. Where a disqualification is imposed under the Road Traffic Offenders Act 1988, s 34 (disqualification for a specific offence), the penalty points previously accumulated will remain effective at the end of the period of disqualification for the specific offence until the expiry of 3 years from the date of the offence for which they were imposed.

Full fixed-penalty notice

Section 54 of the Road Traffic Offenders Act 1988 deals with circumstances in which the fixed-penalty offence involves obligatory endorsement. A constable may give the offender a 'full' fixed-penalty notice if:

(a) he produces his licence and its counterpart for inspection by the constable;
(b) the constable is satisfied, on inspecting the licence and its counterpart, that he would not be liable to be disqualified if he were convicted of that offence (i.e. conviction for the fixed-penalty offence) and the award of the appropriate number of penalty points would not cause the total number of relevant penalty points to number or exceed 12; and
(c) he surrenders his licence and its counterpart to the constable to be retained and dealt with in accordance with the provisions of the Act.

So far as it is permitted by the existing policy applicable to a police force, the decision as to whether or not to issue a fixed-penalty notice is a matter within the discretion of the constable. If the officer decides to deal with the matter by way of a fixed-penalty notice, there is a duty to ensure that the offender is aware of the implications of the procedure. It is suggested that the officer uses a form of words which convey the following message:

> I propose to issue you with a fixed penalty notice for the offence of.... It will be
> necessary for me to examine your driving licence and any penalty points which may

be endorsed on it. If, after examination, I find that it is appropriate to issue you with a fixed-penalty notice it will be necessary to surrender your licence to me.

Police officers must not give the impression that the offender must permit the examination of penalty points endorsed on his licence or its counterpart or that it must be surrendered. The 1988 Act requires constables to do things which they are not empowered to do. There is no power given by the Traffic Acts 1988 to examine penalty points on a licence or to require the surrender of a licence in these circumstances. However, the procedure is such that if a person refuses to permit examination of penalty points or to surrender his licence and its counterpart, that person cannot be dealt with by this procedure. If the licence is surrendered and there is no liability to disqualification, a full fixed-penalty notice may be given. The officer should use words to the effect:

> Your licence indicates that you may have this offence dealt with by fixed-penalty notice. Are you willing to surrender your licence to me?
> You will be given a receipt.

If, after such a question, the driver refuses to surrender the licence and its counterpart, he cannot be given a fixed-penalty notice and should be reported in the usual way for the offence. If the person agrees, a receipt will be made out (it is incorporated in the fixed-penalty notice). The notice also gives the offender details of the procedure to be followed if a court hearing is required. Attention should be drawn to this if any factor associated with the offence is disputed. It is helpful if police officers obtain the full postal code of offenders dealt with under this procedure as this assists the justices' clerk in relation to the registration of the subsequent penalties with the offender's home court.

The receipt which is issued by an officer in respect of a surrendered driving licence and its counterpart is valid for 2 months from the date of issue (or such longer period as may be prescribed). In addition, a fixed-penalty clerk may issue a new receipt on the application of the licence holder, which will expire on such date as is specified in the receipt. Any receipt ceases to be valid on the date the driving licence and its counterpart are returned to the offender. Such a receipt may be produced in place of a licence, subject to the usual conditions applicable to the production of a driving licence under s 164 Road Traffic Act 1988. However, it is provided that, if required to do so, that person must subsequently produce his driving licence and its counterpart at a police station immediately on his return.

Traffic wardens are empowered to require the production of a driving licence where the offence is one concerned with stopping on a pedestrian crossing or leaving a vehicle in a dangerous position and where employed as custodian of impounded vehicles.

Provisional fixed-penalty notice

Section 54 is also concerned with 'provisional fixed-penalty notices'. Such notices may be issued in any case where:

(a) the offence appears to the constable to involve obligatory endorsement; and
(b) the person concerned does not produce his licence and its counterpart for inspection by the constable.

The constable may give such a person a notice that if, within 7 days after the notice is given, he produces the notice together with his driving licence and its counterpart in person to a constable or authorised person at the police station specified in the notice (being a police station chosen by the person concerned), he must then be given a 'full' fixed-penalty notice in respect of the offence if:

(a) the constable or authorised person is satisfied, on inspecting the licence and its counterpart, that the person would not be liable to be disqualified if convicted of the offence; and

(b) he surrenders his licence and its counterpart to the constable or authorised person to be retained and dealt with in accordance with the Act.

In effect, the 'provisional' is made 'full' by completing the driving licence receipt section on the fixed-penalty notice.

An 'authorised person', in relation to a fixed-penalty notice given at a police station, means a person authorised for the purpose of the section by or on behalf of the chief officer of police for the area in which the police station is situated including the British Transport Police.

Fixed-penalty notices are made out in such a way that they contain all of the details of the offence with which they are concerned and will form a basis of any report which may subsequently be required from the officer in the event of court proceedings.

However, no offence is committed by a person who fails to produce his driving licence as a result of a fixed-penalty offer under s 54. If a constable wishes to examine the licence for any other reason, it must be made clear that the requirement is made under the Road Traffic Act 1988, s 164, and that the licence *must* be produced to permit examination of those matters set out in s 164.

Practical points

The procedure does not apply to Scotland and it is therefore not permissible for a constable to issue a provisional fixed-penalty notice with a request to produce a driving licence, together with the notice, at a police station in Scotland.

Fixed-penalty notices should not be given to juveniles as there are other recommended procedures for dealing with juveniles in relation to offences generally. These procedures recognise the particular circumstances of each case.

Where the circumstances within which the issue of a fixed-penalty notice is being considered involve an offence which is associated with a traffic accident, a fixed-penalty notice must not be issued. This may occur where a driver has passed a 'Give way' sign, or some other sign placing upon him a similar demand for action, and has become involved in a collision with another vehicle. In such circumstances it is possible that the prosecutor will wish to prefer additional charges when all of the available evidence is considered. The driver's failure to recognise the requirements of the sign may form the basis of such an additional charge.

Section 2 of the Road Traffic Offenders Act 1988 removes the necessity for an offender to be given notice of intended prosecution for an offence in respect of which a fixed-penalty notice has been given or fixed under any provision of the Act.

Action by offender on receipt of notice

An offender who has received a fixed-penalty notice shall not be subject to proceedings during a 'suspended enforcement period', which is the period of 21 days following the date of the notice, or such longer period as may be specified in the notice. During the suspended enforcement period a person may give notice requesting a court hearing (in which case the fixed penalty notice will be set aside and a court hearing will be arranged), pay the fixed penalty required by the notice (by completing part 2 of the notice and sending it with the fixed penalty required to the justices' clerk at the Fixed Penalty Office) or do nothing. If payment is not made before the end of the suspended enforcement period or notice is not given of the requirement for a hearing, the sum required by way of fixed penalty, plus 50 per cent of that penalty, is registered with the court in the area of residence and becomes recoverable as a fine.

In cases in which a fixed-penalty notice is fixed to a vehicle and the fixed penalty has not been paid and notice requesting a hearing has not been received within the suspended enforcement period, a notice to the owner may be served by or on behalf of the chief officer of police on any person who appears to him to be the owner of the vehicle (or a person authorised to act on such person's behalf). Such a notice shall give particulars of the offence and of the fixed penalty required and indicate the time allowed for response. If the fixed penalty is not paid before the end of that period, the person on whom the notice is served must furnish, before the end of that period, a statutory statement of ownership. The period allowed for response to such a notice is defined by s 63(5) as 21 days from the service of the notice.

If such a person was not the owner of the vehicle at the time of the alleged offence, a statutory statement of ownership may be made stating whether he was ever the owner, or when ownership ceased, or when ownership began after the date of the alleged offence. In the last two circumstances, if the information is in his possession he must give the name and address of the person to or from whom the vehicle was sold/bought together with the date of such transaction. If such a statement is not furnished, proceedings may be taken. These proceedings shall be by way of registering a penalty against that person equal to the fixed penalty concerned, plus 50 per cent. Provision is also made for statutory statements of hiring in the case of hire vehicles.

The Road Traffic Offenders Act 1988 recognises that there will be occasions upon which the person who receives the notice to owner will not have been the driver at the relevant time. The notice therefore indicates that within the period allowed, a hearing may be requested. Alternatively, the person who was actually driving at the time may wish to request a hearing. If this is so, the owner should also provide a statutory statement of facts which has the effect of the actual driver requesting a hearing. (If such a driver is prepared to accept responsibility for the fixed penalty, the Act assumes that this will be done on behalf of the owner to whom the notice is addressed.)

Conditional offer of fixed penalty

In England and Wales, where a constable has reason to believe that a fixed-penalty offence has been committed and no fixed-penalty notice was given at the time or fixed to the vehicle concerned, a notice of 'conditional offer' may be sent to the alleged offender by or on behalf of the chief officer of police including the British Transport Police. A conditional offer must give particulars of the circumstances and give reasonable information about the alleged offence, and state that proceedings cannot be commenced for the offence until the end of 28 days following the date of issue (or such longer period specified). Such a notice must indicate that if, within that period, the alleged offender pays the fixed penalty to the fixed-penalty clerk and, where the offence concerned involved obligatory endorsement and the licence (and its counterpart) is delivered to the clerk at the same time and the clerk is satisfied that the alleged offender if convicted would not be liable to disqualification under the Road Traffic Offenders Act 1988, s 35 (disqualification for repeated offences), liability to conviction shall be discharged. In assessing liability to such disqualification, it is assumed (where penalty points awarded for the offence are in a range) that the number to be attributed for the offence would be the lowest in the range.

A person issuing a conditional offer must notify the fixed-penalty clerk. If payment is made in accordance with the offer and the licence is delivered, no proceedings will be taken for the offence to which the conditional offer relates. The fixed-penalty clerk must endorse the licence or counterpart in appropriate cases and return the licence to the holder. Where the payment of a fixed penalty is made by means of a cheque which is subsequently dishonoured, the validity of the endorsement remains valid, even though the licence holder is then liable to prosecution for the offence. In such circumstances the fixed-penalty clerk must, on the expiry of the period specified in the conditional offer, or (if that period has expired) forthwith, notify the person to whom the conditional offer was made that no payment has been made. Where proceedings are brought against a licence holder after notification that a cheque tendered in payment has been dishonoured, the court must order the removal of the fixed-penalty endorsement from the licence (or counterpart) and may make any competent order of endorsement or disqualification, in addition to sentence.

The fixed-penalty clerk must notify the Secretary of State of any endorsement made on the licence in accordance with these procedures.

Special provisions in relation to fixed-penalty offences

The Road Traffic (Vehicle Emissions) (Fixed Penalty) Regulations 1997 provide for specified local authorities to authorise persons to issue fixed-penalty notices to users of vehicles within their areas who contravene, or fail to comply with, the Road Vehicles (Construction and Use) Regulations 1986, reg. 61 (emission of smoke, vapour, gases, oily substances, etc.) or reg. 98 (stopping engine when stationary).

There are now a number of other Acts of Parliament which specifically authorise the use of fixed-penalty procedures. These are dealt with within the appropriate chapters of this book.

Road vehicles – construction and use

The first horseless carriages to be manufactured were not subject to any form of control during the production process. The 'lethal' nature of the modern vehicle has made regulation essential. The Road Vehicles (Construction and Use) Regulations 1986 now regulate the use of motor vehicles and trailers on roads, their construction, equipment and the conditions under which they may be used. Their purpose is to provide for the safety of drivers and other road users.

Many modern vehicles are exempt from various provisions of the 1986 Regulations because they comply with certain international requirements in relation to the construction and use of motor vehicles. The requirements are commonly referred to as 'Type Approval' requirements. When vehicles are so exempt, this is stated in the particular regulation which refers to the alternative standards which they must meet.

Construction and use offences: general

The Road Traffic Act 1988, ss 40A, 41A and 41B, provides various offences which may be committed in relation to the use of a vehicle in a dangerous condition and/or in contravention of the Regulations.

Section 40A makes it an offence for a person to use, cause or permit another to use a motor vehicle or a trailer on a road when:

(a) the condition of the motor vehicle or trailer or of its accessories or equipment; or
(b) the purpose for which it is used; or
(c) the number of passengers carried by it or the manner in which they are carried; or
(d) the weight, position or distribution of its load or the manner in which it is secured,

is such that the use of the motor vehicle or trailer involves danger of injury to any person.

A tractor was driven on a Class C road with the front link arms of the vehicle in the lowered position. Although the tractor driver was not responsible for the accident, a collision with a car caused the death of the other driver. The tractor driver was charged under s 40A with an offence of using the tractor on a road when the condition of its accessories or equipment were such that the use involved danger of injury to any person. Had the link arms been raised, the protrusion would have been less. The Divisional Court would not interfere with a decision of justices to acquit. They had applied their local knowledge of the area, considered the rural nature of the area and the classification of the road, together with the fact that tractors frequently used the road at that time. It could not be said that their finding was plainly wrong or irrational. The Court said that its decision did not give licence to tractor drivers to proceed along any road at any time with the link arms in the lowered position. However, it was not the law that such use will automatically amount to any offence. While it is easy to sympathise with the driver of the tractor in these circumstances (the other car was out of control at the time of the collision), it is difficult to come to terms with the fact that the use of the tractor in any other condition than its safest condition, does not offend against the section.

Section 41A makes it an offence for a person to:

(a) contravene or fail to comply with a construction and use requirement as to brakes, steering gear or tyres; or
(b) use on a road a motor vehicle or trailer which does not comply with such a requirement, or cause or permit a motor vehicle or trailer to be so used.

Offences against ss 40A and 41A carry discretional disqualification; the endorsement of 3 penalty points is obligatory.

Section 41B punishes offences in relation to weight. A person who:

(a) contravenes or fails to comply with a construction and use requirement as to any description of weight applicable to
  (i) a goods vehicle, or
  (ii) a motor vehicle or trailer adapted to carry more than eight passengers; or
(b) uses on a road a vehicle which does not comply with such a requirement, or causes or permits a vehicle to be so used,

commits an offence against the section. Section 41B(2) provides a defence where the alleged contravention relates to any description of weight applicable to a goods vehicle. It provides that in such a case it is a defence to prove either that the vehicle was going to or coming from a weighbridge or, where the relevant weight limit is not exceeded by more than 5 per cent, that the weight was not exceeded at the time of loading and that the load had not been added to.

Section 42 is concerned with the contravention of a construction and use requirement other than those relating to brakes, steering gear or tyres, or those relating to weight, which are dealt with by ss 41A and 41B. It provides that a person who:

(a) contravenes or fails to comply with such a requirement; or
(b) uses on a road a motor vehicle or trailer which does not comply with such a requirement, or causes or permits a motor vehicle or trailer to be so used,

commits an offence.

Those who contravene s 41B or 42 are not liable to disqualification or to obligatory endorsement under these sections.

An offence of using on a road a trailer which does not comply with regulations is an offence distinct from that of using a defective motor vehicle.

Since the relevant provisions are concerned with persons who *use, cause* or *permit* the use of motor vehicles or trailers in contravention of the Regulations, it is important that police officers understand the meaning of these terms.

To use

The term 'use' should be given its ordinary meaning and indicates absolute liability by persons who are using the motor vehicle. It is obvious that the driver is using the vehicle, but if the journey is being made on an employer's business, the employer is also using it, although he may be many miles distant at the time. The Divisional Court has ruled that a person is the 'user' of a motor vehicle only if he is the owner or driver of the vehicle, but it applies to the owner only if the driver is employed by the owner under a contract of service and, at the material time, he is driving on his employer's business. A self-employed driver who is hired from time to time to drive a company's vehicles is not an employee of that company when work is accepted on its behalf. Where an employment agency provides drivers on a contract basis, the agency remains the employer. In such cases, charges of 'causing' or 'permitting' use should be preferred against the owners. Where two partners jointly own a vehicle, use by one of them of the particular vehicle does not necessarily involve use by the other.

Where a company hired a vehicle together with its driver (who continued to be employed by that company) to a second company for a period of 5 years and the vehicle carried the livery of the company which hired it, the owners of the vehicle were still held to be 'using' the vehicle when it was found to be overloaded. Similarly, where the driver of a vehicle who was employed by company A was ordered by telephone to pick up a load on behalf of another company B, that company being responsible for loading the vehicle, its documentation and the selection of route, the Divisional Court held that company A was using the vehicle when it was found to be overloaded. The Court said that whilst it might be correct to argue that company B was using the vehicle, this did not mean that company A was not. It was their vehicle and their driver and that driver was employed under a contract of service.

The term 'absolute liability' means that we must usually let the facts speak for themselves; if the vehicle is being driven and there is a defect existing in it, then persons using it are guilty of an offence and it is not necessary to prove that they were aware of the defect at the time. In such cases, it is not an 'optional extra' to offer evidence of guilty knowledge. Evidence must be limited to the points which must be proved to show that the offence has been committed. The High Court has advised that in circumstances in which a sudden defect occurs, such as a brake failure, the police should not prosecute. The rule appears to be that if the user is morally guiltless and has not been negligent, no charge should be preferred. An example of the strict liability of users is given by the following circumstance. A driver was convicted of using a motor vehicle with a load which had not been properly secured, although he took no part in the loading, which was carried out by loaders employed for the purpose.

A vehicle is in 'use' when it is stationary on a road for loading or unloading. It has also been held that it is in use even when left with a defective engine and without a battery or petrol, on the grounds that it could still be moved by pushing or releasing the brake. It is, therefore, plain that the term 'use' does not imply that the vehicle must be in motion, or have previously been in motion within a short period of time.

An employee used a motor vehicle with defective brakes, although the owner had told him to take it to a garage whenever it required maintenance. It was held that as the vehicle was being used on the owner's business, he was guilty of using it with defective brakes as the Construction and Use Regulations generally impose absolute liability upon those contravening them. This decision provides a good summary of instances in which persons may be alleged to be using a motor vehicle in contravention of the regulations.

Perhaps the clearest indication of the limitation of charges of 'using' was given when the owner of a stock car was convicted at a magistrates' court of seven offences contrary to the Road Vehicles (Construction and Use) Regulations. There was no evidence to show that the driver of the car was a servant of the owner and it was held that only the driver and his employer could be said to 'use' the vehicle. The Lord Chief Justice said that when an employer–servant relationship could not be proved, a charge of 'permitting' would be correct.

Where a trailer is towed by another vehicle and the offence concerned relates to the trailer, for example, there is a defective part on the trailer, or it carries an insecure load, the information should specify that it was the trailer which was defective or improperly used. This is essential where the tractor unit and the trailer are owned by different persons or companies. However, the Divisional Court refused to quash convictions where offences were alleged to have been committed in relation to a 'motor vehicle', whereas, in fact, those offences related to a trailer, where the trailer and the tractor unit were owned by the same person or company. The correct procedure in such cases is for the information to be amended before the court under the Magistrates' Courts Act 1980, s 123.

To cause

Judges of the High Court have suggested that the term 'causing' in addition to the term 'permitting' deal with offences of being an accessory or aider and abettor, and in circumstances in which one is considering the position of the aider or abettor in respect of Construction and Use offences, one of these terms will fit the appropriate circumstances.

The term 'cause' suggests that the person 'causing' has some authority over the person concerned. The person charged with such an offence must have had the necessary authority to cause the vehicle to be used, and must have directly or indirectly ordered or directed the use of the vehicle. If an employee uses a vehicle without authority, the employer has neither caused nor permitted its use as he has no guilty knowledge, which is now recognised to be essential in such cases. Such guilty knowledge may be proved by showing that he had knowledge of the defect in the vehicle, or wilful blindness towards his responsibilities. There must be some evidence linking the person charged, more or less directly, with the use of the vehicle on the particular occasion. Where a manager was responsible for five vehicle depots, at each of which there was a vehicle superintendent, he was found not guilty of causing it to be used in a defective condition, having no opportunity to exercise local control. It is also possible for the driver of a vehicle to be charged with offences of 'causing' in certain circumstances, as some offences can only be committed by persons causing or permitting them. A bus driver who left his bus and reported off duty without handing over to his relief driver was convicted of causing it to stand so as to cause unnecessary obstruction. A driver who is towing another vehicle is causing it to be used.

To permit

The term 'permit' covers instances in which either a general or a particular permission has been given to use the vehicle. The owner, or any person who has control on the owner's behalf, for example, a company manager, can permit the use of a vehicle. It is necessary to prove that the use of the vehicle in its defective condition was permitted by a responsible officer of the company, and this can be done by allowing it to be used in a known defective condition, or by closing the eyes to the possibility of such use.

A vehicle belonging to a company left its premises in good condition and, while out of the control of the responsible officers of the company, the crew coupled up a trailer in such a manner that the brakes were defective. It was held that the company was not guilty of 'permitting' the use of the vehicle with defective brakes as there was no evidence of any kind of permission by a responsible officer of the company. The observation was made, however, that as the vehicle was on company business at the time, the company could be said to be 'using' it. Similarly, where a man was the owner of a lorry driven on a road by his employee while the brakes were defective, it was held that for a charge of permitting to succeed there must be proof of actual knowledge or recklessness on the part of the owner.

It has been held that the essence of 'permitting' offences is knowledge, and when such knowledge cannot be proved directly, there must be sufficient proof that the person charged had ignored the obvious or there had been recklessness as to whether it was allowed to occur.

The High Court set aside a conviction where a company had been found guilty of permitting a vehicle to be used with inefficient brakes, in that the managing director should have ensured that the vehicle was lubricated more frequently that at 4-weekly intervals and that he should have ensured that it was done correctly. The company employed an experienced foreman fitter, and it was held that the manager had not been sufficiently reckless to justify a charge of permitting.

The position appears to be that if an employee can be shown to be negligent, it is not sufficient to assume that responsible officers of the company are aware of this and, therefore, guilty of permitting. In certain circumstances, if responsibility for maintenance is delegated to an unskilled employee, the officers of the company may be liable.

In relation to offences under the Road Vehicles (Construction and Use) Regulations 1986, charges of permitting should be restricted to instances in which it can be shown that responsible officers of the company were aware of the condition of the vehicle or had closed their eyes to the obvious. Employers are not necessarily guilty of permitting use in instances in which the defect is due to the negligence of a skilled mechanic. Charges of 'using' are better made when the vehicle is being used by a servant on his master's business.

Vehicle classification

The Road Vehicles (Construction and Use) Regulations make references to all forms of motor vehicles but make special references to dual-purpose vehicles and motor cars. These terms have already been considered but it will assist understanding to remember that dual-purpose vehicles can be either shooting brakes or four wheel drive vehicles and that the term 'motor car' embraces certain goods vehicles in addition to passenger-carrying vehicles.

Construction and maintenance of vehicles

The Road Vehicles (Construction and Use) Regulations 1986 create offences in relation to the fitting and maintenance of parts and accessories of motor vehicles. We will examine the provisions of these regulations which create offences most commonly dealt with by police officers.

Audible warning instrument

The regulations deal with the requirements in relation to the fitting of a horn to motor vehicles and also place restrictions upon the use of such instruments in certain circumstances.

Fitting of horn and its use

All motor vehicles which have a maximum speed of more than 20 mph or, in the case of an agricultural vehicle, if it is being driven at more than 20 mph, require a horn. There was once a tendency to fit warning instruments which played the first notes of 'Colonel Bogey' or other ear-catching tunes, and although this will still be lawful in the case of older vehicles, vehicles first used on or after 1 August 1973 must have a horn which gives a continuous and uniform sound.

Motor vehicles used by emergency services, all of which are specified in the regulations and include police, fire brigade, ambulance and the emergency vehicles used by other services for fire fighting or rescue operations, may be fitted with gongs, bells, sirens or two-tone horns. Vehicles used for the sale of goods from the vehicle, e.g. ice cream vans, may be fitted with an instrument, other than a two-tone horn, to advertise their presence. They must, additionally, have a normal warning instrument fitted. Bells, gongs or sirens may be fitted to a vehicle if their purpose is to prevent theft or attempted theft of the vehicle or its contents. They may also be fitted to large passenger-carrying vehicles if the purpose is to summon help for the driver, conductor or an inspector. Such anti-theft alarms must be fitted with a device which switches the alarm off after a period of 5 minutes.

It is an offence for any person to sound or cause or permit the sounding of the warning instrument of a motor vehicle which is stationary on a road at any time other than when there is danger due to another moving vehicle on or near the road. Horns shall not be sounded between the hours of 23.30 and 07.00 hours on a moving vehicle on a restricted road (roads to which a 30 mph speed limit applies). These generally occur in built-up areas and these provisions are to prevent unnecessary annoyance to residents.

Reversing alarms and boarding aid alarms

The regulations permit 'reversing alarms' to be fitted to certain vehicles in addition to horns. These are devices to warn persons that the vehicle is reversing or about to reverse. Some public service vehicles are required to be fitted with a 'boarding aid alarm', which is an alarm for a power-operated lift or ramp fitted to a bus to enable wheelchair users to board or alight and which are designed to warn persons that the lift or ramp is in operation. Such devices are exempted from the requirement that the sound of a warning instrument shall be continuous and uniform and from restrictions affecting restricted roads.

Reversing alarms may be fitted to goods vehicles with a maximum gross weight of not less than 2000 kg, buses, refuse vehicles, engineering plant and works trucks. The sound emitted must be such that it is not likely to be confused with the sound emitted from a pedestrian crossing.

A reversing alarm may only be used on a stationary vehicle if the vehicle's engine is running and it is about to move backwards or the vehicle is in danger from another moving vehicle. A boarding aid alarm may be used on a stationary vehicle.

Maintenance

Horns and other audible warning instruments must be maintained in good and efficient working order at all times.

Brakes

Fitting of brakes

There are a number of regulations which provide for the provision of effective braking systems upon motor vehicles. The common factor is that no matter what system of braking the regulations require to be fitted to particular types of vehicles, every part of the system and its means of operation must be maintained in good and efficient working order and must be properly adjusted. Foot braking systems should be capable of stopping the vehicle within a reasonable distance, and tables of braking distances are set out in the Highway Code. For example, at a speed of 30 mph, the overall stopping distance is 75 feet.

Regulation 15(1) of the Regulations requires that with certain exceptions (generally embracing specialist types of vehicles) all wheeled motor vehicles specified in the table set out within the regulation, which were first used on or after 1 April 1983, must comply with the construction, fitting and performance requirements of Community Directive 79/489, and so must a trailer manufactured on or after 1 October 1982. The vehicles specified include most vehicles on our roads today. The table indicates the vehicle category set out in the Community Directive, specifying the construction, fitting and performance requirement of each type of vehicle. Other similar vehicles used or manufactured before the relevant date may comply with these requirements as an alternative to reg. 16.

Regulations 15(1A) and 15(1B) require that, with certain exceptions, the braking systems of most motor vehicles first used on or after 1 April 1989 (or trailers manufactured on or after 1 October 1988) must comply with the requirements of Community Directive 85/647. Motor cars, buses of a gross weight not exceeding 5000 kg and dual-purpose vehicles must comply if first used on or after 1 April 1990. By reg. 15(1C), other motor vehicles (with certain exceptions) first used on or after 1 April 1992, and trailers manufactured on or after 1 October 1991, must comply with Community Directive 88/194. Regulation 15(1D) requires that all such vehicles as specified above first used on or after 1 April 1995 and trailers manufactured after that date must comply with Community Directive 91/422. Once again, other such vehicles may comply as an alternative to the other Directives specified above. Regulation 15(1E) requires the vehicles referred to below to comply with Community Directive 98/12/EC. It has the effect of extending the categories of vehicles which are required to be fitted with ABS braking systems at the point of manufacture to include all passenger-carrying vehicles with more than eight passenger seats in addition to the driver's seat, all goods vehicles over 3500 kg and all trailers over 3500 kg. Regulation 15(1E) will apply to all motor vehicles of the relevant kinds first used on or after 1 April 2002. Motor vehicles first used before 1 May 2002 or, in the case of a trailer, manufactured before 1 May 2002, may comply with these requirements as an alternative to reg. 15(1), (1A), (1C) or (1D) or with reg. 16 or 17.

For the purposes of reg. 15, the date upon which a trailer was manufactured shall be taken to be the date on which its manufacture was completed except that, in the case of a trailer whose manufacture has been completed for more than 8 years and which has been the subject of a notifiable alteration under reg. 30 of the Goods Vehicles (Plating and Testing) Regulations 1988, it shall be the date on which the notifiable alteration was completed. Such a trailer must comply with all Community Directives which applied to the trailer when the notifiable alteration was completed.

Vehicles first used before 1 April 1983 and those not covered by the Community Directive are dealt with by reg. 16, but such vehicles may, as an alternative, comply with the Community Directive.

Generally, by reg. 16, heavy motor cars and motor cars first used on or after 1 January 1968 must be equipped with one efficient braking system having two means of operation, or an efficient split braking system with one means of operation, or two efficient systems with separate means of operation. Such systems must be so designed that in the event of failure (of other than a fixed member or a brake shoe anchor pin), there shall still be sufficient braking power to bring the vehicle to rest within a reasonable distance. Such brakes must be applied to at least one wheel of a three-wheeler, otherwise to at least half of the wheels of the vehicle. The parking brake must be independent and able to hold the vehicle stationary on a gradient of at least 16 per cent. The full braking system of such vehicles must apply to all the wheels.

The provisions set out above also apply, to a large degree, to a heavy motor cars and motor cars first used before 1 January 1968. There are small variations, perhaps the most significant being that the parking brake must be such that it can be set so as to prevent the rotation of at least one wheel in the case of a three-wheeler, and at least two wheels in the case of a vehicle having more than three wheels, and the requirement that the full braking system must apply to all wheels does not apply to such vehicles.

Two-wheeled motor cycles must have either an efficient braking system with two means of operation, or two efficient independent systems. Trailers, with limited exceptions, require brakes if they have a maximum gross weight exceeding 750 kg. However, where a trailer which does not exceed that maximum gross weight is fitted with a braking system, that system must be maintained in efficient working order, even though it is not *required* to have any brakes. The brakes will apply to all wheels and, in the event of failure, brakes must be left for one wheel in the case of a trailer with two wheels, and for at least two wheels if it has more than two wheels. Brakes may be of the 'overrun' type. They must have a parking brake which can be applied by a person on the ground, by a means of operation fitted to the trailer. There are minor differences if the trailer is pre-1 January 1968, particularly in relation to the main system, in that the brakes need only apply to two wheels if there are no more than four wheels and to at least half of the wheels if there are more than four.

Although the provisions of reg. 16 do not apply to trailers which do not exceed 750 kg, such trailers manufactured on or after 1 January 1997 are required to have a braking device such that the trailer will stop automatically if the coupling separates while the trailer is in motion, or be provided with a secondary coupling (e.g. a chain or cable) which, in the event of separation of the main coupling, can stop the draw bar from touching the ground and provide some residual steering action in the trailer. Such trailers manufactured on or after that date must carry a plate which gives their year of manufacture.

Efficiency and maintenance

Regulation 18 deals with the efficiency of braking systems, requiring that they shall be maintained in good and efficient working order and be properly adjusted. Defects arising within ABS braking systems during the course of a journey, or use whilst the vehicle is being taken to a place of repair, are removed from the requirement that every part of a braking system shall be maintained in good and efficient working order. However, the affected braking system must still meet the braking efficiencies specified in reg. 18(3).

Service and secondary systems are required to meet minimum percentage efficiencies as measured by a testing meter. Most vehicles are required to have a service braking system of 50 per cent efficiency and a secondary system of 25 per cent efficiency. These percentages are usually reduced if the vehicle is drawing a trailer. The regulation also deals with the efficiency of parking brakes, requiring that all vehicles shall have parking brakes so maintained that the brakes are capable, without the assistance of stored energy, of holding the vehicle stationary on a gradient of at least 16 per cent. If a trailer is attached to a vehicle which complies with Community Directive 79/489, this requirement is reduced to 12 per cent.

Mirrors

The requirements of the regulations in relation to mirrors are very much affected by the date of first use of a motor vehicle. The important date is 1 June 1978. As more recent vehicles have more extensive requirements, we will consider them first.

First used on or after 1 June 1978

Every passenger vehicle, goods vehicle or dual-purpose vehicle first used on or after 1 June 1978 must be equipped with an interior rear view mirror and at least one exterior rear view mirror fitted to the offside of the vehicle. If, for any reason, the interior rear view mirror does not provide an adequate view to the rear, the vehicle must also have an exterior rear view mirror fitted to the nearside of the vehicle. If we consider these requirements in relation to the family car, it *must* have an interior mirror and an exterior mirror on the offside, both giving an adequate rearwards view. If, on returning from holiday, the rear of the vehicle has been filled with luggage, etc., the interior mirror may not afford a rearwards view. However, the regulation provides that if the vehicle has an exterior mirror on the nearside, no offence will be committed. The relevant date of first use in the case of Ford Transit vehicles is 10 July 1978.

First used before 1 June 1978

In the case of vehicles first used before 1 June 1978, passenger vehicles adapted to carry more than eight passengers exclusive of the driver, goods vehicles and dual-purpose vehicles (except locomotives and motor tractors) require two mirrors, one fitted externally on the offside of the vehicle and the second *either* internally, or externally on the nearside of the vehicle. However, the remainder of vehicles, including the family car, merely require one mirror fitted either internally or externally in such a way that the driver can become aware of traffic to the rear.

Although this appears to permit the fitting of a mirror anywhere, it must be remembered that its purpose is to allow the driver to become aware of traffic to the rear. Most nearside mirrors would not satisfy this requirement as there would be no view to the offside rear of the vehicle.

Motor cycles and special vehicles

There is no requirement for mirrors in relation to a two-wheeled motor cycle. However, if mirrors are fitted to motor cycles first used on or after 1 October 1978 they must be of a type which complies with the regulations. Other 'excepted vehicles' are motor vehicles drawing trailers upon which there is some person who can communicate to the driver the intentions of other vehicles to the rear, works trucks which afford a clear view to the rear, pedestrian-controlled vehicles and a chassis being driven to a body plant.

Motor tractors, agricultural and forestry tractors, locomotives, works trucks and some vehicles with limited design speed are only required to be fitted with one mirror, fitted on the offside of the vehicle.

Manner of fitting

General provisions contained in the regulations include requirements that mirrors shall be fixed to a vehicle first used on or after 1 June 1978 in such a way that they remain steady under normal driving conditions; each exterior mirror shall be visible to the driver from his driving position, through either a side window or area of the windscreen swept by a wiper blade. Interior mirrors and those fitted to the offside shall be capable of adjustment by the driver from his driving position, except where the exterior mirror is a 'spring back' model. However, the offside mirror may be locked into position from the outside of the vehicle.

If the bottom edge of an exterior mirror is less than 2 m from the road surface when the vehicle is laden, projection must not exceed 20 cm. If drawing a trailer which is wider than the towing vehicle, projection must not exceed the trailer width by more than 20 cm. This proviso permits the use of extended mirrors on motor cars towing caravans. All mirrors fitted after these dates must bear approval marks described in the Motor Vehicles (Designation of Approval Marks) Regulations.

Silencer and exhaust system

All vehicles propelled by an internal combustion engine must be fitted with an exhaust system including a silencer and the exhaust gases from the engine shall not escape into the atmosphere without first passing through the silencer. Most silencers consist of a series of baffle plates which the gases strike, breaking their velocity and so reducing the noise. The removal of plates results in an increase of noise. This can be popular with young motor cyclists. It is an offence to alter any exhaust system in such a way as to increase the noise. Alterations or replacements to exhaust systems are not permitted if they have the effect of increasing the noise.

Anchorage points and seat belts

Regulations 46 and 47 of the Construction and Use Regulations deal with anchorage points and seat belts.

Anchorage points

Regulation 46 provides that, except in the case of an 'excepted vehicle', every bus first used on or after 1 April 1982, every wheeled motor car first used on or after 1 January 1965, every three-wheeled motor cycle the unladen weight of which exceeds 255 kg and which was first used on or after 1 September 1970 and every heavy motor car first used on or after 1 October 1988 must be fitted with anchorage points and seat belts as specified.

Excepted vehicles

The following are excepted vehicles:

(a) a goods vehicle (other than a dual-purpose vehicle) which was first used
  (i) before 1 April 1967; or
  (ii) on or after 1 April 1980 and before 1 October 1988 which has a maximum gross weight exceeding 3500 kg; or

(iii) before 1 April 1980 or, if the vehicle is a model manufactured before 1 October 1979, was first used before 1 April 1982 and, in either case, has an unladen weight exceeding 1525 kg;

(b) an agricultural vehicle;
(c) a motor tractor;
(d) a works truck
(e) an electrically propelled goods vehicle first used before 1 October 1988;
(f) a pedestrian-controlled vehicle;
(g) an imported vehicle, whilst travelling to be fitted, etc.;
(h) a vehicle having a maximum speed not exceeding 16 mph; and
(i) a locomotive.

Where points are to be fitted

The rules are as follows:

(a) A vehicle first used before 1 April 1982 must be equipped with anchorage points for seat belts in respect of the driver's seat and any specified passenger's seat. 'A specified passenger's seat' is a forward-facing front seat. Where there is more than one forward-facing front seat, the term is applied to the one furthest from the driver's seat. A passenger or dual-purpose vehicle (other than a bus) first used on or after 1 April 1982 and not falling within (b) to (h) below must have anchorage points for every forward-facing seat constructed or adapted to accommodate one adult.

(b) A minibus, motor ambulance or motor caravan first used on or after 1 April 1982 but before 1 October 1988 must have anchorage points for the driver's and specified passenger's seats.

(c) A minibus [not being within (g) or (h) below] with a gross weight not exceeding 3500 kg, a motor ambulance or motor caravan first used on or after 1 October 1988 must have anchorage points for the driver's seat and each forward-facing front seat.

(d) A goods vehicle first used on or after 1 October 1988 but before 1 October 2001 which has a maximum gross weight exceeding 3500 kg must have anchorage points for the driver's seat and each forward-facing front seat.

(e) A goods vehicle first used on or after 1 October 2001 which has a maximum gross weight exceeding 3500 kg must have anchorage points for all forward-facing seats.

(f) A coach first used on or after 1 October 1988 but before 1 October 2001 must have anchorage points for all exposed forward-facing front seats.

(g) A bus (other than an urban bus) with a gross vehicle weight of 3500 kg and first used on or after 1 October 2001 must have an anchorage point for every forward-facing seat and every rearward-facing seat.

(h) A bus (other than an urban bus) with a gross vehicle weight *not* exceeding 3500 kg and first used on or after 1 October 2001 must have anchorage points for every forward-facing and every rearward-facing seat.

(i) In every other case a vehicle (other than a bus) first used on or after 1 April 1982 [and not within (b) to (h) above] must have anchorage points for every forward-facing front seat and every non-protected seat. A 'non-protected seat' is one which is not a front seat where the screen zones within the 'protected area' have a combined surface of less than 80 cm^2.

Seat belts

Regulation 47, which deals with seat belts, applies to all vehicles covered by the requirements of reg. 46 in relation to anchorage points. Such vehicles first used before 1 April 1981 must have seat belts for the driver's seat and the specified passenger's seat. They must be of an approved type and, in respect of these vehicles, 'diagonal belts' are approved. Those first used on or after 1 April 1981 must be provided with three-point seat belts for both the driver's seat and the specified passenger's seat.

Every passenger vehicle or dual-purpose vehicle (other than a bus) not falling within (b) to (h) of the text relating to anchorage points, and any other vehicle fitted with anchorage points and not falling within (b) to (i) in the last list, first used on or after 1 April 1987 must additionally be fitted with a three-point belt, lap or disabled person's belt for every forward-facing front seat which is not a specified passenger's seat. Thus, the 'Transit' type of vehicle will be required to have seat belts for all three front seats. Such vehicles must also be fitted with rear seat belts for passengers sitting in the rear of the vehicle who are using a forward-facing seat. Rear seat belts must be provided as follows:

(a) vehicles with not more than two forward-facing seats behind the driver's seat must have *either* an inertia reel belt for *at least one* of those seats, *or* a three-point, lap, disabled person's or child restraint belt for each of those seats;

(b) vehicles having more than two forward-facing seats behind the driver's seat must have either

   (i) an inertia reel belt for one of those seats being an outboard seat, and a three-point, lap, disabled person's or child restraint belt, for *at least one other* of those seats; or

  (ii) a three-point belt for one of those seats and either a child restraint or disabled person's belt for *at least one other* of those seats; or

 (iii) a three-point, lap, disabled person's or child restraint belt for each of those seats.

The rear seat belt provisions become a little easier to understand if one imagines, in terms of providing an opportunity for all rear seat passengers to 'belt up', that an inertia reel will count as two in the case of a vehicle with only two rear seats, and that an inertia reel belt will count as two in the case of a vehicle with more than two rear seats.

The use of a coach or minibus for the purpose of carrying a group of three or more children in connection with an organised trip is prohibited by reg. 48A unless the vehicle has at least as many forward-facing passenger seats as there are children, and each seat is fitted with seat belts. A disabled child in a wheelchair is disregarded for this purpose. For these purposes a child is a person who is 3 years or more but is under the age of 16. In the case of a coach or minibus first used on or after 1 October 2001, a rearward-facing seat is treated as a forward-facing seat if it has the appropriate anchorage point and belt.

Without prejudice to the generality of these requirements, a group of such children will be regarded as being on an organised trip if they are being carried to or from their school or from one part of their school premises to another.

A minibus not exceeding 3500 kg gross weight, motor ambulance or motor caravan first used on or after 1 October 1988 must have three-point belts for the driver's and specified passenger's seats and a three-point or lap belt for any other forward-facing front seat. A coach first used on or after 1 October 1988 but before 1 October 2001 must have three-point, lap or disabled person's belts for all exposed forward-facing front seats. Goods vehicles first used on or after 1 October 2001 and having a maximum gross weight exceeding 3500 kg must have a three-point belt or lap belt for the driver's seat and such a belt or a disabled person's belt for every forward-facing front seat. A bus falling within item (g) in the list relating to anchorage points must be fitted, in respect of every forward- and rearward-facing seat, with an inertia reel belt, a retractable lap belt, a disabled person's belt or a child restraint. In the case of a bus falling within (h) the requirements are the same in respect of every forward- and rearward-facing seat except that a retractable lap belt may not be fitted in respect of a forward-facing seat.

Where lap belts are fitted to a forward-facing seat of a minibus, motor ambulance or motor caravan or to an exposed forward-facing seat of a coach (other than the driver's seat), either the requirements of Annex 4 to ECE Regulation 21 must be met, or padding to a depth of not less than 50 mm must be provided on that part of the surface or edge of any bar or the top or edge of any screen or partition which would be likely to be struck by the head of a passenger wearing the lap belt in the event of an accident. Padding need not be provided on any surface more than 1 m from the centre of the line of intersection of the seat cushion and the back rest, or on the instrument panel of a minibus. The revised provisions concerning padding apply to vehicles registered from 7 September 1989 after 7 September 1990. Such padding must extend for not less than 150 mm on either side of the central point of the seat. Thus, persons who may be thrown forward, and thereby come into contact with obstructions in front of them, are less likely to be seriously injured.

The requirements concerning the fitting of seat belts generally do not apply to vehicles being used under a trade licence or new vehicles in the course of delivery, nor do they apply (except in relation to the driver's seat or a front passenger seat) to vehicles constructed or adapted for the secure transport of prisoners.

Maintenance of seat belts

It is an offence to fail to maintain seat belts and their anchorage points. Buckles must be maintained so that they can be readily fastened and unfastened, and they must be kept free of any obstruction which would prevent them from becoming readily accessible to a person using the seat. Each end of a seat belt must be securely fastened to its anchorage point and the webbing must be free of cuts and other visible faults likely to affect its performance under stress. Within 30 cm of a seat belt anchorage point, the load-bearing members or panelling of the vehicle structure must be maintained in sound condition.

Wearing of seat belts

The circumstances in which seat belts must be worn by passengers in motor vehicle are prescribed in the Motor Vehicles (Wearing of Seat Belts) Regulations 1993 and the Motor Vehicles (Wearing of Seat Belts by Children in Front Seats) Regulations 1993. The 1993 Regulations implement the requirements of Council Directive 91/671/EEC, which only applies to vehicles of less than 3.5 tonnes which have four or more wheels and a design speed of more than 25 kph. The Directive does not apply to passenger vehicles with more than eight passenger seats if they are designed to carry standing passengers. Vehicles within the scope of the Directive with not more than eight seats in addition to the driver's seat are referred to in the Regulations as 'passenger cars'.

The offences committed by breaches of the Regulations are punishable under the Road Traffic Act 1988, ss 14 and 15, as amended by the Road Traffic Act 1988 (Amendment) Regulations 1992. The requirements created by the 1993 Regulations are not always confined to the description of vehicles set out in the Directive.

Front seat adult passengers

Regulation 5 of the Motor Vehicles (Wearing of Seat Belts) Regulations 1993 requires that every person driving or riding in the front seat of a motor vehicle (other than a two-wheeled motor cycle with or without sidecar) must wear an adult seat belt. The regulation does not apply to a person under the age of 14 years, nor does it apply if no seat belt is provided for a driver, or is not available for a front seat passenger. Failure to comply with reg. 5 is an offence under the Road Traffic Act 1988, s 14(3).

Regulation 6 provides the following exemptions from the requirement to wear a seat belt made by reg. 5:

(a) a person holding a medical certificate (including that of a member State);
(b) a person using a vehicle constructed or adapted for the delivery of goods or mail to consumers or addresses, while engaged in making local rounds of deliveries or collections;
(c) a person performing a manoeuvre which includes reversing;
(d) a qualified driver supervising a learner carrying out such a manoeuvre;
(e) a person by whom a test of competence to drive is being conducted where wearing a seat belt would endanger himself or another person;
(f) a person driving or riding in a vehicle being used for fire brigade or police purposes or for carrying a person in lawful custody (this includes the prisoner);
(g) the driver of a licensed taxi whilst being used to seek hire or answer a call, or when carrying a passenger for hire, or a private hire car whilst it is being used to carry a passenger for hire;
(h) a person in a vehicle being used under a trade licence for investigating or remedying a fault;
(i) a disabled person who is wearing a disabled person's belt; or
(j) a person riding in a vehicle whilst it is in a Crown Procession.

In addition to (j), a person who is riding in a vehicle which is taking part in a procession which is being held to commemorate an event if either the procession is one commonly or customarily held in a police area or areas, or notice in respect of the procession has been given in accordance with the Public Order Act 1986, s 11 (see page 483).

Rear seat adult passengers

Regulation 5 also prohibits an adult person (i.e. someone aged 14 or over) from riding in the rear seat of a motor car, or of a passenger car which is not a motor car, if that person is not wearing an adult seat belt provided in the vehicle. Persons who fail to comply offend against the Road Traffic Act 1988, s 14(3).

Front seat child passengers

It is an offence contrary to the Road Traffic Act 1988, ss 15(1) and (2), for a person, without reasonable excuse, to drive a motor vehicle on a road in which a child under the age of 14 is in the front of that vehicle unless the child is wearing a seat belt in conformity with the Motor Vehicles (Wearing of Seat Belts by Children in Front Seats) Regulations 1993. Generally, it is irrelevant that a seat belt is not provided or available for the seat. The Regulations set out the rules with which a driver must conform. A 'front seat' is one which is wholly or partially in the front of the vehicle. The regulations do not apply to two-wheeled motor cycles, with or without sidecars.

The description of the seat belts which satisfy the requirements of the Regulations is prescribed in reg. 5:

(a) in the case of a 'small child' travelling in a passenger car, light goods vehicle (not exceeding 3.5 tonnes) or a small bus (more than eight passenger seats not exceeding 3.5 tonnes) the seat belt must be a child restraint with a marking required under the Road Vehicles (Construction and Use) Regulations 1986, reg. 47(7), or a child restraint approved by another member State;

(b) in the case of a 'small child' in any other vehicle, the seat belt must be a child restraint approved under reg. 47(7);

(c) in the case of a 'large child', the seat belt must be a child restraint approved under reg. 47(7) or an adult belt.

A 'small child' is a child who is under 12 and under 150 cm in height and a 'large child' is a child under 14 who is not a 'small child'.

Regulation 7 exempts from these provisions:

(a) a 'small child' aged three or more if a prescribed seat belt is not available for him *in the front or rear* of the vehicle and he is wearing an adult belt;

(b) a child for whom there is a medical certificate (including one issued in a member State);

(c) a child under the age of one in a carry cot provided that it is restrained by straps;

(d) a disabled child who is wearing a disabled person's belt; or

(e) a child riding in a motor car first used before 1 January 1965 if
  (i) the vehicle has no rear seat; and
  (ii) apart from the driver's seat, no seat in the vehicle is provided with a seat belt which is appropriate for that child.

In addition, the prohibition created by s 15 does not apply in relation to a child riding in a vehicle which is being used to provide a local service within the meaning of the Transport Act 1985 and is neither a motor car nor a passenger car. The prohibition does not apply in relation to a 'large child' if no appropriate seat belt is available for him in the front of the vehicle.

Rear seat child passengers

The Road Traffic Act 1988, ss 15(3) and (3A), make it an offence for a person, without reasonable excuse, to drive a motor vehicle on a road if there is a child of under 14 in the rear of it who is not wearing a seat belt fitted there or, in the case of a 'small child', if there is no rear seat belt and there is an unoccupied seat in the front which is fitted with an appropriate seat belt. Exemption from these requirements is provided by the Motor Vehicles (Wearing of Seat Belts) Regulations 1993, reg. 9. An offence is not committed where the vehicle is neither a motor car nor a passenger car or where the vehicle is a licensed taxi or licensed hire car in which (in each case) the rear seats are separated from the driver by a fixed partition. Further exemptions are provided by reg. 10:

(a) where a seat belt of a description prescribed by reg. 8 (i.e. an approved child restraint) is not available to a 'small child' aged three or more in the front or rear of the vehicle and he is wearing an adult seat belt;
(b) where the child holds an approved medical certificate (including that of a member State);
(c) where a child under the age of one is being carried in a carry cot provided that it is restrained by straps; and
(d) where a disabled child is wearing a disabled person's belt.

The prohibition against the carriage of a child in the rear of a vehicle who is not wearing a seat belt does not apply in relation to a 'small child' in a passenger car if no appropriate seat belt is available to him in the front or rear of the vehicle. Nor does it apply to such a child in the rear of a vehicle other than a passenger car in such circumstances. There is also an exemption in favour of a 'large child' where, in any vehicle, no appropriate seat belt is available to him.

Availability of seat belts

Schedule 2 of the 1993 Regulations describes the circumstances in which a seat belt will be regarded as not being available. They are where:

(a) another person is wearing the relevant belt;
(b) a child is occupying the relevant seat and wearing a child restraint which is an appropriate child restraint for that child and this renders use of the seat belt impracticable;
(c) a person holding a medical certificate is occupying the relevant seat;
(d) a disabled person (not being the person in question) is occupying the relevant seat and wearing a disabled person's belt and this renders use of the seat impracticable;
(e) by reason of his disability, it would not be practicable for the person in question to wear the relevant belt;
(f) the seat is occupied by a carry cot containing a child under one and that cot is secured by straps and it would not be practicable to carry the cot, suitably restrained, elsewhere;
(g) the person in question is prevented from occupying the relevant seat by the presence of a child restraint which could not readily be removed without the use of tools; or
(h) the relevant seat is so designed that it can be adjusted to increase the space available for goods and effects and when it is so adjusted the seat cannot be used.

Steering gear

All steering gear fitted to a motor vehicle shall, at all times when the vehicle is used on a road, be maintained in good and efficient working order and shall be properly adjusted. This regulation is general in nature and there are so many moving parts in a steering system that a defect may exist in many places. Defective steering systems are usually detected by over-stiffness in movement, which indicates lack of lubrication, or by excessive movement at the steering wheel without any movement being transmitted to the appropriate road wheels, which suggests lack of adjustment or excessive wear in joints.

Tyres

Tyre defects

No person shall use, cause or permit to be used on a road, a motor vehicle or trailer of which a tyre:

(a) is unsuitable for the use to which the vehicle, etc., is being put;

(b) is wrongly inflated for that use;

(c) has a cut exceeding 25 mm or 10 per cent of the section width of the tyre, which-ever is the greater, in any direction and reaching the ply or body cords;

(d) has a lump, bulge or tear caused by separation or partial failure of the structure;

(e) has a portion of the ply or cord structure exposed;

(f) possesses any groove which showed in the original tread pattern of the tyre and which is not clearly visible; or

(g) either does not have a depth of 1 mm in the grooves of the tread pattern through-out a continuous band measuring at least three-quarters of the breadth of the tyre and round its entire circumference or, if the grooves of the original tread pattern of the tyre did not extend beyond three-quarters of the breadth of the tread, any groove which showed in the original tread pattern does not have a depth of at least 1 mm (see below for requirement of 1.6 mm on some vehicles); or

(h) is not maintained in such condition as to be fit for the use to which the vehicle or trailer is being put or has a defect which may in any way cause damage to the sur-face of the road or damage to persons on or in the vehicle or to other persons using the road.

This regulation is extremely comprehensive. Any defect in a tyre which may cause danger is covered by these requirements. The contact area of a tyre must have visible tread which must be at least 1 mm deep for three-quarters of the contact area. The regulation makes special provisions to allow the use of a tyre which will operate satis-factorily when deflated. It also prohibits the use of recut pneumatic tyres if the ply or cord has been exposed in the recutting process.

With effect from 1 January 1992:

(i) passenger vehicles other than motor cycles constructed or adapted to carry no more than eight seated passengers in addition to the driver;

(ii) goods vehicles with a maximum gross weight which does not exceed 3500 kg; and

(iii) light trailers not falling within sub-paragraph (ii)

first used on or after 3 January 1933 are not subject to the provisions set out in (f) and (g) above. With regard to such vehicles, these provisions are replaced by a requirement that the grooves of the tread pattern shall be of a depth of at least *1.6 mm* throughout a continuous band comprising the central three-quarters of the breadth of tread and round the entire circumference of the tyre.

Mixture of tyres

No person shall use or cause or permit to be used on a road a vehicle if pneumatic tyres of different types of structure are fitted to the same axle of the vehicle. The regulations mention three types of tyres:

(a) diagonal-ply tyres which are commonly known as cross-ply tyres;
(b) bias-belted tyres which are as above but have a reinforcing band around the outer circumference of the tyre, under the tread, but on top of the cords;
(c) radial-ply tyres.

The regulation also provides that a motor vehicle, having only two axles, must not be fitted with the following combination of tyres: cross-ply or bias-belted tyres on the rear axle and radials on the front; and cross-ply on the rear axle and bias-belted on the front. These provisions are designed to prevent a 'gripping' tyre from being fitted to the steering wheels whilst a tyre which is not so stable is fitted to the rear.

Tyre checks

It can be seen, therefore, that there are many statutory requirements in relation to tyres, and vehicle checks must be thorough. A check might begin with an examination for a mixture of tyres on the same axle and if there are cross-plies on the rear axle a check that radials or bias-belted are not fitted to the front axle. Individual tyres should be examined for depth of tread (gauges are provided for this purpose), and defects such as bulges, cuts, incorrect tyre pressures or exposed cord. The references to the base of any groove showing in the original tread not being visible refer to smooth patches where the tread has disappeared.

Windscreen wipers and washers

All vehicles which are fitted with windscreens must be fitted with at least one automatic efficient windscreen wiper which is capable of clearing the windscreen sufficiently to give an adequate view to the front of both sides of the vehicle and to the front of it. The only exceptions are in respect of vehicles which have a windscreen which opens (now rare) or which it is possible to see over. Windscreen wipers required by the regulation must be properly maintained at all times when the vehicle is used on a road. However, it must be remembered that only one wiper, that for the driver, is required by law and it is not necessarily an offence to fail to maintain a wiper fitted to the passenger side of a vehicle, unless two wipers are necessary to give the driver an adequate view to the front, of both sides of the vehicle and to the front of it.

The provision of wipers would be of little effect if vehicles which are required to have wipers were not also required to have windscreen washers fitted. The washers must be capable of cleaning, with the assistance of the wiper, the area swept by the wiper blade. Washers must be fitted to all such vehicles, except vehicles incapable of exceeding 20 mph, agricultural motor vehicles and vehicles being used to provide a local bus service.

Instrument for measuring and controlling speed

Speedometer

The general rule is that all motor vehicles must be fitted with a speedometer. However, some vehicles are exempt: invalid carriages, motor cycles not exceeding 100 cc and works trucks (provided that in each case they were first used before 1 April 1984), agricultural vehicles which are not driven at more than 20 mph, vehicles which legally or physically cannot exceed 25 mph and those which have an alternative type of approved instrument. Vehicles first used before 1 October 1937 are also exempt.

Speedometers must be kept free of any obstruction which might prevent them from being easily read and must at all times be kept in good working order. It is a defence to prove that a defect arose in the course of the journey then being undertaken or that steps had already been taken to have repairs or replacements effected as soon as possible. These defences eliminate the possibility of charges in all but those cases in which there is an admission of a long-standing defect by the driver or where the condition of the parts indicates that the instrument has not been working for some time.

Speed limiter

Most buses and goods vehicles which exceed 7.5 tonnes maximum gross weight are required to be fitted with speed limiters. Where such requirements exist the vehicle will be fitted with a plate in a conspicuous position in the driving compartment of the vehicle. The plate will be clearly and indelibly marked with the speed at which the speed limiter has been set.

Coaches first used on or after 1 April 1974 and before 1 January 1988 must be fitted with a speed limiter calibrated to a set speed not exceeding 112.65 kph; those first used on or after 1 January 1998 will be limited to 100 kph. Those goods vehicles exceeding 7500 kg but not exceeding 12 000 kg and first used on or after 1 August 1992 will be limited to 60 mph and those exceeding 12 000 kg, first used on or after 1 January 1988 will be limited to 85 kph.

All such speed limiters must be sealed against improper interference or adjustment and against interference with the power supply and must be maintained in good and efficient working order.

Defences exist where a defect has occurred in the course of a journey or where the vehicle is being taken to a place where a speed limiter is to be installed, calibrated, repaired or replaced. Vehicles used by some Crown and emergency services are specifically exempted.

Maintenance of glass

All glass or other transparent material fitted to a motor vehicle shall be maintained in such condition that it does not obscure the vision of the driver while the vehicle is being driven on a road. The provisions of this regulation are frequently ignored by early morning drivers following a severe frost. It is not enough to clear a small portion of glass through which a driver can see. *All* glass or transparent material must be maintained in a suitable condition.

Petrol tank

All fuel tanks must be constructed and maintained so that leakage of any liquid or vapour from the tank is adequately prevented. Where filler caps are lost, vapour will escape from the tank unless it is adequately plugged and this cannot be done with porous material. However, it must be remembered that a driver who loses his filler cap will reasonably expect that he will be allowed to proceed to a garage or accessory shop to replace it provided that reasonable provision has been made to prevent leakage.

Wings

All invalid carriages, heavy motor cars and motor cycles, not being agricultural vehicles or pedestrian-controlled vehicles, shall be fitted with wings or similar fittings to catch, as far as practicable, mud or water thrown up by the wheels, unless adequate protection is afforded by the body of the vehicle. There are certain exceptions, which include unfinished vehicles and articulated vehicles used only for the carriage of round timber.

The rear wheels of trailers must be fitted with wings, where the trailer has more than two wheels.

Duties of drivers and others

Some of the regulations contained in the Road Vehicles (Construction and Use) Regulations 1986 are concerned with prohibiting the driver of a vehicle from carrying out certain actions. We will examine some of these.

Position of driver

A driver must always be in such a position to have proper control of the vehicle and a full view of the road and traffic ahead. It is also an offence for any other person to cause or permit a driver to be in such a position that full control of the vehicle is not retained.

Danger

Reference has already been made on page 375 to the offences under the Road Traffic Act 1988, s 40A, of using, causing or permitting the use of a motor vehicle or trailer which is in a dangerous condition because of the condition of the vehicle's accessories or equipment, the purpose of its use, the number of passengers carried or the manner of their carriage and the weight, or distribution or security of the load, etc. It is submitted that most offences involving dangerous vehicles will now be charged under the Road Traffic Act 1988, s 40A, and not under s 42 (which covers most construction and use offences), since a conviction of an offence under s 40A involves the risk of discretionary disqualification and requires the obligatory endorsement of three penalty points. Where there is a conviction under s 42 for a breach of reg. 100 there can be no disqualification or endorsement of the offender's driving licence.

Regulation 100(1) requires that all motor vehicles and trailer and all parts and accessories must always be in such a condition that no danger is caused or is likely to be caused to persons being carried, or on a road. The regulation is concerned with the correct maintenance of all parts and accessories of vehicles which must always be in good working order. It was, therefore, held that when a ball and socket unit connecting a lorry to a trailer was in good repair, but incorrectly coupled, they were not in efficient working order. It is important to remember that, in any charge alleging failure to maintain a vehicle, the particular defects must be specified in the charge. Separate and distinct offences are involved in using a defective motor vehicle and a defective trailer on a road. This equally applies to articulated vehicles.

A breach of reg. 100(1) is also committed if the number of passengers in a vehicle is excessive, or, because of the manner of their carriage, danger may be caused. When a small car designed to carry four passengers was driven with eight persons aboard, it was found that at any speed other than a low one, the steering of the vehicle was affected and that this constituted an offence of driving in an unsafe or unroadworthy condition.

One of the most common offences committed under reg. 100(1) is that of faulty loading, or security of the load. Unfortunately, these offences often become apparent when the load, or part of it, has fallen from the vehicle. It must be stressed that reg. 100(1) is concerned with badly loaded vehicles which cause danger by the manner in which the load is carried. Regulation 100(2) requires that loads, where necessary, must be secured by physical restraint other than their own weight and that loads must be so positioned that neither danger nor nuisance is likely to be caused to persons or property by reason of the load, or part of it, falling or being blown from the vehicle, or by reason or movement of the load or vehicle. Where two large vats were knocked from a vehicle when it was driven under a pedestrian bridge, the High Court ruled that something 'fell' from a vehicle whether it fell because it was not securely strapped to the vehicle or because it had been knocked off the vehicle. In deciding whether a load was so secured that neither danger nor nuisance was likely to be caused four things must be considered:

(a) the nature of the journey;
(b) the way in which the load was secured;
(c) the way in which the load was positioned; and
(d) the journey to be taken.

What might be secure for one journey in fine weather and on good roads might not be secure for another journey in poor weather and on less good roads.

It is an offence contrary to reg. 100(3) to use a vehicle or trailer for a purpose for which it is unsuitable, so as to cause such danger or nuisance to persons in or on that vehicle or trailer or on a road.

However, where a vehicle or trailer is designed for the purpose of carrying goods and is capable of carrying those goods without danger if properly loaded, it is suitable for that purpose. Thus, if a trailer is loaded with a machine which would pass under a bridge with that load if properly loaded, an offence does not lie under reg. 100(3) if the load strikes the bridge. A charge under reg. 100(2) would be appropriate.

The responsibility of the driver is absolute and it is no defence that the loading was carried out by some other persons, although such person may also be in breach of the regulation. It has been held that where crates fall from a lorry when taking a bend, the driver may be convicted although the crates were loaded by another person. Remember, however, that in all circumstances where danger can be proved the most appropriate charge will probably be one contrary to the Road Traffic Act 1988, s 40A.

Noise

Permitted noise levels of vehicles are prescribed by the Construction and Use Regulations and are measured at the time of manufacture by a device known as a sound level meter. Drivers are also required to prevent the use of vehicles on roads in a manner which causes excessive noise which could reasonably have been avoided. This last offence is committed by those drivers, particularly motor cyclists, who 'rev' up the engines of their vehicles while stationary.

Unnecessary obstruction

A person in charge of a motor vehicle must not cause or permit that vehicle to stand on a road so as to cause unnecessary obstruction. It has been held that to leave a vehicle on a road for an 'unreasonable' time may constitute an unnecessary obstruction, but if the driver has only left his car for a 'reasonable' time, this does not amount to an unnecessary obstruction. The duration of an obstruction, the characteristics of the road at the particular place, the purpose for which the vehicle was parked and the actual degree of obstruction caused are all matters which the court will consider in deciding whether or not an obstruction had been caused.

Exemptions provided by 'no-waiting' orders in favour of loading and unloading have led to many goods vehicle drivers double-parking, often completely blocking a road. This is an obstruction and it will be so where a road, which normally permits two-way traffic, is reduced to a one-way flow.

Doors

No person shall open, or cause to permit to be opened, any door of a motor vehicle or trailer while it is on a road, so as to cause injury or danger to any person.

Quitting

It is an offence for a person to leave or cause or permit a motor vehicle to be left on a road which is unattended by a person who is licensed to drive it unless the engine has been stopped and the brake set. Fire engines at work, or vehicles being used for police or ambulance purposes, are included in the exemptions. The peculiarity of this charge is that the word 'and' is used and it is, therefore, apparent that the driver is required to do two things: to stop the engine and set the handbrake. Failure to do one or the other amounts to an offence.

Reversing

The offence lies in causing or permitting a motor vehicle to travel backwards for a greater distance or time than may be required for the safety or reasonable convenience of the occupants of the vehicle, or other traffic on the road. This regulation is provided to reinforce the common sense assumption that the safest way to propel a motor vehicle is in a forward direction, when the driver has a full view of traffic ahead and to both sides. Reversing is at times necessary, but can only safely be carried out for a limited time owing to the necessity for the driver either to look over his shoulder or to rely upon driving mirrors. If it is unreasonable, and drivers have been known to reverse at fast speeds over considerable distances, then an offence has been committed. The presence of other traffic and pedestrians, combined with other factors such as the passing of possible turning points and the overall distance travelled, can combine to provide good evidence of such an offence. It is always a good guide to respond only to situations which make you fear for the safety of the public.

Tow ropes

Where a motor vehicle is drawing a trailer by means of a rope or chain, the rope or chain shall be of such a length that the nearest points of both vehicles are no more than 4.5 m (15 ft) apart. In assessing this distance, towing attachments shall be disregarded. If a tow rope or chain exceeds 1.5 m (5 ft), it must be made clearly visible to all road users within a reasonable distance on each side.

Testing and inspection

On a road

The powers of constables and examiners to inspect vehicles are contained in the Road Traffic Act 1988 and the Road Vehicles (Construction and Use) Regulations 1986.

The Road Traffic Act 1988, s 67, permits authorised examiners to test a motor vehicle on a road for the purpose of ascertaining whether the requirements relating to construction and use and the requirement that the condition of the vehicle is not such that its use on a road would involve danger of injury to any person are being complied with.

For the purposes of testing a vehicle an examiner may require the driver to comply with his reasonable instructions and may drive the vehicle. The term 'authorised examiners' includes vehicle examiners appointed under s 66A of the Road Traffic Act 1988 by the Secretary of State and constables authorised by their chief officer of police. Only a constable in uniform may stop vehicles for a test. In the case of normal checks, the driver may elect that the test be deferred. In certain circumstances, for example, following an accident on a road or where, in his opinion, the vehicle is apparently so defective that it should not be allowed to proceed without being tested, the constable may require the test to be carried out immediately. If the constable concerned is not himself authorised by his chief officer of police to carry out such tests, the officer may insist that the vehicle is not removed before testing.

However, this does not mean that the provisions of the Road Vehicles (Construction and Use) Regulations 1986 can only be enforced by authorised constables. Particular offences may and should be dealt with by any constable. If this is not done the right to defer examination will be exercised where a full vehicle examination is proposed and the defect will be remedied before that examination takes place. Where a constable who was not an authorised examiner tested the efficiency of a handbrake with the driver's consent, evidence of his findings was admitted. There is a difference between a formal examination of a vehicle and dealing with infringements of the regulations.

Traffic wardens are authorised to stop motor vehicles for the purpose of tests under s 67.

Prohibition of unfit vehicles

The Road Traffic Act 1988, s 69, empowers an authorised constable to issue an immediate prohibition notice, if on inspection under s 41, 45, 49, 61, 67, 68 or 77 it appears to him that owing to any defects in the vehicle, driving it (or driving it for any particular purpose or purposes or for any except one or more particular purposes) would involve a danger of injury to any person. The sections referred to deal with powers in relation to construction and use, test certificates generally, inspections related to plated weights of goods vehicles, public service vehicles and vehicles adapted to carry more than eight passengers which are not public service vehicles and the testing of the condition of used vehicles at sale rooms, etc. A notice under s 69 may prohibit use absolutely, or for one or more specified purposes, or except for one or more specified purposes.

Vehicle examiners appointed under s 66A have a similar power.

The Road Vehicles (Prohibition) Regulations 1992 make provision for a vehicle which is subject to a prohibition issued by an authorised constable or vehicle examiner to be used on a road for the purpose of submitting it, by arrangement, for test with a view to the removal of that prohibition, within 3 miles from where it is being, or has been repaired, solely for the purpose of test or trial, and during any test for the purpose of the removal of the prohibition. Evidence that a vehicle is being driven in contravention of a prohibition order may be some evidence of it being used in contravention of the Road Traffic Act 1988, s 2.

Off-road

The Construction and Use Regulations are concerned with the testing of motor vehicles on premises. Constables in uniform and authorised examiners may carry out such tests with the permission of the owner of the premises. If the owner of the vehicle refuses permission, notice may be served upon him, not less than 48 hours before the time of the proposed test (or 72 hours before if by recorded delivery service), setting out the date and time of the proposed test. However, if the test and inspection are made within 48 hours of an accident which is required to be reported by law, such notice will not be necessary. The owner, for the purpose of this regulation, is the registered owner or, if used under a trade licence, the holder of the licence.

Traffic signs and pedestrian crossings

Traffic signs

Traffic signs are used to control and guide traffic and to promote road safety. The term 'traffic sign' means any object or device (whether fixed or portable) for conveying to traffic on roads or any specified class of traffic warnings, information, requirements, restrictions or prohibitions of any description which are specified by regulations. The bulk of legislation concerning the placing of traffic signs is to be found in the Road Traffic Regulation Act 1984 and the Traffic Signs Regulations and General Directions 2002.

Traffic signs may be placed on or near a road by the highway authority and in certain circumstances police officers may also place signs. There are many types of sign prescribed by statute and it would make the enforcement of the law unnecessarily tedious if, upon each occasion when proceedings were taken against an offender, it was essential to prove that the sign complied in form and content with the regulations. A traffic sign placed on or near a road is deemed to be of the prescribed size, colour and type authorised by the Minister unless the contrary is proved. The burden of proof, therefore, lies upon the defendant to prove that a sign is defective. However, if the issue is raised by the defence it will be for the prosecution to prove that the sign and road markings were in order. Account must therefore be taken of such matters. There is also a presumption that automatic traffic lights are in working order unless the contrary is proved.

In offences of non-compliance with the directions given by a traffic sign, it is no defence for a driver to allege that he did not see the sign, as guilty knowledge is not essential and the requirement to comply is absolute. It may be a defence that a sudden mechanical defect occurred in the vehicle which the driver could not have foreseen. Although various types of sign are described in the regulations, the offences are contrary to s 36 of the Road Traffic Act 1988, which provides the penalty for non-compliance with the directions given by certain traffic signs.

Traffic signs placed by the police

By the Road Traffic Regulation Act 1984, s 66, a constable, or other person acting under instructions (whether general or specific) of a chief officer of police, may place on a highway such authorised traffic signs indicating prohibitions, restrictions or requirements relating to vehicular traffic as may be required to prevent an obstruction on public occasions or near public buildings or at an authorised cycle race. This section authorises police officers to place emergency signs on the road at special events such as air displays. A second power is given by s 67 to a police officer, or a person under instructions (whether general or specific) of a chief officer of police, to place on a highway authorised traffic signs indicating prohibitions, restrictions or requirements to prevent or mitigate congestion or obstruction of traffic, or danger to or from traffic in consequence of extraordinary circumstances. Among other things, this section authorises the police to place emergency signs on a road at the scene of an accident. Such signs may be maintained for a maximum of 7 days. The 'time-clock' in relation to such a period of 7 days starts when the signs are placed so that a sign placed at 9 a.m. on a particular day must be removed by 9 a.m. 7 days after placement.

Failure to comply with such a sign constitutes an offence against the Road Traffic Act 1988, s 36.

Failing to conform to traffic signs

Section 36 of the Road Traffic Act 1988 creates the offence of failing to comply with the indication given by a traffic sign. Section 35 deals with the offence of failing to comply with a signal given by a constable or traffic warden who is engaged in the regulation of traffic on a road. An offence is committed by a driver who neglects or refuses to stop the vehicle, or to make it proceed in, or keep to, a particular line of traffic when directed to do so by a constable or traffic warden in the execution of his duty. The section, therefore, gives statutory backing to the signals given by a constable on point duty.

In addition, s 163 of the Road Traffic Act 1988 requires the drivers of motor vehicles and riders of pedal cycles to stop on being so required by a constable in uniform. It is an offence to fail to do so. Traffic wardens are also permitted to require vehicles to stop.

The police officer observes many failures to comply with traffic signs in the course of his duties and common offences include parking in contravention of emergency signs placed by the police, failing to stop at 'Stop' signs or to give way at 'Give way' signs, failures to comply with stop/go signs at road works, light signals at junctions and at railway crossings, failing to keep left or right as required, failing to comply with double white lines in the middle of the road, and ignoring 'No entry' signs or the signals of a police officer regulating traffic. All of these offences require notice of intended prosecution.

Meaning of certain traffic signs

Traffic lights

The red signal given by a traffic light indicates that traffic shall not proceed beyond the stop line on the carriageway provided in conjunction with the signal. If that line has become obscured or there is no line, traffic must not pass the post or object in which the light signals are contained.

The only exception to the rule that all traffic must halt at a red light relates to vehicles being used for police, fire or ambulance purposes if observance would hinder the use to which the vehicle was then being put, but this exception is not absolute and those vehicles must not proceed beyond such signals in such a manner or at such time as is likely to cause danger to the driver of any other vehicle, on that or any other road controlled by those lights or so as to necessitate the other driver to change speed or course in order to avoid an accident. The exception is, therefore, limited to cautious progress across such a junction when no other traffic will be interfered with.

Amber with red denotes an impending change to green but does not alter the prohibition set out above. It is an offence to pass the red with amber light. Amber on its own conveys a prohibition and vehicles may not pass unless, when the signal first appears the vehicle is so close to the signal that it cannot safely be stopped before passing. This frequently occurs when a continuous stream of traffic is passing the traffic lights. When a sudden change to amber occurs when a moving vehicle is up to the light, the driver must consider the advisability of braking if following traffic is close behind him. Discretion must be used in such instances; there is a considerable difference between the driver who is close to the signal at the time of the change and chooses to proceed because of the presence of following traffic and the driver who chooses to shoot the lights.

A green signal indicates that vehicular traffic may pass the signals and may proceed straight on or to the left or to the right. A green arrow indicates that traffic may proceed in the direction shown by the arrow, regardless of the signals shown by other lights.

'Stop' signs

The modern 'Stop' sign is octagonal and coloured red with the word 'Stop' in white capitals on it. The sign is used in conjunction with two solid white transverse lines marking the point at which a vehicle must stop on the road. The word 'Stop' is also painted on the roadway. The sign requires that every vehicle shall, before entering the major road, stop at the transverse lines at the junction or, if these lines are not visible, at the junction with the major road.

No vehicle shall proceed past the transverse line or the junction as the case may be so as to enter into the major road in such a manner or at such a time as is likely to cause danger to the driver of another vehicle on the major road or to cause the driver to change speed or direction to avoid an accident. It will be seen that it is not sufficient to stop; the vehicle must not proceed at any time at which it is likely to interfere with traffic on the major road.

'Give way' signs

A 'Give way' sign consists of a red inverted triangle with the words 'Give way' in black lettering on a white background. These signs are used in conjunction with two broken white lines at the junction of the road with the major road and an inverted white triangle on the road surface of the minor road at the approach to the junction.

Although there is no requirement to stop, a driver must give way to traffic on the major road and must not enter the major road in such a manner as to be likely to cause danger or a collision with a vehicle on the major road or to cause that vehicle to change its speed or course. The offence is a common one and it is important for a constable to recognise that all that is needed to prove the offence is that the vehicle proceeded beyond the broken white lines or in to the major road and caused danger, etc. On many occasions when accidents occur at such junctions and a plea of not guilty is entered, the defendant experiences great difficulty in explaining how it is that he emerged from the junction safely, but nevertheless an accident occurred. The usual allegation is that he did not see the vehicle which he struck. If it was there and it was not seen, it is submitted that there may also be an offence of careless driving.

'Stop' and 'Give way' signs must be illuminated during the hours of darkness if they are within 50 m of an electric street lamp. Those signs not within 50 m of an electric street lamp and which are not illuminated must be of reflective material. It will be appreciated that it would be impossible to illuminate such signs in the middle of the countryside.

Carriageway markings (double white lines)

The Road Traffic Regulation Act 1984 permits certain lines or marks on the road to be regarded as traffic signs in themselves without necessarily being supported by signs of any description. The single white lines marked on the road are not traffic signs in the sense that they are not connected with offences against s 36 of the Road Traffic Act 1988. However, the presence of such lines on the road might be significant in a prosecution for careless driving.

Regulation 26 of the 2002 Traffic Signs, etc., Regulations authorises the placing of double white lines, which may consist of two continuous white lines or one continuous white line together with a broken white line. Any white unbroken line must be immediately preceded with a white warning arrow painted on the road, otherwise the line is not an authorised traffic sign. If there are two continuous white lines, vehicles travelling in both directions must at all times keep to the nearside of the nearest continuous line. If there is a continuous line with a broken line, the vehicles are required to keep to the nearside of the continuous line when it is the nearer of those two lines to that vehicle. Those drivers who find the broken line nearest to their vehicles must not cross or straddle the line unless it is seen by the driver of the vehicle to be safe to do so.

However, these prohibitions upon crossing a continuous white line shall not apply to a vehicle which has to do so to obtain access to another road, land or premises, therefore, right turns made across the line into other roads, driveways or on to land are not prohibited. Drivers may also cross the line in order to pass stationary vehicles, to overtake a road maintenance vehicle, pedal cycle or horse moving at no more than 10 mph, or in circumstances outside the control of the driver or in order to avoid an accident, or for the purpose of complying with a direction given by a police constable in uniform or a traffic warden in uniform. These are merely common-sense exceptions to allow drivers to turn into their own access roads and to allow broken down or damaged vehicles to be overtaken with care, either by the driver himself or with the assistance of a constable or traffic warden who is controlling traffic.

No vehicle may stop on any length of road along which double white line markings have been placed. There are certain permitted stoppages and they are mainly predictable:

(a) to enable a person to board or alight from the vehicle;
(b) to enable goods to be loaded on to or unloaded from the vehicle;
(c) to enable essential road works;
(d) in connection with building operations or demolition;
(e) police, fire and ambulance usage;
(f) pedal cycles with sidecars (including power assisted);
(g) in circumstances where the driver is required by law to stop, or to avoid an accident, or in circumstances beyond the driver's control;
(h) when permission is given by a police constable in uniform or a traffic warden in uniform;
(i) to overtake a road maintenance vehicle, pedal cycle or horse moving at no more than 10 mph.

The various types of traffic sign

The understanding of the legislation concerning traffic signs is made easier if they are considered in relation to their purpose. Do they set out to inform, direct, warn, regulate or prohibit?

Informatory signs

When undertaking long journeys it can be extremely helpful to have certain points of information available concerning facilities which are provided in particular places. Informatory signs have, therefore, been placed to assist motorists. Examples of such signs, which usually consist of white lettering on a blue background, are the letter 'P' indicating a parking place, 'Dual carriageway ahead', 'Unsuitable for motors', 'Single track road with passing places', 'H' for hospital, 'Road clear', and 'Forton Services ½ m'.

Directional signs

The colouring and types of directional signs vary according to the types of road upon which they are displayed. On primary roads other than motorways, directional signs will carry white letters and symbols on a green background, the classifications of the roads approached being shown in gold letters and figures. To give more local information, other signs will appear at the roadside indicating the direction and the distance of local towns and villages, and these will be black lettering on a white background. Signs show the relative importance of each road by differing widths of the route symbol. Motorway signs consist of white symbols, letters and figures on a blue background. If travelling on a motorway *en route* for some town or village, the first sign to be met will indicate the turn off towards the nearest large town in the vicinity of our destination and will be of white symbols, letters and figures on a blue background. The directional arrow pointing ahead may show 'The North, Sheffield, Leeds', whereas the turn off arrow indicates 'Nottingham A52'. On leaving the motorway and joining the A52, which is a primary road, it is probable that the next sign to be met will be white lettering on a green background, which will indicate the direction of Nottingham and other large towns in the area. Steering towards the nearest town to our destination we may then meet a local sign of black lettering on a white background showing the turn off towards the village which we are seeking. When travelling the journey in reverse, the signs are met in opposite order, but those indicating the approach to primary roads and motorways include this information on the sign. As the A52 is approached the local sign will show its direction and will carry a small green square with the letter and figures 'A52' in gold, below the directional arrow. The approach to a motorway is similarly shown by a blue square with letters and figures in white below the directional arrow.

Other types of directional signs are authorised, many of which provide local information. Examples of these signs are arrowheaded signs carrying such information as 'Public Library', 'Council Offices', 'Free Car Park', 'Toilets'. Only traffic signs which are authorised by statute may be placed on or near a highway, and this control ensures that motorists experience little difficulty in recognising traffic signs as their colour, size and type become familiar.

Warning signs

The Romans probably eliminated the need for warning signs by making all of their roads straight, keeping junctions to a minimum, and thus avoiding many of the hazards which our modern roads provide. If we consider this situation and add to it our modern motor vehicles which are capable of travelling at great speed, a need for warning signs begins to appear. One of the penalties which results from making all roads straight is that they must be taken over ranges of hills rather than around them, and gradients begin to appear. Our first warning signs, therefore, become necessary to indicate steep hills. Warning signs consist of an upright red triangle surrounding black symbols on a white background, the symbols depicting the particular hazard to be met. On occasions letters or figures are also included in the sign to provide additional information. Our first sign, would, therefore, show a hill up or a hill down, supported by the figures 1:10, for example, to inform approaching drivers of the slope to be met.

As road development continues and tributary roads are constructed, the need to warn drivers of the presence of road junctions arises and warning signs appear showing the types of junctions which lie ahead, the presence of roundabouts, double bends, the fact that the road narrows or that there is a hump-backed bridge. In each case, a diagram in black sets out the particular hazard which is to be encountered.

Mandatory signs

This title can be given to both regulatory and prohibitory signs. They must be obeyed and an offence is committed if the driver of a motor car fails either to do what he is told to do or does that which is prohibited.

(a) *Regulatory signs* – The types of action which these signs require motorists to perform are to 'Stop' or 'Give way' and this requirement may be conveyed by a sign or by a light signal. The recognition of a regulatory sign lies in its message, rather than its form, as drivers will also face white arrows on a blue circular background, indicating the direction in which they must proceed, or white arrows with a right angle bend, on the circular background, meaning turn left or right ahead, as the case may be. The common factor is that the driver's actions are regulated by requiring him to do something in order to comply with the sign.

(b) *Prohibitory signs* – 'No right turn', 'No left turn', 'No U turns', 'All motor vehicles prohibited', 'Lorries prohibited', 'No overtaking' are all examples of actions which a motorist can be prohibited from doing by traffic signs. These types of signs are often without written instructions of any kind, the symbol included in the sign being sufficient for identification. The advantage of such signs is that their message is clear to all drivers, whether they are capable of reading the English language or not. The sign itself often consists of a red circle with a symbol contained inside it in black, on a white background. Thus a sign prohibiting right turns would carry a black arrow angled to the right with a red line cutting through the arrow to show that turns in that direction are prohibited. A sign denying access to all motor vehicles would carry diagrams of a motor car and a motor cycle in black, in each case surrounded by a red circle. On occasions, additional information is provided by fixing a plate on the supporting post. In the case of the sign prohibiting the entry of motor vehicles, such a plate may read 'Except for access', indicating that residents in that street and their visitors may enter with motor vehicles. Signs which prohibit waiting include a red outer circle surrounding a blue background with a red band cutting across the face from the top left to the bottom right of the sign as seen by approaching drivers. Information is often provided on a surrounding yellow sign and, on occasions, on a plate attached to the post supporting the sign, giving particular information concerning the nature of the prohibition; for example, a yellow plate with the words 'At any time' painted in black, showing a continuous prohibition on waiting. Similar signs may carry the words '8.00 a.m.–6.00 p.m.' and carry an arrow pointing to the direction in which waiting is prohibited between these hours, or the words 'No loading at any time' in black on a white background. In instances in which waiting is limited, rather than prohibited altogether, the signs will consist of white lettering on a blue background.

There are other signs which may be placed on the roadway to reinforce prohibitions in relation to waiting. A single, continuous, yellow line running parallel with the kerb restricts waiting (other than for loading or unloading) for a period of at least 8 hours between 7.00 a.m. and 7.00 p.m. on a minimum of four weekdays. A double, continuous, yellow line indicates these restrictions, but additionally there are restrictions on occasions which are outside the limits of 7.00 a.m. and 7.00 p.m. Broken yellow lines show waiting restrictions other than these shown by continuous lines, and usually appear for unilateral parking schemes, restricting waiting on certain sides of the road on particular days of the week. However, such road markings are only valid if used in conjunction with a plate of the type referred to above.

Restrictions upon waiting for the purpose of loading or unloading vehicles are shown by the provision of yellow lines running at a right angle to the kerb line: two lines restricting the waiting of goods vehicles in the same ways as the single continuous yellow line for all traffic, three lines having the same meaning as a double continuous line, and a single line to restrict such waiting in any other way, often for unilateral schemes.

Equipment for detection of traffic offences

Section 95A of the Highways Act 1980 permits a highway authority to install and maintain on or near a highway structures and equipment for the detection of traffic offences.

Provision is made by the Road Traffic Offenders Act 1988, s 20, for records produced by prescribed devices to be evidence, and in Scotland sufficient evidence, of a fact related to an offence involving a driver's failure to comply with a traffic sign. The record must provide, in the same or another document, a certificate as to the circumstances in which the record was produced, signed by a constable or person authorised by or on behalf of a chief officer of police for the area in which the offence is alleged to have been committed. The device must be an approved device, and for these purposes the Secretary of State has approved a device designed or adapted for recording by photographic or other image-recording means the position of motor vehicles in relation to light signals.

A copy of such evidence must be served on the person charged not less than 7 days before his trial. If the person charged, not less than 3 days before the hearing or trial, requires the attendance of the person who signed the document, the evidence of the circumstances in which the evidence was produced will not be admissible. The record produced by the device will.

Pedestrian crossings

In times during which an ever-increasing volume of vehicular traffic increases the dangers which pedestrians must face when attempting to cross roads, it becomes essential to provide crossings to safeguard pedestrians. There have been many experiments aimed at discovering the safest forms of pedestrian crossing and currently the three types to be met on our roads are zebra, pelican and puffin crossings. The main purpose of a pedestrian crossing is to safeguard pedestrians.

Zebra crossings

The zebra crossing is easily identifiable by its alternate black and white stripes, its flashing beacons and its zigzag approach lines. The limits of the crossing itself (the walking area for pedestrians) are shown by outer lines of studs, the area between being marked with alternative black and white stripes. The presence of a crossing is indicated to approaching drivers by flashing yellow globes, mounted on posts marked by black and white stripes. There must be flashing globes at each side of the crossing and if there is a central reservation or street refuge on the crossing, one or more globes may also be placed there. Failure of lamps does not prevent the crossing from being a valid zebra crossing, so that the provisions of the Regulations must still be complied with.

On each side of the crossing (or on one side only in the case of one-way traffic) an area is marked out which is known as the 'controlled area'. It is a defensive area before the crossing itself is reached and it is met by the approaching driver first coming to the 'terminal line' which is indicated by white lines situated at each kerb and on the crown of the road on the approaching driver's side. From this 'terminal line' three zigzag lines stretch, until they are halted 1 m from the studs of the pedestrian crossing itself by a broken white line which is known as the 'give way' line.

These regulations are concerned with zebra crossings at which traffic is not for the time being controlled by a police constable in uniform or a traffic warden. Immediately such an officer takes control of the movements of traffic at such a crossing, the crossing ceases to be an uncontrolled crossing and the provisions of the regulations do not apply.

Pelican and puffin crossings

The essential difference between a zebra crossing and pelican and puffin crossings is that, whereas the zebra crossing is uncontrolled, both the pelican and puffin crossings are controlled by a system of lights. A driver who ignores a red light at a pelican or puffin crossing commits an offence against reg. 23 by 'proceeding beyond the stop line' or, if that line is not visible, the post on which the light signal is mounted. At a puffin crossing, a red with amber signal denotes an impending change to green, but it conveys the same prohibition as a red signal. At either type of crossing a steady amber signal when shown alone conveys the same prohibition as a red signal (with the usual proviso applicable to traffic lights), and there may be a green arrow showing which signals that traffic may cross the stop line to proceed in a particular direction. There is an offence of failure to accord precedence when a driver passes a flashing amber light at a pelican crossing, denying precedence to a pedestrian who is on the crossing.

Both pelican and puffin crossings will have 'controlled areas' on each side of the crossing (or on one side in the case of one-way traffic), this controlled area being indicated by two or more zigzag lines stretching from the terminal line to the stop line, a line which is met before the limits of the crossing itself are reached. The primary signals shown to both drivers and pedestrians are by synchronised light signals. Whilst a steady green light is shown to drivers, a steady red light is shown to pedestrians. The light signals to pedestrians are, in the case of pelican crossings, steady red, steady green and flashing green figures reinforced by the illumination of a sign which reads 'WAIT'. Those at puffin crossings are by means of red and green figures and the green figure must only be capable of showing when a red light is indicated to drivers.

Audible signals may be used at pelican crossings to indicate to pedestrians when it is safe to cross.

Precedence at a zebra crossing

Foot passengers on an uncontrolled crossing have precedence over vehicles, and the driver of a vehicle must accord precedence if the foot passenger is within the limits of the crossing before any part of the vehicle has entered these limits. In instances in which a crossing is separated by a street refuge or central reservation, each part becomes a separate crossing so far as precedence is concerned. The driver of a vehicle commits an offence only if the pedestrian is on the carriageway within the limits of the crossing before any part of the vehicle enters the limits. A pedestrian who is waiting on the kerb does not raise the issue of precedence until stepping into the carriageway. Once this has been done, drivers must stop at or before the 'give way' line.

It has been decided that, where a driver is satisfied that persons on the crossing are no longer in danger from his vehicle, that driver may proceed at a reasonable speed. There is, therefore, no need for him to wait until the crossing is absolutely clear. If pedestrians are pushing a pram or baby carriage, precedence must be afforded immediately the carriage enters the crossing.

The duty to accord precedence is absolute, unless control of the vehicle is temporarily taken from the driver, such as would occur if his vehicle was struck from behind while stationary outside the limits of the crossing. It is unnecessary to prove negligence and convictions have been upheld in circumstances in which the view of a driver was obstructed on approach in such a way that he could not see if there were persons on the crossing.

When a driver was approaching a crossing at a reasonable speed and was only 10 yards from it, two children stepped on to the crossing without regard for traffic and he was unable to avoid one of them. He was found guilty of this offence.

It is, therefore, clear that drivers must approach crossings in such a manner that they are able to stop in all circumstances if the issue of precedence is raised. The only circumstances which may excuse such lack of precedence are those involving a sudden defect in the vehicle, where a vehicle is pushed on to a crossing by another vehicle or there is clear evidence that owing to circumstances beyond his control the driver could not discharge his responsibilities. Such instances will be rare.

Precedence at a pelican or puffin crossing

Both pelican and puffin crossings are 'light controlled' and the issue of precedence is determined, to a major extent, by the light signals which are showing at the time. There are specific offences within the Regulations dealing with failure to comply with such signals.

However, at pelican crossings a driver may encounter a flashing amber signal which indicates that pedestrians who are on the carriageway or a central reservation within the limits of the crossing before any part of the vehicle has entered those limits must be accorded precedence. It is an offence for a driver to fail to accord such precedence. The flashing amber signal is peculiar to pelican crossings alone and is not one of the signals shown at a puffin crossing.

Stopping on a crossing

Vehicles are not permitted to stop within the limits of a crossing unless in circumstances beyond the driver's control or when it is necessary to prevent an accident.

▰▰

Pedestrians are also prohibited from remaining in such limits longer than is necessary to cross with reasonable dispatch.

Stopping in a controlled area

The driver of a vehicle shall not cause any part of his vehicle to stop in a controlled area, that is, the part marked by zigzag lines between the terminal and 'give way' line. The object of this regulation is to prevent obstruction of the view of approaching drivers and it is, therefore, not surprising to find that pedal cycles with or without sidecars, whether mechanically assisted or not, are not included. It is also clear that vehicles will have to stop within the controlled area to accord precedence to foot passengers and this is permitted, as is the presence of vehicles of essential services, such as fire, police, ambulance, building, demolition, road construction, gas, sewage, electricity or telephone. Vehicles waiting to make a right turn and public service vehicles which have passed the crossing itself and require to set down or pick up passengers are also permitted to wait.

Overtaking in a controlled area

It is an offence, when approaching a crossing, to overtake another vehicle in the controlled area. Overtaking, for the purpose of this regulation, has been completed when any part of the vehicle moves ahead of the foremost part of another vehicle. The exceptions to the rule are, once again, common sense. If a number of vehicles are coming to a halt at a crossing to allow pedestrians precedence there will be a closing up towards the crossing itself. In these circumstances this offence is only committed if the moving vehicle nearest to the crossing is overtaken. If stationary vehicles are overtaken, it is only an offence if the vehicle overtaken has stopped to allow pedestrians to cross. If this was not so, a vehicle which was illegally parked in the controlled area would prevent other vehicles from proceeding.

School crossing patrols

Local authorities may appoint school crossing patrols for the purpose of assisting children, on their way to or from school, who are crossing or seeking to cross a road. School crossing patrols must wear a uniform approved by the Secretary of State (peaked cap or blue or black beret or yellow turban and a white dustcoat or raincoat which may carry fluorescent material). Arrangements may be made for patrolling such places at such times as the authority thinks fit.

They may require drivers to stop their vehicles by exhibiting a sign carrying the word 'Stop – Children' in black letters, with a black bar on a yellow fluorescent background surrounded by a red fluorescent border. It is an offence to fail to stop before reaching the place of crossing or the point at which the children are waiting to cross, or to set the vehicle in motion again while the sign remains displayed.

The sign must be exhibited in such a way that the word 'Stop' can be read by approaching drivers, who will commit an offence if they move off while the sign remains displayed whether children are crossing or not.

Introduction to statement writing

Introduction

A statement is a document made by or taken from a person containing details of the knowledge that person has of an incident. It is, therefore, a document containing a story told by, or written by, some person with a knowledge of an incident. A police officer recognises that it is necessary to record, in some particular way, most incidents dealt with. An officer will certainly make a record in a pocket notebook. From that record the officer may make out a report. On many occasions the officer will make out a statement of his own evidence, telling his own story of what occurred and the action which was taken. Frequently the officer will record a statement made by some other person. A statement provides a means of informing senior officers and prosecution departments of the evidence which will be given by persons who will later attend a court, and it is, therefore, important that it contains sufficient detail to make the facts clear.

Types of statement

The training of police recruits is fashioned, to some extent, on a need to know basis. Each lesson is examined to ensure that all aspects of law and procedure essential to the efficient discharge of a police officer's duties on the beat are explained. The approach to statement taking should be similar and we will examine different types of statement and their different levels of complexity. One form of statement writing is concerned with the commission of simple offences. It is the officer's statement describing that offence as he saw it committed and detailing the action taken. It will follow the rules of evidence. An occurrence statement contains all of the information concerning an incident which the person concerned can give. Its purpose is to gather all of the relevant information and it does not necessarily recognise the rules of evidence; hearsay and opinion might be included. For ease of reference, we will call each of these types of statement offence statements and occurrence statements.

Offence statements

We will look at the description 'offence statements' in the broadest possible manner by considering every statement which is taken in relation to every type of offence, from the most serious offence to a minor one. However, in introducing the concept of this type of statement, it is helpful to consider the basic level of statement at the outset.

An offence statement is a written record of a person's first-hand knowledge of an incident which as far as practicable contains:

(a) *Factual details* –
  (i) That is, the exact time, day, date and place of the alleged offence, e.g., 'At 10 a.m. on Monday 5 March 1984 I was on duty in High Street, Longtown, when I saw, etc.'. The details given by the officer or witness will be concerned with things which have been perceived by the senses – seen, heard, smelt, felt, or tasted, and it contains
  (ii) the identification of the alleged offender(s). This identification is essential. We are not concerned with formal identification of offenders, we are concerned with what the officer or a witness saw. Someone was driving the car: identify

him, 'At 10 a.m. on Monday 5 March 1984, I was on duty in High Street, Long-town, when I saw John Smith enter the Broadway Garage.' The manner of this identification tends to vary. Some supervisors prefer, in instances where the man was unknown to the officer when the officer first saw him, that the statement reads, 'saw a man enter the Broadway Garage, whom I now know to be John Smith'. The form of identification is not so important as the identification itself. The important fact is that it was John Smith who entered and there is merit in describing that event as directly as possible. Frequently a positive identification cannot be made and it is then important to describe the person concerned as fully as possible to provide every opportunity for an identification to be made. 'The man who stole my handbag was quite tall, about six feet, had brown wavy hair which was greying at the temples and he was wearing a navy blue half-length coat and faded blue jeans.' It may be that such a witness later saw the man being taken into police custody and her statement would then include that fact. 'I later saw the man who stole my handbag with PC Brown.' Assaults are frequently carried out by persons well known to the witness and a direct identification can be recorded in the statement. 'It was James Brown who hit me. I have known him for seven years.'

(b) *The offence details* – Sufficient detail must be included of the evidence which is within the knowledge of the officer, or the particular witness, in any statement. It is essential to prove every aspect of the offence alleged. Often a number of statements are taken from different persons, each of whom can prove some of the points to be proved if that offence is to be established. Police officers frequently witness offences themselves and in such cases the statement of that officer is sufficient to prove all elements of the offence. If the offence is one of failing to stop at a 'Stop' sign, the officer will have to prove that a particular person was driving a certain vehicle, in a particular road, when he failed to cause the vehicle to stop at a stop line at a junction with another specified road. The time, day, date, etc., will introduce the statement. Evidence will also be required of the presence of a 'Stop' sign on the approach to the junction, an estimate of the speed of the vehicle as it passed over the stop line, together with details of the officer's action and the explanation, if any, given by the offender.

Dealing with offences of this nature provides a good opportunity to look at the beginnings of a file of evidence which really exists whenever there is more than one statement of evidence in relation to an offence. It may be that an officer observes a certain motor car drive past a stop sign while not in a position to stop the vehicle. In such a case the officer will be able to supply all of the factual details, i.e. time, day, date, place and particulars of the vehicle, but is unlikely to be able to provide any evidence of the identification of the driver, unless the person was previously known to the officer. Having traced the driver, if the officer is able to interview him personally, an offence statement can then be completed in every respect. The officer may recognise the man as the person who was driving or, more probably, that person will admit that he was driving at the time. However, if the driver lives many miles away it is more likely that he will be seen by another police officer. That officer will have no first-hand knowledge of the offence, as he will not have seen it being committed. His statement will, therefore, be concerned with identifying the man interviewed as being the man who was driving the car when it passed over the stop line. Such an officer will still commence his statement with time, day, date and place, but these will be related to the interview with the alleged driver. His statement will then continue to give details of that interview, for example: I said to John Brown, 'Were you the driver of a Ford Escort motor car registered number, P123 YTN in High Street, Longtown, at 10 a.m. on Monday 5 March 1984?' He replied, 'Yes, I was driving the car at that time.' I cautioned him and said 'At that time the Ford Escort P123 YTN passed over a stop line situated on the junction of Lime Grove with High Street without stopping at that line.' Brown said, 'I don't remember failing to stop at that junction but I was certainly driving the car at that time.' The remainder of the second officer's statement would be concerned with the technicalities of informing Brown that he would be reported, etc. Thus we have two statements to prove the offence. If two police officers had been on duty together and had both observed the original offence, there would have been three statements.

Offence statements are read by supervisory officers and by the Crown Prosecution Service to establish whether or not there is sufficient evidence to justify the prosecution of the alleged offender. If there is and proceedings follow, the statements are used by the prosecutor as a guide to the evidence which each witness will give. When that witness subsequently gives evidence in court, the statement will be used as a guide to the questions which the prosecutor should put to the witness.

Method of approach

A police officer is a trained observer and, therefore, begins to view things and to plan a course of action in an ordered way. An officer witnesses an incident and queries its nature. What is this? What am I dealing with? Do the actions which I see amount to an offence (that is, directing attention towards the necessary points to prove in relation to the particular offence)? What is that offence? How do I prove it? This final question is tied up with the entire concept of an offence statement. Its purpose is to include all of the information essential to prove particular points.

The points to remember are, therefore, logical. Follow the mental processes which are essential to establish whether an offence is being committed and, if so, which courses of action are open; shall I arrest, report, caution, search or seize property?

(a) What is the incident?
(b) Is it an offence?
(c) Which offence is it?
(d) How do I prove that particular offence?

These same steps give a skeleton to the process of statement taking.

Occurrence statement

An occurrence statement is a written record of an incident which contains all the relevant knowledge of that incident, held by the person making it. Such a statement can include hearsay evidence and evidence of opinion and is not subject to the Codes of Practice. Its purpose is merely to collate all of the relevant knowledge of an occurrence held by the person making the statement, so that a reader is aware of the whole picture. Occurrence statements are uncommon as most statements taken by the police tend to refer to the investigation of offences. Nevertheless, it is frequently necessary for a police officer to record all of the facts of an occurrence from a witness to an incident for the information of his or her senior officers. It may be that the officer is recording a statement from a person who witnessed a sudden death. A man walking down the street suddenly suffers a heart attack and falls to the ground. There is no suggestion of an offence by anyone, but a general description of the incident will be helpful to the officer's supervisor and to HM coroner. Disputes frequently occur involving families and neighbours and complaints are made to the police. Frequently there is no offence involved in respect of which the police can take action but, if the issue seems to be complex, the only way in which this can be established is for the officer to record full statements of the particular occurrence from all parties involved.

Occurrence statements generally allow the person concerned to tell his story in his own way, the role of the police officer being confined to recording the events in an ordered way which gives some flow and sequence to the events described. The basic factors remain the same: times, days, dates, etc., must be recorded. The use of hearsay and the inclusion of opinions is immaterial at this stage as the purpose of the statement is merely to record all of the circumstances, including the feelings of the people who are making the statement, so that a reader will be aware of the whole issue as seen through the eyes of the person making the statement. The information so gathered is of interest to supervisors, coroners, perhaps civil courts at some later stage, or insurance companies assessing fire claims. If it was decided that the information contained in an occurrence statement, or statements, disclosed an offence, offence statements which recognise the rules of evidence would then be taken from the witness for use in court by the prosecutor.

Usually civilian witnesses have no previous experience of providing statements following any particular occurrence. They therefore tend to begin in the middle and to describe the occurrence itself rather than to include the events leading up to that occurrence. It is an advantage to allow a witness to describe the event in his or her own words in the beginning and to follow this introduction with a series of questions designed to clarify the picture in your mind. It is almost invariably a mistake to begin writing before a clear picture has developed. The usual results are to obtain a statement which lacks the detail necessary to permit supervisory officers to make a decision as to whether or not proceedings should follow, or, alternatively, to obtain an inaccurate account of events which will differ considerably from the story subsequently related to a court.

Certain basic rules assist in ensuring that a statement is sufficient in detail to describe events accurately, and these include:

(a) the recording of the events in the order in which they occurred;
(b) ensuring that there is sufficient detail to make the account accurate and free from ambiguity;
(c) that the writing is at least legible;
(d) that the words used are clear in meaning and convey the same impression to both the witness and the police officer; and
(e) including only information relevant to the investigation.

It is perhaps an oversimplification to say that only words which are clear in meaning should be used, as it is often possible to use words which are correct, but which are so wide in meaning that the picture in the mind of the reader differs considerably from that in the mind of the writer. Such terms are usually referred to as 'abstract terms' and a simple rule to follow is to ask yourself whether the words used will conjure up a sufficiently clear picture in the mind of the reader. Words have meaning when they represent something that can be readily identified, and communication takes place when the picture represented by those words is shared by two people. There must be a common understanding.

A male refugee from a foreign country arrived late for work at a factory and was told by a colleague that if he did this again he would be 'shot' by the foreman. He has not been seen since! Although the use of the word 'shot' as a replacement for 'reprimanded' is in common usage in this country, it will not always convey the meaning intended. It is also possible to use terms which, although correct in themselves, are capable of a different meaning and for this reason they should be avoided.

Certain words which may be used carry a personal flavour and have a specific identity. Others which are more abstract have a collective meaning which is not so positive. If our children have a pet dog known as Rex, they have a clear picture of a particular animal when the word Rex is used. When they see other dogs outside they tend to identify them all as Rex. This requires an explanation that not all such animals are named Rex, but they are all dogs. When the term 'dog' is subsequently used, the picture in their mind becomes less distinct. A mixture of dogs and cats must be identified as 'pets' and the process of abstraction continues, using terms which are more collective and therefore less specific.

In the course of statement taking, the process tends to appear in reverse order and a witness may say, 'The car approached me from the right', which might be extended by the addition of 'at a speed', which can be further extended to include the adjective 'fast', which still leaves the enquiring officer with a statement which is not very descriptive. Further details are still required concerning the terms 'car' and 'fast' before a clear picture can emerge.

Statement conclusion

All witness statements should include a declaration made by the witness to the effect that they are true to the best of the witness's knowledge or belief, and that it is made in the knowledge that he will be subject to prosecution if it is later given in evidence and it is shown that he has wilfully stated something known to be false, or not believed to be true. The form of this declaration is as follows:

> This statement consisting of … pages, signed by me is true to the best of my knowledge and belief and I make it knowing that, if it is tendered in evidence, I shall be liable to prosecution if I have wilfully stated in it anything which I know to be false or do not believe to be true.

The witness must be required to read this declaration and to sign it if satisfied with the accuracy of the information included. If unable to read it, then it must be read to him and endorsed accordingly by the police officer. Finally, the police officer must record, on the statement form, the time at which the taking of the statement began and ended, the day and date, the place at which it was taken, his signature, rank and number.

Statement writing rules

There are a certain number of general rules to be followed when recording statements and these are as follows:

(a) All statements should be recorded in ink (this prevents unauthorised alterations).

(b) Place names and surnames should be in block capitals (stand out to reader).

(c) Avoid police jargon (the witness's own words should be used as far as is practicable with understanding as this helps the prosecutor to assess the type of witness to be dealt with, but the officer may suggest alternatives to terms which are not generally understood and should marshal the story in logical fashion).

(d) So that the original can still be read, errors should be crossed out with a single line through the words to be removed and these should be initialled by the witness. There must be no erasures.

(e) Where relevant use direct speech ('I said to him,' etc.).

(f) The normal rules of English grammar should apply, that is, spelling, punctuation and paragraphing.

(g) Each page of the statement must be signed by the witness as each part which can be separated must be authenticated.

(h) If the person making the statement is unable to read, it must be read over to him and the fact that this has been done must be noted on the statement by the police officer recording it.

(i) Persons making statements must sign the declaration provided on the statement to the effect that it is true, etc. (see above).

(j) The officer taking a statement must sign it and give his name, rank and number.

Further development of statement writing skills

Introduction

When statements were first considered we looked at offence statements and occurrence statements. A fairly clear separation was made. An offence statement is a written record of a person's first-hand knowledge of an incident which contains factual detail, that is, the exact time, day, date and the place at which the offence occurred together with the identification of the offender, and sufficient evidence to prove the offence. Such a statement confined itself to those facts which were admissible in evidence. At the other extreme, the occurrence statement is a written record of an incident which contains all of the relevant knowledge of the person making it. As it is required to include all detail, it is not bound by the rules of evidence and can virtually include any connected fact as its purpose is really to be fully descriptive of the incident.

On occasions it is desirable to combine some of the features of each, as the laws of evidence on occasions allow matters which would otherwise have been excluded to be given in certain circumstances. This in effect means that when recording statements made by particular people, in particular circumstances, evidence of some other matters might be included.

Evidence of opinion

Generally, the opinion of a witness is inadmissible and it is therefore not included in statements. There are occasions upon which evidence of opinion can be given:

(a) Statement of opinion can be given by recognised experts in science, art or trade, for example, doctors, lawyers, forensic scientists and fingerprint experts, who have knowledge of points outside the knowledge and experience of a jury. In such circumstances, it is necessary to show that the witness has carried out some form of special study or has sufficient skill or experience to be accepted by a court as an expert witness. This must be borne in mind when a statement is being taken. If expert opinion is included, details of the qualifications and experience of the witness must also be shown so that the prosecutor is aware of the grounds upon which the court may consider whether or not to admit the evidence as expert evidence. This is a question which only the court can determine. A police officer with 15 years' experience as a traffic officer who had attended a course on accident investigation and had attended more than 400 fatal road accidents was accepted as an expert by the High Court.

(b) Opinion as to the identity, condition or age of a person or thing may be admitted. To some degree the identification of any person who was previously unknown to the witness must be a matter of opinion and so far as the recording of statements is concerned the police officer should attempt to gather as much information as possible as to identity. This may, on occasions, involve matters of opinion. Witnesses who cannot be sure that it was a particular person whom they saw committing a certain act may be able to express the view that they are almost certain that it was a particular person. When this is done, support that statement with as much information as the witness can give as to why this opinion was formed. The same considerations would apply to property about which a conclusive identification may be possible. Opinions are sometimes expressed concerning the condition or age of persons or things. A witness may say that he formed the opinion that a person was under the influence of drugs. If the witness had previous experience of dealing with drug addicts the court may allow his evidence on the grounds that it was based upon matters within his knowledge. If he had little or no experience in this respect, the court will allow facts to be given as to the way in which the person behaved and concerning his general appearance. The witness may be asked for his conclusions if his evidence of observation is sound. Such conclusions are best included in the statement and it is then a matter for the prosecutor to decide whether to ask the witness to express an opinion and, in the final analysis, for the court to decide whether an answer will be permitted.

(c) Opinion as to appearance of illness or drunkenness may be permitted and should be included in a statement. Police officers frequently express the opinion that a man was drunk but courts accept that constables have considerable experience of dealing with such people and are prepared to accept such evidence, provided that it is supported by evidence of appearance and actions which are consistent with drunkenness.

(d) Opinion as to the speed of a vehicle may be accepted by a court. Although a person may not be convicted of an offence of speeding upon the evidence of witness as to his opinion of the speed at which a vehicle was travelling, this does not affect the general issue of giving evidence as to speed. It is important that drivers involved in motor accidents and witnesses to accidents are asked for their estimate as to the speed of vehicles. It is a matter, once again, for the court to attach weight to that evidence. A factual inclusion as to the length of time a driver has been driving and the extent of his experience can be extremely helpful to a prosecutor. Such an estimate from an experienced lorry driver will obviously be much more reliable than that of an old lady who has never driven. This does not mean that the old lady should not be asked whether she could estimate the speed. She may be able to do so and may be a reliable witness, as she may have had many years of experience of travelling in other people's cars. Record that fact in the statement.

Negative statements

It is occasionally of advantage to record a statement from a person even though that statement amounts to no more than a denial of knowledge of a particular occurrence. Such a record can be helpful if subsequent enquiries reveal that some knowledge must have existed. Passengers in motor cars may allege that they have no knowledge of the circumstances leading up to an accident because they were either asleep or not paying attention. They may subsequently give evidence on behalf of the driver if he is charged with careless driving. It is useful to the prosecutor to be able to show that a person previously denied knowledge of the events. The prosecutor does this by asking the witness if he made the negative statement, shows it to him and asks if it is his signature.

Attendance at court

The accuracy of statements is extremely important as there are times when a written statement may be offered in evidence without the necessity for the witness to attend court and give evidence on oath.

In criminal proceedings, a written statement by any person shall be admissible in evidence to the same extent as oral evidence if:

(a) the statement purports to be signed by the person who made it;

(b) the statement contains a declaration by that person to the effect that it is true to the best of his knowledge and belief and that he made the statement knowing that, if it were tendered in evidence, he would be liable to prosecution if he wilfully stated in it anything which he knew to be false or did not believe to be true;

(c) before the hearing at which the statement is tendered in evidence, a copy of the statement is served, by or on behalf of the party proposing to tender it, on each of the other parties to the proceedings; and

(d) none of the other parties or their solicitors, within 7 days from the service of the copy of the statement, serves a notice on the party so proposing, objecting to the statement being tendered in evidence.

However, the conditions in (c) and (d) can be waived if the parties agree before or during the hearing to allow the statement to be tendered. If made by a person under 18, the age must be given and if read to a person who cannot read, a declaration must be included to that effect. If the statement refers to an exhibit, the defence must have the opportunity to inspect it.

In effect, this means that if the contents of a statement are accepted by both sides as presenting a fair and accurate account, and they agree to its use, a witness need not be called. These provisions are used extensively when evidence is merely of a formal and non-contentious nature.

Linking exhibits with statements

Witnesses will frequently refer to articles when making a statement to a constable and it is essential that the article can be clearly identified so that it may be produced to the court at the appropriate time. To permit this to be done, each exhibit is given a number and this number is shown in the statement at the point at which the witness refers to it. There is no standard way of doing this; sometimes the exhibits are numbered in a continuous way. The important thing is to do so in the manner followed in a particular police force or area and to ensure that each exhibit is individually identifiable. Labels are attached to exhibits at the time at which this identification is made. The labelling procedure does not apply to statements under caution, taken from defendants. If property was recovered from a thief by a police officer, the recovery of that property would be a part of the officer's evidence and he would produce the exhibits.

A police officer, Jane Smith, who arrested a thief who had stolen a ring from jeweller's shop, and subsequently found that ring in the thief's possession could include in her statement, 'I searched the accused's jacket and in the breast pocket I found a diamond ring (J.S.1)'. If later, the thief made a statement under caution, that statement would also become an exhibit to be produced by the officer who took the statement, and may become J.S.2 although it would not be labelled.

Hearsay

The admissibility of hearsay evidence was discussed when the functions of and evidence accepted by courts were examined. In general terms, it is not included in offence statements as it is inadmissible in evidence but there are exceptions to this rule and it must be remembered that oral statements made by an accused and oral statements made in the presence and hearing of the accused may be included in statements as they may be given in evidence. This is also true of evidence of early complaint in sexual offences. However, the circumstances of the admissibility of such statements are worth recalling:

(a) *Oral statements made by the accused* – The general rule is that things said by another person may not be given in evidence if the purpose is to tender them as evidence of the truth of the matters asserted in them, unless they were made by a defendant and constitute admissions of facts relevant to these proceedings. The rule is founded in common sense. If Brown says to Green, 'I saw Smith break a window in High Street', this is obviously not a matter for Green to give in evidence as it has no value. Green did not see the window broken and is not permitted to give evidence of the fact. Brown saw Smith break the window and may give direct evidence of that fact and it should be included in Brown's statement. However, this does not apply to statements made by an accused person and this includes any incriminating statement, whether spoken or written, which is made by an accused person. If an accused says to a police officer, 'OK officer, I was in Woodbine Close that night and I did try to open the door of a blue car', the officer may include the words used by the accused in his statement of evidence and may repeat those words subsequently when giving evidence against the accused in court. The words amount to a verbal admission made to an officer which is relevant to the proceedings before the court.

(b) *Oral statements made in the presence and hearing of the accused* – This exception is better understood if it is considered in the context of facts which might be stated to an accused person in the course of an enquiry. Any such statement is only of value to the enquiry if it provokes some form of response in the accused and it is only in such circumstances that it will be admitted. If a police officer says to an accused, 'Your sister told me that you brought a silver tea set home with you last Monday night', that statement would not normally be admissible as it is the sister who should give that evidence. If the accused then says, 'Yes I did, I may as well admit that I stole the tea set', that statement would be admissible as a statement made by the accused, but it would be strange if the officer could not tell the court what was said to the accused to stimulate that response. Perhaps the accused may not reply at all, but merely shrug his shoulders and nod in the affirmative. In such circumstances, the officer could describe what was said to the accused, because it is a statement made in the presence and hearing of the accused which did result in some form of acknowledgement of its truth.

(c) *Early complaint in sexual offences* – Generally, complaints made to a police officer by a woman who had been the victim of a sexual offence would be inadmissible because those statements would be of matters best described to the court by the woman herself. However, the nature of such a complaint made by the victim of sexual offence should be included in a statement taken by a police officer in relation of an offence. Words may be admitted in evidence by the court, provided that they are not elicited by leading, inductive or intimidatory questions and the complaint was made as soon as possible after the act complained of as was reasonable in the circumstances. Such early complaints are admissible to prove the fact that a complaint was made, which fact is relevant to the question of consent. The words used by the complainant are also of value to the court as they will indicate the nature of the assault alleged and the complainant's reaction to that assault – these issues being, once again, relevant to the question of consent. The words used should be included in the statement made by the police officer receiving the complaint, or by any other witness who receives that complaint, together with details of the distress, etc., shown by the complainant.

If a girl runs into her home and says to her mother, 'Mummy, a man put his hand up my skirt as I was walking home, I was frightened, I've run all the way home', the nature of that complaint and the fact that it was made straightaway are very import-ant to the enquiry and full details must be recorded in the statement of the person who received the complaint.

In many police forces today, the procedure is to require investigating officers to include all information in a statement, whether or not the particular facts are admis-sible in evidence. It is then left to the Crown Prosecution Service to decide what will be given in evidence.

Relevant facts in addition to points to prove

In general terms, a court is concerned with evidence which directly points towards the particular points to prove in an offence but courts will admit relevant facts, that is additional matters which may assist the court, which are related to the offence being considered. The matters are:

(a) introductory and explanatory facts, being matters which prove identity, e.g. the witness himself, the objects, etc., referred to;
(b) facts showing opportunity, that a witness saw the accused in the area in which the crime was committed, if such an accused denies being there;
(c) motive such as expressions of ill will towards a person or threats made against such person;
(d) preparation to commit the crime, e.g. evidence of the purchase of fire-raising materials by an accused charged with arson;
(e) conduct of an accused after a crime is alleged to have been committed, e.g. the burning of clothing by a man charged with rape; or
(f) conduct of the victim of a crime after its commission, i.e. was a complaint made (that is the fact that the person made it, not the terms of the complaint itself)?

In addition to these specific instances of related facts, a person recording such a state-ment from anyone should always ask himself the question, 'Is this information suffi-ciently connected with the offence to be of value to the court in establishing guilt or innocence?' If the answer to this question is 'yes' and the statement made is not specific-ally excluded by the laws of evidence, it will be a related fact. The general bearing, attitude or conduct of an accused before an offence is committed may be important as may the surrounding circumstances. If a man assaults a girl friend causing her bodily harm, the fact that he left a public house in an angry mood having said that he was going to look for her because he suspected that she was with another man is a related fact and may be described by those witnesses who saw and heard these matters.

On many occasions, related facts will explain why certain things occurred and pro-vided that the explanation is relevant to a fact in issue, it may be given in evidence and should be included in a statement. The condition of a road, the condition of a vehicle, the nature of and make up of the area in which a certain type of driving occurred are all issues related to charges of dangerous or careless driving.

Corroboration

A corroboration statement is a statement from another independent source which tends to support in a material particular the truthfulness or accuracy of a statement already obtained. It either confirms, supports or strengthens other evidence. In general circumstances, the English common law merely requires the evidence of one competent witness. There are exceptions to this rule, perjury and speeding, but they are limited in relation to the overall extent of our laws. The practice, however, is for police officers to gather as much corroborative evidence as possible in the circumstances of each case. A statement made by a traffic officer who pursued a motor vehicle which was being driven dangerously over a number of miles can be corroborated by statements from witnesses who observed the manner of the driving at various points along the route. When taking corroborative statements, it is helpful to remember certain desirable points of procedure which will add to the credibility of the evidence when presented to a court:

(a) Take the statements from each witness separately and, where possible, in the absence of other witnesses from the immediate vicinity. Each account of happenings should be independently made without comment or prompting from other witnesses.

(b) The officer taking the statement should take care not to prompt the witness by using information which has already been been gathered in the course of recording other statements. There is nothing wrong with questioning a witness at length, even before commencing to record a statement, provided that those questions are directed towards establishing with certainty the witness's own recollection of the incident.

(c) The corroborative evidence must be set out in detail, including all elements of information which support the truthfulness or accuracy of other statements. Do not set out merely to gain corroboration of one predetermined fact as the witness may have much more evidence to offer if his story is recorded in detail.

Scenes of crime – management

Introduction

Although police officers visit many scenes of crime, they must never relax their attention to detail. Much valuable evidence may be obliterated or lost by the first officer at the scene of a crime through his non-awareness of its significance. In many cases, valuable traces will have been obliterated by other persons who arrived on the scene before the police, and although this may be unavoidable in the present state of public awareness, after the arrival of the first police officer no more useful traces should be lost. It should always be remembered that evidence may be found not only at the scene itself but also on or near the line of approach and departure.

Such evidence will often be undetectable by the human eye, but wherever a criminal has been, there are likely to be traces of his presence.

Action at the scene and specialist assistance

The first police officer at the scene of a crime must take complete control of the situation. Any unnecessary movement should be avoided. The first fact to establish is whether or not a crime has been committed, although this is generally obvious. It is essential to note the time when the crime was committed (if this can be established), the time it came to notice and the time of your arrival.

If the first officer on the scene is not trained in searching the scene of a crime and it is possible to summon a specially trained officer, this should be done as soon as possible, and pending his arrival precautions should be taken to ensure that no unauthorised person approaches the scene. All persons, including witnesses and the inmates of any building concerned, should be warned not to touch or disturb anything and, in cases of serious crime, a guard should if possible be posted to prevent entry. If the scene is in the open, all access to the area should be prevented and care taken to protect from the weather any traces (footprints, stains, etc.) which may be discovered.

It is usually the responsibility of the first officer at the scene of a crime to record the names and addresses of any witnesses present so that they can be seen later if they cannot be prevented from leaving the scene. It will also be his task to identify the complainant if that person is present and to take particulars of the alleged crime and details of any property involved. It will also be helpful if the officer records the identity of all persons visiting the scene, both police and public, together with the times of arrival. All this information will prove invaluable when compiling any subsequent report.

When examining the scene of a crime, an officer should make very careful notes, in writing, of the scene and its condition; memory alone must not be relied upon. Specialist officers such as detective officers, fingerprint officers, photographers and dog handlers are available to assist at the scene of a crime, and where the nature of the crime makes such action appropriate, such specialists should be called to the scene as soon as possible. Consideration will be given by such specialists as to the necessity to take photographs before anything is moved.

Any search for traces should be both thorough and systematic. Such searches will usually be carried out under the directions of a supervisor. It must be kept in mind that very minute quantities of material or small marks may be significant. Nothing capable of bearing a fingerprint or palmprint should be handled without proper precautions. It is said that whenever persons and objects come into contact with one another, traces of one are almost certain to be left on the other. Do not pick things up or move them, or attempt to match up implements with marks or shoes with imprints. Such actions can result in the loss of valuable evidence. Human hairs, blood, saliva, etc., are all likely to provide some evidence of an offender's identity.

Avoid contact with areas with which the criminal may have made contact. Watch particularly where you are walking. In making any form of preliminary examination, attention should be paid to likely points of contact such as doors, windows, light switches, even telephones.

Where the offence concerned is one of burglary, the householder may have already begun to tidy up. Further tidying-up should be discouraged but do not attempt to replace objects in their original positions as this only leads to further handling.

Objects which are commonly touched by thieves include bottles (particularly where the householder has been saving coins), coin boxes, boxes which have contained jewellery and the contents of wardrobes and drawers. Where a considerable time is likely to pass before a scenes of crime specialist can attend, it may be advisable to take some form of action to ensure that any marks are preserved after you leave the scene and that the house is in such a condition that the occupants can be reasonably comfortable. Where coin boxes have been removed from meters they can be put in a safe place. Most have a ring attached which can be used for lifting. It may be replaced within the meter by this method, where it should be safe from interference. Ensure however, that the fitter employed by the public utility concerned is not likely to remove it when fitting a new box, or that he securely replaces the one which has been tampered with. Bottles, or other objects which have a 'neck', can be lifted by placing the fingers, or some object, inside the neck. Where bedrooms have been ransacked, the contents of drawers and wardrobes will probably be heaped upon the bed. In such cases where there is likely to be an overnight delay before an examination can be carried out, all articles which will not carry prints, such as clothing, may be returned to their storage places.

Articles which are suitable for examination should be carefully set aside in a safe place to await examination. However, where the crime which has been committed is a very serious one, such as murder or rape, nothing should be touched as a full examination will take place quickly. Footprints can be adequately protected by covering them with some object such as a box. If such a mark is in soft ground outside a building, it should be similarly protected. Documents which may have been handled by the criminal can be preserved in a polythene bag.

Where stolen vehicles are located, do not enter the vehicle or touch it in any way. Arrange for the vehicle to be examined before removal, or to be removed by specialists for later examination. Not all vehicles which have been taken without consent, as opposed to having been stolen, will be examined in detail. Much will depend upon local procedures.

If a firearm has been left at the scene of a crime it must not be touched or moved in any other way. If circumstances exist which necessitate its removal from its original position, it is best to take hold of the 'grip' itself which usually carries a rough surface. Use no more than two fingers and record the fact that the firearm has been moved. Care must be taken as some modern weapons are extremely sensitive and discharge easily. Television detectives frequently pick up firearms by placing a pencil inside the barrel. Avoid this, as forensic tests may later be carried out to match marks on spent ammunition with irregularities which exist on the surface of the barrel.

In searching vehicles which are suspected of having been used in connection with a crime, particular attention should be given to bumpers, lamps, wings, handles, tyres, etc., as well as the interior, under cushions, carpets, etc. Suspect vehicles should be immediately impounded and kept under cover until they can be examined. Where vehicles have to be moved a long distance, particularly over rough ground, the examination should be done on the spot to prevent the loss of material in transit.

In examining tools and weapons it should be remembered that the colour of blood varies with the action of the atmosphere and sometimes with the action of the chemicals in the article on which the blood lies. If blood is visible on a weapon, its distribution and general appearance should be noted and it should be observed whether or not the weapon has been wiped. Special care should be taken to see that all unevenness of surface joins, etc., is examined. The collection of traces from knives and weapons should be left to the expert, unless the traces are liable to become dislodged by the most careful method of transit. The material on a knife may indicate its previous history, and may also show whether it has been used for making more than one stab wound.

In examining splashes of blood on floors and walls, the shape of the splashes will be particularly noted and photographed in order to establish the direction of fall.

If a suspect is being searched then, after examination of the exposed parts of the body, particular attention should be paid to the fingernails and, where considered advisable, scrapings from under the nails should be taken if the suspect consents. It should also be remembered that the victim of an attack may bear traces left by the assailant during a struggle, e.g. small fragments of skin tissue under the fingernails.

At the scene of every crime, the task of the first officer must be the preservation of any traces. However, where it is left to him to make a preliminary search, all the points above should be clearly borne in mind.

Serious crimes

Supervisory officers must be called to the scene of serious crimes and, pending the arrival of such officers, everything must be done to ensure that there is no disturbance of the scene and that the identity of all persons present at the scene when the officer arrived is known. It is helpful if the first officer at the scene, or a colleague, has talked to as many witnesses as possible, to gather as much information as possible, while at the same time keeping the scene secure.

Police action at scenes of homicides and abortions

It has already been stressed that the actions of the first police officer at the scene of a crime can have an important bearing on any later courses of action. Every care should be taken to preserve the scene and prevent unauthorised persons tampering or interfering in any way.

Homicide

The first consideration must be the possible preservation of life, and in cases of suspected homicide medical assistance should be requested to confirm that life has ceased to exist, unless death is obvious, e.g. decapitation. The time at which the original information was received should be noted, together with the identity of the person from whom it was received. A supervisory officer should be notified at once.

The position of articles at the scene should be carefully noted and measures taken for their security, but they should not be moved without the authority of a senior officer, and then only under his direction. When possible, a rough sketch should be made pinpointing such articles in their relative positions. It is appreciated that photographs will be taken as soon as possible, but such a sketch provides insurance in the event of something being subsequently inadvertently moved. Witnesses at the scene should be identified. They should be asked to remain at the scene until the arrival of a senior officer so that their evidence can be obtained as soon as possible to avoid their recollections becoming distorted by discussing events with other people. It should also be remembered that such a witness may in some way be involved in the offence.

The scene of a homicide must be carefully protected and no unauthorised person should be allowed to approach it. An assurance that the scene has been protected will be required by senior detective officers immediately they arrive, together with precise information concerning the line of approach taken by the police officer, if this was necessary. An approved line of approach will subsequently be marked out by detective officers, and it is essential that this is followed by all specialist personnel who subsequently attend the scene of the crime. If anything has been touched by anyone, inform the supervisory officer as soon as he arrives. Any suspected offender should be detained but should not be questioned at this stage: any such questioning at the scene could lead to complications concerning admissibility of evidence and the non-observance of the Codes of Practice. A note should be made of anything said by such a suspect.

In all cases of this kind, the press will quickly learn of the occurrence and will ask questions of persons at the scene. It is the job of reporters to obtain a story and they cannot be blamed for trying! They should be politely told that full information will be available in due course from the forces press liaison officer or a senior officer. In no circumstances must the press be allowed to approach the scene or any witnesses who are awaiting the arrival of senior officers.

Abortion

Although the general principles outlined above apply equally to cases of abortion, the nature of the incident requires that attention be given to other matters. Medical assistance will be urgently required as it is usually when things go wrong that illegal abortions come to the notice of the police. Many illegal abortions result in the death of the pregnant woman through lack of skill, hygiene and care on the part of the abortionist. The varied nature of articles which can be used to effect an abortion should be recognised in protecting the scene from all except the doctor, who may arrive before specialist police assistance.

Conclusion

It is essential that police officers remain aware of the distress which has been caused to those who are the victims of crime and treat such persons accordingly. It is difficult for those of us who have not experienced that moment when, upon returning home one finds that one's home has been burgled, to imagine the feelings of the lady of the house who sees what remains of her property strewn about the floor. It may be that considerable damage has been done to the property. The standing of the police service depends upon the impression which is created in the minds of such victims. The manner in which they are interviewed, the degree of sympathy shown and the apparent concern of those charged with the task of investigation to do all that is possible to apprehend the offenders are all factors of critical importance. The situation is a test of a police officer's qualities and professionalism, communication skills and ability to handle situations involving stress. Most of all it is a test of leadership.

Loss of memory and illness in the street

Introduction

The police service is one of the few civil agencies which provides a 24-hour service to the community on 7 days of each week. Unlike other agencies, however, the police do not confine themselves to specialist matters such as those provided by hospitals, ambulance brigades and fire brigades, but are available to provide help and guidance on any matter and often liaise with other agencies to ensure maximum efficiency. It is inevitable, therefore, that a police officer will usually make the first contact with persons requiring help, particularly when dealing with persons suffering from loss of memory, who fall ill in the street or who are missing from home, destitute or homeless.

Loss of memory

When a person suffering from loss of memory is found in a street or public place, steps must be taken to obtain medical treatment as soon as possible. Because this condition is usually associated with injury or shock, a police officer must first ascertain whether the person requires first aid treatment, particularly if concussion is suspected to be present, in which case the breathing will be shallow, the patient's face will be pale, the skin cold and clammy and the pulse rapid and weak. The correct first aid treatment in such cases is the same as that for unconsciousness, i.e. to ensure an open airway and obtain urgent medical treatment.

The person should be removed to hospital by ambulance if necessary and any personal property should be safeguarded. If there has been an accident, for example, if the person has fallen or sustained an injury in any way, then the police officer should take the names and addresses of any witnesses present. On arrival at the hospital, the clothing and personal effects of the person should be examined to establish his identity. In the majority of cases personal documents will quickly establish identity, but when a person's identity cannot be established from an examination of his personal effects, a detailed description of the patient should be compiled, including details of any birthmarks, scars or other distinguishing features. Arrangements should also be made to have the patient photographed. An examination of any clothing may reveal name tags or laundry marks which may subsequently lead to an identification.

The officer should inform his immediate supervisor of any case where identity has not been established so that a decision can be made in relation to the circulation of the photograph, description and circumstances of the finding of such a person to other police areas or to the public. The use of newspapers and television can be very helpful in urgent cases. Reports of persons listed as missing from home should be checked to see if the description tallies with that of the person in hospital. A check should be made of the names index with the PNC.

Illness in the street

Where a police officer is called to a person who has been taken ill in a street or public place, the action to be taken is similar to that taken in relation to persons found suffering from loss of memory, the most important consideration being the welfare of such a person. First aid should be administered where necessary and an ambulance or other medical assistance summoned. It is wise to check that an ambulance has been summoned. Many persons who are likely to become ill while outside their homes carry documentary evidence of the medical condition which causes their condition. An identification card, coloured blue, is issued to patients receiving steroid therapy; identification cards are also issued by the British Diabetic Association and by the Multiple Sclerosis Society to persons suffering from those diseases, and the Medic-Alert Foundation supplies, on payment, a metal wrist bracelet indicating a medical condition or allergy together with a serial number and telephone number by means of which information about the medical condition of the wearer can be obtained. The identity of such a person should always be established and his relatives informed of what has happened.

Where a person declines assistance and refuses medical treatment he should be allowed to make his own arrangements, although the police officer should offer to contact a taxi or make other transport arrangements at that person's expense.

As in all cases of this kind, the personal property of any person taken to hospital, etc., should be safeguarded. If necessary, the constable should take possession of the property and, in accordance with local force orders, record each item and the eventual disposal of the property.

A word of caution: never assume that a person is drunk if found unconscious. The symptoms of some illnesses can be very similar. A person who is found alone and unconscious should be taken to hospital even if that person smells of drink or there are other grounds for suspecting a drunken stupor.

Where a person is taken to hospital and detained, any relatives or friends should be notified as soon as possible to avoid any unnecessary concern on their part at the absence of that person.

Mentally vulnerable persons found in public places

Many people who are suffering from some form of mental disability or illness now receive treatment within the community. It is therefore probable that such persons when found in these circumstances are known to suffer from that disability or illness and are receiving treatment whilst continuing to live at home. Where possible, such persons should be taken home if found in distressed circumstances and their medical advisers contacted.

Where a constable finds, in a place to which the public have access, a person who appears to be suffering from mental disorder and to be in immediate need of care or control the officer may, if it is considered necessary to do so in the interests of that person or for the protection of other persons, remove that person to a place of safety.

The Mental Health Act 1983 provides that such a person may be detained for a period not exceeding 72 hours for the purpose of enabling him to be examined by a doctor, to be interviewed by an approved social worker and to make any necessary arrangements for his treatment or care. Such a person should normally be taken directly to a hospital or, if this is not practicable, the assistance of the approved social worker should be sought to advise upon where the person should be taken. When the person cannot be taken to a hospital immediately and is taken to a police station, every endeavour should be made to have that person removed as soon as possible to a more suitable place, preferably an appropriate hospital in the district.

In circumstances in which such a person is suspected of committing an offence, it must be remembered that specific procedures are set out in the Code of Practice for the Detention, Treatment and Questioning of Persons by Police Officers when dealing with the mentally ill and the mentally handicapped.

Missing persons, absconders, deserters and escapees

Introduction

Thousands of people are reported missing from home each year. They frequently leave because of discontent with their existing lives, or because they wish to escape from a situation which they feel to be intolerable. On many occasions the reason for departure will be apparent; on other occasions there may appear to be no reason for a person dropping out of sight. Enquiries are important, particularly where young or other vulnerable people are concerned. It is important to recognise that many murder investigations begin with a report of 'missing from home'. However, it must also be recognised that the vast majority of such reports are concerned with people who had deliberately dropped out of sight. Even where that is so, such persons may, as a result, be exposed to danger.

Persons unlawfully at large

Escape is a common law offence. It is an offence for a person who is lawfully arrested to gain liberty before he is given it within the due processes of law. The offence may be committed by the prisoner himself either by escaping, without the use of force, before being put in hold, or with force, after being restrained. It may also be committed by other persons and may be committed by permitting such a person to escape, or by negligently allowing him to escape or by rescuing such a person from custody.

A constable may arrest such a person without a warrant (but see below in relation to young persons).

Young persons absent from institutions

A child or young person who is absent, without the consent of the responsible person, from a place of safety to which he has been taken after arrest upon a warrant and has been detained there because he cannot be brought immediately before a court, or local authority accommodation in which he was required to live under the provisions of the Powers of Criminal Courts (Sentencing) Act 2000 (residence requirement imposed with supervision order) or to which that person had been remanded under the provisions of the Act of 2000 (remand of person already under supervision), may be arrested by a constable anywhere in the United Kingdom or Channel Islands without a warrant. A person so arrested shall be conducted to the place of safety, local authority accommodation or such other place as may be directed, at the responsible person's expense. The 'responsible person' is the person who made the arrangements under para. 7(4) of Schedule 7 of the Powers of Criminal Courts (Sentencing) Act 2000 or the authority designated under para. 5 of Schedule 6, para. 7(8) of Schedule 7 to that Act or s 23 of the Children and Young Persons Act 1969.

This power is provided by s 32 of the 1969 Act as amended.

Young persons in breach of conditions

Section 23A of the Children and Young Persons Act 1969 provides that a young person who has been remanded or committed to local authority accommodation who is subject to requirements that he will not commit further offences or will not interfere with witnesses or otherwise obstruct the course of justice may be arrested without warrant by a constable if the constable has reasonable grounds for suspecting that the person has broken any of those conditions.

Missing persons

The police receive many reports of persons missing from their homes and police action will depend, to some extent, upon whether the report concerns a child or young person, a woman or girl under 21 years of age or an adult other than such a woman or girl.

On receiving a report of a person missing from home, a police officer should first establish the relationship between the person making the report and the missing person, and the reasons or suspected reasons for disappearance. It is not usual to consider as missing persons adults who have left home or employment intentionally, such as men who have left their wives or women who have left their husbands. In the absence of any special circumstances such as mental or physical illness or disability, suicidal tendencies, injury, loss of memory or senility, no police action is normally taken beyond the recording of the report, unless police action is necessary in the interest of children or young persons who have been left by a parent or guardian.

Where the person reported missing is a child or young person, the steps taken are normally immediate and extensive, whatever the circumstances. Children have been known to travel considerable distances in a relatively short time and this should be borne in mind when considering the extent and circulation of information about the missing child, and the fact that the child may have been a victim of serious assault or murder must not be overlooked. In the event of a woman or girl under 21 years being reported missing, it is usual for the enquiry to be immediate and for the assistance of a detective officer and a policewoman to be enlisted if it is likely that a criminal offence has been committed.

Where it is considered that police action is necessary, the officer receiving a report of a missing person should obtain the following information:

(a) Any previous similar behaviour? A check on the file kept of missing persons will reveal this information. It may be that a person who has been missing previously may be quickly traced using the information from previous reports. Where a person has been missing on previous occasions this is usually a good indication that no harm has befallen him, although enquiries should not be curtailed because of previous conduct.

(b) Is there any suspicion of the missing person being involved in, or the subject of, crime? It may be that a person has left home to avoid arrest or prosecution, particularly in the case of children and young persons. It is also possible that they have left home in consequence of their treatment.

(c) The steps which have already been taken to trace the missing person should be recorded. This will avoid duplication of enquiries. If enquiries have been made of all local relatives, these persons will have been made aware that the person is missing.

(d) Full name, age and address of the missing person together with a full description and, if possible, a recent photograph. A photograph is worth more than the most detailed description and every effort should be made to obtain one.

(e) The usual haunts and acquaintances of the missing person. These include clubs, public houses, dance halls, school friends, boy or girl friends and, if applicable, places of employment. Where the person is in employment, an enquiry at the place of work may reveal that the person has obtained his National Insurance cards and outstanding wages, which would be a good indication that the person intended leaving, and this may dispel any suspicion of foul play.

(f) Places where the person is likely to go. This is coupled with the information at (e) above, but may be more extensive. It may be that a person has discussed going to a particular area, in this country or abroad. This information may assist when deciding upon the extent of any circulation of the report of the missing person.

(g) The wishes of relatives regarding any publicity. Often persons do not wish the press or the news media to be made aware of the fact that a person is missing. The police should abide by the wishes of relatives except where the health and well-being of the person missing are likely to be endangered, in which case the overriding consideration must be the safety of that person and the assistance of the press may then be sought.

When dealing with children and young persons, one of the first places to be searched is the home of the child. Particular attention should be paid to discarded refrigerators, boxes, the luggage compartment of a car, all places where a child may have hidden and then been trapped by the door or lid closing with no means of escape from the inside. The use of police dogs at this stage should be considered. There has been at least one instance where, as a result of the prompt use of a police dog, a young child was found head down in a drum in the garage where the child would have died had it not been found at an early stage of the enquiry.

It may be necessary to check records held on the PNC and within police publications and to arrange for details to be so recorded. The BBC normally will only consider broadcasting particulars of missing persons exceptionally, the decision in this case being made by the chief officer of police of the area concerned.

Announcements concerning missing persons will be issued in the *Police Gazette* only on compassionate grounds such as loss of memory or illness, or if bodily harm is feared.

When a missing person is found, any further police action will depend on the circumstances in which that person is found. A child or young person is normally immediately restored to the parents or guardian or, where the child is in the care of the local authority, to an officer of that local authority. In the case of an older person, the circumstances may be that the individual does not wish his whereabouts to be disclosed. The police should, where advisable, try to persuade the person concerned to return home or, failing that, to inform parents or relatives that the he is safe and well and that there is no cause for anxiety. Care should be taken about revealing the whereabouts of a person unless the express permission of that person has been obtained. The Department of Health and Social Security will assist in tracing persons under 18 years of age reported missing from home. The procedure to be followed is set out in Home Office Circular 212/1978.

Destitute and homeless persons

A destitute and homeless person may be one who has been reported missing. A check should be made with the PNC. If the person appears to be ill and in need of medical care, he should be treated in the same way as a person found in the street.

When a person is not of the vagrant type but appears in need of assistance, the social services department of the local authority should be contacted, particularly if a homeless family is found destitute and sleeping out. If such a family refuses assistance and, because of the way in which it is living, harm or unnecessary suffering is likely to be caused to a child or young person, then consideration should be given to removing the child to a place of safety. This may seem a rather harsh way to deal with a destitute and homeless family, but the interests of the child should be paramount; such a course of action safeguards the health and future of the child and is often the means of obtaining help and assistance for the whole family.

Local authority welfare officers can be of considerable assistance to the destitute and the homeless. It is the responsibility of the DSS to provide temporary board and lodging in such circumstances. The 'Shelter' organisation devotes much time and effort to these problems and is always willing to offer advice and assistance. Other organisations such the Women's Voluntary Service and the Salvation Army allocate much of their time and resources to the comfort of such persons.

Persons who have become 'stranded' by losing travel tickets and money are usually helped by the police. Money may be advanced to such persons, provided that someone deposits a similar sum with the police in the area of that person's residence.

Absentees and deserters from armed forces

Arrest

A constable may arrest any person whom he has reasonable cause to suspect of being an officer, warrant officer, non-commissioned officer or soldier of the regular forces who has deserted or is absent without leave. Persons so arrested must be brought before a summary court as soon as practicable. This power to arrest is provided by the Army Act 1955, Air Force Act 1955 and Naval Discipline Act 1957 and such powers were preserved by the Police and Criminal Evidence Act 1984, s 26 and Schedule 2. The Visiting Forces Act 1952 applies these provisions to members of visiting forces. Such a person is absent without leave if illegally absent from his unit at that time and has deserted if he intends to remain permanently absent or goes absent temporarily to avoid a particular overseas posting or service before the enemy.

Where such persons are brought before a summary court and admit that they are illegally absent and the court is satisfied of the truth of that admission, then, unless in custody for some other offence, the court shall, and notwithstanding that the person is in custody for some other cause, forthwith either cause him to be delivered into military custody or commit him to prison, a police station or other place for the confinement of persons in custody, to be kept there for delivery into military custody. Where the person concerned does not admit such absence the court must consider the evidence and the statement of the accused before coming to a decision.

Surrender

Where a person surrenders to the police as being illegally absent from the armed forces, the constable shall take him to a police station. The officer in charge of the police station, if satisfied that the person is illegally absent, may cause him to be delivered into military custody without bringing him before a court.

Certificate of arrest and surrender

Where, in either case, a person is handed over to a military escort, there shall be handed over with him a certificate signed by either a justice of the peace or clerk of the court or, where appropriate, by the officer of police who causes him to be delivered into military custody, setting out the particulars of his arrest or surrender.

No money for train fare

In circumstances in which service personnel report to the police and claim that they do not have the necessary fare to enable them to rejoin their units they should be referred to a local service establishment or to a service careers information office. Where this cannot be done, railway travel warrants may be issued by the police to such a serviceman, provided that the unit is more than 10 miles distant.

Breath specimens and drinking and driving

Introduction

The driving of motor vehicles by persons adversely affected by drink or drugs has become a social problem not only in this country but throughout the Western world. In 1967, Parliament introduced new legislation creating the offences of driving, attempting to drive and being in charge of a motor vehicle with a blood/alcohol concentration above a prescribed limit. This limit was set at 80 mg of alcohol in 100 ml of blood or 107 mg of alcohol in 100 ml of urine. Prior to the introduction of precise scientific methods of determining a blood/alcohol or urine/alcohol level, successful prosecutions were dependent upon the evidence of the medical practitioner who examined the suspect and subjected him to certain tests, most of which were concerned with co-ordination. It was hoped that these more precise methods would lead to a more effective enforcement of drink/driving legislation.

The early impact of the 1967 legislation, now incorporated in the Road Traffic Act 1988, led to a marked increase in prosecutions and an estimated saving of 1000 lives in the first year. However, complexities within the legislation led to difficulties in enforcement. A clear prescription was set out for the demand and the taking of preliminary breath tests by means of screening devices. To prove an offence, it became necessary to offer proof that procedures had been meticulously followed. Defects led to acquittals in many cases where analysis of blood or urine samples showed high levels of alcohol, and the will to enforce legislation which included so many pitfalls was obviously affected.

The Road Traffic Act 1988 was drafted with a view to eliminating all of the difficulties encountered in enforcement and it has gone some way towards doing so. For example, the reason for many acquittals was seated in a procedural defect which was alleged to have invalidated the arrest. This, in turn, made evidence of alcohol content inadmissible. The 1988 Act does not require an arrest as an essential prerequisite to a successful prosecution. It includes measures to eliminate the need for medical practitioners to become involved in most prosecutions, by introducing a requirement to provide two specimens of breath for analysis by means of a device approved by the Secretary of State. The approved devices accurately measure the alcohol in the breath and the prescribed limit is set at $35\,\mu g$ in 100 ml of breath. Substantive breath testing machines in police stations are operated by trained and approved operators.

However, care is essential in carrying out 'in station' procedures, within which irregularities may still lead to unmeritorious acquittals. There is currently an increasing tendency on the part of the High Court to allow appeals which are based upon the finer points of the procedure to be followed in a police station. The 'game' is once again becoming more important than the question of whether or not the driver was over the limit. Care must be taken in following the correct procedure in the police station.

Breath specimens at scene

Roadside specimens

The enforcement of this legislation must begin with the driving, etc., of a motor vehicle on a road or public place in circumstances in which a police officer suspects that the driver has alcohol in his body. The law allows the officer to demand a specimen of breath in certain circumstances. The suspect, by blowing into one of a number of approved screening devices, which indicate the presence of alcohol in the breath in such quantity that it is suspected that the prescribed limit might be exceeded, either confirms the officer's suspicion or provides evidence that he is not sufficiently affected. The operative word is 'screening device'. At this stage we are taking a breath specimen, measured roughly by a screening device, to confirm or set aside our suspicions. This procedure has nothing to do with the later requirement to provide breath for measurement by an evidential breath testing machine.

Section 6(1) of the Road Traffic Act 1988 provides that:

Where a constable in uniform has reasonable cause to suspect:

(a) that a person driving or attempting to drive or in charge of a motor vehicle on a road or other public place has alcohol in his body or has committed a traffic offence whilst the vehicle was in motion; or

(b) that a person has been driving or attempting to drive or been in charge of a motor vehicle on a road or other public place with alcohol in his body and that that person still has alcohol in his body; or

(c) that a person has been driving or attempting to drive or has been in charge of a motor vehicle on a road or other public place and has committed a traffic offence whilst the vehicle was in motion,

he may, subject to Section 9 (protection for hospital patients), require him to provide a specimen of breath for a breath test.

However, arresting officers must give direct evidence of their suspicion of the presence of alcohol in the accused person at the time at which they require a roadside specimen, where the issue of such suspicion is relevant to the arrest. The Divisional Court has ruled that the justices had the right to exclude the evidence of the subsequent analysis of a specimen, under the provisions of the Police and Criminal Evidence Act 1984, s 78, on the grounds that the defendant had been denied the protection of the Road Traffic Act 1988, s 6 (that a demand could only be made for a roadside specimen where that suspicion existed in the circumstances), and that the prosecutor had, in consequence of that denial, obtained evidence which would not otherwise have been obtained. This resulted in the defendant being significantly prejudiced in resisting the charge. This ruling would appear, to some extent, to negate the purpose behind the phrasing of the Road Traffic Act 1988, s 7 (see below) in its present form.

The constable's reasonable suspicion may arise as a result of an anonymous telephone call.

Special provision is made to prevent conversations between police officers and suspects in relation to procedures under s 7 (providing specimens for analysis) being classed as 'interviews' for the purpose of Code C of the Codes of Practice. There are no such provisions in relation to s 6 procedures. It is therefore advisable that, where there is a conversation between an officer and a suspect which relates to the suspect's condition, the conversation is recorded and read and signed by the suspect. In most cases such conversations will not take place.

Section 6(2) provides that if an accident occurs owing to the presence of a motor vehicle on a road or other public place, a constable may require any person whom he has reasonable cause to believe was driving or attempting to drive or in charge of the vehicle at the time of the accident, to provide a specimen of breath for a breath test, subject to s 9 (at a hospital – special provisions). The fact that an accident has occurred owing to the presence of the motor vehicle on a road or other public place does not entitle a constable to require a specimen under s 6(2) from *anyone*. The requirement may only be made of a person whom he *has reasonable cause to believe was driving or attempting to drive or in charge of the vehicle* at the time of the accident. It is not enough for a constable to 'reasonably suspect', he must 'reasonably believe' that such a person was the driver.

Section 6(3) provides that the specimen may be required to be provided at or near the place where the requirement is made. If made under subsection (2), that is following an accident, and the constable making the requirement thinks fit, the specimen may be provided at a police station specified by the constable.

The power to require a screening breath test does not depend upon a person actually having alcohol in his body or actually having committed a moving traffic offence. It arises when a constable has reasonable cause to suspect such a thing. In addition, the power to require a screening breath test extends to circumstances in which a constable has *reasonable cause to suspect* that a person *has been driving, attempting to drive or is in charge of a vehicle* on any road or public place with *alcohol in his body* and that person still has alcohol in his body or has committed a moving traffic offence. Such a suspicion need not have arisen whilst the vehicle was in motion. Thus, in any case where a constable has stopped a motorist under his common law or statutory powers, and then has reasonable cause to suspect that the driver has alcohol in his body, a screening breath test may be required.

Screening devices

The breath tests provided in accordance with this section are designed solely to assist police officers in deciding whether further action should be taken; the result of a breath test of this nature merely provides evidence on which to found reasonable suspicion that an offence is being committed. The specimen must be in sufficient quantity to enable the test to be carried out. Where a screening device requires the illumination of two lights before a satisfactory specimen has been obtained, there is a failure where only one of those lights is illuminated and a police officer is not required to 'read' such a specimen.

The screening devices used must be those approved by the Home Secretary. At present the Home Secretary has approved certain devices comprising indicator tubes, mouthpieces and inflatable bags and four electronic screening devices. The 'blow in the bag' types are the 'ALCOTEST R80' and R80A and the Alcolyser. The correct assembly and use of the devices demand a special technique which must be mastered. The containers of these devices are marked with a date after which the device must not used, and checks should be made to ensure that any device used has not become dated. The Home Secretary has approved four electronic screening devices, the LION SL2, SL2A, the DRAEGER ALERT and the DRAEGAR ALCOTEST 7410. These devices give an electronic indication by means of lights, whether or not a motorist has provided a positive or negative specimen. Once again, it is important for police officers to master the correct usage of these devices.

The instructions dealing with the operation of screening devices state that the breath test should not be given until at least 20 minutes have elapsed since the consumption of alcoholic drink. If an officer has reason to believe that such a drink may have been taken within the preceding 20 minutes, he should wait for such a period to elapse. This is because even small traces of mouth alcohol can give a positive indication. Breath should be supplied continuously for 10 to 20 seconds in the case of 'blow in the bag' devices, or until indicated in the case of electronic devices. If a driver is smoking, he should be asked to stop and allowed to take two or three breaths to void the lungs of smoke, before taking the test.

Section 9 is referred to above in relation to the taking of breath specimens. It provides that a person who is at a hospital as a patient shall not be required to provide such a breath test unless the medical practitioner in immediate charge of the case has been notified of the proposal to make the requirement. If the requirement is then made, it shall be for provision of a specimen *at the hospital*. If the medical practitioner objects, the requirement shall not be made. The grounds upon which a medical practitioner can object are that the requirement itself, or the provision of the specimen, would be prejudicial to the proper care and treatment of the patient. The same provisions apply to the provision of laboratory specimens (see page 456). A person remains a patient until discharged by a doctor or when that person discharges himself. A person is 'at a hospital' if remaining within a hospital complex, including its car park.

Driving, etc., whilst over the prescribed limit

Section 5 of the 1988 Act is concerned with driving, attempting to drive or being in charge of a motor vehicle with an alcohol concentration above the prescribed limit:

> If a person drives, or attempts to drive a motor vehicle on a road or other public place, or is in charge of a motor vehicle on a road or other public place, after consuming so much alcohol that the proportion of it in his breath, blood or urine exceeds the prescribed limit, he shall be guilty of an offence.

It will be seen that the word 'breath' precedes 'blood or urine'. In order to prove an offence the prosecution must bring evidence that the breath/alcohol concentration, as established by the correct use of an evidential breath testing machine, exceeds 35 µg of alcohol in 100 ml of breath. Only in particular circumstances, in which it has not been possible to obtain evidence of breath/alcohol concentrations, will it become necessary to show that one of the other prescribed limits was exceeded, that is either 80 mg of alcohol in 100 ml of blood or 107 mg of alcohol in 100 ml of urine. However, a police officer's involvement with such offences begins at an earlier stage, when it is suspected that a driver, etc., has alcohol in his body, so it will be of assistance to follow the procedure through from this obvious beginning.

Driving, attempting to drive or in charge of

Generally, we have little difficulty in deciding who is a driver and the term 'driver' is well discussed in other chapters. When a motorist stops before completing his journey, he may still be driving; an obvious example is when halted at traffic lights or a road junction. If a motorist is stopped by a constable in uniform, who immediately forms the suspicion that the motorist has alcohol in his body, the motorist should be regarded as still driving. If an appreciable time has elapsed before such a suspicion is formed, then it will be safer to allege 'in charge'.

In deciding whether or not someone is attempting to drive, a moment must arrive when the acts of the motorist amount to more than mere preparation. If an attempt to drive cannot be safely alleged, then an allegation of 'in charge' should be relied upon.

It would be preparation to search for the ignition keys, whereas it would be an attempt to drive if those keys are used to start the engine. A man who was trying to start the engine of his car with the wrong ignition key and who was not in possession of the correct key was held to be attempting to drive. Similarly, where a police officer found a man with a knife in his hand, fiddling with the wires beneath the steering column, it was held that there was an attempt to drive.

Motor vehicle

The term 'motor vehicle' means a mechanically propelled vehicle intended or adapted for use on roads.

Road

A road, as defined in the Act, is any highway and any other road to which the public have access, and includes bridges over which a road passes. It includes the footway as well as the carriageway. This definition can extend to privately maintained roads, if evidence can be brought to prove that the public have access; a quayside where the public are free to walk and drive, and where there is no notice of hindrance to stop them, is a road. Each case must be considered on its merits, the important factor being, in each case, the extent to which the general public, as opposed to any particular section of the public, have access. Where a road within a housing estate has not been adopted by the local authority, the determining factor is not whether the road is repairable at public expense but whether the public have access to it. If members of the public are seen there and their presence is tolerated, it is a 'road or public place'. As these offences can be committed on a road *or* in a public place, the sometimes difficult distinction between that which is a 'road' as opposed to a 'public place' is avoided.

Public place

The term 'public place' is not defined in the Act and it is a question of fact and degree; if only a restricted class of persons is permitted or invited to have access, the place would be private, but if only a restricted section of the public is excluded, the place would be public. A private field to which members of the public were permitted access to watch racing was held to be a public place at the time. A car park at the side of a public house where members of the public were permitted to park their cars was held to be a public place when it was open for such use, but this decision should be compared with that in which a car park attached to a private club used by members was held not to be a public place; a public house offers its services to the public, but a private club only offers admittance to members and their guests. Justices are entitled to rely on their local knowledge in determining whether a car park is a public place.

Caravan sites which are open to members of the public are public places. It is irrelevant that payment is required for use of the roads and facilities within the site. A site which is owned by a club and where admittance is restricted to members is a private place. However, if members of the public are additionally admitted, the site becomes 'public'. A multi-storey car park is a public place at any time at which members of the public are admitted, and so is the disembarkation lane at a ferry terminal as the persons using it are merely ticket-holding members of the public. In relation to the offence of careless driving, the foyer of the departure lounge at Heathrow Airport terminal was held to be a public place. A driver who drove an electric buggy carelessly in that area was convicted of the offence. Passengers who are about to board aircraft are still members of the public; they do not belong to any exclusive club. In relation to the same offence, the car park of a hospital was held to be a public place. There is no special or particular reason which would cause people to visit the car park which would distinguish them from ordinary members of the public.

The Divisional Court has held that a causeway giving access to an island on which there were four houses, the causeway being covered at high tide, was not a public place. There were notices in place restricting vehicular access to residents and persons having business on the island but pedestrian access was not forbidden by notice. However, no evidence had been offered of usage by members of the public (and this is essential if a place is to be considered a 'public place'), nor was the position in relation to use by residents considered.

Is in charge

This term should be given its ordinary meaning. A person is in charge of a motor vehicle, if in control of it. There is no requirement to be driving or attempting to drive it. However, distinctions must be drawn to be realistic and we must look at journeys and their purposes. A motorist remains in charge of his vehicle throughout a journey. If he sits in it at the end of that journey, then positive control is retained. Should the vehicle be secured when the driver enters a public house, it is submitted that he is no longer sufficiently in control to justify a charge even though the keys are retained. On returning to the vehicle and beginning to enter it, the driver has certainly regained his charge. If, however, the keys have been surrendered to another person with instructions that that person assumes control of the vehicle, then it is clear that 'charge' has been relinquished.

Persons other than the owner or person in lawful possession or control of a vehicle may assume charge of it. In such cases, consideration must be given as to whether and where the person was in the vehicle or how far from it, what he was doing, whether in possession of a suitable ignition key, evidence of intention to take control by driving or otherwise and the position and circumstances of other persons who were also in the vehicle.

Prescribed limit, etc.

The prescribed limits are:

(a) 35 µg of alcohol in 100 ml of *breath*;
(b) 80 mg of alcohol in 100 ml of *blood*;
(c) 107 mg of alcohol in 100 ml of *urine*.

Note that the alcohol level in the breath is measured in *micrograms* – 35 µg in 100 ml of breath is roughly equivalent to the other two levels.

In uniform

The test is whether or not the officer is identifiable as a constable and the fact that he is not wearing a cap does not affect the fact that the officer is in uniform, nor does the fact that a raincoat is being worn loosely over his uniform. Note that this requirement to be in uniform when a breath test, using a screening device, is demanded does not apply to s 6(2), in cases following an accident. A court is entitled to presume that a constable was in uniform unless the contrary is proved.

Suspicion of alcohol

It is clear that the point is not whether the motorist has actually consumed alcohol but whether the constable has reasonable cause to suspect a motorist of having alcohol in his body. All factors will be taken into account in deciding whether actions merited reasonable cause to suspect alcohol. Lack of steering control would generally give cause to such suspicions, while selecting a wrong indicator would be unlikely to be enough standing alone. It is really a question of fact for the magistrates to decide upon the evidence put forward. It is possible that more than one officer may be involved in this process. A motorist whose driving gives rise to such a suspicion may be seen driving erratically by one officer who passes a radio message to a colleague who actually stops the vehicle.

Traffic offence while vehicle in motion

The term 'traffic offence' is defined by s 6(8). It means an offence under:

(a) any provision of Part II of the Public Passenger Vehicles Act 1981 (fitness of vehicles, licences, etc.);
(b) any provision of the Road Traffic Regulation Act 1984;
(c) any provision of the Road Traffic Act 1988 except Part V (driving instruction);
(d) any provision of the Road Traffic Offenders Act 1988 except Part III (fixed penalties).

This includes offences contrary to the various regulations made under those Acts, for example, the Road Vehicles (Construction and Use) Regulations and the Road Vehicles Lighting Regulations. A common fault is to regard all offences committed in a moving vehicle as being included in the term 'moving traffic offence'. All offences under the Vehicle Excise and Registration Act 1994 and the Regulations made under the authority of that Act, e.g. Road Vehicles (Registration and Licensing) Regulations, are not offences for which a motorist can be required to give a specimen of breath for a breath test.

Has been driving, etc.

A sample of breath can be demanded if a constable reasonably suspects that a person has been driving, attempting to drive or has been in charge:

(a) with alcohol in his body and that that person still has alcohol in his body; or
(b) has committed a traffic offence while the vehicle was in motion.

These provisions are extremely helpful.

Difficulties existed in the past when drivers abandoned their vehicles and were later found after they had obviously ceased driving, etc. Now a reasonably held suspicion of the circumstances above, empowers a constable to demand a sample of breath. It should be noted that when the requirement is made following an accident, this provision is only concerned with persons who the constable reasonably believes to have been driving, attempting to drive or in charge of the vehicle at the time of the accident.

Accident

There is no legal definition of the term 'accident' and an objective test should be applied, that is, would a reasonable person, applying everyday descriptions, describe what had occurred as an accident? It has been held that a deliberate motoring act which resulted in damage to a motor car was an accident because that is how a reasonable person would describe it.

Failure to provide a sample of breath

A person who, without reasonable excuse, fails to provide a specimen of breath when required to do in pursuance of s 6(4) Road Traffic Act 1988 commits an offence. Section 6(4) is concerned with the screening test given to suspects by beat officers, using either tube and bag devices or electronic screening devices. There is no statutory requirement that a motorist must be warned that refusal to supply such a specimen will be an offence. Had it been intended, a statutory requirement would have been made, as in the case of a requirement under s 7 (see below).

Reasonable excuse

No excuse can be adjudged a reasonable one unless the person from whom the specimen is required is physically or mentally unable to provide the specimen of breath or its provision would entail a substantial risk to health. For example, a person suffering from chest or lung disorders such as bronchitis or asthma may be unable to provide sufficient breath for screening purposes. It is not a reasonable excuse that the person concerned has not consumed alcohol when a police officer, with reasonable cause, believes that he has alcohol in his body. Nor is it a reasonable excuse that consumption of alcoholic drink took place after an accident, or after immediate driving had ceased or that he mistakenly believed that the request was invalid. The term 'reasonable excuse' is strictly related to mental and physical factors which would prevent such a sample being given. It has been held that there was a reasonable excuse where a driver was concussed and where a foreigner was unable to understand the nature of the requirement.

Fail

The term 'fail' includes a refusal to provide a specimen, and failure shall be construed accordingly. As long as clear words are used to show a person that he is being required to give a sample of breath, that is sufficient. The absence of a full reason for a request to provide a specimen does not render the request unlawful.

It has been held that once a person has been given an opportunity to do something and did not do it, there is a 'failure'. For example, where a motorist refused to wait until the testing device arrived at the scene, having been required by a police officer to provide a specimen, it was held that he had refused the test. On another occasion, a motorist refused a breath test, and later the provision of samples, until his solicitor was present. It was decided that acceptance, subject to a condition, amounted to a refusal.

Where a person refuses to reply to a clear request, there has been a failure and it is no defence to allege that the refusal to reply was consequent upon a previous caution.

A person does not provide a specimen of breath for a breath test or for analysis (see below) unless the specimen is sufficient to enable the test (or analysis) to be carried out and it is provided in such a way as to enable the objective of the test (or analysis) to be satisfactorily achieved.

Arrest and entry

Section 6(5) provides that a constable may arrest a person without warrant if:

(a) as a result of a breath test he has reasonable cause to suspect that the proportion of alcohol in that person's breath or blood exceeds the prescribed limit; or
(b) that person has failed to provide a specimen of breath for a breath test when required to do so in pursuance of this section and the constable has reasonable cause to suspect that he has alcohol in his body.

Where magistrates found that a driver had been given two roadside tests, the first being negative and the second positive, they found that the arrest had been unlawful and exercised their discretion under PACE, s 78, to exclude the evidence of a subsequent analysis of breath. In making their decision, the magistrates recognised that a valid arrest was not a necessary prerequisite of the obtaining of a specimen for analysis. The Divisional Court said although it would not necessarily have agreed with their decision, they could not fault their exercise of discretion in these circumstances.

However, a person must not be arrested by virtue of either of these provisions when he is at a hospital as a patient. These powers are straightforward. Arrest may follow the provision of a positive breath sample or failure to provide a specimen, provided that in the second instance, the constable also believes that the person failing to provide the specimen has alcohol in his body. However, a driver must be requested to provide such a specimen before he can be arrested under this subsection, even if his conduct makes this difficult. Where an officer is assaulted and thus prevented from making a proper request, the driver should be arrested for that assault. The person arrested must be under no illusion as to what is happening to him. An arrest is constituted when any clear form of words is used which conveys to the accused that he is under compulsion and thereafter he submits to that compulsion. The police officer must also make the reason for the arrest clear, and if the wrong reason is given the arrest could be unlawful. In circumstances where a man was in his home and he was required to submit to a breath test and refused, it was ruled that police officers had no power to enter private premises unless this is stated in the statute.

A person who, without reasonable excuse, fails to provide a specimen of breath when required to do so in pursuance of s 6 of the 1988 Act commits an offence contrary to s 6(4).

The offence is not committed where the required procedure has not been followed, such as the use of a defective device, or where the manufacturer's instructions are not followed in relation to assembly. Where a mistake is recognised, a constable may require another breath test to be taken on another device. Provided that a constable acts in good faith and is not negligent, non-compliance with the manufacturer's instructions as to the use of the device does not invalidate the test unless the non-compliance is prejudicial to the accused.

With one exception, police officers do not have power to enter premises without the express or implied consent of the occupier for the purpose of requiring a screening breath test or making an arrest under s 6. Thus, where officers pursued a driver whom they had cause to suspect of driving with excess alcohol and they followed him into the driveway of his house without permission to carry out a breath test, the evidence of the subsequent analysis of a specimen was excluded under the provisions of the Police and Criminal Evidence Act 1984, s 78 because they had acted deliberately outside their powers.

The exceptional case where an officer is authorised to enter without consent to require a screening breath test, or to arrest, is provided by s 6(6), which states:

> A constable may for the purpose of requiring a person to provide a specimen of breath under sub-section (2) [which relates to accidents] in a case where he has reasonable cause to suspect that the accident involved injury to another person or of arresting him in such a case under sub-section (5) [where a person has provided a positive breath test or has failed to do so] enter (if need be by force) any place where that person is or where the constable, with reasonable cause, suspects him to be.

Clearly, the power to enter to require a breath test is limited to cases where the entry is for the purpose of requiring a person to provide a specimen of breath under s 6(2) in a case where a constable has reasonable cause to suspect that the accident involved injury to some other person. However, it is open to question whether the power to enter to effect an arrest under s 6(5) is limited to cases where a constable has reasonable cause to suspect that the accident involved injury to some other person. The use of the words 'in such a case' in the relevant part of s 6(6) is such that it may mean that the power is so limited. That the power under s 6(6) is so limited is supported by the words of Home Office Circular 35/1983 published in 1983. If this is the correct interpretation, a constable will be empowered by s 6(6) to enter premises to breath test a driver involved in an 'injury to another' accident or to arrest under s 6(5) where there has been an 'injury to another' accident, but he will not be empowered by s 6(6) to enter to conduct a breath test or to arrest under s 6(5) in any other case following a positive breath test or a failure to provide a breath specimen. This can hardly be supported as a logical or practical distinction. However, whatever the original intention of those who drafted the legislation, the words of s 6(6) are at least capable of being interpreted in the wider sense that such an entry may be effected to carry out an arrest which would be authorised by s 6(5).

Provision of specimen for analysis

Section 7(1) Road Traffic Act 1988 now provides:

> In the course of an investigation into whether a person has committed an offence under Sections 3A or 4 or 5 of this Act, a constable may, subject to the following provisions of this Section and Section 9 below (hospitals), require him:
>
> (a) to provide two specimens of breath for analysis by means of a device of a type approved by the Secretary of State; or
> (b) to provide a specimen of blood or urine for a laboratory test.

It will be seen that there is no prerequisite for an arrest as the new provisions use the term 'in the course of an investigation...'. It may be that there has been no arrest; a person may have come to a police station to report an accident or for some other cause or he may have been arrested for some other offence. The provision of the words 'in the course of an investigation...' has been added to avoid unmeritorious acquittals when a mistake in procedure has invalidated an arrest and thus made the subsequently acquired evidence of alcohol concentration in breath, blood or urine inadmissible. The new wording separates the arrest from the following station procedures which are independent of arrest. Thus, where a constable, in good faith, had administered a breath test on a public house car park which, at the time, was not a public place, it was held that the subsequent specimen for analysis was properly required 'in the course of an investigation'.

The procedure under s 7 does not constitute an 'interview' for the purpose of Code C of the Codes of Practice.

In addition, a person who alleges that he was a passenger, not the driver, of a car at the time in question may be lawfully required to provide a specimen as a 'person under investigation for an offence'. It is not necessary to show that he was driving.

Requirements under s 7 to provide specimens of breath can only be made at a police station. The requirement to provide two specimens of breath must be made first. By s 7(3) a requirement to provide a blood specimen or urine can only be made at a police station or at a hospital and it cannot be made at a police station unless:

(a) the constable making the requirement has reasonable cause to believe that for medical reasons a specimen of breath cannot be provided (because of inability) or should not be required (for some other reason, such as the taking of a drug which affects blood/alcohol levels). Provided that a reasonable cause to believe that medical reasons exist, it is irrelevant that the constable himself does not believe that for medical reasons a breath specimen cannot be provided or should not be required. The present position does not require the constable to seek medical advice; the question is whether on the facts before the constable he had reasonable cause to believe that medical reasons exist;

(b) at the time the requirement is made an approved device or a reliable approved device is not available at the police station, or it is then for any other reason not practicable to use such a device there; or

(bb) a device of the type mentioned in subsection (1) (a) has been used at the police station but the constable who required the specimen of breath has reasonable cause to believe that the device has not produced a reliable indication of the proportion of alcohol in the breath of the person concerned; or

(c) the suspected offence is one under s 4 of this Act and the constable making the requirement has been advised by a medical practitioner that the condition of the person required to provide the specimen might be due to some drug,

but may then be made notwithstanding that the person required to provide the specimen has already provided or been required to provide two specimens of breath.

Where a specimen is required under (c) above, the section requires that the constable making the requirement has been advised by a medical practitioner that the condition of the person might be due to some drug. This may be proved by oral evidence from the doctor or by the police officer saying what the doctor said to him. Where procedural forms have been completed, including the signed observations of the doctor, the Divisional Court has held that justices are entitled to find that this advice had been given. Whilst the endorsement signed by the doctor is, in its contents, hearsay, the fact that the doctor signed the endorsement which was then followed by words which led the officer to complete the rest of the document in a particular way, indicating that he was concerned with impairment through drugs after medical advice, was a matter to which the justices could have regard. However, it will be sensible to have the doctor give evidence either orally or by a statement under the Criminal Justice Act 1967, s 9.

A suspect must now be asked to provide two specimens of breath in the first instance. Blood or urine is only to be taken if medical reasons, lack of machine availability or suspected drug taking make this course essential. Where a defendant stated that he was taking a prescribed drug which would influence the outcome of a breath test, and this was believed by the constable, the constable had reasonable cause to believe that such a medical reason existed and was entitled to ask for an alternative specimen. On the other hand, where a motorist replied, 'I do take tablets', when asked if there was a medical reason why he could not or should not give blood, this was capable in principle of being a valid reason and the police officer should not have gone on to arrange for a specimen of blood to be taken without making enquiries as to the nature of the medication and seeking medical advice if necessary. Provided that there is reasonable cause to believe that medical reasons exist, it is irrelevant that the constable himself does not believe that for medical reasons, a breath specimen cannot be provided, or should not be required. Where a defendant has provided two specimens of breath on a machine which is then found to be defective, he may lawfully be required to provide two further specimens of breath for analysis by another device instead of being required to provide blood or urine. Where this involves taking such a person to another police station, it will be wise to repeat the statutory warning (see page 445) that failure may render him liable to prosecution. It must be remembered that where a person is charged with failure to provide a specimen of blood for laboratory analysis in circumstances in which a breath testing device was not available, if the validity of the request for a sample of blood is challenged the non-availability of the device must be proved in accordance with the laws of evidence. However, where a defendant contended that there was no direct evidence to show that there was no device available as there could have been a second device at the police station, the Divisional Court ruled that where there was evidence that the accused was told that the machine had failed to operate and that it was not therefore possible to take specimens of breath, this was sufficient. Had there been another device, it would have been possible to take specimens of breath.

For the purpose of this section, a 'reliable device' is one which the police officer concerned reasonably believes to be reliable. It is 'not practicable' to use a device if there is no officer available at the station who has been trained to use the device. A police officer must believe that a device is unreliable, not that it might be unreliable, before he is empowered to require an alternative specimen. Where a police officer thought that the device might be unreliable because the motorist did not appear to be as badly affected as the device indicated and required an alternative specimen, the conviction was quashed on the grounds that a belief that the device might be unreliable is insufficient. In another case where, during the morning and after a positive roadside breath test, a reading which was more than four times the legal limit was obtained and the driver gave no indication that she was so badly affected, the Divisional Court refused to interfere with the justices' conclusion that the intoximeter must have been unreliable even though she had not called expert evidence as to what the reading should have been following her admitted consumption of alcohol. The court said that the decision was very close to the line of perversity. For the officer to have required an alternative specimen he would have had to believe that the device had not produced a reliable reading.

Where a police officer at first reasonably believed that an intoximeter device had failed to calibrate correctly, required a specimen of blood which the motorist refused to supply, then discovered that the device had operated satisfactorily and had given a correct reading, justices were entitled to admit evidence of the analysis of the breath specimen which gave the lower reading. A breath specimen remains potentially admissible unless and until replaced by an admissible blood or urine specimen.

Where defence 'experts' carried out tests on two intoximeter devices by swilling alcohol around their mouths without swallowing it before taking tests on the machines, they found that in some circumstances, mouth alcohol was not detected. The justices dismissed the charges, in one case because they considered the device to be unreliable and in the other because the device had not performed to the same standards as the device approved by the Secretary of State. The Divisional Court said that their reasons were not valid. A challenge could be mounted to the reliability of a particular device if there was a defect which could be linked to an inability to measure deep lung alcohol. There would not have been mouth alcohol or alcohol vapour in the dead space of the upper respiratory tract when the readings which were relied upon were taken.

Section 7(3) (bb) [the substance of which is set out in (c) above] was inserted by the Criminal Procedure and Investigations Act 1996. Section 7(3) (b) requires evidence that the device was unreliable or that it was not practicable to use a reliable device. It is therefore necessary for the prosecution to prove that the officer believed that the device was unreliable and that there was material evidence on which, at the time, he could reasonably have formed that view. Reliance on the guidance contained in procedural instructions about the use of breath testing equipment which leads to the conclusion that an indication is unreliable will mean that the constable has reasonable grounds to believe that the device has not produced a reliable reading.

Whilst decisions of the High Court concerning s 7(3) (b) remain valid, the addition of s 7(3) (bb) makes, in some circumstances, the issue of the reliability of the machine itself irrelevant. An alternative specimen may be required where a breath testing device has been used and the constable who required the specimens has reasonable cause to believe that the device has not produced *a reliable indication* of the proportion of alcohol in the breath of the person concerned. Thus, if the device produces two readings which indicate significant differences in the level of alcohol, it will be open to the constable to require an alternative specimen if he reasonably believes that the device has not produced a reliable indication of the level of alcohol in the breath. These provisions paved the way for the introduction of new devices which indicate the presence of any substance which interferes with the reading, the presence of mouth alcohol and when the difference between the two readings is greater than 15 per cent.

Where only one satisfactory specimen of breath has been obtained owing to a failure of the breath testing machine and an alternative specimen has been, in consequence, obtained and a charge has been preferred alleging an excess of alcohol in that alternative specimen, evidence of the proportion of alcohol found in the one specimen of breath will be inadmissible, as it is not relevant to a charge of excess alcohol in another specimen. However, where the accuracy of the analysis of the alternative specimen is challenged, the prosecution is required to prove beyond reasonable doubt that the blood alcohol analysis was reliable and if the breath test result was broadly equivalent to the analysis of the alternative specimen, then notwithstanding the reason for requiring the alternative specimen, such evidence is at least capable of tending to support the reliability of the analysis of the alternative specimen. Provided that the significance of the relationship between the two analyses is explained by an expert, the Divisional Court has held that the evidence may be relevant.

Section 7(4) provides that if the provision of a specimen other than a specimen of breath may be required in pursuance of the section the question of whether it is to be a specimen of blood or a specimen of urine and, in the case of a specimen of blood, the question of who is to be asked to take it shall be decided [subject to s 7(4A)] by the constable making the requirement. The Police Reform Act 2002 not only amended s 7(4) but also added a new subsection (4A). The existing situation is that if a specimen other than breath may be required in pursuance of s 7 it remains for the constable making the requirement to decide whether the specimen shall be of blood or urine. Subject to s 7(4A), in the case of blood, it is for the constable to decide who is to be asked to take the specimen. Section 7(4A) provides that, where a constable decides for the purposes of s 7 to require the provision of a specimen of blood, there must be no requirement to provide such a specimen if:

(a) the medical practitioner who is asked to take the specimen is of the opinion that, for medical reasons, it cannot or should not be taken; or

(b) the registered health-care professional who is asked to take it is of that opinion and there is no contrary opinion from a medical practitioner;

Section 7(4A) also provides that where by virtue of s 7(4A) there can be no requirement to provide a specimen of blood, the constable may require a specimen of urine instead.

The term 'registered health-care professional' means a person (other than a medical practitioner) who is a registered nurse or a registered member of a health-care profession which is designated for the present purposes by an order made by the Home Secretary.

If a constable requires a specimen of blood or urine under s 7(3), the decision as to whether it should be blood or urine is for the constable and he does not have to invite the motorist to express his own preference before making the decision. However, if the constable intends to require a specimen of blood, under the provisions of s 7(3), there are two mandatory requirements which must be fulfilled:

(a) he must, in accordance with s 7(7), warn the person that a failure to provide a specimen may render him liable to prosecution (if this is not done the evidence of the analysis of the specimen is inadmissible); and

(b) he must inform the person of the reason why specimens of breath could not be taken.

There are further factors which the constable should bring to the attention of the person concerned. Although these factors have been held not to be mandatory by the House of Lords, the House has said that police officers, in order to seek to ensure that a driver is aware of the role of a doctor, should continue to use a formula recommended by Lord Bridge within a previous judgement given by the House. The additional factors included in the formula are:

(a) that the driver is informed that he is required to provide a specimen of blood or urine but that it is for the constable to decide which;

(b) that his only right to object to giving blood will be for medical reasons to be determined by a doctor;

(c) where a driver makes a representation in answer to a question about whether a specimen of blood should be taken, the constable must consider whether the statement proffered is capable of being a medical reason;

(d) if the constable concludes that there is no medical reason, he may require a blood specimen, but if he has doubts about the matter, he should seek the opinion of a medical practitioner.

In relation to these non-mandatory requirements, the House of Lords said that what was necessary is that the driver should be aware, whether or not he was told by a police officer, of the doctor's role *so that he does not suffer prejudice*. If a driver appreciates that a blood specimen would be taken by a doctor and not by a police officer, a charge should not be dismissed merely because a police officer has failed to tell the driver that a specimen would be taken by a doctor. The House said that a court should follow a two-stage process:

(a) It should consider whether all of these matters had been brought to the attention of the driver. If the answer to that question was 'No', it should then consider (b).
(b) In relation to the non-mandatory requirements, the issue was whether the police officer's failure to give the full formula deprived the driver of the opportunity to exercise any option open to him, or caused him to exercise it in a way which he would not have done had everything been said.
   (i) If the answer to (b) is 'Yes', the driver should be acquitted.
   (ii) If the answer to (b) is 'No', the police officer's failure to use the full formula should not be a reason for an acquittal.

The House of Lords said that it would only be in exceptional circumstances that a court would acquit on the grounds that a driver suffered prejudice without having heard evidence from the driver himself which raised the issue of prejudice. These issues are questions of fact. If the court, having heard the driver's evidence, is not satisfied beyond reasonable doubt that he was not prejudiced, he should be acquitted.

The House of Lords also ruled on this occasion that there is no statutory requirement, or any considerations of fairness, which require a police officer to ask a driver if any non-medical reason exists in consequence of which a specimen of blood should not be taken. Any such matter might support 'a reasonable cause for failure to provide a specimen' but that is a matter for a court.

A breath analysing device was inoperative and the sergeant required blood. The motorist's vein collapsed when a police surgeon attempted to take blood and the sergeant then required urine. The Divisional Court ruled that the sergeant's right to change his mind continued up to the time at which blood *was actually given*.

Whether or not there has been a valid requirement to provide a specimen of blood is a question of fact to be determined by a court, having regard to all of the circumstances. The Divisional Court has said that fairness can be achieved without the introduction of rigid judge-made formulae which can so easily mask the statutory language and needlessly complicate its construction. However, it is good practice to ensure that a direct requirement is made and to ensure that there has been a positive refusal.

Section 11(4) of the Road Traffic Act 1988 states that a person provides a specimen of blood if, and only if, he consents to its being taken by a medical practitioner and it is so taken. Subsection (4) was substituted by the Police Reform Act 2002. The new s 11(4) provides that:

A person supplies a specimen of blood if and only if:

(a)   he consents to the taking of such a specimen from him; and
(b)   the specimen is taken from him by a medical practitioner or, if it is taken in a police station, either by a medical practitioner or by a registered health-care professional.

Where a constable requires a specimen of blood and the person refuses but offers urine as an alternative, there has been a 'failure' on the part of the motorist, unless such a medical reason exists. A belief does not amount to a reasonable excuse; thus a refusal to give blood because of a fear of AIDS is not, in normal circumstances, a reasonable excuse, but a medically recognised phobia in relation to contracting AIDS may be. It is advisable, therefore, that where a motorist alleges a genuine fear of AIDS, the opinion of a medical practitioner is sought so that the rare condition of 'phobia' may be eliminated.

Where no reliable intoximeter device was available, a sergeant asked if there was any reason why blood could not, or should not be taken. The motorist replied, 'I do take tablets'. The sergeant asked if he would supply blood and he agreed to do so. The Divisional Court said that the sergeant was faced with a claim for medical immunity which was capable of being valid and that he had usurped the functions of a medical practitioner by holding that it was invalid.

In relation to urine specimens, they must be provided within 1 hour of the requirement being made and after a previous specimen has been provided and discarded. It is a question of fact for the justices to determine as to whether a full period of 1 hour had passed following the requirement. Where a second specimen of urine is accepted outside this time limit as an alternative to charging a person with failure, the Divisional Court has held that the result of the analysis of that specimen is nevertheless admissible. A police officer is not obliged to extend that time, but if he does so, the subsequent specimen will not be rendered inadmissible. Warning that failure to provide a specimen for analysis may result in a prosecution is essential in all cases.

Specimens of blood taken from a person incapable of consenting

The Police Reform Act 2002 inserted a 7A into the Road Traffic Act 1988 to deal with the taking of blood specimens from a person who has been involved in an accident and is, for some reason, incapable of giving a valid consent to the taking of a specimen of blood.

Section 7A(1) provides that a constable may make a request to a medical practitioner for him to take a specimen of blood from a person ('the person concerned') irrespective of whether that person consents if:

(a) that person is a person from whom the constable would (in the absence of any incapacity of that person and of any objection under s 9) be entitled under s 7 to require the provision of a specimen of blood for a laboratory test;
(b) it appears to that constable that that person has been involved in an accident that constitutes or is comprised in the matter that is under investigation or the circumstances of that matter;
(c) it appears to that constable that that person is or may be incapable (whether or not he has purported to do so) of giving a valid consent to the taking of a specimen of blood; and
(d) it appears to that constable that that person's incapacity is attributable to medical reasons.

Under s 7A, a request:

(a) shall not be made to a medical practitioner who for the time being has any responsibility (apart from the request) for the clinical care of the person concerned; and
(b) shall not be made to a medical practitioner other than a police medical practitioner unless

(i) it is not reasonably practicable for the request to be made to a police medical practitioner; or

(ii) it is not reasonably practicable for such a medical practitioner (assuming him to be willing to do so) to take the specimen.

By s 7A(3), it shall be lawful for a medical practitioner to whom a request is made under this section, if he thinks fit:

(a) to take a specimen of blood from the person concerned irrespective of whether that person consents; and

(b) to provide the sample to a constable.

Section 7A(4) states that, if a specimen is taken in pursuance of a request under this section, the specimen shall not be subjected to a laboratory test unless the person from whom it was taken:

(a) has been informed that it was taken; and

(b) has been required by a constable to give his permission for a laboratory test of the specimen; and

(c) has given his permission.

On requiring a person to give his permission for the purposes of s 7A for a laboratory test of a specimen, a constable is required by s 7A(5) to warn that person that a failure to give the permission may render him liable to prosecution.

It is an offence under s 7A(6) for a person, without reasonable excuse, to fail to give permission for a laboratory test of a specimen of blood taken from him under s 7A. It is a defence that a warning was not given under s 7A(5) or has not been understood by the person in question.

In this section, 'police medical practitioner' means a medical practitioner who is engaged under any agreement to provide medical services for purposes connected with the activities of a police force.

Blood samples must be taken by doctors (or registered health-care professionals) and all are aware of the techniques to be employed. The blood specimen kits are provided by the forensic science laboratories and are kept at police stations. When a police surgeon (or other person authorised to take specimens of blood) takes a specimen of blood for analysis, he completes a certificate and signs it, to show that he took the specimen of blood with the consent of the accused. This is evidence of the facts certified and, provided that a copy of such certificate is served on an accused not less than 7 days before the court or trial, and the accused has not within 3 days of the court hearing or trial served notice on the prosecutor that he requires the attendance of the doctor, the certificate may be put in evidence and the police surgeon need not attend court.

When a specimen of blood or urine has been obtained from an accused, care should be taken that the labels are correctly made out and securely attached to the samples to be sent to the forensic science laboratory with the completed form FSL I. The Divisional Court has said that, where there is an allegation of mislabelling, each case must be considered on its own facts. Where the name and initial of the motorist were correct, the date and time of the taking of the specimen were correctly indicated and the name of the police force and the arresting officer were correct, the justices had been correct to be satisfied as to the admissibility of evidence of the analysis of the specimen. Errors in the name of the police station and the exhibit number were not sufficient to invalidate the specimen in these circumstances.

Samples must be positively identified as those of particular defendants. To mark them with the surname of the defendant only is insufficient to ensure positive identification. It should be remembered that continuity must be maintained from the time the sample is taken from an accused to the time it is handed over, or posted, to the forensic science laboratory.

When, at the time of the provision of a specimen of blood or urine, an accused asks to be supplied with a specimen, the specimen taken must be divided into two parts, the other part being supplied to the accused. If this is not done, the evidence of the proportion of alcohol will not be admissible. Where the doctor left the room for about 2 minutes and divided the specimen of blood outside the accused's view, such a division had taken place 'at the time'. 'At the time' means closely linked in time and a part of the same event. It is desirable, however, that the division takes place in the presence of the accused.

The most reliable analysis of a specimen of blood is that which takes place soon after the specimen was provided. There is a continuing loss of alcohol content even where a specimen is stored in controlled conditions.

The use of the evidential breath testing machine

Approved devices may only be operated by trained operators authorised by chief officers of police. Instructors have been trained by the Home Office and authorised to teach the actual machine operators the correct procedures to be followed. The design of the machines is such that most of the likely problems in usage have been eliminated. At the outset the machine is correctly calibrated but its operating procedure is such that the machine checks its correct calibration both before and after a breath sample is provided and provides evidence on the printout slip that this has been done. The accused should be present throughout the running cycle of the machine. The police officer carrying out the test is not obliged to explain to the motorist that the second specimen must be provided within 3 minutes or the test will abort. However, in certain circumstances, it may be relevant to consider whether such a failure can constitute the basis of a reasonable excuse. This could occur where a person was, in good faith, delaying the provision of a second specimen and he was not warned of the consequences of such delay. In such circumstances, it would be a matter for the court to consider.

The operator must sign a certificate to the effect that the machine printout relates to the specimen provided by the accused at the date and time shown. The printout from the machine provides most of the details required and can be incorporated into the statement. The officer certifies all copies of the printout from the machine, declares the reading in respect of the lower proportion of alcohol in the accused's breath specimen to be at the specified level and certifies that copies of the statement were signed by him and signed (or signature refused) by the accused. He also declares that he has handed a copy of the statement to the accused who accepted or declined to accept it. The Road Traffic Offenders Act 1988, s 16(3), requires that a copy is either 'handed to' an accused at the time, or is served upon him not later than 7 days before the hearing. Where an accused signed all three copies but refused to accept one, the Divisional Court held that the provisions of the section had been complied with when the accused was offered a copy although there had been no physical transfer of possession of the document. Nevertheless, it will be good practice in such circumstances subsequently to serve a copy of the statement upon the accused in accordance with the section. Proof of calibration and intoximeter readings is complete when a printout is handed to the operator in court and he confirms its authenticity. It is not essential that the justices examine it. It is before the court.

The intoximeter devices are computers. Previously, the Police and Criminal Evidence Act 1984, s 69, required that a constable certified that such a computer had been properly used, was operating correctly (and if not the defect was not such as would affect the production of the document) and that operating rules had been observed. However, s 69 was repealed by the Youth Justice and Criminal Evidence Act 1999 so there is now no requirement that the reliability of the computer be proved as a matter of course. Nevertheless, where reliability is challenged, such proof will be required. It is therefore desirable that police officers continue to record on the appropriate procedural forms the fact that the computer was operating correctly together with any appropriate observations, as is done at present. The references to the 1984 Act will no doubt be removed. Previous decisions concerning 'computers' will still be relevant in some instances in which reliability is challenged. The ordinary law of evidence will now apply to computer evidence. In the absence of evidence to the contrary, courts will presume that the computer system was working correctly. If there is evidence that it may not have been, the party seeking to introduce the evidence will need to prove that it was working.

Where the procedural form had not been fully completed by filling in the blank spaces in the certificate, the Divisional Court said that the justices were entitled to rely upon other evidence that the computer was operating correctly, the fact that a trained operator was present, that the calibration had been checked and was in order and that the operator had not indicated, at a point where the form provided an opportunity to do so, that the computer was not working. Similarly, where the sergeant had, when deleting a part of the procedural form which did not apply to the procedure which he was following, inadvertently struck out a part of the completed certificate, the Divisional Court said that the justices had been entitled to find that the certificate was valid. No objection had been taken in respect of the forms which had been served on the accused and it was obvious, in view of the fact that proceedings had been taken, that the part of the certificate had been deleted in error.

The fact that the clock on such a device is registering an incorrect time, or that the device registers an incorrect date, is not such a defect as would affect the production of such a document, where satisfactory evidence is offered to that effect. Nor is the fact that a printer omitted the second half of the first character and the second character in every line and printed some parts in smaller print. Provided that the part of the intoximeter device which is a 'computer' was operating correctly at the time and that it was calibrated and correct, the malfunctioning of the printer does not affect in any way the manner in which the intoximeter processes, stores or retrieves the information used to generate the statement offered in evidence.

Where a motorist has opted to replace the analysis of a specimen of breath with that of a specimen of blood (see below), it is not necessary for the prosecution to prove the calibration of the intoximeter. The positive specimen of breath, in such circumstances, is no more than a prerequisite for the supply of a specimen of blood; analysis of the breath specimen ceases to have any probative value in proving the offence.

However, all such decisions will now have to be considered in the light of the fact that there is now no requirement for and no regulated procedure by which proof of reliability may be measured.

Oral evidence is admissible of the results of such a test but in such instances oral evidence must also be given of the calibration of the machine. It will be good practice, in such cases, to serve a copy of the evidence of the police operator on the defendant in accordance with s 9 of the Criminal Justice Act 1967.

The machine provides a timed, dated, identifiable printout which relates to a particular machine operator and a particular accused person. It shows that it has checked its own calibration both before and after samples and gives an immediate and accurate reading of alcohol concentration. Remember that two specimens are required and it is the lower of the two readings which may be given in evidence. This record is a statement within the meaning of s 16 of the Road Traffic Offenders Act 1988 and is admissible in evidence as such.

Defence solicitors have no right to obtain intoximeter documents such as the log, repair reports and memory roll with a view to searching for material which might support a submission that the machine was defective. They must rely upon the prosecution to fulfil its duty to disclose material evidence which might be of assistance to the defence.

An approved device can only be shown to be defective by evidence which goes directly to the defective nature of the machine itself, or by the result of a blood analysis. However, the reliability of all devices of a prescribed type cannot be challenged as the device has been approved by the Home Secretary.

The statutory option

The caution which one would expect in relation to the introduction of such mechanical devices is expressed by the requirement that if the lower of the two readings is no more than $50 \mu g$ of alcohol in $100 ml$ of breath, the accused may require that it may be replaced by a blood or urine sample for analysis. This has become known as the 'statutory option'. He must be informed of his right to exercise it, unless he makes this impossible (as where he refuses to listen and walks away). Similarly, where a defendant's consumption of alcohol had contributed to his inability to comprehend the nature of the offer made to him to replace the specimen, he could not allege that the breath specimen became inadmissible because of that failure to comprehend the procedure.

It is not necessary to invite him to express a preference as to whether the specimen should be of blood or urine (since it suffices that he is told that, if he exercises the right to have a replacement specimen taken, it will be for the police officer to decide whether that specimen is to be of blood or urine). The Divisional Court has held that it is not *strictly* necessary for a police officer to inform such a person that the breath specimen which he has provided exceeds the statutory limit, since the fact that an alternative is being offered must make that fact obvious. Where an officer said that a replacement specimen would be used for *court purposes* the Divisional Court said that whilst those words served no useful purpose they were not misleading.

Where a police officer decides to require an alternative specimen of blood, the House of Lords has ruled that he must inform the person that the specimen of breath which he has given which contains the lower proportion of alcohol does not exceed $50 \mu g$ in $100 ml$ of breath. See page 445 for non-mandatory procedural requirements in relation to the provision of a specimen of blood. In a s 8(2) case, in addition to telling the driver that a specimen of blood 'will be taken by a doctor unless he considers that there are medical reasons for not taking blood', the constable should ask the driver if there are any medical reasons why a specimen of blood could or should not be taken by a doctor. This should be done at the outset of the procedure.

Where procedural forms used by the police were such that the question, 'Are there any reasons why a specimen of blood cannot or should not be taken by a doctor?' should only be asked if the option had been taken, the Divisional Court said that it was bound to follow the procedure approved by the House of Lords which included the fact that the question should be asked at the outset. It was therefore necessary, as this was not one of the mandatory requirements, to consider whether the suspect had suffered prejudice in consequence of the question not being asked. If there had been such prejudice, evidence to that effect would be required.

A suspect has no right to legal advice before deciding whether or not to exercise this option and this applies equally to a driver who is a 'young person'; the suspect's situation is the same as that of a person who is being *required* to provide a specimen for analysis; the procedure may not be delayed. Where the option has been offered and refused, it is for the justices to decide, in accordance with the evidence, whether the procedure has come to an end at the time when the motorist subsequently changed his mind. It is likely that a more or less immediate change of mind will be acceptable as in other similar circumstances such words have been held to be 'relevant words and conduct to be taken into account'. However, once the procedure has moved on to the next stage, justices will have grounds to support a conclusion that the issue of acceptance or refusal had been finalised.

Where a police officer had, at the outset, explained the whole procedure to the driver who exercised this option, it was not essential that he repeat the whole procedure once more when this option was exercised. The information, in such a case, will still be present and effective in the driver's mind. On the other hand, it has been held that the fact that consent would be required if blood were taken by a doctor at a later stage, does not mean that a driver has to be told in terms at an earlier stage that it would be so taken. Follow the procedure as prescribed by the existing forms used by your force. The constable will decide which of these alternatives is to be provided. In such instances, where the suspect chooses to replace the specimen of breath with an alternative, the evidence of the analysis of the breath specimen is not admissible in evidence.

Where an accused initially declined to exercise such an option, but agreed to do so after legal advice 1 hour later, a court was entitled to decide that enough time had passed to bring the statutory procedure to an end, and admit evidence of the proportion of alcohol in his breath. If a motorist, given the statutory option, is asked to provide a blood specimen, but the police officer is unable to contact a doctor, the police officer has the power to ask the motorist to provide a urine specimen instead. If the motorist is unable to do so (e.g. because he has visited the lavatory in the meanwhile), the lower of the two breath specimens can be used in evidence since the statutory option procedure only prohibits either specimen of breath being used if a blood or urine specimen is provided within the procedure.

Where a motorist gives a reason for not giving blood, which may amount to a medical reason, the police officer should ask him for an explanation of that reason as such an enquiry may establish that the reason is without foundation. If the reason advanced is capable of being a 'medical reason' a doctor should be consulted; if the officer is in any doubt, a doctor should be consulted. Where a person who was a diabetic injected himself twice a day, was tattooed and whose ears had been pierced claimed that he did not want other people putting needles into his arm or skin, the Divisional Court ruled that this was a medical reason which should have been referred to a doctor. Such a reference not having been made, he had been deprived of his rights under the section and no requirement 'in pursuance of the section' had been made. On the other hand, where a motorist says that he would prefer to give urine as he does not like needles but accepts that there is no reason why a specimen of blood should not be taken by a doctor and then refuses to supply blood, the police officer is under no obligation to make further enquiries about that person's fear of needles. The House of Lords has ruled that it is a question of fact whether a driver's statement to the effect that he does not like needles raises a potential medical reason for not providing a blood specimen and that a court is entitled to find, on the facts, that a police officer was not obliged to investigate the matter further. Where a person makes it perfectly clear that he is not going to provide a specimen of any description, he cannot suffer prejudice in relation to the nature of such a specimen.

However, where a driver said, 'I do take tablets', when asked if there was a medical reason why he should not or could not give blood, this was capable of being a valid reason and the police officer should not have gone on to make arrangements for a specimen of blood to be taken without making enquiries as to the nature of the medication and seeking medical advice if necessary.

There are two important factors to remember when dealing with evidential breath specimens. If a breath sample is analysed soon after the last drink has been taken the reading will be very high owing to residual mouth alcohol. It is essential that a period of 20 minutes has elapsed since the last drink, to allow mouth alcohol to disperse. A wide variation in levels of alcohol as indicated in the two tests should raise the suspicion of mouth alcohol, which can sometimes be present even after a period of 20 minutes, if the accused has vomited or regurgitated. True measurements must be of deep lung air in sufficient quantity. If less quantity is provided, the machine will not accept it; it will abort and require a fresh specimen. The Divisional Court has held that the innocent failure by a police officer to follow these instructions does not render the result of a subsequent analysis of a specimen by an intoximeter device at a police station, and the arrest, unlawful.

Failure to provide a specimen

A person who, without reasonable excuse, fails to provide a specimen when required to do so in pursuance of these requirements commits an offence. Failure includes refusal. Where a motorist at first refused to provide a specimen but asked some 5 seconds later whether he could change his mind, there was no refusal. The Divisional Court held that his words, said so quickly afterwards, were words which were relevant to the issue and should be taken into account. They were part of the conduct of the accused at the relevant time. It is submitted that this ruling, read with others, suggests that all words and conduct which occur whilst that stage of the procedure is still 'active' are relevant to the issue of refusal. Where a motorist refused to supply breath on the grounds that he suffered from bronchitis and the sergeant, who doubted the validity of his claim, sent for a doctor who certified that the motorist was fit to supply specimens of breath, the Divisional Court ruled that the sergeant was under no obligation to start the procedure again. There had been a failure to supply breath when the person concerned was capable of supplying it.

Where a motorist refuses to supply specimens of breath and it is subsequently found that, because of his limited lung capacity, he would have been unable to supply specimens, this cannot amount to a reasonable excuse. There would have to be a causative link between the refusal and the excuse and this could not be so where the condition was not known to exist at the time of the refusal.

The term 'reasonable excuse' has already been discussed. However, in a case related to the provision of two specimens of breath for analysis, it was held that where a defendant is young, fit and can provide no valid reason for his inability to provide two specimens of breath, justices are not entitled to 'assume', in the absence of direct evidence, that he was under some stress as a result of an accident and his arrest. In addition, in deciding whether or not an excuse is reasonable, justices are not entitled to go beyond the evidence which is before them. They should avoid using whatever knowledge they may have of physical or mental conditions which may have been affecting a motorist.

A Libyan national claimed that his command of the English language was such that he could not understand the requirement itself, or the consequences of failure. This was accepted as a reasonable excuse. In the same way as in screening tests, the imposition of conditions by an accused, for example, presence of a solicitor, or that he requires time to read the Detention Code or time to refer to a law book, amounts to a failure. A divisional court has held that there was no breach of a person's human right to legal advice where a duty solicitor was contacted some 7 minutes after that person's arrival in a police station, at which stage the testing procedure was commenced. Nor was there such a breach where a person had been given a notice which said that he was entitled to legal advice, and thereafter, that person twice refused to provide a specimen for analysis as he had not spoken to a solicitor. He was charged with refusal. A solicitor was then contacted and an hour later he attended and spoke to the accused. The Court said that the public interest had to be weighed against the right to legal advice provided by PACE, s 58, and that although s 58 had been breached, that breach was neither significant nor substantial. However, it would be good practice for someone to contact a solicitor at the time of such a request as this would not involve any significant delay to the testing procedure.

Unreasonable conditions concerning the method by which blood is to be taken shall also amount to refusal. There has also been a refusal where a person fails to give a specimen on the advice of his solicitor.

Stress caused by self-precipitated agitation is not sufficient reasonable excuse, nor is anguish caused by the conduct of a police officer which the driver considered to be oppressive. There would have to be a causal connection between that anguish and the inability to supply breath. Almost invariably, medical evidence will be required for such a defence. However, the Divisional Court would not interfere with a finding of the justices that there had been a reasonable excuse where a driver was said by her doctor to be suffering from a condition in which any stress would cause her to suffer from extremes of agitation which would require chemical intervention. She had not taken medication which controlled her condition within the preceding few days. The justices found that she had been suffering from a panic attack at the police station and this had prevented her from supplying specimens of breath. They noted the doctor's opinion that she would have understood the procedure and that there would be nothing of a physical or mental nature to prevent her from supplying breath, but considered that there was a causative link between her physical condition and her inability to supply breath.

Where a driver is so drunk that he is unable to understand the procedure which is being followed, such an excuse does not relate to his 'capacity' to provide a specimen. In such a case he is unable to respond owing to self-induced drunkenness and this is not a reasonable excuse. However, where a driver failed to provide two specimens of breath and two police officers gave evidence that he appeared to be too drunk to do so, the Divisional Court refused to overturn a decision that the accused had a reasonable excuse due to stress resulting from adverse personal and family circumstances which had led to recent breathlessness, although no medical evidence was offered. It said that the justices had reached their decision on unimpeachable findings of fact and that they would not interfere. It is possible that the court was influenced by the fact that the accused had offered an alternative specimen, thus indicating that he was not attempting to avoid providing a specimen.

The Divisional Court has ruled that justices were entitled to accept that an accused was physically unable to provide the required two specimens of breath where, after providing the first, she broke down, sobbed continuously and experienced difficulty in breathing. She alleged that this was due to post-arrest shock. She was unable to provide a second specimen. The court acknowledged that, having successfully provided one specimen, the case was close to the borderline. It would not accept, in absolute terms, that there was a need for medical evidence to support such a claim. The circumstances of this case differed from that relating to 'stress' in that the woman concerned had been pursued by rowdy youths, had been involved in an accident whilst so pursued and was in an almost hysterical condition.

In addition, the Divisional Court overruled a decision by magistrates that an accused was unable to provide a second specimen of breath owing to pain which he was suffering following an accident. He had already provided a roadside specimen and one specimen at a police station. The magistrates had ignored the fact that expert evidence had been given to the effect that it was more difficult to provide a specimen on the device used for a roadside breath test.

The Divisional Court has recently re-examined all previous decisions relating to what it described as the 'trying one's best excuse' and said that justices should examine whether a defendant had a reasonable excuse by reason of some physical or mental infirmity. A defendant will not satisfy this evidential burden unless he provides medical evidence to support his contention. If such evidence is not forthcoming, that burden will not be satisfied. If it is satisfied, it is for the prosecution to negate it to the criminal standard of proof. However, the court did not go so far as to say that the medical evidence *must* be given by a doctor, but made it clear that this would be so in most circumstances.

Justices accepted that a motorist had a reasonable excuse for failing to provide a specimen for analysis where the constable conducting the roadside test had failed to pass on to the officer conducting the substantive breath tests at a police station a comment made by the driver to the effect that he suffered from bronchitis (a roadside specimen had been provided). At the police station the motorist had made no attempt to provide breath. The Administrative Court would not accept that there had been a reasonable excuse for the non-provision of specimens. Where no attempt was made to provide a specimen there could be no subsequent contention that a reasonable excuse had existed. The sergeant conducting the test had not known of the motorist's condition and the motorist had not made him aware of it. The failure of the arresting constable to tell the custody sergeant of the roadside contention did not affect the investigating officer's statutory obligations within the procedure.

A driver refused to provide specimens of breath because he had a sore ear. The sergeant thereupon decided that, subject to anything which the medical officer might say, he would charge him with failure. The medical officer found that the driver had a slightly swollen ear with impacted hard wax in the outer canal but said that no harm would be caused to the man by blowing into the tube. The driver was charged with failure and claimed 'reasonable excuse' because, after being told of the medical officer's opinion, he was not given another opportunity to provide specimens of breath. The Administrative Court said that the procedure suggested by the appellant was not provided for by Act or regulations. The sergeant's decision to charge failure subject to the opinion of the medical officer was a sensible one. The sergeant was not obliged to accept the appellant's contention. He was not medically qualified.

The section is now simplified in relation to warnings to be given to the accused. It is sufficient to warn him that failure may render him liable to prosecution. Failure to give such warning, however, will be a bar to conviction, as will failure to make the meaning of such a warning sufficiently clear to ensure that it was understood.

There is a failure if insufficient breath is provided for the purpose of analysis. A motorist has a duty, if he knows that a medical condition prevents him from providing sufficient breath, to inform the constable. If he does not do so, he may be found guilty of the offence of failure to provide a specimen.

A police doctor was of the opinion that a man was under the influence of drugs. On being required by the police officer to provide a specimen of blood or urine he refused to be examined by the doctor saying, 'You are not going to examine me'. He was charged with refusal. He was acquitted by justices who considered that his behaviour was probably a consequence of some stimulant drug and this, coupled with his refusal to provide blood, could amount to a medical reason for non-provision of blood and the officer should have requested urine instead. The Divisional Court said that a refusal to be examined, without more, could not possibly amount to a medical reason. It might have been different if the refusal had been qualified with some valid reason.

A person only provides a specimen of blood if he consents to its being taken by a medical practitioner and it is so taken.

Section 7(6), which creates the offence of failing to provide a specimen, creates only one offence, although the punishments provided by the Road Traffic Offenders Act 1988, Schedule 2, provide different penalties for those driving or attempting to drive a motor vehicle, as opposed to being in charge of it. Information framed in terms of s 7(6) alone without reference to the circumstances in which the requirement was made is not bad for duplicity. However, the Divisional Court has pointed out that it will be good practice to inform an accused of the circumstances in which the investigation was taking place at the time when the specimen was demanded, that is, under s 4(1), 4(2), 5(1) (a) or 5(1) (b), driving or attempting to drive whilst unfit, in charge whilst unfit, driving or attempting to drive whilst over the limit, and in charge whilst over the limit, respectively. The decision of the Divisional Court has since been endorsed by the House of Lords.

Section 7A(6) creates the offence of, without reasonable excuse, failing to give permission for a laboratory test of a specimen of blood taken from a person under the section. Section 7A provides a means by which a specimen of blood may be obtained from a person who, at the time, appears to be incapable of consenting to such a specimen being taken, where it appears to a constable that that person has been involved in an accident; see page 447.

Hospital procedure

Section 9(1) requires that while a person is at a hospital as a patient he shall not be required to provide a specimen of breath for a breath test or to provide a specimen for a laboratory test unless the medical practitioner in immediate charge of his case has been notified of the proposal to make the requirement, and:

(a) if the requirement is then made, it shall be for the provision of a specimen at the hospital; *but*
(b) if the medical practitioner objects on the ground specified in subsection (2) below), the requirement should not be made.

Subsection 9(1A) provides that while a person is at a hospital as a patient, no specimen of blood shall be taken from him under s 7A of this Act and he shall not be required to give his permission for a laboratory test of a specimen taken under that section unless the medical practitioner in immediate charge of his case:

(a) has been notified of the proposal to take the specimen or to make the requirement; and
(b) has not objected on the ground specified in subsection (2).

Subsection (2) states that the ground on which the medical practitioner may object is:

(a) in a case falling within subsection (1), that the requirement or the provision of the specimen or (if one is required) the warning required by s 7(7) of this Act would be prejudicial to the proper care and treatment of the patient; and
(b) in a case falling within subsection (1A), that the taking of the specimen, the requirement or the warning required by s 7A(5) of this Act would be so prejudicial.

The Divisional Court held that where a suspect collapsed at a police station during a breath test (which was not completed) and he was removed to hospital, the doctor in charge should have been informed of a comment to the effect that he suffered from 'immune system breakdown' which had been made at the police station. Such a reason had the potential to cause a doctor to prohibit the taking of a specimen of blood.

Let us consider this in stages and from the outset remember that we cannot, in any circumstances, demand a specimen of breath for analysis from a patient at a hospital.

(1) Seek out the medical practitioner in charge of the case.
(2) Seek his consent to the provision of a screening breath test with a tube and bag or electronic screening device, explaining what you intend to ask his patient to do.
(3) Secure that consent. He will give it if the procedure is not prejudicial to care or treatment.
(4) Obtain a screening sample of breath observing usual procedures and warnings as to consequences of failure.
(5) If negative, explain, and take no further action (unless drugs suspected).
(6) If positive, obtain the medical practitioner's consent to the taking of a specimen for laboratory analysis, explaining the procedure. Remember that it must be blood or urine. Ask the driver if there is any reason why a specimen of blood should not be taken.
(7) If consent is obtained, etc., obtain a specimen of blood or urine by the usual means.

However, where the person concerned appears to the constable to have been involved in an accident that constitutes or is comprised in the matter which is under investigation, or the circumstances of that matter, and it appears to the constable that the person is or may be incapable (whether or not he has purported to do so) of giving a valid consent to the taking of a specimen of blood and that incapacity appears to be due to medical reasons, s 7A authorises a constable to request a medical practitioner to take a specimen of blood irrespective of whether that person consents. However, the medical practitioner must not be requested to take such a specimen where he considers that it will be prejudicial to the care or treatment of the patient.

Where a requirement to provide a specimen of blood has been made at a hospital but the patient is discharged before the specimen can be taken, that requirement is not varied or discharged by the mere fact that the person to whom the requirement was made, is then taken to a police station. The specimen may be taken there.

Detention of persons affected by alcohol

A person may be detained until it appears to a constable that by driving he would not commit a further offence. In practice, this means until he provides a negative screening specimen. However, there is no power to detain where there is no likelihood of his driving or attempting to drive while his ability to drive is impaired or the level of alcohol in his breath, blood or urine exceeds the limit. Many accused persons might be taken home by a responsible person in circumstances which would satisfy a constable that there is no likelihood of the accused driving, etc. If drugs are involved, medical advice should be obtained.

Offences of being unfit through drink or drugs

Section 4 of the Road Traffic Act 1988 states that a person who, when driving or attempting to drive or in charge of a mechanically propelled vehicle on a road or other public place, is unfit to drive through drink or drugs is guilty of an offence. He is 'unfit' if his ability to drive properly is for the time being impaired.

'Drug' means any intoxicant other than alcohol, including medicine and glue. However, where a driver's condition is due to hypoglycaemic attack, this may or may not be due to insulin. There must be direct evidence that the attack was the direct result of an injection of insulin either because it was injected in too great a quantity, or because it was still clearly operative at the moment of the attack. Other factors such as neglect of diet, etc., may have been the direct cause of the attack.

Section 4 provides the only means by which we can deal with a person whose ability to drive is impaired by drugs. There is no purpose in requiring the specimens previously described as they will not identify drug content and it becomes necessary to depend upon observation. Witnesses may describe the manner of driving, speech and manner when interrogated by a police officer, the police surgeon's observations and the driver's responses to co-ordination tests carried out by the surgeon. It is submitted that the use of this section in relation to alcoholic drink is likely to be extremely limited. The circumstances in which it is prudent to proceed with a charge of this nature when a subsequent analysis of a laboratory specimen has shown an alcohol concentration below any of the prescribed limits, are likely to be limited, if not non-existent. Some forms circulated to police forces suggest that if an evidential machine indicates less than $35\,\mu g$ per 100 ml, one should call a doctor if there is evidence of drugs, but if not and there is evidence of impairment, the person should be charged with the appropriate s 4 offence. There can be little purpose in proceeding under s 4 unless the evidence of impairment is really compelling and it is submitted that courts would always require evidence of a medical practitioner. It will be good practice to call a doctor in these cases too, should it ever be felt that proceedings are merited when there is little evidence of alcohol. There will be little prospect of a successful prosecution upon evidence unsupported by medical opinion.

Power of arrest and entry

A constable may arrest a person without warrant if he has reasonable cause to suspect that that person is, or has been, committing an offence of driving, attempting to drive or being in charge of a motor vehicle on a road or other public place while unfit through drink or drugs. Where a negative roadside test was carried out but the officers were of the opinion that the driver had not provided a sufficient quantity of breath, the Divisional Court held that the arrest of the motorist under s 4 (the officers being of the opinion that he was unfit to drive) was not unlawful. The power to arrest under s 4 did not fall away simply because a roadside test had been carried out. The justices had excluded the evidence of the analysis of a specimen of breath on the grounds that the specimen had been unlawfully obtained following an unlawful arrest.

For the purpose of arresting a person under s 4, a constable may enter (if need be by force) any place where that person is or where the constable, with reasonable cause, suspects him to be.

To summarise in relation to powers of entry, power to enter, by force if necessary, has been provided in respect of s 5 offences (driving, attempting to drive or in charge while alcohol in the body is above prescribed limits), only following an injury accident for the purpose of obtaining a breath test, but in all cases involving driving, attempting to drive or being in charge *while ability is impaired*, entry is authorised, by force if necessary.

Defence to 'being in charge of' in section 4 and 5 offences

For the purposes of charges relating to being in charge while there is alcohol in the body in excess of prescribed limits or while unfit to drive through drink or drugs, a person shall be deemed *not* to have been in charge of a motor vehicle if he proves that at the material time the circumstances were such that there was no likelihood of his driving it so long as he remained unfit to drive through drink or drugs, but in determining whether there was a likelihood, the court may disregard any injury to him and any damage to the vehicle.

A man who has taken steps to place his vehicle in someone else's charge while he remains affected by drink or drugs is entitled to use this defence. Prior to the final provisions allowing a court to disregard any injury to him or damage to his vehicle, it was possible for an accused to plead that there was no likelihood of his driving as his car had been too severely damaged to use, or that his injuries were such that driving was unlikely. The wording of ss 4 and 5 is now such that a court may disregard these factors if other evidence shows guilt. It has been decided that a man who is in his car who is too drunk to drive it cannot rely upon this defence because he will be able to drive on regaining consciousness, even though he may still be severely affected by alcohol.

Where the accused's car had been wheel-clamped and there was no evidence to show that the clamp could have been removed by any means other than paying for release and the accused had refused to do this, it was held that there was no likelihood of his driving at that time. The fixing of a wheel-clamp does not damage a car; the vehicle itself is not altered in any way.

Evidence in proceedings for offences under sections 3A, 4 and 5

The Road Traffic Offenders Act 1988, s 15, provides that evidence of the proportion of alcohol or a drug in a specimen of breath, blood or urine provided by or taken from an accused shall, in all cases (including cases where the specimen was not provided or taken in connection with the alleged offence), be taken into account and it shall be assumed that the proportion of alcohol was at least that found in the sample. However, in cases involving drink, that assumption shall not be made if the accused proves:

(a) that he had consumed alcohol before he provided the specimen; or had it taken from him; and
   (i) in relation to an offence under s 3A, after the time of the alleged offence; and
   (ii) otherwise, after he had ceased to drive, attempt to drive or be in charge of a vehicle on a road or other public place; and
(b) that had he not done so the proportion of alcohol in his breath, blood or urine would not have exceeded the prescribed limit and, if it is alleged that he was unfit to drive through drink, would not have been such as to impair his ability to drive properly.

It is, therefore, for an accused who alleges that he has taken drink subsequent to the driving, etc., to prove this to the satisfaction of the court and, additionally, that without such subsequent drink or drinks, he would not have been in excess of the limit or impaired. It will be necessary in such cases for a defendant to call expert medical or scientific evidence in order to discharge this burden of proof, unless the nature of non-expert evidence is such that it will enable a court reliably and confidently to reach a sensible conclusion without expert evidence. However, once justices have been given clear evidence from an expert as to the amount of alcohol necessary to cause a particular driver to exceed the legal limit and plausible evidence as to the quantity of alcohol consumed post-incident, then it is open to them, in spite of the fact that apparent discrepancies remain unexplained, to find that the defendant has discharged the burden necessary to establish a defence under s 15(3). However, the burden of proof rests with the accused and it has been held that magistrates are not entitled to find that a defendant has no case to answer without him giving evidence as to his alleged post-incident drinking.

If a specimen of blood is taken, the Road Traffic Offenders Act 1988, s 15(4), provides that a specimen of blood shall be disregarded unless:

(a) it was taken from the accused with his consent and either
   (i) if taken in a police station, was taken by a medical practitioner *or a registered health-care professional*, or
   (ii) if taken elsewhere, by a medical practitioner;
(b) if taken from an accused by a medical practitioner under s 7A of the Road Traffic Act 1988 (which permits the taking of a specimen without valid consent) and the accused subsequently gives his permission for a laboratory test of the specimen.

The requirement that the results of the analysis of a specimen shall always be taken into account eliminates the possibility that such evidence might be excluded by courts on the grounds that there had been an error in procedure prior to the obtaining of a sample. However, the High Court has recently approved the exclusion of such evidence under the provisions of the Police and Criminal Evidence Act 1984, s 78, where the defendant had been wrongfully arrested, in that he was not told by the officer that he suspected him of having alcohol in his body at the time that a roadside specimen was required.

Remember that when, at the time of the provision of a specimen of blood or urine, an accused asks to be supplied with such a specimen, the specimen taken must be divided into two parts, the other part being supplied to the accused. If this is not done, the evidence of the proportion of drug or alcohol found in the specimen will not be admissible. It should be noted, however, that the legislation requires provision of a part of the specimen only if requested by the accused.

Subsection (5A) provides that where a specimen of blood was taken from an accused under s 7A (taken from person incapable of consenting), evidence of the proportion of alcohol or any drug found in the specimen will not be admissible unless any request to be supplied with the other part which was made by the accused at the time when he gave his permission for a laboratory test of the specimen was complied with.

Documentary evidence

The Road Traffic Offenders Act 1988, s 16, provides for documentary evidence to be given of the proportion of alcohol or drug in a specimen of breath, blood or urine. The statement automatically produced by a breath testing device together with a certificate signed by a constable that the statement relates to the specimen provided by the accused at the date and time shown in the statement, and a certificate signed by an authorised analyst as to the proportion of alcohol or drug found in a specimen of blood or urine identified in that certificate, are admissible in evidence. Similarly, certificates of medical practitioners to the effect that a specimen of blood was taken from the accused with his consent are admissible.

Copies must be handed to the accused at the time, or served on him not less than 7 days before trial. However, if an accused, not less than 3 days before the hearing (or lesser time if the court allows), serves notice requiring the attendance of the person producing any such document, the document itself is no longer admissible.

Whilst this legislation permits the use of documentary evidence, it does not require this procedure to be followed. A police officer may give oral evidence of the readings which he saw displayed on the intoximeter, provided that he is also able to testify that the device was working properly and was accurately calibrated.

Police officers frequently give evidence whilst referring to a pro forma completed at the time. Any reference to a person's previous convictions on such a pro forma must be removed or concealed as there is always a possibility that, for one reason or another, the document may be examined by the court.

Evidence that a specimen of blood was taken from the accused with his consent by a medical practitioner or a registered health-care professional may be given by the production of a document purporting to certify that fact and to be signed by a medical practitioner or registered health-care professional.

Alternative verdicts

A person charged with driving or attempting to drive whilst unfit or whilst over the prescribed limit and who is found not guilty of that offence, but the allegations in the information amount to or include an allegation of an offence of 'being in charge' in those circumstances, may be convicted of that offence. A person charged with 'driving' may be convicted of 'attempting to drive'.

Courses for drink/drive offenders

The Road Traffic Offenders Act 1988 as amended by the Road Traffic Act 1991 gives the courts power to order that the period of disqualification imposed for an offence against ss 3A, 4, 5 or 7 of the Road Traffic Act 1988 may be reduced if the person concerned completes a course approved by the Secretary of State. This applies where the disqualification is for a period of not less than 12 months. The reduction may be of not less than 3 months and not more than one quarter of the unreduced period. Consequently, a disqualification of 12 months may be reduced to one of 9 months.

Regulations have provided for course managers to be appointed who may issue certificates of completion in a form approved by the Secretary of State. The areas within which courses are available are specified in schedules to the Courses for Drink-Drive Offenders (Designation of Areas) Order 1997.

Drinking – guided transport systems

The Transport and Works Act 1992 applies to transport systems which are used, or are intended to be used, wholly or partly for the carriage of members of the public. Its provisions are restricted to railways, tramways or other *guided transport systems* specified by the Secretary of State. The guided transport systems at Birmingham International Airport, Merry Hill Centre, West Midlands, and Gatwick and Stansted Airports have been so specified.

The Act creates two offences involving drink or drugs on such transport systems which can be committed by the following workers:

(a) drivers, guards, conductors, signalmen or others who control or affect the movement of vehicles operating under one of these systems; or

(b) persons who couple or uncouple such vehicles or check that they are working properly; or

(c) persons maintaining the permanent way (or other support or guidance structures), signalling systems and power supply used by such vehicles; and

(d) supervisors of, and look-outs for, persons engaged in the functions set out in categories (b) or (c) above.

These two offences are committed where:

(i) a person in one of the above categories carries out his duties when unfit to carry out that work due to drink or drugs;

(ii) a person in one of the above categories carries out his duties after consuming so much alcohol that the proportion of it in his breath, blood or urine exceeds the prescribed limit (which is the same limit as prescribed by the Road Traffic Act 1988).

A constable in uniform is empowered to require a screening breath test where he has reasonable cause to suspect:

(a) that a person working on a transport system has alcohol in his body; or

(b) that a person has been working on a transport system with alcohol in his body and still has alcohol in his body.

This power is extended to circumstances in which there has been an *accident or dangerous incident* and a constable in uniform has reasonable cause to suspect that, at the time of the event, the person was working in one of the above capacities and that his act, or omission, whilst so working may have been the cause of the accident or incident. A 'dangerous incident' means an accident which, in the constable's opinion, involved a danger of death or personal injury.

Similar powers to those under the Road Traffic Act 1988 are provided by the Act in relation to arrest and entry, the provision of specimens for analysis, the option to have a breath specimen replaced if the alcohol content in it does not exceed 50 µg in 100 ml of breath, failure to comply with a request and hospital patients. The penalties for such offences are the same as those provided by the Road Traffic Act 1988, save, of course, that there is no power of disqualification from driving. However, the consent of the Secretary of State, or the Director of Public Prosecutions, is required before proceedings for such offences may be instituted in England and Wales.

The evidential provisions of the Road Traffic Act 1988 in relation to such offences are repeated in this Act.

Operators of such systems may be vicariously liable for some offences committed by employees.

These provisions are important to all police officers. Following a train crash, it is the first police officer on the scene who will be expected to require a screening breath test if it applies.

Pedal cycles – drinks or drugs

The offences set out above under the Road Traffic Act 1988 are concerned with motor vehicles. However, s 30 of that Act deals specifically with cycles which are not motor vehicles. It creates the offence of riding a cycle, not being a motor vehicle, on a road or other public place while unfit to ride through drink or drugs. This means that such a person is sufficiently under the influence of drink or drugs as to be incapable of having proper control of the cycle.

Pedal cycles – drunk in charge

The Licensing Act 1872 states that it is an offence for a person to be drunk while in charge of a carriage on a highway or any other public place. A bicycle is a carriage. A person in charge of a cycle, otherwise than riding it, is liable to be charged with this offence.

Public order

Introduction

Throughout the years, police involvement in the prevention of public disorder has developed from dealing with situations which involved little more than a Saturday night fight involving a number of people to dealing with large-scale, organised protests which quickly degenerate into various forms of public disorder on a massive scale. Not too many years ago, the public would have been astonished if anyone had suggested that our police officers would appear on British streets in riot gear and would be compelled to become proficient in 'extinguishing' colleagues who had been set on fire by petrol bombs. However, no matter what may have caused large numbers of persons to assemble in the first instance, once there is danger, it is the duty of police officers to ensure that the Queen's peace is maintained.

A crowd of people is a difficult thing to deal with. Where large numbers of people gather together for any particular single purpose, there is a possibility of disorder. Even where the gathering is of people who are intent upon making some peaceful form of protest, such a gathering may attract others who are opposed to their beliefs.

Shakespeare's *Julius Caesar* provides a fine example of the emotions which can be built up quickly in a crowd as the 'fever' spreads. Adolf Hitler had the ability to bring about a quick change in temperature within a crowd. Some pop groups have effected a style of performance which, quite apart from their music, tends to build up emotion. Once a 'common purpose' has been established within a group, it quickly grows as individual members of the group become encouraged by the attitude of those surrounding them to believe that they have a 'cause'. Inhibitions which might normally have prevented individuals within the group from committing acts which are outside the law tend to disappear and people become prepared to act in a manner which is completely foreign to their normal pattern of behaviour.

Once a crowd has become unruly, it is difficult to deal with the persons who constitute it; in the absence of someone who can influence the crowd to alter its behaviour, there is no way of making effective contact with such a large number of individuals. When it is seen that a situation is becoming potentially explosive, it may be possible to remove or to influence those who are providing the 'crowd motivation'. Increasingly, in places such as football grounds, visible cameras are used to reinforce the message that individuals who cause disturbances within a crowd may not be able to preserve the anonymity which a crowd provides.

Public meetings

The Public Meeting Act 1908, s 1, makes it an offence for any person, at a lawful public meeting, to act in a disorderly manner for the purpose of preventing the transaction of the business for which the meeting was called. This offence is punishable summarily. A similar offence is committed by any person who incites another to commit this offence. A public meeting is one held to discuss matters of public interest, or for the exchange of views on such matters. It includes any meeting in a public place and any meeting which the public or any section of the public are permitted to attend whether on payment or otherwise. The term 'public place' has its usual meaning.

Police powers

If a constable reasonably suspects any person of committing an offence under this Act he may, if requested to do so by the chairman of the meeting, require that person to give his name and address. If he refuses or fails to do so, or gives a false name and address, he commits an offence.

This Act has as its purpose the correct control of public meetings, the majority of which are likely to be of a political nature. It is not intended that such meetings should pass without comment or interruption by hecklers, and it is necessary for police officers to make their own judgment as to forms of conduct which are no more than protest and those which are purposely intended to prevent the transaction of business. If the person who is guilty of this conduct provides the constable with his name and address when requested to do so, the constable should provide the chairman of the meeting with those particulars. The issue at this stage clearly lies between the organisers and the person breaking up their meeting, and it is only when this information is refused that the constable becomes involved. It is unusual for police officers to be on duty at such meetings and their involvement is usually confined to instances in which they are summoned by the organisers, or events are such that their attention is directed to the meeting.

A constable's power to enter meetings which are held on private premises is restricted to circumstances in which they reasonably apprehend a breach of the peace. A meeting which is held on the highway is not necessarily unlawful, and consideration must be given to whether or not there is likely to be a nuisance or a breach of the peace. The High Court has ruled that it is the duty of the police to prevent any action likely to result in a breach of the peace by any person, and that the refusal of persons to desist from acts which may lead to such consequences amounts to obstructing the police in the execution of their duty.

Industrial disputes

The subject of trade disputes is so important that it merits examination in some depth. The law, from the time of the Industrial Revolution, has been increasingly concerned with finding the correct balance between the freedom of the unions to further their interests by industrial action and the freedom of individuals to exercise a personal choice. The Trade Union and Labour Relations (Consolidation) Act 1992, s 240, makes it an offence for any person wilfully and maliciously to break a contract of service knowing or having reasonable cause to believe that the probable consequence of doing so, either alone or in combination with others, will be:

(a) to endanger life or cause serious bodily injury; or
(b) to expose valuable property, whether real or personal, to destruction or serious injury.

In other circumstances, s 242 of the Act declares that an agreement by two or more persons to do, or to procure to be done, any act in contemplation of furtherance of a trade dispute within the meaning of that Act, shall not amount to a conspiracy if the act itself is a summary offence which is not punishable with imprisonment. Nothing in this section shall affect the law relating to riot, unlawful assembly, breach of the peace, sedition or any offence against the state or the sovereign. As will be seen, there can be a fine distinction between the peaceful picket and an unlawful assembly when the number of the pickets becomes such that their purpose is effected by intimidation.

Section 241 of the 1992 Act deals with forms of intimidation designed to prevent workmen from exercising their right to work if they wish to do so, and provides a penalty of 6 months' imprisonment or a fine or both for any person who, wrongfully and without legal authority:

(a) uses violence to or intimidates such person or his wife or children, or injures his property;
(b) persistently follows him about;
(c) hides his tools, clothes or other property to prevent or hinder his working;
(d) watches or besets his house or place of work, or the approach to it; or
(e) follows him with two or more persons through the street in a disorderly manner,

if such acts are done to compel that person to abstain from doing or to do any act which that person has a legal right to do or abstain from doing.

Although the offence of 'watching and besetting' is normally associated with trade disputes, it is not limited to such disputes. It is concerned with actions aimed at preventing people from doing what they wish to do. Anti-abortionists were found not to be watching and besetting an abortion clinic for the purposes of the section, as verbal abuse and reminders of the physical implications of abortion did not amount to physical force or the threat of physical force.

It has been held that it is intimidation for an assembly to hurl abuse and missiles at a workman while on his way to work. In one case, all 13 men involved were convicted although only two could be proved to have thrown objects.

Police powers

A constable may arrest without warrant anyone he reasonably suspects is committing an offence under this section.

Peaceful picketing

Section 220(1) of the Trade Union and Labour Relations (Consolidation) Act 1992 provides that it shall be lawful for a person in contemplation of or furtherance of a trade dispute to attend:

(a) at or near his own place of work; or
(b) if he is an official of a trade union, at or near the place of work of a member of that union whom he is accompanying and whom he represents,

for the purpose only of peacefully obtaining or communicating information, or peacefully persuading any person to work or abstain from working.

A common-sense approach should be adopted in determining whether picketing is at or near the pickets' place of work. It has been held that pickets who stood at the entrance to a trading estate, 1200 yards distant from their employer's premises on that estate and who would have been trespassing if they had picketed on the estate, were attending near their place of work.

The only persons other than those described above who may lawfully be on a picket line are those employed by the company who do not work at any one particular depot, or it is otherwise impracticable for them to picket their place of work. Such persons may be included in pickets at any premises of the employer. This is interesting when considering the position of 'flying pickets'. Their presence is not authorised by the Act and they are not therefore protected from the 'watching and besetting' provisions of the Act.

Section 220(3) of the 1992 Act allows a person who is not in work, but whose last employment was terminated in connection with the trade dispute, or the termination of his employment was one of the circumstances giving rise to a trade dispute, to picket at his former place of work.

However, in the circumstances in which pickets are lawfully assembled at a particular place, the law must be observed in other respects and breaches of the peace must be prevented. It has been held that when persons who were acting as pickets in connection with an industrial dispute were requested to move by a police officer who was limiting the number of the pickets to a figure which was considered reasonable because of an apprehended breach of the peace, and refused to do so, they were rightly convicted of obstructing a police officer in the execution of his duty. In another instance, where an excessive number of pickets carried on a circling manoeuvre, obstructing the highway in such a way that vehicles were forced to stop, there was a similar conviction for obstruction of a police officer, although there was no threatened breach of the peace.

The effect of what is now s 220 of the 1992 Act was discussed in both the House of Lords and the Court of Queen's Bench Division. In the House of Lords it was ruled that it is wrong to describe what is conferred by s 220 as a 'right'. What was conferred was an immunity from prosecution in certain circumstances. It was held that s 220 gave no right to a picket to stop a vehicle against the driver's will, although it had been widely believed in trade union circles that it did, if it was done for the purpose of persuading the driver to refrain from doing some act contrary to the interest of the pickets and their representative organisation. This ruling clarifies the position in relation to pickets who forcibly prevent vehicles from gaining access to premises during industrial disputes.

The Divisional Court considered the actions of a man who assaulted and obstructed a police officer in the execution of his duty during an industrial dispute involving electricians at St Thomas's Hospital, London. Thirty to forty people had assembled at the entrance to the site, but only four were official pickets and wore armbands to identify themselves. Police officers under the command of a superintendent arrived at the scene and formed a cordon clearing the exit so that a bus containing electrical workers could leave. Although at first the four pickets were left inside the gate, they were finally cleared from the gateway and placed behind the cordon as the superintendent feared that, if the bus was stopped, a breach of the peace might occur. The man charged was an official of another trade union who had been asked to attend to speak to the bus driver, who was probably a member of his union. When the coach attempted to come out, he began to argue with police officers and eventually struck out at one of them. It was observed that it had already been established that pickets had no right to stop vehicles and that, therefore, the police superintendent and all of the officers were acting in the execution of their duty when the entrance was cleared in order to prevent an apprehended breach of the peace, and that the defendant was, therefore, guilty of both offences.

Other offences – Public Order Act 1936

The 1936 Act was passed at the time of vigorous activity by the British Fascist Party and its object was to resist political organisations which wished to fashion themselves on military lines. It prohibited the wearing, at public meetings or in public places, of uniforms signifying an association with a political organisation. The organisation, training or equipping of members for the purpose of enabling them to usurp the functions of the police or the armed services, or to enable them to display or use force in promoting a political object, or to act in such a way that reasonable suspicion is aroused that such is their purpose, was also prohibited. The consent of the Attorney-General is required before proceedings may be taken for these offences.

Fear or provocation of violence

Section 4 of the Public Order Act 1986 states that a person is guilty of an offence if he:

(a) uses towards another person threatening, abusive or insulting words or behaviour; or
(b) distributes or displays to another person any writing, sign or other visible represen-
     tation which is threatening, abusive or insulting,

with intent to cause that person to believe that immediate unlawful violence will be used against him or another by any person, or to provoke the immediate use of unlawful violence by that person or another, or whereby that person is likely to believe that such violence will be used or it is likely that such violence will be provoked.

An important point within this section is that the violence which is intended must be 'immediate'. However, this does not mean instantaneous. Violence will be 'immediate' if it is likely to result within a short period and without any other occurrence intervening.

The section covers a multitude of possibilities, particularly as the offence may be committed in public or in private, with the exception of a dwelling, where all persons concerned are in that dwelling. 'Dwelling' includes any form of dwelling, even including a tent. However, in this respect, communal landings outside individual flats do not form part of a person's home.

Things which are threatening indicate some immediate menace; those which are abusive are rudely addressed; and those which are insulting, in this context, are likely to be scornful, offensive, contemptuous or an affront. Thus we are concerned with words, behaviour, writing, signs or other visible representations which may be said to be one of those things. The words, etc., may be used:

(a) with intent to cause the person towards whom these acts have been done to believe
     that immediate violence will be used against himself or another;
(b) to provoke such immediate use of unlawful violence;
(c) in such a way that the person addressed will believe it will happen; or
(d) in such a way that it is likely that it will happen.

If a man says, 'I am going to beat you up', and he intends that the person addressed will believe that unlawful violence is about to be used, he commits the offence provided the threat is immediate. It would be different if he said that he would do so when a suitable opportunity presented itself as the threatened violence would not be immediate. If he is one of a group and says, 'We are going to beat you up now', and the person threatened is also one of a group, the offence is committed even though the person addressed does not know who is to do the beating or, indeed, who is to be beaten.

The section also covers circumstances in which the person using the words does not intend to strike the first blow. He may say, 'Margaret Dixon says that you are only half a man', intending to provoke the young man so addressed to use unlawful violence. This offence is committed by the person using these words if he used them to provoke violence. The words need not be spoken; if they are written on a banner, or on a leaflet which is handed out, they are covered by the section. In relation to the offence of displaying, etc., of writings, signs or visible representations, the section specifically requires that the acts are done to another person. The acts must therefore be directed at a particular person and this offence will not be committed by a person who leaves leaflets in a shopping precinct or who pastes posters on a wall when there is no one about. A threat made against a person who is out of earshot and only learns of it through a third party who is not under the control or direction of the maker of the threat is insufficient to constitute an offence against this section. However, although it is necessary that the person towards whom the behaviour is directed be present to perceive it, this does not mean that the only means of proving that the victim perceived the behaviour is by hearing evidence from that person. Justices may rely solely upon any admissible evidence from a bystander and may draw the inference that the victim did perceive what was said and done by the accused.

It has been held that a constable, having a common law duty to uphold the peace, is unlikely to respond to threatening, abusive or insulting language by the use of violence. However, an offence will be committed where such conduct is intended to cause a constable to fear that violence will be used against him.

Section 6(3) of the Acts provides that a person shall only be guilty of an offence under s 4 if he intends his words or behaviour, or the writing, sign or other visible representation to be threatening, abusive or insulting or is aware that it may be threatening, abusive or insulting. This means that there are two propositions to consider: first, the intention behind the words, etc., themselves, and second, the result which those words are intended to bring about.

Where a person ran on to a tennis court at Wimbledon and distributed leaflets, he was not guilty of this offence as his behaviour was not threatening, abusive or insulting, even if it was accepted that he caused anger, disgust or distress in spectators. In such circumstances, procedure by way of complaint with a view to obtaining 'surety of good behaviour' would, however, be appropriate. In the same way, if a person in addressing an audience uses words which in ordinary circumstances would be inoffensive but which are heard by persons to whom (unknown to the speaker) they are highly insulting, the speaker is not guilty of an offence against s 4. It would be different where such a speaker ignored the mood of an audience once it was apparent. He must take an audience as he finds it. If he uses words which he knows will insult those persons and that they are likely to provoke violence on their part, it is irrelevant that a reasonable person would not so react.

Intoxication is no defence to such charges unless it is not self-induced or is a by-product of medical treatment.

This section is most likely to be used in circumstances which are direct where threatening behaviour is used and this may be by gestures or blows. Those engaged in fighting so engage with the clear intention of causing at least a belief in the immediate use of violence. It might be said that actions speak louder than words!

Charges under this section may be appropriate in many situations which arise in 'demonstrations'. If members of an unpopular organisation march through the streets, people may gather to protest. If these protesters then threaten or offer immediate violence they commit offences, as they would do if they used insulting words with the clear intention of provoking the use of violence by members of the march. The section does not aim to prevent protest, it aims to prevent violent protest. It punishes threats and acts of violence wherever, and for whatever reason, they occur.

'Violence' for the purpose of this section means any violent conduct against a person or property and includes any violent conduct, e.g. throwing missiles capable of causing injury which miss or fall short of their target. The inclusion of 'unlawful' before 'violence' means that the common law defences to charges of assault (and the replaced common law offence of affray) of self-defence, reasonable defence of another person, and actions which do no more than restore the peace will be valid.

Police powers

A constable may arrest without warrant anyone he reasonably suspects is committing an offence under this section.

Harassment, alarm or distress

Sections 4A and 5 of the Public Order Act 1986 deal with the offences of harassment. Whilst s 4 of the 1986 Act is primarily concerned with immediate threats to the peace, ss 4A and 5 are directed towards distressing forms of antisocial behaviour. The elderly and members of minority groups are particularly vulnerable. In order to provide protection against those who threaten, abuse or insult or who use written displays to cause harassment, alarm or distress, s 5 is drafted in such a way that it draws a fine dividing line between criminal conduct and that which might be dealt with by other means.

A person is guilty of an offence if he:

(a) uses threatening, abusive or insulting words or behaviour, or disorderly behaviour, or
(b) displays any writing, sign or other visible representation which is threatening, abusive or insulting,

within the hearing or sight of a person likely to be caused harassment, alarm or distress thereby.

There are small differences in (a) and (b) when compared with s 4. To (a) there has been added 'disorderly behaviour' and the words 'towards another person' have been omitted. The words used may therefore be generally addressed to an audience without being aimed in particular at anyone or any group. The addition of the words 'disorderly behaviour' may perhaps embrace some situations which would not be covered by behaviour which could be described as threatening, abusive or insulting. Persons who leave night clubs in the early hours of the morning in a disorderly manner might easily cause harassment or distress to persons in the neighbourhood. In (b) the word 'distribution' is omitted in relation to writing, etc.

However, the 'disorderly behaviour' does not have to be such that it is threatening, abusive or insulting. The section separates such conduct from 'disorderly behaviour' by 'or'. Where protesters persistently obstructed a surveyor by standing in the infra-red beam from his theodolite, the Divisional Court supported the Crown Court's finding that such conduct was 'disorderly' and whilst there had been no threat or fear of violence, the surveyor had been inconvenienced and annoyed and the behaviour was likely to cause harassment to the surveyor. There does not need to be an element of violence. Nor need there be a feeling of insecurity, in an apprehensive sense, on the part of a member of the public. It is sufficient that he is harassed.

Whereas s 4 demands some element of unlawful violence or a belief that it will occur, s 5 is merely concerned with the act being 'within the hearing or sight of a person likely to be caused harassment, alarm or distress'. 'Harassment' may be defined as trouble, torment or confusion caused by persistent attacks; 'alarm' may be anxiety, fear, terror aroused by awareness of danger; and 'distress' may be to cause mental pain or to upset badly. It can be, on occasions, easy to use words which 'upset' some people and this section may cause problems for those charged with the enforcement of the law. Complaints may well be made by groups which are sensitive to critical comment.

It has been held that a police constable is a person capable of being subject to 'harassment, alarm or distress' for the purposes of the section. Where a man walked into he middle of the road and police officers and drivers were *seriously* alarmed concerning his safety, this offence was held to have been committed. It is submitted that the use of abusive and insulting words directed at police officers by lager louts and which have the effect of causing distress to police officers constitutes an offence under this section. However, it will be necessary to show clearly that the effect of such words was to cause harassment, alarm or distress. Anger is a different emotion, although it may be that it follows from the type of distress which the section describes.

This offence may be committed in public or in private with the exception of in a dwelling, where all persons concerned are in that dwelling. It is a defence for the accused to prove that he had no reason to believe that there was any person within hearing or sight who was likely to be caused harassment, alarm or distress, or that he was inside a dwelling and had no reason to believe that his words, etc., would be seen or heard by a person outside, or that his conduct was reasonable. Thus, statements made in a dwelling remain free from legal sanctions, as do those made in a private conversation which is accidentally overheard. A man at a bar who makes an insulting remark concerning 'punks' to a friend without knowing that one is in earshot does not commit this offence. Similarly, a man who makes such an offensive comment in his dwelling as a 'punk' passes his window does not commit an offence if he had no reason to believe that he would be heard by that person.

Where a protester had defaced the American flag in the sight of American servicemen, a district judge considered that the protester's right to freedom of expression under article 10.1 of European Convention on Human Rights was necessarily restricted by s 5 for the protection of the rights of others and convicted her of the offence. The Divisional Court held that the judge had given insufficient weight to the presumption in favour of the protester under article 10 and quashed the conviction. It said that the fact that she could have made her point in another way was only one factor to consider when determining the overall reasonableness and proportionality of her behaviour and the state's response to it.

Section 6(4) of the Act requires that the words, etc., must be intended to be threatening, etc., or the person using the words, etc., must be aware that they may be threatening, etc., or that the person intended his conduct to be disorderly or is aware that it may be disorderly.

To commit the offence a person must intend or be aware that his words, etc., will be threatening, abusive or insulting and they must be used, etc., within the hearing or sight of a person likely to be caused harassment, alarm or distress. It is therefore restricted to 'face-to-face' situations. A newspaper editor may comment in his newspaper concerning homosexual acts and their relationship to the disease AIDS. If he does so in an address to a live audience he must avoid any words which might be considered to be 'insulting' and which might cause 'distress' to any member of his audience. Where a trader set up a video camera in an area used by women to try on swim wear he was found to have been properly convicted of an offence against s 5. His guilty 'act' was the setting up of the camera. Letting it run amounted to insulting behaviour.

A person who gives no thought to the nature of his conduct or who honestly believes that there is no risk of it being threatening, etc., does not commit this offence. However, although the accused's conduct must be in the hearing or in the sight of a person likely to be caused harassment, alarm or distress thereby, the accused is not required to intend such a consequence or to be aware that it might occur.

When complaints are received in relation to alleged offences, the following points should be considered before taking action:

(a) the intention of the person using the words, etc.;
(b) their likely effect;
(c) where they were delivered;
(d) whether the use of the words, etc., was reasonable in the circumstances.

Police powers

A constable may arrest a person without warrant if:

(a) he engages in offensive conduct which the constable warns him to stop; and
(b) he engages in further offensive conduct immediately or shortly after the warning.

For the purposes of this power, 'offensive conduct' means conduct that the constable reasonably suspects to constitute an offence under this section. The conduct mentioned in (a) above need not be the same as the 'further conduct' in (b).

For a constable to be 'acting in the execution of his duty' under this section, the offender must be clearly told of the offensive conduct and that the constable required him to stop such conduct. However, where a man made racial remarks and behaved in a threatening manner, a police officer remonstrated with him and asked him to apologise. The man replied, 'Or else you will nick me?' On being told that this was so, he told her to 'get stuffed' and threatened her and the person to whom the racial remarks had been made, before being arrested by the police officer. It was held that, taken as a whole, the conversation was sufficient to convey to him that he should not engage in further offensive conduct and that it served as a warning for the purposes of the section. Nevertheless, the issue is best avoided by giving a direct warning to cease such conduct.

This power of arrest is not limited to the officer who gave the warning.

Offences against s 5 are 'penalty offences' for the purpose of the criminal Justice and Police Act 2001, s 1.

Harassment, etc., with intent

By s 4A of the Public Order Act 1986, it is an offence for a person *with intent* to cause a person harassment, alarm or distress, to:

(a) use threatening, abusive or insulting words or behaviour, or disorderly behaviour; or
(b) display any writing, sign or other visible representation which is threatening, abusive or insulting,

thereby *causing* that or another person harassment, alarm or distress.

This offence differs from that above in that the act is committed *with the intention* of causing harassment, alarm or distress, whereas that against s 5 is concerned with committing such an act within the hearing or sight of a person which are *likely to have* those effects. In addition, in the case of s 4A, the prosecution must prove that one of the effects *was caused*. In the case of s 4A, the power to arrest without warrant exists on these facts. There is no need to give a warning.

The provisions set out above in relation to s 5 which are concerned with dwelling houses also apply to s 4A. The defences (apart from that associated with having no reason to believe that there was a person within hearing or sight, which clearly could not apply to an offence of intent) also apply.

Racially aggravated public order offences

A person commits an offence under the Crime and Disorder Act 1998, s 31, if he commits an offence under the Public Order Act 1986, s 4, 4A or 5, which is racially or religiously aggravated. There are three separate offences under s 31, each based upon one of the three basic offences under the 1986 Act. The same powers of arrest apply to these offences as apply to their respective basic offences.

An offence is racially or religiously aggravated if:

(a) at the time of committing it, or immediately before or after doing so, the offender demonstrates towards the victim of the offence (or in the case of a basic offence under the 1986 Act, s 5, the person likely to be caused harassment, alarm or distress) hostility based on that person's membership (actual or presumed) of a racial or religious group; or

(b) the offence is motivated (wholly or partly) by hostility towards members of a racial or religious group based on their membership of that group.

For this purpose, membership of a racial or religious group includes association with members of that group, and 'presumed' means presumed by the offender. A 'racial group' means a group of persons defined by reference to race, colour, nationality (including citizenship) or ethnic or national origins. A 'religious group' is a group of persons defined by reference to religious belief or lack of religious belief.

The references to 'religious groups' were inserted by the Anti-terrorism, Crime and Security Act 2001, which must be reviewed 2 years after Royal Assent, which was given on 14 December 2001.

Once again, in relation to these aggravated offences, it must be remembered that two major factors have to be proved: the basic offence *and* the racial or religious element.

A man of the same racial group addressed a bus conductress from Sierra Leone as a 'stupid African bitch'. The Court of Appeal held that the term 'African' did describe a racial group and that it was possible for a person to show hostility to another who was of the same racial group.

Harassment by stalkers

The Protection from Harassment Act 1997, s 1, prohibits a person from pursuing a course of conduct:

(a) which amounts to harassment of another; and

(b) which he knows or ought to know amounts to harassment of the other.

The section provides that such a person ought to know that his conduct amounts to harassment of another if a reasonable person in possession of the same information would think the course of conduct amounted to harassment of the other. The forms which such harassment is likely to take will be many and varied and the section is deliberately non-specific concerning the nature of such conduct. However, the Divisional Court has said that the 1997 Act was clearly not intended to be used to clamp down on discussion of matters of public interest or upon the rights of political protest and public demonstration. The Court said that it would resist a wide interpretation of the Act. However, where a group of protesters were forbidden by an injunction to protest against mink farming in a defined area surrounding a farm, the Divisional Court said that it could not be 'reasonable' within the terms of the Act to continue to do so. The correct course of action would be to seek to have the injunction set aside.

The term 'harassment' includes alarming such a person or causing that person distress. A 'course of conduct' must involve conduct on at least two occasions and such conduct may include speech. The offence is made 'arrestable' under the provisions of the Police and Criminal Evidence Act 1984, s 24(2).

The provisions do not apply to conduct for the purpose of preventing or detecting crime, that pursued under any enactment or rule of law or to comply with a condition or requirement lawfully imposed or where, in particular circumstances, the pursuit of the course of conduct was reasonable.

Section 4 of the Act creates the offence of putting people in fear of violence. It is committed where a person whose course of conduct causes another to fear, on at least two occasions, that violence will be used against him, where the perpetrator knows or ought to know that his course of conduct will cause that other person to fear that consequence on each of the occasions in question. 'Course of conduct' bears the same meaning as in s 1. Where there is a prosecution for this offence, it is important that, so far as possible, there should be direct evidence from the victim as to the effect which was caused by the two incidents or more which were relied upon. Although there can be a course of conduct comprising only two incidents, the fewer the incidents and the wider apart they are spread, the less likely it is that a finding of harassment can be made. Nevertheless, incidents as far apart as 1 year can constitute a cause of harassment made once a year on someone's birthday.

There are similar defences with the substitution of 'circumstances in which the pursuit of his course of conduct was reasonable for the protection of himself or another or for the protection of his or another's property', for 'the pursuit of the course of conduct being reasonable in the circumstances'. This is an arrestable offence by reason of its penalty.

A person charged before a jury with an offence against s 4 may be found guilty of an offence against s 2. A sentencing court, in the case of a conviction under s 2 or 4, in addition to any other penalty imposed, may make an order protecting the victim of the offence, or any other person mentioned in the order, from further conduct which amounts to harassment or will cause a fear of violence.

Section 3 of the Act makes provision for a civil claim by the victim of conduct described by s 1. Damages may be awarded for (among other things) any anxiety caused by the harassment and any financial loss occasioned by it. The High Court or a county court may grant an injunction restraining a defendant from pursuing any course of conduct which amounts to harassment and, where a victim considers that such an injunction has been breached, he may apply for a warrant for that person's arrest. Victims should be made aware of these possibilities.

Police directions stopping the harassment, etc., of a person at his home

The Criminal Justice and Police Act 2001, s 42, provides that a constable who is at the scene may give a direction to a person:

(a) who is present outside, or in the vicinity of, a dwelling; and
(b) the constable believes, on reasonable grounds, that the person is there for the purpose (by his presence or otherwise) of representing to the resident or any other person who is not a resident, or for the purpose of persuading such persons
  (i) that they should not do something which they are entitled or required to do, or
  (ii) that they should do something which they are not under any obligation to do,
(c) provided that the constable believes on reasonable grounds that the presence of that person or persons
  (i) amounts to, or is likely to result in, the harassment of the resident,
  (ii) or is likely to cause alarm or distress to the resident.

Such a direction is one which requires that person to do things which the constable considers to be necessary to prevent the harassment of the resident or the causing of alarm or distress to the resident. It may be given orally, to either an individual or a group. A direction may require a person or persons to leave the vicinity of the premises (either immediately or after a period of time). It may include exceptions and may make exceptions subject to conditions, including where persons who are not required to leave the vicinity must remain, and conditions as to numbers, or the identity of particular persons who are authorised to remain in the vicinity.

When there is more than one officer at the scene, only the senior officer present may give the direction, and the power does not include the power to direct that persons refrain from activity which is lawful under the Trade Union and Labour Relations (Consolidation) Act 1992, s 220. Any direction given may be varied or withdrawn.

A person who knowingly contravenes such a direction commits a summary offence. Section 42(8) of the Act of 2001 provides that a constable in uniform may arrest without warrant anyone whom he reasonably suspects to be committing an offence under the section.

Racially aggravated harassment offences

A person commits an offence against the Crime and Disorder Act 1998, s 32, if he commits an offence under the Protection from Harassment Act 1997 which is racially or religiously aggravated. There are two separate offences under s 32, each based on an offence under s 2 or s 4 of the 1997 Act, respectively. The same powers of arrest apply to them as apply to the basic offences under the 1997 Act.

An offence is racially or religiously aggravated for the purposes of s 32 if:

(a) at the time of committing it, or immediately before or after doing so, the offender demonstrated towards the victim hostility based on that person's membership (actual or presumed) of a racial or religious group; or
(b) the offence is motivated (wholly or partly) by hostility towards members of a racial or religious group based on their membership of that group.

For this purpose, 'membership of a racial group' includes association with members of that group, and 'presumed' by the offender. A 'racial group' means a group of persons defined by reference to race, colour, nationality (including citizenship) or ethnic or national origins. A 'religious group' is a group of persons defined by reference to religious belief or lack of religious belief.

The references to 'religious groups' were inserted by the Anti-terrorism, Crime and Security Act 2001, which must be reviewed 2 years after Royal Assent, which was given on 14 December 2001.

Acts intended to stir up racial hatred

For the purposes of the Public Order Act 1986, 'racial hatred' means hatred against a group of persons defined by reference to colour, race or nationality (including citizenship) or ethnic or national origin.

Section 18 of that Act states that a person who uses threatening, abusive or insulting words or behaviour, or displays any written material which is threatening, abusive or insulting, is guilty of an offence if:

(a) he intends thereby to stir up racial hatred; or
(b) having regard to all the circumstances racial hatred is likely to be stirred up thereby.

The offence may be committed in public or in private with the exception of in a dwelling, where all the persons concerned are in that dwelling. The same defences apply as in cases of serious public disorder (see page 479). In addition, a person who is not shown to have intended to stir up racial hatred is not guilty of this offence if he did not intend his words, etc., to be, or was not aware that they might be, threatening, etc.

Previous legislation required such acts to be in a public place or at a public meeting, or to be demonstrated to a section of the public. The offence may now be committed in a private meeting, attendance at which is restricted to members of a society. Thus, remarks made by a member of the Ku Klux Klan to his fellow members at a closed meeting could be punishable under this section if those remarks were made with the necessary intent or in the required circumstances.

Section 18 does not apply to words or behaviour used, or written material displayed, *solely* for the purpose of being included in a television, sound broadcasting or cable service. In such a case, however, an offence may be committed under s 22 when the programme is transmitted.

Police powers

Section 18(3) provides that a constable may arrest without warrant anyone he reasonable suspects is committing an offence under this section. However, the Anti-terrorism, Crime and Security Act 2001 made all offences under Part III arrestable offences by increasing the punishment to 7 years' imprisonment. The Act of 2001 is to be reviewed 2 years after Royal Assent, which was given on 14 December 2001.

Antisocial behaviour orders

Section 1 of the Crime and Disorder Act 1998 empowers a council, chief officer of police (including British Transport Police) or any person registered under s 1 of the Housing Act 1996 as a social landlord who provides or manages any houses or hostel in a local government area to apply by way of complaint to a magistrates' court for an antisocial behaviour order to be made in respect of any person aged 10 or over. A council must consult the local chief officer of police (and vice versa) before making an application. A registered social landlord must consult the council and the chief officer of police before making an application. A chief officer of police can delegate the consultation process and the application for an order to officers in his force. The circumstances in which a complaint may be made are:

(a) that the person has acted in an antisocial manner, that is to say, in a manner that caused or was likely to cause harassment, alarm or distress to one or more persons not of the same household as himself; and

(b) that such an order is necessary to protect relevant persons from further antisocial acts by him.

A 'relevant person' is a person within the areas of the persons entitled to apply for orders, or residents in the premises, or persons in their vicinity. The revised procedure allows a relevant authority additionally to apply for an order within county court proceedings.

In considering whether to make such an order, the court must disregard any acts which are shown to have been reasonable.

The prohibitions which may be included in such an order are those necessary for the purpose of protecting persons (whether relevant persons or persons elsewhere in England and Wales) from further antisocial acts by the defendant. Such an order will be effective for a period specified in the order (not less than 2 years). Variation of an order may be applied for by way of complaint but no order must be discharged before the end of the period of 2 years other than with the consent of both parties.

The House of Lords has held that although proceedings to obtain antisocial behaviour orders are civil (and not criminal) in nature and therefore the laws of evidence which apply in civil cases will apply to such proceedings (so that hearsay evidence is admissible), the standard of proof is the criminal one: proof beyond reasonable doubt. A Divisional Court has held that it is open to a chief constable to delegate or devolve to any officer or officers judged suitable by him the functions involved in an application for an antisocial behaviour order.

Such an order may be made on conviction in criminal proceedings. If a court considers that the conditions set out in s 1 have been fulfilled this may be done whether or not an application has been made. The order must be additional to a sentence for the offence or an order of conditional discharge. They also provide for the making of an interim order before determination of an application. Such an order must be for a fixed period but may be varied, renewed or discharged.

The commission of any act which is prohibited by such an order is an arrestable offence.

The Police Reform Act 2002, s 50, provides that if a constable in uniform has reasonable grounds to believe that a person has been acting in an antisocial manner within the meaning of s 1 of the 1998 Act, he may require that person to give his name and address. Failure to do so, or the provision of a false or inaccurate name and address, is an offence.

On-the-spot penalties for disorderly behaviour

Chapter 1 of Part I of the Criminal Justice and Police Act 2001 provides for the issue of a 'penalty notice' by a constable in uniform who has reason to believe that a person aged 18 or over has committed a 'penalty offence'. The term 'penalty offence' means:

(a) simple drunkenness (Licensing Act 1872, s 12);
(b) throwing fireworks in a thoroughfare (Explosives Act 1875, s 80);
(c) knowingly giving false alarm of fire (Fire Services Act 1947, s 31);
(d) trespassing on a railway (British Transport Commission Act 1949, s 55);
(e) throwing stones, etc., at trains or other things on railways (British Transport Commission Act 1949, s 56);
(f) buying or attempting to buy alcohol in a bar for consumption by person under 18 [Licensing Act 1964, s 169C(3)] (*LA* 2003, s 149(4));
(g) drunk and disorderly in a public place (Criminal Justice Act 1967, s 91);
(h) wasting police time or giving false report [Criminal Law Act 1967, s 5(2)];
(i) false or annoying message conveyed by public telecommunications system [Telecommunications Act 1984, s 43(1)(b)];
(j) behaviour likely to cause harassment, alarm or distress (Public Order Act 1986, s 5);
(k) consuming alcohol in designated public place (Criminal Justice and Police Act 2001, s 12).

However, a penalty notice may be given at a police station by a constable authorised by the chief officer of police and such officer does not need to be in uniform.

A penalty notice offers the opportunity to discharge liability for such specified offences by the payment of a penalty. The amount of such penalty will be prescribed by order but must not be more than one-quarter of the maximum penalty for the offence.

The provision in respect of penalty notices, their effect, their restriction upon proceedings, the payment of penalties, registration of penalties and sums payable in default and enforcement are the same as those provided in relation to fixed penalties for road traffic offences; see page 367.

The Penalties for Disorderly Behaviour (Amount of Penalty) Order 2002 prescribes penalties of £80 for offences of knowingly giving a false alarm to a fire brigade, wasting police time or giving false report, using public telecommunications system for sending false message to cause annoyance and behaviour likely to cause harassment, alarm or distress, and penalties of £40 for the remainder. Further Regulations of 2002 prescribe the forms of penalty notice.

It is not intended that a penalty notice should always be issued in respect of the specified cases; the constable has discretion. Penalty notices are designed for minor and straightforward cases. More serious cases should be dealt with by using the traditional criminal process.

Where the case is a minor and straightforward one involving drunkenness, it is not intended that a penalty notice should be issued in the street. Instead, the miscreant should be arrested and taken to a police station where a penalty notice will be issued once he has sobered up and his identity has been confirmed.

Publishing or distributing racially offensive material

Section 19 provides that a person who publishes or distributes written material which is threatening, abusive or insulting is guilty of an offence if:

(a) he intends thereby to stir up racial hatred; or
(b) having regard to all the circumstances, racial hatred is likely to be stirred up thereby.

However, the section requires that there must be a publication or distribution to the public or to a section of the public. For this to have occurred, the person must have made his written material available to sufficient people for it to be shown that it was made known to the public at large, or least a section of it. Thus, if a man gives out racist leaflets at a National Front meeting to which admission is restricted to members of that organisation, he does not commit an offence against this section. The distribution is to members of a 'club' and not to the public. It would be different if persons other than members of the National Front had been admitted to the meeting and leaflets had been distributed to everyone. If a man hands a cartoon drawing to a friend, the contents of which are racially inflammatory, he does not commit this offence as his distribution is to only one person, and is therefore not 'public'. It would be different if he handed out such drawings to a number of people in a public bar.

Police powers

The offence contrary to s 19 is an arrestable offence.

Similar offences

Offences also exist under this Act in relation to the publication or distribution of written material, the public performance of plays, the distribution or playing of a recording of visual images or sounds or the broadcasting or inclusion in a cable programme service (other than those of BBC or ITV); in each case if there is an inclusion intended to stir up racial hatred, or having regard to all the circumstances racial hatred is likely to be stirred up. Defences exist where there is a lack of intent, or the act was unknown to the person charged and he had no reason to suspect it.

It is an offence contrary to s 23 of this Act to possess written material or a recording which is threatening, abusive or insulting with a view to display, publication, distribution or inclusion in a cable service (other than BBC or ITV), or its playing, etc., if there is an intention to stir up racial hatred or, having regard to all the circumstances, racial hatred is likely to be stirred up thereby.

Police powers

A warrant may be issued by a justice of the peace if he is satisfied by information on oath laid by a constable that there are reasonable grounds for suspecting possession of such material on premises. Reasonable force may be used if necessary.

The Anti-terrorism, Crime and Security Act 2001 made all offences under Part III arrestable offences by increasing the punishment to 7 years' imprisonment. However, the Act of 2001 is to be reviewed 2 years after Royal Assent, which was given on 14 December 2001.

Offences of serious public disorder

The Public Order Act 1986 abolished the common law offences of riot, rout, unlawful assembly and affray. It introduced statutory offences of riot, violent disorder and affray.

Riot

The Public Order Act 1986, s 1, states that a riot takes place where: 12 or more persons (including the accused) who are present together use or threaten unlawful violence for a common purpose and the conduct of them (taken together) is such as would cause a person of reasonable firmness present at the scene to fear for his personal safety, and that the accused's use of unlawful violence was for the common purpose. Each of the persons using unlawful violence for the common purpose is guilty of riot.

There are therefore a number of essential elements:

(a) 12 or more present together;
(b) the use or threat of unlawful violence;
(c) for a common purpose;
(d) *collective* conduct which would cause a person of reasonable firmness present at the scene;
(e) to fear for his personal safety.

If there are 12 or more present it is immaterial whether or not they threaten unlawful violence simultaneously. If there is a 'mob', therefore, and there is a constant threat or use of unlawful violence, this will suffice in relation to (a) and (b). 'Violence' means any violent conduct whether towards persons or property and includes the throwing of missiles capable of causing injury which miss their target or fall short. The mob must have a common purpose. If some are present to injure or inflict damage and others are merely awaiting an opportunity to steal from shops which have been damaged by others, at least 12 must be shown to have been present together and to be using or threatening use of unlawful violence. The common purpose may, of course, be inferred from the conduct of such persons. In addition, it must be the collective conduct of the 12 or more which causes, or would cause, a person of reasonable firmness to fear for his personal safety. The violence or threat must therefore be such that this stout-hearted bystander would fear for himself.

However, the section states that no person of reasonable firmness need actually be, or be likely to be, present at the scene. A court will have to be satisfied that such a person, had he been present, would have feared for his personal safety.

If 12 or more supporters of a football team advance upon supporters of the opposing team, threatening to use unlawful violence against them, they have a common purpose and their collective conduct would undoubtedly cause supporters of the other team, who were of reasonable firmness, to fear for their personal safety. The 12 or more would therefore be guilty of riot. However, should such a group advance upon the empty coach which was to convey the supporters to their home town, threatening to overturn it, although they are offering violence to property, they would not be guilty of this offence unless they additionally posed a threat to the personal safety of some person, whether present or not.

Section 6(1) of the Act adds that a person is guilty of riot only if he intends to use violence or is aware that his conduct may be violent. Therefore, a 'protester' who, in the course of expressing his protest, is waving his arms about and pointing his finger at counter-protesters, or the police, cannot be guilty if he does not intend to use unlawful violence, or is unaware that his conduct may be violent in the eyes of some persons. Intoxication is no defence unless it is not self-induced, or it occurs in the course of medical treatment by taking some substance.

In addition, since the violence must be unlawful, riot will not be committed if the persons are acting in self-defence or in any other circumstances in which the violence which they were using, was legally justified.

Riot is an arrestable offence, triable only on indictment, and is punishable by 10 years' imprisonment. The consent of the DPP is required before a prosecution may be instituted. Unless there has been a true 'riot' situation, it is probable that the DPP will advise proceedings under one of the alternative sections even when all of the requirements of a riot have been fulfilled.

If 'riot' is being considered, it must be remembered in addition to the use or threat of violence for a purpose common to at least 12 alleged offenders, that collective conduct, if taken together, must be such as would cause a person of reasonable firmness to fear for his *personal* safety.

Violent disorder

This offence is committed against s 2 of the 1986 Act where three or more persons who are present together use or threaten unlawful violence and the conduct of them (taken together) is such as would cause a person of reasonable firmness present at the scene to fear for his personal safety. Each person using or threatening unlawful violence is guilty of this offence. It is immaterial whether or not the three or more use or threaten unlawful violence simultaneously.

The ingredients of the offence differ from riot in that only three or more persons need to be present together and there is no requirement to prove a common purpose, although it is still necessary to prove collective conduct which would cause a person of reasonable firmness present at the scene to fear for his personal safety. Where evidence of the involvement of three or more persons is affected by the dismissal of the charges against all but one or two, the one or two may nevertheless be convicted of violent disorder if it is proved that others not charged with the offence were also involved. If it is not so proved, the one or two may be convicted of affray. However, if there is only evidence of violence towards property, a conviction for an offence of affray will not be possible.

The same considerations apply as in the case of riot in relation to intoxication, use or threat not necessarily being simultaneous, the places where the offence may be committed and the fact that the 'firm' person need not necessarily be present.

This is a useful section to police officers and its use need not be restricted to incidents which are on a large scale. Three or more who gather outside a dance hall using or threatening violence against persons may be guilty of this offence if it can be shown that they acted collectively and that their conduct was such that a 'firm' person would fear for his personal safety. In contrast, a person charged with riot must be shown to intend to *use or threaten* violence or be aware that his conduct may be violent or threatening.

This is an arrestable offence being punishable by 5 years' imprisonment if convicted on indictment or by 6 months' imprisonment if convicted summarily.

Affray

Section 3 of the 1986 Act states that a person is guilty of affray if he uses or threatens unlawful violence towards another and his conduct is such as would cause a person of reasonable firmness present at the scene to fear for his personal safety. By s 6(2), a person is guilty of the offence only if he intends to use or threaten violence or is *aware* that his conduct may be violent or threaten violence.

While the common law offence of affray was seldom charged because it was triable only at Crown Court, the statutory offence is likely to be commonly used. We are concerned to a large extent with violent street fights. One person using or threatening unlawful violence towards another person in circumstances in which a person of reasonable firmness fears for his personal safety commits this offence. Once again the offence may be committed in public or in private and the 'firm' person need not be present, although this is unlikely to be the case in most affrays. Usually there will be a direct threat to strike a blow, or a blow will be struck upon a person present.

However, the section would extend to circumstances where a person was beating upon a closed door in an attempt to burst it open, while threatening a person who was inside, but only if that person, or someone else, whether present or not at the scene, would fear for his personal safety. It must always be recognised that in most circumstances courts will be unlikely to accept that persons who were not being threatened, or were not otherwise caught up in the violent situation, were actually in fear for their personal safety. In the situation outlined, it would be insufficient that a bystander feared for the safety of the man behind the door; he must fear for his own safety.

It is helpful when considering a charge of affray to remember that the offence is essentially concerned with three persons: a person using or threatening unlawful violence, a person towards whom the threat or violence is directed *and* a person of reasonable firmness who need not be present at the scene. Thus, where a man attacks a police officer with a knife, it is not a question of whether another person of reasonable firmness, if he had been in the police officer's shoes at the time, would have feared for his personal safety, but whether such a person *if present in the room* at the time with the other two parties would have so feared.

Affray is a serious public order offence and there are other ways of dealing with two people who fight. Where a doorman at a night club assaulted a woman when ejecting her for alleged unruly behaviour by pushing her through the door, the Court of Appeal said that this could not amount to an affray as there was no evidence that a person of reasonable firmness would have been put in fear. If such circumstances were sufficient, every common assault could amount to an affray.

The section demands a threat by *more than words*. Words must be accompanied by some action *which is sufficient to cause the 'firm' person to fear for his personal safety*. Therefore, a small threatening step and a lot of words will be insufficient, whilst a threat to break the nose which is accompanied by a swift rush forward could amount to a 'threat' for the purposes of this section.

Where a man used words to urge an already excited dog to attack police officers, there was an affray as more than words were involved. The combination of those words with the excited condition of the dog would be enough to cause the officers to fear for their personal safety. It would be different if a man merely said, 'Seize him', to a docile dog which was unlikely to take notice. At that stage, there was no reason for any other person to fear for their safety. However, where persons who were sitting in their cars were asked for a lift by a man who used aggressive tones, there was no affray as there was nothing other than words at that stage.

A gang of Asian youths assembled outside a block of flats. Some of its members were carrying petrol bombs. No other persons were present at the scene. They said that they were waiting for a rival gang. Their convictions for 'affray' were quashed and this decision was upheld by the House of Lords on the grounds that although petrol bombs which were not brandished or waved could amount to a threat of unlawful violence, that threat must be directed towards another person. At the time it was not. This does not conflict with the proposition that the presence at the scene of a 'notional person', who feared for his safety, will suffice, it is concerned with the presence of someone against whom the threat is directed.

A person whose awareness is impaired by intoxication must be taken to have been aware of that of which he would have been aware if he had not been intoxicated, unless that intoxication was not self-induced or followed medical treatment.

The offence is punishable by 3 years' imprisonment if convicted on indictment and by 6 months' imprisonment if convicted summarily.

A constable may arrest without warrant anyone he reasonably suspects is committing this offence.

Processions – Public Order Act 1986

The Public Order Act 1986, s 11, requires that written notice must be given to a police station in the police area within which it is proposed to hold a public procession:

(a) to demonstrate support for or opposition to the views or actions of any person or body of persons;
(b) to publicise a cause or campaign; or
(c) to mark or commemorate an event.

The notice, naming the organisers and specifying the times, route, etc., must be delivered 6 days in advance unless it is not practicable to give any advance notice of the procession, i.e. when it is spontaneous. The chief officer of police (or the senior officer present at a spontaneous procession) may impose conditions relating to time, route or circumstances if he reasonably believes that:

(a) such procession may result in serious public disorder, serious damage to property or serious disruption to the life of the community; or
(b) the purpose of the person organising it is the intimidation of others with a view to compelling them not to do an act they have a right to do, or to do an act they have a right not to do.

Summary offences are committed by organisers who do not give notice, or if the details given in the notice differ from the reality, and by organisers and participants who knowingly fail to comply with conditions. Those who incite others to fail to comply with a condition also commit offences.

Chief officer may apply to the council of a district for an order prohibiting, for a period not exceeding 3 months, the holding of all public processions (or processions of a class), within that district. The Commissioners of the Metropolitan and City of London Police Forces may make such orders. All orders are subject to the consent of the Secretary of State.

The provisions of the section do not apply to processions commonly or customarily held (for example, a procession held as part of an annual gala) or to funeral processions.

Police powers

A constable *in uniform* may arrest without warrant anyone he reasonably suspects is committing an offence or organising a public procession and knowingly failing to comply with a condition, or holding a prohibited procession, or a participant who knowingly takes part in a prohibited procession, or who knowingly fails to comply with a condition or a person who incites a participant to commit such an offence.

Assemblies – Public Order Act 1986

The Public Order Act 1986, s 14, permits a chief officer to impose conditions in relation to the place at which any public assembly (an assembly of 20 or more persons in a public place which is wholly or partly in the open air) may be, or continue to be held; its maximum duration or the maximum number of persons who may constitute it as appear to him necessary to prevent serious public disorder, serious damage to property or serious disruption to the life of the community; or the purpose of the persons organising it is the intimidation of others with a view to compelling them not to do an act they have a right to do, or to do an act they have a right not to do.

The Divisional Court has held that a person does not cease to be one of an assembly of 20 or more person merely by detaching himself from the remainder of the group and then ignoring the conditions imposed.

Police powers

A constable in uniform may arrest without warrant anyone he reasonably suspects is committing an offence of organising such an assembly and knowingly failing to comply with a condition, or of participating in such an assembly and so failing to comply or of inciting another to commit such an offence.

Trespassory assemblies

Section 14A of the 1986 Act was added by the Criminal Justice and Public Order Act 1994. It permits a chief officer of police where he reasonably believes that an assembly of 20 or more persons is intended to be held in a district at a place on land in the open air to which the public has no right of access or only a limited right of access and that assembly:

(a) is likely to be held without permission of the occupier of the land, or to conduct itself in such a way as to exceed the limits of any permission given, or the limits of the public's right of access, and
(b) may result
  (i) in serious disruption of the life of the community, or
  (ii) where the land, or a building or monument on it, is of historical, architectural, archaeological or scientific importance, in significant damage to the land, building or monument,

to apply to the council of the district for an order prohibiting the holding of trespassory assemblies in the district or part of it. The Commissioners of the City of London and Metropolitan Police may make similar orders with the consent of the Secretary of State.

Where an order is made it shall not be for a period exceeding 4 days. It may not apply to an area represented by a circle with a radius of 5 miles.

These provisions are intended to prevent disorder at such places as Stonehenge which attract large numbers of persons at particular times.

Where an s 14A order had been made and protesters assembled on a highway which was in the area specified and took part in a peaceful, non-obstructive and static demonstration there, the House of Lords ruled that they committed no offence. The House said that the question was whether modern law should recognise that the public highway was a public place on which all manner of activities might take place. Provided that these activities were reasonable, did not involve the commission of a public or private nuisance and did not amount to an obstruction of the highway which unreasonably impeded the right of the general public to pass and repass, they should not constitute a trespass.

Offences and powers

It is an offence to organise, take part in or incite another to take part in such a prohibited assembly. A constable in uniform may arrest without warrant anyone he reasonably suspects to be committing any of these offences. Where a constable in uniform who is within the prohibited area reasonably believes that a person is on his way to such a prohibited assembly, he may stop that person and direct him not to proceed in the direction of the assembly. A person who fails to comply commits an offence and may be arrested without warrant by the constable.

Trespass or nuisance on land

The Criminal Justice and Public Order Act 1994, s 61, is the result of the tendency of certain groups to trespass upon private property in large numbers. As a result of such trespass, considerable damage is caused to property. 'Peace convoys' which seek places to stay have attracted the attention of the media.

If the senior police officer present at the scene reasonably believes that two or more persons are trespassing on land and are present there with the common purpose of residing there for any period, that reasonable steps have been taken by or on behalf of the occupier to ask them to leave the land and:

(a) that any of those persons has caused damage to the land or to property on the land or used threatening, abusive or insulting words or behaviour towards the occupier, a member of his family or an employee or agent of his; or
(b) that those persons have between them six or more vehicles on the land,

he may direct those persons, or any of them, to leave the land and to remove any vehicles or other property they have with them on the land. Such a direction may be communicated to such persons by any constable, where it is not delivered by the officer giving the direction. The direction must be to leave, etc., immediately or as soon as reasonably practicable, rather than at some future time.

Where the original entry on to land was not trespassory (where campers outstay their welcome, for example), he must be satisfied that these things occurred after such persons became trespassers (after their permission to stay had been withdrawn).

Persons who, knowing that such a direction has been given, fail to leave the land as soon as reasonable practicable, or who, having left, again enter the land as trespassers within 3 months from the date of the direction, commit an offence. This offence is punishable by 3 months' imprisonment, a fine, or both. A person reasonably suspected of committing this offence may be arrested by a constable without warrant.

It is a defence for such a person to prove that he was not trespassing on such land or that he had a reasonable excuse for failing to leave it as soon as reasonably practicable, or as the case may be, for again entering the land as a trespasser.

Such trespass may occur on common land against the commoners' rights. Whilst the offences do not apply to buildings in a general sense they apply to agricultural buildings and scheduled monuments. They cannot be committed on land forming part of a highway unless it is a footpath, bridleway or byway open to all traffic, a restricted byway or a cycle track.

The term 'vehicle' includes a vehicle which is not in a fit state for use on a road and includes any chassis or body with or without wheels, appearing to have formed part of such a vehicle, and any load carried by, and anything attached to, such a vehicle, and a caravan is any structure designed for human habitation which is capable of being moved from one place to another whether by being towed or by being transported on a motor vehicle or trailer, and any motor vehicle so designed and adapted.

Section 62 provides that a constable has power, where such a direction has been given, to seize and remove a vehicle where he reasonably suspects that a person to whom the direction was given has, without reasonable excuse, failed to remove a vehicle which appears to the constable to belong to him or be in his possession or control. The same powers apply where a person has re-entered the land within a period of 3 months.

Raves – police powers of removal from land

A 'rave' is a gathering on land in the open air of 100 or more persons (whether or not as trespassers) at which amplified music is played during the night (with or without intermissions) and as such, by reason of its loudness and duration and the time at which it is played, is likely to cause serious distress to the inhabitants of the locality.

Such a gathering continues throughout intermissions in the music. Where the rave extends over several days, the section applies to those periods during the night when amplified music is played. 'Music' can include the emission of a succession of repetitive beats.

Where a police officer of at least the rank of superintendent reasonably believes that:

(a) two or more persons are making preparations for the holding there of a such a gathering;
(b) 10 or more persons are waiting for such a gathering to begin there; or
(c) 10 or more persons are attending such a gathering which is in progress,

he may give a direction that those persons and any other persons who come, to prepare or wait for, or to attend the gathering are to leave the land and remove any vehicles or other property which they have with them on the land. The direction may be conveyed to the gathering by a constable. If reasonable steps have been taken to convey the direction, it shall be deemed to have been given. It will be appreciated that there may be difficulties in making announcements at such gatherings and these provisions foresee those difficulties.

Offences, defences and powers

An offence is committed against s 63 of the 1994 Act by any person who, knowing that such a direction has been given, fails to leave the land as soon as practicable or, having left, enters the land within 7 days of the direction being given. These offences are punishable by 3 months' imprisonment, a fine or both.

A constable in uniform who reasonably suspects that a person is committing an offence under the section may arrest him without warrant.

It is a defence for a person to show that he had reasonable excuse for failing to leave the land as soon as reasonably practicable or, as the case may be, for again entering the land. In addition, the section does not apply where an entertainment licence has been granted by a local authority. A direction to leave cannot apply to an exempt person, that is, an occupier, member of his family, or his employee or agent, or to any person whose home is situated on the land.

The authorising superintendent, under powers given by s 64, may authorise constables to enter land to establish that such circumstances exist and to exercise powers. Where such a constable reasonably suspects that any person to whom the direction applies has, without reasonable excuse, failed to remove any vehicle or sound equipment on the land which appears to belong to that person or to be in his possession or control, or has entered the land as a trespasser with a vehicle or sound equipment within 7 days of that direction being given, he may seize and remove that vehicle or sound equipment of any person other than an exempt person.

Under powers given by s 65, where a constable in uniform reasonably believes that a person is on his way to such a gathering, he may stop that person and direct him not to proceed in the direction of the gathering. However, this power may only be exercised within 5 miles of the boundary of the site of the gathering. A person who, knowing that such a direction has been given, fails to comply commits an offence punishable by a fine. A constable in uniform who reasonably believes that a person is committing this offence may arrest him without warrant.

The court is empowered in such cases to order the forfeiture of sound equipment.

Aggravated trespass

Section 68 of the 1994 Act introduces an offence of aggravated trespass which is aimed at hunt protesters. Where a person trespasses on land in the open air and, in relation to any lawful activity which persons are engaged in on that or adjoining land in the open air, does there anything which is intended by him to have the effect:

(a) of intimidating those persons or any of them so as to deter them or any of them from engaging in that activity;
(b) of obstructing that activity; or
(c) of disrupting that activity,

he commits an offence.

Some act is required in addition to trespass and that act must be shown to be intended to have one of the effects set out in (a) to (c) above and this must be specified in the charge.

Thus, trespassers who lay false trails or blow hunting horns commit this offence. However, persons who trespass on land or run after a hunt with the intention of getting close enough to disrupt it commit this offence as such actions are sufficient disruption for the purposes of the Act.

The offence does not extend to circumstances in which there is no person present on the land at the time who is engaged in, or about to become engaged in, a lawful activity.

Thus, it does not extend to trespassers who damage crops on a farm when no person is present to be intimidated or obstructed or no activity is taking place which might be disrupted.

For the purposes of the section, an activity is lawful if it is carried out without trespass. The term 'land' does not include highways and roads.

The offence is punishable by 3 months' imprisonment, a fine or both.

Police powers

A constable in uniform who reasonably suspects that a person is committing this offence may arrest him without warrant.

Powers given by s 69 permit the senior police officer present at the scene, where he reasonably believes:

(a) that a person is committing this offence, or intends to commit it; or
(b) that two or more persons are so trespassing and are present there with the common purpose of intimidating persons so as to deter them from engaging in a lawful activity or of obstructing or disrupting a lawful activity,

to direct that person, or persons, or any of them, to leave the land. Any person who, knowing that such a direction has been given which applies to him and who fails to leave the land as soon as practicable or, who having left again enters the land as a trespasser within a period of 3 months of that direction commits an offence punishable by 3 months' imprisonment, a fine or both.

A constable in uniform who reasonably suspects that a person is committing this offence may arrest him without warrant.

Contamination of goods

The Public Order Act 1986, s 38(1), provides that it is an offence for a person to contaminate or interfere with goods, or make it appear that goods have been contaminated or interfered with, or to place goods which have been contaminated or interfered with, or which have that appearance, in a place where goods of that description are consumed, used, sold or otherwise supplied, with the intention:

(a) of causing public alarm or anxiety; or
(b) of causing injury to members of the public consuming or using the goods; or
(c) of causing economic loss to any person by reason of the goods being shunned by members of the public; or
(d) of causing economic loss to any person by reason of steps taken to avoid any such alarm or anxiety, injury or loss.

It is an offence contrary to s 38(2) for a person to threaten that he or another will do, or claim that he or another has done, any of these acts with such an intention as in (a), (c) or (d) above. The possession of contaminated goods, apparently contaminated goods, materials with which to contaminate goods or make it appear that goods have been contaminated is also punishable.

Individuals are attracted to such acts, or threats, as a means of extracting large sums of money from large companies. In addition, groups of activists who think they know better than we do what is good for us, employ such methods in an attempt to ensure that whether we agree, or do not agree, we will not dare to use the products of targeted companies. By making the offence punishable either way, it is possible to separate the prankster from the seriously ill-intentioned. On indictment the offence is punishable by 10 years' imprisonment, a fine or both, and on summary conviction by imprisonment for 6 months or a fine.

It is important to recognise that although this charge may be appropriate, the actions of such persons may be such that a charge of attempted murder may be appropriate. The placing of a poison in an article with the intention of killing is more than a merely preparatory act. If someone actually eats or drinks the product then such a person is guilty of the full offence of murder (should that person die) or causing grievous bodily harm with intent, should that be the case.

Although a defence is provided by the section, it does not relate to such a person as we have described above. It exists in favour of a person who, in good faith, reports or warns that such a danger exists. In this way, the broadcast of a warning is protected, as without that protection, the broadcaster would have, technically, made it appear that goods had been contaminated in circumstances in which he must have known that economic loss would follow by reason of those goods being shunned.

Public order offences and human rights

We dealt on page 81 with the effect of the Human Rights Act 1998 in general terms.

Public order law can interfere with the exercise of the Convention rights, particularly those under articles 10 and 11 referred to below. It remains to be seen how the coming into force of the Human Rights Act 1998 will affect the law which has been examined above in this chapter.

Article 10 is concerned with freedom of expression. It declares that:

1. Everyone has the right to freedom of expression. This right shall include freedom to hold opinions and to receive and impart information and ideas without interference by public authority and regardless of frontiers. This Article shall not prevent States from requiring the licensing of broadcasting, television or cinema enterprises.
2. The exercise of these freedoms, since it carries with it duties and responsibilities, may be subject to such formalities, conditions, restrictions or penalties as are prescribed by law and are necessary in a democratic society, in the interests of national security, territorial integrity or public safety, for the prevention of disorder or crime, for the protection of health or morals, for the protection of the reputation or rights of others, for preventing the disclosure of information received in confidence, or for maintaining the authority or impartiality of the judiciary.

Thus Article 10 begins with a wide declaration concerning an individual's rights in relation to freedom of expression and continues with a progressive list of matters which are excluded from that general right. Some of the matters listed can be described as 'essential', that is, for example, matters affecting national security, public safety and confidentiality where such confidentiality has been required within a contract of employment and an individual has therefore willingly surrendered some part of that basic freedom. Some of the other 'exclusions' are not so clear cut and may give rise to allegations that the State is attempting to impose its own definitions of terms included within the Article, to limit freedom of expression in respect of matters upon which the

State has decided that there is a 'correct belief' and the freedom should be restricted to an expression of support for the proposition.

Within the field of public order offences there are many which limit freedom of expression by forbidding particular types of statements from being made, or forbidding the expression of certain beliefs when in assemblies or in particular places. It is inevitable that freedoms will come into conflict with other competing rights or interests and it is the duty of Parliament to balance the rights of the individual against the needs of society. Inevitably, it is frequently the rights of individuals who seek to act in defiance of the agreed norms of society which appear to be supported, and the needs of society in general which appear to be ignored. One thing is certain: there will be challenges to the validity of some of our laws relating to public order in consequence of the Act.

The following provisions of Article 11, which are concerned with the freedom of assembly and association, are likely to lead to further challenges. It provides:

1. Everyone has the right to freedom of peaceful assembly and to freedom of association with others, including the right to form and join trade unions for the protection of his interests.
2. No restriction shall be placed on the exercise of these rights other than such as are prescribed by law and are necessary in a democratic society in the interests of national security or public safety, for the prevention of disorder or crime, for the protection of health or morals or for the protection of the rights and freedoms of others. This Article shall not prevent the imposition of lawful restrictions upon the exercise of these rights by members of the armed forces, of the police or the administration of the State.

Where someone is able to show that there has been interference with a specific right, it may be shown that the interference was justified, being prescribed by law, having a legitimate aim, being necessary in a democratic society in the interests of a legitimate aim, and that interference must not be discriminatory. To be 'lawful' or 'in accordance with the law', a citizen must have access to the information and the law must be formulated with sufficient degree of precision to enable a citizen to regulate his conduct. It will not be sufficient that an interference is reasonable or desirable, there must be a pressing social need. An interference within a law must be proportionate to the legitimate aim pursued. While such assessment will be made by the State concerned initially, the 'reasonableness' of that assessment will be subject to scrutiny by the European Court of Human Rights if the individual concerned ultimately takes his case there.

The challenges to our public order laws will occur:

(a) by way of an appeal against a criminal conviction in which case the court may hold that a statutory provision is incompatible with a Convention right;
(b) on an application for a declaration in any judicial proceedings that a statutory provision is incompatible with a Convention right.

However, so far as the police service is concerned, the Human Rights Act 1998 will have a considerable effect upon procedure, particularly in relation to public order matters. Contravention of a Convention right may lead to a court holding that the exercise of the police power in question was invalid and therefore unlawful.

Criminal damage

Damage

Damage, or the causing of actual harm to property, is punishable if it is committed without lawful excuse. The Criminal Damage Act 1971 simplified the law by repealing a multiplicity of offences which were only distinguished one from another for the purpose of providing differing penalties. The Law Commission considered that the essence of the offences of criminal damage should be the destruction of, or damage to, the property of another and that such matters as the means used to commit the damage and the nature of the property should not affect the nature of the offence.

The Act creates one basic offence, which covers the whole field of damage to the property of another committed without lawful excuse, being punishable by 10 years' imprisonment, and a further aggravated offence which additionally involves an intention to endanger the life of another recklessly, which is punishable by life imprisonment. There are two further offences which deal with threats to commit damage and the possession of articles with intent to commit damage.

Section 1(1) of the Act provides:

A person who without lawful excuse destroys or damages any property belonging to another intending to destroy or damage any such property, or being reckless as to whether any such property would be destroyed or damaged, shall be guilty of an offence.

If the destruction or damage is by fire, the offence is required by s 1(3) to be charged as arson, which carries a higher punishment. Where persons are charged with offences of minor damage in addition to major damage caused by fire, separate charges must be made.

Lawful excuse

The accused must destroy or damage another's property 'without lawful excuse'. Section 5(2) of the 1971 Act provides that a person is to be treated as having a lawful excuse if he acted with one of two types of belief: belief in consent and defence of property.

Belief in consent

It is possible that a person may genuinely believe (although he is mistaken in that belief) that he has consent to carry out an act which causes damage. This could occur where a demolition contractor made a genuine error in relation to the building which was to be demolished. Although he would undoubtedly be responsible for his act, he could not be said to be criminally liable as he believed that his act was lawful. It would also apply where an employee of such a company made a genuine mistake in relation to his instructions and pulled down a part of premises that were not within the contract. The test is whether the belief is honest. The more reasonable the belief, the more likely it is that a court or jury will find that it existed.

Defence of property

In the same way, a man who breaks down the door of his neighbour's house to extinguish a fire is acting with lawful excuse although the damage is deliberate as he knows that he is acting in defence of his neighbour's property. The act would also be committed with lawful excuse if he broke down the door merely to preserve his own property, and this would probably be so, even if no fire was discovered in his neighbour's house, provided that he had honestly believed this to be so when the door was broken down. Similarly, for example, a car is parked in a field of valuable crops and a farmer damages it in order to gain access and remove it before irreparable damage occurs; provided that the damage to the car is not disproportionate, he may have a lawful excuse, as he is acting in defence of his property.

However, where a vicar claimed that he had lawful excuse for damaging property by writing biblical quotations on a pillar outside the Houses of Parliament because he had done so to protect property in the Gulf States, the Divisional Court held that, even if the accused genuinely believed that he had a lawful excuse, an objective view had to be taken of whether, on the facts as believed by the accused, what he had done had protected, or was capable of protecting, such property. Protection was too remote from his conduct.

In addition, the breaking down of a door to recover a child which is being unlawfully detained does not fall within this defence. A person is not 'property' for the purposes of the 1971 Act.

General

A police officer executing a search warrant may intentionally damage a door in order to gain access. This act is done with lawful excuse as it is backed by a warrant which authorises the use of force. However, damaging property in the belief that the person concerned was carrying out God's laws is not done with lawful excuse.

Property

The term 'property' is defined by s 10 of the Act as meaning property of a tangible nature, whether real or personal, including money and:

(a) wild creatures which have been tamed or are ordinarily kept in captivity, any other wild creatures or their carcasses if, but only if, they have been reduced into posses-sion which has not been lost or abandoned, or are in the course of being reduced into possession; but

(b) *not* including mushrooms growing wild on any land or flowers, fruit or foliage of a plant growing wild on any land.

The term 'mushroom' includes all forms of fungi and the term 'plant' any shrub or tree. The similarity between this definition and the definition of property given in the Theft Act 1968 will be noticed, and this is a useful comparison to make. However, in relation to offences of criminal damage, there is no proviso that an offence will be committed in respect of mushrooms and plants if the damage is done for a commercial purpose. Damage to such articles, whether for a commercial purpose or not, is no offence. The term 'property' is, therefore, widely defined to cover all forms of tangible property except wild mushrooms and the flowers, fruit and foliage of plants.

The reference to animals is interesting as it would normally be anticipated that offences which are concerned with 'damage' to animals would be dealt with as offences of cruelty, but this need not be so. Injuring animals can be punishable under the Criminal Damage Act, and the classes of animals which may be stolen, as described in the text on the subject of theft, are the same as those in respect of which offences may be committed under this Act. All domestic animals are included within the terms 'real or personal property' and are protected because they are owned by some person, and zoo animals would be included in those which have been tamed or are ordinarily kept in confinement. Wild animals, because they have not become the property of any person while they remain in their wild state, are not protected unless they have been reduced into the possession of some person, e.g. a pet hawk.

Belonging to another

Subsection (2) of s 10 states that property shall be treated for the purpose of the Act as belonging to any person:

(a) having the custody or control of it;
(b) having a proprietary right or interest; or
(c) having a charge on it.

When a person hires a motor car, he gains both custody and control of it. If, whilst he has such custody or control another person damages the car, that person can be convicted of damaging *his* property. If a car is owned by two persons, each has a 'proprietary right or interest' in that car. Should the car be unlawfully damaged by one of them, he may be convicted of the offence of damaging property 'belonging to another'. The inclusion of the word 'proprietary' is for the purpose of restricting such ownership rights to those *directly* owning the property and has the effect of excluding bodies such as insurance companies which, although they have an 'interest' in the property, do not have a 'proprietary interest'.

For example, a building society has a 'charge' on property. Thus, where a house is being purchased by way of a mortgage, the house belongs to both the purchaser and the building society. The owner/occupier who recklessly damages the property without lawful excuse commits an offence in respect of property 'belonging to another'.

The mens rea of the basic offence

Damage [Section 1(1), Criminal Damage Act 1971]

A person who, without lawful excuse, destroys or damages any property belonging to another, intending to destroy or damage any such property or being reckless as to whether any such property would be destroyed or damaged shall be guilty of an offence.

It is an offence to destroy or damage any type of tangible property by any means. Property is obviously damaged if it suffers physical harm which involves permanent or temporary impairment of the property's use or value: a car which is scratched, a wall which is scribbled upon or a radio aerial which has been broken from a vehicle has suffered such physical harm and has been damaged. Where a person throws a stone at a passing car and dents it, he commits damage. This is equally true if he aims at one car and hits another. Property which is rendered inoperative has also been damaged as it has been impaired. If a cog wheel is removed from a mill, the mill is inoperative and has been damaged. If the degree of impairment is minimal, for example, requiring no more than the replacement of the cog wheel which was left at the scene, there will be no 'damage' for the purposes of the Act. However, if the cog wheel has been concealed and could not be replaced, there would be a cost involved in rectification, the machine would have been 'impaired', and an offence of criminal damage would have been committed.

In contrast, it has been held that where a person's car is wheel-clamped without his consent, the car is not damaged as there is no intrusion upon the integrity of the vehicle. It has not been altered or affected in any way; the clamp was added to it. By the Computer Misuse Act 1990, s 3(6), a modification of the contents of a computer shall not be regarded as damaging any computer or computer storage medium unless its effect on that computer or computer storage medium impairs its physical condition. However, where unauthorised alterations are made to a computer system which impair its proper use, an offence of criminal damage can be committed, although the damage to the magnetic particles in the disk are not perceptible without using the computer. Tangible property has been damaged, even though the damage itself is not tangible. Impairment of usefulness does not require physical damage to the thing itself.

The offence is restricted to damaging property belonging to some other person and it is no offence under this subsection to damage one's own property, even if it is done with the intention of making a fraudulent claim upon an insurance company. Such acts are punishable, in most circumstances, under the Theft Act. An honestly held belief, by the person committing the damage, that the property concerned belonged to him is sufficient to negate an offence, even though that belief is a mistaken one. A tenant of a flat installed a wiring system for stereo equipment with the landlord's permission. His adaptations included the addition of roofing material, asbestos wallpanels and floorboarding, which when fitted became the property of the landlord. On leaving the flat, the tenant removed the wiring, causing £130 worth of damage in the course of doing so. It was held by the Court of Appeal that no offence was committed if the tenant honestly believed that the property damaged belonged to him. It is not essential to prove that the property belonged to a particular person, provided that it is clearly shown that it is the 'property of another'.

A person is reckless as to whether or not any property would be destroyed or damaged if:

(a) he does an act which in fact creates an obvious risk that property will be destroyed or damaged; and
(b) when he does the act he either has not given any thought to the possibility of there being any such risk or has recognised that there was some risk involved and has nonetheless gone on to do it.

In relation to (a), the question is concerned with whether the risk would have been obvious to the ordinary, prudent person who gave thought to the matter. If it would have been obvious to such a person, it is irrelevant that it was not obvious to the accused because he was too young or mentally retarded.

If a wildfowler is shooting at ducks on a lake and, missing his aim, shoots through the side of a boat tethered behind the ducks, he cannot be said to have intended to damage the boat. However, his act, in the circumstances, created an obvious risk that property would be damaged and he was reckless as to that risk by not giving any thought to the possibility that such damage would occur. If he did recognise the risk, he was reckless in that he carried out the act in any case. On the other hand, if he had carefully considered the risk and concluded that there was none, he would not be guilty of criminal damage as there would be no recklessness as defined above.

The same would apply where a tramp lights a fire in a hay barn to keep warm. If the barn is subsequently burned down, the act of lighting the hay in these circumstances must be looked upon as one which created an obvious risk of damage. It might be different if he could satisfy a court that he had given consideration to risk and had decided that there was none. The age of the offender is irrelevant. Where, similarly, two boys aged 11 and 12 lit newspapers during the night and placed them under a bin at the rear of a shop leading to £1 million of damage to property, the Court of Appeal said that the test to be applied to 'recklessness' was by reference to the 'reasonable man', not the particular defendants.

Racially aggravated criminal damage

A person commits an offence under the Crime and Disorder Act 1998, s 30, if he commits an offence under the Criminal Damage Act 1971, s 1(1), which is racially or religiously aggravated.

An offence of criminal damage is racially or religiously aggravated if:

(a) at the time of committing it, or immediately before or after doing so, the offender demonstrates towards the person to whom the property belongs or is treated as belonging for the purposes of the 1971 Act hostility based on that person's membership (or presumed membership) of a racial or religious group; or

(b) the offence is motivated (wholly or partly) by hostility towards members of a racial or religious group based on their membership of that group.

For this purpose, 'membership' of a racial or religious group includes association with members of that group, and 'presumed' means presumed by the offender. A 'racial group' means a group of persons defined by reference to race, colour, nationality (including citizenship) or ethnic or national origins. A 'religious group' is a group of persons defined by reference to religious belief or lack of religious belief.

The references to 'religious groups' were inserted by the Anti-terrorism, Crime and Security Act 2001, which must be reviewed 2 years after Royal Assent, which was given on 14 December 2001.

Where an offence is charged under this section, the commission of the offence of criminal damage must be proved in the normal way and additional evidence must be offered of the 'racial' element.

Endangering life

Section 1(2) provides that if a person, without lawful excuse, destroys or damages property whether belonging to himself or another person:

(a) intentionally or recklessly; and

(b) intending by the destruction or damage to endanger the life of another or being reckless as to whether the life of another would be thereby endangered, he shall be guilty of an offence punishable by life imprisonment.

This subsection deliberately includes the property of the offender as it is possible that offences of this nature may be committed with the intention of killing or endangering the life of some person within the offender's family, resident within his own property. Indiscriminate bomb attacks upon buildings, which involve the intention of endangering life, or at least a reckless disregard for the life of others, are punishable under this section. The basic offence of criminal damage is aggravated by a disregard for the safety of other people. 'Recklessness' is to be judged in the same way in its relationship to 'endangering life' as in its relationship to offences of criminal damage contrary to s 1(1). Thus, there may be a need to prove recklessness in relation to the destruction or damage and, in addition, similar recklessness in that the accused's act created an obvious risk that the life of another would be endangered, and when he carried out that act, he either had not given any thought to the possibility of there being any such risk or had recognised such a risk but had nevertheless gone on to take it.

It must be proved that there was either an *intention* to endanger life, or *recklessness* in that respect. If it is alleged that the act was carried out with the *intention* of endangering life, voluntary intoxication is relevant and must be treated like any other evidence which tends to show that a defendant lacked a particular state of mind necessary to support the evidence. However, such self-induced intoxication is not relevant where *recklessness* is alleged. If a man, after taking drink and tablets, either lights a fire or drops a cigarette upon papers which are scattered all around a bed, he is reckless in relation to both criminal damage and the endangering of the lives of other residents in the house. Where a woman who was intoxicated started a fire in the kitchen of a shared flat, it was held that the question of her intoxication was relevant to a charge involving *intention* but was not relevant to a charge involving *recklessness*. Self-induced intoxication is no defence. The act, and state of mind, in relation to both the act itself and its consequences, must be viewed as if the person had not been affected by drink or drugs at the time.

The word 'arson' is retained within the law relating to damage by subsection (3), which directs that acts of damage by fire shall be charged as arson. Self-induced intoxication can be relevant to a defence to a charge of arson where intent is alleged. It cannot be relevant to a charge of arson by recklessness.

The questions are, therefore, was the accused 'reckless' in the manner discussed in relation to s 1(1) as to whether property might be destroyed or damaged by his act? Was he, additionally, reckless in that his act created an obvious risk that the life of another person would be endangered *and* that when he carried out his act, he either did not consider the possibility of there being any such risk, or had recognised that there was a risk, but had nevertheless gone on to take it?

The intended or reckless endangering of life must be by the destruction or damaging of property. Thus, if a man fires through a window and the bullet strikes a person inside, he cannot be guilty of this offence. The victim's life was not endangered by the destruction or damage caused to the building.

Threats to destroy or damage property

Threats to destroy or damage property are dealt with by s 2 of the Act of 1971:

A person who without lawful excuse makes to another a threat, intending that that other would fear it would be carried out:

(a) to destroy or damage any property belonging to that other or a third person; or

(b) to destroy or damage his own property in a way which he knows is likely to endanger the life of that other or a third person,

shall be guilty of an offence.

It does not matter how the threat is made, it may be verbal, by means of a letter or by telephone. Nor does it matter if the threat is made for the purposes of a joke, if it is made with the intention of creating fear in the recipient that it will be carried out.

The threat need not be made to the owner of the property; it may be a threat to damage someone else's property. For example, it would be an offence to make a threat to parents to destroy or damage property belonging to one of their children, if it was intended that the parents would fear that the threat would be carried out. If a person makes a threat to cause an explosion and his intention is to cause that person to fear that the threat will be carried out, he commits an offence against s 2 of the 1971 Act. It does not matter whether or not he actually intends to carry out his threat.

The offences which are separately created by s 51, Criminal Law Act 1977, deal particularly with 'bomb hoaxes'. The section creates offences of placing articles anywhere, or dispatching them by any means whatsoever, with the intention of inducing a belief in some other person that they are likely to explode or ignite, thereby causing injury or damage to property. Similarly, communicating information known or believed to be false to some other person with intent to induce a belief in any person that a bomb or other thing likely to explode or ignite is present anywhere is made a specific offence. Thus, the placing or sending of innocent articles, or the communication of false information concerning such articles, becomes punishable if done to induce a belief in another party that such articles are likely to explode, etc. The use of the words 'there is a bomb' by a hoaxer is sufficient to give rise to this offence. It is not necessary that the hoaxer should identify a location.

Possessing anything with intent to destroy or damage property

Section 3 states that a person who has anything in his custody or under his control intending, without lawful excuse, to use it or cause or permit another to use it:

(a) to destroy or damage any property belonging to some other person; or
(b) to destroy or damage his own or the user's property in a way which he knows is likely to endanger the life of some other person,

shall be guilty of an offence.

This section merely creates further offences of possessing articles which are intended to be used for either of the offences of criminal damage, or aggravated criminal damage, described in subsections (1) and (2) of s 1, respectively. The term 'custody' means physical custody and 'control' means having the power to direct what shall be done with the property in question. These terms are more precise than the general term 'possession', which is difficult to define fully. The essential feature of this offence is the intention of the person having custody or the control of the article, rather than the nature of the thing itself. If a walking stick is in the custody of some person who intends to break shop windows with it, his possession of the stick is punishable. A person who is found with an explosive device in his pocket intending to use it to damage property has custody of it, as it is in physical possession. A man who owns a warehouse full of similar devices, if they are there with his knowledge, is in control of them, as he must have some power of direction over them. The possession of such articles would also be punishable under the Explosives Act. A petrol bomb is an explosive substance.

An offence is committed whether or not the person who has custody or control intends to use the article himself, or merely intends to cause or permit some other person to use it, to commit damage. Carrying a hammer which is to be used by another for the purpose of damaging cars is an offence contrary to this section.

Search warrants

A justice of the peace may issue a search warrant following information, on oath, that there is reasonable cause to believe that a person has anything in his custody or control or on his premises, reasonably suspected to have been used, or be intended to be used, to commit offences under the Criminal Damage Act 1971.

If a search warrant is granted, a constable may enter (if need be by force) any premises and search for the thing in question. He may seize anything which he believes to have been used or to be intended to be used for these purposes.

Police powers

All offences of criminal damage are arrestable offences.

Dogs

Dog registration schemes

The requirement that the owner of a dog shall take out a licence authorising him to keep it was removed by the Local Government Act 1988. Section 37 of that Act authorises the Secretary of State to make provision by way of statutory instrument for the establishment and administration of a dog registration scheme by local authorities, or such other organisation as he may, after consulting with them, designate.

Dog collars

The Control of Dogs Order 1992 requires that every dog while on a highway or in a place of public resort must wear a collar with the owner's name and address inscribed upon it, or on a plate or badge attached to it. There are certain exceptions which refer to dogs which are working dogs used in the countryside in conditions which might make the wearing of a collar dangerous, or to other similar circumstances in other working environments. The exceptions apply to:

(a) any pack of hounds;
(b) any dog while being used for sporting purposes;
(c) any dog while being used for the capture or destruction of vermin;
(d) any dog while being used for the driving or tending of cattle or sheep;
(e) any dog while being used on official duties by a member of Her Majesty's Armed Forces or Her Majesty's Customs and Excise or by the police force for any area;
(f) any dog while being used in emergency rescue work; or
(g) any dog registered with the Guide Dogs for the Blind Association.

Where a dog is found in a highway or place of public resort without the requisite collar, the owner or the person in charge of the dog who, without lawful authority or excuse, the proof whereof shall lie on him, causes or permits the dog to be there without a collar, shall be guilty of an offence.

Dogs on leads

Section 27 of the Road Traffic Act 1988 gives power to local authorities to make orders designating certain roads within their areas as roads in which dogs must be held on a lead. The chief officer of police must be consulted before such an order is made; the local authority must publish the making of the order and provide the necessary signs to indicate that particular roads are designated roads. The local authority, for the purposes of this section, means the county council or other area authority.

Any person who causes or permits a dog to be on a designated road without the dog being held on a lead shall be guilty of an offence. The particular orders may contain certain exceptions to the general rule, and the Road Traffic Act permits the following dogs to be on designated roads:

(a) dogs proved to be kept for driving or tending sheep or cattle in the course of a trade or business;
(b) dogs proved to have been, at the time, in use and proper control for sporting purposes.

The Dangerous Dogs Act 1991 requires that designated dogs (see below) be muzzled and kept on a lead in a public place.

Stray dogs

The Environmental Protection Act 1990, s 149, requires every local authority to appoint an officer to deal with stray dogs found in its area. Where the officer has reason to believe that any dog found in a public place or on any other land or premises is a stray dog, he must, where possible, seize it and detain it. Where the place concerned is not a public place, he may only seize and detain the dog with the consent of the owner or occupier of the place. Notice must be served by the officer on the person whose address appears on the dog's collar, or on the owner (if known), stating that the dog will be liable to be disposed of if it is not claimed within 7 clear days and the expenses of its detention met. After the dog has been detained for 7 clear days (or where a notice has been served if it has not been claimed and the expenses paid within 7 clear days), the dog may be disposed of by way of sale or destruction. Where a dog is sold under the provisions of this section to a person acting in good faith, the ownership of the dog is vested in the recipient.

The officer must keep a register giving particulars of all dogs so seized and disposed of. The register must be available, at all reasonable times, for inspection by the public without charge. The officer must ensure that all such dogs are properly fed and looked after.

Section 150 of the Act requires the finder of a stray dog to:

(a) return it to the owner; or
(b) take the dog
    (i) to the appointed officer of the local authority for the area; or
    (ii) to the police station which is nearest to the place where the dog was found,

and to inform the officer of the local authority or the police officer in charge of the station where the dog was found. Failure to comply with these requirements is an offence. Where the dog has been taken to the appointed officer, the finder may keep the dog if he wishes, on informing the officer of this and his name and address. In such a case the finder must keep the dog for at least 1 month; he commits an offence if he fails to do so.

The Dogs Act 1906, s 3, makes similar provisions in relation to the seizure, detention and disposal of stray dogs by the police but it is anticipated that, in consequence of the 1990 Act, such dogs will be detained by the local authority officer. Section 4 of the 1906 Act makes similar provision to that in s 150 of the 1990 Act concerning the situation where the finder takes a stray dog to a police station and wishes to keep it. It provides that, on informing the police officer of this and of his name and address, he must be given a certificate which includes a description of the dog and gives details of its finding. The finder is, in consequence, obliged to keep the dog for a period of 1 month. If he does not he commits an offence. This must be explained to him before he agrees to keep the dog. If the finder does not wish to keep the dog it must be dealt with by the police by sale or destruction in the same way as described above in relation to an appointed local authority officer.

Further offences of 'straying' are discussed below under the heading 'Specific offences in relation to dangerous dogs'.

Dogs fouling land

The Dogs (Fouling of Land) Act 1996 creates an offence which is committed by a person who is in charge of a dog on designated land at the time when it defecates, who fails to remove the faeces from the land forthwith unless:

(a) he has reasonable cause for failing to do so; or
(b) the owner, occupier or other person or authority having control of the land has consented (generally or specifically) to his failing to do so.

A local authority may designate for the purposes of the Act any land in their area which is in the open air and to which the public are entitled or permitted to have access (with or without payment). The 1996 Act does not apply to land comprised in or running alongside a highway which comprises a carriageway unless the driving of motor vehicles on the carriageway is subject, otherwise than temporarily, to a speed limit of 40 mph or less. The Act does not apply to land used for agriculture or woodlands, land which is predominantly marshland, moorland or heath and common land to which the public are entitled or permitted to have access other than by a right to access to urban common land.

For the purposes of the Act, land which is covered, if open to the air on at least one side, is land which is open to the air.

The provisions do not apply to a registered blind person.

For the purposes of the offence, a person who habitually has a dog in his possession shall be taken to be in charge of the dog at any time unless some other person is then in charge. Placing faeces in a receptacle which is provided on the land amounts to removal. Being unaware of the defecation (whether by reason of not being in the vicinity or otherwise), or not having a device for, or other suitable means of removing faeces, shall not be a reasonable excuse for failing to remove faeces.

An authorised officer of the local authority may issue a fixed-penalty notice to a person who he has reason to believe has committed this offence. The effect of giving the notice is that no proceedings may be instituted before the expiration of 14 days following the giving of the notice. A person who pays the fixed pen-alty within that period cannot be convicted of the offence.

Dangerous dogs

General provisions

The Dogs Act 1871 empowers a magistrates' court to hear any complaint concerning a dog which is alleged to be dangerous and not kept under proper control. The Divisional Court held that it is not necessary that the dog is dangerous to mankind; it is enough that it is dangerous to other animals of whatever kind. However, in one case, a dog which killed two pet rabbits was held by the Divisional Court not to be dangerous as it was within the natural instincts of a dog to chase, wound or kill other small animals. This is a surprising view. If followed generally it would undermine the 1871 Act. In contrast, in a more recent case, where a Japanese Akita dog slipped its lead and attacked a Jack Russell terrier which died as a result of its injuries, the Divisional Court held that a dog could be dangerous and not under proper control even if the only danger it presented was to another dog. It held that 'dangerous' was to be given its ordinary everyday meaning and was not limited to danger to mankind or particular species of animals or birds.

In some cases a single act could be sufficient to prove this; in others, further evidence would be required. Much will depend upon the nature of the attack and the circumstances in which it took place.

The court may make an order requiring the owner to keep the dog under proper control or may order that it be destroyed. It may specify the measures to be taken to keep the dog under control and may require neutering of a male dog. A police officer is authorised to prefer a complaint under this Act. The fact that the incident occurred on private property is not relevant if other persons are permitted access, and such proceedings may be taken in relation to attacks upon livestock, even though proceedings are taken for another offence. The owner may appeal to a Crown Court against the decision of the magistrate.

On receipt of such a complaint, a constable should interview the complainant, or person attacked, and should record all relevant details in a statement and in his pocket notebook. If the dog concerned is subsequently traced it should be identified by such person in the presence of the owner, if this can be arranged. The owner should be informed of the nature of the complaint, including the damage or injury caused to persons or animals. It can be helpful in determining the truth of such an allegation if a careful note is made of the attitude of the dog towards the constable's presence, although this is not by itself significant as dogs are usually quiet in the presence of their owner.

The Dangerous Dogs Act 1989 provides that a magistrates' court may appoint a person to undertake the destruction of a dog, when it makes such an order under the 1871 Act, and may require the person who has custody of the dog to deliver it up. It may also disqualify the owner from having custody of a dog for a specified period. There is an appeal to the Crown Court.

The 1989 Act also creates offences of failing to keep a dog under proper control as ordered under the 1871 Act, s 2, and failing to deliver up a dog for destruction as ordered. These offences are punishable by fine and disqualification from having custody of a dog for a specified period.

Specific offences in relation to dangerous dogs

The Dangerous Dogs Act 1991, ss 1 and 3, make further provisions in relation to dangerous dogs.

The most important provision is s 1(3), which makes it an offence for a person to have in his possession or control a dog to which s 1 applies. However, the Dangerous Dogs Compensation and Exemption Schemes Order 1991 provides that this offence does not apply to a dog born before 30 November 1991 if the following conditions are satisfied:

(a) the person wishing to keep the dog must have notified the police of its address, name, age and gender;
(b) the dog must have been neutered;
(c) there must be third party insurance in respect of bodily harm caused by it and a certificate of exemption must have been issued; and
(d) its terms must be complied with.

The section applies to pit bull terriers, Japanese tosas and any dog of a type designated by order of the Secretary of State, currently *Dogo argentino* and *Fila braziliera*. 'Type' is not synonymous with 'breed' and it is a matter of fact to be determined by a court whether a particular dog is of a type specified. In reaching a decision, a court is entitled to refer to works describing breed standards but it is not essential that a dog should have all of the characteristics described. The behavioural characteristics of the dog may be taken into account.

Section 1(2) prohibits breeding, selling, exchanging, giving or offering to give, advertising or exposing of such matters, of the dogs specified above in relation to lead, etc., and makes it an offence for the owner to abandon such a dog, or for the owner or person in charge of it to allow it to stray. Voluntary intoxication is no defence to a charge of allowing a dog of such a type to be in a public place without being muzzled.

Section 3 creates two offences which apply to all dogs.

First, where a dog is dangerously out of control in a public place, the owner or the person for the time being in charge of it is guilty of an offence under s 3(1). The offence is aggravated if the dog, whilst so out of control, injures any person. These are offences of strict liability and there is no need to prove negligence by the owner or handler. The owner has a defence if he can prove that at the time of the offence the dog was in the charge of a person whom he reasonably believed to be a fit and proper person to be in charge of it. Where a woman was looking after a dog on behalf of another person who was in prison and locked the dog in the house and went out, the Court of Appeal ruled that she remained in charge although another occupant of the house had returned when the dog escaped and bit a small boy. This defence, provided by s 3(2), is not intended to lead to, where a dog is kept at home, a minute analysis of who was in charge of it at the time. The fact that a dog was let out of the house by a person other than the owner is not evidence from which it can be inferred that charge of the dog had been transferred to that other person. The defence only applies if there is plain evidence that 'charge' has been transferred.

Second, the owner or person in charge of a dog commits an offence against s 3(3) if he allows it to enter a place which is not a public place but where it is not permitted to be and while it is there, it injures any person, or there are grounds for reasonable apprehension that it will do so. There would be such grounds, for example, if a dog attacks someone without prior warning. Where a dog was chained in a garden, the owner was held to have 'allowed' it to enter a place where it was not permitted to be when it slipped its chain and escaped from the garden. This will be so even where the owner genuinely believes that the dog has been properly secured. The offence can be committed by omission. An aggravated offence is committed if the dog does injure any person in these circumstances.

Where a person is convicted of an offence against s 1 or 3 the court may order destruction of the dog concerned. It must do in the case of an offence against s 1 or an aggravated offence contrary to s 3 unless it is satisfied that the dog would not constitute a danger to public safety and, where the dog was born before 30 November 1991 and is subject to a prohibition on its possession under s 1(3), that there is good reason why the dog has not been exempted from that prohibition.

Section 4A of the 1991 Act provides that where a person is convicted of an offence under s 1 or 3(1) or (3) and the court does not order destruction of the dog under s 4(1)(a), and in the case of an offence under s 1, the dog is subject to the prohibition under s 1(3) (possessing a prohibited breed of dog), the court must order that, unless the dog is exempted from that prohibition within the requisite period, it shall be destroyed. The requisite period, currently 2 months, may be extended by the court.

A person who is convicted of an offence under s 3(1) or (3) may be ordered to keep a dog under proper control and, if he fails to do so, the dog must be destroyed. Such an order, under s 4A(4), may specify the measures to be taken to keep the dog under control, whether by muzzling, keeping on a lead, excluding it from specified places or otherwise and, if it appears to the court that the dog is a male and would be less dangerous if neutered, may require that the dog be neutered.

Section 4B makes provision for an order of destruction which may be made by a justice of the peace in respect of a dog which has been seized under s 5(1) or (2) of the Act (dogs which appear to be prohibited or dangerously out of control or seized under warrant) where there is no prosecution, or where the dog cannot be released without contravention of s 1(3). A justice is not required to make such an order if he is satisfied concerning the factors mentioned above in relation to s 1.

A court may also order a person convicted of any of these offences to be disqualified from keeping a dog for such a period as it thinks fit. Dogs may not be destroyed during the period allowed for notice of, and determination of, any appeal.

Similar provisions are made in the 1991 Act to those set out above in the 1989 Act in relation to the appointment of a person to undertake the destruction of a dog and requiring it to be delivered up for that purpose.

Offences are committed against s 4(8) where a person has custody of a dog whilst so disqualified, or where he fails to deliver up a dog for destruction as ordered.

Dogs owned by young persons

Where a dog is owned by a person who is less than 16 years old, the term 'owner' in the above provisions includes a reference to the head of the household, if any, of which that person is a member.

Police powers

By section 4 of the 1991 Act, a constable (or authorised local authority officer) may seize any dog which appears to him to be a dog to which s 1 applies and which is in a public place when its possession or custody is unlawful by virtue of s 1, or when it is not muzzled or kept on a lead. Such a person may also seize *any* dog in a public place which appears to him to be dangerously out of control.

Public place

It will be noted that some of the provisions of the Act are limited to a public place. The Act defines a 'public place' as any street, road or other place (whether or not enclosed) to which the public have or are permitted to have access. A private garden is not a public place in this context and neither is any other type of place which people enter by express or implied invitation. On the other hand, a dog in a private car on a public highway is in a public place.

Protection of livestock

The Dogs (Protection of Livestock) Act 1953 provides that if a dog worries livestock on any agricultural land, the owner of the dog and, if it is in the charge of some person other than the owner, that person also shall be guilty of an offence.

The term 'worrying livestock' means either attacking livestock, or chasing them in such a way that injury or suffering may reasonably be expected to be caused. The effects of chasing cattle or sheep which are about to give birth can result in the loss of their calf or lamb, and the Act includes such action within the definition of 'worrying' as well as the diminution in produce which is likely to occur when milking cows are pursued by dogs.

The Wildlife and Countryside Act 1981 extended the meaning of the term 'worrying of livestock' to include a dog being at large, that is not on a lead or otherwise under close control, in a field or enclosure in which there are sheep. If livestock are disturbed, with the effects described, this will be an offence if it results from a dog attacking, chasing or being at large. (Dogs of the occupier of the field, police dogs, guide dogs, trained sheep dogs, working gun dogs and packs of hounds are exempted from the 'being at large' provisions.)

'Livestock' includes cattle, sheep, goats, swine, horses or poultry. The term 'cattle' means bulls, cows, oxen, heifers or calves, 'horses' includes asses and mules, and 'poultry' covers domestic fowls, turkeys, geese and ducks. 'Agricultural land' means land used as arable, meadow or grazing land or for the purposes of poultry farming, pig farming, market gardens, allotments, nursery grounds or orchards.

It is a defence for the owner of a dog to prove that, at the time at which the offence was committed, the dog was in the charge of some person whom he reasonably believed to be a fit and proper person to be in charge of the dog. In addition, animals which are straying on the dog owner's land are not protected by this Act, unless the owner urges his dog to attack.

Police officers serving in all forces are likely to receive complaints concerning dogs which have been worrying livestock. The definition of the term 'agricultural land' is so wide that it includes smallholdings and even allotments which appear even within our large cities. Poultry is kept in many places which are protected by this Act and complaints are fairly frequent. A constable is empowered to seize any dog, found on agricultural land, which he has reasonable cause to believe has been worrying livestock there if there is no one present in charge of it. He may deal with it as if it has been taken possession of as a stray.

Proceedings under the Dogs (Protection of Livestock) Act 1953 may be taken by the occupier of the land, by the owner of the livestock, or by the police. If the police take action, the Act requires that the consent of the chief officer of police is obtained and it is the general practice to have the information authorised by the chief constable. It is good practice for the officer reporting to check that this has been done before the date of the hearing.

The owners of livestock which have been killed or injured frequently ask for advice concerning their entitlement to compensation. The Animals Act 1971 places liability upon the keeper of the dog, and compensation can be obtained by way of civil claim. This Act also protects a person charged with killing or injuring a dog, if he acted in protection of his livestock and gave notice to the police of his actions within 48 hours.

Guard dogs

Guard dogs used on premises must be either under the direct control of a 'handler' or so secured that they are not at liberty to go freely about the premises. A man kept three Alsatian dogs in a yard and premises which he owned. The dogs were independently fastened on separate chains 12 feet in length which did not permit them to reach the entry gate to the yard, or all parts of the premises. There was no handler present.

It was held that a person may lawfully use a guard dog on premises without a handler if the dog is properly secured. Whether a chain of 12 feet is to be regarded as 'not at liberty to go freely about the premises' is a question of fact and will vary in differing circumstances. Offences are committed by those who use or permit the use of a guard dog on premises unless it is under control.

Warning notices must be clearly displayed at each entrance to premises upon which guard dogs are used. It is an offence to fail to do so. The term 'guard dog' means a dog which is used to protect premises, property kept on premises or a person guarding such premises or property. 'Premises' means land other than agricultural land and the curtilage of a dwelling house, and buildings other than dwelling houses.

Assaults and woundings

Assaults

An assault is an attempt by force, or violence, to do bodily injury to another. The display of force should be such that the victim believes that force is about to be used against him. There are two important elements in the offence: a display of force by one party, and a genuine fear that force was about to be used in the mind of the person against whom the threat was made. The pointing of an unloaded gun at a person may amount to an assault. The act amounts to a display of force, and if the person at whom the gun is pointed fears that it may be used this is sufficient to constitute the offence. If a man threatens to throw a punch at another person who fears that his threat will be carried out, the assault is complete although the person assaulted has not been touched in any way. An assault has been committed when there is any act which intentionally, or because of the recklessness of the act itself, causes another person to fear immediate unlawful violence.

It is important to consider whether or not such fear could have existed in the mind of the victim. If the threat is made at such a distance from the other party that it could not possibly have been carried out, then it is inconceivable that there was immediate apprehension that physical force was about to be applied. Provided that there is a present ability to carry out the threat, the nature of the act is only restricted in that it must contain an element of hostility. Urging a dog to attack, drawing a knife, throwing a stone or other missile, or raising a stick in a threatening manner each provides an example of the type of act which would cause a person to fear that violence was about to be used against him. If a gang of rowdy youths throw rubble from a building site at people who are passing in the street, a brick deliberately aimed at a particular person is clearly intended to cause that person to fear being hit; bricks showered at passers-by generally indicate a recklessness as to whether passers-by will be put in fear by these actions.

Recently, the nature of the 'immediate' threat has been given a liberal interpretation by the courts. It has been stretched to include a woman put in fear by a 'peeping-tom' who was outside her closed window. Another who was subjected to telephone calls by a caller who 'hung up' was said to have been put in fear of immediate violence, on the grounds that she would not know what the person was going to do next. In another case, where a woman had been caused psychiatric harm after repeated telephone calls and letters from a stalker, the last two of which contained threats, the Court of Appeal held that the jury were entitled to find that the last letter had caused the woman to fear immediate force. It emphasised that the accused, who was known to the woman, lived near her and she thought that something could happen at any time. Strangely, the Court of Appeal accepted the need for apprehension of immediate force but said that it was enough for the prosecution to prove fear of force 'at some time not excluding the immediate future'! In the light of these decision, the requirement seems to mean little. However, conduct such as that just described would now be better dealt with under the Protection from Harassment Act 1997; see page 473.

The law differentiates between an assault and a battery. The term 'battery' means the intentional or reckless application of unlawful force to another, however slight, and whether directly or indirectly. It would be applied directly where a person hits another with his fist or with some object and indirectly if he placed acid in a hand drier which is later blown onto the hands of some other person. Each battery includes the elements of an assault as it amounts to the eventual application of the threatened violence. A person who strikes another with his fist, or beats him with a stick, has both assaulted and beaten him, but the physical contact does not need to be so aggravated. Any hostile touching, pushing, striking with an implement or object which has been thrown will amount to a battery. If a man throws a stone at his neighbour and misses him, he is guilty of an assault; if the stone finds its mark, he is also guilty of battery. However, the causing of psychiatric harm cannot amount to a battery because it does not involve the use of force.

The High Court has ruled that where there has been an assault *by beating*, it should be so charged.

There are many instances in which such forms of physical contact are justified and are, therefore, not punishable, but in all such instances no more force must be used than is necessary upon that particular occasion.

Defences to assault

Questions concerning the nature of an assault usually establish whether or not valid defences may be put forward. Was consent given to the act which constitutes the allegation of assault? Was the assault justified in law?

Consent

Consent may, on certain occasions, be given to acts which would otherwise be an assault and these occasions would include blows exchanged in the course of friendly athletic contests or during innocent horseplay. If the act results in physical injury to another person, his consent is no defence to a charge of wounding. Thus, willing and enthusiastic participation in sado-masochistic acts of violence for the sexual pleasure engendered in the giving and receiving of pain can lead to a conviction for an assault or battery or for a more serious offence. On the other hand, valid consent can be given to ear-piercing, to being tattooed, or even to be branded with one's spouse's initials, as the causing of bodily harm in these forms is not contrary to public policy. If no physical harm amounting to a wounding or bodily harm results from an assault, it is necessary to prove the absence of consent, unless the actions themselves were injurious to the public or were accompanied by a breach of the peace. It has been held that injuries received in the course of a prize fight are injurious to the public and consent is therefore no defence. The distinction is made between the bare-fisted public spectacle and the lawful sport of boxing, which is conducted in such a way that injuries are kept to the minimum possible in this form of contest.

Persons who participate in sports such as soccer or rugby accept that there is a risk of injury from bodily contact permitted by the rules of the game. However, a head-butt or a deliberate kick aimed at a player on the ground would not be excused as no consent is given to such bodily contacts. If excessive violence is used during an assault the question of consent cannot rise as no legal consent can be given to such acts. In addition, the consent obtained must be a true consent and not one which was obtained by means of fear, fraud or ignorance.

Sometimes a consent which has been given will be invalid, for example where the person giving the consent is young or sufficiently mentally impaired to be unable to understand the nature of the act committed. The same would be true if consent had been obtained by duress.

Legally justified

Lawful correction

It is a good defence that the assault was in the course of correction of a child by its parents, or other people *in loco parentis*, provided that it is moderate in manner and quantity, and that the instrument used is reasonable. Obviously, the force used is unreasonable if it is disproportionate to the wrongdoing, and is also unreasonable if the chastisement involved an uncontrolled response to wrongdoing. Such a person may use reasonable force to restrain a child from injuring another person or damaging property or engaging in disorderly behaviour. However, these parental rights are currently under review since a finding by the European Court of Human Rights that such actions contravened the European Convention on Human Rights which did not permit a person to be subjected to torture or inhuman or degrading treatment or punishment. Amending legislation is therefore expected in relation to such matters and defences of this nature will be subjected to narrow limitations.

Teachers are no longer entitled by virtue of their position as such to apply reasonable corporal punishment as a disciplinary measure.

Self-defence

A person may be justified in assaulting another if the assault is carried out in self-defence. The justification is generally limited to circumstances in which the first act of hostility was carried out by the other party, although it is not essential that the other party struck the first blow. The Court of Appeal has ruled that it is both good law and good sense that a person who is attacked may defend himself, but that in doing so, he may only do what is reasonably necessary. In deciding upon his response, the facts as the person concerned believed them to be are the facts to be assessed. If a man raises a stick intending to strike another, the second party is not obliged to await the blow falling before taking action to defend himself. It is important, but not essential, that a person offering this defence is able to show that he did not wish to become involved in a fight. The test to be applied to a defence of 'self-defence' is an objective one, but is assessed on the facts as the person concerned believed them to be.

There is a limit to the action which must be taken to avoid conflict, and this need not include a willingness to run away in order to avoid a confrontation with a person who offers violence. It is not suggested that a man must avoid going to some place at which he knows persons are assembled who may offer him violence, but he must show that it was neither his wish nor his intention to become involved. A failure to retreat when this was possible is merely one factor which may be taken into account by a court when deciding whether the use of force was necessary and reasonable in the particular circumstances. A person may act in self-defence without temporising, disengaging or withdrawing in circumstances in which he will have a good defence.

Defence of wife, husband, parent or child

It has long been recognised that assaults committed in defence of persons who enjoyed these particular relationships may be justified and the common law recognised the special relationship which existed between masters and servants, so that similar defences are acceptable in respect of acts done in defence of one party by the other. In 1967, the Court of Criminal Appeal refused to restrict this defence to these particular relationships.

There is, additionally, a right held by any person to intervene to prevent someone else from being assaulted, and it is permissible to do all that is necessary and reasonable to prevent such an assault. The Criminal Law Act 1967 provides a defence for anyone who commits an assault while acting in the prevention of crime.

Defence of property

Assaults may be justified if they are committed in defence of property. This justification may relate to the unlawful removal of goods, or to the defence of an owner's right of possession of his property. If force is used to remove a trespasser from property, there must be a request made to the trespasser to leave before force may be used, and then it may only be such as is necessary to remove him from the premises. The essential question must always be 'was the force used reasonable in the circumstances? A property owner does not have the right to use force against a trespasser who does not threaten violence.

During a lawful arrest

An arrest can seldom be effected without some form of physical contact and the action of arrest must in some way indicate to the person arrested that he is subject to physical restraint and that he will be forcibly prevented from leaving, should he attempt to do so. The Criminal Law Act 1967, s 3, authorises the use of reasonable force. The amount of force which must be used varies according to the degree of resistance of the prisoner, which can be considerable, particularly when persons are arrested for offences of drunkenness. The use of force by the constable is justified provided that it is reasonable in the circumstances and necessary to effect the arrest.

Certain other defences can reasonably be put forward in answer to a charge of assault. The physical contact may occur by misadventure, for example the accidental discharge of a missile, or in the course of a lawful sport, such as a wrestling bout or a soccer match.

Offences of assault and battery

The Criminal Justice Act 1988, s 39, states that common assault and battery are summary offences. They are punishable by a fine or imprisonment for 6 months, or both. Offences dealt with by the police should be charged as offences of assault or battery depending upon the circumstances. Where a person has merely been 'put in fear', the person responsible should be charged with an assault contrary to this section. Where force has been applied to a person, the person responsible should be charged that he 'did assault by beating' and it is important that these words are used.

Whilst there is a power of arrest for an assault committed in a police officer's presence, or where there is a danger that further violence will be offered, these are powers which will only be exercised where circumstances demand it. If an arrest is made for a breach, or threatened breach of the peace, proceedings must follow for those offences or be discontinued.

Police action

Whilst police action may follow incidents involving an assault, it must be remembered that the circumstances in which such offences can be committed are so wide that prosecution for a criminal offence may not always be the best way forward. Where the nature of the assault is trivial, particularly in instances in which family, friends or neighbours are the only persons involved, it may be more satisfactory, after a cautionary word, to ensure that the parties involved are aware of each other's names and addresses so that they may make a complaint to the justices' clerk with a view to obtaining 'surety of the peace' from the other party. Any such action must be in accordance with force standing orders. An accurate record must be made of any such incident as constables are frequently called as witnesses in such cases.

Victims of criminal assaults may be entitled to receive compensation from the Criminal Injuries Compensation Board. They should be informed of this entitlement.

Assault – police

Section 89(1) of the Police Act 1996 states that any person who assaults a constable in the execution of his duty, or a person assisting a constable in the execution of his duty, shall be guilty of an offence.

Section 89(2) punishes persons who resist or wilfully obstruct a constable in the execution of his duty, or a person assisting him.

These offences can be committed against a constable of a Scottish or Northern Irish Force when he is executing a warrant, or otherwise acting in England and Wales, by virtue of any enactment conferring powers upon him in England and Wales.

This section covers several important points and it is essential to prove that the person assaulted was a police officer and was acting as such, or, in the case of a person assisting him, both of these factors and that the second party was acting in his aid. It must also be shown that the officer was acting in the execution of his duty, and this is the essence of the offence. If an assault is directed at a police officer who is not acting in the execution of his duty, it is merely a common assault. The distinction is often a fine one, as illustrated by the following examples.

A police officer who witnessed an obstruction by a motor lorry followed the vehicle into a garage in order to make enquiries. He did not have permission to enter the garage. The owner told him to leave and the officer refused, claiming that he had the right to remain, and he was assaulted by the owner. It was held that even if the police officer had a right to enter the garage, he had no right to remain after being told to leave and so became a trespasser. As such he was no longer acting in the execution of his duty at the time at which he was assaulted. However, it would have been different if a breach of the peace had been taking place on the premises, as the common law permits a constable both to enter and to *remain* on private premises to deal with an actual or apprehended breach of the peace. Such a constable is acting in the execution of his duty. A police officer, who believed that a breach of the peace would occur if a man addressed people assembled in a street, forbade him to do so but the man persisted and obstructed the officer when he attempted to prevent the meeting from being held. It was decided that as it is one of the duties of the constable to prevent breaches of the peace which he reasonably believes are about to occur, the man was guilty of obstructing him in the execution of his duty.

Where a constable witnessed an argument between a man and his girl friend which resulted in the girl running away, he was entitled, after giving the girl directions to her home, to speak to the man to ensure that he would not follow the girl, as he was acting in the course of his duties to preserve the peace. A sergeant and two constables passed through a garden gate and approached the door of a house at which they wished to make enquiries concerning a crime. The sergeant was invited into the house by the son of the occupier; the occupier immediately ordered him to leave and as the sergeant was doing so he was attacked. The constables came to the assistance of the sergeant and a fight took place. In this case the defendants were convicted of assaulting the officers in the execution of their duty, it being held that they were not trespassers when they passed through the garden gate as they had implied leave to pass through the gate and approach the front door for the purpose of making enquiries. When the constables went to the assistance of the sergeant, they were acting in the execution of their duty by endeavouring to prevent a breach of the peace.

The situation where there has been a 'touching' of the person alleged to have assaulted a constable is an interesting one. Where a man had kicked a constable and used foul language, he started walking away. The constable laid a hand on his shoulder, not with the intention of arresting him, but to detain him for further questioning. The constable was held not to be acting in the execution of his duty. It would have been different if he had been arresting the man. However, in another case, two officers were attempting to give a parking ticket to the driver of a vehicle which was causing an obstruction and that person swore at the officers, pushed one of them and threatened to drive off. One officer took hold of his arm and told him to calm down as 'it was only a ticket'. The man kicked out at one officer and hit the other with his hand. The Divisional Court said that the justices had found that the officer had taken hold of the man's arm merely to draw his attention to what was being said and in an attempt to calm him down. It was a matter for the justices to decide whether *contact had gone beyond what is acceptable by the ordinary standards of everyday life*. The Court said that much depended upon the nature of the 'contact'. If it went on for any length of time it would obviously signify an intention to detain. Much depended, therefore, upon whether the contact could be described as 'social' rather that 'restraining'.

It has been held that in circumstances in which police officers arrested a man and it was not practicable to tell him of the reason for his arrest at the time, the arrest was lawful and the officers were acting in the execution of their duty, even though the arrest was subsequently made unlawful as the reason for arrest was not given when it was practicable to do so. Similarly, where a constable stopped a motor vehicle pursuant to the Road Traffic Act 1988, s 163, and detained it, suspecting it to be stolen, he was acting in the execution of his duty provided that his 'suspicion' was justified.

Many assaults upon police officers take place in police stations. It must be remembered that a person who is not under arrest may leave a police station at any time. Any act carried out by a police officer to prevent such a person from leaving is not carried out in the execution of the officer's duty.

Section 89(1) is an arrestable offence.

An 'obstruction' of a police officer [the offence under s 89(2)] must be 'wilful'. The conduct must therefore have been deliberate and be intended by the person concerned to prevent, or make more difficult, the constable's task of performing his duties. It is not essential that the person concerned be shown to have realised that that would be the likely effect of his actions. There must have been no lawful excuse. Although constables are empowered to obtain names and addresses from offenders, there is, in most instances, no legal requirement upon the person concerned to provide them. If that is so there has been no obstruction. Sometimes the law requires the provision of such information. If that is so then there is an obstruction if the details are not provided. Similarly, it is not an obstruction to advise another person not to answer police questions which he is not obliged to answer, even if this is done in an offensive way. In all offences of obstruction, there is a similar requirement that a police officer is acting in the execution of his duties.

The Police Reform Act 2002, s 46, creates similar offences in relation to assaults on, or the obstruction of, designated and accredited persons acting the execution of their duties.

Assaults occasioning actual bodily harm

The Offences Against the Person Act 1861, s 47, provides that it is an arrestable offence to assault any person causing him actual bodily harm. The term 'actual bodily harm' is any injury calculated to interfere with health or comfort in a more than trifling way. Psychiatric injury (but not mere emotions such as fear, distress or panic, which are not themselves evidence of a clinical condition) can amount to 'actual bodily harm'. Consequently, to cause someone psychiatric injury by a threat of 'immediate' force can amount to an offence under s 47. Expert evidence should be offered of such a condition.

Actual bodily harm may include black eyes, more serious bruising and minor cuts. The Court of Appeal supported the conviction of man who had made repeated telephone calls to women, remained silent when they answered, and this had led to significant psychological symptoms. This decision seems to depart from the previously recognised rule (as discussed above) that the conduct must be such that the persons would fear immediate and unlawful physical violence. It also recognises a continuing act (over a series of telephone calls) as the *actus reus* of the assault.

It will be seen that this offence does not require a specific intent on the part of the accused; it is sufficient if there is an assault and, as a result of it, actual bodily harm is occasioned. There must be a direct causal connection between the assault and the bodily harm. If a man punches his victim, this is apparent. If he chases him so that, in fear, he jumps out of a window and injures himself, there is still a direct causal connection between the assault and the bodily harm. Assaults resulting in serious nervous disorders have been held to be punishable under this section.

The *mens rea* required for this offence is that required for an assault or battery. It is not essential to establish that a defendant intended to cause some bodily harm, or was reckless as to the risk of doing so.

Woundings

Sections 18 and 20 of the Offences Against the Person Act 1861 deal with offences of wounding which are similar in some characteristics. It will be noticed that these offences require that the accused must have acted unlawfully and maliciously. The requirement that the act must have been carried out unlawfully excludes instances in which a constable or citizen may have used force to prevent a crime or to effect a lawful arrest. For an act to have been done maliciously the accused must have foreseen the possibility of the type of injury specified within each section. It is from this point, in the consideration of a charge, that the further facts of the case must be carefully considered as there is some difference in the seriousness of the offences. Offences contrary to s 18, in respect of which specific intentions to effect particular types of harm must be specified, are punishable by life imprisonment, whereas those contrary to s 20, in respect of which particular intentions need not be shown, are punishable by 5 years' imprisonment.

Wounding with intent

Section 18 of the Offences Against the Person Act 1861 states:

> Whosoever shall unlawfully and maliciously, by any means whatsoever, wound or cause any grievous bodily harm to any person, WITH INTENT to do grievous bodily harm to any person, or with intent to resist or prevent the lawful apprehension or detainer of any person, commits an offence.

The section creates two offences and the different intents mentioned in the section specify variations in the method by which the offences may be committed. There are various terms used within this section which require definition:

(a) *Wound* – To constitute a wound the continuity of the skin must be broken. The skin consists of two layers and both must be broken before an injury can be described as a wound. It is not necessary that this must be an outer skin covering; a break inside the cheek or the lip is a wound for the purposes of this Act.

Wounds may be inflicted in a variety of ways: by a kick, or with an instrument resulting in incised, punctured, lacerated, contused or gunshot wounds. A broken bone cannot be a wound unless a part of it pierces the skin.

(b) *Grievous bodily harm* – This term means really serious bodily harm, but it is not necessary that it should be either dangerous or permanent. Where a man cut the private parts of an infant in order to commit rape, the injury not being serious although it caused considerable bleeding, he was convicted of causing grievous bodily harm with that intent. The term may include psychiatric harm but the harm must be serious to fit within this definition. Grievous bodily harm can be caused even though there is no battery. If a person is forced to jump from a window and suffers such harm, that harm has been 'caused' although there was no touching.

(c) *With intent* – It is necessary to prove that the particular type of injury was inflicted with the intention of doing so, or with the intention to resist or prevent detention. It is reasonable to assume that a person intends the consequences of his deliberate acts unless he is able to prove that the result was accidental, but a court must consider all of the evidence available before deciding whether or not a particular intention existed. If a man attacks another in order to rob him and, in the course of doing so, inflicts grievous bodily harm, he may be convicted of this offence. By using violence to effect his purpose he shows an intention to cause grievous bodily harm, which is a natural consequence of his act.

The section specifies an intention to cause grievous bodily harm to any person and a man will be guilty of this offence if he strikes at or shoots at one person with such intent but injures another. In such circumstances the charge should specify that he caused grievous bodily harm to B with intent to cause harm to A. In all instances the particular intent must be shown in evidence. When a man heard an intruder in his house and fired a gun to frighten him away, but hit him and wounded him, it was held that he was not guilty of an offence contrary to this section as his intention had not been to cause harm, and this must be clearly shown before a conviction would be merited. It is not sufficient to establish mere recklessness, the specific intent alleged must be proved.

(d) *Resist or prevent lawful apprehension or detainer of any person* – If a charge alleges this particular intent, it must be shown that the person concerned was told of the officer's intention to arrest him. By including the words 'any person' it is not only the person who is being arrested who may be convicted of this offence, but any person who attempts to prevent the arrest by use of force. Once again the intention of the person concerned is the first factor for consideration. If a man trips a police officer who is chasing a criminal over grass and the officer falls on to broken glass, the presence of which was unknown to the accused, it cannot be said that it was the intention of his attacker to cause grievous bodily harm by means of broken glass or that such a result could be foreseen. If the police officer was tripped while running after a criminal in a street and was seriously injured when he fell, it can be assumed that such injury was intended as the results could be easily foreseen.

Unlawful wounding

Section 20 of the Offences Against the Person Act 1861 states:

> Whosoever shall unlawfully and maliciously wound or inflict grievous bodily harm upon any other person, either with or without any weapon or instrument, shall be guilty of an offence.

The terms used within this section are similar to those used within s 18, but the notable omission is the words 'with intent'. A particular intention to inflict the types of harm specified is, therefore, unnecessary, but it must be shown that the act was done 'maliciously'. It is sufficient to show that the act was such that the accused must have foreseen that he was likely to cause some harm, even if of a minor nature, to some other person. A person acts maliciously if he carries out an act deliberately and he was aware that some physical harm might result. He need not be aware that it *will* result. Nor is it essential that he foresaw harm of the gravity described in the section; foresight that some harm, albeit of a minor character, might result, is sufficient. In most cases with which police officers are involved, the malice is apparent from the circumstances of the case and need not be specified in any particular manner. If a blow is struck with the fist, which results in a wound requiring stitches, it is evident that it was done maliciously and the fact that a wound was inflicted is sufficient to justify a charge.

A wildfowler was using a punt on a river for the purpose of shooting and the accused fired a shot in the direction of the punt for the purpose of frightening the trespasser, but without the intention of hitting him, although the shot did in fact wound him. He was convicted of an offence contrary to this section as the act was malicious, being reckless in the circumstances, and it resulted in grievous bodily harm being caused. The case illustrates clearly the difference between the offences created by ss 18 and 20. For a charge contrary to s 18 to be proved, the prosecution would have had to prove that the shot was fired with the intention of causing that particular type of injury. A similar illustration of this difference is provided by the prosecution of the man who, with the intention of causing panic to the audience in a theatre, extinguished the lights and placed a bar across the exit door of a staircase leading from the theatre. In the resulting confusion, those coming first to the door were forced against the iron bar and seriously injured. The accused was convicted of an offence contrary to s 20, as his act was malicious and resulted in grievous bodily harm to two persons. In such circumstances, an offence contrary to s 18 had not been committed as it could not be said that the practical joker intended specifically to cause those injuries.

Where a man, believing an air rifle to be unloaded, although he had not checked it, aimed the rifle at another man and pulled the trigger, thus wounding him, it was held that, for the act to be malicious, it must be shown that the accused, on the facts known to him, actually foresaw that a particular kind of harm might be done. Malice must be concerned with foresight of the physical harm which is actually occasioned.

It has been held that this offence can be committed where the conduct of a stalker causes a woman psychiatric injury. It may be difficult to prove that a stalker acted with the necessary malice in that he foresaw such consequences of his conduct. The Protection from Harassment Act 1997 provides specific offences of harassment which include these forms of conduct.

A person charged with unlawful wounding may be found guilty by a jury of assault occasioning actual bodily harm.

Police powers

All offences contrary to ss 18 and 20 of the Offence Against the Person Act 1861 are arrestable offences.

Racially aggravated assaults

The Crime and Disorder Act 1998, s 29(1), provides that a person is guilty of an offence if he commits:

(a) an offence under s 20 of the Offences Against the Person Act 1861;
(b) an offence under s 47 of that Act;
(c) common assault (or battery),

which is racially or religiously aggravated for the purposes of the section.

The section therefore creates a number of offences. It must be proved that the accused has committed one of the offences specified in the section at the outset. Additionally it must be proved that that offence was racially or religiously aggravated.

Section 28(1) of the Act provides that such offences will be racially aggravated if:

(a) at the time of committing the offence, or immediately before or after doing so, the offender demonstrates towards the victim of the offence hostility based on the victim's membership (or presumed membership) of a racial or religious group; or
(b) the offence is motivated (wholly or partly) by hostility towards members of a racial or religious group based on their membership of that group.

'Membership' in relation to a religious or racial group includes association with members of that group; 'presumed' means presumed by the offender; and 'racial group' means a group of persons defined by race, colour, nationality (including citizenship) or ethnic or national origins. A 'religious group' is a group of persons defined by reference to religious belief or lack of religious belief.

The references to 'religious groups' were inserted by the Anti-terrorism, Crime and Security Act 2001, which must be reviewed 2 years after Royal Assent, which was given on 14 December 2001.

Domestic disputes

Introduction

A considerable part of a police officer's time is spent in dealing with disputes involving husbands and wives or men and their partners. Additionally, disputes take place between landlords and their tenants. On occasions, especially where such disputes are non-violent, the solution lies in the consideration of advice given on the spot. There will be no intention on either side to involve the use of the criminal law in the resolution of the dispute. It may be that the parties to the dispute will willingly seek the help of the many specialist advisory organisations which exist to help in such matters. On some occasions, however, it will be necessary to resort to the provisions of the criminal law.

As the advice which is to be given to police officers concerning the 'interaction' involving the disputants and police officers is constantly changing as the problems which are encountered during day-to-day policing lead to the identification of new priorities, the information provided in this chapter will be restricted to those matters which involve the enforcement of the law in such situations. The *detailed* social factors involved in such disputes will be dealt with by instructors during probationary training.

Social factors

There are many factors which affect family life in such a way that violent arguments are bound to occur. The human requires reasonable living space and, like many animals, becomes aggressive if crowded by others. This is perhaps the basis upon which domestic disputes, or breakdowns in the day-to-day family relationships, occur and most of the other factors are merely consequences. Disputes are most frequently met within certain social groups and this is not because of the personalities of the persons included in these groups. The need to provide for large families often means residence in a poor neighbourhood, in indifferent housing or in crowded conditions. Occasionally the mother of the family becomes a little discontented with her day-to-day life and father spends a lot of time at his local pub as a means of escape from the home. Such conditions are endured by many without serious conflict arising, but occasionally disputes are bound to occur. It would be incorrect, however, to convey the impression that domestic disputes are restricted to such groups as disputes occur between partners at all social levels. It is frequently more difficult to deal with those arising in the middle and upper classes, as the parties concerned may not so readily accept the advice which is offered by the police officer, even though he has been called to give advice and assistance.

Initial contact

The method of approach adopted by a constable is of the utmost importance, as the first impression that the constable creates will establish his certainty of purpose in the minds of both parties. If the officer appears calm, assured and helpful, a working relationship will be quickly established with the parties involved in the dispute, particularly if he can give the impression of being there to assist rather than to make demands, unless continuing violence necessitates a more immediate form of police action. Most frequently, the physical action has passed and the establishment of degrees of blame within the parties forms the basis of the dispute at the time of police intervention. On occasions, injuries to the parties must be attended to and consideration given to the desirability of charges being preferred because of the nature of those injuries. Frequently a wife will give whole-hearted support to action being taken against her husband for an assault occasioning actual bodily harm in the heat of the moment, but will be found to be unwilling to continue with the matter on the following day when she has had an opportunity to consider the implications. However, in most circumstances no criminal offence has been committed and the police officer's role is strictly that of an adviser.

Police powers of entry

The difficulties of police officers are increased because of the delicate situation in which they find themselves when attending disputes in the home. In English law there is no such thing as a general power of entry, and a constable must have been invited into the premises or no objection must have been raised to the constable's entry. In normal circumstances, the constable must remain no longer than the invitation remains. If entry is to be considered without invitation, it must be made to quell a breach of the peace or to prevent its occurrence. This power of entry to prevent a breach of the peace is invaluable when attending violent domestic disputes as constables will frequently meet circumstances which will not permit their departure at the request of either party because of the danger of a renewal of a breach of the peace at that time. The Court of Appeal has ruled that where a police officer is invited into a house by a wife to resolve a domestic involving her husband, the officer is entitled to remain long enough to ensure the safety of the complainant and her children and to ensure that there is no further danger of a breach of the peace, even though the officer is ordered to leave by the husband.

Landlord/tenant disputes

On occasions police officers are called to disputes involving the owner of furnished accommodation who has let a part of his premises to tenants and wishes to be rid of them for some reason before the expiration of the term of lease. These can be difficult situations as the conduct of the tenants is on occasions the cause of the dispute and it is therefore possible to feel some sympathy for the owner of the property. However, the Protection from Eviction Act 1977 gives a considerable degree of protection to tenants and the effect of the Act should be explained to such landlords.

Section 1(1) of the Act defines the term 'residential occupier' in relation to any premises as a person occupying the premises as a residence whether under a contract or by virtue of any enactment or rule of law which gives a right to remain in occupation, or restricting the right of any other person to recover possession of the premises. It is an offence contrary to s 1(2) unlawfully to deprive or attempt to deprive a residential occupier of his premises or part of them unless it is proved that the person believed, and had reasonable cause to believe, that the residential occupier had ceased to reside in the premises.

By s 1(3) it is an offence to do any act calculated to interfere with the peace or comfort of a residential occupier or his family, or to withhold services reasonably required for the occupation of the premises as a residence with intent to cause such residential occupier to quit, or to refrain from exercising his rights of pursuing a remedy. Such an offence would be committed if a landlord shuts off gas, electricity, water supplies, etc. These offences may only be committed in relation to a 'residential occupier' and this does not include, for example, persons hiring holiday accommodation on a short-term basis other than under a contract. Section 1(3A) creates a similar offence where the act is not done with 'intent' but where the landlord or his agent *has reasonable cause to believe* that the conduct is likely to cause the residential occupier to give up occupation or to refrain from pursuing remedy. However, s 1(3B) provides that a person is not guilty of an offence against s 1(3A) if he proves that he had reasonable grounds for doing the acts or withdrawing or withholding the services in question.

Although the Protection from Eviction Act 1977 creates these offences, it must be noted that the Act specifically authorises councils to institute proceedings. The action to be taken by a police officer should be restricted to preventing a breach of the peace at the time and to giving advice. A landlord should be warned, if it appears that a breach of the provisions of the Act has occurred, and, on all occasions, the officer should submit a full report to be sent to the local housing authority. In appropriate cases, a complainant should be informed in writing by the police that the complaint has been passed to that authority.

Once a person becomes a residential occupier, his lease cannot be forfeit while he is still residing in his premises, otherwise than by proceedings in a county court or, in exceptional circumstances, the High Court. This applies even when the tenancy agreement has come to an end, if the occupier is still on the premises. The owner may only enforce his right to recover the property through the court.

Similar provisions are made to protect the 'residential occupiers' of caravans by the Caravan Sites Act 1968.

Husband/wife

The subject of 'battered wives' is an important one. However, we are not considering here the various offences of assault which may be appropriate as these have been dealt with under that heading. Disputes involving a husband and wife present difficult situations. Whilst a wife who has been assaulted by her husband is both competent and compellable to give evidence, her reluctance to do so, on occasions, can be appreciated. Some women are reluctant to break up such a marriage as, despite its difficulties, it is all that they have. Help is available from social workers.

When dealing with domestic disputes involving husband and wife, one of the parties will frequently request a police officer to remove the other party from the house. A rent book bearing the name of one party may be produced to prove who is the 'occupier'. It must be remembered that the law gives protection to both parties of the marriage, regardless of proprietary interest in the home. A court order is necessary before either party can be deprived of occupation.

Domestic violence

The subject of assaults is considered elsewhere. A woman who has been assaulted by her husband or partner is competent and compellable to give evidence against him in a criminal court in relation to that assault, and may wish to do so. However, it will be appreciated that this is frequently an extremely difficult decision for a wife to make. Many women feel trapped and helpless and, being unable to face up to life on their own, prefer to remain with a husband who treats them badly. In such circumstances they will not wish to give evidence against their husbands because of their fear that this will lead to a final breakdown of the marriage. The social services are experienced in the handling of these situations and will help if the wife will accept such aid.

Where women are being subjected to violence by their husbands or partners, the courts can assist without the necessity for the woman to give evidence against her husband or partner in a criminal court. They can do so by applying for one of the orders under the Family Law Act 1996, described below, which are not limited to proceedings between spouses (or ex-spouses) or cohabitees (or ex-cohabitees).

Non-molestation orders

A non-molestation order is an order containing either or both of the following provisions:

(a) provision prohibiting a person (the respondent) from molesting another person who is associated with the respondent;
(b) provision prohibiting the respondent from molesting a relevant child.

The term 'associated with' is given a wide meaning to include spouses, cohabitees, live-in friends or relatives. A 'relevant child' in relation to such proceedings is any child who is living with or might reasonably be expected to live with either party to the proceedings, or any child in relation to whom an order under the Adoption Act 1976 or the Children Act 1989 is in question in the proceedings, or any other child whose interests the court considers relevant.

Such an order may be made:

(a) on the application (under the Family Law Act 1996, s 42) (whether in other family proceedings or without any other family proceedings being instituted) of a person who is associated with the respondent; or
(b) during family proceedings to which the respondent is a party, if the court considers that such an order will benefit any other party or a relevant child even though no application has been made.

In deciding whether to make a non-molestation order, the court must consider all the circumstances, including the need to secure the health, safety and well-being of the applicant or person for whose benefit the order would be made and of any relevant child.

A non-molestation order may refer to molestation in general, to particular acts of molestation, or both. It may be made for a specified period, or until a further order is made. An order which is made in other family proceedings ceases to have effect if those proceedings are withdrawn or dismissed.

Ex parte *orders*

Where it appears to be just and convenient to do so, a court may make a non-molestation order even though the party against whom the complaint is made has not been given notice of the proceedings. In such cases, the court must consider:

(a) the risk of significant harm if the order is not made immediately;
(b) whether if such an order is not made the applicant will be deterred or prevented from pursuing the application; and
(c) whether there is reason to believe that the party complained against is aware of the proceedings but is deliberately evading service of the notice and the other applicant, or a relevant child, will be seriously prejudiced by the delay involved in effecting service (or substituted service) of the proceedings.

Where an *ex parte* order is made, it must afford the person against whom it is made an opportunity to make representations as soon as just and convenient, at a full hearing.

Undertakings

Where a non-molestation order could be made, a court may accept an undertaking from any party to the proceedings. Where such an undertaking is given it is enforceable in the same way as a court order, but no power of arrest may be attached to it. Where a power to arrest appears to be appropriate, an undertaking should not be accepted by a court.

Arrest for breach of non-molestation order

Where it appears that the person against whom a non-molestation order has been made has used or threatened violence against the applicant or a relevant child, the court must attach a power of arrest to one or more provisions of the order unless satisfied that in all the circumstances of the case the applicant or child will be adequately protected without such a power of arrest.

This does not apply where the order is an *ex parte order*, but a court may attach a power of arrest to one or more of the provisions of the order where it appears that violence has been used or threatened *and there is the risk of significant harm to the applicant or to a relevant child, attributable to the conduct of the person complained against, if such power is not attached*. Where such a power is attached, it may be for a shorter period than the duration of the order generally, but that shorter period may be extended by the court on one or more occasions upon an application to vary or discharge the order.

The power to arrest may be exercised by a constable. He may arrest without warrant any person whom he has reasonable cause for suspecting to be in breach of the provisions of the order to which the power of arrest is attached. An arrested person must be brought before the relevant judicial authority within the period of 24 hours beginning with the time of his arrest. In reckoning the period of 24 hours, no account is to be taken of Christmas Day, Good Friday or any Sunday. If it is not possible for the judicial authority to deal with that person, then it may remand him. If he is remanded on bail, the judicial authority may require him to comply (before release on bail or later) with specified requirements to secure that he does not interfere with witnesses or otherwise obstruct the course of justice.

Breach of non-molestation order where there is no power to arrest

Where breaches occur of the provisions of an order in respect of which no power to arrest has been attached, an applicant may apply for the issue of a warrant to arrest the respondent. Such an application must be on oath and the judicial authority must have reasonable grounds for believing that the respondent has failed to comply with the order.

Rights associated with the matrimonial home

Where domestic disputes occur, regardless of whether or not a non-molestation order has been sought, the issue of occupational rights in relation to the matrimonial home still remains. The Family Law Act 1996 seeks to ensure that all sides to a dispute are protected from eviction.

Where one spouse has no estate, etc.

The Family Law Act 1996, s 30, provides that, where one spouse is legally entitled to occupy a dwelling house and the other spouse has no such legal entitlement, that other spouse has 'matrimonial home rights' which means that:

(a) if that other spouse is in occupation, that spouse has a right not to be evicted or excluded from the dwelling house or any part of it by the other spouse without the leave of the court under s 33 of the 1996 Act;
(b) if that other spouse is not in occupation, that spouse has a right with the leave of the court under s 33 to enter and occupy the dwelling house.

There is, therefore, no lawful way by which one party to a marriage can be removed from the matrimonial home without the circumstances being examined by a court (i.e. the High Court, a county court or a magistrates' court sitting as a family proceedings court). However, s 59 of the 1996 Act provides that a magistrates' court will not be competent to entertain any application, or make any order, where there is a dispute as to a party's entitlement to occupy property by virtue of beneficial estate, interest or contract or by virtue of any enactment giving him the right to remain in occupation, unless it is unnecessary to determine the question in order to deal with the application or make the order. In any case, a magistrates' court may decline jurisdiction if it considers that the application can more conveniently be dealt with by another court. In addition, a magistrates' court has no power to suspend or rescind orders made under the 1996 Act.

Occupation orders

Section 33 of the 1996 Act provides for the making of an occupation order where the applicant has an estate or interest, etc., entitling him to occupy a dwelling house or has matrimonial home rights in it and the dwelling house is or has been the home of the applicant and of someone else with whom he is associated (or was intended by both such people to be their home). If an occupation order is made, it may:

(a) enforce the applicant's occupation rights as against the other person (the respondent);
(b) require the respondent to permit the applicant to enter and remain in that dwelling house or part of it;
(c) regulate the occupation by both parties;
(d) if the respondent is legally entitled to occupy, prohibit, restrict or suspend the exercise by him of his occupation rights;
(e) if the respondent has matrimonial home rights and the applicant is the other spouse, restrict or terminate those rights;
(f) require the respondent to leave the dwelling house or part of it; or
(g) exclude the respondent from a defined area in which the dwelling house is included.

In deciding whether to make an occupation order and (if so) in what manner, the court must have regard to all of the circumstances, including the housing needs and housing resources of both parties and any child, the financial resources of both parties, the likely effect of any order (or of a failure to make an order) on the health, safety and well-being of each party and child, and the conduct of the parties in relation to each other and otherwise.

Former spouse, cohabitee and situations in which neither spouse has an entitlement to occupy

The 1996 Act makes similar provisions in relation to former spouses and cohabitees where one of them is legally entitled to occupy a dwelling house. It also makes provision for circumstances in which neither spouse (or ex-spouse) has a legal entitlement to occupy a dwelling house which is (or was) the matrimonial home. These provisions are set out in ss 35 to 38.

Breaches of occupation order

The provisions described above in relation to arrest without warrant also apply to occupation orders where such a power has been attached to the order. 'Undertakings' and '*ex parte* orders' may be made in respect of these orders in the same way as in the case of non-molestation orders.

Police action

Arrest for other offence

There are many powers of entry and arrest which are associated with incidents involving domestic violence, bearing in mind that offences of assault occasioning actual bodily harm (an arrestable offence), or more serious offences, may have been committed. The powers which exist at common law in relation to breaches of the peace may also be relevant in the circumstances.

Police action – when contact is first made

When a first contact is made with the police, it should be determined whether immediate response is required or whether there is no immediate danger. Such complaints must be recorded bearing in mind that where a crime is alleged, it should be so recorded. Existing records should be checked to establish whether there is any previous record of incidents involving the complainant. Generally, if the victim claims to have been violently assaulted, reconciliation should not be attempted. A woman police officer should attend such incidents where possible as a woman who has been assaulted may prefer to be dealt with by another woman. Any interview at the time should not take place in the presence of the alleged assailant. However, if a complainant wishes to repeat any allegation in the presence of the alleged assailant, she may do so and any reply made by the assailant should be noted.

If hospital treatment is not required, a victim may be taken to a victim examination suite if one is available. A medical examination by a police surgeon or some other doctor with forensic science training is preferable to examination by her own general practitioner. It is important to ensure that children are adequately cared for throughout this procedure. Other members of the family, or neighbours, may prove to be good witnesses in such cases, particularly where the victim is reluctant to become involved.

In domestic violence cases it is essential that the Crown Prosecution Service is fully informed of the circumstances surrounding the family relationships involved, the domestic circumstances and the likely course of future events including whether there is any likelihood of any lasting reconciliation.

It is important to ensure that victims continue to receive help and guidance in such cases. It may also be necessary to remove the victim to a place of shelter before making long-term arrangements with some other social agency. Some police forces have domestic violence units which specialise in such matters. Where it is necessary for the victim to live elsewhere, the police should assist in taking her to a place of refuge. If she subsequently wishes to visit the home for any reason she should be accompanied by a police officer.

The Secretary of State is currently piloting a scheme within which female victims of domestic violence will be spared court appearances which bring them into contact with their attackers.

Where complainant subsequently withdraws complaint

Where a victim subsequently decides to withdraw her complaint and states that she will be unwilling to give evidence in court, she should be asked to make a statement to that effect. This will be taken into account by the Crown Prosecutor who may, but is unlikely to in most circumstances, take steps to compel the complainant to give evidence against her husband.

The Crown Prosecutor will also wish to take into account the views of the officer who recorded that statement concerning the validity of the complainant's reasons and her likely reaction to being compelled to give evidence. Where a victim refuses to give evidence it may be possible to continue the case by offering her statement in evidence in accordance with the Criminal Justice Act 1988, s 23.

Drugs

Purpose – need for control

The Misuse of Drugs Act 1971 both reformed and strengthened the law related to the misuse of drugs. Previous Acts of Parliament had been passed with a view to controlling different types of drugs as they came to be more commonly used. The 1971 Act, by setting up an Advisory Council on the Misuse of Drugs, has established a system whereby trends in drug taking can be quickly identified and measures taken to set up effective forms of control. The Advisory Council has three functions: to keep under review misuse of various forms of drugs which are likely to have a harmful effect and to advise the Secretary of State upon measures which should be taken; to advise the Secretary of State concerning regulations which he may wish to make under the Act; and to act as an advisory body upon all matters relating to drug dependence or the misuse of drugs, which may be referred to the Secretary of State or any other Minister.

There is so much debate concerning the need for the use of drugs to be controlled, as opposed to the rights of the individual to choose his own path, that it will be helpful to study the nature of that path. At the time of writing there are proposals to decriminalise certain offences relating to cannabis.

In the first instance, drugs are essential, as their medical applications are both useful and varied. From the diabetic who needs insulin to the worried businessman who needs something to relax him sufficiently to enable him to sleep, a medical need for the prescription of drugs has become a part of our modern society. Many general titles are applied to different forms of drugs: the sleeping capsules or sedatives, the pain killers or analgesics, and the anti-depressants or tranquillisers. The stimulation gained by various forms of drug taking is known to most of us, from the small uplift given by the caffeine in a cup of tea or coffee, to the effect of the nicotine in a cigarette or the alcohol in a pint of beer.

Addiction

Drug dependence can be socially, physically or mentally related. It frequently develops within those who are too inhibited to enjoy themselves within a modern society, or those who seek new 'experiences'. An inability to face up to social or personal problems can be the initial cause, but the boredom and restlessness which follow the passing of the drug's effect lead to further compulsion for the drug taker. As the body's tolerance towards the drug increases, it becomes necessary to increase the dose to compensate for this resistance. A drug addict is a sick person and should receive medical treatment as a matter of urgency. It is the duty of a police officer to ensure that he receives it, whether such person is identified as a drug user by an officer on patrol or by a custody officer at a police station.

Offences generally

Unlawful possession

The Misuse of Drugs Act 1971, s 5(2), states that it is an offence for a person to have a controlled drug in his possession. Drugs which are controlled are classified as A, B or C controlled drugs but the important factor is that they are all controlled drugs.

Controlled drugs may lawfully be in the possession of certain persons. Regulations made under the Act describe such lawful possession. In addition to forms of possession which are particularly dealt with by regulations, it is a defence for a person to prove that he took possession of a controlled drug for the purpose of preventing someone else from committing an offence and that, as soon as possible, he took steps either to destroy it or deliver it to some person lawfully entitled to take possession of it. The Court of Appeal has held that concealing a controlled drug in the ground is not sufficient even though that drug may be destroyed in the course of time by the forces of nature. There must be an act of destruction. Section 7 of the Act directs that the Secretary of State shall exercise his power to make regulations to ensure that it is not unlawful for doctors, dentists, veterinarians, pharmacists, scientists and other similar persons to possess drugs in the course of their profession. These other persons include police, customs, carriers, forensic scientists and post office employees. In addition, persons who have been prescribed drugs or are conveying them to a person may lawfully possess controlled drugs in those circumstances.

The term 'possession' is defined in s 37(3). For the purposes of the Act, things which a person has in his possession shall be taken to include anything subject to his control which is in the custody of another. 'Possession', therefore, extends to circumstances in which a controlled drug is being held for someone else; for example, by a servant on behalf of his master. In such an instance, both would be in possession of controlled drugs. It has been held that a person is not in possession of drugs if he is unaware that they are in some place over which he has control, for example, his house or room. Guilty knowledge is necessary in relation to possession, and if a drug has been placed in a man's house or in his jacket pocket without his knowledge, he is not in possession of it for the purposes of the Act. Knowledge of the thing's quality is not required. If a person is in possession of tablets which he believes to be aspirin but which are, in fact, heroin, he is in possession of heroin tablets. A person who has a cigarette in his pocket which he believes to contain tobacco is nevertheless in possession of cannabis if that is what it contains. A person in possession of a parcel which contains drugs commits this offence if he knows that he is in control of the parcel and that it contains something, even if he has no reason to believe that the contents are drugs. Police officers executing a search warrant found a letter on a hall table addressed to the defendant. He was invited to open it and amphetamine hydrochloride was found. It was held that the defendant, having given directions to the supplier to send the drug by post, became the possessor when the letter passed through the letter box.

It is not necessary to prove that a minimum quantity of a controlled drug was unlawfully in the possession of the person charged, but it should be measurable. Persons who are found under the influence of a controlled drug cannot be said to be in possession of it, even though traces are found in a urine sample. If a thing is consumed it changes its character and can no longer be considered to be a controlled drug in its true form. However, evidence of the presence of such a drug in a urine sample can be given to support an allegation of possession at some earlier time.

A person may be guilty of an attempt to possess if he takes possession of a substance which he believes to be a controlled drug, but which is in fact a harmless substance.

Supplying and possession with intent to supply

These offences are those which form a part of 'drug trafficking'. Section 4(3) of the 1971 Act states:

It is an offence for a person to supply a controlled drug to another, or to be concerned in the supplying of such a drug to another or to be concerned in the making to another of an offer to supply a controlled drug.

Those persons who may lawfully supply drugs are considered above. However, if such a person offers to supply those drugs to another person he commits this offence even though he was in lawful possession of the drugs. The 'offer' is unlawful.

A person who passes drugs around at a party supplies them contrary to the section. There is no requirement that the act must be for personal gain. Each person who passes a cannabis cigarette to his neighbour supplies a controlled drug. Many people may be concerned in 'supply'. Those who arrange delivery, allow premises to be used or who arrange for young persons to attend a party with a view to making drugs available to them are all 'concerned' in supply.

It is not necessary that controlled drugs are actually supplied. If an offer is made and the person concerned refuses to accept the controlled drug, an offence of 'offering to supply' has been committed. In fact, it does not matter that the substance proves to be other than a controlled drug if the offer is made in the belief that it is a controlled drug. Where a person supplied vitamin C tablets alleging that they were Ecstasy tablets, it was held that he could be properly convicted of offering to supply a controlled drug. In such cases it is not necessary to prove that, pursuant to the offer, a controlled drug would be supplied.

An offer may be made by words or conduct. Where an offer to supply is made in words the nature of the substance is irrelevant, even where the person offering to supply is aware that the substance is not a controlled drug. Where an offer is made by way of conduct, the issue of whether or not the substance is controlled may be relevant as the conduct must have been sufficient to have indicated that it was a controlled drug which was being offered.

Section 5(3) prohibits possession of controlled drugs with intent to supply. A 'pusher' who is found in possession of large quantities of drugs and can be proved to have been supplying to some persons is obviously in possession of the remainder with intent to supply. Where it was alleged that a person had cocaine in his possession with intent to supply it to another person, the Court of Appeal held that all that needed to be established was that the defendant had *that substance* in his possession with intent to supply it. A claim that the defendant believed the substance to be amphetamine was irrelevant.

For the purpose of proving possession with intent to supply, evidence of the possession of large amounts of cash *which can be shown to be likely to be used for the acquisition of drugs* is relevant, but not conclusive, in relation to the issue of intent to supply, but it is not normally relevant to the issue of possession. For example, evidence of frequent, brief visits by different people to premises the occupant of which was long-term unemployed, those people leaving with small packages in their hands, where a search of the premises revealed large sums of money and some drugs, is relevant. It can be admitted as evidence that the occupant was in control of drugs as well as intending to supply them. However, where there is a possibility that the sum of money found was in the accused's possession for a purpose other than drug dealing, such evidence will not be admitted. Where £150 was found in a kettle, the evidence was not admitted as it indicated nothing in relation to drug dealing. However, where £16 000 was found concealed under a cooker, it was held that such a large sum of money was admissible in relation to intent to supply drugs.

In summary, evidence of the possession of cash will often lack probative value as it cannot, by itself, be directly linked to drugs. However, such evidence may not be irrelevant even in a case of simple possession. The different ingredients of the offence should not be compartmentalised. The jury must consider all relevant evidence. Where

£24 815 in cash was found in a defendant's home in close proximity to 4.99 kg of heroin and the defendant had denied possession of drugs, the Court of Appeal said that such evidence was relevant.

Controlled drugs on premises

Section 8 of the 1971 Act is concerned with persons who, being the occupier or concerned in the management of any premises, knowingly permit or suffer any of the following acts to take place on the premises:

(a) unlawful production or attempted production of a controlled drug;
(b) unlawful supply or attempted supply of a controlled drug to another, or offering to supply a controlled drug unlawfully to another;
(c) preparation of opium for smoking; or
(d) administering or using a controlled drug which is unlawfully in any person's possession at or immediately before the time when it is administered or used.

A person is the occupier of premises if he is entitled to exclusive possession of them having sufficient control to exclude persons who would carry out forbidden activities. Thus, we will normally be concerned with owners, tenants, etc., at this level. To be an 'occupier' two factors must be present: legal possession of the premises and control over them. In circumstances in which two sisters aged 20 and 15 years were charged with permitting cannabis smoking as the occupiers of premises whilst their parents were absent on holiday, it was held that there could be no conviction as they were not occupiers, not being, in law, in possession of the premises during the temporary absence of their parents.

In contrast, a person may be 'concerned in management' without having any ownership or tenancy rights. In this category we will find managers, and persons in control of rooms or a part of the premises, provided that all of them have the power to exercise control over activities which take place there.

Persons who occupy premises as trespassers can commit this offence. If drug parties are organised in 'squats', all concerned in the organisation of those parties commit this offence.

The Court of Appeal has held that a belief by an accused that he had taken reasonable steps to prevent drugs being supplied on his premises did not afford a defence. The prosecution must establish actual knowledge, or the closing of the eyes to the obvious, that drugs were being supplied; and an unwillingness to prevent that occurring. This could be inferred from failure to take reasonable steps to prevent it.

Other offences

The Misuse of Drugs Act 1971 is a very comprehensive piece of legislation. It prohibits the unlawful import or export (s 3) and the unlawful production [s 4(2)] of controlled drugs. In relation to importation, where a person believes that a package which he is carrying contains a controlled drug, it is immaterial that it in fact contained snuff rather than heroin or cannabis.

The term 'production' covers the conversion of cocaine hydrochloride into a freebase cocaine, in which form it would vaporise and be capable of being inhaled. The same would be true where cocaine hydrochloride is converted into 'crack' by mixing it with other chemicals.

Statutory defences generally

The Misuse of Drugs Act 1971, s 28, provides a defence which is applicable to charges contrary to s 4(2) (unlawful production), s 4(3) (unlawful supply), s 5(2) (unlawful possession), s 5(3) (possession with intent to supply), s 6(2) (unlawful cultivation of cannabis) and s 9 (opium smoking, frequenting places used for opium smoking or possessing utensils used for opium smoking).

Where a person has been proved to have been in possession of a controlled drug, he may be convicted of that offence even if it has not been proved that he *knew* that he was in possession of a controlled drug. However, an accused may prove, on the balance of probabilities that he *neither knew of, nor suspected, nor had reason to suspect* the existence of some fact alleged by the prosecution which it is necessary for the prosecution to prove to gain a conviction. However, this is subject to the proviso that where the issue is the nature of a controlled drug alleged to have been possessed and the accused proves that he did not know, suspect or have reason to suspect that the thing in question was the particular controlled drug alleged, this is not a sufficient defence in itself. In such circumstances an accused must also prove:

(a) that he neither believed nor suspected, nor had reason to suspect, that the thing in question was a controlled drug at all; or
(b) that he believed that the thing in question was a controlled drug which he was, in fact, legally entitled to possess (or supply or produce as the case may be).

If, therefore, a person is given a packet of powder which he is told is baking powder but is, in fact, cocaine, that person is in possession of cocaine and he is knowingly in possession of the powder. However, he will have a defence to a charge of unlawful possession if he can prove that he did not believe or suspect that the powder was a controlled drug. It would, of course, be no defence to prove that he believed the powder to be heroin as heroin is merely an alternative controlled drug.

The defence provided by (b) is aimed at less common circumstances. A registered addict may be entitled to receive heroin on prescription. If he is provided with an alternative drug by mistake, he is in unlawful possession as the drug is not that prescribed. If he believed that he was in possession of heroin, this part of the defence would apply.

However, although s 28 says that an accused must prove a defence under the section, the House of Lords has held that s 28 should be read as simply imposing an evidential burden on the accused so as to make it compatible with the presumption of innocence under art. 6(2) of the European Convention on Human Rights. The result is that the accused does not have to prove a defence under s 28, despite the clear wording of the section. Provided that sufficient evidence is offered to raise a defence under s 28, the defence will succeed unless the prosecution is able to prove beyond reasonable doubt that the terms of the defence are not satisfied.

Controlled drugs

The misuse of certain drugs is controlled by the Act. These are called 'controlled drugs', and are divided into three categories, depending upon their harmfulness. The 1971 Act allows new drugs to be added to lists of controlled drugs by the passing of an Order in Council. The reason for dividing controlled drugs into three subgroups is that penalties for offences vary according to the type of controlled drug to which the offence relates. Class A drugs can be divided into two groups: narcotic drugs such as cocaine, morphine, opium, pethidine and heroin; and hallucinogenic drugs such as mescaline, LSD and MDMA (methylenedioxymethamphetamine; Ecstasy). Class B drugs include amphetamines (which are stimulant drugs) such as mandrax, cannabis and cannabis resin. Class C drugs include benzphetamine, pipradrol, chlorphentermine, mephentermine, methaqualone and phendimetrazine. The only significance of differing classifications to constables enforcing the provisions of this Act is that the more serious offences are arrestable offences.

The term 'controlled drug' includes preparations or other products containing a substance or product specified as a controlled drug. Possession of a naturally occurring material which contains a controlled drug, for example a mushroom, is not unlawful, but if it is subjected to some process which prepares it for future use as a drug, such as packaging and freezing for later separation of the drug, such possession is unlawful.

Recognition

The most difficult problem which faces the operational police officer is the impossibility of recognising substances found in the possession of persons suspected of drug offences as being particular drugs of certain classes. It would be a simple matter to reproduce coloured representations of the most common forms of controlled drugs in an effort to assist identification, but it would serve little purpose. These drugs appear in many forms and there is no limit to the variations which can be made in an effort to avoid their identification. Recognising that a detailed analysis will have to be carried out by forensic scientists before the type of drug can be established, identification of the substance cannot be taken as the starting point of a police officer's investigation.

A police officer will become suspicious of persons observed to be passing tablets or capsules to one another in discothèques or cafés. Their appearance – persons under the influence of drugs often look as though they are in that state; a condition which has the look of intoxication without its accompanying tendency to become over-verbose – are all factors which give rise to a reasonable suspicion that such persons are in possession of controlled drugs. It is safe to say that if the tablets are the type used by young people looking for kicks, they will be listed in Schedule 2 of the 1971 Act as controlled drugs. In the absence of some medical reason for possession of such tablets, there is every reason to suspect that they are controlled drugs.

Powers to arrest for such offences require suspicion on the part of the arresting officer, and this must be so because of the impossibility of positive recognition of controlled drugs. Provided that there are grounds for such suspicion, the person concerned can be arrested and searched, suspected substances may be taken into possession by the arresting officer, and that person can be taken to a police station and thoroughly searched before being released on bail within the delayed charge procedure, requiring his presence at the police station at a particular time to finalise the proceedings. If subsequent analysis proves possession of a controlled drug, such person will be charged with an offence when he answers his bail, and if it does not he will be told by written notice that his presence at the police station is not required.

The main offences which police officers on the beat are likely to encounter are those of possession of controlled drugs, the unlawful cultivation of cannabis plants, or persons occupying or managing premises knowingly permitting cannabis smoking, or preparing or smoking opium. The possession of controlled drugs has already been discussed.

The cultivation of cannabis plants is not uncommon. They will grow fairly well in most parts of the British Isles and could be found anywhere. The word 'cultivate' indicates some form of labour in order to raise crops and, therefore, some positive act is required by an accused person either by planting or caring for the plant. It is probable that a mere omission on the part of the occupier of land to destroy plants planted by a previous occupier will be insufficient to merit a conviction. In such circumstances, the new occupier has carried out no positive act in the process of cultivation. If, however, he had done as little as to water the plant, this would be evidence of caring for the plant and this amounts to cultivation. Cannabis (except in the expression cannabis resin) means any plant of the genus *Cannabis*, or part of any such plant. The definition does not include the mature stalk, the stalk fibre or seeds once they have been separated from the plant. However, where a person separates those parts of cannabis plants which can be smoked from those which cannot, although he does not 'cultivate' cannabis, he produces a controlled drug by some 'other method' than cultivation or manufacture and this is an offence against s 4 of the 1971 Act.

Police powers

Search, seize and detain

By s 23 of the 1971 Act, if a constable has reasonable grounds to suspect that any person is in possession of a controlled drug in contravention of the provisions of the Act, he may:

(a) search that person and detain him for the purpose of searching him;
(b) search any vehicle or vessel in which the constable suspects that the drug may be found and for that purpose require the person in control to stop it;
(c) seize and detain, for the purpose of proceedings under the Misuse of Drugs Act 1971, anything found in the course of the search which appears to the constable to be evidence of an offence under the Act.

Other powers are given by the Act in relation to entry to inspect documents which are of little concern to most police officers and are well known to those who are concerned with such inspection. A justice of the peace may issue a search warrant authorising entry to premises within 1 month, if satisfied by information on oath that controlled drugs are on the premises in the possession of any person, or there are documents connected with drug dealing.

The powers of the constable are dependent upon the words 'reasonable grounds to suspect' and in no way include the right to stop and search all persons encountered late at night in an effort to discover drug offences. Matters which afford reasonable grounds to suspect possession cannot be defined. There is no general right to search persons who are found by night in areas which drug users frequent. However, if their presence there is noted together with the fact that substances which have the appearance of being drugs are being passed from one to another, this may give rise to a reasonable suspicion in the mind of the police officer concerned. It should be remembered that precise advice is given within the Code of Practice for the Exercise by Police Officers of Statutory Powers to Stop and Search. In essence, the suspicion must arise from the nature of the property observed, coupled with the significance of the time, place and suspicious behaviour of the person concerned. Suspicion must *not* be based upon the fact that that person's membership of a group creates a higher than average chance that he may be in possession of controlled drugs. However, reasonable suspicion may exist as a result of information received from another party but this would depend upon the reliability of the person providing the information and the likelihood of that information being true in all the circumstances. The most important factor to bear in mind is that the Code requires the degree or level of suspicion which would justify arrest in any case.

Infection

Persons who are drug takers may be in the high-risk category in relation to AIDS or hepatitis. Be careful when carrying out searches of such persons. The hand which is placed into a pocket risks being pierced by a dirty needle; the hand which is run over the outside of clothing is similarly at risk. The saliva or blood of an infected person must enter your body in order to contaminate you and this may occur through the eyes, mouth or any cut in the skin. Do not take unnecessary chances and if there is any form of contact about which you are concerned, ask to consult the police surgeon. It is advisable to wash carefully after contact with persons who may be infected.

Arrestable offences

The offences with which police officers are most likely to be concerned, i.e. possession of controlled drugs, possession with intent to supply another (drug pusher), the occupier or manager of premises permitting certain drug-taking activities on premises, supplying controlled drugs, or offering to supply them to another, are all arrestable offences regardless of the class of the controlled drug concerned, with the exception of possession of a Class C drug. (Cannabis is currently a Class B drug but it is proposed to re-classify it as Class C in the near future.) As already discussed, the precise nature of the drug found in the possession of a particular person can only be established by analysis, but reasonable suspicion that an arrestable offence is being committed is sufficient to make an arrest lawful.

Solvent abuse

It is a summary offence contrary to the Intoxicating Substances (Supply) Act 1985 for a person to supply, or offer to supply, a substance other than a controlled drug:

(a) to a person under 18 years whom he knows or has reasonable cause to believe to be under that age; or

(b) to a person who is acting on behalf of someone under 18, and whom he knows or has reasonable cause to believe to be so acting,

if he knows or has reasonable cause to believe that the substance is, or its fumes are, likely to be inhaled by the person under 18 for the purpose of causing intoxication.

A person charged with supplying or offering may offer in defence that at the material time he was under 18 and was not acting in the course of furtherance of a business.

Statutory preventive measures

The law has always recognised that many acts which are in some ways preparatory to the commission of crime should be punishable if persons are found in possession of articles, or in circumstances which suggest that it was their intention to commit crime. Various Acts of Parliament deal with offences of this nature.

Criminal attempts

The offence

Section 1(1) of the Criminal Attempts Act 1981 provides:

> If, with intent to commit an offence to which this section applies, a person does an act which is more than merely preparatory to the commission of the offence, he is guilty of attempting to commit the offence.

Section 1(4) of the Act provides that the section applies to any offence which, if completed, would be triable in England and Wales as an indictable offence, except:

(a) conspiracy (at common law or under s 1 of the Criminal Law Act 1977 or any other enactment);
(b) aiding, abetting, counselling, procuring or suborning the commission of an offence; and
(c) offences under s 4(1) (assisting offenders) or s 5(1) (accepting or agreeing to accept consideration for not disclosing information about an arrestable offence) of the Criminal Law Act 1967.

All attempts to commit indictable offences are therefore offences contrary to s 1, with the exception of those specified. However, it will be seen that attempts to commit summary offences are not made offences under this Act. A number of statutes specifically create offences of 'attempt' and these are unaffected.

The forbidden act

The section requires 'an act which is more than merely preparatory to the commission of the offence' and this relates to the full offence which he intends to commit. That which is 'merely preparatory' is not defined. One thing of which we can be sure is that what is referred to as a 'last act', because it is the last act which the accused could carry out with the necessary intent, represents a stage beyond preparation. We are considering the 'last act' which the accused could carry out, although, on occasions, a further act might be required on the part of some other person. If a man sends a parcel bomb to another with intent to kill or injure him, or places a poison in another's coffee with a similar intent, he has certainly attempted to commit the full offence even though the other party will have to open the parcel before it will explode, or will have to drink from the cup before he becomes poisoned. The act of the perpetrator is certainly more than preparatory. His preparatory acts would be the assembly of the device or the secreting of the phial of poison about his person.

However, the term 'more than merely preparatory' is not limited to such cases. All acts leading to an offence are 'preparatory' but they are not 'merely preparatory'. If a man buys petrol, boots and overalls with the intention of setting fire to a shop he has carried out a number of preparatory acts which are all 'merely' preparatory to the commission of an offence of arson. If he then arrives outside the shop and places the can of petrol on the ground, it is submitted that his act is still merely preparatory. However, his next step, pouring the petrol over the door of the shop, is likely to be held to be more than merely preparatory as it is a positive step on the road to completion of the offence. The striking of a match would certainly constitute an act which is more than merely preparatory. A man who intends to shoot another carries out acts which are merely preparatory when he takes his gun to a point of ambush and lies in wait. Things change as he takes aim; it is submitted that this is more than merely preparatory; and as he takes up pressure on the trigger he has arrived at a stage which allows only one further act before the full offence will be committed.

Where a man pointed a gun at another whom he intended to kill, and when foiled, placed a cord around his neck, it was held that these combined acts amounted to more than mere preparation and were sufficient evidence of attempted murder. In a case in which a man dragged a girl into a secluded spot and threatened her before putting his hand up her skirt in contact with her vaginal area, then moving his hand to the top of her tights, it was held that there was sufficient evidence of attempted rape for consideration by a jury.

At the opposite end of the scale, a man was seen to approach a post office, ride around the area on a motor cycle and walk around that area before putting on sunglasses and placing his hand in a pocket which appeared to contain something heavy. These acts were all held to be merely preparatory to an attempt to rob the post office and this is understandable. They were far removed from an offence of robbery; the suspect had not even arrived at the scene of his intended crime. He was later found to be in possession of an imitation gun and a threatening note but these matters were related to his intentions when he arrived at the scene of his crime. The writing of the note was another 'merely preparatory' matter. Had the note subsequently been handed over the counter, that act would have been more than merely preparatory. In another case, a man was seen in the boys' lavatory block in a school. He was in possession of a rucksack which contained a large kitchen knife, lengths of rope and a roll of masking tape. The Court of Appeal said that there was not much room for doubt about the man's intention and there was clear evidence of preparation, but there was no evidence that he had even put himself in a position to commit an offence and he had had no contact or communication with, nor had he confronted, any pupil. There was therefore no evidence of an act which was more than merely preparatory to an act of wrongful imprisonment. The Court of Appeal has also ruled that where men were found examining the padlock of a barn to see how best to enter, having concealed oxyacetylene cutting equipment nearby, those acts were capable of being considered to be more than *merely* preparatory.

The guilty state of mind

The intention of the person who attempts to carry out a particular act is important in 'attempt' cases. The accused must intend to commit an act or to continue with a series of acts which when completed will amount to or lead to an offence. He must *intend* the consequences of his act, as opposed to being reckless in relation to that consequence, even though recklessness may suffice in respect of the commission of the full offence. For example, for there to be a conviction for attempted murder the accused must be shown to have *intended* to kill. Where the person concerned had been killed as a result of such an act, it would be sufficient to justify a conviction for murder, that he intended his act to cause grievous bodily harm.

However, where the act of the accused is merely forbidden if it occurs with lack of consent, the accused will have sufficient *mens rea* if he knew or believed that that state of affairs existed.

The standard of proof of intention in cases of 'attempt' is thus twofold: there must have been, in a case of attempted theft, for example, an *intention* to appropriate property belonging to another and a *dishonest intention* to deprive the owner permanently of his property, where an offence of attempted theft is preferred.

Impossibility

By s 1(2), a person may be guilty of attempting to commit an offence to which the section applies, even though the facts are such that the commission of the full offence is impossible. Thus, a man who puts his hand into another's pocket intending to steal commits an offence of attempted theft even though the pocket is empty. He who shoots a man who is already dead can be convicted of an offence of attempted murder.

Section 1(3) reinforces this by stating that where apart from s 1(3) a person's intention would not be regarded as having amounted to an intent to commit an offence, but if the facts had been as that person believed them to be, his intention would have been so regarded, he is to be regarded as having an intent to commit that offence. An accused was arrested carrying a package which he had brought from India which he believed contained heroin or cannabis. It in fact contained snuff. It was held by the House of Lords that he had nevertheless attempted to import controlled drugs as he believed that the substance which he was bringing into the country was a controlled drug.

Other statutory offences of 'attempt'

The Criminal Attempts Act 1981, s 3, applies the provisions of the Act to offences of 'attempt' created by other statutes.

Offensive weapons – Prevention of Crimes Act 1953

The 1953 Act was passed at time when the incidence of the possession of offensive weapons was on the increase. Flick knives and gravity knives were two of the types of weapon which were increasingly in evidence at this time.

Section 1 provides:

> Any person who without lawful authority or reasonable excuse, the proof whereof shall lie on him, has with him in any public place any offensive weapon shall be guilty of an offence.

The term 'offensive weapon' means any article made or adapted for use for causing injury to the person, or intended by the person having it with him for such use by him or by some other person. The definition specifies three different types of weapon: those made for causing injury, those adapted for that purpose and others merely intended to be used.

Articles made to cause injury would include knuckledusters, swordsticks, a dagger (as opposed to a sheath knife), flick knives, gravity knives or butterfly knives because they are manufactured for no other purpose than to cause bodily injury. Those adapted to cause injury might include a bottle which is broken to form a weapon, a bicycle chain with sharpened links or a cap the peak of which has been reinforced with metal. Weapons which are intended to be used for the purpose of causing injury can include any object which is ordinarily inoffensive: a walking stick, spanner, shoe or sheath knife. It is at this point that the importance of the three categories of weapons specified in the definition can be observed. If persons are found in possession of weapons which are either made or adapted for the purpose of causing harm, and this fact is proved to the court, the burden of proof shifts to the defence to prove lawful authority or reasonable excuse for possession.

However, if the weapon concerned is merely an article, normally inoffensive, which is intended to be used for the purpose of causing injury, the burden of proof remains with the prosecution to show that the accused had it with him intending it to be so used. If a police officer finds a man in a public place in possession of a swordstick or a chain with sharpened links, he may immediately take action under this section, the responsibility being that of the defendant to establish lawful excuse. In the case of objects normally inoffensive, such as the walking stick, it is necessary to prove an intention to use them before the offence is committed. In normal circumstances the first step in proving that a weapon which an accused had with him was intended to be used for causing injury to the person is that it was used to assault, or attempt to assault, another person.

For many years, the High Court tended to accept that this was so. In 1975 a carpenter on his way home from work took a hammer from his case and assaulted another man with it. He was charged with an assault occasioning bodily harm and possessing an offensive weapon, the hammer. The second charge was dismissed in that the use of the weapon was part of the assault, and the dismissal was upheld by the High Court. It was said that in such circumstances the weapon must have been carried (i.e. the accused had it with him) with the intention to use it offensively *before* the occasion for its use had arisen. Therefore, in the case of a weapon 'intended to be used', it must be carried prior to its use 'without lawful authority or excuse', or such a weapon not previously in lawful possession must be taken up by the accused who must then show an intention to use it. A man who assaulted another in a public street and requested, and was given, a clasp knife by a companion, which he then held to his victim's head intending to cause injury, was held not to be guilty of this offence, having seized the weapon for instant use, rather than to have 'possessed' it for a sufficient length of time.

In the case of articles already lawfully possessed which are used as offensive weapons, such use does not prove the intent by itself. Where a man took hold of a 'Krooklock' which was lawfully in his car and was alleged to have used it immediately to assault the rider of a horse, it was held that although, in these circumstances, the man would clearly form the intention to use the Krooklock as an offensive weapon before he got out of the car, that is not necessarily sufficient. Whether sufficient time had elapsed to be able to say that the purpose of its possession had changed is a matter of fact for a court or jury. Similarly, where a defendant used abusive language to police officers, picked up her dog and put it behind a wall before swinging the metal and leather strap at the officers, the Divisional Court held that there was insufficient evidence to support the submission that her intention to use the lead as an offensive weapon had been formed prior to the occasion of its actual use.

A person may have an offensive weapon 'with him' even though he is not carrying the weapon at the time, but he must be closely linked with it and it must be readily accessible to him. Thus, a man who has an offensive weapon with him in his car still has it with him when he goes into a public convenience. A person does not have something with him when it has been slipped into his bag without his knowledge. If a person is at one time aware that there is a cosh in the glove compartment of his car it is no excuse that at the material time he had forgotten about it.

Circumstances which will be regarded as a reasonable excuse for possession of offensive weapons are restricted. A man was convicted when found in possession of a knuckle-duster and truncheon which he alleged were kept for protection when collecting his firm's wages. The last occasion upon which wages had been collected was some days previously and the divisional court ruled that his possession was unreasonable. A taxi driver who carried a cosh for protection against violent passengers was also convicted. Where a person is proved to have been in possession of a weapon which is offensive *per se*, he cannot allege reasonable excuse for possession. The defence of 'reasonable excuse' can only arise after possession of an offensive weapon has been proved. An accused cannot, therefore, then allege that he did not know that the weapon was offensive. The Act imposes a strict liability where the weapon is offensive *per se*.

Although the statute does not demand proof by the prosecution that those weapons which are made or adapted for use for causing injury to the person are possessed 'knowingly', it has been held that proof should be offered concerning knowledge. If a defendant alleges that he had put a weapon under the seat of his car and forgotten about it, he in effect admits knowledge of its presence. It is no excuse that he has since forgotten about it.

'Lawful authority' refers to those persons in the armed services, police, etc., who are authorised to carry such weapons.

The term 'public place' is given its normal meaning. Hospital grounds to which visitors and their friends were admitted have been held to be a public place. An interesting decision of assistance to police officers was that in which a man who produced a gun in a private dwelling house was convicted on the grounds that the court was entitled to infer that it was brought to the house through the streets and that the defendant must have been in possession of the gun in a public place. Soccer grounds, dance halls and similar places of public entertainment, when open to the public, are 'public places' for the purposes of the Act.

Restriction of Offensive Weapons Act 1959

This Act creates the offences of manufacturing, selling, hiring, offering for sale or hire, exposing for sale, or having in possession for the purpose of sale or hire, or lending or giving to any person, flick knives or gravity knives. The importation of these knives is also prohibited by this Act, which made the transfer of such weapons from one person to another outside the law. Flick knives are those whose blade opens automatically on pressure on a button, and gravity knives those which open by the application of gravitational or centrifugal force.

Flick knives and gravity knives are weapons which are 'made' for the purpose of causing injury. A person who has such a weapon in his possession in a public place is guilty of an offence against the Prevention of Crime Act 1953, which is dealt with above.

Criminal Justice Act 1988

Section 139 of this Act punishes possession in a public place of articles which otherwise escape the definition of those which are made or adapted for use for causing injury.

It declares it to be an offence for a person to have with him in a public place an article which is sharply pointed or with a blade, other than a folding pocket knife with a blade not exceeding 3 inches. A knife which is held in the open position by a locking device and can only be released from that position by pressing a button is not a 'folding pocket knife' for the purposes of this section. A defence of 'lawful authority or good reason' for possession or that he had it with him for use at work, for a religious reason or as part of a national dress is provided by the Act. Where a man was found in possession of a knife 6 days after he had used it at work, it was held that 'forgetfulness' was not a good reason for having it in his possession at the relevant time. The burden of proving 'good reason' is not discharged when an explanation is offered which is not contradicted by the prosecution. The justices were entitled to reject an excuse that a knife was to be used for food preparation later in the evening, as being improbable. This is an arrestable offence.

The Offensive Weapons Act 1996 added s 139A to the Criminal Justice Act 1988. The section makes it an offence for a person to have an article to which s 139 applies with him on school premises. It creates a similar offence in relation to an offensive weapon to which the Prevention of Crimes Act 1953 applies. These are arrestable offences. The term 'school premises' means any land used for the purpose of a school excluding any land occupied solely as a dwelling by a person employed at the school. Similar defences exist; a person who proves that he has good reason or lawful authority for having the article or weapon with him on the premises has a defence; so does a person who proves that he had the article or weapon with him for the purposes set out above in relation to s 139. In addition, he may show possession for 'educational purposes'. The Divisional Court has held that to require a defendant to establish good reason or lawful authority does not constitute a breach of Article 6 of the European Convention on Human Rights.

Section 141 of the 1988 Act also creates offences of manufacture, sale or hire, exposing for sale or hire, or lending or giving to another person any weapon which the Secretary of State has specified in an order made, by statutory instrument. The Secretary of State has since made the Criminal Justice Act 1988 (Offensive Weapons) Order 1988, listing the knuckleduster, swordstick, handclaw, belt-buckle, knife, pushdagger, hollow kubotan (small truncheon with spikes in sides), footclaw, death star, butterfly knife, telescopic truncheon, blow-pipe, Kusari-game (sickle and chain) kyoketushoge (hook, knife and chain) and kusari (weights joined by chain) as weapons to which this offence applies. A further Order of 2002 adds a 'disguised knife', which is one that has a concealed blade or concealed sharp point and is designed to appear to be an everyday object of a kind commonly carried on the person or in a handbag, briefcase or other hand luggage (such as a comb, brush, writing instrument, cigarette lighter, key, lipstick or telephone).

In addition, the Offensive Weapons Act 1996 adds s 141A to the Criminal Justice Act 1988, making it an offence for any person to sell to a person under the age of 16 years a knife, knife blade or razor blade, any axe and any other article which has a blade which is sharply pointed and which is made or adapted for use for causing injury to the person. The section does not apply to articles already controlled by the Restriction of Offensive Weapons Act 1959, or an order made by the Secretary of State under s 141(2) of the 1988 Act or an order made by the Secretary of State under this section. The Secretary of State has made an order in respect of a folding pocket knife with a blade which does not exceed 3 inches and razor blades permanently enclosed in a cartridge or housing.

The section provides a defence for a person who proves that he took all reasonable precautions and exercised all due diligence to avoid the commission of the offence.

Search warrant

A justice may issue a warrant authorising entry and search on the application of a constable if he is satisfied that there are reasonable grounds for believing that there are on those premises knives such as are mentioned in the Restriction of Offensive Weapons Act 1959, s 1(1), or weapons to which the Criminal Justice Act 1988, s 141, applies and that an offence under either of these provisions has been or is being committed in relation to them and that one of the essential conditions exists (see page 537).

Police powers

Section 139B provides a constable with a power of entry, using reasonable force if necessary, into school premises, and the power to search those premises, and any person on those premises, for articles to which s 139 applies, or to which the Prevention of Crimes Act 1953, s 1, applies, if he has reasonable grounds for believing that an offence under s 139A of the 1988 Act is being, or has been, committed. He may seize any articles or weapons discovered in the course of such a search which he reasonably suspects to be such articles or weapons.

Marketing of combat knives

The Knives Act 1997, s 1, represents a further attempt to ban particular types of weapon. It provides that it is an offence to market a knife in a way which:

(a) indicates, or suggests, that it is suitable for combat; or
(b) is otherwise likely to stimulate or encourage violent behaviour involving the use of the knife as a weapon.

The term 'market' includes selling or hiring, offering or exposing for sale or hire, or possession for the purpose of sale or hire. A 'knife' is an instrument which has a blade or is sharply pointed; 'suitable for combat' means suitable for use as a weapon for inflicting injury on a person or causing a person to fear injury; and 'violent behaviour' means an unlawful act inflicting injury on a person or causing a person to fear injury.

The section provides that for the purposes of the Act, an indication or suggestion that a knife is suitable for combat may, in particular, be given or made by a name or description applied to the knife, on the knife or its packaging or in any advertisement which, expressly or by implication, relates to the knife.

Section 2 creates the offence of publishing any written, pictorial or other material in connection with the marketing of any knife which:

(a) indicates, or suggests, that the knife is suitable for combat; or
(b) is otherwise likely to stimulate or encourage 'violent behaviour' involving the use of the knife as a weapon.

Because of the wide range of the provisions of this Act, the defences to such charges are extensive. The marketing of knives for the armed forces, antiques or other types as prescribed are exempted, as is marketing which was reasonable for that knife (otherwise marketing descriptions applied to the sharpness of knives used in kitchens, etc., may have been caught); and it is a defence where there were no reasonable grounds for suspecting that a person into whose possession the knife might come in consequence of the way in which it was marketed would use it for an unlawful purpose. It is also a defence for a person to prove that he did not know or suspect, and had no reasonable grounds for suspecting, that the way the knife was marketed amounted to such an indication or suggestion or that it was so likely to stimulate or encourage violent behaviour.

The Act provides for the issue of search warrants and entry, using reasonable force, together with seizure of knives and publications.

This may turn out to be an extremely complicated offence to prove. The legislation does not seek to prohibit the weapons, merely to outlaw certain descriptions being applied to the weapons.

Trespassing with a weapon of offence

The Criminal Law Act 1977 creates several offences the purpose of which is to prevent unlawful trespass upon buildings. Section 8 states:

> A person who is on any premises as a trespasser, after having entered as such, is guilty of an offence if, without lawful authority or reasonable excuse, he has with him on the premises any weapon of offence.

There are a number of points to consider. We are concerned with persons who enter premises as trespassers with weapons who have no lawful excuse for possession of such weapons. The offender must enter as a trespasser. It is not sufficient to constitute an offence if a person enters lawfully and is subsequently asked to leave, thereby becoming a trespasser once his leave to remain is withdrawn. A thief who has a gun in his possession when he breaks into premises must always be guilty of this offence in addition to any other offence which he may commit. He enters as a trespasser and is unlikely to have any lawful excuse for his possession of a gun in such circumstances. However, persons may enter shops lawfully in circumstances in which they could not be described as trespassers while having knives in their possession. Provided that they remain in the public part of the shop, they can never be trespassers unless required to leave. As they entered the shop lawfully, they do not commit this offence.

A 'weapon of offence' is any article made or adapted for use for causing injury to or incapacitating a person, or intended by the person having it with him for such use. The meaning of the word 'premises' makes it clear that offences can be committed by persons who although lawfully in one part of a building, trespass into another part which is in separate occupation, for example, hotel rooms or office blocks. Land ancillary to buildings is also included.

The extent of the s 8 offence is such that offences may be committed in the course of theft in a very general sense. The other offences with which the Criminal Law Act of 1977 is specifically concerned are those caused by squatters and are strictly phrased to prevent the unlawful occupation of residential premises. The s 8 offence would also deal with armed squatters.

Police powers

A constable in uniform may arrest without warrant anyone who is, or whom he reasonably suspects to be, in the act of committing this offence. For the purpose of effecting such an arrest, he may enter premises without a warrant in accordance with the provisions of s 17 of the Police and Criminal Evidence Act 1984.

Going equipped to steal

Section 25 of the Theft Act 1968 provides that a person shall be guilty of an offence if, when not at his place of abode, he has with him any article for use in the course of or in connection with any burglary, theft or cheat.

Unlike the provisions replaced by this section, this offence can be committed at any time of the day or night. Possession of articles in the home is excepted, but elsewhere it is punishable if the articles are such that they are for use in the course of, or in connection with, any burglary, theft or cheat. Under previous legislation it was held that the possession must be actual rather than constructive, and that actual possession by one of two persons acting in concert is possession by both. It is probable that these decisions will be followed in relation to the Theft Act offences. Once possession of articles has been proved, the burden of proof shifts to the accused, who must satisfy the court that his possession was for a lawful purpose.

The nature of the article carried is of importance from an evidential viewpoint. If it is made or adapted for use in committing burglary or theft, then proof of possession may be enough in itself to prove the charge. Possession of articles such as jemmies, skeleton keys or picklocks can be for no other purpose than the commission of crime in most circumstances, although the exceptional case may arise in which the defendant can establish that they were carried for a lawful purpose. Where a man carried Kenyan five shilling pieces to place in a machine at an amusement arcade and thereby win money and tokens, he was convicted of this offence as the coins were of half the value required. He knew that the arcade owner would not consent to his taking property in this way and that his act involved the assumption of ownership rights and would therefore be theft.

If the nature of the article is such that it can be used for these forms of crime as well as for some lawful purpose, then the court must decide from the evidence available, including the nature of the article and the circumstances in which the accused was in possession of it, the intention of the person concerned. This could apply to a bunch of car keys.

The reference to articles used for the purpose of 'cheat' is first met in this context in the Theft Act 1968, and means obtaining property by deception contrary to s 15 of that Act. Such articles could therefore include false identification documents for the purpose of deceiving households into handing over rent money, in the belief that they were giving money to a representative of the local authority.

The person concerned must be equipped to carry out a burglary, theft or cheat which is to be committed in the future and it need not be proved that his possession related to a particular crime of this nature. Section 25(5) provides that for the purposes of this offence, an offence of taking a conveyance, contrary to the Theft Act 1968, shall be treated as an offence of theft.

Police powers

Going equipped to steal is an arrestable offence.

Found on enclosed premises

Section 4 of the Vagrancy Act 1824 states that it is an offence for any person to be found in or upon any dwelling house, warehouse, coach house, stable or outhouse or in any enclosed yard, garden or area for any unlawful purpose. The influence of the early nineteenth-century situation can be read within this offence. The buildings which are specified are associated with the residences of the middle and upper classes, which it was then necessary to protect from large numbers of vagrants (many of whom had been disabled during the Napoleonic wars) who were wandering throughout the country. However, this legislation is just as effective today in dealing with persons found in certain places in circumstances which suggest that they are about to commit crime.

There are a number of points which must be proved in these cases. Although it is unnecessary to specify the occupier of the building concerned, the address of the premises must be shown in the charge. The word 'enclosed' qualifies the terms 'yard', 'garden' or 'area' and it is, therefore, necessary to show that there was some form of enclosure. It is not necessary to establish that the yard is completely enclosed; there may be a form of access through an open gate, archway or a gap between buildings. This is a common-sense approach adopted by the courts in looking at the usual forms of access to yards which accompany various buildings. A decision to the effect that railway sidings are not an 'area' for the purposes of this section perhaps provides a useful parallel. Most railway sidings do not have the strict form of enclosure envisaged by the legislators. The scope of the section does not extend to a room in a building other than those mentioned in the section; thus the offence cannot be committed in a room used as an office in a university.

The most significant factor for police officers is that the 'unlawful purpose' must be some criminal purpose, as opposed to acts of immorality. It is not an offence contrary to this section to be found in such a place for the purpose of prostitution. Following complaints, men are often found in the grounds of houses and hostels for the purpose of looking through lighted windows, and it is submitted that this is not an offence under this section as the commission of the actual offence would only lead to action by way of complaint, with a view to surety for good behaviour being given by the person concerned. The person committing an offence contrary to s 4 must be found on the premises, but it is not necessary that he be arrested there.

The Vagrancy Act 1824, s 6, provides a power to any person to arrest anyone found committing an offence against the Act. The Court of Appeal has held that this power to 'any person' includes a constable and that a constable's power to arrest was not removed by the Police and Criminal Evidence Act 1984, s 26.

Crossbows

The Crossbows Act 1987 is concerned with crossbows with a draw weight of at least 1.4 kg.

It is an offence for anyone to sell or let on hire a crossbow or part of a crossbow to a person under the age of 17 years. No offence is committed if the seller or hirer believes that the person so acquiring is of or over the age of 17, provided that he has reasonable ground for that belief. It is also an offence for such a person to purchase or hire such a crossbow or part of a crossbow, or for him to have with him a crossbow capable of discharging a missile, or parts which together (and without any other parts) can be assembled to form a complete crossbow, unless in either case he is under the supervision of a person who is 21 years of age or older.

Police powers

Where a constable suspects with reasonable cause that a person is committing or has committed an offence of having with him a crossbow or parts, he may:

(a) search that person for a crossbow or part of a crossbow; or
(b) search any vehicle, or anything in or on a vehicle, in or on which the constable reasonably suspects there is a crossbow or part of a crossbow connected with the offence.

A person or vehicle may be detained by a constable for the purpose of such searches and evidence may be seized. A constable may enter any land other than a dwelling house to exercise these powers.

Intimidation of witnesses, jurors and others

Intimidation, etc., before or during a trial

Section 51(1) provides that a person commits an offence if:

(a) he does an act which intimidates, and is intended to intimidate, another person (the victim);
(b) he does the act knowing or believing that the victim is assisting in the investigation of an offence or is a witness or potential witness or a juror or potential juror in proceedings for an offence; and
(c) he does it thereby intending to cause the investigation or the course of justice to be obstructed, perverted or interfered with.

Thus, all that is required is the doing of an act which intentionally results in another person being intimidated. An act or threat made directly to a witness or juror will suffice but so will, for example, a threat to the wife of such a person to the effect that, unless her husband changes his evidence (or fails to vote for the acquittal of a defendant), her face will be slashed. The person making such a threat clearly intends the husband to be intimidated, in addition to the wife, and has thereby carried out an act to the husband through the medium of his wife. The husband will therefore be 'another person' for the purposes of the section. In addition, s 51(3) makes it clear that it is immaterial that the act is or would be done, or that the threat is made otherwise than in the presence of the victim (or to a person other than the victim).

'Intimidation' includes putting a person in fear by an exhibition of force or violence, whether to persons or property. This interpretation is well established within other parallel legislation. Section 51(1)(a) requires an act which 'intimidates' and thus the person must have been put in fear by a threat. In Scotland, intimidation has been held to be measured by whether the accused's conduct would induce 'serious apprehension of violence in the mind of a man of ordinary courage'. Threats to 'put your windows in', etc., can therefore be effectively dealt with.

Section 51(1) does not require that the person who is intimidated is actually assisting in the investigation of an offence at the time, or is a witness or potential witness, or a juror or potential juror, in proceedings for an offence. By s 51(1)(b), it is sufficient that the accused believes that the person so intimidated is involved in that way. There must, however, be an investigation in progress; it is insufficient that a person believed that such an investigation was taking place. Evidence of that investigation must be before the court. An 'investigation into an offence' means an investigation by the police or other persons charged with the duty of investigating offences or charging offenders.

There must be an intention to intimidate. An attempt to persuade a person to change his testimony without threats will not be sufficient for these offences. The accused must also intend, by the intimidating act done to the other person, to cause the investigation or the course of justice to be perverted, obstructed or interfered with. However, in this respect, s 51(7) provides that if it is proved that such an act was done with the required knowledge of belief, it must be presumed, unless the contrary is proved, that the accused did the act with the required intention. Thus, the onus is upon the accused to show in such circumstances that he did not have such an intention.

Reprisals against witnesses, jurors and others

Section 51(2) provides that a person commits an offence if:

(a) he does an act which harms, and is intended to harm, another person or, intending to cause another person to fear harm, he threatens to do an act which would harm that other person;

(b) he does or threatens to do the act knowing or believing that the person harmed or threatened to be harmed (the victim), or some other person, has assisted in the investigation into an offence or has given evidence or particular evidence in proceedings for an offence, or has acted as a juror or concurred in a particular verdict in proceedings for an offence; and

(c) he does or threatens to do it because of that knowledge or belief.

It must be shown that the accused did (or threatened to do) something to another person, which results in harm (or would result in harm) to that other person. Moreover, by s 51(3) it is immaterial that the act is or would be done, or that the threat is made, otherwise than in the presence of the victim (or to a person other than the victim). There is no requirement that the other person is actually intimidated thereby. As in the case of an s 51(1) offence, such an act may be carried out through the medium of a third party, with the intention of harming the second party. The remaining points which have to be proved are similar to those already discussed in relation to s 51(1). The act carried out or threatened must be intended to harm that person.

Section 51(4) provides that the harm which may be done or threatened may be financial as well as physical (whether to the person or a person's property), and similarly as respects an intimidatory act which consists of threats. The Court of Appeal has held that 'harm', other than financial harm or damage to property, bears the ordinary meaning of physical harm. As a result, it allowed the appeal against conviction under s 51(2) of a man who had spat in the face of a witness and verbally abused her. There had been no proof that the woman had been harmed.

Proof of knowledge or belief that the other person, or some other person, has assisted in an investigation or has given evidence, etc., is also required.

However, a third factor is involved which is not involved in the case of s 51(1). It must be proved that the accused did, or threatened to do, the act because of what he knows or believes about the assisting in an investigation or the giving of evidence, etc. In this respect, s 51(8) provides that if it is proved that within the 'relevant period':

(a) he did an act which harmed and was intended to harm, another person; or
(b) intending to cause another person fear of harm, he threatened to do an act which would harm that other person,

and that he did the act, or (as the case may be) threatened to do the act, and with the knowledge or belief required by s 51(2)(b) he is presumed, unless the contrary is proved, to have done the act, or (as the case may be) threatened to do the act, with the requisite knowledge or belief. Thus, it is clear that where there are threats within the relevant period to harm a witness or juror, there is no need for the prosecution to prove a connection between the threat and the trial.

For the purposes of this presumption, the 'relevant period' in relation to:

(a) a witness or juror begins with the institution of proceedings and ends with the first anniversary of the conclusion of the trial, or of any appeal;
(b) a person who has assisted in the investigation of an offence (or is believed by the accused to have done so) but who was not a witness in proceedings for an offence, is the period of 1 year beginning with the act (or believed act) which assisted the investigation; and
(c) a person in (b) above who was also a witness in proceedings for an offence, is the period beginning with the act (or believed act) which assisted in the investigation and ending with the first anniversary of the conclusion of the trial, or of any appeal.

However, it must be appreciated that the 'relevant period' is only of significance in relation to the presumption which leads to the burden of proof of motive being switched to the accused. It does not prevent a prosecution outside that time; if there is a prosecution outside such time, the presumption will no longer apply and it will be necessary to prove the requisite motive.

Common factors in relation to both offences

Section 51(5) provides that the intention/motive required (in either case) need not be the only or predominating intention/motive with which the act is done or threatened. This should exclude defences based upon the fact that the primary intention of the perpetrator was to avoid a miscarriage of justice.

Police powers

Both offences are arrestable offences.

Sudden death

Introduction

This section is concerned with deaths which are reported to and dealt with by HM Coroner. They are referred to as 'sudden deaths' and this term covers not only a sudden death of which the cause is unknown but also violent or unnatural deaths. The police usually receive the first report of such deaths and investigate the circumstances and notify HM Coroner of their findings. Once a coroner has been informed of a death it is for him to consider whether it will be necessary to hold an inquest or order a post-mortem examination to be made, or whether, after due enquiry, he should notify the Registrar of Births and Deaths that an inquest or post-mortem examination is unnecessary. A police officer investigating a sudden death has to keep two things in mind: the possibility of the death being in consequence of a criminal act, and the necessary information required by the coroner.

Initial action

On receiving a report of a possible sudden death, the first thing is to determine whether or not a death has occurred; if there is any doubt, first aid should be given and medical assistance called for, including an ambulance. It would not be the first time that a police officer has been called to a reported sudden death only to find that there are signs of life, and prompt action by the police officer has resulted in the 'corpse' surviving. This has happened on a number of occasions with persons suffering from a condition of deep coma resembling death.

In the majority of deaths coming to the knowledge of the police, an enquiry with the deceased's doctor will establish the fact that the deceased was suffering from an illness, and was receiving treatment from the doctor, who is prepared to certify the cause of death. Usually the doctor will not issue such a certificate if he has not seen the deceased within the 28 days prior to his death. If there are any suspicious circumstances the coroner should be informed, notwithstanding that the deceased's doctor is prepared to certify the cause of death.

If the circumstances are such that the deceased's doctor is not prepared to issue a death certificate, for whatever reason, the reporting officer should notify his supervising officer via control, and request that the coroner's office be informed. Many forces have a police officer whose sole duty is to act as the coroner's officer for a particular area, and he reports all sudden deaths in that area. If there are any suspicious circumstances, control should be informed as soon as possible and the action taken should follow that for a suspected homicide. Do not move the body or interfere with the scene.

If there are no suspicious circumstances, police action depends on the place where death has occurred. If, as in the majority of cases, a person dies in his own home, the first act after death has been certified is to examine the body for any marks or signs of violence. This will usually be done or directed by the coroner's officer. It is not a very pleasant task but one which should not be overlooked. The procedures to be followed when dealing with bodies are set out in force orders. These may differ from force to force. The essential thing is to take care to avoid any form of contamination which may occur due to the presence of saliva, blood, excreta, etc.

Where death occurs out of doors or on business or industrial premises, there are not the same facilities to examine the body. Make sure that the body is screened from public view and that the property of the deceased person is protected. In such circumstances, if a doctor has not certified death, the body is removed by ambulance to the nearest hospital where the deceased will be certified as dead on arrival and placed in the mortuary. If possible, a cursory examination should be made of a body before it is moved in case there is the slightest possibility of life being present, in which case medical assistance should not be delayed. Where a person has died in suspicious circumstances, it is important for the purposes of identification to have continuity from the scene of the death to the mortuary. If the body has not been moved before the arrival of the police, one police officer should accompany the body to the hospital and to the mortuary. In the event of an inquest, this procedure will obviate the necessity of having statements from the ambulance personnel and the mortuary attendant as well as the police officer reporting the death to provide continuity of identification. On arrival at the mortuary, the body should be thoroughly examined for any marks or signs of violence.

The next step is to identify the deceased. Where death occurs at the home of the deceased it may be possible to have a relative identify the body before it is removed. In situations where death has occurred outside or at a hospital and the body has been removed to the mortuary, the identification should be made at the mortuary. This can be a very distressing experience for the relatives, particularly in cases of fatal accidents or where the death was not expected, and relatives should be treated tactfully and with sympathy. Where the death has resulted from an accident and a police officer is given the task of breaking the news of the death to relatives, he should be both tactful and sympathetic. If the relative lives alone, the assistance of a neighbour should be sought so that the relative is not left alone.

Usually the statement of identification is coupled with a history of the deceased's employment and health. This should include details of any disability pension which a deceased may have been in receipt of, such as a pension for an industrial disease. Where the death has occurred at home, usually one statement will suffice and, in addition to identifying the deceased and giving details of his employment and medical history, it will incorporate details of when, where and by whom the deceased was last seen alive and any other details connected with the death.

Suicide

When the death appears to be a suspected suicide, the reporting officer should immediately notify his supervising officer and if there is the slightest suspicion of another person being involved in the death the police procedures should follow those prescribed for a homicide. An officer must ensure his own safety. Care must be taken with live electric wires, caustic agents, etc.

In uncomplicated cases of suicide, the means employed in the killing should be seized where applicable (e.g. tablets), or noted where seizure is inapplicable (e.g. gas oven). Any letters or suicide notes found should be handed over to the coroner's officer. In no circumstances should a letter addressed to a coroner be opened by the reporting officer. In cases involving hanging, the rope should be cut rather than the knot untied. The type of knot tied might be important.

There should be no delay in notifying the coroner of the death, giving as much information as possible. The coroner will then authorise the removal of the body to a mortuary in cases where the body is not already at a mortuary, and arrange for a post-mortem to be carried out by a pathologist to determine the cause of death.

Essential details for sudden death report

The sudden death report is designed to include all information which is essential to the coroner. It contains the name, address, age, occupation, sex, date and place of birth, etc., of the deceased person, details of the person who identified the deceased, the time and place at which death occurred together with details of the suspected cause, particulars of the person who found the deceased including how, when and where the body was found, the identity of the person who identified the deceased, the identity of the person who last saw the deceased alive and when and where that occurred, any history of illness and the name of the doctor who certified death, evidence of neglect, particularly in the case of children, marks on the body, the names and addresses of any other witnesses who may be able to assist, information as to the location of the body and details of the removal of the body to the place at which it rests to allow continuity of evidence as to the identity of the deceased person at all stages.

Post-mortem

This is arranged by the coroner, although, having ordered a post-mortem, the coroner often leaves the task of liaising with the pathologist to the police officer reporting the death. The body of the deceased must be identified to the pathologist before a post-mortem can be performed, and to ensure continuity the police officer to whom the deceased was identified provides this information. It is not part of a police officer's duty to assist or remain in the mortuary while a post-mortem examination is being carried out, although this is sometimes required.

The pathologist is responsible for informing the coroner of the results of the post-mortem and, in cases where death has resulted from natural causes, the coroner will normally dispense with an inquest and will issue a certificate authorising the Registrar of Births and Deaths to register the death. In connection with the registration of death, the coroner must know whether it is intended to have the deceased buried or cremated in order to issue the correct documents with the correct information for the registration of death.

Property of deceased

The property of a deceased person should be safeguarded by the police until it can be handed over to a relative or personal representative of the deceased against his signature. Where the next of kin cannot be traced and the deceased lived alone, the local authority should be contacted to see whether assistance can be given to store the effects of the deceased until arrangements are made for eventual disposal.

Whenever possible, a police officer should have a witness, either another police officer or a responsible person, when checking any money found on a deceased person. This will protect him from any subsequent complaint from relatives that the deceased was thought to be in possession of more money than was actually found, the implication being that some money had been stolen after death.

In fatal road accidents any property found in the deceased's vehicle should be safeguarded if it cannot be secured in the vehicle itself.

Details of all property coming into the possession of the police should be recorded in detail and the record should be endorsed as to the subsequent disposal of the property.

Coroner's court

The coroner makes the decision whether or not an inquest should be held into the circumstances of a death. He is required to hold an inquest when he is informed that the body of a person is lying within his jurisdiction and that there is reasonable cause to suspect that such person has died a violent or unnatural death, or a sudden death of which the cause is unknown, or has died in prison or in such circumstances as to require an inquest in pursuance of an Act of Parliament. Such inquests may be with or without a jury. The Coroner's Act 1988 authorises him to request the coroner of another district to hold the inquest in his area if it is more expedient to do so.

A coroner may decide to hold an inquest with a jury of not less than seven and not more than 11 persons who are summoned by a warrant addressed to the coroner's officer and to members of the police force for the area, setting out the number of jurors to be summoned. On receipt of the warrant the coroner's officer, or the police officer dealing with the death, makes out the summonses to be served on the persons selected as jurors. These summonses should preferably be served personally, although service by leaving with a person at the juror's house would appear to be sufficient compliance.

A coroner's inquest is not bound by the laws of evidence. In practice, however, the laws of evidence are usually observed by coroners. A witness is not bound to answer any questions which might incriminate him, but this does not entitle a witness to refuse to enter the witness box on the grounds that he may be asked such questions.

Section 56 of the Criminal Law Act 1977 removed the power previously held by coroners to find a person guilty of murder, manslaughter or infanticide, and prohibits any person being charged with any such offence by coroner's inquisition. The section also removed the mandatory requirement for a coroner to sit with a jury in any case involving murder, manslaughter, infanticide or death caused by an accident arising out of the use of a motor vehicle in a street or public highway. In addition, inquests may be adjourned if criminal proceedings are pending. If, at any time before an inquest is concluded, the coroner is informed by a clerk to magistrates that a person has been charged with murder, manslaughter, infanticide, causing death by dangerous driving, or an offence contrary to s 2(1) of the Suicide Act 1961 (aiding and abetting suicide) or is required by the Director of Public Prosecutions to do so, he shall adjourn the inquest.

After the conclusion of the relevant proceedings, a coroner may proceed, if with a jury, with the jury previously convened, or may begin again with a new jury. He may alternatively supply the Registrar of Deaths with the result of the criminal proceedings (by certificate).

Police action generally

Dealing with a sudden death is a distressing experience. People have never been able to come fully to terms with death. The person who was loved and respected by all has now gone; the body which is left behind represents something quite different and this is difficult to come to terms with. If a researcher was to question a large number of long-serving police officers to establish those incidents which occurred during their service which had a lasting effect upon them, it is submitted that most would be concerned with incidents which involved a death.

When dealing with relatives and close friends, the distress of the situation generally, being equally felt by the police officer, tends to ensure that the enquiry is dealt with in a sensitive manner. However, it helps to remember that such persons may appreciate additional help, and offers to contact other persons or associations who will be willing to help may be much appreciated. There are so many things which need to be done following a death and on many occasions close relatives need advice and assistance in this respect.

It is also important to keep an eye on yourself. Such situations can have a considerable effect upon you. If you feel that dealing with the situation has left you with questions which need to be answered, ask them. Other police officers will have moved through the same experiences. You will be surprised at the quality of the advice which can be given by an experienced officer, and perhaps finding that they will readily admit that they have travelled the same journey will provide assurance. If the problem which you have encountered goes beyond this, then seek further help.

Accidents – law

Introduction

Police officers are called upon to deal with many types of accident, but those involving motor vehicles warrant special attention and the Road Traffic Act 1988 contains provisions dealing with the obligations of drivers of mechanically propelled vehicles involved in accidents on roads. Not all road accidents are covered by those statutory provisions, and it is important to distinguish between those to which the Road Traffic Act 1988 applies, referred to as 'reportable accidents', and those outside the Act.

The statutory provisions are concerned with mechanically propelled vehicles. The words 'mechanically propelled' immediately exclude vehicles not propelled by mechanical means such as carts drawn by horses, cycles without motors attached and any other type of vehicle which is not mechanically propelled.

A vehicle does not necessarily cease to be mechanically propelled merely because of a mechanical fault which can be rectified or because the mechanical means of propulsion was not being used at that time. Thus, a motor car with the engine removed remains a mechanically propelled vehicle if there is evidence of the possibility that the engine may shortly be replaced. Similarly, a motor-assisted pedal cycle remains a mechanically propelled vehicle while it is being propelled only by the pedals.

A 'road', for the purpose of the Act, means any length of highway or of any other road to which the public has access, and includes bridges over which a road passes. This definition will embrace the footpath as well as the carriageway, a cul-de-sac made up with houses on both sides and a quayside over which the public walk and motor without a legal right. It is really a question of fact, each case being decided on its own merit. Places which have been held not to have been 'roads' within the terms of the above definition include a car park maintained by a local authority (in special circumstances existing in that particular car park), an occupation road leading to a farm and caravan site where there was no evidence of general use by the public and a yard, not being a thoroughfare, to which the public had access. Car parks at supermarkets do not necessarily include roads. Although it is usual to find that such car parks have 'access roads' a court will consider whether that 'access road' exists merely for the purpose of gaining entry to the car parking bays, as opposed to existing to carry a vehicle on a journey from one place to another. If it exists merely to give access to the parking bays, the whole area, although being a public place, will not be a road. If it is a recognised road which exists to carry traffic from one destination to another, that road may be a road for the purposes of the Road Traffic Acts, but the parking bays themselves will not be a part of it. However, the issue is only important in relation to a charge. Section 170 of the Road Traffic Act 1988 has been amended to extend the requirement for motor vehicle insurance to any public place. The nature of all car parks open to the general public is such that they will be public places for the purpose of the section.

Having briefly examined the basic elements of what constitutes a mechanically propelled vehicle to which the Act applies and where reportable accidents can occur, it is now necessary to examine the statutory provisions relating to reportable accidents.

Road accidents

Section 170 of the Road Traffic Act 1988 applies in a case where, owing to the presence of a mechanically propelled vehicle on a road or other public place, an accident occurs by which personal injury is caused to a person other than the driver of that mechanically propelled vehicle or a trailer drawn by it or to an animal other than an animal in or on it or trailer drawn by that mechanically propelled vehicle or to any other property constructed on, fixed to, growing in or otherwise forming part of the land on which the road or public place in question is situated, or land adjacent to such land, the driver of the mechanically propelled vehicle shall stop and, if required so to do by any person having reasonable grounds for so requiring, give his name and address, and also the name and address of the owner and the identification marks of the vehicle. If, for any reason, such a driver does not give his name and address to any such person as aforesaid, he shall report the accident at a police station or to a constable as soon as reasonably practicable, and in any case within 24 hours of the occurrence thereof.

Note that the mechanically propelled vehicle does not have to be in motion before these provisions apply; the mere presence of the vehicle on a road or other public place could be sufficient. For example, if a person parks his car on the road outside a shop while he goes for cigarettes and because his car is parked there an accident occurs, causing damage or injury to another vehicle or another person, this would be a reportable accident. The word 'driver' means the person who takes out the vehicle and he remains the driver until the journey is complete. A man parked his car on a hill and left it to post a letter. The car was showing hazard warning lights. It subsequently rolled down a hill and collided with a wall which was damaged. He said that a passenger had released the handbrake and had therefore become the driver. The Divisional Court supported the Crown Court's conclusion that, although there had been a break in the actual driving, he had remained the driver for the purposes of the section. He had parked the vehicle for a purpose of his own, had shown an intention to return to driving by showing hazard warning lights and he was still engaged upon his journey.

There must a direct causal connection between the presence of the mechanically propelled vehicle and the occurrence of the accident. Where a driver, who is approaching a pedestrian crossing at a fast speed, causes a pedestrian to turn quickly to regain the pavement and in doing so the pedestrian falls and injures himself, there has been an 'accident' as there is a direct causal link between the mechanically propelled vehicle and the accident. If a cyclist collides with a stationary car there is such a link; the accident could not have occurred without the presence of the motor vehicle. On the other hand, if a cyclist who merely moves to the nearside of the road to allow a car to pass oversteers and, because of his own actions, falls from the cycle, the causal connection with the motor car would be too remote.

It has been held that an 'accident' has occurred where the situation is such that an ordinary person would say that an accident had occurred. Thus, where a driver deliberately drives into another vehicle or property, an 'accident' has occurred because that is how the ordinary man would describe it. It is not necessary that a mechanically propelled vehicle is involved in a collision. If the actions of the driver are such that they cause other vehicles to collide, he is involved in an accident and the obligations imposed by the section apply. There can be an accident where a part of the injury or damage was deliberate. If a person deliberately drives into a wall there has been an accident because that is how an ordinary member of the public would describe it.

Personal injury

Where personal injury is involved as a result of the accident, this means personal injury to any person other than the driver of the mechanically propelled vehicle concerned. It includes any passengers in his mechanically propelled vehicle, the driver and passengers in any other vehicle and pedestrians, etc. It would cover the situation where a public service vehicle loaded with passengers swerved violently, resulting in a number of the passengers being injured, or any circumstances in which there is any direct connection between the presence of the vehicle on a road and the injury. Sometimes it is difficult to decide whether there is an injury; often there is only shock, and a good guide as to whether to class shock as an injury is whether the shock is severe enough to require medical treatment. If this is the case, then shock is classed as personal injury (see also 'Additional information in personal injury accidents', page 555).

Damage to an animal

Where an animal is injured in an accident it must be an animal other than one carried in or on the mechanically propelled vehicle concerned or in or on a trailer drawn by such a motor vehicle. Thus, if the driver of a mechanically propelled vehicle pulling a trailer full of pigs has to brake sharply and, as a result, one of the pigs suffers a broken leg, this would not be a reportable accident. The term 'animal' is defined for the purpose of s 170 as meaning any horse, cattle, ass, mule, sheep, pig, goat or dog. The notable omission is a cat. If the animal injured is a cat, or some other animal not included in the definition, then the accident does not come within the provisions of s 170 of the Act.

Damage

The statutory provisions apply to the driver of a mechanically propelled vehicle involved in a reportable accident, but it should be noted that where owing to the presence of a mechanically propelled vehicle on a road or other public place damage is caused to another vehicle, not necessarily a mechanically propelled vehicle, this is a reportable accident. An example would be where the other vehicle involved was a pedal cycle or a horse and cart; if the cycle or car was damaged, this would be a reportable accident.

Property damage

Damage to property, not being a vehicle, is covered by the Act. Where a mechanically propelled vehicle collides with a lamp standard, the Act places an obligation on the driver of the motor vehicle to report the accident. Similarly, damage to buildings, fences, hedgerows, traffic signs, etc., would be included within the provisions of the section.

Driver's obligations

(a) *Stopping* – Where a mechanically propelled vehicle is involved in an accident to which s 170 applies, the driver must stop. This appears simple enough but it has caused some difficulty, particularly on how long the driver should stop at the scene. It has been held that 'stop' means that the driver should stop and remain where he has stopped for such a period of time as in the prevailing circumstances, having regard in particular to the character of the road or place where the accident happened, will provide sufficient time to enable persons who have the right to do so, and reasonable ground for so doing, to require from the driver directly and personally the information the driver is required to supply under the Act. Thus, where a mechanically propelled vehicle collided with a parked motor vehicle causing damage to that other vehicle and the driver, having stopped, instructed an employee to wait by this vehicle to supply the necessary information and the driver left the scene, it was held that he had failed to stop after the accident, because having stopped he did not remain at the scene for such a period as would have enabled the owner of the other vehicle concerned to require him to supply the information he was obliged to give.

Where a driver collided with a parked vehicle and drove on for a distance of about 80 yards before stopping and returning to the scene of the accident, justices convicted him of an offence of failing to stop. The Divisional Court refused to interfere with that finding, which was one which had been open to the justices on the facts of the case, but said that it was not sure that it would have reached the same conclusion. If a driver who is supervising a learner driver allows the learner to walk away from the scene of an accident without remaining there for the purpose of discharging his duties, he aids and abets the offence if he took no steps to ensure that the driver remained at the scene.

A bus driver braked sharply and a passenger fell and was injured. He was informed of what had occurred but, after making arrangements by radio to meet an ambulance and police officers at a point which he would reach some 15 minutes later, continued with his journey. The Divisional Court held that this was insufficient. There may have been witnesses at the scene who could have helped. The scene of the accident was the place on the roads where the incident had occurred, not the bus itself.

(b) *Supplying information* – Having stopped, the driver of a mechanically propelled vehicle involved in a reportable accident has an obligation to supply certain information at the scene, but only if he is required by some person having reasonable ground for requiring such information. Whilst that person will usually be the driver of the other vehicle or the owner of the property, a relative or friend, or person acting on his behalf, can be such a person. If the requirement is made by any person having such grounds, s 170 obliges the driver to give:

(a) his name and address;

(b) the name and address of the owner of the vehicle; and

(c) the identification mark of the vehicle.

Section 170(2), which requires a driver to stop and to give this information, is concerned with one offence which can be committed in two ways: either by failing to stop or if, having stopped, failing to provide the information which is required to be given.

If at the scene of an accident the driver is not required to supply the necessary information, then s 170 places an obligation on the driver to report the accident at a police station or to a constable as soon as practicable, and in any case within 24 hours. Thus, if he supplies the necessary information at the scene of the accident, this relieves him of any obligation to report the matter to the police. However, this does not mean that if he refuses to supply the information at the scene when required by a person having reasonable grounds for so requiring, and later reports the accident to the police, he has fulfilled his obligations under the Act; an offence is committed if he refuses such information at the scene, even if he later reports the accident to the police. Where a driver is already known by the person reasonably requiring his name and address, he must give the information required.

Where a driver provided the address of his solicitor, as an alternative to his own, it was held that this was sufficient for the purposes of the section. With respect to the court, while accepting that this provided a means of contacting the driver, the solicitor's address could not realistically be described as 'his' (the driver's) address.

(c) *Reporting to the police* – If for any reason the driver of the mechanically propelled vehicle does not give his *name and address* to a person having reasonable grounds for so requiring, he must report the accident at a police station or to a constable as soon as reasonably practicable, and in any case within 24 hours of the occurrence of the accident. The obligation to report arises whenever the driver has not given his name and address at the scene of the accident, whether or not he was required to do so. This does not give a driver leave to report the accident at any time within 24 hours; thus, where a driver involved in an accident is traced and interviewed by police who obtain his name and address, the name and address of the owner of the vehicle and the identification marks of his vehicle, this does not amount to compliance with the provisions of s 170 of the Act, and it may be, having regard to the time which has elapsed since the time of the accident and any opportunity that the driver had of reporting the accident to the police, that the driver has committed an offence of failing to report the accident, notwithstanding that he was interviewed before 24 hours had elapsed from the time of the accident. It should be noted that s 170(3) requires a driver to report an accident, if for any reason he does not give his *name and address*. It does not specify the other particulars required by s 170(2).

The duty to report is a personal one; the report must be made by the driver to a police constable or at a police station. A telephone call will not suffice, nor will informing a friend who happens to be a police officer. What is 'reasonably practicable' is a matter for the court.

Additional information in personal injury accidents

Where a reportable accident involves personal injury to a person other than the driver of the mechanically propelled vehicle involved, then, in addition to his obligations under s 170 of the Act, a driver has to produce evidence of insurance or security. If the driver of the mechanically propelled vehicle does not at the time of the accident produce a certificate of insurance or security to a constable or to some other person who, having reasonable grounds for so doing, has required its production, the driver shall as soon as possible, and in any case within 24 hours of the occurrence of the accident, report the accident at a police station or to a constable. He must then produce a certificate of insurance or security. If he fails to do so he commits an offence.

However, it is important that we recognise that there are no circumstances, therefore, in which a driver must report an accident to the police if he provides all of the necessary information at the scene of the accident and in addition, if personal injury to someone results, he produces a certificate of insurance to a person having reasonable grounds for requiring it. It would not, of course, be sufficient for a driver to wave a certificate of insurance before the eyes of such a person. It must be produced so that a person can take particulars if required and can satisfy himself that proper insurance is in force.

However, if at the time of reporting the accident he is unable to produce a certificate of insurance or security, he may produce it subject to the usual conditions set out in the Road Traffic Act 1988.

General

Whilst the provisions examined above are concerned with legal requirements to report accidents, the high incidence of accident reports has led to force procedures being adapted to meet the situation. It may be that police officers are not required to record all of the details set out above on every occasion. This is equally true of the process of the police investigation of accidents as set out in the following section.

In many areas the Crown Prosecution Service has given guidance as to the types of accidents which are likely to result in proceedings before a court and police action has been adapted to recognise such guidance.

The offence against s 170(4), which consisted of failure to stop and report an accident in circumstances in which the duty to stop and report arose in consequence of an accident causing personal injury, is an arrestable offence.

Accidents – police action

Introduction

Prompt action by the first police officer at the scene of a road accident often prevents further accidents occurring, saves lives and provides evidence of possible offences committed by the drivers of vehicles involved in the accident. No two accidents are exactly the same but certain basic rules will apply to the handling of all accidents, and by following these basic rules a police officer should be competent to deal with any road accident except where a specialist knowledge is required, e.g. accidents on motorways, where special procedures apply.

Receipt of information

When a police officer receives a report of an accident, he should note the time the report is received. If the report is received from a member of the public, the name and address of the informant should also be recorded and as much information about the accident as possible, e.g. the time and place of the accident, the number of vehicles involved and the presence of any injured. The informant should be asked if he witnessed the accident and, if so, arrangements can be made for him subsequently to be interviewed and a statement obtained, if necessary. Speed is essential, however, and these details should be obtained with a minimum of delay.

If the report of an accident is received from a non-police source, then a radio message should be sent to control; it may be that a police officer is nearer to the scene or event or already at the scene, in which case the presence of another police officer may not be required.

Initial action and safety precautions

A police officer's first duty is to preserve life and attend to any injured persons. It is essential to check whether an ambulance has been called; if not, or if there is any doubt, summon an ambulance. Where there is danger of petrol being ignited, warn spectators not to smoke and ensure that the ignition of any motor vehicle is switched off or, where this is not possible, disconnect the battery. If people are trapped in a motor vehicle, the fire service, which is equipped with cutting equipment and lifting apparatus which is specially designed to cope with such situations, will assist. It might also be necessary to have a doctor at the scene to give medical attention to a trapped and injured person, pending his release from the vehicle, although paramedics attending with the ambulance service may be able to cope.

Where injured persons are removed from the scene by ambulance, obtain the name of the hospital to which they will be taken and, if possible, the names and addresses of the injured persons. This information can be passed by radio to control so that relatives can be informed. Where there are a large number of persons requiring medical attention, it may be necessary to warn the hospital as soon as possible so that the hospital staff are in a position to deal with the injured when they arrive.

On arriving at the scene of a road accident, it is a police officer's duty to prevent any further accidents and to safeguard his own life. A fluorescent jacket or white coat should be worn at all times to minimise the risk of being injured by other traffic. This applies particularly at night when a police uniform is hard to distinguish against a dark background.

If particular vehicles are involved which present hazards because of the dangerous loads which they carry, check the markings on the vehicle and inform control giving the details of the hazard warning panel, including the telephone number to be contacted for advice. It is essential to obtain assistance from the fire service when there is a danger from hazardous substances.

Witnesses

Witnesses should be located as soon as possible after arrival at the scene. If any witness is unable to wait at the scene, his name and address should be obtained and arrangements can be made later for the witness to be interviewed and a statement obtained.

When statements are taken from witnesses either at the scene or at a police station, this should be done out of the presence and hearing of other witnesses. It is often a good idea to see whether a witness can indicate on the rough sketch of the scene exactly where he was standing at the time of the accident.

It is often useful to ask a witness about his own driving experience and to endorse this on his written statement. If there is a subsequent prosecution, this information may guide the prosecuting officer, particularly where a witness has estimated the speed of a vehicle. Non-drivers may have very little idea of vehicle speeds; in one instance a speed described as very fast was later put at 45 mph when in fact other evidence indicated a speed of 80 mph.

Position of vehicles

The position of the vehicles involved in a road accident often produces valuable evidence as to the cause of an accident. It is important to ascertain whether any of the vehicles have been moved from the positions they occupied immediately after the accident. If the vehicles have been moved, there is no evidential value in taking measurements fixing their positions. If the vehicles have not been moved after the accident, they should not be moved until their relative positions have been fixed by means of measurements, unless it is essential to move the vehicles to save life or in some other emergency. Where it is necessary to move the vehicles, mark their positions; the yellow sticks of wax crayon used in the tyre industry are very good for marking the position of motor vehicles on a road. Unlike chalk marks which fade very quickly when traffic passes over the marks, yellow crayon marks last some hours and can also be used where the road surface is wet.

It is not only essential to fix the position of vehicles involved in an accident; a record should be made of any other marks or debris which may prove to have evidential value. The point of impact can usually be ascertained by debris on the road where dried mud, etc., has fallen from under the wheel arches at the moment of impact. Black tyre marks on the road should be measured; such skid marks may often be an indication of the speed of a motor vehicle immediately before the accident.

Any measurements taken and notes made should, if possible, be made in the presence of drivers concerned, who then have an opportunity of corroborating the accuracy of the measurements and may have some relevant comment to make about marks found on the road.

The accident report book provides space for a sketch of the scene of the accident which should, where possible, show the relative position of vehicles and the fixed objects from which measurements are taken. As the sketch will perhaps be referred to later by those concerned with conducting prosecutions which arise from such accidents, it should be as accurate as possible in the circumstances existing at the time. Whilst it is usually referred to as a 'rough sketch', 'rough' distinguishes the sketch from a scale plan which may subsequently be prepared. Make sure that everything which is relevant is included in the sketch: the names of roads, the position of traffic signs, hedges, etc., which may affect the line of vision of a driver approaching a junction, the marked positions of vehicles involved in the accident and, additionally, the positions of any other vehicle or vehicles on the road or roads concerned, the presence of which may have some bearing on the cause of the accident.

The measurements which are taken should be taken from at least two fixed points such as lamp posts, the corners of walls or drain covers, anything which will always be there and thus merits the description 'fixed point'. In selecting your fixed points, keep in mind that it is a good idea to select two which are some distance apart, so that the 'triangle' which you produce has a fairly wide base. The triangle will consist of, at its base, your two fixed points, and at its apex, the particular corner of the motor vehicle, or the position of the debris, which you are seeking to fix. The sketch will be easier to follow if you indicate these three points with chosen letters, for example FP 1 or FP 2 for the fixed points, together with letters of the alphabet to mark the apex of the triangle. If this is done, the measurements can then be listed at some place on the plan which is well separated from the actual scene of the impact. The measurements can be listed, for example, as A to FP 1 = 3.6 m. Listing the actual distances in this way, as opposed to attempting to indicate the distance above the line which is drawn between the appropriate part of the vehicle, avoids 'cluttering up' the sketch in the area surrounding the vehicles.

Accident booklet

The accident report booklet is to be used for all original entries at the scene of an accident. The booklet, not the police officer's notebook, is the original record which must be examined when giving evidence in court. The entry made in the officer's notebook should merely itemise brief details of the occurrence and all original entries must be made in the accident report booklet.

If the accident is serious, and particularly if there is a likelihood that a person will die from injuries received, then this information should be passed by radio to control as soon as possible in order that a supervising officer may attend at the scene together with other officers, such as a photographer, to assist the reporting officer.

If there is any suspicion that a mechanical failure in any of the vehicles involved contributed to the accident, then arrangements should be made for the vehicle to be examined. A police officer has the power to detain any vehicle for the purpose of such an examination where such a vehicle has been involved in a road accident.

In the case of hit and run accidents, it is possible that you will be required to take and submit paint samples to the forensic laboratory for examination. Although the taking of such samples is sometimes considered to be a job for a specialist, it will not always be practicable to receive immediate assistance. It must be recognised that this procedure will be restricted to serious accidents which are likely to give rise to serious criminal charges. If it becomes necessary to take samples, there are a number of factors which should be observed:

(a) Take a control sample of paint from the vehicle which has been struck. A control sample is a sample of uncontaminated paint, taken from a point close to the damaged area, but away from an area on which there may be transferred material.

(b) Take a sample from the damaged area, to include some of the vehicle's own paint and some of the transferred material. Even if no transferred material can be seen, take the sample, as the microscope may well pick out transferred material.

(c) It may be possible to take a sample of debris at the scene which might include fittings, glass, paint or filler.

(d) Paint samples should be taken by scraping down to the bare metal to include all layers of paint. Avoid contamination which might occur by using the same scraper on two different spots. You should take enough paint to cover a circle of about 2.5 cm diameter.

(e) Place each paint sample on a separate sheet of plain paper and enclose the sample by wrapping in the manner of a Beecham's powder. Seal it with adhesive tape and place the folded, sealed paper in an envelope or polythene bag, then seal and attach a label giving details of the sample.

(f) Do not put samples directly into envelopes which may leak at the corners. Do not use polybags or fixed-penalty bags as the paint tends to stick to these bags. For the same reasons, adhesive tape lifts should not be used, as the adhesive contaminates the sample.

(g) The following information must be given to the laboratory with the samples:
    (i) time, date and place of occurrence;
    (ii) make, model and registration mark of vehicle(s);
    (iii) the colours of vehicle(s), locations and extent of damage;
    (iv) the name of any suspect or accused; and
    (v) the name, location and telephone number of the OIC case.

Similar samples must be taken from suspect vehicles when traced and submitted to the laboratory in the same way.

Property

Any property found at the scene of an accident should be taken into police custody if it cannot be immediately identified and returned to the owner. Where it is necessary to remove damaged vehicles from the scene, the driver should be asked whether he wishes to have the vehicle removed by any particular garage. If the driver does not nominate a particular garage, or the driver is absent from the scene, control should be asked to arrange for a breakdown truck to remove the vehicle. The driver should be asked to remove any property from the vehicle or to secure any property by locking it in the boot of the car.

Interviewing drivers

There is certain essential information to be obtained when interviewing drivers who have been involved in accidents. Each driver must be identified with a particular vehicle and the direction of travel of the vehicle must be clearly established. It is helpful if a compass direction can be given, but this is not essential. The vehicle must have been travelling along a particular road, from one place to another. The driver's estimate of speed is helpful as it may later establish the reliability of his story, as there are scientific ways of determining the speed of a vehicle when the circumstances of the accident justify a through investigation. The position which the vehicle occupied on the road is most important, as are the manoeuvres of the vehicle immediately prior to the collision, including any avoiding action taken. Any information which helps to establish the point of impact must be recorded, as should information which helps to establish where the vehicle came to rest.

When interviewing a driver of a motor vehicle involved in a road accident, it is necessary to obtain certain details to complete the accident report. These reports usually take the form of a booklet and are self-explanatory. The police officer should go through the report carefully, filling in the necessary information.

General

A police officer must act positively at the scene of an accident. The public expect a sympathetic, competent performance, as no-one else is trained to deal with such situations in their entirety.

It is frequently necessary to use the accident report book and the statements taken from the drivers and witnesses in order to prepare a file of evidence in respect of offences disclosed. This is more effectively done while all of the facts are still fresh in the mind of the reporting officer. The file should be completed without delay.

On some occasions it may be necessary to inform relatives or friends of those injured in road accidents as it will be unlikely that they will be in a position to do so themselves. However, hospitals usually make such contacts, but it is advisable to check. There is nothing to be gained by informing such relatives or friends twice. The question of providing first aid at the scene should be answered in recognition of existing circumstances. Where injuries are of a minor nature and medical help is readily available, there may be more urgent matters to deal with as a first priority if a dangerous situation exists because of the presence of damaged vehicles or debris at the scene.

Many accidents occur in consequence of drivers failing to distinguish road markings which have become faded, or to recognise traffic signs which have been vandalised. Accidents can be avoided if such matters are reported to the highway authority.

Firearms

The Firearms Act 1968 deals with, among other things, the sale, transfer and possession of firearms. Such sales and transfers are prohibited, other than those carried out in accordance with the provisions of the Act. The failure to comply with instructions in a firearm certificate when transferring a firearm to a person other than a registered dealer, or the failure to report that transaction to the police, is an arrestable offence. Within the United Kingdom, only a minority of firearms (mainly air weapons) may be possessed without authority. It is one of the functions of chief officers of police to control possession of firearms by issuing various forms of certificates and permits to those who have sufficient reason to possess firearms.

Explanation of terms

Firearm

A firearm is a lethal barrelled weapon of any description from which any shot, bullet or other missile can be discharged. The term also includes:

(a) any prohibited weapon, whether it is a lethal weapon or not;
(b) any component part of such a lethal or prohibited weapon; and
(c) any accessory designed or adapted to diminish the noise or flash caused by firing the weapon.

The first important word within this definition is 'lethal', and the High Court has ruled that it will include a weapon which is not designed to kill or inflict injury, but is capable of doing so if it is misused. This decision was made after considering the status of a Very light pistol, which is designed to give a distress signal but is capable of killing. Most air weapons are likely to cause only minor injuries, but if they are capable of causing serious injury they may be classified as 'lethal' and if they are so capable, they may be declared to be specially dangerous.

A prohibited weapon is:

(a) any firearm which is so designed or adapted that two or more missiles can be successively discharged without repeated pressure on the trigger;
(b) any self-loading or pump-action rifled gun other than one which is chambered for 0.22 rim-fire cartridges;
(c) any firearm which either has a barrel less than 30 cm in length or is less than 60 cm in length overall, other than an air weapon, a muzzle-loading gun or a firearm designed as signalling apparatus;
(d) any self-loading or pump-action smooth-bore gun which is not an air weapon or chambered for 0.22 rim-fire cartridges and either has a barrel less than 24 inches in length or is less than 40 inches in length overall;
(e) any smooth-bore revolver gun other than one which is chambered for 9-mm rim-fire cartridges or a muzzle-loading gun;
(f) any rocket launcher, or any mortar, for projecting a stabilised missile, other than a launcher or mortar designed for line-throwing or pyrotechnic purposes or as signalling apparatus; and
(g) any weapon of whatever description designed or adapted for the discharge of any noxious liquid, gas or other thing.

The Court of Appeal has held that the words used in (a) above 'so designed or adapted that two or more missiles can be successively discharged without repeated pressure on the trigger' relate to that which is objectively possible and not to the intention of the designer of the weapon.

It is important to remember when considering prohibited weapons of a type used for the discharge of a noxious liquid, gas or other thing, that such weapons, to be prohibited, must have been 'designed or adapted' for that purpose. A water pistol is designed to eject water and its design purpose does not change simply because someone puts acid in it. The same applies to, for example a 'Fairy Liquid' bottle. The fact that a 'stun-gun' designed for the discharge of an electrical charge is not working owing to some unknown fault, does not change its character as a prohibited weapon.

The prohibition set out in (c) is that introduced by the Firearms (Amendment) Act 1997 to restrict the use of hand guns. For the purpose of (c) and (d) above, any detachable, folding, retractable or other movable butt-stock shall be disregarded in measuring the length of any firearm.

References to muzzle-loading guns are references to guns which are designed to be loaded at the muzzle end of the barrel or chamber with a loose charge and a separate ball (or other missile).

Section 5(1A) was added to the 1968 Act and specifically prohibits the sale, transfer, purchase, acquisition or possession of a weapon 'prohibited' by the section, except with the authority of the Secretary of State for Defence. It prohibits any firearm which is *disguised as another object* and any launcher or other projecting apparatus designed to be used with any rocket or ammunition which is designed to explode on or immediately before impact. In relation to these weapons and ammunition, there are a number of exemptions which are concerned primarily with collectors and use in connection with slaughtering animals, sporting purposes, shooting vermin, estate management purposes, and competition and target-shooting purposes.

A component part of a weapon is some part which is essential to its functioning as a firearm. A telescopic sight is not a component part as the weapon would function without it, whereas the trigger mechanism is such a part as the firearm could not function without it. It is for the courts to decide whether or not a particular weapon is a firearm for the purposes of the Act, but a decision of the High Court ruled that a dummy revolver, which could be readily converted into a lethal firearm by boring through a solid barrel, consisted of component parts of a firearm and fell within the definition. Some starting pistols are outside this definition as they are incapable of conversion, whereas others, with small modifications, can be made to kill. Where there may be doubts concerning whether a weapon may be 'lethal barrelled', it is useful to recognise that it is as essential to be authorised to possess a component part as it is to possess the whole weapon.

Noise and flash eliminators would not be a component part of a weapon as defined, because a weapon would function as a firearm without it, and Parliament has, therefore, found it necessary specifically to include such items as 'accessories' because of their nature. They have no other purpose than to allow firearms to be used without the user being detected.

Ammunition

Ammunition means ammunition for any firearm and includes grenades, bombs and other like missiles whether capable of use with a firearm or not; it also includes prohibited ammunition.

This definition is extremely wide and includes all forms of ammunition, including blank cartridges, for use with guns and, because the purpose of the Firearms Act 1968 is to prevent sections of the public from arming themselves in any way (unless they can show cause for doing so), includes other offensive explosive devices such as grenades and bombs. A 'bomb' is any explosive substance in a case, or a case containing poisonous gas, smoke or flammable material which might be dropped from an aircraft, fired from a gun or thrown or placed by hand.

Certain ammunition is 'prohibited':

(a) including bullets which are designed to explode on or immediately before impact (e.g. dum-dum bullet);
(b) ammunition containing or designed or adapted to contain any noxious liquid, gas or other thing; and
(c) if capable of being used with any firearm, any grenade, bomb or other like missile, or a rocket or shell designed to explode on or immediately before impact,

other than ammunition used for treating animals.

Section 5(1A) makes specific prohibitions in respect of similar military rockets and ammunition, military ammunition which ignites on or immediately before impact, military armour-piercing ammunition, expanding bullets for use with pistols and similar prohibited ammunition designed to be projected as a missile.

Public place

A public place for the purposes of this Act includes any highway and any other premises or place to which, at the material time, the public have or are permitted to have access, whether on payment or otherwise.

Classification

The Firearms Act 1968 controls the purchase of and the possession of firearms by members of the public. It can be appreciated that having defined, in the broadest sense, those weapons which are firearms and those things which are ammunition, the law begins to make provisions in respect of different types of firearms. There can be no reason for a member of the public to possess a sub-machine gun, so it is declared to be a prohibited weapon and cannot be possessed by the public. There are many different types of rifles and, although members of the public may not be encouraged to own some of them, there are many sporting uses to which rifles and revolvers can be put, and considerable enjoyment can be experienced by enthusiasts. Ownership of such weapons is not, therefore, prohibited, but it is carefully controlled and persons wishing to possess them must show sufficient reason for doing so.

Shotguns are perhaps less offensive, being primarily designed for sporting purposes, but when it was lawful to buy and possess such weapons without any form of control, they were found to be increasingly used by criminals and control became essential.

Air weapons are not usually a danger to life but can become so in the hands of young people. There is no control over the purchase or possession of such weapons generally, but there are restrictions in relation to young people.

In effecting different forms of control, the Act divides firearms into three groups for practical purposes. We shall examine each in turn.

Firearms and ammunition controlled by Section 1 of the Act

Section 1 applies to all firearms except:

(a) a shotgun within the meaning of this Act, that is to say a smooth-bore gun (not being an airgun) which
  (i) has a barrel not less than 24 inches in length and does not have any barrel with a bore exceeding 2 inches in diameter;
  (ii) either has no magazine or has a non-detachable magazine incapable of holding more than two cartridges; and
  (iii) is not a revolver gun; and
(b) air weapons (air gun, air pistol or air rifle, not declared specially dangerous under rules made by the Secretary of State);

and to all ammunition except:

(a) cartridge containing five or more shot, none of which exceeds 0.36 inch diameter;
(b) ammunition for air weapons; and
(c) blank cartridges not more than 1 inch in diameter.

This section applies to all firearms which are particularly dangerous, merely omitting some shotguns, air weapons and their ammunition. It declares that it is an offence for a person:

(a) to have in his possession, or to purchase or acquire, such a firearm or ammunition without having a firearm certificate in force, or otherwise than as authorised by the certificate; or
(b) to have in his possession, or to purchase or acquire, any ammunition to which the section applies without holding a firearm certificate, or otherwise than as authorised by such a certificate, or in quantities in excess of those authorised.

Possession

It is not essential that a person has physical custody of a firearm to have it in his possession. A person who keeps a firearm in his home, or in a desk at his office, remains in possession of that weapon no matter where he may be. The offence is one of strict liability, so much so that a person can be in possession of a firearm even though he is unaware that he has control of it. If a man briefly has custody of a grip containing a firearm and does not consider the nature of its contents, he is nevertheless in possession of them. Brevity of possession or lack of knowledge of the contents is no defence. The nature of the legislation is deliberately strict.

Control of possession

(a) *A firearm certificate* – A certificate for a firearm controlled by s 1 of the Act is granted by the chief officer of police for the area in which the applicant resides. An applicant must state such particulars as are required by the application form. Information concerning previous names, residences or convictions, other than those for minor traffic offences, must be given. The applicant must sign a statement to the effect that the statements *are* true rather than believed to be true. An applicant must provide up to four photographs and the names and addresses of two persons who have agreed to act as referees. These particulars must be verified, as must the 'likeness' of the photographs, and there must be a statement from each referee to the effect that he knows of no reason why the applicant should not possess a firearm, together with any other prescribed information. It is an offence knowingly or recklessly to make a statement false in any material particular.

Similar provisions and offences apply to applications for shotgun certificates (see below). Chief officers of police must grant certificates if they are satisfied that the applicant is fit to be entrusted with a firearm to which s 1 of the Act applies and that he is not a prohibited person, that he has good reason for possessing, purchasing or acquiring the firearm and ammunition and that in all the circumstances the applicant can be permitted to have the firearm and ammunition in his possession without danger to the public safety or peace.

A person who is under 18 who applies for such a certificate is capable of having a good reason for possessing it *only* if he has no intention of using it for a purpose other than a purpose authorised by the European firearms directive. An authorised purpose is a sporting purpose, the shooting of vermin, a purpose related to estate management activities, competition or target shooting.

The certificate issued by the chief of police will identify the serial number of the particular weapon which the holder may possess, and if this information is not available at the time of application it will be added to the certificate at a later date. Conditions may be imposed restricting the use of the firearm; for example, if it is the applicant's wish to shoot over open land, conditions may be made limiting use to a certain area of land. In such instances, if the area over which the applicant wishes to shoot is to be changed, he must apply to the chief officer of police for variation of this certificate, and this provides a further opportunity to have land assessed with a view to ensuring public safety. It is unusual for conditions to be attached to certificates held by persons who regularly use firearms in the course of their employment, such as gamekeepers, RSPCA inspectors and recognised sportsmen who are used to handling firearms and appreciate the general rules to be observed.

Ammunition is carefully controlled. Applicants for certificates are required to state the total amount of ammunition which they are likely to use in the course of a year, the maximum amount which they would wish to purchase on any occasion and the maximum to be in their possession at any one time. Conditions are attached to the grant of the certificate controlling the sale and use of ammunition. If the amounts applied for appear to a chief officer of police to be excessive, the conditions imposed will limit the purchase, possession and use of ammunition to a reasonable level.

(b) *A shotgun certificate* – Shotguns are controlled in a similar way. The conditions relating to applications for shotgun certificates are not so strict. Similar provisions concerning photographs and referees apply as in the case of firearms certificates. Such a certificate must be granted by a chief officer of police if he is satisfied that the applicant can be permitted to possess a shotgun without danger to the public safety or the peace, unless he has reason to believe that the applicant is prohibited from possessing a shotgun, or is satisfied that the applicant does not have a good reason for possessing, purchasing or acquiring one. The Court of Appeal supported the decision of a chief constable to refuse to renew a shotgun certificate where the holder stored his gun in a safe at his mother's home. His mother was not a certificate holder, but was aware of the location of the key to the safe and had access to the gun at any time.

Section 2 of the Act states that it is an offence for a person to have in his possession, or purchase or acquire, a shotgun without holding a certificate authorising him to do so. A shotgun certificate shall specify the description of the shotguns to which it relates including, if known, the identification numbers of the guns. Although ammunition sales are not strictly controlled in terms of quantity, it is an offence to sell ammunition to a person who is not a registered firearms dealer, or a person who sells such ammunition by way of trade or business, unless that person produces a shotgun certificate, or shows that he is exempt from the necessity to hold one, or produces someone else's certificates with that person's written authority to purchase ammunition on his behalf.

It is an offence to shorten the length of the barrel of any shotgun. When the barrel has been so shortened to less than 24 inches, it is no longer a shotgun for the purposes of the Firearms Act and becomes a firearm to which s 1 applies. A firearm certificate, rather than a shotgun certificate, would then be required to authorise its possession. It is difficult to imagine any lawful use which could be made of such a weapon, and the grant of a firearm certificate is most improbable.

The Firearms (Amendment) Act 1988 creates an offence of shortening the barrel of any smooth-bore gun to which s 1 of the Act of 1968 applies to a length less than 24 inches, other than a gun which has a barrel with a bore exceeding 2 inches in diameter. Therefore, pump-action and revolver-type shotguns are similarly protected.

A person who is under 18 who applies for such a certificate is capable of having a good reason for possessing it *only* if he has no intention of using it for a purpose other than an authorised purpose (see page 565). It has been held that when deciding whether to revoke a shotgun certificate, a chief constable is entitled to take into account irresponsible conduct by the holder which does not involve the use of the shotgun. It is a matter for the chief constable's discretion to what extent he should investigate a particular offence.

(c) *A permit to possess* – On occasions, some form of authority is required for a person to hold a firearm or shotgun for a relatively short period, usually to permit disposal. If the holder of a firearm certificate dies, his widow may wish to sell the weapon, but from the moment she becomes the owner she must have some authority to possess it. Chief officers of police are authorised to issue permits in such circumstances, giving details of the weapon and ammunition. The expiry date must be shown and it is unusual to issue permits valid for longer than 1 month.

Exemptions

There are certain exemptions from the necessity to hold either a firearm certificate or a shotgun certificate:

(a) Persons carrying a weapon belonging to another person who is the holder of a certificate which is to be used for sporting purposes by some other person. Such a person might be described as 'gun bearer'. He is not authorised to use the weapon.

(b) Possession at a miniature rifle range, usually at a side show, provided that only rifles and ammunition not more than 0.23 inch calibre are used.

(c) Starters at athletic meetings may possess firearms without a certificate for the purpose of starting races only but cannot possess ammunition other than blanks not exceeding 1 inch in diameter.

(d) Persons taking part in theatrical performances, rehearsals or films may possess a firearm without a certificate during such events (not ammunition).

(e) Firearms dealers do not require certificates for guns in their possession in the course of business, but if a dealer wished to possess one for his own use for sporting purposes, a certificate would be required. He is required to register as a dealer with the chief officer of police and must keep records of firearms and ammunition in his possession. However, this exemption only applies to firearms and ammunition kept on registered premises.

(f) Persons in the service of the Crown and police may possess firearms in their capacity as such.

(g) Auctioneers, carriers, warehousemen and their servants may frequently be required to handle firearms in the course of their business, and this is permitted without a certificate. They must take reasonable precautions for safe custody and report forthwith to the police any theft or loss.

(h) Slaughtering instruments, and ammunition for them, may be possessed by a licensed slaughterman without the necessity for a firearm certificate.

(i) Firearms may be possessed as part of a ship's equipment without a certificate being in force, and may be removed from the ship on the authority of a police permit.

(j) Signalling apparatus on aircraft or at an aerodrome, for example, Very light pistols, may be held without a certificate.

(k) A member of an approved cadet corps may possess a firearm and ammunition when engaged as such a member in, or in connection with, drill or target shooting.

(l) A member of an approved rifle club, miniature rifle club or pistol club may possess a firearm and ammunition when engaged as such a member in, or in connection with, target shooting. An approval of a club may be subject to limitation to specified weapons.

Although at first sight this list of exemptions appears to be very difficult to memorise, the items are more easily remembered by recalling instances in which firearms have been seen in the possession of various persons in the course of their trade or business. There are further exceptions in relation to shotguns which may be possessed without a shotgun certificate:

(a) guests and other persons who are loaned shotguns by the occupier of private land, for use on that land in the occupier's presence;

(b) clay pigeon shoots approved by the chief officer of police;

(c) visitors to Great Britain who have not been here for more than 30 days in the preceding 12 months.

The Firearms (Amendment) Act 1988 permits a person of or over the age of 17 to borrow a rifle from the occupier of private premises, without such person holding a firearm certificate, for use on those premises in the presence of the occupier or his servant provided that the person accompanying the borrower holds a firearm certificate in respect of that rifle and the borrower's possession and use of it complies with any conditions as to those matters specified in the certificate.

The 1988 Act also makes provision for 'visitors' permits' for both s 1 firearms and shotguns.

In addition, the Firearms Acts (Amendment) Regulations 1992 introduced provisions which permit the issue of a European Firearms Pass to citizens of a member State. The holders of such passes are entitled to be in possession of the firearm or firearms specified within that pass. The pass will record the authorisation given by the State such a person is visiting. Such a pass must be produced on demand by a constable.

Sections 16A and 16B of the Firearms (Amendment) Act 1988 authorise respectively, persons under the supervision of a member of armed forces to possess a firearm and ammunition on service premises and persons being trained or assessed under the supervision of a member of the Ministry of Defence Police to do so on premises used for any purpose of the Ministry of Defence Police.

Police powers

All offences of possession of s 1 firearms or shotguns without having a certificate are arrestable offences, as are offences of possessing or distributing prohibited weapons, and offences selling firearms to another person who does not have a certificate.

Air weapons

Air weapons operate by the release of compressed air. They contain no explosive charge. No form of certificate is required to authorise possession unless the particular weapon has been declared by the Secretary of State to be especially dangerous. If so, the weapon becomes an s 1 firearm. The Firearms (Amendment) Act 1997, s 48, provides that any reference in the Acts of 1968 to 1997 to an air rifle, air pistol or air gun shall include a reference to a rifle, pistol or gun powered by compressed carbon dioxide.

Offences

Carrying a firearm in a public place

A person commits an offence against s 19 of the 1968 Act if, without lawful authority or reasonable excuse (the proof whereof lies upon him), he has with him in a public place a loaded shotgun or loaded air weapon, or any other firearm whether loaded or not, together with ammunition suitable for use in that firearm. A certificate for a firearm and ammunition is not in itself lawful authority for a holder to have the firearm and ammunition in a public place. This is an arrestable offence.

There are certain points which require amplification. Although lawful authority or reasonable excuse for possession must be established by the person charged, this burden is less than that placed upon the prosecution, who are required to prove all matters beyond reasonable doubt. If it appears that a reason put forward by an accused is probably correct, this will be sufficient. There will be occasions upon which there can be a reasonable excuse for carrying a loaded shotgun in a public place and it must be recognised that possession of a shotgun certificate is irrelevant in relation to this offence.

A gamekeeper who is merely crossing a public road in the course of his duties might be considered to have such an excuse, but the courts are unlikely to place any wider interpretation upon the term 'reasonable excuse'. Even in that event, the justices may feel that a professional gamekeeper should have known better and, therefore, did not have a reasonable excuse. While a person who is going to a rifle club for the purpose of target shooting might be considered to have an excuse for possession of his rifle and ammunition, much will depend upon the club rules. If the rules of the club insist that ammunition is left in a secure place within the club premises, a court may consider that such a person did not have a reasonable excuse for such possession. An air weapon is loaded for the purposes of this section if there is a missile which is available for discharge in the weapon, although the necessary compression is *not* yet present, and in the case of either a shotgun or an air weapon having a loaded magazine, it shall be treated as loaded even though there is no round in the breech. The aim of this section is to prevent criminals from having weapons in their possession in public places in a state of readiness. The offence is a serious one if the loaded weapon is a shotgun and is punishable by 5 years' imprisonment if tried on indictment.

This section uses the term 'has with him' not the word 'possession'. However, this does not mean that he has the firearm and/or ammunition on his person, but he must have a close personal link with it and it must be readily accessible to him. This could be so where they are in a bag which he is carrying, or in the glove compartment of a car which he is driving, or where the car has been parked sufficiently close to make the weapon readily accessible. It has been held that a person has a firearm with him if it is readily available to him when he is committing a robbery. The emphasis should not be so much upon the exact distance between the criminals and the guns but rather on the accessibility of those guns judged in a common-sense way in the context of criminals embarking on a joint enterprise.

This section creates an absolute offence. Where a woman knows that there is a parcel in her handbag, the issue of whether or not she knew that it contained a loaded pistol is irrelevant as a matter of law.

Trespassing with a firearm

A person commits an offence against s 20 if, while he has a firearm or imitation firearm with him, he enters or is in any building or part of a building or on any land as a trespasser without reasonable excuse, the proof of which lies on him.

In this offence the words 'lawful authority' are omitted, as such authority would prevent the entry from becoming a trespass. It is immaterial whether or not the firearm is loaded, or if ammunition is carried, as the essence of these offences is that the presence of such a person as a trespasser is made more ominous by his possession of firearms. The expression 'land' includes water. If the trespass is upon buildings, the offence is more serious and can be tried on indictment.

Where the weapon possessed is an air weapon, it is necessary to show that it is one from which a shot could be fired, or was one which could be adapted to do so and that it was 'lethal barrelled'.

The offence is an arrestable offence.

General police powers

Production – handing over of firearms

Section 47 (1) of the Firearms Act 1968 authorises a constable to require any person whom he has reasonable cause to suspect:

(a) of having a firearm, with or without ammunition, with him in a public place; or
(b) to be committing or about to commit, elsewhere than in a public place, an offence of 'having with him' a firearm or imitation firearm with intent to commit an indictable offence or to resist arrest or an offence of trespassing with a firearm,

to hand over the firearm or ammunition for examination. It is an offence to fail to hand over the firearm when required to do so.

The purpose of subsection (1) of s 47 is to enable a constable to require a firearm to be handed over for his examination so that he may establish its type and, therefore, what type of authority should be held to authorise its possession. In the case of a shotgun or air weapon carried in a public place, he will also wish to establish whether or not it is loaded.

Stop and search

Subsection (3) of s 47 authorises a constable to search persons reasonably suspected of having firearms in public places, buildings, parts of buildings or on land and to detain them for that purpose. This power is an extension of that above. After the person concerned has failed to hand over a firearm which he is suspected of possessing, the power to search can be exercised. The power of search is extended by subsection (4) to vehicles, and constables, by subsection (5), may enter any place to exercise these powers.

Production of certificates

Following the probable process of enquiry, a person may fail to hand over a firearm at (1) above which he is suspected of possessing, and his actual possession can only be established by exercising the search powers outlined at (2) above. Having established that the person is in possession of a firearm, the Act must give a constable power to determine whether or not the person is authorised to possess a weapon of the type produced. Section 48 provides:

(a) A constable may demand, from any person whom he believes to be in possession of a firearm or ammunition to which s 1 applies, or of any shotgun, the production of his firearm certificate or shotgun certificate.
(b) If such a person fails to produce his certificate, or to permit the constable to read it, or to show that he is exempt from the necessity to hold a certificate, the constable may seize the firearm or ammunition and require such person to give his name and address.
(c) It is an offence for a person to refuse or fail to give his true name and address.

Section s 48(1A) provides that where a constable has made a demand under s 48 and there is a failure to produce the relevant certificate and that person fails to show that he is not a person entitled to receive a European Firearms Pass, or to show that he is a recognised collector of a another member State, he may demand the production of a European Firearms Pass. It is an offence for the holder of such a document to fail to comply with such a demand. The powers of seizure, etc., then apply.

Search with warrant

A justice of the peace who is satisfied by information on oath that there is reasonable ground for suspecting:

(a) that an offence (other than an offence relating to air weapons or possession of an uncovered shotgun by an unsupervised person under 15) has been, is being or is about to be committed; or

(b) that in connection with a firearm or ammunition, there is a danger to the public safety or to the peace,

he may grant a search warrant authorising a constable or civilian officer to enter premises, if necessary by force, and to search the premises and any persons found there and to seize and detain anything reasonably suspected to be connected with such an offence, or which involves danger to the public safety or peace. Information stored in any electronic form must be made available in a form which is visible and legible and can be taken away. The additional powers of seizure provided by the Criminal Justice and Police Act 2001, s 50, apply where such a search warrant is executed (see page 174).

It is an offence to obstruct a constable or civilian officer carrying out such a search.

Children and young persons

It is an offence for a person under the age of 17 to purchase or hire *any* firearm or ammunition. Persons under 14 years of age may not be granted a firearm certificate in any circumstances. Possession of s 1 firearms is restricted as described below. Persons between 14 and 17 years may be granted firearms certificates but are not permitted to purchase or hire firearms or ammunition, but may acquire them in other ways, for example, as a birthday gift. Such a person could also borrow or receive an air weapon as a gift. In the case of shotguns, persons over 15 years of age but less than 17 years may also accept weapons as a gift, provided that they are in possession of a shotgun certificate. There are a number of restrictions placed upon the possession of firearms by young persons.

The Firearms Acts (Amendment) Regulations 1992 extend the Firearms Act 1968 to create a requirement that the holder of a firearm or shotgun certificate who is under 18 may only use that firearm for a purpose authorised by the European weapons directive. It is an offence to use the weapon for a purpose other than those specified. It is probable that such purposes will be specified in the certificate.

Section 1 firearms and ammunition

A person less than 17 years of age may not purchase or hire any such firearm or ammunition, but may acquire it by way of a gift or loan, if he is 14 years of age or over. In such circumstances he must have been granted a firearm certificate, and if it is the wish of an adult to make such a present, the adult must obtain a firearm certificate to allow him to purchase the weapon, which can then be transferred. The transfer must be notified to the chief officer of police within 48 hours by registered post or recorded delivery service. On occasions in which persons less than 17 years are granted firearms certificates, they are endorsed to the effect that firearms and ammunition must not be sold or let on hire until a given date, which will be the date of the person's 17th birthday.

It is an offence to give or lend s 1 firearms or ammunition to persons under 14 years of age, or for such persons to possess them, except:

(a) when carrying for another, who is the holder of a firearm certificate, for sporting purposes;
(b) as a member of an approved cadet corps, while engaged in target shooting or drill;
(c) at a miniature range or shooting gallery using air weapons or rifles not exceeding 0.23 calibre; or

(d) when, as a member of an approved rifle club, he is engaged in, or in connection with, target shooting.

Shotguns

It is an offence for a person less than 17 years of age to purchase or hire any shotgun and an offence for a person to sell or hire a shotgun to such a person. It is also an offence to make a gift of a shotgun to a person under 15. No one less than 15 years shall possess an assembled shotgun, except:

(a) while under the supervision of a person of 21 years or more; or
(b) while it is securely fastened with a gun cover so that it cannot be fired.

The sale or hire of a shotgun to such a person is an offence. It should be noted that the Act does not prohibit the grant of a shotgun certificate to a person of any age. It is for chief officers of police to decide whether or not a shotgun certificate can be granted to a person under 15 without public safety being endangered. Young persons must have a certificate authorising their possession of shotguns when shooting under supervision or when carrying a covered gun.

A holder of a shotgun certificate who is under 18 may not use the weapon for a purpose which is not authorised by the European weapons directive.

Air weapons

It is an offence for a person less than 17 years to purchase or hire air weapons or ammunition. The seller or person who lets on hire in such a case also commits an offence. He may accept them as a gift or loan, and there being no requirement to possess any form of certificate they may be handed over immediately after purchase by an adult. However, such a gift or loan may not be made to a person under 14. The restrictions in respect of these weapons relate to possession.

A person less than 17 years of age commits an offence if he has with him an air weapon in any public place, except:

(a) as a member of an approved rifle club, for the purpose of target shooting;
(b) at a shooting gallery or miniature range using air weapons or rifles not exceeding 0.23 calibre; or
(c) an air rifle which is so covered with a securely fastened gun cover that it cannot be fired.

The exception in (c) does not apply to air pistols. It is an offence for persons under 17 years of age to possess air pistols in a public place whether or not they are in a gun cover.

It is an offence for persons under the age of 14 years to possess air weapons or ammunition in any circumstances (including on private premises), except:

(a) while shooting under the supervision of a person of 21 years or over on private premises (including land) and provided that the missile is not fired beyond those premises;
(b) at shooting galleries, as above;
(c) as a member of an approved rifle club for the purpose of target shooting.

Offences are committed by persons supervising shooting on private premises if they allow shots to be fired beyond those private premises, and also by those who part with possession of air weapons or ammunition to persons less than 14 years of age.

Criminal use of firearms

Possession of firearm with intent to injure

Section 16 of the 1968 Act states that it is a serious offence, punishable by life imprisonment, for any person to possess any firearm or ammunition with intent to endanger life, or enable any other person to do so, whether any injury has been caused or not. However, possession with intent that another person should by means of the firearm or ammunition endanger life means more than merely making those objects available to known criminals who could, or might, endanger life. If criminals are found in a post office in possession of firearms, that is some evidence to suggest an intention to endanger life. If they produce the firearms in the course of a robbery the inference becomes compelling. A person who carries a firearm for another, intending to hand it to him should it be needed, commits this offence.

It has been held not to be an offence contrary to this section to possess a firearm with intent to endanger one's own life.

Section 16A creates offences which are committed by a person who has in his possession any firearm or imitation firearm with intent by means thereof, or to enable any other person by means thereof, to cause any person to believe that unlawful violence will be used against him or another. These offences are punishable by 10 years' imprisonment.

Use of firearm to resist arrest

It is an offence contrary to s 17(1) to use or attempt to use a firearm or imitation firearm with intent to resist or prevent the lawful arrest or detention of oneself or any other person. It must be proved that the firearm was used intentionally for that purpose. It would not be sufficient if the firearm was used to prevent a search of premises where an arrest was not intended at that time.

To possess a firearm or imitation firearm at the time of arrest for, or when committing any offence mentioned in Schedule 1 of the Firearms Act 1968 is an offence against s 17(2) unless it can be shown that it was possessed for a lawful purpose. In the case of possession at the time of arrest for a specified offence, there is no requirement that it be proved that the defendant actually committed the specified offence. It is sufficient to prove possession when lawfully arrested for a specified offence. These offences include theft, robbery, burglary, blackmail, taking a conveyance, assaulting a constable in the execution of his duty, assaulting a prison custody officer or secure training centre custody officer, rape, abduction of women or children, offences of criminal damage, malicious woundings, assaults occasioning actual bodily harm and assaults with intent to resist arrest. The physical possession of the firearm is not essential. The Court of Appeal has said that the Act distinguishes between the concept of 'having a firearm with him' and 'having a firearm in his possession'. The circumstances which the Court had been considering involved an arrest of an accused for having an air rifle in his possession at the time of his arrest for a Schedule 1 offence where the weapon had been discovered in a nearby van.

For the purposes of both subsections of s 17, a 'firearm' does not include a component part or accessory. These offences are punishable by life imprisonment.

An imitation firearm is anything which has the appearance of being a firearm (other than for the discharge of noxious liquid, gas or other thing), whether or not it is capable of discharging any bullet, shot or other missile. An automatic pistol with the firing pin removed has been held to be an imitation firearm. On many occasions the circumstances of the use of an object will be important in establishing whether or not it was being used as an imitation firearm. A child's plastic gun may be clearly identifiable as such in daylight, but when used in a darkened room it may have the appearance of being a firearm.

Possession at the time of assaulting a prison custody officer at a contracted out prison is now also included under the provisions of the Criminal Justice Act 1991, s 90(2).

Carrying firearms with criminal intent

A person who has with him a firearm or imitation firearm with intent to commit an indictable offence, or to resist arrest, or to prevent the arrest of some other person, commits an offence against s 18. It is necessary to prove:

(a) possession of the firearm or imitation firearm;
(b) an intention to commit an indictable offence, or resist arrest, or prevent the arrest of some other person; and
(c) that he intended to have the firearm with him.

If the first two factors can be proved, it is evidence that he intended to have the weapon with him at the time of committing the indictable offence or of resisting or preventing the arrest. The accused must show that there is a reasonable doubt of his intention to have the firearm at the material time. It need not be proved that the accused had the firearm with him in order to further his criminal intent.

A person 'has a firearm with him' if it is readily available to him when he is committing a robbery. The emphasis should not be so much upon the exact distance between the criminals and the guns but rather on the accessibility of those guns judged in a common-sense way in the context of criminals embarking on a joint enterprise to commit an indictable offence.

This offence is punishable by life imprisonment.

Possession of firearm after conviction

Restriction are placed, by s 21 of the 1968 Act, upon the possession of any firearm or ammunition by a person who has been convicted of a crime and been sentenced to:

(a) custody for life, imprisonment or youth custody or detention in a young offenders' institution for 3 years of more; such a person is banned for life; or
(b) imprisonment or youth custody or detention in a young offenders' institution from 3 months to 3 years; or who has been subject to a secure training order, such a person is banned for 5 years.

For these purposes, suspended sentences are discounted unless they are actually served at a later date. This is an arrestable offence.

An air rifle which is shown to be in working order at the time is a firearm for these purposes. Evidence that the rifle is barrelled and working normally fully justifies a court in making an inference that the weapon was 'lethal' and therefore a firearm for these purposes.

Converting a firearm or shortening the barrel of a shotgun

It is an offence for anyone other than a registered firearms dealer to convert into a firearm anything which, though having the appearance of a firearm, cannot discharge a missile through its barrel.

It is an offence to shorten the barrel of a shotgun or any smooth-bore gun to which s 1 of the 1968 Act applies (other than one which has a bore exceeding two inches in diameter) to a length of less than 24 inches. It is not an offence in either case for a firearms dealer to shorten a barrel for the sole purpose of replacing a defective part so as to produce a barrel not less than 24 inches in length. These are arrestable offences.

Indecent language, exposure and telephone calls

Indecent language

Although the use of language which borders upon the obscene has become almost socially acceptable in our modern society, mainly owing to its use within the mass media, some control is still exercised by the Town Police Clauses Act 1847. Since the passing of the Local Government Act 1972, the provisions of this Act apply generally throughout England and Wales, although there are certain administrative exceptions (e.g. licensing of Hackney carriages, and some other provisions do not apply in London). However, this is probably now of little significance to police officers, as the persons who are found to be using obscene language in places in which use is likely to offend other people, use it in conjunction with other forms of antisocial behaviour while under the influence of drink, and are arrested for being drunk and disorderly. In such circumstances, evidence of the obscene language used is usually given to the magistrates as supporting evidence of their disorderly conduct. Other offences contrary to the Public Order Act 1986 may also be considered, depending upon the circumstances and the place in which the conduct occurs.

Section 28 of the Town Police Clauses Act 1847 lists various street nuisances which may be committed to the annoyance of residents or passengers in a street. For the purpose of this section, the term 'street' includes any road, square, court, alley, thoroughfare or public passage, and a street will be taken to include the carriageway and the footway at its sides. The offence must be committed in the street, but as the annoyance may be to 'residents', it may include the occupiers of houses in that street, although they are not in the street itself at the time.

One of the offences listed is that committed by any person who uses any profane or obscene language or sings any profane or obscene song or ballad in any street, including any place to which the public have a right of access, and any place of public resort, or unfenced ground adjoining a street, to the annoyance of residents or passengers. In the event of action being taken for this offence it is essential that evidence of such annoyance should be given to the court, and it is advisable to secure witnesses who will give evidence to the effect that they were annoyed by this conduct. The terms 'obscene' and 'profane' should be given their ordinary meanings, things 'obscene' being those which are disgusting, filthy, offensive or repulsive and those 'profane' being disrespectful, irreverent, impious or blasphemous. The current trend towards acceptance of many terms which the society of 1847 would not have tolerated should be recognised as it is undesirable that police officers should be seen to interpret things which are offensive in an over-formal manner. The essence of the offence is the annoyance which is caused to residents or passengers and this should either be very apparent or be the subject of a complaint.

Indecent exposure – Vagrancy Act 1824

Section 4 of the Vagrancy Act 1824 as amended states that every person who wilfully, openly, lewdly and obscenely exposes his person with intent to insult any female commits an offence. This offence is one which can only be committed by a male, and the inclusion of the word 'openly' means that the act is done without concealment. It can be committed in any place, whether in public or in private, and the word 'person' means 'penis'. The inclusion of the word 'wilful' in the offence is provided to distinguish those exposures which are not committed deliberately.

Complaints are frequently received from women who have been subjected to this form of conduct on more than one occasion, particularly when the offence is alleged to have been committed by a man living nearby who may expose himself in front of a window or while in his garden. In such circumstances the complainant may give evidence of other occasions upon which exposures have taken place for the purpose of showing that she was not mistaken in her identification of the man, and that the act was wilful and carried out with intent to insult her. In addition, if the accused gives evidence on his own behalf, he may be cross-examined as to whether he has exposed himself to the complainant on other occasions. Generally, evidence of exposure to other women on other occasions is not admissible unless they are acts committed nearby on the same occasions, tending to show a systematic course of conduct. In such cases the evidence must not be offered until a defence of accident, mistake or lack of intention to insult is raised.

Indecent exposure – Town Police Clauses Act 1847

It is an offence contrary to s 28 of the Town Police Clauses Act 1847 for any person wilfully and indecently to expose the person in a public place to the annoyance of residents or passengers. No intention to insult a female needs to be proved; the offence is complete if the exposure is to the annoyance of residents or passengers, and it can be committed by a male or female.

Police officers on specific duties to apprehend persons committing indecent acts are not 'passengers' within the meaning of this section.

Indecent exposure – common law

An offence of indecent exposure also exists at common law but such an offence is rarely charged as, like all such common law nuisances, it is only triable on indictment. Occasions may arise in which no other offence can be charged. The exposure may not have been in a 'street' or done with intent to insult a female. In such circumstances no offence may be charged other than that at common law. Such a charge should allege that the accused unlawfully, wilfully and publicly exposed his naked person.

For an exposure to be public for the purposes of common law, it must be to more than one member of the public. It need not necessarily occur in a public place; it is sufficient if it is made where a number of persons may be offended by it and a number see it. However, the common law offence cannot be committed in a place to which the public have *no* access, for example a private dwelling, even though the exposure may be to more than one person. The common law does not require that the act of indecency disgusted or annoyed anyone; the offence is indictable as a nuisance. It has been held to be an indictable offence for a man to undress himself on the beach and to bathe in the sea near inhabited houses from which he might be distinctly seen. Perhaps the greatest ever common law example of exposure which constituted an indictable nuisance occurred in 1663 when a man appeared naked on a balcony in Covent Garden before a huge assembly below. Today we have the streakers!

'Peeping Toms'

This term is used to describe those individuals who gain pleasure from watching others undress or make love. It is not an offence contrary to any statute to do so, but such conduct may lead to a breach of the peace in the event of discovery. Although a power to arrest without warrant exists at common law where such a breach is imminent, it should seldom be necessary to exercise it. Proceedings should normally be by way of complaint with a view to binding over.

Indecent telephone calls and messages

The incidence of complaints concerning offensive telephone calls is increasing, and this can prove to be one of the most difficult offences to detect. Section 43 Telecommunications Act 1984 states that any person who sends, by means of a public telecommunication service, a message or other matter that is grossly offensive or of an indecent, obscene or menacing character shall be guilty of an offence. If indecent telephone calls are frequently received by a particular woman, it is sometimes only possible to trace the offender if she is willing to engage the speaker in conversation for a sufficient length of time to allow the call to be traced, although at times it may be possible to 'fix' a caller, following the completion of a call. This offence is a 'penalty offence' for the purposes of Part I of the Criminal Justice and Police Act 2001 and may be dealt with under a fixed-penalty procedure; see page 478.

By previous arrangement with the telephone exchange supervisor, it is possible to arrange for all calls to be intercepted for a period of time, either with a view to tracing the call while the caller is engaged in conversation or, alternatively, to prevent nuisance calls from being connected to the complainant's number. It is frequently possible to keep such persons engaged in conversation for some time as they derive considerable pleasure from these conversations. In many cases, the complainant is more concerned about the prevention of further indecent calls, which invariably cease when the caller finds that the exchange supervisor is intercepting the calls. However, new procedures being introduced by the telecommunications industry can lead to a quick identification of the source of the call.

The Malicious Communications Act 1988 makes it an offence for any person to send to another person:

(a) a letter, electronic communication or article of any description which conveys
  (i) a message which is indecent or grossly offensive;
  (ii) a threat; or
  (iii) information which is false and known or believed to be false by the sender; or
(b) any other article or electronic communication which is wholly or partly of an indecent or grossly offensive nature,

if his purpose or one of his purposes in sending it is that the message, threat or information should cause distress or anxiety to the recipient or to any other person to whom he intends that it, or its content or nature, should be communicated.

In relation to the sending of a threat, a defence exists if the threat is to reinforce a demand made by him on reasonable grounds and he believed and had reasonable grounds for believing that it was a proper means of reinforcing the demand.

For the purposes of the Act, the term 'electronic communication' includes any oral or other communication by means of a telecommunication system and any communication (however sent) that is in electronic form.

Where a man made hundreds of indecent telephone calls to 13 women over a period of 5½ years, he was convicted of the common law offence of causing a public nuisance. The Court of Appeal said that it was necessary to look at the cumulative effect of the calls which materially affected the reasonable comfort and convenience of a class of the Queen's subjects. However, a large number of calls made to only one person cannot amount to a public nuisance as they do not affect the 'public' in that they are directed to only one person.

Indecent assault

Introduction

The Sexual Offences Act 1956, s 14, states that it is an offence for a person to make an indecent assault on a woman. An indecent assault is an assault which in itself, or taken in conjunction with the surrounding circumstances, is capable of being considered an indecent assault by right-minded people. Section 15 of the 1956 Act makes it an offence for any person to make an indecent assault on a man.

The elements of an indecent assault

The assault itself

An indecent assault involves the use of, or threats to use, any physical force to commit a sexual act. As can be seen from the provisions of the Sexual Offences Act 1956, it does not matter whether the person assaulted is a male or female, or whether the person committing the assault is male or female. It is as clearly an offence for a woman to commit an indecent assault upon a man as it is for the opposite to occur.

The points to prove

It is necessary to prove two essential points: first, that there has been an assault (the use or threat of use of physical force upon another), and second, that the assault was accompanied by circumstances of indecency. In this way, kissing a girl against her will, accompanied by a suggestion either by words or actions that sexual activity should take place, is an indecent assault as the suggestion itself amounts to circumstances of indecency and the forcible kissing is an assault. Similarly, a man was convicted of an indecent assault when he moved towards a woman with his person exposed, inviting her to have intercourse with him. Here there was a threat to use force, accompanied by indecent circumstances. However, in most cases of indecent assault, the circumstances will be straightforward, involving some form of indecent physical contact.

The prosecution should seek to prove that the defendant intended to lay hands on his victim without her consent in circumstances of indecency. As it is necessary for a woman to have been touched, or put in fear of being immediately touched, an invitation to her to touch the accused person indecently can never be an indecent assault. Thus, where a man is sitting still in a chair with his penis exposed and invites a woman to touch it there is no indecent assault at that stage as he has done nothing to put the woman in fear of immediate bodily contact. There was, therefore, no assault. In the same way where a man exposed his penis to a 9-year-old girl and invited her to touch it, there was no indecent assault as he had made no move towards her. It would be different if the man then took hold of the girl's hand and placed it upon his penis, as he would then have carried out an assault which, combined with the indecency, would become an indecent assault.

On most occasions the assault is indecent in itself and the basic intent sufficient to establish assault is enough. If a man walks up to a woman and places his hand on her breast, both the assault and the circumstances of indecency are direct and apparent. However, if this occurred on a crowded underground train, the circumstances would be such that they would be capable of an innocent, as well as an indecent, interpretation.

Similarly, a man may spank a girl, which amounts to an assault if the spanking was not permitted by law in the particular circumstances, but if he did so because it gave him sexual satisfaction, it could be an indecent assault and evidence of his admission that sexual satisfaction was derived would be admissible. The test of indecency is that there has been a contravention of the standards of decent behaviour in the minds of right-thinking members of society.

Similar considerations apply to assaults committed upon a male. Where a youth was grabbed and forced to masturbate into a condom, there was an indecent assault. The assault was intentional, the circumstances were indecent and there was an intention to commit an assault of that nature. Where a woman induces a boy under 16 to have intercourse with her there will be no indecent assault if she merely permits the act to take place and does not assault the boy in any way. However, if she handles his penis at any time, that will be an indecent assault as consent cannot be given by the boy.

Where an act is committed which amounts to an indecent assault, a defence based upon a submission that the person carrying out the act was too drunk to form the necessary intent cannot succeed.

Consent

If consent is given to the acts which take place then the actions cannot be an assault as an essential element of any assault is lack of consent, with the exception that the Sexual Offences Act 1956 states that if the person assaulted is under 16 years of age, consent is no defence. It is apparent that the legislators intended to offer full protection to persons under the age of 16 years, while still of such an age that they may give consent without fully appreciating the significance of doing so. There must, however, be an assault and the girl must, therefore, have been touched or put in fear. The House of Lords has ruled that where a person is charged with committing an indecent assault upon a girl under the age of 16, the prosecution must establish that, that at the time of the incident, the defendant did not have a genuine belief that the girl was 16 or over. The House said that *mens rea* was not expressly excluded from this offence by statute and therefore must be shown to have existed. This overruled a decision of the Court of Appeal to the effect that there was no such defence available in these circumstances. The House was bound to make this decision in view of a similar ruling which it made in relation to offences of gross indecency with children. The Court of Appeal has since held that this applies equally in the case of an indecent assault on a boy under the age of 16.

A reasonable belief that a girl under 16 is his wife, having gone through a form of marriage, is a defence.

The consent given by a woman of any age must be a true consent, and if the consent is obtained in circumstances involving force or fraud, the act will still amount to an indecent assault. Where an indecent assault occurred under the pretext of a medical operation (which it was not), the man concerned was convicted of an indecent assault. A man may be guilty of an indecent assault upon his wife by causing her to indulge in acts which she finds to be indecent, repellent or abhorrent.

Evidence

The Youth Justice and Criminal Evidence Act 1999 makes extensive provisions in relation to the competence of witnesses, for the protection of child witnesses and the victims of offences involving violence and provides a number of special measures to be taken. These are set out on page 110.

If the person assaulted is a child under 14, his evidence in criminal proceedings shall be given unsworn, and a deposition of such a child's unsworn evidence may be taken for the purpose of criminal proceedings as if that evidence had been given on oath. The question of the competence of the child to give evidence is one to be considered by the court. The Criminal Justice and Public Order Act 1994, abolished the common law duty to give a direction to a jury to the effect that corroboration is required in relation to such sexual offences. Nor need magistrates direct themselves in a similar way. However, perhaps more particularly than in other cases, corroborative evidence will be of value otherwise the issue devolves to evidence of one person against that of another.

Anonymity of complainant

The Sexual Offences (Amendment) Act 1992, s 1, makes provision for the anonymity of complainants in cases of indecent assault. Where an *allegation* has been made that such an offence has been committed, no matter relating to the person shall during that person's lifetime be included in any publication if it is likely to lead members of the public to identify that person as the person against whom the offence is alleged to have been committed. Section 2 of the Act makes similar provisions in the case where a person *has been accused* of such an offence, in relation to the person against whom the offence is alleged to have been committed.

A trial judge has the power to set aside these provisions on an application being made by an accused, if it is necessary to induce persons to come forward as witnesses and that the accused's defence is likely to be substantially prejudiced if such a direction is not given.

Police powers

Indecent assault is an arrestable offence.

Railways

Introduction

The various laws concerned with our railway network in particular have been passed at different times and with different aims and objectives. Some regulate the running of the railway system while others are concerned with the comfort and protection of the travelling public. On occasions specific responsibility for the enforcement of laws protecting railway property and railway practices is given to bodies other than the police forces of England and Wales. A number of Acts authorise the appointment of railway constables. The British Transport Police are responsible for the protection of railway property and the enforcement of legislation which is particularly concerned with the railway system. However, it is only in instances in which particular enforcement problems are of such a nature that they are obviously the concern of the railways that the power to act tends to be restricted to constables of the British Transport Police and, on occasions, to employers of the railway authorities in addition.

Railways pass through the areas of all police forces and on occasions there are miles of railway tracks within a force area. The officers of the British Transport Police tend to be rather thinly spread and they will not always be available, or available in sufficient numbers, to deal with incidents which arise. The football special passing through the area of a police force may present problems throughout its journey, and wherever it may halt, as it progresses through that journey. Damage to the track, the throwing of missiles and trespass upon dangerous sections of the track are all matters which are likely to be reported to any police officer. However, it is only in instances in which particular enforcement problems are of such a nature that they are obviously the concern of the railways that the power to act tends to be restricted to constables of the British Transport Police, and, on occasions, to employees of the railway authorities in addition.

Powers of entry

A constable may enter and remain on railway property to protect life and property and to prosecute offenders. Most offences which occur on railway property are offences in respect of which constables have the power of enforcement. The only exceptions to the general rule that constables may take action for all offences are where powers of enforcement are specially given to some other body. Some Acts dealing with railways restrict enforcement to railway personnel but generally, these offences are of significance to the British Railways Board only. Some forms of trespass and some ticket offences related to production, etc., are restricted in this way.

Trespass on railway property

The British Transport Commission Act 1949, s 55, creates an offence of trespass upon any of the lines of a railway or siding, or in any tunnel or upon any railway embankment, cutting or similar work, or in dangerous proximity to any railway lines or to any electrical apparatus used for or in connection with the working of a railway. No person may be convicted of this offence unless it is proved that public warning has been given to persons not to trespass upon the railway by a notice fixed at the nearest railway station to the point at which the trespass occurred. That notice must be clear and not obliterated or destroyed.

This is a 'penalty offence' for the purposes of Part I of the Criminal Justice and Police Act 2001 and may be dealt with under a fixed-penalty procedure; see page 478.

Police powers

Police officers have a duty to prevent the dangers caused by foolish trespass upon railway property. It should be remembered, however, that the notice must be shown to have been displayed properly before this offence can be committed, although the effect of such a notice upon a trespasser who may be some miles from the station is likely to be limited.

Trespass and refusal to quit

The Railway Regulation Act 1840, s 16, states that it is an offence for a person wilfully to trespass upon any railway, or any of the stations or other works, or premises connected with a railway and to refuse to quit when so requested by an officer or agent of the company. The word 'railway' in this section extends to all railways, constructed under any Act of Parliament, which are intended for the conveyance of passengers. There is no necessity to prove that notices are in place. Constables, other than those of the British Transport Police, are not officers or agents of the railways.

A trespasser is a person who has entered upon or who remains upon land or property without lawful authority.

Causing danger or obstruction – with intent

There are two almost parallel offences created by the Offences Against the Person Act 1861, s 32, and the Malicious Damage Act 1861, s 35. In common the two Acts deal with persons who unlawfully and maliciously commit certain acts, that is, the placing of any obstruction on any part of the railway, the moving of points or similar fittings or machinery, the showing of a false signal or the concealment of a real signal or carrying out any other act with certain intents. The Offences Against the Person Act is concerned with such acts being carried out with intent to endanger the safety of any person travelling or being on the railway. This is reasonable; that Act is concerned with protecting people from injury. If the actions are carried out with the intention of obstructing, upsetting or overthrowing, injuring or destroying any engine, tender, carriage or truck which is using the railway, then the offence contrary to the Malicious Damage Act is committed.

The word 'malicious' can extend to acts done in sport and mischievously with a view to obstruct.

Both of these offences are arrestable offences. It will be a question of proof of actual intention in deciding which of the offences should be preferred. If such an act is carried out with the intention of derailing a train, it is obvious that there must be some intention to damage parts of the train. The additional question of intention to harm passengers will have to be considered before an offence contrary to the Offences Against the Person Act can be considered in the particular circumstances of each case.

Causing danger or obstruction – no intent

It will be appreciated that there will be occasions in which it is impossible in the circumstances to prove a particular intention either to endanger passengers or to damage any part of a train. The reference to 'malice' is removed from the offences which we have already considered above, as is the reference to particular intentions. In all other respects the offences are the same. They are committed by persons who by any unlawful act, or by any wilful omission or neglect (in the case of the offence committed contrary to the Offences Against the Person Act 1861, s 34), do such acts and as a result endanger, or cause to be endangered, the safety of any person conveyed or being in or upon a railway, or aid or assist any such act, etc. In the case of the Malicious Damage Act 1861, s 36, the act or acts must lead to the obstruction of an engine or carriage using the railway. There is one essential difference between these two offences. In the case of the offence of endangering, etc., the placing of the obstruction wilfully, in such way that potential danger is caused, even if that danger is removed by another person, is sufficient. The offence under the Malicious Damage Act requires that an obstruction is actually caused.

These are lesser offences because of the absence of malice and particular intentions and are only punishable by 2 years' imprisonment. They are not arrestable offences.

Throwing objects

In addition, the Offences Against the Person Act 1961, s 33, deals specifically with particular offences of throwing objects at trains. It is an offence unlawfully and maliciously to throw, or cause to fall, or strike at, against, into, or upon any engine, tender, carriage or truck used upon any railway, any wood, stone or other matter or thing with intent to injure or endanger the safety of any person being in or upon such vehicles. This is an arrestable offence punishable by imprisonment for life.

For the purposes of this section an act can be malicious even if it is carried out in sport and mischievously with a view to obstruct.

Although this offence deals with 'stone throwing' in a particular way, acts done which involve throwing missiles may also be punishable under the provisions which we have examined above. The fact that a specific intent need not be proved increases the usefulness of the offences previously discussed. An offence against the British Transport Commission Act 1949, s 56 (throwing stones, etc., at trains or other things on railways), is a 'penalty offence' for the purposes of Part I of the Criminal Justice and Police Act 2001 and may be dealt with under a fixed-penalty procedure; see page 462.

Interviewing railway staff

In normal circumstances, police officers should not attempt to interview such persons as signalmen, guards or look-outs whilst they are carrying out their duties unless the matter is extremely urgent, when arrangements should be made with a supervisor to have such person relieved. It is advisable not to enter a signal box unless extreme danger exists and it is essential to warn the signalman of it.

However, police officers must bear in mind their responsibilities under the Transport and Works Act 1992 in relation to such key railway personnel carrying out their duties when unfit through drink or drugs, or having consumed alcohol in excess of the prescribed limit; see page 462.

Bodies on railway lines

Bodies should be removed from railway lines as soon as possible, unless it is suspected that a crime has been committed. Where a crime is not suspected a police officer should not require that a body be left in position and if photographs are required, perhaps to assist a coroner, the photographs of the body should be taken after it has been removed from the track.

How to give evidence

Introduction

A police officer giving evidence before a court is expected to be a professional witness. It is part of his occupation to be a trained observer, to note facts and to be able to present those facts to a court correctly, impartially and respectfully. The police officer's conduct while in the witness box must be of the highest order and be an example to others who may follow. To assist in attaining this ideal, a police officer should constantly be aware of the importance of the following points.

Appearance

A police officer must look the part, particularly when giving evidence. The officer's bearing and appearance should always reflect the status of the profession which he represents. A police officer is usually required to attend court in uniform unless employed on plain clothes duties.

Punctuality

Not only must a police officer be punctual in attending court, he must ensure that sufficient time is left to ensure that the witnesses for the prosecution are present and that details of any expenses they have incurred are known to the prosecutor so that, in the event of a conviction, the prosecutor may inform the court so that the court may assess costs. A police officer should also be available before the court for consultation with the prosecutor, should this be required.

Witness – exhibits

It is the responsibility of the police officer in the case to ensure that all the witnesses are present. He must inform the prosecutor in the event of a witness not turning up as it may be necessary to apply to the court for an adjournment of the hearing. It is also the officer's responsibility to ensure that all of the exhibits, properly labelled, are present in court.

Place in court

Unless otherwise instructed, the police officer in charge of a case should be present in court before the hearing begins. In the event of a 'not guilty' plea, witnesses will be asked to leave the courtroom and will be called to give their evidence separately.

Evidence

An officer's evidence is concerned with facts within his knowledge. He saw something, said something, heard something said by the defendant, or perhaps did something. These events should be described naturally and not recited in an artificial manner. The pocket notebook may be referred to with the permission of the court but should not be used as a basis for recitation.

Swearing witnesses

Most witnesses giving evidence before a court take the oath or make an affirmation. As a general principle, the oath may be administered in such a form or made as accords with the religion of the witness. Christians are sworn on the New Testament, Jews on the Old Testament and with the head covered if the witness so wishes, Muslims on the Koran and others according to the form prescribed by their particular religion. When it is not reasonably practicable to administer an oath in the manner prescribed by the religion of a witness, he may be permitted to affirm. Similarly, where a person objects to being sworn and states, as the grounds of such objection, that he has no religious belief or that the taking of an oath is contrary to his religious belief, he shall be permitted to make an affirmation and this shall have the same effect as if he had taken an oath.

Form of oath

The form of oath taken in an adult court is as follows:

> I swear by Almighty God that the evidence I give shall be the truth, the whole truth, and nothing but the truth.

In relation to juveniles, the beginning of the oath is changed slightly to read 'I promise before Almighty God'.

Giving evidence

A police officer called to give evidence should enter the witness box, raise the Testament in his right hand and give the oath in a clear voice. He should identify himself to court by giving his name, rank, number, force and the station at which he serves. He should then address the court and give his evidence in a clear voice which can be heard by the court. As far as possible he should give his evidence from memory, referring to his notebook only when necessary to refresh his memory. A witness may refresh his memory by reference to any writing made or verified by himself which is made contemporaneously with the facts about which he is testifying. In this respect, 'contemporaneously' means made or verified at a time when the facts were still fresh in the mind of the witness. The Divisional Court has held that a record made of a conversation which took place 2 hours after it occurred was made 'contemporaneously', where throughout that period the officer had been dealing with a person arrested for the offence with which the person concerned was subsequently charged with aiding and abetting. Being constantly involved with the circumstances of the offence, the court considered that the events which were then recorded must have been fresh in the officer's mind.

When giving evidence a police officer should speak to the magistrates or, in the case of an indictable offence at the Crown Court, the judge and jury. Having completed his evidence he should remain in the witness box to answer any questions the prosecutor may wish to put to him and for the defence to cross-examine him on the evidence he has given to the court. When answering questions put to him in cross-examination, he should face the person asking the question; if he is in doubt about the question, he should ask for it to be repeated. Any answer given should be made to the magistrates or, in the case of the Crown Court, to the judge and jury. A police officer should beware of getting involved in an argument with the defence. Any question asked should be answered to the extent of a police officer's knowledge, and if the officer does not know the answer he should not be afraid to say so. Similarly, if the answer is favourable to the accused it must be given, as the police officer has a duty to serve the court. When answering a question, a police officer should not enlarge on his answer but should confine himself to the answer required.

When a police officer has completed his evidence and has been cross-examined by the defence and re-examined by the prosecution when necessary, he should leave the witness box but remain in the court unless, for some special reason, the court permits him to be released before the end of the hearing.

The officer in charge of a case is responsible for the civilian witnesses who have been called to give evidence. The result of a hearing frequently depends upon the evidence of an independent witness, and if such a witness is neglected and left to fend for himself at court, he will not willingly attend court to give evidence on any further occasion. Nor will he have formed a good opinion of British justice, or the police service. The success of our system of policing is entirely dependent upon the full co-operation of the public. Every police officer bears a heavy burden of responsibility in ensuring that the image of the service does not become tarnished.

There are certain forms of address which a police officer giving evidence in court will be expected to use. Magistrates should be addressed as 'Your Worships', a district judge as 'Your Honour' and a High Court judge as 'My Lord'.

Crime prevention

Introduction

The prevention of crime, in the widest sense, requires the co-operation of many elements in society – parents, schools, churches, the probation service, youth clubs and youth leaders, voluntary organisations, the prison service, the police and many others – all of whom have their part to play in ensuring that crime is not made easy and that people are discouraged from embarking on a life of crime.

The prevention of crime has always been one of the primary functions of the police; all officers have a general responsibility in this field. The following extract from *Instructions to Constables* by Charles Rowan, the first Commissioner of Police of the Metropolis, clearly illustrates this point:

> It should be understood, at the outset, that the principal object to be attained is the Prevention of Crime. To this great end, every effort of the Police is to be directed. The security of person and property, the preservation of the public tranquillity, and all the other objects of a Police Establishment, will thus be better effected, than by the detection and punishment of the offender, after he has succeeded in committing the crime. This should constantly be kept in mind by every member of the Police Force, as the guide for his own conduct. Officers and Police Constables should endeavour to distinguish themselves by such vigilance and activity as may render it extremely difficult for any one to commit a crime within the portion of the town under their charge.

Crime prevention officers

Crime prevention is the anticipation, recognition and appraisal of a crime risk and the initiation of action to remove or reduce it. It has now been recognised as an integral and important part of all police work, and every force has a crime prevention department the members of which make a special study of this field. A Home Office Committee on the Prevention and Detection of Crime considered that the duties of a crime prevention officer should include:

(a) the cultivation of a two-way relationship between beat and patrol officers and the crime prevention officer, and encouragement of beat constables to report matters of crime prevention interest;

(b) the collection, co-ordination and dissemination of crime prevention information on current trends of crime;

(c) the acquiring of a thorough knowledge of technical aids to security, by study of appropriate journals and visits to manufacturers of locks, safes, etc.;

(d) the inspection of property where there are special or difficult security features and the keeping of records of such visits to enable follow-up visits to be made at appropriate times;

(e) maintaining a firm relationship with local bank managers, local authorities and all other bodies to whom advice can be given on crime prevention;

(f) the giving of talks, whenever the opportunity arises, to local bodies on crime prevention;

(g) ensuring that crime prevention literature is used to its best effect and displayed or distributed on all appropriate occasions; the crime prevention officer should always have available a collection of locks and, possibly, burglar alarms for selective display;

(h) the regular giving of lectures at probationer and refresher courses and the issue of a crime prevention booklet for the guidance of all members of all the force;

(i) the co-operation and liaison with children where the force operates a Juvenile Liaison Scheme, with the fire service to ensure that security standards do not conflict with fire safety precautions, with night watchmen in those parts of the country where Mutual Aid Schemes involving night watchmen have been introduced and with burglar alarm companies on matters in respect of the installation of alarms; and

(j) giving advice on security to builders and architects in the planning stages of buildings and, if necessary, to survey premises from plans.

This is a very comprehensive brief for a crime prevention officer and it is essential that all police officers assist in this area of police work. The bulk of the day-to-day crime prevention work inevitably and rightly falls to the operational uniformed police officer; his very presence on patrol is the best deterrent against crime, and any police officer should take every opportunity to give advice and assistance on prevention of crime matters to householders, vehicle owners, car park attendants and other persons with whom a police officer comes into daily contact.

Most crimes are committed because an opportunity suddenly presents itself; few are carefully planned. The eradication of such opportunities is an essential part of a police officer's duties.

Motor vehicles, premises and handbags

Thefts of motor vehicles and theft of property from parked and unattended motor vehicles are common and police officers should advise drivers and owners of motor vehicles to take the following basic steps to minimise the risk of such offences:

(a) Never leave the ignition keys of a parked vehicle in the ignition switch, no matter how brief the time which the driver is likely to be absent from the vehicle.

(b) Never leave expensive articles lying on the seats or back window ledge of the vehicle. If it is not possible or convenient to remove such articles from the vehicle, the property should be placed in the boot of the vehicle, which should be locked.

(c) Never leave motor vehicle unlocked; a determined thief can start a vehicle in seconds if he can gain access to the vehicle quickly and quietly.

(d) The drivers of goods vehicles carrying valuable loads should be advised to park their vehicles off the road during an overnight stay, preferably in a lorry park if available.

(e) Advise drivers of motor vehicles to consider fitting an anti-thief device to their vehicles. Should they wish further details, the crime prevention officer will supply details of the various devices available.

Officers should also check the security of business premises to see if they have been left insecure and should offer advice to women who leave handbags or purses on top of shopping bags, or in perambulators, in crowded places.

Buildings

A patrolling beat officer will often see examples of people's carelessness towards their own property, e.g. notes left for the milkman or tradesman and newspapers or bottles of milk left on the doorstep, all of which indicate to a thief that the occupiers are absent and the house empty. Ladders left in easily accessible places and insecure garage doors make entry into premises and the theft of property a simple matter. A word with the householder will correct such carelessness.

When a person is going away on holiday and seeks advice on the security of the house in his absence, he should be advised to leave a key to the house with a trustworthy neighbour, to take any valuables to the bank, to cancel deliveries of bread, milk and newspapers, to leave curtains undrawn and to leave details at the local police station of the period of absence, and the name and address of the person with whom the key has been left.

If a beat officer is asked for advice on the security of shops or business premises, he should refer the person to the crime prevention officer, whose specialised knowledge will assist. Often a police officer summoned to the scene of a crime will notice that the premises lack security, and in such cases the owners should be advised to contact the local crime prevention officer, who would be only too willing to advise on appropriate security measures. Whether or not the owner follows up this advice, the officer should notify the crime prevention officer of his findings so that he can follow up by visiting the premises himself.

The locks fitted to many dwelling houses and business premises are inadequate. Deadlocks and security catches fitted to windows make it much more difficult for a thief. If such devices are fitted to buildings and, in addition, security lights are installed, it is more likely that a thief will seek an easier target. All householders can use approved marker pens to mark valuable property invisibly. This is best done by marking property with the post code followed by the number of the house. Householders should be advised that it is important to check after a period of time that such marks are still distinguishable.

'Neighbourhood Watch' schemes can play a significant part in efforts to reduce crime, and should be encouraged. The more eyes which are tuned to recognition of the unusual, the more likely the prevention of crime becomes. In addition, those crimes which are committed are much more likely to be detected if public co-operation is encouraged. The success of the various 'crime watch' programmes provided by TV broadcasters gives evidence of the value of full co-operation in every respect.

Local knowledge

A good knowledge of the locality and its residents will always assist a constable in efforts to prevent crime. He should make it his business to know the current crime trends in the area and the most vulnerable premises such as banks, jewellers, lock-up premises and building sites. Such knowledge will enable him to concentrate his efforts and time to the best advantage. It is useful to have knowledge of wanted and suspected persons and any persons believed to be actively engaged in crime in his area. The local intelligence officer will have photographs of convicted criminals.

The provisions of the Crime and Disorder Act 1998

The provisions included within the Crime and Disorder Act 1998 which provide for child curfew schemes, child safety orders and parenting orders represent measures which have been taken to prevent crime and nuisance.

Stage 3

Crime reporting and the *modus operandi* system

The modus operandi *system*

Criminals frequently follow a general pattern of actions when committing crime. If it can be said that crimes have a 'personality' then it is because individual criminals, by the method which they follow, give their crimes noticeable characteristics. The criminal's methods of working is known as the *modus operandi* or MO.

If care is taken when a crime is committed, all of the usual forms of identification of the criminal can be avoided. By wearing gloves a criminal will avoid leaving fingerprints, and by carefully selecting a form of dress will to some degree eliminate fabric traces left at the scene. A mask may make personal identification less likely and if care is taken when disposing of identifiable property, or the stealing identifiable property is avoided, the thief has considerably lessened the chance of being arrested. It is much more difficult to avoid acting in a way which is natural to the individual and, upon this human factor, the strength of the MO system stands. The system tabulates information and the description of known criminals and the pattern of their actions and methods in committing crime. If the MO is correctly reported when a crime is committed, these methods can be compared with similar methods recorded in the system. Suspects can thus be identified and this may limit the extent of the enquiry. It will be appreciated that the use of computers has made the 'matching' of such items of information much more effective.

Collection of information

In order to build up a picture of the criminal's usual method of going about a crime, it is necessary to record accurately details of each crime as it is reported. If a sneak thief is operating in your area and each offence is accurately reported upon by the investigating officer, it will soon become apparent to those who examine reports submitted through your force area that the same person is likely to be responsible for all crimes of this nature which are being committed. When the thief is eventually apprehended, it is then possible to clear up all offences which have been committed.

Much of the information required can be obtained by examination of the scene of the crime. For example, the method of entry in burglary offences can be established in this way, witnesses will be able to repeat the particular lie which was told to them by the confidence trickster, or the criminal, when arrested, may wish to tell you exactly how the crime was committed.

The 10 points of modus operandi

Details of crimes are entered in an index under each of 10 headings.

Classword

Under this heading is described the class of person or property attacked. The purpose of description is to make the person or property as individual as possible. A term such as 'dwelling house' is abstract and describes all forms of dwelling. The word 'bungalow', 'detached villa' or 'farm cottage' is more helpful.

Entry

The actual point of entry must be described. To use the word 'window' is helpful, but not as helpful as 'ground floor window at rear'.

Means

The method used by the criminal in effecting an entry should be explained. The criminal may have used a jemmy, a drill or bodily pressure in order to burst open the door. If entry has been effected through an upstairs window or via the roof, the approach to the point of entry should be described, for example, 'by scaling drainpipe'.

Object

Why did the criminal commit this crime? What was the motive? In instances of theft, it will be for personal gain; in sexual crimes, sexual satisfaction.

Time

The actual time at which the crime was committed will be reported elsewhere. The importance of this factor for the purposes of MO is the occasion, indicating the opportunity which presented itself to the thief, for example, market day, lunchtime (office thefts) or early closing day (afternoon burglaries in shops).

Style

This refers to the criminal's style of approach, alleged trade or profession and is, therefore, used in connection with offences involving deception. The bogus meter reader and alleged local authority rating officer provide examples of the types of person who adopt a 'style'.

Tale

This means the account which a criminal gives of himself and is associated with the previous point, 'style', being applicable to offences of deception. The man who is posing as a vicar will also have some ready account of the reason for being in the area and for approaching members of the public. This is the most important factor to be described in all offences involving an element of criminal deception.

Pal

If there has been more than one person involved in the commission of the crime, details of accomplices should be included. Some criminals prefer to work with accomplices, and this can be an important element in assisting to extract suspects from the index.

Transport

Was a vehicle used in connection with the crime? Tyre marks may have been found at the scene or it may be evident, because of the quantity of property which was removed from the attacked premises, that some form of transport was used. Motor vehicles are becoming an essential part of the equipment of criminals, whose range of activities has thus become extensive.

Trademarks

In the course of committing crime over a number of years, criminals establish their own methods of achieving their aims, which can frequently become second nature. The aggressive type will commit unnecessary damage; the perverted will commit various forms of nuisances on the floor of a room or on a bed; some develop tidy, methodical methods of searching a room for property; and others cannot resist leaving a note for the householder. In instances in which such methods are observed, experienced officers can frequently limit their enquiries to a small number of criminals who are known to act in such a way.

It is not possible on all occasions to complete all 10 points of MO. If the offence does not involve deception, it is unlikely that 'style' or 'tale' will be applicable; there may be no 'trademark', 'pal' or 'transport' involved and in such instances these points should be left blank.

Details of these factors will be recorded in the police officer's pocket notebook at the scene of the crime and transferred to the crime report when submitted.

Crime complaint

A crime complaint is the first written record of a complaint of crime. A crime complaint form must be completed as soon as possible after a report of crime is received, and crime complaint forms are kept at all police stations. Usually the crime complaint form is combined with the crime report form. Copies are self-carbonating. In many forces the records of crime are now contained within electronic storage systems and written methods of storage no longer exist. However, no matter how information is stored, it must first be obtained.

Information to the effect that a crime has been committed may reach police officers in a number of ways:

(a) by personal observation – the officer sees a crime being committed;
(b) by oral complaint at a police station;
(c) by oral complaint to a constable on the beat, or even at home;
(d) by telephone;
(e) by letter;
(f) while another crime is being investigated, information is received that further offences have been committed – for example, in fraud investigations, the examination of a firm's accounts;
(g) by admission – further offences admitted by a person in custody.

Whenever an allegation is made that a crime has been committed, an entry must be made in the crime complaint form (or within the electronic system) even if the police officer concerned doubts the authenticity of the complainant's story. If it subsequently becomes clear that no crime has been committed, a report is submitted to this effect, asking approval to have the entry endorsed 'No crime'.

Contents of a crime complaint

A completed crime complaint, however it is made, should contain:

(a) the nature of complaint (offence as reported);
(b) the time and date the report was received;
(c) the name and number of the police officer receiving the report;
(d) the full name and address of the person making the report;
(e) the action taken and by whom (who was informed and attended to the complaint and at what time);
(f) how report was received, e.g. '999' call.

Crime report

When an investigating police officer has visited a scene of a crime and has made preliminary, on-the-spot enquiries, he will submit a crime report (by whatever means are the order of the day within the force) which provides the details which form a permanent record of the crime. These details are:

(a) name and address of aggrieved person, date and place of birth, occupation and sex;
(b) place of offence and time and date committed;
(c) details of the offence (MO);
(d) injury to victim and type of weapon used (where appropriate);
(e) value of property stolen, recovered or damaged;
(f) property stolen which is identifiable, non-identifiable and any which is recovered;
(g) means of disposal of offence (is crime detected?; was no crime in fact committed?; or other means of disposal);
(h) officers who attended scene;
(i) report of investigating officer;
(j) person wanted for offence, or suspected of it;
(k) information circulated by telephone, bulletin, etc.;
(l) date upon which a supplementary crime report is to be submitted setting out details of further enquiries;
(m) when and by whom complainant informed of result of investigation.

The nature of the 'crime report' and its contents may vary according to the recording system operating within a police force. As in the case of crime complaints, many records are now stored electronically.

Police action

The strength of an investigation lies in the extent of the information gathered and the number of people who are contacted for information. The crime report includes full details of the offence, MO of the criminal and details of suspected and wanted persons. The likelihood of the offender being identified increases with the extent of the information which is gathered from witnesses or the complainant. The accurate completion of a crime report is extremely important as it may have to be referred to months or years after it was completed, when some person is in custody for similar offences. It is important that investigating officers keep the records of particular crimes up to date as reference may be made to those records years after the crime was committed.

Police officers must always ensure that a crime complaint is made out immediately upon a report of a crime being received. If enquiries quickly show that no crime has been committed, it is an easy matter to record that, in fact, no crime has been committed. The crime is, in effect, cancelled. Such action prevents allegations that police forces are 'shelving' crime.

It is extremely important that the complainant is informed of progress in the investigation of the offence. If no progress is made, it is equally important that the complainant is aware of the efforts being made by the police to discover those responsible for the offence. The time spent doing this is small; the gain is large.

Police National Computer

Introduction

The Police National Computer became operational in 1974. It has become known as PNC 2 and is now as essential a part of normal policing operations as the pocket notebook. Police officers on the beat can talk to their computer which is filled with information about vehicles, drivers and wanted, suspected or missing persons, etc. The computer does not sleep and it is available throughout each working day. It provides a reliable source of information but it can be a mistake to rely upon it completely. Computers can only provide the information with which they have been programmed. The vehicle which is being checked may be stolen even though the computer holds no record of it. It may not have been reported as stolen at the time of the check.

Computer terminals are available in every police force in England, Scotland and Wales. Terminals are available at force control rooms and frequently at divisional or area stations. Information can only be obtained from the computer directly. Contact control by personal radio or from any telephone or other internal communication system and the PNC 2 operator will make an instant check with the computer.

PNC 2 was established in 1991 and the system was extended to embrace the Phoenix enhancement to PNC names. QUEST (see page 604) assists in identifying offenders where there is no known name. It is based upon the physical characteristics of persons and the nature of offences.

Confidentiality

The information stored on the PNC is highly confidential and is for police use only. It must not be divulged to any unauthorised person or to another organisation. Disciplinary offences in consequence of improper disclosure of information may be committed by any police officer who provides information obtained from the computer to any external agency. In some cases, offences against the Data Protection Act 1984 may be committed.

Security

Most requests for information will come from a police officer on the beat who will use his personal radio. Although this system is not always secure, most operators at local controls are easily able to identify the voices of their fellow officers and security is easily maintained. However, requests received by telecom lines should be carefully vetted. Once again, if the enquiry is local it is probable that the voice of the caller will be recognised but the PNC operator will require the name, rank and station of the caller so that, if necessary, identity can be verified by means of a return call to a particular police station, before a reply is given. Force orders are always very specific in relation to the correct use of PNC 2 and it is essential that these are studied carefully, as failure to follow the correct procedure could result in a disciplinary offence.

Indexes

Information relating to different matters is stored in different indexes. In relation to vehicles, information is stored concerning owners, those vehicles listed as stolen or suspicious and chassis and engine numbers. Those concerned with persons include criminals, wanted and missing persons and drivers who are disqualified.

Owners' index

The details recorded on the vehicle owners' index are similar to those recorded by the Driver and Vehicle Licensing Agency (DVLA), Swansea. The DVLA computer is of a different type to PNC 2 and is basically designed to store information. The basis of these records is therefore stored in PNC 2 in a different way to permit quick and easy access. Its aim is to give an immediate response to an enquiry, even in relation to special searches when only the description of the vehicle is available, or only part of its registration number. The index contains the names and addresses of the current keepers of all motor vehicles registered in England, Scotland and Wales together with the descriptions of the vehicles. The Road Vehicles (Registration and Licensing) Regulations 2002 have provided for the incorporation of Northern Ireland vehicles into DVLA records.

Computer records are only as strong as the updating system. It must be remembered that not all changes of ownership are notified to DVLA. If they are not, then PNC 2 records cannot be updated and the name and address of the previous owner may be given. Whenever a police officer making an enquiry finds that a change has not been notified, apart from any other action which might be taken, a form V.79, which is concerned with incorrect information found on PNC 2, should be completed. Obviously, the computer does not contain details of foreign vehicles, military vehicles, trade plates or unregistered vehicles. Enquiries concerning the previous keepers of vehicles should be directed to DVLA on form VQ.1. DVLA will reply on form VQ.5.

Stolen and suspect vehicles' index

An index of vehicle registration marks (VRM) is maintained, listing those which are stolen, suspected or of interest to the police for any reason. This index has no relationship to the vehicle owners' index and any index mark may be included as the concern is with vehicles which are stolen or suspect. It therefore does not matter what type of plates they are carrying.

Property index

This contains details of parts of motor vehicles, their trailers, items of plant or equipment, boats, animals and firearms, which have either been stolen or obtained by means of deception. Marine engines which have been reported stolen or found are included in this index, which has become known as the property index because information is always recorded concerning identification marks.

'Plant' includes excavators, bulldozers, dumper trucks, road marking equipment and many other forms of plant. Engines belonging to such plant are also listed, as are motor vehicle engines generally by a system of 'interlink' with the stolen vehicle index. Details recorded are likely to be the manufacturer's number, fleet number, make, type, model, colour and engine capacity. The term 'trailers' embraces all but the small domestic trailer and it includes domestic caravans and sidecars. When checking records of articulated vehicles it is best to check the registered number of the drawing vehicle against the vehicles' index and to carry out a separate check on the property file in relation to the trailer. The property file should hold details of the manufacturer's number, fleet number, container number, ministry number, make, type, model and colour.

A record is maintained of valuable animals which have been in any way indelibly marked. This may be by tattoo, branding or microchip implant. It includes details of dogs, horses, cattle, sheep, pigs, goats, cats, etc., and the identity numbers, species, marker type, marker company and the colour of an animal will be recorded.

There is a separate 'marine' section which includes details of boats, marine engines, jet-skis, etc. Details of numbers of engines and other parts of such sailing craft are included.

The section dealing with firearms includes the make, model, type, calibre and serial number of real or imitation firearms. In providing the PNC with a firearm number, care should be taken to avoid providing the patent number rather than the individual firearm number.

To use this index, start with the serial number where it is known and otherwise give details such as make, type, model and colour as this will provide you with details of all similar items which are recorded. Searches of this file may be limited to force or regional areas.

With all enquiries the response may be that there is no trace of the vehicle on the records required to be searched, although this is highly unlikely in relation to searches of the vehicle owners' index. If the vehicle is recorded, then full information will be provided. Occasionally, the computer will not release information as the vehicle has been 'blocked' for particular reasons, which means that information will not be given over the air or by telephone.

Names index

This index contains the names and descriptive details of persons who have been convicted of crime or who are within the investigative process, that is from the moment of arrest, charge or report for summons, or who are wanted or missing or are disqualified drivers. Thus, it will tell you whether the person you have arrested is on bail for any other offence or is subject to any other form of curfew restriction. A name is required to initiate a search and identification is assisted if information is available concerning date of birth, sex, height, etc. The index contains the names of those persons with a Criminal Record Office (CRO) number in the United Kingdom. It also includes details of all aliases used by such persons, as well as details of personal characteristics such as manner of speech, way of walking, scars and marks and mode of dress. The PNC will also provide details of MO (the way in which that person usually commits offences) as well as a list of previous addresses and the names of known associates. It will also tell you where to find the most recent photograph of that person together with details of the last 10 photographs on record.

There are many other ways in which the PNC can assist. It will help you to get in touch with an officer who knows your suspect well; it will give you driving licence, passport and National Insurance numbers. Where you are interested in a particular person, you can place a 'bookmark' in the file which will alert other users to your interest in that person.

The updating of this index is carried out by means of updated information from Criminal Record Office. It is important to remember that the information given will draw attention to possible matches and can never be taken to be conclusive. It is the responsibility of the police officer making the enquiry to decide whether or not the person being checked is the person recorded in the index.

This index includes the names of persons wanted by the police, suspected of being involved in particular offences or whose whereabouts are to be established for particular reasons, missing persons, found persons, absconders, absentees and deserters from the armed forces and life licensees. It is essential that all police officers are aware of the need to keep this index up to date. If wanted persons are found and dealt with, or missing persons are located and their relatives have been informed, the records must be amended. The enquirers must provide as much information as possible to assist identification.

Up-to-date records are maintained of all persons disqualified from driving by order of a court.

Directory tables

The PNC contains the full postal addresses, telephone numbers, fax numbers and station and force codes of all police forces within England, Scotland, Wales and Northern Ireland police stations and also contains similar information in relation to courts. The force/station code identifies the originator of information contained on the PNC. A search for a police force by name will reveal the locations of all of the courts within that area. Endorsements on driving licences carry the code of the court which imposed the disqualification.

Warning signals

Additional information may be provided on occasions when an enquiry is made which may be of extreme importance. The person about whom the enquiry is made may prove to be wanted, but it may also be known that the person is ill, perhaps suffering from heart disease. In such cases the officer will be informed so that the possibility of aggravation of his condition will be recognised. On other occasions, information may be given concerning weapons which are frequently carried, or a tendency to violence or escape.

Methods of creating/updating or deleting records on PNC 2

The records contained in the computer are the product of an awareness by police officers that certain information may be of use to their colleagues in the fight against crime. The computer records are updated from 'source input documents' which are sometimes referred to locally as descriptive or antecedent forms. Whenever a situation is dealt with in which a person or vehicle is involved in the circumstances described, the officer should ensure that a record is made. On occasions, this will amount to creating a new record; the first time that a particular vehicle has been reported in suspicious circumstances or when a vehicle is reported to have been stolen. At other times additional information will come to hand; further descriptive particulars of a vehicle or person will become available or it will become necessary to delete records as vehicles are recovered or wanted persons are arrested. It is essential that this is done immediately by radio to control, or by telephone to the PNC operator, or by completion of the various forms provided for the purpose. The circumstances in each case will dictate the method to be used.

It is not necessary to complete a full record on each occasion that a person is dealt with for an offence, as most of the information will already be on record. However, the accuracy of recorded information should be checked (the person may have changed appearance) and any new information should be added to the record.

The completion of the various forms used for including information in the various indexes maintained is a matter which requires considerable care. We have all been critical of computers at times, usually when a bill is received which contains errors or that bill has already been settled. Computers do not make mistakes, it is the people who use them who are the weak links.

QUEST

'Query Using Enhanced Search Techniques' or QUEST was introduced in 1998 and provides a means of search where the available information about a suspect is limited to such matters as:

(a) description or other information concerning a suspect, such as nickname, age, sex, height, ethnicity, hair and eye colour, accent, shoe size, nationality, occupation;
(b) postal areas for addresses involving home, office, places frequented, business and other;
(c) tattoos, marks and scars;
(d) type of offence and MO.

The QUEST index contains a lot of information and can permit the production of a useful list of suspects from a small amount of positive information. It must be remembered that the details of all persons who are not first offenders are within the PNC database and it is merely a matter of finding the correct 'prompts' to discover possibilities.

Extent of PNC operations

The use of 'technology' within police work is increasing and will go on increasing. The help which can be received from the PNC, as described above, is confined to the main indexes and systems currently in use. The Police Information and Technology Organisation will ensure that an ever increasing amount of information is immediately to hand.

Recent legislation has made provision for the availability of much additional information, particularly in relation to motor vehicle licensing and insurance. Experimental work is currently being carried out within selected police forces using the 'automatic number plate recognition system'. Cameras scan the number plates of all passing vehicles and these are checked against various databases including the PNC, customs and excise databases and DVLA. Where there may be offences seated in the use of identified motor vehicles on a road, an audio identification alerts a central operator who dispatches a mobile unit to intercept the particular vehicle. Indications are that the system will be most effective.

Identification methods

The Home Secretary is required by the Police and Criminal Evidence Act 1984 (PACE), s 66, to issue a Code of Practice in connection with the identification of persons. The relevant Code of Practice (Code D: the Code of Practice for the Identification of Persons by Police Officers, hereafter referred to as the Identification Code) is concerned with three methods by which identification can be made: identification by witnesses, identification by fingerprints and identification by body samples, swabs and impressions. Code D was revised with effect from 1 April 2003. It is concerned with the principal methods used by police to identify people in connection with the investigation of offences and the keeping of records. Identification may be made by witnesses who saw the crime committed who may make an identification in a video identification, identification parade or similar procedure. There may be an identification by fingerprints or by body samples such as blood or hair to generate a DNA profile. The Code also deals with the taking of photographs of arrested people. The provisions of the Code, together with PACE, are designed to ensure that approved procedures are followed in relation to all matters concerned with identification.

General principles

The Identification Code provides certain general principles which apply to all methods by which identification can be made. It provides that:

(a) where a record is made of any action requiring the authority of an officer of a specified rank, the name (except in the case of terrorism enquiries, where the warrant or other identification number should be given) and rank of the officer must be included in the record. Where the Code requires the prior authority or agreement of an officer of at least the rank of inspector or superintendent, that authority may be given by a sergeant or chief inspector who has been authorised to perform the functions of the higher rank under The Police and Criminal Evidence Act 1984, s 107;

(b) all records must be timed and signed by the maker (or warrant or other identification number given in the case of terrorism enquiries);

(c) in the case of a detained person records must be made in the custody record unless otherwise specified;

(d) where the consent of the suspect to a procedure is required, the consent of a suspect who is mentally disordered or mentally vulnerable is only valid if given in the presence of the appropriate adult; and in the case of a juvenile, the parent or guardian must consent in addition to the juvenile himself (unless under 14, in which case the consent of a parent or guardian suffices in its own right). These provisions follow the general rules of good practice. If there is a suspicion that a suspect is a child or young person or is mentally handicapped etc., the procedure should be followed as a matter of fairness to that individual;

(e) in the case of a person who is blind or seriously visually handicapped or unable to read, the custody officer or identification officer must ensure that his solicitor, relative, the appropriate adult or some other person likely to take an interest (and not involved in the investigation) is available to help in checking any documentation. Where the Code requires written consent or signification, then the person who is assisting may be asked to sign if the detained person so wishes;

(f) if any information concerning the processes of an identification must be given to or sought from a suspect, it must be given or sought in the presence of the appropriate adult if the suspect is mentally disordered or mentally vulnerable, or a juvenile. If the appropriate adult is not present when the information is first given or sought, the procedure must be repeated in his presence when he arrives. If the suspect is deaf or there is doubt about hearing ability or the ability to understand, the information must be given through an interpreter.

(g) any procedure involving the participation of a person who is mentally disordered, mentally vulnerable or a juvenile (whether a suspect or witness) must take place in the presence of the appropriate adult but the adult must not be allowed to prompt any identification of a suspect by a witness.

The terms 'appropriate adult' and 'solicitor' where they appear above have the same meaning as in the Detention Code.

Identification by witnesses

Identification by witnesses arises, for example, if the offender is seen committing the crime and a witness is given an opportunity to identify the suspect in a video identification, identification parade or similar procedure designed to test the ability of a witness to identify the person seen on a previous occasion and to provide safeguards against mistaken identification (persons other than police officers, including designated persons and other civilian support staff, must comply with the Code. Such persons must be employees of the police authority under the control of the chief officer of police or employed by a person contracted to provide services related to persons arrested or otherwise in custody).

A record must be made of the description of the suspect as first given by a potential witness. This must be made and kept in a form which enables details of that description to be accurately produced from it, in a visible and legible form, which can be given to the suspect or the suspect's solicitor in accordance with the Code and, unless otherwise specified, be made before the witness takes part in any identification procedures. A copy must be provided to the suspect or his solicitor before any procedures under the Code are carried out.

Where the suspect is known and available

In a case involving disputed identification evidence, and where the identity of the suspect is known to the police and is available, the methods of identification which may be used are:

(a) video identification (where the witness is shown video images of a known suspect together with images of other people who resemble him; Annex A to the Identification Code governs this);

(b) identification parade (where the witness sees the suspect in a line of other people who resemble the suspect; Annex B to the Identification Code governs this);

(c) group identification (where the witness sees the suspect in an informal group of people; Annex C to the Identification Code governs this); and

(d) a confrontation by a witness (where the suspect is directly confronted by the witness; Annex D to the Identification Code governs this).

A suspect is 'known' for present purposes if there is sufficient information known to the police to justify the arrest of a particular person (the 'suspect') for suspected involvement in the offence. A suspect is 'available' if immediately available to take part in the procedure or will become available in a reasonably short time and is willing to take an effective part in at least one of the identification procedures.

The arrangements for, and conduct of, these four types of identification are the responsibility of an officer *not below the rank of inspector* who must *not be involved in the investigation*; he is called the 'identification officer'. No officer or any other person involved with the investigation may take any part in these procedures beyond the extent required by the procedures or act as the identification officer. Unless otherwise specified, an identification officer may allow another officer or member of civilian staff to make arrangements for and to conduct any of the identification procedures. The identification officer must supervise such persons effectively. However, the identification officer may consult the officer in charge of an investigation to determine which procedure to use. There will be a breach of this prohibition, not only if an officer investigating an offence participates in the actual identification process but also if he takes the witness to the police station at which the identification is to be attempted. This is understandable since such contact permits the transfer of information concerning the identification. However, there is nothing to prevent an identification officer from consulting the officer in charge of the investigation in order to determine which procedure to use.

Circumstances in which an identification procedure must be held

Whenever a witness has identified a suspect or purported to have identified a suspect prior to any identification procedure having been held, or there is a witness available, who expresses an ability to identify the suspect, or where there is a reasonable chance of the witness being able to do so, and that witness has not been given an opportunity to identify the suspect in any procedure and the person disputes being the person the witness claims to have seen, an identification procedure must be held unless it is not practicable or it would serve no useful purpose in proving or disproving whether the suspect was involved in committing the offence, for example, when it is not disputed that the suspect is already well known to the witness who claims to have seen him commit the crime.

An identification procedure may also be held if the officer in charge of an investigation considers that it would be useful.

Identification procedures must be held as soon as practicable.

Selecting an identification procedure

Where it is proposed to hold an identification procedure, the suspect must initially be offered a video identification unless it is not practicable, or an identification parade is practicable and more suitable unless it is considered that in the particular circumstances it is more suitable to hold a group identification and that it is practicable to arrange one. He should discuss with the identification officer which of the two options is the more suitable and practicable. An identification parade may not be practicable because of factors such as the number of witnesses, their state of health, availability and travelling requirements. A video identification would normally be more suitable if, in a particular case, it could be arranged and completed sooner than an identification parade.

Where a suspect refuses the offered identification procedure, he must state the reason for doing so and may obtain advice from his solicitor and appropriate adult if present. All such persons must be allowed to make representations as to why another identification procedure should be used. A record must be made of these matters. After consideration of such reasons and representations, the identification officer must, if appropriate, arrange for the suspect to be offered an alternative which the officer considers to be suitable and practicable. If it is decided that it is not suitable and practicable to offer an alternative, the reasons for that decision must be recorded.

If a suspect refuses or fails to take part in a video identification, or refuses to take part in the only practicable option from that list, the identification officer may make arrangements for a covert video identification or other arrangements to test the ability of a witness to identify the person. The officer may use suitable images of the suspect, whether moving or still, which are available or can be obtained.

Where none of these options is practicable the identification officer may arrange a confrontation.

Information to be given to suspect

Before a video identification, an identification parade or a group identification is arranged, the following must be explained to the suspect:

(a) the purpose of the video identification, identification parade or group identification;
(b) the suspect's entitlement to free legal advice;
(c) the procedures for holding it (including the suspect's right to have a solicitor or friend present);
(d) that the suspect does not have to take part in a video identification, identification parade or group identification;
(e) whether, for the purpose of the video identification procedure, images of the suspect have previously been obtained and if so, that he may co-operate in providing further suitable images which shall be used in place of those previously taken;
(f) where appropriate, the special arrangements for juveniles;
(g) where appropriate, the special arrangements for mentally disordered or otherwise mentally vulnerable persons;
(h) that, if the suspect does not consent to and take part in a video identification, identification parade or group identification, refusal may be given in evidence in any subsequent trial and police may proceed covertly without consent, or make other arrangements to test whether a witness can identify him;
(i) that if the suspect should significantly alter appearance between being offered an identification procedure and any attempt to hold it, this may be given in evidence and the identification officer may consider other forms of identification;
(j) that a moving image or photograph may be taken of the suspect when attending for any identification procedure;
(k) whether the witness has been shown photographs, a computerised or artist's composite likeness or similar likeness or picture by the police during the investigation before the identity of the suspect became known;
(l) that if the suspect changes appearance before an identification parade it may not be practicable to arrange one on the day in question or subsequently and, because of the change of appearance, the identification officer may then consider alternative methods of identification; and

(m) that the suspect or his solicitor will be provided with details of the description of the suspect as first given by any witnesses who are to attend the video identification, identification parade, group identification or confrontation.

The identification officer must also give to the suspect a written notice (the 'Notice to Suspect') containing this information and provide a reasonable opportunity for it to be read. The suspect must then be asked to sign a second copy of the notice to indicate whether or not he is willing to participate in the making of a video or take part in an identification parade or group identification. The signed copy must be retained by the identification officer.

The duties of an identification officer in respect of giving information and the giving of the Notice to Suspect may be performed by the custody officer or any other officer not involved in the investigation if it is proposed to hold an identification procedure at a later date (as where the suspect is bailed to attend an identification parade and an inspector is not available to act as identification officer).

Where it is suspected that the giving of a notice may lead the suspect to take steps to avoid identification

Where the identification officer and the officer in charge of the investigation have reasonable grounds to suspect that if the suspect was given the information and notice as set out above, the suspect would thereafter take steps to avoid being seen by a witness in any identification procedure, the identification officer may arrange for images of the suspect for use in a video identification procedure to be obtained before that information and notice are given. If this is done, the suspect may then co-operate in providing suitable images.

Where a suspect is known but not available

Where a suspect is known but is not available or has ceased to be available, the identification officer may make arrangements for a video identification in accordance with the Code (e.g. by using images they already have of the suspect, or finding the suspect and filming him). If necessary, the identification officer may follow the video identification procedures while using still images. Any suitable moving or still images may be used and these may be obtained covertly if necessary. Covert activity must be limited to that which is necessary. The identification officer may arrange a confrontation where no other option is available. However, the requirements for the giving of notice or the viewing of images prior to their being shown to a witness do not apply where the suspect is not available. The record must indicate the reason for the suspect not being available.

These provisions would apply where a known suspect deliberately makes himself unavailable in order to delay or frustrate arrangements being made for obtaining evidence. They enable any suitable images of the suspect (moving or still) which are available or can be obtained to be used in a video identification.

Where the identity of the suspect is not known

In such cases a witness may be taken to a neighbourhood or place to see whether they can identify the person seen on the relevant occasion. Although it is appreciated that there can be no control over the general mix of people, their age, sex, race and general description or manner of dress, the principles governing formal identification procedures must be followed so far as practicable. For example:

(a) Before asking the witness to make an identification, a record must be made, where practicable, of any description of the suspect given by the witness.

(b) The witness's attention should not be directed towards any individual unless, having regard to the circumstances, this is unavoidable. This does not prevent a witness being told to look carefully at people who are around at the time, or to look towards a group or in a particular direction if this appears to be necessary to ensure that the witness does not overlook a possible suspect simply because the witness is looking in the opposite direction and also to enable a witness to make comparisons between any suspect and others who are in the area at the time.

(c) Where there is more than one witness, every effort should be made to keep them separate and, where practicable, witnesses should be taken to see whether they can identify a person independently.

(d) Once there is sufficient information to justify the arrest of a particular individual, for example after a witness makes a positive identification, formal identification procedures must be adopted for any other witnesses in relation to that individual.

(e) The officer or member of civilian support staff accompanying the witness must record in the pocket book the action taken as soon as practicable and in as much detail as possible. Such a record must include the date, time and place of the previous occasion upon which the witness claims to have seen the suspect, where any identification is made, how it was made and the conditions at the time (for example, the distance which the witness was from the suspect, the weather and light), if the witness's attention was drawn to the suspect, the reason for this and anything said by the witness or the suspect about the identification or the conduct of the procedure.

A witness must not be shown photographs, computerised or artist's composite likenesses or similar likenesses or pictures if the identity of the suspect is known to the police and the suspect is available to take part in a video identification, an identification parade or a group identification. If the identity of a suspect is not known, the showing of such pictures must be in accordance with Annex E to the Identification Code.

Documentation

A record must be made of any identification procedure on the forms provided. Where an identification officer considers that it is not practicable to hold a video identification or identification parade, when either is requested by the suspect, a record must be made and the reasons explained to the suspect. Failure or refusal to co-operate in a video identification, identification parade or group identification must be recorded. If applicable, the grounds for obtaining images where it was reasonably suspected that following notice a suspect would take steps to avoid being seen by a witness must be recorded.

Showing films and photographs of incidents and information released to the media

Films or photographs may be shown to the public at large through the national or local media, or to police officers for the purposes of recognition and tracing suspects.

However, when such material is shown to potential witnesses (including police officers) for the purpose of obtaining identification evidence, it must be shown on an individual basis so as to avoid the possibility of collusion, and the showing must, so far as possible, follow the principles for video identification if the suspect is known (see page 612) or identification by photographs if the suspect is not known (see page 620).

Where a broadcast or publication is made, a copy of the material released by the police to the media must be kept and the suspect or his solicitor must be allowed to see this material before any identification procedure is carried out, provided that it is practicable to do so and would not unreasonably delay the investigation. Each witness must be asked, after taking part in that identification procedure, whether he has seen any broadcast or published films or photographs relating to the offence or seen any description of any person suspected of the offence. Any reply must be recorded. This does not affect any separate requirement under the Criminal Procedure and Investigations Act 1996 to retain material in connection with an investigation.

Taking, destruction and retention of photographs or images taken or used in identification procedures

Section 64A of PACE provides powers to take photographs and images of suspects *detained at police stations* with or without consent where it is withheld or it is not practicable to obtain consent, and allows them to be used or disclosed only for purposes related to the prevention and detection of crime, the investigation of offences or the conduct of prosecutions. Examples of circumstances in which these purposes will exist are set out at Note 5B of Code D. After such use or disclosure, they may be retained but only for those purposes. Thus, s 64A allows photographs or images of suspects detained at police stations to be taken and used for the purpose of the identification procedures. Only constables may take such photographs. The officer may require the person to remove any item or substance worn on, or over, all or any part of the head or face. In the event of non-compliance, the officer may remove the item or substance. In the event of non-co-operation, where it is not possible to take the photograph covertly, reasonable force may be used. A photograph obtained without permission may be obtained by making a copy of an image taken on a camera system installed anywhere in a police station. Such persons must be informed of the reason for taking the photograph and the purpose for which it may be used. This does not apply to the taking of a photograph covertly.

The photographs and images (and negatives and copies) of suspects who have *not been detained* (in such cases force may not be used to take photographs) and any moving images (and copies) of suspects, whether or not they have been detained, which are taken for the purposes of, or in connection with, identification procedures must be destroyed unless the suspect:

(a) is charged with, or informed that he may be prosecuted for, a recordable offence;
(b) is prosecuted for a recordable offence;
(c) is cautioned for a recordable offence or given a warning or reprimand in accordance with the Crime and Disorder Act 1998 for a recordable offence; or
(d) gives informed consent in writing for the photograph or image to be retained for the purposes specified by s 64A.

Full records must be made of the procedure followed, including the reasons for taking action.

A person must be given an opportunity to witness the destruction or to have a certificate confirming destruction if so requested within 5 days of notification that the destruction is required.

Video film identification

The following rules are laid down by Annex A as to how video identification should be carried out.

General

The arrangements for obtaining and ensuring the availability of a suitable set of images to be used in a video identification must be the responsibility of an identification officer or investigation officers who have no direct involvement with the relevant case.

The set of images must include the suspect and at least eight other people who so far as possible resemble the suspect in age, height, general appearance and position in life. Only one suspect may appear on any set unless there are two suspects of roughly similar appearance, in which case they may be shown together with at least 12 other persons.

The images used to conduct a video identification must, so far as possible, show the suspect and other people in the same positions or carrying out the same sequence of movements. They must also show the suspect and other people under identical conditions unless the identification officer reasonably believes:

(a) that because of the suspect's failure or refusal to co-operate or other reasons, it is not practicable for the conditions to be identical; or

(b) that any difference in the conditions would not attract a witness's attention to any individual image.

The reason why identical conditions were not practicable must be recorded on the forms provided.

Provision must be made for each person filmed to be identified by number. If police officers are filmed, any numerals or other identifying badges must be concealed. If a prison inmate is filmed, either as a suspect or not, then either all or none of the persons filmed should be in prison clothing.

The suspect or his solicitor, friend or appropriate adult must be given a reasonable opportunity to see the complete set of images before it is shown to any witness. If the suspect has a reasonable objection to the set of images or any of its participants, he must be asked to state the reason. Steps must, if practicable, be taken to remove the grounds for objection. If this is not practicable, the suspect and/or representative must be told why the objections cannot be met. The objection, the reason given for it and why it cannot be met must be recorded.

Before the images are shown, the suspect or solicitor must be provided with the details of the first description of the suspect by any witnesses who are to attend the video identification. The suspect or solicitor must also be allowed to view any material released to the media by the police for the purpose of recognising or tracing the suspect, provided it is practicable to do so and to do so would not unreasonably delay the investigation.

Where practicable, the suspect's solicitor, or where one is not instructed the suspect himself, must be given reasonable notification of the time and place that it is intended to conduct the video identification in order that a legal representative may attend on behalf of the suspect. The suspect himself may not be present when the film is shown to a witness. In the absence of a person representing the suspect, the viewing itself shall be recorded on video. No unauthorised person may be present.

Conduct of video identification

The identification officer is responsible for ensuring that, before they see the set of images, witnesses are not able to communicate with each other about the case or overhear a witness who has seen the material. There must be no discussion with the witness about the composition of the set of images film and he must not be told whether a previous witness has made any identification.

Only one witness may see the set of images at a time. Immediately before the images are seen, the witness must be told that the person he saw may or may not appear in the images shown and that if a positive identification cannot be made, he should say so. The witness must be advised that at any point he may ask to see a particular part of the set of images or to have a particular image frozen for study. Furthermore, it should be pointed out to the witness that there is no limit on how many times the whole set of images, or any part of them, can be viewed. However, the witness should be asked to refrain from making any decision until the entire set has been seen at least twice.

Once the witness has seen the whole set of images at least twice and has indicated that he does not want to view the images or any part of them again, the witness must be asked to say whether the individual seen in person on an earlier occasion has been shown and, if so, to identify that person by number. The witness will then be shown that image to confirm the identification.

Care must be taken not to direct the witness's attention to any one individual image, or to give any other indication of the suspect's identity. Where a witness has previously made an identification by photographs, or a computerised or artist's composite likeness or similar likeness, the witness must not be reminded of such a photograph or composite likeness once a suspect is available for identification by other means in accordance with the Identification Code. Neither must the witness be reminded of any description of the suspect.

Where video films or photographs have been released to the media by the police, each witness must be asked after the procedure whether he has seen any broadcast or published films or photographs or any description of suspects relating to the offence and any reply must be recorded.

Image security and destruction

It is the responsibility of the identification officer to ensure that all relevant material containing sets of images used for a specific identification procedure is kept securely and its movement accounted for. In particular, no one involved in the investigation against the suspect may be permitted to view the material prior to its being shown to any witness.

Where a video film has been made all copies of it must be destroyed with the exceptions set out on page 619. An opportunity of witnessing the destruction must be given to the suspect if requested within 5 days of being cleared or informed that a prosecution will not follow.

Records

A record must be made of all those participating in or seeing the set of images whose names are known to the police.

A record of the conduct of the video identification must be made on the forms provided. This must include anything said by the witness about the identification or the conduct of the procedure and any reasons why it was not practicable to comply with any provisions of the Identification Code governing the conduct of a video identification.

Identification parades

Identification parades must be carried out in accordance with Annex B to the Identification Code, which provides as follows.

A suspect must be given a reasonable opportunity to have a solicitor or friend present, and the identification officer must ask the suspect to indicate any wishes in this respect on a second copy of the 'Notice to Suspect'. A parade may take place either in a normal room or in one equipped with a screen permitting witnesses to see members of the parade without being seen. The procedures for the composition and conduct of the parade are the same in both cases (except that a parade involving a screen may take place only when the suspect's solicitor, friend or appropriate adult is present or the parade is video recorded). This exception is an obvious safeguard, if the evidence of the identification is to have any value.

Before the parade takes place, the suspect or solicitor must be provided with the details of the first description of the suspect by any witnesses who are to attend the parade. The suspect or solicitor should be allowed to view any material released to the media by the police for the purpose of recognising or tracing the suspect, provided that it is practicable to do so and would not unreasonably delay the investigation.

Cases involving prison inmates

If a prison inmate is required for identification, and there are no security problems about his leaving the establishment, the inmate may be asked to participate in an identification parade or video identification.

A parade may be conducted in a Prison Department establishment. If it is, it must be conducted as far as practicable under normal parade rules. Members of the public must make up the parade unless there are serious security or control objections to their admission to the establishment. In such cases, or if a video or group identification is arranged within the establishment, other inmates may participate.

If an inmate is the suspect, there should be no be requirement to wear prison clothing for the parade unless the other persons taking part are other inmates in prison clothing or are members of the public who are prepared to wear prison clothing for the occasion.

The evidential value of a group identification in a prison could be high. Where prison clothing is worn by all, the similarity of dress of all participants will make identification difficult for witnesses who are not certain of the appearance of a suspect.

Conduct of an identification parade

Immediately before the parade, the suspect must be reminded of the procedure governing its conduct and given the appropriate caution. All unauthorised persons must be excluded from the place where the parade is held.

Once the parade has been formed, everything afterwards in respect of it must take place in the presence and hearing of the suspect and of any interpreter, solicitor, friend or appropriate adult who is present (unless the parade involves a screen, in which case everything said to or by any witness at the place where the parade is held must be said in the hearing and presence of the suspect's solicitor, friend or appropriate adult or be video recorded). No investigating officer should enter the room in which the parade is being held.

The parade must consist of at least eight persons (other than the suspect) who so far as possible resemble the suspect in age, height, general appearance and position in life. Where a suspect has an unusual physical feature, for example, a facial scar or tattoo or distinctive hairstyle or hair colour which cannot be replicated on other members of the identification parade, steps may be taken to conceal the location of that feature on the suspect and other members of the parade if the suspect, solicitor or appropriate adult agrees. The use of a plaster or a hat may achieve such an objective. It is also permissible to take reasonable steps in good faith to make non-suspects resemble the suspect by the use of make-up, but this should not be done if there is an objection.

One suspect only may be included in a parade unless there are two suspects of roughly similar appearance, in which case they may be paraded together with at least 12 other persons. In no circumstances may more than two suspects be included in one parade, and where there are separate parades they must be made up of different persons.

Where all members of a similar group are possible suspects, separate identification parades must be held for each member of the group unless there are two suspects of similar appearance. Where police officers in uniform form an identification parade, numerals or other identifying badges must be concealed. It must be remembered that if a complaint concerns a police officer in uniform who was on duty at a particular time, all those on duty at the time who would have had an opportunity to be in the vicinity of any incident, whether in accordance with instructions or not, should be subjected to the identification procedure.

When the suspect is brought into the place where the parade is to be held, he must be asked whether there are any objections to the arrangements for the parade or to any of the other participants in it and to state reasons for any objections made. The suspect may obtain advice from a solicitor or friend, if present, before the parade proceeds. If a suspect has a reasonable objection to the arrangements or to any of the participants, steps must, where practicable, be taken to remove the grounds for objection. Where it is not practicable to do so, the officer must explain to the suspect why objections cannot be met and a record of the objection, the reason for it and why it cannot be met must be recorded on the forms provided.

The suspect may select a position in the line. Where there is more than one witness, the identification officer must tell the suspect, after each witness has left the room, that he can, if he wishes, change position in the line. Each position in the line must be clearly numbered, whether by means of a numeral laid on the floor in front of each parade member or by other means.

Appropriate arrangements must be made to ensure, before they attend the parade, that witnesses are not able to:

(a) communicate with each other or overhear a witness who has already seen the parade;
(b) see any member of the parade;

(c) see, or be reminded of, any photograph or description of the suspect, nor are given any other indication of identity;

(d) see the suspect, either before or after the parade.

The person conducting a witness to the parade must not discuss the composition of the parade and, in particular, must not disclose whether a previous witness has made any identification.

Witnesses must be brought in one at a time. Immediately before a witness inspects the parade, the identification officer or approved person must say that the person previously seen may or may not be on the parade and that if a positive identification cannot be made, this should be stated. The witness must also be told that a decision should not be made before looking at each member of the parade at least twice. When the identification officer or civilian support staff member is satisfied that the witness has properly looked at each member of the parade, he must ask whether the person observed on an earlier relevant occasion is on the parade and, if so, to indicate the number of the person concerned. Where this takes place behind a screen, it is desirable for the witness to be asked to make a note of the number of the person identified so that direct evidence of that fact may be given. However, if a witness is unable to recall that number at a subsequent trial, evidence from the person who conducted the parade as to the number called out by the witness is admissible as there is statutory authority for its admission. If the witness makes an identification after the parade has ended, the suspect and, if present, his solicitor, interpreter or friend must be informed. Where this occurs, consideration should be given to allowing the witness a second opportunity to identify the suspect.

If a witness wishes to hear any parade member speak, to see them adopt any specified posture or to move, the witness must first be asked whether he can identify any persons on the parade on the basis of appearance only. When the request is to hear members of the parade speak, the witness must be reminded that the participants in the parade have been chosen on the basis of physical appearance only. Members of the parade may then be asked to comply with the witness's request to hear them speak, to see them move or to adopt any specified posture.

If the witness requests that the person indicated remove anything used to conceal the location of an unusual physical feature, that person may be asked to remove it.

Where video films or photographs have been released to the media by the police for the purpose of recognising or tracing the suspect, the investigating officer must ask each witness after the parade whether he has seen any broadcast or published films or photographs relating to the offence and any reply must be recorded.

When the last witness has left, the suspect must be asked for any comments on the conduct of the parade.

A video recording of the parade must be taken. Where this is impracticable a colour photograph must be taken. A copy must be supplied on request to the suspect or solicitor within a reasonable time. The rules about the destruction and retention of such a video photograph are the same as those described on page 619.

If the identification officer or civilian support staff member asks any person to leave the parade because of interference with its conduct, the circumstances must be recorded.

A record must be made of all those present at an identification parade whose names are known to the police and a record of the conduct of the parade must be made on the forms provided, including anything said by the witness or suspect about any identifications or the conduct of the procedure, and any reasons why it was not possible to comply with any provision of the Identification Code.

Group identification

Group identification must be carried out in accordance with Annex C to the Identification Code, which provides as follows.

General

The arrangements must as far as practicable satisfy the requirements of an identification parade. A group identification may take place either with the suspect's consent and co-operation or covertly without consent.

The location is a matter for the identification officer, who may take into account representations made by a suspect, an appropriate adult, a solicitor or a friend. It should be a place in which other people are passing by, or waiting around informally, in groups so that the suspect is able to join them and is capable of being seen at the same time as others in the group.

A group identification could be held, for example where people are leaving an escalator, walking through a shopping centre, passengers at railway or bus stations, waiting in queues or groups, or where people are standing or sitting in groups in other public places. Where identification is carried out covertly, it could take place on a route regularly travelled by the suspect, including buses, trains and public places.

While it is appreciated that the general description of people included in a group identification cannot be controlled, the identification officer must consider the general appearance and number of persons likely to be present. In particular, it must be expected that persons broadly similar to the suspect will appear from time to time during the period of the witness's observation. A group identification need not take place where the identification officer believes that, because of the unusual appearance of the suspect, none of the locations which it would be practicable to use is likely to make the identification fair.

Immediately after a group identification (whether with or without the suspect's consent), a colour photograph or a video should be taken of the scene, where this is practicable, so as to give a general impression of the scene and the number of people present. Alternatively, if it is practicable, the group identification may be video recorded. If it is not practicable to take the photograph or video immediately after the group identification, such a record must be made later where practicable.

If at the time of the identification, the suspect is alone, it remains a group identification.

Before the group identification takes place, the suspect or solicitor should be provided with details of the first description of the suspect by any witness attending it. In addition, the suspect or solicitor must be allowed to view any material released to the media for the purpose of recognising or tracing the suspect, provided that it is practicable to do so and it will not unreasonably delay the investigation. Where such releases have been made, each witness must be asked after the procedure whether they have been seen and any reply must be recorded.

Identification with the consent of the suspect

A suspect must be given a reasonable opportunity to have a solicitor or friend present and must be asked by the identification officer to indicate any requirements on a second copy of the Notice to Suspect. The witness, person carrying out the procedure, suspect's solicitor, appropriate adult, friend and any interpreter for the witness may be concealed from the sight of the persons in the group if this facilitates the identification. The person conducting a witness to the location must not discuss the forthcoming group identification or disclose whether a previous witness has made an identification.

Anything said to or by a witness during the procedure regarding the identification must be said in the presence and hearing of those present at the procedure. Witnesses who have not yet attended the identification must not be able to communicate with each other about the case or overhear a witness who has already been given an opportunity to see the suspect in the group, or see the suspect or see or be reminded of any photograph or description of the suspect or be given any other indication of identity. Witnesses must be brought to the place singly and must be told that the person they saw may or may not be in the group and that if they cannot make a positive identification they should say so. The witness must then be asked to observe the group; the manner of doing so will depend upon whether the group is stationary or moving.

Moving group

The following provisions of Annex C apply when the group in which the suspect is to appear is moving, e.g. leaving an escalator.

If two or more suspects consent to a group identification, they should each be subject to different identification procedures, which may be conducted consecutively. The person conducting the procedure must ask the witness to observe the group and ask the witness to point out any person thought to have been seen on an earlier relevant occasion. The suspect should then be allowed to take up whatever position in the group is preferred. When an identification is made, the witness must, where practicable, be asked to take a closer look to confirm identification. If this is not practicable, or the witness in unable to confirm the identification, the witness must be asked how sure he is that the person is the relevant person. The duration of the identification process must be such that the person conducting the procedure reasonably believes necessary for the witness to be able to make comparisons between the suspect and other individuals of broadly similar appearance.

Stationary group

When the group in which the suspect is to appear is stationary, e.g. people waiting in a queue, the following provisions of Annex C apply.

Where there are two or more suspects who consent to a group identification, there should generally be two separate procedures. However, if they are of broadly similar appearance, they may appear in the same group. Separate stationary group identifications must consist of different people.

The suspect may select a position; where there is more than one witness, the suspect must be told, out of sight and hearing of any witness, that that position may be changed between witnesses. The witness must be asked to pass along or amongst the group and to look at each person at least twice before making an identification. Once the witness has done so, it must be established whether the person seen previously is in the group and to indicate that person by any means considered appropriate by the person conducting the identification. If this is not practicable, the witness will be asked to point out that person and must, where practicable, be asked to take a closer look and confirm identification. If this is not practicable, it must be established how sure he is that the person is the one seen on a previous occasion.

Rules common to moving and stationary groups

An unreasonable delay by the suspect in joining the group, or (having joined the group) a deliberate concealment from the sight of the witness, may be considered as a refusal to co-operate in the identification.

Where a witness identifies someone other than the suspect, that person should be asked, if willing, to give his name and address, but is not obliged to do so. There is no duty to record persons present in the group or at the place where the procedure is conducted.

At the end of the procedure the suspect must be asked to comment on the conduct of the procedure. If not previously informed, the suspect must be told of any identifications made by witnesses.

Group identifications without suspect's consent

These should, so far as possible, follow the rules set out above. As such an identification will take place without the suspect's knowledge, no solicitor, etc., will be present. Any number of suspects may be identified at the same time.

Group identifications in police stations

These may take place for reasons of security or safety, or because it is impracticable to hold them elsewhere. The group identification may be in a room equipped with a one-way screen, or elsewhere in the police station. Safeguards applicable to identification parades must be followed where practicable.

Group identifications involving prison inmates

These may only take place in a prison or police station. They must follow the procedure which is applicable to group identifications in a police station. Where a group identification takes place in a prison, other inmates may participate. If the suspect is in prison clothing, all persons taking part must be so dressed.

Documentation

Where a photograph or video is taken a copy must be supplied on request to the suspect or solicitor within a reasonable time. Such records must be destroyed or wiped clean in accordance with the rules described on page 619. A record of the conduct of the identification must be made on the forms provided and must include anything said by the witness or suspect about any identification or the conduct of the procedure and any reason why it was not practicable to comply with any of the provisions of the Code governing the conduct of group identifications.

Confrontation by a witness

A confrontation may be used when it is not possible to arrange a video identification, an identification parade or a group identification. A confrontation does not require the suspect's consent, although a suspect cannot be compelled to make the face visible to a witness. As with the other identification procedures, the identification officer is responsible for the arrangements for and conduct of any confrontation of a suspect by a witness. The rules concerning confrontation, which are set out in Annex D to the Identification Code, are simple.

Before the confrontation takes place, the witness must be told that the person seen may or may not be the person to be confronted and that if it is not possible to make a positive identification, this should be stated. In addition, before the confrontation, the suspect or solicitor must be provided with the details of the first description of the suspect given by any witness who is to attend the confrontation. The note should be made available for examination at trial to act as a safeguard against the risk of auto-suggestion. Where a broadcast or publication has been made for the purpose of recognition and tracing of suspects, the suspect or solicitor should also be allowed to view any material released by the police to the media, provided that it is practicable to do so and would not unreasonably delay the investigation. The suspect must be confronted independently by each witness, who must be asked 'Is this the person?' If the witness identifies the person but is unable to confirm the identification, it must be established how sure he is that the person is the person seen on the earlier relevant occasion. Confrontation must take place in the presence of the suspect's solicitor, interpreter or friend, where there is one, unless this would cause unreasonable delay.

The confrontation should normally take place in the police station, either in a normal room or in one equipped with a screen permitting a witness to see the suspect without being seen. In both cases the procedures are the same, except that a room equipped with a screen may be used only when the suspect's solicitor, friend or appropriate adult is present or the confrontation is recorded on video. After the confrontation each witness must be asked whether any broadcast or published films, photographs or descriptions of suspects relating to the offence had been seen previously, and any reply must be recorded.

The showing of photographs

Annex E of the Identification Code sets out the procedures to be followed if photographs, or photofit, identikit or similar pictures are shown to a witness for identification purposes where the suspect's identity is not known. Where it is proposed to show photographs to a witness, the officer in charge of the investigation must confirm to the officer responsible for supervising and directing the showing that the first description of the suspect given by the witness has been recorded. If it has not, the Annex E procedure must be postponed.

An officer of the rank of sergeant or above must be responsible for supervising and directing the showing of photographs, but the actual showing may be done by a constable or civilian support staff member. (This means that most of the responsibility remains with the sergeant, etc. The accountability of a constable or approved person will be limited to non-observance of the directions given.) The supervising officer must confirm that the first description of the suspect given by the witness has been recorded before the witness is shown the photographs. If it cannot be confirmed that the description has been recorded, the showing must be postponed.

Only one witness may be shown photographs at any one time. As much privacy as possible must be given and there must not be any possibility to communicate with any other witness in the case. The witness must be shown not less than 12 photographs at a time, which shall, as far as possible, all be of a similar type.

When the witness is shown photographs, he must be told that the photograph of the person said to be previously seen may or may not be amongst them and that if a positive identification cannot be made, this should be stated. The witness must be told not to make a decision until at least 12 photographs have been viewed. There must not be prompting or guidance in any way; the witness must be left to make any selection without help. If a witness makes a positive identification from photographs then, unless the person identified is otherwise eliminated from the enquiries or is not available, other witnesses must not be shown photographs. However, both they and the witness who has made the identification must be asked to attend a video identification, an identification parade or group identification unless there is no dispute about the identification of the suspect. If the witness makes a selection or is unable to confirm the identification the person showing the photographs must ask the witness how sure he is that the photograph indicated is the person seen on a previous occasion.

Where the use of computerised or artist's composite likeness or similar has led to there being a known suspect who can be asked to participate in video identification, appear on an identification parade or participate in a group identification, that likeness shall not be shown to other potential witnesses.

Where a witness attending a video identification, an identification parade or a group identification has previously been shown photographs or computerised or artists's composite likeness or similar likeness, the suspect and solicitor must be informed of this fact before the video identification, identification parade or group identification takes place. The officer in charge of the investigation is responsible for informing the identification officer of this fact.

Any photograph used must be retained for production in court if necessary, whether or not an identification is made.

None of the photographs used shall be destroyed, whether or not an identification is made, since they may be required for production in court. The photographs should be numbered and a separate photograph taken of the frame or part of the album from which the witness made an identification as an aid to reconstituting it.

Documentation

Whether or not an identification is made, a record must be kept of the showing of photographs on forms provided for the purpose. The record must include anything said by the witness about any identification or the conduct of the procedure, any reasons why it was not practicable to comply with any provisions of the Identification Code and the name and rank of the supervising officer, who must sign the record.

Identification by fingerprints

The Police and Criminal Evidence Act 1984, ss 27, 61, 63A and 64, and the Identification Code deal with the taking of fingerprints and the circumstances in which fingerprints must be destroyed.

A person's fingerprints may be taken only with consent (which must be in writing if given at a police station) or in accordance with the provisions of the following paragraph.

Powers to take fingerprints from a person over the age of 10 years without consent are provided by ss 27 and 61 of PACE. Those sections provide that fingerprints may be taken without consent:

(a) from a person detained at a police station, if an officer of at least the rank of inspector authorises them to be taken (which authority may only be given if the officer has reasonable grounds for suspecting the involvement of the person whose fingerprints are to be taken in a criminal offence and for believing that the finger-prints will tend to confirm or disprove his involvement *or will facilitate the ascertainment of his identity within the meaning of s 54A (authorisation of search and examination to ascertain identity) or both*; see below;

(b) or where

 (i) if the detained person has been charged with a recordable offence (see below) or informed that he will be reported for such an offence; and

(ii) he has not had his fingerprints taken in the course of the investigation by the police. If a set of fingerprints has been taken in consequence of a person's being charged with, or told that he would be reported for, a recordable offence, this does not prevent a second set of prints from being taken if the first did not constitute a full set or is of unsatisfactory quality for their purpose; or

(c) if that person has been convicted of a recordable offence, or has been cautioned for an admitted recordable offence, or is a child or young person and has been warned or reprimanded under the crime and Disorder Act 1998, s 65, for an admitted recordable offence.

'Recordable offence' is defined on page 625.

Paragraphs (a) and (b) do not apply to a person detained under the legislation relating to terrorism; special provision is made under the Terrorism Act 2000.

The words in italics in (a) were added by the Anti-terrorism, Crime and Security Act 2001, the provisions of which are subject to review on 14 December 2003. An authorisation under s 54A of PACE may only be given where there has been a refusal by a person to identify himself, or the officer has reasonable grounds for suspecting that the person is not who he claims to be. The section allows a detainee at a police station to be searched or examined or both, to establish whether there are any marks, features or injuries that would tend to identify the detainee as a person involved in the commission of an offence and to photograph any identifying marks. Such a search may only be carried out without the detainee's consent if authorised by an officer of at least the rank of inspector. Where it is done to establish identity, the authorising officer must be satisfied that the detainee has refused to identify himself or is reasonably suspected of giving a false identity.

The Police and Criminal Evidence Act 1984, s 27(1B), authorises the taking of fingerprints in circumstances in which a person has been cautioned for an admitted recordable offence, or where that person has been warned or reprimanded under s 65 of the Crime and Disorder Act 1998. The Criminal Justice and Police Act 2001 also added subsections (4A) and (4B) to s 61, which provide that the fingerprints of a person who has answered to bail at a court or police station may be taken without the appropriate consent if the court, or an officer of at least the rank of inspector, authorises them to be taken. This may be done where the court or officer reasonably believes that a person who has surrendered to bail is not the person admitted to bail and the person bailed has been previously fingerprinted, or the person who has answered to bail claims to be a different person from the person who had his fingerprints taken on a previous occasion.

In all cases, an authorisation for fingerprinting may be given orally or in writing, but if given orally it must be confirmed in writing as soon as practicable. A person whose fingerprints are to be taken with or without consent must be told the reason before the fingerprints are taken and must be told that the prints may be the subject of a speculative search against other fingerprints and a record must be made of this. This means that a check may be made against other fingerprints contained in records held by or on behalf of the police or held in connection with or as a result of an investigation into that offence.

Section 64(1A) of PACE provides that where fingerprints or samples are taken from a person in connection with the investigation of an offence and s 64(3) (see below) does not require them to be destroyed, they may be retained after they have fulfilled the purpose for which they were taken but may not be used other than for purposes related to the prevention or detection of crime, the investigation of an offence or the conduct of a prosecution. However, by s 64(3) where fingerprints or samples are taken from someone who is not suspected of having committed the offence in question (elimination prints), they must be destroyed as soon as they have served their purpose, and neither the fingerprints nor sample, nor anything derived from the sample, may be used in evidence against the suspect, or for the investigation of any offence. Samples and fingerprints are not required to be destroyed under s 64(3):

(a) where the non-suspected person consents in writing to the retention of the fingerprints or sample. Where this is done the use of the fingerprint or sample and the information gained from it is not restricted. Such consent cannot later be withdrawn;

(b) where the fingerprint or sample was taken for the purpose of the same investigation of an offence for which a person from whom such a fingerprint or sample was taken has been convicted. This provision was introduced because there were found to be scientific reasons for processing some fingerprints or samples together and it is not technologically possible to separate them afterwards. This could occur where the fingerprints of a number of suspects were all found on a gun and were photographed together. However, the information derived from such a fingerprint or sample must not be used in evidence against that person, or for the purpose of any investigation of an offence. This restriction does not apply in cases where a written consent has been given under (a).

The Court of Appeal has held that s 64(1A) of PACE does not contravene the right to a private life under art. 8 of the European Convention on Human Rights, or the right not to be discriminated against under art. 14. The reason was that the rule that fingerprints and samples could only be used for the purpose of 'the prevention or detection of crime, the investigation of an offence, or the conduct of a prosecution' meant that the interference with the right to privacy was not substantial and could be justified as necessary for that purpose. So far as discrimination is concerned, once such fingerprints or samples had been lawfully obtained, there was a clear and objective distinction between the individuals from whom these had been taken and those persons who had not been lawfully required to provide them.

Where fingerprints are destroyed, any copies must also be destroyed, and access to relevant computer data must be made impossible, as soon as it is practicable to do so. A person must be allowed to witness the destruction of fingerprints where a request is made. In addition, if the fingerprints are destroyed or rendered inaccessible, that person is entitled to a certificate, to be issued within 3 months of the application, certifying destruction or that access to the data has been made impossible.

The Police and Criminal Evidence Act 1984, s 63A(1), provides that, where a person has been arrested on suspicion of being involved in a recordable offence, or has been charged with a recordable offence, or has been informed that he will be reported for a recordable offence, fingerprints or samples or the information derived from samples taken under any power conferred by the Act from the person may be checked against:

(a) other fingerprints or samples to which the person seeking to check has access and which are held by or on behalf of a police force, or are held in connection with or as a result of an investigation of an offence;

(b) information derived from other samples if the information is contained in records to which the person seeking to check has access and which are held as described in (a).

The Identification Code deals with the taking of fingerprints for the purposes of Immigration Service enquiries in accordance with powers and procedures other than PACE and for which the Immigration Service (and not the police) is responsible. Although the relevant legislation empowers police officers, in addition to immigration officers, to take fingerprints, immigration officers will, almost without exception, be concerned. However, should it be necessary for a police officer to take such fingerprints, an officer is empowered to take such fingerprints with or without consent provided that the person is informed of the reason for which they are taken.

Where public co-operation is being sought in relation to an investigation, it is important to minimise the risk of confusion in relation to the effect of giving consent to the provision of fingerprints or a DNA sample. A DNA sample may be requested for the purpose of elimination or as a part of an intelligence-led screen and to be used only for that purpose. On other occasions it may be required to be retained on the National DNA database and used in the future. The same applies to fingerprints. Annex F to Code D contains specimen endorsements in relation to the appropriate consent.

Documentation

A record must be made as soon as possible of the reason for taking a person's fingerprints (or palm prints) without consent and of their destruction. If that person is detained at a police station when they are taken, the reason must be recorded on the custody record. If force is used a record must be made of the circumstances and those present.

A record must be made when a person has been informed that his fingerprints may be the subject of a speculative search.

Fingerprints (or a DNA sample) taken from a person *suspected of committing a recordable offence but not arrested, charged or informed that he will be prosecuted for it* may only be subjected to a speculative search if consent is given in writing. The Identification Code suggests a basic form of words for such written permission:

> I consent to my fingerprints/DNA sample and information derived from it being retained and used only for the purposes related to the prevention and detection of crime, the investigation of an offence or the conduct of a prosecution either nationally or internationally. I understand that my fingerprints or this sample may be checked against other fingerprints and DNA records held by or on behalf of relevant law enforcement authorities, either nationally or internationally.

I understand that once I have given my consent for a sample to be retained and used I cannot withdraw that consent.

Recordable offences are those which follow:

(a) convictions for and cautions, reprimands and warnings given in respect of any offence punishable with imprisonment (to be construed without regard to any prohibition or restriction imposed by or under any enactment on the punishment of young offenders);

(b) loitering or soliciting for the purposes of prostitution (Street Offences Act 1959, s 1);

(c) improper use of public telecommunications system (Telecommunications Act 1984);

(d) tampering with a motor vehicle (Road Traffic Act 1988, s 25);

(e) sending letters, etc., with intent to cause distress or anxiety (Malicious Communications Act 1988, s 1);

(f) having an article with a blade or point in a public place [Criminal Justice Act 1988, s 139(1)];

(g) giving intoxicating liquor to a child under 5, exposing children under 12 to risk of burning, failing to provide for safety of children at entertainments (Children and Young Persons Act 1933, ss 5, 11 and 12);

(h) drunkenness in a public place (Criminal Justice Act 1967, s 91);

(i) failing to deliver up authority to possess prohibited weapon or ammunition, possession of assembled shotgun by an unsupervised person under 15, possession of an air weapon or ammunition for air weapon by an unsupervised person under 14, possession of an air weapon in public place by an unsupervised person under 17 [Firearms Act 1968, ss 5(6), 22(3), 22(4) and 22(5)];

(j) trespassing in daytime on land in search of game, refusal by such trespasser to give name and address, five or more found armed in daytime in search of game and using violence or refusing name and address (Game Act 1831, ss 30, 31 and 32);

(k) being drunk in a highway or public place (Licensing Act 1972, s 12);

(l) obstructing a constable or local authority officer inspecting premises for use as registered club, permitting drunkenness on licensed premises, failing to leave licensed premises when requested to do so, allowing prostitutes to assemble in a brothel, allowing a constable to remain on licensed premises when on duty, supplying intoxicants or refreshments to a constable or bribing a constable (Licensing Act 1964, ss 45, 172, 174, 175, 176 and 178);

(m) making a false statement in relation to an application for a sex establishment licence [Local Government (Miscellaneous Provisions) Act 1982];

(n) falsely claiming a professional qualification (Nurses, Midwives and Health Visitors Act 1997);

(o) taking or destroying game or rabbits by night (Night Poaching Act 1828, s 1);

(p) wearing police uniform with intent to deceive, unlawful possession of police uniform (Police Act 1996, s 90);

(q) harassment, alarm or distress, failing to give notice of

(r) public procession, failing to comply with condition imposed on a public procession, taking part in a prohibited public procession, failing to comply with a condition imposed on a public assembly, taking part in a prohibited assembly and failing to comply with directions [Public Order Act 1986, ss 5, 11, 12(5), 13(8), 14(5), 14B(2) and 14C(3)];

(s) failing to provide a roadside specimen of breath (Road Traffic Act 1988, s 6);

(t) kerb crawling, persistently soliciting women (Sexual Offences Act 1985, ss 1 and 2);

(u) in connection with sporting events, allowing alcohol to be carried on public vehicles, allowing alcohol to be drunk on such vehicles or persons being drunk on such a vehicle, trying to enter designated sports ground while drunk, unauthorisedly drinking (or supplying) alcohol at a designated sports ground [Sporting Events (Control of Alcohol Etc.) Act 1985, ss 1(2), 1(4), 1A(2), 2(2), 5B(3), 5C(4), 5C(5) and 5D(3)] and throwing missiles, indecent or racist chanting, or going on to the playing area [Football (Offences) Act 1991, ss 2, 3 and 4];

(v) taking or riding a pedal cycle without the owner's consent [Theft Act 1968, s 12(5)]; and

(w) purchasing or hiring a crossbow (or part) or unsupervised possession by a person under 17 (Crossbows Act 1987, ss 2 and 3).

Photographs

The Identification Code provides that the photograph of a person who has been arrested may be taken at a police station only with *written consent* or, without consent, *in one of the following cases*:

(a) if arrested at the same time as other persons, or at a time when it is likely that other persons will be arrested, and a photograph is necessary to establish who was arrested, at what time and at what place; or

(b) if charged with or reported for a recordable offence and has not yet been released or brought before a court; or

(c) if convicted of such an offence and his photograph is not already on record as a result of (a) or (b). There is no power of arrest to take a photograph in pursuance of this provision which applies only where the person is in custody as a result of the exercise of another power (e.g. an arrest for fingerprinting under the Police and Criminal Evidence Act 1984, s 27, discussed on page 624); or

(d) if a superintendent (or above) authorises it, having reasonable grounds for suspecting the involvement of the person in a criminal offence and where there is identification evidence in relation to that offence.

Case (a) above will cover situations when multiple arrests are made in public order situations; if used in such a situation, it will ease the identification of offenders at a later stage.

Force may not be used to take a photograph; this is not surprising, as it should always be possible to take a photograph without resorting to force.

Whether or not consent has been given to a photograph being taken, a suspect must be told that if he should significantly alter in appearance between the taking of the photograph and any attempt to hold an identification procedure, this may be given in evidence if the case comes to trial.

Whether or not a photograph is taken with consent, a person whose photograph is taken must be informed of the reason for taking it, that the photograph, negatives and all copies will be destroyed if he is cleared (unless he has a previous conviction for a recordable offence) or is not prosecuted (unless he admits the offence and is cautioned for it or he has a previous conviction for a recordable offence) and that he may witness its destruction or be provided with a certificate confirming its destruction if he asks to do so within 5 days of being cleared or informed that there will be no prosecution.

All references to photographs include computer images.

Photographs must be kept in a secure manner to ensure that a potential witness in an identification procedure is unable to view them before any such procedure. The admissibility and value of identification evidence may be compromised if a potential witness in an identification procedure sees any photograph of the suspect otherwise than in accordance with the Identification Code.

The Anti-terrorism, Crime and Security Act 2001 (which is subject to review on 14 December 2003) inserted s 64A into PACE dealing with the photographing of *suspects*. It provides that a person detained at a police station may be photographed (with appropriate consent or if such consent is withheld, or it is not practicable to obtain it, without consent). A person being so photographed may be required to remove any item or substance worn on or over the whole or any part of the head or face and if he does not comply with such a request, the item may be removed. Photographs may be taken by constables or appointed persons who may use reasonable force for this purpose if necessary.

A photograph so taken may be used by or disclosed to any person for any purpose related to the prevention or detection of crime, the investigation of an offence or the conduct of a prosecution and may be retained thereafter but may only be used for such a related purpose. The term 'crime' includes conduct which constitutes one or more criminal offences whether under United Kingdom law or that of a country or territory outside the United Kingdom, or is conduct, or corresponds to conduct, which, if it took place in the United Kingdom, would so constitute one or more criminal offences.

Documentation

A record must be made as soon as practicable of the reason for taking a person's photograph under the above provisions without consent and of the destruction of any photograph.

Identification by body samples, swabs and impressions

The Police and Criminal Evidence Act 1984, ss 62 to 64, contains the basic provisions in this area, but (within the terms of these sections) it is the Identification Code which sets out the detailed procedures. The powers set out below are concerned with cases other than terrorism.

Intimate samples

An intimate sample means a sample of *blood, semen or any other tissue fluid, urine, pubic hair, a dental impression, or a swab taken from a person's body orifice other than the mouth*. Section 62 of PACE is the relevant provision.

An intimate sample may be taken from a person in police detention only with written consent. In the case of any procedure requiring a person's consent, the consent of a person who is mentally disordered or mentally handicapped is only valid if given in the presence of an appropriate adult; and in the case of a juvenile the consent of the parent or guardian is required in addition (unless under 14, in which case the consent of the parent or guardian is sufficient in its own right). An intimate sample may also be taken from a person not in police detention if, in the course of an investigation into an offence, two or more non-intimate samples have been taken which have proved unsuitable or insufficient for a particular form of analysis and such an officer as is mentioned below authorises it to be taken and the person concerned (or an appropriate adult) gives written consent.

In these two cases, an intimate sample may only be taken if an officer of at least the rank of inspector authorises it to be taken because of reasonable grounds of suspicion of the involvement of the person from whom the sample is to be taken in a recordable offence and for believing that the sample will tend to confirm or disprove involvement.

A record must be made of the authorisation by virtue of which the sample was taken, the grounds for giving the authorisation and the fact that the appropriate consent was given. This must be done as soon as is practicable after the sample is taken.

Before a person is asked to provide an intimate sample, he must be informed that it may be the subject of a speculative search (a check against other samples or against information derived from other samples) and the fact that this has been done must be recorded as soon as practicable after the sample has been taken. Where an intimate sample is taken from a person detained at a police station, the records referred to above must be made in the custody record.

Where a person refuses, without good cause, to consent to the taking of an intimate sample, in any proceedings for an offence, a court may draw such inferences from the refusal as appear proper.

An intimate sample, other than a sample of urine, may only be taken from a person by a registered medical practitioner or a registered health-care professional (a registered nurse or a registered member of a health-care profession designated by regulations). A dental impression may only be taken by a registered dentist.

Before a person is asked to provide one of these samples or swabs, he must be warned that a refusal may be treated, in any proceedings against him, as corroborating relevant prosecution evidence. The Code suggests the use of the following words:

> You do not have to provide this sample/allow this swab or impression to be taken, but I must warn you that if you refuse without good cause, your refusal may harm your case if it comes to trial.

The person must also be reminded of the entitlement to free legal advice and that the sample taken may be the subject of a speculative search against other samples. A record must be made of the giving of this warning and this reminder.

Non-intimate samples

There are separate provisions, contained in s 63 of PACE, for the taking of a *non-intimate sample*. A non-intimate sample means hair (other than pubic hair) which includes hair plucked by the root, a sample taken from a nail or under a nail, swabs taken from parts of the body including the mouth but not any other body orifice, saliva or a skin impression, which means any record, other than a fingerprint, which is a record, in any form and produced by any method, of the skin pattern and any other physical characteristics or features of the whole, or any part of a person's foot or any other part of the body. Where hair samples are taken for the purpose of DNA analysis (rather than for other purposes such as making a visual match), the suspect should be permitted a reasonable choice as to which part of the body the hairs are to be taken from. When hairs are plucked they should be plucked individually unless the suspect prefers otherwise and no more should be plucked than the person taking them reasonably considers necessary for a sufficient sample.

Except in the following three cases, a non-intimate sample may be taken from a suspect only with written consent. The three exceptional cases are:

(a) A non-intimate sample may be taken from a person without the appropriate consent if
  (i) he is in police detention or is being held in custody by the court or on the authority of a court; and
  (ii) an officer of the rank of inspector (or above) has authorised it to be taken without consent.

  Such authorisation may only be given where the inspector (or above) has reasonable grounds to suspect that the offence in question is a recordable offence and that the sample will tend to confirm or disprove the suspect's involvement in it. An authorisation must not be given if the non-intimate sample concerned consists of a skin impression and such an impression has already been taken in the course of the investigation of the offence and that impression did not prove to be insufficient. Where such an impression is taken electronically it must be taken in the approved manner by an approved device.

  Where an authorisation is given for the taking of a non-intimate sample, the suspect must be informed, before it is taken, of the grounds on which the authorisation has been given, including the nature of the suspected offence, and must also be told that any sample taken may be the subject of a speculative search.

(b) A non-intimate sample may be taken without the appropriate consent from any person (whether or not in custody or detained) if
  (i) charged with a recordable offence or informed that he will be reported for such an offence, and that person has not had a non-intimate sample taken in the course of the investigation, or, if a sample has been taken, it has proved unsuitable or insufficient for a particular form of analysis. An *unsuitable sample* is one which, by its nature, is not suitable for a particular form of analysis. An *insufficient sample* is one which is not sufficient either in quantity or quality for the purpose of enabling information to be provided for the purpose of a particular form of analysis such as DNA analysis.

(c) A non-intimate sample may be taken without the appropriate consent if the person has been *convicted* of a recordable offence. However, this does not apply to any person convicted before 10 April 1995 unless he is a person to whom the Criminal Evidence (Amendment) Act 1997 applies (persons imprisoned or detained by virtue of a pre-existing conviction for a sexual offence or an offence of violence or potential violence, listed in Schedule 1 to the Act), and at the relevant time such person is serving a sentence of imprisonment in respect of that offence.

(d) A non-intimate sample may be taken without appropriate consent from a person detained following acquittal on the grounds of insanity or a finding of unfitness to plead.

Provision is made by s 63A of PACE, for a constable to require a person convicted of a recordable offence to attend a police station in order that non-intimate samples may be taken.

Section 63A of PACE permits a constable within 1 month from the date of charge or conviction (as the case may be) or from the date of being informed that a sample is not suitable or is insufficient (as the case may be), to require a person who is neither in police detention, nor held in custody by the police on the authority of a court, to attend a police station in order to have a sample taken. While the section does not require this requirement to be in writing, as arrest may follow refusal, it is submitted that it would be wise to do so.

Reasonable force may be used to take a non-intimate sample without the suspect's consent under the above provisions.

General

A record must be made as soon as practicable of the reasons for taking a sample or impression and the warnings given. If force is used a record shall be made of the circumstances and those present. If written consent is given to the taking of a sample or impression, the fact must be recorded in writing. A record must be made of the giving of a warning that a refusal without reasonable cause to provide an intimate sample may harm the suspect's case if it comes to trial. A record must also be made that the subject has been warned that a sample may be the subject of a speculative search.

Where clothing needs to be removed in circumstances likely to cause embarrassment to the person, no person of the opposite sex who is not a medical practitioner or nurse shall be present (unless, in the case of a juvenile or a mentally disordered or mentally handicapped person, that person specifically requests the presence of a particular adult of the opposite sex who is readily available), nor shall anyone whose presence is unnecessary. However, in the case of a juvenile this is subject to the overriding proviso that such a removal of clothing may take place in the absence of the appropriate adult only if the juvenile signifies such a preference in the presence of the appropriate adult, for the search to be done in his absence and the appropriate adult agrees.

A sample or an impression must be destroyed as soon as practicable if the suspect is prosecuted and acquitted or not prosecuted (unless the offence is admitted and there is a caution). However, although information derived from a sample which should have been destroyed must not be used in evidence against the suspect or for the purpose of any investigation of an offence, the House of Lords has held that evidence obtained by matching with that sample a sample taken from the suspect in another investigation is admissible at the trial judge's discretion.

Samples need not be destroyed if they were taken for the purpose of an investigation of an offence for which someone has been convicted, and from whom a sample was also taken.

Showing of video recordings taken by security cameras

The Court of Appeal has held that in the following circumstances, subject to judicial discretion to exclude such evidence in particular circumstances, evidence that a person has committed an offence based upon photographic images from the scene of crime is admissible in the following cases:

(a) where the photographic image was sufficiently clear and the jury could compare it with the defendant;
(b) where the witness knows the defendant sufficiently well to recognise the defendant as the person depicted;

(c) where a witness who did not know the defendant had spent time viewing and analysing such photographic images, thus acquiring a special knowledge that the jury did not have, such a witness could give evidence of identification based on a comparison of those images with a reasonably contemporary photograph of the defendant, provided that both were available to the jury; and

(d) where a witness qualified in 'facial mapping' could give opinion evidence of identification based on a comparison of images from the scene (whether expertly enhanced or not) with a reasonably contemporary photograph, provided that both were available to the jury.

Voice identification

The Court of Appeal has ruled that the Identification Code does not apply to identification by voice, and therefore there is no need for an identification parade (or presumably any other identification procedure) to be held. However, there is currently a difference of opinion between the judges about the relative values of 'auditory phonetic analysis' and 'quantitative acoustic analysis' as methods of identification. It would seem that the former is more valuable, because it tells one of the acoustic properties of the speech which depend on the individual's vocal tract, mouth and throat, whereas the latter tells one principally about the dialect or accent of the speaker.

Stage 5

Major incidents – fires and carriage of dangerous substances

Initial action – fire

There are a number of ways in which the presence of fire in buildings, or in other places at which there is a threat to public safety, may come to the attention of a police officer. In all circumstances, initial action must recognise the duty to protect life and property. While patrolling a beat at night, police officers frequently discover fires and, because they are so easily visible in their early stages, it is often possible to take effective action immediately to extinguish or at least control the outbreak. It is, therefore, inadvisable to offer a list of rules which must be strictly observed; the constable must exercise discretion and decide upon the most effective action to be taken at the time.

Difficulties can be encountered when reports are made to police officers by telephone, or orally, by members of the public who are usually highly excited and are not trained to give concise, essential information. It is important to establish whether or not the fire service has been informed, and it can be dangerous to assume that any telephone message passed to the fire service by a member of the public is sufficiently complete to ensure the arrival of tenders at the correct location. Many members of the public use a telephone badly in times of emergency and may have reported the fire, impressing upon the recipient of their message the need for speedy assistance, without giving the details of its location. It is much safer to pass the correct information and to check that the fire service telephone operator has all the information necessary to allow effective action to be taken. When initial reports of this nature are received, it will be possible to decide whether other emergency services should be alerted. If it appears likely that people are trapped in the building, or will have difficulty in escaping, a request for the attendance of an ambulance is advisable to avoid unnecessary delay in their removal from the scene of the incident. Immediate medical attention is essential to persons suffering from severe burns or suffocation.

Usually, the radio message to control requesting confirmation that the fire service operator has received a full report will ensure that supervisory officers and a keyholder are informed, but if the incident appears likely to be a serious one it is advisable that their attendance is specifically requested. As much information as possible should be obtained concerning persons who are likely to be in the building from the person making the report, from neighbours, or from the owners of the premises. It will be of considerable assistance to those responsible for the rescue of trapped people if information is also gathered concerning the likely places in which such persons may be located. If a fire is spreading rapidly, it is frequently impossible to search an entire building and it is preferable that limited search time is spent to the best advantage.

Duties and responsibilities

A police officer's first duty is always to preserve life, and if fire is discovered in a building the occupants should be warned and removed as speedily as possible, as should those occupying buildings in dangerous proximity. It may, in some circumstances, be possible to take some steps to extinguish or at least contain the outbreak. As police assistance arrives measures may be taken to ensure that easy access is maintained for rescue services. The Fire Services Act 1947 empowers the senior police officer present, or in the absence of the police, the senior fire officer, to close any street to traffic or to stop or regulate traffic in any street whenever, in the opinion of such officer, it is necessary or desirable to do so. If the fire is one which is likely to spread quickly, such measures will have to be considered and action taken quickly if chaos is to be avoided.

Members of the public will arrive in considerable numbers – even in the early hours of the morning – if there is something unusual to look at. Their presence can seriously hinder effective fire-fighting operations. Major outbreaks of fire involve the presence of a large number of pumping appliances, and hose reels are likely to be laid across sections of the roadway in considerable numbers. The fire service frequently provides ramps which can be laid in conjunction with their hose pipes to allow traffic to pass cautiously, but it is often more efficient to divert traffic and this becomes essential if there is any danger of building collapse.

Police problems are increased if it becomes necessary to pump water from rivers or canals over considerable distances as complex operations to control traffic movement become necessary. It is on occasions such as these that individual police officers carrying out traffic control duties some distance from the scene of the incident may question the necessity for their presence for lengthy periods of time performing functions for which the reasons are not apparent.

Some incidents involve danger to members of the public over a considerable area, and where buildings used for the storage of highly flammable or explosive substances are involved, a complex scheme of evacuation must be planned and put into effect. Having ensured the removal of all persons from buildings, the preservation of animal life and property may be considered and during incidents which involve evacuation of certain areas, it must be remembered that the police are responsible for the safety of the property of those removed and that looting must be prevented. Causes of fire are always of relevance to the police, and the observations of the fire prevention officer when the outbreak has been finally controlled can be extremely important in subsequent enquiries to determine whether or not an offence of arson has been committed. Some police forces have formed special arson units in conjunction with the fire service.

The owners, occupiers or keyholders of affected premises must be informed as soon as possible in all instances of fire and asked to attend as quickly as possible. Their knowledge of the inside of buildings can be of major assistance to the senior fire officer present.

The senior police officer present is in charge of police operations and is responsible for the control of the area surrounding the fire; in the same way, the senior fire officer is in charge of fire-fighting operations. The Fire Services Act 1947 provides this power and gives sole charge and control of any operations for the extinguishing of fire, including the fixing of positions of fire engines and apparatus and the attaching of hose to any water pipes, to that officer. Any person who wilfully obstructs or interferes with any member of a fire brigade who is engaged in operations for fire-fighting purposes shall be guilty of an offence.

It is essential for the police to liaise closely with the senior officer present at every stage. If at any point there is the slightest doubt concerning the origin of the fire, or a hint that it may not have been an accident, a supervisory officer must be informed.

Rescue procedure

Most casualties are probably caused by smoke, fumes and heat rather than by the flames themselves and it is important that all rescue personnel, including police officers, observe elementary safety procedures. On entering buildings one must shield against the impact of hot gases and smoke. These will be released instantly when a door is opened or entry is forced and a rescuer must keep out of line. Shelter should be taken behind the wall as the door is opened. Because of this surge effect, it is essential to keep as many doors and windows closed as is possible in the circumstances. It is also sensible to break in as far away from the seat of the fire as possible, unless there is a clear access closer to it which has proved to be safe. The opening of an access door, etc., will allow air to rush in, which will accelerate the spread of the fire by feeding it with oxygen. Smouldering material will often burst into flames immediately a door is opened.

In smoke-filled rooms, cleaner air is always to be found closer to the floor and it can, therefore, be better to enter on all fours or to crawl on the stomach. If it is possible, keep close to walls as the floor joists are at their strongest at this point. They may have been weakened by fire closer to the centre of the room. A wet handkerchief placed over the mouth and nose will assist as it will exclude a proportion of the irritant fumes. If the hands are being used to attempt to locate casualties, use the back of the hand to feel around the room. If the open palm touches live electric wires, the fingers will automatically clasp the live wires.

Buildings should be searched methodically. The first task should be to examine the area in greatest danger quickly, so that casualties can be removed before the situation there becomes impossible. In all other circumstances search the top of the building where people will be in the greatest danger from rising smoke. Observe the rules and ensure your own safety at all times; you are of no use to the public if you make yourself a casualty. When the rescue of persons is obviously beyond you, ensure that the senior fire officer is quickly informed of places in the building where people are known to be, the number of persons who are likely to be there and their probable location.

Persons with their clothing on fire should be laid flat to prevent flames creeping up towards their faces. Panic may have deprived them of their reason and it may be necessary to execute a flying rugby tackle to save their lives. When in the prone position the flames should be smothered with some heavy material such as woollen garments, coats or jackets. Fires caused by oil or electricity leaks present special hazards as the use of water is absolutely prohibited. When it can be done, the source of supply should be shut off.

Particular action when fire of doubtful origin

Collect as much information as possible from the senior fire officer and inform control and a supervisory officer of your concern and give the reasons for that concern. A senior police officer will then attend the scene. Immediately the fire is under control, ensure that the scene is preserved for a careful and thorough examination by experts. No one must be allowed access to the scene unless authorised. Identify and take the names of persons present who were witnesses to the outbreak, or of any persons showing particular interest in the fire. Persons acting in any way suspiciously should be identified and if there are reasonable suspicions of implication, such persons should be detained.

Particulars to note

A comprehensive report will be required at the conclusion of any major incident involving fire, and on all occasions it will be necessary to make every effort to trace the cause of the fire. Fatalities will necessitate an inquest and accurate records of events as they occurred are essential. A simple rule to follow is to record the times of arrival of all persons and services and to record immediately the full particulars of the person who first reported the fire and any witnesses who may be present. In cases of extreme urgency, it may be difficult to record the personal details of the informant. In such circumstances, the person reporting should be asked to accompany the constable to the scene. Details should be recorded of all persons who have left the building. The last to leave is of particular importance as that person will be able to give a more accurate account of the spread of fire, the parts of the building affected and persons who are likely to be there.

When the fire has been extinguished, enquiries should be made of witnesses in an attempt to establish as clearly as possible the time of the outbreak, and an assessment of the extent of the damage should be made. The identity of the senior fire officer present and any fire prevention officer who may be called to the scene should be established. These officers will ultimately be able to provide a fairly accurate estimate of the extent of the damage and be able to give useful information as to the possible cause. If arson is suspected, detailed statements should be taken from such experts and any material they may discover which indicates the likelihood of the fire having been started deliberately should be preserved and packed for laboratory examination by trained officers at the scene. All forms of police fire reports require information concerning the insurance cover of the buildings damaged.

Force orders should be studied before reports are submitted as they are not always required following minor fires.

Police powers

The powers of the senior police officer at the scene of a fire have already been described. In addition, the Fire Services Act 1947 authorises constables to enter, if necessary by breaking in, any premises or place in which fire has, or is reasonably believed to have, broken out. Such an entry may also be made of adjoining premises in order to protect them from acts done for fire-fighting purposes, or for rescuing persons. The consent of the owner or occupier of premises is not required on any of these occasions.

False alarms of fire

Any person who knowingly gives, or causes to be given, a false alarm of fire to any fire brigade shall be guilty of an offence. This offence, contrary to the Fire Services Act 1947, s 31, is a 'penalty offence' for the purposes of Part I of the Criminal Justice and Police Act 2001 and may be dealt with under a fixed-penalty procedure; see page 478.

Incidents involving dangerous substances

The Carriage of Dangerous Goods by Road Regulations 1996 are concerned with the conveyance by road of various substances which, in the event of an accident, or a leak in a storage tank, would be dangerous. The Regulations require the approval and publication by the Health and Safety Commission of documents entitled 'Approved Carriage Lists', 'Approved Tank Requirements' and 'Approved Vehicle Requirements' and place duties on the operator of, and other specified persons concerned with, any tank or vehicle used for the carriage of dangerous goods.

No operator of a container, tank or vehicle shall cause or permit to be carried thereon any dangerous goods unless a consignor's declaration has been obtained in relation to those goods and he has taken all reasonable steps to ensure that the goods are in a fit condition for carriage. No passengers (other than a crew member) may be carried in such a vehicle.

The operator of any container, tank or vehicle used for the carriage of dangerous goods must ensure that information as specified in the regulations is displayed on the container, tank or vehicle in accordance with the regulations.

The driver of such vehicles will carry the Transport Documentation (consignor's information, details of the total mass or volume of dangerous goods to be carried, the emergency action code where applicable, the prescribed temperature where appropriate and the emergency information) and keep that information readily available. These documents must be produced at the request of a constable or vehicle examiner. Where a trailer which is being used for the carriage of dangerous goods becomes detached from the motor vehicle, the driver must give the Transport Documentation to the occupier of the premises on which the trailer is parked. The occupier must ensure that the documentation is kept readily available at those premises, or the driver of the vehicle must attach the Transport Documentation to the trailer in a readily visible position.

Where such a vehicle is no longer being used for the carriage of dangerous goods, the driver must ensure that any documentation relating solely to dangerous goods which have been carried is either removed from the vehicle or placed in a securely closed container clearly marked to show that it does not relate to any dangerous goods which are being carried.

The operator of a vehicle which is used for the transportation of dangerous goods must keep a record of the information contained in the Transport Documentation for a period of at least 3 months.

The Transport of Dangerous Goods (Safety Advisers) Regulations 1999 prohibit the transport of dangerous goods by road, railway or inland waterway by an employer unless a safety officer has been appointed. The adviser will advise the employer as to health, safety and environmental matters in connection with the transport of such goods. A self-employed person may appoint himself as safety officer.

Explosives

The Carriage of Explosives by Road Regulations 1996 lay down additional provisions in relation to the carriage of explosives. The carriage of certain explosives in a vehicle is prohibited. The carriage of any form of explosives in a vehicle used to carry passengers for hire and reward is prohibited, other than strict conditions. The Regulations also deal with the suitability of vehicles and freight containers and with the quantities of explosives which may be carried.

When explosives are carried, vehicles must carry at the front and rear reflectorised orange plates with a black border. They must also carry side-marker plates on each side of the vehicle, trailer, semi-trailer or freight container in which explosives are carried, of diamond shape, which are orange in colour with a black border, bearing certain letters in black according to the type of explosives carried. The letters may be 1.2E (with a symbol of an explosion above), or 1.4 with the letter 'E' below. If the explosives carried have not yet been classified, such plates may only carry the symbol of an explosion.

Police powers

Chief constables may appoint certain officers, in writing, to be inspectors for the purposes of the Health and Safety at Work Act. An officer so appointed has the power to detain a road tanker or tank container for the purpose of examining its contents.

Training of drivers and police powers

The operators of vehicles used for the carriage of dangerous goods, including radioactive material, are required by the Carriage of Dangerous Goods by Road (Driver Training) Regulations 1996 to ensure that drivers of such vehicles are properly trained. Drivers must hold 'vocational training certificates' which must be carried in the vehicle and produced to a police constable or a goods vehicle examiner on request. Drivers may only be issued with vocational training certificates where they have completed training in the carriage of the dangerous goods concerned and they have passed the appropriate examination approved by the Secretary of State.

Stage 6

Licensed premises, registered clubs, refreshment houses and drunkenness

Licensed premises

General

The term 'licensed premises' is defined by s 200 of the Licensing Act 1964. This definition includes premises for which a justices' licence (or an occasional licence) is in force for the sale of intoxicating liquor to members of the public. Justices' licences are granted at the annual general licensing sessions or at transfer sessions that must be held at least four times a year. Licences are valid for a period of 3 years. There is a general renewal date every 3 years.

A full on-licence authorises sale of intoxicating liquor for consumption on or off the premises. An off-licence authorises sale for consumption off the premises only. The term 'intoxicating liquor' means spirits, wine, beer, cider, and any other fermented, distilled or spirituous liquor of a strength of 0.5 per cent or more. Low alcohol drinks are, therefore, intoxicating liquor. Generally, any form of liquor which does not require an excise licence to permit sale by wholesale, is not intoxicating liquor – the exception being cider.

At the time at which proofs were being set for this edition, the Licensing Act 2003 received Royal Assent. However, the provisions of the Act are to be brought into force by statutory instrument when the administrative procedure essential for the maintenance of the new system has been put in place. The new system removes 'justices' licences' and replaces them with premises licences, club premises certificates and temporary events notices. The first will cover the existing licensed premises, the second represents a new approach to the authorisation of clubs, and temporary event notices deal with those events which are 'occasional'. The issue of these forms of authorisation will be placed in the hands of local authorities. 'Permitted hours' are dispensed with. Applicants for licences and certificates will select their own hours and if there are no sustainable objections, those hours will be accepted. Local authorities will maintain a register of premises and the hours which currently apply. These may be varied by further application. Chief officers of police will be consulted at all stages of these procedures and may object to any proposals. The Act also introduces 'personal licences' which are granted by a licensing authority to an individual and authorise him to supply alcohol, or authorise the supply of alcohol, in accordance with the premises licence.

When the 2003 Act is brought into force, please ignore this chapter and refer to the material in the Appendix.

Restaurant and residential licences

Restaurant licences may be granted for premises which are structurally adapted and bona fide used, or intended to be used, for the purpose of providing the customary main meal at midday, or in the evening, or both, for the accommodation of persons frequenting the premises. We are therefore considering establishments which provide either, or both of, the main meals of the day. Sale and supply of intoxicants is permitted to persons taking table meals on the premises, the drinks being consumed as an ancillary to the meal. Persons who are not eating there may not drink there. Where a restaurant licence is in force which serves alcohol with meals until midnight on weekdays and 11.30 p.m. on Sundays there is no need for the licensee to apply for a supper hour certificate; see page 646. This also applies where the licence is a combined residential and restaurant licence.

Residential licences are granted to private hotels or boarding houses which provide breakfast and at least one of the customary main meals. Sale or supply of intoxicants is restricted to residents or their private friends who must be entertained at their expense. If meals are offered to the general public and drinks are to be supplied with those meals, a combined restaurant/residential licence would be required.

Occasional licence

The definition includes premises in respect of which an occasional licence is in force. These licences are granted at magistrates' courts to allow intoxicating liquor to be sold at certain special events and are granted only to the holder of justices' on-licences (permitting sale of intoxicating liquor for consumption on the premises), allowing them to sell elsewhere than on their licensed premises the forms of liquor specified in their licence. An occasional licence may be valid for a period not exceeding 3 weeks. Such a licence may not be granted in respect of Good Friday, Christmas Day or any other appointed day of public fast or thanksgiving. At race meetings, sporting events, flower shows, dances and other social events, beer tents or occasional bars may have been set up by an on-licence holder who is temporarily selling intoxicating liquor at premises other than his established licensed premises. In such circumstances, the hours during which liquor may be sold are specified in the occasional licence and normal permitted hours do not apply. During the validity of the licence, the premises are licensed premises and the various offences which may be committed by the holder of a justices' licence may also be committed by the holder of an occasional licence. Thus, a licence holder may not permit drunkenness, violence or unlawful gaming to take place on the premises, or unlawful sales to be made to persons who are under age.

However, drinking-up time provisions (explained below) cannot apply to occasional licences because the licence expires at a given time and when that occurs the premises are no longer licensed. If a sale takes place outside the hours specified in the licence, it is a sale other than as authorised by a justices' licence.

Occasional permission

Licensing justices can grant to an officer of any organisation not carried on for the purpose of private gain, occasional permission to sell intoxicating liquor during any period not exceeding 24 hours, in respect of a function held by the organisation which is allied to its activities. Such permissions must specify the place, type of intoxicants to be sold and the hours. An organisation may not have more than 12 occasional permissions in any year. The justice may attach conditions to such permissions should they consider it proper to do so.

The Licensing (Occasional Permissions) Act 1983 was introduced to remove some on the inconsistencies within the system of occasional licensing. Before this procedure was set up, a non-licensed (registered or proprietary) club was compelled to ask a licensee to obtain an occasional licence whenever it held a function upon the premises at which non-members would be allowed to purchase drinks, as such clubs are not permitted to sell to non-members.

Where the profits made from sales under the authority of occasional permissions go to the club or organisation, there is no *private gain*. Thus, a club may operate its own bar at a function to which non-members are admitted.

Section 3 of the Act provides for a number of offences the details of which are contained in the Schedule to the Act. These include permitting drunkenness and sales, etc., to persons under 18. The same powers of exclusion and expulsion are given as are given to licensees and the same powers are given to constables in this respect (see below). A power of entry exists for a constable at any time during the hours specified in the occasional permission.

Public entry

A public house with open doors inviting the public to enter is a public place. The fact that certain people are excluded by law from entering and that others may be excluded at the will of the landlord does not prevent it from being public. A 'bar' in licensed premises is any place mainly or exclusively used for the sale *and* consumption of intoxicating liquor.

Licensing hours

A licensee, servant or agent shall not sell or supply any intoxicating liquor, whether to be consumed on or off the licensed premises, outside the general licensing hours described in the Licensing Act 1964. The hours prescribed are:

(a) weekdays (other than Christmas Day or Good Friday or New Year's Eve), 11.00 to 23.00;
(b) Sundays (other than Christmas Days or New Year's Eve) and on Good Friday, 12.00 to 22.30;
(c) Christmas Day, 12.00 to 22.30 with a break of 4 hours beginning at 15.00;
(d) New Year's Eve, 11.00 to 23.00 (12.00 to 22.30 on a Sunday); in addition, unless a special occasions restriction order is in force, special occasion licensing hours apply between 23.00 (22.30 on a Sunday) and the beginning of permitted hours on New Year's Day (in other words, an all-night party).

The hours prescribed in relation to off-licensed premises are from 08.00 to 23.00 on weekdays. On Sundays, they are from 10.00 to 22.30.

There are a number of reasons for which the licensing justices may vary these hours.

Special requirements of the district

On weekdays, the licensing justices for any licensing district, if satisfied that the requirements of the district make it desirable, may by order modify the hours for the district so that the permitted hours begin at a time earlier than 11.00 but not earlier than 10.00.

Meals

In instances in which intoxicating liquor is supplied during the permitted hours, if supplied for consumption as an ancillary to a meal, it may be consumed during the half hour following permitted hours.

The legal meaning of the term 'meal' has never been strictly defined. In general circumstances it does not necessarily mean table meals. If meals are being served in premises which are fully on-licensed, advantage may be taken of this extended drinking-up time without full table meals being provided, but if the licence has been granted in respect of a restaurant it will be upon the condition that either the main midday meal, or evening meal, or both such meals will be provided. What constitutes a meal is a matter for the justices. It is unlikely that toasted sandwiches from a machine would be considered sufficient. The consumption of drink as an ancillary to a meal does not mean that it must be supplied at the same time as the meal or drunk with the meal. It can be taken as an aperitif prior to the meal or as a drink to follow a meal, and in either case can be taken in the separate room usually set apart for such purpose. It is a question of fact to be determined by the magistrates when drinking away from the table ceases to be ancillary to the meal.

Apart from this general provision in respect of premises supplying meals, in instances in which premises are structurally suitable and are bona fide used for providing substantial table meals with an ancillary supply of liquor, licensed premises or registered clubs may be granted a supper hour extension of 1 hour to the evening permitted hours. This extension will only apply to the part of the premises set apart for table meals as specified in the order. There is no requirement to obtain a supper hour extension in the case of premises in respect of which there is a restaurant or combined restaurant and residential licence and which serves alcohol with meals until midnight on weekdays and 23.30 on Sundays. The provisions permitting 'drinking-up' time of half an hour following a meal apply to premises with a supper hour extension, so that drinking with a meal can lawfully continue until 00.30. A lunch hour extension permits such premises to serve intoxicants with a meal throughout the period between the first and second parts of licensing hours on Sundays, Christmas Day and Good Friday.

Entertainment

The Licensing Act 1964, s 70, states that justices may, by order, extend permitted hours until 01.00 on weekdays for premises in respect of which a supper hour certificate has been granted. Musical or other entertainment must be provided by persons who are actually present (which excludes recorded music) and the premises must be suitable for such entertainment and for the supply of meals. The sale and supply of intoxicants must be ancillary to the provision of meals and entertainment. The extension will only apply to the part of the premises set aside for these purposes.

Although the section permits extended hours until 01.00 (if the order applies to permitted hours on a Sunday they may extend to 00.30), the justices may limit the order to a time earlier than 01.00 (or 00.30) if it appears to them to be reasonable to do so having regard to all the circumstances, particularly in relation to the comfort and convenience of those in nearby premises. If the licensing justices make an extended hours order in spite of objections from the relevant local authority based on the residential character of the area where the premises are situated, they must state their reasons for doing so.

Such an order, in effect, permits the sale and supply of intoxicating liquor up to the time at which the availability of meals or the provision of entertainment ceases and to allow the consumption of those intoxicants within the terms of the normal half-hour drinking-up time following the end of permitted hours or where meals are being taken. Thus, if no meals or entertainment are offered after 23.30, licensing hours end then and drinking must cease at midnight.

Special hours certificates

Sections 76 to 83 of the 1964 Act deal with various types of premises in respect of which there may be a 'special hours certificate'. Where the licensed premises are casino premises or a music and dancing licence is in force for them, and the premises (or part of them) are structurally adapted and bona fide used, or intended to be used, for gaming facilities and substantial refreshment (in the case of casino premises) or the provision of music and dancing and substantial refreshment (in the case of other premises), to which the sale of intoxicants is merely ancillary, the licensing justices may grant, with or without limitations, a special hours certificate. The requirement in the case of premises other than casino premises relating to the provision of music and dancing and substantial refreshment is not framed as alternatives. All three things must be provided (or be intended to be provided) on the premises, although it is not necessary that their provision should be at the same time throughout the licensing hours permitted by the certificate. No doubt a corresponding interpretation applies in the case of casino premises.

Where a registered club holds a certificate of suitability for music and dancing and its premises are, in whole or in part, structurally adapted and bona fide used, or intended for use, for the provision of music and dancing and substantial refreshment to which the supply of intoxicants is merely ancillary, a magistrates' court may grant, with or without limitations, a special hours certificate.

A special hours certificate may restrict the hours to a part of the premises. Many premises to which a special hours certificate may be issued are also referred to loosely as night clubs but, unlike extended hours orders, a special hours certificate does not include a requirement for live entertainment with meals, although there is a requirement that music and dancing will be available with meals.

Where a certificate is in force, the permitted hours on *weekdays* extend until 02.00 the next morning [03.00 in those parts of the metropolis specified in the Licensing (Metropolitan Special Area) Order 1961].

Permitted hours on a weekday:

(a) must end at midnight on any weekday on which music and dancing or (in the case of casinos) gaming facilities are not provided after midnight;
(b) must end when the music and dancing, or the gaming, end on a weekday on which music and dancing, or (in the case of casinos) gaming, end between midnight and 02.00.

Certificates may be limited to particular times of the day, days of the week or periods of the year.

However, existing certificate holders must apply for their certificates to be extended to Sundays. New applicants must request the inclusion of Sundays within the permitted hours. Provision is made by an added s 81AA of the 1964 Act for application to be made to the licensing justices or magistrates' court for the imposition of a limitation excluding Sunday on the grounds that it is desirable to avoid or reduce disturbance or annoyance on Sundays to persons living or working in the neighbourhood or customers or clients of any business, or the occurrence in the vicinity of the premises of disorderly conduct on the part of persons resorting to the premises. Such affected persons, a chief officer of police or a local authority may make such an application. These provisions do not apply to a Sunday.

An hour is not lost on days upon which clocks go forward. An hour is added.

Sales out of hours

An offence is committed against s 59 of the Act by any person who, himself or by his servant or agent, sells or supplies intoxicating liquor in licences premises or in a registered club, whether to be drunk on or off the premises, outside permitted hours. An offence is also committed by any person who drinks on the premises, or takes intoxicants away from such premises, outside permitted hours.

General and special orders of exemption

The holder of a justices' on-licence or the secretary of a registered club may be granted a 'general order of exemption' when the premises in question are situated in the immediate neighbourhood of a public market or place where people follow a particular trade or calling. Many market towns have a market day on which farmers and residents gather from a large catchment area. The influx of such a large number of people makes it desirable that places of refreshment are open and available to them. The licensing hours are as specified in the order of exemption and registers are kept in police stations in which details of such orders are recorded. Orders are made in respect of named licensed premises.

The same persons may apply to a magistrates' court for a 'special order of exemption'. Here we are concerned with the extension of licensing hours in particular premises on a special occasion. That which is a special occasion has not been defined but the Divisional Court has indicated that the more frequently a particular 'occasion' arises, the less likely it is to be special. Weekly debates at the Oxford Union which were held over a period of 8 weeks were held not to be special occasions. Special occasions are usually associated with weddings, 21st birthday parties and annual dinners. Each of these occasions is 'special' to the person or organisation concerned. Football matches during the World Cup have been held to be 'special occasions'. Once it is granted, a special order automatically applies to the whole of the premises and is not restricted to the room in which the function is held. As a result, the justices frequently demand an undertaking that normal licensing hours will be observed in other parts of the premises. Nevertheless, if that undertaking is ignored, no offence is committed in relation to sales. Such an order may be valid for more than one day.

Exemptions to licensing hours

The permitted hours do not prohibit or restrict drinking in certain circumstances:

(a) A resident in licensed premises may drink outside permitted hours and may entertain guests at his own expense. Such guests must be private friends.
(b) These provisions extend to the licence holder and any servants who are resident on the premises. Whether such persons are true, as opposed to pretended, friends and were truly entertained at the resident's expense are matters to be determined by the magistrates.

(c) 'Drinking-up' time of 20 minutes is allowed at the end of normal permitted hours so that glasses may be emptied when sales have ended. Bottles purchased before the end of permitted hours may be taken from the premises during this time.

Police entry

For the purposes of preventing and detecting the commission of any of these offences against the Licensing Act 1964, a constable is empowered by s 186 of the Act to enter licensed premises, a licensed canteen (licensed by the Secretary of State), or premises for which (or any part of which) a special hours certificate is in force:

(a) in the case of licensed premises or licensed canteens, during permitted hours and during the first half hour after the end of any period of permitted hours;
(b) where an occasional licence is in force, during the hours specified in the licence; and
(c) where a special hours certificate is in force, during the period between 23.00 and half an hour after the end of permitted hours for those premises.

These powers of entry might be described as the 'general' powers of entry as they are obviously concerned with inspections during and immediately after permitted hours. However, in respect of licensed premises and licensed canteens an entry may be made *at any time* outside these hours where a constable suspects with reasonable cause that an offence against the Act is being or is about to be committed. This power enables entry to deal with 'lock-in' after-hours drinkers.

It is an offence to fail to admit a constable who identifies himself as such. An employer commits an offence if an employee, or any other person acting with consent, fails to admit a constable.

The orders issued by most chief constables require that entry into licensed premises should normally only be effected in the presence of a supervisory rank. There are, however, many occasions upon which the urgency of the matter requires an immediate entry to be made, and it is good practice to make an accurate record of such entry, and the action which was taken, in the official pocket notebook.

Expulsion from licensed premises and exclusion

A constable is required to help to expel from licensed premises any person who is drunk, violent, quarrelsome or disorderly or whose presence would subject the licence holder to a penalty, on being requested to assist by the licensee, his agent or employee. A person who refuses to leave on being so required by the licensee, his servant or agent, or any constable, commits an offence. There is no power to arrest without warrant for this offence, but the Act authorises the use of such force as is necessary to expel such a person from the licensed premises.

The Licensed Premises (Exclusion of Certain Persons) Act 1980 allows courts to make orders in respect of persons convicted of offences involving violence or threats of violence on licensed premises, prohibiting that person from entering specified licensed premises without the express consent of the licensee, his servant or agent. A person who enters in breach of an order commits an offence. A licensee, his servant or agent may expel a person who has entered, or whom he reasonably suspects of entering, in breach of an order. A constable shall, on demand of such licensee, servant or agent, help to expel any person whom the constable reasonably suspects of being in breach of an exclusion order.

Restriction orders and licensed premises

Restriction orders may apply to licensed premises or registered clubs, specifying any time between 14.30 and 17.30 (15.00 and 19.00 on Sundays and Good Fridays) as being non-permitted hours. They may apply to particular days of the week and to particular periods of the year and must not remain in force for more than 12 months.

An application for such an order may be made by a chief officer of police, persons living in the neighbourhood (or their representative), neighbouring businessmen or their managers or head teachers. Such an order may be made on the grounds of avoiding or reducing annoyance or disturbance to local residents or workers, to customers of businesses in the locality, or to people at schools. They may also be made on the grounds that it is desirable to avoid or reduce the incidence of disorderly conduct on the premises or in their vicinity.

Persons under 18

Sales for consumption 'on' the premises

Section 169 of the Licensing Act 1964 was substituted by the Licensing (Young Persons) Act 2000. The section was, in effect, broken up into parts, each of which dealt with a particular aspect of sale of intoxicants to persons under 18.

Section 169A(1) provides that a person commits an offence by selling intoxicating liquor to a person under 18. Subsections (2) and (3) provide defences: where a person is charged by reason of his own act, to prove belief that the person was not under 18 and either that all reasonable steps had been taken to establish the person's age or that nobody could reasonably have suspected from appearance that the person was under 18 years of age. A person will be treated as having taken all reasonable steps to establish another person's age if evidence of age is requested unless it is shown that the evidence was such that no reasonable person would have been convinced by it. Where charged by reason of the act or default of someone else, it is a defence to prove that he exercised all due diligence to avoid the commission of such an offence.

Section 169B provides that it is an offence for a person who works in licensed premises in a capacity, whether paid or unpaid, which carries authority to prevent a sale if he knowingly allows any person to sell intoxicating liquor to a person under 18.

It is an offence, by s 169C, for a person under 18, in licensed premises, to buy or attempt to buy intoxicating liquor (other than where the purchase or attempted purchase is at the instigation of a constable or weights and measures inspector). This is a 'penalty offence' for the purposes of Part I of the Criminal Justice and Police Act 2001 and may be dealt with under a fixed-penalty procedure. In addition, it provides that it is an offence for any person, in licensed premises, to buy or attempt to buy intoxicating liquor on behalf of a person under 18 or for such a person to buy or attempt to buy intoxicating liquor for consumption in a bar in licensed premises by a person under 18. In the case of these last two offences (committed by someone other than the person under 18), it is a defence for such a person to prove that there was no reason to suspect that the person was under 18. The offence against s 169(C) (3) (person under 18 buying or attempting to buy alcohol for consumption in a bar) is a 'penalty offence' for the purposes of Part I of the Criminal Justice and Police Act 2001 and may be dealt with under a fixed-penalty procedure; see page 478.

However, s 169D exempts from these offences such purchases where the person has attained the age of 16 and the liquor in question is beer, porter or cider and its sale or purchases is for consumption at a meal in a part of the licensed premises which is not a bar and is usually set apart for the service of meals.

Thus, the offences we have considered so far are all related to the purchase or attempted purchase of intoxicants. It goes on to deal with offences associated with the drinking of intoxicants.

Section 169E provides that a person under 18 will be guilty of an offence if he consumes intoxicating liquor in a bar in licensed premises. In addition, it provides that a person who works in the licensed premises, whether paid or unpaid, in a capacity which carries authority to prevent such consumption, commits an offence if knowingly allowing a person under 18 to drink intoxicants in a bar in licensed premises.

Sales for consumption 'off' the premises

By s 169F, a person who works in licensed premises, whether paid or unpaid, commits an offence by knowingly delivering to a person under 18 intoxicants for consumption off the premises. Such a person, if authorised to prevent the delivery, will also commit an offence by knowingly allowing any person to deliver to a person under 18 intoxicants sold in licensed premises for consumption off the premises. However, these offences do not apply in circumstances involving delivery to the residence or work place of the purchaser, or where the person under 18 works in the licensed premises, whether paid or unpaid, in a capacity which includes the delivery of intoxicating liquor.

Section 169G makes it an offence for a person knowingly to send a person under 18 (other than where the purchase or attempted purchase is at the instigation of a constable or weights and measures inspector) for the purpose of obtaining intoxicating liquor sold, or to be sold, in licensed premises for consumption off the premises. This applies whether the liquor is to be obtained from the licensed premises, or from other premises from which it is delivered in consequence of the sale. Once again, the section does not apply in respect of persons under 18 who work as delivery boys.

Forfeiture of licence following conviction for selling, etc., to a person under 18

Where the holder of a justices' licence is convicted of any of these offences associated with the licensed premises, the court may order forfeiture of the licence if he already has one or more convictions for any of these offences, or the similar offences which existed under s 169 of the 1964 Act.

The possibility of forfeiture of a justices' licence in these circumstances reflects the determination of the legislators to prevent drinking in public places by those who are 'under age'.

General nature of these offences

In deciding the offences which have been committed in circumstances involving young persons who are drinking on licensed premises, it is helpful first to consider the question of where the drinking is taking place. If it has taken place in a bar then offences of 'consumption' may be charged. If it has not, the appropriate charges will be of sale and purchase, if these can be proved. When reporting offenders for offences involving consumption, the fact that they took place in a bar must be mentioned.

John, aged 17, is in a bar with his friend, David, who is 18. If John orders a pint of beer and is served by the licensee, the licensee commits an offence by selling the beer. At this stage the issue of whether or not it takes place in a bar is unimportant as the offence of 'sale', unless specifically permitted in the circumstances, can take place anywhere. In addition to the liability of the licensee, John commits the offence of 'purchasing'.

Once John begins to drink from the glass he is guilty of an offence of 'consumption', provided that this takes place in a bar. At this time the licensee and the barman, if they are aware of the situation, may become guilty of knowingly allowing consumption in a bar. The word 'knowingly' in these circumstances applies to the age of the customer, not to the act of the sale. It can be applied to situations in which a licensee deliberately closes his eyes to the obvious. If David had bought the drink, or had attempted to buy it, for consumption in a bar by John, he would have committed an offence.

If the purchase had been made by David with the intention of taking the drink outside so that John might consume it, he would not have committed an offence as it was not bought for John to drink in a bar. The taking outside of drinks purchased on licensed premises is not uncommon and it is quite lawful.

The term 'bar' is defined by the Licensing Act 1964 as including any place exclusively or mainly for sale or consumption of intoxicating liquor. It does not apply to rooms exclusively used for table meals in which the sale of intoxicants is restricted to persons taking meals as an ancillary to such meals. In all other instances the matter to be considered is the room's use. If it is mainly or exclusively used for the sale and consumption of intoxicants, it is a bar.

Where it is necessary to prove that offences were committed 'knowingly', that is, in the knowledge that the person served, or drinking, was under the age of 18, it may be possible to show that the licensee or the servants positively knew the age of the person concerned, but such occasions will be rare. Most frequently the offences will come to light because the person concerned appears to be under the age of 18 and is in fact under the age of 18. An accused will have sufficient knowledge if he suspects that the person is under 18 and deliberately fails to make enquiries. This will be apparent to the justices. Within many police areas there are schemes the purpose of which is to provide 18-year-olds with identity documents.

Section 170 prohibits a licensee from employing a person under 18 in a bar of licensed premises at any time when the bar is open for the sale or consumption of intoxicating liquor. This does not apply to persons who are employed to work elsewhere on the premises who may pass through a bar or deliver messages to persons in a bar. Equally, it would not apply to dining room waiters who were asked by customers to deliver their coffee and brandy to an adjoining bar. The term 'employment' is given its general meaning of use and there is no necessity to prove payment of wages.

Confiscation of alcohol – young persons

The Confiscation of Alcohol (Young Persons) Act 1997 provides that where a constable reasonably suspects that a person in any public place other than licensed premises; or any place, other than a public place, to which a person has unlawfully gained access, is in possession of alcohol and that either:

(a) he is under the age of 18; or
(b) he intends that any of the liquor should be consumed by a person under the age of 18 in that or another similar place; or
(c) a person under the age of 18 who is, or has recently been, with him, has recently consumed intoxicating liquor in that or another similar place,

the constable may require that person to surrender anything which he possesses which is, or the constable reasonably believes to be, intoxicating liquor, or a container for such liquor (or a sealed container reasonably believed for use for such a purpose) and to state his name and address. A person who, without reasonable excuse, fails to comply with such a requirement commits an offence. A constable who makes such a requirement must inform the person concerned of the suspicion and that failing without reasonable excuse to comply with the requirement is an offence.

The Act provides a means by which the nuisance caused by young people assembling in public places and drinking from cans may be removed. The terms of s 1 of the Act are such that all persons who are included in such a group who have intoxicating liquor in their possession may be required to surrender it.

Police powers

A constable may dispose of anything surrendered in such a manner as he considers appropriate.

The section provides a power to arrest without warrant a person who fails to comply with such a requirement made under the 1997 Act.

Persons under 14 years

By s 168 of the 1964 Act, the holder of a justices' licence shall not allow a person under 14 years to be in the bar of the licensed premises during permitted hours. No other person shall cause or procure, or attempt to cause or procure, any such person to be in a bar during permitted hours.

The previous offences which we considered were concerned with drinking intoxicants on premises, but we are now examining the question of those persons who may be present. It is no offence for a 14-year-old to be in a bar on licensed premises drinking soft drinks. It is an offence for a 13-year-old to be there whether drinking anything or not. However, there are certain exceptions to the general rule that persons under 14 shall not be in a bar during permitted hours.

The licence holder's children are exempt, as are those of residents on the premises, provided that they are not children of resident employees. Children who are simply passing through a bar where there is no other means of access to another part of the premises are also exempt, and these provisions do not apply to railway refreshment rooms or premises in respect of which the holding of a justices' licence is merely ancillary to some other main purpose.

A licensee may prove due diligence to prevent the person under 14 from being admitted, but if unable to do so, must be convicted of the offence if such a person is found there.

There is no offence where the persons under 14 is in the company of someone of 18 or over and one or both of them is consuming a meal in the bar provided that there is in force a children's certificate relating to the bar. Such a certificate is obtainable from the licensing justices, who must be satisfied that the premises are a suitable environment for children to be present and that meals and non-alcoholic drinks will be available. If a non-authorised child is in a bar, the licensee is guilty of an offence unless he exercised all due diligence to prevent the admission of a child or that the child had apparently reached 14. In addition to the licensee, a person who causes or procures a child under 14 to be in a bar during permitted hours, or attempts to do so, is guilty of an offence. The child itself commits no offence.

A notice must be displayed stating that such a certificate is in force.

Licensed clubs

Clubs may be licensed or registered. The legal aspects of registered clubs are examined below. The term 'club' has not been defined but it can be described as a voluntary association of a number of people for a common object or purpose, for example, recreation, art, science, politics or social welfare. When such an association has been formed and it is intended to serve drinks in the club, the members must decide whether to license or register the premises which are to be occupied and habitually used for the purposes of the club. If the decision is to apply for a justices' licence and it is subsequently granted, the licence will authorise the sale of intoxicants on the premises. A nominated officer of the club must apply for the justices' licence and, when it is issued in his name, he assumes the right and the obligations of a licence holder. The club must restrict sales to normal permitted hours and the legal restrictions which apply to the sale or supply of liquor to persons under 18 years of age will apply. In addition, conditions may be attached to the licence, prohibiting or restricting the sale of liquor to non-members. In this way, although a justices' licence is in force which would normally permit the licence holder to sell liquor to all members of the public, conditions attached to the licence probably restrict sales to members and, perhaps, their guests.

Registered clubs

We have already considered licensed clubs and other forms of licensed premises, and the common factor has been that a justices' licence is required before intoxicating liquor may be sold. A justices' licence is not required for the supply of liquor in a registered club which, to meet the conditions for registration, must consist of members who jointly own the property of the club, including the drinks. In this way, the profits of the club are also shared by the membership and there is no direct profit to any individual. It is considered, therefore, that there is no sale of liquor in a registered club as the members actually own all of the intoxicating liquor in the first instance, it having been bought with money which they have paid as membership dues. When drinks are supplied in such a club, it is merely a release to a member of his own property.

The permitted hours in respect of the premises of a registered club shall be:

(a) on days other than Christmas Day, the general licensing hours; and
(b) on Christmas Day, the hours fixed by or under the rules of the club in accordance with the following conditions:
   (i) the hours fixed shall not be longer than 6½ hours and shall not begin earlier than 12.00 or end later than 22.30;

(ii) there shall be a break in the afternoon of not less than 2 hours, which shall include the hours from 15.00 to 17.00; and

(iii) there shall not be more than 3½ hours after 17.00.

So that the permitted hours which have been fixed by the rules of a registered club may be known, written notice of the hours fixed must be given to the justices' clerk. In most police stations a record of licensed premises and registered clubs is maintained, in which the permitted hours are recorded. If offences of supplying intoxicating liquor during non-permitted hours are suspected in the premises of any registered club, the hours can be checked by reference to such records or by checking with the justices' clerk.

There is no general power of entry into the premises of a registered club. If a special hours certificate is in force then the Licensing Act authorises entry to any part of the premises in respect of which the certificate applies during the period between 23.00 and half an hour after the end of permitted hours for those premises. Generally, entry into a registered club in which it is suspected that offences are being committed is effected under the authority of two search warrants issued under ss 54 and 187 of the Licensing Act 1964, authorising the seizure of documents and intoxicating liquor if sales to non-members and other unauthorised persons are suspected.

Late-night refreshment houses

A late-night refreshment house is a house, room, shop or building which is kept open for public refreshment, resort and entertainment at any time between the hours of 22.00 and 05.00, other than premises licensed for the sale of intoxicants. All such refreshment houses must be licensed by the county or district council and it is an offence for any person to keep a late-night refreshment house without a licence.

It is a question of fact as to whether or not a particular building is kept as a refreshment house, and it is not essential that seating is provided for customers provided that refreshment is consumed on the premises. In most cases it is evident, as the premises involved will be late-night cafes and restaurants.

Police powers

A constable may at any time enter a licensed late-night refreshment house. It is an offence for the licensee, or any person acting on his behalf, to fail or refuse to admit a constable who demands admittance. On the demand of the occupier of such a house, a constable must assist in expelling drunken, riotous, quarrelsome and disorderly persons.

Drunkenness

Drunkenness is not in itself an offence, but becomes punishable when it is accompanied by aggravating circumstances which interfere with other people. The most common offences of drunkenness are contained in the Licensing Act 1872 and in s 91 of the Criminal Justice Act 1967:

(a) Any person who is found drunk in any highway or other public place, whether a building or not, or on any licensed premises, is guilty of an offence. The term 'public place' includes any place to which the public have access, whether on payment or otherwise.

(b) Any person who, while drunk in a public place, is guilty of disorderly behaviour, is guilty of an offence.

Both of the above offences are 'penalty offences' for the purposes of Part I of the Criminal Justice and Police Act 2001 and may be dealt with under a fixed-penalty procedure; see page 478.

Where there is an intercom system and locks on the entrance to a block of flats, the landing area outside the flats is not a public place for the purposes of the offence of being drunk and disorderly.

Other offences, now rare, are also contained in the 1872 Act and include being drunk while in charge, on any highway or other public place, of any carriage (which includes bicycles), horse, cattle or loaded firearm. The term 'loaded firearm' includes an air weapon.

The term 'drunkenness' is not defined, nor is the form of disorderly conduct which accompanies this condition. It has been held that an offence will be committed if the conduct is honestly believed to have been such disorderly conduct, if that belief is based upon reasonable grounds. The offence is most usually met in circumstances which involve disturbances by fighting or rowdy conduct involving persons who are obviously under the influence of drink.

The words 'found drunk' mean perceived to be drunk. When a person is expelled from a private place and is then perceived to be drunk on a highway, this offence is committed. In practice, prosecutions for simple drunkenness are confined to circumstances in which the person concerned is incapable of taking care of himself. Often such persons are found lying in the street, having drunk themselves into a state of unconsciousness, or staggering through traffic with little control over their actions, causing danger both to themselves and to the drivers who are forced to take avoiding action.

A person who is drunk on a public service vehicle or railway passenger vehicle which is being used for the principal purpose of carrying passengers for the whole or part of a journey to or from a designated sporting event, commits an offence against s 1(3) of the Sporting Events (Control of Alcohol, etc.) Act 1985. A person who is drunk in a designated sports ground at any time during the period of a designated sporting event at that ground, offends against s 2(2) of that Act (see page 665).

Police powers

The general power of arrest which is provided by s 25 of the Police and Criminal Evidence Act 1984 will usually be applicable to offences of drunkenness, where an arrest may be necessary for a number of reasons. A person who is 'found drunk' may often be in such a condition that he cannot establish identity to the satisfaction of the constable, or arrest may be necessary to prevent a person from causing injury to himself, or suffering physical injury. The person who is guilty of disorderly behaviour while drunk may be arrested without warrant by any person, including a constable. The conduct in any case will invariably involve a breach of the peace.

Care must be taken in dealing with all persons who appear to be drunk. If there is any suggestion that they may be ill, or may have injured themselves because of their condition, medical assistance should be provided. It must be remembered that persons who are very drunk are likely to be sick, and if they are not carefully watched while in custody, are likely to choke if this should occur while they are lying on their backs. Frequent visits must be made by police officers responsible for the care and custody of prisoners.

Opinion

A necessary ingredient of these offences is that the person concerned was drunk, and this should be stated clearly by the constable in evidence. Although a statement to the effect that a man was drunk is largely a matter of opinion, the courts have always accepted the testimony of a police officer in this respect. The statement must be supported by evidence of the factors which caused the police officer to form the opinion that the man was drunk, and observable symptoms might include lack of co-ordination of movements, manner of speech and the fact that the breath of the offender smelled of intoxicating liquor.

Particular offences involving police officers

The Licensing Act 1964, s 178, provides that the holder of a justices' licence commits an offence where that person:

(a) knowingly suffers any constable to remain on the licensed premises during any part of the time appointed for the constable's being on duty, except for the purpose of the execution of the constable's duty; or

(b) supplies any liquor or refreshment whether by way of gift or sale, to any constable on duty except by authority of a superior officer of the constable; or

(c) bribes or attempts to bribe any constable.

The holder of an occasional licence is the holder of a justices' licence for the purposes of this section. It must be proved that the licensee knew that person to be a constable *and* to be on duty. A constable is in the execution of his duty for the purposes of the section if assisting in the exclusion of drunkards or detecting offences under the Act.

Alcohol consumption in designated public places

Sections 12 to 16 of the Criminal Justice and Police Act 2001 give a constable certain powers (set out below) where he reasonably believes that a person is, or has been, consuming intoxicating liquor in a designated public place, or intends to consume intoxicating liquor in such a place.

The powers of a constable just referred to are to require the person concerned not to consume, in the designated place, anything which is or the constable reasonably believes to be intoxicating liquor, and to surrender such liquor or a container for such liquor. Anything so surrendered may be disposed of by the constable in a manner considered to be appropriate. Failure without reasonable excuse to comply with such a requirement is an arrestable offence. However, the constable making the requirement must inform the person concerned that failing without reasonable excuse to comply with the requirement is an offence.

As can be seen, it is not essential that in order for a requirement to be made that an officer sees a person consuming alcohol. If such a person has intoxicating liquor in a glass or an open container it raises the inference of an intention to drink it. Where liquor is in a sealed container, notice will have to be taken of the surrounding circumstances. Possession of a 'four-pack' by a person who is walking home differs from possession by groups of persons assembled at that place for the purpose of drinking.

Section 13 provides that a 'designated public place' is a public place within the area of a local authority which is identified in an order made by that authority. A local authority may make such an order where it is satisfied that:

(a) nuisance or annoyance to members of the public, or a section of the public; or
(b) disorder,

has been associated with the consumption of intoxicating liquor in that place. The making of Orders is controlled by the Local Authorities (Alcohol Consumption in Designated Public Places) Regulations 2001.

By s 14, a place is not a designated place if it is:

(a) licensed premises or a registered club;
(b) a place within the curtilage of any licensed premises or registered club;
(c) a place where the sale of intoxicating liquor is for the time being authorised by an occasional permission or was so authorised within the last 20 minutes;
(d) a place where the sale of intoxicating liquor is not for the time being authorised by an occasional licence but was so authorised within the last 20 minutes; or
(e) a place where facilities or activities relating to the sale or consumption of intoxicating liquor are for the time being permitted by virtue of a permission granted under s 115E of the Highways Act 1980 (council permission to set up objects and structures on a highway for the purpose of producing income).

Closure of licensed premises due to disorder or disturbance

Section 17 of the 2001 Act inserted new sections into the Licensing Act 1964 to deal with this.

The making of an order: s 179A

Section 179A provides that a senior police officer (i.e. of or above the rank of inspector) may make a closure order in relation to licensed premises (other than off-licensed premises or those which have occasional licences) if he reasonably believes that:

(a) there is likely to be disorder on, or in the vicinity of and related to, the premises and the closure of the premises is necessary in the interests of public safety;
(b) there is disorder on, or in the vicinity of and related to, the premises and the closure of the premises is necessary in the interests of public safety; or
(c) a disturbance is being caused to the public by excessive noise emitted from the premises and the closure of the premises is necessary to prevent the disturbance.

A closure order requires the premises to be closed for a period not exceeding 24 hours. An officer making a closure order must consider, in particular, any conduct of the holder of the justices' licence or the manager of the premises in relation to the disorder or disturbance. A closure order is effective as soon as notice of it has been given to the licensee or a manager of the premises.

Procedure following the making of an order, s 179B

As soon as reasonably practicable after the making of the order, the responsible senior police officer (he who made the order or another senior officer designated for the purpose by the chief officer of police) must apply to the licensing justices (or other justices if the licensing justices are not available within a reasonable time) for them to consider the order and any extension of it. The justices may:

(a) revoke the order and any extension of it;
(b) order that closure continues until the matter is considered at the next licensing sessions;
(c) make any other order they think fit.

Extension of closure order, s 179C

The responsible senior officer may extend the closure order for a further period of 24 hours where there is reasonable belief that the conditions which made the closure order necessary still exist and the justices have not yet had an opportunity to consider the order. Any notice of extension must be given before the end of the original period of closure.

Cancellation of closure order, s 179D

The responsible senior officer may cancel any order or an extension of it at any time where there is reasonable belief that the conditions which made it necessary no longer exist.

Revocation of justices' licence following closure order, s 179E

Licensing justices must consider at the next licensing sessions all closure orders and may revoke a justices' licence or attach conditions to that licence. The power to revoke is exercisable on any ground which would merit refusal to renew a licence. At least 7 days' notice must be given to the holder of a licence of a proposal to exercise such powers. Where licensing justices have decided to revoke a licence, or attach conditions to a licence, they must allow time for an appeal to a Crown Court and they may make any order which they consider necessary in relation to a closure order or any extension of it.

Persons failing to leave premises after the making of a closure order, s 179H

It is an offence for any person, without reasonable excuse, to fail to leave such premises when asked to do so by the holder of the justices' licence or manager of the premises, for the purpose of securing compliance with the order or extension concerned.

A constable, at the request of such a person or the agent or servant of such a person, must assist to remove such persons from the premises. Reasonable force may be used. Neither a constable nor the chief officer of police will be liable for any damage which occurs in the course of such duties unless the act or omission is shown to have been in bad faith or to be unlawful because of the Human Rights Act 1998.

Other offences

A person who, without reasonable excuse, permits premises to be open in contravention of a closure order made by a senior officer, or in contravention of an order under s 179B that the premises remain closed until the matter is dealt with by an order of the licensing justices or in contravention of any other order made by the justices under that section, or in contravention of a requirement under s 179E that the premises remain closed until the expiry of the appropriate time for appeal or the determination of that appeal, commits an offence.

Closure of unlicensed premises

Where a constable or a local authority is satisfied that premises are being, or within the last 24 hours have been, used for the unlicensed sale of intoxicating liquor for consumption on, or in the vicinity of the premises, s 19 of the 2001 Act provides that he or it must serve a closure notice on a person having control of, or responsibility for, the activities carried on at the premises. A closure notice must also be served on any person occupying any other part of the building whose access would be impeded by the order. It may also be served on *any other* person with control of or responsibility for, the activities on the premises, or any person with an interest in the premises. A closure notice must specify the nature of the alleged use of the premises, state the effect of s 20 and set out the steps which may be taken to ensure that the alleged use of the premises ceases or (as the case may be) does not recur. Closure notices issued by a constable or a local authority may be cancelled at any time.

Section 20 of the 2001 Act provides that when a closure notice has been served, the constable or local authority may seek an order from the justices, not less than 7 days and not more than 6 months after the service of the notice. An order should not be sought where the constable or local authority is satisfied that the offending use of the premises has ceased and that there is no reasonable likelihood of resumption. Where the justices on hearing the case are satisfied that a notice was properly served under s 19, and that the premises and/or the vicinity of those premises continue to be used for the offending purpose or that there is a reasonable likelihood that there will be such use, they may make a closure order, requiring in particular:

(a) immediate closure of the premises to the public until the constable or local authority (as the case may be) has certified that the need for the order has ceased (such an order may include conditions relating to admission and access to other parts of the building);
(b) any offending use to be discontinued immediately;
(c) any defendant to pay into court a sum of money which will not be released until the other requirements of the order have been complied with.

The constable or local authority (as the case may be) must fix a copy of the order to the premises.

An appeal against the making of such an order may be made to a Crown Court. Affected persons may seek discharge of the order. If the justices are satisfied that the need for the order has ceased, they may discharge it.

A person who, without reasonable excuse, permits premises to be open in contravention of a closure order or who otherwise fails to comply with it, commits an offence.

Police powers

Where a closure order has been made a constable or an authorised person, who identifies himself if so required, may enter the premises at any reasonable time, if need be by reasonable force, and do anything reasonably necessary to secure compliance with the order.

It is an offence for a person intentionally to obstruct such a person in the exercise of these powers.

Control of alcohol at sporting events

Introduction

Dealing with crowds of people who could be described, at best, as being somewhat indifferent towards the laws of the land and towards the well-being of other members of the public, is perhaps the most difficult task which faces the police officer today. A person who shows little individual courage within day-to-day life, becomes all that he would really like to be when submerged in the anonymity of a crowd of pretended football supporters. All of the advice and training offered to police officers, which are concerned with dealing with the individual and the group, are of little purpose when the group has reached its fever pitch of excitement and has engaged itself within a course of conduct which at the best could be described as a 'massive breach of the peace' and at worst a 'riot'. When such a stage has been reached, only the effective use of force will prevent a bad situation from becoming an impossible one.

Parliament has therefore directed its attention towards preventive measures calculated to decrease the likelihood of such a large-scale breach of the peace occurring at soccer matches. The provisions of the Sporting Events (Control of Alcohol, etc.) Act 1985 are aimed at the soccer hooligan.

Designation of grounds and events

The Act is concerned with 'designated sporting events' which occur at 'designated sports grounds'.

A 'designated sports ground' is any place:

(a) used (wholly or partly) for sporting events where accommodation is provided for spectators; and
(b) for the time being designated, or of a class designated, by order made by the Home Secretary.

The Home Secretary has designated the home grounds of all football clubs which are members of the Football Association or the Football Association of Wales, and any other ground in England and Wales used occasionally or temporarily by such a club, grounds used for international matches, Wembley Stadium (which is not solely a football ground) and the ground of Berwick Rangers (specially mentioned because the Club plays in the Scottish League).

A 'designated sporting event' is any one of the following classes:

(a) (i) Association Football matches in which one or both teams represent a Football League or a Football Association Premier League club;
    (ii) International Association Football matches (including semi-professional and schoolboy matches);
    (iii) Association Football matches in the European Champion Clubs Cup, European Cup Winners or UEFA Cup,
    provided that in each case the match takes place at the ground of an Association Football club which is a member of the Football Association or the Football Association of Wales, or at Wembley Stadium;

(b) Association Football matches within the jurisdiction of the Scottish Football Association;

(c) Association Football matches outside Great Britain:
  (i) in which one or both teams represent the Football Association or Football Association of Wales or a Football League club (whether a full or associate member); or
  (ii) in competition for the European Champion Clubs Cup, European Cup Winners Cup or UEFA Cup and one or both teams represent a club which is a member of the Football Association or the Football Association of Wales.

All matches in the Scottish Football League, all matches in the Highland Football League, all Scottish Football League and Association cup matches, all football matches in the three European cups and soccer internationals, provided that in each case they take place at a designated ground, have been designated by the Sports Grounds and Sporting Events (Designation) (Scotland) Order. The grounds designated by the Order are Hampden Park and the grounds of members of the Scottish Football League or of the Highland League. Rugby internationals at Murrayfield are also designated sporting events.

Permitted hours within designated sports grounds

The following provisions (underlined) are prospectively reported by the Licensing Act 2003 which, when in force, will introduce a new form of licensing by local authorities.

Section 3(1) of the 1985 Act states that permitted hours within licensed premises or registered clubs which are situated in designated sports grounds shall not include any part of the period of a designated sporting event at the ground, nor must there be any off-supply during that period. The period of a designated sporting event is the period beginning 2 hours before the start of the event or, if earlier, 2 hours before the time at which it is advertised to start, and ending 1 hour after that event. If a match is postponed or cancelled, the period includes the period in the day on which it is advertised to take place, beginning 2 hours before and ending 1 hour after that time. Thus, the Act prevents bars within these sports grounds from being open pre-match and after-match. However, a magistrates' court is authorised by s 3(2) to allow by order, supply in the premises (or part of those premises) subject to any conditions which the court may impose. Such an order must not apply to any part of the premises from which the designated sporting event may be directly viewed. There must be a condition requiring that a person must be in attendance throughout, who is responsible for compliance with the order. Such an order may be cancelled or varied and it expires on the coming into force of a further order, or after 12 months.

In an emergency situation, where there is no time to refer the matter to a magistrates' court, the order may be temporarily cancelled or varied by written notice from a police inspector (or above) if of the opinion that such sale or supply is likely to be detrimental to the orderly conduct or safety of spectators at a particular designated sports event.

These provisions ensure that there is no public, or near-public bar open while spectators are present in designated grounds and attending designated events, other than bars from which there is no view of the match. Therefore, a 'directors' bar', for example, could be open in a part of the ground from which the match could not be directly viewed. It could be watched on closed-circuit television.

However, s 5A permits variations in the case of private facilities for viewing these events. Sale, supply or possession of intoxicants is permitted in a room from which the event may be viewed, which is not open to the general public, at times other than within a 'restricted period' which is defined by that Act as a period which begins 15 minutes before the start of the event (or advertised start of the event if earlier) and ends 15 minutes after the end of the event. The same considerations apply in relation to postponed fixtures. The Secretary of State may by order shorten this restricted period or may abolish it. Drinking in the directors' box is, by these means, partially restored and may be fully restored by order.

Offences of selling, etc.

A person who sells or supplies or authorises the sale or supply of intoxicating liquor at a time which is excluded from the permitted hours by s 3 of this Act, or in contravention of conditions imposed under s 3(2), does not commit an offence under the Licensing Act 1964, s 59(1)(a). The offence is against the Sporting Events (Control of Alcohol etc.) Act 1985, s 3(10), if the holder of a justices' licence or an officer of the club. Any other person who sells or supplies in these circumstances is guilty of a similar offence if he knows or has reasonable cause to believe the sale or supply to be such a contravention.

Police powers

Section 6(1) of the Act provides that if at any time during the period of a designated sporting event at a designated sports ground, it appears to a constable in uniform that the sale or supply of intoxicating liquor at any bar within the ground is detrimental to the orderly conduct or safety of spectators, that constable may require the person having control of the bar, to close it and keep it closed until the end of that period. It is an offence to fail to comply with such a requirement.

A constable may enter *any part* of a designated sports ground during the period of a designated sporting event for the purpose of enforcing the provisions of the Act.

Travel to and from the ground

The vehicles concerned

The provisions set out above are provided to prevent spectators from becoming intoxicated while at these sporting events. The Act also seeks to control the behaviour of supporters who are travelling to and from these grounds.

A person who knowingly causes or permits intoxicating liquor to be carried on a public service vehicle or railway passenger vehicle which is being used for the principal purpose of carrying passengers for the whole, or part of a journey, to or from a designated sporting event is guilty of an offence against s 1 of the 1985 Act. These provisions apply to the operators of public service vehicles, their servants or agents and to the hirer of such vehicles, the servant or agent. Each person who is on such a vehicle and who has intoxicating liquor in his possession in such circumstances commits an offence. It is also an offence to be drunk on such a public service or railway passenger vehicle. The prohibition created by the Act is concerned with travel to and from a designated sporting event, wherever it may be held. Thus, travel to soccer matches which are being played abroad are subject to these provisions if the match is one of those specified, i.e. one of the teams involved represents the Football Association (including that of Wales) or a Football League club, or the match is in competition for one of the European cups and one of the teams represents those Football Associations. As Association Football matches within the jurisdiction of the Scottish Football Association are also designated sporting events, the 'travel' provisions also apply to such matches.

Section 1A applies these provisions to motor vehicles which:

(a) are not public service vehicles, but are adapted to carry more than eight passengers; and
(b) are being used for the principal purpose of carrying *two or more* passengers for the whole or part of a journey to or from a designated sporting event.

The same offences apply; but it is the driver or keeper or the servant or agent of the keeper, or the person to whom the vehicle is made available (by hire, loan or otherwise), or his servant or agent who commits the offence of causing or permitting intoxicating liquor to be carried. This extension is to embrace the use of owned or hired 'Transit'-type vehicles which are used for the conveyance of soccer supporters.

Possession of intoxicants by an individual within the vehicle is an offence by that individual. A person who is drunk on such a vehicle is guilty of an offence.

The person who 'causes or permits'

Section 1(2) provides that a person who knowingly causes or permits intoxicating liquor to be carried on a vehicle to which s 1 applies is guilty of an offence:

(a) if the vehicle is a public service vehicle and he is the operator of the vehicle or the employee or agent of the operator; or
(b) if the vehicle is hired (e.g. a chartered train or football special) and he is the person to whom it is hired or the employee or agent of that person.

It can be seen, therefore, that the secretary of a supporters' club or some other person who hires a vehicle on the club's behalf is guilty of an offence by permitting intoxicating liquor to be carried on the vehicle or passenger train.

Section 1(2A) provides that a person who *knowingly* causes or permits intoxicating liquor to be carried on a motor vehicle to which s 1A applies is guilty of an offence:

(a) if the driver; or
(b) if not the driver but its keeper, the servant or agent of its keeper, a person to whom it is made available (by hire, or loan or otherwise) by its keeper or the keeper's servant or agent, or the servant or agent of the person to whom it is made available.

The act must be carried out *knowingly* and it must therefore be proved that the accused actually knew of the presence of intoxicating liquor or was wilfully blind to the fact. In the case of responsible persons present in the vehicle, the open carriage or drinking of intoxicants will provide such proof.

Police powers

Section 7 permits a constable to stop a vehicle to which s 1 or s 1A applies and to search that vehicle or a railway passenger vehicle if there are reasonable grounds to suspect that an offence of possession of intoxicants, or one of drunkenness, is being or has been committed in respect of the vehicle. Thus, a 'football special' upon which there is seen to be drinking, or upon which such drinking is suspected, may be stopped and searched. The power to search vehicles is restricted to a search *for intoxicants*. This is important. The Act also provides a power to arrest without warrant for offences under the Act. It would not be an offence under this Act to possess 'articles' (see below) on such a vehicle. A constable may therefore arrest those who are drunk or those who are in possession of intoxicants upon such a vehicle. 'Reasonable grounds to suspect' such offences will be those as described in the Code of Practice.

At the ground

Possession of articles

Section 2 of the 1985 Act is concerned with the designated sports ground itself and its provisions are mainly related to intoxicating liquor or 'articles' as defined by the Act. (See page 661 for the meaning of a designated sports ground.)

An article is, for the purposes of the Act, any article capable of causing injury to a person struck by it, being:

(a) a bottle, can or other portable container (including such an article when crushed or broken) which
  (i) is holding any drink; and
  (ii) is of a kind which, when empty, is normally discarded or returned to, or left to be recovered by, the supplier; or
(b) part of any article described above.

However, the definition expressly does not apply to anything which is for holding any medicinal product.

Section 2A(1) extends the definition of 'article' to include articles or substances whose main purpose is the emission of a flare for purposes of illuminating or signalling (as opposed to igniting or heating) or the emission of smoke or visible gas, and in particular to distress flares, fog signals and pellets or capsules intended to be used as fumigators or for testing pipes but *not* matches, cigarette lighters or heaters. It is a defence to prove 'lawful authority'.

Offences of possession

By s 2, it is an offence for a person while entering or trying to enter a designated sports ground at any time during the period of a designated sporting event to have intoxicating liquor or an article to which the Act refers in his possession. Similarly, it is an offence to have intoxicating liquor or an article in one's possession at any time during the period of a designated sporting event when in any area of a designated sports ground from which the event may be directly viewed. The only places in which intoxicants could be lawfully possessed, therefore, are those bars such as 'directors' bars', from which there is no direct view of the game, or where there are private viewing facilities.

These are useful provisions. Any form of intoxicating liquor is banned from spectator areas, as are 'articles capable of causing injury' if they are 'empties' of a disposable kind and most pyrotechnic devices. An empty beer bottle is certainly capable of causing injury, but it is doubtful if an empty beer can (which is made of aluminium) would do so in its original form. If such a can is crushed, it becomes a more effective and harmful missile and may well be capable of causing injury. The article must be of a disposable kind, so that the spectator who is in possession of an expensive 'hip flask' is not in possession of an article within the meaning of this Act. However, if the flask contains intoxicants, the offence is one of possessing intoxicants. Pyrotechnic devices include all those which cause danger or nuisance to persons.

Police powers

A constable may search a person he has reasonable grounds to suspect is committing or has committed *an offence under the Act* and may arrest such a person. The Act therefore provides wide powers of search and arrest. It must be remembered that the term 'reasonable grounds to suspect' is now precisely defined in the Code of Practice for the Exercise by Police Officers of Statutory Powers to Stop and Search. Although reasonable suspicion does not amount to certainty, it must be founded on fact. There must be a concrete basis for the officer's suspicion which is related to the individual concerned. A constable is not entitled to search soccer supporters who are entering a sports ground because it is suspected that football fans, generally, take intoxicants into football matches. However, if the constable noticed the distinctive bulge of a 'four-pack' in a spectator's pocket, it is submitted that this would be reasonable. The suspicion is related to an individual and there is a concrete basis for the officer's suspicion. Paragraph 1.5 of Stop and Search Code provides that an officer must not search a person, even with his consent, where no power to search is applicable. It excepts from this rule and provides that an officer does not require a specific power in relation to searches of persons entering sports grounds or other premises carried out with their consent given as a condition of entry.

There is no doubt that this special provision exists in view of public concern over soccer hooliganism. A search as a condition of entry into the ground must be a matter between the proprietor of the ground and the intended customer. As such, any search should be carried out by some person other than a police officer in any case. It is no part of an officer's duty to enforce the rights of proprietors of places of entertainment.

The police powers under this Act are very wide, extending to the stopping of 'football specials' where there is reasonable suspicion of there being intoxicants, or drunken persons, aboard. Search powers extend to those occasions, to entry or attempted entry to the ground, and within the ground itself (for both intoxicating liquor *and* articles in relation to the ground itself). The power to arrest extends to reasonable grounds to suspect that *any* offence under the Act is being committed or has been committed.

Banning orders

The Football (Disorder) Act 2000 substituted ss 14 to 17 of the Football Spectators Act 1989. The new sections deal with 'regulated football matches' which are Association Football matches (whether in England or Wales or elsewhere) which are a prescribed match or a match of a prescribed description. The Football Spectators (Prescription) Order 2000 prescribes in Schedules 2 and 3, respectively, 'regulated football matches in England and Wales' and 'regulated football matches outside England and Wales'. The amendments have the effect of permitting the making of banning orders which combine the effect of the previous domestic football banning orders and international football banning orders.

Regulated football matches in England and Wales

This is an Association Football match:

(a) in which one or both of the participating teams represents a club which is for the time being a member (whether a full or associate member) of the Football League, the Football Association Premier League or the Football Conference, or represents a club from outside England and Wales, or represents a country or territory; and

(b) which is played

    (i) at a sports ground which is designated by order under s 1(1) of the Safety of Sports Grounds Act 1975, or registered with the Football League or the Football Association premier League as the home ground of a club which is a member of the Football league or the Football Association Premier League at the time the match is played; or

    (ii) in the Football Association Cup (other than in a preliminary or qualifying round).

Regulated football matches outside England and Wales

This is an Association Football match involving:

(a) a national team appointed by the Football Association to represent England or the Football Association of Wales to represent Wales; or

(b) a team representing a club which is, at the time the match is played, a member (whether a full or associate member) of the Football League or the Football Association Premier League.

Banning orders following a conviction for a relevant offence

Section 14A is concerned with a situation in which an offender is convicted of a 'relevant offence'. Relevant offences are set out in Schedule 1 to the Act. They are:

(a) offences contrary to the Sporting Events (Control of Alcohol, etc.) Act 1985, ss 1, 2 or 2A (possession of alcohol, containers or fireworks committed at a regulated match or while entering or trying to enter the ground);

(b) offences involving harassment, alarm or distress or racial hatred committed during a period relevant to a regulated football match, while at, entering or leaving the ground, or while on a journey to or from the match, in respect of which the court declares that the offence relates to football matches 'a declaration of relevance' or involving the use, carrying or possession of an offensive weapon or firearm;

(c) offences involving violence or threats of violence against persons or property, or committed during such a period, while at, entering or leaving the ground, or while on a journey to or from the match, in respect of which the court makes a 'declaration of relevance';

(d) offences of drunkenness committed while on such a journey (found drunk or drunk and disorderly, in respect of which the court makes a declaration of relevance);

(e) offences contrary to the Sporting Events (Control of Alcohol, etc.) Act 1985, s 1 (alcohol on coaches or trains), committed on a journey to or from a regulated match, in respect of which the court makes a declaration of relevance;

(f) offences of the type referred to in (b) and (c) committed during a period relevant to a regulated football match, in respect of which the court makes a declaration of relevance;

(g) offences contrary to the Road Traffic Act 1988, s 4 or 5 (drink and driving, etc.), committed while the accused was on a journey to or from a designated football match, in respect of which the court makes a declaration of relevance;

(h) offences contrary to the Football (Offences) Act 1991;

(i) ticket touting in relation to football matches (Criminal Justice and Public Order Act 1994, s 166).

An attempt, conspiracy, incitement or aiding, abetting, counselling or procuring the commission of any such offence is included within these provisions. A person may be regarded as having been on a journey to or from a football match whether or not he attended or intended to attend the match. A journey includes breaks (including overnight breaks). References to 'football matches' are references to a 'regulated football match' for the purposes of Part II of the Act of 1989. Offences involving violence, threats and offensive weapons committed during a period relevant to a football match are also 'relevant offences'.

If, upon conviction for such an offence, a court is satisfied that there are reasonable grounds to believe that making a banning order would help to prevent violence or disorder at, or in connection with, any regulated football match, it must make such an order in respect of the offender. If it is not so satisfied, it must state its reasons in open court. A banning order is in addition to a sentence or order of conditional discharge.

Banning orders made on complaint

Under s 14B, the chief officer of police of an area in which a person resides, or appears to reside, may make a complaint to a magistrates' court that the respondent has at some time contributed to violence or disorder in the United Kingdom or elsewhere. If the court is satisfied as to the substance of the complaint and has reasonable grounds for believing that making a banning order would help to prevent violence or disorder at or in connection with any regulated football match, it must make a banning order. In deciding these matters a court may take into account (among other things):

(a) any decision of a court or tribunal outside the United Kingdom;

(b) deportation or exclusion from a country outside the United Kingdom;

(c) removal or exclusion from football grounds in the United Kingdom or elsewhere; or

(d) conduct recorded by video or by any other means.

However, a court may only take note of matters occurring within the 10 years preceding the application. It must also consider any statement or reasons made by a court when, in relation to a relevant offence, it did not make a banning order. In this respect, the terms 'violence' and 'disorder' carry their usual meanings, embracing violence against persons and property, threats of violence and endangering life, stirring up racial hatred, threatening, abusive and insulting behaviour or displaying any such material. The terms, in dealing with these matters, are not restricted to such acts in connection with football.

The Court of Appeal has held that the making of such a banning order under s 14B is compatible with European Community law as it is justified on the grounds of public policy in order to prevent violence or disorder at foreign football matches. If operated correctly, the scheme satisfies the requirements of proportionality. So far as the standard of proof is concerned, the Court described it as an exacting one which would be hard in practice to distinguish from the criminal standard of proof beyond reasonable doubt. This high standard is imposed because of the serious restraints on an individual's freedom which a banning order imposes.

An appeal lies to a Crown Court against any banning order made following such a complaint.

No application may be made under s 14B after the end of the 'initial period', which is a period of 5 years beginning on 28 August 2002.

Banning order under s 22

Section 22 of the 1989 Act governs the making of a banning order as a result of a conviction for a 'corresponding offence' outside England and Wales. A 'corresponding offence' is an offence under the law of a country specified outside England and Wales in an Order in Council. At the time that this book went to press, Orders have been made in respect of Italy, Scotland, Sweden, Norway, the Republic of Ireland, France, Belgium and The Netherlands.

The effect of a banning order

A 'banning order' means an order made by a court under Part II of the 1989 Act which:

(a) in relation to regulated football matches in England and Wales, prohibits the person who is subject to the order from entering premises for the purpose of attending such matches; and

(b) in relation to regulated football matches outside England and Wales, requires that person to report at a police station in accordance with Part II.

An order will apply to the whole range of matches which are prescribed, whatever the venue and whatever the club. This is sensible. Clearly, a banning order would not be very effective if it barred a person only from the ground at which the offence was committed.

The effect of a banning order must be explained by the court.

A banning order must require the person subject to the order to report to a police station specified in the order, within 5 days beginning with the day upon which the order is made. Unless there are exceptional circumstances, it must contain a requirement as to the surrender of a passport of the person subject to the order, in accordance with the requirements of the Act, in connection with regulated football matches. Such exceptional circumstances, if found, must be stated in open court. If the person concerned is detained in custody, the requirements apply upon release.

The court may impose additional requirements upon a person subject to such an order and may subsequently vary an order so as to impose, replace or omit requirements on the application of the person subject to the order or the person who applied for the order or the prosecutor. In addition, the court has power to require a constable to photograph the person or cause that person to be photographed.

Duration of banning order

Where a banning order is made under s 14A (following conviction for a relevant offence) and is in addition to a sentence of imprisonment (the term includes any form of detention) taking immediate effect, the maximum may be for 10 years and the minimum is 6 years. In any other case under s 14A, the maximum is 5 years and the minimum

3 years. Orders which are made under s 14B (following complaint) may be for a maximum of 3 years and a minimum of 2 years.

Termination of an order

After two-thirds of the period of the ban has passed, the person subject to it may apply to the court by which the order was made to terminate it. The court, in considering whether or not to terminate the ban, must have regard to a person's character, conduct since the order was made, the nature of the offence or conduct concerned and any other relevant circumstances.

Functions of the enforcing authority and local police forces

Reporting at a police station

When a banned person initially reports at a police station, the officer responsible for that station may make such requirements of that person as are determined by the enforcing authority to be necessary or expedient for giving effect to the banning order, so far as matters are related to regulated football matches outside England and Wales. The 'enforcing authority' is a police common service established by the Home Secretary. If that authority considers that a requirement to report is necessary or expedient to reduce the likelihood of violence or disorder at or in connection with the match, the authority must give the person subject to the order a notice in writing to report as instructed and, if the match is outside the United Kingdom, to surrender his passport as instructed. In the case of a regulated football match there may be a demand to comply with additional requirements.

A requirement to report at a police station is restricted to the 'control period' in relation to a regulated football match outside England and Wales or an external tournament and a requirement to surrender a passport in such circumstances must also be so restricted. The control period in relation to such a regulated football match is the period commencing 5 days before the date of the match and ending when the match is concluded or cancelled. In relation to an external tournament it means any period described in an order made by the Secretary of State beginning 5 days before the first match outside England and Wales and ending when the last match outside England and Wales has been concluded or cancelled. However, qualifying matches do not count in determining the start of the tournament.

Section 22A(2) of the 1989 Act empowers the Secretary of State, if he considers it necessary or expedient to do so in order to secure the effective enforcement of these provisions, to make an order extending the 'control period' in relation to any regulated football match to a maximum of not more than 10 days.

Failure to comply with the requirements

It is an offence contrary to s 14J(1), for a person subject to a banning order to fail to comply with:

(a) any requirement imposed by the order; or
(b) any requirement imposed by s 19(2B) or s 19(2C), that is, to report at a police station specified in a notice at a time, or between the times, specified and, if the match is outside

the United Kingdom and the order requires the surrender of a passport, to surrender it at a police station specified in the notice at the required time, or between the required times, s 19(2B), and a requirement made in relation to a regulated football match by the enforcing authority, s 19(2C).

Police powers

Sections 21A and 21B of the 1989 Act underpin the procedure for the application by way of complaint for a banning order. They provide for a constable in uniform to exercise powers of detention and of reference to a court in specified circumstances. The powers under ss 21A and 21B may be exercised only in relation to a British citizen.

Section 21A provides a constable in uniform with the power to detain a person in custody if, during any 'control period' in relation to a regulated football match outside England and Wales or an external tournament:

(a) he has reasonable grounds to suspect that the person has at any time caused or contributed to any violence or disorder in the United Kingdom or elsewhere; and
(b) he has reasonable grounds to believe that making a banning order in his case would help to prevent violence or disorder at, or in connection with, any regulated football matches.

Such a person may be detained until the constable has decided whether or not to issue a notice under s 21B requiring that person:

(a) to appear before a magistrates' court at a specified time;
(b) not to leave England and Wales before that time; and
(c) if the control period relates to a regulated football match outside the United Kingdom or to an external tournament which includes such matches, to surrender his passport to the constable,

and stating the grounds upon which the decision is based.

Such detention may not exceed 4 hours or, with the authority of an officer of at least the rank of inspector, 6 hours. A person so detained may not be further detained within the same control period unless new information becomes available.

The notice referred to above may be issued where the officer is authorised to do so by an officer of at least the rank of inspector. The time at which such a person must appear before a magistrates' court must be within 24 hours of receiving the notice or that person's detention, whichever is the earlier. Such a notice will be treated as an application for a banning order by way of complaint. A constable may arrest a person to whom he is giving such a notice if there are reasonable grounds to believe that it is necessary to do so in order to secure that the person complies with the notice.

Where a person to whom such a notice has been given appears before a magistrates' court, the court may remand him. If that person is remanded on bail, there may be a requirement not to leave England and Wales before the appearance before the court and, if the control period relates to a regulated football match outside the United Kingdom or to an external tournament which includes such matches, may be required to surrender his passport to a constable.

It is an arrestable offence to fail to comply with a notice under s 21B.

Applications for banning orders by way of complaint and the exercise of the police powers under s 21A or 21B are restricted to an 'initial period'. No application may be made after the end of the 'initial period', which is a period of 5 years beginning on 28 August 2002.

Misbehaviour at a designated football match

The Football (Offences) Act 1991 creates a number of offences. They can only be committed at a 'designated football match'. Such matches are designated by the Football (Offences) (Designation of Football Matches) Order 2000. They are Association Football matches:

(a) in which one or both of the participating teams represents a club which is for the time being a member (whether a full or associate member) of the Football League, the Football Association Premier League or the Football Conference, or represents a club from outside England and Wales, or represents a country or territory; and
(b) which is played
    (i) at a sports ground which is designated by order under s 1(1) of the Safety at Sports Grounds Act 1975, or registered with the Football League or the Football Association Premier League as the home ground of a club which is a member of the Football League or the Football Association Premier League at the time the match is played; or
    (ii) in the Football Association Cup (other than in a preliminary or qualifying round.

References in the Act to things done at a designated football match include anything done there in the period beginning 2 hours before the start of the match or (if earlier) 2 hours before the advertised start time and ending 1 hour after the end of the match. If the match does not take place, the period is 2 hours before the advertised start time until 1 hour after that time.

Throwing objects

The Football Offences Act 1991, s 2, creates offences of throwing anything at or towards:

(a) the playing area or any area adjacent to the playing area to which spectators are not generally admitted; or
(b) any area in which spectators or other persons are or may be present,

without lawful authority or excuse (which it is for the accused to prove).

Thus, those who throw objects on to the pitch, into the players' tunnel, etc., or into spectator areas, will commit offences. Those who may prove 'lawful authority or excuse' would include vendors who throw packets of crisps, etc., into the crowd, or spectators who throw money to such persons.

Chanting

Section 3 of the 1991 Act makes it an offence to engage or take part in chanting of an indecent or racist nature. 'Chanting' means the repeated uttering of words or sounds whether alone or in concert with one or more others and 'racist nature' means consisting of or including matter which is threatening, abusive or insulting to a person by reason of colour, race, nationality (including citizenship) or ethnic or national origin.

Pitch invasion

By s 4, it is an offence for a person to go on to the playing area, or any area adjacent to the playing area to which spectators are not generally admitted, without lawful authority or lawful excuse (which it is for the accused to prove).

   This offence could be interesting in circumstances in which spectators surge forward on to the pitch. Most will contend that they were carried forward unwillingly by the momentum of the crowd. However, if this is so, it is submitted that they should be able to establish that they retreated from the playing area at the first opportunity. However, such an incident is not likely where all spectators are seated. Those who would have lawful excuse for going on to the pitch would include trainers and official first aiders.

Ticket touts at designated football matches

The Criminal Justice and Public Order Act 1994, s 166, provides that it is an offence for an unauthorised person to sell, or offer or expose for sale, a ticket for a designated football match in any public place, place to which the public has access or in any other place in the course of a trade or business. An authorised person must be authorised in writing by the home club or the organisers of the match. The section also provides that the powers of search of persons and premises (including vehicles) upon arrest under the Police and Criminal Evidence Act 1984 shall apply as if the power to enter and search any vehicle extended to any vehicle which the constable has reasonable grounds to suspect was being used for a purpose connected with the offence.

   This is an arrestable offence under the amended provisions of s 24(2) of the 1984 Act.

'Street offences'

Introduction

The offences which are concerned with various activities associated with 'prostitution' are made punishable more because of the fact that those engaged in such activities constitute a nuisance than that they commit offences which are blameworthy in the normal sense. The actual sexual activities in which the people concerned engage are not, where those acts take place with consent, etc., criminal offences. They usually become criminal offences where the 'contact' which precedes such activities takes place in public places. The nature of the offences is such that cautions are given in respect of many of them; it is when the persons concerned persist in their conduct that the criminal law is invoked.

Common prostitute

The term 'prostitute' is not defined but is now used to describe a woman (or a man) who offers her (or his) body commonly for sexual intercourse or other acts of a sexual nature, in return for payment. It is immaterial that the woman (or man) is dishonest and does not intend to provide the services offered. The term 'other acts of a sexual nature' covers all of the other activities which are associated with prostitution, such as masturbation and whipping. Thus, 'massage parlours' can offer the types of sexual activity which are associated with prostitution if the service extends to masturbation. A virgin may therefore be a prostitute.

For a woman to be a *common* prostitute she must offer her services commonly, that is, to more than one man. A girl who adopts a 'sugar daddy' who sets her up in a luxury flat and pays all of the expenses involved does not thereby become a prostitute as she limits the services which she 'sells' to one man. She who offers herself commonly for no other reasons than that she enjoys intercourse is not a prostitute as she does not do so for payment.

However, it is not an offence to be a prostitute *per se*, but it becomes an offence in certain circumstances.

Loitering or soliciting

The Street Offences Act 1959, s 1, creates the offence committed by a common prostitute who loiters or solicits in a street or public place. To prove that such an offence is committed, there must be evidence of the accused's recent behaviour in a street or public place. She should have been seen on at least two previous occasions accosting men in a street or public place and she should have been seen to leave with them. The fact that she leaves with them will frequently eliminate the possibility of an innocent explanation. Whilst a woman may approach different men in an effort to find out the location of a particular place, she is unlikely to leave with them and this increases the likelihood that she is soliciting.

However, it is not necessary that a woman should approach men. Many prostitutes dress in a manner which leaves little doubt concerning the reason for their presence on the street. They may be approached by men who see them as 'loitering' for the purposes of prostitution. There may be soliciting from a slowly moving vehicle and soliciting need not involve the use of words. A deaf and dumb prostitute solicited by making grunting noises accompanied by a gesture involving the right arm being bent and then straightened. No one ever doubted what she had for sale!

Solicitation may take place even though the prostitute is not in the street or public place. Standing, scantily dressed in front of a lighted window whilst indicating with the fingers the price charged, tapping on the window and indicating the door of the house or placing a card in the window offering services are all forms of solicitation. The test is whether it is clear to those men that they are being offered sex for money.

Cautions

In practice, at least two cautions are given before proceedings are taken against a woman in these circumstances. Particulars of cautions given are entered in an official cautions register maintained at the police station. A woman so cautioned, who wishes to deny that her actions were such that she merited a caution, can apply to a court within 14 days for an order directing that the caution be expunged. The procedure is as follows:

(a) On the first occasion that a woman is suspected of this offence, obtain the assistance of a colleague as a witness (joint observation).
(b) Tell her what you have seen and caution her. Obtain name, date of birth, address and description to aid later observation. Check the name and address, if possible from documents. There is no power to use or threaten force to detain a woman for these purposes; consequently, the use or threat of force in such circumstances is unlawful.
(c) Ask her if she is willing to be put in touch with a welfare, social or probation service or help organisation, or attend at a police station to see a policewoman, at her convenience.
(d) If seen on a second occasion, the same procedure should be followed.
(e) All cautions must be officially recorded.
(f) If seen loitering or soliciting after having been cautioned twice, she may be arrested and charged. A custody officer must satisfy himself that two cautions have been so recorded and that they are sufficiently recent (some forces require that they must have been given within the preceding 12 months) before accepting the charge.
(g) A complaint from a woman to the effect that she has been cautioned without cause requires investigation in the same way as any other complaint. If the complaint is justified it may be expunged without the need to refer the matter to a court.
(h) When a hearing is in progress it is not necessary to mention cautions. However, the conduct which occasioned those cautions will probably have to be given to prove that she is a common prostitute.

What is a street or public place?

For the purposes of the Act, a street includes any bridge, lane, footway, subway, square, court, alley or passage, whether a thoroughfare or not, which is for the time being open to the public, and doorways and entrances to premises abutting upon a street and the ground adjoining and open to a street are treated as forming part of the street. The terms of this definition therefore prohibit loitering and soliciting in places which are on private property if they open on to streets. Prostitutes who solicit from balconies or from behind closed windows are therefore caught by the Act. The mischief which the Act seeks to prevent is the molestation of persons who merely wish to walk along a street and a form of solicitation which is 'projected' into a street is forbidden.

The Act does not define 'public place' but it is a place where the public go, no matter whether they have a right to go or not. Places which are 'private' for most of the time may be 'public' at other times, for example, where the grounds of a private house are opened to members of the public.

Police powers

A constable may arrest without warrant anyone found in a street or public place suspected, with reasonable cause, to be committing an offence against the Act.

Child prostitutes

Although those under 18 who engage in prostitution are subject to the above offences penalising the activities of a prostitute, a Home Office Circular issued in 2000 states that they are almost invariably victims and should be treated as such. Criminal justice action should only be taken against them (as opposed to those who abuse them or seek to exploit them) if all the relevant local agencies are satisfied that the child is involved in prostitution of her own free will, and attempts to divert the child out of prostitution have failed.

Placing of advertisements relating to prostitution

The Criminal Justice and Police Act 2001, s 46, creates an offence of placing on, or in the immediate vicinity of, a public telephone, an advertisement relating to prostitution intending that the advertisement should come to the attention of any other person. The advertisement is one covered by the section if it is for the services of a prostitute, whether male or female, or indicates that such services are available at premises. Any advertisement which a reasonable person would consider to be such an advertisement shall be presumed to be so.

For the purposes of this section, 'public telephone' means any telephone which is located in a public place for public use together with any structure in which it is housed. A 'public place' means any place to which the public have, or are permitted to have, access, whether on payment or otherwise, other than any place to which children under the age of 16 years are not permitted to have access, whether by law or otherwise, and any premises which are wholly or mainly used for residential purposes.

This is an arrestable offence specified in the Police and Criminal Evidence Act (PACE) 1984, s 24(2).

Section 47 permits the Secretary of State to extend these provisions to other public structures by order.

Brothels

Premises become a brothel if they are used by persons of opposite sexes for illicit intercourse or other indecent behaviour. The Sexual Offences Act 1956, s 33, makes it an offence for a person to keep or manage a brothel, or to act or assist in its management.

The offence is not associated with those relating to prostitutes and it is not necessary to show that the women in a brothel were prostitutes. It is not therefore necessary to prove that the women concerned received payment for their services. The premises must be used by at least two women before the premises can be a brothel, but it does not matter that only one of them uses the premises at any one time. Where many flats in one building are so used, if each is used by only one woman, none are brothels. However, where a number of single rooms in one building are so used, it is probable that the whole building will be looked upon as a brothel housing a number of women.

A residential landlord is likely to be a 'keeper', a day-to-day manager (or a madame) is likely to be a manager and all other persons associated with the 'trade' will be assisting in the management of the premises. To assist in the management of a brothel does not necessarily involve any element of 'control' but it must involve some element of 'management'. Thus, a person who arranges for advertisements to be placed in respect of the premises assists in management, but a person who cleans out the rooms does not.

Kerb crawling

The Sexual Offences Act 1985, s 1, makes it an offence for a man persistently to solicit a woman, or different women, for the purpose of prostitution, from a motor vehicle while that motor vehicle is in a street or public place, or for a man persistently to solicit a woman, or different women, for the purpose of prostitution, in a street or public place while in the immediate vicinity of a motor vehicle which he has just got out of or off. The offences are designed to remove the nuisance caused to respectable women who are mistaken for prostitutes in areas which become 'red light' districts.

The man must indicate to the woman or women by words or actions that he requires her or their services as a prostitute. Men who drive through such districts persistently addressing such requests to women, where the vehicle is in a street or public place, commit the offence. If a man travels to the general district in a vehicle, parks and leaves it, and persistently solicits a woman or women in the immediate vicinity of the place where he has parked the vehicle, he similarly commits an offence. It does not matter that the vehicle was parked in an official car park; if it was parked and left there whilst the driver or an occupant solicited a woman or women in the immediate vicinity, an offence is committed. The test to be applied is whether the vehicle was used directly for, or was connected with, the solicitation.

There are alternative charges under s 1 which are useful where 'persistent' soliciting cannot be proved. It is an offence if there is soliciting in such a manner or in such circumstances as to be likely to cause annoyance to the woman (or any of the women) solicited, or nuisance to other persons in the neighbourhood. Justices are entitled to use their local knowledge of the area in which the offence is alleged to have occurred when considering whether particular behaviour was likely to cause nuisance to other members of the public.

Section 2 of the Act deals with the offence of a man persistently soliciting a woman, or different women, in a street or public place for the purpose of prostitution. There is no mention of the use of a motor vehicle within this section. Where there is a doubt concerning whether the solicitation occurred 'in the immediate vicinity' of a motor vehicle, it will be preferable to charge under s 2.

Police powers

The offences under the Sexual Offences Act 1985, s 1, are arrestable offences. The general power to arrest provided by PACE 1984, s 25, applies to other offences.

Male importuning

It is an offence contrary to the Sexual Offences Act 1956, s 32, for a man persistently to solicit or importune in a public place for immoral purposes.

In this sense 'immoral' does not indicate that the conduct must be contrary to law. However, it must be associated with sexual activity whether of a homosexual or heterosexual nature. The standards of ordinary, right-thinking people should be applied when considering the circumstances and the nature of the overtures being made. Persistently suggesting homosexual acts between consenting adults in private is an 'immoral' purpose and it is irrelevant that no offence would be committed by those who took up those suggestions. This is true also in relation to women prostitutes. What they eventually do is not an unlawful act, the essence of the crime lies in the way in which they arrange that activity.

The offences under the Sexual Offences Act 1985 do not include male prostitutes soliciting women for the purposes of prostitution, but such conduct would be punishable under the 1956 Act, s 32.

Sexual offences including rape

Indecent conduct towards young children

The Indecency with Children Act 1960 was passed to remedy a defect in the law, where the High Court ruled that there could be no indecent assault where a child had merely accepted the accused's invitation to touch him in an indecent manner. It is an offence for any person to commit an act of gross indecency with or towards a child under the age of 16 years, or to incite any child to commit such an act with that person or another.

The term 'gross indecency' is limited to activities involving indecent contact with the genitalia including contact through clothing. A person incites another to commit an act if he, by any form of arrangement, promise, inducement or invitation, encourages him to commit that act. The words of the section extended the offence to circumstances in which the accused incited the child to commit the act of gross indecency. An act of gross indecency with or towards a child is committed if a person does something grossly indecent against or directed towards a child, or if that person co-operates in or invites some act of that nature which is done by the child. If a man masturbates in the presence of a child and gains his 'thrill' by the fact that the child is watching, he is guilty, whether or not he has attracted the child's attention towards his act. Alternatively, if he was doing this secretly while looking at the child, the offence would not have been committed as the act was not directed towards the child, nor was there any form of co-operation. Where a man encourages a child to touch his genitalia and the circumstances are such that he can be said to permit the child to touch him in this way, he commits the offence.

An act of incitement must be judged on its own. Where a man left notes in a public lavatory inviting boys to be his 'pretend son' those notes in themselves did not amount to incitement to commit acts of gross indecency. Entries in a diary kept by such a man disclosing his desire for sexual activity with such boys were held merely to relate to 'intention' and to be inadmissible in evidence. It is submitted that there is an alternative view; that the diary entries were sufficiently 'related' to the alleged offence to be admissible in evidence.

Whereas it was previously assumed that proof concerning knowledge that a child was under 16 was unnecessary, the House of Lords has ruled that there is nothing in this statute to replace the common law presumption that *mens rea* is relevant. The necessary mental element with regard to the age ingredient in an offence against s 1 of the 1960 Act is the absence of genuine belief by the accused that the victim is 16 or above. The effect of the decision is that the prosecution must show, should such circumstances arise, that the mature paedophile charged with such an offence could not possibly have believed that the young person involved was 16, as opposed to 15 years and 11 months!

Police powers

Offences of indecent conduct towards children are not arrestable offences. However, the circumstances of the offence, if current, may be such that a breach of the peace is immediately apprehended. If not, the general power to arrest under PACE, s 25, will apply.

Unnatural sexual offences

The Sexual Offences Act 1956, s 12, makes it an offence, other than in certain circumstances, for a person to commit buggery with another person or an animal. Because of the reference to persons and animals, the offence is frequently described as either sodomy or bestiality.

(a) Sodomy is committed where sexual intercourse takes place per anum between males or between a male and a female per anum.
(b) Bestiality is committed where either a man or a woman has sexual intercourse with an animal in any manner, which could involve a man with an animal per vagina or per anum, or an animal with a man per anum, or a woman with an animal per vagina or per anum.

The exceptional circumstances referred to above are that the act of buggery takes place in private and both parties have attained the age of 16.

Such an act of buggery by one man with another shall not be treated as taking place in private if it takes place:

(a) when more than two persons take part or are present; or
(b) in a lavatory to which the public have or are permitted to have access whether on payment or otherwise.

At the time of writing, the European Court of Human Rights has criticised the provision of the Act which prohibits acts of gross indecency where two or more persons are present, on the grounds that the legislation is discriminatory in that there is no similar prohibition upon heterosexual sex. In consequence, the section will be, at some stage, amended and prosecutions are unlikely in the interim.

By s 12AA of the 1956 Act, a boy under the age of 16 does not commit buggery if the other party has attained that age, whether or not the buggery is in private.

Offences of buggery, or attempted buggery, are arrestable offences if committed by a person of or over the age of 21, where the other person is under the age of 16. If the other person is under the age of 16, the punishment is life imprisonment. An assault with intent to commit buggery is also an arrestable offence. It is for the prosecutor to prove that the act took place otherwise than in private or that one of the parties to it had not attained the age of 16. Buggery with a boy under 16 is a serious arrestable offence for the purposes of the law relating to search warrants.

Where buggery remains an offence, both the active and passive parties are guilty if both consent to the act.

Prior to the Criminal Justice and Public Order Act 1994, intercourse per anum with a female was always punishable as an offence of buggery, but that Act decriminalised such acts committed with consent and in private. If the woman does not consent, the appropriate charge is rape.

Gross indecency

Section 13 of the Sexual Offences Act 1956 creates another complex series of offences by providing that it is an offence for a man to commit an act of gross indecency with another man other than in specified circumstances, whether in public or in private, or to be a party to the commission of such an act, or to procure it. The term 'gross indecency' has never really been defined other than to declare that there is no need for physical contact if two men behave in an indecent manner in concert. The offence usually takes one of three forms: mutual masturbation, bodily intertwining and oral–genital contact. All of these acts are included in the 1967 Act as 'homosexual acts' which are lawful in the circumstances described above in relation to buggery. Thus, if committed in private, by no more than two consenting males who have attained the age of 16 years, such acts are lawful.

A boy under 16 does not commit an act of gross indecency with someone of 16 or over, whether or not the conduct occurs in private. If someone commits an offence under s 13, we must consider not only those who are directly committing such acts, but also those who may be party to such acts without physically participating. Such a person may have procured the act by arranging for it to take place. A person who is present when the act is committed and who encourages it will also be a party to its commission. Gross indecency committed by a man of or over the age of 21 with a man under the age of 16 is an arrestable offence; so is an attempt to procure such an offence.

Restriction on prosecution

The Director of Public Prosecutions must consent to the prosecution of a man for buggery or gross indecency with another man where either was under 16 at the time of the offence.

Procuring

Any person who procures an unlawful act of buggery or gross indecency is guilty of an offence of buggery as an accomplice. In addition, the 1967 Act created a new offence of procuring another man to commit an act of buggery or gross indecency with a third man, which by virtue of the Act is not unlawful. It must be emphasised that this offence is only committed if the procurer, or male pimp, procures on behalf of someone else.

Abuse of position of trust

The Sexual Offences (Amendment) Act 2000, s 3, provides that it shall be an offence for a person aged 18 or over:

(a) to have sexual intercourse (whether vaginal or anal) with a person under that age; or
(b) to engage in any other sexual activity with or directed towards such a person,

if (in either case) that person is in a position of trust in relation to that person.

It is a defence for such a person to prove that at the time of the intercourse or activity:

(a) he did not know, and could not reasonably have been expected to know, that the person was under 18;
(b) he did not know, and could not reasonably have been expected to know, that the other was a person in relation to whom that person was in a position of trust.

This is an arrestable offence.

Section 4 of the Act fully defines the nature of the 'trust' referred to. It covers those caring for people detained in an institution in consequence of a court order, care homes provided under the Children Act 1989, or a hospital, residential care home, community home, voluntary home, children's home or residential establishment, a home provided under the Children Act 1989, s 82(5), or an educational institution where that person looks after persons under 18 who are in full-time education.

Section 5 of the Act of 2000 adds offences contrary to s 3 to the list of offences to which the provisions of the 1997 Act apply.

Rape

The Sexual Offences Act 1956, s 1(1), as amended by the Criminal Justice and Public Order Act 1994 states that it is an offence for a man to rape a woman or another man. A man commits rape if:

(a) he has sexual intercourse with a person (whether vaginal or anal), who at the time of the intercourse does not consent to it; and
(b) at the time he knows that the person does not consent to the intercourse or is reckless as to whether that person consents to it.

For this offence to be committed, per vagina, with a woman, it is necessary to prove penetration of the female organ but it is not necessary to prove rupture of the hymen, should the girl attacked be a virgin, or that there was any emission of seed. Evidence of penetration can be given by the complainant herself, supported by the evidence of a doctor who conducted a medical examination as soon as possible following the commission of the offence. Absence of consent is an essential factor, and the consent obtained must have been a true consent and not one obtained by intimidation or fraud. Where non-consensual intercourse, whether vaginal or anal, is alleged, it must be charged as rape with, if appropriate, an alternative charge of buggery.

There is no requirement that the sexual intercourse be 'unlawful' in the sense that it is extra-marital intercourse. A husband can be convicted of raping his wife if the elements of the offence can be proved. Section 1(2) of the Act provides that a man who induces a woman to have sexual intercourse with him by impersonating her husband is guilty of rape. Thus, if a man climbs into bed with a sleeping woman and induces her to respond to his sexual advances by pretending to be her husband, he commits rape, as any form of consent given is negatived by s 1(2). This only applies to impersonation of a *husband*. If, of course, the woman responds because she believes it to be her husband without any pretence on the part of the man, it will still be rape because there is no consent to the act. It is not necessary that there be some form of objection; it is sufficient that there was no form of consent.

Where consent is gained in consequence of violence or threats of violence, there can be no true consent. However, threats of the exposure of an extra-marital affair will not suffice for the offence of rape, but such a person would commit an alternative offence under s 2 of the 1956 Act.

Consent gained by fraud *as to the nature of the act* is not a true consent; thus a doctor can commit rape by gaining consent to intercourse by falsely claiming that the act is a recognised part of medical procedure. However, where full consent is given following other fraudulent claims, an offence of rape is not committed, but an alternative offence, discussed below, will be committed.

In addition, a consent gained from a woman who is mentally deficient or drunk is not a true consent.

The Court of Appeal has said that there is a difference between consent and submission. A woman who submits to intercourse does not necessarily consent to it. If this finding is taken in its widest sense, it may lead to a broadening of the circumstances in which rape can be committed. It is submitted that there must be some recognisable form of objection, even it is merely circumstantial, before there can be rape.

The definition of the offence of rape was amended by the Criminal Justice and Public Order Act 1994 to extend the offence to the rape, by a man, of another man.

A man commits rape if he has sexual intercourse with a person who at the time of the intercourse does not consent to it and at the time, he knows that there is no consent or he is reckless as to whether there is such consent. To show such recklessness it is necessary to prove that the man was indifferent and gave no thought to the possibility that the person might not be consenting, or being aware that the person was probably not consenting in the circumstances, he persisted regardless. It must be remembered that there is a difference between consent and submission induced by fear of physical harm.

The question of consent can be a difficult one for the jury. If a girl permits a casual acquaintance to take her to a remote spot and then to kiss and fondle her, the man concerned may be encouraged to attempt to have intercourse with her. If she refuses, no matter how far the preliminaries have gone, it will be rape to proceed with the act. Bearing in mind recent decisions of the High Court, if the intercourse is proceeding, it will be rape to continue after a request to desist.

'Recklessness' in its relationship to consent in a case of rape is concerned with the state of mind of the accused on the occasion in question, not some hypothetical reasonable person.

Sexual intercourse may also be without consent where a prostitute, although consenting to intercourse, does not consent to unprotected sex and unprotected sex is forced upon her.

Offences of procurement

The Sexual Offences Act 1956, ss 2 and 3, deal with further offences which are similar to rape in many respects.

By s 2 it is an offence for a person to procure a woman, by threats or intimidation, to have sexual intercourse in any part of the world.

By s 3 it is an offence to procure a woman, by false pretences or false representations, to have sexual intercourse in any part of the world.

For the purpose of s 2, the words 'threats or intimidation' do not have the same meaning as they do when considering rape. For the purposes of the present offence, threats to expose a woman's unfaithfulness to her husband unless she consents to intercourse would suffice, whereas they would not suffice in relation to rape as they do not constitute a threat of bodily harm. On the other hand, a threat not to buy a girl a further drink unless she consents to intercourse could never be construed as a threat for the purpose of the section.

Because it has already been said that it will be rape if consent is obtained by fraud, these offences appear to be unnecessary. However, we were then considering a fraud as to the nature of the act which was taking place. Section 3 requires a misrepresentation of an existing fact. There was a conviction under replaced legislation where a man obtained consent to intercourse following a false offer of marriage. However, in such cases it is submitted that it would be essential to prove that the man was not in a position, nor was he likely to be in a position, in which he could marry the girl.

In these cases intercourse must have taken place. Although these offences can be committed by a man who procures a woman to have intercourse with himself, they may also be committed by those who procure a woman for the purpose of intercourse with some other person. Both of these offences are such that the intercourse may take place 'in any part of the world' but the 'procuring' must have taken place within the jurisdiction of the court.

Administering drugs to obtain or facilitate intercourse

An offence, contrary to s 4 of the 1956 Act, is committed by any person who applies, administers to, or causes to be taken by, a woman any drug, matter or thing with intent to stupefy or overpower her so as to enable any man to have sexual intercourse with her.

This offence is complete when the substance has been taken with this intention in the mind of the person responsible, and it is immaterial whether he intends to seek intercourse himself or to facilitate matters for some other person. The words 'drug, matter or other thing' are wide enough to include intoxicating liquor where the intention can be established.

Evidence in rape cases

Early complaint

Although it would normally be inadmissible as hearsay, the terms of an early complaint by the man or woman who alleges that he has been raped are admissible evidence on the part of the person to whom it was made, provided the complaint was made at the first opportunity and was not made in response to an inducement or a leading question. Provided that these conditions are satisfied, the terms of an early complaint are also admissible in evidence given by that person. Where evidence of an early complaint is admissible, it is admissible to prove consistency of the complainant's conduct with the story told by him in court and as something to negative consent when that is in issue.

Police powers

Rape is an arrestable offence. The offences of procurement by threats, false pretences or the administration of drugs to facilitate intercourse are not arrestable offences.

Rape is a serious arrestable offence for the purpose of the law relating to search warrants.

Unlawful sexual intercourse with young girls

It is an offence contrary to s 5 of the 1956 Act for a man to have unlawful sexual intercourse with a girl under 13. A further offence under s 6 is concerned with such intercourse with a girl under 16. If a man marries a girl who has not reached the age of 16 and genuinely believes that his marriage is valid, he commits no offence if he has intercourse with her.

For the purposes of 'intercourse', proof of penetration is sufficient. A certified copy of a birth certificate, supported by proof of the identity of the girl, is sufficient for the purposes of the sections. 'Unlawful' in such cases means 'illicit', outside the bonds of matrimony.

In the case of an s 6 offence, it is provided that a man shall not be guilty of an offence under this section if, at the time of commission, he is under the age of 24 and has not been previously *charged* with such an offence, and he believes the girl to be 16 or more and has reasonable cause for such belief. An accused must satisfy a court of his belief and that it was reasonable. The law recognises the possibility that girls not yet 16 may frequently appear to be much older. It at the same time recognises that males of 24 or more should be able to identify, or at least suspect, their true age.

Police powers

It is an arrestable offence to have unlawful sexual intercourse with a girl not yet 13 years. It is also a serious arrestable offence for the purposes of the law relating to search warrants. Although the imprisonment to be awarded for an offence in respect of a girl who is 13 but not yet 16 is only 2 years and it is therefore not an arrestable offence, it should be remembered that an indecent assault upon a woman is an arrestable offence. Such offences will almost invariably involve an indecent assault.

In relation to both offences the question of consent does not arise, but if the act is done without consent, the man would be additionally guilty of rape.

General

It is essential to obtain assistance when these offences are reported and to ensure that the place at which a rape is alleged to have occurred is protected. An accurate record must be made of the actual complaint made by the person concerned, as evidence of early complaint, and the nature of that complaint, are important in relation to the question of consent. It is admissible (although hearsay) if it was made to someone at the first opportunity and was not made in response to leading questions. It is admissible to prove consistency of the complainant's conduct with the story told in court and as tending to negative consent when that is in issue. It is not evidence of the facts complained of.

On occasions it may be found that the victim has returned to her home and she may have changed her clothing and be preparing to wash her undergarments. These will be required for forensic examination.

Evidence

Unsworn evidence will be given where the person concerned is under 14. A deposition of such a child's unsworn evidence may be taken for the purposes of criminal proceedings as if that evidence had been given on oath.

Restrictions on evidence or questions about complainant's sexual history

Section 41 of the Youth Justice and Criminal Evidence Act 1999 imposes such restrictions where a person is charged with a 'sexual offence'. For the purposes of s 41, a 'sexual offence' is an offence of rape, burglary with intent to rape, procuring intercourse by threats or false pretences, administration of drugs to facilitate intercourse, under-age intercourse, intercourse with a defective (or procuring such), incest, buggery, indecent assault, forcible abduction, etc., intercourse with a mental patient by a member of hospital staff, etc., grossly indecent conduct with or towards a child under 16 and incitement of a child under 16 to incest. Attempting, conspiring, aiding, abetting, counselling, procuring or inciting any of these offences is also a 'sexual offence'.

Section 41 requires that where someone is charged with a sexual offence then, except with the leave of the court, no evidence may be adduced, and no questions may be asked in cross-examination, by or on behalf of any accused about the 'sexual behaviour' of the complainant. 'Sexual behaviour' means any sexual behaviour or other sexual experience, whether or not involving any accused or other persons.

If the defence wishes to introduce evidence or ask question about such matters, it must apply to the court. The court will decide the application in private and in the absence of the complainant, after the prosecution has had the chance to oppose the application. The court can only grant leave when two conditions are satisfied. The first is that a refusal of leave might have the result of rendering unsafe a conclusion of the jury or (as the case may be) of the court on any relevant issue in the case. The second condition is that:

(a) the evidence in question relates to a relevant issue in the case and either

  (i) that issue is not an issue of consent (for example, as the Court of Appeal has held, if the defence is that the accused believed the victim was consenting, evidence of recent consensual activity between them is admissible in relation to the issue of the accused's belief, but not as to whether the victim had consented); or

  (ii) it is an issue of consent and the complainant's sexual behaviour to which the evidence or question relates is alleged to have occurred at or about the same time as the event which is the subject of the matter of the charge against the accused (for example, that the complainant had consented to intercourse with the accused a couple of hours earlier but not, according to the Court of Appeal, days or weeks before); or

  (iii) it is an issue of 'consent' and the complainant's sexual behaviour to which the evidence or question relates is *so similar either* to any sexual behaviour of the complainant which (according to the defence) took place as part of the event which is the subject matter of the charge, *or* to any other sexual behaviour of the complainant which, according to the defence, took place at or about the same time as that event, so that the similarity cannot reasonably be explained as a coincidence; or

(b) the evidence or question relates to any evidence adduced by the prosecution about any sexual behaviour of the complainant, and would go no further than necessary to enable the evidence adduced by the prosecution to be rebutted or explained by the accused.

To be admitted under the above provisions, the evidence must relate to a specific instance, or instances, of sexual behaviour. If the court considers that the purpose (or main purpose) of the evidence which the defence seeks to have admitted is to undermine or diminish the complainant's credibility, it will not allow the evidence to be given.

The House of Lords has held that (a)(iii) above must be construed, like any other statutory provision impinging upon a Convention right, so as to give effect to that right so far as is possible. It held, therefore, that under (a)(iii) the test of admissibility was whether the evidence, and the questioning relating to it, was so relevant to the issue of consent that to exclude it would endanger the fairness of the trial, contrary to the accused's right to a fair trial under Art. 6 of the European Convention on Human Rights. If that test was satisfied, the sexual behaviour evidence should not be excluded.

Complainants and other witnesses who are children

In relation to an offence to which it applies, s 35 of the 1999 Act makes similar provisions concerning a 'protected witness'. A 'protected witness' is a witness who:

(a) is either a complainant or a witness to the offence; and

(b) is either a child or falls to be cross-examined after giving evidence-in-chief as a child (even if by the time of the cross-examination he is no longer a child).

Section 35 applies to any offence under the Sexual Offences Act 1956, the Indecency with Children Act 1960, the Protection of Children Act 1978 (indecent photographs, etc., of a child) and the Criminal Law Act 1977, s 54 (incitement to incest). It also includes kidnapping, false imprisonment, child abduction, cruelty to children or any offence involving an assault on or injury (or a threat of injury) to any person.

For the purposes of s 35, where an offence is under one of the pieces of legislation just specified, a 'child' is someone under 17. For the purposes of the other specified offences, a 'child' is someone under 14.

Direction prohibiting cross-examination

Section 36 of the 1999 Act permits a court to prohibit an unrepresented defendant from cross-examining witnesses in other cases, where the provisions of ss 34 and 35 do not apply. This may be done where the court is satisfied that the quality of the evidence given by the witness on cross-examination is likely to be diminished if cross-examination is undertaken or continued by the accused in person, and would be likely to be improved if a direction was given, and that such a prohibition will not be contrary to the interests of justice. The court may discharge such a direction at any time.

A direction may be made on application by the prosecutor, or on the court's own motion.

The term 'witness' does not include any other person who is charged with an offence within the proceedings.

Representation of such persons for the purpose of cross-examination

Where a defendant is prohibited from cross-examining a witness under the provisions of s 34, 35 or 36, the court must invite the accused to appoint a legal representative to cross-examine on his behalf. If no such appointment is made within the prescribed time limits, the court must consider whether it is necessary, in the interests of justice, for the witness to be cross-examined by a legal representative. If the court considers that it is necessary, it must appoint a legal representative. Such a court-appointed representative will not have been instructed by the accused and will not, therefore, be responsible to him. Material relating to the proceedings must be made available to an appointee.

In such a case, the judge must give the jury such warning as is considered necessary to ensure that the accused is not prejudiced:

(a) by any inferences which might be drawn from the fact that he has been prevented from carrying out a cross-examination in person;
(b) where the witness has been cross-examined by a legal representative appointed by the court, by the fact that such cross-examination was carried out by a representative other than a person acting as the accused's own legal representative.

Incest

The history of the offence of incest begins with society's (and the church's) desire to ensure that children were not affected by the close blood ties of the parents. The ingredients of the offence therefore become predictable. If we are to prevent a male from siring children of closely related females of child-bearing age, sexual intercourse with the mother, daughter, granddaughter and sister must be prohibited. A 'grandmother' is not included as it is extremely unlikely that a liaison between the two would produce a child.

They say that 'it takes two to tango', so we must look at the other side of the bed. Women who have intercourse which is likely to result in the birth of a child must be of child-bearing age and the law currently requires that they must be 16 or more before they can be guilty of the offence. When we consider the males within her close family who are likely to make her pregnant, her grandfather must be included as males remain sexually potent into late life. The banned relationships are therefore with her grandfather, father, brother or son. There is no purpose in including 'grandson' as, by the time he reaches sexual maturity, grandmother will be past child-bearing age.

The terms 'brother' and 'sister' include 'half-brother' and 'half-sister'. The offence being concerned with blood relationship, it is immaterial that the relationship is illegitimate, provided that at the time that the intercourse took place, the accused was aware of the relationship.

The Criminal Law Act 1977, s 54, makes it an offence for a man to incite a girl under 16 who he knows to be his granddaughter, daughter or sister to have sexual intercourse with him.

Anonymity of complainants

The law provides for the anonymity of complainants (male or female) in the following cases: rape, burglary with intent to rape, procurement of a woman by threats or false pretences, administering drugs to obtain intercourse, intercourse with girls under 13 or under 16 and intercourse with, or procurement of, mentally handicapped persons, incest, buggery, indecent assault, assault with intent to commit buggery or abduction of a woman by force, offences by hospital staff against mental patients, indecent conduct towards children, incitement to incest, or attempts, conspiracies or incitement to commit those offences.

Where an allegation is made that one of these offences has been committed against a person, no matter relating to that person may, during that person's lifetime, be included in any publication if it is likely to lead members of the public to identify that person as the person against whom the offence was committed. These matters include particularly (if their inclusion in any publication is likely to have such a result):

(a) the person's name;
(b) the person's address;
(c) the identity of any school or other educational establishment attended by the person;
(d) the identity of any place of work; and
(e) any still or moving picture of the person.

For the above purpose, and for the purpose of the next paragraph but one, 'publication' is widely defined. It includes, for example, a television or radio programme, a film, a written communication or a speech, addressed to the public at large or a section of the public.

This prohibition ceases to apply once a person has been accused of an offence. In such a case, the law thereafter is as set out in the next paragraph.

Where a person has been accused of one of the above offences, no matter whatsoever which is likely to lead to the identification of the complainant may be included in any publication during the complainant's lifetime. Provision is made for the requirements of the Act to be set aside on application being made to the trial judge where it is considered necessary to induce persons to come forward as witnesses and that the applicant's defence will be substantially prejudiced if the direction is not given. The judge also has a 'public interest' discretion to set aside these provisions.

If any matter is published in breach of the above rules, an offence is committed:

(a) in the case of a newspaper or periodical, by any proprietor, editor or publisher of it;
(b) in the case of any other publication, by its publisher; or
(c) in the case of a programme, by any body corporate engaged in providing the service and by anyone involved in the programme corresponding to an editor of a newspaper.

The provisions of the Act do not apply to the 'other party' in cases of incest and buggery where that other person is alleged to have committed a similar offence as a part of a joint enterprise; in other words, that person can be identified.

Sex offender orders

Section 2 of the Crime and Disorder Act 1998 deals with these. If it appears to a chief officer of police that the following conditions are satisfied with respect to any person believed to be in, or intending to come to, his police area, namely:

(a) that person is a sex offender; and
(b) that person has acted in such a way as to give reasonable cause to believe that an order under the section is necessary to protect the public in the United Kingdom, or any particular members of the public from serious harm by him.

An application under s 2 must be made to any magistrates' court whose area includes any place where the defendant is alleged to have acted in such a way as mentioned in (b) or whose area includes any part of the applicant chief officer's police area. A 'sex offender' is someone who has been convicted of a sexual offence to which the Sex Offenders Act 1997, Part I, applies.

The court may make an order prohibiting the person concerned from doing any act specified in the order. The order will remain in force for a period specified in the order (not less than 5 years). While such an order is in force, Part I of the Sex Offenders Act 1997 will have effect as if the defendant were subject to its notification requirements. If, without reasonable excuse, a person does an act prohibited by a sex offender order, that person is guilty of an offence.

The defendant may apply by way of complaint for variation or discharge of the order but it may not be discharged without the consent of both parties before the end of a period of 5 years.

There may be an application for an interim order pending determination of an application.

Indecent literature through the post

Sending indecent, etc., matter through post

The Postal Services Act 2000, s 85, provides an offence which is concerned with sending a postal packet which encloses any indecent or obscene matter, or which has on the packet indecent or obscene words, marks or designs.

The Malicious Communications Act 1988 makes it an offence for any person to send to another person:

(a) a letter, electronic communication or article of any description which conveys
   (i) a message which is indecent or grossly offensive;
   (ii) a threat; or
   (iii) information which is false and known or believed to be false by the sender; or
(b) any other article or electronic communication which is wholly or partly of an indecent or grossly offensive nature;

if the purpose or one of the purposes in sending it is that the message, threat or information should cause distress or anxiety to the recipient or to any other person to whom it is intended that it, or its content or nature, should be communicated.

In relation to the sending of a threat, a defence exists if the threat is to reinforce a demand made on reasonable grounds and there is a belief, for which there were reasonable grounds, that it was a proper means of reinforcing the demand.

For the purposes of the Act, the term 'electronic communication' includes any oral or other communication by means of a telecommunication system and any communication (however sent) that is in electronic form.

Indecent literature for sale

The Obscene Publications Act 1959 creates the offence of:

(a) publishing an obscene article, whether for gain or not; or
(b) having an obscene article for publication for gain, whether for himself or another.

Therefore, a person who publishes such an article commits an offence whether or not the question of gain arises. Those who merely possess, must so possess with a view to publication for gain. An article for the purposes of the Act is anything to be read, looked at or both, any sound record or film or other picture record (such as a photograph, video cassette or computer disc). 'Article' for the purposes of the Act also includes any matter included in a television or sound broadcast or in a cable programme service. Such an article is published if it is distributed, circulated, sold, hired, given or lent, or so offered. In relation to films, sounds, etc., they are published if they are shown, played, projected or, where the matter is data stored electronically, when they are transmitted.

An article is obscene if its effect is to deprave or corrupt those likely to read, see or hear it. Those who distribute child pornography on the Internet by means of images held in digital form 'publish' obscene material for the purposes of the Act. Whether or not it is obscene is a matter to be determined by the jury. Where matter or data are stored electronically, a person 'publishes' it if he transmits those data and 'transmit' includes where the recipient downloads the obscene matter from the accused's computer.

A photographer who develops obscene pictures publishes them when he distributes or sells them. The photographs are 'records of a picture' and are articles for the purposes of the Act.

Whether or not an article is obscene is determined by measuring its effects in the light of the standards of ordinary, decent people and the jury need not have regard to that which is available and permissible elsewhere in deciding what society at large currently considers to be acceptable.

It is a defence for a person to prove that he had not examined the article and had no reasonable cause to suspect that it was of such a nature that publication of it, or possession of it, would make him liable under the Act. There is also a defence of 'public good' on the grounds that it is in the interests of science, literature, art or learning, or of other objectives of general concern. Expert evidence is frequently given in relation to such matters.

Proceedings must be approved by the Director of Public Prosecutions as such prosecutions lead to complexities because of conflicting expert evidence which tends to be offered in relation to that which is obscene and that which is not.

Police powers

This offence is an arrestable offence. It is also a serious arrestable offence for the purpose of searches.

A justice of the peace may issue a warrant authorising search and seizure of articles considered to be obscene.

Indecent displays

The Indecent Displays (Control) Act 1981 makes it an offence to display publicly any indecent matter. An offence is committed by the person who makes the display and any other person who causes or permits the display to be made. If matter is visible from any public place, it is deemed to be publicly displayed. The term 'public place' has its usual meaning, that is, a place to which the public have or are permitted to have access (whether on payment or otherwise), at the time at which the matter is displayed. To protect certain art exhibitions, premises are exempt when the payment taken includes payment for the display, and shops, or parts of shops, to which the public can only gain access by passing beyond an adequate warning notice, provided in both instances persons under 18 are not admitted while the display is in progress. The warning notice must read, 'WARNING. Persons passing beyond this notice will find material on display which they may consider indecent. No admittance to persons under 18 years of age.'

The provisions do not apply to BBC or ITV broadcasts, art galleries, museums, Crown or local authority buildings, theatres and cinematograph exhibitions under the appropriate regulating legislation.

Police powers

A constable may seize any article in respect of which there are reasonable grounds for believing it to be, or to contain, indecent matter and to have been used in the commission of an offence under the Act.

Indecent photographs of children

The Protection of Children Act 1978, s 1, states that it is an offence for a person to take, or permit to be taken or made, any indecent photograph, or pseudo-photograph of a child. A 'child' for the purposes of the Act means a person under the age of 16. Thus, the person who takes such a photograph and anyone who permits it to be taken (perhaps a parent or guardian) commit offences.

The term 'photograph' includes a negative and data stored on a computer disc or by other electronic means which are capable of conversion into a photograph. A 'pseudo-photograph' is an image, whether made by computer graphics or otherwise in any way, which appears to be a photograph. The definition of 'photograph' was extended by, and the term 'pseudo-photograph, was introduced by, the Criminal Justice and Public Order Act 1994. These provisions are aimed at the trade in indecent material which is read by a computer, such material being concerned with paedophile activities. Copies of indecent photographs are covered by the Act, as are data stored in a computer disc or by other electronic means which are capable of conversion into a pseudo-photograph.

The 1978 Act also prohibits the distribution, possession with a view to distribution or showing, and publication or causing publication of an advertisement for photographs or pseudo-photographs.

The Court of Appeal has held that images held in digital form on the Internet are copies of photographs for the purposes of s 1 of the 1978 Act and are distributed or shown by being made available for access by other computer users. It has also held that a person who downloads indecent images of children from the Internet on to a disc, or who prints out such images, 'makes' an indecent photograph or pseudo-photograph for the purposes of the 1978 Act. Even if those images originated outside the United Kingdom, the downloading or printing would create new material which had been *made* inside the United Kingdom. In addition, a person who voluntarily downloads an indecent image from a web page on to a computer screen 'makes' a photograph or pseudo-photograph and if that act is deliberate and intentional, with knowledge that the image was, or was likely to be, an indecent photograph or pseudo-photograph of a child, an offence is committed. It is irrelevant whether or not the motive is sexual gratification.

Where, in response to an advertisement, a firm distributed pornographic videotapes showing very young girls, the Court of Appeal supported the conviction of the person who ordered the tapes of an offence of attempting to incite another to distribute indecent photographs of children. The offer to buy the photographs amounted to an inducement to commit that offence.

For an offence of 'showing' to be committed under these provisions, a person must be in possession with a view to showing the indecent photographs to a third party; it is not sufficient that there is an intention to show a film to himself.

The term 'indecent' means offending against recognised standards of propriety. The Court of Appeal has held that in relation to an offence of making indecent photographs of children, the offence consisted of deliberately making a photograph which was considered indecent by right-thinking people.

Police powers

Under s 4 of the 1978 Act, a justice may issue a warrant to authorise entry, search for and seizure of such photographs or pseudo-photographs on information laid on oath by a constable or by or on behalf of the Director of Public Prosecutions. The additional powers of seizure provided by s 50 of the Criminal Justice and Police Act 2001 apply where a search warrant under s 4 of the 1978 Act is executed.

An offence against s 1 of the 1978 Act is an arrestable offence and also a 'serious arrestable offence' for the purposes of the law relating to search warrants under s 8 of PACE.

Possession of indecent photographs of children

The Criminal Justice Act 1988, s 160, creates the arrestable offence of possession of an indecent photograph or pseudo-photograph of a child. It is a matter for a court or jury to decide whether an unknown person depicted in an indecent photograph was under the age of 16. There is no need for expert evidence concerning age: the court or jury is as well placed as an expert to assess any argument concerning the age of the person depicted. Expert evidence would therefore be inadmissible. A person shall be taken to be a child at the material time if it appears from the evidence as a whole that that person was under 16. If the impression conveyed by a pseudo-photograph is that the person shown is a child, it shall be treated as showing a child and so shall a pseudo-photograph where the predominant impression conveyed is that the person shown is a child, notwithstanding that some of the physical characteristics shown are those of an adult. This represents a commendable attempt to deal with the problem of 'computer images' in their relationship to 'photographs'. No matter how these images are presented, it is the overall impression which will be important.

A male employee who was in charge of a shop selling pornographic videos depicting sex acts with young boys was convicted of an offence of possession. The videos were part of the stock of the shop and by reason of his employment he had agreed to sell them. They were under his control and that amounted to possession. However, such an employee could take advantage of the defence afforded by s 1(4)(b) of the 1978 Act (that he had not seen the film and had no cause to suspect that it was obscene), but that would be a matter for the court or jury to decide.

Defences

Both Acts provide defences if there is proof of a legitimate reason for distribution, showing or possession, as the case may be, or proof that the person concerned had not seen the photograph and did not know, or have reason to suspect, the photograph to be indecent.

The term 'showing' includes 'making available', as where a person gives another a key to a cupboard containing indecent photographs. The same would apply where a person made available a 'password' which enabled another to download such material from a computer.

A justice may issue a warrant to authorise entry, search for and seizure of such photographs or pseudo-photographs on information laid on oath by a constable or by or on behalf of the Director of Public Prosecutions.

Goods vehicles – plating and testing: driving licences and operators' licences

Introduction

A 'goods vehicle' is a motor vehicle or trailer constructed or adapted for the carriage of goods. The carriage of goods includes haulage. If a vehicle is adapted it is 'altered physically so as to make fit for the purpose'. If the seats are taken out of a minibus which is then fitted out as a mobile shop, the vehicle has been adapted as a goods vehicle. On the other hand, the mere removal of the rear seats of an estate car to permit it to carry more goods does not amount to an adaptation. The seats can easily be replaced. There has been no substantial and dramatic alteration to the vehicle. The test is to ask oneself whether, if the motor vehicle had been originally constructed in the form in which it then exists, it would have been classified as a goods vehicle.

The driver of a goods vehicle

Minimum age for driving goods vehicles

Different minimum ages are prescribed for different vehicles. A goods vehicle may be a small, medium or large goods vehicle for this purpose.

(a) A *small vehicle* is a motor vehicle (other than a motor cycle or invalid carriage, moped or motor bicycle) which:
   (i) is not constructed or adapted to carry more than nine persons inclusive of the driver, and
   (ii) has a maximum gross weight not exceeding 3.5 tonnes, and includes a combination of such a motor vehicle and trailer.
   Persons of 17 or over (16 if in receipt of a disability living allowance) may drive small goods vehicles.
(b) A *medium-sized goods* vehicle is a motor vehicle which is constructed or adapted to carry or haul goods, *and* which is not adapted to carry more than nine persons inclusive of the driver, *and* the permissible maximum weight of which exceeds 3.5 tonnes but does not exceed 7.5 tonnes and includes a combination of such a motor vehicle and a trailer where the relevant maximum weight of the trailer does not exceed 750 kg. Persons of 18 or over may drive medium-sized goods vehicles.
(c) A *large goods vehicle* (not being a medium-sized goods vehicle) is a motor vehicle which is constructed or adapted to carry or haul goods and the permissible maximum weight of which exceeds 7.5 tonnes. Persons of 21 or over may drive large goods vehicles.

   The carriage of passengers is referred to in these definitions of goods vehicles because of the existence of Transit-type vehicles, which although constructed for the carriage of goods, retain a quantity of seats. Such vehicles are frequently used for the carriage of goods in addition to the transport of workers to a site.
   The 'permissible maximum weight' of a vehicle is usually the relevant maximum weight of the vehicle and this will be shown on the plate of the vehicle (see below). In the case of an articulated goods vehicle, the permissible maximum weight will be its

relevant maximum train weight which is the gross weight of the unladen motor vehicle and its unladen trailer plus the maximum weight which the combination is permitted to carry. Again, this will be shown on the 'plate' in the column marked 'gross train weight'.

The Goods Vehicles (Authorised Weight) Regulations 1998 apply to most buses, goods vehicles and trailers in excess of 3500 kg. Regulation 4 of those Regulations states that no vehicle to which the Regulations apply which is of a description specified in a schedule to the regulations shall be used on a road if the weight of the vehicle, vehicle combination or any axle exceeds the maximum specified in that schedule. Such weights will be shown on plates as 'maximum authorised weights' which are, in relation to a vehicle, vehicle combination or axle, the maximum authorised weight for that vehicle, combination or axle. The Road Vehicles (Construction and Use) Regulations 1986, reg. 66, have been amended so that plates fitted to motor vehicles first used after 31 December 1998 may show particulars of the maximum authorised weights as determined by the 1998 Regulations, as alternatives to the weights at present required to be shown on such plates. The definition of the term 'Ministry plate' in reg. 70 has been amended to permit plates fitted under the 1998 Regulations to show particulars of 'maximum authorised weights'. However, reg. 4(2) of the 1998 Regulations provides that a vehicle to which the Road Vehicles (Construction and Use) Regulations 1986, regs 75 to 79, apply and which is being used in accordance with those provisions, shall be taken to comply with the 1998 Regulations.

It is important to recognise that whilst persons of less than 21 may be permitted to drive certain types of goods vehicle, the addition of a trailer to the vehicle can make a difference. A person of 17 may drive a goods vehicle of a permissible maximum weight of 3.5 tonnes but if a trailer is attached which has a relevant maximum weight of 1 tonne, the sum of the weights exceeds 3.5 tonnes and the combination becomes a medium-sized goods vehicle.

There are some exceptions to these rules in relation to age which are set out in the Motor Vehicles (Driving Licences) Regulations 1999, reg. 9. Medium and large goods vehicles owned and used by naval, military or air force authorities may be driven by persons aged 17. In addition, there is a large goods vehicle training scheme; if a person is registered and employed by an employer who is also registered in the large goods vehicle training scheme, a person may, at 18, drive, in accordance with the training scheme, a large goods vehicle, provided that it is of a class approved by the training agreement. Such a person may also drive vehicles used by a registered large goods vehicle training establishment. Regulation 54 of the 1999 Regulations permits the issue of large goods vehicle trainee driver's licences to such persons.

Large goods vehicle drivers' licences

It is an offence contrary to the Road Traffic Act 1988, s 87, for a person to drive a large goods vehicle (LGV) on a road otherwise than in accordance with a DVLA driving licence granted for that class of vehicle. However, the Road Traffic Act 1988, Part IV, imposes additional requirements upon the drivers of large goods vehicles. The Secretary of State may only grant such a licence in accordance with Part IV of the Act. Part IV requires that a traffic commissioner for an area shall exercise the functions concerned with the conduct of applicants for, and holders of, large goods vehicle drivers' licences and LGV Community licence holders.

The provisions of the 1988 Act in relation to the licensing of drivers of large goods vehicles are extended by the Motor Vehicles (Driving Licences) Regulations 1999. Schedule 2 to the Regulations provides a multiplicity of categories and sub-categories of vehicles. The various forms of goods vehicle are included in variations of category C types of vehicles. However, reg. 50(1) of the 1999 Regulations provides that Part IV of the Act shall not apply to vehicles of sub-category C1 + E (8.25 tonnes). That category is a sub-category of C + E, a category which includes vehicles of a maximum authorised mass of 12 tonnes.

For the purposes of the Regulations, the term 'maximum authorised mass' has the same meaning, in relation to goods vehicles, as 'permissible maximum weight' as defined in the Road Traffic Act 1988, s 108(1). In relation to other vehicles or trailers, it has the same meaning as 'maximum gross weight' as defined by the Road Vehicles (Construction and Use) Regulations 1986, reg. 3(2). Such weights are indicated on the 'plate' attached to the vehicle (see below).

The provisions of Part IV of the 1988 Act which are concerned with driver licensing, and the provisions of the 1999 Regulations, regs 54–57 (large goods vehicle drivers' licences issued to persons under 21; revocation of large goods vehicle drivers' licences and removal of disqualification), do not apply to large goods vehicles of a class included in categories F, G or H (some tractors, road rollers and track-laying vehicles) or C1 + E (8.25 tonnes), or exempted vehicles (including military vehicles). The list of other exempted vehicles is extensive, covering a variety of vehicles used in public works, industry, agriculture, articulated vehicles the unladen weight of which does not exceed 3.5 tonnes, forces vehicles and emergency vehicles.

Trainee drivers

The 1999 Regulations permit persons (including those of 18 or over 18 years who have training agreements) to be issued with provisional driving licences. They are of two types, one concerned with such persons and the other with those issued with a standard provisional driving licence for large goods vehicles.

Regulation 19 sets out details of certain full licences which do not carry provisional entitlement to drive other categories of vehicles. The table included within this regulation sets out details of categories of full licences together with the provisional entitlement which is included within that licence. Most significant to issues surrounding large goods vehicles is the provision that a category C licence carries provisional entitlement to drive vehicles of categories C1 + E and C + E.

Regulation 54(5) provides that the holder of an LGV trainee driver's full licence authorising the driving of a vehicle of category C (other than vehicles included in sub-category C1 + E the maximum authorised mass of which does not exceed 7.5 tonnes) may not drive a large goods vehicle of a class included in category C + E as if authorised by a provisional licence to do so before the expiration of 2 years commencing on the date on which a test for category C was passed. Thus, a trainee driver could pass a test for category C vehicles (exceeding 3.5 tonnes + trailer not exceeding 750 kg) but would be unable to use the full licence for category C vehicles as a provisional licence in respect of category C + E vehicles (combinations of motor vehicles and trailers which fall outside category C) until a full licence has been held for a period of 2 years. This has the effect of preventing young trainee drivers from progressing to the driving of very heavy lorries whilst well below the age of 21.

The driving test

Goods vehicle drivers will be in possession of driving licences issued under Part III of the 1988 Act for differing categories of vehicles as described in Schedule 2 to the 1999 Regulations. In order to obtain those licences they will have been tested on different types of vehicles. The table sets out the various categories of goods vehicles and gives details of the 'minimum test vehicle' which would have been used in the relevant test.

Category or sub-category	Weight	Specification
C1	3.5 tonnes but not exceeding 7.5 tonnes + trailer not exceeding 750 kg	C1 vehicle of 4000 kg capable of 80 kph, at least 5 m long
C1 + E	C1 tractor, trailer exceeds 750 kg but not the unladen weight of the tractor and combination not exceeding (evening – after 6.30 pm)	C1 vehicle + trailer having maximum authorised mass of 2000 kg, overall length of 8 m and capable of 80 kph (combination must be 4000 kg)
C	Exceeding 3.5 tonnes + trailer not exceeding 750 kg	C vehicle other than an articulated goods vehicle of maximum authorised mass of 12 000 kg and a length of 8 m, capable of 80 kph
C + E	Tractor category C but the combination does not fall within that category	Either an articulated combination having a maximum authorised mass of 20 000 kg and a length of 14 m and capable of 80 kph *or* C + trailer having a length of 7.5 m and a maximum authorised mass of 4 tonnes, in aggregate being of 20 000 kg, an overall length of 14 m and capable of 80 kph

Where a test vehicle was first used on a road before 1 October 2003, the requirements in relation to weights and lengths are slightly less.

Conditions applicable to both types of provisional licence

Holders of provisional licences to drive large goods vehicles may not drive an authorised vehicle unless they comply with the general conditions prescribed by reg. 16 of the 1999 Regulations relating to supervision, learner plates and the general restrictions placed upon vehicles being used to draw a trailer. However, the supervisor of a learner driver of a large goods vehicle must have held a licence authorising the driving of a vehicle of the same class for a continuous period of not less than 3 years or for periods amounting in aggregate to not less than 3 years, or where supervising a driver in a category C, D, C + E or D + E vehicle, held a relevant licence on 6 April 1998 and has held it continuously since that date, in addition to having held a full category B licence for a total of not less than 3 years. In addition, reg. 54 provides that where a person holds an LGV trainee driver's full licence, that person will still be subject to the requirement that he must drive as a registered employee of a registered employer, vehicles to which the training agreement applies, which are owned or operated by that employer or by a registered LGV training establishment.

Such a licence which authorises the driving of a class of vehicles included in category C and is a full licence, is subject to the condition that its holder shall not drive a large goods vehicle of a class included in category C + E, other than vehicles included in sub-category C1 + E the maximum authorised mass of which does not exceed 7.5 tonnes, as if authorised to do so by a provisional licence before the expiration of a period of 6 months from the date of passing the test for that licence.

Drivers from abroad

The Road Traffic Act 1988, Part III, as amended by the Driving Licences (Community Driving Licences) Regulations 1996 permits holders of Community licences authorising them to drive large goods vehicles to drive large goods vehicles in the United Kingdom. Those who become resident in the United Kingdom *may* exchange those licences for British ones, but are in any case required to submit to the Secretary of State details of driving entitlement and other information which is prescribed within a year of becoming resident. Such licences are referred to in the 1988 Act as LGV Community licences.

Holders of convention or domestic driving permits who are resident in the Isle of Man, Guernsey or Jersey may drive any large goods vehicle which they are authorised to drive by that permit during a period of 12 months from the date of their last entry into the United Kingdom. Holders who are not residents of an EEA State, or the Isle of Man, Guernsey or Jersey, may only drive a large goods vehicle brought temporarily into Great Britain.

Plating and testing of goods vehicles

Manufacturer's plate

The Road Vehicles (Construction and Use) Regulations require the following vehicles to be fitted with a manufacturer's plate:

(a) every heavy motor car and motor car first used on or after 1 January 1968, which is not a passenger vehicle or dual-purpose vehicle; and

(b) every bus (whether or not it is an articulated bus) and first used on or after 1 April 1982; and

(c) every locomotive and motor tractor first used on or after 1 April 1973; and

(d) every trailer manufactured on or after 1 January 1968 which exceeds 1020 kg unladen weight (although living vans not exceeding 2040 kg are exempted if fitted with pneumatic tyres); and

(e) every trailer which is a converter dolly manufactured on or after 1 January 1979.

There are the usual exceptions in favour of land, works, pedestrian-controlled and plant, etc., vehicles.

Motor tractors and locomotives are 'pulling' vehicles which do not themselves carry a load. All such vehicles must be plated. Motor cars and heavy motor cars are vehicles which will themselves carry a load and if they are goods vehicles, unless they are exempted, they must carry a plate. Converter dollies are trailers used to support the front of a trailer which is normally attached to an articulated vehicle, when it is not so attached.

A manufacturer's plate must be fitted in a conspicuous and readily accessible position. The particulars which the plate must contain are prescribed in Schedule 2 to the Regulations. In some instances, the only plate to be carried by a goods vehicle during the first year of its life will be the manufacturer's plate. However, vehicles to which the Motor Vehicles (Type Approval for Goods Vehicles) (Great Britain) Regulations 1982 apply will be examined and fitted with a 'Ministry plate' within 14 days.

For practical purposes, all such vehicles will be fitted with a plate which contains details of authorised weights, etc. These weights may be shown as 'gross weights'. The maximum gross weight of a vehicle is the unladen weight of the vehicle plus its maximum permitted load, thus it represents the weight transmitted to the road surface. A vehicle of 5 tonnes unladen weight which is permitted to carry 4 tonnes of cargo would have a maximum gross weight of 9 tonnes. The term 'permissible maximum weight' which is used to establish whether goods vehicles are small, medium or large for the purpose of determining the minimum age at which they may be driven is the vehicle's 'relevant maximum weight' which in turn, is the maximum gross weight which is shown on the plate. In addition, and by way of further complication, the Road Vehicles (Authorised Weight) Regulations 1998, which came into force on 1 January 1998 and apply to vehicles which are in effect, buses, goods vehicles and trailers in excess of 3500 kg, may have the weights shown on the plate expressed as 'maximum authorised weights' and where this is so, the plating has been carried out under the 1998 Regulations and the vehicle is being used in accordance with those Regulations. The weights which are shown on the plate are the weights which we look at for enforcement purposes when goods vehicles are being examined. The helpful factor is that however the weight may be described, it will be expressed as a total weight under each heading shown on the plate. See page 695 for further details of 'authorised weights'.

Ministry plate

The Goods Vehicles (Plating and Testing) Regulations 1988 require that most goods vehicles and trailers are subject to annual testing. The first examination is for the purpose of both plating and testing. Goods vehicles subject to type approval will be fitted with a Ministry plate within 14 days and the requirement to have a first examination no longer applies to a motor vehicle where a certificate of conformity or a Minister's approval certificate has been issued. The plating examination includes assessment of the vehicle's axle and gross weights, in addition to a test of roadworthiness. These weights are recorded on a 'Ministry plate'.

Every motor vehicle which meets the following requirements, namely:

(a) a plating certificate is in force for the vehicle; and
(b) that plating certificate is a certificate of conformity or a Minister's approval certificate that is treated as a plating certificate by virtue of s 59(4) of the RTA 1988,

shall be submitted for a goods vehicle test on or before the appropriate day. Other motor vehicles, and every trailer, shall be submitted for both a plating examination and a goods vehicle test on or before the appropriate day. The term 'appropriate day' means:

(a) in relation to a vehicle which is a motor vehicle, the last day of the calendar month in which falls the anniversary of the date on which it was registered; and
(b) in relation to a vehicle which is a trailer, the last day of the calendar month in which falls the anniversary of the date on which it was first sold or supplied by retail.

However, the prescription of such dates does not prevent the Secretary of State authorising the submission of a vehicle after the appropriate day.

Some vehicles are exempt from these requirements, e.g. dual-purpose vehicles not constructed or adapted to form part of an articulated vehicle (although they are subject to MOT testing). In addition, breakdown, firefighting or snow-clearance vehicles are exempt, as are living vans whose unladen weight does not exceed 3500 kg, police vehicles and those temporarily in Great Britain.

The requirements set out under the heading 'manufacturer's plate' are in respect of certain vehicles *at the time of manufacture*. The requirements at the time of plating are concerned with annual tests and are prescribed by the 1988 Testing Regulations.

The first examination, unless the vehicle has already received a Ministry plate, is a joint exercise leading to the affixing of a Ministry plate and the issue of the first goods vehicle test certificate. Those vehicles which were subject to the Motor Vehicles (Type Approval for Goods Vehicles) (Great Britain) Regulations 1982 would be issued with a certificate of conformity or approval and this must be produced.

The nature of the plate

The manufacturer's plate is a metal plate fixed to the vehicle at the time of manufacture. Once a Ministry plate has been attached, the manufacturer's plate is of no significance. The weights, etc., shown on the Ministry plate are those with which we are concerned. The Ministry plate is a paper plate which is fixed in a conspicuous place in the cab of the vehicle or elsewhere in a trailer. Where the vehicle is an articulated vehicle, plates will be attached to both parts of it.

In addition to the plates which are attached to vehicles, a 'plating certificate' is issued in respect of the vehicle. A plating certificate carries some additional details, such as the types of tyres fitted to the vehicle at the time of its examination.

Offences in connection with plating

It is an offence for a person to use, or to cause or permit a goods vehicle to be used, on a road which is of a class required to have been submitted for an examination with a view to plating, where no *plating certificate* is in force in respect of that vehicle. This certificate will normally be held at the company office. A constable may demand its production in the same circumstances as apply to the production of other vehicle documents.

A Ministry plate will specify the maximum laden weight of any trailer which may be drawn by the vehicle. It is an offence to draw a trailer other than one which complies with the plated requirements of the vehicle.

If alterations are made to a vehicle after it has been plated, the nature of those alterations must be notified to the Ministry and it is an offence to fail to do so. However, alterations to plated particulars may be made without the necessity for a further examination where a plating certificate is in force for the vehicle and the alterations applied for would not affect the safety of the vehicle on a road.

Goods vehicle testing

The examination of a goods vehicle with a view to plating is solely concerned with establishing its safe operating weights, etc. It must also be submitted for testing at the same time and it is, thereafter, subject to the requirement that it shall be tested annually. Vehicles submitted for a first examination during the 2 months preceding the appropriate day may be issued with a certificate which expires on the next but one appropriate day. It is an offence to use a goods vehicle on a road, at any time after the relevant date upon which it was required to be tested, where no test certificate is in force. A person who causes or permits such a vehicle to be so used also commits an offence. Computer-generated test certificates can now be produced.

Trailers will carry a disc which shows the date upon which a test is due.

Exemption is afforded to vehicles and trailers which are going, by previous appointment, to (and from) a testing station, while it is undergoing a test or, where the vehicle is refused a certificate, it is going to or from a place of repair or to the breakers.

A goods vehicle test certificate must be produced to a constable in the same instances as a certificate of insurance and within the same time limitations. It is an offence to fail to produce it.

Operators' licences

The nature of goods vehicles and the tasks which they undertake make it essential that there is a strict form of regulation in respect of their use on a road. The traffic commissioner for the area is responsible for goods vehicle licensing.

The Goods Vehicles (Licensing of Operators) Act 1995, s 2, states that no person shall use a goods vehicle on a road for the carriage of goods for hire or reward, or for or in connection with any trade or business carried on by him, except under the authority of an operator's licence. Section 2(5) provides that it is an offence to do so.

For licensing purposes, where a person who owns a vehicle, or has it in his possession under an agreement for hire, hire purchase or loan, is driving it on a road, that person is deemed to be the owner. In other cases, the owner will be the person whom the driver is serving or whose agent he is at the time. The offence of using a goods vehicle without an operator's licence is therefore one which is committed by anyone who owns, has hired, or in some other way is 'operating' the vehicle. However, where a company leases vehicles with their drivers from a second company and the second company prescribes the drivers' duties, pays their wages, allocates their holidays and is responsible for driver discipline, the second company is operating those vehicles and must hold the appropriate licences. Thus, if a man drives his own vehicle on a road for the carriage of goods for hire or reward without an operator's licence he commits this offence. If another person is driving the vehicle for him in these circumstances it makes no difference; the owner commits the offence of using the vehicle without an operator's licence; the driver does not, as he is not the operator of the goods vehicle.

Hire or reward

The best example of a use of a goods vehicle for hire or reward is where the vehicle and its driver are hired to another person. This occurs where a person hires a firm of furniture removers as, in effect, the proprietor hires both the vehicle and the driver to the person who is to move house. Firms which 'rent-a-van' do so for hire or reward. Where earth is removed from a site by contractors for a fixed fee, there is such a use and this is also so where septic tanks are emptied and the effluent dumped on land elsewhere, if this is done on a contract basis.

For or in connection with a trade or business

If, in the last two examples above, these tasks had been carried out by, in the first instance, the firm which was engaged in the earth removal, for example an open-cast mining company, the removal would have been in connection with the remover's trade or business and, in the last, if the septic tank had been that of the company itself, the removal would also have been connected with the trade or business. There would be no element of 'hire or reward'. Supermarket chains operate their own fleets of vehicles for delivering goods to their retail outlets. Such deliveries are made for or in connection with a trade or business carried on by them.

A local authority is carrying on a business for the purposes of this legislation and requires operators' licences in respect of its vehicles.

Types of operators' licence

Standard operators' licences

These licences authorise a holder to carry goods for hire or reward or in connection with a trade or business carried on by him. Where a licence is held by a company, a restricted licence may be used to carry goods for hire or reward instead of a standard licence, but only if the goods are the property of a subsidiary or holding company.

A standard licence may authorise operations both nationally and internationally, but may be limited to national operations. Transport operators who have dealings throughout the EU require a standard licence which authorises international operations. If they do not hold one, they will be restricted to delivery of goods to a port for dispatch.

Restricted licences

These licences are restricted in that they merely authorise the use of the vehicle for, or in connection with, a trade or business carried on by the holder of the licence, other than that of carrying goods for hire or reward.

General points in relation to licences

An operator's licence is issued to the operator of the vehicles and will be kept at the office of the operator. The licence may authorise the operator to use any specified vehicles and the registration numbers will be set out in the licence. Trailers will be identified by type and the number which may be used will be specified. A substitute s 5(6) of the Goods Vehicles (Licensing of Operators) Act 1995, provided by the Transport Act 2000, s 263 (which has not been brought into force at the time of writing), provides that a motor vehicle which is not specified in an operator's licence is not authorised to be used under that licence unless the licence holder has notified the traffic commissioner who issued the licence and has paid a fee. The existing s 5(6) permits a vehicle which is not specified in an operator's licence to be used by the operator for a period of 1 month after the vehicle first came into possession, provided that the traffic commissioner is notified at some time within that period of 1 month, with a view to specifying that vehicle in the licence held by the operator.

So that it is possible to establish, on the spot, that a vehicle is being operated under a licence, an identity disc is issued for each vehicle and must be fixed to the vehicle in a waterproof container next to the vehicle excise licence. An identity disc will specify the type of licence which is in force, that is, whether it is 'standard' or 'restricted' and whether it is 'national' or 'international'.

It is an offence if a licence holder does not cause a disc to be displayed at all times whether the vehicle is being used under the licence or not.

The holder of a licence must produce it at any time if required to do so by a constable, vehicle examiner or person authorised by the licensing authority. A holder may elect whether to produce it at his operating centre, head office or principal place of business within the traffic area of the licensing authority by whom the licence was granted.

Exceptions to the rule that licences must be in force

The Goods Vehicles (Licensing of Operators) Act 1995, s 2(2), exempts small goods vehicles as defined by Schedule 2 and vehicles of a class specified in regulations.

A 'small goods vehicle' is a goods vehicle:

(a) which does not form part of a vehicle combination and has a relevant plated weight not exceeding 3.5 tonnes or (not having a relevant plated weight) has an unladen weight not exceeding 1525 kg; or
(b) which forms part of a vehicle combination (not being an articulated combination) which is such that the total plated weight of the combination (except any small trailer) does not exceed 3.5 tonnes (or, if one or more of the vehicles in the combination, other than a small trailer, is not plated, if the total unladen weight of those vehicles, excluding such a trailer does not exceed 1525 kg); or
(c) which forms part of an articulated combination which is such that the total of the unladen weight of the tractive unit and the plated weight of the trailer does not exceed 3.5 tonnes (or, if the trailer does not have a plated weight, the total of their unladen weights does not exceed 1525 kg).

This appears to be terribly complex until it is realised that we are only concerned with 3.5 tonnes and 1525 kg, which is 30 cwt; 3.5 tonnes applies to vehicles and combinations where plated weights are available and 1525 kg applies where there is no plated weight and we therefore have to deal with unladen weight.

Certain vehicles are exempted from these provisions by the Goods Vehicles (Licensing of Operators) Regulations 1995. Schedule 3 to those Regulations lists a large number of vehicles which are exempt but generally they fall within what might be described as 'public services'. Defence force, firefighting, rescue and ambulance vehicles are exempt, and so are vehicles used for snow clearance, gritting and refuse disposal. Outside the description 'public services' we have agricultural tractors or machines, dual-purpose vehicles, showmen's goods vehicles, recovery vehicles, cement mixer lorries, hackney carriages and vehicles used for funerals.

Vehicles temporarily in Great Britain

The Goods Vehicles (Community Authorisations) Regulations 1992 established a Community-wide authorisation allowing goods vehicles access to the market in the carriage of goods by road between member States. The Goods Vehicles (Licensing of Operators) Act 1995, s 2, together with the Regulations consolidate the provisions of Council Regulation No. 881/92, which requires that each member State must issue a

Community authorisation to any haulier established in that State who is entitled to carry out international carriage of goods by road for hire or reward. Holders of such authorisations do not require operators' licences in other Community countries. The Community Regulation provides for the appointment of 'authorised inspecting officers' who are empowered to demand the production of a certified copy of the authorisation which must be carried on each vehicle operating under its authority. The 1992 Regulations appoint police constables and examiners appointed under the Road Traffic Acts as authorised inspecting officers. The Road Traffic (Foreign Vehicles) Act 1972 has been amended to permit an examiner who is exercising the functions of an authorised inspecting officers to prohibit the driving of a motor vehicle on a road where it appears that there may have been a contravention of the 1992 Regulations involving the vehicle's use without a Community authorisation or a failure to comply with the conditions governing the use of Community authorisations.

The Goods Vehicles (Licensing of Operators) (Temporary Use in Great Britain) Regulations 1996, in consequence, define a 'foreign goods vehicle' as one:

(a) which is operated by a person who is not established in the United Kingdom and has been brought temporarily into Great Britain;
(b) which is not being used for international carriage by a haulier who is established in a member State other than the United Kingdom;
(c) which is engaged in carrying goods by road on a journey some part of which has taken place, or will take place, outside the United Kingdom; and
(d) which is not used at any time during the said journey for the carriage of goods loaded at one place in the United Kingdom and delivered at another place in the United Kingdom.

EU Regulations lay down the conditions under which non-resident carriers may operate national road haulage services within a member State.

The 1996 regulations, in addition, provide specific exemptions in favour of goods vehicles of named countries, in specified circumstances.

Seizure of vehicle and load where a vehicle is used without an operator's licence

The Goods Vehicles (Enforcement Powers) Regulations 2001 are made under Schedule 1A of the Goods Vehicles (Licensing of Operators) Act 1995 and permit an 'authorised person' to detain a heavy goods vehicle and its contents in circumstances where the person using the vehicle does not have an operator's licence for that or any other vehicle. Schedule 1A defines the term 'authorised person' as an examiner appointed by the Secretary of State under the Road Traffic Act 1988, s 66A, or a person acting under the direction of such a person.

Regulation 3 provides that where an authorised person has reason to believe that a vehicle is being or has been used on a road in contravention of s 2 of the 1995 Act (no operator's licence), that authorised person may detain the vehicle and its contents. However, no one other than a constable may stop a vehicle on a road. The release of such a detained vehicle is provided for by reg. 4. A vehicle shall be returned when it transpires that at the time that the vehicle was being used, the person using it had an operator's licence (whether or not it authorised the use of the vehicle concerned), or where it transpires that at the time of the detention of the vehicle, it was not, and had not been, used in contravention of s 2. Detained vehicles may be immobilised either at the place of detention or elsewhere and a notice must be affixed to the vehicle explaining what has occurred and giving details of the release procedure. The removal of an immobilisation device or a notice, other than under the direction of an authorised person, is an offence.

The Regulations also provide procedures for the return of the contents of such a vehicle.

An authorised person must publish a notice in the London (England or Wales) or Edinburgh (Scotland) Gazette giving details of the detention and the procedure for claiming the vehicle and its contents. In addition, not less than 21 days before the expiry of the period given in the notice (also 21 days), a copy must be served upon the owner, traffic commissioner and chief officer of police in whose areas the vehicle was detained, the Association of British Insurers and the British Vehicle Rental and Leasing Association.

The Regulations also make provision for the owner of a vehicle so detained to apply in writing, within 21 days, to the traffic commissioner for the area in which the detention took place for the return of the vehicle. An application may be made on the grounds that the person using the vehicle held a licence (whether or not authorising the use of the particular vehicle), that the vehicle was not being, and had not been, used in contravention of s 2, or that the owner did not know that the vehicle was being used or had been so used. It must also state whether the applicant requires a hearing. Any determination of a traffic commissioner must be notified in writing. There is an appeal to a Transport Tribunal. Notice of such an appeal must be given before the expiry of 28 days from that determination. Where the traffic commissioner or a Transport Tribunal finds that one of the grounds specified above is made out, they must order the authorised person to return the vehicle to the owner.

The Regulations provide for the disposal of vehicles where no application for return has been made or, where such an application has been made but the traffic commissioner or Transport Tribunal determines, on appeal, that none of the grounds set out in the paragraph above exist. An authorised person is empowered to sell or destroy the vehicle as considered fit. Notice of such disposal must be given to the persons and bodies to whom notice of detention is required to be sent, as set out above.

It is an offence against reg. 20 for a person intentionally to obstruct an authorised person in the exercise of powers under reg. 3 (detention of vehicle) or 8 (removal). Regulation 21 creates the offence of making a declaration with a view to securing the return of a vehicle where that declaration is to the effect that the vehicle was not being, or had not been, used in contravention of s 2 of the 1995 Act and that declaration is to the person's knowledge either false or in any material respect misleading.

Forgery, etc., of documents and powers of seizure

The Goods Vehicles (Licensing of Operators) Act 1995, s 38, provides offences of forgery, alteration, use, lending, allowing to be used, making or having in possession a document or other thing to which the section applies. In the case of 'making or possessing' the offences also apply to things so closely resembling such document, etc., as to be calculated to deceive. Section 39 is concerned with false statements which are knowingly made in order to obtain, vary, prevent the issue or variation, procure the imposition of a condition or limitation upon an operator's licence or obtain the issue of a certificate or diploma under the Act.

A vehicle examiner, a person appointed or a police constable may at any reasonable time enter any premises of an applicant for an operator's licence or the holder of such a licence and inspect the facilities for maintaining vehicles. It is an offence to obstruct such a person. Where such persons have reason to believe that a document carried on or by a driver or a document produced under the Act is such a document (or a consignment note) they may seize the document or article.

The making of, or causing to be made, a consignment note, which the person knows to be false, or a person who, with intent to deceive, alters or causes to be altered such a document, offends against Schedule 5, para. 4.

Dangerous and careless driving and exceeding speed limits

Speed limits

The maximum speed limit at which a motor vehicle can be lawfully driven on public roads depends on two factors, the first of which is the motor vehicle concerned. Motor vehicles are classified according to their weight, construction and use, e.g. motor car, heavy motor car, goods vehicle or public service vehicle, and a maximum speed limit may be applied to the vehicle itself.

The second factor to consider is the road and particular restrictions which may be imposed in relation to a road which are of a temporary nature. Speed limits apply to public roads and these can be divided into classes, the most important of which is the restricted road.

All of the offences of speeding which we will consider are offences in respect of which there is discretionary disqualification; the endorsement of 3–6 or 3 (if fixed penalty) penalty points is obligatory.

Restricted road

By the Road Traffic Regulation Act 1984, s 82, the general rule is that a road is restricted if there is provided thereon a system of street lighting furnished by means of lamps placed not more than 200 yards apart. However, a direction may be given that a road which has such street lighting shall cease to be a restricted road, or that a road which is not provided with such lighting shall be a restricted road. If this is so, de-restriction signs (including repeater signs) shall be in place in the first instance, and restriction signs (including repeater signs) shall be in place in the second. If roads with such street lighting are subject to a 30 mph limit they will not necessarily show signs to that effect. The absence of any signs is an indication that such a limit is in force. If it is otherwise, the piece of road will show signs indicating any other speed limit which applies, or de-restriction signs, indicating that no speed limit applies. Other roads, which have no street lighting, may have speed limits applied by order.

Roads other than restricted roads

The general rule is that where a road is not a restricted road then no speed limit applies to the road itself, although a motor vehicle may be limited because of its weight, construction or use. However, the appropriate authority, i.e. the Minister or local authority, may, after giving public notice of the intention to do so, make an order prohibiting either generally or during certain periods specified in the order, the driving of motor vehicles at a speed exceeding that specified in the order. Thus, where there is a 40 or 50 mph speed limit in force, this is because the appropriate authority has made an order imposing such a speed limit. The restriction is indicated by signs showing the restriction, e.g. 50 mph, erected at the point where the restriction commences, together with repeater signs at set intervals along the road to indicate the length of road affected. Such orders are made under the Road Traffic Regulation Act 1984, s 84, and may prohibit exceeding a specified speed limit at all times, during specified periods or whilst a limit is for the time being indicated by traffic signs in accordance with the order.

Where speed limit signs had been wrongfully placed, in that they indicated that the length of road affected by the restriction was longer than that actually restricted by the order, the Divisional Court said that the signs gave adequate guidance of the speed limit to be observed on the part of the road which was properly subject to that speed limit order. The wrongful placing of the signs did not invalidate the speed limit order.

Speed limits for particular classes of vehicle

The Road Traffic Regulation Act 1984, Schedule 6, sets out speed limits which apply to particular classes of motor vehicle. The limits apply apart from the limits which apply to roads. The restrictions imposed by the Schedule relate generally to those vehicles which are larger or heavier than most vehicles (it does not deal with any vehicles, other than invalid carriages, which are less than 3.05 tonnes unladen weight, or goods vehicles which are less than 7.5 tonnes unless the particular vehicle is drawing a trailer).

Buses exceeding 12 m in length, goods vehicles (other than those up to 7.5 tonnes maximum laden weight, not drawing a trailer) and passenger vehicles or dual-purpose vehicles drawing one trailer are generally restricted to a maximum speed of 60 mph on a motorway or dual carriageway (but articulated and other goods vehicles over 7.5 tonnes are restricted to 50 mph on a dual carriageway) and to 50 mph on other roads (but articulated and other goods vehicles over 7.5 tonnes are restricted to 40 mph on other roads).

Temporary speed limits

Under the Road Traffic Regulation Act 1984, s 88, orders may be made to impose temporary maximum speed limits. Where the Secretary of State considers that, in the interests of safety or to facilitate the movement of traffic, such an order is desirable, he may impose a temporary maximum speed limit. In relation to such temporary limits, the order is deemed to have been made under s 88. The 70 mph, 60 mph and 50 mph (Temporary Speed Limit) Order 1977 has been given indefinite validity. The effect of the Order is that the maximum limit is 70 mph for any vehicle using an unrestricted dual carriageway and 60 mph for unrestricted carriageways unless a lower limit is particularly specified. (Schedules to the Order impose limits of 60 mph on certain specified lengths of dual carriageway and of 50 mph on certain specified lengths of single carriageway. Signs must be provided on such roads.)

Section 88 also permits orders to be made imposing minimum speed limits but conviction for offences under such an order may not lead to disqualification or endorsement.

Motorways

Because of the special nature of motorways and the absence of junctions, traffic lights, etc., the speed limits placed on various classes of motor vehicle differ from those imposed on other roads, and these limits are laid down in the Motorways (Speed Limit) Regulations 1974. The maximum permitted speed on a motorway at present is 70 mph. There is no requirement for signs to be placed indicating the 70 mph limit. If any lower speed limit is imposed on any section of motorway, that section must bear the appropriate signs.

Offences

It is an offence for any person to drive a motor vehicle on a restricted road at a speed greater than 30 mph (ss 81 and 89 of the Road Traffic Regulation Act 1984). Similarly, it is an offence to drive a motor vehicle at a speed which is in excess of that prescribed by a particular order (ss 84 and 89), a motor vehicle of any class at a speed greater than the speed specified in Schedule 6 of the Road Traffic Regulation Act 1984 as the maximum speed for that class of vehicle (ss 86 and 89 of the Road Traffic Regulation Act 1984) and in excess of a limit prescribed by a temporary order (ss 88 and 89).

In addition, the Road Traffic Regulation Act 1984, ss 14 and 15 [as replaced by the Road Traffic (Temporary Restrictions) Act 1991], is concerned with temporary prohibitions or restrictions made in consequence of the likelihood of danger to the public or serious damage to a road, or to enable cleaning or litter clearance. Such restrictions may be brought into force by notice in urgent cases. They may be concerned with regulating the use of roads, waiting, loading, direction of travel, restrictions on overtaking, *speed limits*, etc. Where such restrictions are in force, an offence is committed by any person who drives a motor vehicle at a speed in excess of that specified as the maximum.

Section 17 of the Act empowers the Minister to make regulations in relation to motorways and a person who drives a motor vehicle on a motorway in excess of 70 mph commits an offence against s 17(4).

A person prosecuted for exceeding a speed limit is not liable to conviction on the evidence of one witness who states that, in his opinion, the accused was driving at a speed greater than the specified limit. This does not necessarily mean that there must be more than one witness. A person can be convicted on the evidence of one witness who is able to state as a fact, not an opinion, the exact speed at which the vehicle was being driven. In such cases, a police officer giving such factual evidence is supported by the reading of a speedometer or other mechanical or electronic device which indicated the speed of the offending vehicle, supported in the case of speedometers, by evidence of their accuracy. Similarly, evidence of speed given by a single police officer, which is based upon calculations made from skid marks existing at the scene of an accident, is factual evidence based upon objectively detectable phenomena, not opinion.

The law also recognises that pressure can be applied to persons who are employed as drivers and who, in order to comply with any timetable, schedule or directions given by their employers, are forced to exceed the speed limit. In such cases, the publication or issue of any such timetable or schedule, or the giving of such directions, may be produced to a court as prima facie evidence that the employer, as the case may be, procured or incited the employee to drive vehicles to exceed the speed limit.

Notice of intended prosecution

The provisions contained in s 1 of the Road Traffic Offenders Act 1988, relating to notice of intended prosecutions, apply to an offence of exceeding a speed limit. It is important, therefore, to ensure that the provisions of that section are complied with when dealing with an offence of exceeding a speed limit, otherwise a subsequent prosecution may fail.

Exemptions from speed limit

Where a motor vehicle is being used for fire brigade, ambulance or police purposes, any provision imposing a speed limit will not apply if the observance of such a provision would be likely to hinder the use of the vehicle on that occasion. This does not mean that a police officer is free to ignore the speed limit. An officer should, in fact, set an example to other road users by strict observance of all traffic laws; it is only in exceptional circumstances that a speed limit should be exceeded, and the utmost caution must be exercised. Exemption from the speed limit does not affect a police officer's liability to prosecution for dangerous or careless driving. The life of a police officer and that of any other road user is much more valuable than the arrest of a thief or an intruder.

Evidence

The Road Traffic Offenders Act 1988, s 20, provides that records produced by prescribed devices are evidence of a fact related to any offence of speeding. The record must provide (in the same or another document) a certificate as to the circumstances in which the record was produced, signed by a constable or a person authorised by the chief officer of police for the police area in which the offence is alleged to have been committed. The device must be of a type proved to have been approved by the Secretary of State and must be used in accordance with conditions subject to which the approval was given. The Road Traffic Offenders (Prescribed Devices) Order 1992 gave approval to devices designed or adapted for measuring by radar the speed of motor vehicles. An identically named order in 1993 approved devices designed or adapted for measuring speeds by way of cables or sensors on or near the surface of a highway and those activated by means of a light beam or beams. An order of 1999 authorises the use of cameras which take photographs of vehicles at each of two predetermined positions and calculate the speed of the vehicle over that distance.

A copy of evidence obtained by means of an approved device must be served on the person charged with the offence not less that 7 days before the hearing or trial. If the person charged, not less than 3 days before the hearing or trial, requires the attendance of the person who signed the document, the evidence of the circumstances in which the record was produced will not be admissible, although the record produced by the device will. Notices may be sent under the Road Traffic Act 1988, s 172, requiring the owner of the vehicle to identify the driver within 28 days. The Divisional Court supported a finding by justices that an unsigned notice sent by a Central Ticket Office Manager 'For the Chief Constable' which was clearly identified as emanating from the Central Ticket Office of the Thames Valley Police had all the hallmarks of authenticity. The requirement that the notice had been sent by or on behalf of the chief officer of police had been satisfied.

Radar meters are extremely accurate devices and the courts will accept evidence of speed which is based upon meter readings provided that there is evidence of use by a trained operator. Hand-held radar guns are similarly accurate (provided that the batteries are fully charged). They should not be operated within a quarter of a mile of powerful VHF or UHF transmissions or within 100 yards of high-voltage cables. All such devices (and others which are in common use) are approved by the Secretary of State.

Evidence of the approval of the particular device may be required and should be offered in the absence of judicial notice having been taken of its existence. This is usually done by the production of a valid copy of the statutory instrument concerned, but the Divisional Court has said that the burden of proof may be satisfied by oral evidence from a constable who has knowledge of that approval, and notice can be taken of an entry in a work such as Wilkinson's Road Traffic Offences giving details of the instrument signifying approval.

Introduction to dangerous and careless driving

It was recognised as long ago as the Motor Act 1903 that legislation was necessary to prevent misconduct in the management of motor vehicles on a highway. The relevant provisions are now contained in the Road Traffic Act 1988, covering both motor vehicles and pedal cycles. These provisions are concerned with standards, and it should be noted that there is only one standard of driving and this is an objective one, fixed and impersonal, governed by the essential needs of the public and fixed in relation to the safety of other road users. There is no distinction drawn between the person learning to drive and the professional driver who earns a living by driving all day. Invariably it is a question of facts whether, in particular circumstances, a person is guilty of driving or riding dangerously or carelessly, and it is the job of a police officer to present all the facts of a case to the court to enable the court to arrive at the correct decision. In connection with motor vehicles only, s 1 of the Road Traffic Act 1988 creates the offence of causing death by dangerous driving. This offence is not intended to be an alternative to manslaughter, but is intended to be used as a substitute. Charges of manslaughter arising out of the driving of a motor vehicle are only preferred in the most serious cases where there is a high degree of negligence.

Driving

The word 'driving' in connection with these offences does not have an extended meaning as in other traffic offences. A person is driving if the vehicle, when moving, is subject to his control and direction and he has something to do with the propulsion of the vehicle. If a person is sitting in the driving seat of a stationary vehicle parked in such a manner as to be dangerous to other road users and an accident occurs in which a person is fatally injured, the person sitting in the driving seat of the parked vehicle will not be liable for the offence of causing death by dangerous driving, although such a person may be guilty of other traffic offences. A man steering a car being towed by a tow rope is driving because he can both steer and operate the brakes. This would not necessarily be so on a fixed tow bar provided that the tow bar was such that the 'driver' of the towed vehicle took no part in the steering of the towed vehicle. However, where two vehicles were attached by means of a rigid tow bar which was attached to the towing vehicle by means of a ball hitch, and to the vehicle being drawn by means of a shackle, the Divisional Court held that such a combination requires the 'driver' of the towed vehicle to keep it in line with the towing vehicle by means of the steering wheel and that such a person was 'driving'. A person who momentarily takes hold of a steering wheel whilst a motor vehicle is being driven by someone else does not 'drive' that vehicle. 'Driving' involves more than such minimal action.

It must be proved that the person alleged to be driving at the time of the incident was, in fact, driving. There can be evidential problems where a witness provides a police officer with a vehicle registration number and states that that was the vehicle involved in an incident. The police officer subsequently cannot say in evidence that he was told that the number of the car involved in the incident was that given by the witness, as this is hearsay. In such cases it would be good practice for the officer to record the registration number in the pocket note book and to have the witness endorse and sign the entry to the effect that it is correct. Such a record then becomes 'joint' and may be referred to by either. The witness's statement should also include the fact that the particular number was given to the officer and that it was the number of the vehicle seen on that occasion.

Dangerous driving

The offence of dangerous driving is provided in the Road Traffic Act 1988, s 2. The section provides that a person who drives a mechanically propelled vehicle dangerously on a road or other public place is guilty of an offence. Section 2A of the 1988 Act provides that, for the purposes of ss 1 and 2, a person is to be regarded as driving dangerously if, and only if:

(a) the way that he drives falls far below what would be expected of a competent and careful driver; and
(b) it would be obvious to a competent and careful driver that driving in that way would be dangerous.

The significant factors are the words 'falls far below' and the words 'would be obvious' in their relationship to 'danger'. This standard applies to all drivers regardless of their experience. It will be no defence for an accused to claim that he was doing his incompetent best. The objective standard against which driving will be measured will vary according to the prevailing conditions and to exceptional circumstances which may have existed at the time. In fog, the competent and careful driver would drive differently than if in clear conditions. High speed in a built-up area may amount to dangerous driving but is less likely to be so on a dual carriageway which is unobstructed. If the high-speed driving in a built-up area occurred in the middle of the night when there were no other vehicles or pedestrians about, the element of 'danger' is not so apparent as it would be had that driving occurred in the middle of the day.

The Court of Appeal was asked by the Attorney-General to consider circumstances in which the male driver of a public service vehicle had pressed the accelerator pedal rather than the brake, causing the vehicle to collide with pedestrians. Was the driver 'driving' the vehicle if he caused it to behave in a dangerous manner by unintentionally pressing the wrong pedal? It had been submitted that the driver's act was not voluntary in the sense that he intended to press one pedal and instead pressed a different one. The Court of Appeal said that the *actus reus* of the offence is the act of driving dangerously. The driver had been conscious of the act he was performing. He was aware that he was pressing the pedal and the fact that it was the wrong pedal was irrelevant.

Section 2A(2) provides that a person shall be regarded as driving dangerously for the purposes of ss 1 and 2 if it would be obvious to a competent and careful driver that driving the vehicle in its current state would be dangerous. Thus, a person who drives a vehicle, for example, with obviously defective brakes, drives dangerously if those defects would be obvious to a competent and careful driver. A driver took a lorry on to a motorway after having been warned that the brake air pressure gauges were not working. The hand brake system was operated owing to loss of air pressure. The trailer unit blocked the nearside lane of the motorway and shortly afterwards a lorry collided with it and the driver of that lorry was killed. The Court of Appeal ruled that the consequences of dangerous driving are capable of outlasting time at the wheel. The dangerous driving (due to the condition of the vehicle) had played a part in creating both the occasion and the event. The consequences of the person's driving were not 'spent' or too remote from the event which occurred so proximately to the event causing the death of another person.

He who drives a goods vehicle and is aware that the vehicle's heavy load may fall off and kill or injure another road user drives dangerously if the danger would be obvious to a competent and careful driver. A vehicle which was defective because of serious corrosion underneath the vehicle was held not to be such that a competent and careful driver would necessarily be aware of the defects. Similarly, where a wheel came off a lorry and killed another driver and it was proved that visual checks were made daily and that a physical check was carried out once a week, the Court of Appeal said that 'obvious' meant something which can be seen and realised at first glance. It would be wrong to expect a driver to do more than he had been instructed to do in the absence of evidence that those instructions are inadequate. A man was the driver of a goods vehicle which was fitted with a crane which in turn was fitted with outriggers for stabilisation when the crane was in use. The vehicle was fitted with devices for securing the crane and it was possible to see whether or not these securing devices were in position if they were examined (as they protruded slightly). The arm of the crane broke free and struck two pedestrians, killing one of them. The defence submitted that there was no case to answer as there had been no evidence to show that it would have been obvious to a competent driver that the arm was not properly secured. It had not been used that day. The Court of Appeal said that he had been the only person to use the vehicle since he last secured the riggers. In the absence of any explanation, it was clearly open to a jury to conclude that it should have been obvious that they were not properly secured.

To return to circumstances of *driving* dangerously, when it has been established that the actual driving fell far below such standards, it becomes necessary to consider whether it would be obvious to a competent and careful driver that such driving would be dangerous. In this context, 'dangerous' refers to danger either of injury to any person or of serious damage to property. In determining what would be expected of, or obvious to, a competent and careful driver, regard shall be had not only to the circumstances of which he could be expected to be aware, but also to any circumstances shown to have been within the knowledge of the accused. A police driver had pursued another car at speeds up to 100 mph on an urban dual carriageway along which junctions had been screened by police cars. He passed over another junction against a red traffic light and collided with a vehicle emerging from a side road which had not been so screened on both sides. The Court of Appeal said that the officer's genuine belief that the junction had been screened was not a relevant factor in such a case. The beliefs of the driver are irrelevant in deciding how a *competent and careful driver* would have behaved in the existing circumstances.

Where, for example, a rope securing a load was seriously weakened, this may be shown to have been within the knowledge of the accused, although it may not have been obvious to a competent and careful driver in a general sense. A person drove while fully aware that he was prone to hypoglycaemic attacks which occurred without warning. This was held to be 'circumstances of which he could be expected to be aware' and of which he had knowledge. The Court of Appeal said that it would be strange if Parliament had intended making the driving of a vehicle which was in a dangerously defective state an offence, but not the driving of a motor vehicle by a person who was in a dangerously defective state.

The Court of Appeal has ruled that where a charge of dangerous driving (in the particular case one of causing death by dangerous driving) involves the use of a vehicle in a defective condition, proof of guilt depends upon an objective test as to the standard of driving, namely, what would have been obvious to a competent and careful driver. The state of mind of the accused is relevant only if, and to the extent that, it attributes additional knowledge to the notional competent and careful driver. The standard of proof is high. It must be shown that the defect was 'obvious' to the 'competent and careful driver'. It is not enough to show that a driver, had he examined the vehicle by going underneath it, would have seen the defect. *Mens rea* plays no part in the offence as it is concerned with defective vehicles.

In determining the state of a vehicle, regard may be had to anything attached to it or carried on or in it and to the manner in which it is attached or carried.

Causing death by dangerous driving

This is the most serious offence that the driver of a motor vehicle can commit and is contained in s 1 of the Road Traffic Act 1988, which reads:

> A person who causes the death of another person by driving a mechanically propelled vehicle dangerously on a road or other public place shall be guilty of an offence.

This offence is punishable on indictment with 10 years' imprisonment and, consequently, is an arrestable offence. It was created because of the reluctance of juries to convict a person of manslaughter in motor accident cases – a charge of manslaughter now being preferred only when there is clear evidence of criminal negligence. For an explanation of the term 'public place', see page 436.

Causes the death of another person

This does not mean that dangerous driving must be the sole cause of death; the prosecution need only prove that the driving was a cause of the death. It is not necessary to show that the dangerous driving was the sole cause of death, since it is sufficient that it is more than a trifling cause. Where two drivers were engaged in a high-speed chase and one of them was killed when she collided with an oncoming car, the other driver engaged in the chase was convicted of this offence. His dangerous driving had been a cause of the death of the other driver and that 'cause' had been more than 'slight or trifling'.

Where a fatal accident occurs, one of the important points to remember is the continuity of identification from the scene of the accident to the hospital and later the mortuary. If the person is not certified dead at the scene by a doctor, the usual practice is to convey the victim by ambulance to the nearest hospital where death is certified on arrival, before the victim is conveyed to the mortuary where a post-mortem will be carried out later. To avoid the necessity of having a number of witnesses to provide the chain of identification, a police officer will usually accompany the body from the scene to the mortuary via the hospital, and later will identify the body to the pathologist who performs the post-mortem examination.

The question of clothing worn by the deceased may be an important factor in any subsequent court proceedings, particularly where the person killed was a pedestrian. A note should be made of the top clothing worn by the deceased. If the accident occurred during the hours of darkness, one of the questions which will be asked is whether or not the pedestrian could have been easily seen by the driver of a motor vehicle. Similarly, if the motor vehicle concerned in the death failed to stop after the accident, an examination of the clothing may yield valuable evidence connecting the vehicle with the accident.

The death must be of another person; this includes a passenger in the motor vehicle involved in the accident. However, when a prosecution is being considered for causing death by dangerous driving and the person, or all of the persons killed, were relatives of the driver but police nevertheless believe that in the light of all circumstances a prosecution should be brought, the case should be referred to the Director of Public Prosecutions before a decision is made to institute proceedings. Where the deceased is not a relative in a legal sense, but has a close connection with the driver, the case may still be referred to the Director where advice is required.

Road or public place

The meaning of the term 'road' is defined by the Road Traffic Act 1988, s 192, and has been previously examined. While this is also true of 'public place', there are some specific matters which are additionally helpful.

By the Road Traffic Act 1988, s 13A, a person is not guilty of an offence involving dangerous or careless driving by virtue of driving a vehicle in a public place other than a road if it is shown that the driving was in accordance with an authorisation for a motoring event given under the Motor Vehicles (Off Road Events) Regulations 1995. These Regulations empower prescribed bodies to issue authorisations.

It has been held that the foyer of the departure lounge at a Heathrow Airport terminal is a public place for the purposes of an offence of careless driving. The offender was driving an electric buggy in a congested foyer containing seated passengers and walking passengers. Although this occurred in an area to which access was restricted to passengers who had boarding passes and had passed through passport control, it was held to be a public place in that the persons who were there were members of the public, not a special group of persons subjected to any form of screening process which might have endowed them with some special characteristic. A similar decision was made in relation to a hospital car park.

Evidence of drink

Evidence that the driver was adversely affected by drink is relevant where the issue is whether the person was driving dangerously. To be admissible, such evidence must tend to show that the amount of drink taken would adversely affect a driver or, alternatively, that the driver was in fact adversely affected. Thus, where it could be given that the alcohol content of the blood of a driver exceeded 80 mg per 100 ml of blood, that would be evidence tending to show that the amount of drink taken was such that it would adversely affect the driving of the person concerned. However, there must be evidence of the manner of driving. Consumption of alcohol is not, by itself, sufficient to justify conviction for dangerous driving. The section requires evidence of 'the way he drives' (as compared with the competent and careful driver) and evidence of the fact that it would be obvious to such a driver that driving in that way would be dangerous. The consumption of alcohol may be relevant to the first point; it cannot be relevant to the second as in that case we are concerned with the competent and careful driver, not with the accused in a direct sense. However, evidence of the consumption of alcohol will always be relevant to 'the way he drives' as it is a related fact.

Evidence of the quantity of alcohol in a specimen of blood which was too small to be divided into two parts may be admissible in a case of dangerous driving where it is relevant to the nature of the driving. The limitations placed by the Road Traffic Offenders Act 1988, s 15, apply only to proceedings under s 3A, 4 or 5 of the Road Traffic Act 1988.

Defences

Once it is proved that a person was in the driving seat of a moving vehicle, there is an irresistible inference that that person was driving, and if the driving was dangerous then that is likely to be regarded as conclusive evidence that the person in the driving seat was driving in a dangerous manner. However, a person cannot be said to be driving if he suffers a sudden mischance for which he is no longer to blame and which renders that person unconscious or otherwise prevents him from controlling the movements of the vehicle. Examples of such situations are a sudden epileptic fit or coma, a blow on the head from a stone or an attack by a swarm of bees.

This defence, now generally referred to as 'automatism', will only apply if the deprivation of all thought, which is caused by the affliction, was not connected with any deliberate act or conduct of the driver and arose from a cause which a reasonable man would have no reason to expect, and which the driver did not think might occur. In the absence of medical evidence, the defence of automatism can only succeed in rare circumstances.

A good defence can be put forward when the driver of a vehicle is suddenly deprived of control due to some defect in the vehicle suddenly manifesting itself. Such a defect may be a defence if, because of it, the danger was created by a sudden total loss of control in no way due to fault on the part of the driver, but the defence has no application where the defect is known to the driver or should have been discovered had that driver exercised reasonable prudence.

Where a motor car is being hotly pursued by an armed gang or where it has been hijacked by an armed gang who order the driver to drive in a particular way, the driver may have a defence if it can be proved that he drove dangerously in order to avoid a threat of death or serious injury.

Aiding and abetting

Although the offence of causing death by dangerous driving can only be committed by the person driving a vehicle, this does not preclude any other person who aided, abetted, counselled or procured the offence from being punished. In relation to indictable offences, the relevant legislation is contained in s 8 of the Accessories and Abettors Act 1861, which states:

> Whosoever aids and abets, counsels or procures the commission of an indictable offence either at common law or by virtue of any Act passed or to be passed, is liable to be tried, indicted and punished as a principal.

Thus, where a qualified accompanying driver is charged with aiding and abetting a provisional licence holder who was driving a motor vehicle when it was involved in a fatal accident, the accompanying driver could be convicted of aiding and abetting the provisional licence holder in causing death by dangerous driving if it could be shown that the provisional licence holder had been driving the car dangerously for a sufficient time to enable the accompanying driver to try to stop the driver from driving dangerously, and that he had not done so.

Alternative verdicts

The Road Traffic Offenders Act 1988, s 24, provides that where a person is found not guilty of an offence of causing death by dangerous driving he may be found guilty of dangerous driving or careless or inconsiderate driving, and that a person found not guilty of an offence of dangerous driving may be found guilty of careless or inconsiderate driving, provided that the allegations in the indictment or information amount to or include an allegation of an offence under the appropriate alternative provision.

Careless and inconsiderate driving

The relevant provisions are now contained in s 3 of the Road Traffic Act 1988, as follows:

> If a person drives a mechanically propelled vehicle on a road or other public place without due care and attention, or without reasonable consideration for other persons using the road or place, he shall be guilty of an offence.

A person commits an offence of careless driving if not exercising that degree of care and attention that a reasonable and prudent driver would exercise in those circumstances. No allowances are made for learner drivers; there is only one standard of care.

It is difficult to draw a distinction between dangerous driving and driving without due care and attention, or without reasonable consideration. The view most often taken is that where a driver has been merely careless, or momentarily inattentive, he is guilty of careless driving. Some examples will serve to illustrate the point. A driver who mounted the verge, hitting a pole almost 3 feet from the edge of the road, was held to be driving carelessly; similarly, it was careless driving where a driver gave misleading signals. Examples of driving without reasonable consideration include driving with brilliant headlights which were not dipped for oncoming traffic and driving through puddles at speed, drenching pedestrians.

Sometimes the situation in which a vehicle is found raises a prima facie case of driving without due care and attention, for example, where a car left the road, mounted the footpath on its nearside, and collided with a structure on the other side of the footpath. Another example was where a car collided with a lamp standard and a shop, and although there were no eye witnesses there were tyre marks showing that the vehicle had been driven for 100 yards on the wrong side of the road and partly on the footpath. Paint of the same colour as the car was found on the lamp standard and the shop, and the position where the car, which was also badly damaged, came to rest was noted; these were all facts which were so eloquent in themselves that the court was entitled to find that the driver was guilty of driving without due care and attention.

On occasions a driver will have carried out an act which is contrary to the indications given by a traffic sign. This would be so if the requirement imposed by road markings which accompany signs such as 'Stop' and 'Give way', that no vehicle shall pass the line markings on the road concerned in circumstances which will impede other traffic on the main road, were ignored. Whilst an offence of failing to comply with the indications given by the sign will always apply, a charge of careless driving may also lie where a collision or near-collision occurs owing to the driver's actions. It is submitted that the driver who impedes traffic by unreasonably remaining in the overtaking lane of a motorway or dual carriageway and the driver who irresponsibly uses full-beam headlamps are driving without reasonable consideration for other road users.

The Divisional Court has said that the actions of the party charged with careless driving must be judged separately from the actions of the other party to the issue, who may also be guilty of such an offence.

The section creates two separate offences: careless driving and driving without reasonable consideration for other road users. Both cannot be charged in a single information.

Vehicle involved in careless driving used in manner causing alarm, distress or annoyance

The Police Reform Act 2002, s 59(1), provides that where a constable in uniform has reasonable grounds for believing that a motor vehicle (mechanically propelled vehicle for these purposes) is being used on any occasion in a manner which contravenes s 3 of the Road Traffic Act 1988 (careless and inconsiderate driving) and is causing, or is likely to cause, alarm, distress or annoyance to members of the public, that constable has the power:

(a) if the vehicle is moving, to order the person driving it to stop the vehicle;
(b) to seize and remove the vehicle;
(c) for the purposes of exercising a power falling within para. (a) or (b) to enter any premises (other than a dwelling house, but this term does not include any garage or other structure occupied with the dwelling house, or any land appurtenant to the dwelling house) on which there are reasonable grounds for believing the vehicle to be;
(d) to use reasonable force, if necessary, in the exercise of any power conferred by (a) to (c).

A constable additionally has the powers set out in (a) to (d) above where there are reasonable grounds for believing that a motor vehicle has been used on any occasion in a manner falling within s 59(1).

The power of seizure shall not be exercised unless:

(a) the constable has warned the person appearing to him to be the person whose use falls within s 59(1) that he will seize the vehicle if that use continues or is repeated; and
(b) it appears that the use has continued or been repeated after the warning.

However, a warning need not be given if the constable would otherwise have the power to seize the vehicle under the s 59 if:

(a) the circumstances make it impracticable for him to give the warning;
(b) the constable has already on that occasion given a warning under s 59(4) in respect of any use of that or of another mechanically propelled vehicle by that person or any other person;
(c) the constable has reasonable grounds for believing that such a warning has been given on that occasion otherwise than by him; or
(d) the constable has reasonable grounds for believing that the person whose use of that mechanically propelled vehicle on that occasion would justify the seizure is a

person to whom a warning under s 59(4) has been given (whether or not by that constable or in respect of the same vehicle or the same or a similar use) on a previous occasion in the previous 12 months.

It is an offence to fail to comply with an order under s 59(3) to stop a motor vehicle.

The Police (Retention and Disposal of Motor Vehicles) Regulations 2002 provide for the removal, retention, release or disposal of such vehicles. Regulation 4 provides that the authority having custody of any such vehicle is obliged to take steps to give a notice to a person who owns the vehicle requiring him to claim it within 21 days. The notice must indicate that charges may be payable by that person and that the vehicle may be retained until these charges have been paid. The charges are currently £105 for removal and £12 for each period of 24 hours or part thereof, during which the vehicle has been in the custody of the authority. Regulation 7 lays down strict rules in relation to the disposal of vehicles seized to ensure that time is available for sufficient enquiries to be made. The date specified in the seizure notice must not be less than 21 days from the date upon which the notice was given to the person and, generally, disposal will not be permitted before a period of 3 months has passed since seizure.

Regulation 5(3) provides that a person who would otherwise be liable to charges shall not be liable to pay if the use which caused the seizure was not a use by him and he did not know of the use of the vehicle in the manner which led to its seizure, had not consented to its use in that manner and could not, by the taking of reasonable steps, have prevented its use in that manner.

These powers additionally apply where offences against s 34 of the Road Traffic Act 1988 (prohibition of off-road driving) have been committed; see page 352.

Causing death by careless driving when under the influence of drink or drugs

Section 3A of the 1988 Act provides:

> If a person causes the death of another person by driving a mechanically propelled vehicle on a road or other public place without due care and attention, or without reasonable consideration for other persons using the road or place, and:
>
> (a) he is, at the time when he is driving, unfit to drive through drink or drugs; or
> (b) he has consumed so much alcohol that the proportion of it in his breath, blood or urine at that time exceeds the prescribed limit; or
> (c) he is, within 18 hours after that time, required to provide a specimen in pursuance of s 7 of this Act, but without reasonable excuse fails to provide it, he is guilty of an offence.

The term 'causing the death of another person' is discussed above. The terms 'unfit to drive through drink or drugs', 'exceeds the prescribed limit' and 'without reasonable excuse fails to provide it' are explained in the section entitled 'Breath specimens and drinking and driving' on pages 437–439.

It is important to be able to establish clearly *careless driving* in the first instance, and:

(a) that at the time the driver is either
    (i) unfit to drive through drink or drugs;
    (ii) driving while over the prescribed limit; or

(b) that within 18 hours of that careless driving, the driver fails, without reasonable excuse, to provide a specimen for analysis; and that the careless driving was a cause of the death of another person.

Alternative verdicts

A person who is found not guilty of this offence may be convicted of an offence of careless or inconsiderate driving, driving when unfit to drive through drink or drugs, driving with excess alcohol in breath, blood or urine, or failing to provide a specimen for analysis, if the allegations in the indictment or information amount to or include an allegation of such an offence.

Identification

As in all criminal cases, the identification of the driver and the linking of the driver to the alleged offence are most important. If the driver cannot be identified with the alleged offence, then a charge will generally fail.

Defences

As in dangerous driving, the defences of 'automatism' and 'mechanical defect' and perhaps 'necessity' apply to a person charged with an offence under s 3 of the Act.

Aiding and abetting

Both the offences under s 3 (careless and inconsiderate driving) are summary offences and, therefore, a person who is charged with aiding, abetting, counselling or procuring the commission of an offence under s 3 of the Act is dealt with under the Magistrates' Courts Act 1980, which states:

> A person who aids, abets, counsels or procures the commission by another person of a summary offence shall be guilty of the like offence and may be tried (whether or not he is charged as a principal) either by a court having jurisdiction to try that other person or by a court having, by virtue of his own offence, jurisdiction to try him.

The test to be applied in aiding and abetting cases is that if a person knows that the acts which constitute an offence are being done and he helps in any way, he is guilty of aiding and abetting that offence. It should be noted, however, that the passive conduct of the supervisor of a learner driver in circumstances which called for action could render the supervisor liable for aiding and abetting an offence committed by the learner driver.

Dangerous and careless cycling

The offences of dangerous and careless cycling are covered by ss 28 and 29 of the Road Traffic Act 1988, and in each case the wording is similar to the corresponding sections of the Act relating to motor vehicles. What has been said about 'dangerous' for the purposes of dangerous driving also applies to the offence of dangerous cycling. Where a person is charged with dangerous cycling and is found not guilty of that offence and the allegations in the information amount to or include an allegation of careless cycling, there may be a conviction for that offence.

Notice of intended prosecution

The provisions contained in s 1 of the Road Traffic Offenders Act 1988 relating to notice of intended prosecution apply to all the offences with which we have dealt, with the notable exception of the offence of causing death by dangerous driving. It is, therefore, important when dealing with an offence of dangerous or careless driving or cycling that the provisions of s 1 of the Act are complied with. In practice, notice of intended prosecution is sometimes sent for the offence of dangerous driving, when a charge of causing death by dangerous driving is being considered.

However, s 2 of the Road Traffic Offenders Act 1988 states that the requirements of s 1 do not apply in relation to an offence if, at the time of the offence or immediately thereafter, an accident occurs owing to the presence on a road of the vehicle in respect of which the offence was committed. If, therefore, the dangerous or careless manner of the driving results immediately in an accident, there is no requirement to comply with the provisions of this section.

Police powers

The offence of causing death by dangerous driving is punishable with 10 years' imprisonment and is, therefore, an arrestable offence. However, it should seldom be necessary to exercise such a power unless the driver is uncooperative.

Foreign citizens in the United Kingdom

Introduction

The Immigration Act 1971 is concerned with persons who are not British citizens.

It is concerned with those who have a right of abode within the United Kingdom and with ensuring that such persons shall be allowed to live in the United Kingdom freely, and to come and go into and from, the United Kingdom without let or hindrance, except such as may be required under and in accordance with the Act.

Second, it is concerned that persons not having such a right of abode, may live, work and settle in the United Kingdom by permission, subject to such regulation and control of their entry into, stay in, and departure from the United Kingdom, as may be imposed. The Act provides that rules laid down by the Secretary of State dealing with such persons shall include provision for admitting persons coming for the purpose of taking employment, or for the purpose of study, or as visitors, or as dependants of persons lawfully in or entering the United Kingdom. Indefinite leave to enter and remain in the United Kingdom shall be treated as having been given to those who were in the United Kingdom under these conditions at the time of the 1971 Act coming into force.

Right of abode in the United Kingdom

A person has a right of abode if:

(a) he is a British citizen; or
(b) he is a Commonwealth citizen who
  (i) immediately before the commencement of the British Nationality Act 1981 was a Commonwealth citizen having the right of abode in the United Kingdom at the time at which the 1971 Act was passed; and
  (ii) has not ceased to be a Commonwealth citizen in the meantime.

The British Nationality Act 1981 is now the principal Act dealing with citizenship. It deals with three categories of citizen:

(a) those who have British citizenship because of a right which is associated with descent, birth, adoption, naturalization, etc.;
(b) persons who are citizens of British Overseas Territories which are set out in Schedule 6 to the Act, for example, Gibraltar, Falkland Islands and Bermuda; and
(c) persons who are British Overseas Citizens and became such, having been a citizen of the United Kingdom and Colonies, whilst not becoming a British citizen or a citizen of the British Overseas Territories, at the commencement of the British Nationality Act 1981.

Any person who immediately before 21 May 2002 was a British Overseas Territories citizen automatically became a British citizen on that day, except someone who became a British Overseas Territories citizen solely through a connection with the Sovereign-Base Areas in Cyprus. Those within (b) and (c) above are categorised as Commonwealth citizens.

There are no restrictions upon the movements of persons who are classed as *British citizens*.

Immigration controls

Control over immigration is exercised in the first instance by immigration officers, who have the power to give or refuse leave to enter the United Kingdom. Thereafter, the power to give leave to remain in the United Kingdom, or to vary the original leave granted by the immigration officer, is exercised by the Secretary of State. Generally, the Secretary of State exercises his powers by notice in writing to the person concerned.

The 1971 Act also empowers the Secretary of State to make regulations requiring some person who have been permitted entry to the United Kingdom to register with the police. The regulations which have been made include a requirement that such persons shall be issued with a police registration certificate. In connection with the purpose of this Act, the Secretary of State is also permitted to make regulations requiring records to be made and kept of persons staying in hotels and at other premises where lodging or sleeping accommodation is provided.

Common travel area

Arrival and departure from the United Kingdom from or to any of the Islands (Channel Islands and Isle of Man) or the Republic of Ireland are within this area and are not subject to the controls effected by this Act if they are connected with a 'local journey'.

A 'local journey' is one which begins and ends in the common travel area and is not made by a ship or aircraft which began its journey outside the common travel area, or is due to end its journey at a place outside that area.

Conditional leave to enter the United Kingdom

Persons not having a right of abode in the United Kingdom may be admitted subject to such restrictions as may be provided by rules of the Secretary of State which may provide that such entry shall be subject to conditions as to length of stay or otherwise. A person's leave to enter may be varied by altering its limits, or by adding, varying or revoking conditions.

Breach of conditions and deportation

A person who is in the United Kingdom in breach of such conditions is liable to deportation and the Secretary of State may make a deportation order against him.

In addition, a person who is not a British citizen is liable to deportation if, after he has attained the age of 17, he is convicted of an offence punishable with imprisonment and such deportation is recommended at the time of the conviction.

The Secretary of State may also order deportation if he deems it conducive to the public good, if another person to whose family he belongs is, or has been ordered to be, deported or where a person has obtained leave to remain by deception.

Illegal entry and similar offences

The Immigration Act 1971, s 24(1) states that a person who is not a British citizen is guilty of an offence if:

(a) contrary to the Act such person knowingly enters the United Kingdom in breach of a deportation order or without leave;

(b) having only a limited leave to enter or remain in the United Kingdom that person knowingly either
   (i) remains beyond the time limited by the leave; or
   (ii) fails to observe a condition of the leave;

(c) if, having lawfully entered the United Kingdom without leave by virtue of s 8(1) of the Act (crew member of ship or aircraft), that person remains without leave beyond the time allowed by that section;

(d) without reasonable excuse, that person fails to comply with any requirement imposed under Schedule 2 of the Act to report to a medical officer of health, or to attend or submit to a test or examination, as required by such an officer;

(e) without reasonable excuse, such a person fails to observe any restriction imposed under Schedule 2 or 3 of the Act as to residence, as to employment or occupation or as to reporting to the police or to an immigration officer;

(f) that person disembarks in the United Kingdom from a ship or aircraft after being placed on board under Schedule 2 or 3 with a view to his removal from the United Kingdom;

(g) that person embarks in contravention of a restriction imposed by or under an Order in Council under s 3(7) of the Act (provisions aimed at preventing persons from going to specified places on the grounds of safety).

Section 24(1A) provides that a person who commits an offence under (b) above by remaining beyond the time limited by the leave commits that offence on the day when he first knows that the time limited by his leave has expired and continues to commit it throughout any period during which that person is in the United Kingdom thereafter. However, a person may not be prosecuted under (b) more than once in respect of the same limited leave.

It is an offence contrary to the Immigration Act 1971, s 24A, for a person who is not a British citizen to obtain or seek to obtain leave to enter or remain in the United Kingdom, or to secure or to seek to secure the avoidance, postponement or revocation of enforcement action against him, by means which include deception. The offence of deception has been expanded to include claims made by asylum seekers which are blatantly deceitful. The further extension to include deceit in relation to enforcement measures recognises that a claim for asylum represents a claim that it would be contrary to the Refugee Convention for that person to be removed from or required to leave the United Kingdom. Thus, the offence embraces claims made by those who seek to remain on the basis of unfounded asylum claims involving the use of deceit.

Section 26 of the 1971 Act includes summary offences which can be committed in relation to statements or representations made to an immigration officer during examination which are known to be false, or are not believed to be true, and in relation to alterations to documents and the possession of documents known, or reasonably believed, to be false.

A constable or an an immigration officer may arrest without warrant anyone who has committed or attempted to commit, or whom he has reasonable grounds for suspecting has committed or attempted to commit, an offence under s 24 or 24A other than an offence under (d) above.

Assisting illegal entry and harbouring

Section 25(1) of the 1971 Act provides that a person who is knowingly concerned in making or carrying out arrangements for securing or facilitating:

(a) the entry into the United Kingdom of anyone whom he knows, or has reasonable cause for believing, to be an illegal entrant;
(b) the entry into the United Kingdom of anyone whom he knows or has reasonable cause to believe to be an asylum claimant; or
(c) the obtaining by anyone of leave to remain in the United Kingdom by means which he knows or has reasonable cause for believing to include deception,

commits an offence. These are arrestable offences. Immigration officers are given statutory power to arrest in these circumstances by s 28A.

The offence set out in (b) does not apply in relation to anything done by a person who has been detained under para. 16 of Schedule 2 (detention of persons liable to examination or removal) or has been granted temporary admission under para. 21 (temporary admission or release of persons liable to detention). Nor does the offence in (b) apply to anything done by a person otherwise than for gain, or to an employee of a bona fide organisation designed to assist persons who are asylum claimants. An 'asylum claimant' is a person who intends to make a claim that it would be contrary to the United Kingdom's obligations under the Refugee Convention or the Human Rights Convention for him to be removed from, or required to leave, the United Kingdom.

Section 25(2) makes it an offence for a person knowingly to harbour any person whom he knows or has reasonable cause for believing to be either an illegal entrant or a person who has committed an 'overstaying' offence under (b) or (c) of s 24. This is not an arrestable offence but an immigration officer is given statutory power to arrest.

EU nationals

EU nationals are admitted on proof of European citizenship.

Registration with police

The Immigration (Registration with Police) Regulations 1972 deals with the registration of aliens. An 'alien' is a person who is neither a Commonwealth citizen, nor a British protected person nor a citizen of the Irish Republic. Such persons may be required to register with the chief officer of police for the area in which they reside. They will have been granted limited leave to enter which will be subject to a condition of registration and their passports will have been endorsed accordingly. If, in any circumstances, EU nationals are required to register, the Home Office will notify the appropriate police force. Where this occurs, the residence permit will be endorsed in the space provided and this endorsement fulfils the purpose of a police registration certificate.

In respect of other persons who must register with the police, a police registration certificate will be issued which carries the photograph of the person concerned. Police forces maintain records of aliens living within their areas who are subject to registration requirements. Changes of residence must be reported within 7 days and changes in other registered particulars within 8 days. This may be done by post but personal attendance may be required.

An immigration officer or constable may require an alien to whom the Regulations apply either to produce a certificate of registration or to give to the officer or constable a satisfactory reason for failure to produce it, forthwith. Where alterations are being made in registered particulars, a registration officer may require the alien concerned to produce his certificate of registration so that necessary amendments can be made. Where there is a failure to produce at the time, the officer or constable may require that person to produce a certificate of registration at a police station specified by the officer or constable within the following 48 hours.

A person who fails to register as required or to comply with any registration requirement offends against s 26(1) of the 1971 Act.

Asylum seekers

The Immigration and Asylum Act 1999 represents a far-reaching attempt to regularise immigration procedures by streamlining the process for those who have a genuine reason for wishing to enter the United Kingdom, and by providing measures to combat illegal entry and 'overstaying'. Formal arrangements are made for the welfare of genuine asylum seekers and the procedure is tightened in respect of bogus asylum seekers. Most of the changes which are important to police officers have been achieved by the amendment of provisions of the Immigration Act 1971. So far as police officers are concerned, those persons who have entered the United Kingdom without leave may be arrested under the amended provisions of the 1971 Act and detained for examination by an immigration officer. The various offences which can be committed under the provisions of the Acts of 1971 or 1999 are likely to be prosecuted by the Immigration Service.

However, it is important to appreciate the additional heavy penalties introduced by the 1999 Act for those involved in smuggling immigrants or asylum seekers into the United Kingdom. By s 32, a person is classed for the purposes of the Act as a clandestine entrant if:

(a) he arrives in the United Kingdom concealed in a vehicle, ship or aircraft;
(b) he passes, or attempts to pass, through immigration control concealed in a vehicle; or
(c) he arrives in the United Kingdom on a ship or aircraft, having embarked
   (i) concealed in a vehicle; and
   (ii) at a time when the ship or aircraft was outside the United Kingdom,

and claims, or indicates that he intends to seek, asylum in the United Kingdom, or evades, or attempts to evade, immigration control. Where this occurs, the person responsible for the clandestine entrant is liable to a penalty for that person and the same penalty for each person concealed with the claimant. The penalty set out in current Regulations is £2000 but is subject to a maximum aggregate of £4000. The 'person responsible' is the owner or captain of a ship, the owner, hirer or driver of a vehicle (but not a detached trailer), and, if it is a detached trailer, the owner, hirer or operator of the trailer. Section 34 provides defences of duress; a defence where the carrier can show that he did not know, and had no reasonable grounds for suspecting, that a clandestine entrant was, or might be, concealed in the transporter, an effective system was in operation for preventing such carriage and, on the occasion is question, the person or persons responsible for carrying out the system had done so correctly.

Penalties will be imposed by notice and provision is made for the submission of a 'notice of objection'. Power is given to a senior officer of the Immigration Service to detain any relevant vehicle, small ship (500 tonnes) or small aircraft (5700 kg) where such notice has been given, until all penalties and expenses reasonably incurred by the Secretary of State have been paid. This power to detain will only be exercised where there is a significant risk of non-payment. The Secretary of State has extended some of these provisions to rail freight wagons by the Carriers' Liability (Clandestine Entrants) (Application to Rail Freight) Regulations 2001.

It is important, therefore, when such persons are found by a police officer, either wandering around the countryside after having been set down by a vehicle, or aboard such a vehicle, that the necessary details are obtained so that these penalties may be applied. These penalties are in addition to penalties provided by the Immigration and Asylum Act 1999, ss 40 to 42, which are concerned with persons arriving by such means who do not have proper documents. In such circumstances, the Secretary of State may charge the owner of the ship, aircraft or vehicle or the train operator, in respect of that person, the sum of £2000 or any other sum prescribed. The section provides a number of defences.

In 2002, a majority of the Court of Appeal made a declaration that the regime under the 1999 Act in respect of the liability of carriers for clandestine entrants was incompatible with Art. 6 of the European Convention on Human Rights, although they differed in their reasons. Since, the Carriers' Liability Regulations 2002 have effected changes in procedure.

Immigration generally

Leave to enter

As has been seen above, the 1971 Act provides an element of control in respect of non-British citizens. Leave to enter the country must be obtained from an immigration officer and leave may be limited and may be subject to restrictions. Registration with the police may be one of the conditions which is imposed. On the other hand, unlimited leave to enter may be granted and such leave cannot be subject to conditions. The Immigration (Leave to Enter and Remain) Order 2000 introduced a system which allows entry to a person who produces an 'entry clearance' which specifies the purpose for which that person is entering the United Kingdom and the permitted duration of the stay. The Order provides quick entry to persons where there has been an opportunity to examine their reasons for coming to the United Kingdom, in advance of arrival. However, the important factor is that leave and conditions will be endorsed on the passport or travel document of the person concerned. EU nationals are admitted on proof of European citizenship. Endorsements which are made on such documents are authenticated by a date stamp which shows the immigration officer's identity number and the port of entry. Where entry is refused, the date stamp is applied to the document by means of a cross.

Police officers are often asked to assist immigration officers with their enquiries (it makes a change from others assisting police officers with their enquiries). Such enquiries are frequently urgent and merit a speedy reply by telephone. Confirmation may be required.

No immigration controls are imposed upon persons entering the United Kingdom from the Republic of Ireland but the Home Secretary may exclude or deport persons in certain circumstances. Conditions which are imposed where a person enters at another place within the 'common travel area' apply elsewhere within it. The Immigration (Control of Entry through the Republic of Ireland) Order 1972 applies special provisions in relation to leave to enter, and, in respect of certain foreign nationals and police registration, in the case of entry via the Republic of Ireland.

The Immigration Act 1971, Schedule 2, para. 16, provides that a person who may be required to submit to examination under para. 2 of the schedule (a person who has arrived in the United Kingdom by ship or aircraft) may be detained under the authority of an immigration officer pending examination and a decision in relation to entry. A person liable to be so detained may be arrested without warrant by a constable or immigration officer. This power is useful where the police have been notified that persons intending to seek entry to the United Kingdom have been discovered on a ship and are to be brought into a port. Such persons may be detained under these provisions for interview by an immigration officer.

Suspected international terrorists

The Anti-terrorism, Crime and Security Act 2001 makes special provisions in relation to suspected international terrorists. Where the Secretary of State reasonably believes that a person's presence in the United Kingdom is a risk to national security and he suspects that the person is a terrorist, s 21 permits him to issue a certificate to this effect. A terrorist for the purposes of the Act is a person who is, or has been, concerned in the commission, preparation or instigation of acts of terrorism, is a member of or belongs to an international terrorist group or has links with an international terrorist group. A group is an international terrorist group for these purposes if it is subject to the control or influence of persons outside the United Kingdom and the Secretary of State suspects that it is concerned in the commission, preparation or instigation of acts of international terrorism.

When a certificate is issued, reasonable steps must be taken to notify the person concerned and the Special Immigration Appeals Commission. An appeal against such certification lies to that Commission under s 25. The Commission is also under a duty to review certificates after a period of 6 months.

Section 23 permits the detention of a suspected international terrorist under para. 16 of Schedule 2 to the Immigration Act 1971 (detention of persons liable to examination or removal), or para. 2 of Schedule 3 (pending deportation). Such a suspected international terrorist may be detained regardless of the fact that removal or departure from the United Kingdom is prevented (whether temporarily or indefinitely) by some point of law which wholly or partly relates to an international agreement, or a practical consideration.

Section 28 requires that these provisions must be reviewed after a period of 14 months from the Act coming into force. In addition, s 122 requires a review of the Act by a committee of privy councillors. Their report must be submitted to the Secretary of State not later than 2 years from the Act coming into force (14 December 2001) and it may recommend that certain provisions cease to have effect.

Fingerprinting

Persons who may be fingerprinted on arrival

The Immigration and Asylum Act 1999, s 141, applies to:

(a) any person who, on arrival in the United Kingdom, fails to produce a valid passport with a photograph or some other document satisfactorily establishing identity and nationality;

(b) any person who has been refused leave to enter but has been temporarily admitted pending removal if an immigration officer reasonably suspects that the individual will not comply with a reporting or residence requirement;

(c) an illegal entrant subject to a direction under Schedule 2 to the Immigration Act 1971 or subject to a deportation order where a direction has been given for his removal;

(d) a person about whom a decision to give leave to enter has not yet been made, who has been arrested;

(e) an asylum seeker; and

(f) a dependent of anyone in (a) to (e).

The taking of fingerprints and powers to enforce

Fingerprints may be taken by an 'authorised person' and this term includes a constable, an immigration officer, a prison officer or an officer appointed for the purpose or a person employed under a contract at a detention centre.

Section 142 of the 1999 Act makes provision for requiring the attendance of a person to whom s 141 applies at a specified place for the purpose of fingerprinting. The section gives a constable or an immigration officer a power of arrest without warrant where a person fails to comply with such a requirement.

A constable or an immigration officer may arrest without warrant someone who fails to comply with a requirement made under s 142.

Wildlife and countryside

Introduction

Until the passing of the Wildlife and Countryside Act 1981, very little protection was given to wild creatures and wild plants. Although game birds, etc., were protected, little existed to prevent interference with other wild birds. Game birds were primarily given protection because so many of them were reared or 'encouraged' by land owners, who demanded that that which they saw as their property was protected from the attentions of poachers. In the same way, plants which were grown by farmers were protected by law, but those which grew wild were largely ignored as they were not seen as being sufficiently identified as anyone's property.

Wild birds

It is an offence (arrestable if committed in respect of a bird listed in Schedule 1 to the Act) contrary to s 1 of the Act intentionally to kill, injure or take any wild bird, or intentionally to take, damage or destroy the nest of such a bird while the nest is in use or being built, or intentionally to take or destroy an egg of such a bird.

The possession of a wild bird, whether alive or dead (including one which has been stuffed and mounted), or any part of it, or an egg (or part of an egg) of such a bird is also an arrestable offence if committed in respect of a Schedule 1 bird. Offences of possession are offences of strict liability.

The term 'wild bird' includes all wild birds which are resident in, or are visitors to, Great Britain, with the exception of poultry (which could not in any case be truly described as wild) and game birds (protection for which is provided by other Acts, see below). However, the provisions of the Act which are concerned with the prohibition of certain methods of killing or taking wild birds (s 5) and the power to grant licences for certain activities (s 16) may apply to game birds.

The foremost problem in relation to the enforcement of this legislation has been the fact that the term 'wild bird' does not include a wild bird bred in captivity. For a bird to be bred in captivity, the parent birds must have been in captivity when the egg was laid. Licensed keepers of birds of prey frequently take eggs or chicks from the nests of protected birds of prey and have the eggs hatched under captive birds, and in either case, offer the chicks for registration in due course. In this way the number of captive birds for the sport of falconry is increased.

It is also an arrestable offence against s 1(5) intentionally or recklessly to disturb any wild bird mentioned in Schedule 1 to the Act whilst it is building a nest, or is in or near such a nest containing eggs or young birds. Schedule 1 contains all but the commonest of birds. It includes all resident birds of prey with the exception of the more common kestrel and sparrow hawk. Nest robbers target the nests of peregrine falcons, goshawks, kites and eagles. If chicks are found in the possession of persons suspected of offences against this Act, assistance should be obtained from the RSPB, who can establish, by means of DNA testing, whether the young birds could have been bred from captive adult birds which are lawfully being kept.

If persons are found killing wild birds, or in possession of their eggs, it is almost certain that they will have committed offences against the Act. However, some birds may be killed or taken outside their close season (generally their nesting season) and predictably they are the commoner species of duck, goose, plover, snipe and woodcock. These birds are listed in Part I of Schedule 2 to the Act.

On occasions, the Secretary of State may wish to provide special protection to birds within an area. Section 3 of the 1981 Act empowers him to make an order with respect to any area. Such an order may include provisions prohibiting any person from intentionally killing, injuring or taking a wild bird (or one specified), and from taking, damaging or destroying the nest of any such bird while it is in use or being built, or the taking or destroying of any egg of such a bird, or disturbing a bird which is building a nest or is in, on or near a nest containing eggs or young, or disturbs the dependent young of any such bird. Offences may also be committed by persons entering such an area at a time or during a period specified in the order.

Sale of wild birds or their eggs

Section 6 of the Act of 1981 prohibits the sale, or offer or exposure for sale, or the possession of any wild bird (other than those included in Part I of Schedule 3 which lists birds which may be ringed and bred in captivity, such as the usual cage birds) or an egg (or part of an egg) of such a wild bird. It is an arrestable offence if committed in respect of a bird listed in Schedule 1 to the Act. It also creates offences of publishing or causing to be published an advertisement concerning such sales, etc.

Wild animals

The wild animals which are protected by the 1981 Act are listed in Schedule 5 to the Act. It is an offence against s 9 intentionally to kill, injure or take any animal so listed, or to possess such an animal alive or dead (in whole or in part), without lawful authority. These provisions of the Act are more difficult to enforce. It is fairly safe to assume that any wild animal will be protected. There are narrow exceptions. The animals listed in Schedule 5 include most of the less common butterflies, moths, frogs, lizards and newts, porpoises and dolphins, red (but not grey) squirrels and the common otter.

The section also provides protection for places which animals use for shelter by prohibiting the damage or destruction, or the obstruction of any access to, any such structure or place. It is also an offence to disturb any such animal while it is occupying such a structure or place. The sale, exposing or offering for sale, possession for sale or advertising for sale of a wild animal listed in Schedule 5 (alive or dead) is prohibited as in the case of birds.

The offences against s 9 are arrestable offences being listed in Schedule 1A to PACE which contains those offences declared to be arrestable.

Wild plants

By s 13, it is an offence for anyone intentionally to *uproot any wild plant*. 'Authorised persons' are excepted and the term includes owners of land or persons authorised by them, or local authority officers or those of the Department of the Environment, Farming and Rural Affairs. A person who is digging up wild daffodils and primroses is committing an offence unless that person is the land owner or properly authorised.

However, it is more likely that persons will be found intentionally *picking* the flowers from such plants. The picking of such flowers is only an offence if the plant concerned is one which is listed in Schedule 8 to the Act. Many wild plants are protected even from 'pickers' and the list contains all but the commonest of our wild flowers and plants.

The offences against s 13(1)(a) (intentionally picking, uprooting or destroying a wild plant included in Schedule 8) or 13(2) (selling, offering for sale, possessing, transporting for the purpose of sale a Schedule 8 plant) are arrestable offences being listed in Schedule 1A to PACE which contains those offences declared to be arrestable.

Additional police powers

If a constable suspects, with reasonable cause, that any person has committed or is committing these offences, that constable may, without warrant, stop and search that person and search and examine anything which that person may then be using or have in his possession. In each case, if the constable with reasonable cause suspects that evidence of the offence is to be found, he may seize and detain for the purpose of proceedings under the Act anything which may be evidence of the commission of the offence or may be liable to be forfeited.

For the purpose of exercising these powers, or for the purpose of arresting a person under PACE, s 25, for any of the offences under the 1981 Act, a constable may enter onto any land other than a dwelling house. A justice may issue a search warrant subject to the usual conditions in respect of the offence disclosed.

The Protection of Badgers Act

The Protection of Badgers Act 1992, s 1, creates offences of wilfully killing, injuring or taking any badger, or attempting to do any of these things. The Act provides that if there is evidence from which it could be reasonably concluded that at the material time the accused was doing so, he shall be presumed to have been doing so, unless the contrary is shown. It is an offence to be found in possession of a dead badger, or any part of it, unless the person concerned can show that the badger had not been killed in contravention of the Act, or that it, or the part, had been sold (whether to him or another) and, at the time of the purchase, that person had no reason to believe that the badger had been killed in contravention of the Act.

Licences may be granted by the Ministry of Agriculture to permit badgers to be killed or taken where they are causing serious damage to crops, or where it is necessary to prevent the spread of disease, or it is for scientific purposes.

Where dogs are used in the taking or destruction of badgers, a court may order their destruction.

Section 2(1) of the Act makes it an offence cruelly to ill-treat, use badger tongs or dig for badgers. By s 2(2), a person found digging for badgers is presumed to have been doing so in contravention of the Act, unless the contrary is shown. The use of firearms, other than smooth-bore weapons of not less than 20 bore or a rifle using ammunition having a muzzle energy not less than 160 footpounds and a bullet weighing less than 38 grains, is prohibited.

Section 3 makes it an offence to interfere with a badger sett by intentionally or recklessly damaging it, destroying it, obstructing access to it or causing a dog to enter it or disturbing a badger when it is occupying that sett. Fox hunters are permitted to obstruct entrances to keep their hounds out of the setts. The section also makes it an offence to sell, offer for sale or have a badger in one's possession or control.

Mercy killings and taking for the purpose of caring for an injured badger are exempted by the Act. Farmers, etc., are exempted if they kill or take badgers to prevent serious damage to land, crops, poultry or other property but this is subject to conditions. If it was apparent before the act was carried out that it would be necessary to prevent such damage (i.e. there is no urgency), such a person is not exempted if there has been no application for a licence as soon as reasonably practicable after it became apparent, or if an application for such a licence was under consideration at the time.

Police powers

Where a constable has reasonable grounds for suspecting that a person is committing an offence under this Act, or has committed such an offence, and that evidence is to be found on that person, or in any vehicle or article that person has with him, the constable may without warrant stop and search that person, vehicle or article and may seize and detain anything which may be evidence of the commission of such an offence.

Poaching

Day poaching

The offence of poaching by day is contrary to the Game Act 1931, s 30. Anyone who trespasses by entering or being upon land in the daytime in search or pursuit of game, woodcocks, snipes or rabbits commits an offence. 'Game' includes hares and pheasants, partridges, grouse, heath or moor game and black game, for the purposes of this Act. 'Daytime' begins 1 hour before sunrise and ends 1 hour after sunset.

A person trespasses on land if there without authority. The occupier of that land is empowered to order that person to leave at once and is authorised to use reasonable force to eject such a trespasser who refuses to go. For an offence to be committed under this section, there must also be evidence of a search for or the pursuit of game. The Act exempts persons who trespass on land when coursing or hunting with hounds or greyhounds.

Where five or more persons so trespass together, the offence attracts a higher penalty under s 31. There is a threat offered to land owners or occupiers by the presence of such a large party. Section 32 creates a further offence. If any of these persons is armed with a gun and uses violence, intimidation or menaces to prevent any person from exercising powers under the Act, that person and those with him commit a further offence. In addition, s 4A of the Game Laws (Amendment) Act 1960 provides that where a person is convicted as one of five or more persons so liable and the court is satisfied that any vehicle belonging to him or in possession or under control at the relevant time has been used for the purpose of committing or facilitating the commission of the offence, the court may make an order for forfeiture in respect of that vehicle. This may be done regardless of any other way in which the court deals with the offender and without regard to any restriction on forfeiture in any enactment.

Police powers

A constable has power to require trespassers in search or pursuit of game to quit and give their names and addresses. If a constable has reasonable cause for suspecting that the person is committing the offence of trespassing in pursuit of game in the daytime, the constable may enter on to land for the purpose of exercising this power.

Night poaching

Poaching by night is covered by the Night Poaching Act 1828. 'Night' commences 1 hour after sunset and continues until 1 hour after sunrise. There are two specific offences under s 1:

(a) unlawfully taking or destroying by night any game or rabbits on land, open or enclosed (including a public road, highway or path); and
(b) by night unlawfully entering or being on any land, open or enclosed, with any gun, net, engine or other instrument for the purpose of taking or destroying game.

'Game' as defined under this Act includes hares, pheasants, partridges, grouse, heath or moor game, black game or bustards; it does not include rabbits, but it will be noted that rabbits are added to the offence under (a).

A person who commits an offence under (a), i.e. killing or taking, commits it in respect of game *or rabbits* killed or taken anywhere; in a field, street or public place. Anyone who commits an offence under (b), i.e. trespass with instruments, etc., for the purpose of taking or killing, must commit it on land, open or enclosed. The offence cannot be committed in a street or public place. Anyone who commits an offence under s 1, who assaults or offers violence with a gun or other offensive weapon towards any person authorised to apprehend him is liable to an increased penalty.

By s 9, if three or more people together enter or are on land at night to take or destroy game or rabbits, and one of them is armed with a gun or other offensive weapon, all are guilty of an aggravated offence.

Police powers

A constable who has reasonable grounds for suspecting that one of these offences is being committed may enter land to deal with the offences.

Game licences

Whether authorised to take game or not, all persons who kill or take game must have a game licence. Game licences are required in respect of game, woodcocks, snipe, rabbits or deer. Exemption is limited to coursing and hunting, the authorised killing of deer and the killing of rabbits by landowners. The occupiers of land, and persons authorised, do not need licences for the taking of hares. The Game Act 1831 requires that a licence be held if a person searches for game, but 'game' for the purposes of that Act does not include rabbits.

Close season for game

The taking or killing of game is prohibited on Sundays or Christmas Day by the 1831 Act, which also prohibits the killing or taking of game during their close seasons, which are as follows:

(a) partridges – 1 February–1 September;
(b) pheasants – 1 February–1 October;
(c) black game – 10 December–20 August;
(d) grouse – 10 December–12 August.

Animals

Cruelty to animals

The Protection of Animals Act 1911 sets out various offences involving cruelty to animals and states that the offences may be committed by any person carrying out any act, causing or procuring an act to be committed or, in the case of the owner, permitting such an act.

The offences include cruelty, kicking, beating, ill-treating, over-riding, overdriving, overloading, torturing, infuriating or terrifying any animal, as well as acts of commission or omission which cause unnecessary suffering. Each of the terms used creates a separate offence, and if we consider all instances in which we have witnessed an animal being ill-treated in the past, it is probable that one of these words will describe the particular form of unpleasantness. The owner who savagely corrects a dog, the itinerant collector who overloads or overworks a horse and the owner or keeper of animals who neglects them are all guilty of offences contrary to this Act. Where it is alleged that there has been an unreasonable omission to act, the test to be applied is concerned with what a reasonably caring and reasonably competent owner would do in the circumstances. The tethering of horses, asses and mules under conditions or in such a manner as to cause unnecessary suffering is also punishable under this section.

Offences of cruelty can also be committed by transporting animals in a manner which causes suffering, by carrying out careless or inhumane operations, by administering poisonous or injurious drugs or by fighting or baiting animals. In this way, amateur operations and such sports as bull fighting are made illegal. Cockfighting is still arranged in some parts of the United Kingdom and those concerned with its organisation are punishable under these provisions. In addition, the Cockfighting Act 1952 punishes the possession of instruments or appliances for use in this connection.

For the purposes of the Protection of Animals Act, the term 'animal' means any domestic or captive animal. 'Domestic animals' include fowl and all other animals which are tame or are being sufficiently tamed to serve some purpose useful to humans. 'Captive animals' are those which are in captivity or confinement or are subjected to any contrivance to prevent escape. This Act is not intended in normal circumstances to protect wild animals, and it has been held that wild rabbits caught and kept in confinement for a few days before being released for the purpose of being coursed are not captive animals, nor is a hunted stag which is temporarily unable to escape before being killed. Similarly, it has been held that the cruel maiming of a hedgehog by repeatedly beating it with a stick does not make that animal a 'captive animal' and that the trapping of a wild squirrel in a tree does not make it 'captive' for the purposes of the Act. However, where wild animals have been found to be subjected to cruelty, see 'Cruelty to wild mammals' below.

The Abandonment of Animals Act 1960 punishes the owner, or person who has charge or control of any animal, if he, without reasonable excuse, abandons it, whether permanently or not, in circumstances likely to cause unnecessary suffering. The offence is one of cruelty as set out in the Act of 1911 and carries the same penalty. Publicity is frequently given to the abandonment of puppies given as Christmas presents to children.

'Abandonment' in the present context does not require permanent abandonment, although it means something more than merely leaving unattended. For abandonment, there must be a leaving unattended of the animal in circumstances where suffering is likely and where there is sufficient evidence to prove that the accused had relinquished, wholly disregarded, or given up a duty of care for the animal. Where a person has made, or attempted to make, arrangements for the animal's welfare during a period where he cannot look after it himself, there is no abandonment.

Persons who, without reasonable excuse, are present when animals are placed together for the purpose of fighting each other, commit an offence. Those who publish, or cause to be published, an advertisement for such a fight, knowing that it is such an advertisement, also commit an offence. The offences are particularly relevant to dog fights.

Further protection is given to animals by the Pet Animals Act 1951, which requires pet shops to be licensed and prescribes conditions under which animals must be kept.

Police powers

A constable may arrest without warrant any person whom he reasonably believes to be guilty of an offence contrary to s 1 of the Protection of Animals Act 1911 (the offences listed under Cruelty to animals, above), whether:

(a) in his own view; or
(b) on the complaint of a third person who gives his name and address.

The power of arrest does not extend to offences under s 1(2), which is concerned with owners who permit cruelty by failing to exercise reasonable care and supervision in protecting an animal from cruelty. A constable is also empowered to take charge of the animal and vehicle, where applicable, and to arrange for custody and care. If veterinary treatment is needed, the cost, in addition to the cost of custody, must be paid as costs of the case upon the owner's conviction. If some other person is convicted, such expenses may be recovered from the owner as a civil debt.

Arrests for these offences are now rare as it is usually possible to establish the offender's identity and to proceed by way of summons. The itinerant collector, who is often of no fixed abode, may have to be arrested to ensure appearance before a court.

Cruelty to wild mammals

The Wild Mammals (Protection) Act 1996, s 1, makes it an offence for any person to mutilate, kick, beat, nail or otherwise impale, stab, burn, stone, crush, drown, drag or asphyxiate any wild mammal with intent to inflict unnecessary suffering upon it.

Section 2 exempts an attempted mercy killing of a wild mammal which has been so seriously disabled by someone else's act that there is no chance of recovery; the reasonably swift and humane killing of a wild mammal injured or taken in the course of lawful shooting, hunting, coursing or pest control; acts authorised under any enactment, an act made unlawful by s 1 if it was by means of a snare, trap, dog or bird lawfully used for the purpose of killing or taking any wild mammal; or the lawful use of a poison or noxious substance.

For the purposes of the Act, a 'wild mammal' is one which is not a domestic or captive animal within the meaning of the Protection of Animals Act 1911.

The 1996 Act seals the gap left by other legislation whilst exempting acts which are either humane or authorised under other legislation. Perhaps the precise specification of some of the exempted acts is unnecessary as the methods described in s 1 would be unlikely to be used in any case, and the acts described within the exemptions could scarcely be described as being carried out 'with intent to inflict unnecessary suffering'. However, the terms of s 2 place the issues beyond doubt.

Police powers

Section 4 of the 1996 Act provides that where a constable has reasonable grounds for suspecting that a person has committed an offence under the provisions of the Act and that evidence of the commission of the offence may be found on that person or in or on any vehicle which he may have with him, the constable may:

(a) without warrant, stop and search that person and any vehicle or article he may have with him; and
(b) seize and detain for the purposes of proceedings under any of those provisions anything which may be evidence of the commission of the offence or may be liable to be confiscated under s 6 of the Act (a convicting court may order confiscation of any vehicle or equipment used in the commission of the offence).

Section 5 of the 1996 Act provides that the maximum fine will apply to each animal so injured, where more than one animal is affected. It is therefore essential that police officers specify in their report the number of animals subjected to such cruelty.

Animals ill or injured

The section of the Protection of Animals Act 1911, which gives a constable power to deal with animals which are ill or injured, defines the term 'animal' as including a horse, mule, ass, bull, cow, sheep, goat or pig. It is concerned with farm animals and, by exclusion of dogs and cats, eliminates the most likely instances which a constable will meet. However, to ensure that correct veterinary attention is given, most police forces follow a similar procedure when these animals are injured in road accidents.

When a constable finds an animal in such a condition through disease or injury that it cannot be removed without cruelty, the constable shall, if the owner is absent or refuses to have the animal destroyed:

(a) send for a veterinary surgeon, who may
(b) certify in writing giving the reasons why it would be cruel to keep the animal alive, and then
(c) arrange for the animal to be humanely destroyed, and
(d) if on a highway, removed.

If the veterinary surgeon certifies that the animal may be moved without causing unnecessary suffering, it is the owner's responsibility to arrange it, but if the owner cannot be found, or fails to do so, the constable may make the necessary arrangements. All expenses may be recovered from the owner as a civil debt.

Animals straying

The keeper, or person in whose possession animals may be, is guilty of an offence contrary to s 155 of the Highways Act 1980 if horses, cattle, sheep, goats or swine are found, at any time, straying on the highway or lying at the side of a highway. The provisions of this section do not apply to highways passing over any common, waste or unenclosed land. Such highways usually carry signs which warn drivers that their way passes over unenclosed land and that animals are likely to be encountered.

Police officers who find animals straying on the highway may return them to the owner's or keeper's land, or to any other place provided for the safe custody of animals. Many years ago, common pounds were provided for the purpose of containing animals found straying, but are now extremely rare. Police officers, in instances in which the owner is not known, are compelled to make some arrangements for the security of the animals, but it is advisable to avoid securing them in any field in which other animals are already grazing. If non-tested cattle are placed in a field of tested cattle, a claim may lie against the police in respect of the expense involved in re-testing cattle.

When animals are impounded in this way, the person doing so is responsible for their well-being and must ensure that they are properly fed and watered until the owner is traced. When traced, the owner should be reported for the offence. The owner is responsible for any expenses involved in the care of the animals.

Rabies

The Rabies (Importation of Dogs, Cats and Other Mammals) Order 1974 prohibits the landing of such animals in Great Britain if brought from a place outside Great Britain. However, the prohibition does not apply if the animal has been detained and isolated in quarantine for a period of at least 6 months before being landed in Great Britain. Otherwise, landing will only be permitted if it is in accordance with a licence granted by the Minister of Agriculture. One of the conditions of such a licence will be that it is similarly quarantined on arrival in Great Britain. In certain restricted circumstances, the importation of dogs and cats from another member State of the EU is permitted without a licence in accordance with the terms of Council Directive 92/65/EEC. The Directive is concerned with commercial transactions and requires vaccination and that the animals concerned were born on a registered holding and have remained there, in captivity, with no contact with wild animals susceptible to rabies. Certificates will be in existence authorising such importation.

However, the Pet Travel Scheme (Pilot Arrangements) (England) Order 1999 creates exemptions, in limited circumstances, from the requirement that pet cats and pet dogs imported into England be placed in quarantine under the Rabies (Importation of Dogs, Cats and Other Mammals) Order 1974. While the Order does not currently extend to Scotland or Wales, an animal brought into England in accordance with the Order may then be taken into Scotland or Wales. The exemptions are restricted to authorised carriers operating on specified routes and the animals concerned must be identified by a microchip, be vaccinated against rabies and must have had a blood test demonstrating that the vaccination was successful. The animal must be accompanied by a health certificate relating to rabies and containing information relating to the microchip number and its location, together with a declaration from a veterinary surgeon. The carrier of such an animal, having checked the documentation, etc., in relation to such an animal, will issue a foot passenger with a certificate stating that the animal has been checked and where the animal is being carried in a car, a sticker or hanger suitable for display on a windscreen will be issued.

The 'permitted routes' are currently the sea routes of Calais/Dover, Cherbourg/Portsmouth, Caen/Portsmouth, Le Havre/Portsmouth and St Malo/Portsmouth, the air routes from approved countries (set out in Schedule 2 to the Order), or any route originating in Australia or New Zealand, to London Heathrow in either case, and the Channel Tunnel Coquilles/Cheriton route.

Police powers

The Animal Health Act 1981, s 61, provides that a constable may arrest without warrant any person whom he, with reasonable cause, suspects to be in the act of committing or to have committed an offence to which s 61 applies. Section 61 applies to:

(a) the landing or attempted landing of any animal or importation or attempted importation through the tunnel system as defined in the Channel Tunnel Act 1987 of any animal in contravention of an order made under this Act, and expressed to be made for the purpose of preventing the introduction of rabies into Great Britain; or
(b) the failure by the person having the charge or control of any vessel or boat to discharge any obligation imposed on him in that capacity by such an order; or
(c) the movement, in contravention of an order under s 17 or 23 of the Act, of any animal into, within or out of a place or area declared to be infected with rabies. (Section 17 is concerned with powers which relate to infected areas or places and s 23 with Orders made in relation to such areas or places.)

In addition, s 62 of the Act provides that for the purpose of arresting a person under the power conferred by s 61 a constable may enter (if need be by force) and search any vessel, boat, aircraft or vehicle of any other description in which that person is or in which the constable, with reasonable cause, suspects him to be.

For the purpose of exercising any power to seize an animal or to cause an animal to be seized, and:

(a) where that power is conferred on constables by an order made under this Act; and
(b) where that power is expressed to be made for the purpose of preventing the introduction of rabies into Great Britain,

a constable may enter (if need be by force) and search any vessel, boat, aircraft or vehicle of any other description in which there is, or in which he, with reasonable cause, suspects that there is, an animal to which that power applies.

Children and young persons

Purpose of law

The law of the land shows considerable tolerance towards offences committed by children and young persons and, additionally, gives them special protection by including offences which are only offences if committed by adults against them. There are also provisions for ensuring that, in certain circumstances, special arrangements can be made for their care by removing them from an unstable family background. Juvenile courts were not established until 1908, and before this date there was little distinction between the methods by which adults and juveniles were tried, although an Act of 1879 did allow indictable offences committed by young people, in certain circumstances, to be tried summarily. When juvenile courts were set up in 1908, the legislation merely provided for separate courts but did not prescribe rules for their constitution. The matter was remedied in the metropolis in 1920, but was not resolved in relation to the remainder of the country until an Act of 1932 introduced a system of selecting, for juvenile court work, justices who were qualified to deal with young people. The Criminal Justice Act 1991 renamed the juvenile courts as 'youth courts'.

Ages

A 'child' for most purposes relevant to a police officer is a person under the age of 14 years, and a 'young person' is one who has attained the age of 14 but is not yet 18 years of age.

It is frequently necessary to establish the age of young people appearing before the court and the best evidence available, when strict proof is required, is the production of a birth certificate with evidence from the mother to the effect that the child before the court is the child specified in the birth certificate. However, when such persons are appearing as defendants before a court, the issue seldom arises as the person concerned is prepared to give his age to the proper officer of the court on request. The parents of such an offender are always aware of the proceedings as they are also served with a copy of any summons or sent notice by the police in other circumstances, and almost invariably are present in court if the issue of age should arise. The court is entitled to determine the age of an offender appearing before it by making enquiries and making its own ruling. If the age of the offender is later established and found to be different from that determined by the court, any order or judgment made will not be invalidated.

Liability of young offenders

The Children and Young Persons Acts 1933 and 1963 say that it shall be conclusively presumed that no child under the age of 10 years can be guilty of an offence. Conclusive presumptions permit no argument in law and it is a fact that no matter what a child under the age of 10 years may do, or why it is done, the act is not punishable as that child is beyond the law. However, a child under the age of 10 years, who is guilty of conduct which in an older person would constitute an offence, may be brought before a court under care proceedings.

Until 30 September 1998, children between the ages of 10 and 14 were presumed to be incapable of committing crime, but this presumption could be rebutted by proof beyond reasonable doubt that when the child did the act charged he knew that it was seriously wrong. This rule was abolished in relation to anything done or after 30 September 1998, by the Crime and Disorder Act 1998, s 34.

Parents, guardians and their responsibilities

Where an application is made to a court by an individual, the court may by order appoint that individual to be the child's (for these purposes under 18) guardian if:

(a) the child has no parent with parental responsibility for him; or
(b) a residence order has been made with respect to the child in favour of a parent or guardian who has died whilst the order was in force.

Such an order may be made during family proceedings in a court even though no individual has applied for it to be made. Existing parents or guardians may appoint another to assume those responsibilities in the event of their death.

A court may, and in the case of a child under the age of 16 who is charged with an offence must, require the parent or guardian to attend court unless it would be unreasonable, in the circumstances, to do so. A local authority which has such responsibility for a child may be so ordered. The Powers of Criminal Courts (Sentencing) Act 2000 provides that parents or guardians *must* be required to pay any fine, costs or compensation awarded against a child who is under the age of 16. They *may* be so required where the child is 16 years or more. There are exceptions, where the parent or guardian cannot be found, or where it would be unreasonable to make such an order.

Courts are also empowered to require a parent or guardian to enter, with consent, into a recognisance to take proper care of the child and to exercise proper control over him. If a parent or guardian refuses, and the court considers the refusal unreasonable, it may order him to pay a fine not exceeding £1000. In the case of a child or young person who has not attained the age of 16 years, it is the duty of the court to exercise these powers where it is satisfied, having regard to all the circumstances of the case, that it is desirable, to prevent him from committing further offences. If it does not so order, in these circumstances, it must give its reasons for not making such an order in open court.

Such orders may not be made in respect of the binding over of a parent or guardian where a referral order is made under the Youth Justice and Criminal Evidence Act 1999.

Where a court has passed a community sentence, it may include in such a recognisance a condition that the minor's parent or guardian ensures that the minor complies with the requirements of that sentence.

Offences

Cruelty, etc.

Section 1 of the Children and Young Persons Act 1933 provides that if any person who has attained the age of 16 years, who has responsibility for any person under the age of 16 years, wilfully:

(a) assaults;
(b) ill-treats;
(c) neglects;

(d) abandons; or

(e) exposes

him in a manner likely to cause unnecessary suffering or injury to health, that person commits an offence. The offences outlined in this section are arrestable offences.

The section requires that these acts are done 'wilfully', and the term means deliberately, intentionally or by reckless act or failure, as opposed to accidentally or by mistake. The offence, however, should not be judged against that which a reasonable parent would have done. It must be judged against the person responsible, allowing for stupidity, ignorance or inadequacy. It has been held that the term 'ill-treats' covers most, if not all, forms of neglect which form a continuous course of conduct. 'Neglect' means the absence of such reasonable care as an ordinary parent would use for the care and protection of his child, and the terms 'abandon or expose' are concerned with leaving a child to its fate. Once a child has been so abandoned (e.g. being left on a doorstep), it is from that moment exposed.

A person is presumed to have responsibility for a child or young person if:

(a) he has parental responsibility for him under the Children Act 1989 [which the mother and the father will both have if they were married to each other when the child or young person was born, or which only the mother will have if the mother and father were not so married, or which another person (including a father in the instance just given) or a local authority may acquire by operation of law]; or

(b) he is otherwise liable to maintain him; or

(c) he has care of him.

In this way, a burden of responsibility for the proper care of young people is placed firmly upon all persons of 16 years or more who have responsibility for them. Such persons include parents, foster parents, relatives who may be permanently or temporarily caring for children or even baby sitters who have the care of the children for only a few hours, and all are responsible for the well-being of persons under 16 years of age in their care. If young people are not provided with adequate food, clothing, medical aid or lodging, the parent or other person legally responsible for their maintenance shall be deemed to be guilty of neglecting them in a manner likely to cause unnecessary suffering, and where it is proved that a child under 3 years was suffocated by being over-lain by a person of 16 years or over who went to bed under the influence of drink, the same shall apply.

These offences may be encountered in a number of ways, from the incident involving the father who beats his child with a buckled leather belt to the mother who abandons her baby on a doorstep or in an underground station.

Other offences under the 1933 Act

Other offences include allowing children between 4 and 16 years to reside in or frequent a brothel, causing children under 16 years to be used for begging, taking articles in pawn from persons under 14 years, giving intoxicating liquor to children under the age of 5 years unless in a medical emergency, exposing children under the age of 12 years to risk of burning or employing a child under 13 years in circumstances other than those permitted by local by-laws, etc. In offences of exposing children under the age of 12 years to the risk of burning, the fact that such children were left in a room with an open fire or with an unguarded appliance and are burned so as to suffer death or serious injury is sufficient to prove the offence.

Tobacco

The selling of tobacco or cigarette papers to a person under the age of 16 is prohibited by s 7 of the 1933 Act, whether the tobacco is for his own use or not. The term 'tobacco' includes cigarettes and any product containing tobacco intended for oral or nasal use and smoking mixtures intended as a substitute for tobacco. The offence is one of strict liability and the proprietor of a shop is guilty even when he has played no part in the transaction by him and he knows nothing about it. However, s 7 provides that it is a defence for an accused to prove that all reasonable precautions were taken and due diligence exercised to avoid the commission of the offence.

A constable in uniform may seize any tobacco or cigarette papers from a person apparently under 16 who is found smoking in any street or public place.

Where a cigarette machine is extensively used by persons under 16, a court may order the owner to take precautions to prevent such use or, if necessary, to remove the machine.

The Children and Young Persons (Protection from Tobacco) Act 1991 prohibits the sale of unpackaged cigarettes by a person carrying on a retail business and requires notices to be displayed on premises and machines concerning the illegality of sales to persons under 16.

The provisions of the Children Act 1989 and other Acts in relation to child welfare

Care proceedings

We have already examined the conclusive presumption that a child under the age of 10 years is incapable of committing any offence. Although such persons may escape punishment for offences that they commit, the Children Act 1989 makes various provisions for children and young persons to be brought into the care of a local authority. For the purpose of these provisions, the use of the term 'child' is a reference to a person under 18. Local authorities are required to make provision for the reception and accommodation of children, including children who are in police protection and those whom they are requested, by a custody officer, to receive, where that custody officer has authorised an arrested juvenile to be kept in police detention.

Care and supervision orders

On the application of a local authority or an authorised person (from the NSPCC or other body authorised by the Secretary of State), a family proceedings court (i.e. that part of a magistrates' court hearing proceedings under the 1989 Act) may make an order:

(a) placing the child with respect to whom the application is made in the care of a designated local authority; or
(b) putting him under the supervision of a designated local authority or of a probation officer.

A court may only make a care or supervision order if it is satisfied:

(a) that the child concerned is suffering, or is likely to suffer, significant harm; and
(b) that the harm, or likelihood of harm, is attributable to
    (i) the care given to the child, or likely to be given to him if the order were not made, not being what it would be reasonable to expect a parent to give to him; or
    (ii) the child being beyond control.

Such an order may not be made with respect to a child who has reached the age of 17 (or 16 in the case of a child who is married). On an application for a care order, the court may make a supervision order and vice versa. 'Harm' means ill-treatment or the impairment of health or development.

It can be seen, therefore, that where a child has been the victim of an offence of cruelty or sexual abuse or neglect, an application may be made by a local authority or an authorised person for either of the above orders. In addition, the provision at (b)(ii) above provides a means of obtaining a care order in circumstances in which a child who is below the age of criminal responsibility habitually commits crime, or where a child who is receiving adequate care from parents but is so out of control that he is likely to harm himself.

Child assessment orders

The Children Act 1989, s 43, permits a local authority or an authorised person to apply to the High Court or a county court or magistrates' court sitting as a family proceedings court for such an order where difficulties are being experienced in making an assessment of the needs of such a child. This may be due to the lack of co-operation by those who have parental responsibility for the child. Such an order permits assessment to be made over a period not exceeding 7 days and may require any person to produce the child to a person named in the order and to comply with specified instructions. However, a court should not make such an order if it is satisfied that there are grounds for making an emergency protection order and that it ought to do so rather than make an assessment order.

Emergency protection orders

There will be occasions upon which action must be taken immediately to protect a child. Section 44 of the 1989 Act empowers the High Court, a county court or magistrates' court, on the application of any person, to make an emergency order for the protection of a child. It may do so if it is satisfied that:

(a) there is reasonable cause to believe that the child is likely to suffer significant harm if
    (i) he is not removed to accommodation provided by or on behalf of the applicant; or
    (ii) he does not remain in the place in which he is then being accommodated;
(b) in the case of an application made by a local authority
    (i) enquiries are being made with respect to the child under the authority's duty to investigate where a child is suffering, or is unlikely to suffer, significant harm; and
    (ii) those enquiries are being frustrated by access to the child being unreasonably refused to a person authorised to seek access and that the applicant has reasonable cause to believe that access to the child is required as a matter of urgency; or

(c) in the case of an application made by an authorised person
   (i) the applicant has reasonable cause to believe that the child is suffering, or is likely to suffer, significant harm;
   (ii) the applicant is making enquiries with respect to the child's welfare; and
   (iii) those enquiries are being frustrated by access to the child being unreasonably refused to a person authorised to seek access and the applicant has reasonable cause to believe that access to the child is required as a matter of urgency.

An emergency protection order directs a person to produce a child and authorises the child's removal to accommodation provided by or on behalf of the applicant or prevents the removal of the child from a hospital or another place. It also gives the applicant parental responsibility for the child. An emergency protection order has effect for such period, not exceeding 8 days, as is specified by the court, but the court has power (on one occasion only) to extend it for up to a further 7 days. An emergency protection order can include an exclusion requirement in specified circumstances. Such a requirement enables a child to stay in its home by excluding someone else, such as a suspected child abuser, from it.

Removal and accommodation of children by police in emergencies

Section 46 of the 1989 Act empowers police officers to take a child into 'police protection' in prescribed circumstances. It also places responsibilities upon 'designated police officers', that is, officers designated by their chief officers of police to conduct enquiries into such cases. The details are as follows. Where a constable has reasonable cause to believe that a child would otherwise be likely to suffer significant harm, he may:

(a) remove the child to suitable accommodation and keep him there; or
(b) take such steps as are reasonable to ensure that the child's removal from any hospital, or other place, in which he is then being accommodated is prevented.

As soon as is reasonably practicable after taking the child into police protection, as above, the constable shall:

(a) inform the local authority within whose area the child was found of the steps that have been, or are proposed to be taken, with respect to the child and the reason for taking them;
(b) give details to the local authority within whose area the child is ordinarily resident (the appropriate authority) of the place at which the child is being accommodated;
(c) inform the child (if he appears to be capable of understanding)
   (i) of the steps that have been taken with respect to him and of the reasons for taking them; and
   (ii) of the further steps which may be taken with respect to him under this section;
(d) take such steps as are reasonably practicable to discover the wishes and feelings of the child;
(e) secure that the case is enquired into by a designated officer; and
(f) where the child was taken into police protection by being removed to accommodation which is not provided
   (i) by or on behalf of a local authority; or
   (ii) as a 'refuge', i.e. a voluntary home or registered children's home certified as a refuge,
   secure that he is removed to accommodation which is so provided.

He must also, as soon as practicable, inform:

(a) the child's parents;
(b) every person who is not a parent but has parental responsibility for him; and
(c) any other person with whom the child was living immediately before being taken into police protection,

of the steps that he has taken under this section with respect to the child, the reasons for taking them and the further steps that may be taken with respect to him under the section.

When the case has been enquired into by the designated officer, he must release the child from police protection unless it is considered that there is still reasonable cause for believing that the child would be likely to suffer significant harm if released.

No child may be kept in police protection for more than 72 hours. However, at any time while the child is in police protection, the designated officer may apply *on behalf of the appropriate authority* for an emergency protection order to be made with respect to the child. Such an application may be made whether or not the authority knows of it or agrees to its being made.

While a child is in police protection, the designated officer must do what is reasonable in all the circumstances of the case for the purpose of safeguarding or promoting the child's welfare (having regard in particular to the length of the period during which the child will be so protected).

The designated officer must allow:

(a) parents;
(b) any other person with parental responsibility;
(c) any person with whom the child was living immediately before that child was taken into police protection;
(d) where there is a 'contact order' (an order permitting contact by named persons), any such person; and
(e) any person acting on behalf of any of these persons,

to have such contact (if any) with the child as, in the opinion of the designated officer, is both reasonable and in the child's best interests. However, if a child taken into police protection is in accommodation provided by, or on behalf of, the appropriate authority, these contact responsibilities are those of the authority rather than the designated officer.

Police powers

An emergency protection order may include a requirement directed to a person to disclose the whereabouts of the child and it may authorise an applicant to enter premises specified by the order and search for the child. Such a warrant may authorise a constable to assist an applicant where entry is being, or is likely to be, denied. It may also direct that a constable be accompanied by a registered medical practitioner, registered nurse or registered health visitor.

If a child or young person is absent without the consent of the responsible person:

(a) from a place of safety to which that child or young person has been taken under the Powers of Criminal Courts (Sentencing) Act 2000 (supervised person arrested on warrant and so placed); or

(b) from local authority accommodation in which that child or young person was required to live as a condition of a supervision order; or

(c) from accommodation to which that child or young person had been remanded by a court either awaiting trial or an offence, or having been convicted of such an offence,

the Children and Young Persons Act 1969, s 32, as amended by Schedule 12 to the 1989 Act, continues to authorise a constable to arrest such a child or young person without a warrant. When so arrested he must be conducted to a place of safety, local authority accommodation or such other place as the responsible person may direct.

The Children and Young Persons Act 1969, s 23A, provides that a constable may arrest without warrant a young offender who has been remanded or committed to local authority accommodation in respect of any breach of a condition of that remand or committal if the constable has reasonable grounds for suspecting that the offender has broken any of those conditions. The arrested person must be brought before a justice as soon as is practicable and in any event within 24 hours of the arrest. In reckoning any period of 24 hours, no account shall be taken of Christmas Day, Good Friday or any Sunday.

Local child curfew schemes

Section 14 of the Crime and Disorder Act 1998 permits local authorities or chief officers of police to set up child curfew schemes for children under 16. An authority or a chief officer of police may give notice that, for a specified period, there is a ban on children of specified ages (under 16) being in a public place within a specified area:

(a) during specified hours (between 9 p.m. and 6 a.m.);

(b) and otherwise than under the effective control of a parent (of whatever age) or of a responsible person aged 18 or over.

A 'public place' means 'any highway and any place at which at the material time the public or any section of the public has access, on payment or otherwise, as of a right by virtue of express or implied permission'. The definition therefore covers shopping centres, parks, communal areas of residential blocks, amusement arcades, etc.

Before such a scheme is made, the local authority must consult:

(a) every chief officer of police any part of whose area lies within its area); and

(b) such other persons or bodies as it thinks appropriate, such as social services departments, voluntary agencies and the local community (e.g. residents' groups).

Similarly, before making a scheme, a chief officer of police must consult:

(a) every local authority any part of whose area lies within the area to be specified; and

(b) such other persons or bodies as the chief officer considers appropriate.

A scheme does not have effect until confirmed by the Home Secretary.

Curfew notices

Curfew notices may specify different hours in relation to children of different ages. Such notices must be posted in the area affected and publicised in any other way which the local authority considers to be desirable. The maximum period of such an order is

90 days. If it is necessary that it should continue, a fresh order must be made after the procedure has been followed once again.

Where a constable has reasonable cause to believe that an unaccompanied child is in such a place in breach of an order, he is empowered by s 15 of the 1998 Act to remove that child to the child's place of residence unless there is reasonable cause to believe that the child would, if removed there, be likely to suffer significant harm. There is no requirement that the child, if taken home, must be handed over to a responsible person. However, s 46 of the Children Act 1989 does provide a power for a constable, in appropriate circumstances, to remove a child to other suitable accommodation, but there would have to be much more involved than the temporary absence of a parent from the home. Where such action is a possibility, it is submitted that there should be consultation with other agencies.

The constable is required to inform the local authority of the contravention of the order. The local authority must then arrange for a social worker to interview the family to discover the reason why the child was found in that place in breach of the order.

Child safety orders

The Crime and Disorder Act 1998, ss 11 to 13, makes provision for a child safety order which:

(a) places a child, for a period specified in the order, under the supervision of the responsible officer; and
(b) requires the child to comply with such requirements as are specified.

Such an order may continue in force for 3 months, unless the court is satisfied that the circumstances are exceptional (in which case it may continue for 12 months).

The 'requirements' are those which the court considers desirable in the interests of:

(a) securing that the child receives appropriate care, protection and support and is subject to proper control; or
(b) preventing any repetition of the kind of behaviour which led to the child safety order being made.

The officers responsible for supervision will be a social worker of a local authority social services department and a member of a youth offending team.

Such a child safety order is directed to the child and requires or prohibits conduct specified in it. However, if such an order requires that a child should be home by 8 p.m., an associated parenting order could require a parent to ensure that this was so.

Such orders will be made by magistrates' courts sitting as family proceedings courts. An order may only be made where the court is satisfied, with respect to a child under 10, that one or more of the following conditions is satisfied:

(a) that the child has committed an act which, if that child had been 10 or over, would have constituted an offence;
(b) that a child safety order is necessary to prevent the child committing such an act;
(c) that the child has contravened a ban imposed by a curfew order; or
(d) that the child has acted in a manner which caused or was likely to cause harassment, alarm or distress to one or more persons not of the same household as himself.

Proceedings for a breach of such an order must be brought by the responsible officer. If it is proved that the order has been breached, the court may:

(a) discharge the order and of its own motion make in respect of the child a care order under s 31 of the Children Act 1989 (see above); or
(b) make an order varying the order in the same way as on a variation after an application for discharge.

Such a breach may also result in the making of a parenting order.

Parenting orders

A 'parenting order' is a court order under the Crime and Disorder Act 1998, ss 8 to 10, requiring the parent of a child (i.e. someone under 14) or, in some cases, a young person (14 or over but under 18):

(a) to comply, for up to 12 months, with such requirements as are specified in the order; and
(b) to attend, for a concurrent period not exceeding 3 months, and not more than once in any week, such counselling and guidance sessions as may be specified in directions given by the responsible officer.

The provisions at (b) need not apply if the parent has previously attended for such guidance but they may do so. A 'responsible officer' may be a probation officer, a social worker of the local authority social services department or a member of a youth offending team.

The court may attach under (a) any conditions which it considers to be necessary to prevent a repetition of the conduct which caused the making of the order. They may include requirements that a child must be accompanied to school every day by a responsible adult, a requirement to exercise control, and a requirement to ensure that the child is home at a certain time at night. They may be made against one or both parents, i.e. biological parents. As it is not essential that a parent should have parental responsibility, an order may be made against the father of a child or young person, who was not married to the mother when the child was born and has not acquired parental responsibility under the Children Act 1989. It may also be made against a guardian (a person who, in the opinion of the court, has for the time being the care of a child or young person). The term 'parent' includes such a person when it used below.

Parenting orders may be made in any court proceedings where:

(a) a child safety order is made in respect of a child;
(b) an antisocial behaviour order or sex offender order is made in respect of a child or young person (someone aged under 18);
(c) a child or young person is convicted of an offence; or
(d) a person is convicted of an offence under the Education Act 1996, s 443 (failure to comply with a school attendance order) or s 444 (failure to secure regular attendance at school of registered pupil).

Thus, orders under (a) will be made by a magistrates' court sitting as a domestic proceedings court, an order under (b) or (d) by a magistrates' court and an order under (c) by a youth court or (where the conviction is in a Crown Court) the Crown Court.

Courts are not bound to make such orders with the exception that, where the relevant condition is (c) and the offender is under 16, there is a statutory presumption in favour of making a parenting order.

Where such an order is in force, it is an offence for a parent to fail, without reasonable excuse, to comply with any of its requirements, or a requirement specified in directions given by a responsible officer.

The making of a parenting order requiring instruction in parenting techniques does not contravene art. 8 of the European Convention on Human Rights.

Reprimands and warnings

The circumstances in which they may be given

Where a constable has evidence that an offence, in respect of which there is a realistic prospect of conviction, has been committed by a child or young person who has not been previously convicted of an offence, the offence is admitted, and the constable is satisfied that it is not in the public interest to prosecute that child or young person, the provisions of s 65 of the Crime and Disorder Act 1998 relating to reprimand and warning apply.

Reprimand

Where the circumstances are as set out above, the constable may reprimand the offender if that offender has not been previously reprimanded or warned (see below).

Warning

The constable may warn the offender if:

(a) he has not been previously warned; or
(b) he has been previously warned, the offence was committed more than 2 years after the date of the previous warning and the constable considers that the offence is not so serious as to merit prosecution. However, this special additional warning may only be given once.

Although a warning will not normally be given to an offender who has not previously been reprimanded, it may be given to such an offender if the constable considers the offence to be so serious as to require a warning.

Procedure

A reprimand or warning under s 65 must be given at a place approved by the Home Secretary. Where the offender is under 17, an appropriate adult must be present.

A constable giving a reprimand or warning must explain that it may be cited in criminal proceedings in the same circumstances as a conviction. In the case of a warning, the constable must refer the offender to a youth offending team as soon as practicable; the constable must explain this to the offender.

Removal of truants to schools or designated premises

Section 16 of the Crime and Disorder Act 1998 authorises a local education authority to designate premises to which children and young persons of compulsory school age may be removed. It must inform the chief constable or commissioner for the area of the designation. Where this has been done, a police officer of or above the rank of superintendent may direct that powers conferred under s 16 are to be exercisable within the area. The powers will only be exercisable during hours specified in the direction. This equally applies to areas in the vicinity of any policed premises, together with those premises, policed by the British Transport Police.

Where a police officer has reasonable cause to believe that a child or young person found in a public place in a specified area during specified hours:

(a) is of compulsory school age; and
(b) is absent from a school without lawful authority,

he may remove the child or young person to designated premises, or to the school from which he is absent. These powers are exercisable only in a public place. There is no power to remove a truanting child from his home. An absence is deemed to be without lawful authority unless the child is absent with leave, or because attendance at school is prevented by sickness or any unavoidable cause, or because the absence is on a day exclusively set aside for religious observance by the religious body to which the parent belongs. Although no specific power to arrest without warrant is provided by the section, the power of removal must have inherent in it the power to deprive a juvenile of liberty, and to use reasonable force to do so.

Record of persons unsuitable for employment in child-care positions

The Protection of Children Act 1999 set up a system within which the identity of persons who are unsuitable to work with children may be established. Child-care organisations *must*, and other organisations *may*, refer an individual to the Secretary of State if that individual has been employed in a child-care position and the organisation considers that he has been guilty of misconduct which harmed a child, or placed a child at risk of such harm.

The 'Consultancy Index List' which was maintained by the Department of Health (a list including the names of persons considered unsuitable for work with children) is given statutory recognition. The 'List 99' which was maintained by the Department of Education and Employment (a list of persons who are not considered fit and proper persons to be employed as teachers or in work involving regular contact with children) already enjoyed statutory recognition and the 1999 Act gives statutory authority for access, in prescribed circumstances, to the appropriate part of these records.

The 1999 Act amends the Police Act 1997 to permit the 'Criminal Records Bureau' established under that Act to include such information in addition to the criminal records of such persons. In this way, a check upon the suitability of a person applying for a job in child care can be carried out through one agency. The Police Act 1997 (Criminal Records) Regulations 2002 make provision for the issue of various forms of criminal record certificates in relation to convictions, or cautions, reprimands or warnings given under the Crime and Disorder Act 1998. They also specify the information drawn from lists kept under specified pieces of legislation which will appear on criminal records certificates.

Child-care organisations are required by the 1999 Act, where they propose to employ someone in a child-care position, to check that person against the records held by the Criminal Records Bureau. They must not employ persons identified on such records as being included on the 'Consultancy Index List' or the part of 'List 99' held by the Bureau under these provisions.

Section 1 of the 1999 Act requires that the Secretary of State establishes a list of those persons who are considered unsuitable to work with children. Section 2(1) requires that 'child-care organisations' (providing accommodation, social services or health-care services to children or the supervision of children, etc.) refer to the Secretary of State, for possible inclusion on the list, the names of persons who are or have been employed in child-care positions and are eligible for such referral. Other organisations are permitted to do so.

Eligibility for referral under the provisions of the Act includes circumstances where a persons has been dismissed, transferred or suspended on the grounds of misconduct (whether or not in the course of their employment), that misconduct being such that it harmed a child, or placed a child at risk of harm. The provisions also embrace a person who would have been dismissed, or would have been considered for dismissal for such conduct had that person not resigned or retired. In addition, a referral should or may be made where an organisation has dismissed a person, that person has resigned or retired, or has been transferred by the organisation to a position within that organisation which is not a child-care position. In circumstances where information which was not available to the organisation at the time of any such dismissal, resignation, retirement or transfer has since become available and the organisation is of the opinion that, if that information had been available at the time and, in applicable circumstances that person had not resigned or retired, the organisation would have dismissed him or would have considered doing so, on the grounds of such misconduct, these provisions apply.

In the case of employment agencies, or agencies supplying nurses, the requirements are modified so that they refer to circumstances in which the organisation has refused to do business with the individual on the grounds of misconduct (whether or not in the course of employment) which harmed a child or placed a child at risk.

The 1999 Act requires that the Secretary of State, after considering observations from appellants and employers, must confirm the inclusion of an individual's name on the list. An appeal lies to a Tribunal established under s 9. A person who is included on the list (otherwise than provisionally) may appeal against inclusion in the list or, with the leave of the Tribunal, against a decision not to remove his name from the list.

Disqualification order

Part II of the Criminal Justice and Court Services Act 2000 provides for an order to be made by the Crown Court, the Court of Appeal, a court martial or the Courts Martial Appeal Court, where a person is convicted of specified offences committed against a child, disqualifying that person from working with children. The specified offences consist generally of those offences against a child which are of a sexual nature or involve cruelty, assault, abduction, prostitution, supplying drugs to children or aiding, abetting, etc., such offences. 'Child' for the purposes of Part II means a person under the age of 18.

Where the person is convicted of an offence which was committed when that person was 18 or over, the court must make an order unless, having regard to all the circumstances, it considers it unlikely that the individual will commit any further offences against a child. Reasons for not making an order must be stated and recorded. If the offence for which the individual is convicted was committed before reaching 18, the court must order disqualification if it is satisfied that, having regard to all of the circumstances, it is likely that the individual will commit a further offence against a child.

Interrogation of children and young persons

The Code of Practice for the Detention, Treatment and Questioning of Persons by Police Officers makes special provisions for persons who are particularly at risk in interview situations. Juveniles are persons considered to be at risk.

If anyone appears to be under the age of 17 then he shall be treated as a juvenile for the purposes of the Code and all other Codes of Practice issued under the Police and Criminal Evidence Act 1984, in the absence of clear evidence to show that he is older.

A juvenile, whether suspected of crime or not, must not be interviewed or asked to provide a written statement in the absence of 'the appropriate adult' unless an officer of the rank of superintendent or above considers that delay will involve an immediate risk of harm to persons or serious loss of or damage to property. However, in these exceptional circumstances questioning may not continue once sufficient information to avert the immediate risk has been obtained. A record must be made of the grounds for any decision to interview a juvenile in these circumstances. These instances must be exceptional to minimise the risk of interviews producing unreliable information.

Other than in these exceptional circumstances, all interviews with juveniles must take place in the presence of the 'appropriate adult'. The 'appropriate adult' in the case of a juvenile is the parent or guardian (or, if in care, the care authority or voluntary organisation) or a social worker or, failing the attendance of these persons, another responsible adult aged 18 or over who is not a police officer or employed by the police. The parent or guardian of a juvenile should be the appropriate adult unless suspected of involvement in the offence, or is a witness, or is involved in the investigation or has received admissions. In such circumstances it will be desirable for the appropriate adult to be someone else. If the parent or guardian is estranged from the juvenile, he should not be asked to be the appropriate adult if the juvenile expressly or specifically objects to that person's presence. If a child in care admits an offence to a social worker, another social worker must be the appropriate adult.

If a juvenile has been cautioned before the arrival of the 'appropriate adult', the caution must be repeated in the adult's presence (unless the interview has by then already finished if conducted in the urgent situation described above). The 'appropriate adult' should also be informed of the juvenile's right to legal advice and, if such adult feels that it is desirable, advice must be obtained.

Juveniles may only be interviewed at their place of education in exceptional circumstances and then only where the principal or a nominee agrees. Every effort should be made to contact both the parents, or other person responsible for the juvenile's welfare and the 'appropriate adult' (if a different person) and a reasonable time should be allowed to enable the 'appropriate adult' to attend. Where this would cause undue delay and unless the offence is against the educational establishment, the principal or a nominee can act as the 'appropriate adult' for the purposes of the interview.

Juveniles are particularly prone in certain circumstances to provide information which is unreliable, misleading or self-incriminating. It is necessary to exercise special care in questioning such a person. It is also good practice to obtain corroboration of any facts admitted in such an interview. The 'appropriate adult' is present to advise the person being questioned and to satisfy himself that the interview is being conducted fairly as well as to facilitate communication with the person being interviewed.

There will be few occasions upon which the arrest of a juvenile at his place of education could be justified. If, exceptionally, this must be done, the head teacher or a nominee must be informed.

Detention of juveniles

Where an arrested person is a juvenile, that person must be released on bail if the name and address are known, if it is not necessary to keep him in detention for protection or to prevent him from causing physical injury to another person or causing loss of or damage to property, there are no reasons for believing that such a person will fail to appear in answer to bail, it is not necessary to detain him to prevent interference with the administration of justice or the investigation of offences and the custody officer does not have reasonable grounds for believing that the juvenile ought to be detained in his own interests.

Section 38 of the Police and Criminal Evidence Act 1984 requires that where a custody officer authorises an arrested juvenile to be kept in police detention, the officer must secure that the arrested juvenile is moved to local authority accommodation, unless that officer certifies:

(a) that, by reason of such circumstances as are specified in the certificate, it is impracticable to do so; or

(b) in the case of an arrested juvenile who has attained the age of 12 years, that no secure accommodation is available and that keeping him in other local authority accommodation would not be adequate to protect the public from serious harm from him.

'Secure accommodation' is that provided for the purposes of restricting liberty. In the case of arrested juveniles who are charged with a violent or sexual offence (as defined by the Act; see below), the reference in (b) to protecting the public from serious harm is to protection from death or serious personal injury, whether physical or psychological, occasioned by further such offences. The term 'sexual offence' in this context means an offence under one of the following Acts:

(a) the Sexual Offences Act 1956 (other than living on immoral earnings, woman exercising control over a prostitute or offences connected with brothels);

(b) the Mental Health Act 1959, s 128 (sexual intercourse with patient);

(c) the Indecency with Children Act 1960;

(d) the Theft Act 1968, s 9 (burglary with intent to commit rape);

(e) the Criminal Law Act 1977, s 54 (inciting incest with girl under 16);

(f) the Protection of Children Act 1978 (indecent photographs of children); or

(g) conspiracy, incitement or attempt to commit any of these offences.

'Violent offence' means an offence which leads, or is intended or likely to lead, to a person's death or to physical injury to a person, and includes an offence which is required to be charged as arson (whether or not it would otherwise fall within this definition).

Except as provided above, neither a juvenile's behaviour nor the nature of the offence charged provides grounds for the custody officer to retain him in police custody rather than to seek to arrange for the transfer to the care of the local authority on the grounds of impracticability. Similarly, the lack of secure local authority accommodation does not make it impracticable for the custody officer to transfer him. The availability of secure accommodation is only one factor in relation to a juvenile aged 12 or over for whom other local authority accommodation would not be adequate to protect the public from serious harm from the juvenile.

Evidence given by children

The question whether a witness in criminal proceedings may be sworn, whether raised by a party to the proceedings or by the court of its own motion, is determined by the court as follows in accordance with s 55 of the Youth Justice and Criminal Evidence Act 1999.

A witness may not be sworn unless he has attained the age of 14 and has sufficient appreciation of the solemnity of the occasion and of the particular responsibility to tell the truth which is involved in taking an oath. If the witness is able to give intelligible testimony, he is presumed to have sufficient appreciation if no evidence is offered to the contrary. If such evidence is adduced, the issue of competence must be decided on the balance of probabilities.

Such issues must be dealt with in the absence of the jury.

Section 57 of the 1999 Act provides that it is an offence for a person wilfully to give false evidence in such circumstances that, had the evidence been given on oath, that person would have been guilty of perjury. The offence applies to all persons giving unsworn evidence, including those under 14.

Offences of entering and remaining on property

The offences themselves

The Criminal Law Act 1977 creates several offences, the purpose of which is to prevent unlawful occupation of residential premises. These offences are as follows:

(a) for a person without lawful authority to use or threaten violence for the purpose of securing entry into premises for himself or another person provided that there is someone present on the premises at the time who is opposed to entry and the person seeking entry knows that to be the case, s 6;
(b) for a person to fail to leave premises on which he is trespassing and which he entered as a trespasser, when required to do so by a displaced residential occupier or by a protected intending occupier of the premises, s 7;
(c) for a person to resist or intentionally obstruct an officer of a court in the execution of a High Court or county court judgment or order for the recovery of any premises or for the delivery of possession of any premises, s 10.

We are concerned with premises, and 'premises' for the purposes of the Act includes any building, any part of a building under separate occupation, any land ancillary to the building, and the site comprising any building or buildings together with any land ancillary thereto. The definition would therefore cover a block of flats, a single flat or even the grounds within which the block has been erected. The term 'building' includes any immovable structure, and any movable structure, vehicle or vessel designed or adapted for residential use. Thus, caravans, houseboats, etc., are covered by the Act.

Violence for securing entry

The offence

By s 6 of the Act, it is an offence for any person, without lawful authority, to use or threaten violence for the purpose of securing entry into any premises either for himself or any other person, provided that:

(a) there is someone present on those premises at the time who is opposed to the entry which the violence which the entry is intended to secure; and
(b) the person using or threatening the violence knows that to be the case.

However, this does not apply to a person who is a 'residential occupier' or a 'protected intending occupier' of the premises in question or who is acting on behalf of such an occupier. Where a person who is accused of such an offence adduces sufficient evidence that he was, or was acting on behalf of, such an occupier, that person shall be presumed to be, or to be acting on behalf of, such an occupier unless the contrary is proved. These terms are explained below.

Use or threat of violence

The essence of the offence is the use or threat of violence for the purpose of securing entry into premises upon which is present, a person who is opposed to entry. An intention to secure possession is not an issue.

The violence used or threatened may be directed against persons or property. The section requires the use of 'violence' which differs from 'force'. The press of a crowd may force entry into premises without any of the persons, thus forced into the premises, intending or threatening violence.

Entry

Actual entry is not required; it is the use or threat of violence for the purpose of securing entry into premises upon which a person opposed to entry is present that is the essence of the offence. The section does not require that the violence is for the purpose of securing possession of the property. Persons who used or threatened violence to gain entry to the annual hunt ball would commit this offence if they were aware that there were people inside who opposed their entry. Similarly, protesters who tried to secure entry to premises upon which animals were kept in captivity would commit offences in the same circumstances.

To kick down a door to secure entry amounts to violence directed against property, but it is submitted that the use of a key to gain unlawful entry would not involve a violent entry, although it would amount to a forceful one.

Person on premises who is opposed to entry

There must be someone on the premises who is opposed to entry. If squatters attempt, by violence, to take possession of premises which are guarded by a watchman who is opposed to their entry, they commit this offence.

However, once they have gained occupation of the premises, the owner of the premises may commit this offence if, by violence, he seeks to regain occupation of the premises. This does not apply where person concerned is a displaced residential occupier or a protected intending occupier or a person acting on their behalf. In the case of business premises there can be no displaced residential occupier or protected intending occupier.

Without lawful authority

The offence contrary to s 6 must be committed *without lawful authority*. Obviously those executing orders of the courts would have lawful authority for such entry and, in the case of s 6, this is as far as this may go. It would be reasonable to assume that an owner of property would always have lawful authority to reoccupy his property, but this is not so. Section 6(2) states clearly that the fact that a person has any interest or right to possession or occupation of any premises does not give him lawful authority to use or threaten the use of violence for the purpose of securing entry into those premises.

The section recognises the need to ensure the keeping of the peace as opposed to an owner's right of occupation of property. Thus, where business premises are taken over by squatters, the owner of those premises has no right to repossession other than that which might be established by other means. It may be, however, that such an owner or occupier might gain entry to property by means other than the use or threat of violence and if such a person does so he will not offend against the section by evicting those who are trespassing upon the premises.

Displaced residential occupier and protected intending occupier

The provisions of the section do not apply to displaced residential occupiers or protected intending occupiers.

A 'displaced residential occupier' is:

> any person who was occupying any premises as a residence immediately before being excluded from occupation by anyone who entered those premises, or any access to those premises, as a trespasser is a displaced residential occupier of the premises as long as he continues to be excluded from occupation of the premises by the original trespassers or by any subsequent trespasser.

The section makes clear, however, that a person who was occupying the premises as a trespasser before being excluded is *not* a displaced residential occupier.

A 'protected intending occupier' is a person who:

(a) has in those premises a freehold interest or a leasehold interest with not less than 2 years still to run;

(b) requires the residence for his own occupation as a residence;

(c) is excluded from occupation of the premises by a person who entered them, or any access to them, as a trespasser; and

(d) has, or a person acting on his behalf holds a written statement which specifies his interest in the premises, states that he requires the premises for occupation as a residence for himself and it is signed in the presence of a magistrate or commissioner for oaths, who has subscribed his name as a witness to that signature.

Tenants and those holding a licence to occupy premises granted by an authority (local authority, housing corporation, etc.) are similarly protected in the circumstances set out above.

Adverse occupation of residential premises

The offence

Section 7 gives a residential occupier or an individual who is a protected intending occupier of premises a quicker remedy in relation to reoccupation than would be afforded by civil process. He, or a person acting on his behalf, may require the trespassers to leave. They commit an offence if they fail to do so.

Defences to charges under s 7

There are three defences provided by s 7. The burden of proof in each case is upon the accused:

(a) where the accused believed that the person requiring him to leave was not a displaced residential occupier or a protected intending occupier of the premises, or someone acting on his behalf, he has a defence. However, it is of limited effect when one recognises that there is a requirement that protected intending occupiers will be in possession of a written statement or certificate to this effect. Most displaced residential occupiers will be in possession of documentary proof of ownership and residence;

(b) where the accused proves that, although asked to do so by the accused at the time the accused was requested to leave, the person requesting him to leave failed at the time to produce a written statement or certificate as required by the Act;

(c) that the premises in question are or form part of premises used mainly for non-residential purposes and that the accused was not on any part of the premises used wholly or mainly for residential purposes. This ensures that strikers, or protesters who are upon private property do not commit the offence if they fail to leave when required to do so, provided that they are not in occupation of any part of the premises which might be used, for example, by a resident watchman.

Police powers generally

A constable in uniform may arrest without warrant anyone who is, or whom he with reasonable cause suspects to be, in the act of committing these offences. For this purpose the police officer may enter (by force if need be) and search any premises where he has reasonable grounds for believing the person to be.

A similar offence of entering diplomatic missions and similarly inviolable premises is included and the power to arrest persons committing that offence is extended to constables in uniform. However, proceedings for this offence require the consent of the Attorney-General and the question of action by a constable on personal initiative does not arise.

Offences related to interim possession orders

The Criminal Justice and Public Order Act 1994, ss 75 and 76, deals with 'interim possession orders' which are to be made under rules of court for the bringing of summary proceedings for possession of premises which are occupied by trespassers. Where such an order has been made and served in accordance with rules of the court, a person who is present on the premises as a trespasser at any time during the currency of the order commits an offence. However, no offence will be committed if such a person leaves the premises within 24 hours of service of the order, or where a copy of the order was not fixed to the premises in accordance with the rules of court.

A person who was in occupation of the premises at the time of the service of the order, commits an offence if he re-enters, or attempts to re-enter as a trespasser within one year of service of the order.

Police powers

A constable in uniform may arrest without warrant anyone who is, or whom he reasonably suspects to be, guilty of this offence.

Powers to remove unauthorised campers

The Criminal Justice and Public Order Act 1994, s 77, empowers local authorities to give a direction to persons residing in a vehicle or vehicles within their area on land forming part of a highway, unoccupied land or occupied land without consent, and to other persons with them, to leave the land and remove the vehicle or vehicles and any other property from the land and not to return within 3 months of the date of the direction.

Persons who fail to do so as soon as reasonably practicable commit an offence. Within proceedings for such an offence, it is a defence for an accused to show that failure to leave or to remove the vehicle or other property as soon as practicable or re-entry with a vehicle was due to illness, mechanical breakdown or other immediate emergency. The term 'vehicle' includes any vehicle, whether or not it is in a fit state for use on a road, and includes any body, with or without wheels, appearing to have formed part of such a vehicle, and any load carried by, and anything attached to, such a vehicle, and a caravan.

Section 78 permits a magistrates' court to make an order, on complaint made by a local authority, where it is satisfied that persons are in contravention of such a direction, requiring the removal of any vehicle or other property and any person residing in that vehicle. It is an offence wilfully to obstruct any person in the exercise of any power conferred by the order. Such action will be taken by officers and servants of the local authority who are required to give land owners 24 hours' notice of their intention to enter the land.

Appendix:
Licensed premises, licensed persons, clubs, places of entertainment and offences of drunkenness

The material included in this Appendix deals with the situation when the provisions of the Licensing Act 2003 are brought into force by statutory instrument. When this occurs, the chapter commencing on page 643 entitled: 'Licensed premises, registered clubs, refreshment houses and drunkenness' becomes redundant.

Introduction

Prior to the Licensing Act 2003, the licensing of premises for the sale and supply of intoxicating liquor was in the hands of the licensing justices. In addition, such sale and supply was restricted to times of the day allowed by the provisions of the repealed Licensing Act 1964, the 'permitted hours'. The Act of 2003 introduced a system of licensing operated by local authorities who are empowered to issue various types of authorisation by means of personal licences, premises licences, club premises certificates and temporary events notices. The provisions of the Act are not restricted to matters involving the sale and supply of intoxicating liquor; they extend to the control of various forms of entertainment and to the provision of late-night refreshment. Schedule 8 to the Act makes transitional arrangements in respect of the transfer of the licensing functions from the justices to the relevant licensing authorities.

All of the 'sections' referred to in this chapter are references to sections of the Licensing Act 2003 unless otherwise stated. On certain occasions it is an offence to obstruct an officer of the licensing authority who shares powers with a constable. On each of these occasions it will be an offence against the Police Act 1996 to obstruct a constable in the execution of his duties.

The Act is concerned with licensable activities which are:

(a) the sale by retail of alcohol;
(b) the supply of alcohol by or on behalf of a club to, or to the order of, a member of the club;
(c) the provision of regulated entertainment; and
(d) the provision of late-night refreshment.

There are various forms of 'authorisations' which are a premises licence, a club premises certificate or a temporary events notice. The authorities will be issued by a 'licensing authority' which is a council of a district in England, the council of a county in England in which there are no district councils, the council of a county or county borough in Wales, the council of a London borough, the Common Council of the City of London, the Sub-Treasurer of the Inner Temple, the Under-Treasurer of the Middle Temple, or the Council of the Isles of Scilly. Such council must carry out their duties under the Act with a view to promoting the licensing objectives which are the prevention of crime and disorder, public safety, the prevention of public nuisance, and the protection of children from harm.

Many of the offences under the Licensing Act 2003 are committed 'knowingly'. Where such knowledge is required, it is required in relation to the act which is prohibited. It may be knowledge as to the age of the person carrying out an act; it may be knowledge of a condition such as drunkenness. The onus of proving that such knowledge existed lies with the prosecution but a licence holder may not wilfully shut his eyes to the obvious. A person may act knowingly if, intending to do the act prohibited, he deliberately looks the other way, but evidence that the form of supervision was such that under-age drinking was almost inevitable is not sufficient. The particular incident should be related to the particular person.

Before considering the authorisations in respect of premises, we will take a look at the need for certain persons to have a 'personal licence' which is granted by a licensing authority to an individual under Part 6 of the Act.

Personal licences

A personal licence is required in the case of some persons involved in the sale or supply of intoxicating liquor. Such licences are in addition to the requirement for the premises to be licensed. They are granted by the local authority for the area in which the applicant is normally resident. A personal licence authorises an individual to sell or supply alcohol, or authorise the sale or supply of alcohol, for consumption on or off the premises (in respect of which there is a 'premises licence', see below). For a person to be granted a personal licence he must:

(a) be aged 18 or over;
(b) possess a recognised qualification (awarded by an accredited body or a comparable qualification granted before the coming into force of the 2003 Act); and
(c) be in a position to show the licensing authority that he has not been convicted of 'relevant offences' and 'foreign offences'.

Where a person has been convicted of a relevant or a foreign offence and notification of such a conviction has been given to the chief officer of police, and consideration has been given to any objections received from the police, a licence may be granted unless it is considered that doing so would undermine the crime prevention objective of the legislation.

A personal licence is valid for 10 years and there is a presumption in favour of renewal if the licence holder has not been convicted of a relevant offence.

The provision of personal licences, in addition to premises licences, permits licensed persons to move from one set of premises to another. The personal licence concerned is one which relates solely to the supply of alcohol and has no relationship to other activities regulated by the 2003 Act such as regulated entertainment or late-night refreshment. In either of those cases, no personal licence is required.

A personal licence authorises sale or supply of alcohol from premises in respect of which there is a premises licence. On any such premises, the person nominated for the day-to-day running of the licensed premises must hold a personal licence and is known as the 'designated premises supervisor'. There may be more than one personal licence holder on licensed premises, although it is not necessary for all members of staff to have personal licences. However, all supplies of alcohol under a premises licence must be made by or under the authority of a personal licence holder.

The relevant licensing authority for the purpose of personal licences is the authority which granted it. It does not matter that the holder moves or works elsewhere. However, any change of name or address must be notified.

Relevant offences

For the purposes of Part 6 of the Act, 'relevant offences' are set out in Schedule 4 to the Act and are, in general terms:

(a) offences under the 2003 Act or the similar offence under the previous legislation;

(b) offences in relation to the licensing of entertainments under previous legislation or the licensing of late-night refreshment houses;

(c) most firearms offences;

(d) false trade description of alcoholic goods;

(e) offences related to stealing or which incorporate elements of stealing under the Theft Act 1968;

(f) production, supplying or possessing controlled drugs or permitting drug activities on premises;

(g) related offences of possessing smuggled goods;

(h) most offences of forgery or counterfeiting, breaches of related copyright laws;

(i) offences against s 3A (causing death by careless driving while under the influence of drink), s 4 (driving, etc., a vehicle when under the influence of drink or drugs) or s 5 (driving, etc., a vehicle with alcohol concentration above prescribed limit);

(j) selling food or drink not of nature or quality demanded or falsely describing such products;

(k) a sexual or violent offence as described by the Powers of Criminal Courts (Sentencing) Act 2000; and

(l) engaging in certain activities relating to security without a licence, s 3 of the Private Security Industry Act 2001.

Foreign offence

A foreign offence is an offence (other than a relevant offence) under the law of anywhere outside England and Wales.

Significance of a relevant or foreign offence

A relevant offence, or an offence which is considered to be a comparable foreign offence, must be taken into account on an application for the grant or renewal of a personal licence. A licensing authority must grant or renew a personal licence if the applicant is aged 18 or over, no personal licence has been forfeited in the preceding 5 years and he has not been convicted of any relevant offence or any foreign offence. It must reject an application if the applicant is under 18 or does not possess the required qualification, or has had a licence forfeited.

Notice of an application must be given to the chief officer of police who, if having regard to a conviction for a relevant offence or a foreign offence which he considers to be comparable to a relevant offence, is satisfied that the grant of a licence would undermine the crime prevention objective, must give notice to the licensing authority within 14 days, giving his reasons for reaching that conclusion.

Where a licence holder is convicted for a relevant offence his licence may be forfeited. However, such convictions must be disregarded if spent in terms of the Rehabilitation of Offenders Act 1974. Where, on an application for grant or renewal of a personal licence, an applicant is convicted of a relevant or foreign offence in the period between application and determination, but knowledge of the conviction came to notice after grant or renewal, the licence may be revoked by the licensing authority after consultation with the police. Provision is made for a record of convictions for relevant or foreign offences to be shown within a licence.

Duties of various bodies when personal licence holder charged with a relevant offence

A personal licence holder, when charged with a relevant offence, must produce his licence to a court before the case against him is first heard in court. If for any reason he does not do so, he must explain why. If he is granted a personal licence after being charged he must produce the licence to the court or explain why he is unable to do so. He must also notify the court if, after having first produced his licence, it is renewed, surrendered or revoked. Section 128 makes it an offence to fail, without reasonable excuse, to comply with these requirements.

If a court convicts a personal licence holder of a relevant offence, it may forfeit the licence or suspend it for up to 6 months, but such an order may be suspended pending an appeal. The court must notify the relevant licensing authority of the holder's name and address, the nature and date of the conviction and the details of the sentence passed. Where a conviction is quashed or a sentence altered on appeal, the court must notify the relevant licensing authority. In circumstances in which a court was not aware of the existence of a personal licence at the time of the conviction for a relevant offence or a foreign offence, the holder must notify the licensing authority as soon as possible concerning the conviction and the outcome of any appeal. It is an offence against s 132 to fail, without reasonable excuse, to comply with these requirements.

Where the holder of a personal licence is on premises to sell or authorise the sale of alcohol by virtue of a premises licence or temporary event notice, he may be required by a constable or officer of the licensing authority to produce his licence. Failure to do so, without reasonable excuse, is an offence against s 135.

Premises licence

A premises licence is granted by the licensing authority for the area in which the premises are situated and authorises its holder to use the premises to which the licence relates for licensable activities.

There are four licensable activities:

(a) sale by retail of alcohol, but 'business to business' sales are outside the provisions of the Act ('alcohol' means spirits, beer, wine, cider or any other fermented, distilled or spirituous liquor, not including any liquor of 0.5% strength or below);
(b) supply of alcohol by clubs;
(c) the provision of regulated entertainment;
(d) the provision of late-night refreshment.

A licence will set out the conditions subject to which it is issued, and remains in force unless revoked or suspended. However, an applicant may request a licence with a time limitation. Representations may be made to the licensing authority by local residents or businesses, the police, the fire authority and public environmental agencies. Following the grant of a licence, such persons may seek reconsideration of its conditions. It is an offence against s 136 to carry out any licensable activity relating to alcohol otherwise than in accordance with a premises licence, club premises certificate or temporary event notice.

Licensed premises selling alcohol

Part 3 of the Act requires that in relation to such premises there will be a 'designated premises supervisor' and that person must hold a personal licence. Representations as to the identity of the designated supervisor may only be made by the police.

Such premises may also be covered by its licence to provide specified forms of entertainment.

A constable or authorised person may enter the premises to which an application relates, before that application has been determined, in order to assess the likely effect on the promotion of the licensing objectives of the grant of the application, or as the case may be, the effect of the activities authorised by the licence which is applied for. Reasonable force may be used if necessary. It is an offence against s 59 intentionally to obstruct an authorised person.

Applications for a premises licence must be accompanied by an operating schedule, a plan of the premises and (if the application proposes that the licence will authorise the supply of alcohol) a form containing the consent of the individual whom it is proposed will be specified as the designated premises supervisor. The operating schedule must show the licensable activities to be carried out, the proposed hours of opening, etc., the duration of the licence (if it has a fixed term), details about the individual who is to act as the designated premises supervisor, details of whether alcohol is to be supplied for on-sales, off-sales or both, and a statement of how the applicant intends to promote the licensing objective (for instance the security arrangements). If the application is approved these factors will be incorporated into the licence. Regulations will provide for advertisements and the specification of when interested parties can make representations to the authority.

If no representations are made, a licensing authority is obliged to grant the application. The licence will be subject to conditions consistent with those listed in the operating schedule. Where it is a condition that door supervision be provided anyone carrying out these duties must be licensed by the Security Industry Authority established under the Private Security Industry Act 2001.

Clubs

Club premises certificates will be granted by the licensing authority for the area in which the club is situated and will authorise the use of club premises for permitted club activities such as the supply of intoxicating liquor to a member (there is no sale to a member of a club as he is deemed to be an owner of the liquor supplied to him and the transfer of the property to him is merely a release to him of his own property), the sale by retail of alcohol by the club to a guest of a member for consumption on the premises, and the provision of regulated entertainment to members and their guests. Representations may be made by the same persons as is the case in respect of a premises licence.

It is an offence against s 136 to carry out a licensable activity within a club otherwise than in accordance with a club premises certificate.

A club may wish to provide entertainment to members of the public on certain occasions and in consequence it may hold a club premises certificate in respect of its day-to-day activities and a premises licence authorising the provision of entertainment.

The 2003 Act is not solely concerned with club activities involving the supply of alcohol. It covers many other forms of activity in respect of which licensing is desirable. Part 4 of the Act deals with arrangements for 'qualifying clubs':

(a) no one may be admitted as a member without an interval of at least 2 days after his nomination or application for membership;
(b) a person who is admitted as a member other than by prior nomination or application must wait at least 2 days before enjoying the privileges of membership;
(c) the club is established and conducted in good faith as a club;
(d) the club has at least 25 members;
(e) no alcohol is supplied, or intended to be supplied, on the club premises except by or on behalf of the club.

In relation to whether or not the club is established and conducted in good faith, account must be taken of the club's freedom to purchase alcohol, how money or property belonging to the club is used, giving members information about club finances, the club's accounts and the nature of its premises.

If a club at any time ceases to meet these criteria its certificate will be withdrawn. A justice may issue a search warrant authorising a constable to enter club premises (if necessary by force) and to search them if he is satisfied that a club holding a club premises certificate ceases to meet the criteria necessary to be a qualifying club and evidence of that fact may be obtained at the club premises. The provisions of the Criminal Justice and Police Act 2001, s 50 (seizure of material which cannot be separated), apply to such a search.

If alcohol is to be supplied by a club the purchase and supply must be managed by a committee; no commission or percentage deriving from the purchase of alcohol should be paid to any person at the expense of the club and no one must receive a pecuniary benefit from the supply of alcohol by the club to its members.

An application for a club premises certificate must be advertised. It must be accompanied by similar information to that required in respect of a premises licence.

A club premises certificate may authorise the supply of alcohol to its members for consumption off the premises. Sale by retail for off-consumption to a guest is not authorised by the certificate. In general:

(a) a club premises certificate may not authorise the supply of alcohol for consumption off the premises unless it also authorises its supply to members for consumption on the premises;
(b) a club premises certificate authorising the supply of alcohol for consumption off the premises must include three conditions:
  (i) the supply must be made at a time when the premises are open for the purposes of supplying alcohol, in accordance with the club premises certificate, to members of the club for consumption on the premises;
  (ii) any alcohol supplied for consumption off the premises must be in a sealed container;
  (iii) any supply of alcohol for consumption off the premises must be made to a member of the club in person.

No conditions attached to a club premises certificate must prevent the sale by retail of alcohol or the provision of regulated entertainment to associate members of a club or their guests if those are permitted activities.

A club premises certificate has effect until it is withdrawn or it is surrendered. The certificate must be produced at the request of the licensing authority. It is an offence against s 93 to fail, without reasonable excuse, to do so. A police officer or an authorised person may require production of a certificate. Failure to do so, without reasonable excuse, or to produce a certified copy, is an offence against s 94. Clubs must ensure that the certificate is held on relevant premises, and that a summary of the certificate and notice of the nominated individual responsible for it on the premises are prominently displayed.

Inspection of club premises

A constable authorised by the chief officer of police or an authorised person may enter and inspect premises in respect of which an application has been made for the grant, variation or review of a certificate. Forty-eight hours' notice must have been given to the club. It is an offence to obstruct an authorised person exercising these powers.

By s 97 a constable may enter and search club premises where he has reasonable cause to believe that an offence in respect of controlled drugs has been, is being, or is about to be committed there, or there is likely to be a breach of the peace. If necessary, reasonable force may be used.

Temporary events

Part 5 of the Act deals with permitted temporary activities. It permits a 'premises user' (the individual who gave the notice) to carry out licensable activities on a temporary basis (a period not exceeding 96 hours) subject to conditions and limitations.

A personal licence holder may wish to carry out licensable activities at premises which are not licensed. He may wish to provide bar facilities at a wedding reception or he may wish to set up a disco in premises which, although licensed for the sale of alcohol, are not licensed for the provision of entertainment. A licence holder may be permitted to provide temporary activities on not more than 50 occasions in any one year.

A person who is not the holder of a personal licence may wish to carry out licensable activities on premises regardless of whether they are covered by a premises licence in respect of the proposed activities. This might occur where a person wishes to celebrate a particular anniversary and to provide bar facilities and dance music. This may be done on not more than five occasions in any calendar year.

The temporary activities covered by Part 5 apply to events attended by fewer than 500 persons. No premises may be used more than 12 times in a calendar year, with an overall maximum of 15 days in any year on which temporary events may take place at any particular premises.

A 'permitted temporary activity' is one which is carried on in accordance with a temporary events notice given to the relevant authority which satisfies the following conditions:

(a) the temporary event notice has been duly acknowledged by the licensing authority and notified to the police;
(b) the temporary event notice has not been subsequently withdrawn by the individual giving the notice; and
(c) the licensing authority has not issued a counter-notice which would be issued, if necessary, following a hearing of any objections raised by the police to the effect that the crime prevention objective would be undermined by allowing the activity

to go ahead or if the permitted limits attaching to the applicant or the premises would be exceeded.

Temporary event notice

The system of temporary event notices reverses the procedure which it replaces. Under previous legislation application had to be made to and formal approval given before the event took place. Now, notice must be given to the relevant licensing authority, as prescribed by Part 5 of the Act, of an intention to hold an event and this may go ahead provided that no counter-notice is issued by the licensing authority.

A 'premises user', who must be 18 or over, who proposes to carry out a licensable activity for a temporary period of not more than 96 hours, must give notice to the licensing authority no later than 10 working days before the proposed event. The licensing authority must acknowledge receipt no later than the day after receipt of the notice. The form of the notice is to be prescribed by regulations which will require details including:

(a) the licensable activities which are to be carried out;
(b) the total length of the event which must not exceed 96 hours;
(c) the times during the event at which the licensable activities are to be carried out (bar facilities may be limited during a 4-day event);
(d) the maximum number of people to be allowed on the premises at any one time and this must be less than 500;
(e) whether any alcohol sales are to be made for consumption on or off the premises (or both);
(f) any other information prescribed by regulations.

If the proposed licensable activities include the supply of alcohol, the notice must include the condition that all supplies will be made by, or under the authority of, the premises user. The temporary event notice must be given to the licensing authority and the chief officer of police at least 10 working days before the event. The police may object and if they do the authority must, if necessary, arrange a hearing to decide whether to issue a counter-notice.

There must be at least 24 hours between temporary events held on the same premises by a premises user, or by him and another person who is related to, associated with, or in business with that user.

A premises user can withdraw a temporary event notice up to 24 hours before the event is scheduled to take place. Once so withdrawn, the notice does not count towards the limitation upon numbers of notices which may be given.

Where the police consider that if the temporary event should proceed it would undermine the crime prevention objective, the premises user and the relevant licensing authority must be informed by an objection notice, setting out the reasons, not later than 48 hours after receiving the temporary event notice. If there is a police objection there must be a hearing unless all parties agree that it is unnecessary. Where the licensing authority accepts the objection it must issue to the premises user a counter-notice preventing the event from taking place and this must be done at least 24 hours before the proposed event. If the notice is not sent as required, the premises user may proceed with the event. However, at any time before a hearing the chief officer of police may, with the consent of the premises user, modify the terms of the temporary event notice.

In addition to the circumstances in which an objection is accepted, a licensing authority must issue a counter-notice where the premises user holds a personal licence and has already given 50 such notices in the calendar year, where no personal licence is held and the premises user has already given five notices in that year, where 12 notices have been given in respect of the same premises in that year, or notices for events at the same premises have already covered 15 days in a year.

Police powers in relation to temporary events

Section 108 provides that a constables or an officer of the licensing authority may, at any reasonable time, enter premises to assess the probable impact of the proposed event upon the crime prevention objective. The officer of the licensing authority must produce evidence of his authority, if requested. It is an offence to obstruct such an officer.

The premises user must ensure that the notice is displayed on the premises or is kept there under his control or that of a nominated person. Where the notice is in the custody of a nominated person, the premises user must ensure that a notice to that effect is prominently displayed on the premises. It is an offence against s 109 for a premises user, without reasonable excuse, to fail to comply. Where a temporary event notice is not displayed and there is no such notice, a constable or authorised officer may require the premises user to produce the temporary event notice. Such a person may also require production of the actual notice where a notice relating to a 'nominated person' is displayed on the premises. It is also an offence for a person who holds the premises licence under such arrangements to fail, without reasonable excuse, to produce that licence to a constable or an officer of the licensing authority when requested to do so.

Entertainments

Schedule 1 to the Act is concerned with regulated entertainment provided solely or partly for members of the public, or exclusively to members of a club and their guests, or for which a charge is made, which is provided for profit (which includes raising money for charity). It is also concerned with the provision of entertainment facilities for the participation in entertainment. Thus, a show staged to raise funds for famine relief would fall within the Act, while a show provided without charge by a company for business clients would not.

The entertainments concerned include the performances of plays, film shows and all indoor sporting events (events which takes place inside a building for spectators in that building). A venue with an opening/closing roof is not an indoor event, even if the roof is closed. 'Sport' is related to a physical skill and thus includes indoor bowls, tennis and indoor athletics, but would not include a bridge competition or a 'sports quiz'. Outdoor boxing and wrestling matches are included but no other form of outdoor sport. Live music, the playing of recorded music and the performance of dance, where the entertainment takes place in the presence of an audience and is provided for its entertainment, are activities included in the schedule.

Schedule 1 to the Act provides that the following are not 'regulated entertainments':

(a) live TV and radio programmes within the meaning of the Broadcasting Act 1990;
(b) incidental music in a lift or a piano in a restaurant;
(c) films used for product demonstration, advertisement, information, education or instruction (such as in schools or shopping centres);

(d) incidental to a religious service or at a place of religious worship;

(e) entertainment at a garden fete;

(f) Morris dancing or dancing of similar type; and

(g) entertainment provided on vehicles in motion.

Premises licences which are issued to authorise the exhibition of films must include a condition requiring the admission of children to be restricted in accordance with recommendations given either by a body designated under the Video Recordings Act 1984 or by the licensing authority. At the time of writing the only body so designated is the British Board of Film Classification.

No condition relating to the nature of the play or the manner of its performance may be attached to a club premises certificate authorising the performance of a play, unless such conditions are justified as a matter of public safety.

The procedures to be followed in relation to securing permission to hold licensable activities which consist of forms of entertainment are the same as those to be followed in respect of such activities which involve the supply of alcohol.

Late-night refreshment

Section 1 lists the provision of late-night refreshment within the four activities which constitute licensable activities.

Schedule 2 provides that late-night refreshment means the supply of hot food or hot drink to the public for consumption on or off the premises, between 11 p.m. and 5 a.m. It includes such supply on premises to which the public has access. 'Hot' for the purposes of the Act means food or drink which is heated on the premises or elsewhere or that which, after it is supplied, may be heated on the premises.

There are exemptions:

(a) supply to guests of hotels or similar premises such as guest houses, lodging houses, caravan or camping sites or other premises supplying accommodation as their main purpose;

(b) supply to members of recognised clubs;

(c) supply to employees of particular employers (works canteens, etc.);

(d) premises already licensed under other Acts – 'near beer' premises in London in which non-alcoholic beverages are sold.

The supply of food or drink free of charge by a registered charity is exempted, as is provision by way of a vending machine where money is inserted by members of the public.

Register of authorisations

Section 8(1) requires each licensing authority to maintain a register containing the details of all authorisations which it issues, temporary event notices which it receives, any other notices and applications and any other prescribed information. The Secretary of State is empowered to make regulations. This register must be made available for inspection by the public during office hours free of charge. A charge may be made for a copy of such information. The legislation provides for the keeping of one or more central registers to be established by regulations.

Opening hours of licensed premises

The Act does not prescribe 'permitted hours' within which alcohol may be sold or supplied for consumption on or off the premises. In addition, there are no general restrictions placed upon any other licensable activity. An applicant for a premises licence or a club premises certificate may choose the hours within which it would like to be authorised to carry out the licensed activities. The licence will be granted on those terms unless, following representations, the authority considers it necessary to reject the application or alter its terms bearing in mind the 'licensing objectives', which are:

(a) the prevention of crime and disorder;
(b) public safety;
(c) the prevention of public nuisance; and
(d) the protection of children from harm.

Licensing offences

Part 7 of the Act deals with the various offences associated with licensing.

Unauthorised licensable activities

It is an offence against s 136 for a person to carry on, or attempt to carry on, a licensable activity without having the authorisation provided by a:

(a) premises licence;
(b) club premises certificate; or
(c) temporary event notice.

It is also an offence for such a person knowingly to allow such an activity to take place. In the case of regulated entertainment, a person does not commit an offence if his only involvement is that as a performer. Conviction is punishable summarily by imprisonment for 6 months or to a fine not exceeding £20 000, or both.

Section 173 exempts activities which would otherwise be licensable activities if carried on in particular places, for example on board a vessel on an international journey or the examination station of an international airport (area beyond security check-in). Premises permanently or temporarily used for the purpose of the armed forces, aircraft, hovercraft and railway vehicles engaged on a journey are also exempted, together with royal palaces. Cabinet ministers or the Attorney-General may grant a certificate on the grounds of national security where inspection of the premises would involve a security risk.

Section 175 provides that the giving of a sealed container of alcohol as a prize in a lottery will not be a licensable activity if:

(a) the lottery is promoted as incidental to a bazaar, sale of work, fête, dinner, dance, sporting or athletic event or other entertainment of a similar character;
(b) after the deduction of all relevant expenses, none of the proceeds is used for private gain;
(c) none of the prizes is a money prize;
(d) the tickets or chances are sold or issued and the result of the draw is announced at the time of, and in the same place as, the entertainment;
(e) the lottery or draw is not the only or main inducement to attend the entertainment.

The expenses which are relevant are those incurred in arranging and holding the entertainment and those in connection with the lottery or draw, including the printing of tickets and the purchase of prizes.

Exposing alcohol for unauthorised sale

It is an offence against s 137 to expose alcohol for sale by retail in circumstances in which the sale is not under and in accordance with a premises licence, club premises certificate or temporary event notice. It is not therefore essential that there has been a sale, or an attempted sale, provided that the alcohol is there to be sold and exposed to potential customers. A court which convicts a person of such an offence may order the confiscation of the alcohol for destruction or to be dealt with in some other way.

The offence is punishable as in the case of carrying on an unlawful licensing activity.

Keeping alcohol on premises for unlawful sale

Section 138 creates the offence of possessing, or having under control, alcohol, with the intention of selling it by retail, or supplying it, unless that sale or supply would be in accordance with an authorisation (premises licence in the case of a sale and a club premises certificate in the case of supply). A court has the same powers of confiscation as set out in the previous paragraph.

Defence of due diligence

Section 139 provides a defence where a person is charged with carrying on an unauthorised licensable activity, exposing alcohol for unauthorised sale, or keeping alcohol on premises for unlawful sale or supply if:

(a) his act or omission was mistaken;
(b) it was due to his relying on information given to him;
(c) it was the fault of another person; or
(d) it was due to some cause beyond his control,

and he took all reasonable steps and exercised all due diligence to avoid committing the offence.

Allowing disorderly conduct on licensed premises, etc.

Section 140 makes it an offence knowingly to allow disorderly conduct on licensed premises. The offence can be committed by any person who works on the premises in a capacity which gives him the authority to prevent such conduct, or a premises licence holder or designated premises supervisor. In the case of a club it might be an officer or member of the club who is present when the disorderly conduct takes place and who has the authority to prevent it. Members of a club committee would obviously be in such a position. In the case of a temporary event the main responsibility will fall upon the premises user.

Sale of alcohol to a person who is drunk or obtaining alcohol for such a person

It is an offence, contrary to s 141, knowingly to sell, or attempt to sell alcohol to a person who is drunk, or to allow alcohol to be sold to such a person, on relevant premises. The section also applies to the supply of alcohol by or on behalf of a club. The offence may be committed by the same category of persons to which s 140 applies.

By s 142, it is an offence for a person knowingly to obtain, or attempt to obtain, alcohol for consumption on relevant premises by a person who is drunk.

Failure to leave licensed premises, etc.

A person commits an offence against s 143 if he is drunk and disorderly and fails, without reasonable excuse, at the request of a police constable or:

(a) any person who works at the premises in a capacity which gives him the authority to make that request;
(b) a premises licence holder or designated premises supervisor;
(c) an officer or member of a club who is present at the time and has authority to make that request; or
(d) a premises user who has given a temporary event notice in respect of the premises,

to leave those premises. Such a person also commits an offence if he enters, or tries to enter such premises when requested not to do so by any such persons.

No offence will be committed where the person concerned has a reasonable excuse for not leaving the premises. It could be that such a person was suffering from leg injuries which prevented his leaving until transport arrived.

The section requires a constable to assist in the expulsion of persons who are drunk and disorderly from relevant premises, or to help to prevent such a person from entering if requested to do so by any of the persons described above.

Keeping of smuggled goods

Section 144 creates an offence committed by a person who knowingly keeps, or allows to be kept, on relevant premises any goods which have been imported without payment of duty or which have otherwise been unlawfully imported. The persons who may commit this offence are:

(a) any person who works at the premises in a capacity which gives him the authority to prevent those goods from being on the premises;
(b) a premises licence holder or designated premises supervisor;
(c) an officer or member of a club who is present at a time when the goods are kept on the premises and has authority to prevent them being so kept; and
(d) a premises user who has given a temporary event notice in respect of the premises.

A court which convicts a person of such an offence may order the confiscation of the goods in question and their containers which may then be destroyed or dealt with in some other way prescribed by the court.

This offence is aimed at those suppliers who obtain cheap supplies from smugglers who arrange for large quantities of liquor and tobacco to be imported into Great Britain. Currently, HM Customs and Excise and ferry operators provide advice concerning the quantities of excisable goods which will looked upon favourably by HM Customs officers. There is no legal limit, as EU law prevents restrictions where duty has been paid within an EU State. HM Customs are obliged to prove that excisable goods bought within an EU State are not for personal use. Thus, any excisable goods bought within the EU which are then passed to some other person for sale within premises or supply within a club will be unlawfully imported goods upon which UK duty has not been paid.

Unaccompanied children prohibited from certain premises

It is an offence against s 145 to allow children under 16 to be on certain categories of relevant premises if they are not accompanied by an adult (18 or over) and the premises are open for the supply of alcohol for consumption on the premises. The premises concerned are:

(a) those exclusively or primarily used for the supply of alcohol for consumption on the premises; or
(b) those open for the purpose of being used for the supply of alcohol for consumption on the premises by virtue of Part 5 (permitted temporary activities) and, at the time the temporary event notice in question has effect, they are exclusively or primarily used for such supplies.

It is also an offence against the section to allow an unaccompanied child under 16 to be on the relevant premises at a time between the hours of midnight and 5 a.m. when the premises are open for the supply of alcohol for consumption there.

These offences may be committed by a person working on the premises with the authority to ask the child to leave, a premises licence holder or designated premises supervisor, an officer or member of a club with that authority, or a premises user who has given temporary notice in respect of the premises.

The section provides a defence where the person was charged by reason of his own conduct and he believed the child to be 16 or over, or the accompanying adult to be 18 or over and had either taken all reasonable steps to establish the individual's age, or no one could reasonably have suspected from the individual's appearance that they were aged under 16 or 18. A person will be treated as having taken all reasonable steps to establish an individual's age if he asked for evidence of it and the evidence would have convinced a reasonable person. Where a person is charged because of the default of some other person, it is a defence to show that he had exercised all due diligence to avoid committing the offence.

No offence is committed where the unaccompanied child is merely passing through the premises, where this is the only route.

Sale of alcohol to persons under 18

Section 146 prohibits the sale of alcohol to an individual aged under 18 anywhere. It additionally prohibits the supply of alcohol in a club to, or to the order of, a person under 18 who is a member of the club, or to any such person on the order of a member of a club. The repealed legislation dealt with the sale to such persons on licensed premises but did not prohibit supply in a club. The new provisions have simplified the law as the place where a sale took place is no longer relevant.

The section provides a defence where the person charged believed that the purchaser was 18 or over and either:

(a) took all reasonable steps to establish the purchaser's age; or
(b) no one could reasonably have suspected from the purchaser's appearance that he was under 18.

An accused will be deemed to have taken all reasonable steps if he asked the individual for evidence of his age and the evidence would have convinced a reasonable person. However, the prosecution may show that the evidence of age produced was such that no reasonable person would have been convinced by it (it may be an obvious forgery or obviously belong to some other person).

Where a sale or supply was made by some person other than the person charged (as where a barman supplies a drink on behalf of a manager) it is a defence to show that the person charged exercised all due diligence to avoid committing the offence.

It is an offence against s 147 for a person knowingly to allow the sale or supply of alcohol to a person under 18 on relevant premises. The persons who can commit this offence are those workers with authority to prevent sale or supply or an officer or a member of a club with that authority.

By s 148 it is an offence to sell liqueur confectionery to a person under the age of 16, or for a club or person on behalf of a club to supply to, or to the order of a person under 16. It is good to know that in these dangerous times our children are protected from this evil! The same defences apply as in the case of unlawful sales under s 146.

Purchase of alcohol by persons under 18 or on their behalf

Section 149(1) makes it an offence for a child to buy or attempt to buy alcohol (whether or not on licensed premises) or, if he is a member of a club, for him to have alcohol supplied to him by the club in circumstances in which he actively initiates the supply, or for him to attempt to do so. Test purchasing on behalf of a constable or trading standards officer is excepted from these provisions.

Subsection (3) makes it an offence for a person to act as an agent for a child in purchasing, or attempting to purchase alcohol. A person under 18 may ask a stranger to purchase alcohol from an off-licence on his behalf and provide that person with the money, in the same way as children request adults to take them into a cinema when a film is being shown which requires an accompanying adult. Subsection (4) provides an offence which is committed on licensed premises, by prohibiting a person from buying or attempting to buy alcohol for consumption by a person under 18 on those premises. This would cover any relative or friend of a child who buys a drink for a child, or tries to do so, on licensed premises. However, the offence is not committed by anyone who buys beer, wine or cider for a person aged 16 or 17 to consume with a meal taken on those premises in the company of an adult.

These offences are 'penalty offences' for the purpose of the Criminal Justice and Police Act 2001, see page 478.

Consumption by, delivering to and sending a child to obtain alcohol

It is an offence against s 150(1) for a child knowingly to consume alcohol on relevant premises. Because of the presence of 'knowingly' the offence will not be committed where a child accidentally consumes alcohol, being unaware of the nature of his drink, or where something has been furtively added to it. Subsection (2) makes it an offence for a person knowingly to allow such consumption to take place. The offence can be committed, once again, by those responsible persons on licensed premises and officers and members of a club. The offence does not apply to persons of 16 or 17 who consume beer, wine or cider with a table meal (eaten by a person seated at a table, counter or other structure used as a table by seated persons) on relevant premises and are accompanied by a person of 18 or over.

Section 151(1) is concerned with the delivery of alcohol to a person under 18. Delivery is a term which avoids 'sale or supply'. The offence lies where a person who works on relevant premises, knowingly delivers to a person under 18, alcohol which is sold on the premises or supplied by a club. It may be that his mother has bought and paid for a quantity of drink and has left it at the off-licence to be picked up. If a child goes to pick up the alcoholic liquor and it is handed over to that child, there has been a delivery. Once again, it is an offence for a person working there with the necessary authority to prevent the delivery, to allow it to take place. The offence also applies to clubs, where a person in authority allows such delivery. However, no offence is committed if alcohol is delivered to a home and handed over to a child who acknowledges receipt of his mother's order, nor does it apply where the job of a minor involves messages on behalf of his employer and alcohol is delivered to the order of the employer, nor where alcohol is sold or supplied for consumption on the relevant premises, as other offences are committed in those circumstances.

In view of the offences involving delivery to a person under 18, it is not surprising to find that 'sending' such a person to obtain alcohol is an offence against s 152. Thus, where a parent orders by telephone from an off-licence and sends a child to seek the order, an offence against the section is committed. The section provides that the offence is committed whether or not the child is sent to the actual off-licence. If the 'order' has been sent to a distribution centre and it is collected from those premises, the offence is still committed. No offence is committed where the minor works at the premises, or if the child is assisting a constable or trading standards officer.

Unsupervised sales by persons under 18

It is an offence against s 153 knowingly to allow a person under the age of 18 to sell, or in the case of a club supply, alcohol unless each sale or supply has been specifically approved. The offence may be committed, once again, by those persons with authority to prevent the sale or supply whether upon licensed premises, within a club, or at a temporary permitted activity. Many of the check-out personnel in supermarkets which are authorised to sell for off-consumption are under 18, but provided that each sale is specifically approved (to prevent their young friends from conveniently going through their check-out) no offence is committed. Such youngsters are seen to gain the approval of more senior personnel. In addition, the section exempts sales in a restaurant of alcohol to be taken with a meal. Thus waiters and waitresses under 18 may serve drinks in such a part of the premises.

Confiscation of alcohol – young persons

The Confiscation of Alcohol (Young Persons) Act 1997 provides that where a constable reasonably suspects that a person in any public place other than licensed premises; or any place, other than a public place, to which a person has unlawfully gained access, is in possession of alcohol and that either:

(a) he is under the age of 18; or

(b) he intends that any of the liquor should be consumed by a person under the age of 18 in that or another similar place; or

(c) a person under the age of 18 who is, or has recently been, with him, has recently consumed intoxicating liquor in that or another similar place,

the constable may require that person to surrender anything which he possesses which is, or the constable reasonably believes to be, alcohol, or a container for such liquor and to state his name and address. A person who, without reasonable excuse, fails to comply with such a requirement commits an offence. A constable who makes such a requirement must inform the person concerned of the suspicion and that failing without reasonable excuse to comply with the requirement is an offence. However, a constable may not require a person to surrender any sealed container unless the constable reasonably believes that the person is, or has been, consuming, or intends to consume, alcohol in any relevant place.

The Act provides a means by which the nuisance caused by young people assembling in public places and drinking from cans may be removed. The terms of s 1 of the Act are such that all persons who are included in such a group who have alcohol in their possession, may be required to surrender it.

Police powers

A constable may dispose of anything surrendered in such a manner as he considers appropriate.

The section provides a power to arrest without warrant a person who fails to comply with such a requirement made under the 1997 Act.

Prohibition of sale of alcohol on moving vehicles

Section 156 of the 2003 Act creates the offence of selling alcohol by retail on or from a vehicle which is not permanently or temporarily parked. It is a defence where the sale was mistaken, was due to the seller relying on information given to him, was the fault of another person or was due to some cause beyond his control and he took all reasonable precautions and exercised due diligence to avoid committing the offence. This could occur where it was believed that the refreshment served was non-alcoholic and there was some reason for a person to have held that belief.

While the section does not apply to trains, s 157 provide for the prohibition of sales of alcohol at specified stations or on trains travelling between specified stations for a particular period. A prohibition order may be made by magistrates on the application of a police officer of at least the rank of inspector, if the magistrates are satisfied than an order is necessary for the prevention of disorder. A copy of the order must be served by the police upon the operator or operators concerned. Thus provision is made for 'dry' soccer specials, at least so far as the operating companies are concerned.

Making of false statements in applications for licences and certificates and in notices

It is an offence against s 158 for a person knowingly or recklessly to make a false statement in or in connection with the grant, variation, transfer or review of a premises licence or club premises certificate, or in any provisional statement, temporary event notice or any other notice under the Act, or for any personal licence. For the purposes of the section a person will be treated as making a false statement if he produces, furnishes, signs or otherwise makes use of a document that contains a false statement. Thus there is no limitation to signed statements made by an applicant. It will be sufficient if he includes with his application any document which he knows to be false.

Alcohol consumption in designated public places

Sections 12 to 16 of the Criminal Justice and Police Act 2001 give a constable certain powers (set out below) where the constable reasonably believes that a person is, or has been, consuming alcohol in a designated public place, or intends to consume alcohol in such a place.

The powers of a constable just referred to are to require the person concerned not to consume, in the designated place, anything which is or the constable reasonably believes to be, alcohol, and to surrender such liquor or a container for such liquor. Anything so surrendered may be disposed of by the constable in a manner considered to be appropriate. Failure without reasonable excuse to comply with such a requirement is an arrestable offence. However, the constable making the requirement must inform the person concerned that failing without reasonable excuse to comply with the requirement is an offence.

As can be seen, it is not essential in order for a requirement to be made that an officer sees a person consuming alcohol. If such a person has alcohol in a glass or an open container it raises the inference of an intention to drink it. Where liquor is in a sealed container, notice will have to be taken of the surrounding circumstances. Possession of a 'four-pack' by a person who is walking home differs from possession by groups of persons assembled at that place for the purpose of drinking.

Section 13 provides that a 'designated public place' is a public place within the area of a local authority which is identified in an order made by that authority. A local authority may make such an order where it is satisfied that:

(a) nuisance or annoyance to members of the public, or a section of the public; or
(b) disorder

has been associated with the consumption of intoxicating liquor in that place. The making of orders is controlled by the Local Authorities (Alcohol Consumption in Designated Public Places) Regulations 2001.

By s 14, a place is not a designated place if it is:

(a) premises in respect of which a premises licence or club premises certificate under the Licensing Act 2003 has effect;
(b) a place within the curtilage of premises within paragraph (a);
(c) premises which by virtue of Part 5 of the Licensing Act 2003 may for the time being be used for the supply of alcohol or which, by virtue of that Part, could have been so used within the last 20 minutes;
(d) a place where facilities or activities relating to the sale or consumption of alcohol are for the time being permitted by virtue of a permission granted under s 115E of the Highways Act 1980 (council permission to set up objects and structures on a highway for the purpose of producing income).

Closure of licensed premises due to disorder or disturbance

The making of a closure order

Section 161 provides that a senior police officer (i.e. of or above the rank of inspector) may make a closure order in relation to any relevant premises if he reasonably believes that:

(a) there is, or is likely imminently to be, disorder on, or in the vicinity of and related to, the premises and closure is necessary in the interests of public safety; or

(b) a public nuisance is being caused by noise coming from the premises and the closure of the premises is necessary to prevent that nuisance.

A closure order requires the premises to be closed for a period not exceeding 24 hours. An officer making a closure order must consider, in particular, any conduct of each appropriate person in relation to the disorder or nuisance. A closure order is effective as soon as notice of it has been given to the licensee or a manager of the premises.

A person who permits relevant premises (premises in respect of which there is a premises licence or a temporary events notice) to be open, without reasonable excuse, commits an offence which attracts a penalty of 3 months' imprisonment or a £20 000 fine, or both.

Extension of a closure order

Where, before the end of the closure period the responsible senior police officer reasonably believes that:

(a) a magistrates' court will not have determined what to do about the order in terms of s 165(2) (see below) before the end of the closure period; and

(b) the conditions for an extension are satisfied,

he may extend the closure period for a further 24 hours. The conditions for an extension are:

(a) in the case of an order made on the grounds of public safety because of disorder, that those conditions still exist,

(b) in the case of an order made on the grounds of nuisance, that those conditions still exist.

To have effect, such a notice of extension must be given before the original period has expired.

Cancellation of a closure order

The responsible senior officer may cancel a closure order or any extension of it at any time between the making of the appropriate order and determination by the magistrates. Such an officer must cancel an order if he does not believe that the original conditions which merited its making continue to exist. Notice of cancellation must be given.

Procedure following the making of an order

As soon as reasonably practicable after the making of the order, the responsible senior police officer (he who made the order or another senior officer designated for the purpose by the chief officer of police) must apply to a relevant magistrates' court for it to consider the order. The magistrates' court must as soon as reasonably practicable hold a hearing and may:

(a) revoke the order and any extension of it;
(b) order that closure continues until the matter is considered by the relevant licensing authority;
(c) order the premises to remain closed until a time specified in an order subject to any stated exceptions; or
(d) order closure until a stated time unless prescribed conditions are satisfied.

An appeal lies to a Crown Court against any such decision by the magistrates.

The magistrates must notify the licensing authority of their decision in relation to any premises in respect of which a premises licence is in force. The licensing authority is required to review the premises licence within 28 days of receiving notification from the justices. Regulations are to be made concerning notification to the holder of a premises licence. Where it has been ordered that premises remain closed an offence is committed by a person who, without reasonable excuse, allows the premises to remain open. Such premises are open if a person (other than a licence holder or person living there) enters the premises and is supplied with food or drink, or while he is there the premises are used for entertainment. Entries to premises which are not associated with licensable activities sit outside these provisions.

Police powers

A constable may use such force as may be necessary for the purpose of closing premises in compliance with a closure order. Neither a constable nor the chief officer of police will be liable for any damage which occurs in the course of such duties unless the act or omission is shown to have been in bad faith or to be unlawful because of the Human Rights Act 1998.

Closure of all premises in an identified area

Section 160 deals with situations in which there is, or there is expected to be, disorder in any petty sessional area. In such cases, a magistrates' court acting for that area may make a closure order for a period not exceeding 24 hours, in relation to all premises situated at or near the place of the disorder, or expected disorder, and in respect of which a premises licence or a temporary event notice has effect. Application for such an order must be made by an officer of at least superintendent rank and it must not be made unless the court is satisfied that it is necessary to prevent disorder.

It is an offence for a manager of premises, the holder of a premises licence, the designated premises supervisor or the premises user in the case of a temporary event knowingly to keep premises to which the order relates open, or to allow any such premises to be kept open during the currency of that order.

A constable may use such force as may be necessary to close such premises.

Closure of unlicensed premises

Where a constable or a local authority is satisfied that premises are being, or within the last 24 hours have been, used for unauthorised sale of alcohol for consumption on or in the vicinity of the premises, s 19 of the 2001 Act provides that the constable or local authority must serve a closure notice on a person having control of, or responsibility for the activities carried on at the premises. A closure notice must also be served on any person occupying any other part of the building whose access would be impeded by the order. It may also be served on *any other* person with control of or responsibility for the activities on the premises, or any person with an interest in the premises. A closure notice must specify the nature of the alleged use of the premises, state the effect of s 20 and set out the steps which may be taken to ensure that the alleged use of the premises ceases or (as the case may be) does not recur. Closure notices issued by a constable or a local authority may be cancelled at any time.

Section 20 of the 2001 Act provides that when a closure notice has been served the constable or local authority may seek an order from the justices, not less than 7 days, and not more than 6 months after the service of the notice. An order should not be sought where the constable or local authority is satisfied that the offending use of the premises has ceased and that there is no reasonable likelihood of resumption. Where the justices on hearing the case are satisfied that a notice was properly served under s 19, and that the premises and/or the vicinity of those premises continue to be used for the offending purpose or that there is a reasonable likelihood that there will be such use, they may make a closure order, requiring in particular:

(a) immediate closure of the premises to the public until the constable or local author-ity (as the case may be) has certified that the need for the order has ceased (such an order may include conditions relating to admission and access to other parts of the building);
(b) any offending use to be discontinued immediately;
(c) any defendant to pay into court a sum of money which will not be released until the other requirements of the order have been complied with.

The constable or local authority (as the case may be) must fix a copy of the order to the premises.

An appeal against the making of such an order may be made to a Crown Court. Affected persons may seek discharge of the order. If the justices are satisfied that the need for the order has ceased, they may discharge it.

A person who, without reasonable excuse, permits premises to be open in contraven-tion of a closure order or who otherwise fails to comply with it, commits an offence.

Police powers

Where a closure order has been made a constable or an authorised person, who identi-fies himself if so required, may enter the premises at any reasonable time, if need be by reasonable force, and do anything reasonably necessary to secure compliance with the order.

It is an offence for a person intentionally to obstruct such a person in the exercise of these powers.

Miscellaneous matters

Part 9 of the Act contains provisions of interest to the police.

Opening hours

The Secretary of State is empowered by s 172 to make an order to provide for premises with a premises licence or a club premises certificate to open for specified, generally extended hours, on special occasions.

Prohibition of sales of alcohol at service areas, garages, etc.

Section 176 provides that no premises licence, club premises certificate or temporary event notice has effect to authorise the sale by retail or supply of alcohol on or from excluded premises. These are premises on the land of a special road authority being used for the provision of facilities at service stations catering for traffic of class 1 (with or without other classes) or premises used primarily as a garage or which form part of such premises. The nature of prohibited premises may be altered by order. However, the prohibition is not limited to motorways, trunk roads, etc. It may be that the Secretary of State may wish to exempt certain premises in rural areas where the business concerned with the provision of petrol, etc., is only a part of the business concerned.

Dancing and live music in certain small premises

Section 177 is concerned with where a premises licence or a club premises certificate authorises the sale of alcohol for consumption on the premises, the provision of musical entertainment which may consist of live music or dancing, and the relevant premises are used primarily for the sale of alcohol for consumption on the premises and have a capacity limit of up to 200. Any conditions imposed in respect of musical entertainment imposed by the licensing authority, other than those set out in the licence holder's operating schedule, will be suspended unless they were imposed for public safety or the prevention of crime and disorder.

Where a premises licence or a club premises certificate authorises the provision of musical entertainment and the premises have a capacity limit of less than 200, between the hours of 8 a.m. and midnight, if the premises are being used for live unamplified music but no other form of regulated entertainment, conditions imposed by the licensing authority, other than those set out in the operating schedule, will be suspended.

This section may be disapplied in relation to conditions in respect of particular premises following a review of the licence or certificate. There are exceptions where a licensing authority believes that a condition must continue to apply in the interests of the prevention of the prevention of crime and disorder or the maintenance of public safety.

Powers of entry to investigate licensable activities

Section 179 provides for a police officer or another authorised person to enter premises where he has reason to believe that the premises are being, or are about to be, used for a licensable activity to ensure that the activities are being carried on under and in accordance with the appropriate authorisation (premises licence, club premises certificate or temporary event notice). Reasonable force may be used if necessary. It is an offence to obstruct an authorised person.

Section 180 provides that a police officer may enter and search premises where there is reason to believe an offence under the Act has been, is being or is about to be committed, and may use reasonable force to gain entry.

Drunkenness

Drunkenness is not in itself an offence, but becomes punishable when it is accompanied by aggravating circumstances which interfere with other people. The most common offences of drunkenness are contained in the Licensing Act 1872 and in s 91 of the Criminal Justice Act 1967:

(a) any person who is found drunk in any highway or other public place, whether a building or not, or on any licensed premises, is guilty of an offence. The term 'public place' includes any place to which the public have access, whether on payment or otherwise;

(b) any person who, while drunk in a public place, is guilty of disorderly behaviour, is guilty of an offence.

Both of the above offences are 'penalty offences' for the purposes of Part I of the Criminal Justice and Police Act 2001 and may be dealt with under a fixed-penalty procedure (see page 478).

Where there is an intercom system and locks on the entrance to a block of flats, the landing area outside the flats is not a public place for the purposes of the offence of being drunk and disorderly.

Other offences, now quite rare, are also contained in the 1872 Act and include being drunk while in charge, on any highway or other public place, of any carriage (which includes bicycles), horse, cattle or loaded firearm. The term 'loaded firearm' includes an air weapon.

The term 'drunkenness' is not defined, nor is the form of disorderly conduct which accompanies this condition. It has been held that an offence will be committed if the conduct is honestly believed to have been such disorderly conduct, if that belief is based upon reasonable grounds. The offence is most usually met in circumstances which involve disturbances by fighting or rowdy conduct involving persons who are obviously under the influence of drink.

The words 'found drunk' mean perceived to be drunk. When a person is expelled from a private place and is then perceived to be drunk on a highway, this offence is committed. In practice prosecutions for simple drunkenness are confined to circumstances in which the person concerned is incapable of taking care of himself. Often such persons are found lying in the street, having drunk themselves into a state of unconsciousness, or staggering through traffic with little control over their actions, causing danger both to themselves and to the drivers who are forced to take avoiding action.

A person who is drunk on a public service vehicle or railway passenger vehicle which is being used for the principal purpose of carrying passengers for the whole or part of a journey to or from a designated sporting event, commits an offence against s 1(3) of the Sporting Events (Control of Alcohol, etc.) Act 1985. A person who is drunk in a designated sports ground at any time during the period of a designated sporting event at that ground, offends against s 2(2) of that Act.

Police powers

The general power of arrest which is provided by s 25 of the Police and Criminal Evidence Act 1984 will usually be applicable to offences of drunkenness, where an arrest may be necessary for a number of reasons. A person who is 'found drunk' may often be in such a condition that he cannot establish identity to the satisfaction of the constable, or arrest may be necessary to prevent a person from causing injury to himself, or suffering physical injury. The person who is guilty of disorderly behaviour while drunk may be arrested without warrant by any person, including a constable. The conduct in any case will invariably involve a breach of the peace.

Care must be taken in dealing with all persons who appear to be drunk. If there is any suggestion that they may be ill, or may have injured themselves because of their condition, medical assistance should be provided. It must be remembered that persons who are very drunk are quite likely to be sick, and if they are not carefully watched while in custody, are likely to choke if this should occur while they are lying on their backs. Frequent visits must be made by police officers responsible for the care and custody of prisoners.

Opinion

A necessary ingredient of these offences is that the person concerned was drunk, and this should be stated clearly by the constable in evidence. Although a statement to the effect that a man was drunk is largely a matter of opinion, the courts have always accepted the testimony of a police officer in this respect. The statement must be supported by evidence of the factors which caused the police officer to form the opinion that the man was drunk, and observable symptoms might include lack of co-ordination of movements, manner of speech, and the fact that the breath of the offender smelled of intoxicating liquor.

Index

Absentees from HM Forces, 430
Abstracting electricity, 232
Accidents, motor vehicle, 551
   accident booklet, 559
   damage to animal, 553
   damage to property, 553
   driver's obligations, 553
   interviewing drivers, 560
   law, 551
   personal injury, 552, 555
   police action, 488
   position of vehicle, 558
   reportable, 554
Accused, character of, 119
Acts, Parliamentary, 78
Actual bodily harm, 513
Advance disclosure of evidence 88
Affray, 481
Aggravated burglary, 238
Aggravated vehicle taking, 261
Air weapons, 569
Alcohol
   in blood of driver, 441
   sports grounds, 661
   vehicles/sports grounds, 663
Alcotest
Aliens, *see* Foreign citizens
Ammunition
   auctioneers, 568
   certificate, 565
   definition, 563
Analyst, certificate of, 461
Animals, and the law, 735
   cruelty offences – domestic, 735
   cruelty offences – wild, 736
   injuries in road accidents, 737
   rabies, 738
   straying, 737
   theft, 227
Anonymity of complainants, 688
Appeals, 78
'Appropriates', definition, 183
Arrest
   action following, 185
   action upon, 185
   and common law, 150
   arrestable offences, 151
   arrival at police station, 218
   bail after 138
   category of police station, 134
   conditional powers, 155
   cross-border, 158
   driving while disqualified, 309
   enquiries prior to, 183
   entry to effect, 140
   factors for consideration, 131
   inform someone of, 211

   object of, 131
   on warrant, 135
   other than at police station, 131
   plain clothes, 133
   preliminary search after, 216
   release of detained persons 137
   search on, 136
   statutory powers, 157
   truncheon, use of 133
   violence during, 132
   visits and phone calls, 211
   without warrant, 150
Arrestable offences, 151
Arson, 496
Articulated vehicles, 277
Assaults, 507
   affray, 481
   battery, 510
   consent, 508
   defence of others, 509
   defence of property, 510
   indecent, 580
   justifications for, 509
   occasioning actual bodily harm, 513
   on police, 511
   racially aggravated, 516
   self defence, 509
Attempt, 533
Audible warning instruments in vehicles, 324

Badgers, 732
Battery, definition, 510
'Belonging to another', definition, 229
Belts, seat, 386
Bicycles
   Brakes on, 345
   Drinking, 463
   on footpaths, 345
   passengers on, 344
   unauthorised taking, 262
Binding over, 87
Brakes
   cycles, 345
   motor vehicles, 380
Breach of peace
   arrest, 150
   binding over, 87
   entry into premises, 140
Breath test, drivers, 432
   failure to provide specimen, 439
   substantive, 453
Broken down vehicles, 348
Brothels
   children in, 742
   generally, 676
Buggery, 679
Builder's skips, 340

Buildings
    burglary, 234
    crime prevention, 590
    entry, 234
    explosive used in burglary, 239
    part of, 235
    theft in, 237
    trespass, 236
Built-up area, restricted roads, 707
Burglary, 234
    aggravated, 238
    forms, 237
Business records as evidence, 114

Captive animals, 736
Care proceedings, children, 743
Careless cycling, 720
Careless driving, 717
Careless driving and harassment, 718
Careless driving and notice of intended
      prosecution, 721
Case
    for defence, 96
    for prosecution, 95
Causing danger to road users, 347
Causing death by careless driving, 719
Causing death by dangerous driving, 714
Certificates
    evidence by, 112
    extended hours, 646
    firearm, 565
    insurance, 329
    of analysis, alcohol tests, 461
    of security, 329
    shotgun, 566
    special hours, 647
    test, 331
Charge, decision to do so, 194
Cheats, 541
Children and young persons
    abandoning, 742
    absent from institution etc, 428
    ages, 740
    air weapons, 572
    assessment orders, 744
    begging, 741
    brothels, 742
    care proceedings, 743
    care and supervision orders, 743
    cruelty, 741
    curfew schemes, 747
    detention, 754
    disqualification orders of carers, 752
    emergency protection orders, 744
    employment records of carers, 751
    evidence by, 755
    exposure, 743
    firearms, 572
    indecency with, 679
    indecent photographs, 692

    interrogation of, 753
    intoxicants, 742
    liability of, 740
    neglect, 742
    parents, guardians etc, 741
    parenting orders, 749
    removal by police, 745
    reprimands, 750
    responsibility for, 741
    safety orders, 748
    shotguns, 572
    supervision orders, 743
    tobacco, 743
    truants, 750
    warnings, 750
Classification
    of motor vehicles, 273
    of offences, 151
    of offenders, 277
Clubs, 654
Collars on dogs, 499
Committal proceedings, 104
    transfer, 105
Common law 77
Common law   arrest, 150
Competency, in evidence, 117
Complaints
    Action following final reports 29
    crime, 597
    dispensation by Commission 25
    double jeopardy 51
    foundation of complaints procedure 22
    final reports on investigations 29
    handling of complaints, police against, 23, 25
    handling of conduct matters 26
    investigations by Commission 27
    other investigations 28
    police, local resolution, 25
    public interest immunity, 31
    reference of complaints to Commission 24
    reviews of investigation 30
Computer misuse, 10
Conditional offer – fixed penalty, 373
Conduct Regulations and Complaints
    appeal tribunal, 50
    appropriate officer 36
    appropriate standard 34
    code of conduct, 41–43
    conduct matter 27
    disciplinary hearing, 36
    efficiency and attendance 43
    hearing 37
    Independent Police Complaints Commission 22
    investigating officer, 35
    investigations, 35
    legal representation, 36
    notice of hearing, 37
    punishments, 34
    record of hearing, 40
    regulations, 34

remission of case, 39
review of hearing, 39
special cases, 40
standard of proof 38
supervising officer, 35
Confessions, 120
Consent
    homosexual acts, 680
    indecent assault, 581
    rape, alleged, 682
    taking conveyances, 259
Constitutional position of the police 59
Construction and use, motor vehicles, 375
Contamination of goods, 488
Controlled drugs, 529
Conveyances, defined,259
    taking, 259
Coroners' inquests, 549
Coroner's court, 549
Corroboration, 119, 420
Court
    Appeal, Criminal division, 92
    Crown, 92
    European Court 94
    Functions of 94
    House of Lords, 94
    Magistrates', 84
    procedure, magistrates' courts, guilty plea
        94
    Queens Bench Division, 93
    Youth, 91
    witness out of, 95
Crime
    attempts at, 533
    complaints of, 597
    reports, 598
    scenes of, 442
Crime prevention, 589
    buildings, 590
    local knowledge, 591
    motor vehicles, premises, handbags,
        590
Criminal damage, 491
    arson, 496
    belief in consent, 491
    belonging to another, 493
    defence of property, 491
    endangering life, 495
    lawful excuse, 491
    mens rea, 493
    possession of implements, 497
    property, 492
    racially aggravated, 495
    threats to damage, 496
    warrant, 498
Criminal deception, 242
    definition, 242
Crossbows, 542
Cross-examination, 95
Crossing, pedestrian, 405

Cruelty
    animals, 735
    children, 741
Cycles, *see* Bicycles

Dangerous cycle riding, 720
Dangerous dogs, 501
Dangerous driving, 711
    aiding and abetting, 716
    alternative verdicts, 717
    causing death by, 714
    driving, 711
    definition and proof, 715
    evidence of drink, 715
Dangerous loads, 394
Dangerous substances, 638
Data protection, 12
Deaths, sudden, 546
Deception, criminal, 242
    deception, nature of 244
    electronic transfer, 246
    evasion of liability, 250
    exemption or abatement, 252
    making off without payment, 252
    money transfer, 246
    obtains, 242
    pecuniary advantage, 247
    remission of liability, 250
    services obtained by, 249
    wait for payment, 251
Declaration, dying, 113
Desborough Committee, 53
Deserters from HM Forces, 430
Destitute persons, 429
Detention, conditions of, 197, 219
Detention, juveniles, 206, 745
Direction indicators, 358
Directional signs, 403
'Dishonestly', definition, 220, 222
Disputes, domestic, 519
Disqualification from driving, 309
Documentary evidence, 107
Documents
    business, 114
    evidence, 107
    privilege, 118
Dogs, 499
    and livestock, 504
    collars, 499
    dangerous, 501
    fouling land, 501
    guard, 505
    registration, 499
    leads, 499
    stray, 500
    young persons, owned by, 504
Domestic animals, cruelty, 735
Domestic orders and rights
    domestic violence, 519
    ex parte orders, 520

Domestic orders and rights (*cont'd*)
  husband/wife disputes, 519
  landlord/tenant disputes, 518
  matrimonial home/rights, 521
  non-molestation orders, 520
  occupation orders, 522
  undertakings, 521
Double jeopardy/discipline, 51
Double white lines, 401
Drink, *see* Alcohol; Drunkenness
Drinking and driving
  alternative verdicts, 461
  arrest and entry, 440, 459
  attempting to drive, 437
  breath specimens at scene, 432
  charge of, 437
  constable in uniform, 437
  courses for offenders, 462
  detention of affected driver, 458
  documentary evidence, 461
  driving, 435
  driving while over prescribed limit, 435
  evidence, 460
  evidential testing devices, 449
  failure/roadside, 439
  failure/for analysis, 453
  guided transport systems, 462
  hospital procedure, 456
  moving traffic offence, 438
  prescribed limit, 437
  public place, 436
  reasonable excuse, 439, 455
  road, 436
  roadside specimens, 432
  screening devices, 434
  specimen for analysis, 441
  specimen from person incapable of consenting, 447
  statutory option, 451
  suspicion of alcohol, 438
  unfit through drink or drugs, 458
Drivers
  alcohol in blood, 441
  duties, 394
  eyesight, 324
  identity of, 353
  learner, 318
  licences, 313
  minimum age, 307
  obligations at accidents, 553
  position of, 558
Driving
  and drink, 436
  careless, 717
  causing death by, 719
  defined, 711
  disqualified from, 309
  elsewhere than on road, 352
  endorsement of licence, 310
  footpath, on, 352

  licence, 313
  motor cycles, 319
  production of licence, 334
  provisional licence, 318
  while disqualified, 312
Driving licence, 306
  examination of, 324
  provisional and conditions, 318
  types of, 313
Drugs
  and driving, 458
  arrest, 532
  charging prisoner, taking of specimen
  controlled, 529
  defences, 529
  facilitate intercourse, 683
  infection, 532
  possession, 525
  premises, on, 528
  recognition, 530
  search, seize and detain, 531
  supplying, 526
  trafficking, 526
Drunkenness
  arrest, 656
  at late night refreshment house, 655
  offences, 656
  on bicycles, 463
Dual purpose vehicles, 277
Dying, declaration by, 113

Edmund Davies Committee, 55
Efficiency Regulations
  first interview, 43
  inefficiency hearing, 47
  performance after interviews, 49
  records, 44, 50
  reviews, 49
  second interview, 44
Electricity, abstracting, 232
Enclosed premises, found on, 542
Endorsement of licence, 310
Entering and remaining on property, 756
  adverse occupation of residential premises, 758
  campers-unauthorised, power to remove, 759
  interim possession orders, 759
  violence for securing entry, 756
  without lawful authority, 757
European Convention on Human Rights 80
Evasion of liability, 250
Evidence
  accused person giving, 115
  advance disclosure of, 88
  blood tests, 441
  breath specimens, 460
  breath tests, 432
  business records, 114
  case for defence 96
  certificates, 112
  character, 119

children by, 755
circumstantial, 107
compellability, 117
competency, 117
computers, 115
corroboration, 119, 420
deceased persons, statements of, 113
defence, case for, 96
depositions, 104
direct, 107
disclosure, 88
documentary, 107
dying declarations, 113
examination of witness, 95
exclusion if unfair, 120
expert, 116
first-hand hearsay 114
functions of 106
giving, 587
handling stolen goods, 265
hearsay, 112, 417
how to give, 586
husband and wife, 117
inference from silence, 97–101
leading questions, 95
no case to answer 96
opinion, 116
oral, 107
plea of guilty by post 102
presenting, 107
privilege, 118
public documents, 116
prosecution, case for, 95
real, 107
rebutting, 101
recent complaint, 113
re-examination, 95
res gestae, 113
special measures 108
speeding, 710
statements in presence and hearing of accused 116
statements voluntary, 201
tape recordings, 188
TV link, by, 111
unfair, exclusion, 120
unsworn statement by accused 101
written statements 96
Examination in chief, 95
Examining justices, 104
Execution of warrants, 127
Explosives
  in burglary, 239
  conveyance of, 639
Exposure, indecent, 577
Eyesight, drivers', 324

False alarms, fires, 638
Fear of provocation/violence,
  468

Firearms
  air weapons, 569
  ammunition, *see* Ammunition
  auction, 568
  carriers, 568
  carrying in a public place, 569
  certificates, 565
  children and, 572
  classification of, 564
  converting, 576
  criminal intent and use, 575
  definition, 562
  exemptions from certificates, 567
  in burglary, 238
  intention to injure, 574
  on ships, 568
  permit, 567
  police powers, 569
  possession, 565
  possession after conviction, 575
  production of certificates, 571
  prohibited weapons, 562
  public place, 564
  resist arrest, 570
  search for, 571
  section 1 control, 565
  silencers, 562
  shotguns, 566
  stop and search, 571
  trespass, 570
  warrant, 571
  see also Offensive weapons
Fires
  duties and responsibilities of police, 635
  false alarms, 638
  initial action, 635
  on highways, 338
  reporting of, 635
  rescue procedure, 636
Fireworks on highways, 338
Fixed penalty procedure, 367
Flick knives, 535
Flowers, theft, 227
Football
  banning orders 666
  misbehaviour 672
  ticket touts 673
Footrests, on motor cycles, 344
Foreign citizens, 722
  asylum seekers, 726
  abode, 722
  common travel area, 723
  conditional leave to enter, 723
  deportation, 723
  fingerprinting, 729
  illegal entry, 724, 725
  immigration controls, 723
  registration with police, 725
  terrorist suspects, 728
Found on enclosed premises, 542

Found property, 7

Game
   close season, 734
   licences, 734
Games, on highways, 338
Give way sign, 401
Glue sniffing, 532
Going equipped to steal, 541
Goods vehicles
   age for driving, 694
   driving test 697
   foreign drivers, 698
   forgery of documents, 705
   large goods vehicle driver's licence, 695
   learner drivers, 696
   operators' licences, 702
   plating, 698
   seizure 704
   testing, 700
   vehicles temporarily in Great Britain 704
Goods
   defined, 266
   handling stolen, 265
Gravity knives, 535
Gross indecency, 680
Guilty plea by post, 102
Guns, *see* Firearms

Handling stolen goods, 265
   benefit of another, 270
   goods ceasing to be stolen, 266
   goods representing those originally stolen 267
   forms of handling 269
   guilty knowledge, 270
   powers, 271
   receiving, 269
   stolen goods, 265
   undertaking and assisting, 270
   wrongful credit, 268
Harassment, alarm, etc., 470
Harassment of tenants, 518
Hearsay, evidence, 112, 417
Heavy locomotives, 276
Heavy motor cars, 275
Highways
   builders' skips on, 340
   definition, 337
   fires and fireworks on, 338
   games on, 338
   litter on, 339
   loudspeakers, 341
   obstruction, 337
   parking by disabled persons 341
   powers 338
   see also Roads
Homeless persons, 429
Homosexual acts, 679
Hospital procedure, drinking and driving, 456
Hours

of darkness, 355
extended licences, 646
late night refreshment houses, 655
permitted, 645
restrictions to permitted, 650
special, 647
House of Lords, 94
Husband and wife
   evidence of, 117
   privilege, 118
   see also Disputes, domestic

Identification
   Avoiding action by suspect 609
   confrontation, 619
   fingerprints, 621
   first description by witness, 612
   generally, 605
   group, 617
   identification procedure must be held, 607
   information to be given to suspect, 608
   information given to media, 610
   intimate samples, 627
   methods, 605
   non-intimate samples, 628
   parades, 614
   photographs, 620, 626
   pictures by security camera, 630
   prison inmates, 614
   recordable offences, 625
   retention of photographs, 611
   selecting an identification procedure, 607
   suspect known, 606
   suspect not known, 609
   video, 612
   voice, 631
   witnesses, 606
   see also Description
Illness in street, 425
Importuning – males, 678
Incest, 687
Inconsiderate driving, 717
Indecency
   between males, 680
   gross, 680
   with children, 679
Indecent
   Anonymity of complainant, 582
   assault, 580
   displays, 691
   exposure, 577
   literature, 690, 691
   photographs of children, 692, 693
   telephone calls, 570
Index marks, motor registration, 287
Indictable offences committal, 70
Informatory signs, 402
Inhabited vessels or vehicles, 235
Inquests, 549
Insurance, motor vehicles, 272

exemptions, 330
proof of, 329
Interference with vehicles, 263#
Interrogation
deaf persons, 170
mentally handicapped, 205
of foreigners, 208
tape recording, 188
Interviews, tape recorded, 188
Blind, 207
breaks, 191
broken tapes, 192
changing tapes, 191
cautions 191
complaints during, 199
conclusion, 192
deaf, 207
decision to charge, procedure, 194
equipment failure, 192
foreigners, 207
juveniles, 206
nature of taped record 189
oppression during, 197
persons at risk, 205
police stations 196
security of tapes, 198
significant silence 190
significant statement 190
special caution 188
solicitor, 190, 209
urgent, 206, 208
visual recording 192
written records, 193
Interviews, non-taped, 193
Interviews, urgent, 206
Interviews, records of, 192
Intimidation, witnesses, jurors etc, 543
Intoxicants
licences for sale of, 643

Justices of the peace
and binding over, 87
examining, 104
Juveniles
care proceedings, 743
definition, 740
interviewing, 753
liability of, 740
smoking by, 743
see also Children and young people

Kerb crawling, 677

Lamps, *see* Lights on vehicles
Land, theft, 226
Late night refreshment houses, 655
Learner driver, *see* Drivers
Legislation of European Union 80
Licences
driving, *see* Driving licences

excise licences, vehicles, 293
forged, 325
Justices', 643
occasional, 644
provisional driving, 318
trade, 300
Licensed clubs, 654
Licensed premises, 643
Licensing, liquor laws, 643 Appendix p 761 when
LA 2003 in force)
closure due to disorder, 658
closure of unlicensed premises, 660
clubs, 654
confiscation, young persons, 652
designated public places, alcohol consumption,
657
drunkenness, 655
entertainment, 646
exemptions from hours, 648
expulsion from premises, 649
justices, 557
Licensing Act 2003, 643 and Appendix
meals, 645
occasional, 644
occasional permission, 644
permitted hours, 645, 654
persons under 18, 650
persons under 14, 653
refreshment houses, 655
residential, 643
restaurant, 643
restriction orders, 650
sales out of hours, 648
special hours certificate, 647
variations in hours, 559
Light locomotives, 276
Lights on vehicles, 355
control on parking at night, 365
daytime hours, 355
direction indicators, 358
end-outline marker lamps, 362
fitting, lamps and reflectors, 366
front fog lamps, 360
front position lamps, 357
hazard warning, 360
headlamps, 356
hours of darkness, 355
maintenance of lights and reflectors, 365
obligatory lights, 356
optional lamps and reflectors, 356
overhanging loads, 363
pedal cycles, 364
rear fog lamps, 359
rear markings, 363
rear position lamps, 357
rear registration lamps, 358
rear retro reflector, 359
reversing lamps, 360
side marker lamps, 362
side retro reflectors, 362

Lights on vehicles (*cont'd*)
    stop lamps, 358
    trailers, 361
    use of during darkness, 364
    warning beacons, 361
Litter, abatement, 284
Livestock
    and dogs, 504
    ill or injured, 737
    see also Animals
Local authorities, and builders' skips, 340
Loss of memory, 425
Lost property, 7
Loudspeakers on highways, 341

Major incidents, 635
Making off without payment, 252
Mandatory signs, 404
Marks, registration, 267
Mechanically propelled vehicles;
    registration and licensing, 281
    trade licences, 300
Mental disorder, 426
Missing persons, 428
Modus operandi, index, 595
Motor cars
    definition, 383
    learner driver, 321
    minimum age for driving, 307
    reversing, 396
Motor cycles
    definition, 274
    foot rests,344
    learner drivers, 318
    minimum age for driving, 307
    passengers on, 344
    protective headgear, 344
Motor tractors, 276
Motor vehicles
    abandonment, 293
    accidents, 551
    ages for driving, 307
    aid or abet offences, 279
    anchorage points, 384
    articulated, 277
    audible warning instruments, 379
    brakes, 380
    broken down, 348
    cause use of, 278, 378
    change of ownership/address, 283
    classification, 273
    construction and use, 375
    direction indicators, 356
    doors opening, 396
    driving licences, *see* Driving licences
    dual purpose, 277
    examination, 332
    excise duty, 293
    glass, maintenance of, 393
    heavy locomotive, 276

    heavy motor car, 275
    horns, 379
    immobilisation/unlicensed, 300
    insurance, 326
    interference, 263
    invalid carriages, 274
    lights, 355
    light locomotive, 276
    mechanically propelled, 282
    mirrors, 383
    motor car, 274
    motor cycle, 274
    motor tractor, 276
    noise, 395
    obstruction, 396
    permit use of, 277, 378
    petrol tank, 393
    position at accidents, 558
    prohibition of unfit, 397
    quitting, 396
    registration, 281
    registration document, 282
    registration marks, 287
    registration plates, 291
    removal of, 348
    reversing of, 396
    reversing alarms, 380
    salvage operators, 285
    seat belts, 386
    silencer, 384
    speed limits, 707
    speedometer, 392
    speed limiter, 393
    steering gear, 390
    stop, power to 280
    taking of, 259
    tampering with, 353
    testing, 331, 397
    tow ropes, 397
    trade licences, 300
    trade plates, 301
    tyres, 390
    use, 277, 376
    used or kept, 282
    windscreen wipers and washers, 392
    wings, 394
    see also Motor cars
Moving traffic offences, 438
National Crime Intelligence Service, 66
National Crime Squad, 67
Noise, motor vehicles, 395
Notebooks, police, 3
Not guilty procedure, 70
Notice of prosecution, 350
    offences requiring, 350

Oaksey Committee, 54
Oath, form of, 587
Obscene telephone calls, 510
Obscenity, *see* Indecency

Obstruction
    builders' skips, 340
    highways, 337
    motor vehicles, 396
    police, 512
'Obtains', definition, 242
Obtains services by deception, 249
Occurrence reports, 254
Offence reports, 254
Offences
    arrestable, 151
    classification, 151
    common law, 77
    fixed penalty, 367
    indictable, 85
    summary, 85
    triable either way, 86
Offensive weapons, 535
    restriction, 537
    under CJ Act 1988, 537
Open court 87
'On-the-spot' penalties – disorderly behaviour, 477
Opinion, evidence, 116
Oral evidence, 107
Overtaking near crossings, 408
Owner's index, 601

Parking
    brakes, 380
    dangerous position, 347
    disabled persons, 341
    footways by heavy vehicles, 349
    removal of vehicles, 348
    without lights, 364
Passengers, conduct of
    on bicycles, 344
    on motor cycles, 344
Peace, breach of, *see* Breach of peace
Pecuniary advantage by deception, 247
Pedal cycles, *see* Bicycles
Pedestrian crossing, *see* Crossings
Pelican crossing, 406
Penalty points, 310
Permits, firearms, 567
Picketing, 466
Pleas, magistrates' court, by post, 86
Poaching, 733
Pocket notebooks, *see* Notebooks
Police
    assaulting, 511
    complaints against, 22
    conditions of service, 16
    discipline hearing, 36
    discipline of, 33
    notebooks of, 3
    obstruction of, 512
    personal records, 18
    probationary period, 19
    promotion, 20
    punishment for offences, 34

    sick leave, 18
    support personnel
    Police Advisory Board, 55
Police authorities, 68
Police College, 65
Police Council, 54
Police Federation, 52
Police Federation Regulations 1969, 57
Police force
    areas of responsibility, 64
    borough, 62
    collective responsibility, 59
    county police, 62
    formation of, 61
    history, 59
    Home Secretary & control, 65
    Metropolitan 61
    modern, 63
    objectives, local & central, 65
    organisation of, 65
    rank structure, 69
    community support officers etc 71
    type of, 64
Police National Computer, 600
    creating & updating, 603
    direction tables, 603
    names index, 602
    owners index, 601
    property index, 601
    quest, 604
    stolen and suspect vehicles, 601
    warning signals, 603
Police Promotion Examinations Board, 20
Police (Promotion) Regulations 1996, 20
Police Regulations, 16
Police service, *see* Police force
Possession
    of drugs, 525
    of firearms, 565
    of offensive weapons, 537
Precedence on zebra crossings, 407
Precedence at Pelican or Puffin crossing,
    407
Premises
    adverse occupation, 758
    violence to enter, 756
Prescribed limits, alcohol, 437
Prisoners
    access to solicitors, 190, 209
    arrival at police station, 218
    cautioning, 191
    searching, 148
    transporting, 217
    visits, letters and telephone calls,
    211
Privilege, 118
Processions, 483
Procuration in rape cases, 683
Prohibited uniform, 467
Prohibitory signs, 404

Property
  belonging to another, 229
  criminal damage, 492
  defence of, 481
  entering and remaining on, 756
  found, 7
  in public service vehicles, lost or found, 8
  lost, 7
  obtaining by deception, 242
  seizure of, 147, 174
Prostitution, 674
  advertisements, 676
  brothels, 676
  common prostitute, 675
  cautions, 675
  kerb crawling, 677
  loitering, 674
  male importuning, 678
  soliciting, 674
Protective headgear, 344
Provisional driving licences, 318
Public meetings, 465
Public order, 464
  Act of 1936, 467
  affray, 481
  aggravated trespass, 487
  anti-social behaviour orders, 476
  assemblies, 484
  contamination of goods, 488
  fear or provocation of violence, 468
  harassment, alarm or distress, 470
  harassment at home, 475
  human rights, 489
  industrial disputes, 465
  on-the-spot penalties – disorderly behaviour,
    471
  peaceful picketing, 466
  processions, 483
  public meetings 465
  publishing racially sensitive material, 478
  racial hatred, 476
  raves, 486
  racially aggravated offences, 473, 475
  riot, 480
  stalkers, 473
  trespassory assemblies, 484
  trespass or nuisance on land, 485
  violent disorder, 481
Public records, as evidence, 116
Public roads, 282
  see also Roads
Puffin Crossing, 406

Queen's Bench Division, 93
Quitting motor vehicles, 396

Railways
  causing danger, etc., 584
  throwing objects, 585
  trespass on, 583

Rape
  evidence in, 684
  police powers, 684
  the offence, 682
Real evidence, 107
Receiving stolen goods, 269
Refreshment houses, 655
Refuse Disposal (Amenity) Act 1978, 340
Registered clubs, 654
Registration of vehicles, 281
Regulation of investigatory powers 176
Removal of articles, (Theft Act), 240
Removal of vehicles, 348
Report writing, 254
Res gestae, 113
Restitution of found property, 9
Restricted road, 707
Restriction of Offensive Weapons Act, 537
Restriction orders, licensed premises, 650
Reversing alarms, 396
Reversing motor vehicles, 396
Riot, 480
Road checks
  authorisation, 213
  common law powers, 215
  records, 215
  searches, 215
  statutory powers, 213
  time limits, 214
Roads, definition, 282
Robbery, 257
  see also Theft and robbery

Safe custody of prisoners, 216
Scenes of crime, 421
School, crossing patrols, 408
Search
  action after, 148, 216
  action on, 169
  arrest, to effect, 140
  arrest, after entry, 141
  alcohol – sports grounds, 664
  CJ Act 1994, 163
  detained persons of, 136
  entry after arrest, 141
  for drugs, 531
  for firearms, 571
  force to effect 143
  location of personal search, 167
  of accused
  power to stop and, 159
  premises – consent, 143
  premises – no consent, 145
  premises, notice of powers etc 144
  reasonable suspicion to, 160
  records, 170
  removal of clothing, 172
  seizure of articles, 147, 173
  sports grounds, 168
  stolen or prohibited articles, 168

stop and, 159
street, 173
Terrorism Act 2000, 164
unattended vehicles, 172
Search warrants
criminal damage, 498
firearms, 571
Seat belts, 386, 387
Service of summons, 122
Sexual offences
abuse of position of trust, 681
anonymity of complainants, 688
complainants, witnesses who are children, 686
generally, 679
unnatural, 679
restrictions on evidence of sexual history, 685
sex offender orders, 689
Sheehy Inquiry, 55
Shotguns, 566
certificate, 565
children and, 572
Sick leave, police, 18
Signs, traffic, 399
Silence, inference drawn from, 97–101
Silencers, 384
Solicitors, communication with, 186
Solvent abuse, 532
Special hours certificates, 647
Special reasons, and disqualification of drivers, 309
Speed limits, 707
class of vehicle, 708
evidence, 710
exemptions, 709
motorways, 708
notice of intended prosecution, 709
other than restricted roads, 707
restricted roads, 707
temporary limits, 708
Sports grounds
articles, possession of, 665
chanting, 672
designation of, 661
banning order, 666
permitted hours, 662
pitch invasion, 673
throwing objects, 672
ticket touts, 673
unlawful sale of liquor, 663
vehicles travelling to, 663
Squatters, 756
Statements
by accused, 201
by co-accused, 205
by deaf, 207
by mentally ill, 205
by foreigner, 208
caution, 201
committal proceedings, 104
conclusion, 413
corroboration 420

exhibits, 417
hearsay 417
negative, 416
occurrence, 411
offence, 409
opinion 415
persons at risk 205
rules 413
types of, 410
voluntary, 201
witness, 415
writing rules, 413
written by police, 202
see also Evidence
Statute law, 78
Statutory preventive measures, 533
criminal attempts, 533
found on enclosed premises, 542
going equipped to steal, 541
offensive weapons, 535
Steering gear, motor vehicles, 390
Stolen goods, handling, 265
guilty knowledge, 270
Stop and search 159
Stop signs, 401
Stopping, at accidents, 553
Stopping at crossing, 407
Stopping in controlled area, 408
Straying animals, 737
dogs, 500
Street offences, 674
cautions to prostitutes, 675
common prostitute, 674
loitering or soliciting, 674
powers, 676
public place, 675
street, 675
Subordinate legislation, 79
Sudden deaths, 546
continuity of police attendance, 547
Coroner's court, 549
examination of bodies, 547
identification, 547
inquests, 549
post mortem, 548
property, 548
suicide, 547
Summary cases
procedure and trials, 95
Summonses, 122
Supervision orders, 743
Sureties
good behaviour, 87
peace, breach of, 87
Swearing witnesses, 587

Taking conveyances, 259
Tampering with motor vehicle, 353
Telephone calls, indecent, 579

Testing
   bicycles, 345
   eyesight, 324
   vehicles, 331
Theft, 220
   appropriation, 223
   belief in lawful right to deprive, 220
   belief owner cannot be found, 221
   belief owner would have consented, 221
   belonging to another, 229
   consent, 221
   deer, 228
   definition,220
   dishonesty, 220, 222
   electronic transfer, 246
   evasion of liability by deception, 250
   fish, 228
   intention, 231
   land etc, 226
   making off without payment, 252
   obtaining services by deception, 249
   property, definition, 225
   removal from public buildings, 231
   wild animals, 227
   wild, things growing, 227
Theft Act 1978, 248
Threat to destroy, 496
Threats to commit damage, 496
Tobacco and children, 743
Tow-ropes, motor vehicle, 397
Trade disputes, 465
Trade licences, motor vehicles, 300
   carriage of goods, 304
   carriage of passengers, 302
   offences, 304
   permitted purposes, 302
   use by holder, 301
Trade plates, 301
Traffic
   lights, 400
   signs, 399
   wardens, 71
Transport of prisoners, 217
Treasure, 9
Trespass
   aggravated, 487
   armed, 570
   burglary, 234
   firearms, 570
   weapon of offence, 540
Truncheons, use of, 133
Two-tone horns, 379
Tyres, motor vehicle, 390

Undertaking and assisting, 270
Uniforms, political, 467

Vehicles
   brakes, *see* Brakes
   broken down, 348
   construction and use, 375
   dangerous driving, 347
   dangerous position, 347
   dual purpose, 277
   excise licence, 293
   exempt from licence duty, 294
   interference, 263
   lighting, 355
   obstruction, 396
   registration, 281
   removal, 348
   speed limits, 707
   use in commission of crime, 311
   see also Motor vehicles
Violent disorder, 481
Voluntary statements, 201

Warning instrument, 379
Warning signs, 403
Warrants, 124
   arrest, 127
   arrest without, 150
   bail, 126
   commitment, 126
   cross-border 130
   default, 126
   execution of, 127
   search, 124, 128
Wife, *see* Husband and Wife; Disputes, domestic
Wild animals and flowers, theft, 227
Wild animals, 731
Wild birds, 730
Wild plants, 731
Wildlife and countryside, 730
Windscreen washers and wipers, 392
Witness
   competency, 117
   intimidation, 543
   privilege, 118
   refreshing memory 120
   statements, 415
   special measures
   swearing, 587
Woundings, 513
   unlawful, 515
   with intent, 514
Written statements
   in evidence, 96

Young persons, *see* Children and young persons
Youth court, 91
Zebra crossings, 405